Fourth Conference on Machine Translation (WMT)

Volume 2: Shared Task Papers, Day 1

Florence, Italy
1-2 August 2019

ISBN: 978-1-5108-9290-3

WMT 2019

**Fourth Conference on
Machine Translation**

Proceedings of the Conference

August 1-2, 2019
Florence, Italy

Introduction

The Fourth Conference on Machine Translation (WMT 2019) took place on Thursday, August 1 and Friday, August 2, 2019 in Florence, Italy, immediately following the 57th Annual Meeting of the Association for Computational Linguistics (ACL 2019).

This is the fourth time WMT has been held as a conference. The first time WMT was held as a conference was at ACL 2016 in Berlin, Germany, the second time at EMNLP 2017 in Copenhagen, Denmark, and the third time at EMNLP 2028 in Brussels, Belgium. Prior to being a conference, WMT was held 10 times as a workshop. WMT was held for the first time at HLT-NAACL 2006 in New York City, USA. In the following years the Workshop on Statistical Machine Translation was held at ACL 2007 in Prague, Czech Republic, ACL 2008, Columbus, Ohio, USA, EACL 2009 in Athens, Greece, ACL 2010 in Uppsala, Sweden, EMNLP 2011 in Edinburgh, Scotland, NAACL 2012 in Montreal, Canada, ACL 2013 in Sofia, Bulgaria, ACL 2014 in Baltimore, USA, and EMNLP 2015 in Lisbon, Portugal.

The focus of our conference is to bring together researchers from the area of machine translation and invite selected research papers to be presented at the conference.

Prior to the conference, in addition to soliciting relevant papers for review and possible presentation, we conducted 8 shared tasks. This consisted of four translation tasks: Machine Translation of News, Biomedical Translation, Robust Machine Translation, and Similar Language Translation, two evaluation tasks: Metrics and Quality Estimation, as well as the Automatic Post-Editing and Parallel Corpus Filtering tasks.

The results of all shared tasks were announced at the conference, and these proceedings also include overview papers for the shared tasks, summarizing the results, as well as providing information about the data used and any procedures that were followed in conducting or scoring the tasks. In addition, there are short papers from each participating team that describe their underlying system in greater detail.

Like in previous years, we have received a far larger number of submissions than we could accept for presentation. WMT 2019 has received 48 full research paper submissions (not counting withdrawn submissions). In total, WMT 2019 featured 12 full research paper oral presentations and 102 shared task poster presentations.

The invited talk was given by Marine Carpuat from the University of Maryland, College Park, USA. It was titled "Semantic, Style & Other Data Divergences in Neural Machine Translation".

We would like to thank the members of the Program Committee for their timely reviews. We also would like to thank the participants of the shared task and all the other volunteers who helped with the evaluations.

Ondřej Bojar, Rajen Chatterjee, Christian Federmann, Mark Fishel, Yvette Graham, Barry Haddow, Matthias Huck, Antonio Jimeno Yepes, Philipp Koehn, André Martins, Christof Monz, Matteo Negri, Aurélie Névéol, Mariana Neves, Matt Post, Marco Turchi, and Karin Verspoor

Co-Organizers

Organizers:

Ondřej Bojar (Charles University in Prague)
Rajen Chatterjee (FBK)
Christian Federmann (MSR)
Mark Fishel (University of Tartu)
Yvette Graham (DCU)
Barry Haddow (University of Edinburgh)
Matthias Huck (LMU Munich)
Antonio Jimeno Yepes (IBM Research Australia)
Philipp Koehn (University of Edinburgh / Johns Hopkins University)
André Martins (Unbabel)
Christof Monz (University of Amsterdam)
Matteo Negri (FBK)
Aurélie Névéol (LIMSI, CNRS)
Mariana Neves (German Federal Institute for Risk Assessment)
Matt Post (Johns Hopkins University)
Marco Turchi (FBK)
Karin Verspoor (University of Melbourne)

Invited Speaker:

Marine Carpuat (University of Maryland, College Park)

Program Committee:

Tamer Alkhouli (RWTH Aachen University)
Antonios Anastasopoulos (Carnegie Mellon University)
Yuki Arase (Osaka University)
Mihael Arcan (INSIGHT, NUI Galway)
Duygu Ataman (Fondazione Bruno Kessler - University of Edinburgh)
Eleftherios Avramidis (German Research Center for Artificial Intelligence (DFKI))
Amittai Axelrod (Didi Chuxing)
Parnia Bahar (RWTH Aachen University)
Ankur Bapna (Google AI)
Petra Barancikova (Charles University in Prague, Faculty of Mathematics and Physics)
Joost Bastings (University of Amsterdam)
Rachel Bawden (University of Edinburgh)
Meriem Beloucif (University of Hamburg)
Graeme Blackwood (IBM Research AI)
Frédéric Blain (University of Sheffield)
Chris Brockett (Microsoft Research)
Bill Byrne (University of Cambridge)
Elena Cabrio (Université Côte d'Azur, Inria, CNRS, I3S, France)

Marine Carpuat (University of Maryland)
Francisco Casacuberta (Universitat Politècnica de València)
Sheila Castilho (Dublin City University)
Rajen Chatterjee (Apple Inc)
Boxing Chen (Alibaba)
Colin Cherry (Google)
Mara Chinea-Rios (Universitat Politècnica de València)
Chenhui Chu (Osaka University)
Ann Clifton (Spotify)
Marta R. Costa-jussà (Universitat Politècnica de Catalunya)
Josep Crego (SYSTRAN)
Raj Dabre (NICT)
Steve DeNeefe (SDL Research)
Michael Denkowski (Amazon)
Mattia A. Di Gangi (Fondazione Bruno Kessler)
Miguel Domingo (Universitat Politècnica de València)
Kevin Duh (Johns Hopkins University)
Marc Dymetman (Naver Labs Europe)
Hiroshi Echizen'ya (Hokkai-Gakuen University)
Sergey Edunov (Faceook AI Research)
Marcello Federico (Amazon AI)
Yang Feng (Institute of Computing Technology, Chinese Academy of Sciences)
Andrew Finch (Apple Inc.)
Orhan Firat (Google AI)
George Foster (Google)
Alexander Fraser (Ludwig-Maximilians-Universität München)
Atsushi Fujita (National Institute of Information and Communications Technology)
Juri Ganitkevitch (Google)
Mercedes García-Martínez (Pangeanic)
Ekaterina Garmash (KLM Royal Dutch Airlines)
Jesús González-Rubio (WebInterpret)
Isao Goto (NHK)
Miguel Graça (RWTH Aachen University)
Roman Grundkiewicz (School of Informatics, University of Edinburgh)
Mandy Guo (Google)
Jeremy Gwinnup (Air Force Research Laboratory)
Thanh-Le Ha (Karlsruhe Institute of Technology)
Nizar Habash (New York University Abu Dhabi)
Gholamreza Haffari (Monash University)
Greg Hanneman (Amazon)
Christian Hardmeier (Uppsala universitet)
Eva Hasler (SDL Research)
Yifan He (Alibaba Group)
John Henderson (MITRE)
Christian Herold (RWTH Aachen University)
Felix Hieber (Amazon Research)
Hieu Hoang (University of Edinburgh)

Vu Cong Duy Hoang (The University of Melbourne)

Bojie Hu (Tencent Research, Beijing, China)

Junjie Hu (Carnegie Mellon University)

Mika Hämäläinen (University of Helsinki)

Gonzalo Iglesias (SDL)

Kenji Imamura (National Institute of Information and Communications Technology)

Aizhan Imankulova (Tokyo Metropolitan University)

Julia Ive (University of Sheffield)

Marcin Junczys-Dowmunt (Microsoft)

Shahram Khadivi (eBay)

Huda Khayrallah (Johns Hopkins University)

Douwe Kiela (Facebook)

Yunsu Kim (RWTH Aachen University)

Rebecca Knowles (Johns Hopkins University)

Julia Kreutzer (Department of Computational Linguistics, Heidelberg University)

Shankar Kumar (Google)

Anoop Kunchukuttan (Microsoft AI and Research)

Surafel Melaku Lakew (University of Trento and Fondazione Bruno Kessler)

Ekaterina Lapshinova-Koltunski (Universität des Saarlandes)

Alon Lavie (Amazon/Carnegie Mellon University)

Gregor Leusch (eBay)

William Lewis (Microsoft Research)

Jindřich Libovický (Charles University)

Patrick Littell (National Research Council of Canada)

Qun Liu (Huawei Noah's Ark Lab)

Samuel Läubli (University of Zurich)

Pranava Madhyastha (Imperial College London)

Andreas Maletti (Universität Leipzig)

Saab Mansour (Apple)

Sameen Maruf (Monash University)

Arne Mauser (Google, Inc)

Arya D. McCarthy (Johns Hopkins University)

Antonio Valerio Miceli Barone (The University of Edinburgh)

Paul Michel (Carnegie Mellon University)

Aaron Mueller (The Johns Hopkins University)

Kenton Murray (University of Notre Dame)

Tomáš Musil (Charles University)

Mathias Müller (University of Zurich)

Masaaki Nagata (NTT Corporation)

Toshiaki Nakazawa (The University of Tokyo)

Preslav Nakov (Qatar Computing Research Institute, HBKU)

Graham Neubig (Carnegie Mellon University)

Jan Niehues (Maastricht University)

Nikola Nikolov (University of Zurich and ETH Zurich)

Xing Niu (University of Maryland)

Tsuyoshi Okita (Kyushuu institute of technology)

Daniel Ortiz-Martínez (Technical University of Valencia)

Myle Ott (Facebook AI Research)
Santanu Pal (Saarland University)
Carla Parra Escartín (Unbabel)
Pavel Pecina (Charles University)
Stephan Peitz (Apple)
Sergio Penkale (Lingo24)
Mārcis Pinnis (Tilde)
Martin Popel (Charles University, Faculty of Mathematics and Physics, UFAL)
Maja Popović (ADAPT Centre @ DCU)
Matīss Rikters (Tilde)
Annette Rios (Institute of Computational Linguistics, University of Zurich)
Jan Rosendahl (RWTH Aachen University)
Raphael Rubino (DFKI)
Devendra Sachan (CMU / Petuum Inc.)
Elizabeth Salesky (Carnegie Mellon University)
Hassan Sawaf (Amazon Web Services)
Jean Senellart (SYSTRAN)
Rico Sennrich (University of Edinburgh)
Patrick Simianer (Lilt)
Linfeng Song (University of Rochester)
Felix Stahlberg (University of Cambridge, Department of Engineering)
Dario Stojanovski (LMU Munich)
Katsuhito Sudoh (Nara Institute of Science and Technology (NAIST))
Felipe Sánchez-Martínez (Universitat d'Alacant)
Aleš Tamchyna (Charles University in Prague, UFAL MFF)
Gongbo Tang (Uppsala University)
Jörg Tiedemann (University of Helsinki)
Antonio Toral (University of Groningen)
Ke Tran (Amazon)
Marco Turchi (Fondazione Bruno Kessler)
Ferhan Ture (Comcast Applied AI Research)
Nicola Ueffing (eBay)
Masao Utiyama (NICT)
Dušan Variš (Charles University, Institute of Formal and Applied Linguistics)
David Vilar (Amazon)
Ivan Vulić (University of Cambridge)
Ekaterina Vylomova (University of Melbourne)
Wei Wang (Google Research)
Weiyue Wang (RWTH Aachen University)
Taro Watanabe (Google)
Philip Williams (University of Edinburgh)
Hua Wu (Baidu)
Joern Wuebker (Lilt, Inc.)
Hainan Xu (Johns Hopkins University)
Yinfei Yang (Google)
François Yvon (LIMSI/CNRS)
Dakun Zhang (SYSTRAN)
Xuan Zhang (Johns Hopkins University)

Table of Contents

Conference Program

Thursday, August 1, 2019

8:45–9:00   *Opening Remarks*

9:00–10:30   **Session 1: Shared Tasks Overview Presentations I (chair: Barry Haddow)**

9:00–9:35   *Findings of the 2019 Conference on Machine Translation (WMT19)*
Loïc Barrault, Ondřej Bojar, Marta R. Costa-jussà, Christian Federmann, Mark Fishel, Yvette Graham, Barry Haddow, Matthias Huck, Philipp Koehn, Shervin Malmasi, Christof Monz, Mathias Müller, Santanu Pal, Matt Post and Marcos Zampieri

9:35–9:50   *Test Suites*

9:50–10:10   *Results of the WMT19 Metrics Shared Task: Segment-Level and Strong MT Systems Pose Big Challenges*
Qingsong Ma, Johnny Wei, Ondřej Bojar and Yvette Graham

10:10–10:30   *Findings of the First Shared Task on Machine Translation Robustness*
Xian Li, Paul Michel, Antonios Anastasopoulos, Yonatan Belinkov, Nadir Durrani, Orhan Firat, Philipp Koehn, Graham Neubig, Juan Pino and Hassan Sajjad

10:30-11:00   *Coffee Break*

11:00–12:30   **Session 2: Shared Task Poster Session I**

11:00–12:30   *Shared Task: News Translation*

The University of Edinburgh's Submissions to the WMT19 News Translation Task
Rachel Bawden, Nikolay Bogoychev, Ulrich Germann, Roman Grundkiewicz, Faheem Kirefu, Antonio Valerio Miceli Barone and Alexandra Birch

GTCOM Neural Machine Translation Systems for WMT19
Chao Bei, Hao Zong, Conghu Yuan, Qingming Liu and Baoyong Fan

Machine Translation with parfda, Moses, kenlm, nplm, and PRO
Ergun Biçici

Neural Machine Translation for English–Kazakh with Morphological Segmentation and Synthetic Data
Antonio Toral, Lukas Edman, Galiya Yeshmagambetova and Jennifer Spenader

The LMU Munich Unsupervised Machine Translation System for WMT19
Dario Stojanovski, Viktor Hangya, Matthias Huck and Alexander Fraser

Combining Local and Document-Level Context: The LMU Munich Neural Machine Translation System at WMT19
Dario Stojanovski and Alexander Fraser

IITP-MT System for Gujarati-English News Translation Task at WMT 2019
Sukanta Sen, Kamal Kumar Gupta, Asif Ekbal and Pushpak Bhattacharyya

The University of Helsinki Submissions to the WMT19 News Translation Task
Aarne Talman, Umut Sulubacak, Raúl Vázquez, Yves Scherrer, Sami Virpioja, Alessandro Raganato, Arvi Hurskainen and Jörg Tiedemann

Microsoft Research Asia's Systems for WMT19
Yingce Xia, Xu Tan, Fei Tian, Fei Gao, Di He, Weicong Chen, Yang Fan, Linyuan Gong, Yichong Leng, Renqian Luo, Yiren Wang, Lijun Wu, Jinhua Zhu, Tao Qin and Tie-Yan Liu

The En-Ru Two-way Integrated Machine Translation System Based on Transformer
Doron Yu

DFKI-NMT Submission to the WMT19 News Translation Task
Jingyi Zhang and Josef van Genabith

11:00–12:30 *Shared Task: Test Suites*

Linguistic Evaluation of German-English Machine Translation Using a Test Suite
Eleftherios Avramidis, Vivien Macketanz, Ursula Strohriegel and Hans Uszkoreit

A Test Suite and Manual Evaluation of Document-Level NMT at WMT19
Kateřina Rysová, Magdaléna Rysová, Tomáš Musil, Lucie Poláková and Ondřej Bojar

Evaluating Conjunction Disambiguation on English-to-German and French-to-German WMT 2019 Translation Hypotheses
Maja Popović

The MuCoW Test Suite at WMT 2019: Automatically Harvested Multilingual Contrastive Word Sense Disambiguation Test Sets for Machine Translation
Alessandro Raganato, Yves Scherrer and Jörg Tiedemann

SAO WMT19 Test Suite: Machine Translation of Audit Reports
Tereza Vojtěchová, Michal Novák, Miloš Klouček and Ondřej Bojar

11:00–12:30   *Shared Task: Metrics*

WMDO: Fluency-based Word Mover's Distance for Machine Translation Evaluation
Julian Chow, Lucia Specia and Pranava Madhyastha

Meteor++ 2.0: Adopt Syntactic Level Paraphrase Knowledge into Machine Translation Evaluation
Yinuo Guo and Junfeng Hu

YiSi - a Unified Semantic MT Quality Evaluation and Estimation Metric for Languages with Different Levels of Available Resources
Chi-kiu Lo

EED: Extended Edit Distance Measure for Machine Translation
Peter Stanchev, Weiyue Wang and Hermann Ney

Filtering Pseudo-References by Paraphrasing for Automatic Evaluation of Machine Translation
Ryoma Yoshimura, Hiroki Shimanaka, Yukio Matsumura, Hayahide Yamagishi and Mamoru Komachi

11:00–12:30   *Shared Task: Robustness*

Naver Labs Europe's Systems for the WMT19 Machine Translation Robustness Task
Alexandre Berard, Ioan Calapodescu and Claude Roux

NICT's Supervised Neural Machine Translation Systems for the WMT19 Translation Robustness Task
Raj Dabre and Eiichiro Sumita

System Description: The Submission of FOKUS to the WMT 19 Robustness Task
Cristian Grozea

Thursday, August 1, 2019 (continued)

11:00–12:30   Session 2: Shared Task Poster Session I

USAAR-DFKI – The Transference Architecture for English–German Automatic Post-Editing
Santanu Pal, Hongfei Xu, Nico Herbig, Antonio Krüger and Josef van Genabith

APE through Neural and Statistical MT with Augmented Data. ADAPT/DCU Submission to the WMT 2019 APE Shared Task
Dimitar Shterionov, Joachim Wagner and Félix do Carmo

Effort-Aware Neural Automatic Post-Editing
Amirhossein Tebbifakhr, Matteo Negri and Marco Turchi

UdS Submission for the WMT 19 Automatic Post-Editing Task
Hongfei Xu, Qiuhui Liu and Josef van Genabith

11:00–12:30   *Shared Task: Biomedical Translation*

Terminology-Aware Segmentation and Domain Feature for the WMT19 Biomedical Translation Task
Casimiro Pio Carrino, Bardia Rafieian, Marta R. Costa-jussà and José A. R. Fonollosa

Exploring Transfer Learning and Domain Data Selection for the Biomedical Translation
Noor-e- Hira, Sadaf Abdul Rauf, Kiran Kiani, Ammara Zafar and Raheel Nawaz

Huawei's NMT Systems for the WMT 2019 Biomedical Translation Task
Wei Peng, Jianfeng Liu, Liangyou Li and Qun Liu

UCAM Biomedical Translation at WMT19: Transfer Learning Multi-domain Ensembles
Danielle Saunders, Felix Stahlberg and Bill Byrne

BSC Participation in the WMT Translation of Biomedical Abstracts
Felipe Soares and Martin Krallinger

11:00–12:30   *Shared Task: Similar Languages*

The MLLP-UPV Spanish-Portuguese and Portuguese-Spanish Machine Translation Systems for WMT19 Similar Language Translation Task
Pau Baquero-Arnal, Javier Iranzo-Sánchez, Jorge Civera and Alfons Juan

14:00–15:30   Session 7: Invited Talk (chair: Matt Post)

14:00–15:30   *Marine Carpuat (University of Maryland): Semantic, Style and Other Data Divergences in Neural Machine Translation*

15:30–16:00   *Coffee Break*

16:00–17:30   Session 8: Research Papers on Applications (chair: Marco Turchi)

16:00–16:15   *Hierarchical Document Encoder for Parallel Corpus Mining*
Mandy Guo, Yinfei Yang, Keith Stevens, Daniel Cer, Heming Ge, Yun-hsuan Sung, Brian Strope and Ray Kurzweil

16:15–16:30   *The Effect of Translationese in Machine Translation Test Sets*
Mike Zhang and Antonio Toral

16:30–16:45   *Customizing Neural Machine Translation for Subtitling*
Evgeny Matusov, Patrick Wilken and Yota Georgakopoulou

16:45–17:00   *Integration of Dubbing Constraints into Machine Translation*
Ashutosh Saboo and Timo Baumann

17:00–17:15   *Widening the Representation Bottleneck in Neural Machine Translation with Lexical Shortcuts*
Denis Emelin, Ivan Titov and Rico Sennrich

17:15–17:30   *A High-Quality Multilingual Dataset for Structured Documentation Translation*
Kazuma Hashimoto, Raffaella Buschiazzo, James Bradbury, Teresa Marshall, Richard Socher and Caiming Xiong

Findings of the 2019 Conference on Machine Translation (WMT19)

Loïc Barrault
Le Mans Université

Ondřej Bojar
Charles University

Marta R. Costa-jussà
UPC

Christian Federmann
Microsoft Cloud + AI

Mark Fishel
University of Tartu

Yvette Graham
Dublin City University

Barry Haddow
University of Edinburgh

Matthias Huck
LMU Munich

Philipp Koehn
JHU / University of Edinburgh

Shervin Malmasi
Harvard Medical School

Christof Monz
University of Amsterdam

Mathias Müller
University of Zurich

Santanu Pal
Saarland University

Matt Post
JHU

Marcos Zampieri
University of Wolverhampton

Abstract

This paper presents the results of the premier shared task organized alongside the Conference on Machine Translation (WMT) 2019. Participants were asked to build machine translation systems for any of 18 language pairs, to be evaluated on a test set of news stories. The main metric for this task is human judgment of translation quality. The task was also opened up to additional test suites to probe specific aspects of translation.

1 Introduction

The Fourth Conference on Machine Translation (WMT) held at ACL 2019[1] hosts a number of shared tasks on various aspects of machine translation. This conference builds on 13 previous editions of WMT as workshops and conferences (Koehn and Monz, 2006; Callison-Burch et al., 2007, 2008, 2009, 2010, 2011, 2012; Bojar et al., 2013, 2014, 2015, 2016, 2017, 2018).

This year we conducted several official tasks. We report in this paper on the news and similar translation tasks. Additional shared tasks are described in separate papers in these proceedings:

- biomedical translation (Bawden et al., 2019b)
- automatic post-editing (Chatterjee et al., 2019)
- metrics (Ma et al., 2019)
- quality estimation (Fonseca et al., 2019)
- parallel corpus filtering (Koehn et al., 2019)
- robustness (Li et al., 2019b)

In the news translation task (Section 2), participants were asked to translate a shared test set, optionally restricting themselves to the provided training data ("constrained" condition). We held 18 translation tasks this year, between English and each of Chinese, Czech (into Czech only), German, Finnish, Lithuanian, and Russian. New this year were Gujarati↔English and Kazakh↔English. Both pose a lesser resourced data condition on challenging language pairs. System outputs for each task were evaluated both automatically and manually.

This year the news translation task had two additional sub-tracks: an unsupervised language pair (German→Czech) and a language pair not involving English (German↔French). Both sub-tracks were included into the general list of news translation submissions and are described in more detail in the corresponding subsections of Section 2.

The human evaluation (Section 3) involves asking human judges to score sentences output by anonymized systems. We obtained large numbers of assessments from researchers who contributed evaluations proportional to the number of tasks they entered. In addition, we used Mechanical Turk to collect further evaluations. This year, the official manual evaluation metric is again based on judgments of adequacy on a 100-point scale, a method we explored in the previous years with convincing results in terms of the trade-off between annotation effort and reliable distinctions between systems.

The primary objectives of WMT are to evaluate the state of the art in machine translation, to disseminate common test sets and public training data with published performance numbers, and to refine evaluation and estimation methodologies for machine translation. As before, all of the data, translations, and collected human judgments are publicly available.[2] We hope these datasets serve as a valuable resource for research into data-

---

[1] http://www.statmt.org/wmt19/

[2] http://statmt.org/wmt19/results.html

Proceedings of the Fourth Conference on Machine Translation (WMT), Volume 2: Shared Task Papers (Day 1) pages 1–61
Florence, Italy, August 1-2, 2019. ©2019 Association for Computational Linguistics

driven machine translation, automatic evaluation, or prediction of translation quality. News translations are also available for interactive visualization and comparison of differences between systems at `http://wmt.ufal.cz/` using MT-ComparEval (Sudarikov et al., 2016).

In order to gain further insight into the performance of individual MT systems, we organized a call for dedicated "test suites", each focussing on some particular aspect of translation quality. A brief overview of the test suites is provided in Section 4.

2 News Translation Task

The recurring WMT task examines translation between English and other languages in the news domain. As in the previous year, we include Chinese, Czech, German, Finnish and Russian (into and out of English, except for Czech were only out of English was included). New language pairs for this year were Gujarati, Lithuanian and Kazakh (to and from English), and French-German. We also used German-Czech (joining the corresponding parts of the English-X test sets) for the unsupervised subtask.

2.1 Test Data

The test data for this year's task (except for the French-German set) was selected from online news sources, as in previous years, with translation produced specifically for the task. For language pairs that had appeared before at WMT (and so had previous years' data for development testing) we selected approximately 2000 sentences in each of the languages in the pair and translated them into the other language. The source English sentences were common across all test sets. For the new language pairs (i.e. English-Gujarati, English-Kazakh and English-Lithuanian) we released development sets at the start of the campaign, consisting of approximately 1000 sentences in each language in the pair, translated into the other language. For Gujarati-English the development set was selected from online news in the same way as the test set, whereas for Kazakh-English the development set was selected (and removed) from the news-commentary training set. The test sets for these new language pairs was half the size of the test sets of the existing language pairs.

Different to previous years, all test sets (ex-

cept for French-German and German-Czech) only included naturally occurring text on the source side. In previous years, the way we produced an English-X test set was to take 1500 sentences of English text, translate these into language X, then take 1500 sentences in language X, and translated them into English. These 3000 translation pairs were then used for the English-X task, and for the X-English task, meaning that 50% of the sentences in each test has "translationese" on the source side, potentially leading to distortions in automatic and human evaluation (Graham et al., 2019a). This year, we did not include such "flipped" test data in the test sets, meaning that the English-X and X-English sets were non-overlapping.

The composition of the test documents is shown in Table 1, the size of the test sets in terms of sentence pairs and words is given in Figure 2.

The translation of the test sets was sponsored by the EU H2020 projects Bergamot and GoURMET (English-Czech and Gujarati-English respectively), by Yandex (Kazakh-English and Russian-English), Microsoft (Chinese-English and German-English), Tilde (Lithuanian-English), the University of Helsinki (Finnish-English) and Lingua Custodia[3] (a part of French-German test set).

The translations into Czech were carried out by the agency Překlady textu, s.r.o.[4] with the instructions for translators as given to all agencies:

- preserve line and document boundaries,

- translate from scratch, without post-editing,

- translate as literally as possible, but ensure that the translation is still a fluent sentence in the target language,

- do not add or remove information from the translations, and do not add translator's comments.

- The point is to have a linguistically nice document, but to be matching the original text as closely as possible in terms of segmentation into sentences (e.g. we don't want 3 English sentences combined into 1 long Czech complex sentence).

---

[3]`http://www.linguacustodia.finance/`
[4]`http://www.preklady-textu.cz/`

Europarl Parallel Corpus

	Czech ↔ English		Finnish ↔ English		German ↔ English		Lithuanian ↔ English		French ↔ German	
Sentences	645,241		1,835,071		1,825,741		631,309		1,726,419	
Words	14,948,882	17,380,337	35,766,351	50,233,589	48,125,049	50,506,042	13,448,546	17,070,302	46,014,903	41,000,331
Distinct words	172,450	63,287	677,673	112,751	371,743	113,958	237,740	62,885	388,613	616,702

News Commentary Parallel Corpus

	Czech ↔ English		German ↔ English		Russian ↔ English	
Sentences	240,243		329,506		281,184	
Words	5,372,690	5,938,908	8,363,213	8,295,418	7,132,754	7,447,684
Distinct words	172,215	68,966	197,056	80,623	194,808	76,953

	Chinese ↔ English		Kazakh ↔ English		French ↔ German	
Sentences	311,922		7,475		256,226	
Words	–	7,926,131	157,171	193,101	8,049,218	6,607,025
Distinct words	–	75,955	24,676	13,982	82,740	171,410

Common Crawl Parallel Corpus

	German ↔ English		Czech ↔ English		Russian ↔ English		French ↔ German	
Sentences	2,399,123		161,838		878,386		622,288	
Words	54,575,405	58,870,638	3,529,783	3,927,378	21,018,793	21,535,122	13,991,973	12,217,457
Distinct words	1,640,835	823,480	210,170	128,212	764,203	432,062	676,725	932,137

ParaCrawl Parallel Corpus

	German ↔ English		Czech ↔ English		Lithuanian ↔ English	
Sentences	31,358,551		5,862,521		1,368,691	
Words	559,348,288	598,362,329	89,066,831	93,943,773	20,992,360	23,111,861
Distinct Words	8,081,990	4,888,665	1,477,399	1,108,068	723,940	495,311

	Finnish ↔ English		Russian ↔ English		French ↔ German	
Sentences	3,944,929		12,061,155		7,222,574	
Words	55,245,472	66,352,625	182,325,667	210,770,856	145,190,707	123,205,701
Distinct Words	1,787,403	944,140	2,958,831	2,385,075	1,534,068	2,368,682

EU Press Release Parallel Corpus

	German ↔ English		Finnish ↔ English		Lithuanian ↔ English	
Sentences	1,480,789		583,223		213,173	
Words	29,458,773	30,097,541	8,052,607	11,244,602	4,097,713	4,817,655
Distinct words	399,545	165,084	315,394	94,979	106,603	53,239

Chinese Parallel Corpora

	casia2015	casict2011	casict2015	datum2011	datum2017	neu2017
Sentences	1,050,000	1,936,633	2,036,834	1,000,004	999,985	2,000,000
Words (en)	20,571,578	34,866,598	22,802,353	24,632,984	25,182,185	29,696,442
Distinct words (en)	470,452	627,630	435,010	316,277	312,164	624,420

Yandex 1M Parallel Corpus

	Russian ↔ English	
Sentences	1,000,000	
Words	24,121,459	26,107,293
Distinct	701,809	387,646

CzEng v1.7 Parallel Corpus

	Czech ↔ English	
Sentences	57,065,358	
Words	667,091,440	751,312,654
Distinct	2,592,850	1,639,658

WikiTitles Parallel Corpus

	Czech ↔ English		German ↔ English		Finnish ↔ English		Gujarati ↔ English	
Sentences	362,014		1,305,135		376,572		11,670	
Words	862,719	924,948	2,817,660	3,271,223	761,213	912,044	23,780	24,098
Distinct	197,743	168,449	618,723	525,023	232,236	183,285	11,557	10,400

	Kazakh ↔ English		Lithuanian ↔ English		Russian ↔ English		Chinese ↔ English	
Sentences	117,041		132,182		1,032,343		765,674	
Words	189,565	231,166	286,837	304,043	2,786,728	2,793,609	–	2,031,512
Distinct	94,525	86,587	95,004	83,404	481,018	410,112	–	341,166

United Nations Parallel Corpus

	Russian ↔ English		Chinese ↔ English	
Sentences	23,239,280		15,886,041	
Words	482,966,738	524,719,646	–	372,612,596
Distinct	3,857,656	2,737,469	–	1,981,413

Figure 1: Statistics for the training sets used in the translation task. The number of words and the number of distinct words (case-insensitive) is based on the provided tokenizer and IndicNLP (https://github.com/anoopkunchukuttan/indic_nlp_library) for Gujarati.

Crawled Kazakh Parallel Data

	Kazakh ↔ English		Russian ↔ English	
Sentences	97,654		5,063,666	
Words	1,224,971	1,524,384	111,492,772	115,950,305
Distinct	89,500	39,704	1,022,853	774,991

Crawled Gujarati-English Parallel Data

	The Bible		Localisation		Indian Govt.		Wikipedia	
Sentences	7,807		107,637		10,650		18,033	
Words	228,113	206,440	763,521	750,659	154,364	177,141	370,972	373,491
Distinct	15,623	5,945	15,406	8,549	23,489	16,361	57,431	32,227

Monolingual Wikipedia Data

	Gujarati	Kazakh	Lithuanian
Sentences	384,485	2,179,180	2,059,198
Words	6,779,645	28,130,741	31,006,475
Distinct words	373,840	1,115,320	970,696

News Language Model Data

	English	German	Czech	Russian	Finnish
Sentences 199,900,557		275,690,481	72,157,988	80,148,714	16,834,066
Words	4,611,843,099	4,922,055,629	1,193,459,840	1,461,279,309	213,048,421
Distinct words	6,910,887	34,747,433	4,668,868	4,771,311	5,084,937

	Gujarati	Kazakh	Lithuanian	French	Chinese
Sentences	244,919	772,892	375,206	76,848,192	1,749,968
Words	3,776,100	13,172,313	6,782,918	1,858,333,964	–
Distinct words	183,425	506,923	288,266	3,376,105	–

Document-Split News LM Data (not dedudped)

	English	German	Czech
Sentences	419,796,579	533,619,919	92,388,432
Words	9,305,189,308	9,520,383,021	1,512,084,445
Distinct words	6,813,799	34,668,232	4,582,601

Common Crawl Language Model Data

	English	German	Czech	Russian	Finnish
Sent.	3,074,921,453	2,872,785,485	333,498,145	1,168,529,851	157,264,161
Words	65,128,419,540	65,154,042,103	6,694,811,063	23,313,060,950	2,935,402,545
Dist.	342,760,462	339,983,035	50,162,437	101,436,673	47,083,545

	Chinese	Lithuanian	Kazakh	Gujarati	French
Sent.	1,672,324,647	103,103,449	10,862,371	3,729,406	
Words	–	2,907,519,260	261,518,626	80,120,267	
Dist.	–	25,343,195	4,381,617	2,068,064	

Test Sets

	Chinese → EN		EN → Chinese		EN → Czech		Finnish → EN		EN → Finnish		German → EN	
Sentences.	2000		1997		1997		1996		1997		2000	
Words	–	80,666	48,021	–	48,021	43,860	24,797	36,809	48,021	38,068	36,141	39,561
Distinct words	–	7,939	7,372	–	7,372	11,537	10,454	5,763	7,372	12,789	8,763	6,764

	EN → German		Gujarati → EN		EN → Gujarati		Kazakh → EN		EN → Kazakh		Lithuanian→ EN	
Sentences.	1997		1016		998		1000		998		1000	
Words	48,021	49,069	15,691	17,950	24,074	22,285	16,259	20,376	24,074	19,142	20,027	26,020
Distinct words	7,372	9,659	5,013	3,388	4,772	6,558	6,200	3,761	4,772	7,113	7,178	4,424

	EN→ Lithuanian		Russian → EN		EN → Russian		German → Czech		French ↔ German	
Sentences.	998		2000		1997		1997		1701	
Words	24,074	20,603	35,821	43,158	48,021	48,298	49,779	43,860	46,216	36,563
Distinct words	4,772	7,046	10,564	6,311	7,372	12,385	9,502	11,537	5,942	7,042

Figure 2: Statistics for the training and test sets used in the translation task. The number of words and the number of distinct words (case-insensitive) is based on the provided tokenizer and IndicNLP (https://github.com/anoopkunchukuttan/indic_nlp_library) for Gujarati.

Language	Sources (Number of Documents)
Chinese	Chinanews (111), Macao Govt. (4), QQ (10), Reuters (31), RFI (2), Tsrus (5)
English I	ABC News (3), BBC (12), CBS News (2), CNBC (3), CNN (3), Daily Mail (9), Euronews (3), Guardian (3), Independent (3), News Week (6), NY Times (4), Reuters (3), Russia Today (1), The Scotsman (3), The Telegraph (2), UPI (2)
English II	ABC News (3), BBC (6), CBS News (4), CNBC (2), CNN (3), Daily Mail (2), Euronews (2), Fox News (1), Guardian (2), Independent (1), News Week (5), NY Times (4), Reuters (9), Russia Today (4), The Scotsman (6), The Telegraph (4), The Local (1), UPI (2)
Finnish	ESS (8), Helsinginsanomat (12), Iltalehti (33), Iltasanomat (34), Kaleva (19), Kansanuutiset (1), Karjalainen (26), Kotiseutu Uutiset (1)
German	Abdendzeitung München (9), Abendzeitung Nürnberg (1), Aachener Nachrichten (7), Augsburger Allgemine (2), Bergdorfer Zeitung (2), Braunschweiger Zeiting (2), Cuxhavener Nachrichten (1), Come On (2), Der Standart (9), Deutsche Welle (1), Duelmener Zeitung (7), Euronews (2), Frankfurter Neue Presse (2), Frankfurter Rundschau (4), Freipresse (1), Geinhaüser Tageblatt (1), Gmünder Tagespost (1), Göttinger Tageblatt (2), Handelsblatt (3), Hannoversche Allgemeine Zeitung (1), Hersfelder Zeitung (2), HNA (2), Infranken (5), In Süd Thüringen (3), Kieler Nachrichten (6), Merkur Online (5), Morgen Post (1), Nachrichten (4), N TV (3), NW News (1), NZZ (6), OE24 (5), PAZ Online (1), Passauer Neue Presse (1), Rhein Zeitung (1), Rheinische Poste (1), Salzburg (3), Schwarzwälder Bote (2), Söster Anzeiger (2), Südkurier (1), Usinger Anzeiger (1), Westfaelischer Anzeige (2), Welt (2), Wienerzeitung (2), Westfaelische Nachrichten (18), Zeit (1), Zeitungsverlag Waiblingen (2)
Gujarati	ABP Asmita (13), BBC (3), Divya Bhaskar (20), Global Gujarati News (13), Web Dunia (21)
Kazakh	7Kun (4), Aktobe Gazeti (3), Alkyn (4), Astana Akshamy (6), Atyray (1), Kazakh Adabieti (1), Egemen (5), Jaskazaq (11), Akorda/Kazinform (34), SN.kz (5), Zamedia (1)
Lithuanian	Delfi (22), Diena (25), Lietuvos Zinios (7), TV3 (12), Voruta (2), VZ (8)
Russian	AIF.ru (14), Altapress (4), Argumenti (3), Euronews (13), Fakty (9), Gazeta (7), Infox (3), Izvestiya (38), Kommersant (12), Lenta (14), Nezavisimaya Gazeta (8), Moskovskij Komsomolets (19), Parlamentskaya Gazeta (1), Rossiskaya Gazeta (1), ERR (1), Sovetskij Sport (31), Vedomosti (1), Nasha Versiya (1), Vesti (14), Za Rulyom (2)

Table 1: Composition of the test sets. English I was used for all language pairs, whereas English II was used for all except Gujarati, Kazakh and Lithuanian. For more details see the XML test files. The `docid` tag gives the source and the date for each document in the test set, and the `origlang` tag indicates the original source language.

2.2 Training Data

As in past years we provided parallel corpora to train translation models, monolingual corpora to train language models, and development sets to tune system parameters.

This year, we proposed document-level evaluation for the English-German and English-Czech tasks. We therefore attempted to provide training corpora with document boundaries intact wherever possible. We produced new versions of the Europarl corpora with document boundaries, an updated version of news-commentary with document boundaries, and a release of the Rapid corpus for German-English with document boundaries intact. The CzEng[5] already included context for each sentence, so we did not update it. We also produced a WikiTitle corpus this year for all language pairs, and allowed the use of a new ParaCrawl corpus (v3). The UN, Common-Crawl and Yandex corpora were unchanged since last year.

For Gujarati-English, we allowed several extra parallel corpora (the Bible, a localisation corpus from Opus, the Emille corpus, a Wikipedia corpus and a crawled corpus specifically for this task),

as well as encouraging participants to experiment with the HindEnCorp[6] for transfer learning.

For Kazakh-English, we released a crawled corpus (from KazakhTV) prepared by Bagdat Myrzakhmetov of Nazarbayev University as well as a much larger Kazakh-Russian corpus for transfer learning or pivoting.

We released new monolingual news crawls for each of the languages used in the task. For German and Czech, we released versions of these with the document boundaries intact, for participants wishing to experiment with document-level models.

Some statistics about the training materials are given in Figures 1 and 2.

2.3 Unsupervised Sub-Task

Following up on the unsupervised learning challenge from last year, we again invited participants to build *unsupervised machine translation* systems without the use of any parallel training corpora.

While WMT has been (and is) providing considerable amounts of bitext for most of the language pairs covered in its shared tasks on machine translation of news, there is however still a shortage of available parallel resources between

---

[5]http://ufal.mff.cuni.cz/czeng/czeng17

[6]http://ufallab.ms.mff.cuni.cz/~bojar/hindencorp/

lots of combinations of two human languages. Bridging through a global hub language—such as English—can be a solution in scenarios where no bitext exists between two languages but parallel corpora with the hub language are at hand for each of the two. This "pivot translation" approach of cascading source–English and English–target MT is well-established. More recent research on unsupervised translation, on the other hand, seeks to altogether eliminate the need for parallel training data. Unsupervised translation techniques should be capable of learning translation correspondences from only monolingual data in two different languages, thus potentially offering a solution to machine translation between each and every possible pair of written human languages.

Previous year's evaluation had indicated that, unsurprisingly, unsupervised translation clearly lags behind supervised translation. But we had also seen promising early-stage research results which seemed to suggest that the difficult task of unsupervised learning in machine translation may not be impossible to solve in the long run. When acceptable quality can be reached with unsupervised methods, these methods will likely not directly compete with supervised translation, but rather be deployed to cover language pairs where supervised translation is inapplicable due to a lack of parallel data.

The language pair for the WMT19 unsupervised sub-task was German–Czech. Only the German→Czech translation direction was evaluated, not the Czech→German direction. German is a compounding language, and German and Czech are both morphologically rich. Linguistic peculiarities on both the source *and* the target side impose difficulties other than for last year's languages, where we paired Turkish, Estonian, and German each with English for the unsupervised sub-task. By choosing German–Czech, we hope to simulate practical application scenarios for fully unsupervised translation. However, note that there actually is German–Czech parallel data, e.g. from European parliamentary proceedings. German–English and English–Czech bitexts likewise exist in large amounts. We asked the participants to avoid any of these corpora, as well as any monolingual or parallel data for other languages and language pairs. Permissible training data for the unsupervised sub-task were only the monolingual corpora from the constrained monolingual WMT

News Crawls of German and Czech. Last years' parallel dev and test sets (from the development tarball[7]) were allowed for bootstrapping purposes. Since they contain a few thousand sentences of high-quality German–Czech parallel text, we advised participants to make only very moderate use of this data. Using it directly as a training corpus was strongly discouraged, but we wanted to provide system builders with a means to evaluate and track progress internally during system development. We also did not prohibit its use for lightweight (hyper-)parameter optimization.

Seven German→Czech unsupervised machine translation systems were submitted and marked as primary submissions by the participating teams. The unsupervised system submissions were evaluated along with four online systems for the German→Czech language pairs, which we assume are all supervised MT engines. The official results of the human evaluation are presented in Table 12 (Section 3).

2.4 EUElections German→French and French→German Sub-Tasks

The second new sub-task this year included translating news data between French and German (both directions) on the topic of the European Elections. We collected a development and test set from online news websites. Articles were originally in French or in German. Statistics of the corpora a presented in the following table. In or-

	#lines	#token FR	#token DE
dev2019 FULL	1512	33833	28733
- source FR	462	11081	10890
- source DE	1050	22752	17843
test2019 FULL	1701	38154	31560
- source FR	335	7678	7195
- source DE	1366	30476	24365

Table 2: Statistics of the French↔German dev and test sets with breakdown statistics based on the source language.

der to analyse the impact of the original source language of document on systems' performance, we computed the METEOR scores on the full corpus (FULL), on the sentences from articles initially written in French (second column) or in German (third column). Results are shown in the Tables 3 and 4. One can notice some differences depending on the language direction. While the performance of the systems when translating from French to German seems to heavily depend on the

---

[7]http://data.statmt.org/wmt19/
translation-task/dev.tgz

Systems	FULL	source FR	source DE
MSRA.MADL	47.3	38.3	50.0
eTranslation	45.4	37.4	47.8
LIUM	43.7	37.5	45.5
MLLP-UPV	41.5	36.4	43.0
onlineA	40.8	35.4	42.3
TartuNLP	39.2	34.8	40.5
onlineB	39.1	35.3	40.2
onlineY	39.0	34.7	40.2
onlineG	38.5	34.6	39.7
onlineX	38.1	35.6	38.8

Table 3: French→German Meteor scores.

Systems	FULL	source FR	source DE
MSRA.MADL	52.0	51.9	52.0
LinguaCustodia	51.3	52.5	51.0
MLLP_UPV	49.5	49.9	49.4
Kyoto_University_T2T	48.8	49.7	48.6
LIUM	48.3	46.5	48.7
onlineY	47.5	43.7	48.4
onlineB	46.4	43.7	47.0
TartuNLP	46.3	45.0	46.7
onlineA	45.3	43.7	45.8
onlineX	42.7	41.6	42.9
onlineG	41.7	40.9	41.9

Table 4: German→French Meteor scores. Green cells highlight the systems performing equally when source text is in either language. The gray cells show that the TartuNLP system performs better with French source text relatively to its overall score.

original language of the document, this is less the case for the German to French direction. These results suggest that the German text produced by translating French documents is somewhat different from the German text originally produced even though native German translators were involved in the process. This is of course not new and is related to *translationese* (Koppel and Ordan, 2011). As shown in Table 2, only one fifth of the test corpus originates from French documents. With this in mind, Table 4 suggests that the *translationese* is less obvious for French text.

For next year, we plan to produce additional data with documents created during and after the elections.

2.5 Submitted Systems

In 2019, we received a total of 153 submissions. The participating institutions are listed in Table 5 and detailed in the rest of this section. Each system did not necessarily appear in all translation tasks. We also included online MT systems (originating from 5 services), which we anonymized as ONLINE-A,B,G,X,Y.

For presentation of the results, systems are treated as either *constrained* or *unconstrained*, depending on whether their models were trained only on the provided data. Since we do not know how they were built, the online systems are treated as unconstrained during the automatic and human evaluations.

In the rest of this sub-section, we provide brief details of the submitted systems, for those in cases where the authors provided such details.

2.5.1 AFRL

AFRL-SYSCOMB19 (**Gwinnup et al., 2019**) is a system combination of a Marian ensemble system, two distinct OpenNMT systems, a Sockeye-based Elastic Weight Consolidation system, and one Moses phrase-based system.

AFRL-EWC (**Gwinnup et al., 2019**) is a Sockeye Transformer system trained with the default network configuration as described in Vaswani et al. (2017). The model is trained using the prepared parallel corpus used in other AFRL systems. A fine-tuning corpus is created from the 2014–2017 WMT Russian–English test sets. EWC is applied as described in Thompson et al. (2019). The final submission is an ensemble decode of the four best-performing checkpoints from a single training run when scoring newstest2018.

2.5.2 APERTIUM-FIN-ENG (**Pirinen, 2019**)

APERTIUM-FIN-ENG is a standard shallow rule-based machine translation using Apertium.

2.5.3 APPRENTICE-C (**Li and Specia, 2019**)

APPRENTICE-C is a RNN-based encoder-decoder with pre-trained embedding enhanced by character information. The system is trained on 10.38M Chinese-English sentence pairs after tokenization, filtering by alignment and BPE . Pre-trained embedding is trained on monolingual data for 5 iterations and used as an initialization for the RNN model.

2.5.4 AYLIEN_MULTILINGUAL (**Hokamp et al., 2019**)

The Aylien research team built a Multilingual NMT system which is trained on all WMT2019 language pairs in all directions, then fine-tuned for a small number of iterations on Gujarati-English data only, including some self-backtranslated data.

2.5.5 BAIDU (**Sun et al., 2019**)

Baidu systems are based on the Transformer architecture with several improvements. Data selection, back translation, data augmentation, knowledge distillation, domain adaptation, model ensemble and re-ranking are employed and proven effective in our experiments.

Team	Institution
AFRL	Air Force Research Laboratory (Gwinnup et al., 2019)
APERTIUM-FIN-ENG	Apertium (Pirinen, 2019)
APPRENTICE-C	Apprentice (Li and Specia, 2019)
AYLIEN_MULTILINGUAL	Aylien Ltd. (Hokamp et al., 2019)
BAIDU	Baidu (Sun et al., 2019)
BTRANS	(no associated paper)
BASELINE-RE-RERANK	(no associated paper)
CAiRE	(Liu et al., 2019)
CUNI	Charles University (Popel et al., 2019; Kocmi and Bojar, 2019) and (Kvapilíková et al., 2019)
DBMS-KU	Kumamoto University, Telkom University, Indonesian Institute of Sciences (Budiwati et al., 2019)
DFKI-NMT	DFKI (Zhang and van Genabith, 2019)
ETRANSLATION	eTranslation (Oravecz et al., 2019)
FACEBOOK FAIR	Facebook AI Research (Ng et al., 2019)
GTCOM	GTCOM (Bei et al., 2019)
HELSINKI NLP	University of Helsinki (Talman et al., 2019)
IIITH-MT	IIIT Hyderabad (Goyal and Sharma, 2019)
IITP	IIT Patna (Sen et al., 2019)
JHU	Johns Hopkins University (Marchisio et al., 2019)
JUMT	(no associated paper)
JU_SAARLAND	University of Saarland (Mondal et al., 2019)
KSAI	Kingsoft AI (Guo et al., 2019)
KYOTO UNIVERSITY	University of Kyoto (Cromieres and Kurohashi, 2019)
LINGUA CUSTODIA	Lingua Custodia (Burlot, 2019)
LIUM	LIUM (Bougares et al., 2019)
LMU-NMT	LMU Munich (Stojanovski and Fraser, 2019; Stojanovski et al., 2019)
MLLP-UPV	MLLP, Technical University of Valencia (Iranzo-Sánchez et al., 2019)
MS TRANSLATOR	Microsoft Translator (Junczys-Dowmunt, 2019)
MSRA	Microsoft Research Asia (Xia et al., 2019)
NIUTRANS	Northeastern University / NiuTrans Co., Ltd. (Li et al., 2019a)
NICT	National Institute of Information and Communications Technology (Dabre et al., 2019; Marie et al., 2019b)
NRC	National Research Council of Canada (Littell et al., 2019)
PARFDA	Boğaziçi University (Biçici, 2019)
PROMT-NMT	PROMT LLC (Molchanov, 2019)
RUG	University of Groningen (Toral et al., 2019)
RWTH AACHEN	RWTH Aachen (Rosendahl et al., 2019)
TALP_UPC_2019	TALP Research Center, Universitat Politècnica de Catalunya (Casas et al., 2019)
TARTUNLP-C	University of Tartu (Tättar et al., 2019)
TILDE-NC-NMT	Tilde (Pinnis et al., 2019)
UALACANT	Universitat d'Alacant (Sánchez-Cartagena et al., 2019)
UCAM	University of Cambridge (Stahlberg et al., 2019)
UDS-DFKI	Saarland University, DFKI (España-Bonet and Ruiter, 2019)
UEDIN	University of Edinburgh (Bawden et al., 2019a)
UMD	University of Maryland (Briakou and Carpuat, 2019)
USTC-MCC	(no associated paper)
USYD	University of Sydney (Ding and Tao, 2019)
XZL-NMT	(no associated paper)

Table 5: Participants in the shared translation task. Not all teams participated in all language pairs. The translations from the online systems were not submitted by their respective companies but were obtained by us, and are therefore anonymized in a fashion consistent with previous years of the workshop.

2.5.6 BTRANS

Unfortunately, no details are available for this system.

2.5.7 BASELINE-RE-RERANK (no associated paper)

BASELINE-RE-RERANK is a standard Transformer, with corpus filtering, pre-processing, post-processing, averaging and ensembling as well as n-best list reranking.

2.5.8 CAiRE (Liu et al., 2019)

CAiRE is a hybrid system that took part only in the unsupervised track. The system builds upon phrase-based MT and a pre-trained language model, combining word-level and subword-level NMT. A series of pre-processing and post-processing steps improves the performance, e.g. placeholders for numbers and dates, recasing and quotes normalization.

2.5.9 Charles University (CUNI) Systems

CUNI-T2T-TRANSFER (Kocmi and Bojar, 2019) are Transformer neural machine translation systems (as implemented in Tensor2tensor) for Kazakh↔English, Gujarati↔English. CUNI-T2T-TRANSFER focused on transfer learning from a high-resource language pair (Russian-English and Czech-English, respectively) followed by iterative back-translation.

CUNI-DocTransformer-T2T2019 and CUNI-Transformer-T2T2019 (Popel et al., 2019) are trained in the T2T framework following the last year submission (Popel, 2018), but training on WMT19 document-level parallel and monoliongual data. During decoding, each document is split into overlapping multi-sentence segments, where only the "middle" sentences in each segment are used for the final translation. CUNI-Transformer-T2T2019 is the same system as CUNI-DocTransformer-T2T2019, just applied on separate sentences during decoding.

CUNI-DocTransformer-Marian (Popel et al., 2019) is a Transformer model as implemented in Marian and trained in a context-aware ("document-level") fashion. The training started with the same technique as the last year's submission but it was finetuned on document-level parallel and monolingual data by translating triples of adjacent sentences at once. If possible, only the middle sentence was considered for the final translation hypothesis, otherwise shorter context of two sentences or just a single sentence was used.

CUNI-Transformer-T2T2018 (Popel, 2018) is the exact same system as used last year.

CUNI-Transformer-Marian (Popel et al., 2019) is a "reimplementation" of the last year's system (Popel, 2018) in Marian (Junczys-Dowmunt et al., 2018).

CUNI-Unsupervised-NER-post (Kvapilíková et al., 2019) follows the strategy of Artetxe et al. (2018), creating a seed phrase-based system where the phrase table is initialized from cross-lingual embedding mappings trained on monolingual data, followed by a neural machine translation system trained on synthetic parallel corpus. The synthetic corpus is produced by the seed phrase-based MT system or by a such a model refined through iterative back-translation. CUNI-Unsupervised-NER-post further focuses on the handling of named entities, i.e. the part of vocabulary where the cross-lingual embedding mapping suffer most.

2.5.10 DBMS-KU (Budiwati et al., 2019)

The system DBMS-KU INTERPOLATION uses Linear Interpolation and Fillup Interpolation method with different language models, i.e., 3-gram and 5-gram. It combines a direct phrase table with pivot phrase table, pivoting through the Russian language.

2.5.11 DFKI-NMT (Zhang and van Genabith, 2019)

DFKI-NMT is a Transformer model trained using various techniques including data selection (using custom Transformer-based language models), back-translation and in-domain fine-tuning.

2.5.12 EN-DE-TASK

Unfortunately, no details are available for this system.

2.5.13 ETRANSLATION (Oravecz et al., 2019)

ETRANSLATION En-De ETRANSLATION's En-De system is an ensemble of 3 base Transformers and a Transformer-type language model, trained from all available parallel data (cleaned up and filtered with dual conditional cross-entropy filtering) and with additional back-translated data generated from monolingual news. Each Transformer model is fine tuned on previous years' test sets.

ETRANSLATION **Fr-De** The Fr-De system is an ensemble of 2 big Transformers (with size 8192 FFN layers). Back-translation data was selected using topic modelling techniques to tune the model towards the domain defined in the task.

ETRANSLATION **En-Lt** The En-Lt system is an ensemble of 2 big Transformers (as for Fr-De) and a Transformer type language model. The training data contains the Rapid corpus and the news domain back-translated data sets 2 times oversampled.

ETRANSLATION **Ru-En** The Ru-En system is a single base Transformer trained only on true parallel data (including ParaCrawl but excluding the UN corpus) filtered in the same way as in the other submissions and fine tuned on previous test sets.

2.5.14 FACEBOOK FAIR (Ng et al., 2019)

Facebook FAIR system is a pure sentence level system, it is an ensemble of 3 Big Transformer models with FFN layers of size 8192. Trained on the mix of bitext and back-translated newscrawl data, oversampling was used to keep the effective ratio of bitext and back-translated data the same. Sampling from an ensemble of 3 models trained on bitext only was used to generate back-translations. The models were fine-tuned on in-domain data and a final noisy channel reranking was applied. All the training data (bitext and monolingual) was cleaned using langid filtering.

2.5.15 FRANK-S-MT

Unfortunately, no details are available for this system.

2.5.16 GTCOM (Bei et al., 2019)

GTCOM's systems (sysNameGTCOM-Primary) mainly focus on backtranslation, knowledge distillation and reranking to build a competitive model with transformer architecture. Also, the language model is applied to filter monolingual data, back-translated data and parallel data. The techniques for data filtering include filtering by rules, language models. Furthermore, they apply knowledge distillation techniques and right-to-left (R2L) reranking.

2.5.17 HELSINKI NLP (Talman et al., 2019)

HELSINKI NLP is a Transformer (Vaswani et al., 2017) style model implemented in OpenNMT-py using a variety of corpus filtering techniques, truecasing, BPE (Sennrich et al., 2016), back-translation, ensembling and fine-tuning for domain adaptation.

2.5.18 IIITH-MT (Goyal and Sharma, 2019)

IIITH-MT for Gujarati-English first experimented with attention-based LSTM encoder-decoder architecture, but later found the results to be more promising by using Transformer architecture. The paper documents that with Hindi-English as an assisting language pair in a joint training, the multilingual system obtains significant BLEU improvements for a low resource language pair like Gujarati-English.

2.5.19 IITP (Sen et al., 2019)

IITP-MT is a Transformer based NMT system trained using original parallel corpus and synthetic parallel corpus obtained through backtranslation of monolingual data. All the experiments are performed at subword-level using BPE with 10K merge operations.

2.5.20 JHU (Marchisio et al., 2019)

JHU's English-German system is an ensemble of 2 Transformer base models, improved by filtered backtranslation with restricted sampling (like Edunov+ 2018), filtered ParaCrawl and CommonCrawl (Junczys-Dowmunt, 2018a), continued training on newstest15-18 (like JHU's submission to WMT18, Koehn et al., 2018), reranking with R2L models (like Sennrich et al., 2017 or Junczys-Dowmunt, 2018b) and fixing quotation marks to match the German style (as many other teams did).

English-German was the same, with a 3 Transformer base ensemble, no fixed quotation marks, and reranking additionally included a language model (inspired by Junczys-Dowmunt, 2018a).

2.5.21 JUMT (no associated paper)

For the training purpose, the preprocessed Lithuanian-English sentence pairs were fed to Moses toolkit (Koehn et al., 2007). This created an SMT translation model with Lithuanian as the source language and English as the target language. After that, the Lithuanian side of a parallel corpus of 2,00,000 Lithuanian-English sentence pairs was re-translated into English with the

SMT model. These 2,00,000 machine translated English sentences and the respective 2,00,000 gold standard Lithuanian sentences (from the Lithuanian-English sentence pairs) were given as input to a word embedding based NMT model. This resulted in the hybrid model submitted for manual evaluation.

2.5.22   JU_SAARLAND (Mondal et al., 2019)

The systems JU_SAARLAND and JU_SAARLAND_CLEAN_NUM_135_BPE used additional backtranslated data and were trained using phrase-based and BPE-based attention models.

2.5.23   KSAI (Guo et al., 2019)

Kingsoft's submissions were based on various NMT architectures with Transformer as the baseline system. Several data filters and backtranslation were used for data cleaning and data augmentation, respectively. Several advanced techniques were added to the baseline system such as Linear Combination and Layer Aggregation. Fine-tuning methods were applied to improve the in-domain translation quality. The final model was a system combination through multi-model ensembling and reranking, post-processed.

2.5.24   KYOTO UNIVERSITY (Cromieres and Kurohashi, 2019)

KYOTO UNIVERSITY used the now standard Transformer model (with 6 layers for each of encoder/decoder, hidden size of 1024, 16 attention heads, dropout of 0.3). Training data was carefully cleaned and the 2018 monolingual data was used through back-translation, as it turned out to be necessary for correctly translating recent news items. No ensemble translation was performed but a small BLEU improvement was obtained by taking a "majority vote" on the final translations for different checkpoints.

2.5.25   LINGUA CUSTODIA (Burlot, 2019)

The German-to-French system LINGUA-CUSTODIA-PRIMARY is an ensemble of eight Transformer *base* models, fine-tuned on monolingual news data back-translated with constrained decoding for specific terminology control.

2.5.26   LIUM (Bougares et al., 2019)

LIUM introduced two new translation directions involving two European languages: French and German. The training data was created by cross-matching the training data from previous WMT shared tasks. Development and test sets have been manually created from news articles Focusing on EU elections topics. LIUM participated in both directions for German-French language pairs. LIUM systems are based on the self-attentional Transformer networks using "small" and "big" architectures. We also used monolingual data selection and synthetic data through backtranslation.

2.5.27   LMU-NMT

LMU Munich provided two systems.

LMU-NMT (Stojanovski and Fraser, 2019) The LMU Munich system for En-De translation is based on a context-aware Transformer. We first train a baseline big Transformer on filtered ParaCrawl and an oversampled version of the remaining parallel data and then continue training with NewsCrawl backtranslations. We use the baseline to initialize the context-aware Transformer which uses fine-grained modeling of local and coarse-grained modeling of large context.

LMU-UNSUP (Stojanovski et al., 2019) The LMU Munich system for German-Czech translation is based on BWEs, cross-lingual LM, SMT and NMT, all trained in an unsupervised way. We train a cross-lingual Masked LM (Lample et al., 2019) and use it to initialize the NMT model. The NMT model is trained with denoising autoencoding and online backtranslation. We also include backtranslations from an unsupervised SMT. German data is compound-split and for NMT we further apply BPE splitting.

2.5.28   MLLP-UPV (Iranzo-Sánchez et al., 2019)

MLLP-UPV submitted systems for the German↔English and German↔French language pairs, participating in both directions of each pair. The systems are based on the Transformer architecture and make ample use of data filtering, synthetic data and domain adaptation through fine-tuning.

2.5.29   MS TRANSLATOR (Junczys-Dowmunt, 2019)

MS Translator systems (MICROSOFT-WMT19-SENT-DOC, MICROSOFT-WMT19-DOC-LEVEL and MICROSOFT-WMT19-SENT-LEVEL) explore the use of document-level context in large-scale settings. We build 12-layer Transformer-Big systems: a) on the sentence-level, b) with large document-level context (training on full documents with up to 1024 subwords) and c) hybrid models via 2nd-pass decoding and ensembling. The models are trained on filtered parallel data, large amounts of back-translated documents and augmented fake and true parallel documents.

2.5.30 MSRA (Xia et al., 2019)

MSRA was submitted by Microsoft Research Asia. This system covers also the following sub-systems: MSRA.MADL, MSRA.MASS, MSRA.NAO and MSRA.SCA.

MSRA.MADL is based on Transformer (i.e., the standard transformer_big setting with 6 layers, embedding dimension 1024 and hidden state dimension 4096) and trained with multi-agent dual learning (Wang et al., 2019) scheme (briefly, MADL). The core idea of dual learning is to leverage the duality between the primal task (mapping from domain $\mathcal{X}$ to domain $\mathcal{Y}$) and dual task (mapping from domain $\mathcal{Y}$ to $\mathcal{X}$) to boost the performances of both tasks. MADL extends the dual learning framework by introducing multiple primal and dual models. It was integrated into the submitted system MSRA.MADL for German↔English and German↔French translations.

MSRA.SCA is a combination of Transformer network, back translation, knowledge distillation, soft contextual data augmentation (Zhu et al., 2019), and model ensembling. The Transformer big architecture is trained using soft contextual data augmentation to further enhance the performance. Following the above procedures, 5 different models are trained and ensembled for final submission.

MSRA.MASS is based on Transformer (i.e., the standard transformer_big setting with 6 layers, embedding dimension 1024 and hidden state dimension 4096) and pre-trained with MASS: masked sequence to sequence pre-training for language generation (Song et al., 2019). MASS leverages both monolingual and bilingual sentences for pre-training, where a segment of the source sentence is masked in the encoder side, and the decoder predicts this masked segment in the monolingual setting and predicts the whole target sentence in the bilingual setting. After pre-training,

back-translation and ensemble/reranking are further leveraged to improve the accuracy of the system. MSRA.MASS handles Chinese→English and English↔Lithuanian translations in the submission

MSRA.NAO is a system whose architecture is obtained by neural architecture optimization (briefly, NAO; Luo et al., 2018). NAO leverages the power of a gradient-based method to conduct optimization and guide the creation of better neural architecture in a continuous and more compact space given the historically observed architectures and their performances. The search space includes self attention, convolutional networks, LSTMs, etc. It was applied in English↔Finnish translations in the submitted systems.

2.5.31 NıuTrans **providing the system** NEU **(Li et al., 2019a)**

The NıuTrans submissions are based on Deep-Transformer-DLCL and its variants, we used back-translation with beam search and sampling methods for data augmentation. Iterative ensemble knowledge distillation was employed to enhance single systems by various teachers. Ensembling and reranking facilitated further system combination.

2.5.32 NICT

NICT **(Dabre et al., 2019)** submitted supervised neural machine translation (NMT) systems developed for the news translation task for Kazakh↔English, Gujarati↔English, Chinese↔English, and English→Finnish translation directions.

NICT focused on leveraging multilingual transfer learning and back-translation for the extremely low-resource language pairs: Kazakh↔English and Gujarati↔English translation. For the Chinese↔English translation, back-translation, fine-tuning, and model ensembling were found to work the best. For English→Finnish, NICT submission from WMT18 remains a strong baseline despite the increase in parallel corpora for this year's task.

NICT **(Marie et al., 2019b)** submitted also an unsupervised neural machine translation system developed for the news translation task for German→Czech translation direction, focussing on language model pre-training, n-best list reranking, fine-tuning, and model ensembling technologies. The final primary submission to this task is the result of a simple combination of the unsupervised neural and statistical machine translation systems.

2.5.33 NRC (Littell et al., 2019)

The National Research Council Canada (NRC-CNRC) Kazakh-English news translation system is a multi-source, multi-encoder NMT system that takes Russian as the additional source. The constrained Kazakh-Russian parallel corpora is used to train NMT systems for "cross-translation" of resources between the languages, and the final Kazakh/Russian-to-English system is trained on a combination of genuine, back-translated, and cross-translated synthetic data. The submitted model is a partially trained single run system.

2.5.34 PARFDA (Biçici, 2019)

Biçici (2019) reports on the use of parfda system, Moses, KenLM, NPLM, and PRO, including the coverage of the test sets and the upper bounds on the translation results using the constrained resources.

2.5.35 PROMT-NMT (Molchanov, 2019)

This is an unconstrained, transformer-based single system, built using Marian and using BPE.

2.5.36 RUG

RUG_KKEN_MORFESSOR (Toral et al., 2019) uses (i) unsupervised morphological segmentation given the agglutinative nature of Kazakh, (ii) data from an additional language (Russian), given the scarcity of English–Kazakh data and (iii) synthetic data for the source language filtered using language-independent sentence similarity.

RUG_ENKK_BPE (Toral et al., 2019) uses data from an additional language (Russian), given the scarcity of English–Kazakh data and synthetic data (for both source and target languages) filtered using language-independent sentence similarity.

2.5.37 RWTH AACHEN (Rosendahl et al., 2019)

The systems by RWTH AACHEN are all based on Transformer architecture and aside from careful corpus filtering and fine tuning, they experiment with different types of subword units.

For English-German, no gains over the last year setup are observed. Small improvements are reached in Chinese-English. The highest gain of 11.1 BLEU is obtained for Kazakh-English, also thanks to transfer learning techniques.

2.5.38 TALP_UPC_2019_KKEN and TALP_UPC_2019_ENKK (Casas et al., 2019)

The TALP-UPC system was trained on a combination of the original Kazakh-English data (oversampled 3x) together with synthetic corpora obtained by translating with a BPE-based Moses the Russian side of the Kazakh-Russian data to English for the en-kk direction, and the Russian side of the English-Russian data to Kazakh for the kk-en direction. For the final systems, a custom model consisting in a self-attention Transformer decoder that learns joint source-target representations (with BPE tokenization) was used, implemented on the fairseq library.

2.5.39 TARTUNLP-C (Tättar et al., 2019)

TARTUNLP-C is a multilingual multi-domain neural machine translation, achieved by specifying the output language and domain via input word features (factors). The system was trained using all the parallel data for latin alphabet languages and used self-attention (Transformer) as the base architecture.

2.5.40 TILDE-NC-NMT and TILDE-NC-NMT (Pinnis et al., 2019)

Tilde developed both constrained and unconstrained NMT systems for English-Lithuanian and Lithuanian-English using the Marian toolkit. All systems feature ensembles of four to five transformer models that were trained using the quasi-hyperbolic Adam optimiser (Ma and Yarats, 2018). Data for the systems were prepared using TildeMT filtering (Pinnis, 2018) and preprocessing (Pinnis et al., 2018) methods. For unconstrained systems, data were additionally filtered using dual conditional cross-entropy filtering (Junczys-Dowmunt, 2018a). All systems were trained using iterative back-translation (Rikters, 2018) and feature synthetic data that allows training NMT systems to support handling of unknown phenomena (Pinnis et al., 2017). During translation, automatic named entity and nontranslatable phrase post-editing were performed. For constrained systems, named entities and nontranslatable phrase lists were extracted from the parallel training data. For unconstrained systems,

WikiData[8] was used to acquire bilingual lists of named entities.

2.5.41 Universitat d'Alacant

UALACANT-NMT (Sánchez-Cartagena et al., 2019) is an ensemble of two RNN and two transformer models. They were trained on a combination of genuine parallel data, synthetic data generated by means of pivot backtranslation (from the available English-Russian and Kazakh-Russian parallel data) and backtranslated monolingual data. The Kazakh text was morphologically segmented with Apertium.

UALACANT-NMT+RBMT (Sánchez-Cartagena et al., 2019) is an ensemble of two RNN and two Transformer models. They were trained on a combination of genuine parallel data, synthetic data generated by means of pivot backtranslation (from the available English-Russian and Kazakh-Russian parallel data) and backtranslated monolingual data. The Kazakh text was morphologically segmented with Apertium. The RNN models were multi-source models with two inputs: the original SL text and its translation with the Apertium RBMT English-Kazakh system.

2.5.42 UCAM (Stahlberg et al., 2019)

The Cambridge University Engineering Department's entry to the WMT19 evaluation campaign focuses on fine-tuning and language modelling. Fine-tuning on former WMT test sets is regularized with elastic weight consolidation (Kirkpatrick et al., 2017). Language models are used on both the sentence-level and the document-level, with a modified Transformer architecture for document-level language modelling. An SMT system is integrated via a minimum Bayes-risk formulation (Stahlberg et al., 2017).

2.5.43 UDS-DFKI (España-Bonet and Ruiter, 2019)

The UdS-DFKI English→German system uses a standard Transformer architecture where data is enriched with coreference information gathered at document level. The training is still done at the sentence level.

The English↔Gujarati systems are phrase-based SMT systems enriched with parallel sentences extracted from comparable corpora with a

[8]www.wikidata.org

self-supervised NMT system. In this case, also back-translations are used.

2.5.44 UEDIN (Bawden et al., 2019a)

The UEDIN systems are supervised NMT systems based on the transformer architecture and trained using Marian (Junczys-Dowmunt et al., 2018). For English↔Gujarati, synthetic parallel data from two sources, backtranslation and pivoting through Hindi, is produced using unsupervised and semi-supervised NMT models, pre-trained using a cross-lingual language objective (Lample and Conneau, 2019) For German→English, the impact of vast amounts of back-translated training data on translation quality is studied, and some additional insights are gained over (Edunov et al., 2018). Towards the end of training, for German→English and Chinese↔English, the mini-batch size was increased up to fifty-fold by delaying gradient updates (Bogoychev et al., 2018) as an alternative to learning rate cooldown (Smith, 2018). For Chinese↔English, a comparison of different segmentation strategies showed that character-based decoding was superior to the translation of subwords when translating into Chinese. Pre-processing strategies were also investigated for English→Czech, showing that pre-processing can be simplified without loss to MT quality.

UEDIN's main findings on the Chinese↔English translation task are that character-level model on the Chinese side can be used when translating into Chinese to improve the BLEU score. The same does not hold when translating from Chinese.

2.5.45 UMD (Briakou and Carpuat, 2019)

UMD NMT models are Sequence-2-Sequence attentional with Long-Short Term Memory units; words are segmented using BPEs jointly learned on the concatenation of Turkish and Kazakh data. The submitted model is an ensemble obtained by averaging the output distributions of 4 models trained on Kazakh, Turkish and back-translated data using different random seeds.

2.5.46 UNSUPERVISED-6929 and UNSUPERVISED-6935

Unfortunately, no details are available for these systems.

2.5.47 USTC-MCC (no associated paper)

USTC-MCC is a Transformer model implemented in Fairseq-py. Tokenization and BPE were used and the training data were augmented with back-translation.

2.5.48 USYD (Ding and Tao, 2019)

The University of Sydney's system is based on the self attentional Transformer networks, into which they integrated the most recent effective strategies from academic research (e.g., BPE, back translation, multi-features data selection, data augmentation, greedy model ensemble, reranking, ConMBR system combination, and post-processing). Furthermore, they proposed a novel augmentation method Cycle Translation and a data mixture strategy Big/Small parallel construction to entirely exploit the synthetic corpus.

2.5.49 XZL-NMT (no associated paper)

XZL-NMT is an ensembled Transformer model as implemented in Marian, using Moses tokenizer and subword units.

2.6 Submission Summary

An overview of techniques used in the submitted systems was obtained in a poll. The full details are available on-line.[9] Including manually entered data rows, we had more than 60 responses, some of which describe more MT systems at once.

Overall, most of the submitted systems were standard bilingual MT systems, optimized to translate one language pair, even in the case when data from other languages are used to support this pair. Truly multilingual systems were TARTUNLP-C covering 7 of the tested language pairs, DBMS-KU INTERPOLATION (bidirectional Kazakh-English) and AYLIEN_MT_MULTILINGUAL which was unfortunately tested only on the very low-resource Gujarati-English and not all the language pairs it covers. In the highly competitive task of news translation, these systems ended up on lower ranks, so aiming at multi-linguality seems rather as a distraction, except for supporting low-resource languages.

As already in the previous year, the Transformer architecture (Vaswani et al., 2017) domi-

Feature	#	[%]
Dropout	42	69
Back-translation	39	64
Ensembling	37	61
Careful corpus filtering	35	57
Tied source and target word embeddings	24	39
Fine-tuning for domain adaptation	22	36
Back-translation more than once	20	33
Averaging	17	28
Oversampling	14	23
Extra languages used (e.g. some form of pivoting or multi-lingual training)	12	20
Pre-trained model parts (e.g. word embeddings)	10	16
Total	61	100

Table 6: Model and training features frequently reported for submitted systems.

nates with more than 80% of submissions[10] reporting to include it. Some diversity is seen at least in the actual implementation of the model, with Marian (Junczys-Dowmunt et al., 2018) being by far the most popular (more than 30%), followed by fairseq (18%), OpenNMT-py (16%) and Tensor2tensor and Sockeye (14% each). Phrase-based MT (primarily Moses, Koehn et al., 2007) is still often in use, with 15–25% submissions using it in some way.

Subword processing is very frequent: BPE (Sennrich et al., 2016) taking the lead (two thirds) and SentencePiece (Kudo and Richardson, 2018) following (a quarter of submissions). More than 90% of submissions use tokenization (Moses tokenizer being used in 40% of cases) before subword splitting while more language-specific tools such as morphological segmenters are rare. Unicode characters were used only exceptionally (4 mentions) and with rather experimental systems, except for UEDIN, see Section 2.5.44.

More than 40% of submissions used language identification to clean the provided training data. Truecasing or recasing was also quite popular.

Common NMT model and training features are listed in Table 6, documenting that back-translation, ensembling and corpus filtering are a must.

3 Human Evaluation

A human evaluation campaign is run each year to assess translation quality and to determine the final ranking of systems taking part in the competition.

---

[9]https://tinyurl.com/
wmt19-systems-descr-summary

[10]The percentages are indicative only. They are based on the total number of responses in the poll, with only an inexact correspondence to the number of evaluated primary submissions.

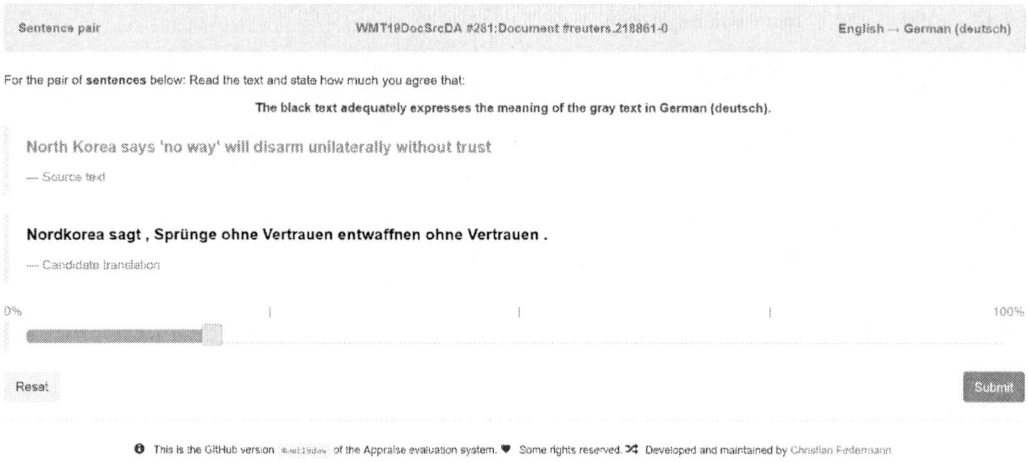

Figure 3: Screen shot of segment-rating portion of document-level direct assessment in the Appraise interface for an example English to German assessment from the human evaluation campaign. The annotator is presented with the machine translation output segment randomly selected from competing systems (anonymized) and is asked to rate the translation on a sliding scale.

This section describes how preparation of evaluation data, collection of human assessments, and computation of the official results of the shared task was carried out this year.

3.1 Direct Assessment

Work on evaluation over the past few years has provided fresh insight into ways to collect *direct assessments* (DA) of machine translation quality (Graham et al., 2013, 2014, 2016), and three years ago the evaluation campaign included parallel assessment of a subset of News task language pairs evaluated with *relative ranking* (RR) and DA. DA has some clear advantages over RR, namely the evaluation of absolute translation quality and the ability to carry out evaluations through quality controlled crowd-sourcing. As established in 2016 (Bojar et al., 2016), DA results (via crowd-sourcing) and RR results (produced by researchers) correlate strongly, with Pearson correlation ranging from 0.920 to 0.997 across several source languages into English and at 0.975 for English-to-Russian (the only pair evaluated out-of-English). Since 2017, we have thus employed DA for evaluation of systems taking part in the news task and do so again this year.

Human assessors are asked to rate a given translation by how adequately it expresses the meaning of the corresponding reference translation or source language input on an analogue scale, which corresponds to an underlying absolute 0–100 rating scale. No sentence or document length restriction is applied during manual evaluation.

3.2 Styles of Direct Assessment Tested in WMT19

In previous year's evaluation translated segments for all language pairs were evaluated independent of the wider document context. However, since recent MT evaluations address the question of comparison of system and human performance, evaluation within document context has become more relevant (Läubli et al., 2018; Toral et al., 2018). Therefore, for a selection of language pairs, human evaluation was carried out within the document context. We denote the two options "+DC" (with document context) and "−DC" (without document context) in the following.

Additionally in past years, test data included text that was created in the opposite direction to testing, in order to achieve a larger test set with limited resources. Inclusion of test data has been shown to introduce inaccuracies in evaluations particularly in terms of BLEU scores however (Graham et al., 2019b) and for this reason, this year we only test systems on data that was originally written in the source language.

In previous years we have employed only monolingual human evaluation (denoted "M" in the following for official results. Last year we trialled source-based evaluation for English to Czech translation, i.e. a bilingual configuration ("B") in which the human assessor is shown the source input and system output only (with no reference

Figure 4: Screen shot of document-rating portion of document-level direct assessment in the Appraise interface for an example English to German assessment from the human evaluation campaign. The annotator is presented with the machine translation output document randomly selected from competing systems (anonymized) and is asked to rate the translation on a sliding scale.

translation shown). This approach has the advantage of freeing up the human-generated reference translation so that it can be included in the evaluation as another system and provide an estimate of human performance. Since we would like to restrict human assessors to only evaluate translation *into* their native language, we restricted bilingual/source-based evaluation to evaluation of translation for out-of-English language pairs. This is especially relevant since we have a large group of volunteer human assessors with native language fluency in non-English languages and high fluency in English, while we generally lack the reverse, native English speakers with high fluency in non-English languages. A summary of the human evaluation configurations run this year in the news task is provided in Table 7, where configurations that correspond to official results are highlighted in bold.

The style of official evaluation used in the past recent years of WMT corresponds to M SR−DC (Segment Rating without Document Context) i.e. evaluating individual segments against the reference translation and independently of each other.

For language pairs for which our original style SR−DC evaluation was run this year, the SR−DC configuration was kept as the source of the official results with additional configurations provided for the purpose of comparison. For the remaining language pairs, official results are based on the SR+DC evaluation, i.e. the assessment of individual segments which are nevertheless provided in their natural order as they appear in the document. Fully document-level evaluation (DR+DC)

	Doc Rating + Doc Context (DR+DC)	Seg Rating + Doc Context (SR+DC)	Seg Rating − Doc Context (SR−DC)
de-cs			**M**
de-fr			**M**
fr-de			**M**
de-en	M	M	
en-cs	B	**B**	B
en-de	B	**B**	
en-fi	B	**B**	
en-gu	B	**B**	
en-kk	B	**B**	
en-lt	B	**B**	
en-ru	B	**B**	
en-zh	B	**B**	
fi-en			**M**
gu-en			**M**
kk-en			**M**
lt-en			**M**
ru-en			**M**
zh-en	M	M	**M**

Table 7: Summary of human evaluation configurations; M denotes reference-based/monolingual human evaluation in which the machine translation output was compared to human-generated reference; B denotes bilingual/source-based evaluation where the human annotators evaluated MT output by reading the source language input only (no reference translation present); configurations comprising official results highlighted in bold.

as trialled this year where we asked for a single score given the whole document is problematic in terms of statistical power and inconclusive ties, as shown in Graham et al. (2019b).

In order to maximize the number of human annotations collected while minimizing the amount of reading required by a given human assessor, we combined two evaluation configurations, Document Rating + Document Context (DR+DC) and Segment Rating + Document Context (SR+DC), shown in Table 7 and ran them as a single task. In this configuration, human annotators were shown each segment of a given document (produced by a single MT system) in original sequential order and the human assessor rated each segment in turn. Figure 3 shows a screenshot of this part of the annotation process. This was followed by a screen where the human assessor rated the entire document as a whole comprising the most recently rated segments. Figure 4 shows this later part of the same evaluation set-up. Subsequently when sufficient data is collected, SR+DC results are arrived at by combining ratings attributed to segments, while DR+DC results are a combination of document ratings.

For some language pairs the standard configuration from past years in which segments are evaluated in isolation from the wider document context, which we call Segment Rating − Document Context (SR−DC) and a screenshot of this configuration is shown in Figure 5.

As in previous years, the standard SR−DC annotation is organized into "HITs" (following the Mechanical Turk's term "human intelligence task"), each containing 100 such screens and requiring about half an hour to finish. For the additional configuration that included both DR+DC and SR+DC, HITs were simply made up of a random sample of machine translated *documents* as opposed to segments.

3.3 Evaluation Campaign Overview

In terms of the News translation task manual evaluation, a total of 263 individual researcher accounts were involved, and 766 turker accounts.[11] Researchers in the manual evaluation contributed judgments of 242,424 translations, while 487,674 translation assessment scores were submitted in total by the crowd, of which 224,046 were provided by workers who passed quality control.

Under ordinary circumstances, each assessed translation would correspond to a single individual scored segment. However, since distinct systems can produce the same output for a particular input sentence, in previous years we were often able to take advantage of this and use a single assessment for multiple systems. For example, last year we combined human assessment of identical translations produced by multiple systems and were able to get up to 17% saving in terms of evaluation resources. However, since our evaluation now includes document context, deduplication of system outputs was not possible for most of the configurations run this year.

3.4 Data Collection

System rankings are produced from a large set of human assessments of translations, each of which indicates the absolute quality of the output of a system. Annotations are collected in an evaluation campaign that enlists the help of participants in the shared task. Each team is asked to contribute 8 hours annotation time, which we estimated at 16 100-translation HITs per primary system submitted. We continue to use the open-source Appraise[12] (Federmann, 2012) tool and Turkle2 for

---

[11]Numbers do not include the 1,005 workers on Mechanical Turk who did not pass quality control.

[12]https://github.com/cfedermann/Appraise

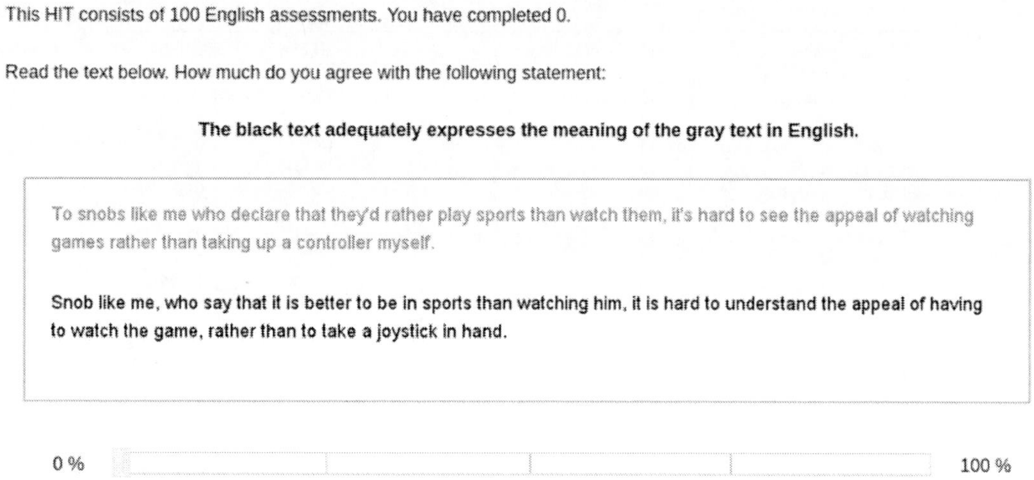

Figure 5: Screen shot of Direct Assessment as carried out by workers for the standard Segment Rating − Document Context (SR−DC) Human Evaluation Configuration.

our data collection, in addition to Amazon Mechanical Turk.[13] Table 8 shows total numbers of human assessments collected in WMT19 contributing to final scores for systems.[14]

The effort that goes into the manual evaluation campaign each year is impressive, and we are grateful to all participating individuals and teams. We believe that human annotation provides the best decision basis for evaluation of machine translation output and it is great to see continued contributions on this large scale.

3.5 Crowd Quality Control

In order to trial document-level evaluation, in addition to our standard segment-level human evaluation, we ran two additional evaluations combined into a single HIT structure. Firstly, we collected segment ratings with document context (SR+DC) and secondly document ratings with document context (DR+DC). We refer to our original segment-level evaluation where assessors are shown segments in isolation from the wider document context as segment rating − document context (SR−DC). We describe all three methods of ranking systems in detail below.

3.5.1 Standard DA HIT Structure (SR−DC)

In the standard DA HIT structure (Segment Rating − Document Context), three kinds of quality control translation pairs are employed as described

in Table 9: we repeat pairs (expecting a similar judgment), damage MT outputs (expecting significantly worse scores) and use references instead of MT outputs (expecting high scores).

In total, 60 items in a 100-translation HIT serve in quality control checks but 40 of those are regular judgments of MT system outputs (we exclude assessments of bad references and ordinary reference translations when calculating final scores). The effort wasted for the sake of quality control is thus 20%.

Also in the standard DA HIT structure, within each 100-translation HIT, the same proportion of translations are included from each participating system for that language pair. This ensures the final dataset for a given language pair contains roughly equivalent numbers of assessments for each participating system. This serves three purposes for making the evaluation fair. Firstly, for the point estimates used to rank systems to be reliable, a sufficient sample size is needed and the most efficient way to reach a sufficient sample size for all systems is to keep total numbers of judgments roughly equal as more and more judgments are collected. Secondly, it helps to make the evaluation fair because each system will suffer or benefit equally from an overly lenient/harsh human judge. Thirdly, despite DA judgments being absolute, it is known that judges "calibrate" the way they use the scale depending on the general observed translation quality. With each HIT including all participating systems, this effect is averaged out. Furthermore apart from quality con-

---

[13]https://www.mturk.com

[14]Number of systems for WMT19 includes ten "human" systems comprising human-generated reference translations used to provide human performance estimates.

Language Pair	Systems	Comps	Comps/Sys	Assessments	Assess/Sys
Chinese→English	15	–	–	20,199	1,346.6
German→English	17	–	–	39,556	2,326.8
Finnish→English	12	–	–	23,301	1,941.8
Gujarati→English	11	–	–	17,147	1,558.8
Kazakh→English	11	–	–	18,339	1,667.2
Lithuanian→English	11	–	–	18,807	1,709.7
Russian→English	14	–	–	27,836	1,988.3
English→Chinese	13	–	–	28,801	2,215.5
English→Czech	12	–	–	29,207	2,433.9
English→German	23	–	–	49,535	2,153.7
English→Finnish	13	–	–	22,310	1,716.2
English→Gujarati	12	–	–	11,223	935.2
English→Kazakh	13	–	–	15,039	1,156.8
English→Lithuanian	13	–	–	14,069	1,082.2
English→Russian	13	–	–	24,441	1,880.1
German→Czech	11	–	–	16,900	1,536.4
German→French	11	–	–	6,700	609.1
French→German	10	–	–	4,000	400.0
Total Appraise	112	–	–	194,625	1,737.7
Total MTurk	76	–	–	144,986	1,907.7
Total Turkle	47	–	–	47,799	1,017.0
Total WMT19	243	–	–	387,410	1,594.3
WMT18	150	–	–	302,489	2,016.6
WMT17	153	–	–	307,707	2,011.2
WMT16	138	569,287	4,125.2	284,644	2,062.6
WMT15	131	542,732	4,143.0	271,366	2,071.5
WMT14	110	328,830	2,989.3	164,415	1,494.7
WMT13	148	942,840	6,370.5	471,420	3,185.3
WMT12	103	101,969	999.6	50,985	495.0
WMT11	133	63,045	474.0	31,522	237.0

Table 8: Amount of data collected in the WMT19 manual evaluation campaign (after removal of quality control items). The final eight rows report summary information from previous years of the workshop.

Repeat Pairs:	Original System output (10)	An exact repeat of it (10);
Bad Reference Pairs:	Original System output (10)	A degraded version of it (10);
Good Reference Pairs:	Original System output (10)	Its corresponding reference translation (10).

Table 9: Standard DA HIT structure quality control translation pairs hidden within 100-translation HITs, numbers of items are provided in parentheses.

trol items, HITs are constructed using translations sampled from the entire set of outputs for a given language pair.

3.5.2 Document-Level DA HIT Structure (SR+DC and DR+DC)

As mentioned previously, collection of segment-level ratings with document context (Segment Rating + Document Context) and document ratings with document context (Document Rating + Document Context) assessments were combined into a single evaluation set-up to save annotator time. This involved constructing HITs so that each sentence belonging to a given document (produced by a single MT system) were displayed to and rated by the human annotator before he/she was shown the same entire document again and asked to rate it.

Quality control items for this set-up was carried out as follows with the aim of constructing a HIT with as close to 100 segments in total:

1. All documents produced by all systems are pooled;[15]

2. Documents are then sampled at random (without replacement) and assigned to the current HIT until the current HIT comprises

[15] If a "human" system is included to provide a human performance estimate, it is also considered a system during quality control set-up.

no more than 70 segments in total;

3. Once documents amounting to close to 70 segments have been assigned to the current HIT, we select a subset of these documents to be paired with quality control documents; this subset is selected by repeatedly checking if the addition of the number of the segments belonging to a given document (as quality control items) will keep the total number of segments in the HIT below 100; if this is the case it is included; otherwise it is skipped until the addition of all documents has been checked. In doing this, the HIT is structured to bring the total number of segments as close as possible to 100 segments in total within a HIT but without selecting documents in any systematic way such as selecting them based on fewest segments, for example.

4. Once we have selected a core set of original system output documents and a subset of them to be paired with quality control versions for each HIT, quality control documents are automatically constructed by altering the sentences of a given document into a mixture of three kinds of quality control items used in the original DA segment-level quality control: bad reference translations, reference translations and exact repeats, see Section 3.5.3 for details of bad reference generation;

5. Finally, the documents belonging to a HIT are shuffled.

3.5.3 Construction of Bad References

In all set-ups employed in the evaluation campaign, and as in previous years, bad reference pairs were created automatically by replacing a phrase within a given translation with a phrase of the same length, randomly selected from n-grams extracted from the full test set of reference translations belonging to that language pair. This means that the replacement phrase will itself comprise a fluent sequence of words (making it difficult to tell that the sentence is low quality without reading the entire sentence) while at the same time making its presence highly likely to sufficiently change the meaning of the MT output so that it causes a noticeable degradation. The length of the phrase to be replaced is determined by the number of words in the original translation, as follows:

Translation Length (N)	# Words Replaced in Translation
1	1
2–5	2
6–8	3
9–15	4
16–20	5
>20	$\lfloor N/4 \rfloor$

3.6 Annotator Agreement

When an analogue scale (or 0–100 point scale, in practice) is employed, agreement cannot be measured using the conventional Kappa coefficient, ordinarily applied to human assessment when judgments are discrete categories or preferences. Instead, to measure consistency we filter crowd-sourced human assessors by how consistently they rate translations of known distinct quality using the bad reference pairs described previously. Quality filtering via bad reference pairs is especially important for the crowd-sourced portion of the manual evaluation. Due to the anonymous nature of crowd-sourcing, when collecting assessments of translations, it is likely to encounter workers who attempt to game the service, as well as submission of inconsistent evaluations and even robotic ones. We therefore employ DA's quality control mechanism to filter out low quality data, facilitated by the use of DA's analogue rating scale.[16]

Assessments belonging to a given crowd-sourced worker who has not demonstrated that he/she can reliably score bad reference translations significantly lower than corresponding genuine system output translations are filtered out. A paired significance test is applied to test if degraded translations are consistently scored lower than their original counterparts and the p-value produced by this test is used as an estimate of human assessor reliability. Assessments of workers whose p-value does not fall below the conventional 0.05 threshold are omitted from the evaluation of systems, since they do not reliably score degraded translations lower than corresponding MT output translations.

Table 10 shows the number of workers who met our filtering requirement by showing a signif-

---

icantly lower score for bad reference items compared to corresponding MT outputs, and the proportion of those who simultaneously showed no significant difference in scores they gave to pairs of identical translations.

Numbers in Table 10 of workers passing quality control criteria (A) varies across language pairs and this is in-line with passed DA evaluations. Language pairs were run in the following order on Mechanical Turk: fi-en, gu-en, kk-en, lt-en ru-en, zh-en, de-en. We observe that the amount of low quality data we received (with one exception at the beginning) steadily decreases as data collection proceeded from $(100-31=)$ 69% low quality data for fi-en to $(100-71=)$ 29% for de-en, the last language pair to be evaluated. This is likely due to the active rejection of low quality HITs and word spreading among unreliable workers to avoid our HITs. The assessors were least reliable for gu-en, with only 60 out of 301 workers passing the quality control. We removed the data from the non-reliable workers in all language pairs.

In terms of numbers of workers who passed quality control who also showed no significant difference in exact repeats of the same translation, the two document-level runs, zh-en and de-en, showed lower reliability than the original DA standard sentence-level set-up. Overall the reliability is still relatively high however with the lowest language pair being de-en still reaching 88% of workers showing no significant difference in scores for repeat assessment of the same translation. In sum, we confirmed this year again that the check on bad references is sufficient and not many more workers would be ruled out if we also demanded similar judgements for repeated inputs.

3.7 Producing the Human Ranking

The data belong to each individual human evaluation run were compiled individually to produce either one of our official system rankings or a ranking that we would like to compare with official rankings.

In all set-ups, similar to previous years, system rankings were arrived at in the following way. Firstly, in order to iron out differences in scoring strategies of distinct human assessors, human assessment scores for translations were first standardized according to each individual human assessor's overall mean and standard deviation score. For rankings arrived at via segment ratings

(SR−DC as well as SR+DC), average standardized scores for individual segments belonging to a given system were then computed, before the final overall DA score for a given system is computed as the average of its segment scores (Ave z in Table 11). For rankings arrived at via document ratings (DR+DC), average standardized scores for individual documents belonging to a given system were then computed, before the final overall DA score for a given system was computed as the average of its document scores (Ave z in Table 11). Results are also reported for average scores for systems, computed in the same way but without any score standardization applied (Ave % in Table 11).

Tables 11, Tables 12 and 13 include the official results of the news task and Tables 14 and 15 include results for alternate human evaluation configurations.[17] Human performance estimates arrived at by evaluation of human-produced reference translations are denoted by "HUMAN" in all tables. Clusters are identified by grouping systems together according to which systems significantly outperform all others in lower ranking clusters, according to Wilcoxon rank-sum test. Appendix A shows the underlying head-to-head significance test official results for all pairs of systems.

3.8 Human Parity

In terms of human parity, as pointed out by Graham et al. (2019b), fully document-level evaluations incur the problem of low statistical power due to the reduced sample size of documents. The many ties in our DR+DC evaluation results cannot be used to draw conclusions of human parity with MT therefore. In addition, as highlighted by Toral et al. (2018), Läubli et al. (2018) and also us Bojar et al. (2018), a tie of human and machine in an evaluation of isolated segments cannot be used to draw conclusions of human parity. Given a wider context, human evaluators may draw different conclusions.[18]

Our SR+DC human evaluation configuration is an attempt to draw the right balance between making it possible to assess a sufficient sample size of translations but importantly keeping the docu-

---

[17]See Table 7 for human evaluation configuration details of each language pair

[18]The only setting where segment-level evaluation could serve in human-parity considerations would be when both humans and machines were translating isolated segments but this setting is not very interesting from the practical point of view.

Order		All	(A) Sig. Diff. Bad Ref.	(B) (A) & No Sig. Diff. Exact Rep.
1	Finnish→English	443	137 (31%)	135 (99%)
2	Gujarati→English	301	60 (20%)	59 (98%)
3	Kazakh→English	217	73 (34%)	70 (96%)
4	Lithuanian→English	233	90 (39%)	85 (94%)
5	Russian→English	321	137 (43%)	136 (99%)
6	Chinese→English	440	208 (47%)	186 (89%)
7	German→English	380	268 (71%)	236 (88%)
	Total	**1,706**	**766 (45%)**	**711 (93%)**

Table 10: Number of crowd-sourced workers taking part in the reference-based SR−DC campaign; (A) those whose scores for bad reference items were significantly lower than corresponding MT outputs; (B) those of (A) whose scores also showed no significant difference for exact repeats of the same translation. The language pairs were submitted for evaluation one after another in the reported order.

ment context available to human assessors, a configuration highlighted as suitable for human-parity investigations by Graham et al. (2019b) and already employed by Toral et al. (2018) (although our overall evaluation differs in other respects). According to the power analysis provided in Graham et al. (2019b), the sample size of translations evaluated in the set-up is large enough to safely conclude statistical ties between pairs of systems in our SR+DC configurations. In addition our evaluation meets all requirements included on the MT evaluation checklist of Graham et al. (2019b).

The results that can be relied upon for drawing conclusions of human parity therefore include the following from our SR+DC configurations:

✓ German to English: many systems are tied with human performance;

× English to Chinese: all systems are outperformed by the human translator;

× English to Czech: all systems are outperformed by the human translator;

× English to Finnish: all systems are outperformed by the human translator;

✓ English to German: Facebook-FAIR achieves super-human translation performance; several systems are tied with human performance;

× English to Gujarati: all systems are outperformed by the human translator;

× English to Kazakh: all systems are outperformed by the human translator;

× English to Lithuanian: all systems are outperformed by the human translator;

✓ English to Russian: Facebook-FAIR is tied with human performance.

Even with all our precautions, the indications of human parity should not be overvalued. For instance, the super-human performance observed with Facebook-FAIR on English to German is based on standardized scores (Ave z.). Without the standardization (Ave.), Facebook-FAIR is on par with the reference and two systems by Microsoft score higher. The same mismatch of Ave. and Ave. z happens for English-Czech within the second performance cluster and also a couple of times in German-English and other language pairs. This has happened in the past already but the English-German case seems to be the first one where the Wilcoxon test claims a significant difference.

3.9 Comparing the Different English-Czech Results

Table 16 reproduces English-to-Czech official SR+DC scores and the full-document DR+DC, to compare them with two additional runs of the bilingual SR−DC style, i.e. the exact same context-less setting used in source-based evaluation of en2cs in WMT18 where the quality of the reference has been significantly surpassed.

The results "SR−DC WMT" are based on 6,225 judgements (518 per system) collected by the same set of annotators as the official SR+DC scores and the "SR−DC Microsoft" are based on 21,918 judgements (1,826 per system) sponsored and carried out by Microsoft.

English→German

Ave.	Ave. z	System
90.3	0.347	Facebook-FAIR
93.0	0.311	Microsoft-WMT19-sent-doc
92.6	0.296	Microsoft-WMT19-doc-level
90.3	0.240	HUMAN
87.6	0.214	MSRA-MADL
88.7	0.213	UCAM
89.6	0.208	NEU
87.5	0.189	MLLP-UPV
87.5	0.130	eTranslation
86.8	0.119	dfki-nmt
84.2	0.094	online-B
86.6	0.094	Microsoft-WMT19-sent-level
87.3	0.081	JHU
84.4	0.077	Helsinki-NLP
84.2	0.038	online-Y
83.7	0.010	lmu-ctx-tf-single
84.1	0.001	PROMT-NMT
82.8	−0.072	online-A
82.7	−0.119	online-G
80.3	−0.129	UdS-DFKI
82.4	−0.132	TartuNLP-c
76.3	−0.400	online-X
43.3	−1.769	en-de-task

Gujarati→English

Ave.	Ave. z	System
64.8	0.210	NEU
61.7	0.126	UEDIN
59.4	0.100	GTCOM-Primary
60.8	0.090	CUNI-T2T-transfer
59.4	0.066	aylien-mt-multilingual
59.3	0.044	NICT
51.3	−0.189	online-G
50.9	−0.192	IITP-MT
48.0	−0.277	UdS-DFKI
47.4	−0.296	IIITH-MT
41.1	−0.598	Ju-Saarland

English→Gujarati

Ave.	Ave. z	System
73.1	0.701	HUMAN
72.2	0.663	online-B
66.8	0.597	GTCOM-Primary
60.2	0.318	MSRA
58.3	0.305	UEDIN
55.9	0.254	CUNI-T2T-transfer
52.7	−0.079	Ju-Saarland-clean-num-135-bpe
35.2	−0.458	IITP-MT
38.8	−0.465	NICT
39.1	−0.490	online-G
33.1	−0.502	online-X
33.2	−0.718	UdS-DFKI

Kazakh→English

Ave.	Ave. z	System
72.2	0.270	online-B
70.1	0.218	NEU
69.7	0.189	rug-morfessor
68.1	0.133	online-G
67.1	0.113	talp-upc-2019
67.0	0.092	NRC-CNRC
65.8	0.066	Frank-s-MT
65.6	0.064	NICT
64.5	0.003	CUNI-T2T-transfer
48.9	−0.477	UMD
32.1	−1.058	DBMS-KU

Lithuanian→English

Ave.	Ave. z	System
77.4	0.234	GTCOM-Primary
77.5	0.216	tilde-nc-nmt
77.0	0.213	NEU
76.4	0.206	MSRA-MASS
76.4	0.202	tilde-c-nmt
73.8	0.107	online-B
69.4	−0.056	online-A
69.2	−0.059	TartuNLP-c
62.8	−0.284	online-G
62.4	−0.337	JUMT
59.1	−0.396	online-X

German→English

Ave.	Ave. z	System
81.6	0.146	Facebook-FAIR
81.5	0.136	RWTH-Aachen
79.0	0.136	MSRA-MADL
79.9	0.121	online-B
79.0	0.086	JHU
80.1	0.067	MLLP-UPV
79.0	0.066	dfki-nmt
78.0	0.066	UCAM
76.6	0.050	online-A
78.4	0.039	NEU
79.0	0.027	HUMAN
77.4	0.011	uedin
77.9	0.009	online-Y
74.8	0.006	TartuNLP-c
72.9	−0.051	online-G
71.8	−0.128	PROMT-NMT
69.7	−0.192	online-X

English→Czech

Ave.	Ave. z	System
91.2	0.642	HUMAN
86.0	0.402	CUNI-DocTransformer-T2T
86.9	0.401	CUNI-Transformer-T2T-2018
85.4	0.388	CUNI-Transformer-T2T-2019
81.3	0.223	CUNI-DocTransformer-Marian
80.5	0.206	uedin
70.8	−0.156	online-Y
71.4	−0.195	TartuNLP-c
67.8	−0.300	online-G
68.0	−0.336	online-B
60.9	−0.594	online-A
59.3	−0.651	online-X

Finnish→English

Ave.	Ave. z	System
78.2	0.285	MSRA-NAO
77.8	0.265	online-Y
77.6	0.261	GTCOM-Primary
76.4	0.245	USYD
72.5	0.107	online-B
73.3	0.105	Helsinki-NLP
69.2	0.012	online-A
68.4	−0.044	online-G
68.0	−0.053	TartuNLP-c
67.3	−0.071	online-X
61.9	−0.209	parfda
53.3	−0.516	apertium-uc

English→Finnish

Ave.	Ave. z	System
94.8	1.007	HUMAN
82.6	0.586	GTCOM-Primary
80.2	0.570	MSRA-NAO
70.9	0.275	online-Y
65.8	0.199	NICT
65.7	0.09	Helsinki-NLP
63.1	0.072	online-G
63.0	0.037	online-B
54.5	−0.125	TartuNLP-c
48.3	−0.384	online-A
47.1	−0.398	online-X
47.9	−0.522	Helsinki-NLP-rule-based
16.9	−1.260	apertium-uc

English→Kazakh

Ave.	Ave. z	System
81.5	0.746	HUMAN
67.6	0.262	UAlacant-NMT
63.8	0.243	online-B
63.8	0.222	UAlacant-NMT-RBMT
63.3	0.126	NEU
63.3	0.108	MSRA
60.4	0.097	CUNI-T2T-transfer
61.7	0.078	online-G
55.2	−0.049	rug-bpe
49.0	−0.328	talp-upc-2019
41.4	−0.493	NICT
11.6	−1.395	DBMS-KU

English→Lithuanian

Ave.	Ave. z	System
90.5	1.017	HUMAN
72.8	0.388	tilde-nc-nmt
69.1	0.387	MSRA-MASS-uc
68.0	0.262	tilde-c-nmt
68.2	0.259	MSRA-MASS-c
67.7	0.155	GTCOM-Primary
62.7	0.036	eTranslation
59.6	−0.054	NEU
57.4	−0.061	online-B
47.8	−0.383	TartuNLP-c
38.4	−0.620	online-A
39.2	−0.666	online-X
32.6	−0.805	online-G

English→Russian

Ave.	Ave. z	System
89.5	0.536	HUMAN
88.5	0.506	Facebook-FAIR
83.6	0.332	USTC-MCC
82.0	0.279	online-G
80.4	0.269	online-B
79.0	0.223	NEU
80.2	0.219	PROMT-NMT
78.5	0.156	online-Y
71.7	−0.188	rerank-er
67.9	−0.268	online-A
68.8	−0.310	TartuNLP-u
62.1	−0.363	online-X
35.7	−1.270	NICT

English→Chinese

Ave.	Ave. z	System
82.5	0.368	HUMAN
83.0	0.306	KSAI
83.3	0.280	Baidu
80.5	0.209	NEU
80.3	0.052	online-A
79.9	0.042	xzl-nmt
79.0	0.017	UEDIN
77.8	0.009	BTRANS
76.9	0.000	NICT
74.6	−0.125	online-B
75.6	−0.218	online-Y
72.6	−0.262	online-G
69.5	−0.553	online-X

Russian→English

Ave.	Ave. z	System
81.4	0.156	Facebook-FAIR
80.7	0.134	online-G
80.4	0.122	eTranslation
80.1	0.121	online-B
81.4	0.115	NEU
80.4	0.102	MSRA-SCA
79.8	0.084	rerank-re
79.2	0.076	online-Y
79.0	0.029	online-A
76.8	0.012	afrl-syscomb19
76.8	−0.039	afrl-ewc
76.2	−0.040	TartuNLP-u
74.5	−0.097	online-X
69.3	−0.303	NICT

Chinese→English

Ave.	Ave. z	System
83.6	0.295	Baidu
82.7	0.266	KSAI
81.7	0.203	MSRA-MASS
81.5	0.195	MSRA-MASS
81.5	0.193	NEU
80.6	0.186	BTRANS
80.7	0.161	online-B
79.2	0.103	BTRANS-ensemble
77.9	0.054	UEDIN
78.0	0.049	online-Y
77.4	0.001	NICT
75.3	−0.065	online-A
72.4	−0.202	online-G
66.9	−0.483	online-X
56.4	−0.957	Apprentice-c

Table 11: Official results of WMT19 News Translation Task. Systems ordered by DA score z-score; systems within a cluster are considered tied; lines indicate clusters according to Wilcoxon rank-sum test $p < 0.05$; grayed entry indicates resources that fall outside the constraints provided.

German→Czech

Ave.	Ave. z	System
63.9	0.426	online-Y
62.7	0.386	online-B
61.4	0.367	NICT
59.8	0.319	online-G
55.7	0.179	NEU-KingSoft
54.4	0.134	online-A
47.8	−0.099	lmu-unsup-nmt
46.6	−0.165	CUNI-Unsupervised-NER-post
41.7	−0.328	Unsupervised-6929
39.1	−0.405	Unsupervised-6935
28.4	−0.807	CAiRE

Table 12: Official results of WMT19 German to Czech Unsupervised News Translation Task. Systems ordered by DA score z-score; systems within a cluster are considered tied; lines indicate clusters according to Wilcoxon rank-sum test $p < 0.05$; grayed entry indicates resources that fall outside the constraints provided (in particular the use of parallel training data).

German→French

Ave.	Ave. z	System
77.0	0.249	MSRA-MADL
76.8	0.230	MLLP-UPV
74.8	0.164	Kyoto-University-T2T
75.5	0.160	lingua-custodia-primary
74.4	0.129	LIUM
72.7	0.038	online-B
71.7	0.019	online-Y
68.8	−0.104	TartuNLP-c
66.0	−0.194	online-A
65.0	−0.240	online-G
58.9	−0.456	online-X

French→German

Ave.	Ave. z	System
82.4	0.267	MSRA-MADL
81.5	0.246	eTranslation
78.5	0.082	LIUM
76.8	0.037	MLLP-UPV
76.0	0.001	online-Y
76.6	−0.018	online-G
75.2	−0.034	online-B
74.8	−0.039	online-A
73.9	−0.098	TartuNLP-c
66.5	−0.410	online-X

Table 13: Official results of WMT19 German to French and French to German News Translation Task for which the topic was restricted to EU Elections. Systems ordered by DA score z-score; systems within a cluster are considered tied; lines indicate clusters according to Wilcoxon rank-sum test $p < 0.05$; grayed entry indicates resources that fall outside the constraints provided.

German→English

Ave.	Ave. z	System
75.4	0.283	MSRA-MADL
77.5	0.243	online-B
75.9	0.227	Facebook-FAIR
75.1	0.202	JHU
71.3	0.192	UCAM
77.3	0.171	RWTH-Aachen
76.8	0.166	HUMAN
73.8	0.164	dfki-nmt
77.9	0.162	MLLP-UPV
75.1	0.150	NEU
73.1	0.137	online-Y
72.1	0.103	online-A
71.2	0.009	TartuNLP-c
73.2	−0.052	uedin
67.0	−0.183	online-G
69.0	−0.194	PROMT-NMT
62.8	−0.299	online-X

English→Czech

Ave.	Ave. z	System
84.0	0.915	HUMAN
76.4	0.537	CUNI-Transformer-T2T-2019
76.7	0.528	CUNI-Transformer-T2T-2018
73.7	0.474	CUNI-DocTransformer-T2T
69.7	0.299	CUNI-DocTransformer-Marian
70.0	0.234	uedin
60.0	−0.098	TartuNLP-c
59.9	−0.169	online-Y
57.3	−0.314	online-B
54.7	−0.368	online-G
47.7	−0.619	online-A
47.4	−0.763	online-X

English→German

Ave.	Ave. z	System
82.6	0.530	Facebook-FAIR
81.0	0.335	HUMAN
78.6	0.334	MSRA-MADL
81.3	0.314	Microsoft-WMT19-sent-doc
78.6	0.313	NEU
81.4	0.312	Microsoft-WMT19-doc-level
79.0	0.282	UCAM
77.3	0.268	MLLP-UPV
76.4	0.250	online-Y
78.1	0.200	eTranslation
74.0	0.198	online-B
76.3	0.176	JHU
74.1	0.169	lmu-ctx-tf-single
73.4	0.169	Helsinki-NLP
76.9	0.158	dfki-nmt
76.0	0.156	Microsoft-WMT19-sent-level
73.3	0.101	online-A
73.2	0.058	PROMT-NMT
74.8	0.008	online-G
70.1	−0.027	UdS-DFKI
71.1	−0.087	TartuNLP-c
67.3	−0.285	online-X
40.1	−1.555	en-de-task

English→Finnish

Ave.	Ave. z	System
86.2	1.225	HUMAN
72.9	0.776	GTCOM-Primary
71.0	0.745	MSRA-NAO
57.1	0.293	NICT
57.3	0.237	online-Y
55.1	0.127	Helsinki-NLP
52.2	0.070	online-B
49.6	0.038	online-G
46.2	−0.006	TartuNLP-c
38.0	−0.405	online-A
37.9	−0.433	online-X
39.3	−0.462	Helsinki-NLP-rule-based
14.0	−1.156	apertium-uc

English→Gujarati

Ave.	Ave. z	System
67.1	1.119	HUMAN
57.5	0.759	GTCOM-Primary
63.7	0.737	online-B
54.0	0.561	UEDIN
54.1	0.431	MSRA
47.2	0.146	CUNI-T2T-transfer
44.5	−0.178	Ju-Saarland-clean-num-135-bpe
35.0	−0.481	online-G
33.1	−0.495	IITP-MT
33.0	−0.496	NICT
27.1	−0.724	online-X
29.7	−0.791	UdS-DFKI

English→Kazakh

Ave.	Ave. z	System
73.7	0.883	HUMAN
64.1	0.471	UAlacant-NMT
59.9	0.269	UAlacant-NMT-RBMT
57.9	0.228	MSRA
56.5	0.223	online-B
55.7	0.166	NEU
56.6	0.138	online-G
53.5	0.071	CUNI-T2T-transfer
51.0	−0.039	rug-bpe
45.9	−0.342	talp-upc-2019
37.3	−0.550	NICT
12.2	−1.472	DBMS-KU

English→Lithuanian

Ave.	Ave. z	System
81.2	1.176	HUMAN
63.0	0.548	tilde-nc-nmt
55.4	0.367	MSRA-MASS-uc
58.6	0.342	MSRA-MASS-c
56.9	0.331	tilde-c-nmt
54.6	0.157	GTCOM-Primary
54.3	0.121	eTranslation
51.1	0.040	NEU
48.4	0.017	online-B
39.5	−0.338	TartuNLP-c
28.5	−0.738	online-A
28.8	−0.768	online-X
23.8	−0.797	online-G

English→Russian

Ave.	Ave. z	System
78.9	0.699	HUMAN
78.3	0.645	Facebook-FAIR
72.8	0.449	USTC-MCC
70.8	0.362	online-B
70.8	0.335	online-G
69.4	0.314	NEU
68.0	0.248	PROMT-NMT
65.2	0.157	online-Y
62.7	−0.099	rerank-er
59.9	−0.142	TartuNLP-u
56.8	−0.262	online-A
48.6	−0.389	online-X
32.8	−1.156	NICT

English→Chinese

Ave.	Ave. z	System
70.3	0.486	HUMAN
71.0	0.421	KSAI
69.4	0.303	Baidu
65.6	0.245	NEU
64.7	0.156	BTRANS
65.4	0.146	UEDIN
62.4	0.116	NICT
65.4	0.094	online-A
64.6	0.057	xzl-nmt
59.6	−0.081	online-B
60.5	−0.09	online-Y
58.0	−0.141	online-G
55.3	−0.346	online-X

Chinese→English

Ave.	Ave. z	System
77.7	0.278	Baidu
76.5	0.220	NEU
78.0	0.217	online-B
77.8	0.181	BTRANS-ensemble
74.5	0.169	MSRA-MASS
73.8	0.141	BTRANS
75.6	0.138	KSAI
73.4	0.070	UEDIN
75.6	0.051	online-Y
74.6	0.050	NICT
74.9	0.015	MSRA-MASS
73.4	−0.043	online-A
71.4	−0.104	online-G
67.7	−0.333	online-X
57.8	−0.915	Apprentice-c

Table 14: Document Rating+Document Context (DR+DC) results of WMT19 News Translation Task for subset of language pairs. Systems ordered by DA score z-score; systems within a cluster are considered tied; lines indicate clusters according to Wilcoxon rank-sum test $p < 0.05$; grayed entry indicates resources that fall outside the constraints provided.

Ave.	Ave. z	System
79.1	0.142	NEU
80.9	0.142	KSAI
79.0	0.139	MSRA-MASS
79.5	0.130	online-B
79.5	0.125	Baidu
77.9	0.076	MSRA-MASS
76.0	0.073	BTRANS
77.6	0.051	BTRANS-ensemble
78.0	0.047	online-Y
76.5	−0.015	online-A
75.1	−0.019	UEDIN
75.3	−0.033	NICT
73.3	−0.095	online-G
69.2	−0.276	online-X
58.4	−0.609	Apprentice-c

Table 15: Segment Rating+Document Context (SR+DC) results of WMT19 News Translation Task for Chinese to English. Systems ordered by DA score z-score; systems within a cluster are considered tied; lines indicate clusters according to Wilcoxon rank-sum test $p < 0.05$; grayed entry indicates resources that fall outside the constraints provided.

In contrast to the previous year, reference translations were scored significantly higher than MT systems in all these settings. It is thus not clear if the super-human quality observed last year was due to lower quality of last year's references, different set of documents or the segment-level style of evaluation as thoroughly discussed by Bojar et al. (2018).

The good news is that all the different types of evaluation correlate very well, with Pearson correlation coefficient ranging from .978 (Ave. of DR+DC vs. SR−DC Microsoft) to .998 (Ave. vs. Ave. z of SR+DC). The document-level ranking (DR+DC) correlates with all variants of segment-level ranking with Pearson of .981 to .996.

4 Test Suites

Following our practice since last year, we issued a call for "test suites", i.e. test sets focussed on particular language phenomena, to complement the standard manual and automatic evaluations of WMT News Translation system.

Each team in the test suites track provides source texts (and optionally references) for any language pair that is being evaluated by WMT News Task. We shuffle these additional texts into the inputs of News Task and ship them jointly with the regular news texts. MT system developers may decide to skip these documents based on their ID but most of them process test suites along with the main news texts. After collecting the output translations from all WMT News Task Partic-

ipants, we extract translated test suites, unshuffle them and send them back to the corresponding test-suite team. It was up to the test-suite team to evaluate MT outputs and some did this automatically, some manually and some both.

When shuffling, test suites this year closely observed document boundaries. If a test suite was marked as sentence-level only by their authors, we treated individual sentences as if they were one-sentence documents. This lead to a very high number of input documents for some language pairs but all News Task participants managed to handle this additional burden.

As in the previous year, we have to note that test suites go beyond the news domain. If News Task systems are too heavily optimized for news, they may underperform on these domains.

The primary motivation in 2018 was to cut through the opacity of evaluations. We wanted to know more details than just which systems perform better or worse *on average*. This motivation remains also this year but one more reason for people providing test suites was to examine the *human parity* question from additional viewpoints beyond what Bojar et al. (2018) discuss for English→Czech and Hassan et al. (2018) for Chinese→English.

4.1 Test Suite Details

The following paragraphs briefly describe each of the test suites. Please refer to the respective paper for all the details of the evaluation.

4.1.1 Audits and Agreements (Vojtěchová et al., 2019)

The test suite provided by the ELITR project (Vojtěchová et al., 2019) focuses on document-level qualities of two types of documents, audit reports and agreements (represented with only one document, in fact), for the top-performing English-to-Czech systems and some English↔German systems.

The English-to-Czech systems were found as matching or perhaps even surpassing the quality of news reference translations in WMT18 (Bojar et al., 2018) and they also perform very well this year on news. The test suite wanted to validate if this quality transfers (without any specific domain adaptation) also to the domain of reports of supreme audit institutions, which is much more sensitive to terminological choices, and the domain of agreements, where term consistence is

Official SR+DC

Ave.	Ave. z	System
91.2	0.642	HUMAN
86.0	0.402	CUNI-DocTransformer-T2T
86.9	0.401	CUNI-Transformer-T2T-2018
85.4	0.388	CUNI-Transformer-T2T-2019
81.3	0.223	CUNI-DocTransformer-Marian
80.5	0.206	uedin
70.8	−0.156	online-Y
71.4	−0.195	TartuNLP-c
67.8	−0.300	online-G
68.0	−0.336	online-B
60.9	−0.594	online-A
59.3	−0.651	online-X

SR−DC WMT

Ave. z	System
0.62538	HUMAN
0.40505	CUNI-Transformer-T2T-2018
0.39463	CUNI-DocTransformer-T2T
0.35678	CUNI-Transformer-T2T-2019
0.31261	CUNI-DocTransformer-Marian
0.26538	uedin
-0.17006	TartuNLP-c
-0.18841	online-Y
-0.26188	online-B
-0.36871	online-G
-0.67123	online-A
-0.72614	online-X

DR+DC

Ave.	Ave. z	System
84.0	0.915	HUMAN
76.4	0.537	CUNI-Transformer-T2T-2019
76.7	0.528	CUNI-Transformer-T2T-2018
73.7	0.474	CUNI-DocTransformer-T2T
69.7	0.299	CUNI-DocTransformer-Marian
70.0	0.234	uedin
60.0	−0.098	TartuNLP-c
59.9	−0.169	online-Y
57.3	−0.314	online-B
54.7	−0.368	online-G
47.7	−0.619	online-A
47.4	−0.763	online-X

SR−DC Microsoft

Ave. z	System
0.39909	HUMAN
0.30170	CUNI-DocTransformer-T2T
0.28599	CUNI-Transformer-T2T-2018
0.27254	CUNI-Transformer-T2T-2019
0.21186	uedin
0.19160	CUNI-DocTransformer-Marian
-0.05716	TartuNLP-c
-0.09987	online-Y
-0.21633	online-B
-0.29386	online-G
-0.40917	online-A
-0.58836	online-X

Table 16: English-Czech translation: A comparison of SR+DC (official), DR+DC (doclevel) and two versions of segments-evaluation (SR−DC): by WMT annotators and Microsoft annotators.

critical.

The main findings are that also for precise texts (even if intended for the general public and written in a relatively simple language), current NMT systems are close to matching human translation quality. Terminological choices are a little worse but syntax and overall understandability was scored on par or better than the human reference (mixed among the system in an anonymous way). This can be seen as an indication of human parity even out of the original domain of the systems, although the official evaluation on news this year ranks the reference significantly higher.

A very important observation is that (single) reference translations are insufficient because they don't reflect the truly possible term translations. Manual non-expert evaluation would also not be sufficiently reliable because non-experts do not realize the subtle meaning differences among the terms.

On the other hand, the micro-study on agreements reveals that even these very good systems produce practically useless translations of agreements because none of them handles document-specific terms and their consistent translations whatsoever.

4.1.2 Linguistic Evaluation of German-to-English (Avramidis et al., 2019)

The test suite by DFKI covers 107 grammatical phenomena organized into 14 categories. The test suite is very closely related to the one used last year (Macketanz et al., 2018), which allows an evaluation over time.

The test suite is evaluated semi-automatically on a large set of sentences (over 25k) illustrating each of the examined phenomenon and equipped with automatic checks for anticipated good and bad translations. The outputs of these checks are manually verified and refined.

The cross-year comparison is naturally affected by the different set of systems participating in each of the evaluations, but some trends are still observed, namely the improvement in function words, non-verbal agreement and punctuation. The least improvement is seen in terminology and named entities.

Overall, MT system still translate on average about 25% of the tested sentences wrongly. The worst performance is seen for idioms (88% wrong) and complex German verbal grammar (72–77% wrong). Specific terminology and some grammatical phenomena reach about 50%. The paper also indicates phenomena with error rate below 10%, e.g. negation or several cases of verb conjugation.

4.1.3 Document-Level Phenomena (Rysová et al., 2019)

The English-to-Czech test suite by Rysová et al. (2019) builds upon discourse linguistics and manually evaluates three phenomena related to document-level coherence, namely topic-focus articulation (information structure), discourse connectives and alternative lexicalizations of connectives (essentially multi-word discourse connectives). Co-reference is deliberately not included.

The 101 test suite documents (3.5k source sentences in total) come from Penn Discourse Treebank and are speficically the "essay" or "letter" type. The manual evaluation by trained linguists considered always the whole document: the source English text and one of the MT outputs. Targetted phenomena were highlighted in the source and the annotators marked whether they agree with the source annotation and (if yes) whether the respective source phenomenon is also refleted in the target. The reference translation comes from Prague Czech-English Dependency Treebank (Hajič et al., 2012) and it was included in the annotation in a blind way, as if it was one of the MT systems.

The results indicate that the examined phenomena are also handled by the MT systems exceptionally well, matching human quality or even negligibly outperforming humans, e.g. in the mutli-word discourse connectives. Interestingly, the English-Czech systems trained in some document-level way this year do not seem any better than the segment-level ones.

4.1.4 Producing German Conjuctions from English and French (Popović, 2019)

The test suite by Popović (2019) contains approximately 1000 English and 1000 individual French sentences that were included in the English→German and French→German tasks. The sentences focus on the translation of the English "but" and French "mais" which should be disambiguated into German "aber" or "sondern".

Except for 1–2% of cases (when no conjunction or both possibilities are found in the target), the outputs can be evaluated automatically. The results indicate that the situation when "aber" is needed is recognized almost perfectly by all the system but the situation which requires "sondern" is sometimes mishandled and the (generally more frequent) "aber" is used. The error rate ranges from 3% (TARTUNLP-C) to 14% (ONLINE-X) or 22% (the unclear system called EN-DE-TASK)

4.1.5 Out-of-Domain Check of Formal Language for German→English (Biçici, 2019)

A small test suite by Biçici (2019) contains 38 sentences from texts by Prussian Cultural Heritage Foundation, checking the performance of MT systems on the domain of cross-cultural international relations.

The test suite is evaluated only with a few automatic measures with no clear conclusion.

4.1.6 Word Sense Disambiguation (Raganato et al., 2019)

Raganato et al. (2019) present the MuCoW (multilingual contrastive word sense disambiguation) test suite which contains a relatively large set of sentences (69–4268 depending on the language pair) mined from parallel corpora to illustrate words which are particularly ambiguous for the given translation pair.

Originally, the test suite relies on MT systems scoring candidate pairs of sentences. Raganato et al. (2019) adapt it for the use case of WMT test suites where the black-box MT systems only provide their translation output. Due care is taken in sentence selection, in particular any overlap with WMT constrained training data is avoided.

The test suite covers from German, Finnish, Lithuanian and Russian into English and from English into these four langauges and Czech.

The ambiguous words were identified with the help of BabelNet (Navigli and Ponzetto, 2012) multilingual synsets and the granularity was reduced with the help of word embeddings to ensure that the meaning distinctions are reliably big. For the WMT use case, there are dozens or a few hundreds of ambiguous source words (except Lithuanian with only very few words) with slightly more than 2 distinct word senses per examined source word on average.

The results show that overall, WMT systems perform quite well word-sense disambiguation when evaluated in the "in-domain" setting (word senses not too common in subtitle corpora), with precision (examples with correct target words over examples with either correct or incorrect target words) in the ranges 64–80% (e.g. Finnish→English or English→German) up to 95–97% (English→Czech) depending on the language pair. The recalls (examples with correct target words over all examples) are similarly high, 65–91 across the board.

The "out-of-domain" evaluation was directed at word senses common in colloquial speech and in general, research WMT news system perform a little worse than online systems in these scores except for English-Czech.

5   Similar Language Translation

Within the MT and NLP communities, English is by far the most resource-rich language. MT systems are most often trained to translate texts from and to English or they use English as a pivot language to translate between resource-poorer languages. The interest in English is reflected, for example, in the WMT translation tasks (e.g. News, Biomedical) which have always included language pairs in which texts are translated to and/or from English.

With the widespread use of MT technology, there is more and more interest in training systems to translate between languages other than English. One evidence of this is the need of directly translating between pairs of similar languages, varieties, and dialects (Zhang, 1998; Marujo et al., 2011; Hassani, 2017; Costa-jussà et al., 2018). The main challenge is to take advantage of the similarity between languages to overcome the limitation given the low amount of available parallel data to produce an accurate output.

Given the interest of the community in this topic we organize, for the first time at WMT, a shared task on "Similar Language Translation" to evaluate the performance of state-of-the-art translation systems on translating between pairs of languages from the same language family. We provide participants with training and testing data from three language pairs: Spanish - Portuguese (Romance languages), Czech - Polish (Slavic languages), and Hindi - Nepali (Indo-Aryan languages). Evaluation will be carried out using automatic evaluation metrics and human evaluation.

5.1   Data

Training   We have made available a number of data sources for the Similar Language Translation shared task. Some training datasets were used in the previous editions of the WMT News Translation shared task and were updated (Europarl v9, News Commentary v14), while some corpora were newly introduced (Wiki Titles v1, JRC Acquis). For the Hi–Ne language pair, parallel corpora have been collected from Opus (Tiedemann and Nygaard, 2004)[19]. We used the Ubuntu, KDE, and Gnome corpus available at OPUS for this shared task.

Development and Test Data   The creation of development and test sets for Czech and Polish involved random extraction of 30 TED talks for the development and 30 TED talks for the test set in each language. Then unique sentences were extracted and cleaning of lines containing meta-data information was performed which resulted in 4.7k sentences in the development sets and 4.8k sentences in the test sets. Further cleaning of the corpus to retain only sentences between 7 and 100 words limited the number of the sentences in the dev and test sets to 3050 and 3412 sentences respectively.

The development and test sets for Spanish and Portuguese were created from a corpus provided by AT Language Solutions [20]. First, the extraction of unique sentences and cleaning of lines containing meta-data information was performed which narrowed the number of sentences to 11.7k sentences. Then cleaning of the corpus to retain only sentences between 7 and 100 words limited the number of the sentences to 6.8k. Finally, 3k randomly selected sentences were used for the development set and other 3k random sentences were extracted to form the test set. For HI–NE, all data was initially combined and randomly shuffled. From the combined corpus, we randomly extracted 65,505 sentences for the training set, 3,000 sentences for development set and 3,567 for the test set. Finally, the test set was split into two different test sets: 2,000 sentences used for HI to NE and 1,557 sentences were used for NE to HI.

5.2   Participants

The first edition of the WMT Similar Language Translation task attracted more participants than we anticipated. There were 35 teams who signed up to participate in the competition and 14 of them submitted their system outputs to one of the three language pairs in any translation direction. In the

---

[19]http://opus.nlpl.eu/
[20]https://www.at-languagesolutions.com/en/

Table 17: Europarl v9 Parallel Corpus

	Czech ↔ Polish		Spanish ↔ Portuguese	
sentences	631372		1811977	
words	12526659	12641841	47832025	46191472

Table 18: Wiki Titles v1 Parallel Corpus

	Czech ↔ Polish		Spanish ↔ Portuguese	
sentences	248645		621296	
words	551084	554335	1564668	1533764

Table 19: JRC-Acquis Parallel Corpus

	Czech ↔ Polish		Spanish ↔ Portuguese	
sentences	1311362		1650126	
words	21409363	21880482	35868080	33474269

Table 20: News Commentary v14 Parallel Corpus

	Spanish ↔ Portuguese	
sentences	48168	
words	1271324	1219031

Table 21: GNOME, Ubuntu, KDE Parallel Corpus

	Hindi ↔ Nepali	
sentences	65505	
words	253216	222823

Table 22: Europarl v9 Monolingual Corpus

	Czech	Polish	Spanish	Portuguese
sentences	665433	382726	2019336	2015290
words	13199347	7087267	52157546	50462045

Table 23: News Crawl Monolingual Corpus

	Czech	Polish	Spanish	Portuguese
sentences	72157988	814754	43814290	8301536
words	1019497060	12370354	1159300825	160477593

Table 24: News Commentary v14 Monolingual Corpus

	Czech	Spanish	Portuguese
sentences	266705	424063	59502
words	4922572	10724738	1443204

end of the competition, 10 teams submitted system description papers which are referred to in this report. Table 25 summarizes the participation across language pairs and translation directions and includes references to the 10 system description papers.

We observed that the majority of teams contain only members which work in universities and research centers (12 teams) whereas only two teams contain members who work in the industry. The participants were distributed across different continents with a higher participation of European teams (7 European) with two teams based on the Americas, and five Asian teams.

As follows we provide summaries for each of the entries we received:

BSC: Team BSC (Barcelona SuperComputing Center) participated with a Transfomer-based approach in the Spanish-Portuguese track. As pre-processing, SentencePiece [21] was applied after concatenating and shuffling the data. For the Portuguese to Spanish language direction, BSC made use of back-translation.

CFILT_IITB: The CFILT_IITB submission (Khatri and Bhattacharyya, 2019) is based on unsupervised neural machine translation described in Artetxe et al. (2018) in the task Hindi ↔ Nepali, where encoder is shared and following bidirectional recurrent neural network architecture. They used 2 hidden layers for both encoder and decoder.

CMUMEAN: The is system is based on standard

---

[21] https://github.com/google/sentencepiece

transformer based NMT model for the Hindi ↔ Nepali shared task. To compensate the insufficient released parallel data, they utilized 7M monolingual data for both Hindi and Nepali taken from CommonCrawl. They augmented the monolingual data by constructing pseudo-parallel datasets. The pseudo-parallel sentences were constructed by word substitutions, based on a mapping of the embedding spaces of the two languages. These mapping were learned from all data and a seed dictionary based on the alignment of the parallel data.

Incomslav: Team INCOMSLAV (Chen and Avgustinova, 2019) by Saarlad University participated in the Czech to Polish translation task only. The team's primary submission builds on a transformer-based NMT baseline with back translation which has been submitted one of their contrastive submission. Incomslav's primary system is a phoneme-based system re-scored using their NMT baseline. A second contrastive submission builds our phrase-based SMT system combined with a joint BPE model.

JUMT: This submittion used phrase based statistical machine translation model for Hindi → Nepali task. They used 3-gram language model and MGIZA++ for word alignment. However, their system achieved poor performance in the shared task.

MLLP-UPV: Team MLLP-UPV (Baquero-Arnal et al., 2019) by Universitat Politècnica de València (UPV) participated with a Transformer (implemented with FairSeq (Ott et al., 2019)) and a fine-tuning strategy for domain adaptaion in the task of Spanish-Portuguese. Fine-tunning on the development data provide improvements of almost 12 BLEU points, which may explain their clear best performance in the task for this language pair. As a contrastive system authors provided only for the Portuguese-to-Spanish a novel 2D alternating RNN model which did not respond so well when fine-tunning.

KYOTOUNIVERSITY: Kyoto University's submission, listed simply as KYOTO in Table 25 for PT → ES task is based on transformer NMT system. They used difference word segmentation strategies during preprocessing. Additionally they used optional reverse feature in their prepro-

cessing step. Their submission achieved average scores in the shared task.

NICT: The NICT team (Marie et al., 2019a) participated with the a system combination between the Transformer (implemented in Marian (Junczys-Dowmunt et al., 2018) and Phrase-based machine translation system (implemented with Moses) and for the Spanish-Portuguese task. The system combination included features formerly presented in (Marie and Fujita, 2018), including scores left-to-right and right-to-left, sentence level translation probabilities and language model scores. Also authors provide contrastive results with an unsupervised phrase-based MT system which achieves quite close results to their primary system. Authors associate high performance of the unsupervised system to the language similarity.

NITS-CNLP: The NITS-CNLP team (Laskar et al., 2019) by the National Institute of Technology Silchar in India submitted results to the HI-NE translation task in both directions. The NITS-CNLP systems are based on Marian NMT (Junczys-Dowmunt et al., 2018) and Open NMT implementations of sequence-to-sequence RNNs with attention mechanisms. Their contrastive submissions were ranking first in both Hindi to Nepali and Nepali to Hindi translation.

Panlingua-KMI: The Panlingua-KMI team (Ojha et al., 2019) tested phrase-based SMT and NMT methods for HI-NE translation in both directions. The PBSMT systems have been trained using Moses (Koehn et al., 2007) and KenLM. Their two NMT systems were built using OpenNMT. The first system was built with 2 layers using LSTM model while the second system was built with 6 layers using the Transformer model.

UBC-NLP: Team UBC-NLP from the University of British Columbia in Canada (Przystupa and Abdul-Mageed, 2019) compared the performance of the LSTM plus attention (Bahdanau et al., 2015) and Transformer (Vaswani et al., 2017) (implemented in OpenNMT toolkit[22]) perform for the three tasks at hand. Authors use backtranslation to introduce monolingual data in their systems. LSTM plus attention outperformed Transformer for Hindi-Nepali, and viceversa for the other two tasks. As reported by the authors, Hindi-Nepali task provides much more shorter sentences than

---

[22] http://opennmt.net/

the other two-tasks. Additionally, authors in their system description report interesting insights on how similar are languages in each of the 3 different tasks.

UDS-DFKI: The UDS-DFKI team (Pal et al., 2019) is formed by researchers from Saarland University (UDS), the German Research Foundation of Artificial Intelligence (DFKI), and the University of Wolverhampton. They submitted a *transference* model that extends the original transformer model to multi-encoder based transformer architecture. The *transference* model contains two encodes, the first encoder encodes word form information of the source (CS), and a second encoder to encode sub-word (byte-pair-encoding) information of the source (CS). The results obtained by their system in translating from Czech→Polish and comment on the impact of out-of-domain test data in the performance of their system. UDS-DFKI ranked second among ten teams in Czech–Polish translation.

UHelsinki: The University of Helsinki team (Scherrer et al., 2019) participated with the Transformer (Vaswani et al., 2017) implemented in the OpenNMT toolkit. They focused on word segmentation methods and compared a cognate-aware segmentation method, Cognate Morfessor (Grönroos et al., 2018), with character segmentation and unsupervised segmentation methods. As primary submission they submitted this Cognate Morfessor that optimizes subword segmentations consistently for cognates. They participated for all translation directions in Spanish-Portuguese and Czech-Polish, and this Cognate Morfessor performed better for Czech-Polish, while character-based segmentations (Costa-jussà and Fonollosa, 2016), while much more inefficient, were superior for Spanish-Portuguese.

UPC-TALP: The UPC-TALP team (Biesialska et al., 2019) by the Universitat Politècnica de Catalunya submitted a Transformer (implemented with Fairseq (Ott et al., 2019)) for the Czech-to-Polish task and a Phrase-based system (implemented with Moses (Koehn et al., 2007)) for Spanish-to-Portuguese. They tested adding monolingual data to the NMT system by copying the same data on the source and target sides, with negative results. Also, their system combination based on sentence-level BLEU in back-translation

did not succeed. Authors provide interesting insights on language distance based on previous work by (Gamallo et al., 2017) and their results show that the Phrase-based compared to NMT achieves better results when the language distance between source and target language is lower.

5.3 Results

We present results for the three language pairs, each of them in the two possible directions. For this first edition of the Similar Translation Task and differently from News task, evaluation was only performed on automatic basis using BLEU (Papineni et al., 2002) and TER (Snover et al., 2006) measures. Each language direction is reported in one different table which contain information of the team; type of system, either contrastive (C) or primary (P), and the BLEU and TER results. In general, primary systems tend to be better than contrastive systems, as expected, but there are some exceptions.

Even if we are presenting 3 pairs of languages each pair belonging to the same family, translation quality in terms of BLEU varies signficantly. While the best systems for Spanish-Portuguese are above 64 BLEU and below 21 TER (see Tables 26 and 27), best systems for Czech-Polish do not reach the 8 BLEU and the 79.6 TER for the direction with lowest TER (Polish-to-Czech). The case of Hindi-Nepali is in between, with BLEU of 53.7 and TER of 36.3 for the better direcion Hindi-to-Nepali. Also, we noticed that BLEU and TER do not always correlate and while some systems performed better in BLEU, the ranking is different if ordered by TER. In any case, we chose BLEU as the official metric for ranking.

The highest variance of system performance can be found in Hindi-Nepali (both directions), where the best performing system is around 50 BLEU (53 for Hindi-to-Nepali and 49.1 for Nepali-to-Hindi), and the lowest entry is 1.4 for Hindi-to-Nepali and 0 for Nepali-to-Hindi. The lowest variance is for Polish-to-Czech and it may be because only two teams participated.

5.4 Conclusion of Similar Language Translation

In this section we presented the results of the WMT Similar Language Translation shared task 2019. The competition featured data in three language pairs: Czech-Polish, and Hindi-Nepali, and Portuguese-Spanish.

Team	CS→PL	PL→CS	HI→NE	NE→HI	PT→ES	ES→PT	Paper
BSC					✓	✓	
CFILT_IITB			✓	✓			Khatri and Bhattacharyya (2019)
CMUMEAN			✓	✓			
Incomslav	✓						Chen and Avgustinova (2019)
JUMT			✓				
KYOTO					✓		
MLLP-UPV					✓	✓	Baquero-Arnal et al. (2019)
NICT					✓		Marie et al. (2019a)
NITS-CNLP			✓	✓			Laskar et al. (2019)
Panlingua-KMI			✓	✓			Ojha et al. (2019)
UBC-NLP	✓	✓	✓	✓	✓	✓	Przystupa and Abdul-Mageed (2019)
UDS-DFKI	✓						Pal et al. (2019)
UHelsinki	✓	✓			✓	✓	Scherrer et al. (2019)
UPC-TALP	✓					✓	Biesialska et al. (2019)
Total	5	2	6	5	6	5	10

Table 25: The teams that participated in the Similar Translation Task.

Team	Type	BLEU	TER
MLLPUPV	P	66.6	19.7
NICT	P	59.9	25.3
Uhelsinki	C	59.1	25.5
Uhelsinki	C	58.6	25.1
Uhelsinki	P	58.4	25.3
KYOTOUNIVERSITY	P	56.9	26.9
NICT	C	54.9	28.4
BSC	P	54.8	29.8
UBC-NLP	P	52.3	32.9
UBC-NLP	C	52.2	32.8
MLLPUPV	C	51.9	30.5
MLLPUPV	C	49.7	32.1
BSC	C	48.5	35.1

Table 26: Results for Portuguese to Spanish Translation

Team	Type	BLEU	TER
NITS-CNLP	C	53.7	36.3
Panlingua-KMI	P	11.5	79.1
CMUMEAN	P	11.1	79.7
UBC-NLP	P	08.2	77.1
UBC-NLP	C	08.2	77.2
NITS-CNLP	P	03.7	-
NITS-CNLP	C	03.6	-
CFILT_IITB	C	03.5	-
Panlingua-KMI	C	03.1	-
CFILT_IITB	P	02.8	-
CFILT_IITB	C	02.7	-
Panlingua-KMI	C	01.6	-
JUMT	P	01.4	-

Table 28: Results for Hindi to Nepali Translation

Team	Type	BLEU	TER
MLLPUPV	P	64.7	20.8
UPC-TALP	P	62.1	23.0
NICT	P	53.3	29.1
Uhelsinki	C	52.8	28.6
Uhelsinki	P	52.0	29.4
Uhelsinki	C	51.0	33.1
NICT	C	47.9	33.4
UBC-NLP	P	46.1	36.0
UBC-NLP	C	46.1	35.9
MLLPUPV	C	45.5	35.3
BSC	P	44.0	37.5

Table 27: Results for Spanish to Portuguese Translation

Team	Type	BLEU	TER
NITS-CNLP	C	49.1	43.0
NITS-CNLP	P	24.6	69.1
CMUMEAN	P	12.1	76.2
Panlingua-KMI	P	09.8	91.3
UBC-NLP	P	09.1	88.3
UBC-NLP	C	09.1	88.4
Panlingua-KMI	C	04.2	-
Panlingua-KMI	C	03.6	-
CFILT_IITB	P	02.7	-
NITS-CNLP	C	01.4	-
CFILT_IITB	C	0	-
CFILT_IITB	C	0	-

Table 29: Results for Nepali to Hindi Translation

For the future it is worth investigating why languages from the same family, like Czech-Polish have extremely low performance. Authors in (Biesialska et al., 2019), with the best performing system in Czech-to-Polish, hypothesize that one of the reasons is the different in alphabets from both languages. Additionally, they refer to

Team	Type	BLEU	TER
UPC-TALP	P	7.9	85.9
UDS-DFKI	P	7.6	87.0
Uhelsinki	P	7.1	87.4
Uhelsinki	C	7.0	87.3
Incomslav	C	5.9	88.4
Uhelsinki	C	5.9	88.4
Incomslav	P	3.2	-
Incomslav	C	3.1	-
UBC-NLP	C	2.3	-
UBC-NLP	P	2.2	-

Table 30: Results for Czech to Polish Translation

Team	Type	BLEU	TER
Uhelsinki	C	7.2	79.6
Uhelsinki	P	7.0	79.4
UBC-NLP	P	6.9	86.5
UBC-NLP	C	6.9	86.2
Uhelsinki	C	6.6	80.2

Table 31: Results for Polish to Czech Translation

Gamallo et al. (2017) and provide big language distances for Czech-Polish compared to Spanish-Portuguese.

6 Conclusion

We presented the results of the WMT18 News Translation Shared Task. Our main findings rank participating systems in their sentence-level translation quality, as assessed in a large-scale manual evaluation using the method of Direct Assessment (DA).

The novelties this year include (1) avoiding effects of translationese by creating reference translations always in the same directions as the MT systems are run, (2) providing human assessors with the context of the whole document when assessing individual segments for a large portion of language pairs, (3) extending the set of languages which are evaluated given the *source*, not the reference translation, and (4) scoring also whole documents, not only individual segments.

Our results indicate which MT systems perform best across the 18 examined translation pairs, as well as what features are now commonly used in the field. The test suites complement this evaluation by focussing on particular language phenomena such as word-sense disambiguation, document-level coherence or terminological correctness.

As in the previous year, MT systems seem to reach the quality of human translation in the news domain for some language pairs. This result has to be regarded with a great caution and considering the technical details of the (document-aware) DA evaluation method as well as the outcomes of complementary evaluations, such as those included in the test suites. Importantly, the language pairs where the parity was reached last year were not confirmed by the evaluation this year and a similar situation can repeat. As one of the test suites (Vojtěchová et al., 2019) suggests, there are aspects of texts which are wrongly handled by even the best translation systems.

The task on similar language translation indicated that the performance in this area is extremely varied across language pairs as well as across participating teams.

Acknowledgments

This work was supported in part by funding from the European Union's Horizon 2020 research and innovation programme under grant agreement Nos. 825299 (GoURMET) and 825303 (Bergamot), and from the Connecting Europe Facility under agreement No. NEA/CEF/ICT/A2016/1331648 (ParaCrawl).

The human evaluation campaign was very gratefully supported by Apple, Microsoft, and Science Foundation Ireland in the ADAPT Centre for Digital Content Technology (`www.adaptcentre.ie`) at Dublin City University funded under the SFI Research Centres Programme (Grant 13/RC/2106) co-funded under the European Regional Development Fund.

We are grateful to the large number of anonymous Mechanical Turk workers who contributed their human intelligence to the human evaluation.

Ondřej Bojar would like to acknowledge also the grant no. 19-26934X (NEUREM3) of the Czech Science Foundation.

The organizers of the similar languages task want to thank Magdalena Biesialska for her support in the compilation of the Czech-Polish data set as well as her valuable support as a Polish native speaker. This work is supported in part by the Spanish Ministerio de Economía y Competitividad, the European Regional Development Fund and the Agencia Estatal de Investigación, through the postdoctoral senior grant Ramón y Cajal, through the travel grant José Castillejo, CAS18/00223, the contract TEC2015-69266-P

(MINECO/FEDER,EU) and the contract PCIN-2017-079 (AEI/MINECO). The authors also want to thank German research foundation (DFG) under grant number GE 2819/2-1 (project MMPE) and the German Federal Ministry of Education and Research (BMBF) under funding code 01IW17001 (project Deeplee).

References

Mikel Artetxe, Gorka Labaka, Eneko Agirre, and Kyunghyun Cho. 2018. Unsupervised neural machine translation. In *Proceedings of the Sixth International Conference on Learning Representations*.

Eleftherios Avramidis, Vivien Macketanz, Ursula Strohriegel, and Hans Uszkoreit. 2019. Linguistic Evaluation of German-English Machine Translation Using a Test Suite. In *Proceedings of the Fourth Conference on Machine Translation*, Florence, Italy. Association for Computational Linguistics.

Dzmitry Bahdanau, Kyunghyun Cho, and Yoshua Bengio. 2015. Neural machine translation by jointly learning to align and translate. In *3rd International Conference on Learning Representations, ICLR 2015, San Diego, CA, USA, May 7-9, 2015, Conference Track Proceedings*.

Pau Baquero-Arnal, Javier Iranzo-Sánchez, Jorge Civera, and Alfons Juan. 2019. The MLLP-UPV Spanish-Portuguese and Portuguese-Spanish Machine Translation Systems for WMT19 Similar Language Translation Task. In *Proceedings of the Fourth Conference on Machine Translation*, Florence, Italy. Association for Computational Linguistics.

Rachel Bawden, Nikolay Bogoychev, Ulrich Germann, Roman Grundkiewicz, Faheem Kirefu, Antonio Valerio Miceli Barone, and Alexandra Birch. 2019a. The University of Edinburgh's Submissions to the WMT19 News Translation Task. In *Proceedings of the Fourth Conference on Machine Translation*, Florence, Italy. Association for Computational Linguistics.

Rachel Bawden, Kevin Bretonnel Cohen, Cristian Grozea, Antonio Jimeno Yepes, Madeleine Kittner, Martin Krallinger, Nancy Mah, Aurelie Neveol, Mariana Neves, Felipe Soares, Amy Siu, Karin Verspoor, and Maika Vicente Navarro. 2019b. Findings of the WMT 2019 Biomedical Translation Shared Task: Evaluation for MEDLINE Abstracts and Biomedical Terminologies. In *Proceedings of the Fourth Conference on Machine Translation*, Florence, Italy. Association for Computational Linguistics.

Chao Bei, Hao Zong, Conghu Yuan, Qingming Liu, and Baoyong Fan. 2019. GTCOM Neural Machine Translation Systems for WMT19. In *Proceedings of the Fourth Conference on Machine Translation*, Florence, Italy. Association for Computational Linguistics.

Magdalena Biesialska, Lluis Guardia, and Marta R. Costa-jussà. 2019. The TALP-UPC System for the WMT Similar Language Task: Statistical vs Neural Machine Translation. In *Proceedings of the Fourth Conference on Machine Translation*, Florence, Italy. Association for Computational Linguistics.

Ergun Biçici. 2019. Machine Translation with parfda, Moses, kenlm, nplm, and PRO. In *Proceedings of the Fourth Conference on Machine Translation*, Florence, Italy. Association for Computational Linguistics.

Nikolay Bogoychev, Marcin Junczys-Dowmunt, Kenneth Heafield, and Alham Fikri Aji. 2018. Accelerating asynchronous stochastic gradient descent for neural machine translation. In *Proceedings of the 2018 Conference on Empirical Methods in Natural Language Processing*, Brussels, Belgium.

Ondřej Bojar, Christian Buck, Christian Federmann, Barry Haddow, Philipp Koehn, Johannes Leveling, Christof Monz, Pavel Pecina, Matt Post, Herve Saint-Amand, Radu Soricut, Lucia Specia, and Aleš Tamchyna. 2014. Findings of the 2014 Workshop on Statistical Machine Translation. In *Proceedings of the Ninth Workshop on Statistical Machine Translation*, pages 12–58, Baltimore, Maryland, USA. Association for Computational Linguistics.

Ondřej Bojar, Rajen Chatterjee, Christian Federmann, Yvette Graham, Barry Haddow, Matthias Huck, Philipp Koehn, Varvara Logacheva, Christof Monz, Matteo Negri, Matt Post, Raphael Rubino, Lucia Specia, and Marco Turchi. 2017. Findings of the 2017 Conference on Machine Translation (WMT17). In *Proceedings of the Second Conference on Machine Translation*, Copenhagen, Denmark. Association for Computational Linguistics.

Ondřej Bojar, Christian Federmann, Mark Fishel, Yvette Graham, Barry Haddow, Philipp Koehn, and Christof Monz. 2018. Findings of the 2018 conference on machine translation (WMT18). In *Proceedings of the Third Conference on Machine Translation: Shared Task Papers*, pages 272–303, Belgium, Brussels. Association for Computational Linguistics.

Ondřej Bojar, Christian Buck, Chris Callison-Burch, Christian Federmann, Barry Haddow, Philipp Koehn, Christof Monz, Matt Post, Radu Soricut, and Lucia Specia. 2013. Findings of the 2013 Workshop on Statistical Machine Translation. In *Proceedings of the Eighth Workshop on Statistical Machine Translation*, pages 1–44, Sofia, Bulgaria. Association for Computational Linguistics.

Ondřej Bojar, Rajen Chatterjee, Christian Federmann, Yvette Graham, Barry Haddow, Matthias Huck, Antonio Jimeno Yepes, Philipp Koehn, Varvara

Logacheva, Christof Monz, Matteo Negri, Aurelie Neveol, Mariana Neves, Martin Popel, Matt Post, Raphael Rubino, Carolina Scarton, Lucia Specia, Marco Turchi, Karin Verspoor, and Marcos Zampieri. 2016. Findings of the 2016 Conference on Machine Translation. In *Proceedings of the First Conference on Machine Translation*, pages 131–198, Berlin, Germany. Association for Computational Linguistics.

Ondřej Bojar, Rajen Chatterjee, Christian Federmann, Barry Haddow, Matthias Huck, Chris Hokamp, Philipp Koehn, Varvara Logacheva, Christof Monz, Matteo Negri, Matt Post, Carolina Scarton, Lucia Specia, and Marco Turchi. 2015. Findings of the 2015 Workshop on Statistical Machine Translation. In *Proceedings of the Tenth Workshop on Statistical Machine Translation*, pages 1–46, Lisbon, Portugal. Association for Computational Linguistics.

Fethi Bougares, Jane Wottawa, Anne Baillot, Loïc Barrault, and Adrien Bardet. 2019. LIUM's Contributions to the WMT2019 News Translation Task: Data and Systems for German-French Language Pairs. In *Proceedings of the Fourth Conference on Machine Translation*, Florence, Italy. Association for Computational Linguistics.

Eleftheria Briakou and Marine Carpuat. 2019. The University of Maryland's Kazakh-English Neural Machine Translation System at WMT19. In *Proceedings of the Fourth Conference on Machine Translation*, Florence, Italy. Association for Computational Linguistics.

Sari Dewi Budiwati, Al Hafiz Akbar Maulana Siagian, Tirana Noor Fatyanosa, and Masayoshi Aritsugi. 2019. DBMS-KU Interpolation for WMT19 News Translation Task. In *Proceedings of the Fourth Conference on Machine Translation*, Florence, Italy. Association for Computational Linguistics.

Franck Burlot. 2019. Lingua Custodia at WMT'19: Attempts to Control Terminology. In *Proceedings of the Fourth Conference on Machine Translation*, Florence, Italy. Association for Computational Linguistics.

Chris Callison-Burch, Cameron Shaw Fordyce, Philipp Koehn, Christof Monz, and Josh Schroeder. 2007. (Meta-) Evaluation of Machine Translation. In *Proceedings of the Second Workshop on Statistical Machine Translation*, pages 136–158, Prague, Czech Republic. Association for Computational Linguistics.

Chris Callison-Burch, Cameron Shaw Fordyce, Philipp Koehn, Christof Monz, and Josh Schroeder. 2008. Further Meta-Evaluation of Machine Translation. In *Proceedings of the Third Workshop on Statistical Machine Translation*, pages 70–106, Columbus, Ohio. Association for Computational Linguistics.

Chris Callison-Burch, Philipp Koehn, Christof Monz, Kay Peterson, Mark Przybocki, and Omar Zaidan. 2010. Findings of the 2010 Joint Workshop on Statistical Machine Translation and Metrics for Machine Translation. In *Proceedings of the Joint Fifth Workshop on Statistical Machine Translation and MetricsMATR*, pages 17–53, Uppsala, Sweden. Association for Computational Linguistics.

Chris Callison-Burch, Philipp Koehn, Christof Monz, Matt Post, Radu Soricut, and Lucia Specia. 2012. Findings of the 2012 Workshop on Statistical Machine Translation. In *Proceedings of the Seventh Workshop on Statistical Machine Translation*, pages 10–48, Montreal, Canada. Association for Computational Linguistics.

Chris Callison-Burch, Philipp Koehn, Christof Monz, and Josh Schroeder. 2009. Findings of the 2009 Workshop on Statistical Machine Translation. In *Proceedings of the Fourth Workshop on Statistical Machine Translation*, pages 1–28, Athens, Greece. Association for Computational Linguistics.

Chris Callison-Burch, Philipp Koehn, Christof Monz, and Omar Zaidan. 2011. Findings of the 2011 Workshop on Statistical Machine Translation. In *Proceedings of the Sixth Workshop on Statistical Machine Translation*, pages 22–64, Edinburgh, Scotland. Association for Computational Linguistics.

Noe Casas, José A. R. Fonollosa, Carlos Escolano, Christine Basta, and Marta R. Costa-jussà. 2019. The TALP-UPC Machine Translation Systems for WMT19 News Translation Task: Pivoting Techniques for Low Resource MT. In *Proceedings of the Fourth Conference on Machine Translation*, Florence, Italy. Association for Computational Linguistics.

Rajen Chatterjee, Christian Federmann, Matteo Negri, and Marco Turchi. 2019. Findings of the WMT 2019 Shared Task on Automatic Post-Editing. In *Proceedings of the Fourth Conference on Machine Translation*, Florence, Italy. Association for Computational Linguistics.

Yu Chen and Tania Avgustinova. 2019. Machine Translation from an Intercomprehension Perspective. In *Proceedings of the Fourth Conference on Machine Translation*, Florence, Italy. Association for Computational Linguistics.

Marta R. Costa-jussà and José A. R. Fonollosa. 2016. Character-based neural machine translation. In *Proceedings of the 54th Annual Meeting of the Association for Computational Linguistics (Volume 2: Short Papers)*, pages 357–361, Berlin, Germany. Association for Computational Linguistics.

Marta R. Costa-jussà, Marcos Zampieri, and Santanu Pal. 2018. A Neural Approach to Language Variety Translation. In *Proceedings of VarDial*.

Fabien Cromieres and Sadao Kurohashi. 2019. Kyoto University Participation to the WMT 2019 News

Shared Task. In *Proceedings of the Fourth Conference on Machine Translation*, Florence, Italy. Association for Computational Linguistics.

Raj Dabre, Kehai Chen, Benjamin Marie, Rui Wang, Atsushi Fujita, Masao Utiyama, and Eiichiro Sumita. 2019. NICT's Supervised Neural Machine Translation Systems for the WMT19 News Translation Task. In *Proceedings of the Fourth Conference on Machine Translation*, Florence, Italy. Association for Computational Linguistics.

Liang Ding and Dacheng Tao. 2019. The University of Sydney's Machine Translation System for WMT19. In *Proceedings of the Fourth Conference on Machine Translation*, Florence, Italy. Association for Computational Linguistics.

Sergey Edunov, Myle Ott, Michael Auli, and David Grangier. 2018. Understanding Back-Translation at Scale. In *Proceedings of the 2018 Conference on Empirical Methods in Natural Language Processing (EMNLP)*, Brussels, Belgium. Association for Computational Linguistics.

Cristina España-Bonet and Dana Ruiter. 2019. UdS-DFKI Participation at WMT 2019: Low-Resource (en-gu) and Coreference-Aware (en-de) Systems. In *Proceedings of the Fourth Conference on Machine Translation*, Florence, Italy. Association for Computational Linguistics.

Christian Federmann. 2012. Appraise: an open-source toolkit for manual evaluation of mt output. *The Prague Bulletin of Mathematical Linguistics*, 98:25–35.

Erick Fonseca, Lisa Yankovskaya, André F. T. Martins, Mark Fishel, and Christian Federmann. 2019. Findings of the WMT 2019 Shared Task on Quality Estimation. In *Proceedings of the Fourth Conference on Machine Translation*, Florence, Italy. Association for Computational Linguistics.

Pablo Gamallo, José Ramom Pichel, and Iñaki Alegria. 2017. From language identification to language distance. *Physica A: Statistical Mechanics and its Applications*, 484:152 – 162.

Vikrant Goyal and Dipti Misra Sharma. 2019. The IIIT-H Gujarati-English Machine Translation System for WMT19. In *Proceedings of the Fourth Conference on Machine Translation*, Florence, Italy. Association for Computational Linguistics.

Yvette Graham, Timothy Baldwin, Alistair Moffat, and Justin Zobel. 2013. Continuous Measurement Scales in Human Evaluation of Machine Translation. In *Proceedings of the 7th Linguistic Annotation Workshop and Interoperability with Discourse*, pages 33–41, Sofia, Bulgaria. Association for Computational Linguistics.

Yvette Graham, Timothy Baldwin, Alistair Moffat, and Justin Zobel. 2014. Is Machine Translation Getting Better over Time? In *Proceedings of the 14th Conference of the European Chapter of the Association for Computational Linguistics*, pages 443–451, Gothenburg, Sweden. Association for Computational Linguistics.

Yvette Graham, Timothy Baldwin, Alistair Moffat, and Justin Zobel. 2016. Can machine translation systems be evaluated by the crowd alone. *Natural Language Engineering*, pages 1–28.

Yvette Graham, Barry Haddow, and Philipp Koehn. 2019a. Translationese in machine translation evaluation. *CoRR*, abs/1906.09833.

Yvette Graham, Barry Haddow, and Philipp Koehn. 2019b. Translationese in machine translation evaluation and mt checklist. *CoRR*.

Stig-Arne Grönroos, Sami Virpioja, and Mikko Kurimo. 2018. Cognate-aware morphological segmentation for multilingual neural translation. *CoRR*, abs/1808.10791.

Xinze Guo, Chang Liu, Xiaolong Li, Yiran Wang, Guoliang Li, Feng Wang, Zhitao Xu, Liuyi Yang, Li Ma, and Changliang Li. 2019. Kingsoft's Neural Machine Translation System for WMT19. In *Proceedings of the Fourth Conference on Machine Translation*, Florence, Italy. Association for Computational Linguistics.

Jeremy Gwinnup, Grant Erdmann, and Tim Anderson. 2019. The AFRL WMT19 Systems: Old Favorites and New Tricks. In *Proceedings of the Fourth Conference on Machine Translation*, Florence, Italy. Association for Computational Linguistics.

Jan Hajič, Eva Hajičová, Jarmila Panevová, Petr Sgall, Ondřej Bojar, Silvie Cinková, Eva Fučíková, Marie Mikulová, Petr Pajas, Jan Popelka, Jiří Semecký, Jana Šindlerová, Jan Štěpánek, Josef Toman, Zdeňka Urešová, and Zdeněk Žabokrtský. 2012. Announcing Prague Czech-English Dependency Treebank 2.0. In *Proceedings of the Eighth International Language Resources and Evaluation Conference (LREC'12)*, pages 3153–3160, Istanbul, Turkey. ELRA, European Language Resources Association.

Hany Hassan, Anthony Aue, Chang Chen, Vishal Chowdhary, Jonathan Clark, Christian Federmann, Xuedong Huang, Marcin Junczys-Dowmunt, William Lewis, Mu Li, Shujie Liu, Tie-Yan Liu, Renqian Luo, Arul Menezes, Tao Qin, Frank Seide, Xu Tan, Fei Tian, Lijun Wu, Shuangzhi Wu, Yingce Xia, Dongdong Zhang, Zhirui Zhang, and Ming Zhou. 2018. Achieving Human Parity on Automatic Chinese to English News Translation. https://www.microsoft.com/en-us/research/uploads/prod/2018/03/final-achieving-human.pdf.

Hossein Hassani. 2017. Kurdish Interdialect Machine Translation. *Proceedings of VarDial*.

Chris Hokamp, John Glover, and Demian Gholipour Ghalandari. 2019. Evaluating the Supervised and Zero-shot Performance of Multilingual Translation Models. In *Proceedings of the Fourth Conference on Machine Translation*, Florence, Italy. Association for Computational Linguistics.

Javier Iranzo-Sánchez, Gonçal Garcés Díaz-Munío, Jorge Civera, and Alfons Juan. 2019. The MLLP-UPV Supervised Machine Translation Systems for WMT19 News Translation Task. In *Proceedings of the Fourth Conference on Machine Translation*, Florence, Italy. Association for Computational Linguistics.

Marcin Junczys-Dowmunt. 2018a. Dual Conditional Cross-Entropy Filtering of Noisy Parallel Corpora. In *Proceedings of the Third Conference on Machine Translation*, Brussels, Belgium. Association for Computational Linguistics.

Marcin Junczys-Dowmunt. 2018b. Microsoft's Submission to the WMT2018 News Translation Task: How I Learned to Stop Worrying and Love the Data. In *Proceedings of the Third Conference on Machine Translation*, Brussels, Belgium. Association for Computational Linguistics.

Marcin Junczys-Dowmunt. 2019. Microsoft Translator at WMT 2019: Towards Large-Scale Document-Level Neural Machine Translation. In *Proceedings of the Fourth Conference on Machine Translation*, Florence, Italy. Association for Computational Linguistics.

Marcin Junczys-Dowmunt, Roman Grundkiewicz, Tomasz Dwojak, Hieu Hoang, Kenneth Heafield, Tom Neckermann, Frank Seide, Ulrich Germann, Alham Fikri Aji, Nikolay Bogoychev, André F. T. Martins, and Alexandra Birch. 2018. Marian: Fast Neural Machine Translation in C++. In *Proceedings of ACL 2018, System Demonstrations*, pages 116–121. Association for Computational Linguistics.

Jyotsana Khatri and Pushpak Bhattacharyya. 2019. Utilizing Monolingual Data in NMT for Similar Languages: Submission to Similar Language Translation Task. In *Proceedings of the Fourth Conference on Machine Translation*, Florence, Italy. Association for Computational Linguistics.

James Kirkpatrick, Razvan Pascanu, Neil C. Rabinowitz, Joel Veness, Guillaume Desjardins, Andrei A. Rusu, Kieran Milan, John Quan, Tiago Ramalho, Agnieszka Grabska-Barwinska, Demis Hassabis, Claudia Clopath, Dharshan Kumaran, and Raia Hadsell. 2017. Overcoming catastrophic forgetting in neural networks. *Proceedings of the National Academy of Sciences of the United States of America*, 114 13:3521–3526.

Tom Kocmi and Ondřej Bojar. 2019. CUNI Submission for Low-Resource Languages in WMT News 2019. In *Proceedings of the Fourth Conference on Machine Translation*, Florence, Italy. Association for Computational Linguistics.

Philipp Koehn, Kevin Duh, and Brian Thompson. 2018. The JHU Machine Translation Systems for WMT 2018. In *Proceedings of the Third Conference on Machine Translation*, Brussels, Belgium. Association for Computational Linguistics.

Philipp Koehn, Francisco Guzmán, Vishrav Chaudhary, and Juan Pino. 2019. Findings of the WMT 2019 Shared Task on Parallel Corpus Filtering for Low-Resource Conditions. In *Proceedings of the Fourth Conference on Machine Translation*, Florence, Italy. Association for Computational Linguistics.

Philipp Koehn, Hieu Hoang, Alexandra Birch, Chris Callison-Burch, Marcello Federico, Nicola Bertoldi, Brooke Cowan, Wade Shen, Christine Moran, Richard Zens, Christopher J. Dyer, Ondřej Bojar, Alexandra Constantin, and Evan Herbst. 2007. Moses: Open Source Toolkit for Statistical Machine Translation. In *Proceedings of the 45th Annual Meeting of the Association for Computational Linguistics Companion Volume Proceedings of the Demo and Poster Sessions*, pages 177–180, Prague, Czech Republic. Association for Computational Linguistics.

Philipp Koehn and Christof Monz. 2006. Manual and Automatic Evaluation of Machine Translation between European Languages. In *Proceedings on the Workshop on Statistical Machine Translation*, pages 102–121, New York City. Association for Computational Linguistics.

Moshe Koppel and Noam Ordan. 2011. Translationese and its dialects. In *Proceedings of the 49th Annual Meeting of the Association for Computational Linguistics: Human Language Technologies - Volume 1*, HLT '11, pages 1318–1326, Stroudsburg, PA, USA. Association for Computational Linguistics.

Taku Kudo and John Richardson. 2018. Sentencepiece: A simple and language independent subword tokenizer and detokenizer for neural text processing. *CoRR*, abs/1808.06226.

Ivana Kvapilíková, Dominik Macháček, and Ondřej Bojar. 2019. CUNI Systems for the Unsupervised News Translation Task in WMT 2019. In *Proceedings of the Fourth Conference on Machine Translation*, Florence, Italy. Association for Computational Linguistics.

Guillaume Lample and Alexis Conneau. 2019. Cross-lingual language model pretraining. *CoRR*, abs/1901.07291.

Sahinur Rahman Laskar, Partha Pakray, and Sivaji Bandyopadhyay. 2019. Neural Machine Translation: Hindi-Nepali. In *Proceedings of the Fourth Conference on Machine Translation*, Florence, Italy. Association for Computational Linguistics.

Samuel Läubli, Rico Sennrich, and Martin Volk. 2018. Has Neural Machine Translation Achieved Human Parity? A Case for Document-level Evaluation. In *EMNLP 2018*, Brussels, Belgium. Association for Computational Linguistics.

Bei Li, Yinqiao Li, Chen Xu, Ye Lin, Jiqiang Liu, Hui Liu, Ziyang Wang, Yuhao Zhang, Nuo Xu, Zeyang Wang, Kai Feng, Hexuan Chen, Tengbo Liu, Yanyang Li, Qiang Wang, Tong Xiao, and Jingbo Zhu. 2019a. The NiuTrans Machine Translation Systems for WMT19. In *Proceedings of the Fourth Conference on Machine Translation*, Florence, Italy. Association for Computational Linguistics.

Xian Li, Paul Michel, Antonios Anastasopoulos, Yonatan Belinkov, Nadir Durrani, Orhan Firat, Philipp Koehn, Graham Neubig, Juan Pino, and Hassan Sajjad. 2019b. Findings of the First Shared Task on Machine Translation Robustness. In *Proceedings of the Fourth Conference on Machine Translation*, Florence, Italy. Association for Computational Linguistics.

Zhenhao Li and Lucia Specia. 2019. A Comparison on Fine-grained Pre-trained Embeddings for the WMT19Chinese-English News Translation Task. In *Proceedings of the Fourth Conference on Machine Translation*, Florence, Italy. Association for Computational Linguistics.

Patrick Littell, Chi-kiu Lo, Samuel Larkin, and Darlene Stewart. 2019. Multi-Source Transformer for Kazakh-Russian-English Neural Machine Translation. In *Proceedings of the Fourth Conference on Machine Translation*, Florence, Italy. Association for Computational Linguistics.

Zihan Liu, Yan Xu, Genta Indra Winata, and Pascale Fung. 2019. Incorporating Word and Subword Units in Unsupervised Machine Translation Using Language Model Rescoring. In *Proceedings of the Fourth Conference on Machine Translation*, Florence, Italy. Association for Computational Linguistics.

Renqian Luo, Fei Tian, Tao Qin, Enhong Chen, and Tie-Yan Liu. 2018. Neural architecture optimization. In *Advances in neural information processing systems*, pages 7816–7827.

Jerry Ma and Denis Yarats. 2018. Quasi-hyperbolic momentum and Adam for deep learning. *arXiv preprint arXiv:1810.06801*.

Qingsong Ma, Johnny Wei, Ondřej Bojar, and Yvette Graham. 2019. Results of the WMT 2019 Metrics Shared Task: Segment-Level and Strong MT Systems Pose Big Challenges. In *Proceedings of the Fourth Conference on Machine Translation*, Florence, Italy. Association for Computational Linguistics.

Vivien Macketanz, Eleftherios Avramidis, Aljoscha Burchardt, and Hans Uszkoreit. 2018. Fine-grained evaluation of German-English Machine Translation based on a Test Suite. In *Proceedings of the Third Conference on Machine Translation*, Brussels, Belgium. Association for Computational Linguistics.

Kelly Marchisio, Yash Kumar Lal, and Philipp Koehn. 2019. Johns Hopkins University Submission for WMT News Translation Task. In *Proceedings of the Fourth Conference on Machine Translation*, Florence, Italy. Association for Computational Linguistics.

Benjamin Marie, Raj Dabre, and Atsushi Fujita. 2019a. NICT's Machine Translation Systems for the WMT19 Similar Language Translation Task. In *Proceedings of the Fourth Conference on Machine Translation*, Florence, Italy. Association for Computational Linguistics.

Benjamin Marie and Atsushi Fujita. 2018. A smorgasbord of features to combine phrase-based and neural machine translation. In *Proceedings of the 13th Conference of the Association for Machine Translation in the Americas (Volume 1: Research Papers)*, page 111–124, Boston, MA. Association for Machine Translation in the Americas.

Benjamin Marie, Haipeng Sun, Rui Wang, Kehai Chen, Atsushi Fujita, Masao Utiyama, and Eiichiro Sumita. 2019b. NICT's Unsupervised Neural and Statistical Machine Translation Systems for the WMT19 News Translation Task. In *Proceedings of the Fourth Conference on Machine Translation*, Florence, Italy. Association for Computational Linguistics.

Luís Marujo, Nuno Grazina, Tiago Luís, Wang Ling, Luísa Coheur, and Isabel Trancoso. 2011. BP2EP–Adaptation of Brazilian Portuguese texts to European Portuguese. In *Proceedings of EAMT*.

Alexander Molchanov. 2019. PROMT Systems for WMT 2019 Shared Translation Task. In *Proceedings of the Fourth Conference on Machine Translation*, Florence, Italy. Association for Computational Linguistics.

Riktim Mondal, Shankha Raj Nayek, Aditya Chowdhury, Santanu Pal, Sudip Kumar Naskar, and Josef van Genabith. 2019. JU-Saarland Submission to the WMT2019 English–Gujarati Translation Shared Task. In *Proceedings of the Fourth Conference on Machine Translation*, Florence, Italy. Association for Computational Linguistics.

Roberto Navigli and Simone Paolo Ponzetto. 2012. Babelnet: The automatic construction, evaluation and application of a wide-coverage multilingual semantic network. *Artif. Intell.*, 193:217–250.

Nathan Ng, Kyra Yee, Alexei Baevski, Myle Ott, Michael Auli, and Sergey Edunov. 2019. Facebook FAIR's WMT19 News Translation Task Submission. In *Proceedings of the Fourth Conference on Machine Translation*, Florence, Italy. Association for Computational Linguistics.

Atul Kr. Ojha, Ritesh Kumar, Akanksha Bansal, and Priya Rani. 2019. Panlingua-KMI MT System for Similar Language Translation Task at WMT 2019. In *Proceedings of the Fourth Conference on Machine Translation*, Florence, Italy. Association for Computational Linguistics.

Csaba Oravecz, Katina Bontcheva, Adrien Lardilleux, László Tihanyi, and Andreas Eisele. 2019. eTranslation's Submissions to the WMT 2019 News Translation Task. In *Proceedings of the Fourth Conference on Machine Translation*, Florence, Italy. Association for Computational Linguistics.

Myle Ott, Sergey Edunov, Alexei Baevski, Angela Fan, Sam Gross, Nathan Ng, David Grangier, and Michael Auli. 2019. fairseq: A fast, extensible toolkit for sequence modeling. In *Proceedings of the 2019 Conference of the North American Chapter of the Association for Computational Linguistics (Demonstrations)*, pages 48–53, Minneapolis, Minnesota. Association for Computational Linguistics.

Santanu Pal, Marcos Zampieri, and Josef van Genabith. 2019. UDS–DFKI Submission to the WMT2019 Czech–Polish Similar Language Translation Shared Task. In *Proceedings of the Fourth Conference on Machine Translation*, Florence, Italy. Association for Computational Linguistics.

Kishore Papineni, Salim Roukos, Todd Ward, and Wei-Jing Zhu. 2002. BLEU: A Method for Automatic Evaluation of Machine Translation. In *Proceedings of the 40th Annual Meeting on Association for Computational Linguistics*, ACL '02, pages 311–318, Philadelphia, Pennsylvania.

Mārcis Pinnis. 2018. Tilde's Parallel Corpus Filtering Methods for WMT 2018. In *Proceedings of the Third Conference on Machine Translation*, Brussels, Belgium. Association for Computational Linguistics.

Mārcis Pinnis, Rihards Krišlauks, Daiga Deksne, and Toms Miks. 2017. Neural Machine Translation for Morphologically Rich Languages with Improved Sub-word Units and Synthetic Data. In *Proceedings of the 20th International Conference of Text, Speech and Dialogue (TSD2017)*, volume 10415 LNAI, Prague, Czechia.

Marcis Pinnis, Rihards Krišlauks, and Matiss Rikters. 2019. Tilde's Machine Translation Systems for WMT 2019. In *Proceedings of the Fourth Conference on Machine Translation*, Florence, Italy. Association for Computational Linguistics.

Mārcis Pinnis, Andrejs Vasiļjevs, Rihards Kalniņš, Roberts Rozis, Raivis Skadiņš, and Valters Šics. 2018. Tilde MT Platform for Developing Client Specific MT Solutions. In *Proceedings of the Eleventh International Conference on Language Resources and Evaluation (LREC 2018)*, Miyazaki, Japan. European Language Resources Association (ELRA).

Tommi Pirinen. 2019. Apertium-fin-eng–Rule-based Shallow Machine Translation for WMT 2019 Shared Task. In *Proceedings of the Fourth Conference on Machine Translation*, Florence, Italy. Association for Computational Linguistics.

Martin Popel. 2018. CUNI Transformer Neural MT System for WMT18. In *Proceedings of the Third Conference on Machine Translation*, Brussels, Belgium. Association for Computational Linguistics.

Martin Popel, Dominik Macháček, Michal Auersperger, Ondřej Bojar, and Pavel Pecina. 2019. English-Czech Systems in WMT19: Document-Level Transformer. In *Proceedings of the Fourth Conference on Machine Translation*, Florence, Italy. Association for Computational Linguistics.

Maja Popović. 2019. Evaluating Conjunction Disambiguation on English-to-German and French-to-German WMT 2019 Translation Hypotheses. In *Proceedings of the Fourth Conference on Machine Translation*, Florence, Italy. Association for Computational Linguistics.

Michael Przystupa and Muhammad Abdul-Mageed. 2019. Neural Machine Translation of Low-Resource and Similar Languages with Backtranslation. In *Proceedings of the Fourth Conference on Machine Translation*, Florence, Italy. Association for Computational Linguistics.

Alessandro Raganato, Yves Scherrer, and Jörg Tiedemann. 2019. The MuCoW Test Suite at WMT 2019: Automatically Harvested Multilingual Contrastive Word Sense Disambiguation Test Sets for Machine Translation. In *Proceedings of the Fourth Conference on Machine Translation*, Florence, Italy. Association for Computational Linguistics.

Matīss Rikters. 2018. Impact of Corpora Quality on Neural Machine Translation. In *In Proceedings of the 8th Conference Human Language Technologies - The Baltic Perspective (Baltic HLT 2018)*, Tartu, Estonia.

Jan Rosendahl, Christian Herold, Yunsu Kim, Miguel Graça, Weiyue Wang, Parnia Bahar, Yingbo Gao, and Hermann Ney. 2019. The RWTH Aachen University Machine Translation Systems for WMT 2019. In *Proceedings of the Fourth Conference on Machine Translation*, Florence, Italy. Association for Computational Linguistics.

Kateřina Rysová, Lucie Rysová, Magdaléna Poláková, Tomáš Musil, and Ondřej Bojar. 2019. Manual Evaluation of Discourse Relations Translation Accuracy in Document Level NMT. In *Proceedings of the Fourth Conference on Machine Translation*, Florence, Italy. Association for Computational Linguistics.

Yves Scherrer, Raúl Vázquez, and Sami Virpioja. 2019. The University of Helsinki Submissions to the WMT19 Similar Language Translation Task. In *Proceedings of the Fourth Conference on Machine Translation*, Florence, Italy. Association for Computational Linguistics.

Sukanta Sen, Kamal Kumar Gupta, Asif Ekbal, and Pushpak Bhattacharyya. 2019. IITP-MT System for Gujarati-English News Translation Task at WMT 2019. In *Proceedings of the Fourth Conference on Machine Translation*, Florence, Italy. Association for Computational Linguistics.

Rico Sennrich, Alexandra Birch, Anna Currey, Ulrich Germann, Barry Haddow, Kenneth Heafield, Antonio Valerio Miceli Barone, and Philip Williams. 2017. The University of Edinburgh's Neural MT Systems for WMT17. In *Proceedings of the Second Conference on Machine Translation*, Copenhagen, Denmark. Association for Computational Linguistics.

Rico Sennrich, Barry Haddow, and Alexandra Birch. 2016. Neural Machine Translation of Rare Words with Subword Units. In *Proceedings of the 54th Annual Meeting of the Association for Computational Linguistics (Volume 1: Long Papers)*, pages 1715–1725, Berlin, Germany. Association for Computational Linguistics.

Leslie N. Smith. 2018. A disciplined approach to neural network hyper-parameters: Part 1 - learning rate, batch size, momentum, and weight decay. *CoRR*, abs/1803.09820.

Matthew Snover, Bonnie Dorr, Richard Schwartz, Linnea Micciulla, and John Makhoul. 2006. A study of translation edit rate with targeted human annotation. In *Proceedings of association for machine translation in the Americas*, pages 223–231.

Kaitao Song, Xu Tan, Tao Qin, Jianfeng Lu, and Tie-Yan Liu. 2019. Mass: Masked sequence to sequence pre-training for language generation. In *International Conference on Machine Learning*, pages 5926–5936.

Felix Stahlberg, Adrià de Gispert, Eva Hasler, and Bill Byrne. 2017. Neural machine translation by minimising the Bayes-risk with respect to syntactic translation lattices. In *Proceedings of the 15th Conference of the European Chapter of the Association for Computational Linguistics: Volume 2, Short Papers*, pages 362–368, Valencia, Spain. Association for Computational Linguistics.

Felix Stahlberg, Danielle Saunders, Adrià de Gispert, and Bill Byrne. 2019. CUED@WMT19:EWC&LMs. In *Proceedings of the Fourth Conference on Machine Translation*, Florence, Italy. Association for Computational Linguistics.

Dario Stojanovski and Alexander Fraser. 2019. Combining Local and Document-Level Context: The LMU Munich Neural Machine Translation System at WMT19. In *Proceedings of the Fourth Conference on Machine Translation*, Florence, Italy. Association for Computational Linguistics.

Dario Stojanovski, Viktor Hangya, Matthias Huck, and Alexander Fraser. 2019. The LMU Munich Unsupervised Machine Translation System for WMT19. In *Proceedings of the Fourth Conference on Machine Translation*, Florence, Italy. Association for Computational Linguistics.

Roman Sudarikov, Martin Popel, Ondřej Bojar, Aljoscha Burchardt, and Ondřej Klejch. 2016. Using MT-ComparEval. In *Translation Evaluation: From Fragmented Tools and Data Sets to an Integrated Ecosystem*, pages 76–82.

Meng Sun, Bojian Jiang, Hao Xiong, Zhongjun He, Hua Wu, and Haifeng Wang. 2019. Baidu Neural Machine Translation Systems for WMT19. In *Proceedings of the Fourth Conference on Machine Translation*, Florence, Italy. Association for Computational Linguistics.

Víctor M. Sánchez-Cartagena, Juan Antonio Pérez-Ortiz, and Felipe Sánchez-Martínez. 2019. The Universitat d'Alacant Submissions to the English-to-Kazakh News Translation Task at WMT 2019. In *Proceedings of the Fourth Conference on Machine Translation*, Florence, Italy. Association for Computational Linguistics.

Aarne Talman, Umut Sulubacak, Raúl Vázquez, Yves Scherrer, Sami Virpioja, Alessandro Raganato, Arvi Hurskainen, and Jörg Tiedemann. 2019. The University of Helsinki Submissions to the WMT19 News Translation Task. In *Proceedings of the Fourth Conference on Machine Translation*, Florence, Italy. Association for Computational Linguistics.

Brian Thompson, Jeremy Gwinnup, Huda Khayrallah, Kevin Duh, and Philipp Koehn. 2019. Overcoming catastrophic forgetting during domain adaptation of neural machine translation. In *Proceedings of the 2019 Conference of the North American Chapter of the Association for Computational Linguistics: Human Language Technologies, Volume 1 (Long and Short Papers)*, pages 2062–2068, Minneapolis, Minnesota. Association for Computational Linguistics.

Jörg Tiedemann and Lars Nygaard. 2004. The opus corpus-parallel and free: http://logos.uio.no/opus. In *Proceedings of LREC*.

Antonio Toral, Sheila Castilho, Ke Hu, and Andy Way. 2018. Attaining the Unattainable? Reassessing Claims of Human Parity in Neural Machine Translation. In *Proceedings of the Third Conference on Machine Translation*, Brussels, Belgium. Association for Computational Linguistics.

Antonio Toral, Lukas Edman, Galiya Yeshmagambetova, and Jennifer Spenader. 2019. Neural Machine Translation for English–Kazakh with Morphological

Segmentation and Synthetic Data. In *Proceedings of the Fourth Conference on Machine Translation*, Florence, Italy. Association for Computational Linguistics.

Andre Tättar, Elizaveta Korotkova, and Mark Fishel. 2019. University of Tartu's Multilingual Multidomain WMT19 News Translation Shared Task Submission. In *Proceedings of the Fourth Conference on Machine Translation*, Florence, Italy. Association for Computational Linguistics.

Ashish Vaswani, Noam Shazeer, Niki Parmar, Jakob Uszkoreit, Llion Jones, Aidan N Gomez, Ł ukasz Kaiser, and Illia Polosukhin. 2017. Attention is All you Need. In I. Guyon, U. V. Luxburg, S. Bengio, H. Wallach, R. Fergus, S. Vishwanathan, and R. Garnett, editors, *Advances in Neural Information Processing Systems 30*, pages 5998–6008. Curran Associates, Inc.

Tereza Vojtěchová, Michal Novák, Miloš Klouček, and Ondřej Bojar. 2019. SAO WMT19 Test Suite: Machine Translation of Audit Reports. In *Proceedings of the Fourth Conference on Machine Translation*, Florence, Italy. Association for Computational Linguistics.

Yiren Wang, Yingce Xia, Tianyu He, Fei Tian, Tao Qin, Cheng Xiang Zhai, and Tie-Yan Liu. 2019. Multiagent dual learning. In *International Conference on Learning Representations*.

Yingce Xia, Xu Tan, Fei Tian, Fei Gao, Weicong Chen, Yang Fan, Linyuan Gong, Yichong Leng, Renqian Luo, Yiren Wang, Lijun Wu, Jinhua Zhu, Tao QIN, and Tie-Yan Liu. 2019. Microsoft Research Asia's Systems for WMT19. In *Proceedings of the Fourth Conference on Machine Translation*, Florence, Italy. Association for Computational Linguistics.

Jingyi Zhang and Josef van Genabith. 2019. DFKI-NMT Submission to the WMT19 News Translation Task. In *Proceedings of the Fourth Conference on Machine Translation*, Florence, Italy. Association for Computational Linguistics.

Xiaoheng Zhang. 1998. Dialect MT: A Case Study Between Cantonese and Mandarin. In *Proceedings of ACL*.

Jinhua Zhu, Fei Gao, Lijun Wu, Yingce Xia, Tao Qin, Wengang Zhou, Xueqi Cheng, and Tie-Yan Liu. 2019. Soft contextual data augmentation for neural machine translation. *CoRR*, abs/1905.10523.

	BAIDU-SYSTEM	KSAI-SYSTEM	MSRA	MSRA	NEU	BTRANS	ONLINE-B	BTRANS-ENSEMBLE	UEDIN	ONLINE-Y	NICT	ONLINE-A	ONLINE-G	ONLINE-X	APPRENTICE-C
BAIDU-SYSTEM	-	0.03	0.09★	0.10★	0.10†	0.11†	0.13‡	0.19‡	0.24‡	0.25‡	0.29‡	0.36‡	0.50‡	0.78‡	1.25‡
KSAI-SYSTEM	-0.03	-	0.06	0.07	0.07	0.08★	0.10†	0.16‡	0.21‡	0.22‡	0.27‡	0.33‡	0.47‡	0.75‡	1.22‡
MSRA	-0.09	-0.06	-	0.01	0.01	0.02	0.04	0.10‡	0.15‡	0.15‡	0.20‡	0.27‡	0.41‡	0.69‡	1.16‡
MSRA	-0.10	-0.07	-0.01	-	0.00	0.01	0.03	0.09†	0.14‡	0.15‡	0.19‡	0.26‡	0.40‡	0.68‡	1.15‡
NEU	-0.10	-0.07	-0.01	0.00	-	0.01	0.03	0.09†	0.14‡	0.14‡	0.19‡	0.26‡	0.39‡	0.68‡	1.15‡
BTRANS	-0.11	-0.08	-0.02	-0.01	-0.01	-	0.02	0.08†	0.13‡	0.14‡	0.19‡	0.25‡	0.39‡	0.67‡	1.14‡
ONLINE-B	-0.13	-0.10	-0.04	-0.03	-0.03	-0.02	-	0.06★	0.11‡	0.11†	0.16‡	0.23‡	0.36‡	0.64‡	1.12‡
BTRANS-ENSEMBLE	-0.19	-0.16	-0.10	-0.09	-0.09	-0.08	-0.06	-	0.05	0.05	0.10†	0.17‡	0.30‡	0.59‡	1.06‡
UEDIN	-0.24	-0.21	-0.15	-0.14	-0.14	-0.13	-0.11	-0.05	-	0.01	0.05★	0.12‡	0.26‡	0.54‡	1.01‡
ONLINE-Y	-0.25	-0.22	-0.15	-0.15	-0.14	-0.14	-0.11	-0.05	-0.01	-	0.05★	0.11‡	0.25‡	0.53‡	1.01‡
NICT	-0.29	-0.27	-0.20	-0.19	-0.19	-0.19	-0.16	-0.10	-0.05	-0.05	-	0.07★	0.20‡	0.48‡	0.96‡
ONLINE-A	-0.36	-0.33	-0.27	-0.26	-0.26	-0.25	-0.23	-0.17	-0.12	-0.11	-0.07	-	0.14†	0.42‡	0.89‡
ONLINE-G	-0.50	-0.47	-0.41	-0.40	-0.39	-0.39	-0.36	-0.30	-0.26	-0.25	-0.20	-0.14	-	0.28‡	0.76‡
ONLINE-X	-0.78	-0.75	-0.69	-0.68	-0.68	-0.67	-0.64	-0.59	-0.54	-0.53	-0.48	-0.42	-0.28	-	0.47‡
APPRENTICE-C	-1.25	-1.22	-1.16	-1.15	-1.15	-1.14	-1.12	-1.06	-1.01	-1.01	-0.96	-0.89	-0.76	-0.47	-
score	0.29	0.27	0.20	0.20	0.19	0.19	0.16	0.10	0.05	0.05	0.00	-0.07	-0.20	-0.48	-0.96
rank	1–7	1–7	1–7	1–7	1–7	1–7	1–7	8–10	8–10	8–10	11	12	13	14	15

Table 32: Head to head comparison for Chinese→English systems

A   Differences in Human Scores

Tables 32–49 show differences in average standardized human scores for all pairs of competing systems for each language pair. The numbers in each of the tables' cells indicate the difference in average standardized human scores for the system in that column and the system in that row.

Because there were so many systems and data conditions the significance of each pairwise comparison needs to be quantified. We applied Wilcoxon rank-sum test to measure the likelihood that such differences could occur simply by chance. In the following tables ★ indicates statistical significance at $p < 0.05$, † indicates statistical significance at $p < 0.01$, and ‡ indicates statistical significance at $p < 0.001$, according to Wilcoxon rank-sum test.

Each table contains final rows showing the average score achieved by that system and the rank range according according to Wilcoxon rank-sum test ($p < 0.05$). Gray lines separate clusters based on non-overlapping rank ranges.

	HUMAN	KSAI-SYSTEM	BAIDU-SYSTEM	NEU	ONLINE-A	XZL-NMT	UEDIN	BTRANS	NICT	ONLINE-B	ONLINE-Y	ONLINE-G	ONLINE-X
HUMAN	-	0.06†	0.09‡	0.16‡	0.32‡	0.33‡	0.35‡	0.36‡	0.37‡	0.49‡	0.59‡	0.63‡	0.92‡
KSAI-SYSTEM	-0.06	-	0.03	0.10†	0.25‡	0.26‡	0.29‡	0.30‡	0.31‡	0.43‡	0.52‡	0.57‡	0.86‡
BAIDU-SYSTEM	-0.09	-0.03	-	0.07	0.23‡	0.24‡	0.26‡	0.27‡	0.28‡	0.40‡	0.50‡	0.54‡	0.83‡
NEU	-0.16	-0.10	-0.07	-	0.16‡	0.17‡	0.19‡	0.20‡	0.21‡	0.33‡	0.43‡	0.47‡	0.76‡
ONLINE-A	-0.32	-0.25	-0.23	-0.16	-	0.01	0.04	0.04	0.05	0.18‡	0.27‡	0.31‡	0.60‡
XZL-NMT	-0.33	-0.26	-0.24	-0.17	-0.01	-	0.03	0.03	0.04	0.17‡	0.26‡	0.30‡	0.60‡
UEDIN	-0.35	-0.29	-0.26	-0.19	-0.04	-0.03	-	0.01	0.02⋆	0.14‡	0.23‡	0.28‡	0.57‡
BTRANS	-0.36	-0.30	-0.27	-0.20	-0.04	-0.03	-0.01	-	0.01	0.13‡	0.23‡	0.27‡	0.56‡
NICT	-0.37	-0.31	-0.28	-0.21	-0.05	-0.04	-0.02	-0.01	-	0.12‡	0.22‡	0.26‡	0.55‡
ONLINE-B	-0.49	-0.43	-0.40	-0.33	-0.18	-0.17	-0.14	-0.13	-0.12	-	0.09⋆	0.14‡	0.43‡
ONLINE-Y	-0.59	-0.52	-0.50	-0.43	-0.27	-0.26	-0.23	-0.23	-0.22	-0.09	-	0.04	0.34‡
ONLINE-G	-0.63	-0.57	-0.54	-0.47	-0.31	-0.30	-0.28	-0.27	-0.26	-0.14	-0.04	-	0.29‡
ONLINE-X	-0.92	-0.86	-0.83	-0.76	-0.60	-0.60	-0.57	-0.56	-0.55	-0.43	-0.34	-0.29	-
score	0.37	0.31	0.28	0.21	0.05	0.04	0.02	0.01	0.00	-0.13	-0.22	-0.26	-0.55
rank	1	2–4	2–4	2–4	5–9	5–9	5–9	5–9	5–9	10	11–12	11–12	13

Table 33: Head to head comparison for English→Chinese systems

	HUMAN	CUNI-DOCTRANSFORMER-T2T	CUNI-TRANSFORMER-T2T-2018	CUNI-TRANSFORMER-T2T-2019	CUNI-DOCTRANSFORMER-MARIAN	UEDIN	ONLINE-Y	TARTUNLP-C	ONLINE-G	ONLINE-B	ONLINE-A	ONLINE-X
HUMAN	-	0.24‡	0.24‡	0.25‡	0.42‡	0.44‡	0.80‡	0.84‡	0.94‡	0.98‡	1.24‡	1.29‡
CUNI-DOCTRANSFORMER-T2T	-0.24	-	0.00	0.01	0.18‡	0.20‡	0.56‡	0.60‡	0.70‡	0.74‡	1.00‡	1.05‡
CUNI-TRANSFORMER-T2T-2018	-0.24	0.00	-	0.01	0.18‡	0.20‡	0.56‡	0.60‡	0.70‡	0.74‡	1.00‡	1.05‡
CUNI-TRANSFORMER-T2T-2019	-0.25	-0.01	-0.01	-	0.17‡	0.18‡	0.54‡	0.58‡	0.69‡	0.72‡	0.98‡	1.04‡
CUNI-DOCTRANSFORMER-MARIAN	-0.42	-0.18	-0.18	-0.17	-	0.02	0.38‡	0.42‡	0.52‡	0.56‡	0.82‡	0.87‡
UEDIN	-0.44	-0.20	-0.20	-0.18	-0.02	-	0.36‡	0.40‡	0.51‡	0.54‡	0.80‡	0.86‡
ONLINE-Y	-0.80	-0.56	-0.56	-0.54	-0.38	-0.36	-	0.04	0.14†	0.18‡	0.44‡	0.49‡
TARTUNLP-C	-0.84	-0.60	-0.60	-0.58	-0.42	-0.40	-0.04	-	0.10⋆	0.14‡	0.40‡	0.46‡
ONLINE-G	-0.94	-0.70	-0.70	-0.69	-0.52	-0.51	-0.14	-0.10	-	0.04⋆	0.29‡	0.35‡
ONLINE-B	-0.98	-0.74	-0.74	-0.72	-0.56	-0.54	-0.18	-0.14	-0.04	-	0.26‡	0.31‡
ONLINE-A	-1.24	-1.00	-1.00	-0.98	-0.82	-0.80	-0.44	-0.40	-0.29	-0.26	-	0.06⋆
ONLINE-X	-1.29	-1.05	-1.05	-1.04	-0.87	-0.86	-0.49	-0.46	-0.35	-0.31	-0.06	-
score	0.64	0.40	0.40	0.39	0.22	0.21	-0.16	-0.20	-0.30	-0.34	-0.59	-0.65
rank	1	2–4	2–4	2–4	5–6	5–6	7–8	7–8	9	10	11	12

Table 34: Head to head comparison for English→Czech systems

	FACEBOOK-FAIR	RWTH-AACHEN-SYSTEM	MSRA	ONLINE-B	JHU	MLLP-UPV	DFKI-NMT	UCAM	ONLINE-A	NEU	HUMAN	UEDIN	ONLINE-Y	TARTUNLP-C	ONLINE-G	PROMT-NMT-DE-EN	ONLINE-X
FACEBOOK-FAIR	-	0.01†	0.01	0.03	0.06†	0.08‡	0.08‡	0.08†	0.10‡	0.11‡	0.12‡	0.13‡	0.14‡	0.14‡	0.20‡	0.27‡	0.34‡
RWTH-AACHEN-SYSTEM	-0.01	-	0.00	0.02	0.05	0.07†	0.07	0.07	0.09	0.10	0.11★	0.12‡	0.13‡	0.13‡	0.19‡	0.26‡	0.33‡
MSRA	-0.01	0.00★	-	0.02	0.05★	0.07‡	0.07†	0.07†	0.09‡	0.10‡	0.11‡	0.12‡	0.13‡	0.13‡	0.19‡	0.26‡	0.33‡
ONLINE-B	-0.03	-0.02	-0.02	-	0.03	0.05‡	0.05★	0.05	0.07†	0.08†	0.09†	0.11‡	0.11‡	0.11‡	0.17‡	0.25‡	0.31‡
JHU	-0.06	-0.05	-0.05	-0.03	-	0.02★	0.02	0.02	0.04	0.05	0.06	0.08†	0.08‡	0.08‡	0.14‡	0.21‡	0.28‡
MLLP-UPV	-0.08	-0.07	-0.07	-0.05	-0.02	-	0.00	0.00	0.02	0.03	0.04	0.06	0.06	0.06	0.12†	0.20‡	0.26‡
DFKI-NMT	-0.08	-0.07	-0.07	-0.05	-0.02	0.00	-	0.00	0.02	0.03	0.04	0.06★	0.06★	0.06†	0.12‡	0.19‡	0.26‡
UCAM	-0.08	-0.07	-0.07	-0.05	-0.02	0.00	0.00	-	0.02	0.03	0.04	0.05★	0.06†	0.06†	0.12‡	0.19‡	0.26‡
ONLINE-A	-0.10	-0.09	-0.09	-0.07	-0.04	-0.02	-0.02	-0.02	-	0.01	0.02	0.04	0.04★	0.04★	0.10‡	0.18‡	0.24‡
NEU	-0.11	-0.10	-0.10	-0.08	-0.05	-0.03	-0.03	-0.03	-0.01	-	0.01	0.03	0.03★	0.03★	0.09‡	0.17‡	0.23‡
HUMAN	-0.12	-0.11	-0.11	-0.09	-0.06	-0.04	-0.04	-0.04	-0.02	-0.01	-	0.02	0.02★	0.02★	0.08‡	0.16‡	0.22‡
UEDIN	-0.13	-0.12	-0.12	-0.11	-0.08	-0.06	-0.06	-0.05	-0.04	-0.03	-0.02	-	0.00	0.00	0.06★	0.14‡	0.20‡
ONLINE-Y	-0.14	-0.13	-0.13	-0.11	-0.08	-0.06	-0.06	-0.06	-0.04	-0.03	-0.02	0.00	-	0.00	0.06	0.14‡	0.20‡
TARTUNLP-C	-0.14	-0.13	-0.13	-0.11	-0.08	-0.06	-0.06	-0.06	-0.04	-0.03	-0.02	0.00	0.00	-	0.06	0.13‡	0.20‡
ONLINE-G	-0.20	-0.19	-0.19	-0.17	-0.14	-0.12	-0.12	-0.12	-0.10	-0.09	-0.08	-0.06	-0.06	-0.06	-	0.08‡	0.14‡
PROMT-NMT-DE-EN	-0.27	-0.26	-0.26	-0.25	-0.21	-0.20	-0.19	-0.19	-0.18	-0.17	-0.16	-0.14	-0.14	-0.13	-0.08	-	0.06★
ONLINE-X	-0.34	-0.33	-0.33	-0.31	-0.28	-0.26	-0.26	-0.26	-0.24	-0.23	-0.22	-0.20	-0.20	-0.20	-0.14	-0.06	-
score	0.15	0.14	0.14	0.12	0.09	0.07	0.07	0.07	0.05	0.04	0.03	0.01	0.01	0.01	-0.05	-0.13	-0.19
rank	1–3	1–3	1–3	4–15	4–15	4–15	4–15	4–15	4–15	4–15	4–15	4–15	4–15	4–15	4–15	16	17

Table 35: Head to head comparison for German→English systems

	FACEBOOK-FAIR	MICROSOFT-SENT-DOC	MICROSOFT-DOC	HUMAN	MSRA	UCAM	NEU	MLLP-UPV	ETRANSLATION	DFKI-NMT	ONLINE-B	MICROSOFT-SENT	JHU	HELSINKI-NLP	ONLINE-Y	LMU-CTX-TF-SINGLE-EN-DE	PROMT-NMT-EN-DE	ONLINE-A	ONLINE-G	UdS-DFKI	TARTUNLP-C	ONLINE-X	EN-DE-TASK
FACEBOOK-FAIR	-	0.04‡	0.05‡	0.11‡	0.13‡	0.13‡	0.14‡	0.16‡	0.22‡	0.23‡	0.25‡	0.25‡	0.27‡	0.27‡	0.31‡	0.34‡	0.35‡	0.42‡	0.47‡	0.48‡	0.48‡	0.75‡	2.12‡
MICROSOFT-SENT-DOC	-0.04	-	0.02	0.07	0.10‡	0.10†	0.10‡	0.12‡	0.18‡	0.19‡	0.22‡	0.22‡	0.23‡	0.23‡	0.27‡	0.30‡	0.31‡	0.38‡	0.43‡	0.44‡	0.44‡	0.71‡	2.08‡
MICROSOFT-DOC	-0.05	-0.02	-	0.06	0.08⋆	0.08	0.09⋆	0.11‡	0.17‡	0.18‡	0.20‡	0.20‡	0.21‡	0.22‡	0.26‡	0.29‡	0.29‡	0.37‡	0.41‡	0.42‡	0.43‡	0.70‡	2.06‡
HUMAN	-0.11	-0.07	-0.06	-	0.03⋆	0.03	0.03⋆	0.05‡	0.11‡	0.12‡	0.15‡	0.15‡	0.16‡	0.16‡	0.20‡	0.23‡	0.24‡	0.31‡	0.36‡	0.37‡	0.37‡	0.64‡	2.01‡
MSRA	-0.13	-0.10	-0.08	-0.03	-	0.00	0.01	0.03	0.08⋆	0.10‡	0.12†	0.12⋆	0.13‡	0.14†	0.18‡	0.20‡	0.21‡	0.29‡	0.33‡	0.34‡	0.35‡	0.61‡	1.98‡
UCAM	-0.13	-0.10	-0.08	-0.03	0.00	-	0.00	0.02⋆	0.08†	0.09‡	0.12‡	0.12†	0.13‡	0.14‡	0.17‡	0.20‡	0.21‡	0.29‡	0.33‡	0.34‡	0.34‡	0.61‡	1.98‡
NEU	-0.14	-0.10	-0.09	-0.03	-0.01	0.00	-	0.02	0.08⋆	0.09‡	0.11†	0.11⋆	0.13‡	0.13‡	0.17‡	0.20‡	0.21‡	0.28‡	0.33‡	0.34‡	0.34‡	0.61‡	1.98‡
MLLP-UPV	-0.16	-0.12	-0.11	-0.05	-0.03	-0.02	-0.02	-	0.06	0.07‡	0.09⋆	0.09	0.11‡	0.11⋆	0.15‡	0.18‡	0.19‡	0.26‡	0.31‡	0.32‡	0.32‡	0.59‡	1.96‡
ETRANSLATION	-0.22	-0.18	-0.17	-0.11	-0.08	-0.08	-0.08	-0.06	-	0.01⋆	0.04	0.04	0.05⋆	0.05	0.09‡	0.12†	0.13‡	0.20‡	0.25‡	0.26‡	0.26‡	0.53‡	1.90‡
DFKI-NMT	-0.23	-0.19	-0.18	-0.12	-0.10	-0.09	-0.09	-0.07	-0.01	-	0.02	0.02	0.04	0.04	0.08†	0.11	0.12†	0.19‡	0.24‡	0.25‡	0.25‡	0.52‡	1.89‡
ONLINE-B	-0.25	-0.22	-0.20	-0.15	-0.12	-0.12	-0.11	-0.09	-0.04	-0.02	-	0.00	0.01	0.02	0.06‡	0.08⋆	0.09‡	0.17‡	0.21‡	0.22‡	0.23‡	0.49‡	1.86‡
MICROSOFT-SENT	-0.25	-0.22	-0.20	-0.15	-0.12	-0.12	-0.11	-0.09	-0.04	-0.02	0.00	-	0.01⋆	0.02	0.06‡	0.08†	0.09‡	0.17‡	0.21‡	0.22‡	0.23‡	0.49‡	1.86‡
JHU	-0.27	-0.23	-0.21	-0.16	-0.13	-0.13	-0.13	-0.11	-0.05	-0.04	-0.01	-0.01	-	0.00	0.04⋆	0.07	0.08⋆	0.15‡	0.20‡	0.21‡	0.21‡	0.48‡	1.85‡
HELSINKI-NLP	-0.27	-0.23	-0.22	-0.16	-0.14	-0.14	-0.13	-0.11	-0.05	-0.04	-0.02	-0.02	0.00	-	0.04†	0.07	0.08†	0.15‡	0.20‡	0.21‡	0.21‡	0.48‡	1.85‡
ONLINE-Y	-0.31	-0.27	-0.26	-0.20	-0.18	-0.17	-0.17	-0.15	-0.09	-0.08	-0.06	-0.06	-0.04	-0.04	-	0.03	0.04	0.11	0.16‡	0.17†	0.17‡	0.44‡	1.81‡
LMU-CTX-TF-SINGLE-EN-DE	-0.34	-0.30	-0.29	-0.23	-0.20	-0.20	-0.20	-0.18	-0.12	-0.11	-0.08	-0.08	-0.07	-0.07	-0.03	-	0.01	0.08†	0.13‡	0.14‡	0.14‡	0.41‡	1.78‡
PROMT-NMT-EN-DE	-0.35	-0.31	-0.29	-0.24	-0.21	-0.21	-0.21	-0.19	-0.13	-0.12	-0.09	-0.09	-0.08	-0.08	-0.04	-0.01	-	0.07	0.12‡	0.13†	0.13‡	0.40‡	1.77‡
ONLINE-A	-0.42	-0.38	-0.37	-0.31	-0.29	-0.29	-0.28	-0.26	-0.20	-0.19	-0.17	-0.17	-0.15	-0.15	-0.11	-0.08	-0.07	-	0.05‡	0.06	0.06†	0.33‡	1.70‡
ONLINE-G	-0.47	-0.43	-0.41	-0.36	-0.33	-0.33	-0.33	-0.31	-0.25	-0.24	-0.21	-0.21	-0.20	-0.20	-0.16	-0.13	-0.12	-0.05	-	0.01	0.01	0.28‡	1.65‡
UdS-DFKI	-0.48	-0.44	-0.42	-0.37	-0.34	-0.34	-0.34	-0.32	-0.26	-0.25	-0.22	-0.22	-0.21	-0.21	-0.17	-0.14	-0.13	-0.06	-0.01⋆	-	0.00	0.27‡	1.64‡
TARTUNLP-C	-0.48	-0.44	-0.43	-0.37	-0.35	-0.34	-0.34	-0.32	-0.26	-0.25	-0.23	-0.23	-0.21	-0.21	-0.17	-0.14	-0.13	-0.06	-0.01	0.00	-	0.27‡	1.64‡
ONLINE-X	-0.75	-0.71	-0.70	-0.64	-0.61	-0.61	-0.61	-0.59	-0.53	-0.52	-0.49	-0.49	-0.48	-0.48	-0.44	-0.41	-0.40	-0.33	-0.28	-0.27	-0.27	-	1.37‡
EN-DE-TASK	-2.12	-2.08	-2.06	-2.01	-1.98	-1.98	-1.98	-1.96	-1.90	-1.89	-1.86	-1.86	-1.85	-1.85	-1.81	-1.78	-1.77	-1.70	-1.65	-1.64	-1.64	-1.37	-
score	0.35	0.31	0.30	0.24	0.21	0.21	0.21	0.19	0.13	0.12	0.09	0.09	0.08	0.08	0.04	0.01	0.00	-0.07	-0.12	-0.13	-0.13	-0.40	-1.77
rank	1	2–20	2–20	2–20	2–20	2–20	2–20	2–20	2–20	2–20	2–20	2–20	2–20	2–20	2–20	2–20	2–20	2–20	2–20	2–20	21	22	23

Table 36: Head to head comparison for English→German systems

	MSRA	ONLINE-Y	GTCOM-PRIMARY	USYD	ONLINE-B	HELSINKI-NLP	ONLINE-A	ONLINE-G	TARTUNLP-C	ONLINE-X	PARFDA	APERTIUM-FIN-ENG-UNCONSTRAINED-FIEN
MSRA	-	0.02⋆	0.02⋆	0.04⋆	0.18‡	0.18‡	0.27‡	0.33‡	0.34‡	0.36‡	0.49‡	0.80‡
ONLINE-Y	-0.02	-	0.00	0.02	0.16‡	0.16‡	0.25‡	0.31‡	0.32‡	0.34‡	0.47‡	0.78‡
GTCOM-PRIMARY	-0.02	0.00	-	0.02	0.15‡	0.16‡	0.25‡	0.31‡	0.31‡	0.33‡	0.47‡	0.78‡
USYD	-0.04	-0.02	-0.02	-	0.14‡	0.14‡	0.23‡	0.29‡	0.30‡	0.32‡	0.45‡	0.76‡
ONLINE-B	-0.18	-0.16	-0.15	-0.14	-	0.00	0.09‡	0.15‡	0.16‡	0.18‡	0.32‡	0.62‡
HELSINKI-NLP	-0.18	-0.16	-0.16	-0.14	0.00	-	0.09‡	0.15‡	0.16‡	0.18‡	0.31‡	0.62‡
ONLINE-A	-0.27	-0.25	-0.25	-0.23	-0.09	-0.09	-	0.06	0.06⋆	0.08†	0.22‡	0.53‡
ONLINE-G	-0.33	-0.31	-0.31	-0.29	-0.15	-0.15	-0.06	-	0.01	0.03	0.17‡	0.47‡
TARTUNLP-C	-0.34	-0.32	-0.31	-0.30	-0.16	-0.16	-0.06	-0.01	-	0.02	0.16‡	0.46‡
ONLINE-X	-0.36	-0.34	-0.33	-0.32	-0.18	-0.18	-0.08	-0.03	-0.02	-	0.14‡	0.45‡
PARFDA	-0.49	-0.47	-0.47	-0.45	-0.32	-0.31	-0.22	-0.17	-0.16	-0.14	-	0.31‡
APERTIUM-FIN-ENG-UNCONSTRAINED-FIEN	-0.80	-0.78	-0.78	-0.76	-0.62	-0.62	-0.53	-0.47	-0.46	-0.45	-0.31	-
score	0.28	0.27	0.26	0.24	0.11	0.10	0.01	-0.04	-0.05	-0.07	-0.21	-0.52
rank	1	2–4	2–4	2–4	5–6	5–6	7–10	7–10	7–10	7–10	11	12

Table 37: Head to head comparison for Finnish→English systems

	HUMAN	GTCOM-PRIMARY	MSRA	ONLINE-Y	NICT	HELSINKI-NLP	ONLINE-G	ONLINE-B	TARTUNLP-C	ONLINE-A	ONLINE-X	HELSINKI-NLP–RULE-BASED-	APERTIUM-FIN-ENG-UNCONSTRAINED-EN-FI
HUMAN	-	0.42‡	0.44‡	0.73‡	0.81‡	0.92‡	0.93‡	0.97‡	1.13‡	1.39‡	1.40‡	1.53‡	2.27‡
GTCOM-PRIMARY	-0.42	-	0.02	0.31‡	0.39‡	0.50‡	0.51‡	0.55‡	0.71‡	0.97‡	0.98‡	1.11‡	1.85‡
MSRA	-0.44	-0.02	-	0.29‡	0.37‡	0.48‡	0.50‡	0.53‡	0.69‡	0.95‡	0.97‡	1.09‡	1.83‡
ONLINE-Y	-0.73	-0.31	-0.29	-	0.08★	0.19‡	0.20‡	0.24‡	0.40‡	0.66‡	0.67‡	0.80‡	1.54‡
NICT	-0.81	-0.39	-0.37	-0.08	-	0.11‡	0.13‡	0.16‡	0.32‡	0.58‡	0.60‡	0.72‡	1.46‡
HELSINKI-NLP	-0.92	-0.50	-0.48	-0.19	-0.11	-	0.02	0.05★	0.21‡	0.47‡	0.49‡	0.61‡	1.35‡
ONLINE-G	-0.93	-0.51	-0.50	-0.20	-0.13	-0.02	-	0.04	0.20‡	0.46‡	0.47‡	0.59‡	1.33‡
ONLINE-B	-0.97	-0.55	-0.53	-0.24	-0.16	-0.05	-0.04	-	0.16‡	0.42‡	0.43‡	0.56‡	1.30‡
TARTUNLP-C	-1.13	-0.71	-0.69	-0.40	-0.32	-0.21	-0.20	-0.16	-	0.26‡	0.27‡	0.40‡	1.14‡
ONLINE-A	-1.39	-0.97	-0.95	-0.66	-0.58	-0.47	-0.46	-0.42	-0.26	-	0.01	0.14‡	0.88‡
ONLINE-X	-1.40	-0.98	-0.97	-0.67	-0.60	-0.49	-0.47	-0.43	-0.27	-0.01	-	0.12‡	0.86‡
HELSINKI-NLP–RULE-BASED-	-1.53	-1.11	-1.09	-0.80	-0.72	-0.61	-0.59	-0.56	-0.40	-0.14	-0.12	-	0.74‡
APERTIUM-FIN-ENG-UNCONSTRAINED-EN-FI	-2.27	-1.85	-1.83	-1.54	-1.46	-1.35	-1.33	-1.30	-1.14	-0.88	-0.86	-0.74	-
score	1.01	0.59	0.57	0.28	0.20	0.09	0.07	0.04	-0.13	-0.38	-0.40	-0.52	-1.26
rank	1	2–3	2–3	4	5	6–8	6–8	6–8	9	10–11	10–11	12	13

Table 38: Head to head comparison for English→Finnish systems

	NEU	UEDIN	GTCOM-PRIMARY	CUNI-T2T-TRANSFER-GUEN	AYLIEN-MT-GU-EN-MULTILINGUAL	NICT	ONLINE-G	IITP-MT	UDS-DFKI	IIITH-MT	JU-SAARLAND
NEU	-	0.08†	0.11‡	0.12‡	0.14‡	0.17‡	0.40‡	0.40‡	0.49‡	0.51‡	0.81‡
UEDIN	-0.08	-	0.03	0.04	0.06	0.08⋆	0.31‡	0.32‡	0.40‡	0.42‡	0.72‡
GTCOM-PRIMARY	-0.11	-0.03	-	0.01	0.03	0.06	0.29‡	0.29‡	0.38‡	0.40‡	0.70‡
CUNI-T2T-TRANSFER-GUEN	-0.12	-0.04	-0.01	-	0.02	0.05	0.28‡	0.28‡	0.37‡	0.39‡	0.69‡
AYLIEN-MT-GU-EN-MULTILINGUAL	-0.14	-0.06	-0.03	-0.02	-	0.02	0.25‡	0.26‡	0.34‡	0.36‡	0.66‡
NICT	-0.17	-0.08	-0.06	-0.05	-0.02	-	0.23‡	0.24‡	0.32‡	0.34‡	0.64‡
ONLINE-G	-0.40	-0.31	-0.29	-0.28	-0.25	-0.23	-	0.00	0.09†	0.11†	0.41‡
IITP-MT	-0.40	-0.32	-0.29	-0.28	-0.26	-0.24	0.00	-	0.08†	0.10†	0.41‡
UDS-DFKI	-0.49	-0.40	-0.38	-0.37	-0.34	-0.32	-0.09	-0.08	-	0.02	0.32‡
IIITH-MT	-0.51	-0.42	-0.40	-0.39	-0.36	-0.34	-0.11	-0.10	-0.02	-	0.30‡
JU-SAARLAND	-0.81	-0.72	-0.70	-0.69	-0.66	-0.64	-0.41	-0.41	-0.32	-0.30	-
score	0.21	0.13	0.10	0.09	0.07	0.04	-0.19	-0.19	-0.28	-0.30	-0.60
rank	1	2–6	2–6	2–6	2–6	2–6	7–8	7–8	9–10	9–10	11

Table 39: Head to head comparison for Gujarati→English systems

	HUMAN	ONLINE-B	GTCOM-PRIMARY	MSRA	UEDIN	CUNI-T2T-TRANSFER-ENGU	JU-SAARLAND-CLEAN-NUM-135-BPE	IITP-MT	NICT	ONLINE-G	ONLINE-X	UDS-DFKI
HUMAN	-	0.04⋆	0.10‡	0.38‡	0.40‡	0.45‡	0.78‡	1.16‡	1.17‡	1.19‡	1.20‡	1.42‡
ONLINE-B	-0.04	-	0.07⋆	0.34‡	0.36‡	0.41‡	0.74‡	1.12‡	1.13‡	1.15‡	1.16‡	1.38‡
GTCOM-PRIMARY	-0.10	-0.07	-	0.28‡	0.29‡	0.34‡	0.68‡	1.06‡	1.06‡	1.09‡	1.10‡	1.31‡
MSRA	-0.38	-0.34	-0.28	-	0.01	0.06	0.40‡	0.78‡	0.78‡	0.81‡	0.82‡	1.04‡
UEDIN	-0.40	-0.36	-0.29	-0.01	-	0.05	0.38‡	0.76‡	0.77‡	0.79‡	0.81‡	1.02‡
CUNI-T2T-TRANSFER-ENGU	-0.45	-0.41	-0.34	-0.06	-0.05	-	0.33‡	0.71‡	0.72‡	0.74‡	0.76‡	0.97‡
JU-SAARLAND-CLEAN-NUM-135-BPE	-0.78	-0.74	-0.68	-0.40	-0.38	-0.33	-	0.38‡	0.39‡	0.41‡	0.42‡	0.64‡
IITP-MT	-1.16	-1.12	-1.06	-0.78	-0.76	-0.71	-0.38	-	0.01	0.03	0.04†	0.26‡
NICT	-1.17	-1.13	-1.06	-0.78	-0.77	-0.72	-0.39	-0.01	-	0.02	0.04†	0.25‡
ONLINE-G	-1.19	-1.15	-1.09	-0.81	-0.79	-0.74	-0.41	-0.03	-0.02	-	0.01⋆	0.23‡
ONLINE-X	-1.20	-1.16	-1.10	-0.82	-0.81	-0.76	-0.42	-0.04	-0.04	-0.01	-	0.22‡
UDS-DFKI	-1.42	-1.38	-1.31	-1.04	-1.02	-0.97	-0.64	-0.26	-0.25	-0.23	-0.22	-
score	0.70	0.66	0.60	0.32	0.30	0.25	-0.08	-0.46	-0.47	-0.49	-0.50	-0.72
rank	1	2	3	4–6	4–6	4–6	7	8–10	8–10	8–10	11	12

Table 40: Head to head comparison for English→Gujarati systems

	GTCOM-PRIMARY	TILDE-NC-NMT	NEU	MSRA	TILDE-C-NMT	ONLINE-B	ONLINE-A	TARTUNLP-C	ONLINE-G	JUMT	ONLINE-X
GTCOM-PRIMARY	-	0.02	0.02	0.03	0.03⋆	0.13‡	0.29‡	0.29‡	0.52‡	0.57‡	0.63‡
TILDE-NC-NMT	-0.02	-	0.00	0.01	0.01	0.11‡	0.27‡	0.28‡	0.50‡	0.55‡	0.61‡
NEU	-0.02	0.00	-	0.01	0.01	0.11‡	0.27‡	0.27‡	0.50‡	0.55‡	0.61‡
MSRA	-0.03	-0.01	-0.01	-	0.00	0.10†	0.26‡	0.27‡	0.49‡	0.54‡	0.60‡
TILDE-C-NMT	-0.03	-0.01	-0.01	0.00	-	0.09†	0.26‡	0.26‡	0.49‡	0.54‡	0.60‡
ONLINE-B	-0.13	-0.11	-0.11	-0.10	-0.09	-	0.16‡	0.17‡	0.39‡	0.44‡	0.50‡
ONLINE-A	-0.29	-0.27	-0.27	-0.26	-0.26	-0.16	-	0.00	0.23‡	0.28‡	0.34‡
TARTUNLP-C	-0.29	-0.28	-0.27	-0.27	-0.26	-0.17	0.00	-	0.22‡	0.28‡	0.34‡
ONLINE-G	-0.52	-0.50	-0.50	-0.49	-0.49	-0.39	-0.23	-0.22	-	0.05	0.11†
JUMT	-0.57	-0.55	-0.55	-0.54	-0.54	-0.44	-0.28	-0.28	-0.05	-	0.06†
ONLINE-X	-0.63	-0.61	-0.61	-0.60	-0.60	-0.50	-0.34	-0.34	-0.11	-0.06	-
score	0.23	0.22	0.21	0.21	0.20	0.11	-0.06	-0.06	-0.28	-0.34	-0.40
rank	1–5	1–5	1–5	1–5	1–5	6	7–8	7–8	9–10	9–10	11

Table 41: Head to head comparison for Lithuanian→English systems

	HUMAN	TILDE-NC-NMT	MSRA	TILDE-C-NMT	MSRA	GTCOM-PRIMARY	ETRANSLATION	NEU	ONLINE-B	TARTUNLP-C	ONLINE-A	ONLINE-X	ONLINE-G
HUMAN	-	0.63‡	0.63‡	0.75‡	0.76‡	0.86‡	0.98‡	1.07‡	1.08‡	1.40‡	1.64‡	1.68‡	1.82‡
TILDE-NC-NMT	-0.63	-	0.00	0.13★	0.13†	0.23‡	0.35‡	0.44‡	0.45‡	0.77‡	1.01‡	1.05‡	1.19‡
MSRA	-0.63	0.00	-	0.13†	0.13†	0.23‡	0.35‡	0.44‡	0.45‡	0.77‡	1.01‡	1.05‡	1.19‡
TILDE-C-NMT	-0.75	-0.13	-0.13	-	0.00	0.11†	0.23‡	0.32‡	0.32‡	0.65‡	0.88‡	0.93‡	1.07‡
MSRA	-0.76	-0.13	-0.13	0.00	-	0.10†	0.22‡	0.31‡	0.32‡	0.64‡	0.88‡	0.92‡	1.06‡
GTCOM-PRIMARY	-0.86	-0.23	-0.23	-0.11	-0.10	-	0.12†	0.21‡	0.22‡	0.54‡	0.77‡	0.82‡	0.96‡
ETRANSLATION	-0.98	-0.35	-0.35	-0.23	-0.22	-0.12	-	0.09†	0.10†	0.42‡	0.66‡	0.70‡	0.84‡
NEU	-1.07	-0.44	-0.44	-0.32	-0.31	-0.21	-0.09	-	0.01	0.33‡	0.57‡	0.61‡	0.75‡
ONLINE-B	-1.08	-0.45	-0.45	-0.32	-0.32	-0.22	-0.10	-0.01	-	0.32‡	0.56‡	0.60‡	0.74‡
TARTUNLP-C	-1.40	-0.77	-0.77	-0.65	-0.64	-0.54	-0.42	-0.33	-0.32	-	0.24‡	0.28‡	0.42‡
ONLINE-A	-1.64	-1.01	-1.01	-0.88	-0.88	-0.77	-0.66	-0.57	-0.56	-0.24	-	0.05	0.19‡
ONLINE-X	-1.68	-1.05	-1.05	-0.93	-0.92	-0.82	-0.70	-0.61	-0.60	-0.28	-0.05	-	0.14†
ONLINE-G	-1.82	-1.19	-1.19	-1.07	-1.06	-0.96	-0.84	-0.75	-0.74	-0.42	-0.19	-0.14	-
score	1.02	0.39	0.39	0.26	0.26	0.15	0.04	-0.05	-0.06	-0.38	-0.62	-0.67	-0.81
rank	1	2–3	2–3	4–5	4–5	6	7	8–9	8–9	10	11–12	11–12	13

Table 42: Head to head comparison for English→Lithuanian systems

	ONLINE-B	NEU	RUG-KKEN-MORFESSOR	ONLINE-G	TALP-UPC-2019-KKEN	NRC-CNRC	FRANK-S-MT	NICT	CUNI-T2T-TRANSFER-KKEN	UMD	DBMS-KU-KKEN
ONLINE-B	-	0.05	0.08⋆	0.14‡	0.16‡	0.18‡	0.20‡	0.21‡	0.27‡	0.75‡	1.33‡
NEU	-0.05	-	0.03	0.08†	0.10‡	0.13‡	0.15‡	0.15‡	0.21‡	0.69‡	1.28‡
RUG-KKEN-MORFESSOR	-0.08	-0.03	-	0.06⋆	0.08⋆	0.10‡	0.12†	0.12‡	0.19‡	0.67‡	1.25‡
ONLINE-G	-0.14	-0.08	-0.06	-	0.02	0.04	0.07	0.07⋆	0.13‡	0.61‡	1.19‡
TALP-UPC-2019-KKEN	-0.16	-0.10	-0.08	-0.02	-	0.02	0.05	0.05	0.11†	0.59‡	1.17‡
NRC-CNRC	-0.18	-0.13	-0.10	-0.04	-0.02	-	0.03	0.03	0.09⋆	0.57‡	1.15‡
FRANK-S-MT	-0.20	-0.15	-0.12	-0.07	-0.05	-0.03	-	0.00	0.06⋆	0.54‡	1.12‡
NICT	-0.21	-0.15	-0.12	-0.07	-0.05	-0.03	0.00	-	0.06	0.54‡	1.12‡
CUNI-T2T-TRANSFER-KKEN	-0.27	-0.21	-0.19	-0.13	-0.11	-0.09	-0.06	-0.06	-	0.48‡	1.06‡
UMD	-0.75	-0.69	-0.67	-0.61	-0.59	-0.57	-0.54	-0.54	-0.48	-	0.58‡
DBMS-KU-KKEN	-1.33	-1.28	-1.25	-1.19	-1.17	-1.15	-1.12	-1.12	-1.06	-0.58	-
score	0.27	0.22	0.19	0.13	0.11	0.09	0.07	0.06	0.00	-0.48	-1.06
rank	1–3	1–3	1–3	4–9	4–9	4–9	4–9	4–9	4–9	10	11

Table 43: Head to head comparison for Kazakh→English systems

	HUMAN	UALACANT—NMT	ONLINE-B	UALACANT—N	RBMT	NEU	MSRA	CUNI-T2T-TRANSFER-ENKK	ONLINE-G	RUG-ENKK-BPE	TALP-UPC-2019-ENKK	NICT	DBMS-KU-ENKK
HUMAN	-	0.48‡	0.50‡	0.52‡	0.52‡	0.62‡	0.64‡	0.65‡	0.67‡	0.79‡	1.07‡	1.24‡	2.14‡
UALACANT—NMT	-0.48	-	0.02	0.04	0.04	0.14‡	0.15‡	0.16‡	0.18‡	0.31‡	0.59‡	0.75‡	1.66‡
ONLINE-B	-0.50	-0.02	-	0.02	0.02	0.12†	0.14†	0.15†	0.17‡	0.29‡	0.57‡	0.74‡	1.64‡
UALACANT—N	-0.52	-0.04	-0.02	-	0.00	0.10†	0.11†	0.13⋆	0.14‡	0.27‡	0.55‡	0.72‡	1.62‡
RBMT	-0.52	-0.04	-0.02	0.00	-	0.10†	0.11†	0.13⋆	0.14‡	0.27‡	0.55‡	0.72‡	1.62‡
NEU	-0.62	-0.14	-0.12	-0.10	-0.10	-	0.02	0.03	0.05	0.18‡	0.45‡	0.62‡	1.52‡
MSRA	-0.64	-0.15	-0.14	-0.11	-0.11	-0.02	-	0.01	0.03	0.16‡	0.44‡	0.60‡	1.50‡
CUNI-T2T-TRANSFER-ENKK	-0.65	-0.16	-0.15	-0.13	-0.13	-0.03	-0.01	-	0.02	0.15‡	0.42‡	0.59‡	1.49‡
ONLINE-G	-0.67	-0.18	-0.17	-0.14	-0.14	-0.05	-0.03	-0.02	-	0.13†	0.41‡	0.57‡	1.47‡
RUG-ENKK-BPE	-0.79	-0.31	-0.29	-0.27	-0.27	-0.18	-0.16	-0.15	-0.13	-	0.28‡	0.44‡	1.35‡
TALP-UPC-2019-ENKK	-1.07	-0.59	-0.57	-0.55	-0.55	-0.45	-0.44	-0.42	-0.41	-0.28	-	0.17‡	1.07‡
NICT	-1.24	-0.75	-0.74	-0.72	-0.72	-0.62	-0.60	-0.59	-0.57	-0.44	-0.17	-	0.90‡
DBMS-KU-ENKK	-2.14	-1.66	-1.64	-1.62	-1.62	-1.52	-1.50	-1.49	-1.47	-1.35	-1.07	-0.90	-
score	0.75	0.26	0.24	0.22	0.22	0.13	0.11	0.10	0.08	-0.05	-0.33	-0.49	-1.40
rank	1	2–5	2–5	2–5	2–5	6–9	6–9	6–9	6–9	10	11	12	13

Table 44: Head to head comparison for English→Kazakh systems

	FACEBOOK-FAIR	ONLINE-G	ETRANSLATION	ONLINE-B	NEU	MSRA	RERANK-RE	ONLINE-Y	ONLINE-A	AFRL-SYSCOMB19	AFRL-EWC	TARTUNLP-U	ONLINE-X	NICT
FACEBOOK-FAIR	-	0.02⋆	0.03⋆	0.04	0.04	0.05⋆	0.07‡	0.08‡	0.13‡	0.14‡	0.20‡	0.20‡	0.25‡	0.46‡
ONLINE-G	-0.02	-	0.01	0.01	0.02	0.03	0.05⋆	0.06	0.11†	0.12‡	0.17‡	0.17‡	0.23‡	0.44‡
ETRANSLATION	-0.03	-0.01	-	0.00	0.01	0.02	0.04	0.05	0.09⋆	0.11‡	0.16‡	0.16‡	0.22‡	0.43‡
ONLINE-B	-0.04	-0.01	0.00	-	0.01	0.02	0.04⋆	0.04⋆	0.09†	0.11‡	0.16‡	0.16‡	0.22‡	0.42‡
NEU	-0.04	-0.02	-0.01	-0.01	-	0.01	0.03⋆	0.04⋆	0.09†	0.10‡	0.15‡	0.15‡	0.21‡	0.42‡
MSRA	-0.05	-0.03	-0.02	-0.02	-0.01	-	0.02	0.03	0.07⋆	0.09†	0.14‡	0.14‡	0.20‡	0.41‡
RERANK-RE	-0.07	-0.05	-0.04	-0.04	-0.03	-0.02	-	0.01	0.05	0.07⋆	0.12‡	0.12‡	0.18‡	0.39‡
ONLINE-Y	-0.08	-0.06	-0.05	-0.04	-0.04	-0.03	-0.01	-	0.05	0.06⋆	0.12‡	0.12‡	0.17‡	0.38‡
ONLINE-A	-0.13	-0.11	-0.09	-0.09	-0.09	-0.07	-0.05	-0.05	-	0.02	0.07†	0.07†	0.13‡	0.33‡
AFRL-SYSCOMB19	-0.14	-0.12	-0.11	-0.11	-0.10	-0.09	-0.07	-0.06	-0.02	-	0.05⋆	0.05	0.11‡	0.32‡
AFRL-EWC	-0.20	-0.17	-0.16	-0.16	-0.15	-0.14	-0.12	-0.12	-0.07	-0.05	-	0.00	0.06†	0.26‡
TARTUNLP-U	-0.20	-0.17	-0.16	-0.16	-0.15	-0.14	-0.12	-0.12	-0.07	-0.05	0.00	-	0.06†	0.26‡
ONLINE-X	-0.25	-0.23	-0.22	-0.22	-0.21	-0.20	-0.18	-0.17	-0.13	-0.11	-0.06	-0.06	-	0.21‡
NICT	-0.46	-0.44	-0.43	-0.42	-0.42	-0.41	-0.39	-0.38	-0.33	-0.32	-0.26	-0.26	-0.21	-
score	0.16	0.13	0.12	0.12	0.12	0.10	0.08	0.08	0.03	0.01	-0.04	-0.04	-0.10	-0.30
rank	1–12	1–12	1–12	1–12	1–12	1–12	1–12	1–12	1–12	1–12	1–12	1–12	13	14

Table 45: Head to head comparison for Russian→English systems

	HUMAN	FACEBOOK-FAIR	USTC-MCC	ONLINE-G	ONLINE-B	NEU	PROMT-NMT-EN-RU	ONLINE-Y	RERANK-ER	ONLINE-A	TARTUNLP-U	ONLINE-X	NICT
HUMAN	-	0.03	0.20‡	0.26‡	0.27‡	0.31‡	0.32‡	0.38‡	0.72‡	0.80‡	0.85‡	0.90‡	1.81‡
FACEBOOK-FAIR	-0.03	-	0.17‡	0.23‡	0.24‡	0.28‡	0.29‡	0.35‡	0.69‡	0.77‡	0.82‡	0.87‡	1.78‡
USTC-MCC	-0.20	-0.17	-	0.05†	0.06‡	0.11‡	0.11‡	0.18‡	0.52‡	0.60‡	0.64‡	0.69‡	1.60‡
ONLINE-G	-0.26	-0.23	-0.05	-	0.01	0.06★	0.06†	0.12‡	0.47‡	0.55‡	0.59‡	0.64‡	1.55‡
ONLINE-B	-0.27	-0.24	-0.06	-0.01	-	0.05	0.05★	0.11‡	0.46‡	0.54‡	0.58‡	0.63‡	1.54‡
NEU	-0.31	-0.28	-0.11	-0.06	-0.05	-	0.00	0.07†	0.41‡	0.49‡	0.53‡	0.59‡	1.49‡
PROMT-NMT-EN-RU	-0.32	-0.29	-0.11	-0.06	-0.05	0.00	-	0.06★	0.41‡	0.49‡	0.53‡	0.58‡	1.49‡
ONLINE-Y	-0.38	-0.35	-0.18	-0.12	-0.11	-0.07	-0.06	-	0.34‡	0.42‡	0.47‡	0.52‡	1.43‡
RERANK-ER	-0.72	-0.69	-0.52	-0.47	-0.46	-0.41	-0.41	-0.34	-	0.08‡	0.12‡	0.17‡	1.08‡
ONLINE-A	-0.80	-0.77	-0.60	-0.55	-0.54	-0.49	-0.49	-0.42	-0.08	-	0.04	0.09‡	1.00‡
TARTUNLP-U	-0.85	-0.82	-0.64	-0.59	-0.58	-0.53	-0.53	-0.47	-0.12	-0.04	-	0.05‡	0.96‡
ONLINE-X	-0.90	-0.87	-0.69	-0.64	-0.63	-0.59	-0.58	-0.52	-0.17	-0.09	-0.05	-	0.91‡
NICT	-1.81	-1.78	-1.60	-1.55	-1.54	-1.49	-1.49	-1.43	-1.08	-1.00	-0.96	-0.91	-
score	0.54	0.51	0.33	0.28	0.27	0.22	0.22	0.16	-0.19	-0.27	-0.31	-0.36	-1.27
rank	1–2	1–2	3	4–7	4–7	4–7	4–7	8	9	10–11	10–11	12	13

Table 46: Head to head comparison for English→Russian systems

	ONLINE-Y	ONLINE-B	NICT	ONLINE-G	NEU-KINGSOFT	ONLINE-A	LMU-UNSUP-NMT-DE-CS	CUNI-UNSUPERVISED-NER-POST	UNSUPERVISED	UNSUPERVISED	CAIRE
ONLINE-Y	-	0.04	0.06⋆	0.11‡	0.25‡	0.29‡	0.53‡	0.59‡	0.75‡	0.83‡	1.23‡
ONLINE-B	-0.04	-	0.02	0.07⋆	0.21‡	0.25‡	0.49‡	0.55‡	0.71‡	0.79‡	1.19‡
NICT	-0.06	-0.02	-	0.05	0.19‡	0.23‡	0.47‡	0.53‡	0.69‡	0.77‡	1.17‡
ONLINE-G	-0.11	-0.07	-0.05	-	0.14‡	0.19‡	0.42‡	0.48‡	0.65‡	0.72‡	1.13‡
NEU-KINGSOFT	-0.25	-0.21	-0.19	-0.14	-	0.05	0.28‡	0.34‡	0.51‡	0.58‡	0.99‡
ONLINE-A	-0.29	-0.25	-0.23	-0.19	-0.05	-	0.23‡	0.30‡	0.46‡	0.54‡	0.94‡
LMU-UNSUP-NMT-DE-CS	-0.53	-0.49	-0.47	-0.42	-0.28	-0.23	-	0.07⋆	0.23‡	0.31‡	0.71‡
CUNI-UNSUPERVISED-NER-POST	-0.59	-0.55	-0.53	-0.48	-0.34	-0.30	-0.07	-	0.16‡	0.24‡	0.64‡
UNSUPERVISED	-0.75	-0.71	-0.69	-0.65	-0.51	-0.46	-0.23	-0.16	-	0.08⋆	0.48‡
UNSUPERVISED	-0.83	-0.79	-0.77	-0.72	-0.58	-0.54	-0.31	-0.24	-0.08	-	0.40‡
CAIRE	-1.23	-1.19	-1.17	-1.13	-0.99	-0.94	-0.71	-0.64	-0.48	-0.40	-
score	0.43	0.39	0.37	0.32	0.18	0.13	-0.10	-0.17	-0.33	-0.41	-0.81
rank	1–4	1–4	1–4	1–4	5–6	5–6	7	8	9	10	11

Table 47: Head to head comparison for German→Czech systems

	MSRA	MLLP-UPV	KYOTO-UNIVERSITY-T2T	LINGUA-CUSTODIA-PRIMARY	LIUM	ONLINE-B	ONLINE-Y	TARTUNLP-C	ONLINE-A	ONLINE-G	ONLINE-X
MSRA	-	0.02	0.09	0.09★	0.12★	0.21‡	0.23‡	0.35‡	0.44‡	0.49‡	0.71‡
MLLP-UPV	-0.02	-	0.07	0.07	0.10★	0.19‡	0.21‡	0.33‡	0.42‡	0.47‡	0.69‡
KYOTO-UNIVERSITY-T2T	-0.09	-0.07	-	0.00	0.04	0.13†	0.15†	0.27‡	0.36‡	0.40‡	0.62‡
LINGUA-CUSTODIA-PRIMARY	-0.09	-0.07	0.00	-	0.03	0.12†	0.14†	0.26‡	0.35‡	0.40‡	0.62‡
LIUM	-0.12	-0.10	-0.04	-0.03	-	0.09†	0.11†	0.23‡	0.32‡	0.37‡	0.58‡
ONLINE-B	-0.21	-0.19	-0.13	-0.12	-0.09	-	0.02	0.14★	0.23‡	0.28‡	0.49‡
ONLINE-Y	-0.23	-0.21	-0.15	-0.14	-0.11	-0.02	-	0.12★	0.21‡	0.26‡	0.47‡
TARTUNLP-C	-0.35	-0.33	-0.27	-0.26	-0.23	-0.14	-0.12	-	0.09	0.14	0.35‡
ONLINE-A	-0.44	-0.42	-0.36	-0.35	-0.32	-0.23	-0.21	-0.09	-	0.05	0.26‡
ONLINE-G	-0.49	-0.47	-0.40	-0.40	-0.37	-0.28	-0.26	-0.14	-0.05	-	0.22‡
ONLINE-X	-0.71	-0.69	-0.62	-0.62	-0.58	-0.49	-0.47	-0.35	-0.26	-0.22	-
score	0.25	0.23	0.16	0.16	0.13	0.04	0.02	-0.10	-0.19	-0.24	-0.46
rank	1–5	1–5	1–5	1–5	1–5	6–7	6–7	8–10	8–10	8–10	11

Table 48: Head to head comparison for German→French systems

	MSRA	ETRANSLATION	LIUM	MLLP-UPV	ONLINE-Y	ONLINE-G	ONLINE-B	ONLINE-A	TARTUNLP-C	ONLINE-X
MSRA	-	0.02	0.19†	0.23‡	0.27‡	0.29‡	0.30‡	0.31‡	0.37‡	0.68‡
ETRANSLATION	-0.02	-	0.16⋆	0.21⋆	0.24‡	0.26‡	0.28‡	0.29‡	0.34‡	0.66‡
LIUM	-0.19	-0.16	-	0.04	0.08⋆	0.10	0.12⋆	0.12⋆	0.18‡	0.49‡
MLLP-UPV	-0.23	-0.21	-0.04	-	0.04	0.06	0.07	0.08⋆	0.14†	0.45‡
ONLINE-Y	-0.27	-0.24	-0.08	-0.04	-	0.02	0.03	0.04	0.10	0.41‡
ONLINE-G	-0.29	-0.26	-0.10	-0.06	-0.02	-	0.02	0.02	0.08⋆	0.39‡
ONLINE-B	-0.30	-0.28	-0.12	-0.07	-0.03	-0.02	-	0.01	0.06	0.38‡
ONLINE-A	-0.31	-0.29	-0.12	-0.08	-0.04	-0.02	-0.01	-	0.06	0.37‡
TARTUNLP-C	-0.37	-0.34	-0.18	-0.14	-0.10	-0.08	-0.06	-0.06	-	0.31‡
ONLINE-X	-0.68	-0.66	-0.49	-0.45	-0.41	-0.39	-0.38	-0.37	-0.31	-
score	0.27	0.25	0.08	0.04	0.00	-0.02	-0.03	-0.04	-0.10	-0.41
rank	1–2	1–2	3–9	3–9	3–9	3–9	3–9	3–9	3–9	10

Table 49: Head to head comparison for French→German systems

Results of the WMT19 Metrics Shared Task: Segment-Level and Strong MT Systems Pose Big Challenges

Qingsong Ma
Tencent-CSIG, AI Evaluation Lab
qingsong.mqs@gmail.com

Johnny Tian-Zheng Wei
UMass Amherst, CICS
jwei@umass.edu

Ondřej Bojar
Charles University, MFF ÚFAL
bojar@ufal.mff.cuni.cz

Yvette Graham
Dublin City University, ADAPT
graham.yvette@gmail.com

Abstract

This paper presents the results of the WMT19 Metrics Shared Task. Participants were asked to score the outputs of the translations systems competing in the WMT19 News Translation Task with automatic metrics. 13 research groups submitted 24 metrics, 10 of which are reference-less "metrics" and constitute submissions to the joint task with WMT19 Quality Estimation Task, "QE as a Metric". In addition, we computed 11 baseline metrics, with 8 commonly applied baselines (BLEU, SentBLEU, NIST, WER, PER, TER, CDER, and chrF) and 3 reimplementations (chrF+, sacreBLEU-BLEU, and sacreBLEU-chrF). Metrics were evaluated on the system level, how well a given metric correlates with the WMT19 official manual ranking, and segment level, how well the metric correlates with human judgements of segment quality. This year, we use direct assessment (DA) as our only form of manual evaluation.

1 Introduction

To determine system performance in machine translation (MT), it is often more practical to use an automatic evaluation, rather than a manual one. Manual/human evaluation can be costly and time consuming, and so an automatic evaluation metric, given that it sufficiently correlates with manual evaluation, can be useful in developmental cycles. In studies involving hyperparameter tuning or architecture search, automatic metrics are necessary as the amount of human effort implicated in manual evaluation is generally prohibitively large. As objective, reproducible quantities, metrics can also facilitate cross-paper compar-

isons. The WMT Metrics Shared Task[1] annually serves as a venue to validate the use of existing metrics (including baselines such as BLEU), and to develop new ones; see Koehn and Monz (2006) through Ma et al. (2018).

In the setup of our Metrics Shared Task, an automatic metric compares an MT system's output translations with manual reference translations to produce: either (a) *system-level* score, i.e. a single overall score for the given MT system, or (b) *segment-level* scores for each of the output translations, or both.

This year we teamed up with the organizers of the QE Task and hosted "QE as a Metric" as a joint task. In the setup of the Quality Estimation Task (Fonseca et al., 2019), no human-produced translations are provided to estimate the quality of output translations. Quality estimation (QE) methods are built to assess MT output based on the source or based on the translation itself. In this task, QE developers were invited to perform the same scoring as standard metrics participants, with the exception that they refrain from using a reference translation in production of their scores. We then evaluate the QE submissions in exactly the same way as regular metrics are evaluated, see below. From the point of view of correlation with manual judgements, there is no difference in metrics using or not using references.

The source, reference texts, and MT system outputs for the Metrics task come from the News Translation Task (Barrault et al., 2019, which we denote as Findings 2019). The texts were drawn from the news domain and involve translations of English (en) to/from

---

[1] http://www.statmt.org/wmt19/metrics-task.html

62

Proceedings of the Fourth Conference on Machine Translation (WMT), Volume 2: Shared Task Papers (Day 1) pages 62–90
Florence, Italy, August 1-2, 2019. ©2019 Association for Computational Linguistics

Czech (cs), German (de), Finnish (fi), Gujarati (gu), Kazakh (kk), Lithuanian (lt), Russian (ru), and Chinese (zh), but excluding cs-en (15 language pairs). Three other language pairs not including English were also manually evaluated as part of the News Translation Task: German→Czech and German↔French. In total, metrics could participate in 18 language pairs, with 10 target languages.

In the following, we first give an overview of the task (Section 2) and summarize the baseline (Section 3) and submitted (Section 4) metrics. The results for system- and segment-level evaluation are provided in Sections 5.1 and 5.2, respectively, followed by a joint discussion Section 6.

2 Task Setup

This year, we provided task participants with one test set for each examined language pair, i.e. a set of source texts (which are commonly ignored by MT metrics), corresponding MT outputs (these are the key inputs to be scored) and a reference translation (held out for the participants of "QE as a Metric" track).

In the system-level, metrics aim to correlate with a system's score which is an average over many human judgments of segment translation quality produced by the given system. In the segment-level, metrics aim to produce scores that correlate best with a human ranking judgment of two output translations for a given source segment (more on the manual quality assessment in Section 2.3). Participants were free to choose which language pairs and tracks (system/segment and reference-based/reference-free) they wanted to take part in.

2.1 Source and Reference Texts

The source and reference texts we use are *newstest2019* from this year's WMT News Translation Task (see Findings 2019). This set contains approximately 2,000 sentences for each translation direction (except Gujarati, Kazakh and Lithuanian which have approximately 1,000 sentences each, and German to/from French which has 1701 sentences).

The reference translations provided in *newstest2019* were created in the same direction as the MT systems were translating.

The exceptions are German→Czech where both sides are translations from English and German↔French which followed last years' practice. Last year and the years before, the dataset consisted of two halves, one originating in the source language and one in the target language. This however lead to adverse artifacts in MT evaluation.

2.2 System Outputs

The results of the Metrics Task are affected by the actual set of MT systems participating in a given translation direction. On one hand, if all systems are very close in their translation quality, then even humans will struggle to rank them. This in turn will make the task for MT metrics very hard. On the other hand, if the task includes a wide range of systems of varying quality, correlating with humans should be generally easier, see Section 6.1 for a discussion on this. One can also expect that if the evaluated systems are of different types, they will exhibit different error patterns and various MT metrics can be differently sensitive to these patterns.

This year, all MT systems included in the Metrics Task come from the News Translation Task (see Findings 2019). There are however still noticeable differences among the various language pairs.

- **Unsupervised MT Systems.** The German→Czech research systems were trained in an unsupervised fashion, i.e. without the access to parallel Czech-German texts (except for a couple of thousand sentences used primarily for validation). We thus expect the research German-Czech systems to be "more creative" and depart further away from the references. The online systems in this language directions are however standard MT systems so the German-Czech evaluation could be to some extent bimodal.

- **EU Election.** The French↔German translation was focused on a sub-domain of news, namely texts related EU Election. Various MT system developers may have invested more or less time to the domain adaptation.

- **Regular News Tasks Systems.** These

are all the other MT systems in the evaluation; differing in whether they are trained only on WMT provided data ("Constrained", or "Unconstrained") as in the previous years. All the freely available web services (online MT systems) are deemed unconstrained.

Overall, the results are based on 233 systems across 18 language pairs.[2]

2.3 Manual Quality Assessment

Direct Assessment (DA, Graham et al., 2013, 2014a, 2016) was employed as the source of the "golden truth" to evaluate metrics again this year. The details of this method of human evaluation are provided in Findings 2019.

The basis of DA is to collect a large number of quality assessments (a number on a scale of 1–100, i.e. effectively a continuous scale) for the outputs of all MT systems. These scores are then standardized per annotator.

In the past years, the underlying manual scores were reference-based (human judges had access to the same reference translation as the MT quality metric). This year, the official WMT19 scores are reference-based (or "monolingual") for some language pairs and reference-free (or "bilingual") for others.[3]

Due to these different types of golden truth collection, reference-based language pairs are in a closer match with the standard reference-based metrics, while the reference-free language pairs are better fit for the "QE as a metric" subtask.

Note that system-level manual scores are different than those of the segment-level. Since for segment-level evaluation, collecting enough DA judgements for each segment is infeasible, so we resort to converting DA judgements to

golden truth expressed as relative rankings, see Section 2.3.2.

The exact methods used to calculate correlations of participating metrics with the golden truth are described below, in the two sections for system-level evaluation (Section 5.1) and segment-level evaluation (Section 5.2).

2.3.1 System-level Golden Truth: DA

For the system-level evaluation, the collected continuous DA scores, standardized for each annotator, are averaged across all assessed segments for each MT system to produce a scalar rating for the system's performance.

The underlying set of assessed segments is different for each system. Thanks to the fact that the system-level DA score is an average over many judgments, mean scores are consistent and have been found to be reproducible (Graham et al., 2013). For more details see Findings 2019.

2.3.2 Segment-level Golden Truth: daRR

Starting from Bojar et al. (2017), when WMT fully switched to DA, we had to come up with a solid golden standard for segment-level judgements. Standard DA scores are reliable only when averaged over sufficient number of judgments.[4]

Fortunately, when we have at least two DA scores for translations of the same source input, it is possible to convert those DA scores into a relative ranking judgement, if the difference in DA scores allows conclusion that one translation is better than the other. In the following, we denote these re-interpreted DA judgements as "DARR", to distinguish it clearly from the relative ranking ("RR") golden truth used in the past years.[5]

---

[2]This year, we do not use the artificially constructed "hybrid systems" (Graham and Liu, 2016) because the confidence on the ranking of system-level metrics is sufficient even without hybrids.

[3]Specifically, the reference-based language pairs were those where the anticipated translation quality was lower or where the manual judgements were obtained with the help of anonymous crowdsourcing. Most of these cases were translations into English (fi-en, gu-en, kk-en, lt-en, ru-en and zh-en) and then the language pairs not involving English (de-cs, de-fr and fr-de). The reference-less (bilingual) evaluations were those where mainly MT researchers themselves were involved in the annotations: en-cs, en-de, en-fi, en-gu, en-kk, en-lt, en-ru, en-zh.

[4]For segment-level evaluation, one would need to collect many manual evaluations of the exact same segment as produced by each MT system. Such a sampling would be however wasteful for the evaluation needed by WMT, so only some MT systems happen to be evaluated for a given input sentence. In principle, we would like to return to DA's standard segment-level evaluation in future, where a minimum of 15 human judgements of translation quality are collected per translation and combined to get highly accurate scores for translations, but this would increase annotation costs.

[5]Since the analogue rating scale employed by DA is marked at the 0-25-50-75-100 points, we use 25 points as the minimum required difference between two system scores to produce DARR judgements. Note that we

	DA>1	Ave	DA pairs	DARR
de-en	2,000	16.0	239,220	85,365
fi-en	1,996	9.5	83,168	38,307
gu-en	1,016	11.0	55,880	31,139
kk-en	1,000	11.0	55,000	27,094
lt-en	1,000	11.0	55,000	21,862
ru-en	1,999	11.9	131,766	46,172
zh-en	2,000	10.1	95,174	31,070
en-cs	1,997	9.1	75,560	27,178
en-de	1,997	19.1	347,109	99,840
en-fi	1,997	8.1	59,129	31,820
en-gu	998	6.9	21,854	11,355
en-kk	998	9.0	37,032	18,172
en-lt	998	9.0	36,435	17,401
en-ru	1,997	8.7	69,503	24,334
en-zh	1,997	9.8	87,501	18,658
de-cs	1,997	8.5	65,039	35,793
de-fr	1,605	4.1	12,055	4,862
fr-de	1,224	3.0	4,258	1,369
newstest2019				

Table 1: Number of judgements for DA converted to DARR data; "DA>1" is the number of source input sentences in the manual evaluation where at least two translations of that same source input segment received a DA judgement; "Ave" is the average number of translations with at least one DA judgement available for the same source input sentence; "DA pairs" is the number of all possible pairs of translations of the same source input resulting from "DA>1"; and "DARR" is the number of DA pairs with an absolute difference in DA scores greater than the 25 percentage point margin.

From the complete set of human assessments collected for the News Translation Task, all possible pairs of DA judgements attributed to distinct translations of the same source were converted into DARR better/worse judgements. Distinct translations of the same source input whose DA scores fell within 25 percentage points (which could have been deemed equal quality) were omitted from the evaluation of segment-level metrics. Conversion of scores in this way produced a large set of DARR judgements for all language pairs,

rely on judgements collected from known-reliable volunteers and crowd-sourced workers who passed DA's quality control mechanism. Any inconsistency that could arise from reliance on DA judgements collected from low quality crowd-sourcing is thus prevented.

shown in Table 1 due to combinatorial advantage of extracting DARR judgements from all possible pairs of translations of the same source input. We see that only German-French and esp. French-German can suffer from insufficient number of these simulated pairwise comparisons.

The DARR judgements serve as the golden standard for segment-level evaluation in WMT19.

3 Baseline Metrics

In addition to validating popular metrics, including baselines metrics serves as comparison and prevents "loss of knowledge" as mentioned by Bojar et al. (2016).

Moses scorer[6] is one of the MT evaluation tools that aggregated several useful metrics over the time. Since Macháček and Bojar (2013), we have been using Moses scorer to provide most of the baseline metrics and kept encouraging authors of well-performing MT metrics to include them in Moses scorer.[7]

The baselines we report are:

BLEU and NIST The metrics BLEU (Papineni et al., 2002) and NIST (Doddington, 2002) were computed using `mteval-v13a.pl`[8] from the OpenMT Evaluation Campaign. The tool includes its own tokenization. We run `mteval` with the flag `--international-tokenization`.[9]

TER, WER, PER and CDER. The metrics TER (Snover et al., 2006), WER, PER and CDER (Leusch et al., 2006) were produced by the Moses scorer, which is used in Moses model optimization. We used the standard tokenizer script as available in Moses toolkit for tokenization.

sentBLEU. The metric SENTBLEU is computed using the script `sentence-bleu`, a part of the Moses toolkit. It is a

[6]`https://github.com/moses-smt/mosesdecoder/blob/master/mert/evaluator.cpp`

[7]If you prefer standard BLEU, we recommend sacre-BLEU (Post, 2018a), found at `https://github.com/mjpost/sacreBLEU`.

[8]`http://www.itl.nist.gov/iad/mig/tools/`

[9]International tokenization is found to perform slightly better (Macháček and Bojar, 2013).

	Metric	Features	Learned?	Seg	Sys	Citation/Participant	Availability
Baselines	sentBLEU	n-grams		•	—		(mosesdecoder) mert/sentence-bleu
	BLEU	n-grams		—	•	Papineni et al. (2002)	(mosesdecoder) scripts/generic/mteval-v13a.pl
	NIST	n-grams		—	•	Doddington (2002)	(mosesdecoder) scripts/generic/mteval-v13a.pl
	WER	Levenshtein distance		—	•	Leusch et al. (2006)	(mosesdecoder) mert/evaluator
	TER	edit distance, edit types		—	•	Snover et al. (2006)	(mosesdecoder) mert/evaluator
	PER	edit distance, edit types		—	•	Leusch et al. (2003)	(mosesdecoder) mert/evaluator
	CDER	edit distance, edit types		—	•	Leusch et al. (2006)	(mosesdecoder) mert/evaluator
	chrF	character n-grams		•	⊘	Popović (2015)	http://github.com/m-popovic/chrF
	chrF+	character n-grams		•	⊘	Popović (2017)	http://github.com/m-popovic/chrF
	sacreBLEU-BLEU	n-grams		—	•	Post (2018a)	http://github.com/mjpost/sacreBLEU
	sacreBLEU-chrF	n-grams		—	•	Post (2018a)	http://github.com/mjpost/sacreBLEU
Metrics	BEER	char. n-grams, permutation trees	yes	•	⊘	Univ. of Amsterdam, ILCC (Stanojević and Sima'an, 2015)	http://github.com/stanojevic/beer
	BERTr	contextual word embeddings		•	⊘	Univ. of Melbourne (Mathur et al., 2019)	http://github.com/nitikam/mteval-in-context
	characTER	char. edit distance, edit types		•	⊘	RWTH Aachen Univ. (Wang et al., 2016a)	http://github.com/rwth-i6/CharacTER
	EED	char. edit distance, edit types		•	⊘	RWTH Aachen Univ. (Stanchev et al., 2019)	http://github.com/rwth-i6/ExtendedEditDistance
	ESIM	learned neural representations	yes	•	⊘	Univ. of Melbourne (Mathur et al., 2019)	http://github.com/nitikam/mteval-in-context
	LEPORa	surface linguistic features		•	⊘	Dublin City University, ADAPT (Han et al., 2012, 2013)	http://github.com/poethan/LEPOR
	LEPORb	surface linguistic features		•	⊘	Dublin City University, ADAPT (Han et al., 2012, 2013)	http://github.com/poethan/LEPOR
	Meteor++_2.0 (syntax)	word alignments		•	⊘	Peking University (Guo and Hu, 2019)	—
	Meteor++_2.0 (syntax+copy)	word alignments		•	⊘	Peking University (Guo and Hu, 2019)	—
	PReP	psuedo-references, paraphrases		•	⊘	Tokyo Metropolitan Univ. (Yoshimura et al., 2019)	http://github.com/kokeman/PReP
	WMDO	word mover distance		•	⊘	Imperial College London (Chow et al., 2019a)	—
	YiSi-0	semantic similarity		•	⊘	NRC (Lo, 2019)	http://github.com/chikiulo/YiSi
	YiSi-1	semantic similarity		•	⊘	NRC (Lo, 2019)	http://github.com/chikiulo/YiSi
	YiSi-1_srl	semantic similarity		•	⊘	NRC (Lo, 2019)	http://github.com/chikiulo/YiSi
QE Systems	IBM1-morpheme	LM log probs., IBM1 lexicon		•	⊘	Dublin City University, ADAPT (Popovic, 2012)	—
	IBM1-pos4gram	LM log probs., IBM1 lexicon		•	⊘	Dublin City University, ADAPT (Popovic, 2012)	—
	LP	contextual word emb., MT log prob.	yes	•	⊘	Univ. of Tartu (Yankovskaya et al., 2019)	—
	LASIM	contextual word embeddings	yes	•	⊘	Univ. of Tartu (Yankovskaya et al., 2019)	—
	UNI	?	?	•	⊘	?	?
	UNI+	?	?	•	⊘	?	?
	USFD	?	?	•	⊘	Univ. of Sheffield	?
	USFD-TL	?	?	•	⊘	Univ. of Sheffield	?
	YiSi-2	semantic similarity		•	⊘	NRC (Lo, 2019)	http://github.com/chikiulo/YiSi
	YiSi-2_srl	semantic similarity		•	⊘	NRC (Lo, 2019)	http://github.com/chikiulo/YiSi

Table 2: Participants of WMT19 Metrics Shared Task. "•" denotes that the metric took part in (some of the language pairs) of the segment- and/or system-level evaluation. "⊘" indicates that the system-level scores are implied, simply taking arithmetic (macro-)average of segment-level scores. "−" indicates that the metric didn't participate the track (Seg/Sys-level). A metric is learned if it is trained on a QE or metric evaluation dataset (i.e. pretraining or parsers don't count, but training on WMT 2017 metrics task data does). For the baseline metrics available in the Moses toolkit, paths are relative to http://github.com/moses-smt/mosesdecoder/.

smoothed version of BLEU for scoring at the segment-level. We used the standard tokenizer script as available in Moses toolkit for tokenization.

chrF and chrF+. The metrics CHRF and CHRF+ (Popović, 2015, 2017) are computed using their original Python implementation, see Table 2. We ran `chrF++.py` with the parameters `-nw 0 -b 3` to obtain the CHRF score and with `-nw 1 -b 3` to obtain the CHRF+ score. Note that CHRF intentionally removes all spaces before matching the n-grams, detokenizing the segments but also concatenating words.[10]

sacreBLEU-BLEU and sacreBLEU-chrF. The metrics SACREBLEU-BLEU and SACREBLEU-CHRF (Post, 2018a) are re-implementation of BLEU and chrF respectively. We ran SACREBLEU-CHRF with the same parameters as CHRF, but their scores are slightly different. The signature strings produced by sacreBLEU for BLEU and chrF respectively are `BLEU+case.lc+lang.de-en+numrefs.1+smooth.exp+tok.intl+version.1.3.6` and `chrF3+case.mixed+lang.de-en+numchars.6+numrefs.1+space.False+tok.13a+version.1.3.6`.

The baselines serve in system and segment-level evaluations as customary: BLEU, TER, WER, PER, CDER, SACREBLEU-BLEU and SACREBLEU-CHRF for system-level only; SENTBLEU for segment-level only and CHRF for both.

Chinese word segmentation is unfortunately not supported by the tokenization scripts mentioned above. For scoring Chinese with baseline metrics, we thus pre-processed MT outputs and reference translations with the script `tokenizeChinese.py`[11] by Shujian Huang, which separates Chinese characters from each other and also from non-Chinese parts.

---

[10] We originally planned to use the CHRF implementation which was recently made available in Moses Scorer but it mishandles Unicode characters for now.

[11] `http://hdl.handle.net/11346/WMT17-TVXH`

4 Submitted Metrics

Table 2 lists the participants of the WMT19 Shared Metrics Task, along with their metrics and links to the source code where available. We have collected 24 metrics from a total of 13 research groups, with 10 reference-less "metrics" submitted to the joint task "QE as a Metric" with WMT19 Quality Estimation Task.

The rest of this section provides a brief summary of all the metrics that participated.

4.1 BEER

BEER (Stanojević and Sima'an, 2015) is a trained evaluation metric with a linear model that combines sub-word feature indicators (character n-grams) and global word order features (skip bigrams) to achieve a language agnostic and fast to compute evaluation metric. BEER has participated in previous years of the evaluation task.

4.2 BERTr

BERTr (Mathur et al., 2019) uses contextual word embeddings to compare the MT output with the reference translation.

The BERTr score of a translation is the average recall score over all tokens, using a relaxed version of token matching based on BERT embeddings: namely, computing the maximum cosine similarity between the embedding of a reference token against any token in the MT output. BERTr uses `bert_base_uncased` embeddings for the to-English language pairs, and `bert_base_multilingual_cased` embeddings for all other language pairs.

4.3 CharacTER

CHARACTER (Wang et al., 2016b,a), identical to the 2016 setup, is a character-level metric inspired by the commonly applied translation edit rate (TER). It is defined as the minimum number of character edits required to adjust a hypothesis, until it completely matches the reference, normalized by the length of the hypothesis sentence. CHARACTER calculates the character-level edit distance while performing the shift edit on word level. Unlike the strict matching criterion in TER, a hypothesis word is considered to match a reference word and could be shifted, if the edit distance between them is below a threshold value. The Levenshtein distance between the reference and the shifted hypothesis sequence is computed on the character level. In addition, the lengths of hypothesis sequences instead of reference sequences are used for normalizing the edit distance, which effectively counters the issue that shorter translations normally achieve lower TER.

Similarly to other character-level metrics, CHARACTER is generally applied to non-tokenized outputs and references, which also holds for this year's submission with one exception. This year tokenization was carried out for en-ru hypotheses and references before calculating the scores, since this results in large improvements in terms of correlations. For other language pairs, no tokenizer was used for pre-processing.

4.4 EED

EED (Stanchev et al., 2019) is a character-based metric, which builds upon CDER. It is defined as the minimum number of operations of an extension to the conventional edit distance containing a "jump" operation. The edit distance operations (insertions, deletions and substitutions) are performed at the character level and jumps are performed when a blank space is reached. Furthermore, the coverage of multiple characters in the hypothesis is penalised by the introduction of a coverage penalty. The sum of the length of the reference and the coverage penalty is used as the normalisation term.

4.5 ESIM

Enhanced Sequential Inference Model (ESIM; Chen et al., 2017; Mathur et al., 2019) is a neural model proposed for Natural Language Inference that has been adapted for MT evaluation. It uses cross-sentence attention and sentence matching heuristics to generate a representation of the translation and the reference, which is fed to a feedforward regressor. The metric is trained on singly-annotated Direct Assessment data that has been collected for evaluating WMT systems: all WMT 2018 to-English data for the to-English language pairs, and all WMT 2018 data for all other language pairs.

4.6 hLEPORb_baseline, hLEPORa_baseline

The submitted metric HLEPOR_BASELINE is a metric based on the factor combination of length penalty, precision, recall, and position difference penalty. The weighted harmonic mean is applied to group the factors together with tunable weight parameters. The system-level score is calculated with the same formula but with each factor weighted using weight estimated at system-level and not at segment-level.

In this submitted baseline version, HLEPOR_BASELINE was not tuned for each language pair separately but the default weights were applied across all submitted language pairs. Further improvements can be achieved by tuning the weights according to the development data, adding morphological information and applying n-gram factor scores into it (e.g. part-of-speech, n-gram precision and n-gram recall that were added into LEPOR in WMT13.). The basic model factors and further development with parameters setting were described in the paper (Han et al., 2012) and (Han et al., 2013).

For sentence-level score, only HLEPORA_BASELINE was submitted with scores calculated as the weighted harmonic mean of all the designed factors using default parameters.

For system-level score, both HLEPORA_BASELINE and HLEPORB_BASELINE were submitted, where HLEPORA_BASELINE is the the average score of all sentence-level scores, and HLEPORB_BASELINE is calculated via the same sentence-level hLEPOR equation but replacing each factor value with its system-level counterpart.

4.7 Meteor++_2.0 (syntax), Meteor++_2.0 (syntax+copy)

METEOR++ 2.0 (Guo and Hu, 2019) is a metric based on Meteor (Denkowski and Lavie, 2014) that takes syntactic-level paraphrase knowledge into consideration, where paraphrases may sometimes be skip-grams. i.e. (protect...from, protect...against). As the original Meteor-based metrics only pay attention to consecutive string matching, they perform badly when reference-hypothesis pairs contain skip n-gram paraphrases. ME-TEOR++ 2.0 extracts the knowledge from the Paraphrase Database (PPDB; Bannard and Callison-Burch, 2005) and integrates it into Meteor-based metrics.

4.8 PReP

PREP (Yoshimura et al., 2019) is a method for filtering pseudo-references to achieve a good match with a gold reference.

At the beginning, the source sentence is translated with some off-the-shelf MT systems to create a set of pseudo-references. (Here the MT systems were Google Translate and Microsoft Bing Translator.) The pseudo-references are then filtered using BERT (Devlin et al., 2019) fine-tuned on the MPRC corpus (Dolan and Brockett, 2005), estimating the probability of the paraphrase between gold reference and pseudo-references. Thanks to the high quality of the underlying MT systems, a large portion of their outputs is indeed considered as a valid paraphrase.

The final metric score is calculated simply with SentBLEU with these multiple references.

4.9 WMDO

WMDO (Chow et al., 2019b) is a metric based on distance between distributions in the semantic vector space. Matching in the semantic space has been investigated for translation evaluation, but the constraints of a translation's word order have not been fully explored. Building on the Word Mover's Distance metric and various word embeddings, WMDO introduces a fragmentation penalty to account for fluency of a translation. This word order extension is shown to perform better than standard WMD, with promising results against other types of metrics.

4.10 YiSi-0, YiSi-1, YiSi-1_srl, YiSi-2, YiSi-2_srl

YiSi (Lo, 2019) is a unified semantic MT quality evaluation and estimation metric for languages with different levels of available resources.

YiSi-1 is a MT evaluation metric that measures the semantic similarity between a machine translation and human references by aggregating the idf-weighted lexical semantic similarities based on the contextual embeddings extracted from BERT and optionally incorporating shallow semantic structures (denoted as YiSi-1_srl).

YiSi-0 is the degenerate version of YiSi-1 that is ready-to-deploy to any language. It uses longest common character substring to measure the lexical similarity.

YiSi-2 is the bilingual, reference-less version for MT quality estimation, which uses the contextual embeddings extracted from BERT to evaluate the crosslingual lexical semantic similarity between the input and MT output. Like YiSi-1, YiSi-2 can exploit shallow semantic structures as well (denoted as YiSi-2_srl).

4.11 QE Systems

In addition to the submitted standard metrics, 10 quality estimation systems were submitted to the "QE as a Metric" track. The submitted QE systems are evaluated in the same settings as metrics to facilitate comparison. Their descriptions can be found in the Findings of the WMT 2019 Shared Task on Quality Estimation (Fonseca et al., 2019).

5   Results

We discuss system-level results for news task systems in Section 5.1. The segment-level results are in Section 5.2.

5.1   System-Level Evaluation

As in previous years, we employ the Pearson correlation (r) as the main evaluation measure for system-level metrics. The Pearson correlation is as follows:

$$r = \frac{\sum_{i=1}^{n}(H_i - \overline{H})(M_i - \overline{M})}{\sqrt{\sum_{i=1}^{n}(H_i - \overline{H})^2}\sqrt{\sum_{i=1}^{n}(M_i - \overline{M})^2}} \quad (1)$$

where H_i are human assessment scores of all systems in a given translation direction, M_i are the corresponding scores as predicted by a given metric. $\overline{H}$ and $\overline{M}$ are their means, respectively.

Since some metrics, such as BLEU, aim to achieve a strong positive correlation with human assessment, while error metrics, such as TER, aim for a strong negative correlation we compare metrics via the absolute value $|r|$ of a

	de-en	fi-en	gu-en	kk-en	lt-en	ru-en	zh-en
n	16	12	11	11	11	14	15
Correlation	$|r|$	$|r|$	$|r|$	$|r|$	$|r|$	$|r|$	$|r|$
BEER	0.906	**0.993**	0.952	0.986	0.947	0.915	0.942
BERTr	**0.926**	0.984	0.938	0.990	0.948	**0.971**	0.974
BLEU	0.849	0.982	0.834	0.946	0.961	0.879	0.899
CDER	0.890	**0.988**	0.876	0.967	**0.975**	0.892	0.917
CharacTER	0.898	**0.990**	0.922	0.953	0.955	0.923	0.943
chrF	**0.917**	**0.992**	0.955	0.978	0.940	0.945	0.956
chrF+	**0.916**	**0.992**	0.947	0.976	0.940	0.945	0.956
EED	0.903	**0.994**	0.976	0.980	0.929	0.950	0.949
ESIM	**0.941**	0.971	0.885	0.986	**0.989**	0.968	**0.988**
hLEPORa_BASELINE	–	–	–	0.975	–	–	0.947
hLEPORb_BASELINE	–	–	–	0.975	0.906	–	0.947
Meteor++_2.0(SYNTAX)	0.887	**0.995**	0.909	0.974	0.928	**0.950**	0.948
Meteor++_2.0(SYNTAX+COPY)	0.896	**0.995**	0.900	0.971	0.927	**0.952**	0.952
NIST	0.813	0.986	0.930	0.942	0.944	0.925	0.921
PER	0.883	**0.991**	0.910	0.737	0.947	0.922	0.952
PReP	0.575	0.614	0.773	0.776	0.494	0.782	0.592
sacreBLEU.BLEU	0.813	0.985	0.834	0.946	0.955	0.873	0.903
sacreBLEU.chrF	0.910	**0.990**	0.952	0.969	0.935	0.919	0.955
TER	0.874	**0.984**	0.890	0.799	0.960	0.917	0.840
WER	0.863	0.983	0.861	0.793	0.961	0.911	0.820
WMDO	0.872	**0.987**	0.983	**0.998**	0.900	0.942	0.943
YiSi-0	0.902	**0.993**	**0.993**	0.991	0.927	**0.958**	0.937
YiSi-1	**0.949**	0.989	0.924	0.994	0.981	**0.979**	**0.979**
YiSi-1_SRL	**0.950**	0.989	0.918	0.994	**0.983**	**0.978**	0.977
QE as a Metric:							
IBM1-MORPHEME	0.345	0.740	–	–	0.487	–	–
IBM1-POS4GRAM	0.339	–	–	–	–	–	–
LASIM	0.247	–	–	–	–	0.310	–
LP	0.474	–	–	–	–	0.488	–
UNI	0.846	0.930	–	–	–	0.805	–
UNI+	0.850	0.924	–	–	–	0.808	–
YiSi-2	0.796	0.642	0.566	0.324	0.442	0.339	0.940
YiSi-2_SRL	0.804	–	–	–	–	–	0.947

newstest2019

Table 3: Absolute Pearson correlation of to-English system-level metrics with DA human assessment in newstest2019; correlations of metrics not significantly outperformed by any other for that language pair are highlighted in bold.

	en-cs	en-de	en-fi	en-gu	en-kk	en-lt	en-ru	en-zh
n	11	22	12	11	11	12	12	12
Correlation	$|r|$	$|r|$	$|r|$	$|r|$	$|r|$	$|r|$	$|r|$	$|r|$
BEER	**0.990**	0.983	**0.989**	0.829	0.971	**0.982**	0.977	0.803
BLEU	0.897	0.921	**0.969**	0.737	0.852	**0.989**	0.986	0.901
CDER	0.985	0.973	**0.978**	0.840	0.927	**0.985**	**0.993**	0.905
CHARACTER	**0.994**	**0.986**	0.968	**0.910**	0.936	0.954	**0.985**	0.862
CHRF	0.990	0.979	**0.986**	**0.841**	**0.972**	**0.981**	0.943	0.880
CHRF+	**0.991**	0.981	**0.986**	**0.848**	**0.974**	**0.982**	0.950	0.879
EED	**0.993**	**0.985**	**0.987**	**0.897**	**0.979**	0.975	0.967	0.856
ESIM	–	**0.991**	0.957	–	**0.980**	**0.989**	**0.989**	0.931
HLEPORA_BASELINE	–	–	–	0.841	0.968	–	–	–
HLEPORB_BASELINE	–	–	–	0.841	0.968	0.980	–	–
NIST	0.896	0.321	0.971	0.786	0.930	**0.993**	0.988	0.884
PER	0.976	0.970	**0.982**	0.839	0.921	0.985	0.981	0.895
SACREBLEU.BLEU	**0.994**	0.969	**0.966**	0.736	0.852	**0.986**	0.977	0.801
SACREBLEU.CHRF	0.983	0.976	0.980	0.841	**0.967**	0.966	**0.985**	0.796
TER	0.980	0.969	**0.981**	**0.865**	0.940	**0.994**	**0.995**	0.856
WER	0.982	0.966	**0.980**	**0.861**	0.939	**0.991**	**0.994**	0.875
YISI-0	**0.992**	0.985	**0.987**	0.863	0.974	0.974	0.953	0.861
YISI-1	0.962	**0.991**	0.971	**0.909**	**0.985**	0.963	**0.992**	**0.951**
YISI-1_SRL	–	**0.991**	–	–	–	–	–	**0.948**
QE as a Metric:								
IBM1-MORPHEME	0.871	0.870	0.084	–	–	0.810	–	–
IBM1-POS4GRAM	–	0.393	–	–	–	–	–	–
LASIM	–	0.871	–	–	–	–	0.823	–
LP	–	0.569	–	–	–	–	0.661	–
UNI	0.028	0.841	0.907	–	–	–	0.919	–
UNI+	–	–	–	–	–	–	0.918	–
USFD	–	0.224	–	–	–	–	0.857	–
USFD-TL	–	0.091	–	–	–	–	0.771	–
YISI-2	0.324	0.924	0.696	0.314	0.339	0.055	0.766	0.097
YISI-2_SRL	–	0.936	–	–	–	–	–	0.118

newstest2019

Table 4: Absolute Pearson correlation of out-of-English system-level metrics with DA human assessment in newstest2019; correlations of metrics not significantly outperformed by any other for that language pair are highlighted in bold.

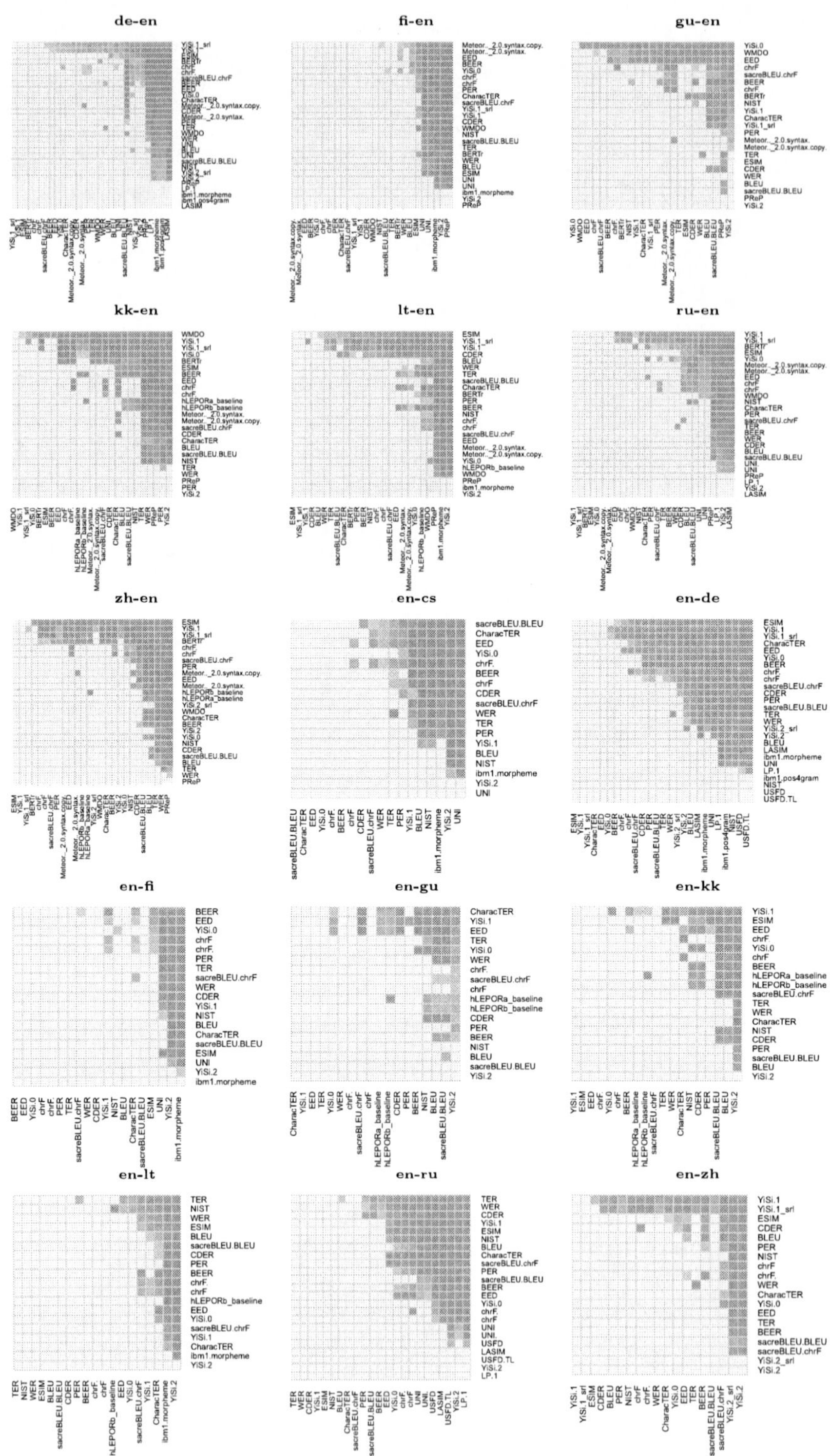

Figure 1: System-level metric significance test results for DA human assessment for into English and out-of English language pairs (newstest2019): Green cells denote a statistically significant increase in correlation with human assessment for the metric in a given row over the metric in a given column according to Williams test.

given metric's correlation with human assessment.

5.1.1 System-Level Results

Tables 3, 4 and 5 provide the system-level correlations of metrics evaluating translation of newstest2019. The underlying texts are part of the WMT19 News Translation test set (newstest2019) and the underlying MT systems are all MT systems participating in the WMT19 News Translation Task.

As recommended by Graham and Baldwin (2014), we employ Williams significance test (Williams, 1959) to identify differences in correlation that are statistically significant. Williams test is a test of significance of a difference in dependent correlations and therefore suitable for evaluation of metrics. Correlations not significantly outperformed by any other metric for the given language pair are highlighted in bold in Tables 3, 4 and 5.

Since pairwise comparisons of metrics may be also of interest, e.g. to learn which metrics significantly outperform the most widely employed metric BLEU, we include significance test results for every competing pair of metrics including our baseline metrics in Figure 1 and Figure 2.

This year, the increased number of systems participating in the news tasks has provided a larger sample of system scores for testing metrics. Since we already have sufficiently conclusive results on genuine MT systems, we do not need to generate hybrid system results as in Graham and Liu (2016) and past metrics tasks.

5.2 Segment-Level Evaluation

Segment-level evaluation relies on the manual judgements collected in the News Translation Task evaluation. This year, again we were unable to follow the methodology outlined in Graham et al. (2015) for evaluation of segment-level metrics because the sampling of sentences did not provide sufficient number of assessments of the same segment. We therefore convert pairs of DA scores for competing translations to DARR better/worse preferences as described in Section 2.3.2.

We measure the quality of metrics' segment-level scores against the DARR golden truth using a Kendall's Tau-like formulation, which is an adaptation of the conventional Kendall's Tau coefficient. Since we do not have a total order ranking of all translations, it is not possible to apply conventional Kendall's Tau (Graham et al., 2015).

Our Kendall's Tau-like formulation, τ, is as follows:

$$\tau = \frac{|Concordant| - |Discordant|}{|Concordant| + |Discordant|} \quad (2)$$

where $Concordant$ is the set of all human comparisons for which a given metric suggests the same order and $Discordant$ is the set of all human comparisons for which a given metric disagrees. The formula is not specific with respect to ties, i.e. cases where the annotation says that the two outputs are equally good.

The way in which ties (both in human and metric judgement) were incorporated in computing Kendall τ has changed across the years of WMT Metrics Tasks. Here we adopt the version used in WMT17 DARR evaluation. For a detailed discussion on other options, see also Macháček and Bojar (2014).

Whether or not a given comparison of a pair of distinct translations of the same source input, s_1 and s_2, is counted as a concordant (Conc) or disconcordant (Disc) pair is defined by the following matrix:

		Metric		
		$s_1 < s_2$	$s_1 = s_2$	$s_1 > s_2$
Human	$s_1 < s_2$	Conc	Disc	Disc
	$s_1 = s_2$	–	–	–
	$s_1 > s_2$	Disc	Disc	Conc

In the notation of Macháček and Bojar (2014), this corresponds to the setup used in WMT12 (with a different underlying method of manual judgements, RR):

		Metric		
WMT12		<	=	>
Human	<	1	-1	-1
	=	X	X	X
	>	-1	-1	1

The key differences between the evaluation used in WMT14–WMT16 and evaluation used in WMT17–WMT19 were (1) the move from RR to daRR and (2) the treatment of ties. In the years 2014-2016, ties in metrics scores were not penalized. With the move to daRR, where the quality of the two candidate translations

	de-cs	de-fr	fr-de
n	11	11	10
Correlation	$|r|$	$|r|$	$|r|$
BEER	**0.978**	**0.941**	0.848
BLEU	**0.941**	0.891	0.864
CDER	0.864	**0.949**	0.852
CharacTER	0.965	0.928	0.849
chrF	**0.974**	0.931	0.864
chrF+	0.972	0.936	0.848
EED	**0.982**	**0.940**	0.851
ESIM	**0.980**	**0.950**	**0.942**
hLEPORa_BASELINE	0.941	0.814	—
hLEPORb_BASELINE	**0.959**	0.814	—
NIST	**0.954**	**0.916**	0.862
PER	0.875	0.857	**0.899**
sacreBLEU-BLEU	0.869	0.891	0.869
sacreBLEU-chrF	**0.975**	**0.952**	0.882
TER	0.890	**0.956**	0.895
WER	0.872	**0.956**	0.894
YiSi-0	**0.978**	**0.952**	0.820
YiSi-1	0.973	**0.969**	0.908
YiSi-1_SRL	—	—	0.912
QE as a Metric:			
IBM1-MORPHEME	0.355	0.509	0.625
IBM1-POS4GRAM	—	0.085	0.478
YiSi-2	0.606	0.721	0.530
newstest2019			

Table 5: Absolute Pearson correlation of system-level metrics for language pairs not involving English with DA human assessment in newstest2019; correlations of metrics not significantly outperformed by any other for that language pair are highlighted in bold.

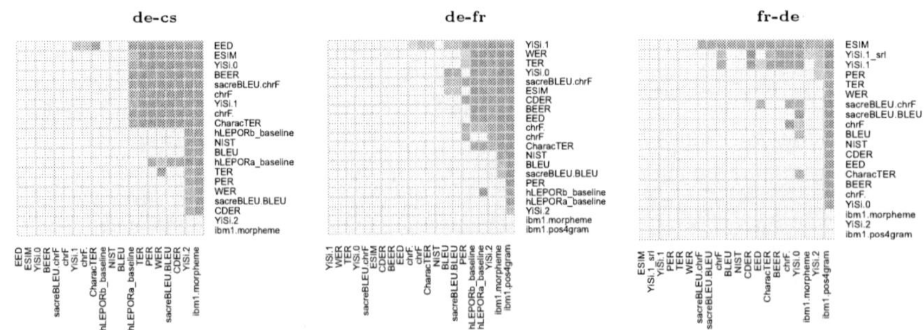

Figure 2: System-level metric significance test results for DA human assessment in newstest2019 for German to Czech, German to French and French to German; green cells denote a statistically significant increase in correlation with human assessment for the metric in a given row over the metric in a given column according to Williams test.

	de-en	fi-en	gu-en	kk-en	lt-en	ru-en	zh-en
Human Evaluation	DARR	DARR	DARR	DARR	DARR	DARR	DARR
n	85,365	38,307	31,139	27,094	21,862	46,172	31,070
BEER	0.128	0.283	0.260	0.421	0.315	0.189	0.371
BERTr	0.142	0.331	0.291	0.421	0.353	0.195	0.399
CharacTER	0.101	0.253	0.190	0.340	0.254	0.155	0.337
chrF	0.122	0.286	0.256	0.389	0.301	0.180	0.371
chrF+	0.125	0.289	0.257	0.394	0.303	0.182	0.374
EED	0.120	0.281	0.264	0.392	0.298	0.176	0.376
ESIM	0.167	**0.337**	**0.303**	**0.435**	0.359	0.201	0.396
hLEPORa_BASELINE	—	—	—	0.372	—	—	0.339
Meteor++_2.0(SYNTAX)	0.084	0.274	0.237	0.395	0.291	0.156	0.370
Meteor++_2.0(SYNTAX+COPY)	0.094	0.273	0.244	0.402	0.287	0.163	0.367
PReP	0.030	0.197	0.192	0.386	0.193	0.124	0.267
sentBLEU	0.056	0.233	0.188	0.377	0.262	0.125	0.323
WMDO	0.096	0.281	0.260	0.420	0.300	0.162	0.362
YiSi-0	0.117	0.271	0.263	0.402	0.289	0.178	0.355
YiSi-1	0.164	**0.347**	**0.312**	**0.440**	**0.376**	**0.217**	**0.426**
YiSi-1_SRL	**0.199**	0.346	0.306	**0.442**	**0.380**	**0.222**	**0.431**
QE as a Metric:							
IBM1-MORPHEME	−0.074	0.009	—	—	0.069	—	—
IBM1-POS4GRAM	−0.153	—	—	—	—	—	—
LASIM	−0.024	—	—	—	—	0.022	—
LP	−0.096	—	—	—	—	−0.035	—
UNI	0.022	0.202	—	—	—	0.084	—
UNI+	0.015	0.211	—	—	—	0.089	—
YiSi-2	0.068	0.126	−0.001	0.096	0.075	0.053	0.253
YiSi-2_SRL	0.068	—	—	—	—	—	0.246
newstest2019							

Table 6: Segment-level metric results for to-English language pairs in newstest2019: absolute Kendall's Tau formulation of segment-level metric scores with DA scores; correlations of metrics not significantly outperformed by any other for that language pair are highlighted in bold.

	en-cs	en-de	en-fi	en-gu	en-kk	en-lt	en-ru	en-zh
Human Evaluation	DARR	DARR	DARR	DARR	DARR	DARR	DARR	DARR
n	27,178	99,840	31,820	11,355	18,172	17,401	24,334	18,658
BEER	0.443	0.316	0.514	0.537	0.516	0.441	0.542	0.232
CharacTER	0.349	0.264	0.404	0.500	0.351	0.311	0.432	0.094
CHRF	0.455	0.326	0.514	0.534	0.479	0.446	0.539	0.301
CHRF+	**0.458**	0.327	0.514	0.538	0.491	**0.448**	0.543	0.296
EED	0.431	0.315	0.508	**0.568**	0.518	0.425	0.546	0.257
ESIM	—	0.329	0.511	—	0.510	0.428	**0.572**	**0.339**
HLEPORA_BASELINE	—	—	—	0.463	0.390	—	—	—
SENTBLEU	0.367	0.248	0.396	0.465	0.392	0.334	0.469	0.270
YISI-0	0.406	0.304	0.483	0.539	0.494	0.402	0.535	0.266
YISI-1	**0.475**	0.351	**0.537**	**0.551**	**0.546**	**0.470**	**0.585**	**0.355**
YISI-1_SRL	—	**0.368**	—	—	—	—	—	**0.361**
QE as a Metric:								
IBM1-MORPHEME	−0.135	−0.003	−0.005	—	—	−0.165	—	—
IBM1-POS4GRAM	—	−0.123	—	—	—	—	—	—
LASIM	—	0.147	—	—	—	—	−0.24	—
LP	—	−0.119	—	—	—	—	−0.158	—
UNI	0.060	0.129	0.351	—	—	—	0.226	—
UNI+	—	—	—	—	—	—	0.222	—
USFD	—	−0.029	—	—	—	—	0.136	—
USFD-TL	—	−0.037	—	—	—	—	0.191	—
YISI-2	0.069	0.212	0.239	0.147	0.187	0.003	−0.155	0.044
YISI-2_SRL	—	0.236	—	—	—	—	—	0.034

newstest2019

Table 7: Segment-level metric results for out-of-English language pairs in newstest2019: absolute Kendall's Tau formulation of segment-level metric scores with DA scores; correlations of metrics not significantly outperformed by any other for that language pair are highlighted in bold.

	de-cs	de-fr	fr-de
Human Evaluation	DARR	DARR	DARR
n	35,793	4,862	1,369
BEER	0.337	0.293	**0.265**
CharacTER	0.232	0.251	**0.224**
CHRF	0.326	0.284	**0.275**
CHRF+	0.326	0.284	**0.278**
EED	0.345	0.301	**0.267**
ESIM	0.331	0.290	**0.289**
HLEPORA_BASELINE	0.207	0.239	—
SENTBLEU	0.203	0.235	0.179
YISI-0	0.331	0.296	**0.277**
YISI-1	**0.376**	**0.349**	0.310
YISI-1_SRL	—	—	0.299
QE as a Metric:			
IBM1-MORPHEME	0.048	−0.013	−0.053
IBM1-POS4GRAM	—	−0.074	−0.097
YISI-2	0.199	0.186	0.066

newstest2019

Table 8: Segment-level metric results for language pairs not involving English in newstest2019: absolute Kendall's Tau formulation of segment-level metric scores with DA scores; correlations of metrics not significantly outperformed by any other for that language pair are highlighted in bold.

is deemed substantially different and no ties in human judgements arise, it makes sense to penalize ties in metrics' predictions in order to promote discerning metrics.

Note that the penalization of ties makes our evaluation asymmetric, dependent on whether the metric predicted the tie for a pair where humans predicted <, or >. It is now important to interpret the meaning of the comparison identically for humans and metrics. For error metrics, we thus reverse the sign of the metric score prior to the comparison with human scores: higher scores have to indicate better translation quality. In WMT19, the original authors did this for CharacTER.

To summarize, the WMT19 Metrics Task for segment-level evaluation:

- ensures that error metrics are first converted to the same orientation as the human judgements, i.e. higher score indicating higher translation quality,

- excludes all human ties (this is already implied by the construction of DARR from DA judgements),

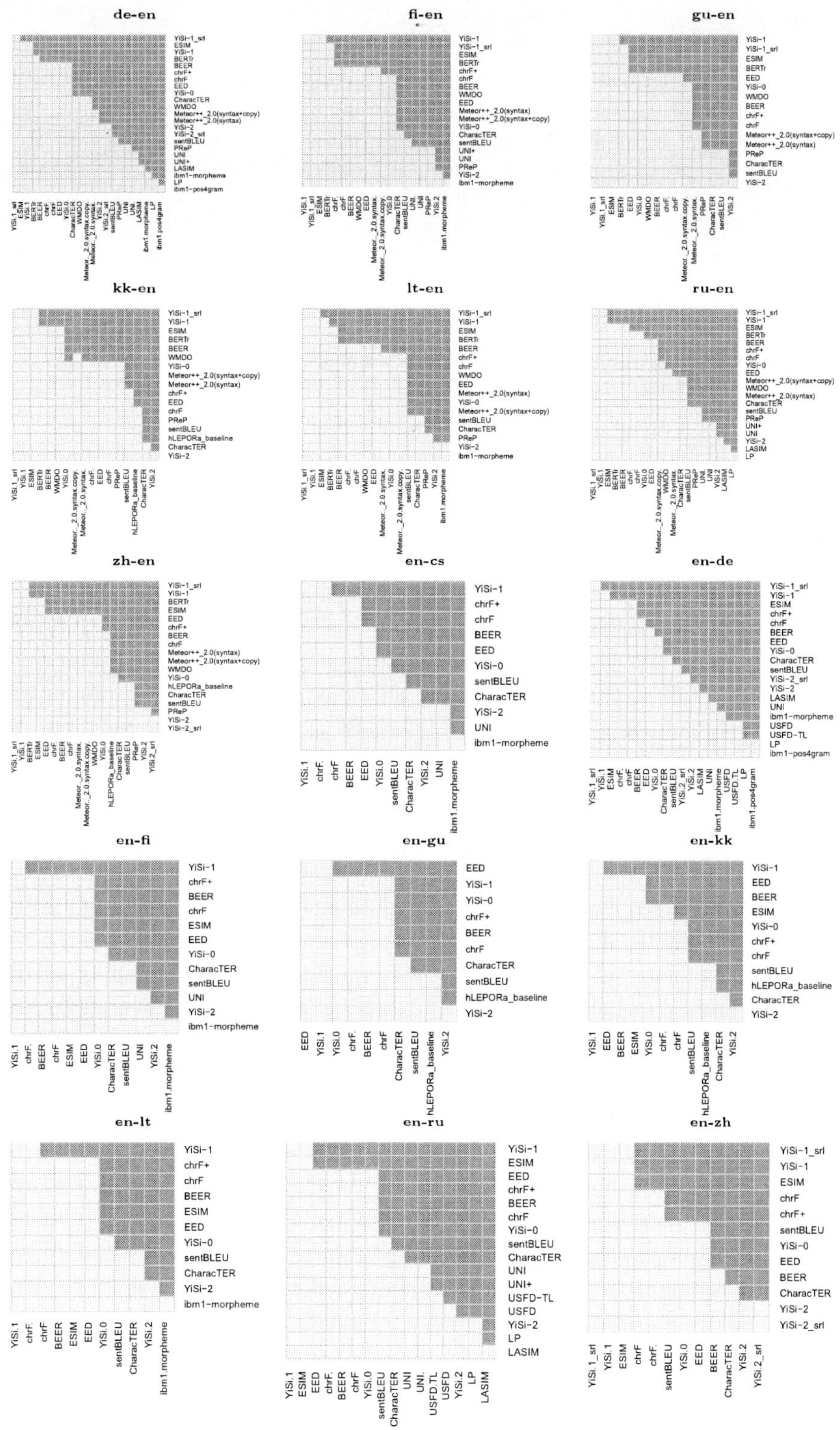

Figure 3: DARR segment-level metric significance test results for into English and out-of English language pairs (newstest2019): Green cells denote a significant win for the metric in a given row over the metric in a given column according bootstrap resampling.

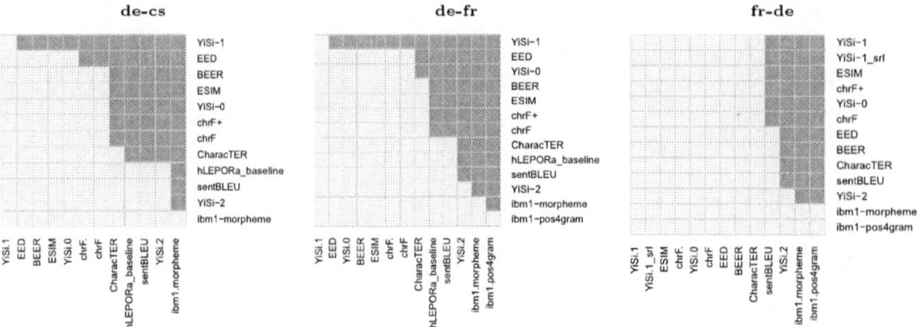

Figure 4: DARR segment-level metric significance test results for German to Czech, German to French and French to German (newstest2019): Green cells denote a significant win for the metric in a given row over the metric in a given column according bootstrap resampling.

- counts metric's ties as a *Discordant* pairs.

We employ bootstrap resampling (Koehn, 2004; Graham et al., 2014b) to estimate confidence intervals for our Kendall's Tau formulation, and metrics with non-overlapping 95% confidence intervals are identified as having statistically significant difference in performance.

5.2.1 Segment-Level Results

Results of the segment-level human evaluation for translations sampled from the News Translation Task are shown in Tables 6, 7 and 8, where metric correlations not significantly outperformed by any other metric are highlighted in bold. Head-to-head significance test results for differences in metric performance are included in Figures 3 and 4.

6 Discussion

This year, human data was collected from reference-based evaluations (or "monolingual") and reference-free evaluations (or "bilingual"). The reference-based (monolingual) evaluations were obtained with the help of anonymous crowdsourcing, while the reference-less (bilingual) evaluations were mainly from MT researchers who committed their time contribution to the manual evaluation for each submitted system.

6.1 Stability across MT Systems

The observed performance of metrics depends on the underlying texts and systems that participate in the News Translation Task (see Section 2). For the strongest MT systems, distinguishing which system outputs are better is

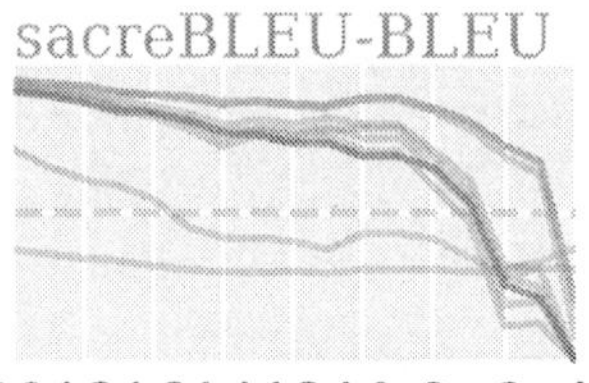

Figure 5: Pearson correlations of SACREBLEU-BLEU for English-German system-level evaluation for all systems (left) down to only top 4 systems (right). The y-axis spans from -1 to +1, baseline metrics for the language pair in grey.

hard, even for human assessors. On the other hand, if the systems are spread across a wide performance range, it will be easier for metrics to correlate with human judgements.

To provide a more reliable view, we created plots of Pearson correlation when the underlying set of MT systems is reduced to top n ones. One sample such plot is in Figure 5, all language pairs and most of the metrics are in Appendix A.

As the plot documents, the official correlations reported in Tables 3 to 5 can lead to wrong conclusions. SACREBLEU-BLEU correlates at .969 when all systems are considered, but as we start considering only the top n systems, the correlation falls relatively quickly. With 10 systems, we are below .5 and when only the top 6 or 4 systems are considered, the correlation falls even to the negave values. Note that correlations point estimates (the value in the y-axis) become noiser with the decreasing number of the underlying MT systems.

Figure 6 explains the situation and illus-

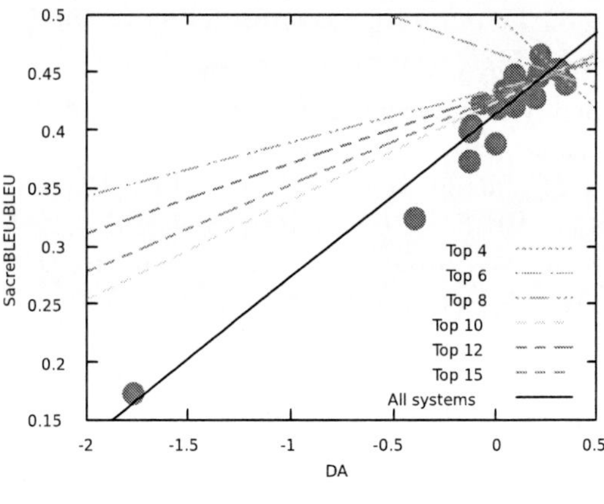

Figure 6

trates the sensitivity of the observed correlations to the exact set of systems. On the full set of systems, the single outlier (the worst-performing system called EN__DE__TASK) helps to achieve a great positive correlation. The majority of MT systems however form a cloud with Pearson correlation around .5 and the top 4 systems actually exhibit a negative correlation of the human score and SACREBLEU-BLEU.

In Appendix A, baseline metrics are plotted in grey in all the plots, so that their trends can be observed jointly. In general, most baselines have similar correlations, as most baselines use similar features (n-gram or word-level features, with the exception of CHRF). In a number of language pairs (de-en, de-fr, en-de, en-kk, lt-en, ru-en, zh-en), baseline correlations tend towards 0 (no correlation) or even negative Pearson correlation. For a widely applied metric such as SACREBLEU-BLEU, our analysis reveals weak correlation in comparing top state-of-the-art systems in these language pairs, especially in en-de, de-en, ru-en, and zh-en.

We will restrict our analysis to those language pairs where the baseline metrics have an obvious downward trend (de-en, de-fr, en-de, en-kk, lt-en, ru-en, zh-en). Examining the top-n correlation in the submitted metrics (not including QE systems), most metrics show the same degradation in correlation as the baselines. We note BERTR as the one exception consistently degrading less and retaining positive correlation compared to other submitted metrics and baselines, in the language pairs where it participated.

For QE systems, we noticed that in some instances, QE systems have upward correlation trends when other metrics and baselines have downward trends. For instance, LP, UNI, and UNI+ in the de-en language pair, YISI-2 in en-kk, and UNI and UNI+ in ru-en. These results suggest that QE systems such as UNI and UNI+ perform worse on judging systems of wide ranging quality, but better for top performing systems, or perhaps for systems closer in quality.

If our method of human assessment is sound, we should believe that BLEU, a widely applied metric, is no longer a reliable metric for judging our best systems. Future investigations are needed to understand when BLEU applies well, and why BLEU is not effective for output from our state of the art models.

Metrics and QE systems such as BERTR, ESIM, YISI that perform well at judging our best systems often use more semantic features compared to our n-gram/char-gram based baselines. Future metrics may want to explore a) whether semantic features such as contextual word embeddings are achieving semantic understanding and b) whether semantic understanding is the true source of a metric's performance gains.

It should be noted that *some* language pairs do not show the strong degrading pattern with top-n systems this year, for instance en-cs, en-gu, en-ru, or kk-en. English-Chinese is particularly interesting because we see a clear trend towards *better* correlations as we reduce the set of underlying systems to the top scoring ones.

6.2 Overall Metric Performance

6.2.1 System-Level Evaluation

In system-level evaluation, the series of YISI metrics achieve the highest correlations in several language pairs and it is not significantly outperformed by any other metrics (denoted as a "win" in the following) for almost all language pairs.

The new metric ESIM performs best on 5 language languages (18 language pairs) and obtains 11 "wins" out of 16 language pairs in which ESIM participated.

The metric EED performs better for language pairs out-of English and excluding English compared to into-English language pairs, achieving 7 out of 11 "wins" there.

6.2.2 Segment-Level Evaluation

For segment-level evaluation, most language pairs are quite discerning, with only one or two metrics taking the "winner" position (of not being significantly surpassed by others). Only French-German differs, with all metrics performing similarly except the significantly worse SENTBLEU.

YISI-1_SRL stands out as the "winner" for all language pairs in which it participated. The excluded language pairs were probably due to the lack of semantic information required by YISI-1_SRL. YISI-1 participated all language pairs and its correlations are comparable with those of YISI-1_SRL.

ESIM obtain 6 "winners" out of all 18 languages pairs.

Both YISI and ESIM are based on neural networks (YISI via word and phrase embeddings, as well as other types of available resources, ESIM via sentence embeddings). This is a confirmation of a trend observed last year.

6.2.3 QE Systems as Metrics

Generally, correlations for the standard reference-based metrics are obviously better than those in "QE as a Metric" track, both when using monolingual and bilingual golden truth.

In system-level evaluation, correlations for "QE as a Metric" range from 0.028 to 0.947 across all language pairs and all metrics but they are very unstable. Even for a single metric, take UNI for example, the correlations range from 0.028 to 0.930 across language pairs.

In segment-level evaluation, correlations for QE metrics range from -0.153 to 0.351 across all language pairs and show the same instability across language pairs for a given metric.

In either case, we do not see any pattern that could explain the behaviour, e.g. whether the manual evaluation was monolingual or bilingual, or the characteristics of the given language pair.

6.3 Dependence on Implementation

As it already happened in the past, we had multiple implementations for some metrics, BLEU and CHRF in particular.

The detailed configuration of BLEU and SACREBLEU-BLEU differ and hence their scores and correlation results are different.

CHRF and SACREBLEU-CHRF use the same parameters and should thus deliver the same scores but we still observe some differences, leading to different correlations. For instance for German-French Pearson correlation, CHRF obtains 0.931 (no win) but SACREBLEU-CHRF reaches 0.952, tying for a win with other metrics.

We thus fully support the call for clarity by Post (2018b) and invite authors of metrics to include their implementations either in Moses scorer or sacreBLEU to achieve a long-term assessment of their metric.

7 Conclusion

This paper summarizes the results of WMT19 shared task in machine translation evaluation, the Metrics Shared Task. Participating metrics were evaluated in terms of their correlation with human judgement at the level of the whole test set (system-level evaluation), as well as at the level of individual sentences (segment-level evaluation).

We reported scores for standard metrics requiring the reference as well as quality estimation systems which took part in the track "QE as a metric", joint with the Quality Estimation task.

For system-level, best metrics reach over 0.95 Pearson correlation or better across several language pairs. As expected, QE systems are visibly in all language pairs but they can also reach high system-level correlations, up to .947 (Chinese-English) or .936 (English-German) by YISI-1_SRL or over .9 for multiple language pairs by UNI.

An important caveat is that the correlations are heavily affected by the underlying set of MT systems. We explored this by reducing the set of systems to top-n ones for various ns and found out that for many language pairs, system-level correlations are much worse when based on only the better performing systems. With both good and bad MT systems participating in the news task, the metrics results can be overly optimistic compared to what we get when evaluating state-of-the-art systems.

In terms of segment-level Kendall's τ results, the standard metrics correlations varied between 0.03 and 0.59, and QE systems obtained even negative correlations.

The results confirm the observation from the last year, namely metrics based on word or sentence-level embeddings (YISI and ESIM), achieve the highest performance.

Acknowledgments

Results in this shared task would not be possible without tight collaboration with organizers of the WMT News Translation Task. We would like to thank Marcin Junczys-Dowmunt for the suggestion to examine metrics performance across varying subsets of MT systems, as we did in Appendix A.

This study was supported in parts by the grants 19-26934X (NEUREM3) of the Czech Science Foundation, ADAPT Centre for Digital Content Technology (`www.adaptcentre.ie`) at Dublin City University funded under the SFI Research Centres Programme (Grant 13/RC/2106) co-funded under the European Regional Development Fund, and Charles University Research Programme "Progres" Q18+Q48.

References

Colin Bannard and Chris Callison-Burch. 2005. Paraphrasing with bilingual parallel corpora. In *Proceedings of the 43rd Annual Meeting on Association for Computational Linguistics*, ACL '05, pages 597–604, Stroudsburg, PA, USA. Association for Computational Linguistics.

Loïc Barrault, Ondřej Bojar, Marta R. Costa-jussà, Christian Federmann, Mark Fishel, Yvette Graham, Barry Haddow, Matthias Huck, Philipp Koehn, Shervin Malmasi, Christof Monz, Mathias Müller, Santanu Pal, Matt Post, and Marcos Zampieri. 2019. Findings of the 2019 Conference on Machine Translation (WMT19). In *Proceedings of the Fourth Conference on Machine Translation*, Florence, Italy. Association for Computational Linguistics.

Ondřej Bojar, Christian Federmann, Barry Haddow, Philipp Koehn, Matt Post, and Lucia Specia. 2016. Ten Years of WMT Evaluation Campaigns: Lessons Learnt. In *Proceedings of the LREC 2016 Workshop "Translation Evaluation – From Fragmented Tools and Data Sets to an Integrated Ecosystem"*, pages 27–34, Portorose, Slovenia.

Ondřej Bojar, Yvette Graham, and Amir Kamran. 2017. Results of the WMT17 metrics shared task. In *Proceedings of the Second Conference on Machine Translation, Volume 2: Shared Tasks Papers*, Copenhagen, Denmark. Association for Computational Linguistics.

Qian Chen, Xiaodan Zhu, Zhen-Hua Ling, Si Wei, Hui Jiang, and Diana Inkpen. 2017. Enhanced lstm for natural language inference. In *Proceedings of the 55th Annual Meeting of the Association for Computational Linguistics (Volume 1: Long Papers)*, pages 1657–1668.

Julian Chow, Pranava Madhyastha, and Lucia Specia. 2019a. Wmdo: Fluency-based word mover's distance for machine translation evaluation. In *Proceedings of Fourth Conference on Machine Translation*.

Julian Chow, Lucia Specia, and Pranava Madhyastha. 2019b. WMDO: Fluency-based Word Mover's Distance for Machine Translation Evaluation. In *Proceedings of the Fourth Conference on Machine Translation*, Florence, Italy. Association for Computational Linguistics.

Michael Denkowski and Alon Lavie. 2014. Meteor Universal: Language Specific Translation Evaluation for Any Target Language. In *Proceedings of the Ninth Workshop on Statistical Machine Translation*, pages 376–380, Baltimore, Maryland, USA. Association for Computational Linguistics.

Jacob Devlin, Ming-Wei Chang, Kenton Lee, and Kristina Toutanova. 2019. BERT: Pre-training of deep bidirectional transformers for language understanding. In *Proceedings of the 2019 Conference of the North American Chapter of the Association for Computational Linguistics: Human Language Technologies, Volume 1 (Long and Short Papers)*, pages 4171–4186, Minneapolis, Minnesota. Association for Computational Linguistics.

George Doddington. 2002. Automatic Evaluation of Machine Translation Quality Using N-gram Co-occurrence Statistics. In *Proceedings of the Second International Conference on Human Language Technology Research*, HLT '02, pages 138–145, San Francisco, CA, USA. Morgan Kaufmann Publishers Inc.

William B. Dolan and Chris Brockett. 2005. Automatically constructing a corpus of sentential paraphrases. In *Proceedings of the Third International Workshop on Paraphrasing (IWP2005)*.

Erick Fonseca, Lisa Yankovskaya, André F. T. Martins, Mark Fishel, and Christian Federmann. 2019. Findings of the WMT 2019 Shared

Task on Quality Estimation. In *Proceedings of the Fourth Conference on Machine Translation*, Florence, Italy. Association for Computational Linguistics.

Yvette Graham and Timothy Baldwin. 2014. Testing for Significance of Increased Correlation with Human Judgment. In *Proceedings of the 2014 Conference on Empirical Methods in Natural Language Processing (EMNLP)*, pages 172–176, Doha, Qatar. Association for Computational Linguistics.

Yvette Graham, Timothy Baldwin, Alistair Moffat, and Justin Zobel. 2013. Continuous Measurement Scales in Human Evaluation of Machine Translation. In *Proceedings of the 7th Linguistic Annotation Workshop & Interoperability with Discourse*, pages 33–41, Sofia, Bulgaria. Association for Computational Linguistics.

Yvette Graham, Timothy Baldwin, Alistair Moffat, and Justin Zobel. 2014a. Is Machine Translation Getting Better over Time? In *Proceedings of the 14th Conference of the European Chapter of the Association for Computational Linguistics*, pages 443–451, Gothenburg, Sweden. Association for Computational Linguistics.

Yvette Graham, Timothy Baldwin, Alistair Moffat, and Justin Zobel. 2016. Can machine translation systems be evaluated by the crowd alone. *Natural Language Engineering*, FirstView:1–28.

Yvette Graham and Qun Liu. 2016. Achieving Accurate Conclusions in Evaluation of Automatic Machine Translation Metrics. In *Proceedings of the 15th Annual Conference of the North American Chapter of the Association for Computational Linguistics: Human Language Technologies*, San Diego, CA. Association for Computational Linguistics.

Yvette Graham, Nitika Mathur, and Timothy Baldwin. 2014b. Randomized significance tests in machine translation. In *Proceedings of the ACL 2014 Ninth Workshop on Statistical Machine Translation*, pages 266–274. Association for Computational Linguistics.

Yvette Graham, Nitika Mathur, and Timothy Baldwin. 2015. Accurate Evaluation of Segment-level Machine Translation Metrics. In *Proceedings of the 2015 Conference of the North American Chapter of the Association for Computational Linguistics Human Language Technologies*, Denver, Colorado.

Yinuo Guo and Junfeng Hu. 2019. Meteor++ 2.0: Adopt Syntactic Level Paraphrase Knowledge into Machine Translation Evaluation. In *Proceedings of the Fourth Conference on Machine Translation*, Florence, Italy. Association for Computational Linguistics.

Aaron L.-F. Han, Derek F. Wong, and Lidia S. Chao. 2012. Lepor: A robust evaluation metric for machine translation with augmented factors. In *Proceedings of the 24th International Conference on Computational Linguistics (COLING 2012)*, pages 441–450. Association for Computational Linguistics.

Aaron L.-F. Han, Derek F. Wong, Lidia S. Chao, Liangye He, Yi Lu, Junwen Xing, and Xiaodong Zeng. 2013. Language-independent model for machine translation evaluation with reinforced factors. In *Machine Translation Summit XIV*, pages 215–222. International Association for Machine Translation.

Philipp Koehn. 2004. Statistical significance tests for machine translation evaluation. In *Proc. of Empirical Methods in Natural Language Processing*, pages 388–395, Barcelona, Spain. Association for Computational Linguistics.

Philipp Koehn and Christof Monz. 2006. Manual and Automatic Evaluation of Machine Translation Between European Languages. In *Proceedings of the Workshop on Statistical Machine Translation*, StatMT '06, pages 102–121, Stroudsburg, PA, USA. Association for Computational Linguistics.

Gregor Leusch, Nicola Ueffing, and Hermann Ney. 2003. A novel string-to-string distance measure with applications to machine translation evaluation. In *Proceedings of Mt Summit IX*, pages 240–247.

Gregor Leusch, Nicola Ueffing, and Hermann Ney. 2006. CDER: Efficient MT Evaluation Using Block Movements. In *In Proceedings of EACL*, pages 241–248.

Chi-kiu Lo. 2019. YiSi - a Unified Semantic MT Quality Evaluation and Estimation Metric for Languages with Different Levels of Available Resources. In *Proceedings of the Fourth Conference on Machine Translation*, Florence, Italy. Association for Computational Linguistics.

Qingsong Ma, Ondřej Bojar, and Yvette Graham. 2018. Results of the WMT18 metrics shared task: Both characters and embeddings achieve good performance. In *Proceedings of the Third Conference on Machine Translation, Volume 2: Shared Task Papers*, Brussels, Belgium. Association for Computational Linguistics.

Matouš Macháček and Ondřej Bojar. 2014. Results of the WMT14 metrics shared task. In *Proceedings of the Ninth Workshop on Statistical Machine Translation*, pages 293–301, Baltimore, MD, USA. Association for Computational Linguistics.

Matouš Macháček and Ondřej Bojar. 2013. Results of the WMT13 Metrics Shared Task. In *Proceed-*

ings of the Eighth Workshop on Statistical Machine Translation*, pages 45–51, Sofia, Bulgaria. Association for Computational Linguistics.

Nitika Mathur, Tim Baldwin, and Trevor Cohn. 2019. Putting evaluation in context: Contextual embeddings improve machine translation evaluation. In *Proc. of ACL (short papers)*. To appear.

Kishore Papineni, Salim Roukos, Todd Ward, and Wei-Jing Zhu. 2002. BLEU: A Method for Automatic Evaluation of Machine Translation. In *Proceedings of the 40th Annual Meeting on Association for Computational Linguistics*, ACL '02, pages 311–318.

Maja Popovic. 2012. Morpheme- and POS-based IBM1 and language model scores for translation quality estimation. In *Proceedings of the Seventh Workshop on Statistical Machine Translation, WMT@NAACL-HLT 2012, June 7-8, 2012, Montréal, Canada*, pages 133–137.

Maja Popović. 2015. chrF: character n-gram F-score for automatic MT evaluation. In *Proceedings of the Tenth Workshop on Statistical Machine Translation*, Lisboa, Portugal. Association for Computational Linguistics.

Maja Popović. 2017. chrF++: words helping character n-grams. In *Proceedings of the Second Conference on Machine Translation, Volume 2: Shared Tasks Papers*, Copenhagen, Denmark. Association for Computational Linguistics.

Matt Post. 2018a. A call for clarity in reporting BLEU scores. In *Proceedings of the Third Conference on Machine Translation: Research Papers*, pages 186–191, Belgium, Brussels. Association for Computational Linguistics.

Matt Post. 2018b. A call for clarity in reporting bleu scores. In *Proceedings of the Third Conference on Machine Translation*, Belgium, Brussels. Association for Computational Linguistics.

Matthew Snover, Bonnie Dorr, Richard Schwartz, Linnea Micciulla, and John Makhoul. 2006. A study of translation edit rate with targeted human annotation. In *In Proceedings of Association for Machine Translation in the Americas*, pages 223–231.

Peter Stanchev, Weiyue Wang, and Hermann Ney. 2019. EED: Extended Edit Distance Measure for Machine Translation. In *Proceedings of the Fourth Conference on Machine Translation*, Florence, Italy. Association for Computational Linguistics.

Miloš Stanojević and Khalil Sima'an. 2015. BEER 1.1: ILLC UvA submission to metrics and tuning task. In *Proceedings of the Tenth Workshop on Statistical Machine Translation*, Lisboa, Portugal. Association for Computational Linguistics.

Weiyue Wang, Jan-Thorsten Peter, Hendrik Rosendahl, and Hermann Ney. 2016a. Character: Translation edit rate on character level. In *ACL 2016 First Conference on Machine Translation*, pages 505–510, Berlin, Germany.

Weiyue Wang, Jan-Thorsten Peter, Hendrik Rosendahl, and Hermann Ney. 2016b. CharacTer: Translation Edit Rate on Character Level. In *Proceedings of the First Conference on Machine Translation*, Berlin, Germany. Association for Computational Linguistics.

Evan James Williams. 1959. *Regression analysis*, volume 14. Wiley New York.

Elizaveta Yankovskaya, Andre Tättar, and Mark Fishel. 2019. Quality Estimation and Translation Metrics via Pre-trained Word and Sentence Embeddings. In *Proceedings of the Fourth Conference on Machine Translation*, Florence, Italy. Association for Computational Linguistics.

Ryoma Yoshimura, Hiroki Shimanaka, Yukio Matsumura, Hayahide Yamagishi, and Mamoru Komachi. 2019. Filtering Pseudo-References by Paraphrasing for Automatic Evaluation of Machine Translation. In *Proceedings of the Fourth Conference on Machine Translation*, Florence, Italy. Association for Computational Linguistics.

A Correlations for Top-N Systems

A.1 de-cs

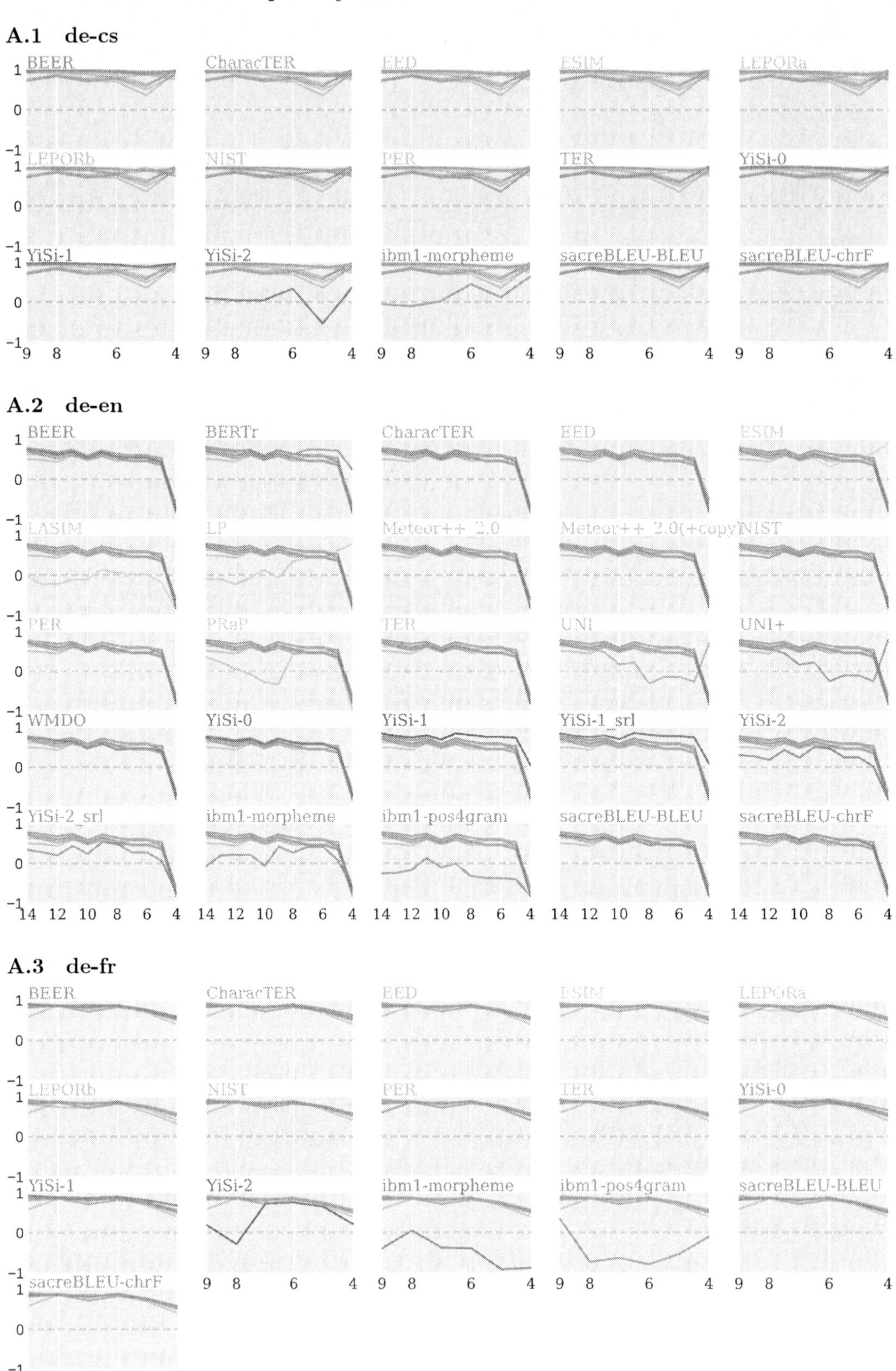

A.2 de-en

A.3 de-fr

A.4 en-cs

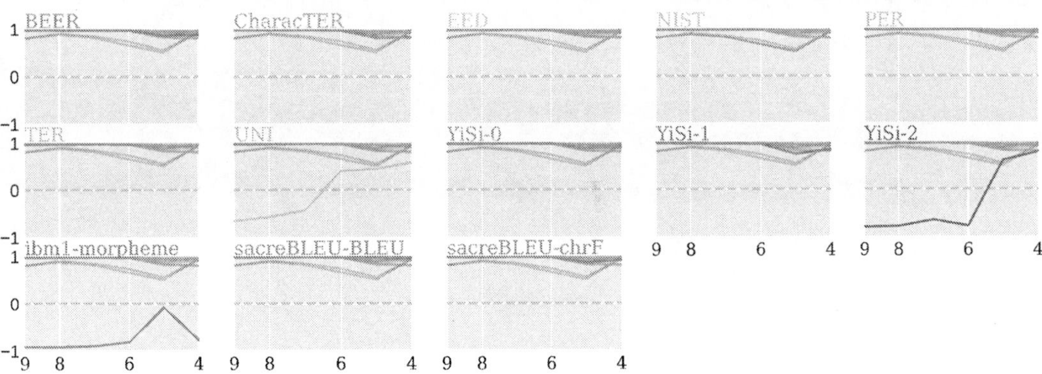

A.5 en-de

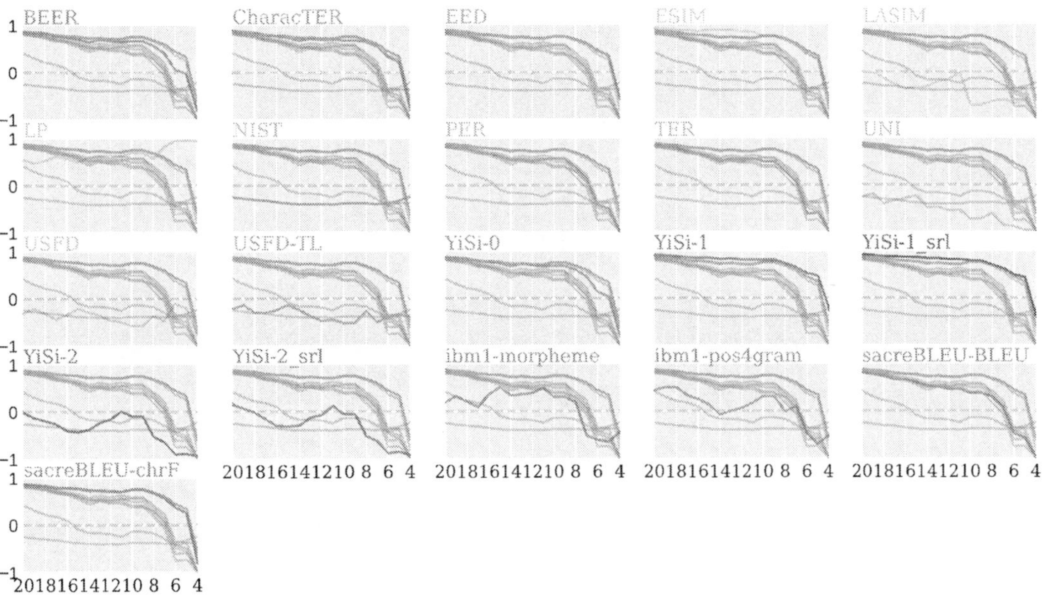

A.6 en-fi

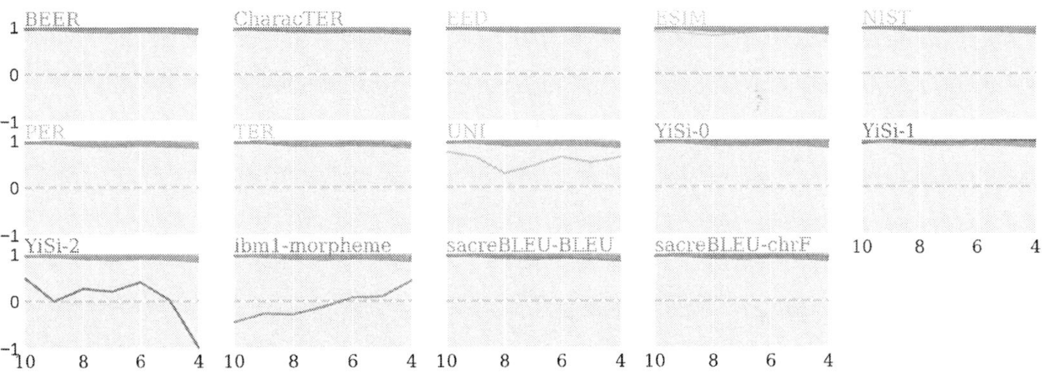

A.7 en-gu

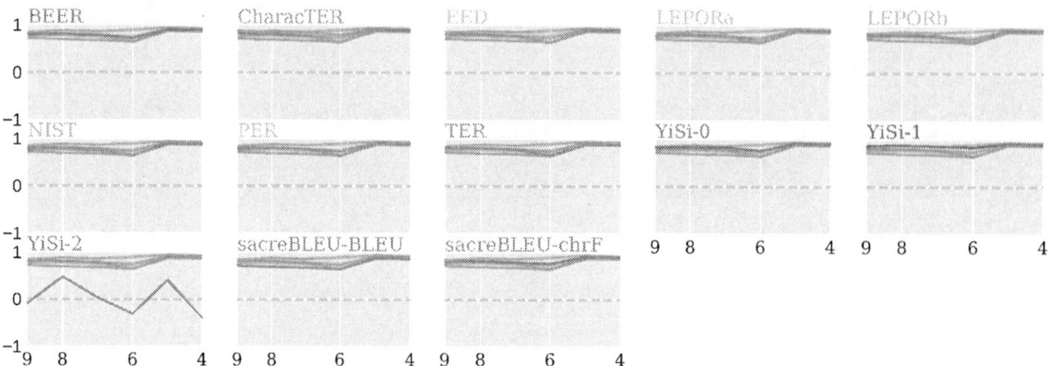

A.8 en-kk

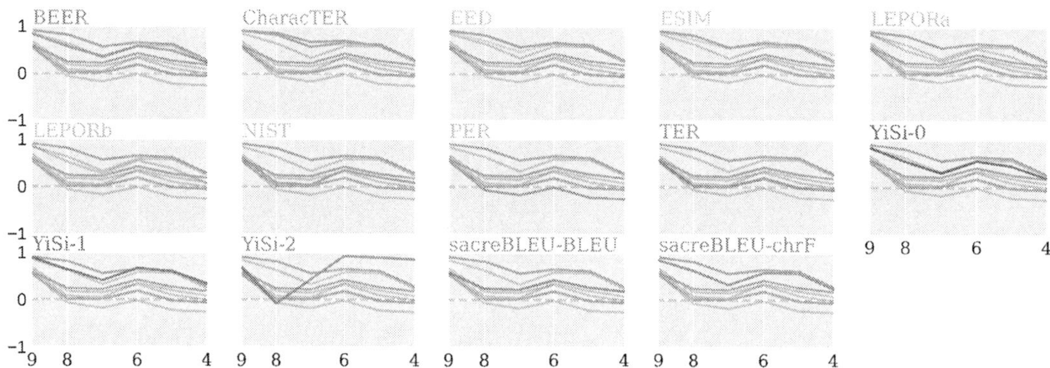

A.9 en-lt

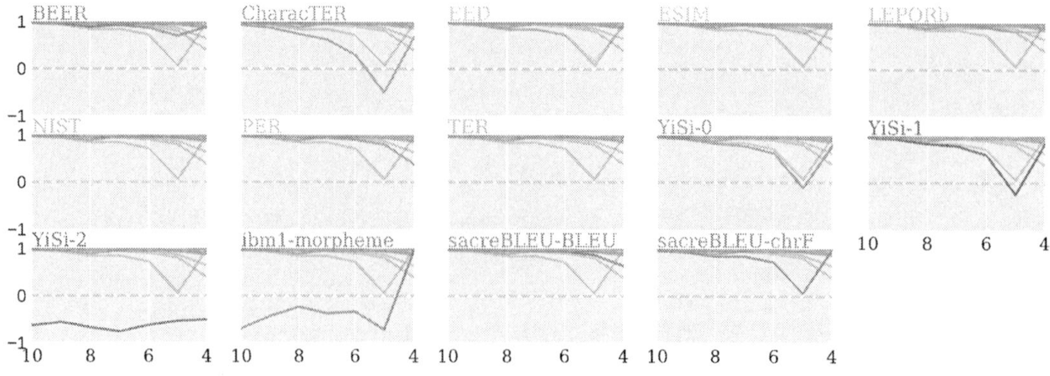

A.10 en-ru

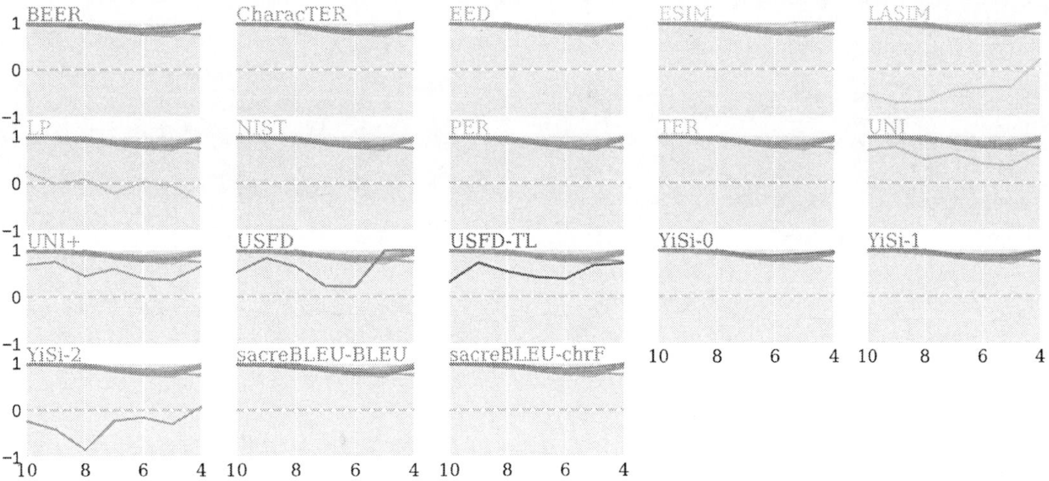

A.11 en-zh

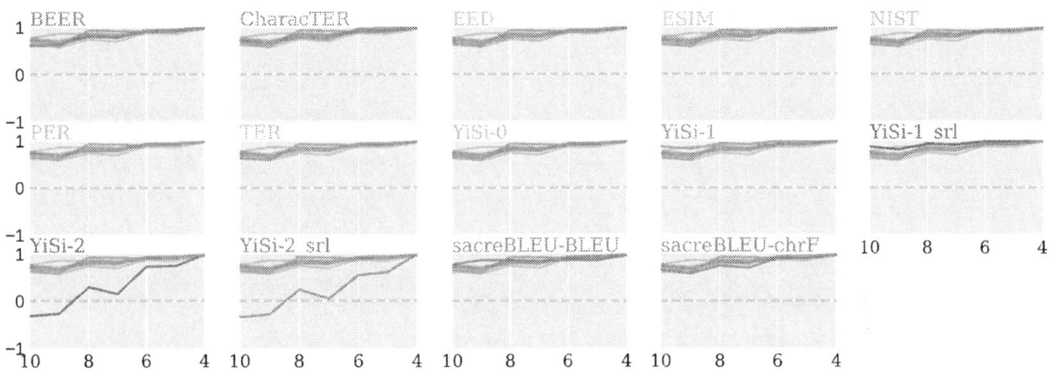

A.12 fi-en

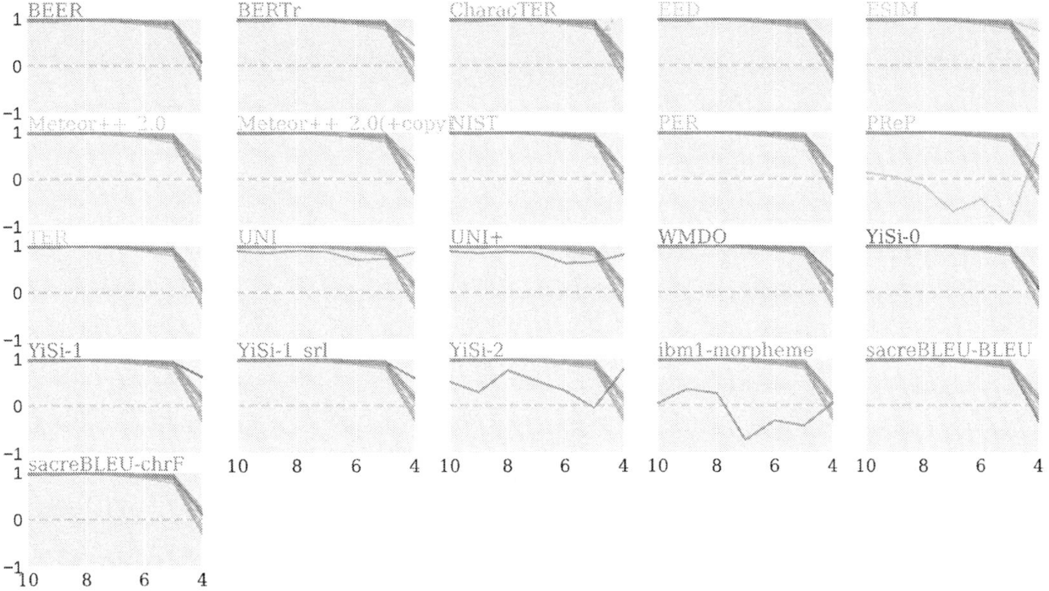

87

A.13 fr-de

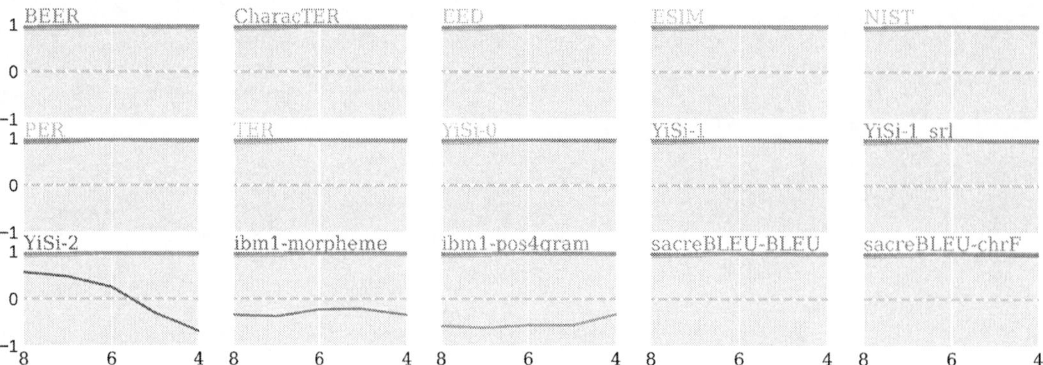

A.14 gu-en

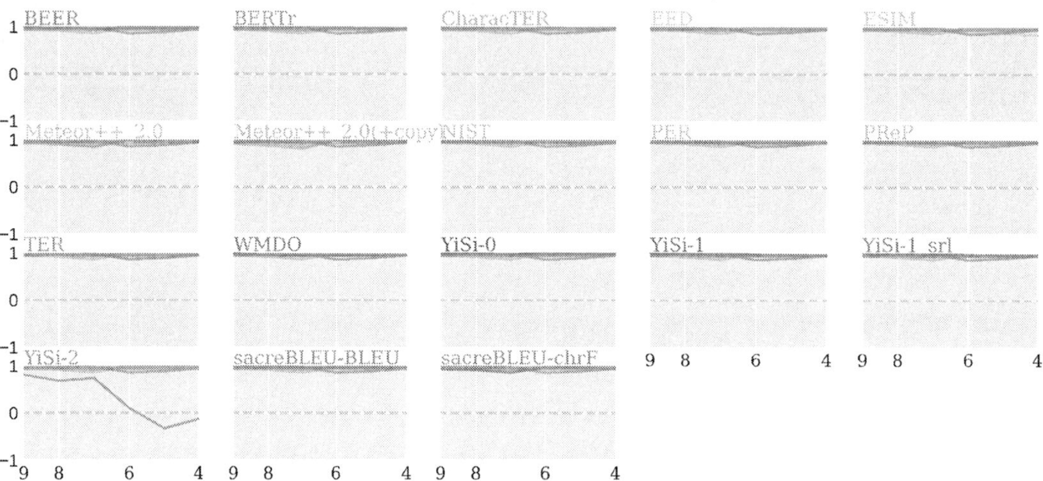

A.15 kk-en

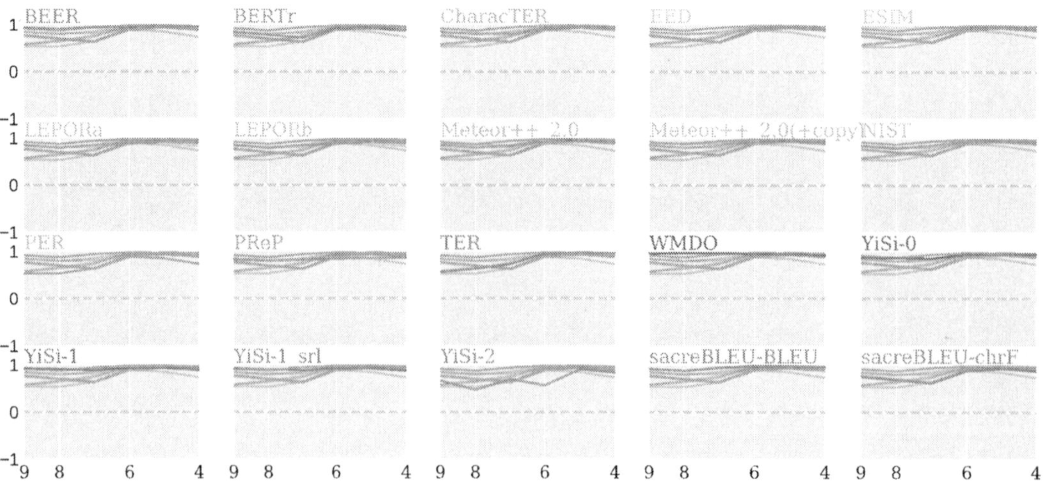

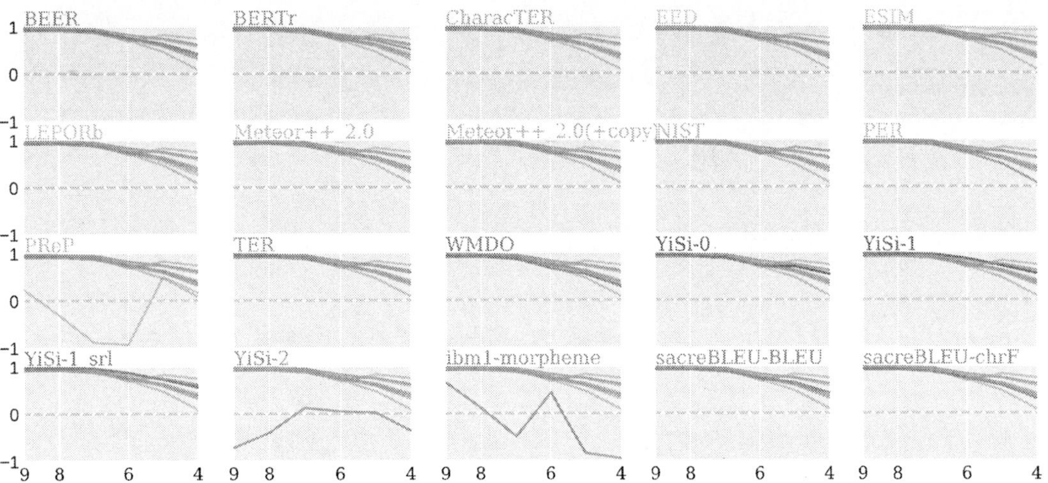

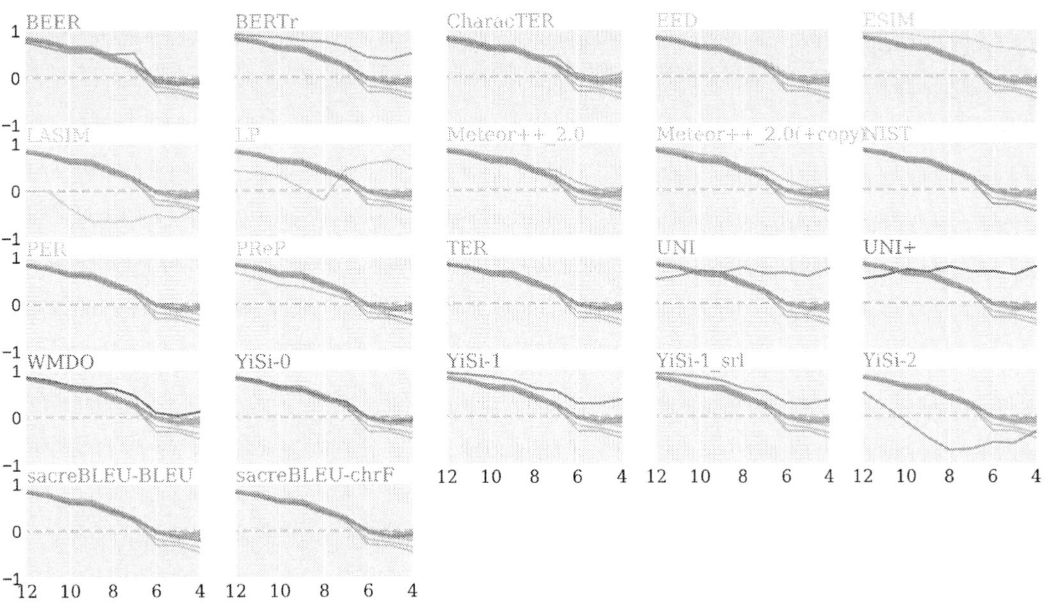

A.18 zh-en

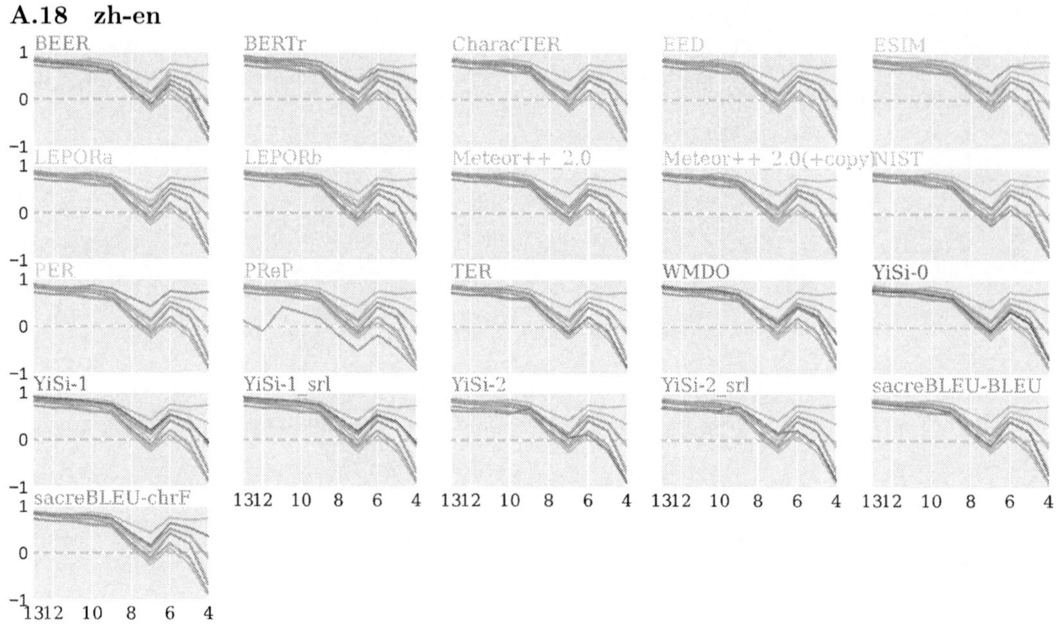

Findings of the First Shared Task on
Machine Translation Robustness

Xian Li[1], Paul Michel[2], Antonios Anastasopoulos[2], Yonatan Belinkov[3], Nadir Durrani[4],
Orhan Firat[5], Philipp Koehn[6], Graham Neubig[2], Juan Pino[1], Hassan Sajjad[4]

[1]Facebook AI, [2]Carnegie Mellon University, [3]Harvard University and MIT,
[4]Qatar Computing Research Institute, [5]Google AI, [6]Johns Hopkins University

Abstract

We share the findings of the first shared task on improving robustness of Machine Translation (MT). The task provides a testbed representing challenges facing MT models deployed in the real world, and facilitates new approaches to improve models' robustness to noisy input and domain mismatch. We focus on two language pairs (English-French and English-Japanese), and the submitted systems are evaluated on a blind test set consisting of noisy comments on Reddit[1] and professionally sourced translations. As a new task, we received 23 submissions by 11 participating teams from universities, companies, national labs, etc. All submitted systems achieved large improvements over baselines, with the best improvement having +22.33 BLEU. We evaluated submissions by both human judgment and automatic evaluation (BLEU), which shows high correlations (Pearson's $r = 0.94$ and 0.95). Furthermore, we conducted a qualitative analysis of the submitted systems using `compare-mt`[2], which revealed their salient differences in handling challenges in this task. Such analysis provides additional insights when there is occasional disagreement between human judgment and BLEU, e.g. systems better at producing colloquial expressions received higher score from human judgment.

1 Introduction

In recent years, Machine Translation (MT) systems have seen great progress, with neural models becoming the *de-facto* methods and even approaching human quality in news domain (Hassan et al., 2018). However, like other deep learning models, neural machine translation (NMT) models are found to be sensitive to synthetic and natural noise in input, distributional shift, and adversarial

examples (Koehn and Knowles, 2017; Belinkov and Bisk, 2018; Durrani et al., 2019; Anastasopoulos et al., 2019; Michel et al., 2019). From an application perspective, MT systems need to deal with non-standard, noisy text of the kind which is ubiquitous on social media and the internet, yet has different distributional signatures from corpora in common benchmark datasets.

The goal of this shared task is to provide a testbed for improving MT models' robustness to orthographic variations, grammatical errors, and other linguistic phenomena common in user-generated content, via better modelling, training, adaptation techniques, or leveraging monolingual training data. Specifically, the shared task aims to bring improvements on the following challenges:

- To improve NMT's robustness to orthographic variations, grammatical errors, informal language, and other linguistic phenomena or noise common on social media.

- To explore effective approaches to leverage abundant out-of-domain parallel data.

- To explore novel approaches to leverage abundant monolingual data on the Web (e.g., tweets, Reddit comments, commoncrawl, etc.).

- To thoroughly investigate and understand the overall challenges in translating social media text and identify major themes of efforts which needs more research from the community.

In this first iteration, the shared-task used the MTNT dataset (Michel and Neubig, 2018) that contains noisy social media texts and their translations between English (Eng) and French (Fra) and English and Japanese (Jpn), in four translation directions: Eng→Fra, Fra→Eng, Eng→Jpn, and

---

[1]`www.reddit.com`
[2]`https://github.com/neulab/compare-mt`

Proceedings of the Fourth Conference on Machine Translation (WMT), Volume 2: Shared Task Papers (Day 1) pages 91–102
Florence, Italy, August 1-2, 2019. ©2019 Association for Computational Linguistics

Jpn→Eng. We describe the dataset and the task setup in Section 3. The shared-task attracted a total of 23 submissions from 11 teams. The teams employed a variety of methods to improve robustness. A specific challenge was the small size of the in-domain noisy parallel dataset. We summarize the participating systems in Section 4 and the notable methods in Section 5. The contributions were evaluated both automatically and via a human evaluation. The results demonstrate a significant progress of the state-of-the-art in MT robustness, with multiple teams surpassing the shared-task baseline by a large margin. These results are discussed in Section 6.

We hope that this task leads to more efforts from the community in building robust MT models.

2 Related Work

The fragility of neural networks (Szegedy et al., 2013) has been shown to extend to neural machine translation models (Belinkov and Bisk, 2018; Heigold et al., 2017) and recent work focused on various aspects of the problem. From the identification of the causes of this brittleness, to the induction of (adversarial) inputs that trigger the unwanted behavior (attacks) and making such models robust against various types of noisy inputs (defenses); improving robustness has been receiving increasing attention in NMT.

While Koehn and Knowles (2017) mentioned domain mismatch as a challenge for neural machine translation, Khayrallah and Koehn (2018) addressed noisy training data and focus on the types of noise occurring in web-crawled corpora. Michel and Neubig (2018) proposed a new dataset (MTNT) to test MT models for robustness to the types of noise encountered in the Internet and demonstrated that these challenges cannot be overcome by simple domain adaptation techniques alone.

Belinkov and Bisk (2018) and Heigold et al. (2017) showed that NMT systems are very sensitive to slightly perturbed input forms, and hinted at the importance of injecting noisy examples during training, also known as adversarial examples. Further research proposed several methods of generating and using noisy examples as NMT input to advance the understanding and improve the translation quality. Following machine vision, two major branches being explored when generating noisy examples, *i)* white box methods, where adversarial

examples are generated with access to the model parameters (Ebrahimi et al., 2018; Cheng et al., 2018a,b, 2019) and *ii)* black-box attacks, where examples are generated without accessing model internals (Zhao et al., 2018; Lee et al., 2018; **?**; Anastasopoulos et al., 2019; Vaibhav et al., 2019); see Belinkov and Glass (2019) for a categorization of such work. In particular, some have focused on specific variations of naturally-occurring noise, such as grammatical errors produced by non-native speakers (Anastasopoulos et al., 2019) or errors extracted from Wikipedia edits (Belinkov and Bisk, 2018). It has also been shown that adding synthetic noise does not trivially increase robustness to natural noise (Belinkov and Bisk, 2018) and may require specific recipes (Karpukhin et al., 2019).

Michel et al. (2019) recently emphasized the importance of meaning-preserving perturbations and along with Cheng et al. (2019) demonstrated the utility of adversarial training without significantly impairing performance on clean data and domain. Durrani et al. (2019) showed that character-based representations are more robust towards noise compared to such learned using BPE-based sub-word units in the task of machine translation.

3 Task

This is the first year we introduce the robustness task. The goal of the task setup is to examine MT systems' performance on non-standard, noisy, user-generated text, which often resemble mixed challenges around orthographic variations, grammar errors, domain shift and stylistic lexical choice, etc. We use the MTNT dataset (Michel and Neubig, 2018) as a testbed for the above-mentioned robustness challenges. To give readers an idea of the natural "noise" present in the MTNT dataset, and the challenges for MT systems to robustly understand and translate them, we provide some examples of input variations:

- **Spelling/typographical errors:** accross (across), recieve (receive), tant (temps)

- **Grammatical errors:** a tons of, there are less people

- **Spoken language and internet slang:** wanna, chais pas, tbh, smh, mdr

- **Code switching:** This is so kawaii, C'est trop mainstream

- **Profanity/slurs:** f*ck, m*rde

Readers are encouraged to refer to Michel and Neubig (2018) for more details. This year's task probes MT robustness for two language pairs, French to/from English and Japanese to/from English.

3.1 Task Setup

The task includes two tracks, *constrained* and *unconstrained* depending on whether the system is trained on a predefined training datasets or not. The two tracks are evaluated by the same automatic and human evaluation protocol, however, they are compared separately.

For the constrained system track, the task specifies two types of training data in addition to MTNT train set:

- **"Out-of-domain" parallel data:** This facilitates MT model's capability to perform supervised learning from examples with different distribution such as lexical choice, language style, genre etc. For example, parallel corpora from WMT news translation task, subtitles and TED talks are specified.

- **Monolingual data:** We encourage participants to develop novel solutions to learn from unlabelled data, improve existing semi-supervised approach such as backtranslation. We provide both in-domain (MTNT) and out-of-domain (News Commentary, News Crawl, etc) monolingual data.

3.2 Training Data

In the constrained setting, participants were allowed to use the WMT15 training data[3] for Eng↔Fra and any of the KFTT (Neubig, 2011), JESC (Pryzant et al.) and TED talks (Cettolo et al., 2012) corpora for Jpn↔Eng. Additionally, the use of the MTNT corpus (Michel and Neubig, 2018) was allowed in order to adapt models on limited in-domain data.

3.3 Test Data

The test sets were collected following the same protocol as the MTNT dataset, *i.e.* collected from Reddit, filtered out for noisy comments using a sub-word language modeling criterion and translated by professional translators. The statistics of the test sets are reported in Table 1.

3.4 Evaluation protocol

The system outputs were evaluated by professional translators. The translators were presented the original source sentence, the reference and the system output side by side. The order between the reference and the system output was randomized by the user interface. The translators rated both the reference and the translation on a scale from 1 to 100. For both the original source sentence and the reference, the original text was presented except for Eng-Jpn where the Japanese reference tokenized with KyTea was presented in order to be consistent with the systems' outputs. The user interface for annotation is illustrated in Figure 1.

We also evaluated BLEU (Papineni et al., 2002) for each system using SacreBLEU (Post, 2018). For all language pairs except Eng-Jpn, we used the original reference and SacreBLEU with the default options. In the case of Eng-Jpn, we used the reference tokenized with KyTea and the option `--tokenize none`.

4 Participants and System Descriptions

We received 23 submissions from 11 teams. Except two submissions on the Eng-Fra language pair, all systems used the *constrained* setup. Below we briefly describe the systems from the 8 teams which submitted corresponding system description papers:

Baidu & Oregon State University's submission (Zheng et al., 2019): Their system is based on the Transformer implementation in OpenNMT-py (Klein et al., 2017). The main methods applied in their submission are: domain-sensitive data mixing and data augmentation with back-translation. For data mixing, they used a special symbol on the source side to indicate the data domain. For data augmentation, they back-translate from a target language to its noisy source. The intuition, also observed by Michel and Neubig (2018), is that the source sentences are noisier than their target translations. They include out-of-domain clean data during this step and differentiate data types with a special symbol on the target side. In addition, they also run a model ensemble.

---

[3] `http://www.statmt.org/wmt15/translation-task.html`

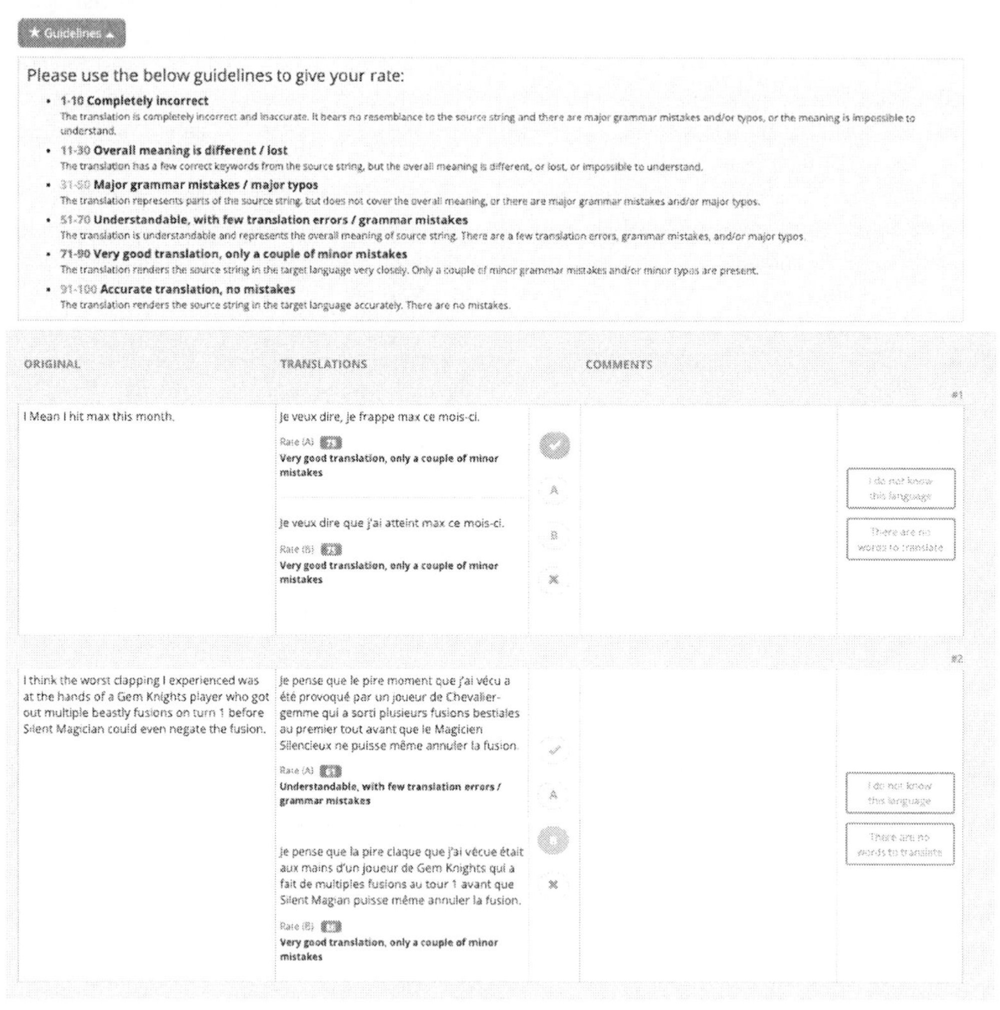

Figure 1: Annotation interface for human evaluations.

	Eng-Fra	Fra-Eng	Eng-Jpn	Jpn-Eng
# samples	1,401	1,233	1,392	1,111
# source tokens	20.0k	19.8k	20.0k	18.7k
# target tokens	22.8k	19.2k	33.6k	13.4k

Table 1: Statistics of the test sets.

The team experimented with the Fra→Eng and Eng→Fra translation directions, obtaining 43.6 and 36.4 BLEU-cased, respectively (3rd place in both). Their ablations show significant benefit from domain-sensitive training (+3 BLEU), with additional improvements from back-translation and ensembling.

CMU's submission (Zhou et al., 2019): This submission only participated in the Fra→Eng direction. They proposed the use of tied multitask learning, where the noisy source sentences are first decoded by a same-language denoising decoder, and both information is passed on to the translation decoder. This approach requires data triples of noisy source, clean source, translation, which they created by data augmentation over the provided data, using tag-informed translation systems trained on either noisy (MTNT) or clean (Europarl) data. As the participants point out though, their performance improvements seems to be attributed to data augmentation and not to the intermediate denoising decoder.

CUNI's submission (Helcl et al., 2019): They participated in Eng→Fra and Fra→Eng directions, following a classical two stage approach, i) training of a base model using a mix of parallel (WMT15 Eng-Fra News Translation) and back-translated monolingual data (from News Crawl and Europarl - excluding News Discussions), ii) fine-tuning of the base model using the training portion of the MTNT dataset. All models follow the Transformer-Big architecture, with the hyper-parameters and optimization recipe from the 2018 WMT News Translation shared task submission of CUNI, without ensembles. For both Eng-Fra and Fra-Eng directions, fine-tuning brought about 2+ BLEU points on top of the base models with the Transformer-Big architecture, whereas improvements were substantially larger when the base models were RNN-Based MTNT baselines, about 8+ BLEU points. Participants emphasized the importance of their strong Transformer-Big base model which was already 10+ BLEU points better than the MTNT baseline provided by the shared task. The effect of individual partitions of the base model training set (parallel and backtranslated-mono) on final system quality is not experimented. Finally, participants point out one peculiarity they've noticed in the train/validation partitioning of the original MTNT dataset; validation source sentences being started with the letter "Y" followed by alphabetically sorted sentences (test partition not effected).

FOKUS' submission (Grozea, 2019): This team participated in three directions: Eng→Fra, Fra→Eng and Jpn→Eng. For the Eng→Fra and Fra→Eng language pairs, the submissions are *unconstrained* systems, where the model was trained on the medical domain corpus provided by the WMT biomedical shared task [4]. Despite the training data being out-of-domain, removing "low-quality" parallel data such as "Subtitles" as the author hypothesized helped to bring 2 to 4 BLEU points improvement over the baseline models. Their Jpn→Eng submission is a *constrained* system, using the same model architecture as the Eng→Fra language pair. To improve robustness, they introduced synthetic noise (omitting and duplicating letters) in the training data to both source and target sentences.

JHU's submission (Post and Duh, 2019): This submission participated in the Fra→Eng and Jpn↔Eng tasks. The participants used data dual cross-entropy filtering for reducing the monolingual data, then back-translate these, and train their Transformer models (Vaswani et al., 2017). They compared Moses tokenization+Byte Pair Encoding (BPE) (Sennrich et al., 2016), and sentence-piece (Kudo and Richardson, 2018) (without any pre-processing) and found the two comparable, and that using larger sentence-piece models improved over smaller ones. For Jpn↔Eng (both di-

---

[4]http://www.statmt.org/wmt19/biomedical-translation-task.html

rections) they first used both in-domain (MTNT) and out-of-domain data (other constrained), and then continued training (fine-tune) using MTNT only. They also reported many results from their hyper-parameter search (albeit without a clear recommendation). The final submission is an ensemble of 4 models.

NaverLabsEurope(NLE)' submission (Bérard et al., 2019): The participants carried substantial effort to clean the CommonCrawl data, applying length filtering (length ratio threshold), language identification-based filtering, and attention based filtering. They used the Transformer-Big architecture for Fra→Eng and Jpn→Eng, and Transformer-Base for the Eng→Jpn direction.

The participants incorporated several methods to encourage robustness (detailed ablations on the effect of each method were not provided). They lowercase all data. However in order to preserve casing information in the input, they propose a technique called *inline casing* which adds additional casing tags (one per non-lowercased subword) in the sequence. Emojis were replaced with a special symbol. Natural noise based on manually defined noise rules was added on the source side of the training data. Lastly, MTNT monolingual data was back-translated to be used during training of the final system. They trained their system on all available data with special tags for each domain and for each data type e.g. real, back-translated, or noisy data. They found that adding tags is as good as fine-tuning the system, allowing for more flexibility at test time. Their final submission with an ensemble of 6 systems for Eng→Jpn and ensembles of 4 systems for the other language directions performed the best in the evaluation campaign.

NICT's submission (Dabre and Sumita, 2019): The authors used Transformer models to train their systems and employed two strategies namely: i) mixed fine-tuning and ii) multilingual models for making the systems robust. The former helps as the in-domain data is available in a very small quantity. Using a mix of in-domain and out-domain data for fine-tuning helps overcome the problem of adjusting learning rate, applying better regularization and other complicated strategies. It is not clear how these two methods contributed towards making the models more robust. According to the authors, mixed fine-tuning and multilingual training (bidirectional) helped. In the error analysis, they found that their system performs poorly in translating emojis. The segmentation errors generated by KyTea resulted in further errors in the translation.

NTT's submission (Murakami et al., 2019): The participants submitted systems for the Eng→Jpn and Jpn→Eng directions in the constrained setting. Their techniques include the placeholder mechanism for copying non-standard tokens (emojis, emoticons, etc), back-translation, fine-tuning on in-domain corpus, and ensemble. Especially, the placeholder mechanism provides +1.4 BLEU and +0.7 BLEU points for Jpn→Eng and Eng→Jpn respectively. Finetuning provides a larger improvement for Eng→Jpn (+1.2 BLEU) than Jpn→Eng (-0.3 BLEU). Their model is Transformer-Base configuration, where they demonstrated its capacity to noise-robustness can be further improved by the above-mentioned techniques.

5 Summary of Methods

In this section, we give a common theme and summary of methods applied by the various participants.

Data Cleaning Data cleaning played an important part in training successful MT systems in this campaign. Unlike other participants, the winning team Naver Labs Bérard et al. (2019) and NTT (Murakami et al., 2019) applied data cleaning techniques in order to filter noisy parallel sentences. They filtered i) identical sentences on source and target side, ii) sentences that belonged to a language other than the source and target language, iii) sentences with length mismatch, and iv) also applied attention-based filtering. Data cleaning gave an improvement of more than 5 BLEU points with substantial reduction in the hallucination of the model for the winning team.

Placeholders Training and test data contained tokens (such as emoticons) which do not require translation. Murakami et al. (2019) and Bérard et al. (2019) preserved these in a preprocessing step using special placeholders and copied them in the translation output. Murakami et al. (2019) reported a gain of up to 1.4 BLEU points by using placeholders.

Data Augmentation Other than handling noisy data, one of the challenges related to this task was data sparsity. All the participants back-translated in-domain monolingual data and used synthetic data as part of their training pipeline. In addition, Bérard et al. (2019) created a noisy version of all the available in-domain and out-of-domain data by randomly replacing words with their noisy variants. For training, they appended source sentences with a tag <noisy> to distinguish them from the original data. Zhou et al. (2019) used translation systems using placeholders in order to create both clean versions of the noisy in-domain datasets, as well as noisy versions of the clean out-of-domain dataset. To get additional data, other than back-translation, the JHU team (Post and Duh, 2019) used cross-entropy based filtering to select top 1 million sentences from Gigaword, CommonCrawl and the UN corpus. Adding large filtered data gave then an improvement of +5.8 BLEU points.

Domain-aware Training   In order to differentiate different data, real from synthetic, in-domain from out-domain, several participants used additional tags. Zheng et al. (2019); Bérard et al. (2019) used domain tags during training to indicate data domain. Bérard et al. (2019) additionally included data type tags (real or back-translated) for further categorization of the training data. Compared to fine-tuning, adding tags provides them additional flexibility, resulting in a generalized system, robust towards a variety of input data.

Fine-tuning   Along with the noisy in-domain MTNT data, general domain data typically made available for WMT campaign was also allowed for this task. Most participants (Murakami et al., 2019; Dabre and Sumita, 2019; Helcl et al., 2019) trained on general domain data and fine-tuned the models towards the task. Murakami et al. (2019) did not see a consistent improvement with fine-tuning. Due to the small size of the in-domain data, Dabre and Sumita (2019) fine-tuned on a mix of in-domain and a subset of the out-of-domain data.

Ensembles   To benefit from the different trained models and to make the performance more stable, many participants performed `ensemble` over their models. Murakami et al. (2019), Bérard et al. (2019), Zheng et al. (2019), and Post and Duh (2019) ensembled between 4 and 6 checkpoints of their model for the final submission. They observed a consistent performance improvement over using a single model.

6   Results

In this section we describe quantitative results, and also perform a qualitative analysis of the results.

6.1   Quantitative Results

The quantitative analysis of the submitted systems yields fairly consistent results. On automatic evaluation (BLEU) the best system across all translation directions is the NaverLabsEurope(NLE) one. The same system received also the highest human judgment scores, with the exception of the Eng→Jpn task, where the NTT system was ranked higher. Overall, the correlation between human judgments and BLEU is very high. For Eng→Fra, the Pearson's correlation coefficient is 0.94, while for the other three tasks it is over 0.97.

Human Evaluation   The results of human evaluation following the evaluation protocol described in Section 3.4 are outlined in Table 2.

Automatic Evaluation   The automatic evaluation (BLEU) results of the Shared Task are summarized in Table 3.

6.2   Qualitative Analysis

In order to discover salient differences between the methods, we performed analysis using `compare-mt` (Neubig et al., 2019), and present a few of the salient findings below.

Stronger Submissions were Stronger at Everything: The submissions to the track achieved a wide range of BLEU and human evaluation scores. In our analysis we found that the systems at the higher end of the spectrum with regards to BLEU also tended to be the best by most other measures (human evaluation, word F-measure by various frequency buckets, sentence-level scores, etc.). Because of this, we limit our remaining analysis to the top three systems in the Fra→Eng and Eng→Fra tracks, and the top two systems in the Eng→Jpn and Jpn→Eng tracks.

Generalization to Words not in Adaptation Data is Essential: The MTNT corpus provides a small amount of training data that can be used to adapt systems to the task of translating social media. One large distinguishing factor between the best-performing system by Naver Labs Europe (NLE) and the second- or third-place systems was

System	Human judgment scores (RANK)			
	Eng→Fra	Fra→Eng	Eng→Jpn	Jpn→Eng
Constrained				
Baidu+OSU	71.5 (2)	80.6 (3)	–	–
CMU	–	58.2 (6)	–	–
CUNI	66.3 (3)	82.0 (2)	–	–
FOKUS	–	–	–	48.5 (5)
JHU	–	76.3 (4)	58.5 (3)	65.4 (3)
NaverLabs	**75.5** (1)	**85.3** (1)	63.9 (2)	**74.1** (1)
NTT	–	–	**66.5** (1)	71.3 (2)
NICT	–	–	44.7 (4)	49.1 (4)
Unconstrained				
FOKUS	52.5 (4)	62.6 (5)	–	–

Table 2: Average human judgments over all submitted systems (the higher the better). The systems' rank for each translation direction is shown in parentheses. The best system is **highlighted**.

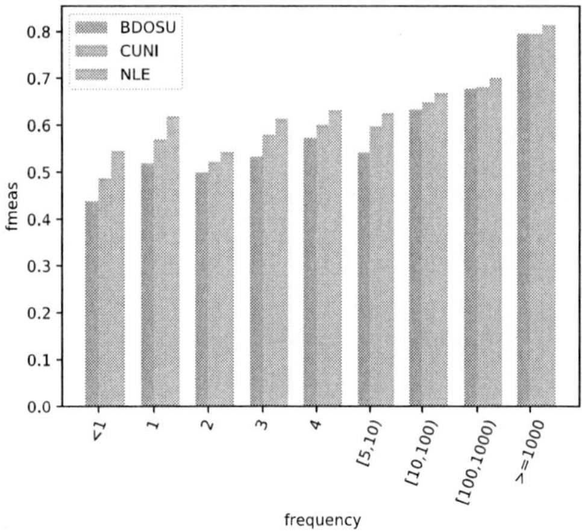

Figure 2: Word F-measure by frequency in the MTNT training data for Fra-Eng.

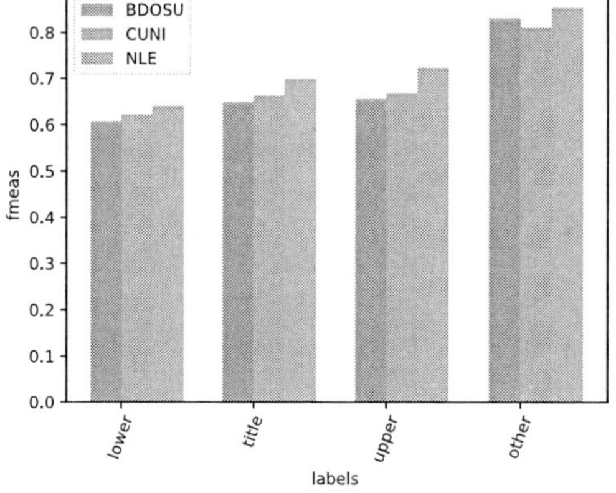

Figure 3: Word F-measure by casing of the words in the target: all lower-case, title case, all upper-case, or other.

performance on words that were *not* included in this training data that nonetheless appeared in the test set. We show the example of word-level F-measure bucketed by frequency of the words in the MTNT test set for Fra→Eng in Figure 2. From this figure we can see that the NLE system does a bit better in all frequency categories, but the difference is particularly stark for words that appear only once or not at all in the MTNT training set.

Proper Handling of Casing is Important: One other innovation performed by the NLE team was lowercasing of words and separate prediction of casing information. This modeling decision apparently resulted in significantly better results partic-

ularly on words that were written in all upper-case, as demonstrated in the results of word F-measure by casing in the target language, demonstrated for Eng→Fra in Figure 3. In addition, we show an example for Fra→Eng in Table 4, where the NLE system translates upper-case characters perfectly, but the CUNI system struggles.

Special Handling of Special Characters is Beneficial: Special characters such as Emojis or symbols were difficult for some systems. Interestingly, even among the top systems, some systems were better at handling different varieties of these characters than others. As an example, in Jpn→Eng, the NTT system performed better on Japanese-style smileys written with standard char-

System	BLEU (RANK)			
	Eng→Fra	Fra→Eng	Eng→Jpn	Jpn→Eng
Baseline	22.1	25.6	8.4	5.8
Constrained				
Baidu+OSU	36.39 (3)	43.59 (3)	–	–
CMU	–	32.25 (5)	–	–
CUNI	38.49 (2)	44.83 (2)	–	–
FOKUS	–	–	–	6.42 (5)
JHU	–	40.24 (4)	14.67 (3)	12.01 (3)
NaverLabs	**41.39** (1)	**47.93** (1)	**17.73** (1)	**16.41** (1)
NTT	–	–	16.86 (2)	14.82 (2)
NICT	–	–	11.09 (4)	7.56 (4)
Unconstrained				
FOKUS	24.22 (4)	29.94 (6)	–	–

Table 3: Automatic evaluation (BLEU, cased) over all submitted systems, with the system's rank in parentheses. The best system is **highlighted**.

	Output	BLEU+1
Ref	From Sri Lanka , to Russia , to the United States , to Japan I mean it 's a market THAT GOES EVERYWHERE .	
CUNI	from sri lanka , to russia , to the united states , to japon I mean it 's a market QUI VA PARTOUT .	33.0
NLE	From Sri Lanka , to Russia , to the United States , to Japan I mean it 's a market THAT GOES EVERYWHERE .	100

Table 4: An example of handling of casing in two Fra→Eng systems

	Output	BLEU+1
Ref	Kawaii ♪ (* · ω · 人)	
NTT	Cute (* · ω · 人)	76.0
NLE	It 's cute .	0.0
Ref	👉 ✴ 👩 ♂	
NTT		0.0
NLE	👉 ✴ 👩 ♂	100

Table 5: Examples of translation results on special characters.

acters, while the NLE system performed better on Unicode-standard Emojis, as shown in Table 5.

Non-standard Sentence Structure can be Difficult: Some systems also found sentences with unusual structures, including brackets or other types of punctuation interspersed with actual text, particularly difficult. For example, Table 6 shows an example of Jpn→Eng sentences where the NTT system had trouble generating the appropriate number of symbols in the appropriate places, while the NLE system was more robust in this regard.

Colloquial Expressions are Key: There was also a marked difference among the top systems in their ability to produce the more informal register reflected in the MTNT test data. We show an example in Table 7 of n-grams that the NTT system was better at producing than the NLE system. All of these are relatively colloquial ways of expressing common function word phrases (1. "is not doing", 2. "but", 3. "lots", 4. "right?", 5. "but,") that can also be expressed with more formal expressions. Clearly the NTT system is producing a slightly less formal register than the NLE system, although a manual examination of the outputs found that even the NTT system was still commonly producing register that was more formal than is commonly found on social media. This may be attributed to the fact that the NTT system

	Output	BLEU+1
Ref	* *] (# mm-e9) [* * Because there 's now protection * *] (# mm-e4)	
NTT	* * * *) (# m-e9) [* * * * * * * * * * * * * * * * * -e4 because there is more protection .)	14.3
NLE	* * * (# mm-e9) [* * Because there is already protection * *] (# mm-e4)	72.0

Table 6: An example of translation results on as sentence with an unusual number of special symbols.

	n-gram	NTT	NLE
1.	ていない	5	0
2.	だけど	4	0
3.	多くの	4	0
4.	ね	3	0
5.	だけど、	3	0

Table 7: Examples of n-grams where one the NTT Eng→Jpn system was more accurate than the NLE system

performed fine-tuning on the MTNT data, moving it towards a more appropriately colloquial register.

7   Conclusions

As a new WMT shared task, this year we focused on building MT systems which are robust to input variations commonly observed in informal language, social media text etc.

From a methodological perspective, the "constrained" setup of the task encouraged participants to leverage both out-of-domain parallel data and in-domain monolingual data to improve performance. Some techniques were utilized by multiple participants and proved their effectiveness in boosting MT models' robustness to noisy input and domain mismatch, including data cleaning, domain-aware training, data augmentation (including backtranslation and copying place-holder tags), finetuning, etc.

In terms of evaluation, we found an automatic metric (BLEU) to be roughly consistent with human judgment. Qualitative analysis found that strong baseline systems were important, but on top of this additional methods specifically aimed at trying to handle various types of noise found in social media text were effective and necessary to further improve within the upper echelons of systems submitted to the shared task.

There are several directions to be explored in the future editions of the task. First, it can exhibit a separate track for "probing" models' robustness so as to understand current models' weaknesses. Second, it could further disentangle improvements for different challenges, e.g., due to noise in training data or due to distribution shift at test time. Controlling the kind of noise introduced, e.g. natural vs. artificial, may be useful in this regard.

Acknowledgements

We thank Facebook for funding the human evaluation and blind test set creation.

References

Antonios Anastasopoulos, Alison Lui, Toan Q. Nguyen, and David Chiang. 2019. Neural machine translation of text from non-native speakers. In *Proc. NAACL HLT*.

Yonatan Belinkov and Yonatan Bisk. 2018. Synthetic and natural noise both break neural machine translation. In *International Conference on Learning Representations (ICLR)*.

Yonatan Belinkov and James Glass. 2019. Analysis methods in neural language processing: A survey. *Transactions of the Association for Computational Linguistics (TACL)*, 7:49–72.

Alexandre Bérard, Ioan Calapodescu, and Claude Roux. 2019. Naver Labs Europe's Systems for the WMT19 Machine Translation Robustness Task. In *Proceedings of the 2019 Shared task on Machine Translation Robustness, Conference on Machine Translation (WMT)*.

Mauro Cettolo, Christian Girardi, and Marcello Federico. 2012. Wit^3: Web inventory of transcribed and translated talks. In *Proceedings of the 16th Conference of the European Association for Machine Translation (EAMT)*, pages 261–268.

Minhao Cheng, Jinfeng Yi, Huan Zhang, Pin-Yu Chen, and Cho-Jui Hsieh. 2018a. Seq2sick: Evaluating the robustness of sequence-to-sequence models with adversarial examples. *CoRR*, abs/1803.01128.

Yong Cheng, Lu Jiang, and Wolfgang Macherey. 2019. Robust neural machine translation with doubly adversarial inputs. In *ACL*. Association for Computational Linguistics.

Yong Cheng, Zhaopeng Tu, Fandong Meng, Junjie Zhai, and Yang Liu. 2018b. Towards robust neural machine translation. *CoRR*, abs/1805.06130.

Raj Dabre and Eiichiro Sumita. 2019. NICT's Supervised MT Systems for the Translation Robustness Task in WMT19. In *Proceedings of the 2019 Shared task on Machine Translation Robustness, Conference on Machine Translation (WMT)*.

Nadir Durrani, Fahim Dalvi, Hassan Sajjad, Yonatan Belinkov, and Preslav Nakov. 2019. One size does not fit all: Comparing NMT representations of different granularities. In *Proceedings of the 2019 Conference of the North American Chapter of the Association for Computational Linguistics: Human Language Technologies, Volume 1 (Long and Short Papers)*, pages 1504–1516, Minneapolis, Minnesota. Association for Computational Linguistics.

Javid Ebrahimi, Daniel Lowd, and Dejing Dou. 2018. On adversarial examples for character-level neural machine translation. In *Proceedings of the 27th International Conference on Computational Linguistics*, Santa Fe, New Mexico, USA. Association for Computational Linguistics.

Cristian Grozea. 2019. The submission of FOKUS to the WMT 19 robustness task. In *Proceedings of the 2019 Shared task on Machine Translation Robustness, Conference on Machine Translation (WMT)*.

Hany Hassan, Anthony Aue, Chang Chen, Vishal Chowdhary, Jonathan Clark, Christian Federmann, Xuedong Huang, Marcin Junczys-Dowmunt, William Lewis, Mu Li, et al. 2018. Achieving human parity on automatic chinese to english news translation. *arXiv preprint arXiv:1803.05567*.

Georg Heigold, Günter Neumann, and Josef van Genabith. 2017. How robust are character-based word embeddings in tagging and mt against wrod scramlbing or randdm nouse? *arXiv preprint arXiv:1704.04441*.

Jindřich Helcl, Jindřich Libovický, and Martin Popel. 2019. CUNI System for the WMT19 Robustness Task. In *Proceedings of the 2019 Shared task on Machine Translation Robustness, Conference on Machine Translation (WMT)*.

Vladimir Karpukhin, Omer Levy, Jacob Eisenstein, and Marjan Ghazvininejad. 2019. Training on synthetic noise improves robustness to natural noise in machine translation. *CoRR*, abs/1902.01509.

Huda Khayrallah and Philipp Koehn. 2018. On the impact of various types of noise on neural machine translation. In *Proceedings of the 2nd Workshop on Neural Machine Translation and Generation*, pages 74–83, Melbourne, Australia. Association for Computational Linguistics.

Guillaume Klein, Yoon Kim, Yuntian Deng, Jean Senellart, and Alexander M. Rush. 2017. OpenNMT: Open-source toolkit for neural machine translation. In *Proc. ACL*.

Philipp Koehn and Rebecca Knowles. 2017. Six challenges for neural machine translation. *arXiv preprint arXiv:1706.03872*.

Taku Kudo and John Richardson. 2018. SentencePiece: A simple and language independent subword tokenizer and detokenizer for neural text processing. In *Proceedings of the 2018 Conference on Empirical Methods in Natural Language Processing: System Demonstrations*, pages 66–71, Brussels, Belgium. Association for Computational Linguistics.

Katherine Lee, Orhan Firat, Ashish Agarwal, Clara Fannjiang, and David Sussillo. 2018. Hallucinations in neural machine translation. In *Interpretability and Robustness in Audio, Speech, and Language Workshop Conference on Neural Information Processing Systems*.

Paul Michel, Xian Li, Graham Neubig, and Juan Miguel Pino. 2019. On evaluation of adversarial perturbations for sequence-to-sequence models. In *Proc. NAACL HLT*.

Paul Michel and Graham Neubig. 2018. MTNT: A testbed for Machine Translation of Noisy Text. In *Proceedings of the 2018 Conference on Empirical Methods in Natural Language Processing (EMNLP)*.

Soichiro Murakami, Makoto Morishita, Tsutomu Hirao, and Masaaki Nagata. 2019. NTT's Machine Translation Systems for WMT19 Robustness Task. In *Proceedings of the 2019 Shared task on Machine Translation Robustness, Conference on Machine Translation (WMT)*.

Graham Neubig. 2011. The Kyoto free translation task. http://www.phontron.com/kftt.

Graham Neubig, Zi-Yi Dou, Junjie Hu, Paul Michel, Danish Pruthi, and Xinyi Wang. 2019. compare-mt: A tool for holistic comparison of language generation systems. In *Proceedings of the 2019 Conference of the North American Chapter of the Association for Computational Linguistics (Demonstrations)*, pages 35–41, Minneapolis, Minnesota. Association for Computational Linguistics.

Kishore Papineni, Salim Roukos, Todd Ward, and Wei-Jing Zhu. 2002. Bleu: a method for automatic evaluation of machine translation. In *Proceedings of 40th Annual Meeting of the Association for Computational Linguistics*, pages 311–318, Philadelphia, Pennsylvania, USA. Association for Computational Linguistics.

Matt Post. 2018. A call for clarity in reporting BLEU scores. In *Proceedings of the Third Conference on Machine Translation: Research Papers*, pages 186–191, Belgium, Brussels. Association for Computational Linguistics.

Matt Post and Kevin Duh. 2019. JHU 2019 Robustness Task System Description. In *Proceedings of the 2019 Shared task on Machine Translation Robustness, Conference on Machine Translation (WMT)*.

R. Pryzant, Y. Chung, D. Jurafsky, and D. Britz. Jesc: Japanese-english subtitle corpus. *ArXiv e-prints*.

Rico Sennrich, Barry Haddow, and Alexandra Birch. 2016. Neural machine translation of rare words with subword units. In *Proceedings of the 54th Annual Meeting of the Association for Computational Linguistics (Volume 1: Long Papers)*, pages 1715–1725, Berlin, Germany. Association for Computational Linguistics.

Christian Szegedy, Wojciech Zaremba, Ilya Sutskever, Joan Bruna, Dumitru Erhan, Ian Goodfellow, and Rob Fergus. 2013. Intriguing properties of neural networks. *arXiv preprint arXiv:1312.6199*.

Vaibhav Vaibhav, Sumeet Singh, Craig Stewart, and Graham Neubig. 2019. Improving robustness of machine translation with synthetic noise. In *Proceedings of the 2019 Conference of the North American Chapter of the Association for Computational Linguistics: Human Language Technologies, Volume 1 (Long and Short Papers)*, pages 1916–1920, Minneapolis, Minnesota. Association for Computational Linguistics.

Ashish Vaswani, Noam Shazeer, Niki Parmar, Jakob Uszkoreit, Llion Jones, Aidan N Gomez, Łukasz Kaiser, and Illia Polosukhin. 2017. Attention is all you need. In *Advances in neural information processing systems*, pages 5998–6008.

Zhengli Zhao, Dheeru Dua, and Sameer Singh. 2018. Generating natural adversarial examples. In *International Conference on Learning Representations*.

Renjie Zheng, Hairong Liu, Mingbo Ma, Baigong Zheng, and Liang Huang. 2019. Robust Machine Translation with Domain Sensitive Pseudo-Sources: Baidu-OSU WMT19 MT Robustness Shared Task System Report. In *Proceedings of the 2019 Shared task on Machine Translation Robustness, Conference on Machine Translation (WMT)*.

Shuyan Zhou, Xiangkai Zeng, Yingqi Zhou, Antonios Anastasopoulos, and Graham Neubig. 2019. Improving Robustness of Neural Machine Translation with Multi-task Learning. In *Proceedings of the 2019 Shared task on Machine Translation Robustness, Conference on Machine Translation (WMT)*.

The University of Edinburgh's Submissions to the WMT19 News Translation Task

Rachel Bawden   Nikolay Bogoychev   Ulrich Germann   Roman Grundkiewicz
Faheem Kirefu   Antonio Valerio Miceli Barone   Alexandra Birch

School of Informatics, University of Edinburgh, Scotland
rachel.bawden@ed.ac.uk

Abstract

The University of Edinburgh participated in the WMT19 Shared Task on News Translation in six language directions: English↔Gujarati, English↔Chinese, German→English, and English→Czech. For all translation directions, we created or used back-translations of monolingual data in the target language as additional synthetic training data. For English↔Gujarati, we also explored semi-supervised MT with cross-lingual language model pre-training, and translation pivoting through Hindi. For translation to and from Chinese, we investigated character-based tokenisation vs. sub-word segmentation of Chinese text. For German→English, we studied the impact of vast amounts of back-translated training data on translation quality, gaining a few additional insights over Edunov et al. (2018). For English→Czech, we compared different pre-processing and tokenisation regimes.

1 Introduction

The University of Edinburgh participated in the WMT19 Shared Task on News Translation in six language directions: English-Gujarati (EN↔GU), English-Chinese (EN↔ZH), German-English (DE→EN) and English-Czech (EN→CS). All our systems are neural machine translation (NMT) systems trained in constrained data conditions with the Marian[1] toolkit (Junczys-Dowmunt et al., 2018). The different language pairs pose very different challenges, due to the characteristics of the languages involved and arguably more importantly, due to the amount of training data available.

Pre-processing For EN↔ZH, we investigate character-level pre-processing for Chinese compared with subword segmentation. For EN→CS, we show that it is possible in high resource settings to simplify pre-processing by removing steps.

Exploiting non-parallel resources For all language directions, we create additional, synthetic parallel training data.

For the high resource language pairs, we look at ways of effectively using large quantities of backtranslated data. For example, for DE→EN, we investigated the most effective way of combining genuine parallel data with larger quantities of synthetic parallel data and for CS→EN, we filter backtranslated data by re-scoring translations using the MT model for the opposite direction. The challenge for our low resource pair, EN↔GU, is producing sufficiently good models for back-translation, which we achieve by training semi-supervised MT models with cross-lingual language model pre-training (Lample and Conneau, 2019). We use the same technique to translate additional data from a related language, Hindi.

NMT Training settings In all experiments, we test state-of-the-art training techniques, including using ultra-large mini-batches for DE→EN and EN↔ZH, implemented as optimiser delay.

Results summary Automatic evaluation results for all final systems on the WMT19 test set are summarised in Table 1. Throughout the paper, BLEU is calculated using SACREBLEU[2] (Post, 2018) unless otherwise indicated. A selection of our final models are available to download.[3]

2 Gujarati ↔ English

One of the main challenges for translation between English↔Gujarati is that it is a low-resource language pair; there is little openly available parallel data and much of this data is domain-specific and/or noisy (cf. Section 2.1). Our aim was therefore to experiment how additional available data

---

[1] https://marian-nmt.github.io

[2] https://github.com/mjpost/sacreBLEU
[3] See data.statmt.org/wmt19_systems/ for our released models and running scripts.

Proceedings of the Fourth Conference on Machine Translation (WMT), Volume 2: Shared Task Papers (Day 1) pages 103–115
Florence, Italy, August 1-2, 2019. ©2019 Association for Computational Linguistics

Lang. direction	BLEU	Ranking
EN→GU	16.4	1
GU→EN	21.4	2
EN→ZH	34.4	7
ZH→EN	27.7	6
DE→EN	35.0	9
EN→CS	27.9	3

Table 1: Final BLEU score results and system rankings amongst constrained systems according to automatic evaluation metrics.

can help us to improve translation quality: large quantities of monolingual text for both English and Gujarati, and resources from Hindi (a language related to Gujarati) in the form of monolingual Hindi data and a parallel Hindi-English corpus. We applied semi-supervised translation, backtranslation and pivoting techniques to create a large synthetic parallel corpus from these resources (Section 2.2), which we used to augment the small available parallel training corpus, enabling us to train our final supervised MT models (Section 2.3).

2.1 Data and pre-processing

We trained our models using only data listed for the task (cf. Table 2). Note that we did not have access to the corpora provided by the Technology Development for Indian Languages Programme, as they were only available to Indian citizens.

Lang(s)	Corpus	#sents	Ave. len.
	Parallel data		
EN-GU	Software data	107,637	7.0
	Wikipedia	18,033	21.1
	Wiki titles v1	11,671	2.1
	Govin	10,650	17.0
	Bilingual dictionary	9,979	1.5
	Bible	7,807	26.4
	Emille	5,083	19.1
GU-HI	Emille	7,993	19.1
EN-HI	Bombay IIT	1.4M	13.4
	Monolingual data		
EN	News	200M	23.6
GU	Common crawl	3.7M	21.9
	Emille	0.9M	16.6
	Wiki-dump	0.4M	17.7
	News	0.2M	15.4
HI	Bombay IIT	45.1M	18.7
	News	23.6M	17.0

Table 2: EN-GU Parallel training data used. Average length is calculated in number of tokens per sentence. For the parallel corpora, this is calculated for the first language indicated (i.e. EN, GU, then EN)

We pre-processed all data using standard scripts

from the Moses toolkit (Koehn et al., 2007): normalisation, tokenisation, cleaning (of training data only, with a maximum sentence length of 80 tokens) and true-casing for English data, using a model trained on all available news data. The Gujarati data was additionally pre-tokenised using the IndicNLP tokeniser[4] before Moses tokenisation was applied. We also applied subword segmentation using BPE (Sennrich et al., 2016b), with joint subword vocabularies. We experimented with different numbers of BPE operations during training.

2.2 Creation of synthetic parallel data

Data augmentation techniques such as backtranslation (Sennrich et al., 2016a; Edunov et al., 2018), which can be used to produce additional synthetic parallel data from monolingual data, are standard in MT. However they require a sufficiently good intermediate MT model to produce translations that are of reasonable quality to be useful for training (Hoang et al., 2018). This is extremely hard to achieve for this language pair. Our preliminary attempt at parallel-only training yielded a very low BLEU score of 7.8 on the GU→EN development set using a Nematus-trained shallow RNN with heavy regularisation,[5] and similar scores were found for a Moses phrase-based translation system.

Our solution was to train models for the creation of synthetic data that exploit both monolingual and parallel data during training.

2.2.1 Semi-supervised MT with cross-lingual language model pre-training

We followed the unsupervised training approach in (Lample and Conneau, 2019) to train two MT systems, one for EN↔GU and a second for HI→GU.[6] This involves training unsupervised NMT models with an additional supervised MT training step. Initialisation of the models is done by pre-training parameters using a masked language modelling objective as in Bert (Devlin et al., 2019), individually for each language (MLM, which stands for *masked language modelling*) and/or cross-lingually (TLM, which stands for *translation language modelling*). The TLM objective is the MLM objective

---

[4] anoopkunchukuttan.github.io/indic_nlp_library/

[5]Learning rate: 5×10^{-4}, word dropout (Gal and Ghahramani, 2016): 0.3, hidden state and embedding dropout: 0.5, batch tokens: 1000, BPE vocabulary threshold 50, label smoothing: 0.2.

[6]We used the code available at https://github.com/facebookresearch/XLM

applied to the concatenation of parallel sentences. See (Lample and Conneau, 2019) for more details.

2.2.2 EN and GU backtranslation

We trained a single MT model for both language directions EN→GU and GU→EN using this approach. For pre-training we used all available data in Table 2 (both the parallel and monolingual datasets) with MLM and TLM objectives. The same data was then used to train the semi-supervised MT model, which achieved a BLEU score of 22.1 for GU→EN and 12.6 for EN→GU on the dev set (See the first row in Table 5). This model was used to backtranslate 7.3M of monolingual English news data into Gujarati and 5.1M monolingual Gujarati sentences into English.[7]

System and training details We use default architectures for both pre-training and translation: 6 layers with 8 transformer heads, embedding dimensions of 1024. Training parameters are also as per the default: batch size of 32, dropout and attention dropout of 0.1, Adam optimisation (Kingma and Ba, 2015) with a learning rate of 0.0001.

Degree of subword segmentation We tested the impact of varying degrees of subword segmentation on translation quality (See Figure 1). Contrary to our expectation that a higher degree of segmentation (i.e. with a very small number of merge operations) would produce better results, as is often the case with very low resource pairs, the best tested value was 20k joint BPE operations. The reason for this could be the extremely limited shared vocabulary between the two languages[8] or that training on large quantities of monolingual data turns the low resource task into a higher one.

2.2.3 HI→GU translation

Transliteration of Hindi to Gujarati script We first transliterated all of the Hindi characters into Gujarati characters to encourage vocabulary sharing. As there are slightly more Hindi unicode characters than Gujarati, Hindi characters with no corresponding Gujarati characters and all non-Hindi characters were simply copied across.

Once transliterated, there is a high degree of overlap between the transliterated Hindi (HG) and the corresponding Gujarati sentence, which is demonstrated by the example in Figure 2.

[7]We were unable to translate all available monolingual data due to time constraints and limits to GPU resources.

[8]Except for occasional Arabic numbers and romanised proper names in Gujarati texts.

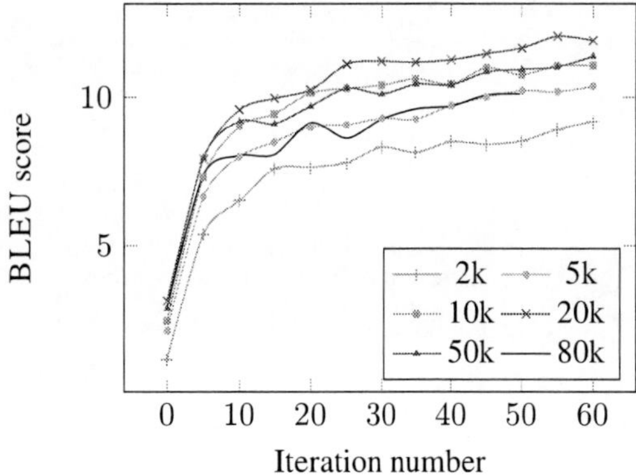

Figure 1: The effect of the number of subword operations on BLEU score during training for EN→GU (calculated on the *newsdev2019* dataset).

Our parallel Gujarati-Hindi data consisted of approximately 8,000 sentences from the Emille corpus. After transliterating the Hindi, we found that 9% of Hindi tokens (excluding punctuation and English words) were an exact match to the corresponding Gujarati tokens. However, we did have access to large quantities of monolingual data in both Gujarati and Hindi (see Table 2), which we pre-processed in the same way.

The semi-supervised HI↔GU system was trained using the MLM pre-training objective described in Section 2.1 and the same model architecture as the EN↔GU model in Section 2.2.2. For the MT step, we trained on 6.5k parallel sentences, reserving the remaining 1.5k as a development set. As with the EN↔GU model, we investigated the effect of different BPE settings (5k, 10k, 20k and 40k merge operations) on the translation quality. Surprisingly, just as with EN↔GU, 20k BPE operations performed best (cf. Table 3), and so we used the model trained in this setting to translate the Hindi side of the IIT Bombay English-Hindi Corpus, which we refer to as HI2GU-EN.

BPE	5k	10k	20k	40k
BLEU	15.4	16.0	16.3	14.6

Table 3: The influence of number of BPE merge operations on HI→GU BLEU score measured using BLEU scores on the development set

2.2.4 Finalisation of training data

The final training data for each model was the concatenation of this parallel data, the HI2GU-EN

105

GU: એમને સાવધાનીપૂર્વક સાફ કરો અને દન્ત ચિકિત્સક ની જોડે નિયમિત જાવો .

HI: उनको सावधानीपूर्वक साफ करें और दन्त चिकित्सक के पास नियमित जायें ।

HG: ઉનકો સાવધાનીપૂર્વક સાફ કરેં ઔર દન્ત ચિકિત્સક કે પાસ નિયમિત જાયેં .

Gloss: THEM CAREFULLY CLEAN DO AND TEETH DOCTOR POSS TO REGULARLY GO .

'Carefully clean them and go to the dentist regularly.'

Figure 2: Illustration of Hindi-to-Gujarati transliteration (we refer to the result as HG), with exact matches indicated in red and partial matches in blue.

translated data and the back-translated data for that particular translation direction (See Table 4).

All synthetic data was cleaned by filtering out noisy sentences with consecutively repeated characters or tokens. As for the genuine parallel data, we choose only to use the following corpora, which contain an average sentence length of 10 tokens or more: Emille, Govin, Wikipedia and the Bible (a total of approximately 40k sentences). All data was pre-processed using FastBPE[9] with 30k BPE merge operations.

Training data source	#sents	
	EN→GU	GU→EN
Genuine parallel data	42k	42k
HI2GU-EN parallel data	1.1M	1.1M
Backtranslated monolingual	4.5M	7.1M
Total	5.6M	8.2M

Table 4: Summary of EN→GU and GU→EN training data, once filtering has been applied to synthetic data.

2.3 Supervised MT training

We trained supervised RNN (Miceli Barone et al., 2017) and transformer models (Vaswani et al., 2017) using the augmented parallel data augmented described in Section 2.2.4. For both model types, we train until convergence and then fine-tuned them on the 40k sentences of genuine parallel data, since synthetic parallel data accounted for more than 99% of total training data in both translation directions. Results are shown in Table 5, our final model results being shown in bold.

2.3.1 RNN

Our RNN submission was a BiDeep GRU sequence-to-sequence model (Miceli Barone et al., 2017) with multi-head attention. The implementation and configuration are the same as in our submission to WMT 2018 (Haddow et al., 2018), except that we use 1 attention hop with 4 attention

heads, with a linear projection to dimension 256 followed by layer normalisation. Other model hyperparameters are encoder and decoder stacking depth: 2, encoder transition depth: 2, decoder base level transition depth: 4, decoder second level transition depth: 2, embedding dimension: 512, hidden state dimension: 1024. Training is performed with Adam in synchronous SGD mode with initial learning rate: 3×10^{-4}, label smoothing 0.1, attention dropout 0.1 and hidden state dropout 0.1. For the final fine-tuning on parallel data we increase the learning rate to 9×10^{-4} and hidden state dropout to 0.4 in order to reduce over-fitting.

2.3.2 Transformer

We trained **transformer base** models as defined in (Vaswani et al., 2017), consisting of 6 encoder layers, 6 decoder layers, 8 heads, with a model/embedding dimension of 512 and feedforward network dimension of 2048.

We used synchronous SGD, a learning rate of 3×10^{-4} and a learning rate warm-up of 16,000. We used a transformer dropout of 0.1.

Our final primary systems are ensembles of four transformers, trained using different random seed initialisations. We also experimented with adjusting the weighting of the models,[10] providing gains for EN→GU but not for GU→EN, for which equal weighting provided the best results. Our final translations are produced using a beam of 12 for EN→GU and 60 for GU→EN.

2.4 Experiments and results

We report results in Table 5 on the official development set (1998 sentences) and on the official test sets (998 sentences for EN→GU and 1016 sentences for GU→EN). Our results indicate that both the additional synthetic data as well as fine-tuning provide a significant boost in BLEU.

---

[9]github.com/glample/fastBPE.git

[10]The weights for EN→GU the were manually chosen guided by the individual BLEU scores of the models.

System	EN→GU		GU→EN	
	Dev	Test	Dev	Test
Semi-sup.	12.6	11.8	22.1	15.5
RNN				
+ synth. data	14.2	11.4	23.4	14.7
+ fine-tuning	15.2	11.7	24.3	15.7
Transformer				
+ synth. data	15.0	14.3	23.8	18.6
+ fine-tuning	16.9	15.1	25.9	20.6
+ Ensemble-4	17.9	16.5	27.2	**21.4**
+ Weighted Ensemble	18.1	**16.4**	-	-

Table 5: BLEU scores on the development and test sets for EN→GU. Our final submissions are marked in bold. Synthetic data is the HI2GU-EN corpus plus backtranslated data for that translation direction and fine-tuning is performed on 40k sentences of genuine parallel data.

3 Chinese ↔ English

Chinese↔English is a high resource language pair with 23.5M sentences of parallel data. The language pair also benefits from a large amount of monolingual data, although compared to English, there is relatively little in-domain (i.e. news) data for Chinese. Our aim for this year's submission was to test the use of character-based segmentation of Chinese compared to standard subword segmentation, exploiting the properties of the Chinese writing system.

3.1 Data and pre-processing

For ZH↔EN we pre-processed the parallel data, which consists of NewsCommentary v13, UN data and CWMT, as follows. The Chinese side of the original parallel data is inconsistently segmented across different corpora so in order to get a consistent segmentation, we desegmented all the Chinese data and resegmented it using the Jieba tokeniser with the default dictionary.[11] We then removed any sentences that did not contain Chinese characters on the Chinese side or contained only Chinese characters on the English side. We also cleaned up all sentences containing links, sentences longer than 50 words, as well as sentences in which the number of tokens on either side was > 1.3 times the number of tokens on the other side, following Haddow et al. (2018). After pre-processing, the corpus size was 23.6M sentences. We applied BPE with 32,000 merge operations to the English side of the corpora and then removed any tokens appearing fewer than 10 times (which were mostly noise),

ending up with a vocabulary size of 32,626. For the Chinese side we attempted two different strategies: A character-level BPE model and a word-level BPE model.

Character-level Chinese A Chinese character-level model is not the same as an English character level model, as it is relatively common for Chinese characters to represent whole words by themselves (in the PKU corpus used for the 2005 Chinese segmentation bakeoff (Emerson, 2005), a Chinese word contains on average 1.6 characters). As such, a Chinese character-level model is much more similar to using a BPE model with very few merge operations on English. We hypothesised that using raw Chinese characters in tokenised text makes sense as they form natural subword units.

We segmented all Chinese sentences into characters, but kept non-Chinese characters unsegmented in order to allow for English words and numbers to be kept together as individual units. We then applied BPE with 1,000 merges, which splits the English words in the corpora into mostly trigrams and numbers as bigrams. From the resulting vocabulary we dropped characters occurring fewer than 10 times, resulting in a vocabulary of size 8,535.

We found that this segmentation strategy was successful for translating into Chinese, however produces significantly worse results when translating from Chinese into English.

Word-level Chinese For word-level Chinese, we took the traditional approach to Chinese pre-processing, where we applied BPE on top of the tokenised dataset. We used 33,000 merge operations and removed tokens occurring fewer than 10 times, resulting in a vocabulary size of 44,529.

3.2 Iterative backtranslation

We augmented our parallel data with the same backtranslated ZH↔EN as used in Sennrich et al. (2017), which consists of 8.6M sentences for EN→ZH from LDC and 9.7M sentences taken from Newscrawl for ZH→EN. After training the initial systems, we added more backtranslations for both language pairs. For the Chinese side, we used Newscrawl (2.1M sentences) as well as a re-translation of a section of LDC, ending up with 9.5M sentences. For the English side we translated an additional section of Newscrawl, ending up 38M sentences in total. Much to our disappointment, we found that the extra backtranslation is not very effective at increasing the BLEU score, likely because we did not perform any specific domain adaptation for the news domain.

3.3 Architecture

We used the transformer architecture and three separate configurations.

Transformer-base   This is the same architecture as described in Section 2.3.2.

Transformer-big   6 encoder layers, 6 decoder layers decoder, 16 heads, a model/embedding dimension of 1024, a feedforward network dimension of 4096 and a dropout of 0.1. For character-level Chinese, the number of layers was increased to 8 on the Chinese side. We found transformer-big to be quite fiddly to train and requires significant hyperparameter exploration. Unfortunately we were unable to find hyperparameters that work effectively for the ZH-EN direction.

Transfomer-base with larger feed-forward network   We test Wang et al.'s (2018) recommendation to use the base transformer architecture and increase the feed-forward network (FFNN) size to 4096 instead of using a transformer-big model.

Ultra-large mini-batches   We follow Smith et al.'s (2018) recommendation to dramatically increase the mini-batch size towards the end of training in order to improve convergence.[12] Once our model stopped improving on the development set, we increased the mini-batch size 50-fold by delaying the gradient update (Bogoychev et al., 2018) to avoid running into memory issues. This increases the average mini-batch size to 13,500 words.

3.4 Results

We identified the best single system for each language direction (Tables 6 and 7) and ensembled four models trained separately using different random seeds. We also trained right-to-left models, but they got lower scores on the development set and also did not seem to help with ensembling. Our final submission to the competition achieved 28.9 for ZH→EN and 34.4 for EN→ZH.

4   German → English

Following the success of Edunov et al. (2018) in WMT18, we decided to focus on the use of large amounts of monolingual data in the target language.

System	BLEU
Word-level segmentation for ZH	
Transformer-base	34.8
Character-level segmentation for ZH	
Transformer-base	35.1
+ Larger FFNN	35.6
Transformer-big	35.7
+ Ultra-large mini-batches	36.1

Table 6: EN→ZH results on the development set.

System	BLEU
Word-level segmentation for ZH	
Transformer-base	24.1
+ Larger FFNN	23.7
+ Ultra-large mini-batches	24.4
+ Ultra-large mini-batches	24.2
Transformer-big	11.3
Character-level segmentation for ZH	
Transformer-base	20.4

Table 7: ZH→EN results on the development set.

In addition, we performed fine tuning on data selected specifically for the test set prior to translation, similar to the method suggested by Farajian et al. (2017), but with data selection for the entire test set instead of individual sentences.

4.1   Approach

Our approach this year is summarised as follows.

1. Back-translate all available mono-lingual English NewsCrawl data (after filtering out very long sentences). As can be seen in Table 8, the amount of monolingual data vastly outweighs the amount of parallel data available.

2. Train multiple systems with different blends of genuine parallel, out-of-domain data and back-translated in-domain data.   We did not use any data from CommonCrawl or Paracrawl to train these base models.

3. For a given test set, select suitable training data from the pool of all available training data (including CommonCrawl and Paracrawl) for fine-tuning, based on n-gram overlap with the source side of the test set, focusing on rare n-grams that occur fewer than 50 times in the respective sub-corpus[13] of training data.

---

[12] We thank Elena Voita for alerting us to this work.

[13] For practical reasons, we sharded the training data based on provenance. In addition, each year of the backtranslated news data was treated as a separate sub-corpus.

Corpus	Type	# of sent. pairs	# of tokens[1] (DE)	# of tokens (EN)
Europarl v9	parallel	1.82 M	48.66 M	51.15 M
Rapid 2019	parallel	1.48 M	30.56 M	30.95 M
News Commentary	parallel	0.33 M	8.51 M	8.51 M
CommonCrawl[1]				
as distributed	parallel	2.40 M	56.87 M	60.83 M
filtered	parallel	0.87 M	19.54 M	20.23 M
ParaCrawl v3[2]				
as distributed	parallel	31.36 M	596.66 M	630.50 M
filtered	parallel	16.66 M	328.14 M	343.68 M
News Crawl 2007–2018	English[3]	199.74 M	4,764.26 M	4,805.45 M

[1] continuous sequences of letters, digits, or repetitions of the same symbol; otherwise, a single symbol.
[2] used for fine-tuning but not for training the base models, filtered as described in Section 4.4.
[3] German side obtained by back-translation with a model from our participation in WMT18.

Table 8: Training data used for German→English translation.

4. Finally, we translate with an ensemble over several check-points of the same training run (best BLEU prior to fine-tuning, fine-tuned, best mean cross-entropy per word if different from best BLEU, etc.).

4.2 Data Preparation

4.2.1 Tokenisation Scheme

For tokenisation and sub-word segmentation, we used SentencePiece[14] (Kudo and Richardson, 2018) with the BPE segmentation scheme and a joint vocabulary of 32,000 items.

4.3 Back-translation

We back-translated all of the available English NewsCrawl data using one of the models from our participation in the WMT18 shared task.

4.4 Data Filtering

The CommonCrawl and ParaCrawl datasets consist of parallel data automatically extracted from web pages from systematic internet crawls. These datasets contain considerable amounts of noise and poor quality data. We used dual conditional cross-entropy filtering (Junczys-Dowmunt, 2018) to rank the data in terms of estimated translation quality, and only retained data that scored higher than a threshold determined by cursory inspection of the data by a competent bilingual at various threshold levels. Table 8 shows the amounts of raw and filtered data. For training, we limited the training data to sentence pairs of at most 120 SentencePiece tokens on either side (source or target).

4.5 Model Training

4.5.1 Initial Training

To investigate the effect of the blend of genuine parallel and back-translated news data on translation quality, we trained five transformer-big models (cf. Section 3.3) with different blends of back-translated and genuine parallel data.

We used a dropout value of 0.1 between transformer layers and no dropout for attention and transformer filters. We used the Adam optimiser with a learning rate of 0.0002 and linear warm-up for the first 8K updates, followed by inverted squared decay.

Figure 3 shows the learning curves for these five initial training runs as validated against the WMT18 test set. Note that the BLEU scores are inflated, as they were computed on the sub-word units rather than on de-tokenised output. The curves suggest that adding large amounts of training data does improve translation quality in direct comparison between the different training runs. However, compared to last year's top system submissions, these systems were still lagging behind.

4.5.2 Continued training with increased batch size

Similar to our EN↔ZH experiments, we experiment with drastically increasing the mini-batch size by increasing optimiser delay (cf. Section 3.3). Figure 4 shows the effect of increased mini-batch sizes of ca. 9K, 13K, and 22K sentence pairs, respectively. The plot shows drastic improvements in the validation scores achieved.

[14] https://github.com/google/sentencepiece

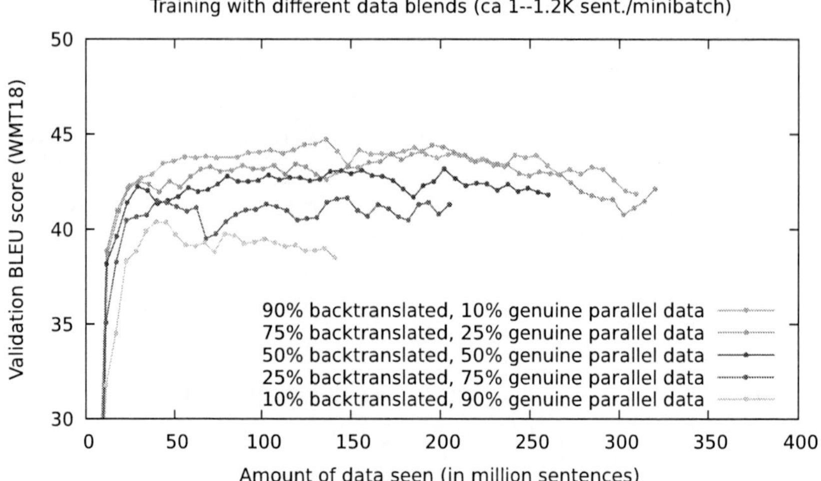

Figure 3: Learning curve for different blends of genuine parallel and synthetic back-translated data. Note that the BLEU scores are inflated with respect to SACREBLEU as they are calculated on BPE-segmented data.

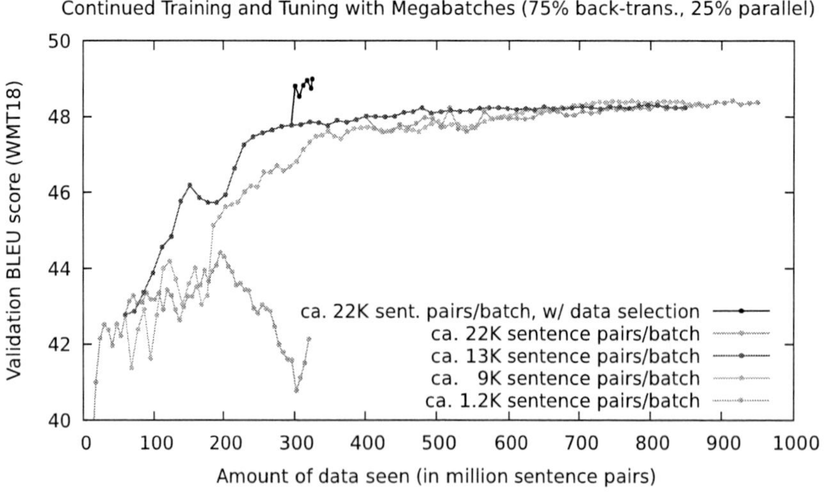

Figure 4: Effect of increased batch size for training and of tuning on data selected for the test set. The red line shows the learning curve for the original training settings (mini-batches of ca. 1,200 sentence pairs). The other lines are the learning curves for models that were initialised with the model parameters of another model at some point in its training process (specifically: at the point where the new learning curve branches off), and then trained with increased batch sizes on the same data (blue and magenta lines), or on data specifically selected to contain rare n-grams that also occur in the test / validation set.

4.5.3 Fine-tuning on selected data

As a last step, we selected data specifically for the test set and continued training on this data for one epoch of this data. For the WMT18 test set, this gives a significant boost over the starting point, as the black line in Figure 4 shows.

4.6 Results and Analysis

Due to resource congestion, we were not able to train our models to convergence in time for submission. The point where the black line in Figure 4 branches off shows the state of our models prior to tuning for a specific test set.

For our submission to the shared task, we ensembled four models:

- an untuned model trained on a blend of 75% back-translated data and 25% genuine parallel data

- checkpoint models after 500, 2000, and 3000 updates with batches of ca. 13K sentences on data selected specifically for the WMT19 test set. This data included data from Common-Crawl and Paracrawl.

With a BLEU score of 36.7 (35.0 cased) — as opposed to 44.3 (42.8 cased) for the top-performing system — our results were disappointing. Apart from a probably suboptimal choice of training hyperparameters, what else went wrong?

Post-submission analysis In order to understand the effect of back-translations better, we evaluated our systems on a split of test sets from past years into "forward" (German is the original source language) and "reverse" (the source side of the test set are German translations of texts originally written in English). The results are shown in Table 9. As we can see, most of the gains from using back-translations are concentrated in the "reverse" section of the test sets. The same also holds for Edunov et al.'s (2018) results on the WMT18 test sets for en→de. Notice how it outperforms the top-performing system (Microsoft Marian) on the reverse translation direction but lags behind in the forward translation.[15]

We see two possible reasons for this phenomenon. The first is that back-translations produce synthetic data that is closer to the reverse

scenario: translating back from the translation into the source. The second reason is that the reverse scenario offers a better domain match: newspapers tend to report relatively more on events and issues relating to their local audience. A newspaper in Munich will report on matters relating to Munich; the Los Angeles time will focus on matters of interest to people living in Southern California.

This became evident when we investigated some strange translation errors that we observed in our submission to the shared task. For example, our system often translates "Münchnerin" (woman from Munich) as 'miner', 'minder', or 'mint' and "Schrebergarten" (allotment garden) as 'shrine' (German: Schrein). When we checked our back-translated training data for evidence, we noticed that these are systematic translation errors in our back-translations. While the word "Münchnerin" is frequent in our German data, women from Munich are rarely mentioned as such in English newspapers. With BPE breaking up rare words into smaller units, the system learned to translate "min" (possibly from "min|t" (as in the production facility for coins), which is "Mün|ze" or "Mün|zprägeanstalt" in German) into "Mün". Once "Mün" was chosen in the decoder of the MT system, the German language model favored the sequence *Mün|ch|nerin* over *Mün|ze* or the even rarer *Münzprägeanstalt*.

These findings suggest that back-translated data as well needs curation for domain match and systematic translation errors.

Since this year's test sets consist only of the (more realistic) "forward" scenario, we were not able to replicate the gains we observed for previous test sets when adding more back-translated data.

5 English → Czech

English-Czech is a high-resource language pair in the WMT News Translation shared task. For our submission to the EN→CS track, we investigated the effects of simplifying the data pre-processing and training data filtering, and experimented with larger architectures of the Transformer model.

5.1 Data and pre-processing

For English→Czech experiments we use all parallel corpora available to build a constrained system except CommonCrawl, which is noisy and relatively small compared to the CzEng 1.7 corpus[16]

---

[15]We thank Barry Haddow for pointing this out to us and for providing us with the split test sets and the split numbers for the Microsoft and Facebook systems.

[16]`https://ufal.mff.cuni.cz/czeng/czeng17`

| | | WMT15 | | WMT16 | | WMT17 | | WMT18 | |
System	batch[1]	fwd	rev	fwd	rev	fwd	rev	fwd	rev
10% back-translated, 90% parallel	1.2K	20.4	34.9	27.7	44.4	25.1	37.8	28.5	46.7
25% back-translated, 75% parallel	1.2K	20.0	37.7	27.5	47.5	24.9	39.8	27.5	49.4
50% back-translated, 50% parallel	1.2K	20.2	38.3	28.2	48.8	25.9	40.8	28.3	51.3
75% back-translated, 25% parallel	1.2K	20.9	39.0	29.4	49.7	26.6	41.7	29.6	52.4
90% back-translated, 10% parallel	1.2K	21.2	38.6	29.0	49.6	26.8	41.5	29.7	52.8
75% back-translated, 25% parallel	1.2K	20.9	39.0	29.4	49.7	26.6	41.7	29.6	52.4
75% back-translated, 25% parallel	9K	23.2	41.2	31.8	51.8	28.7	44.2	32.6	56.3
75% back-translated, 25% parallel	13K	23.2	40.9	31.8	51.3	28.6	44.1	32.4	56.2
75% back-translated, 25% parallel	22K	23.2	41.2	31.8	51.3	28.7	44.2	32.4	56.2
75/25, with tuning for WMT18	22K	23.6	41.3	32.5	51.6	28.9	44.0	33.2	56.7
Microsoft Marian 2018 (en→de)								52.5	41.6
Edunov et al. (2018) (en→de)								45.8	46.1

[1] batch size in sentence pairs

Table 9: Contrastive evaluation (BLEU scores) of performance on genuine German → English (fwd) translation vs. English source restoration from text originally translated from English into German (rev).

(Bojar et al., 2016). We clean the data following Popel (2018) by removing sentence pairs that do not contain at least one Czech diacritic letter. Duplicated sentences, sentences with <3 or >200 tokens, and sentences with the ratio of alphabetic to non-alphabetic characters <0.5 are also removed. The final parallel training data contains 44.93M sentences. For back-translation we use approximately 80M English and Czech monolingual sentences from NewsCrawl (Bojar et al., 2018), which we cleaned in a similar manner.

Preprocessing	Dev	2017	2018
Tc + Tok + BPE	26.8	23.0	22.2
Tc + Tok + ULM	26.7	22.9	22.3
ULM (raw text)	26.7	22.9	**22.9**
+ Resampling	26.7	22.2	21.8

Table 10: Comparison of different pre-processing pipelines for EN→CS according to BLEU. *Tc* stands for truecasing, *Tok* for tokenisation.

We aimed to explore whether, in a high-resource setting, the common pre- and post-processing pipelines that usually include truecasing, tokenisation and subword segmentation using byte pair encoding (BPE) (Sennrich et al., 2016b) can be simplified with no loss to performance. We replace BPE with the segmentation algorithm based on a Unigram Language Model (ULM) from Sentence-Piece, which is built into Marian. In both cases we learn 32k subword units jointly on 10M sampled English and Czech sentences. We gradually remove the elements of the pipeline and find no significant difference between the two segmentation algorithms (Table 10). We do observe a performance drop when subword resampling is used, but this has been shown to be more effective particularly for Asian languages (Kudo, 2018). For the following English-Czech experiments, we use ULM segmentation on raw text.

5.2 Experiment settings

We use the transformer-base and transformer-big architectures described in Section 3.3. Models are regularised with dropout between transformer layers of 0.2 and in attention of 0.1 and feed-forward layers of 0.1, label smoothing and exponential smoothing: 0.1 and 0.0001 respectively. We optimise with Adam with a learning rate of 0.0003 and linear warm-up for first 16k updates, followed by inverted squared decay. For Transformer Big models we decrease the learning rate to 0.0002. We use mini-batches dynamically fitted into 48GB of GPU memory on 4 GPUs and delay gradient updates to every second iteration, which results in mini-batches of 1-1.2k sentences. We use early stopping with a patience of 5 based on the word-level cross-entropy on the *newsdev2016* data set. Each model is validated every 5k updates, and we use the best model checkpoint according to uncased BLEU score.

Decoding is performed with beam search with a beam size of 6 with length normalisation. Additionally, we reconstruct Czech quotation marks using regular expressions as the only post-processing step (Popel, 2018).

5.3 Experiments and Results

Results of our models are shown in Table 11.

Lang.	System	Dev	2017	2018
EN-CS	Transformer-base	26.7	22.9	22.9
	+ Data filtering	27.1	23.4	22.6
CS-EN	Transformer-base	32.6	28.8	30.3
	+ Back-translation	37.3	31.9	32.4
EN-CS	Base + Back-transl.	28.4	25.1	25.1
	$\rightarrow$ Transformer-big	29.6	26.3	26.2
	+ Ensemble x2	29.6	26.5	26.3

Table 11: BLEU score results for EN-CS experiments.

We first trained single transformer-base models for each language direction to serve as our baselines. We then re-score the EN$\rightarrow$CS training data using the CS$\rightarrow$EN model and filter out the 5% of data with the worst cross-entropy scores, which is a one-directional version of the dual conditional cross-entropy filtering, which we also used for our EN$\rightarrow$DE experiments. This improves the BLEU scores on the development set and *newstest2017*. Next, we back-translate English monolingual data and train a CS$\rightarrow$EN model, which in turn is used to generate back-translations for our final systems. The addition of back-translated data improves the Transformer Base model by 1.7-2.5 BLEU, which is less than the improvement from iterative back-translations reported by (Popel, 2018). A Transformer Big model trained on the same data is ca. 1.1 BLEU better.

Due to time and resource constraints we train and submit a EN$\rightarrow$CS system (this was the only language direction for English-Czech this year) consisting of just two transformer-big models trained with back-translated data. Our system achieves 28.3 BLEU on *newstest2019*, 2.1 BLEU less then the top system, which ranks it in third position.

6   Summary

This paper reports the experiments run in developing the six systems submitted by the University Edinburgh to the 2019 WMT news translation shared task. Our main contributions have been in different exploitation of additional non-parallel resources, in investigating different pre-processing strategies and in the testing of a variety of NMT training techniques. We have shown the value of using additional monolingual resources through pre-training and semi-supervised MT for our low-resource language pair EN-GU. For the higher resource language pairs, we also exploit monolingual resources in the form of backtranslation. For GU$\rightarrow$EN in particular we study the effect on translation quality of varying the ratio between between genuine and synthetic parallel training data. For EN$\rightarrow$ZH, we showed that character-based decoding into Chinese produces better results than the standard subword segmentation approach. In EN$\rightarrow$CS, we also studied the effects of pre-processing, by showing that in such a high resource setting, a simplified pre-processing pipeline can be highly successful.

Our low resource language pairs, EN$\rightarrow$GU and GU$\rightarrow$EN systems were ranked 1st and 2nd respectively out of the constrained systems according to the automatic evaluation. For the high resource pairs, our EN$\rightarrow$CS system ranked 3rd, EN$\rightarrow$ZH and ZH$\rightarrow$EN ranked 7th and 6th respectively and DE$\rightarrow$EN ranked 9th.

Acknowledgements

This work was supported by funding from the European Union's Horizon 2020 research and innovation programme under grant agreements No 825299 (GoURMET), 825303 (Bergamot), and 825627 (European Language Grid).

It was also supported by the UK Engineering and Physical Sciences Research Council (EPSRC) fellowship grant EP/S001271/1 (MTStretch).

It was performed using resources provided by the Cambridge Service for Data Driven Discovery (CSD3) operated by the University of Cambridge Research Computing Service (http://www.csd3.cam.ac.uk/), provided by Dell EMC and Intel using Tier-2 funding from the Engineering and Physical Sciences Research Council (capital grant EP/P020259/1), and DiRAC funding from the Science and Technology Facilities Council (www.dirac.ac.uk).

We express our warmest thanks to Kenneth Heafield, who provided us with access to the computing resources.

References

Nikolay Bogoychev, Marcin Junczys-Dowmunt, Kenneth Heafield, and Alham Fikri Aji. 2018. Accelerating asynchronous stochastic gradient descent for neural machine translation. In *Proceedings of the 2018 Conference on Empirical Methods in Natural Language Processing*, EMNLP'18, pages 2991–2996, Brussels, Belgium.

Ondřej Bojar, Ondřej Dušek, Tom Kocmi, Jindřich Libovický, Michal Novák, Martin Popel, Roman Sudarikov, and Dušan Variš. 2016. CzEng 1.6: Enlarged Czech-English Parallel Corpus with Processing Tools Dockered. In *Text, Speech, and Dialogue: 19th International Conference, TSD 2016*, number 9924 in Lecture Notes in Computer Science, pages 231–238, Brno, Czech Republic.

Ondřej Bojar, Christian Federmann, Mark Fishel, Yvette Graham, Barry Haddow, Matthias Huck, Philipp Koehn, and Christof Monz. 2018. Findings of the 2018 Conference on Machine Translation (WMT18). In *Proceedings of the 3rd Conference on Machine Translation, Volume 2: Shared Task Papers*, WMT'18, pages 272–307, Belgium, Brussels.

Jacob Devlin, Ming-Wei Chang, Kenton Lee, and Kristina Toutanova. 2019. Bert: Pre-training of deep bidirectional transformers for language understanding. In *Proceedings of the 2019 Conference of the North American Chapter of the Association for Computational Linguistics; Human Language Technologies*, NAACL-HLT'19, Minneapolis, Minnesota.

Sergey Edunov, Myle Ott, Michael Auli, and David Grangier. 2018. Understanding Back-Translation at Scale. In *Proceedings of the 2018 Conference on Empirical Methods in Natural Language Processing*, EMNLP'18, pages 489–500, Brussels, Belgium.

Thomas Emerson. 2005. The Second International Chinese Word Segmentation Bakeoff. In *Proceedings of the 4th SIGHAN Workshop on Chinese Language Processing*, Jeju Island, Korea.

M. Amin Farajian, Marco Turchi, Matteo Negri, and Marcello Federico. 2017. Multi-domain neural machine translation through unsupervised adaptation. In *Proceedings of the 2nd Conference on Machine Translation*, pages 127–137, Copenhagen, Denmark. Association for Computational Linguistics.

Yarin Gal and Zoubin Ghahramani. 2016. A theoretically grounded application of dropout in recurrent neural networks. In *Advances in Neural Information Processing Systems*, pages 1019–1027.

Barry Haddow, Nikolay Bogoychev, Denis Emelin, Ulrich Germann, Roman Grundkiewicz, Kenneth Heafield, Antonio Valerio Miceli Barone, and Rico Sennrich. 2018. The University of Edinburgh's Submissions to the WMT18 News Translation Task. In *Proceedings of the 3rd Conference on Machine Translation*, WMT'18, pages 399–409, Brussels, Belgium.

Cong Duy Vu Hoang, Philipp Koehn, Gholamreza Haffari, and Trevor Cohn. 2018. Iterative Back-Translation for Neural Machine Translation. In *Proceedings of the 2nd Workshop on Neural Machine Translation and Generation*, WNMT'18, pages 18–24, Melbourne, Australia.

Marcin Junczys-Dowmunt. 2018. Microsoft's submission to the WMT2018 news translation task: How I learned to stop worrying and love the data. In *Proceedings of the Third Conference on Machine Translation: Shared Task Papers*, pages 425–430, Belgium, Brussels. Association for Computational Linguistics.

Marcin Junczys-Dowmunt, Roman Grundkiewicz, Tomasz Dwojak, Hieu Hoang, Kenneth Heafield, Tom Neckermann, Frank Seide, Ulrich Germann, Alham Fikri Aji, Nikolay Bogoychev, André F. T. Martins, and Alexandra Birch. 2018. Marian: Fast Neural Machine Translation in C++. In *Proceedings of the 56th Annual Meeting of the Association for Computational Linguistics*, ACL'18, pages 116–121, Melbourne, Australia.

Diederik Kingma and Jimmy Ba. 2015. Adam: A method for stochastic optimization. In *Proceedings of the 3rd International Conference on Learning Representations*, ICLR'15, San Diego, California, USA.

Philipp Koehn, Hieu Hoang, Alexandra Birch, Chris Callison-Burch, Marcello Federico, Nicola Bertoldi, Brooke Cowan, Wade Shen, Christine Moran, Richard Zens, Chris Dyer, Ondřej Bojar, Alexandra Constantin, and Evan Herbst. 2007. Moses: Open Source Toolkit for Statistical Machine Translation. In *Proceedings of the 45th Annual Meeting of the Association for Computational Linguistics*, ACL'07, pages 177–180, Prague, Czech Republic.

Taku Kudo. 2018. Subword regularization: Improving neural network translation models with multiple subword candidates. In *Proceedings of the 56th Annual Meeting of the Association for Computational Linguistics (Volume 1: Long Papers)*, pages 66–75, Melbourne, Australia. Association for Computational Linguistics.

Taku Kudo and John Richardson. 2018. SentencePiece: A simple and language independent subword tokenizer and detokenizer for neural text processing. In *Proceedings of the 2018 Conference on Empirical Methods in Natural Language Processing: System Demonstrations*, pages 66–71, Brussels, Belgium.

Guillaume Lample and Alexis Conneau. 2019. Cross-lingual Language Model Pretraining. In *arXiv:1901.07291*.

Guillaume Lample, Myle Ott, Alexis Conneau, Ludovic Denoyer, and Marc'Aurelio Ranzato. 2018. Phrase-Based & Neural Unsupervised Machine Translation. In *Proceedings of the 2018 Conference on Empirical Methods in Natural Language Processing*, EMNLP'18, pages 5039–5049, Brussels, Belgium.

Antonio Valerio Miceli Barone, Jindřich Helcl, Rico Sennrich, Barry Haddow, and Alexandra Birch. 2017. Deep Architectures for Neural Machine Translation. In *Proceedings of the 2nd Conference on Machine Translation, Volume 1: Research Papers*, Copenhagen, Denmark. Association for Computational Linguistics.

Martin Popel. 2018. CUNI transformer neural mt system for WMT18. In *Proceedings of the Third Conference on Machine Translation, Volume 2: Shared Task Papers*, pages 486–491, Belgium, Brussels. Association for Computational Linguistics.

Matt Post. 2018. A call for clarity in reporting BLEU scores. In *Proceedings of the 3rd Conference on Machine Translation: Research Papers*, pages 186–191, Belgium, Brussels.

Rico Sennrich, Alexandra Birch, Anna Currey, Ulrich Germann, Barry Haddow, Kenneth Heafield, Antonio Valerio Miceli Barone, and Philip Williams. 2017. The University of Edinburgh's Neural MT Systems for WMT17. In *Proceedings of the 2nd Conference on Machine Translation, Volume 2: Shared Task Papers*, pages 389–399, Copenhagen, Denmark.

Rico Sennrich, Barry Haddow, and Alexandra Birch. 2016a. Improving Neural Machine Translation Models with Monolingual Data. In *Proceedings of the 54th Annual Meeting of the Association for Computational Linguistics*, ACL'16, pages 86–96, Berlin, Germany.

Rico Sennrich, Barry Haddow, and Alexandra Birch. 2016b. Neural Machine Translation of Rare Words with Subword Units. In *Proceedings of the 54th Annual Meeting of the Association for Computational Linguistics*, ACL'16, pages 1715–1725, Berlin, Germany.

Samuel L. Smith, Pieter-Jan Kindermans, Chris Ying, and Quoc V. Le. 2018. Don't decay the learning rate, increase the batch size. In *Proceedings of the 6th International Conference on Learning Representations*, ICLR'18, Vancouver, Canada.

Ashish Vaswani, Noam Shazeer, Niki Parmar, Jakob Uszkoreit, Llion Jones, Aidan N. Gomez, Łukasz Kaiser, and Illia Polosukhin. 2017. Attention is all you need. In *Advances in Neural Information Processing Systems 30*, pages 5998–6008. Curran Associates, Inc.

Qiang Wang, Bei Li, Jiqiang Liu, Bojian Jiang, Zheyang Zhang, Yinqiao Li, Ye Lin, Tong Xiao, and Jingbo Zhu. 2018. The NiuTrans Machine Translation System for WMT18. In *Proceedings of the 3rd Conference on Machine Translation: Shared Task Papers*, WMT'18, pages 528–534, Belgium, Brussels.

GTCOM Neural Machine Translation Systems for WMT19

Chao Bei, Hao Zong, Conghu Yuan, Qingming Liu, Baoyong Fan

Global Tone Communication Technology Co., Ltd.

{beichao, zonghao, yuanconghu, liuqingming, fanbaoyong}@gtcom.com.cn

Abstract

This paper describes the Global Tone Communication Co., Ltd.'s submission of the WMT19 shared news translation task. We participate in six directions: English to (Gujarati, Lithuanian and Finnish) and (Gujarati, Lithuanian and Finnish) to English. Further, we get the best BLEU scores in the directions of English to Gujarati and Lithuanian to English (28.2 and 36.3 respectively) among all the participants. The submitted systems mainly focus on back-translation, knowledge distillation and reranking to build a competitive model for this task. Also, we apply language model to filter monolingual data, back-translated data and parallel data. The techniques we apply for data filtering include filtering by rules, language models. Besides, We conduct several experiments to validate different knowledge distillation techniques and right-to-left (R2L) reranking.

1 Introduction

We participated in the WMT shared news translation task and focus on the bidirections: English and Gujarati, English and Lithuanian, as well as English and Finnish. Our neural machine translation system is developed as transformer (Vaswani et al., 2017a) architecture and the toolkit we used is Marian (Junczys-Dowmunt et al., 2018). Since BLEU (Papineni et al., 2002) is the main ranking index for all submitted systems, we apply BLEU as the evaluation matrix for our translation system. In addition to data filtering, which is basically the same as the techniques we applied in WMT 2018 last year, we verify different knowledge distillation and reranking techniques to improve the performance of all our systems.

For data preprocessing, the basic methods include punctuation normalization, tokenization, truecase and byte pair encoding(BPE) (Sennrich et al., 2015b). Besides, human rules and language

model are also involved to clean English parallel data, monolingual data and synthetic data. Regard to the techniques on model training, back-translation (Sennrich et al., 2015a), knowledge distillation and R2L reranking (Sennrich et al., 2016) are applied to verify whether these techniques could improve the performance of our systems.

In order to explore the application of knowledge distillation technology in the field of neural machine translation, we conduct a number of experiments for sequence-level knowledge distillation and sequence-level interpolation (Kim and Rush, 2016). Another, R2L reranking didn't get the better performance in last year experiment. In order to improve the performance of R2L reranking, we increase the beam size step by step, and explore the effect of any combination for R2L models with every step.

This paper is arranged as follows. We firstly describe the task and provided data information, then introduce the method of data filtering, mainly in the application of language model. After that, we describe the techniques on transformer architecture and show the conducted experiments in detail of all directions, including data preprocessing, model architecture, back-translation and knowledge distillation. At last, we analyze the results of experiments and draw the conclusion.

2 Task Description

The task focuses on bilingual text translation in news domain and the provided data is show in Table 1, including parallel data and monolingual data. For the direction between English and Lithuanian, the parallel data is mainly from Europarl v9, ParaCrawl v3, Wiki Titles v1 and Rapid corpus of EU press releases (Rozis and Skadiņš, 2017). For the direction between English

Proceedings of the Fourth Conference on Machine Translation (WMT), Volume 2: Shared Task Papers (Day 1) pages 116–121
Florence, Italy, August 1-2, 2019. ©2019 Association for Computational Linguistics

direction	number of sentence
en-lt parallel data	4.21M
en-gu parallel data	155K
en-fi parallel data	9.17M
en monolingual data	18M
lt monolingual data	3.09M
gu monolingual data	4.35M
fi monolingual data	18M
en-gu unconstrained data	4.63M

Table 1: Task Description.

direction	number of cleaned data
en-lt parallel data	4.08M
en-gu parallel data	77K
en-fi parallel data	9M
en monolingual data	17.6M
lt monolingual data	2.92M
gu monolingual data	4.28M
fi monolingual data	15M
en-gu unconstrained data	4.55M

Table 2: Number of cleaned data.

and Gujarati the parallel data is from Wiki Titles v1, Bible Corpus, OPUS (Tiedemann, 2012) and govin crawled corpus, as well as our own parallel data. Thus, this direction is unconstrained. The Corpus, from Europarl v9, ParaCrawl v3, Wiki Titles v1 and Rapid corpus of EU press releases, are used to the directions between English and Finnish. Another, monolingual data we used are News crawl, Europarl and Europarl v9. All directions we participated are new for this year, we use newsdev2019 as our development set.

3 Data Filtering

The methods of data filtering by human rules are mainly the same as we did in English to Chinese(Bei et al., 2018) last year, but language models are used to clean all data, including monolingual data, parallel data and synthetic data. We use Marian to train the transformer language model for each language (i.e. English, Gujarati, Lithuanian and Finnish). We introduce this section in two condition:

- For monolingual data and synthetic data (i.e. back-translate data from target side and knowledge distillation from source side), Every sentence are scored by language model, and the score for sentence is calculated as follows:

$$Score_{sentence} = \frac{Score_{lm}}{\sqrt{L_{sentence}}}$$

Here $Score_{lm}$ is score of language model for sentence, and $L_{sentence}$ is length of sentence in token level.

- For parallel data, considering scores of two sides, we combine the two side score of parallel data with liner:

$$Score_{combine} = \lambda * Score_{src} + (1-\lambda) Score_{tgt}$$

Here, λ is 0.5. According the sorted score for each sentence or sentence pair, we clean the sentences that is obviously not influence. Table 2 shows the number of cleaned data.

4 Back-translation

It has been proved that back translation (Sennrich et al., 2015a) is an effective way to improve the translation quality, especially in low-resource condition. Same as we did in last year, we firstly train models from target to source, then we use these model to translate the provided monolingual data in target side onto source side. Besides, the target parallel data is also translated to source side. It should be noticed that the ratio of parallel data and synthetic data is 1:1.

Joint-training (Zhang et al., 2018) is another method which has been proved that it can improve the performance of back-translation. In another perspective, back-translation is the first step of joint-training. When getting the best model from back-translation, we consecutively translate the monolingual data from the target side of parallel data and mix parallel data and synthetic data with the ratio of 1:1. Then the new training set is used to train a new model until there is no improvement. We only repeated this procedure twice due to the time limitation.

5 Knowledge Distillation

5.1 Sequence-level Knowledge Distillation

Sequence-level Knowledge distillation describes the method of training a smaller student network to perform better by learning from a teacher network. Knowledge distillation suggests training by matching the student's predictions to the teacher's predictions. We consider two different kinds of methods to improve the performance for NMT:

- **Ensemble Teacher** As according (Freitag et al., 2017), we translate the source side sentences of parallel data with ensemble models and get the synthetic target side sentences. The synthetic data is applied to training.

- **R2L Teacher** Inspired by (Wang et al., 2018) (Hassan et al., 2018), we translate the source side sentences of parallel data to target side with R2L model to improve L2R model.

To avoid bad translation, we filter the synthetic data with BLEU score lower than 30.

5.2 Sequence-level Interpolation

After sequence-level Knowledge distillation, the trained models are fine-tuned with n-best knowledge distillation data. The n-best knowledge distillation data is from the n-best translation from sequence-level knowledge distillation with different kinds of teachers. For every translation with the same source side sentence in an n-best translation, we extract the highest BLEU score and get the n-best knowledge distillation data.

6 R2L Reranking

Last year we didn't get better result with applying R2L reranking technique from English to Chinese. And we found out that the reason is we didn't increase the beam size step by step and didn't use all combination of R2L models. Therefore, to increase search space and get better translation, we applied the above procedure this time.

7 Experiment

This section describes the all experiments we conducted and illustrates how we get the evaluation result step by step.

7.1 Model Architecture

We use transformer big model to train our model with Marian according (Vaswani et al., 2017b). The model configuration and the training parameters are show in Table 3 and Table 4 respectively.

7.2 Date preprocessing

Both of parallel data and monolingual data are fully filtered. After that, we normalize

configuration	value
architecture	transformer
word embedding	1024
Encoder depth	6
Decoder depth	6
transformer heads	16
size of FFN	4096
transformer dropout attention	0.1
transformer dropout FFN	0.1

Table 3: The main model configuration.

parameters	value
maximum sentence length	100
learning rate	0.0003
label-smoothing	0.1
optimizer	Adam
learning rate warmup	16000
clip gradient	5

Table 4: The main training parameters.

the punctuation of all sentences by normalize-punctuation.perl in Moses toolkit (Koehn et al., 2007). We apply tokenizer and truecaser in Moses toolkit for English, Lithuanian and Finnish sentences and use polyglot [1] to tokenize Gujarati sentences. Finally, BPE is applied on tokenized English, Lithuanian, Finnish and Gujarati sentences respectively. Here, the BPE merge operation is set to 30000, and the vocabulary size is 30500.

7.3 Training Step

Here we introduce the training step in detail.

- **Baseline model** We use transformer big model to train our baseline model with only parallel data cleaned by human rules and language model. Besides, R2L models are trained with the same data with 4 different seeds.

- **Back-translation** When getting the baseline model, we decode monolingual data in target side to source side with ensemble models trained from source side to target side. For example, if we want to train an English to Gujarati model with synthetic data, using Gujarati-to-English baseline model to translate Gujarati sentences to English. Then, the translated English sentences are filtered by

---

[1] https://github.com/aboSamoor/polyglot

language model. The synthetic data and parallel data, which are mixed with ratio of 1:1, are applied to train back-translation model.

- **Joint Training** When getting the back-translation model, repeat back-translation step until there is no improvement. We repeated this step twice.

- **Sequence-level Knowledge Distillation** Different from back-translation, we use different teachers of source-to-target model to translate the source sentence of parallel data to target side. For example, we use English-to-Gujarati model to translate English sentences to Gujarati. Compared with golden reference, each translation with the BLEU score lower than 30 will be removed. Considering the low-resource condition, we mix parallel data, synthetic data and knowledge distillation data with ratio of 1:1:1 to train the new model.

- **Sequence-level Interpolation** After sequence-level knowledge distillation, the best models are fine-tuned with the n-best knowledge distillation data.

- **Ensemble Decoding** To get the best performance over all models efficiently, we use GMSE Algorithm (Deng et al., 2018) to select models.

- **R2L Reranking** To enlarge search space, we increase the beam size step by step and rescore it with all combination of R2L models for each step. Here, the step size is 10 and maximum beam size is 200.

8 Result and analysis

Table 5, Table 6, Table 7, Table 8, Table 9 and Table 10 show the BLEU score we evaluated on development set for English to Lithuanian, Lithuanian to English, English to Gujarati, Gujarati to English, English to Finnish and Finnish to English respectively.

For back-translation, we observe that it is the most effective method with an improvement from 1.54 to 4.87 BLEU score, especially in low-resource condition. And joint training can improve the BLEU score slightly from 0.12 to 0.29. For knowledge distillation, sequence-level knowledge distillation gets an improvement of BLEU

model	BLEU score
baseline	22.56
back-translation	27.43
joint training	27.72
sequence-level KD	27. 83
sequence-level interpolation	27.97
ensemble decoding	28.22
R2L reranking	28.37

Table 5: The case-insensitive BLEU score of English to Lithuanian.

score ranging from 0.09 to 1.03, and sequence-level interpolation has 0.12 to 0.21 BLEU score improvement. When ensemble decoding, GMSE algorithm gets the improvement ranging from 0.22 to 0.55. After increasing search space and combining the R2L models, reranking can still improve the result by 0.1 to 0.17 BLEU score.

9 Summary

This paper describes GTCOM's neural machine translation systems for the WMT19 shared news translation task. For all translation directions, we build systems mainly from data aspect, including acquiring more quantities and higher quality data. Besides, decoding strategies such as GSME algorithm and R2L reranking give us more robust and high quality translation. Finally, the directions of English to Gujarati (unconstrained) and Lithuanian to English get the best case-sensitive BLEU score of all systems.

Acknowledgments

This work is supported by 2020 Cognitive Intelligence Research Institute[2] of Global Tone Communication Technology Co., Ltd.[3]

References

Chao Bei, Hao Zong, Yiming Wang, Baoyong Fan, Shiqi Li, and Conghu Yuan. 2018. An empirical study of machine translation for the shared task of wmt18. In *Proceedings of the Third Conference on Machine Translation: Shared Task Papers*, pages 340–344.

Yongchao Deng, Shanbo Cheng, Jun Lu, Kai Song, Jingang Wang, Shenglan Wu, Liang Yao, Guchun Zhang, Haibo Zhang, Pei Zhang, et al. 2018.

[2]http://www.2020nlp.com/
[3]http://www.gtcom.com.cn/

model	BLEU score
baseline	29.76
back-translation	32.53
joint training	32.7
sequence-level KD	33.73
sequence-level interpolation	33.94
ensemble decoding	34.59
R2L reranking	34.69

Table 6: The case-insensitive BLEU score of Lithuanian to English.

model	BLEU score
baseline	23.93
back-translation	25.62
joint training	25.74
sequence-level KD	26.17
sequence-level interpolation	26.39
ensemble decoding	27.28
R2L reranking	27.44

Table 7: The case-insensitive BLEU score of English to Gujarati.

model	BLEU score
baseline	24.42
back-translation	27.58
joint training	27.79
sequence-level KD	28.05
sequence-level interpolation	28.21
ensemble decoding	28.54
R2L reranking	28.71

Table 8: The case-insensitive BLEU score of Gujarati to English.

model	BLEU score
baseline	18.04
back-translation	21.29
joint training	21.49
sequence-level KD	21.58
sequence-level interpolation	21.79
ensemble decoding	22.01
R2L reranking	22.12

Table 9: The case-insensitive BLEU score of English to Finnish.

Alibaba's neural machine translation systems for wmt18. In *Proceedings of the Third Conference on Machine Translation: Shared Task Papers*, pages 368–376.

model	BLEU score
baseline	25.55
back-translation	27.09
joint training	27.38
sequence-level KD	27.67
sequence-level interpolation	27.79
ensemble decoding	28.22
R2L reranking	28.34

Table 10: The case-insensitive BLEU score of Finnish to English.

Markus Freitag, Yaser Al-Onaizan, and Baskaran Sankaran. 2017. Ensemble distillation for neural machine translation. *arXiv preprint arXiv:1702.01802*.

Hany Hassan, Anthony Aue, Chang Chen, Vishal Chowdhary, Jonathan Clark, Christian Federmann, Xuedong Huang, Marcin Junczys-Dowmunt, William Lewis, Mu Li, et al. 2018. Achieving human parity on automatic chinese to english news translation. *arXiv preprint arXiv:1803.05567*.

Marcin Junczys-Dowmunt, Roman Grundkiewicz, Tomasz Dwojak, Hieu Hoang, Kenneth Heafield, Tom Neckermann, Frank Seide, Ulrich Germann, Alham Fikri Aji, Nikolay Bogoychev, Andr F. T. Martins, and Alexandra Birch. 2018. Marian: Fast neural machine translation in c++. *arXiv preprint arXiv:1804.00344*.

Yoon Kim and Alexander M Rush. 2016. Sequence-level knowledge distillation. *arXiv preprint arXiv:1606.07947*.

Philipp Koehn, Hieu Hoang, Alexandra Birch, Chris Callison-Burch, Marcello Federico, Nicola Bertoldi, Brooke Cowan, Wade Shen, Christine Moran, Richard Zens, et al. 2007. Moses: Open source toolkit for statistical machine translation. In *Proceedings of the 45th annual meeting of the ACL on interactive poster and demonstration sessions*, pages 177–180. Association for Computational Linguistics.

Kishore Papineni, Salim Roukos, Todd Ward, and Wei-Jing Zhu. 2002. Bleu: a method for automatic evaluation of machine translation. In *Proceedings of the 40th annual meeting on association for computational linguistics*, pages 311–318. Association for Computational Linguistics.

Roberts Rozis and Raivis Skadiņš. 2017. Tilde model-multilingual open data for eu languages. In *Proceedings of the 21st Nordic Conference on Computational Linguistics*, pages 263–265.

Rico Sennrich, Barry Haddow, and Alexandra Birch. 2015a. Improving neural machine translation models with monolingual data. *arXiv preprint arXiv:1511.06709*.

Rico Sennrich, Barry Haddow, and Alexandra Birch. 2015b. Neural machine translation of rare words with subword units. *arXiv preprint arXiv:1508.07909*.

Rico Sennrich, Barry Haddow, and Alexandra Birch. 2016. Edinburgh neural machine translation systems for WMT 16. *CoRR*, abs/1606.02891.

Jörg Tiedemann. 2012. Parallel data, tools and interfaces in opus. In *Lrec*, volume 2012, pages 2214–2218.

Ashish Vaswani, Noam Shazeer, Niki Parmar, Jakob Uszkoreit, Llion Jones, Aidan N Gomez, Łukasz Kaiser, and Illia Polosukhin. 2017a. Attention is all you need. In *Advances in Neural Information Processing Systems*, pages 5998–6008.

Ashish Vaswani, Noam Shazeer, Niki Parmar, Jakob Uszkoreit, Llion Jones, Aidan N. Gomez, Lukasz Kaiser, and Illia Polosukhin. 2017b. Attention is all you need. *CoRR*, abs/1706.03762.

Mingxuan Wang, Li Gong, Wenhuan Zhu, Jun Xie, and Chao Bian. 2018. Tencent neural machine translation systems for wmt18. In *Proceedings of the Third Conference on Machine Translation: Shared Task Papers*, pages 522–527.

Zhirui Zhang, Shujie Liu, Mu Li, Ming Zhou, and Enhong Chen. 2018. Joint training for neural machine translation models with monolingual data. In *Thirty-Second AAAI Conference on Artificial Intelligence*.

Machine Translation with `parfda`, Moses, `kenlm`, `nplm`, and PRO

Ergun Biçici

`ergun.bicici@boun.edu.tr`

Electrical and Electronics Engineering Department, Boğaziçi University

`orcid.org/0000-0002-2293-2031`

Abstract

We build `parfda` Moses statistical machine translation (SMT) models for most language pairs in the news translation task. We experiment with a hybrid approach using neural language models integrated into Moses. We obtain the constrained data statistics on the machine translation task, the coverage of the test sets, and the upper bounds on the translation results. We also contribute a new testsuite for the German-English language pair and a new automated key phrase extraction technique for the evaluation of the testsuite translations.

1 Introduction

Parallel feature weight decay algorithms (`parfda`) (Biçici, 2018) is an instance selection tool we use to select training and language model instances to build Moses (Koehn et al., 2007) phrase-based machine translation (MT) systems to translate the test sets in the news translation task at WMT19 (Bojar et al., 2019). The importance of `parfda` increase with the increasing size of the parallel and monolingual data available for building SMT systems. In the light of last year's evidence that shows that `parfda` phrase-based SMT can obtain the $2nd$ best results on a testsuite in the English-Turkish language pair (Biçici, 2018) when generating the translations of key phrases that are important for conveying the meaning, we obtain phrase-based Moses results and its extension with a neural LM in addition to the n-gram based LM that we use. We experiment with neural probabilistic LM (NPLM) (Vaswani et al., 2013). We record the statistics of the data and the resources used.

Our contributions are:

- a test suite for machine translation that is out of the domain of news task to take the chance of taking a closer look at the current status of

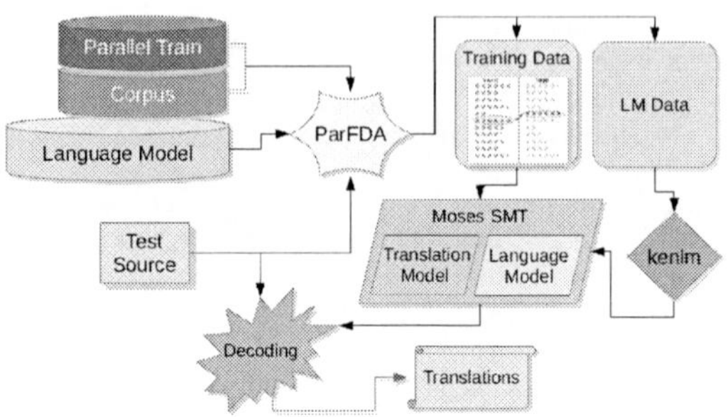

Figure 1: `parfda` Moses SMT workflow.

SMT technology used by the task participants when translating 38 sentences about international relations concerning cultural artifacts,

- `parfda` Moses phrase-based MT results and data statistics for the following translation directions:

    - English-Czech (en-cs)
    - English-Finnish (en-fi), Finnish-English (fi-en),
    - English-German (en-de), German-English (de-en),
    - English-Kazakh (en-kk), Kazakh-English (kk-en),
    - English-Lithuanian (en-lt), Lithuanian-English (lt-en),
    - English-Russian (en-ru), Russian-English (ru-en),

- upperbounds on the translation performance using lowercased coverage to identify which models used data in addition to the parallel corpus.

The sections that follow discuss the instance selection model (Section 2), the machine translation model (Section 3), the testsuite used for evaluating MT in en-de and de-en, and the results.

Proceedings of the Fourth Conference on Machine Translation (WMT), Volume 2: Shared Task Papers (Day 1) pages 122–128
Florence, Italy, August 1-2, 2019. ©2019 Association for Computational Linguistics

$S \to T$	Data	Training Data				LM Data	
		#word S (M)	#word T (M)	#sent (K)	tcov	#word (M)	tcov
en-cs	C	587.2	659.8	44436	0.758	1439.6	0.835
en-cs	parfda	111.4	98.4	2474	0.693	371.3	0.779
en-de	C	832.6	879.0	39959	0.792	4252.0	0.864
en-de	parfda	139.0	130.7	2467	0.736	450.8	0.795
de-en	C	879.0	832.6	39959	0.865	12382.8	0.92
de-en	parfda	132.6	141.3	2441	0.827	487.8	0.871
en-fi	C	96.2	125.3	5657	0.528	1598.9	0.746
en-fi	parfda	73.9	56.1	2168	0.512	419.1	0.676
fi-en	C	130.1	100.4	6254	0.783	12382.8	0.926
fi-en	parfda	51.1	66.4	2021	0.771	416.8	0.869
en-kk	C	1.6	1.9	204	0.262	173.5	0.576
en-kk	parfda	1.9	1.5	202	0.242	175.0	0.576
kk-en	C	1.9	1.6	204	0.591	12382.8	0.907
kk-en	parfda	1.5	1.9	202	0.584	337.7	0.835
en-lt	C	38.2	45.0	2191	0.532	1523.4	0.539
en-lt	parfda	45.0	38.2	2191	0.532	310.7	0.539
lt-en	C	45.0	38.2	2191	0.794	12382.8	0.933
lt-en	parfda	34.1	40.5	1877	0.754	383.5	0.89
en-ru	C	212.0	181.9	9296	0.738	11459.4	0.888
en-ru	parfda	92.3	80.0	2260	0.713	469.0	0.803
ru-en	C	181.7	211.8	9287	0.857	12382.8	0.937
ru-en	parfda	78.2	90.5	2212	0.839	437.0	0.894

Table 1: Statistics for the training and LM corpora in the constrained (C) setting compared with the `parfda` selected data. #words is in millions (M) and #sents in thousands (K). tcov is target 2-gram coverage.

	scov					tcov				
	1	2	3	4	5	1	2	3	4	5
en-cs	0.9762	0.8399	0.5686	0.2809	0.1085	0.9792	0.7557	0.3985	0.1646	0.0618
en-de	0.9673	0.8683	0.6288	0.3301	0.1296	0.96	0.7916	0.5102	0.2438	0.0898
en-fi	0.9535	0.779	0.4829	0.2122	0.0745	0.9009	0.5283	0.2337	0.0849	0.0229
en-kk	0.8399	0.4643	0.1623	0.0363	0.0075	0.7404	0.262	0.0648	0.0104	0.0017
en-lt	0.9519	0.7214	0.3896	0.1374	0.0355	0.909	0.5324	0.2125	0.0663	0.0156
en-ru	0.9743	0.8251	0.5362	0.2434	0.0813	0.9606	0.7384	0.4102	0.1794	0.0673

Table 2: Constrained training data lowercased source feature coverage (scov) and target feature coverage (tcov) of the test set for n-grams.

2 Instance Selection with `parfda`

`parfda` parallelize feature decay algorithms (FDA) (Biçici and Yuret, 2015), a class of instance selection algorithms that decay feature weights, for fast deployment of accurate SMT systems. Figure 1 depicts `parfda` Moses SMT workflow.

We use the test set source sentences to select the training data and the target side of the selected training data to select the LM data. We decay the weights for both the source features of the test set and the target features that we already select to increase the diversity. We select about 2.2 million instances for training data and about 12 million sentences for each LM data not including the selected training set, which is added later. Table 1 shows size differences with the constrained dataset (C).[1] We use 3-grams to select training data and 2-grams for LM data and split the hyphenated words

using the "-a" option of the tokenizer used in Moses (Sennrich et al., 2017). tcov lists the target coverage in terms of the 2-grams of the test set. The maximum sentence length is set to 126. Table 2 lists the lowercased coverage of the test set by the constrained training data of WMT19.

3 Machine Translation with Moses, `kenlm` and `nplm`, and PRO

We train 6-gram LM using `kenlm` (Heafield et al., 2013). For word alignment, we use mgiza (Gao and Vogel, 2008) where GIZA++ (Och and Ney, 2003) parameters set max-fertility to 10, the number of iterations to 7,5,5,5,7 for IBM models 1,2,3,4, and the HMM model, and learn 50 word classes in three iterations with the mkcls tool during training. We use "-mbr" option when decoding the test set.[3] The development set con-

---

[1] Available at `https://github.com/bicici/parfdaWMT2019`

[3] As practiced in the parallel corpus filtering task `http://www.statmt.org/wmt19/`

BLEU	de-en	fi-en	kk-en	lt-en	en-cs	en-de	en-fi	en-kk	en-lt
kenlm	0.309	0.202	0.105	0.225	0.152	0.235	0.127	0.029	
nplm	0.292	0.18		0.215	0.142		0.119	0.029	0.073
bilingual nplm			0.102					0.03	
kenlm + nplm	0.307			0.226	0.156	0.238		0.03	0.078
kenlm with hyphen splitting	0.3074	0.2024	0.0999	0.2245	0.1522	0.2395	0.1294	0.03	0.0828

Table 3: `parfda` BLEU cased results with different LM on text that is not hyphen splitted compared with after hyphen splitting.

BLEU	de-en	fi-en	kk-en	lt-en	ru-en	en-cs	en-de	en-fi	en-kk	en-lt	en-ru
parfda	0.3074	0.2024	0.0999	0.2245	0.3179	0.1522	0.2395	0.1294	0.03	0.0828	0.1846
topC	0.428	0.33	0.305	0.365	0.401	0.299	0.449	0.274	0.111	0.191	0.363
-parfda avg diff	0.1405										

Table 4: `parfda` results compared with the top results in WMT19 and their difference.[2]

tains up to 5000 sentences randomly sampled from previous years' development sets (2013-2018) and remaining come from the development set for WMT19. We obtain robust optimization results using monotonically increasing n-best list size in the beginning of tuning with pairwise ranking optimization (PRO) (Hopkins and May, 2011; Biçici, 2018). This allows us to find parameters whose tuning score reach 1% close to the best tuning parameter set score in only 4 iterations but we still run tuning for 21 iterations. Truecasing updates the casing of words according to the most common form. We truecase the text before building the SMT model as well as after decoding and then detruecase before preparing the translation, which provided better results than simply detruecasing after decoding (Biçici, 2018).

We trained `nplm` LM in 10 epochs. We also experimented with bilingual nplm, which uses nplm in a bilingual setting to use both the source and the target context and builds a LM on the training set (Devlin et al., 2014). Both `nplm` and bilingual `nplm` can be used with Moses as a feature within its configuration file.[4] On average, results in Table 3 shows that using only `nplm` decrease the scores and improvements are obtained when both `nplm` and `kenlm` are used. However, the gain from splitting hyphenated words is more and it is a less computationally demanding option. `kenlm` takes about 20 minutes whereas building a single `nplm` model took us 11.5 to 14.25 days or 1000 times longer and it takes about 56 GB space on the disk.

`parfda` results at WMT19 are in Table 4 using BLEU over tokenized text where we compare with the top constrained submissions (topC). All top models use NMT in 2019 and most use back-translations, which means that their tcov is upper bounded by LM tcov. topC is 14.05 BLEU points on average better than `parfda` in 2019 and the difference was 12.88 in 2018.

4 Translation Upper Bounds with tcov

We obtain upper bounds on the translation performance based on the target coverage (tcov) of n-grams of the test set found in the selected `parfda` training data using lowercased text. For a given sentence T', the number of OOV tokens are identified:

$$OOV_r = \text{round}((1 - \text{tcov}) * |T'|) \quad (1)$$

where $|T'|$ is the number of tokens in the sentence. We obtain each bound using 500 such instances and repeat for 10 times. tcov BLEU bound is optimistic since it does not consider reorderings in the translation or differences in sentence length. Each plot in Figure 2 locates tcov BLEU bound obtained from each n-gram and from n-gram tcovs combined up to and including n and ▩ locates the `parfda` result and ⋆ locates the top constrained result. Based on the distance between the top BLEU result and the bound, we can obtain a sorting of the difficulty of the translation directions in Table 5.

5 German-English Testsuite

We prepared a MT test suite that is out of the domain of news translation task to take a closer

parallel-corpus-filtering.html
[4]http://www.statmt.org/moses/?n=
FactoredTraining.BuildingLanguageModel#
ntoc32

---

[4]We use the results from matrix.statmt.org.

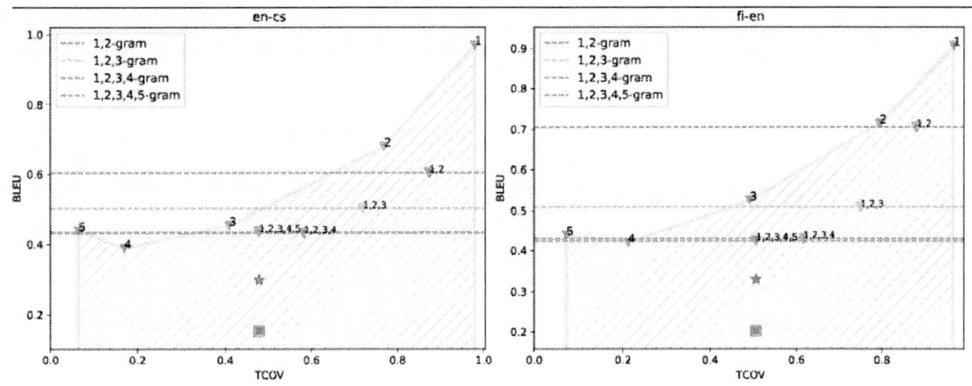

Figure 2: `parfda` results (■) and OOV_r tcov BLEU upper bounds for kk and lt.

BLEU distance	translation direction
0.0041	en-de
0.0092	en-kk
0.0277	en-ru
0.0296	en-fi
0.0372	de-en
0.0407	kk-en
0.0594	lt-en
0.0722	en-lt
0.0849	ru-en
0.0943	fi-en
0.1365	en-cs

Table 5: Difficulty of translation directions based on the distance of the top result to the upper bound.

			bits	% info.
word	order	$\log_2 25!$	83.7	16.8%
	choice	$\log_2 10^{125}$	415.2	83.2%
	total	$\log_2 25! \times 10^{125}$	498.9	100.0%
phrase	order	$\log_2 10!$	21.8	8.6%
	choice	$\log_2 10^{70}$	232.5	91.4%
	total	$\log_2 10! \times 10^{70}$	254.3	100.0%
BPE	order	$\log_2 50!$	214.2	24.4%
	choice	$\log_2 10^{200}$	664.4	75.6%
	total	$\log_2 50! \times 10^{200}$	878.6	100.0%
char	order	$\log_2 125!$	695.2	80.7%
	choice	$\log_2 10^{50}$	166.1	19.3%
	total	$\log_2 125! \times 10^{50}$	861.3	100.0%

Table 6: Information contribution from granular parts of a sentence.

look at the current status of SMT technology used by the task participants to translate 38 sentences about international relations concerning cultural artifacts in German and English. The sentences and their translations are available at `https://github.com/bicici/SMTData` sourced from the press releases of the Prussian Cultural Heritage Foundation.[5] The scores of participants are in Table 10 in terms of BLEU (Papineni et al., 2002) and F_1 (Biçici, 2011) scores. However, such automatic evaluation metrics treat the features or n-grams equivalently or group them based on their length, without knowledge about their frequency in use or significance in conveying the meaning.

Word order in a sentence does not contain the majority of information (Landauer, 2002) for vocabulary size $|V| \geq n$ where n is the average sentence length. For $n = 25$ words with $|V| = 10^5$ with equivalent representation using $n = 10$ phrases with $|V| = 10^7$ or using $n = 50$ BPE tokens with $|V| = 10^4$ or using $n = 125$ chars

with $|V| = 10^2$ have differing contribution to the information of the sentence in bits from token order or choice (Table 6). If we use keyword subsequences for F_1 based evaluation, we would cover about 91% of the information in a sentence whereas if we include punctuation characters, they will contribute at most 19.3%.

Key phrase identification is important since when scores are averaged, important phrases that are missing only decrease the score by $\frac{1}{|p|N_{|p|}}$ for BLEU calculation for a phrase of length $|p|$ over $N_{|p|}$ phrases with length $|p|$. We extend our evaluation of the testsuite translations using keywords (Biçici, 2018).

We automate key phrase identification within a reference set of N sentences by selecting among N_X candidate n-grams that:

- are representative and few

[5]`http://www.preussischer-kulturbesitz.de`

$$\min \ \mathbf{X}^T(\alpha \mathbf{X}_p \cdot \mathbf{X}_l \cdot \frac{1}{-\beta \mathbf{X}_c} + \mathbf{1}_{N_X})$$

$$\text{s.t.} \quad \mathbf{X}_d(\mathbf{X} \cdot \mathbf{L}) \geq 0.5 \ \mathbf{L}_N \qquad \text{min. coverage}$$
$$0 \leq \mathbf{X} \leq 1$$
$$\alpha = 1, \beta = 2$$

Variables:

$\mathbf{X} \in \mathrm{R}^{N_X}$	phrase selection vector
$\mathbf{X}_p \in \mathrm{R}^{N_X}$	phrase probability vector
$\mathbf{X}_c \in \mathrm{R}^{N_X}$	phrase count vector
$\mathbf{L} \in \mathrm{R}^{N_X}$	phrase length vector
$\mathbf{L}_N \in \mathrm{R}^{N}$	sentence length vector
$\mathbf{X}_d \in \mathrm{R}^{N \times N_X}$	phrase distribution matrix

Table 7: Optimization constraints.

system	F_1	# match	# in reference
online-B	0.869	63	82
Facebook_FAIR	0.8531	61	82
NEU	0.8286	58	82
MLLP-UPV	0.8286	58	82
online-Y	0.8286	58	82
MSRA	0.8201	57	82
RWTH_Aachen	0.8201	57	82
UCAM	0.8201	57	82
online-A	0.8029	55	82
online-G	0.7941	54	82
parfda	0.7761	52	82
PROMT_NMT	0.7761	52	82
TartuNLP-c	0.7761	52	82
uedin	0.7761	52	82
dfki-nmt	0.7481	49	82
JHU	0.6557	40	82
online-X	0.4381	23	82

Table 8: de-en testsuite F_1 scores with key phrases.

- cover significant portion of the text

- are frequent ($\mathbf{X}_c$ for counts of phrases)

- are less likely to be found ($\mathbf{X}_p$ for the probability of phrases)

and formulate the task as a linear program in Table 7. We use up to 6-grams and set minimum coverage of each sentence to 0.5. We removed some stop words from the phrases: 'of', 'the', 'and', 'of the', 'a', 'an' and replaced those parts with '.*?' and obtained regular expressions. The key phrases we obtain are listed in Table 9. The key phrases are used to evaluate using the F_1 score (Table 10). We plan to extend this work towards more objective key phrase evaluation methods.

6 Conclusion

We use `parfda` for building task specific MT systems that use less computation overall and release our engineered data for training MT systems.

We also contribute a new testsuite for the German-English language pair and a new automated key phrase extraction technique for evaluation.

Acknowledgments

The research reported here received financial support from the Scientific and Technological Research Council of Turkey (TÜBİTAK).

References

Ergun Biçici. 2011. *The Regression Model of Machine Translation*. Ph.D. thesis, Koç University. Supervisor: Deniz Yuret.

Ergun Biçici. 2018. Robust parfda statistical machine translation results. In *Third Conf. on Statistical Machine Translation (WMT18)*, Brussels, Belgium.

Ergun Biçici and Deniz Yuret. 2015. Optimizing instance selection for statistical machine translation with feature decay algorithms. *IEEE/ACM Transactions On Audio, Speech, and Language Processing (TASLP)*, 23:339–350.

Ondřej Bojar, Christian Federmann, Mark Fishel, Yvette Graham, Barry Haddow, Matthias Huck, Philipp Koehn, Christof Monz, Mathias Müller, and Matt Post. 2019. Findings of the 2019 conference on machine translation (wmt19). In *Proc. of the Fourth Conf. on Machine Translation*, Florence, Italy. Association for Computational Linguistics.

Jacob Devlin, Rabih Zbib, Zhongqiang Huang, Thomas Lamar, Richard Schwartz, and John Makhoul. 2014. Fast and robust neural network joint models for statistical machine translation. In *Proceedings of the 52nd Annual Meeting of the Association for Computational Linguistics (Volume 1: Long Papers)*, pages 1370–1380, Baltimore, Maryland. Association for Computational Linguistics.

Qin Gao and Stephan Vogel. 2008. *Software Engineering, Testing, and Quality Assurance for Natural Language Processing*, chapter Parallel Implementations of Word Alignment Tool.

Kenneth Heafield, Ivan Pouzyrevsky, Jonathan H. Clark, and Philipp Koehn. 2013. Scalable modified Kneser-Ney language model estimation. In *51st Annual Meeting of the Assoc. for Computational Linguistics*, pages 690–696, Sofia, Bulgaria.

Mark Hopkins and Jonathan May. 2011. Tuning as ranking. In *Conf. on Empirical Methods in Natural Language Processing*, pages 1352–1362.

Philipp Koehn, Hieu Hoang, Alexandra Birch, Chris Callison-Burch, Marcello Federico, Nicola Bertoldi, Brooke Cowan, Wade Shen, Christine Moran, Richard Zens, Chris Dyer, Ondrej Bojar, Alexandra Constantin, and Evan Herbst. 2007. Moses: Open source toolkit for statistical machine translation. In *45th Annual Meeting of the Assoc. for Computational Linguistics Companion Volume Demo and Poster Sessions*, pages 177–180.

Thomas K. Landauer. 2002. On the computational basis of learning and cognition: Arguments from LSA. 41:43–84.

Franz Josef Och and Hermann Ney. 2003. A systematic comparison of various statistical alignment models. *Computational Linguistics*, 29(1):19–51.

Kishore Papineni, Salim Roukos, Todd Ward, and Wei-Jing Zhu. 2002. BLEU: a method for automatic evaluation of machine translation. In *40th Annual Meeting of the Assoc. for Computational Linguistics*, pages 311–318, Philadelphia, PA, USA.

Rico Sennrich, Alexandra Birch, Anna Currey, Ulrich Germann, Barry Haddow, Kenneth Heafield, Antonio Valerio Miceli Barone, and Philip Williams. 2017. The university of edinburgh's neural mt systems for wmt17. In *Proceedings of the Second Conference on Machine Translation, Volume 2: Shared Task Papers*, pages 389–399, Copenhagen, Denmark. Association for Computational Linguistics.

Ashish Vaswani, Yinggong Zhao, Victoria Fossum, and David Chiang. 2013. Decoding with large-scale neural language models improves translation. In *Proceedings of the 2013 Conference on Empirical Methods in Natural Language Processing*, pages 1387–1392, Seattle, Washington, USA. Association for Computational Linguistics.

A de-en Testsuite Sentences

They live in seven communities
been granted by .*? community
Southwestern Alaska has been inhabited
Hermann Parzinger
speaking groups .*? Indians immigrated
Ethnological Museum
aim .*? building up
Chugach Alaska Corporation
objects
Chugach
exhibition module in
northwest coast
ethnographic observations than by tales
goods from Chenega Island
to protect people from danger
were therefore removed unlawfully from
indications are that
graves were opened solely for
Ethnological
are two broken masks
cultural heritage
Indians immigrated
items concerned are grave goods
origin .*? history
contacts with Europe existed since
Prince William Sound
grave goods identified in
color on these ones indicates
live in seven communities
Chugach people exist today
journey is .*? impressive
consent had been granted by
virtual presentation .*? all
proposal to this effect from
President
museum at
nineteenth century for
diplomatic note in support
it was decided to return
Corporation asked .*? Ethnological Museum
indigenous peoples
Memorandum .*? Understanding with
has been inhabited for thousands
American northwest coast
now be returning them to

Table 9: Key phrases for the de-en testsuite.

| | BLEU lc | | | | BLEU | | | | F_1 lc | | | | F_1 | | | |
model	1	2	3	4	1	2	3	4	1	2	3	4	1	2	3	4
online-B	0.6976	0.6828	0.6042	0.5889	0.54	0.525	0.4892	0.4745	0.6419	0.6279	0.5756	0.5625	0.5264	0.514	0.4865	0.4746
Facebook_FAIR	0.7169	0.7073	0.6143	0.6037	0.5391	0.5279	0.4764	0.464	0.6311	0.6228	0.5591	0.5505	0.5039	0.4948	0.4596	0.4504
RWTH_Aachen	0.7005	0.6814	0.5889	0.573	0.5132	0.4994	0.4517	0.4385	0.6135	0.5996	0.5416	0.5295	0.4876	0.4762	0.4458	0.4349
NEU	0.7072	0.6913	0.5971	0.5805	0.5195	0.5032	0.4563	0.4396	0.6129	0.5992	0.5401	0.5274	0.4852	0.4727	0.4416	0.4292
UCAM	0.6975	0.6795	0.5943	0.5748	0.5168	0.4958	0.4513	0.4283	0.6127	0.5969	0.5389	0.5219	0.4806	0.4623	0.4346	0.4159
MSRA	0.6894	0.6746	0.5769	0.564	0.4954	0.4844	0.4296	0.4196	0.6034	0.5942	0.5278	0.5196	0.4708	0.4632	0.4263	0.4193
online-A	0.6884	0.6651	0.5822	0.5559	0.5011	0.4728	0.4338	0.4036	0.6133	0.5879	0.5348	0.5092	0.4738	0.4481	0.4265	0.4007
JHU	0.7067	0.6705	0.5923	0.5539	0.5084	0.47	0.4411	0.4025	0.6027	0.5628	0.5231	0.4848	0.4634	0.4261	0.4173	0.3816
online-Y	0.6583	0.6414	0.5413	0.525	0.4597	0.444	0.3952	0.3797	0.5838	0.5682	0.5053	0.4911	0.4469	0.4333	0.4017	0.3884
MLLP-UPV	0.6872	0.6671	0.5666	0.5428	0.4794	0.4562	0.4106	0.3884	0.5888	0.567	0.5067	0.4861	0.447	0.4275	0.4012	0.3829
dfki-nmt	0.6864	0.6503	0.5723	0.5312	0.4902	0.4442	0.4233	0.3737	0.5915	0.5463	0.5133	0.4675	0.4545	0.4082	0.4085	0.362
uedin	0.6493	0.6304	0.5309	0.5116	0.4509	0.4303	0.3862	0.3646	0.5751	0.5585	0.4945	0.4775	0.4344	0.4173	0.3888	0.3718
online-G	0.6536	0.6281	0.5269	0.5008	0.4429	0.4161	0.3809	0.3545	0.5642	0.535	0.4846	0.456	0.4284	0.4005	0.3849	0.3571
PROMT_NMT	0.6565	0.6374	0.5289	0.5074	0.4374	0.4153	0.3642	0.343	0.5529	0.5329	0.4704	0.4512	0.4094	0.3918	0.3617	0.3455
TartuNLP-c	0.6295	0.6137	0.5064	0.4911	0.4186	0.4039	0.3479	0.3339	0.5371	0.5228	0.455	0.442	0.3941	0.382	0.3472	0.3364
parfda	0.6096	0.5969	0.4642	0.4521	0.3686	0.3591	0.2994	0.2931	0.515	0.5021	0.4264	0.4159	0.3658	0.3579	0.3218	0.3153
online-X	0.6316	0.567	0.4837	0.4052	0.3828	0.2997	0.3031	0.2222	0.5149	0.4362	0.4253	0.3464	0.3601	0.2849	0.3113	0.2413

de-en

Table 10: Testsuite BLEU and F_1 results.

LIUM's Contributions to the WMT2019 News Translation Task: Data and Systems for German↔French Language Pairs

Fethi Bougares
LIUM, Le Mans Université
`fethi.bougares@univ-lemans.fr`

Jane Wottawa
LIUM, Le Mans Université
`jane.wottawa@univ-lemans.fr`

Anne Baillot
3L.AM, Le Mans Université
`anne.baillot@univ-lemans.fr`

Loïc Barrault
LIUM, Le Mans Université
`loic.barrault@univ-lemans.fr`

Abstract

This paper describes the neural machine translation (NMT) systems of the LIUM Laboratory developed for the French ↔ German news translation task of the Fourth Conference on Machine Translation (WMT 2019). The chosen language pair is included for the first time in the WMT news translation task. We describe how the training and the evaluation data was created. We also present our participation in the French ↔ German translation directions using self-attentional Transformer networks with small and big architectures.

1 Introduction

Since the start of the WMT translation shared tasks in 2006, English has been involved in the majority of translation directions. Few exceptions have been seen in 2012 and 2013 where Czech was also proposed as source and target for several language pairs. This overwhelming disparity is due to the fact that English is available in large quantity, in both monolingual and bilingual corpora.

We think that this may be problematic for research purposes since considering English (either as source or target language) may hide many linguistic problems. For example, considering gender agreement, which does not exist in English, translating from English is harder because of the lack of source side information, and translating towards English is simpler since the agreement should be ignored. Generally speaking, English is a rather morphologically impoverished language, for instance having few gender agreement cases or conjugated verb forms. This contrasts with French and German where number and gender agreements are very frequent. That is why we introduced two new translation directions involving two European languages, namely French and German.

2 DE↔FR language pair

Training data

The training data for this language pair was created by cross-matching the training data from the previous WMT shared tasks for the EN-FR and EN-DE language pairs. The details of the corpora are provided in Table 1 in which we provide the original sizes of EN-FR and EN-DE corpora and the extracted parallel corpora in DE-FR. Overall, we were able to create a German-French parallel corpus with **153.2M** and **171.1M** words respectively.

Development and test data

The data collected for the FR↔DE language pair has been created from several online news websites. The development and test sets have been created from news articles in both French and German. The development set is the fruit of a collaboration with the Faculty of Literature and Humanities of the University of Le Mans during several Digital Humanities (DH) lab sessions. The purpose of these quality sessions is twofold: on the first hand, students would learn and comprehend the inherent concepts of using a computer assisted translation (CAT) tool in the context of DH classes (Baillot et al., 2019). On the other hand, the translated data is intended to be used for Machine Translation research purposes. This process led to a 1512 sentences[1] development corpus distributed during the WMT2019 shared task. While creating the development data we intentionally mixed (to some degree) the translation directions, therefore 462 sentences were translated from French to German and the reverse for the remaining 1050 sentences. The same process has

---

[1]The translations have been revised by professors from the Faculty of Literature and Humanities in order to reach the desired quality

129

Proceedings of the Fourth Conference on Machine Translation (WMT), Volume 2: Shared Task Papers (Day 1) pages 129–133
Florence, Italy, August 1-2, 2019. ©2019 Association for Computational Linguistics

	FR-EN	DE-EN	FR-DE
europarl-v7	2M (52.5M/50.3M)	1.9M (44.6M/47.9M)	1.7M (46M / 41M)
Common Crawl	3.2M (76.6M/70.7M)	2.4M (47M/51.3M)	622k (14M/12.2M)
ParaCrawl	40.4M (663M/640M)	31.8M (467M/502M)	7.2M (110.6M/99.6M)
dev08-14	–	–	18k (417.1k/369.5k)

Table 1: Training corpora statistics (number of sentences) for FR↔DE News translation shared task. The second line of each cell corresponds to the number of tokens in French followed by the number of tokens in German.

been followed for the test set creation: 335 of the 1701 test sentences have been produced from French documents and the 1366 remaining pairs from German documents. We note that 756 out of the German 1366 German sentences in the test set have been translated into French by professional translators[2]. The dev and test sets are freely distributed and available for download[3].

	#lines	#token FR	#token DE
dev2019	1512	33833	28733
test2019	1701	38138	31560

Table 2: FR-DE dev and test set statistics.

3 LIUM Submissions

All our systems are constrained as we only used the supplied parallel data (described in table 1) with additional back-translations created from a subset of the monolingual news data made available by the shared task organizers.

3.1 Model Description

For our submissions we used the Transformer (Vaswani et al., 2017) sequence-to-sequence model as implemented in fairseq (Ott et al., 2019). Transformer is the state of the art NMT model which rely on a multi-headed attention applied as self-attention to source and target sentences. Our models are based on both small and big Transformer configurations. All experiments with the big transformer are models with 6 blocks in the encoder and decoder networks following the configuration described in (Ott et al., 2018). With respect to the small transformer model, we also used

a 6 blocks encoder and decoder network with an embedding layer of size 512, a feed-forward layer with an inner dimension of 1024, and a multi-headed attention with 4 attention heads.

We use a vocabulary of 35K units based on a joint source and target byte pair encoding (Sennrich et al., 2016). We set the batch size to 2048 tokens and maximum sentence length to 150 BPE units, in order to fit the big Transformer configuration to our GPUs (NVIDIA GeForce GTX 1080 Ti with 11 GB RAM).

3.2 Data Preparation

Our preparation pipeline consists of a preprocessing step performed using scripts from Moses (Koehn et al., 2007). We replace the unicode punctuation, normalize the punctuation and remove the non-printing characters before the tokenization. After the tokenization step, we perform a cleaning stage where all source and target sentences with an overlapping rate higher than 65% are deleted. Statistics of the training corpora after the cleaning process are presented in table 2. These values should be contrasted with those of table 1 to assess the effect of the cleaning process. As it can be seen from tables 1 and 2, the effect of the cleaning step is more pronounced for the noisy parallel corpora (*i.e.* ParaCrawl and Common Crawl). For the europarl-v7 corpus, more than a thousand lines are removed after cleaning which mainly corresponds to English sentences in both languages: FR and DE as well as sentences with long lists of numbers.

In addition to the available parallel data, we have used monolingual News Crawl articles as additional synthetic bilingual data. We used only news 2018 from which we selected a subpart based on cross-entropy data selection method

---

[2]This was carried out by LinguaCustodia

[3]dev and test sets can be downloaded from `https://github.com/lium-lst/euelections`

	#lines	#token FR	#token DE
europarl-v7	1.7M	45.9M	40.9
Common Crawl	585k	13M	11M
ParaCrawl	6.7M	107M	95M
dev08-14	18k	417.1k	369.5k

Table 3: Training corpora statistics for FR↔DE systems after the cleaning process.

(Moore and Lewis, 2010). Data selection was performed with the *europarl* corpus as in-domain data and using the XenC Toolkit (Rousseau, 2013). By doing this, we were able to extract 3.4M German sentences out of the 38.6M sentences of the monolingual German 2018 News Crawl corpus. Similarly, 3.3M sentences were extracted out of the 8.2M monolingual French 2018 News Crawl.

4 Experiments and Results

In this section, we first present the results for German to French translation direction followed by the French to German direction. We use BLEU as evaluation metric (Papineni et al., 2002) and all reported scores are calculated using case-sensitive detokenized BLEU with multi-bleu.pl. All results use beam search with a beam width of 12 and length penalty of 1.

4.1 German to French

In this section we present the results for German to French direction. We have tried three different configurations differentiated by the training data used to create the NMT system. For each of these configurations, we trained a small and a big transformer model.

Given the prior knowledge about the noisy quality of the ParaCrawl corpus, we first tried to train some NMT systems with all available parallel data from table 3 except ParaCrawl. Table 4 contains the results for this setting. We report the results with the best checkpoint and an ensemble-decoding with 2 and 5 checkpoints for small and big Transformer versions. As expected, the big transformer outperforms the small version and we obtain an improvement of 1.69 BLEU point for the ensemble-decoding of 5 checkpoints.

Table 5 shows the BLEU scores when the ParaCrawl corpus is used. We obtain almost the same results for small transformer version while there is a small improvement of 0.46 BLEU point

de → fr	dev (BLEU)
1. Small Transformer (x1)	25.39
+Ensemble (x2)	25.81
+Ensemble (x5)	**25.92**
2. Big Transformer (x1)	26.27
+Ensemble (x2)	27.04
+Ensemble (x5)*	**27.61**

Table 4: BLEU results for DE→FR NMT systems using all training data but ParaCrawl corpus.

for the big model compared to the results reported in table 4 (without ParaCrawl).

de → fr	dev (BLEU)
1. Small Transformer (x1)	25.18
+Ensemble (x2)	25.59
+Ensemble (x5)	**25.93**
2. Big Transformer (x1)	26.83
+Ensemble (x2)	27.80
+Ensemble (x5)	**28.07**

Table 5: BLEU results for DE →FR NMT systems with all training data including ParaCrawl.

Table 6 contains our results for WMT2019 training data with back-translation[4]. As expected, adding back-translations improves the results for both configurations: an increase of about 1% BLEU point is observed for small and big transformer models compared to the same systems without back-translation (see systems labeled "+Ensemble (x5)" in Table 4).

de → fr	dev (BLEU)
1. Small Transformer (x1)	26.64
+Ensemble (x2)	26.95
+Ensemble (x5)	**26.99**
2. Big Transformer (x1)	27.65
+Ensemble (x2)	28.40
+Ensemble (x5)	**28.63**

Table 6: BLEU results for DE →FR NMT systems with back-translation training data and without ParaCrawl parallel data.

---

[4]The FR→DE back-translations have been created using the small transformer (x1) system from table 7

Asterisk (*) in Table 4 marks our submitted model for German to French official evaluation. This model obtains a BLEU score of **33.4**. Our best system with back-translation was also submitted after the evaluation deadline and obtain a BLEU score of **34.6**.

4.2 French to German

We performed the same set of experiments as German to French. Table 7 shows the BLEU scores when NMT systems are trained without the ParaCrawl corpus. Unlike the German to French direction, only a small improvement is observed by using the big transformer architecture compared to the small one (21.18 with big model and 21.08 for small model).

fr $\rightarrow$ de	dev (BLEU)
1. Small Transformer (x1)	20.28
+Ensemble (x2)	20.73
+Ensemble (x5)	**21.09**
2. Big Transformer (x1)	20.42
+Ensemble (x2)	21.03
+Ensemble (x5)	**21.18**

Table 7: Results in terms of BLEU for FR $\rightarrow$DE NMT systems using all the available training data except the ParaCrawl corpus.

As for the DE$\rightarrow$Fr direction, we also trained systems by adding ParaCrawl data and results are presented in Table 9. As was formerly the case with DE$\rightarrow$Fr, no improvement is observed by adding the Paracrawl corpus to the small transformer model. The model works less well than without Paracrawl and a drop of 0.4% BLEU points is observed when we compare the "+Ensemble (x5)" of small transformer models from tables 7 and 8. For the big transformer model there is an improvement of 0.76 BLEU point when the Paracrawl corpus is included in the training data.

Table 9 presents the results when the training set is extended with back-translated data[5]. Results shows a consistent improvement with back-translated data. We note an improvement of 0.4 BLEU points in comparison with the best small and big transformer models without back-translation. Asterisk (*) in Table 9 marks our submitted model for French to German official evaluation.

[5]The DE$\rightarrow$FR back-translations have been created using the small transformer (x1) system from Table 4

fr $\rightarrow$ de	dev (BLEU)
1. Small Transformer (x1)	20.15
+Ensemble (x2)	20.29
+Ensemble (x5)	**20.65**
2. Big Transformer (x1)	21.37
+Ensemble (x2)	21.80
+Ensemble (x5)	**21.94**

Table 8: Results in terms of BLEU for FR $\rightarrow$DE NMT systems using all the available training data including ParaCrawl corpus.

fr $\rightarrow$ de	dev (BLEU)
1. Small Transformer (x1)	21.15
+Ensemble (x2)	21.45
+Ensemble (x5)	**21.50**
2. Big Transformer (x1)	21.82
+Ensemble (x2)*	22.03
+Ensemble (x5)	**22.34**

Table 9: Results in terms of BLEU for the FR$\rightarrow$DE NMT systems with back-translation training data but without ParaCrawl parallel data.

5 Conclusion

In this paper, we presented the LIUM participation to the WMT2019 news translation shared task. This year we have added for the first time the French-German language pair to the WMT news translation task. The parallel training data were created by cross-matching the EN-FR and EN-DE training data from previous WMT shared tasks. The LIUM has participated in the German $\leftrightarrow$ French translation task with an ensemble of neural machine translation models based on the Transformer architecture. Our models were trained using a cleaned subset of the provided training dataset, and synthetic parallel data generated from the provided monolingual corpora.

Acknowledgments

We thank Franck Burlot and LinguaCustodia for translating part of the DE$\rightarrow$FR test set. This work was supported by the French National Research Agency (ANR) through the CHIST-ERA M2CR project[6], under the contract number ANR-15-CHR2-0006-01.

[6]http://m2cr.univ-lemans.fr

References

Anne Baillot, Loïc Barrault, and Fethi Bougares. 2019. Cat tools in dh training. In *Proceedings of the 2019 Digital Humanities Conference*, Utrecht, The Netherlands. Poster.

Philipp Koehn, Hieu Hoang, Alexandra Birch, Chris Callison-Burch, Marcello Federico, Nicola Bertoldi, Brooke Cowan, Wade Shen, Christine Moran, Richard Zens, Chris Dyer, Ondřej Bojar, Alexandra Constantin, and Evan Herbst. 2007. Moses: Open source toolkit for statistical machine translation. In *Proceedings of the 45th Annual Meeting of the ACL on Interactive Poster and Demonstration Sessions*, ACL '07, pages 177–180, Prague, Czech Republic. Association for Computational Linguistics.

Robert C. Moore and William Lewis. 2010. Intelligent selection of language model training data. In *Proceedings of the ACL 2010 Conference Short Papers*, ACLShort '10, pages 220–224, Uppsala, Sweden. Association for Computational Linguistics.

Myle Ott, Sergey Edunov, Alexei Baevski, Angela Fan, Sam Gross, Nathan Ng, David Grangier, and Michael Auli. 2019. fairseq: A fast, extensible toolkit for sequence modeling. In *Proceedings of NAACL-HLT 2019: Demonstrations*.

Myle Ott, Sergey Edunov, David Grangier, and Michael Auli. 2018. Scaling neural machine translation. In *WMT*, pages 1–9. Association for Computational Linguistics.

Kishore Papineni, Salim Roukos, Todd Ward, and Wei-Jing Zhu. 2002. Bleu: A method for automatic evaluation of machine translation. In *Proceedings of the 40th Annual Meeting on Association for Computational Linguistics*, ACL '02, pages 311–318, Philadelphia, Pennsylvania. Association for Computational Linguistics.

Anthony Rousseau. 2013. Xenc: An open-source tool for data selection in natural language processing. *Prague Bull. Math. Linguistics*, 100:73–82.

Rico Sennrich, Barry Haddow, and Alexandra Birch. 2016. Improving neural machine translation models with monolingual data. In *Proceedings of the 54th Annual Meeting of the Association for Computational Linguistics (Volume 1: Long Papers)*, pages 86–96, Berlin, Germany. Association for Computational Linguistics.

Ashish Vaswani, Noam Shazeer, Niki Parmar, Jakob Uszkoreit, Llion Jones, Aidan N Gomez, Ł ukasz Kaiser, and Illia Polosukhin. 2017. Attention is all you need. In I. Guyon, U. V. Luxburg, S. Bengio, H. Wallach, R. Fergus, S. Vishwanathan, and R. Garnett, editors, *Advances in Neural Information Processing Systems 30*, pages 5998–6008. Curran Associates, Inc.

The University of Maryland's Kazakh–English Neural Machine Translation System at WMT19

Eleftheria Briakou and **Marine Carpuat**
Department of Computer Science
University of Maryland
College Park, MD 20742, USA
ebriakou@cs.umd.edu, marine@cs.umd.edu

Abstract

This paper describes the University of Maryland's submission to the WMT 2019 Kazakh to English news translation task. We study the impact of transfer learning from another low-resource but related language. We experiment with different ways of encoding lexical units to maximize lexical overlap between the two language pairs, as well as back-translation and ensembling. The submitted system improves over a Kazakh–only baseline by +5.45 BLEU on *newstest*2019.

1 Introduction

Neural Machine Translation (NMT) outperforms traditional phrase-based statistical machine translation provided that large amounts of parallel data are available (Bahdanau et al., 2014; Sennrich et al., 2017; Vaswani et al., 2017). However, it performs poorly under low-resource conditions (Koehn and Knowles, 2017).

While much work addresses this problem via semi-supervised learning from monolingual text (Sennrich et al., 2016; He et al., 2016), we focus on transfer learning from another language pair (Zoph et al., 2016; Nguyen and Chiang, 2017; Lakew et al., 2018). In this setting, an NMT system is firstly trained using auxiliary parallel data from a so-called "parent" language pair and then the trained model is used to initialize a "child" model which is further trained on a low-resource language pair. Similar approaches that support cross-lingual transfer learning for Multi-lingual NMT train a model on the concatenation of all data instead of employing sequential training (Gu et al., 2018; Zhou et al., 2018; Wang et al., 2019).

Transfer learning has been found effective in submissions to WMT in previous years: Kocmi et al. (2018) reported improvements of +2.4 BLEU on the low-resource Estonian→English translation task by transfer learning from Finnish→English. Interestingly, Kocmi and Bojar (2018) observed that the transfer learning approach is still effective when there is no relatedness between the "child" and "parent" language-pairs and also hypothesize that the size of the parent training set is the most important factor leading to translation quality improvements. However, previous work has also empirically validated that transfer learning benefits most when "child"-"parent" languages belong to the same or linguistically similar language family (Dabre et al., 2017). Specifically, Nguyen and Chiang (2017) showed consistent improvements in two Turkic languages via transfering from another related, low-resource language.

Taking those recent results into consideration, our main focus at WMT19 is to examine transfer learning for the Kazakh–English language pair using additional parallel data from Turkish–English. While using distinct writing systems, both source languages belong to the Turkic language family and preserve many morphological and syntactic features common for that group (Kessikbayeva and Cicekli, 2014). As a result, they constitute a suitable "child"-"parent" language-pair choice for exploring transfer learning between related low-resource languages. In this direction, we conduct experiments to address the following questions:

- How can we represent lexical units to exploit vocabulary overlap between languages? We compare bilingual and monolingual byte-pair encoding models with the recently proposed soft decoupled encoding model.

- How can we leverage both "child" and "parent" parallel data to obtain synthetic back-translated data from monolingual resources?

Proceedings of the Fourth Conference on Machine Translation (WMT), Volume 2: Shared Task Papers (Day 1) pages 134–140
Florence, Italy, August 1-2, 2019. ©2019 Association for Computational Linguistics

2 Approach

Our method follows a simple strategy used in Wang et al. (2019) for multilingual training: we directly train NMT models on the concatenation of parallel data covering both the "child" and "parent" languages with no metadata to distinguish between them.[1]

Within this framework, we study the impact of (a) different lexical representations that attempt to maximize parameter sharing across related languages, (b) romanization to increase overlap between Turkish and Kazakh which are originally written in distinct scripts, (c) synthetic training data obtained by back-translation.

2.1 Lexical Units

How can we define lexical units to maximize information sharing across related source languages? We compare different configurations of sub-word segmentations using different variants of the standard Byte-Pair Encoding (BPE) framework (Sennrich et al., 2016), and compare them with the Soft Decoupled Encoding framework that exploits character n-gram representations of words instead of sub-words (Wang et al., 2019).

Joint BPEs (JBPEs) BPEs are learned jointly from the concatenation of "child" and "parent" parallel data. The advantage of this strategy is that the sub-word segmentations of related words in the two languages are encouraged to be more aligned; thus enabling the sharing of their representations on the source side due to a larger vocabulary overlap. Although, the "child" language might be "overwhelmed" by the "parent" language when there is a significant difference in the amount of their data (Neubig and Hu, 2018). This could lead to over-segmentation of the "child" language and subsequently limit the expressive power of the NMT system.

Separate BPEs (SBPEs) BPEs are learned separately for each language. This framework was found to be effective in the multilingual setting, especially for translation from extremely low-resource languages (Neubig and Hu, 2018). However, learning the merging operations separately might lead to unaligned sub-units between the two languages that fail to exploit relationships between their lexical representations.

Soft Decoupled Encoding (SDE) Small discrepancies in the spelling of words that share the same semantics across the two languages could lead to different segmented sub-units and hinder the lexical-level sharing between them. To take into account those spelling differences, we further experiment with the SDE encoding framework that is not based on any pre-processing segmentation. Specifically, SDE represents a word as a decomposition of two components: a character encoding that models the language-specific spelling of the word and a latent semantic embedding that captures its language-agnostic semantics. Following, we briefly summarize the main SDE components as proposed in Wang et al. (2019):

Lexical embedding Each word w is first decomposed to its bag of character n-grams (BoN(w)). Let C be the number number of character n-grams in the vocabulary and D be the dimension of the corresponding character n-gram embeddings. To acquire a lexical representation $c(w)$, the word is looked up to an embedding matrix $W_c \in \mathbb{R}^{C \times D}$ as shown below:

$$c(w) = \tanh(\text{BoN}(w) \cdot W_c) \qquad (1)$$

Language Specific Transformation Next each word is passed through a language dependent transformation. For each language L_i a matrix $W_{L_i} \in \mathbb{R}^{D \times D}$ is learned and the transformed embeddings $c_i(w)$ is computed:

$$c_i(w) = \tanh(c(w) \cdot W_{L_i}) \qquad (2)$$

Latent Semantic Embedding The shared semantic concepts among languages are represented by a matrix $W_s \in \mathbb{R}^{S \times D}$, where S corresponds to the number of semantic concepts a language can express. The latent embeddings of a word w is then given as:

$$e_{\text{latent}}(w) = \text{Softmax}(c_i(w) \cdot W_s^T) \cdot W_s \qquad (3)$$

Finally, the SDE embedding of word w is extracted as a combination of the language-dependent lexical encoding and the latent embedding:

$$e_{\text{SDE}}(w) = e_{\text{latent}}(w) + c_i(w) \qquad (4)$$

---

[1] We did not experiment with sequential training of the "parent" and "child" language pairs to establish a fair comparison between our BPE-based models and the SDE model that opts for joint training.

Encoding	Original		Romanized	
Word	molekül	молекула	molekuel	molekula
SBPEs	m_ol_ek_ül	мол_ек_ул_а	m_ol_ek_uel	mol_ek_ul_a
JBPEs	mol_ek_ül	мол_ек_ ул_а	mol_ek_uel	mol_ek_ula
Word	fosfor	фосфор	fosfor	fosfor
SBPEs	f_os_for	ф_ос_фор	f_os_for	f_os_for
JBPEs	fos_for	ф_ос_фор	fos_for	fos_for
Word	kalamar	кальмар	kalamar	kalmar
SBPEs	kal_am_ar	к_аль_ мар	kal_am_ar	kalm_ar
JBPEs	kal_am_ar	к_аль_ мар	kalam_ar	kal_mar

Table 1: Examples of words sharing significant lexical overlap in Kazakh and Turkish among with their corresponding sub-words segmentations.

2.2 Romanization

Given that the provided Kazakh and Turkish data are written in the Cyrillic and Latin scripts respectively, we investigate the impact of mapping text in the two languages into a common orthography. We transliterate both the "child" and the "parent" data using a transliteration tool[2] that applies the same romanization rules to encourage more overlap between child and parent data. Table 1 illustrates how romanization makes shared vocabulary and similarity between the two languages more explicit than using the original scripts.

Table 2 summarizes the statistical overlap on the source side vocabularies between the two languages for different lexical encodings with and without romanization. This analysis indicates that using the original script can be seen as an attempt to explore transfer learning when the lexical-level sharing between the two languages is limited. On the other hand, the vocabulary overlap between them is significantly increased once we romanize the data.

2.3 Synthetic Data

We further explore different ways to incorporate target-side English monolingual data provided by the competition into low-resource NMT. Following the widely used back-translation approach (Sennrich et al., 2016), we create synthetic parallel data and then train new NMT models on the mixture of real and synthetic parallel data.

Empty source baseline The source side of each monolingual example sentence is linked to an

Method	Romanization	# Merge op.	Overlap
JBPEs	✓	32K	0.44
	✗		0.13
	✓	64K	0.33
	✗		0.11
SBPEs	✓	32K	0.18
	✗		0.04
	✓	64K	0.13
	✗		0.04
		n-gram	**Overlap**
SDE	✓	4	0.67
	✓	5	0.62

Table 2: Statistical overlap results between the vocabularies of the "child" and "parent" languages on the source sides for different encoding schemes. # Merge op. refers to the number of merge operations when BPEs are explored. For the SDE method we compute the overlap between the n-gram character vocabularies (e.g., n-gram=4 corresponds to $n=\{1,2,3,4\}$).

empty sentence (denoted by an artificial <null> token).

Back-translation We create synthetic source sentences from automatically back-translating each target (English) sentence into the source language (Kazakh). Within this setting, we only use the original English-Kazakh parallel data to train a model that translates in the opposite direction.

Back-translation+transfer Given the data scarcity of the Kazakh parallel data we also attempt to incorporate both Kazakh and Turkish data to train a model that translates in the opposite direction. In order to produce output that is more similar to our main language of interest, we

---

[2]https://www.isi.edu/~ulf/uroman.html

introduce two artificial tokens (<2kk>, <2tr>) at the beginning of the input sentence to indicate the target language the model should translate to (Johnson et al., 2017). After the reversed system is trained we back-translate each target sentence to a Kazakh synthetic sentence.[3]

3 Model Configuration

Our NMT systems are built upon the publicly available code[4] of Wang et al. (2019) and are sequence-to-sequence 1-layer attentional long-short term memory units (LSTMs) with a hidden dimension of 512 for both the encoder and the decoder. The word embedding dimension is kept at 128, and all other layer dimensions are set to 512. We use a dropout rate of 0.3 for the word embedding and the output vector before the decoder Softmax layer. The batch size is set to be 1500 words. We evaluate by development set BLEU score (Papineni et al., 2002) for every 2500 training batches. For training, we use the Adam optimizer with a learning rate of 0.001. We use learning rate decay of 0.8, and stop training if the model performance on development set doesn't improve for 5 evaluation steps. We run each experiment with 3 different random seeds.

4 Data and Pre-processing

Parallel Data   We use all the parallel data available for the Kazakh–English shared task except for the Wikipedia Titles as they consist of very short sentences (approximately 3 words each). Specifically, the "child" training data consist of about 7.5K sentence pairs from the News Commentary Corpus, and 98K sentence pairs from the English-Kazakh crawled corpus[5]. Additionally, we used approximately 200K Turkish–English sentence-pairs from the Setimes2 Corpus that are provided by the WMT18 competition.

Monolingual   For the *Empty source* and *Back-translation* methods of creating synthetic data we used the target-side of the Turkish–English parallel corpus as monolingual data. For the *Back-Translation+transfer* experiment we used 100K randomly selected sentences from the News Commentary corpus, excluding sentences with less than 5 words and more than 50 words.

---

[3]Each English sentence of the monolingual corpus is augmented with a <2kk> token at the beginning.

[4]`https://github.com/cindyxinyiwang/SDE`

[5]We didn't filter out any sentence pairs from this corpus.

Pre-processing   We process all corpora consistently. We tokenize the sentences and perform truecasing with the Moses scripts (Koehn et al., 2007). For all the experiments we consistently use 8K BPEs on the English target side. We experiment with $\{32, 64\}$K merge operations for the models using BPE encoding and $\{4, 5\}$ n-grams for the SDE framework. To establish a fair comparison between the source language representations, we consistently use the same encoding for English words (target side) using BPEs learned on the concatenation of all the English data.

Tuning and Testing Data   The official news-dev2019 is used as the validation set, and news-test2019 is used as the test set.

5 Experiments

Starting from *Baseline* BPE-based NMT systems trained using only the Kazakh data provided by the competition, we conduct the following experiments.

5.1 Byte Pair Encoding

Table 3 presents our results of 3 runs using $\{32, 64\}$K merge operations in total for each experiment. Generally, both Joint and Separate BPE segmentation strategies, with and without romanization improve BLEU over the *Baseline*. Previous empirical results on transfer learning for extremely low-resource languages indicated that training the BPE operations separately for the "child" and "parent" languages has a large positive effect on the performance of the model (Wang et al., 2019). By contrast, JBPEs and SBPEs perform comparably well in almost all configurations here. This could be attributed to our less imbalanced setting where the ratio of "child"-"parent" data is $1 : 2$, and the child language therefore contributes more to sub-word segmentation rules.

The best BLEU score is achieved using 32K JBPEs on the romanized data which is consistent with the configuration with the largest vocabulary overlap, according to Table 2. However, using $\{32, 64\}$K SBPEs on the original data only hurts BLEU by 0.5 and 1.24, despite the lack of lexical overlap. This suggests that most of the improvement does not come from the shared encoder vocabulary.

Method	32K BPEs		64K BPEs	
	Original	Romanized	Original	Romanized
Baseline	4.33 ± 0.16	4.49 ± 0.02	4.35 ± 0.13	4.21 ± 0.28
JBPEs	$\mathbf{9.35 \pm 0.10}$	$\mathbf{9.89 \pm 0.14}$	$\mathbf{8.65 \pm 0.27}$	8.77 ± 0.09
SBPEs	7.10 ± 0.26	9.70 ± 0.28	8.41 ± 0.08	$\mathbf{8.85 \pm 0.34}$

Table 3: Kazakh $\rightarrow$ English BLEU score results on news-test2019 for different BPE configurations and versions of data.

N-gram	*Lexical*	*Latent*	*Specific*	**BLEU**
	✓			$\mathbf{9.12 \pm 0.27}$
4	✓	✓		8.76 ± 0.29
	✓	✓	✓	6.57 ± 0.20
	✓			$\mathbf{9.17 \pm 0.21}$
5	✓	✓		8.69 ± 0.21
	✓	✓	✓	6.21 ± 0.18
Baseline-BPE				8.65 ± 0.27

Table 4: SDE Experiments using 64K n-grams of the concatenated corpora. The last line refers to the best BLEU score using 64K BPEs for comparison.

5.2 Soft-Decoupled Encoding

We compare the BPE results with different configurations of the SDE model. Table 4 presents average results of 3 runs with different random seeds, where we use 64K character n-grams as our vocabulary. The *Language Specific Transformation* consistently harms the BLEU score for both $n = 4, 5$. This result validates the empirical observations of Wang et al. (2019); the separate projection does not help when the "child"-"parent" languages have a significant surface lexical overlap. We also observe comparable BLEU results when we use SDE embeddings or lexical embeddings (where the latent embedding is not taken into account) to encode the semantics of words. The best BLEU scores are achieved for the lexical encoding using either 4-grams or 5-grams of words.

In both cases we observe that the n-gram models perform sligthly better than the best BPE model that uses the same number of merge operations as the n-gram vocabulary size (we refer to that model as *Baseline-BPE* on Table 4). However, we do not adopt SDE in our submitted system as the small BLEU score improvement comes with higher computational cost when compared to the BPE models.

5.3 Synthetic Data

Finally we experiment with back-translation of monolingual English corpora. All experiments used romanized text segmented with 32K BPE merge operations. Table 5 compares 3 different ways of using the same English data extracted from the target side of the Turkish–English parallel corpus. Each target sentence is coupled with a synthetic Kazakh sentence (*Back-translation*), an empty source sentence as a control (*Empty*) or a real Turkish sentence (*Transfer*). The ratio of real to additional data is kept to $1 : 2$ in all cases.

NMT training does not benefit from the back-translated data as it achieves nearly the same BLEU as the baseline model. Suprisingly empty source sentences yield better results than back-translation, suggesting that the synthetic back-translations are of low quality. Translating into Kazakh is challenging given the small amount of data available, especially for translating from a morphologically poor to a morphologically rich language. Finally, using real Turkish data on the source side achieves the best improvement over the baseline system ($+4.4$ BLEU).

Method	Synthetic	BLEU
Baseline		4.49
Empty	✓	5.26
Back-Translation	✓	4.64
Transfer		**9.89**

Table 5: Experiments using 200K monolingual data extracted from the target side of Turkish–English parallel corpus. The *Baseline* system is trained only on Kazakh data.

Given that in all these 3 experiments the decoder model was trained on the exact same English data, these results suggest that the transfer learning benefits both the encoder and decoder models.

Method	Synthetic	BLEU
Baseline-Transfer		**9.89**
Empty	✓	9.17
Back-Translation	✓	9.38
+ ensemble(4)*	✓	**9.94**

Table 6: Experiments using additional 100K News Commentary monolingual data. The Baseline system is trained on the concatenation of Kazakh–Turkish parallel data. The ⋆ symbol denotes our primary submission for human evaluation.

Finally, we attempt to combine Kazakh and Turkish parallel data to back-translate 100K additional monolingual data to Kazakh via training a NMT model that has control over the output language, as can be seen in Table 6. In this experiment our *Baseline-Transfer* system refers to the best model trained on the concatenation of "child" and "parent" data. In contrast to the previous experiment we now combine Kazakh, Turkish and synthetic data with a ratio 1 : 2 : 1. We observe that in both cases (*Back-translation*, *Empty*) the BLEU score of the system trained on the augmented data fails to outperform the *Baseline-Transfer* performance, possibly due to the fact that the real Kazakh data have been "overwhelmed" by the auxiliary ones (Poncelas et al., 2018). However, we could assume that the quality of the back-translated data is slightly better once we utilized the Turkish data (given that it performs better than the *Empty* experiment).

Finally, the last row of Table 6 reports the BLEU score of our **primary submission**.[6] Specifically, the submitted model is an ensemble obtained by averaging the output distributions of 4 models trained on Kazakh, Turkish and Back-Translated using different random seeds.

6   Conclusion

This paper presents the University of Maryland's NMT system for WMT 2019 Kazakh → English news translation task. Specifically, we explored how to improve neural machine translation of a low-resource language by incorporating parallel data from a related, also low-resource language.

---

[6]The *Baseline-Transfer* model slightly under-performed the *Baseline-Transfer+Back-Translation* model on the development set. Given that we did not have access to test data during evaluation time, our primary submission was based on evaluation on the development set.

Our empirical results validate that transfer learning benefits BLEU even when transfering from a low-resource language pair. Furthermore, our results suggest that translation quality (in terms of BLEU score) of the language-pair of focus is most benefited when the surface-level parameter sharing between the lexical representations of the two related languages is maximized. Finally, we observed that NMT training with synthetic data is sensitive to the quality of the back-translation.

References

Dzmitry Bahdanau, Kyunghyun Cho, and Yoshua Bengio. 2014. Neural machine translation by jointly learning to align and translate. *arXiv e-prints*, abs/1409.0473.

Raj Dabre, Tetsuji Nakagawa, and Hideto Kazawa. 2017. An empirical study of language relatedness for transfer learning in neural machine translation. In *Proceedings of the 31st Pacific Asia Conference on Language, Information and Computation*, pages 282–286. The National University (Phillippines).

Jiatao Gu, Hany Hassan, Jacob Devlin, and Victor O.K. Li. 2018. Universal neural machine translation for extremely low resource languages. In *Proceedings of the 2018 Conference of the North American Chapter of the Association for Computational Linguistics: Human Language Technologies, Volume 1 (Long Papers)*, pages 344–354, New Orleans, Louisiana. Association for Computational Linguistics.

Di He, Yingce Xia, Tao Qin, Liwei Wang, Nenghai Yu, Tie-Yan Liu, and Wei-Ying Ma. 2016. Dual learning for machine translation. In *Proceedings of the 30th International Conference on Neural Information Processing Systems*, pages 820–828, USA. Curran Associates Inc.

Melvin Johnson, Mike Schuster, Quoc V. Le, Maxim Krikun, Yonghui Wu, Zhifeng Chen, Nikhil Thorat, Fernanda Viégas, Martin Wattenberg, Greg Corrado, Macduff Hughes, and Jeffrey Dean. 2017. Google's multilingual neural machine translation system: Enabling zero-shot translation. *Transactions of the Association for Computational Linguistics*, 5:339–351.

Gulshat Kessikbayeva and Ilyas Cicekli. 2014. Rule based morphological analyzer of kazakh language. In *Proceedings of the 2014 Joint Meeting of SIGMORPHON and SIGFSM*, pages 46–54, Baltimore, Maryland. Association for Computational Linguistics.

Tom Kocmi and Ondřej Bojar. 2018. Trivial transfer learning for low-resource neural machine translation. In *Proceedings of the Third Conference on Machine Translation: Research Papers*, pages 244–252, Belgium, Brussels. Association for Computational Linguistics.

Tom Kocmi, Roman Sudarikov, and Ondřej Bojar. 2018. CUNI submissions in WMT18. In *Proceedings of the Third Conference on Machine Translation: Shared Task Papers*, pages 431–437, Belgium, Brussels. Association for Computational Linguistics.

Philipp Koehn, Hieu Hoang, Alexandra Birch, Chris Callison-Burch, Marcello Federico, Nicola Bertoldi, Brooke Cowan, Wade Shen, Christine Moran, Richard Zens, Chris Dyer, Ondrej Bojar, Alexandra Constantin, and Evan Herbst. 2007. Moses: Open source toolkit for statistical machine translation. In *Proceedings of the 45th Annual Meeting of the Association for Computational Linguistics Companion Volume Proceedings of the Demo and Poster Sessions*, pages 177–180, Prague, Czech Republic. Association for Computational Linguistics.

Philipp Koehn and Rebecca Knowles. 2017. Six challenges for neural machine translation. In *Proceedings of the First Workshop on Neural Machine Translation*, pages 28–39, Vancouver. Association for Computational Linguistics.

Surafel Melaku Lakew, Aliia Erofeeva, Matteo Negri, Marcello Federico, and Marco Turchi. 2018. Transfer learning in multilingual neural machine translation with dynamic vocabulary. In *Proceedings of the 15th International Workshop on Spoken Language Translation (IWSLT 2018)*, pages 54–62, Brussels, Belgium.

Graham Neubig and Junjie Hu. 2018. Rapid adaptation of neural machine translation to new languages. In *Proceedings of the 2018 Conference on Empirical Methods in Natural Language Processing*, pages 875–880, Brussels, Belgium. Association for Computational Linguistics.

Toan Q. Nguyen and David Chiang. 2017. Transfer learning across low-resource, related languages for neural machine translation. In *Proceedings of the Eighth International Joint Conference on Natural Language Processing (Volume 2: Short Papers)*, pages 296–301, Taipei, Taiwan. Asian Federation of Natural Language Processing.

Kishore Papineni, Salim Roukos, Todd Ward, and Wei-Jing Zhu. 2002. Bleu: A method for automatic evaluation of machine translation. In *Proceedings of the 40th Annual Meeting on Association for Computational Linguistics*, ACL '02, pages 311–318, Stroudsburg, PA, USA. Association for Computational Linguistics.

Alberto Poncelas, Dimitar Shterionov, Andy Way, Gideon Maillette de Buy Wenniger, and Peyman Passban. 2018. Investigating backtranslation in neural machine translation. *CoRR*, abs/1804.06189.

Rico Sennrich, Alexandra Birch, Anna Currey, Ulrich Germann, Barry Haddow, Kenneth Heafield, Antonio Valerio Miceli Barone, and Philip Williams. 2017. The university of Edinburgh's neural MT systems for WMT17. In *Proceedings of the Second Conference on Machine Translation*, pages 389–399, Copenhagen, Denmark. Association for Computational Linguistics.

Rico Sennrich, Barry Haddow, and Alexandra Birch. 2016. Improving neural machine translation models with monolingual data. In *Proceedings of the 54th Annual Meeting of the Association for Computational Linguistics (Volume 1: Long Papers)*, pages 86–96, Berlin, Germany. Association for Computational Linguistics.

Ashish Vaswani, Noam Shazeer, Niki Parmar, Jakob Uszkoreit, Llion Jones, Aidan N Gomez, Ł ukasz Kaiser, and Illia Polosukhin. 2017. Attention is all you need. In I. Guyon, U. V. Luxburg, S. Bengio, H. Wallach, R. Fergus, S. Vishwanathan, and R. Garnett, editors, *Advances in Neural Information Processing Systems 30*, pages 5998–6008. Curran Associates, Inc.

Xinyi Wang, Hieu Pham, Philip Arthur, and Graham Neubig. 2019. Multilingual neural machine translation with soft decoupled encoding. *CoRR*, abs/1902.03499.

Zhong Zhou, Matthias Sperber, and Alexander Waibel. 2018. Massively parallel cross-lingual learning in low-resource target language translation. In *Proceedings of the Third Conference on Machine Translation: Research Papers*, pages 232–243, Belgium, Brussels. Association for Computational Linguistics.

Barret Zoph, Deniz Yuret, Jonathan May, and Kevin Knight. 2016. Transfer learning for low-resource neural machine translation. In *Proceedings of the 2016 Conference on Empirical Methods in Natural Language Processing*, pages 1568–1575, Austin, Texas. Association for Computational Linguistics.

DBMS-KU Interpolation for WMT19 News Translation Task

Sari Dewi Budiwati[1,2], Al Hafiz Akbar Maulana Siagian[1,3],
Tirana Noor Fatyanosa[1], Masayoshi Aritsugi[4],

[1]Computer Science and Electrical Engineering
Graduate School of Science and Technology, Kumamoto University, Japan
[2]School of Applied Science, Telkom University, Indonesia
[3]Indonesian Institute of Sciences, Indonesia
[4]Big Data Science and Technology
Faculty of Advanced Science and Technology, Kumamoto University, Japan
{saridewi, fatyanosa, alha002}@st.cs.kumamoto-u.ac.jp, aritsugi@cs.kumamoto-u.ac.jp

Abstract

This paper presents the participation of DBMS-KU Interpolation system in WMT19 shared task, namely, Kazakh-English language pair. We examine the use of interpolation method using a different language model order. Our Interpolation system combines a direct translation with Russian as a pivot language. We use 3-gram and 5-gram language model orders to perform the language translation in this work. To reduce noise in the pivot translation process, we prune the phrase table of source-pivot and pivot-target. Our experimental results show that our Interpolation system outperforms the Baseline in terms of BLEU-cased score by +0.5 and +0.1 points in Kazakh-English and English-Kazakh, respectively. In particular, using the 5-gram language model order in our system could obtain better BLEU-cased score than utilizing the 3-gram one. Interestingly, we found that by employing the Interpolation system could reduce the perplexity score of English-Kazakh when using 3-gram language model order.

1 Introduction

This paper describes our participation in the WMT19 shared task. We call our system DBMS-KU (Database Management System - Kumamoto University) Interpolation as we use our laboratory and university name, as well as we utilize Interpolation method in our experiments. We choose news translation task and focus on Kazakh-English (and vice versa) language pair.

Kazakh-English is a new shared task for this year, that is, no experience system description from previous WMT. Kazakh-English could be considered as low resource language pair due to the limitation of parallel corpora and morphological tools. Another challenge is the difference in the writing system between Kazakh and English languages. Kazakh uses Cyrillic letters, while English uses the alphabet. Different writing system

between language pair needs specific attention in the tokenization step because of its segmentation results that affect the BLEU-cased score. Thus, we are motivated to solve this intriguing and challenging task.

Kazakh to English machine translation has been explored in Statistical Machine Translation (SMT) (Assylbekov and Nurkas, 2014; Kuandykova et al., 2014; Kartbayev, 2015a,b) and Neural Machine Translation (NMT) (Myrzakhmetov and Kozhirbayev, 2018). Assylbekov and Nurkas (2014) have shown an interesting result that different n-gram and neural LSTM-based language models were able to reduce the perplexity score, i.e., giving better translation result. For this reason, we consider investigating different n-gram language model order in this work.

Interpolation has been used in Language Model (LM) (Allauzen and Riley, 2011; Liu et al., 2013; Heafield et al., 2016) and in Translation Model (TM) (Bisazza et al., 2011; Sennrich, 2012; Rosa et al., 2015). Also, the interpolation has been used in pivot language as a strategy to overcome the limitation of parallel corpora (Dabre et al., 2015; Hoang and Bojar, 2016; Kunchukuttan et al., 2017). Pivot strategy arises as a preliminary assumption that there are enough parallel corpora between source-pivot (SRC-PVT) and pivot-target (PVT-TRG) languages. Currently, English as lingua franca has more datasets compared to other languages. Thus, pivot researchers commonly use English as a bridge between source to target (Paul et al., 2013; El Kholy et al., 2013; Ahmadnia et al., 2017; Dabre et al., 2015; Trieu, 2017). However, Paul et al., (2013) and Dabre et al., (2015) have shown that using non-English as pivot language could be a better option to improve the translation results for particular language pair. Since Kazakh-English is categorized as low resource language pair, we adopt the pivot and interpolation strategies in our translation model.

Proceedings of the Fourth Conference on Machine Translation (WMT), Volume 2: Shared Task Papers (Day 1) pages 141–146
Florence, Italy, August 1-2, 2019. ©2019 Association for Computational Linguistics

In this work, we consider examining two systems, namely, Baseline and Interpolation. The Baseline system is a direct translation between each language pair, while Interpolation one is a combination of pivot and direct translation models. We use Russian as our pivot language with 3-gram and 5-gram language model orders in each system. Our experimental results are encouraging and indicate that using Interpolation system could obtain better BLEU-cased score than employing Baseline one when translating both Kazakh to English (KK-EN) and English to Kazakh (EN-KK).

This paper is organized as follows. Section 2 explains the data preprocessing and experiment setup for each system. Section 3 shows and discusses the obtained results. Section 4 provides the conclusion and future direction of this work.

2 Case Study and Experiment Setup

In this section, we describe the case study, dataset, and experiment of this study.

2.1 Kazakh to English Machine Translation

Kazakh language is an agglutinative and highly inflected language that belongs to the Turkic group (Makhambetov et al., 2013). This rich morphology leads to a different length of phrases when translating from English to Kazakh (Assylbekov and Nurkas, 2014). Therefore, the translation of KK-EN and vice versa is a challenging task. Moreover, the KK-EN is considered as low resource language pair due to the limitation of parallel corpora and morphological tools.

2.2 Data and preprocessing

We used a dataset provided by WMT19 organizer. Thus, our system was considered as a constrained system. To prepare parallel datasets, we cleaned the dataset by using our script because the original dataset had blank lines and unsynchronized sentences between source and target parallel corpora. In the Interpolation system, we used Russian-English dataset from WMT18. The dataset statistics of training *(train)* and development *(dev)* for Baseline and Interpolation systems are given in Table 1.

After cleaning the dataset, we followed dataset preprocessing as in (Myrzakhmetov and Kozhirbayev, 2018), namely, tokenizing, normalizing punctuation, recasing, and filtering the sentences. Tokenizing was used to separate the token and punctuation by inserting spaces. Our tokenization results were based on words. Thus, the obtained sentences of the tokenization results were longer than the original sentences. Since long sentences could cause problems in the training process, we removed the sentences with a length of more than 80 words. This process was called filtering the sentences. Normalizing punctuation was to convert the punctuation for being recognized by the decoder system. Recasing was to change the initial words into their most probable casing in order to reduce the data sparsity. All preprocessing steps were done by using scripts from Moses (Koehn et al., 2007).

2.3 Experiment setup

We used open source Moses decoder (Koehn et al., 2007) and Giza++ for word alignment, Ken-LM (Heafield, 2011) for language model, and MERT (Och, 2003) for tuning the weight. The translation results were measured by five automatic evaluations provided by the organizer, namely BLEU, BLEU-cased, TER, BEER 2.0, and CharacTER. However, in this paper, we used the BLEU-cased because it is the main comparison metric in the evaluation system[1].

We built two systems, namely, Baseline and Interpolation. The Baseline system is a direct translation between KK-EN and vice versa. Meanwhile, the Interpolation system is the combination of direct translation with pivot phrase table. Pivot phrase table was produced by merging the source to pivot (SRC-PVT) and pivot to target (PVT-TRG) by using Triangulation method (Hoang and Bojar, 2015). We built the Interpolation phrase table as follows:

- Constructing a phrase table from SRC-PVT and PVT-TRG systems and pruning the phrase table with *filter-pt* (Johnson et al., 2007). The pruning activity was intended to minimize the noise of SRC-PVT and PVT-TRG phrase tables.

- Merging two pruned phrase tables by using the Triangulation method (Hoang and Bojar, 2015). The result was called `TmTriangulate` phrase table.

- Combining `TmTriangulate` and direct translation model with *dev* phrase table as

---

[1]http://matrix.statmt.org/

Dataset	Sentences	Average Sentence Length	Vocab
Baseline system			
Train			
news-commentary-v14.en-kk.kk	9,619	18.0857	29,142
news-commentary-v14.en-kk.en	9,619	22.1487	16,742
Dev			
newsdev2019-enkk.kk	2,068	18.0164	11,389
newsdev2019-enkk.en	2,068	22.2316	7,726
Language Model			
news-commentary-v14.kk	12,707	17.2109	-
news-commentary-v14.en	532,560	21.5762	-
Interpolation system			
Train			
news-commentary-v14.kk-ru.ru	7,230	23.6836	27,819
news-commentary-v14.kk-ru.kk	7,230	20.1187	24,627
news-commentary-v14.en-ru.en	97,652	23.0416	51,566
news-commentary-v14.en-ru.ru	97,652	21.3508	126,476
Dev			
news-commentary-v14.kk-ru.ru	2,000	20.8755	11,841
news-commentary-v14.kk-ru.kk	2,000	18.048	10,561
newstest2018-ruen.dev.en	3,000	20.975	10,108
newstest2018-ruen.dev.ru	3,000	17.3293	17,091
Language Model			
news-commentary-v14.kk	12,707	17.2109	
news-commentary-v14.en-ru.ru	114,375	21.2678	
news-commentary-v14.en-ru.en	114,375	22.9811	

Table 1: Dataset statistic for Baseline and Interpolation systems

Language Pair	3-gram LM	5-gram LM
KK-EN		
1. Baseline system	2.6	2.9
2. Interpolation system	2.7	3.4
EN-KK		
1. Baseline system	0.8	0.8
2. Interpolation system	0.9	0.9

Table 2: BLEU-cased score results

references. We used linear interpolation with backoff mode and exploited *combine-ptables* tools (Bisazza et al., 2011). The result was called `Interpolation` phrase table.

3 Results and Discussions

In this section, we show the obtained automatic evaluation results using BLEU-cased score. We also discuss the effect of the different language model order with the BLEU-cased score. Furthermore, we analyze the perplexity score on Interpolation system.

3.1 Language model effects on BLEU-cased score

In this paper, we conducted experiments for two language model orders, i.e., 3-gram and 5-gram, and two systems, viz., Baseline, and Interpolation. As shown in Table 2, the 5-gram language model order had more significant influence than the 3-gram one on the BLEU-cased score for KK-EN translation in both Baseline and Interpolation systems. The improvement in KK-EN was obtained by +0.3 and +0.7 points for Baseline and Interpolation systems, respectively. However, the BLEU-cased score for EN-KK could not be improved in terms of the language model order. These results might indicate that the language model order influenced the BLEU-cased score.

In terms of the translation system, the Interpolation system obtained higher BLEU-cased score than the Baseline one for all language model and translation directions. The improvement of BLEU-cased score from Baseline to Interpolation system for KK-EN using 3-gram and 5-gram was +0.1 and +0.5 points, respectively. Meanwhile, the improvement from Baseline to Interpolation System for EN-KK was +0.1 for both 3-gram and 5-gram orders. These results indicated that the use of pivot language in the Interpolation system combined with longer language model also had a significant influence on the BLEU-cased score.

Also, we found that the KK-EN obtained higher BLEU-cased score than the EN-KK in terms of the translation direction. This result might be influenced by the number of target LM datasets in each translation direction. As shown in Table1, KK-EN had 532,560 sentences, while EN-

KK had 12,707 sentences. The translation direction of KK-EN, that is, having almost 42 times larger number of sentences than EN-KK, could obtain a higher BLEU-cased score than that of EN-KK. This result indicated that the number of the target LM dataset in the experiments might be able to improve the BLEU-cased score.

Although our obtained BLEU-cased score was relatively low, we showed that by combining Baseline and pivot parallel corpora with different LM order was a valuable effort compared with using direct parallel corpora only. Moreover, the improvement of BLEU-cased score could be influenced by the language model order, the translation system, and the target monolingual LM dataset.

3.2 Perplexity effects on Interpolation system

Language model (LM) is one of the SMT components to ensure how good is the model by using perplexity as measurement. Lower perplexity score indicates better language models, while high perplexity score represents that the language model has poor quality. We show the perplexity score of the target language test dataset according to each n-gram language model trained on the respective training dataset in Table 3.

As shown in Table 3, the lowest perplexity score for KK-EN was obtained by the 5-gram Baseline system, i.e., 45.51. Thus, the best model for KK-EN was 5-gram Baseline system. However, we found that the difference of perplexity score for 5-gram model between Baseline and Interpolation systems was not quite significant, i.e., 5.42. Specifically, the perplexity of 5-gram of Baseline was 45.51, while the perplexity of 5-gram of Interpolation was 50.93. This finding might indicate that pivot language with interpolation system could be a beneficial approach in the translation process.

In EN-KK, the lowest perplexity score was obtained by 5-gram Baseline system, i.e., 77.18. Thus, the best model for EN-KK was 5-gram Baseline system. However, we found that the difference of perplexity score between 5-gram Baseline and 3-gram Interpolation systems was not quite significant, i.e., 2.16. Specifically, the perplexity of 5-gram of Baseline was 77.18, while the perplexity of 3-gram of Interpolation was 79.34. This finding might indicate that using the interpolation system with 3-gram model only could reduce the perplexity score of EN-KK that using the longer n-gram language model, i.e., 5-gram. Nevertheless, it would be better to study further the cause of this finding in the future.

4 Conclusion and future work

We examined the effect of different LM order with linear interpolation method for participating in WMT19 shared task, namely, Kazakh-English language pair. Our Interpolation system utilized the combination of direct translation, i.e., Baseline, with Russian as our pivot language. We used 3-gram and 5-gram language model orders in our Baseline and Interpolation systems. The BLEU-cased score of using Interpolation system could outperform that of utilizing Baseline one. This good performance of Interpolation system was obtained by using 3-gram and 5-gram language model orders for both Kazakh to English (KK-EN) and English to Kazakh (EN-KK) translations. We found that the Interpolation system indicated a different effect on each of KK-EN and EN-KK in terms of the perplexity score. In KK-EN, the pivot language with interpolation system could be an option in the translation process because the difference of perplexity score between Baseline and Interpolation was not quite significant. Interestingly, we found that the Interpolation system using 3-gram language model order could reduce the perplexity score compared with utilizing longer n-gram one in EN-KK.

In this shared task, we used standardized tokenizer from Moses. In the future, it must be worthwhile to use specific Kazakh and Russian tokenizers as their results will affect the BLEU-case scored. Another pivot language that has the same language family or has the same word order with the Kazakh language could also be a valuable effort. In addition, the use of different n-gram can also be taken into account for the next future research. Furthermore, the utilization of morph-based language modeling can also be applied to the system. Finally, the different interpolation scheme in another MT model, i.e., NMT, with out-domain dataset should be investigated to overcome the sparse of Kazakh resources.

Acknowledgments

A. H. A. M. Siagian would like to express his gratitude for the scholarship support from RISET-Pro (Research and Innovation in Science and Technology Project) KEMENRISTEKDIKTI (Ministry of

Language pair	3-gram LM	5-gram LM
KK-EN		
1. Baseline system	- Incl OOVs: 829.59 - Excl OOVs: 77.79	- Incl OOVs: 617.36 - Excl OOVs: 45.51
2. Interpolation system	- Incl OOVs: 1034.50 - Excl OOVs: 94.72	- Incl OOVs: 762.79 - Excl OOVs: 50.93
EN-KK		
1. Baseline system	- Incl OOVs: 328.940 - Excl OOVs: 103.27	- Incl OOVs: 256.138 - Excl OOVs: 77.185
2. Interpolation system	- Incl OOVs: 256.13 - Excl OOVs: 79.34	- Incl OOVs: 276.85 - Excl OOVs: 85.40

Table 3: Perplexity results

Research, Technology and Higher Education of the Republic of Indonesia).

References

Benyamin Ahmadnia, Javier Serrano, and Gholamreza Haffari. 2017. Persian-spanish low-resource statistical machine translation through english as pivot language. In *Proceedings of the International Conference Recent Advances in Natural Language Processing, RANLP 2017, Varna, Bulgaria, September 2 - 8, 2017*, pages 24–30.

Cyril Allauzen and Michael Riley. 2011. Bayesian language model interpolation for mobile speech input. In *INTERSPEECH 2011, 12th Annual Conference of the International Speech Communication Association, Florence, Italy, August 27-31, 2011*, pages 1429–1432.

Zhenisbek Assylbekov and Assulan Nurkas. 2014. Initial explorations in kazakh to english statistical machine translation. In *Proceedings of the The First Italian Conference on Computational Linguistics CLiC-it 2014*, page 12.

Arianna Bisazza, Nick Ruiz, and Marcello Federico. 2011. Fill-up versus interpolation methods for phrase-based SMT adaptation. In *2011 International Workshop on Spoken Language Translation, IWSLT 2011, San Francisco, CA, USA, December 8-9, 2011*, pages 136–143.

Raj Dabre, Fabien Cromieres, Sadao Kurohashi, and Pushpak Bhattacharyya. 2015. Leveraging small multilingual corpora for smt using many pivot languages. In *Proceedings of the 2015 Conference of the North American Chapter of the Association for Computational Linguistics: Human Language Technologies*, pages 1192–1202. Association for Computational Linguistics.

Ahmed El Kholy, Nizar Habash, Gregor Leusch, Evgeny Matusov, and Hassan Sawaf. 2013. Language independent connectivity strength features for phrase pivot statistical machine translation. In *Proceedings of the 51st Annual Meeting of the Association for Computational Linguistics (Volume 2: Short Papers)*, pages 412–418. Association for Computational Linguistics.

Kenneth Heafield. 2011. KenLM: faster and smaller language model queries. In *Proceedings of the EMNLP 2011 Sixth Workshop on Statistical Machine Translation*, pages 187–197, Edinburgh, Scotland, United Kingdom.

Kenneth Heafield, Chase Geigle, Sean Massung, and Lane Schwartz. 2016. Normalized log-linear interpolation of backoff language models is efficient. In *Proceedings of the 54th Annual Meeting of the Association for Computational Linguistics, ACL 2016, August 7-12, 2016, Berlin, Germany, Volume 1: Long Papers*.

Duc Tam Hoang and Ondrej Bojar. 2015. Tmtriangulate: A tool for phrase table triangulation. *Prague Bull. Math. Linguistics*, 104:75–86.

Duc Tam Hoang and Ondrej Bojar. 2016. Pivoting methods and data for czech-vietnamese translation via english. In *Proceedings of the 19th Annual Conference of the European Association for Machine Translation, EAMT 2017, Riga, Latvia, May 30 - June 1, 2016*, pages 190–202.

Howard Johnson, Joel Martin, George Foster, and Roland Kuhn. 2007. Improving translation quality by discarding most of the phrasetable. In *Proceedings of the 2007 Joint Conference on Empirical Methods in Natural Language Processing and Computational Natural Language Learning (EMNLP-CoNLL)*.

Amandyk Kartbayev. 2015a. Learning word alignment models for kazakh-english machine translation. In *Integrated Uncertainty in Knowledge Modelling and Decision Making - 4th International Symposium, IUKM 2015, Nha Trang, Vietnam, October 15-17, 2015, Proceedings*, pages 326–335.

Amandyk Kartbayev. 2015b. SMT: A case study of kazakh-english word alignment. In *Current Trends in Web Engineering - 15th International Conference, ICWE 2015 Workshops, NLPIT, PEWET, SoWEMine, Rotterdam, The Netherlands, June 23-26, 2015. Revised Selected Papers*, pages 40–49.

Philipp Koehn, Hieu Hoang, Alexandra Birch, Chris Callison-Burch, Marcello Federico, Nicola Bertoldi, Brooke Cowan, Wade Shen, Christine Moran,

Richard Zens, Chris Dyer, Ondrej Bojar, Alexandra Constantin, and Evan Herbst. 2007. Moses: Open source toolkit for statistical machine translation. In *Proceedings of the 45th Annual Meeting of the Association for Computational Linguistics Companion Volume Proceedings of the Demo and Poster Sessions*, pages 177–180. Association for Computational Linguistics.

Ayana Kuandykova, Amandyk Kartbayev, and Tannur Kaldybekov. 2014. English -kazakh parallel corpus for statistical machine translation. In *International Journal on Natural Language Computing (IJNLC)*, page 65.

Anoop Kunchukuttan, Maulik Shah, Pradyot Prakash, and Pushpak Bhattacharyya. 2017. Utilizing lexical similarity between related, low-resource languages for pivot-based SMT. In *Proceedings of the Eighth International Joint Conference on Natural Language Processing (Volume 2: Short Papers)*, pages 283–289, Taipei, Taiwan. Asian Federation of Natural Language Processing.

Xunying Liu, Mark John Francis Gales, and Philip C. Woodland. 2013. Use of contexts in language model interpolation and adaptation. *Computer Speech & Language*, 27(1):301–321.

Olzhas Makhambetov, Aibek Makazhanov, Zhandos Yessenbayev, Bakhyt Matkarimov, Islam Sabyrgaliyev, and Anuar Sharafudinov. 2013. Assembling the Kazakh language corpus. In *Proceedings of the 2013 Conference on Empirical Methods in Natural Language Processing*, pages 1022–1031, Seattle, Washington, USA. Association for Computational Linguistics.

Bagdat Myrzakhmetov and Zhanibek Kozhirbayev. 2018. Extended language modeling experiments for kazakh. In *Proceedings of 2018 International Workshop on Computational Models in Language and Speech, CMLS 2018*. CEUR-WS.

Franz Josef Och. 2003. Minimum error rate training in statistical machine translation. In *Proceedings of the 41st Annual Meeting of Association for Computational Linguistics - Volume 1*, ACL '03, pages 160–167, Stroudsburg, PA, USA. Association for Computational Linguistics.

Michael Paul, Andrew Finch, and Eiichiro Sumita. 2013. How to choose the best pivot language for automatic translation of low-resource languages. *ACM Trans. Asian Lang. Inf. Process.*, 12(4):14:1–14:17.

Rudolf Rosa, Ondrej Dusek, Michal Novak, and Martil Popel. 2015. Translation model interpolation for domain adaptation in tectomt. In *Proceedings of the 1st Deep Machine Translation Workshop (DMTW 2015)*, volume 27, pages 89–96.

Rico Sennrich. 2012. Perplexity minimization for translation model domain adaptation in statistical machine translation. In *Proceedings of the 13th Conference of the European Chapter of the Association for Computational Linguistics*, EACL '12, pages 539–549, Stroudsburg, PA, USA. Association for Computational Linguistics.

Hai-Long Trieu. 2017. *A Study on Machine Translation for Low-Resource Languages*. Ph.D. thesis, Japan Advanced Institute of Science and Technology.

Lingua Custodia at WMT'19:
Attempts to Control Terminology

Franck Burlot
Lingua Custodia
Montigny-le-Bretonneux, France
`franck.burlot@linguacustodia.com`

Abstract

This paper describes Lingua Custodia's submission to the WMT'19 news shared task for German-to-French on the topic of the EU elections. We report experiments on the adaptation of the terminology of a machine translation system to a specific topic, aimed at providing more accurate translations of specific entities like political parties and person names, given that the shared task provided no in-domain training parallel data dealing with the restricted topic. Our primary submission to the shared task uses backtranslation generated with a type of decoding allowing the insertion of constraints in the output in order to guarantee the correct translation of specific terms that are not necessarily observed in the data.

1 Introduction

A sub-task of the WMT'19 News Translation shared task has been jointly organized by the University of Le Mans and Lingua Custodia: the translation of news articles dealing with the topic of the 2019 European Parliament elections for the French-German language pair. This brings back French, a language absent from the News Translation task since 2015, and pairs it with German, a morphologically richer language than English. Finally, the EU election topic brings new challenges to the task.

Such a restriction of the domain to a single topic makes the task very different from the translation of any news data. We propose to roughly define a domain according to two majors dimensions:

- **Syntactic structure**. The European election topic probably has no or few syntactic and stylistic differences with the general news domain, since we are in both cases dealing with news articles with the same characteristics. On the other hand, sentences in newspapers are generally longer than in casual discourse.

- **Terminology**. A specific topic implies a specific terminology. For instance, the system should not attempt a literal translation of the German politician's name *Wagenknecht*. It should also be aware of the specific translations of political party names in the press of the target language: the French party *France Insoumise* should not be translated into German. Furthermore, the French movement *gilets jaunes* (yellow vests) is refered to in the German press as *Gelbwesten*, and a literal translation, such as *gelbe Westen*, is inaccurate.

There exist efficient methods for domain adaptation in neural MT (Luong and Manning, 2015; Chu and Wang, 2018). The experiments introduced in this paper attempt to explore techniques that help to specifically adapt the terminology of a system to a restricted topic. However, a serious difficulty stands in the way: among the parallel data provided for the task, only 1,701 sentence pairs deal with the EU elections (development set). Recent monolingual data in German and French is available and contains several sentences using the required terminology, but we then lack the correct translations of the terms of interest.

This paper describes Lingua Custodia's attempts to specifically control the terminology generated by a Machine Translation (MT) system, using only the data provided at the Conference. The resulting German-to-French system was submitted at WMT'19.

In the first section, we provide an overview of our baselines and point out several terminology issues. We then describe our experiments with constrained decoding to control terminology. The last section introduces an attempt to relax the hard constraints applied to the decoder.

Proceedings of the Fourth Conference on Machine Translation (WMT), Volume 2: Shared Task Papers (Day 1) pages 147–154
Florence, Italy, August 1-2, 2019. ©2019 Association for Computational Linguistics

2   Baseline

The training parallel data provided for the task consisted of nearly 10M sentences, including *Europarl* (Koehn, 2005), *Common-crawl*, *News-commentary* and *Bicleaner07*. The former was the biggest (over 7M sentences) and also the noisiest corpus, containing bad characters, short phrases with only numbers, lists of products, sentences in the wrong language, obviously machine translated sentences, etc.

2.1   Data selection

We have performed a filtering of the *Bicleaner07* corpus in order to reduce the impact of noisy samples on the MT system, using *LC_Pruner*, a in-house system that was submitted at the First Automatic Translation Memory Cleaning Shared Task (Barbu et al., 2016). The system extracts several monolingual and bilingual features that are fed to a random forest classifier aimed at predicting if a sentence pair is a good translation and whether each sentence is well formed. It is based on the following features:

- Total sentence pair length

- Source/target length ratio

- Average token length

- Uppercase token count comparison

- Source/target punctuation comparison

- Source/target number comparison

- Language identification using *langid.py* (Lui and Baldwin, 2012)

- Cognates

- Source and target language model scores

- Hunalign scores (Varga et al., 2007)

- Zipporah adequacy scores (Xu and Koehn, 2017), using a probabilistic bilingual dictionary computed on Europarl.

Random forest parameters are optimized using expert feedback on a set of parallel sentences automatically selected by the model across several iterations. We have run 3 iterations, assessing the quality of 20 sentence pairs each time. The result is a binary classification of each sentence pair based on a score between 0 and 1. We have experimented with two selection criteria, keeping sentence pairs scoring above 0.5 and above 0.8, which led to respectively nearly 4M and 2M finally accepted sentences. The results are introduced in Section 2.3.

2.2   System setup

German and French pre-processing was performed using in-house normalization and tokenization tools. Truecasing models were learnt, using Moses scripts (Koehn et al., 2007), on the monolingual news data provided at the Conference, on all 2017-2018 data for French and 10M sentences from 2018 for German. A shared French-German BPE vocabulary (Sennrich et al., 2016b) was built with 30k merge operations on all the parallel data available for the task, except *Bicleaner07*.

We have trained baseline systems for French-German in both directions. Transformer *base* (Vaswani et al., 2017) models were trained using the Sockeye toolkit (Hieber et al., 2017) on two Nvidia 1080Ti GPU cards. Most of the standard hyper-parameters have been used. The model dimension included 512 units. The initial learning rate was set to 0.0003 with a warmup on for $30k$ updates. Due to the small quantity of training data available, we decided to slightly increase dropout between layers (0.2) and label smoothing (0.2). Validations were performed every $20k$ updates and patience was set to 15. Since this setup contained no training data relevant to the EU election topic, we decided to hold out the provided development set for another purpose, and used a general news domain test set: *Newstest-2012*. We finally wished to sample more sentence pairs from news-related corpora during training. Since no such method is implemented in the Sockeye toolkit for minibatch generation, we simply trained the baselines on a single copy of *Bicleaner07* and *Common-crawl*, and took two copies of *Europarl* and 6 of *News-commentary*.

2.3   Results and terminology issues

The systems were tested on the official development set, *Euelections-dev-2019*, as well as *Newstest-2013* and the official test set *Newstest-2019*. BLEU scores were computed with *Sacre-BLEU* (Post, 2018) and are shown in Table 1.

Experiments with different data filtering criteria for the *Bicleaner07* corpus were introduced in subsection 2.1. We observe that keeping a bigger

	French-to-German		
	Euelections-dev-2019	Newstest-2013	Newstest-2019
Baseline	25.98	23.48	26.94
	German-to-French		
	Euelections-dev-2019	Newstest-2013	Newstest-2019
LC_Pruner $2M$	31.07	27.49	33.04
LC_Pruner $4M$	30.96	27.29	33.16

Table 1: BLEU scores for French-German baselines

set of data does not lead to any clear improvements, at least in terms of BLEU. Thus we have *kept LC_Pruner* $2M$ as the main baseline for further training in Section 4.1.

The translation from English into German of *Euelections-dev-2019* by our baseline shows consistent terminology issues. The systems has difficulties translating the name of the movement *gilets jaunes* (yellow vests). Out of the 19 occurrences of the expression in the French source, only 4 are correctly translated as the compound *Gelbwesten*. We noted several translations as *gelbe Westen*, the translation of the adjective *jaunes* only, as well as full omissions. We also noted that the French party *France Insoumise* was translated litterally as *unbeugsame Frankreich*, instead of simply being copied, the name of the politician *Nicolas Dupont-Aignan* was translated as *Nicolas Dumont-Aignan*, etc. Our best baseline translates the German side of this test into French with the same kind of difficulties: *Gelbwesten* is sometimes translated as *la veste jaune*, etc.

3 Terminology control

We argue that a system specialized in a specific topic should be able to provide the right translations for terms that are relevant to this topic. The baselines we have just introduced fail to translate important terminology. We now seek to adapt these baselines to the EU election terminology.

3.1 Constrained decoding

One way to integrate such knowledge of a specific terminology into the MT system is by using *constrained decoding* (Hokamp and Liu, 2017). The *Grid Beam Search* algorithm guarantees the presence of one or several given phrases in the MT output. This method does not require any change in the model or its parameters, thus the algorithm does not model any sort of token-level source-to-target relation, but simply forces the beam search to go through the target constraint. The challenge

for the decoder is then to correctly insert the constrained phrase in the rest of the sentence.

Post and Vilar (2018) proposed a variant of this algorithm with a significant lower computational complexity. We used their implementation available in the Sockeye toolkit.

3.2 Lexicon extraction

We have extracted bilingual lexicons from two sources: the official development set provided for the task (*Euelections-dev-2019*), and the monolingual French and German data made available at WMT.

3.2.1 Parallel EU election data

We have decided to use the official development set (*Euelections-dev-2019*) as the main source of terminology, for the simple reason that it is the only parallel data available containing the specific terminology of the EU elections with reliable human translations.

Alignments were learnt using Fastalign (Dyer et al., 2013) on a concatenation of *Newscommentary* and *Euelections-dev-2019*, and we used them to extract a phrase table from the former with the Moses toolkit. We removed a phrase pair whenever the probability of the German side, given the French side, was below 0.5. This ensured that we never keep more than one translation for a French phrase[1].

The resulting phrases were furthermore filtered according to their domain. We computed Moore-Lewis (Moore and Lewis, 2010) scores of the source French phrases. The out-of-domain language model was computed on the French side of the parallel data (section 2), and the in-domain model on the French monolingual news data 2018 available at WMT. Although this corpus does not contain exclusively articles about the EU elections, we believe its terminology distribution may

---

[1]Since there can be several French translations for one German phrase, the current terminology can only be used for translation into German.

be closer to what is observed in *Euelections-dev-2019*, because the corpus relates more recent news. We kept the best 2000 phrase pairs according to their Moore-Lewis score.

Finally, we kept the phrase pairs for which the German side appeared at least once in the German monolingual news 2018 corpus, in order to filter out obviously bad expressions that remained. We ended up with 773 phrase pairs, among which could be found the correct translation of *gilets jaunes* (yellow vests).

3.2.2 Monolingual news data

As an attempt to address the issue of person name mistranslations, we extracted named entities from the French monolingual news 2018 corpus. First, we tagged the corpus with an in-house French named entity recognizer. We then computed the tagged named entity occurrence counts over the same corpus and removed the ones occurring less than 9 times. The translations of the extracted expressions into German are unknown, so we looked for the named entities that are not translated, but copied into German. We therefore kept the entries that had an occurrence count higher than 9 in the German news monolingual 2018 corpus. As a result, the name *Poutine* in French would be removed because it translates into a different word in German (*Putin*), whereas *Dupont-Aignan* would be kept, as it stays the same in both languages. This procedure produced nearly 20k phrase pairs.

Prior to inference, constraints extracted from the development set are applied every time a source-side constraint is found in the source sentence to be translated. Named Entity constraints extracted from monolingual data are applied in a different way. The same named entity classifier as above is used to tag the source sentence and a constraint is applied when: 1. the source constraint matches a part of the sentence ; 2. the matched sentence part has been tagged as a named entity.

We are well aware that bilingual terminology extraction is a complex task and that more sophisticated models need to be investigated. We chose to employ these simple heuristics only because we lacked time. We did run experiments with tools, allowing us to extract bilingual lexicons from monolingual data, namely *Muse* (Conneau et al., 2017) and *BiLex* (Zhang et al., 2017). However, we found them not suited for our requirements, because 1. the global quality of the lexicons was too low to be inserted in a MT decoder as hard constraints, and 2. only single-word phrases were extracted and we wished to extract multi-word expressions as well. Future work should include methods for phrase pair extraction from monolingual data (Marie and Fujita, 2018; Artetxe et al., 2019).

3.3 Constrained French-to-German baseline

The scores of the French-to-German baseline with and without constraints are shown in Table 2. We used a beam size of 20 for constrained decoding, as recommended in the Sockeye documentation [2], and a default beam size of 5 for the unconstrained decoding. The final models are averages of the 4 best checkpoints in terms of BLEU on the validation set. Applying constraints to *Euelections-dev-2019* adds 2 BLEU points to the baseline, but this should not be considered as an improvement, since parts of the reference translations were inserted as constraints. We observe that constrained decoding has nearly no impact on the BLEU score for *Newstest-2013*, and that it even slightly degrades the score for *Newstest-2019*.

The low impact of the constraints on *Newstest-2013* may be explained by the fact that this set is irrelevant with regard to the EU election topic, leading to the insertion of few constraints: 465 constraints were inserted in 3000 sentences. As a comparison, 751 constraints were inserted in the 1701 sentences of *Newstest-2019*. Looking more closely at the outputs of the different systems, we observed several cases where : 1. the constraint was erroneously inserted in the sentence; 2. the insertion of a constraint seemed to disturb the decoder, which resulted in broken sentences. Table 3 illustrates a case where the constraint helped to correct a mistranslation, but both issues occurred. The French party *France Insoumise* was translated litterally by the baseline into *Ununterwürfiges Frankreich*, and one of our constraints successfully forced the right translation of this expression. First, the subject of the first clause (*les populistes de gauche*) has been replaced by the constraints, which should have been inserted in the end of the sentence, like in the baseline. Second, the constrained output ignores the whole section about the raise of classical populist parties.

Although several constraints may potentially

---

[2] https://awslabs.github.io/sockeye/inference.html

	Euelections-dev-2019	Newstest-2013	Newstest-2019
Baseline	25.98	23.48	26.94
+ Constraints	27.87	23.42	26.66

Table 2: BLEU scores for French-to-German with constrained decoding

Source	Même si les populistes de gauche ont bien moins de succès en Europe que les acteurs d'extrême-droite, ils peuvent encore s'imposer, comme le montre l'ascension de partis classiques d'opposition tels que **Podemos** en Espagne et **La France Insoumise** en France.
Constraints	Podemos, France Insoumise
English	Even if left-wing populists have far less success in Europe than right-wing actors, they can still prevail, as evidenced by the rise of classic opposition parties such as **Podemos** in Spain and **France Insoumise** in France.
Baseline	Obwohl die Linkspopulisten in Europa deutlich weniger erfolgreich sind als die Rechtsextremen, können sie sich immer noch durchsetzen, wie der Aufstieg klassischer Oppositionsparteien wie **Podemos** in Spanien und Frankreichs **Ununterwürfiges Frankreich** zeigt.
+ Constraints	**Podemos** in Spanien und **France Insoumise** in Frankreich haben zwar deutlich weniger Erfolg als rechtsextreme Populisten, aber sie können sich noch immer durchsetzen.
Reference	Auch wenn die Linkspopulisten in Europa weitaus weniger erfolgreich sind als die Rechts-außen-Player, können sie sich durchaus Geltung verschaffen, wie der Aufstieg klassischer Herausforderer-Parteien wie **Podemos** in Spanien und **La France Insoumise** in Frankreich zeigt.

Table 3: Example of French-to-German translation with and without constrained decoding (*Newstest-2019*)

help the adaptation of a MT system to the specific terminology of the EU elections, it may be possible that the positive impact it could have on BLEU is mitigated by the broken translations the constraints tend to produce.

4 Relaxed use of constraints

We assume that the strict insertion of terminology through constrained decoding sometimes breaks output sentences, partly because the decoder would have never generated such an expression by itself. More specifically, the decoder assigns a low probability to the constrained phrase, which leads to a harmful disruption during the beam search.

Using parallel data containing the required terminology to fine-tune a system is an obvious good way to adapt a system, and it has the advantage to leave the decoder unchanged. Although we have no such data available for training, we do have monolingual French data that contains at least a big part of the EU election terminology we wish to acquire: the monolingual news 2018 corpus released within the shared task. We could use our French-to-German baseline to backtranslate these sentences (Sennrich et al., 2016a), but this would have the effect of introducing mistranslations in the source, which would break the strict source-target mapping we need to learn. For instance, if the French phrase *gilets jaunes* is backtranslated as *gelbe Westen*, the final German-to-French system would learn to translate *gelbe Westen* into French, but could very well still produce erroneous translations of the correct source expression *Gelbwesten*.

To address this issue, we propose to apply the strict constraints (section 3.1) to the French-to-German baseline used for backtranslation. Although we condemn ourselves to certain broken translated outputs, we have the guarantee that the extracted constraints will be learnt by the system. Another advantage of this strategy is that the constraints are inserted in different contexts, which should help the decoder learn to insert constrained terms in the output sentences more correctly.

4.1 Synthetic parallel datasets

The French news monolingual corpus 2018 comes under the general news domain. We attempted to extract the sentences dealing with the EU election topic using Moore-Lewis data selection strategy (Moore and Lewis, 2010). We chose the French side of *Euelections-dev-2019* as our in-domain corpus, with the hope that it will favor sentences containing the constraints we have extracted from it, in order to maximize the presence of constraint pairs in the backtranslated data. We finally selected the best 2M sentences in terms of Moore-Lewis score.

We provide both constrained and unconstrained translations for the resulting French sentences, using the same beam sizes as in Section 3.3. The constrained setup inserted 673,670 phrases in 2M German sentences.

4.2 Results

We used the German-to-French baseline trained on 2M sentences from *Bicleaner07* (section 2.3) as a starting point for fine-tuning using the constrained

	Euelections-dev-2019	Newstest-2013	Newstest-2019
Baseline	31.07	27.49	33.04
Unconstrained	34.06	28.07	35.64
Constrained	34.04	27.99	35.45
Ensemble	34.31	28.10	35.62

Table 4: BLEU scores for German-to-French systems fine-tuned on backtranslated data

and unconstrained versions of the backtranslation. The backtranslated data was mixed with *Europarl* and *News-commentary* corpora. We first tried to use *Newstest-2012* for validation, but only a slight improvement was observed throughout the training in terms of BLEU. In order to avoid stopping the training too early, we finally decided to run validation on *Euelections-dev-2019*. This most certainly led to overestimated BLEU scores, since the backtranslation data has been selected according to its proximity to this development set (section 4.1). However, it allowed the stopping criterion to fire later during training.

The final models we introduce are averages of the 4 best checkpoints in terms of BLEU on *Euelections-dev-2019*. We also provide results for an ensemble of 8 checkpoints (4 best constrained and 4 best unconstrained). We kept the same hyper-parameters as described in Section 2.2, except we lowered the learning rate from 0.0003 to 0.0001, used no warmup, and ran more frequent validations (every 10k updates).

The result of these fine-tuning procedures are shown in Table 4. Both backtranslation setups provide the best improvements we observed on *Newstest-2019* (+2.5). However, we see no significant difference between the constrained and unconstrained setups. This could be expected, since our experiment was focused on a small set of terms we wished the systems to generate, which can only lead to local improvements with low impact on the BLEU score. The ensemble of 8 models combining both setups is our primary submission to the shared task.

We have run a small analysis of the outputs given by both setups for *Newstest-2019*. We observed that the constrained system correctly copied the German name *Alexander Gauland*[3], whereas the unconstrained system erroneously translated the first name into *Alexandre*. The constrained system also translated *europäischen Vermögenssteuer* (European wealth tax) into the acronym *ISF européen*[4], which seems more usual in the press about the EU elections, compared to the litteral translation of the unconstrained system as *impôt européen sur la fortune*. Several phrases that were in our extracted constraints were correctly translated by the unconstrained system as well. Unconstrained backtranslation (Sennrich et al., 2016a) thus seems to be sufficient to adapt the terminology of a system to a specific system, at least in our setup with few low-quality automatically extracted lexical constraints. However, both systems produce consistent errors on terms that we failed to capture in constraints, which leads us to think that higher quality constraints should have a bigger positive impact on terminology adaptation.

5   Conclusions

We have described Lingua Custodia's submission to WMT'19 News Translation shared task. We attempted to adapt the terminology of a MT system to the EU election topic without relevant parallel training data. Forcing the decoder to generate specific terms can help, although it disturbs the decoder, which may lead to broken output sentences. Using hard constraint insertion to generate backtranslated target monolingual data showed no improvement in terms of BLEU scores, but we have observed local improvements in the generated terminology. The system that has been submitted to the shared task is an ensemble of both constrained and unconstrained models.

Lexically constrained decoding is highly dependent on the quality of the bilingual constraints available. In future work, we plan to search for other techniques for automatic lexical constraint extraction in order to improve recall and reach a better terminology coverage. We also plan to investigate new techniques to relax the hard constraints applied to the decoder, in order to impose less disturbance to the beam search and avoid broken output sentences.

---

[3]Constraint: *Alexander Gauland → Alexander Gauland*

[4]Constraint: *Vermögenssteuer → ISF*

References

Mikel Artetxe, Gorka Labaka, and Eneko Agirre. 2019. An effective approach to unsupervised machine translation. *CoRR*, abs/1902.01313.

Eduard Barbu, Carla Parra Escartín, Luisa Bentivogli, Matteo Negri, Marco Turchi, Constantin Orasan, and Marcello Federico. 2016. The first automatic translation memory cleaning shared task. *Machine Translation*, 30(3-4):145–166.

Chenhui Chu and Rui Wang. 2018. A survey of domain adaptation for neural machine translation. In *Proceedings of the 27th International Conference on Computational Linguistics*, pages 1304–1319, Santa Fe, New Mexico, USA. Association for Computational Linguistics.

Alexis Conneau, Guillaume Lample, Marc'Aurelio Ranzato, Ludovic Denoyer, and Hervé Jégou. 2017. Word translation without parallel data. *CoRR*, abs/1710.04087.

Chris Dyer, Victor Chahuneau, and Noah A. Smith. 2013. A simple, fast, and effective reparameterization of IBM model 2. In *Proceedings of the 2013 Conference of the North American Chapter of the Association for Computational Linguistics: Human Language Technologies*, pages 644–648, Atlanta, Georgia. Association for Computational Linguistics.

Felix Hieber, Tobias Domhan, Michael Denkowski, David Vilar, Artem Sokolov, Ann Clifton, and Matt Post. 2017. Sockeye: A toolkit for neural machine translation. *CoRR*, abs/1712.05690.

Chris Hokamp and Qun Liu. 2017. Lexically constrained decoding for sequence generation using grid beam search. In *Proceedings of the 55th Annual Meeting of the Association for Computational Linguistics (Volume 1: Long Papers)*, pages 1535–1546, Vancouver, Canada. Association for Computational Linguistics.

Philipp Koehn. 2005. A parallel corpus for statistical machine translation. In *Proc. MT-Summit*, Phuket, Thailand.

Philipp Koehn, Hieu Hoang, Alexandra Birch, Chris Callison-Burch, Marcello Federico, Nicola Bertoldi, Brooke Cowan, Wade Shen, Christine Moran, Richard Zens, Chris Dyer, Ondřej Bojar, Alexandra Constantin, and Evan Herbst. 2007. Moses: Open source toolkit for statistical MT. In *Proc. ACL:Systems Demos*, pages 177–180, Prague, Czech Republic.

Marco Lui and Timothy Baldwin. 2012. langid.py: An off-the-shelf language identification tool. In *Proceedings of the ACL 2012 System Demonstrations*, pages 25–30, Jeju Island, Korea. Association for Computational Linguistics.

Minh-Thang Luong and Christopher D. Manning. 2015. Stanford neural machine translation systems for spoken language domain. In *International Workshop on Spoken Language Translation*, Da Nang, Vietnam.

Benjamin Marie and Atsushi Fujita. 2018. Phrase table induction using monolingual data for low-resource statistical machine translation. *ACM Trans. Asian Low-Resour. Lang. Inf. Process.*, 17(3):16:1–16:25.

Robert C. Moore and William Lewis. 2010. Intelligent selection of language model training data. In *Proceedings of the ACL 2010 Conference Short Papers*, ACLShort '10, pages 220–224, Stroudsburg, PA, USA. Association for Computational Linguistics.

Matt Post. 2018. A call for clarity in reporting BLEU scores. In *Proceedings of the Third Conference on Machine Translation: Research Papers*, pages 186–191, Belgium, Brussels. Association for Computational Linguistics.

Matt Post and David Vilar. 2018. Fast lexically constrained decoding with dynamic beam allocation for neural machine translation. In *Proceedings of the 2018 Conference of the North American Chapter of the Association for Computational Linguistics: Human Language Technologies, Volume 1 (Long Papers)*, pages 1314–1324, New Orleans, Louisiana. Association for Computational Linguistics.

Rico Sennrich, Barry Haddow, and Alexandra Birch. 2016a. Improving neural machine translation models with monolingual data. In *Proceedings of the 54th Annual Meeting of the Association for Computational Linguistics (Volume 1: Long Papers)*, pages 86–96, Berlin, Germany. Association for Computational Linguistics.

Rico Sennrich, Barry Haddow, and Alexandra Birch. 2016b. Neural machine translation of rare words with subword units. In *Proceedings of the 54th Annual Meeting of the Association for Computational Linguistics (Volume 1: Long Papers)*, pages 1715–1725. Association for Computational Linguistics.

Dániel Varga, Péter Halácsy, Andras Kornai, Viktor Nagy, László Németh, and Viktor Trón. 2007. *Parallel corpora for medium density languages*, pages 247–258. John Benjamins.

Ashish Vaswani, Noam Shazeer, Niki Parmar, Jakob Uszkoreit, Llion Jones, Aidan N Gomez, Ł ukasz Kaiser, and Illia Polosukhin. 2017. Attention is all you need. In I. Guyon, U. V. Luxburg, S. Bengio, H. Wallach, R. Fergus, S. Vishwanathan, and R. Garnett, editors, *Advances in Neural Information Processing Systems 30*, pages 5998–6008. Curran Associates, Inc.

Hainan Xu and Philipp Koehn. 2017. Zipporah: a fast and scalable data cleaning system for noisy web-crawled parallel corpora. In *Proceedings of the 2017*

Conference on Empirical Methods in Natural Language Processing, pages 2945–2950, Copenhagen, Denmark. Association for Computational Linguistics.

Meng Zhang, Haoruo Peng, Yang Liu, Huan-Bo Luan, and Maosong Sun. 2017. Bilingual lexicon induction from non-parallel data with minimal supervision. In *Proceedings of the Thirty-First AAAI Conference on Artificial Intelligence, February 4-9, 2017, San Francisco, California, USA.*, pages 3379–3385.

The TALP-UPC Machine Translation Systems for WMT19 News Translation Task: Pivoting Techniques for Low Resource MT

Noe Casas, José A. R. Fonollosa, Carlos Escolano, Christine Basta, Marta R. Costa-jussà
{noe.casas,jose.fonollosa,carlos.escolano}@upc.edu,
{christine.raouf.saad.basta,marta.ruiz}@upc.edu
TALP Research Center
Universitat Politècnica de Catalunya, Barcelona

Abstract

In this article, we describe the TALP-UPC research group participation in the WMT19 news translation shared task for Kazakh-English. Given the low amount of parallel training data, we resort to using Russian as pivot language, training subword-based statistical translation systems for Russian-Kazakh and Russian-English that were then used to create two synthetic pseudo-parallel corpora for Kazakh-English and English-Kazakh respectively. Finally, a self-attention model based on the decoder part of the Transformer architecture was trained on the two pseudo-parallel corpora.

1 Introduction

Attention-based models like the Transformer architecture (Vaswani et al., 2017) or the Dynamic Convolution architecture (Wu et al., 2019) are currently the dominant approaches for Machine Translation (MT). Nevertheless, these architectures offer best results when trained on large training corpora. When faced with a low-resource scenario, other supporting techniques are needed in order to obtain good translation results. In the WMT19 news translation shared task, two low-resourced language pairs where proposed, namely Gujarati-English and Kazakh-English.

In this report, we describe the participation of the TALP Research Group at Universitat Politècnica de Catalunya (UPC) at the WMT19 news translation shared task (Barrault et al., 2019) in Kazakh→English and English→Kazakh translation directions.

The amount of available parallel Kazakh-English data is very low. In order to overcome this problem in the frame of the shared task, we made use of Russian as an pivot language. This way, we used English-Russian and Kazakh-Russian data to train intermediate translation systems that we then used to create synthetic pseudo-parallel Kazakh-English data. This data enabled us to train the final Kazakh-English translation systems.

This work is organized as follows: in section 2 we describe some techniques normally used in low-resource scenarios, to frame our proposal; in section 3 we provide an overview of other works addressing Kazakh-English as language pair for translation; in section 4 we study the available data sets, both in terms of amount and quality of the data, and describe the processing performed over it; in section 5 we describe the proposed system, together with the details about, including the data augmentation techniques used and the final NMT model trained; in section 6 we describe the experiments carried out to evaluate the translation quality prior to submitting and the obtain results; finally, in section 7 we describe the conclusions drawn from this work.

The source code used for the data download, data preparation and training of the pivot and final systems is available at https://github. com/noe/wmt19-news-lowres.

2 Low-resource NMT

There are several different approaches that can improve translation quality in under-resourced scenarios. In this section, we provide an overview of some of the dominant techniques and justify their application in the frame of this shared task.

While for low resource languages there is limited parallel data, monolingual data is often available in greater quantities. A common strategy to integrate this monolingual data into the NMT system is back-translation (Sennrich et al., 2016a), which consists in generating synthetic data by translating monolingual data of the target language into the source language that would be then fed to the system to further train it.

Proceedings of the Fourth Conference on Machine Translation (WMT), Volume 2: Shared Task Papers (Day 1) pages 155–162
Florence, Italy, August 1-2, 2019. ©2019 Association for Computational Linguistics

Another common scenario is that few or no parallel data is available between the source and target languages but there is a third language or pivot. for which there is parallel data to both source and target. In this case, two systems can be trained, one from the source to the pivot language and another from the pivot to the target language. Inference will be performed as a cascade using the source to pivot system output as synthetic data to input to the pivot to the target system, obtaining a source to target translation.

An alternative to this approach could be the generation of a synthetic pseudo-parallel corpus of translated data between the source and target language through the pivot, and train a system as done in the back translation approach.

Finally, multilingual systems are recently showing nice improvements. Among the different types of multilingual systems there are the many-to-one approaches and the many-to-many approaches. The former is aiming to translate to one single language and can simply concatenate source languages (Zoph and Knight, 2016; Tubay and Costa-jussà, 2018). However, the latter either needs to use independent encoders and decoders (Schwenk and Douze, 2017; Firat et al., 2016; Escolano et al., 2019) or when using universal encoder and decoders (Johnson et al., 2017) needs to add a tag in the source input to let the system know to which language it is translating. This many-to-many systems are an alternative to pivot systems. However, most these multilingual systems are not able to achieve the level of performance of pivot systems yet.

In the frame of the WMT19 news translation shared task several of the aforementioned techniques are applicable.

An English+Russian→Kakakh multilingual system could be trained, but the amount of Kazakh-Russian data is much larger than Kazakh-English, which would bias the encoder toward Russian; as Russian is not similar to English this would decrease the effectiveness of the approach, as opposed to what happens for similar languages (Casas et al., 2018b).

Back-translation could also be applied in this context, but the amount of Kazakh monolingual data is not very large and it is crawled data, with presumably low quality. It could have been used additionally to other techniques, though.

Finally, pivoting approaches are also applicable to this scenario. The cascade approach, however, would not allow to profit from the existing parallel English-Kazakh data, making the pseudo-parallel corpus approach the most sensible option.

3 Related Work

In this section we provide an overview of the different approaches proposed in the literature for Kazakh-English machine translation.

The Apertium Rule-based Machine Translation (RBMT) system (Forcada et al., 2011) offers a generic platform to implement transfer-based rule systems for translation. This platform was used by Assem and Aida (2013) and Sundetova et al. (2014) to implement transfer rules for English→Kazakh and Kazakh→English respectively.

Assylbekov and Nurkas (2014) and Bekbulatov and Kartbayev (2014) studied the effectiveness of Statistical Machine Translation (SMT) of Kazakh to English with different segmentation strategies, trying to cope with the large amount of surface forms of Kazakh in relation to the low amount of available training data. Kartbayev (2015) studied the influence of different alignment models in SMT for Kazakh to English SMT.

Finally, Tukeyev et al. (2019) study the application of NMT to Kazakh to English translation by augmenting the training data with synthetically sentences generated with a rule-based procedure that computes variations of surface forms over simple sentence templates.

4 Corpora and Data Preparation

In order to train our MT systems, we used the data made available by the shared task organizers, including the not only Kazakh-English data but also the English-Russian and Kazakh-Russian data to train pivot translation systems. In this section we describe the data used for each language pair and the processing applied to each of them in order to compile appropriate training datasets.

4.1 Kazakh-English

The available parallel Kazakh-English corpora for the shared task included News Commentary v14, Wiki Titles v1 and a crawled corpus prepared by Bagdat Myrzakhmetov of Nazarbayev University.

Wiki Titles accounts for half of the available parallel segments, but its sentences are around 2 tokens long in average. Therefore, we decided not to include it in the training data, to avoid biasing the trained systems toward short translations.

After concatenating the training corpora, we used the standard Moses scripts to preprocess them, including tokenization, truecasing and cleaning. The statistics of the resulting training data are shown in table 1.

Table 1: Summary statistics of the Kazakh-English training data.

Lang.	Sents.	Words	Vocab.	L_{max}	L_{mean}
Kazakh	99.6K	1.2M	139.6K	85	11.7
English		1.5M	85.3K	102	14.9

The WMT organization split a part of News Commentary to use as development[1]. From this data, we left 500 parallel sentences as hold-out to assess final system translation quality and left the remaining 1566 segments as development data.

4.2 English-Russian

The available parallel English-Russian corpora for the shared task included News Commentary v14, Wiki Titles v1, Common Crawl corpus, ParaCrawl v3, Yandex Corpus and the United Nations Parallel Corpus v1.0 (Ziemski et al., 2016).

Following the rationale exposed for the English-Kazakh Wiki Titles data, we also dropped the English-Russian Wiki Titles data.

Among the other corpora, some are of very large size. In order to assemble a manageable final training dataset and taking into account the high presence of garbage in the crawled datasets, before combining the individual corpora, we filtered each corpus and selected from each a random sample of segments.

For the filtering, we applied heuristic criteria based on our visual inspection of the data, including elimination of lines with repeated separation characters (like ++++ or ----), elimination of fixed expressions (like `The time is now`, which appeared several times in some corpora) and eliminating lines with high ratio of numbers and punctuation characters.

For the random sample, from UN Corpus we took 2M segments out of 23M, from Common Crawl we took 200K out of 900K, from ParaCrawl we took 4M out of 12M and from the Yandex Corpus we took all the 1M segments. These sam-

ples were then combined and went through standard processing with Moses scripts, including tokenization, truecasing and cleaning. After combining them, we applied Moses corpus cleaning with more aggressive settings (sentences between 5 and 80 words and a maximum length ratio of 3.0 between source and target). From the combined corpus, we extracted 4000 random lines as development data and 1000 segments as hold out test set, leaving the rest for training. The statistics of the resulting training data are shown in table 2.

Table 2: Summary statistics of the English-Russian training data.

Lang.	Sents.	Words	Vocab.	L_{max}	L_{mean}
Russian	6.1M	125.6M	3.2M	80	20.7
English		144.9M	2.0M	80	23.9

4.3 Kazakh-Russian

The available parallel Kazakh-Russian corpora for the shared task included News Commentary v14 and a crawled Russian-Kazakh corpus prepared by Bagdat Myrzakhmetov of Nazarbayev University.

After concatenating the training corpora, we used the Moses scripts for preprocessing, including tokenization, truecasing and cleaning, using the same settings as for the aggressive English-Russian data cleaning described before. From the combined corpus, we extracted 4000 lines as development data and 1000 segments as hold out test set, leaving the rest for training. The statistics of the resulting training corpus are shown in table 3.

Table 3: Summary statistics of the Russian-Kazakh training data.

Lang.	Sents.	Words	Vocab.	L_{max}	L_{mean}
Russian	4.2M	78.8M	1.4M	96	18.9
Kazakh		75.3M	1.6M	70	18.0

5 System Description

The amount of available parallel training data for English-Kazakh is scarce. When an NMT system is directly trained on this data, the resulting translation quality is very low, as shown in section 6.

Given the amount of available English-Russian and Kazakh-Russian parallel training data, we decided to use Russian as pivot language. Taking into account the availability of some parallel Kazakh-English data, the pivoting approach that best suits this case is to prepare pseudo-parallel English-Kazakh and Kazakh-English cor-

---

[1] The part of News Commentary provided as development data was excluded from the training set.

pora based on the Russian data and then combine it with the parallel English-Kazakh data. Further justification of the technique used can be found in section 2.

In pivoting approaches, the final translation quality does not get influenced significantly if synthetic data is used for the source language side; on the other hand, using synthetic data for the target language side results in degraded translation quality in the final system (Casas et al., 2018a; Costa-Jussà et al., 2019). Therefore, we will create two different pseudo-parallel corpora for English→Kazakh and Kazakh→English.

In order to create the English→Kazakh synthetic data, we translated the Russian side of the Russian-Kazakh corpus into English. To perform this translation, we need an intermediate Russian→English system. We made use of the Russian-English corpus to train this pivot system.

In order to create the Kazakh→English synthetic data, we translated the Russian side of the Russian-English corpus into Kazakh. To perform this translation, we need an intermediate Russian→Kazakh system. We made use of the Russian-Kazakh corpus to train this pivot system.

The preparation and training of the two pivot translation systems is further described in section 5.1

Once the synthetic data was prepared by means of the pivot translation systems, we combined each synthetic corpus with the parallel data, obtaining the respective training datasets for the two translation directions. This is further described in section 5.2.

Finally, we trained the English→Kazakh and Kazakh→English translation systems on the previously described mix of parallel and synthetic corpora. The NMT model used is presented in section 5.3.

5.1 Pivot SMT Systems

For the Russian→English and Russian→Kazakh pivot translation systems we decided to use Moses (Koehn et al., 2007), a popular phrase-based Statistical Machine Translation (SMT) software package. The use of pivot approaches for SMT has been studied previously, like the works by De Gispert and Marino (2006), Wu and Wang (2007) or Utiyama and Isahara (2007).

Another option would have been to use a Neural Machine Translation (NMT) approach, but this would have required large amounts of GPU time to translate the pseudo-parallel corpora.

While the English language presents simple morphology, Russian is morphologically rich and Kazakh is agglutinative. Therefore, the amount of surface forms in a word-level vocabulary of the two latter languages is very high. This way, we decided to apply subword-level tokenization before training the SMT systems. For this, we used Byte-Pair Encoding (BPE) (Sennrich et al., 2016b) to extract a vocabulary of subword parts based on frequency statistics. We prepared separate BPE vocabularies for each language, with 32K merge operations each. Although not frequent, there are some precedents for subword tokenization in SMT, like the work by Kunchukuttan and Bhattacharyya (2016, 2017).

The use of subword tokenization leads to longer token sequence lengths compared to the usual word-based vocabularies of SMT systems. In order to cope with this fact, we configured the subword-based SMT systems to have longer n-gram order for their Language Models (LM) and phrase tables: the typical n-gram order used is 3 and we used 6. All other Moses configuration settings are the standard ones, using KenLM as language model (Heafield, 2011; Heafield et al., 2013) and MGIZA++ (Gao and Vogel, 2008) for alignment.

The data used to create the respective target-side LMs consisted of the target side of the parallel data used for training. Some improvement could have been gained by using the available extra monolingual English and Kazakh data for the LMs.

5.2 Combination of Parallel and Synthetic Data

The process followed to combine the parallel data with the synthetic data was the same for English-Kazakh and for Kazakh-English: we oversampled at 300% the parallel data and concatenated it with the synthetic data, obtaining the final training datasets on which the translation systems for the submissions were trained.

5.3 Joint Source-Target Self-Attention NMT

The translation system trained on the augmented Kazakh-English data and used for the final WMT submissions is based on the architecture proposed by (He et al., 2018; Fonollosa et al., 2019). This approach is based on the self-attention blocks from (Vaswani et al., 2017), but breaks from the

Table 4: BLEU scores (cased) of the Rule-based baseline (**RBMT**), the Moses system trained on the parallel Kazakh-English data with word-level tokenization (**SMT(w)**), the Moses system trained on the parallel Kazakh-English data with subword-level tokenization (**SMT(sw)**), the **NMT** system trained on the parallel Kazakh-English data, and the final systems trained on the augmented pseudo-parallel corpus data (**NMT pseudo-p.**)

Direction	RBMT	SMT (w)	SMT (sw)	NMT	NMT pseudo-p.
Kazakh→English	1.51	6.34	7.48	2.32	21.00
English→Kazakh	1.46	3.53	3.82	1.42	15.47

encoder-decoder structure and has only a single decoder block that is fed both the source and target sentences, therefore learning joint source-target representations from the initial layers. This model resembles how a language modeling architecture is trained and used for inference.

The positional encodings are applied separately to source and target. An extra embedded vector representation is added to the combination of token and position in order to distinguish source and target parts.

The attention weights can be masked to control the receptive fields (Fonollosa et al., 2019). Both source-source and target-target receptive fields are constrained to a local window around each token, while target-source receptive fields are unconstrained.

The hyperparameter configuration used was the same as the one originally used by the authors for WMT'14 English-German (14 layers, 1024 as embedding dimensionality, feedforward expansion of dimensionality 4096 and 16 attention heads).

For Kazakh-English we used separate BPE vocabularies with 32K merge operations, while for English-Kazakh we used a joint BPE vocabulary with 32K merge operations, together with shared source-target embeddings.

6 Experiments and Results

In order to assess the translation quality of the systems, we computed the BLEU score (Papineni et al., 2002) over the respective held out test sets.

As there is not much literature of current NMT approaches being applied to English-Kazakh, we prepared different baselines to gauge the range of BLEU values to expect:

- Rule-based machine translation system (RBMT): we used the Apertium system (Forcada et al., 2011; Sundetova et al., 2014; Assem and Aida, 2013), which is based on transfer rules distilled from linguistic knowledge. Using the BLEU score to compare an RBMT system with data-driven systems is not fair (see (Koehn, 2010) §8.2.7) but we included it to have a broader picture.

- Statistical Machine Translation with word-level tokenization (SMT(w)): we trained a Moses system on the parallel Kazakh-English data, using normal word-level tokenization

- Statistical Machine Translation with subword-level tokenization (SMT(sw)): we trained a Moses system on the parallel Kazakh-English data, using BPE tokenization with 10K merge operations[2]. Moses default values were used for the rest of configuration settings .

- Neural Machine Translation (NMT): we trained a Transformer model on the parallel Kazakh-English data, using BPE tokenization with 10K merge operations, separately for source and target. We used the fairseq (Ott et al., 2019) implementation with the same hyperparameters as the IWSLT model, namely an embedding dimensionality of 512, 6 layers of attention, 4 attention heads and 1024 for the feedwordward expansion dimensionality.

The translation quality BLEU scores of the aforedescribed baselines were very low, as shown in table 4.

In order to evaluate the pivot translation systems described in section 5.1, we also measured the BLEU scores in the respective held out test sets, obtaining 36.05 BLEU for the Russian→English system and 21.06 for the Russian→Kazakh system. With these pivot systems, we created two pseudo-parallel synthetic corpora, merged them with the parallel data and trained a self-attention NMT model that obtained BLEU scores one order of magnitude above the chosen baselines, as shown in table 4.

---

[2]The low number of BPE merge operations is justified with the low amount of training data

When we tested the final Kazakh→English system on the shared task test set, we identified several sentences that remained completely in Cyrillic script. In order to mitigate this problem, we trained a SMT system on the augmented Kazakh-English data and used it for the sentences that had a large percentage of Cyrillic characters. This lead to a mere 0.1 increase in the case-insensitive BLEU score and no change for the uncased one.

7 Conclusion

In this article we described the TALP-UPC submissions to the WMT19 news translation shared task for Kazakh-English. Our experiments showcase the effectiveness of pivoting approaches for low resourced scenarios, making use of SMT to support the data augmentation process, while using the more effective attention-based NMT approaches for the final translation systems.

Acknowledgments

We would like to thank Lluis Guardia for his help in the news task human evaluation.

This work is partially supported by Lucy Software / United Language Group (ULG) and the Catalan Agency for Management of University and Research Grants (AGAUR) through an Industrial PhD Grant.

This work is supported in part by a Google Faculty Research Award

This work is supported in part by the Catalan Agency for Management of University and Research Grants (AGAUR) through the FI PhD Scholarship.

This work is also supported in part by the Spanish Ministerio de Economía y Competitividad, the European Regional Development Fund and the Agencia Estatal de Investigación, through the postdoctoral senior grant Ramón y Cajal, contract TEC2015-69266-P (MINECO/FEDER,EU) and contract PCIN-2017-079 (AEI/MINECO).

References

S. Assem and S. Aida. 2013. Machine translation of different systemic languages using a apertium platform (with an example of english and kazakh languages). In *2013 International Conference on Computer Applications Technology (ICCAT)*, pages 1–4.

Zhenisbek Assylbekov and Assulan Nurkas. 2014. Initial explorations in kazakh to english statistical machine translation. In *The First Italian Conference on Computational Linguistics CLiC-it 2014*, page 12.

Loïc Barrault, Ondřej Bojar, Marta R. Costa-jussà, Christian Federmann, Mark Fishel, Yvette Graham, Barry Haddow, Matthias Huck, Philipp Koehn, Shervin Malmasi, Christof Monz, Mathias Müller, Santanu Pal, Matt Post, and Marcos Zampieri. 2019. Findings of the 2019 conference on machine translation (wmt19). In *Proceedings of the Fourth Conference on Machine Translation, Volume 2: Shared Task Papers*, Florence, Italy. Association for Computational Linguistics.

Eldar Bekbulatov and Amandyk Kartbayev. 2014. A study of certain morphological structures of kazakh and their impact on the machine translation quality. In *2014 IEEE 8th International Conference on Application of Information and Communication Technologies (AICT)*, pages 1–5. IEEE.

Noe Casas, Marta R. Costa-jussà, and José A. R. Fonollosa. 2018a. English-catalan neural machine translation in the biomedical domain through the cascade approach. In *Proceedings of the 11th Language Resources and Evaluation Conference of the European Language Resources Association*.

Noe Casas, Carlos Escolano, Marta R. Costa-jussà, and José A. R. Fonollosa. 2018b. The TALP-UPC machine translation systems for WMT18 news shared translation task. In *Proceedings of the Third Conference on Machine Translation: Shared Task Papers*, pages 355–360, Belgium, Brussels. Association for Computational Linguistics.

Marta R. Costa-Jussà, Noé Casas, Carlos Escolano, and José A. R. Fonollosa. 2019. Chinese-catalan: A neural machine translation approach based on pivoting and attention mechanisms. *ACM Transactions on Asian and Low-Resource Language Information Processing (TALLIP)*, 18(4):43.

Adrià De Gispert and Jose B Marino. 2006. Catalan-english statistical machine translation without parallel corpus: bridging through spanish. In *Proc. of 5th International Conference on Language Resources and Evaluation (LREC)*, pages 65–68. Citeseer.

Carlos Escolano, Marta R. Costa-jussà, and José A. R. Fonollosa. 2019. Learning joint multilingual sentence representations with neural machine translation. *arXiv preprint arXiv:1905.06831*.

Orhan Firat, Baskaran Sankaran, Yaser Al-Onaizan, Fatos T. Yarman Vural, and Kyunghyun Cho. 2016. Zero-resource translation with multi-lingual neural machine translation. In *Proceedings of the 2016 Conference on Empirical Methods in Natural Language Processing*, pages 268–277, Austin, Texas. Association for Computational Linguistics.

José A. R. Fonollosa, Noe Casas, and Marta R. Costa-jussà. 2019. Joint source-target self attention with locality constraints. *arXiv preprint arXiv:1905.06596*.

Mikel L. Forcada, Mireia Ginestí-Rosell, Jacob Nord-falk, Jim O'Regan, Sergio Ortiz-Rojas, Juan Antonio Pérez-Ortiz, Felipe Sánchez-Martínez, Gema Ramírez-Sánchez, and Francis M. Tyers. 2011. Apertium: a free/open-source platform for rule-based machine translation. *Machine Translation*, 25(2):127–144.

Qin Gao and Stephan Vogel. 2008. Parallel implementations of word alignment tool. In *Software Engineering, Testing, and Quality Assurance for Natural Language Processing*, pages 49–57, Columbus, Ohio. Association for Computational Linguistics.

Tianyu He, Xu Tan, Yingce Xia, Di He, Tao Qin, Zhibo Chen, and Tie-Yan Liu. 2018. Layer-wise coordination between encoder and decoder for neural machine translation. In S. Bengio, H. Wallach, H. Larochelle, K. Grauman, N. Cesa-Bianchi, and R. Garnett, editors, *Advances in Neural Information Processing Systems 31*, pages 7955–7965. Curran Associates, Inc.

Kenneth Heafield. 2011. KenLM: faster and smaller language model queries. In *Proceedings of the EMNLP 2011 Sixth Workshop on Statistical Machine Translation*, pages 187–197, Edinburgh, Scotland, United Kingdom.

Kenneth Heafield, Ivan Pouzyrevsky, Jonathan H. Clark, and Philipp Koehn. 2013. Scalable modified Kneser-Ney language model estimation. In *Proceedings of the 51st Annual Meeting of the Association for Computational Linguistics*, pages 690–696, Sofia, Bulgaria.

Melvin Johnson, Mike Schuster, Quoc V Le, Maxim Krikun, Yonghui Wu, Zhifeng Chen, Nikhil Thorat, Fernanda Viégas, Martin Wattenberg, Greg Corrado, et al. 2017. Google's multilingual neural machine translation system: Enabling zero-shot translation. *Transactions of the Association for Computational Linguistics*, 5:339–351.

Amandyk Kartbayev. 2015. Learning word alignment models for kazakh-english machine translation. In *Integrated Uncertainty in Knowledge Modelling and Decision Making*, pages 326–335, Cham. Springer International Publishing.

Philipp Koehn. 2010. *Statistical Machine Translation*, 1st edition. Cambridge University Press, New York, NY, USA.

Philipp Koehn, Hieu Hoang, Alexandra Birch, Chris Callison-Burch, Marcello Federico, Nicola Bertoldi, Brooke Cowan, Wade Shen, Christine Moran, Richard Zens, Chris Dyer, Ondřej Bojar, Alexandra Constantin, and Evan Herbst. 2007. Moses: Open source toolkit for statistical machine translation. In *Proceedings of the 45th Annual Meeting of the ACL on Interactive Poster and Demonstration Sessions*, ACL '07, pages 177–180. Association for Computational Linguistics.

Anoop Kunchukuttan and Pushpak Bhattacharyya. 2016. Orthographic syllable as basic unit for SMT between related languages. In *Proceedings of the 2016 Conference on Empirical Methods in Natural Language Processing*, pages 1912–1917, Austin, Texas. Association for Computational Linguistics.

Anoop Kunchukuttan and Pushpak Bhattacharyya. 2017. Learning variable length units for SMT between related languages via byte pair encoding. In *Proceedings of the First Workshop on Subword and Character Level Models in NLP*, pages 14–24, Copenhagen, Denmark. Association for Computational Linguistics.

Myle Ott, Sergey Edunov, Alexei Baevski, Angela Fan, Sam Gross, Nathan Ng, David Grangier, and Michael Auli. 2019. fairseq: A fast, extensible toolkit for sequence modeling. In *Proceedings of NAACL-HLT 2019: Demonstrations*.

Kishore Papineni, Salim Roukos, Todd Ward, and Wei-Jing Zhu. 2002. BLEU: a method for automatic evaluation of machine translation. In *Proceedings of the 40th annual meeting on association for computational linguistics*, pages 311–318. Association for Computational Linguistics.

Holger Schwenk and Matthijs Douze. 2017. Learning joint multilingual sentence representations with neural machine translation. In *Proceedings of the 2nd Workshop on Representation Learning for NLP*, pages 157–167, Vancouver, Canada. Association for Computational Linguistics.

Rico Sennrich, Barry Haddow, and Alexandra Birch. 2016a. Improving neural machine translation models with monolingual data. In *Proceedings of the 54th Annual Meeting of the Association for Computational Linguistics (Volume 1: Long Papers)*, pages 86–96, Berlin, Germany. Association for Computational Linguistics.

Rico Sennrich, Barry Haddow, and Alexandra Birch. 2016b. Neural machine translation of rare words with subword units. In *Proceedings of the 54th Annual Meeting of the Association for Computational Linguistics, ACL 2016, August 7-12, 2016, Berlin, Germany, Volume 1: Long Papers*.

Aida Sundetova, Aidana Karibayeva, and Ualsher Tukeyev. 2014. Structural transfer rules for kazakh-to-english machine translation in the free/open-source platform apertium. *Türkiye Bilişim Vakfı Bilgisayar Bilimleri ve Mühendisliği Dergisi*, 7(2):48–53.

Brian Tubay and Marta R. Costa-jussà. 2018. Neural machine translation with the transformer and multi-source romance languages for the biomedical WMT 2018 task. In *Proceedings of the Third Conference on Machine Translation: Shared Task Papers*, pages 667–670, Belgium, Brussels. Association for Computational Linguistics.

Ualsher Tukeyev, Aidana Karibayeva, and Balzhan Abduali. 2019. Neural machine translation system for the kazakh language based on synthetic corpora. In *MATEC Web of Conferences*, volume 252, page 03006. EDP Sciences.

Masao Utiyama and Hitoshi Isahara. 2007. A comparison of pivot methods for phrase-based statistical machine translation. In *Human Language Technologies 2007: The Conference of the North American Chapter of the Association for Computational Linguistics; Proceedings of the Main Conference*, pages 484–491.

Ashish Vaswani, Noam Shazeer, Niki Parmar, Jakob Uszkoreit, Llion Jones, Aidan N Gomez, Łukasz Kaiser, and Illia Polosukhin. 2017. Attention is all you need. In I. Guyon, U. V. Luxburg, S. Bengio, H. Wallach, R. Fergus, S. Vishwanathan, and R. Garnett, editors, *Advances in Neural Information Processing Systems 30*, pages 6000–6010. Curran Associates, Inc.

Felix Wu, Angela Fan, Alexei Baevski, Yann Dauphin, and Michael Auli. 2019. Pay less attention with lightweight and dynamic convolutions. In *International Conference on Learning Representations*.

Hua Wu and Haifeng Wang. 2007. Pivot language approach for phrase-based statistical machine translation. *Machine Translation*, 21(3):165–181.

Michał Ziemski, Marcin Junczys-Dowmunt, and Bruno Pouliquen. 2016. The united nations parallel corpus v1.0. In *Proceedings of the Tenth International Conference on Language Resources and Evaluation (LREC 2016)*, Paris, France. European Language Resources Association (ELRA).

Barret Zoph and Kevin Knight. 2016. Multi-source neural translation. In *Proceedings of the 2016 Conference of the North American Chapter of the Association for Computational Linguistics: Human Language Technologies*, pages 30–34, San Diego, California. Association for Computational Linguistics.

Kyoto University participation to the WMT 2019 news shared task

Fabien Cromieres
Graduate School of Informatics
Kyoto University
fabien@nlp.ist.i.kyoto-u.ac.jp

Sadao Kurohashi
Graduate School of Informatics
Kyoto University
kuro@i.kyoto-u.ac.jp

Abstract

We describe here the experiments we performed for the news translation shared task of WMT 2019. We focused on the new German-to-French language direction, and mostly used current standard approaches to develop a Neural Machine Translation system. We make use of the Tensor2Tensor implementation of the Transformer model. After carefully cleaning the data and noting the importance of the good use of recent monolingual data for the task, we obtain our final result by combining the output of a diverse set of trained models through the use of their "checkpoint agreement".

1 Introduction

The 2019 edition of WMT's news translation shared tasks was proposing the German-French pair for the first time. The inclusion of two not-so-closely related languages which both have a richer morphology than English is interesting and can in theory provide additional challenges to the more English-X pairs most frequently used for Machine Translation. Due to the rather large computation time investment required by the training of a modern Neural Machine Translation system, we focused on the German-to-French direction.

Overall, our submission mostly relied on carefully following current best practices for Neural MT, while trying to analyze results and find simple ways to improve them. We used a Transformer sequence-to-sequence model (Vaswani et al., 2017) as our base system. After cleaning and selecting data, we ran experiments with different settings, and finally tried to combine the results of all of these models. In these combination, we tried to use what we dubbed "checkpoint agreement" as a proxy to measure the confidence of a system in its translation.

We could obtain a final improvement of more than +3.5 BLEU over the baseline trained only on bilingual data. However, the greater part of this improvement was simply due to the addition of relevant monolingual data.

2 Basic setting

All of our experiments are based on the Transformer sequence-to-sequence model (Vaswani et al., 2017). We used the `Tensor2Tensor` implementation[1] (Vaswani et al., 2018). For hyperparameters, we used the predefined "big" setting of Tensor2Tensor:

- 6 layers for the encoder

- 6 layers for the decoder

- Hidden size of 1024

- Feed-forward hidden size of 4096

- 16 attention heads

A dropout of 0.3 was used during training. Training was done with the Adam (Kingma and Ba, 2014) algorithm.

Like Popel and Bojar (2018), we also observed that parallel training on a large number of GPUs (thus with a larger effective batch size) was leading to a better final results than only using one or two GPUs at once. We therefore always ran training on five to eight GPUs in parallel[2]. Using a per-GPU batch size of 2048 tokens, this means our effective batch-size was in the range of 10 000 to 16 000 tokens.

Except when indicated otherwise, training was run for at least 500 000 iterations on 8 GPUs (with more iterations when using fewer GPUs to keep the number of training epochs roughly equivalent).

---

[1] https://github.com/tensorflow/tensor2tensor

[2] Since we are using a shared computation environment, it was not practical to always have a batch of 8 GPUs available for training.

Proceedings of the Fourth Conference on Machine Translation (WMT), Volume 2: Shared Task Papers (Day 1) pages 163–167
Florence, Italy, August 1-2, 2019. ©2019 Association for Computational Linguistics

3 Data preprocessing

3.1 Data used

For bilingual data, we used the provided corpora: europarl ($\approx$ 1.7M sentence pairs), common crawl($\approx$ 620k sentence pairs) and news-commentary ($\approx$ 255k sentence pairs). We did not use the paracrawl corpus.

In addition, we also used the 2018 set of the news crawl corpus ($\approx$ 8M sentences) as additional monolingual data.

3.2 Data cleaning

Inspecting the training data exposed some minor issues, most notably of encoding and mixed languages (eg. Spanish and English sentences in the French part of the corpus).

Encoding issues were mostly due to sentences encoded in the "Latin-1" character set being mixed with "UTF-8" encoded sentences. Encoding was fixed using the convenient Python library `ftfy`[3] (Speer, 2019). In addition, we removed all uncommon[4] special unicode characters: such characters waste embeddings/softmax capacity for no benefits.

In order to remove non-French/German sentences from the corpus, we chose to apply a simple heuristic that was fast enough to be applied to millions of sentences. Comparing corpuses of French, German, English, Spanish and Portuguese, we selected "characteristics" words and characters that were frequent in French or German but rare or inexistent in other languages (eg. character "ç" or words "mais", "donc" for French). We then filtered out any sentence longer than 4 words that did not contain any of these characteristics words/characters. A few dozen thousands sentences were filtered out this way, with a rate of false positive empirically estimated at less than 1%.

3.3 Subwords units

As is now common practice, we tokenized all data with subwords units. We relied on the subword tokenization algorithm implemented in Tensor2Tensor. This algorithm is different from the popular BPE tokenization algorithm (Sennrich

et al., 2015b), but is expected to be similarly efficient. We targeted a joint subword vocabulary of 32 000 units. In other experiments we had observed that smaller subword vocabulary size can work better for language pairs with many common prefixes (such as Spanish and Portuguese); this did not seem to be the case here.

4 The importance of recent news data

4.1 Baseline Experiment and Error Analysis

We ran a first baseline experiment using the setting described in section 2 and the cleaned bilingual data of section3. We obtained a cased BLEU score of 33.18.

Manual inspection of the results showed us that the trained model could have serious trouble translating terms or personal names who had only recently appeared in the news. A typical example would be the translation of German "Gelbwesten" ("Yellow vests") into French "Gibiers jaunes" ("Yellow game[5]"), instead of the correct "Gilets jaunes". The "Yellow vests" are a French protest movement that appeared during 2018 fall, and has received much attention in news from that time into 2019. The collocation "Gilets jaunes" is therefore unlikely to appear in the bilingual training data (which is typically older), which explains why the model seems to prefer the similar (in terms of subwords units) "Gibiers jaunes".

Another common problem was the literal translation of German terms that are normally quoted as-is in French News. For example, the German political Party "Die Linke" ("The Left") was translated as "le parti de gauche" ("the left-wing party"), even though French journalists usually refer to it with its German name ("le parti Die Linke").

4.2 Backtranslating recent news

The problem above prompted us to make use of the provided monolingual data, which includes more recent pieces of news. We used backtranslation (Sennrich et al., 2015a), which is currently the most popular approach for using monolingual data in NMT. Concretely, we trained a French-to-German model with the sam bilingual data, and backtranslated into German the 2018 section of the news crawl data. We expect that using the data from previous years would have been useful as well, but we focused on the year 2018, first out

---

[3]https://github.com/LuminosoInsight/python-ftfy

[4]our definition for uncommon was any character whose frequency rank was beyond 500 and that was not appearing in any sentence of the dev set.

[5]with the meaning of "hunted animal", not (board) game.

of concern with time constraints, and second considering the most recent pieces of news should be by far the most relevant to translate the development set and the test set (which are mostly made of recent news).

We added the backtranslated data to the bilingual data and trained a new model. The new model had a cased BLEU score of 35.92, almost a 3 BLEU improvement. Manual inspection showed a large improvement in the translation of recent terms (eg. "Gelbwesten" was now correctly translated as "Gilets jaunes"). However, the problem of litterally translating terms such as "Die Linke" remained.

4.3 Checkpoint Averaging

In order to improve results further, we tried checkpoint averaging[6]. Averaging was done over 20 checkpoints, each checkpoint being taken with a one hour interval. This led to a modest improvement of +0.2 BLEU.

5 Output combination

An efficient technique for improving the results of a given Neural MT system is to train several models and to compute their ensemble translations. The ensemble translation is obtained by letting each model predict the probability of the next words to be generated, and then combine these probabilities to choose which word is actually generated to create the final translation. The price for the improved translation quality is an increase in training time, decoding time and memory usage proportional to the number of models used.

In the course of this shared task, we trained several different models, but could not use classic ensemble techniques to combine them, due to several factors: absence of a ready-made ensemble implementation in Tensor2Tensor and models being trained with different preprocessing (eg. different subword units). This is why we considered a simple system combination algorithm that proved to be useful.

5.1 Checkpoint agreement

While we could have used some more advanced system combination techniques, such as (Freitag et al., 2014), we experimented with the idea that what we call "checkpoint agreement" gives us useful indication about the reliability of a given translation.

The idea is, essentially, to keep many checkpoints for each models (as in section 4.3). Each checkpoint can be used to generate a translation candidate. If all checkpoints generate the same translation candidate, we can have higher confidence in the translation than if they all generate different translation candidates. Further, if twenty checkpoints lead to a set of, say, three different translations, we can have more confidence in the translation that was generated by the most checkpoint. This provides us with a model-independent and implementation-independent way to estimate the confidence we can have in the output of a model. We empirically check to which extent this is true in section 5.2.

Then, in section 5.3, we make use of this checkpoint agreement to simply combine the output of different systems.

5.2 Empirical evaluation of checkpoint agreement

We first evaluate this idea with the checkpoints of a single model. The first thing to verify is whether different checkpoints actually produce different translations. Using the same checkpoints as in section 4.3 (ie. 20 one-hour-spaced checkpoints), we compute the translations they generate for the development set. We find that for 9% of the input sentences, the 20 checkpoints generate the same translation. For 2% of the input sentences, they all produce distinct translations. For the remaining 89% of inputs, there therefore exists at least one translation candidate generated by at least two checkpoints.

If, for each input, we select the most often generated translation candidate, we obtain a BLEU score improvement of +0.3 ("selection by checkpoint agreement" in table 1). This is a bit better than simply doing checkpoint averaging, but of course it takes 20 times more decoding time to obtain a translation.

5.3 Models output combination through checkpoint agreement

Given that we now have a model-independent way of estimating the reliability of a translation, we can use this to combine the output of different models. This is what we try here.

Model	Dev cased BLEU	Improvement
Baseline (bilingual data only)	33.18	-
+2018 news data (monolingual)	35.92	+2.74
Checkpoint averaging	36.12	+0.2
Selection through checkpoint agreement	36.23	+0.31
All Models combined with Checkpoints agreement	**36.73**	+0.81

Table 1: Cased-BLEU score on the development set for the different experiments. Improvements of checkpoint averaging and checkpoint agreement combination are computed with respect to the "Baseline+2018 monolingual data" BLEU.

5.3.1 Combined models

The additional models we trained include:

- A model with a subword vocabulary size of 8000

- A model with a subword vocabulary size of 512

- A model trained with a reversed French-side word order

The models with alternative vocabulary size were trained to evaluate the effect of the coarseness of the subword segmentation on the final quality. We had observed this can have an important impact on language pairs with many common substrings (like Spanish and Portuguese), but did not find it to give better results for German-French.

The model trained with a reversed French-side order was to evaluate if the model could produce better results by generating the translation from right-to-left. Again, we did not find this to lead to better results in our case.

Note that we could not combine these models with a "classic" ensemble of models: due to different subwords units or word order generation, these models cannot compute consistent "next-word" probabilities that could be easily combined.

5.3.2 Results

We combine the results of our models through a simple "majority vote" weighted by the confidence deduced from the checkpoint agreement. We could possibly obtain better results by integrating the confidence score given by checkpoint agreement in a more complex system combination algorithm such as Freitag et al. (2014).

We obtain an improvement of +0.8 BLEU ("All Models Checkpoints combination" in table 1).

6 Conclusion

We experimented with the translation of German into French in the context of the WMT 2019 shared tasks. Our approach mostly followed the currently known best practices. We detailed how we cleaned an pre-processed the training data, and, in particular, we found it crucial for the task to make good use of recent monolingual data. We also evaluated the idea that a set of checkpoints from a given training run can be used to evaluate the confidence in the quality of the output of a model. We used this to combine simply the output of a set of different models.

References

Markus Freitag, Matthias Huck, and Hermann Ney. 2014. Jane: Open source machine translation system combination. In *Proceedings of the Demonstrations at the 14th Conference of the European Chapter of the Association for Computational Linguistics*, pages 29–32.

Diederik P Kingma and Jimmy Ba. 2014. Adam: A method for stochastic optimization. *arXiv preprint arXiv:1412.6980*.

Martin Popel and Ondřej Bojar. 2018. Training tips for the transformer model. *The Prague Bulletin of Mathematical Linguistics*, 110(1):43–70.

Rico Sennrich, Barry Haddow, and Alexandra Birch. 2015a. Improving neural machine translation models with monolingual data. *arXiv preprint arXiv:1511.06709*.

Rico Sennrich, Barry Haddow, and Alexandra Birch. 2015b. Neural machine translation of rare words with subword units. In *WMT2015*.

Robyn Speer. 2019. ftfy. Zenodo. Version 5.5.

Ashish Vaswani, Samy Bengio, Eugene Brevdo, Francois Chollet, Aidan N. Gomez, Stephan Gouws, Llion Jones, Łukasz Kaiser, Nal Kalchbrenner, Niki Parmar, Ryan Sepassi, Noam Shazeer, and Jakob

Uszkoreit. 2018. Tensor2tensor for neural machine translation. *CoRR*, abs/1803.07416.

Ashish Vaswani, Noam Shazeer, Niki Parmar, Jakob Uszkoreit, Llion Jones, Aidan N Gomez, Łukasz Kaiser, and Illia Polosukhin. 2017. Attention is all you need. In *Advances in neural information processing systems*, pages 5998–6008.

NICT's Supervised Neural Machine Translation Systems for the WMT19 News Translation Task

Raj Dabre[*] and **Kehai Chen**[*] and **Benjamin Marie**[*] and **Rui Wang**[*] and
Atsushi Fujita and **Masao Utiyama** and **Eiichiro Sumita**
National Institute of Information and Communications Technology, Kyoto, Japan
{raj.dabre,khchen,bmarie,wangrui}@nict.go.jp
{atsushi.fujita,mutiyama,eiichiro.sumita}@nict.go.jp

Abstract

In this paper, we describe our supervised neural machine translation (NMT) systems that we developed for the news translation task for Kazakh↔English, Gujarati↔English, Chinese↔English, and English→Finnish translation directions. We focused on leveraging multilingual transfer learning and back-translation for the extremely low-resource language pairs: Kazakh↔English and Gujarati↔English translation. For the Chinese↔English translation, we used the provided parallel data augmented with a large quantity of back-translated monolingual data to train state-of-the-art NMT systems. We then employed techniques that have been proven to be most effective, such as back-translation, fine-tuning, and model ensembling, to generate the primary submissions of Chinese↔English. For English→Finnish, our submission from WMT18 remains a strong baseline despite the increase in parallel corpora for this year's task.

1 Introduction

Neural machine translation (NMT) (Cho et al., 2014; Sutskever et al., 2014; Bahdanau et al., 2015) has enabled end-to-end training of a translation system without needing to deal with word alignments, translation rules, and complicated decoding algorithms, which are the characteristics of phrase-based statistical machine translation (PB-SMT) (Koehn et al., 2007). NMT performs well in resource-rich scenarios but badly in resource-poor ones (Zoph et al., 2016). With the aid of multilingualism, transfer learning, and monolingual corpora, researchers have shown that the translation quality in a low-resource scenario can be significantly boosted (Zoph et al., 2016; Firat et al., 2016; Sennrich et al., 2016a). Furthermore, unsupervised NMT (Lample et al., 2018) has enabled

translation in a scenario where only monolingual corpora are available.

In this paper, we describe all the systems for Kazakh↔English, Gujarati↔English, Chinese↔English, and English→Finnish, that we developed and submitted for WMT 2019 under the team name "NICT." In particular our observations can be summarized as follows:

Kazakh→English translation heavily benefits from the existence of Russian as a pivot language in the form of a Russian–Kazakh corpus which can be used to generate a pseudo-parallel Kazakh–English corpus from the Russian–English corpus.

Gujarati→English translation can be drastically improved by training a robust Hindi→English model and fine tuning it on the Gujarati–English corpus.

Chinese↔English translation can benefit from back-translation, model ensembling, and fine-tuning based on the development data.

English→Finnish translation generated by our WMT18's NMT system (Marie et al., 2018) remains a strong baseline despite the availability of larger bilingual corpora for training this year.

Noisy parallel corpora for back-translation leads to poor quality pseudo-parallel data which leads to poor translations.

Kindly refer to the overview paper (Bojar et al., 2019) for additional details about the tasks, comparisons to other submissions, human analyses and insights.

2 The Transformer NMT Model

The Transformer (Vaswani et al., 2017) is the current state-of-the-art model for NMT. It is a

---

[*]equal contribution

Proceedings of the Fourth Conference on Machine Translation (WMT), Volume 2: Shared Task Papers (Day 1) pages 168–174
Florence, Italy, August 1-2, 2019. ©2019 Association for Computational Linguistics

sequence-to-sequence neural model that consists of two components: the *encoder* and the *decoder*. The encoder converts the input word sequence into a sequence of vectors. The decoder, on the other hand, produces the target word sequence by predicting the words using a combination of the previously predicted word and relevant parts of the input sequence representations. The reader is encouraged to read the original paper (Vaswani et al., 2017) for a deeper understanding.

3 Kazakh↔English Task

3.1 Use of Pseudo-Parallel Data

In this paper, we rely on a highly reliable data-augmentation technique known as back-translation (Sennrich et al., 2016a). This technique relies on a L2→L1 model to translate an L2 monolingual corpus, thereby yielding a large L1–L2 pseudo-parallel corpus for L1→L2 translation. The final L1→L2 translation quality depends on the quality of the pseudo-parallel corpus which in turn depends on L2→L1 translation quality. For a low-resource L1–L2 pair, this approach is rather infeasible.[1] However, the existence of a pivot-language, L3, can prove beneficial. In this situation, we can assume large L3–L1 and L3–L2 corpora. Using a robust L3→L1 model, we can translate the L3 side of the L3–L2 corpus to obtain a high quality L1–L2 pseudo-parallel corpus (Firat et al., 2016).

In our participation, we regard Russian as the helping language, L3.

3.2 Datasets

We used the official Kazakh–English, Kazakh–Russian, and Russian–English datasets provided by WMT. All three datasets belong to the news domain. After filtering the Kazakh–English parallel corpus using the "clean-corpus.perl" script in Moses (Koehn et al., 2007),[2] we obtained 98,602 (noisy) sentence pairs.

We filtered the Kazakh–Russian corpus of 5,063,666 lines according to the scores provided with the corpus files. The real-valued scores ranged from 0 to a maximum value of 11. Since higher scores meant better pairs, we filtered the corpora using the thresholds 1, 2, 3, 4, and 5 and

trained NMT models on the filtered corpora. We found out that a threshold of a score of at least 1 gave a corpus of 2,905,538 lines and performs the best on a development set.[3] Using scores of 2, 3, and 4 gave slightly lower BLEU scores on the development set and thus we decided to use as large a corpus as possible.

We used 4,596,000 lines[4] of Russian sentences, randomly selected from the 12,061,155 sentences Russian–English corpus, for back-translation. No other type of pre-processing was performed.

3.3 Systems

We used the tensor2tensor[5] version 1.6 implementation of the Transformer (Vaswani et al., 2017) model. We used the default hyper-parameters in tensor2tensor for all our models with the exception of the number of training iterations. Unless mentioned otherwise we used the Transformer "base" model hyper-parameter settings with a $2^{15} = 32,768$ sub-word vocabulary which was learned using tensor2tensor's internal tokenization and sub-word segmentation mechanism. We learned separate sub-word vocabularies for the source and target languages.

During training, a model checkpoint was saved every 1000 iterations. All models were trained till convergence on the WMT19's official development set BLEU score. We averaged the last N model checkpoints and used it for decoding the test sets. N is 20 for Kazakh↔English. The choice of N depended on the number of iterations for convergence which in turn depended on the size and quality of the data used to train models. We chose the beam size and length penalty by tuning on the development set. We did not ensemble multiple models although it could possibly improve the translation quality even further.

We first trained Russian→Kazakh and Russian→English models for back-translation purposes. The Russian→Kazakh model was trained for 300,000 iterations on one GPU with a batch size of 2048 words and the

---

[1] We had initially experimented with the large Kazakh and English monolingual corpora for back-translation but observed no benefits.

[2] https://github.com/moses-smt/mosesdecoder

[3] We chose a set of 2,000 sentences, not included in the training set, to monitor convergence.

[4] Due to lack of time, we were unable to back-translate all Russian sentences before the task deadline. After the deadline we experimented with back-translating all Russian sentences but did not observe any appreciable improvements in translation quality.

[5] https://github.com/tensorflow/tensor2tensor

Task	BLEU	BLEU cased	IGNORE BLEU (11b)	IGNORE BLEU-cased (11b)	IGNORE BLEU-cased-norm	TER	BEER 2.0	CharactTER	Rank
Kazakh→English	28.1	26.2	28.1	26.2	26.2	0.670	0.555	0.701	3/9
English→Kazakh	6.4	6.4	6.4	6.4	7.8	0.926	0.418	0.841	8/9
Gujarati→English	18.6	17.2	18.6	17.2	17.3	0.733	0.508	0.705	5/10
English→Gujarati	10.5	10.5	10.5	10.5	10.6	0.856	0.448	0.785	6/8

Table 1: Results for Kazakh↔English and Gujarati↔English tasks. These scores are simply copied from the official runs list.

Russian→English for 100,000 iterations[6] on two GPUs with a batch size of 4096 words. We used the Russian→English model to translate the Russian side of the Russian–Kazakh corpus into English. On the other hand, we used the Russian→Kazakh model to translate the Russian side of the Russian–English corpus into Kazakh. We used greedy decoding (to save time) with a length penalty of 1.0 in both cases.

Both Kazakh→English and English→Kazakh models were trained only on the pseudo-parallel data, using two GPUs with a batch size of 4096 words, till the convergence of BLEU on the development set. As a result, the Kazakh→English model was trained for 200,000 iterations, whereas the English→Kazakh model was trained for 220,000 iterations. For both translation directions, decoding was done using a beam of size 10 and length penalty of 0.8 (determined by tuning on the development set).

3.4 Results

Refer to rows 1 and 2 of Table 1 for the various automatic evaluation scores. For Kazakh→English our submitted system achieved a cased BLEU score of 26.2 placing our system at 3rd rank out of 9 primary systems. On the other hand, our English→Kazakh performed poorly with its system achieving a BLEU score of 6.4 placing it at 8th out of 9 primary systems.

Initially, we had experimented with back-translating English monolingual corpora to Kazakh using models trained on the Kazakh–English parallel corpora. However, this led to a BLEU score of less than 15. After repeated experimentation we realized that the Kazakh–English parallel corpus was of extremely poor quality and hence decided to experiment with Russian as a pivot language. We trained a multilingual English–Russian–Kazakh model

and pivot translation (Firat et al., 2016) gave a BLEU of around 18 which motivated us to exploit the Russian–Kazakh data. The main lesson we learned was: always exploit a pivot language whenever possible instead of relying on a parallel corpus of bad quality. Note once again that our submissions did not involve the use of the Kazakh–English corpus provided by the organizers.

4 Gujarati↔English Task

4.1 Fine-Tuning for Transfer Learning

In addition to the approaches in Section 3.1, we also use fine-tuning for transfer learning. Zoph et al. (2016) proposed to train a robust L3→L1 parent model using a large L3–L1 parallel corpus and then fine-tune it on a small L2–L1 corpus to obtain a robust L2→L1 child model. The underlying assumption is that the pre-trained L3→L1 model contains prior probabilities for translation into L1. The prior information is divided into two parts: language modeling information (strong prior) and cross-lingual information (weak or strong depending on the relationship between L3 and L2). Dabre et al. (2017) have shown that linguistically similar L3 and L2 allow for better transfer learning. As such, we transliterate L3 to L2 before pre-training a parent model. This could help in faster convergence, ensure cognate overlap, and potentially lead to a better translation quality.

In this participation, we used Hindi as the helping language, L3.

4.2 Datasets

We used the official Gujarati–English and Hindi–English datasets provided by WMT. The Gujarati–English corpus contains 28,683 sentence pairs belonging to the news and Wiki domains. We also used the ILCI Gujarati–English corpus (Jha, 2010) of 44,777 sentence pairs belonging to the tourism and health domains. In total the size

---

[6]Given that the Russian–English corpus contains over 12M sentence pairs, training for more iterations could give better results.

of the Gujarati–English parallel corpus is 73,460
sentence pairs. The Hindi–English corpus of
1,492,827 sentence pairs contains sentence pairs
belonging to multiple domains.

We used around 2,700,919 lines of Gujarati
monolingual corpora (of which approximately
244,919 lines were from the news domain) for
back-translation.[7] We mapped the script on the
Hindi side of the Hindi–English corpus to Gujarati
using the Indic languages toolkit.[8] No other type
of pre-processing was performed.

We had initially experimented with a large English monolingual corpus for back-translation but
observed no benefits.

4.3 Systems

Most training details, including the size of subword vocabulary, are same as those in Section 3.3.
The only exception is the number of checkpoints
we averaged before decoding which is 10 instead
of 20. This is because Gujarati↔English models converged rather quickly and hence were not
trained for a long period of time.

We first trained a bi-directional
Gujarati↔English model[9] using the parallel
corpora mentioned above, for 60,000 iterations on
one GPU with a batch size of 2048 words. We
then used this model to translate Gujarati monolingual data into English using greedy decoding
with a length penalty of 1.0. We also pre-trained
a Hindi→English model where the scripts on the
Hindi side was mapped to those in Gujarati. This
model was trained for 90,000 iterations on one
GPU with a batch size of 4096 words.

We then trained a Gujarati→English model
by fine-tuning the Hindi→English model on the
Gujarati→English data for an additional 15,000 iterations[10] on one GPU with a batch size of 4096
words. We also trained a English→Gujarati model
using the pseudo-parallel corpus by training for
60,000 iterations[11] on one GPU with a batch size

of 2048 words. For both cases, decoding was done
using a beam of size 10 and length penalty of 0.8.

4.4 Results

Refer to rows 3 and 4 of Table 1 for the various automatic evaluation scores. For Gujarati→English
our submitted system run achieved a cased BLEU
score of 17.2 placing our system at 5th position
out of 10 primary systems. On the other hand, our
English→Gujarati performed poorly with its system run achieving a BLEU score of 10.6 placing it
at 6th position out of 8 primary systems.

Similar to our experience in Kazakh↔English,
using the NMT models trained using Gujarati–
English parallel corpora for back-translation, led
to poor translation quality. Our Gujarati→English
system achieved less than 10 BLEU when relying on a naive back-translation approach. As
such, we decided to rely on transfer learning
by fine-tuning a Hindi–English model on the
Gujarati–English corpus. In WMT19, Hindi
was the only language linguistically similar to
Gujarati and hence we did not explore other
resource-rich language pairs. Other participants
used Czech–English for transfer learning and
achieved similar success. On the other hand, only
the pseudo English–Gujarati corpus was available for developing the English→Gujarati system.
Due to lack of time, we did not try using our
transfer learning based Gujarati→English model
for back-translation. Given that our submitted
Gujarati→English system is over 8 BLEU points
higher than the naive back-translation based system, we expect that English→Gujarati has a huge
potential for improvement.

As in the case of Kazakh↔English, we noted
that it is extremely beneficial to leverage a helping
language, such as Hindi, for improving translation
quality.

5 Chinese↔English Tasks

5.1 Datasets

The training data for the Chinese↔English
(ZH↔EN) translation tasks consists of two parts:
1) we selected the first 10 million lines of the
News Crawl 2016 English corpus according to our
last year's finding (Marie et al., 2018), 2) the corresponding synthetic data was generated through
back-translation (Sennrich et al., 2016a). We applied tokenizer and truecaser of Moses (Koehn

---

[7]During back-translation, some parts of the monolingual corpus remained untranslated due to out-of-memory errors caused by very long input sentences.

[8]https://github.com/anoopkunchukuttan/indic_nlp_library

[9]We chose a bi-directional model because we observed higher BLEU scores on the development set compared to a unidirectional model.

[10]Fine-tuning converges quickly.

[11]Given the size of the pseudo-parallel corpus we expected to train for much longer but observed convergence rather quickly. It is likely that our generated corpus was quite noisy and hence the models had limited learning potential.

Task	System	BLEU	BLEU cased	IGNORE BLEU (11b)	IGNORE BLEU-cased (11b)	IGNORE BLEU-cased-norm	TER	BEER 2.0	CharactTER
ZH→EN	Single model	24.1	23.3	24.1	23.3	23.5	0.667	0.574	0.643
	+back-translation	26.6	25.3	26.6	25.3	25.5	0.652	0.585	0.632
	+fine-tuning	28.7	27.5	28.7	27.5	27.7	0.621	0.599	0.613
	+ensemble five models	32.3	31.0	32.3	31.0	31.3	0.599	0.615	0.569
EN→ZH	Single model	30.3	30.3	0.4	0.4	2.2	0.999	0.304	0.839
	+back-translation	31.8	31.8	0.6	0.6	2.6	0.999	0.315	0.765
	+fine-tuning	33.1	33.1	0.0	0.0	2.3	1.000	0.319	0.747
	+ensemble five models	34.5	34.5	0.7	0.7	2.6	0.999	0.326	0.734

Table 2: Results for ZH↔EN translation task. "Single model" denotes that it was trained by only using the first 10M lines of the News Crawl-2016 English corpus as training data. These scores are simply copied from the official runs list.

et al., 2007) to the English sentences. Jieba[12] was used to tokenize the Chinese sentence. For cleaning, we filtered out sentences longer than 80 tokens in the training data.

5.2 Systems

We used Marian toolkit (Junczys-Dowmunt et al., 2018)[13] to build competitive NMT systems based on the Transformer (Vaswani et al., 2017) architecture. We used the byte pair encoding (BPE) algorithm (Sennrich et al., 2016b) for obtaining the sub-word vocabulary whose size was set to 50,000. The number of dimensions of all input and output layers was set to 512, and that of the inner feed-forward neural network layer was set to 2048. The number of attention heads in each encoder and decoder layer was set to eight. During training, the value of label smoothing was set to 0.1, and the attention dropout and residual dropout were set to 0.1. The Adam optimizer (Kingma and Ba, 2014) was used to tune the parameters of the model. The learning rate was varied under a warm-up strategy with warm-up steps of 16,000. All NMT models for ZH↔EN tasks were consistently trained on four P100 GPUs. We validated the model with an interval of 5,000 batches on the development set and selected the best model according to BLEU (Papineni et al., 2002) score on the newsdev2018 data set.

We performed the following training run independently for five times to obtain the models for ensembling. First, an initial model was trained on the provided parallel data and used to generate pseudo-parallel data through back-translation. A new model was then trained from scratch on the mixture of the original parallel data and the pseudo-parallel data. The new model was further

fine-tuned on the concatenation of newsdev2017 and newstest2017 data sets for 20 epochs. Finally, we decoded the newstest2019 test set with an ensemble of the five fine-tuned models to generate the primary submissions for the ZH↔EN task.

5.3 Results

Table 2 shows the results of ZH↔EN tasks. It is obvious that the back-translation, fine-tuning, and ensemble methods are greatly effective for the ZH↔EN tasks. In particular, the ensemble gave more improvements on the ZH→EN task over the "Single model+back-translation+fine-tuning" model than the EN→ZH task. In addition, these three methods can incrementally improve translation performance of the Transformer NMT.

6 English→Finnish Task

For the translation direction English→Finnish, we used the exactly same NMT models and system used to generate our last year's submission (Marie et al., 2018). We did not exploit the new larger parallel data provided for this year. For this year, we only submitted the output produced by the ensemble of our three NMT models. Our system was ranked third for the task according to BLEU-cased, at 23.2 BLEU points, which is 4.2 BLEU points below the best system submitted to the task.

7 Conclusion

In this paper, we have described our primary systems whose translations we have submitted to WMT2019. In general, we found that back-translation, fine-tuning, and ensembling are the most effective means of maximizing the translation quality for all language pairs. In addition to this, we have observed that leveraging a helping language, such as Russian for Kazakh↔English

---

[12]https://github.com/fxsjy/jieba
[13]https://marian-nmt.github.io

translation and Hindi for Gujarati→English translation, can lead to large benefits as compared to using only parallel corpora and back-translation.

Acknowledgments

We thank the organizers for providing the datasets and the reviewers for their valuable suggestions in improving this paper. This work was conducted under the program "Research and Development of Enhanced Multilingual and Multipurpose Speech Translation Systems" of the Ministry of Internal Affairs and Communications (MIC), Japan.

References

Dzmitry Bahdanau, Kyunghyun Cho, and Yoshua Bengio. 2015. Neural machine translation by jointly learning to align and translate. In *Proceedings of the 3rd International Conference on Learning Representations*, San Diego, USA.

Ondřej Bojar, Christian Federmann, Mark Fishel, Yvette Graham, Barry Haddow, Matthias Huck, Philipp Koehn, Christof Monz, Mathias Müller, and Matt Post. 2019. Findings of the 2019 conference on machine translation (WMT19). In *Proceedings of the Fourth Conference on Machine Translation, Volume 2: Shared Task Papers*, Florence, Italy. Association for Computational Linguistics.

Kyunghyun Cho, Bart van Merriënboer, Çaglar Gülçehre, Dzmitry Bahdanau, Fethi Bougares, Holger Schwenk, and Yoshua Bengio. 2014. Learning phrase representations using RNN encoder–decoder for statistical machine translation. In *Proceedings of the 2014 Conference on Empirical Methods in Natural Language Processing*, pages 1724–1734, Doha, Qatar.

Raj Dabre, Tetsuji Nakagawa, and Hideto Kazawa. 2017. An empirical study of language relatedness for transfer learning in neural machine translation. In *Proceedings of the 31st Pacific Asia Conference on Language, Information and Computation*, pages 282–286. The National University (Phillippines).

Orhan Firat, Kyunghyun Cho, and Yoshua Bengio. 2016. Multi-way, multilingual neural machine translation with a shared attention mechanism. In *NAACL HLT 2016, The 2016 Conference of the North American Chapter of the Association for Computational Linguistics: Human Language Technologies*, pages 866–875, San Diego, USA.

Girish Nath Jha. 2010. The TDIL program and the Indian Language Corpora Initiative (ILCI). In *Proceedings of the Seventh International Conference on Language Resources and Evaluation (LREC'10)*, pages 982–985, Valletta, Malta. European Language Resources Association (ELRA).

Marcin Junczys-Dowmunt, Roman Grundkiewicz, Tomasz Dwojak, Hieu Hoang, Kenneth Heafield, Tom Neckermann, Frank Seide, Ulrich Germann, Alham Fikri Aji, Nikolay Bogoychev, André F. T. Martins, and Alexandra Birch. 2018. Marian: Fast neural machine translation in C++. In *Proceedings of ACL 2018, System Demonstrations*, pages 116–121, Melbourne, Australia.

Diederik P. Kingma and Jimmy Ba. 2014. Adam: A method for stochastic optimization. *CoRR*, abs/1412.6980.

Philipp Koehn, Hieu Hoang, Alexandra Birch, Chris Callison-Burch, Marcello Federico, Nicola Bertoldi, Brooke Cowan, Wade Shen, Christine Moran, Richard Zens, Chris Dyer, Ondrej Bojar, Alexandra Constantin, and Evan Herbst. 2007. Moses: Open source toolkit for statistical machine translation. In *Proceedings of the 45th Annual Meeting of the Association for Computational Linguistics Companion Volume Proceedings of the Demo and Poster Sessions*, pages 177–180, Prague, Czech Republic.

Guillaume Lample, Alexis Conneau, Ludovic Denoyer, and Marc'Aurelio Ranzato. 2018. Unsupervised machine translation using monolingual corpora only. In *Proceedings of the 6th International Conference on Learning Representations*.

Benjamin Marie, Rui Wang, Atsushi Fujita, Masao Utiyama, and Eiichiro Sumita. 2018. NICT's neural and statistical machine translation systems for the WMT18 news translation task. In *Proceedings of the Third Conference on Machine Translation: Shared Task Papers*, pages 449–455, Belgium, Brussels.

Kishore Papineni, Salim Roukos, Todd Ward, and Wei-Jing Zhu. 2002. BLEU: A method for automatic evaluation of machine translation. In *Proceedings of the 40th Annual Meeting on Association for Computational Linguistics*, pages 311–318, Philadelphia, USA.

Rico Sennrich, Barry Haddow, and Alexandra Birch. 2016a. Improving neural machine translation models with monolingual data. In *Proceedings of the 54th Annual Meeting of the Association for Computational Linguistics (Volume 1: Long Papers)*, pages 86–96, Berlin, Germany.

Rico Sennrich, Barry Haddow, and Alexandra Birch. 2016b. Neural machine translation of rare words with subword units. In *Proceedings of the 54th Annual Meeting of the Association for Computational Linguistic*, pages 1715–1725, Berlin, Germany.

Ilya Sutskever, Oriol Vinyals, and Quoc V. Le. 2014. Sequence to sequence learning with neural networks. In *Proceedings of the 27th International Conference on Neural Information Processing Systems*, pages 3104–3112, Montréal, Canada.

Ashish Vaswani, Noam Shazeer, Niki Parmar, Jakob Uszkoreit, Llion Jones, Aidan N. Gomez, Łukasz Kaiser, and Illia Polosukhin. 2017. Attention is all you need. In *Proceedings of 30th Advances in Neural Information Processing Systems*, pages 5998–6008.

Barret Zoph, Deniz Yuret, Jonathan May, and Kevin Knight. 2016. Transfer learning for low-resource neural machine translation. In *Proceedings of the 2016 Conference on Empirical Methods in Natural Language Processing*, pages 1568–1575, Austin, USA.

The University of Sydney's Machine Translation System for WMT19

Liang Ding   **Dacheng Tao**

UBTECH Sydney AI Center, School of Computer Science, FEIT

University of Sydney, Australia

`ldin3097@uni.sydney.edu.au, dacheng.tao@sydney.edu.au`

Abstract

This paper describes the University of Sydney's submission of the WMT 2019 shared news translation task. We participated in the Finnish→English direction and got the best BLEU(33.0) score among all the participants. Our system is based on the self-attentional Transformer networks, into which we integrated the most recent effective strategies from academic research (*e.g.*, BPE, back translation, multi-features data selection, data augmentation, greedy model ensemble, reranking, ConMBR system combination, and postprocessing). Furthermore, we propose a novel augmentation method **Cycle Translation** and a data mixture strategy $Big/Small$ **parallel construction** to entirely exploit the synthetic corpus. Extensive experiments show that adding the above techniques can make continuous improvements of the BLEU scores, and the best result outperforms the baseline (Transformer ensemble model trained with the original parallel corpus) by approximately 5.3 BLEU score, achieving the state-of-the-art performance.

1 Introduction

Neural machine translation (NMT), as a succinct end-to-end paradigm, has resulted in massive leap in state-of-the-art performances for many language pairs (Kalchbrenner and Blunsom, 2013; Sutskever et al., 2014; Bahdanau et al., 2015; Gehring et al., 2017; Wu et al., 2016; Vaswani et al., 2017). Among these encoder-decoder networks, the Transformer (Vaswani et al., 2017), which solely uses along attention mechanism and eschews the recurrent or convolutional networks, leads to state-of-the-art translation quality and fast convergence speed (Ahmed et al., 2017). Although many Transformer-based variants are proposed (*e.g.*, DynamicConv (Wu et al., 2019), sparse-transformer (Child et al., 2019)), our preliminary experiments show that their performances are unstable compared to the traditional

#	cycle translated sample sentence pair
1	*She stuck to her principles even when some suggest that in an environment often considered devoid of such thing there are little point.*
2	*She insists on her own principles, even if some people think that it doesn't make sense in an environment that is often considered to be absent.*

Table 1: Example of difference between original sentence (line 1) and cycle translated result (line 2). Pretrained BERT model using all available English corpora show that the $\mathcal{L}oss$ decreased from 6.98 to 1.52.

Transformer. Traditional Transformer therefore was employed as our baseline system. In this paper, we summarize the USYD NMT systems for the WMT 2019 Finnish→English (FI→EN) translation task.

As the limitation of time and computation resources, we only participated in one challenging task FI→EN, which lags behind other language pairs in translation performance (Bojar et al., 2018). We introduce our system with three parts.

First, at data level, we find that the data quality of both parallel and monolingual is unbalanced (*i.e.*, contains a large number of low quality sentences). Thus, we apply several features to select the data after pre-processing, for example, language models, alignment scores etc. Meanwhile, in order to fully utilize monolingual corpus, not only back translation (Sennrich et al., 2015) is adopted to back translate the high quality monolingual sentences with target-to-source(T2S) model, we also propose **Cycle Translation** to improve the low-quality sentences, in turn resulting in corresponding high-quality back translation results. Note that unlike text style transfer task (Shen et al., 2017; Fu et al., 2018; Prabhumoye et al., 2018) which transfers text to specific style (*e.g.*, political

Proceedings of the Fourth Conference on Machine Translation (WMT), Volume 2: Shared Task Papers (Day 1) pages 175–182

Florence, Italy, August 1-2, 2019. ©2019 Association for Computational Linguistics

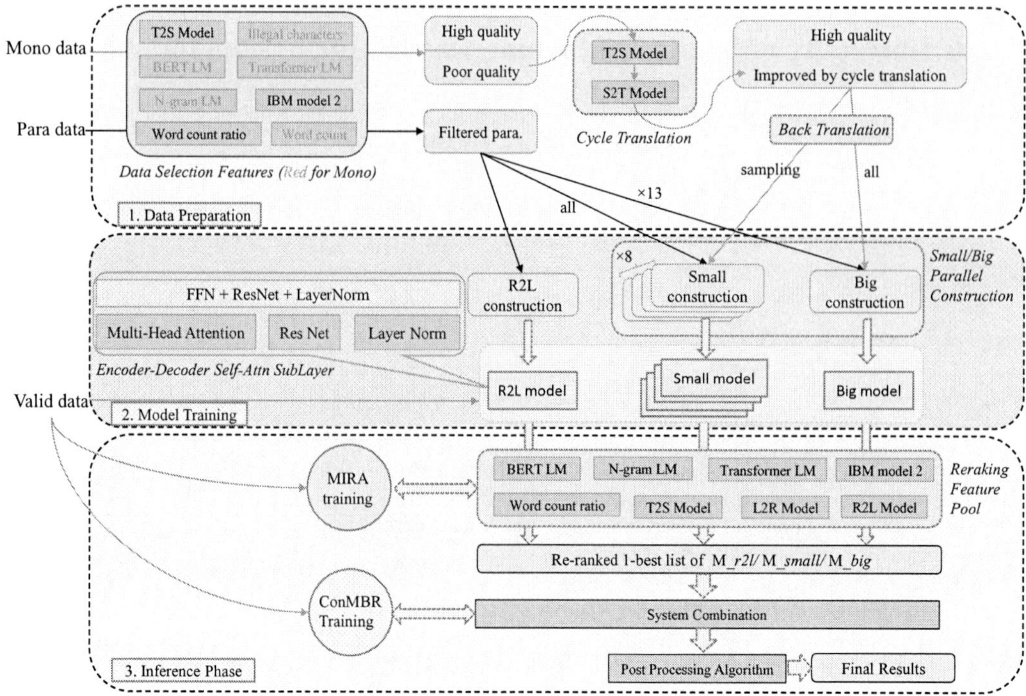

Figure 1: The schematic structure of the three main stages of the USYD-NMT. They are data preparation stage, model training stage and inference phrase. For brevity, here Mono, Para, and Valid represent the monolingual, parallel and validation data respectively.

slant, gender), we aim to improve the fluency of sentences, for instance, through cycle translation, low quality sentence in Table 1 becomes more fluent in terms of language model score. The top diagram of Figure 1 depicts data preparation process concretely.

As to model training in the middle part of Figure 1, we empirically introduced **Big/Small parallel construction** strategy to construct training data for different models. The intuition is all the data are advantageous and can be fully exploited by different models, thus we train 8 Transformer_base models ($\mathcal{M}_{small} \times 8$) by using different small scale corpus constructed by small parallel construction method and a Transformer_big model ($\mathcal{M}_{big} \times 1$) based on the big parallel construction method. In the meantime, a right-to-left model ($\mathcal{M}_{r2l}$) is trained.

In addition, in inference phrase, we comprehensively consider the ensemble strategies at model level, sentence level and word level. For model level ensemble, while brutal ensemble top-N or last-M models may improve translation performance, it is difficult to obtain the optimal result. Hence we employ Greedy Model Selection based Ensembling (GMSE) (Partalas et al., 2008; Deng et al., 2018). For sentence level ensemble, we keep top n-best for multi-features reranking. And for word aspect, we adopt the confusion network decoding (Bangalore et al., 2001; Matusov et al., 2006; Sim et al., 2007) with using the consensus network minimum Bayes risk (MBR) criterion (Sim et al., 2007). After combination, a post-processing algorithm is employed to correct inconsistent number and years between the source and target sentences. The bottom part of Figure 1 shows the inference process.

Our omnivorous model achieved the best BLEU (Papineni et al., 2002) scores among submitted systems, demonstrating the effectiveness of the proposed approach. Theoretically, our approach is not specific to the Finnish→English language pair, *i.e.*, it is universal and effective for any language pairs. The remainder of this article is organized as follows: Section 2 will describe each component of the system. In Section 3, we introduce the data preparing details. Then, the experimental results are showed in Section 4. Finally, we conclude in Section 5.

model_parameters	$\mathcal{M}$_small	$\mathcal{M}$_big
num_stack	6	6
hidden_size	512	1024
FFN_size	2048	4096
num_heads	8	16
p_dropout	0.1	0.3

Table 2: Model differences between base and big.

Category	Features
NMT Features	T2S score (Sennrich et al., 2016)
LM Features	BERT LM (Devlin et al., 2018)
	Transformer LM (Bei et al., 2018)
	N-gram LM (Stolcke, 2002)
Alignment Features	IBM model 2 (Dyer et al., 2013)
Rule-based features	Illegal characters (Bei et al., 2018)
Count Features	Word count
	Word count ratio

Table 3: Features for data selection.

2 Approach

2.1 Neural Machine Translation Models

Given a source sentence $X = x_1, ..., x_{T'}$, NMT model factors the distribution over target sentence $Y = y_1, ..., y_T$ into a conditional probabilities:

$$p(Y|X; \theta) = \prod_{t=1}^{T+1} p(y_t|y_{0:t-1}, x_{1:T'}; \theta) \quad (1)$$

where the conditional probabilities are parameterized by neural networks.

The NMT model consists of two units: an encoder and a decoder. The encoder is assumed that it can adequately represent the source sentence. Then, the decoder can recursively predict each target word. Parameters of encoder, decoder and attention mechanism are trained to maximize the likelihood with a cross-entropy loss applied:

$$\mathcal{L}_{ML} = \log p(Y|X; \theta)$$
$$= \sum_{t=1}^{T+1} \log p(y_t|y_{0:t-1}, x_{1:T'}; \theta) \quad (2)$$

Concretely, an self-attentional encoder-decoder architecture (Vaswani et al., 2017) was selected to capture the causal structure. For training with different size of corpus, we employ the Transformer_base ($\mathcal{M}$_**base**) and Transformer_big ($\mathcal{M}$_**big**) in our structure, see Table 2.

2.2 Data Selection Features

Inspired by (Bei et al., 2018), where their system shows data selection can obtain substantial gains, we deliberately design criteria for parallel and monolingual corpus. Both of them employ rule-based features, count features, language model features. And for parallel data, word alignment-based features, T2S translation model score features are applied. The feature types are described in Table 3. Our BERT language model used here is trained from scratch by the open-source tool[1] with target side data.

According to our observations, by using above multiple data selection filters, issues like misalignment, translation error, illegal characters, over translation and under translation in terms of length could be significantly reduced.

2.3 Cycle Translation for Low-quality Data

Although the data selection procedure has preserved relatively high quality monolingual data, there are still a large batch of data is incomplete or grammatically incorrect. To address this problem, we proposed Cycle Translation (denoted as $\mathcal{CT}(\cdot)$, as Figure 2) to improve the mono-lingual data that below the quality-threshold (According to our empirical ablation study in section 4, the latter 50% will be cycle translated in our submitted system).

2.4 Back Translation for monolingual corpus

Back-translation (Sennrich et al., 2015; Bojar et al., 2018), translating the large scale monolingual corpus to generate synthetic parallel data by Target-to-Source pretrained model, has been widely utilized to improve the translation quality since adding the synthetic data into parallel data can enhance the in-domain information over the original corpus distributions, allowing the translation model to be more robust and deterministic.

2.5 Greedy Model Selection Based Ensemble

Model ensemble is a typical boosting technique, which refers to combining multiple models to reduce stochastic differences in the output that may not be avoided at a single run. Also normally, ensemble model outperforms the the best single one.

---

[1] `https://github.com/huggingface/pytorch-pretrained-BERT`

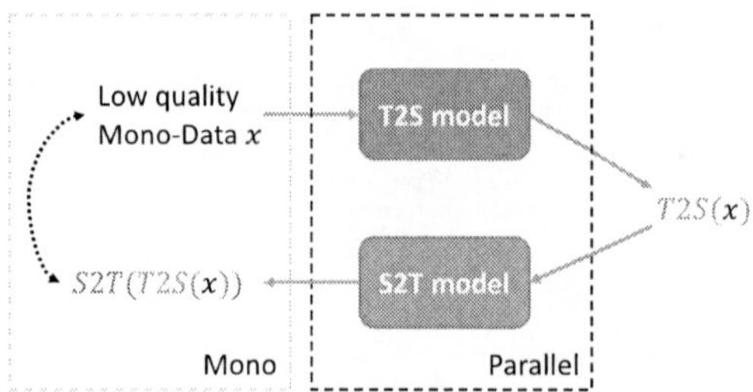

Figure 2: The Cycle Translation process, into which we feed the low quality monolingual data x, and then correspondingly obtain the improved data $\mathcal{CT}(x)$ (denoted as $S2T(T2S(x))$ in figure). Note that models marked in red and green represent the T2S and S2T model trained by $\mathcal{M}_{small}$ with the processed given parallel corpus, the red arrows indicate the data flows of the opposite language type of the inputs. The dotted double-headed arrow between the input x and the final output $\mathcal{CT}(x)$ means that they share the semantics but differs in fluency.

In neural machine translation, we generally ensemble several checkpoints saved during a single model training. However, our preliminary experiments show that both top-N or last-M ensembling approaches could only bring very insignificant improvements but consume a lot of GPU resources.

To overcome this issue, we adopt greedy model selection based ensembling(GMSE), which technically follows the instruction of (Deng et al., 2018).

2.6 Reranking n-best Hypotheses

As the NMT decoding being generally from left to right, this leads to label bias problem (Lafferty et al., 2001). To alleviate this problem, we rerank the n-best hypotheses through training a k-best batch MIRA ranker (Cherry and Foster, 2012) with multiple features on validation set. The feature pool we integrated include left-to-right (L2R) translation model, (right-to-left) R2L translation model, (target-to-source) T2S translation model, language model, IBM model 2 alignment score, and word count ratio. After multi-feature reranking, the best hypothesis of each model ($\mathcal{M}_{big} \times 1$, $\mathcal{M}_{small} \times 8$ and R2L model) was retained for system combination.

2.6.1 Left-to-right NMT model

The L2R feature refers to the original translation model that could generate the n-best list. During reranking training, we keep the original perplexity score evaluated by this L2R model as L2R feature.

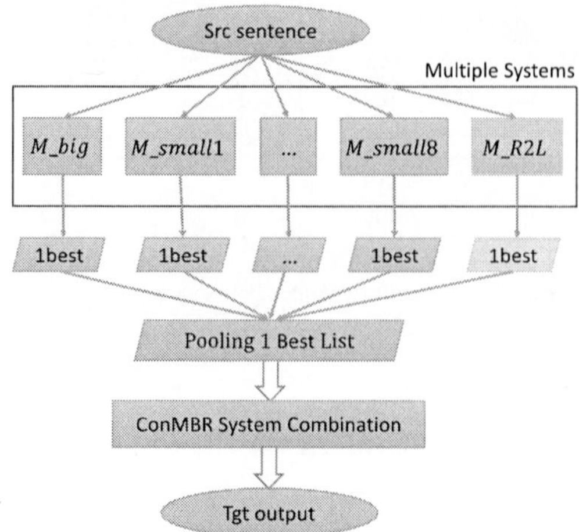

Figure 3: The System Combination process, into which we feed each system/model with the source sentence x, in turn obtain corresponding 1-best result $\mathcal{M}_{big}(x)$, $\mathcal{M}_{small1}(x)$, ... ,$\mathcal{M}_{small2}(x)$,$\mathcal{M}_{R2L}(x)$ (Note that the 1-best result here of each system was already reranked). After pooling all system results, we can perform the ConMBR system combination decoding and obtain the final target side results.

2.6.2 Right-to-Left NMT Model

The R2L NMT model using the same training data but with inverted target sentences (*i.e.*, reverse target side characters "a b c d"→"d c b a"). Then, inverting the hypothesis in the n-best list such that each sequence can be given a perplexity score by R2L model.

2.6.3 Target-to-Source NMT Model

The T2S model was initially trained for back-translation, we can employ this model to assess the translation adequacy as well by adding the T2S feature to reranking feature pool.

2.6.4 Language Model

Besides above features, we employ language models as an auxiliary feature to give the fluent sentences better scores such that the results are easier to understand by human.

2.6.5 Word Count Ratio

To alleviate over-translation or under-translation in terms of length, we set the optimal ratio of $\mathcal{L}_{fi} : \mathcal{L}_{en}$ to 0.76 according to the corpus-based statistics. We use the deviation between the ratio of each sentence pair and this optimal ratio as the score.

src	*Siltalan edellinen kausi liigassa oli 2006-07*
pred	*Siltala's previous season in the league was 2006 at 07*
+post	*Siltala's previous season in the league was 2006-07*

Table 4: Example of the effectiveness of post-processing in handling inconsistent number translation.

Data	Sentences
filtered parallel corpus	5,831,606
reconstructed mono	82,773,126
filtered synthetic parallel	75,940,978
small construction($\times 8$)	11,663,212
big construction	151,751,856

Table 5: Data statistics after data preparation

2.7 System Combination

As is shown in Figure 3, in order to take full advantages of different models($\mathcal{M}_{big}\times 1$, $\mathcal{M}_{small}\times 8$ and R2L model), we adopted word-level combination where confusion network was built. Concretely, our method follows Consensus Network Minimum Bayes Risk (ConMBR) (Sim et al., 2007), which can be modeled as

$$E_{ConMBR} = \operatorname{argmin}_{E'}\mathcal{L}(E', E_{con}) \quad (3)$$

where E_{con} was obtained as backbone through performing consensus network decoding.

2.8 Post-processing

In addition to general post-processing strategies (*i.e.*, de-BPE, de-tokenization and de-truecase [2]), we also employed a post-processing algorithm (Wang et al., 2018) for inconsistent number, date translation, for example, *"2006-07"* might be segmented as *"2006 -@ @ 07"* by BPE, resulting in the wrong translation *"2006 at 07"*. Our post-processing algorithm will search for the best matching number string from the source sentence to replace these types of errors, see Table 4.

3 Data Preparation

We used all available parallel corpus [3] for Finnish→English except the "Wiki Headlines"

due to the large number of incomplete sentences, and for monolingual target side English data, we selected all besides the "Common Crawl" and "News Discussions". The criteria is inspired by (Marie et al., 2018), who won the first place in this direction at WMT18. Table 5 shows the final corpus statistics. More details are as follows:

Parallel Data: We use the criteria in section 2.2, the overall criteria are following:

- Remove duplicate sentence pairs.

- Remove sentence pairs containing illegal characters.

- Retain sentence pairs between 3 and 80 in length.

- Remove sentence pairs that are too far from the best ratio($\mathcal{L}_{fi} : \mathcal{L}_{en}$=0.76)

- Remove pairs containing influent English sentences according to a series of LM features.

- Remove inadequate translation sentence pairs according to $\mathcal{M}_{T2S}$ score.

- Remove sentence pairs with poor alignment quality according to IBM model 2.

After data selection, there are approximately 5.8M parallel sentences.

Monolingual Data: For our Finnish→English system, back translation was performed for monolingual English data. Before back-translation, we filter them according to the aforementioned criteria in section 2.2 and concurrently, the scores of each sentence is obtained. After monolingual selection, there are 82M sentences remained, which is still a gigantic scale. We *cycle translate* the last 25%, 50% and 75% of it in terms of the LM scores to empirically identify the optimal threshold and improve the fluency of monolingual corpora. In doing so, all monolingual corpus is kept at relatively high quality.

Synthetic Parallel Data: The synthetic parallel data also needs to be filtered by alignment score and word count ratio to alleviate poor translation. Further filtration retains 75M synthetic data.

On the other hand, previous works have shown that the maximum gain can be obtained by mixing

#	Models	news-test18	news-test19	Δ_{ave}
1	Baseline(original_parallel + ensemble)	21.8	27.3	—
2	$\mathcal{M}_{small}$(selected_parallel)	22.6	27.9	+0.70
3	+synthetic	23.9	28.8	
4	+GMSE	24.2	29.2	
5	+reranking	24.6	29.5	
6	+post processing	24.8	29.6	+2.65
7	Cycle translation + B/S construction	25.3	30.9	+3.55
8	+GMSE	25.9	31.7	
9	+reranking	26.3	32.4	
10	+system combination	26.6	32.8	
11	+post processing	**26.7**	**33.0**	**+5.30**

Table 6: FI→EN Results on newstest2018 and newstest2019. The submitted system is the last one.

#	$\mathcal{CT}$ **Ratio**	**Val.**	Δ
1	[0%]	22.62	-
2	[25%]	23.18	+0.56
3	[50%]	**23.70**	**+1.08**
4	[75%]	23.07	+0.45

Table 7: Different experimental settings that employed different cycle translation thresholds. Val. denotes that the results are reported on validation set.

the sampled synthetic and original corpus in a ratio of 1:1 (Sennrich et al., 2015, 2016). The size of the synthetic corpus is generally larger than the parallel corpus, thus partial sampling is required to satisfy the 1-1 ratio. However, such sampling leads to waste of enormous synthetic data. To address this issue, we argue that a better construction strategy can be introduced to make full use of the synthetic corpus, subsequently leading to better translation quality.

Small Parallel Construction: We randomly sampled approximate 5.8M corpus from the shuffled synthetic data for 8 times and mix them with parallel data respectively.

Big Parallel Construction: The aim of big construction is to fully utilize the synthetic data. To achieve this, we repeated the parallel corpus 13 times and then mixed it with all synthetic corpora.

4 Experiments

The metric we employed is detokenized case-sensitive BLEU score. news-test2018 is utilized as validation set and test set is officially released news-test2019. Training set, validation set and test set are processed consistently. Both Finnish and English sentences are performed tokenization and truecasing with Moses scripts (Koehn et al., 2007). In order to limit the size of vocabulary of NMT models, we adopted byte pair encoding (BPE) (Sennrich et al., 2016) with 50k operations for each side. All the model we trained are optimized with Adam (Kingma and Ba, 2014). Larger beam size may worsen translation quality (Koehn and Knowles, 2017), thus we set beam_size=10 for each model. All models were trained on 4 NVIDIA V100 GPUs.

In order to find the optimal threshold in cycle translation procedure, we first report our experimental results on validation data set with different thresholds, which ranges from [0%, 25%, 50%, 75%]. Intuitively, the quality improvement of monolingual sentences afforded by cycle translation could bring better synthetic parallel data, subsequently leading to more accurate translation model. Thus, this ablation experiment was trained with synthetic parallel corpus only with different cycle translation ratios on Transformer_base model. As is shown in Table 7, when cycle translation threshold is 50%, the model could achieve the relatively best performance. We therefore set the cycle translation ratio to 50% in our following main experiment.

Our main experiment is shown in Table 6, our baseline system is developed with the $\mathcal{M}_{small}$ configuration using the original parallel corpus and last-20 ensemble strategy. Unsurprisingly, the baseline system relatively performs the worst in Table 6. The $\mathcal{M}_{small}$ configuration trained with selected parallel data improves BLEU by

+0.7 points. According to *exp.*[3-6], adding these components can lead to continuous improvements. Notably, with Cycle Translation and Big/Small parallel construction strategy, our system could obtains +3.55 significant improvement. And *exp.*[8-11] show that with performing GMSE, multi-features reranking, ConMBR system combination and post-processing, our system further improved the BLEU score from 30.9 to 33.0 on the official data set `news-test2019`, which substantially outperforms the baseline by 5.3 BLEU score.

5 Conclusion and Future Work

This paper presents the University of Sydney's NMT systems for WMT2019 Finnish→English news translation task. We leveraged multi-dimensional strategies to improve translation quality in three levels: 1) At data level, in addition to using various data selection criteria, we proposed cycle translation to improve monolingual sentence fluency. 2) For model training, we trained multiple models with R2L corpus and big/small parallel construction corpus respectively. 3) As for inference, we prove the effectiveness of multi-features rescoring, ConMBR system combination and post-processing. We find that cycle translation and B/S construction approach bring the most significant improvement for our system.

In future work, we will apply the beam+noise method (Edunov et al., 2018) to generate robust synthetic data during back translation, we assume that this method combined with our proposed cycle translation strategy can bring greater improvement. Also, we would like to investigate hyper-parameter optimization for neural machine translation to avoid empirical settings.

Acknowledgments

This research was supported by Australian Research Council Projects FL-170100117, DP-180103424 and IH-180100002. We would also thank anonymous reviewers for their comments.

References

Karim Ahmed, Nitish Shirish Keskar, and Richard Socher. 2017. Weighted transformer network for machine translation. *arXiv preprint arXiv:1711.02132*.

Dzmitry Bahdanau, KyungHyun Cho, and Yoshua Bengio. 2015. Neural machine translation by jointly learning to align and translate. In *Proceedings of ICLR 2015*.

B Bangalore, German Bordel, and Giuseppe Riccardi. 2001. Computing consensus translation from multiple machine translation systems. In *IEEE Workshop on Automatic Speech Recognition and Understanding, 2001. ASRU'01*. IEEE.

Chao Bei, Hao Zong, Yiming Wang, Baoyong Fan, Shiqi Li, and Conghu Yuan. 2018. An empirical study of machine translation for the shared task of WMT18. In *Proceedings of the Third Conference on Machine Translation: Shared Task Papers*. Association for Computational Linguistics.

Ondřej Bojar, Christian Federmann, Mark Fishel, Yvette Graham, Barry Haddow, Philipp Koehn, and Christof Monz. 2018. Findings of the 2018 conference on machine translation (WMT18). In *Proceedings of the Third Conference on Machine Translation: Shared Task Papers*. Association for Computational Linguistics.

Colin Cherry and George Foster. 2012. Batch tuning strategies for statistical machine translation. In *Proceedings of NAACL 2012*. Association for Computational Linguistics.

Rewon Child, Scott Gray, Alec Radford, and Ilya Sutskever. 2019. Generating long sequences with sparse transformers.

Yongchao Deng, Shanbo Cheng, Jun Lu, Kai Song, Jingang Wang, Shenglan Wu, Liang Yao, Guchun Zhang, Haibo Zhang, Pei Zhang, Changfeng Zhu, and Boxing Chen. 2018. Alibaba's neural machine translation systems for WMT18. In *Proceedings of the Third Conference on Machine Translation: Shared Task Papers*. Association for Computational Linguistics.

Jacob Devlin, Ming-Wei Chang, Kenton Lee, and Kristina Toutanova. 2018. Bert: Pre-training of deep bidirectional transformers for language understanding. *arXiv preprint arXiv:1810.04805*.

Chris Dyer, Victor Chahuneau, and Noah A. Smith. 2013. A simple, fast, and effective reparameterization of IBM model 2. In *Proceedings of the 2013 Conference of the North American Chapter of the Association for Computational Linguistics: Human Language Technologies*. Association for Computational Linguistics.

Sergey Edunov, Myle Ott, Michael Auli, and David Grangier. 2018. Understanding back-translation at scale. In *Proceedings of EMNLP 2019*.

Zhenxin Fu, Xiaoye Tan, Nanyun Peng, Dongyan Zhao, and Rui Yan. 2018. Style transfer in text: Exploration and evaluation. In *Proceedings of AAAI 2018*.

Jonas Gehring, Michael Auli, David Grangier, Denis Yarats, and Yann N Dauphin. 2017. Convolutional sequence to sequence learning. In *Proceedings of ICML 2017*.

Nal Kalchbrenner and Phil Blunsom. 2013. Recurrent continuous translation models. In *Proceedings of EMNLP 2013*.

Diederik P Kingma and Jimmy Ba. 2014. Adam: A method for stochastic optimization. *arXiv preprint arXiv:1412.6980*.

Philipp Koehn, Hieu Hoang, Alexandra Birch, Chris Callison-Burch, Marcello Federico, Nicola Bertoldi, Brooke Cowan, Wade Shen, Christine Moran, Richard Zens, Chris Dyer, Ondrej Bojar, Alexandra Constantin, and Evan Herbst. 2007. Moses: Open source toolkit for statistical machine translation. In *Proceedings of ACL 2007*.

Philipp Koehn and Rebecca Knowles. 2017. Six challenges for neural machine translation. In *Proceedings of the First Workshop on Neural Machine Translation*. Association for Computational Linguistics.

John D. Lafferty, Andrew McCallum, and Fernando C. N. Pereira. 2001. Conditional random fields: Probabilistic models for segmenting and labeling sequence data. In *Proceedings of ICML 2001*. Morgan Kaufmann Publishers Inc.

Benjamin Marie, Rui Wang, Atsushi Fujita, Masao Utiyama, and Eiichiro Sumita. 2018. NICT's neural and statistical machine translation systems for the WMT18 news translation task. In *Proceedings of the Third Conference on Machine Translation: Shared Task Papers*. Association for Computational Linguistics.

Evgeny Matusov, Nicola Ueffing, and Hermann Ney. 2006. Computing consensus translation for multiple machine translation systems using enhanced hypothesis alignment. In *Proceedings of EACL 2006*.

Kishore Papineni, Salim Roukos, Todd Ward, and Wei-Jing Zhu. 2002. Bleu: a method for automatic evaluation of machine translation. In *Proceedings of ACL 2002*. Association for Computational Linguistics.

Ioannis Partalas, Grigorios Tsoumakas, and Ioannis P Vlahavas. 2008. Focused ensemble selection: A diversity-based method for greedy ensemble selection. In *ECAI*.

Shrimai Prabhumoye, Yulia Tsvetkov, Ruslan Salakhutdinov, and Alan W Black. 2018. Style transfer through back-translation. *arXiv preprint arXiv:1804.09000*.

Rico Sennrich, Barry Haddow, and Alexandra Birch. 2015. Improving neural machine translation models with monolingual data.

Rico Sennrich, Barry Haddow, and Alexandra Birch. 2016. Edinburgh neural machine translation systems for WMT 16. In *Proceedings of the First Conference on Machine Translation*. Association for Computational Linguistics.

Tianxiao Shen, Tao Lei, Regina Barzilay, and Tommi Jaakkola. 2017. Style transfer from non-parallel text by cross-alignment. In *Proceedings of NIPS 2017*.

Khe Chai Sim, William J Byrne, Mark JF Gales, Hichem Sahbi, and Philip C Woodland. 2007. Consensus network decoding for statistical machine translation system combination. In *2007 IEEE International Conference on Acoustics, Speech and Signal Processing-ICASSP'07*. IEEE.

Andreas Stolcke. 2002. Srilm-an extensible language modeling toolkit. In *Seventh international conference on spoken language processing*.

Ilya Sutskever, Oriol Vinyals, and Quoc V Le. 2014. Sequence to sequence learning with neural networks. In *Proceedings of NIPS 2014*.

Ashish Vaswani, Noam Shazeer, Niki Parmar, Jakob Uszkoreit, Llion Jones, Aidan N Gomez, Lukasz Kaiser, and Illia Polosukhin. 2017. Attention is all you need. In *Proceedings of NIPS 2017*.

Qiang Wang, Bei Li, Jiqiang Liu, Bojian Jiang, Zheyang Zhang, Yinqiao Li, Ye Lin, Tong Xiao, and Jingbo Zhu. 2018. The NiuTrans machine translation system for WMT18. In *Proceedings of the Third Conference on Machine Translation: Shared Task Papers*. Association for Computational Linguistics.

Felix Wu, Angela Fan, Alexei Baevski, Yann Dauphin, and Michael Auli. 2019. Pay less attention with lightweight and dynamic convolutions. In *Proceedings of ICLR 2019*.

Yonghui Wu, Mike Schuster, Zhifeng Chen, Quoc V. Le, Mohammad Norouzi, Wolfgang Macherey, Maxim Krikun, Yuan Cao, Qin Gao, Klaus Macherey, Jeff Klingner, Apurva Shah, Melvin Johnson, et al. 2016. Google's neural machine translation system: Bridging the gap between human and machine translation. In *Proceedings of NIPS 2016*.

UdS-DFKI Participation at WMT 2019:
Low-Resource (en–gu) and Coreference-Aware (en–de) Systems

Cristina España-Bonet
Saarland University
DFKI GmbH

Dana Ruiter
Saarland University

Josef van Genabith
Saarland University
DFKI GmbH

druiter@lsv.uni-saarland.de
{cristinae,Josef.Van_Genabith}@dfki.de

Abstract

This paper describes the UdS-DFKI submission to the WMT2019 news translation task for Gujarati–English (low-resourced pair) and German–English (document-level evaluation). Our systems rely on the on-line extraction of parallel sentences from comparable corpora for the first scenario and on the inclusion of coreference-related information in the training data in the second one.

1 Introduction

This document describes the systems and experiments conducted to participate in the news translation tasks of WMT 2019 for Gujarati–English (gu–en, low-resourced language pair) and German–English (de–en, document-level evaluation). We use different approaches to tackle each setting.

Machine translation (neural, statistical or rule-based), usually operates on a sentence-by-sentence basis. However, when translating a coherent document, surrounding sentences may contain information that needs to be reflected in a local sentence. In our experiments for the **document-level** task in $en2de$, we explore how the information beyond sentence level can be made available to a neural machine translation (NMT) system by modifying —tagging— the data in order to include this knowledge. In a similar way, multilingual NMT systems have already been successfully built by only tagging the source data with the knowledge of the target language (Johnson et al., 2017; Ha et al., 2016). With this approach, we incorporate the knowledge that carries coreferences through a text in every sentence. We expect to improve the translation of ambiguous items such as pronouns in English, so we just tackle a specific number of problems and not translation quality in general.

The approach for the **low-resource** setting is completely different. In this case, we use a neural architecture that allows us to extract parallel data from comparable corpora and filter noise from the available parallel data. The additional data obtained in this way is then used to train SMT models, which we compare to a baseline trained on the available parallel data only to observe the effects of the extraction and filtering.

Below, we describe our coreference-aware system for $en2de$ (Section 2) and our low-resourced approach for en–gu (Section 3). Finally we summarise our findings in Section 4.

2 Coreference-Aware English-to-German System

2.1 Data Preparation

Our system makes use of the annotation of coreference mentions through documents in the source side of the corpus. Documents are annotated with coreference chains using a neural-network-based mention-ranking model as implemented by the `Stanford CoreNLP` tool (Manning et al., 2014)[1]. The tool detects pronominal, nominal and proper names as mentions in a chain. For every mention, `CoreNLP` extracts its gender (male, female, neutral, unknown), number (singular, plural, unknown), and animacy (animate, inanimate, unknown). This information is not added directly but used to enrich the MT training data by applying a set of heuristics implemented in `DocTrans`[2]:

- We enrich *pronominal mentions* with the head of the chain

---

[1] This system achieves a precision of 80% and recall of 70% on the CoNLL 2012 English Test Data (Clark and Manning, 2016).

[2] https://github.com/cristinae/DocTrans/

Proceedings of the Fourth Conference on Machine Translation (WMT), Volume 2: Shared Task Papers (Day 1) pages 183–190
Florence, Italy, August 1-2, 2019. ©2019 Association for Computational Linguistics

- Pronoun "I" is not enriched with any coreference information

- We clean the head by removing articles and Saxon genitives and we only consider heads with less than 4 tokens in order to avoid enriching a word with a full sentence

- We enrich *nominal mentions* including *proper names* with the gender of the head

- The head itself is enriched with she/he/it/they depending on its gender and animacy

The example below shows how we tag the cleaned version of the head of the chain (*fish skin*) before a pronominal mention (*it*):

baseline:
I never cook with it.
coref:
I never cook with *<b_crf> fish skin <e_crf>* it.

In order to be able to do this processing, we need documents and that limits the amount of corpora we can use. Even though all the corpora made available for the shared task have document boundaries, ParaCrawl, for instance, has a mean of 1.06 sentences per document which makes it useless within our approach.

2.2 Corpus

Monolingual corpora. We use a subset of the NewsCrawl corpus in English and German (years 2014, 2017 and a part of 2018, named as *ss-NewsCrawl* in Table 1) to calculate word embeddings as explained in Section 2.3. We first use *langdetect*[3] to extract only those sentences that are in the desired language and compile the final corpora to have a similar number of subword units (Sennrich et al., 2016a) in both languages and years ($\sim 4.10^9$). The corpus is further cleaned, tokenised, truecased (with Moses scripts[4]) and BPEd (with subword-nmt[5]). The vocabulary of the BPE model depends on the system and is detailed in Section 2.3.

Parallel corpora. Due to the restrictions explained in Section 2.1, we use the parallel corpora made available for the shared task in different proportions. Our *base* system uses CommonCrawl,

[3]`https://pypi.org/project/langdetect/`
[4]`https://github.com/moses-smt/`
`mosesdecoder/tree/master/scripts`
[5]`https://github.com/rsennrich/`
`subword-nmt`

	# lines	Small	Large
Monolingual			
ssNewsCrawl *en*	176,220,479	x1	x1
ssNewsCrawl *de*	220,443,585	x1	x1
Parallel			
CommonCrawl	2,394,878	x1	x4
Europarl	1,775,445	x1	x4
NewsCommentary	328,059	x4	x16
Rapid	1,105,651	x1	x4
ParaCrawlFiltered	12,424,790	x0	x1

Table 1: Number of lines of the monolingual and parallel corpora used in the *en2de* translation systems for the *base* and *large* configurations. The second and third columns show the amount of oversampling (or dilution) used in both cases.

Europarl, News Commentary and Rapid Corpus. Our *large* system also uses the ParaCrawl corpus but in a diluted way. The purpose of the dilution is to try to minimise the fact that due to the nature of our system we cannot use single sentences (intrasentence dependencies are already learned by an NMT system) or back-translations (quality is not good enough to extract coreference chains in a source sentence that is an automatic translation).

CommonCrawl, Europarl and News Commentary are cleaned, tokenised, truecased and BPEd with the same tools as the monolingual corpus. For the Rapid corpus, we performed an additional cleaning: since some German sentences were missing umlauts, we removed all the sentences that contained any word clearly missing an umlaut such as *europishen* or *erklrte*. For ParaCrawl, we first removed sentence pairs that were not detected as English and German sentences by *langdetect* and afterwards we removed sentences with emoji, bullets, and specific tokens such as *http, pdf, €*, or *hotel*, etc. With this, we reduce the corpus size by more than half of the sentences. The final number of sentences for all the corpora used for training are provided in Table 1. Notice that we do oversampling for the News Commentary corpus as it is supposed to have a similar domain to the test set.

2.3 Neural Machine Translation Systems

Our NMT systems are trained using the transformer architectures implemented in the `Marian` toolkit (Junczys-Dowmunt et al., 2018). We use two architectures *base* and *big* as defined in

Vaswani et al. (2017):

Transformer base. 6-layer encoder–decoder with 8-head self-attention, a 2048-dim hidden feed-forward, and 512-dim word vectors. Growing learning rate from 0 to 0.0003 till update 16,000 (warmup). Decaying learning rate afterwards. Adam optimisation with β_1=0.9, β_2=0.98 and ϵ=1e-09. Tied target embeddings.

Transformer big. As *Transformer base* but with word embeddings with 1024-dim, 4096-dim hidden feed-forward layers, learning rate of 0.0002 with the same warmup and decay. β_2=0.998.

Using these architectures as basis, we train several models on 4 TITAN X GPUs using an adaptive batch size that differ on:

- Corpus size. Small vs. Large as defined in Table 1

- Vocabulary. Joint *en–de* BPE with 40K subword units (*join*) vs. separated vocabularies with 50K subword units each (all the other models).

- Initial word embeddings. Source and target initialisation with monolingual embeddings estimated with word2vec[6] (Mikolov et al., 2013) (*Emb*) vs. source and target initialisation with bilingual embeddings mapped using vecmap[7] (Artetxe et al., 2017) (*EmbMap*) vs. no initialisation (all the other models).

- Annotation. No annotation (*Baseline*) vs. tags with coreference information (all the other models).

- Ensembling. Combinations of the previous models at decoding time.

The terms in parenthesis refer to the models in Table 2. Model names are structured as `architectureVocabulary-Annotation -Embeddings-Corpus`.

2.4 Results

Table 2 shows the BLEU scores of the different models and ensembles on newstest-2017 (validation) and news-test2018 (test). The first block presents the results of a baseline system without any document-level information; the second block shows the models explored to determine the best configuration; and the third block summarises

[6]`https://github.com/tmikolov/word2vec`
[7]`https://github.com/artetxem/vecmap`

Model	news17	news18
Baseline		
M01:trBig-Baseline-Small	25.82	37.62
M02:trBig-Baseline-Large	27.07	40.38
Coreference-Aware		
M03:trBase-Join-Small	20.00	29.08
M04:trBase-Small	24.74	36.56
M05:trBase-Large	26.35	38.74
M06:trBase-Emb-Large	16.15	22.20
M07:trBase-EmbMap-Large	26.72	39.12
M08:trBig-Small	25.85	37.55
M09:trBig-Large	26.38	38.53
M10:trBig-EmbMap-Large	26.33	39.12
M11:trBig-2-Large	27.42	40.07
M12:trBig-2-EmbMap-Large	27.28	40.28
Ensembling		
M05-M07-M10	27.18	40.92
M07-M09	27.29	40.10
M05-M07-M09	27.24	40.56
M05-M07-M09-M10	27.31	40.98
M05-M07-M10-M11	27.58	41.58
M07-M10-M11-M12	**27.62**	**42.82**

Table 2: BLEU scores of the models trained for the *en2de* translation task. The boldfaced ensembled model was submitted as the primary submission; the best performing model with boldfaced BLEU scores was not ready at submission time.

the ensembling combinations explored in order to chose our primary submission.

The first thing to notice is that in terms of BLEU systems with and without **coreference annotations** are not significantly different (M01 vs. M08; M02 vs. M09/M11). Since we are modifying only specific aspects of the translation —few words in a document—, we do not obtain large improvements according to automatic evaluation measures, but we expect differences in translation quality according to human evaluators.

The **vocabulary** turned out to be critical. A system with a joint vocabulary of 40K subword units (M03) is 5-6 BLEU points below its counterpart with 50k units and independent vocabularies (M04).

Embeddings are not that decisive. An initialisation of the system using bilingual embeddings slightly improves the results (M07 vs. M05; M10 vs. M09; M12 vs.M11). Using monolingual embeddings implies a very slow training. M06 in

Table 2 is 10 BLEU points below its counterpart with bilingual embeddings (M07), but the training was far from converging even when running for more days.

As expected, increasing the **size of the corpus** and the number of parameters of the **architecture** is beneficial for the final translation quality. The former has the only disadvantage of needing more time and computing power. The latter even if achieving around 2 BLEU points of improvement (M04 vs. M05; M08 vs. M09) does not allow us to use document level information during training for part of the data.

An **ensemble** of different high performing models showed better results than the combination of the last check-points of the best model. Different combinations are reported in Table 2, all of them using a beam search of size 10 which also performed better than the default value of 6. The best ensemble comes from the combination of the four best performing individual models, but unfortunately the two best performing models were not ready at submission time. M11 and M12 are the same as M09 and M10 before convergence and were the ones used in the ensembled translation as our primary submission.

3 English–Gujarati Systems

3.1 Corpus

Monolingual corpora. The monolingual corpora were used mainly as additional data for training word-embeddings in en and gu. For English we use the same *NewsCrawl* selection as for en–de (ssNewsCrawl). For Gujarati we use the 2018 version of *NewsCrawl* and *CommonCrawl*.

To further increase the available data size for training Gujarati embeddings as well as to add similar content to the English word embeddings, we crawled additional Gujarati news pages and, if existent, their English counterparts. This yielded an increase of about 2 M monolingual Gujarati sentences. While crawling for the news articles, articles written during the period from which the test corpus *newstest2019* was created[8] were not included in the creation of these data sets. The number of sentences and tokens extracted from each news outlet is shown in Table 3.

Wikipedia (WP) is a popular source for comparable documents. In order to later extract paral-lel sentences from it, the WP dumps[9] for English and Gujarati are downloaded. Only the subset of articles that are linked across both languages using Wikipedia's *langlinks* are extracted. That is, an article is only taken into account if there is a linked article in the other language. For these purposes, we use `WikiTailor` (Barrón-Cedeño et al., 2015)[10] to obtain the intersection of articles of both languages. We additionally use the en–gu WP *reference* which was made available for WMT 2019. The monolingual WP in Gujarati is added to the monolingual data for training the embeddings.

Parallel corpora. We use the concatenation of several parallel corpora available for the en–gu news translation task to train the base model. Firstly, the *bible* corpus[11] as well as two corpora specially made for WMT2019[12] are used, namely a crawled corpus (WMT19 Crawl) and a localisation corpus extracted from OPUS[13] (WMT Localisation). Lastly, the *Translation Quality Estimation* (TQE) dataset for Indian languages (Nisarg et al., 2018), which essentially is the concatenation of two corpora by the *Indian Languages Corpora Initiative*, which focus on the health and tourism domain each. For development, we use the first 999 sentences from the English-Gujarati version of *newsdev2019*. Further, we report results on the final *newstest2019* corpus.

Pre-processing. All English corpora (excluding the evaluation corpora) undergo the same pre-processing. After being sentence split, the corpora are normalized, tokenized and truecased using standard Moses scripts (Koehn et al., 2007a). A byte-pair-encoding (BPE) (Sennrich et al., 2016b) of $40\,k$ merge operations trained jointly on en–gu data respectively is applied accordingly. Duplicates are removed and sentences with more than 50 tokens are discarded. In order to enable a multilingual setup, language tokens indicating the designated target language are prepended to each source sentence. As the English–Gujarati setting is bilingual, this reduces to each Gujarati sentence starting with the language token `<en>`, and each English sentence with `<gu>`.

Gujarati corpora are normalized and romanized

---

[8]September-November 2018

[9]Downloaded from `https://dumps.wikimedia.org/` on January 2019.

[10]`https://github.com/cristinae/WikiTailor`

[11]`http://christos-c.com/bible/`

[12]`http://www.statmt.org/wmt19/translation-task.html`

[13]`http://opus.nlpl.eu/`

	# sentences
Monolingual	
ssNewsCrawl *en*	176,220,479
CommonCrawl *gu*	3,729,406
NewsCrawl *gu*	244,919
WP Edition *gu*	4,280,531
Crawled	
Divya Bhaskar *gu*	563,072
News18 *en*	460,097
News18 *gu*	193,455
Gujarat Samachar *gu*	121,349
Sandesh *gu*	892,196
Zeenews *en*	466,449
Zeenews *gu*	244,191
Parallel	
Bible *en–gu*	7,807
WMT19 Crawl *en–gu*	10,650
WMT19 Localisation *en–gu*	107,637
TQE *en–gu*	50,000
WP Reference *en–gu*	18,033
Comparable	
WP Comparable *en*	546,924
WP Comparable *gu*	143,120

Table 3: Size of the corpora used for the *en–gu* models.

using the `Indic NLP Library`.[14] The romanized corpora are then tokenized using Moses. As the romanization is case sensitive, no true-casing is performed. The shared BPE is applied.

Cross-lingual word embeddings. We initialize the unsupervised NMT model using *cross-lingual embeddings*. These are trained using monolingual data only. For the English embeddings, we use *ssNewsCrawl*, as well as the English crawled data. For Gujarati all Gujarati data available in Table 3 is used. The initial monolingual embeddings (of size 512) are trained using `word2vec`[15]. The two embeddings are then projected into a common multilingual space using `vecmap`[16] (Artetxe et al., 2017) . We extract all numerals that occur in both monolingual corpora in order to supply a small seed dictionary for training that is not linguistically motivated. After having projected the embeddings into the same space, they are merged into a single cross-lingual embedding. Whenever a word in the two languages is a homograph, one of the two was chosen randomly.

3.2 Neural Machine Translation System

For training our models, we use both SMT and a transformer architecture. While the SMT is used

to provide a first model for back-translations as well as to train the final model submitted, the transformer is used in-between to extract additional data from Wikipedia.

The transformer is trained using `OpenNMT-py` (Klein et al., 2017) and is defined as follows: 6-layer encoder-decoder with 8-head self-attention and 2048-dim hidden feed-forward layers. Adam optimization with λ=2 and *beta2*=0.998; *noam* learning rate decay (as defined in Vaswani et al. (2017)) with 8000 warm-up steps. Labels are smoothed (ϵ=0.1) and a dropout mask (p=0.1) is applied. As is common for transformers, position encodings and *Xavier* parameter initialization (Glorot and Bengio, 2010) are used.

3.3 Statistical Machine Translation System

The second family of systems we use in this setting is statistical machine translation (SMT). We expect these systems to perform better when the number of parallel sentences is small. SMT systems are trained using standard freely available software. We estimate a 5-gram or 4-gram language model using interpolated Kneser–Ney discounting with `SRILM` (Stolcke, 2002) depending on the language and the size of the monolingual corpus. Word alignment is done with `GIZA++` (Och and Ney, 2003) and both phrase extraction and decoding are done with the `Moses` package (Koehn et al., 2007b). The optimisation of the feature weights of the model is done with Minimum Error Rate Training (MERT) (Och, 2003) against the BLEU (Papineni et al., 2002) evaluation metric. Our model considers the language model, direct and inverse phrase probabilities, direct and inverse lexical probabilities, phrase and word penalties, and a lexicalised reordering.

3.4 Results

We train our SMT and NMT in four steps, yielding the following models:

1. **SMT**$_{base}$: Train an SMT model on the concatenation of all parallel training data listed in Table 3 ($\sim$194 k pairs). This is then used to back-translate 4 k (2 k per language direction) pairs of the monolingual data available.

2. **NMT**$_{extract}$: Initialize Transformer with the pre-trained word-embeddings. The transformer is used to extract additional data from *en–gu* Wikipedias as well as the crawled

[14]https://github.com/anoopkunchukuttan/indic_nlp_library

[15]https://github.com/tmikolov/word2vec

[16]https://github.com/artetxem/vecmap

| | BLEU dev | | BLEU nt2019 | |
Reference	*en2gu*	*gu2en*	*en2gu*	*gu2en*
NMT$_{\text{extract}}$	4.65	10.64	3.10	8.60
SMT$_{\text{base}}$	8.77	12.90	6.90	10.20
SMT$_{\text{extract}}$	9.15	13.08	**6.90**	10.50
SMT$_{\text{all}}$	8.93	14.08	7.10	**10.80**

Table 4: BLEU scores achieved on the internal development set and the official *newstest2019*. Scores on the development set are calculated using `multi-bleu` on the tokenized outputs, while the results on *newstest2019* are those calculated by the WMT matrix. Primary system submissions are in bold.

Zeenews and *News18* articles. It is also used to filter the back-translations produced by SMT$_{\text{base}}$ as well as the parallel corpus available. The extraction is performed using the joint NMT learning and extraction framework described in Ruiter et al. (2019). There, we use the margin-based function (Artetxe and Schwenk, 2018) for scoring both word embedding and hidden-state representations. This results in an extracted and filtered corpus of $\sim$275 k sentences; a slight increase to the original parallel data available to us despite the filtering of less useful pairs.

3. **SMT$_{\text{extract}}$**: SMT model, trained on the corpus that resulted from the extraction and filtering performed by NMT$_{\text{extract}}$.

4. **SMT$_{\text{all}}$**: SMT model, trained on both the extracted and filtered corpus by NMT$_{\text{extract}}$, as well as the parallel data available, resulting in $\sim$475 k training pairs used.

Due to time constraints we could not apply any system combination technique on the individual systems. However, due to the big gap in performance between SMT and NMT we do not expect significant improvements.

Table 4 shows translation quality as measured by BLEU for both the neural and statistical systems with the different data configurations.

The filtering and extraction performed by NMT$_{\text{extract}}$ led to a small increase in BLEU for SMT$_{\text{extract}}$ and SMT$_{\text{all}}$, indicating that the filtering was based on positive decisions. However, when taking into account that the average number of extracted pairs from WP was steadily around 1.6 k pairs, and comparing them with the 18 k pairs in the *en–gu* WP reference, it becomes clear that extraction did not obtain high recall. This is most likely due to three difficulties that the system encounters in this setting: i) Not enough comparable data was available to adapt the internal representations (word embeddings and hidden states) to the data, meaning that the extraction performance, which is bound to the extraction decisions of the representations, stays below its potential. ii) The lack of monolingual data to train high-quality *gu* embeddings as well as iii) the rareness of homographs in this rather distant language pair makes the initialization difficult. Extraction in the first epochs is usually dependent on such homographs and a lack thereof reduces the number of identifiable pairs in the initialization phase of the model.

4 Conclusions

We presented two approaches for the WMT 2019 news translation shared task. We participated in the *en2de* task with a data-based coreference-aware NMT system. The corpus is enriched with this document-level information at sentence level so that the standard training procedure can be used. However, the amount of data we can use is smaller than in the standard pipeline and therefore the global quality can be damaged. We expect the manual evaluation to show improvements on the tackled phenomena such as gender translation.

For the *en-gu* task, we used a NMT architecture that can be trained on comparable corpora. In this case we downloaded news web pages as well as linked Wikipedia articles in Gujarati and English to extract and train on. Our experiments show that very few sentences could be used from this corpus and our results are close to the baseline one can get with the available parallel resources. Given the final amount of data, our state-of-the-art SMT system performed clearly better than our NMT one.

Acknowledgments

The project on which this paper is based was partially funded by the German Federal Ministry of Education and Research under the funding code 01IW17001 (Deeplee) and by the Leibniz Gemeinschaft via the SAW-2016-ZPID-2 project (CLuBS). Responsibility for the content of this publication is with the authors.

References

Mikel Artetxe, Gorka Labaka, and Eneko Agirre. 2017. Learning bilingual word embeddings with (almost) no bilingual data. In *Proceedings of the 55th Annual Meeting of the Association for Computational Linguistics (Volume 1: Long Papers)*, pages 451–462.

Mikel Artetxe and Holger Schwenk. 2018. Margin-based parallel corpus mining with multilingual sentence embeddings. *arXiv preprint arXiv:1811.01136.*

Alberto Barrón-Cedeño, Cristina España-Bonet, Josu Boldoba, and Lluís Màrquez. 2015. A Factory of Comparable Corpora from Wikipedia. In *Proceedings of the Eighth Workshop on Building and Using Comparable Corpora*, pages 3–13. Association for Computational Linguistics.

Kevin Clark and Christopher D. Manning. 2016. Deep reinforcement learning for mention-ranking coreference models. In *Proceedings of the 2016 Conference on Empirical Methods in Natural Language Processing*, pages 2256–2262, Austin, Texas. Association for Computational Linguistics.

Xavier Glorot and Yoshua Bengio. 2010. Understanding the difficulty of training deep feedforward neural networks. In *Proceedings of the thirteenth international conference on artificial intelligence and statistics*, pages 249–256.

Thanh-Le Ha, Jan Niehues, and Alexander H. Waibel. 2016. Toward Multilingual Neural Machine Translation with Universal Encoder and Decoder. In *Proceedings of the International Workshop on Spoken Language Translation*, Seattle, WA.

Melvin Johnson, Mike Schuster, Quoc V. Le, Maxim Krikun, Yonghui Wu, Zhifeng Chen, Nikhil Thorat, Fernanda B. Viégas, Martin Wattenberg, Greg Corrado, Macduff Hughes, and Jeffrey Dean. 2017. Google's Multilingual Neural Machine Translation System: Enabling Zero-Shot Translation. *Transactions of the Association for Computational Linguist*, 5:339–351.

Marcin Junczys-Dowmunt, Roman Grundkiewicz, Tomasz Dwojak, Hieu Hoang, Kenneth Heafield, Tom Neckermann, Frank Seide, Ulrich Germann, Alham Fikri Aji, Nikolay Bogoychev, André F. T. Martins, and Alexandra Birch. 2018. Marian: Fast neural machine translation in C++. In *Proceedings of ACL 2018, System Demonstrations*, pages 116–121, Melbourne, Australia. Association for Computational Linguistics.

Guillaume Klein, Yoon Kim, Yuntian Deng, Jean Senellart, and Alexander M. Rush. 2017. OpenNMT: Open-source toolkit for neural machine translation. In *Proceedings of the 55th Annual Meeting of the Association for Computational Linguistics, System Demonstrations*, pages 67–72.

Philipp Koehn, Hieu Hoang, Alexandra Birch, Chris Callison-Burch, Marcello Federico, Nicola Bertoldi, Brooke Cowan, Wade Shen, Christine Moran, Richard Zens, Chris Dyer, Ondrej Bojar, Alexandra Constantin, and Evan Herbst. 2007a. Moses: Open source toolkit for statistical machine translation. In *Proceedings of the 45th Annual Meeting of the Association for Computational Linguistics Companion Volume Proceedings of the Demo and Poster Sessions*, pages 177–180. Association for Computational Linguistics.

Philipp Koehn, Hieu Hoang, Alexandra Birch Mayne, Christopher Callison-Burch, Marcello Federico, Nicola Bertoldi, Brooke Cowan, Wade Shen, Christine Moran, Richard Zens, Chris Dyer, Ondrej Bojar, Alexandra Constantin, and Evan Herbst. 2007b. Moses: Open source toolkit for statistical machine translation. In *Annual Meeting of the Association for Computation Linguistics (ACL), Demonstration Session*, pages 177–180.

Christopher D. Manning, Mihai Surdeanu, John Bauer, Jenny Finkel, Steven J. Bethard, and David McClosky. 2014. The Stanford CoreNLP natural language processing toolkit. In *Association for Computational Linguistics (ACL) System Demonstrations*, pages 55–60.

Tomas Mikolov, Kai Chen, Greg Corrado, and Jeffrey Dean. 2013. Efficient estimation of word representations in vector space. In *International Conference on Learning Representations (ICLR)*.

Jhaveri Nisarg, Manish Gupta, and Vasudeva Varma. 2018. Translation quality estimation for indian languages. *Proceedings of the 21st Annual Conference of the European Association for Machine Translation*, pages 159–168.

Franz Josef Och. 2003. Minimum error rate training in statistical machine translation. In *Proceedings of the 41st Annual Meeting on Association for Computational Linguistics - Volume 1*, pages 160–167, Stroudsburg, PA, USA. Association for Computational Linguistics.

Franz Josef Och and Hermann Ney. 2003. A systematic comparison of various statistical alignment models. *Computational Linguistics*, 29(1):19–51.

Kishore Papineni, Salim Roukos, Todd Ward, and Wei-Jing Zhu. 2002. Bleu: a method for automatic evaluation of machine translation. In *Proceedings of the Association of Computational Linguistics*, pages 311–318.

Dana Ruiter, Cristina España-Bonet, and Josef van Genabith. 2019. Self-supervised neural machine translation. In *Proceedings of the 57th Annual Meeting of the Association for Computational Linguistics, Volume 2: Short Papers*, Florence, Italy. Association for Computational Linguistics.

Rico Sennrich, Barry Haddow, and Alexandra Birch. 2016a. Neural Machine Translation of Rare Words with Subword Units. In *Proceedings of the 54th Annual Meeting of the Association for Computational Linguistics, (ACL 2016), Volume 1: Long Papers*, pages 1715–1725, Berlin, Germany.

Rico Sennrich, Barry Haddow, and Alexandra Birch. 2016b. Neural Machine Translation of Rare Words with Subword Units. *Proceedings of the 54th Annual Meeting of the Association for Computational Linguistics, (ACL 2016), Volume 1: Long Papers*, pages 1715–1725.

A. Stolcke. 2002. SRILM – An extensible language modeling toolkit. In *Proceedings of the 7th International Conference on Spoken Language Processing*, pages 901–904.

Ashish Vaswani, Noam Shazeer, Niki Parmar, Jakob Uszkoreit, Llion Jones, Aidan N Gomez, Ł ukasz Kaiser, and Illia Polosukhin. 2017. Attention is all you need. In *Advances in Neural Information Processing Systems 30*, pages 5998–6008. Curran Associates, Inc.

The IIIT-H Gujarati-English Machine Translation system for WMT19

Vikrant Goyal
IIIT Hyderabad
vikrant.goyal@research.iiit.ac.in

Dipti Misra Sharma
IIIT Hyderabad
dipti@iiit.ac.in

Abstract

This paper describes the Neural Machine Translation system of IIIT-Hyderabad for the Gujarati→English news translation shared task of WMT19. Our system is based on encoder-decoder framework with attention mechanism. We experimented with Multilingual Neural MT models. Our experiments show that Multilingual Neural Machine Translation leveraging parallel data from related language pairs helps in significant BLEU improvements upto 11.5, for low resource language pairs like Gujarati-English.

1 Introduction

Neural Machine Translation (Luong et al., 2015; Bahdanau et al., 2014; Johnson et al., 2017; Wu et al., 2017; Vaswani et al., 2017) has been receiving considerable attention in the recent years, given its superior performance without the demand of heavily hand crafted engineering efforts. NMT often outperforms Statistical Machine Translation (SMT) techniques but it still struggles if the parallel data is insufficient like in the case of Indian languages.

The bulk of research on low resource NMT has focused on exploiting monolingual data or parallel data from other language pairs. Some recent methods to improve NMT models that exploit monolingual data ranges from back-translation (Sennrich et al., 2015a), dual NMT (He et al., 2016) to Unsupervised MT models (Lample et al., 2017; Artetxe et al., 2017; Lample et al., 2018). Transfer Learning is also a promising approach for low resource NMT which exploits parallel data from other language pairs (Zoph et al., 2016; Nguyen and Chiang, 2017; Kocmi and Bojar, 2018). Typically it is achieved by training a parent model in a high resource language pair, then using some of the trained weights as the initialization for a child

model and further train it on the low-resource language pair. Other promising approach for improving translation performance for low resource languages is Multilingual Neural Machine Translation. It has been shown that exploiting data from other language pairs & joint training helps in improving the translation performance of NMT models. (Ha et al., 2016; Firat et al., 2016; Johnson et al., 2017).

This paper describes the NMT system of IIIT-H for WMT19 evaluation. We participated in the Gujarati→English news translation task. We used an attention-based encoder-decoder model as our baseline system and used Byte Pair Encoding (BPE) to enable open vocabulary translation. We then leverage Hindi-English parallel corpus in a multilingual setting so as to improve our baseline system. We basically combined Hindi-English and Gujarati-English parallel corpus and use it as our training corpus. Our multilingual system is similiar to Johnson et al. (2017) but we don't use any artificial token at the start of source sentences to indicate the target language. The reason is trivial, that is we have only English as our target language. We also provide results of our experiments conducted post WMT19 shared task involving Transformer models.

2 Neural MT Architecture

Our NMT model consists of an encoder and a decoder, each of which is a Recurrent Neural Network (RNN) as described in (Luong et al., 2015). The model directly estimates the posterior distribution $P_\theta(y|x)$ of translating a source sentence $x = (x_1, .., x_n)$ to a target sentence $y = (y_1, .., y_m)$ as:

$$P_\theta(y|x) = \prod_{t=1}^{m} P_\theta(y_t|y_1, y_2, .., y_{t-1}, x) \qquad (1)$$

191

Proceedings of the Fourth Conference on Machine Translation (WMT), Volume 2: Shared Task Papers (Day 1) pages 191–195
Florence, Italy, August 1-2, 2019. ©2019 Association for Computational Linguistics

Each of the local posterior distribution $P(y_t|y_{1,2},..,y_{t-1},x)$ is modeled as a multinomial distribution over the target language vocabulary which is represented as a linear transformation followed by a softmax function on the decoder's output vector $\tilde{h}_t^{dec}$:

$$c_t = AttentionFunction(h_{1:n}^{enc}, h_t^{dec}) \quad (2)$$

$$\tilde{h}_t^{dec} = tanh(W_o[h_t^{dec}; c_t]) \quad (3)$$

$$P(y|y_1, y_2, .., y_{t-1}, x) = softmax(W_s \tilde{h}_t^{dec}; \tau) \quad (4)$$

where c_t is the context vector, h^{enc} and h^{dec} are the hidden vectors generated by the encoder and decoder respectively, AttentionFunction(. , .) is the attention mechanism as shown in (Luong et al., 2015) and [. ; .] is the concatenation of two vectors.

An RNN encoder first encodes x to a continuous vector, which serves as the initial hidden vector for the decoder and then the decoder performs recursive updates to produce a sequence of hidden vectors by applying the transition function f as:

$$h_t^{dec} = f(h_{t-1}^{dec}, [\tilde{h}_{t-1}^{dec}; e(y_t)]) \quad (5)$$

where e(.) is the word embedding operation. Popular choices for mapping f are Long-Short-Term Memory (LSTM) units and Gated Recurrent Units (GRU), the former of which we use in our models.

An NMT model is typically trained under the maximum log-likelihood objective:

$$\max_\theta J(\theta) = \max_\theta \mathrm{E}_{(x,y)\sim D}[\log P_\theta(y|x)] \quad (6)$$

where D is the training set. Our NMT model uses a bi-directional RNN as an encoder and a uni-directional RNN as a decoder with global attention (Luong et al., 2015) .

3   Multilingual Neural Machine Translation

Most of the practical applications in Machine Translation have focused on individual language pairs because it was simply too difficult to build a single system that translates to and from many language pairs. But Neural Machine Translation was shown to be an end-to-end learning approach and was quickly extended to multilingual machine translation in several ways. In Dong et al. (2015), the authors modify the attention-based encoder-decoder approach by introducing separate decoder

and attention mechanism for each target language. In Zoph and Knight (2016), multi-source translation was proposed where the model has different encoders and different attention mechanisms for different source languages. In Firat et al. (2016), the authors proposed a multi-way multilingual NMT model using a single shared attention mechanism but with multiple encoders/decoders for each source/target language. In this paper, we adopted the approach proposed in Johnson et al. (2017), where a single NMT model is used for multilingual machine translation. We used Hindi-English as our assisting language pair and combined it with Gujarati-English parallel data to form a multi source translation system.

4   Experimental setup

4.1   Dataset

In our experiments, we use the Gujarati-English training data provided by the organisers namely Wiki Titles, Bible corpus, Localisation Opus, Wikipedia corpus & crawled corpus. It consists of around 155K parallel sentences. We used news-dev2019 as our development corpus. For building our multilingual model, we used IIT-Bombay parallel data (Kunchukuttan et al., 2017) as our Hindi-English parallel corpus. The top level statistics of the data used is provided in Table 1.

Table 1: Statistics of our processed parallel data.

Dataset	Sentences	Tokens
IITB Hi-En Train	15,28,631	21.5M / 20.3M
Gu-En Train	1,55,767	1.68M / 1.58M
Gu-En Dev	1,997	51.3K / 47.4K
Gu-En Test	1,998	51.5K / 47.5K

4.2   Data Processing

We used Moses (Koehn et al., 2007) toolkit for tokenization and cleaning the English side of the data. Gujarati and Hindi sides of the data is first normalized with Indic NLP library[1] followed by tokenization with the same library. As our preprocessing step, we removed all the sentences of length greater than 80 from our training corpus.

4.3   Subword Segmentation for NMT

Neural Machine Translation relies on first mapping each word into the vector space, and tradi-

---

[1]https://anoopkunchukuttan.github.io/indic_nlp_library/

tionally we have a word vector corresponding to each word in a fixed vocabulary. Addressing the problem of data scarcity and the hardness of the system to learn high quality representations for rare words, (Sennrich et al., 2015b) proposed to learn subword units and perform translation at a subword level. With the goal of open vocabulary NMT, we incorporate this approach in our system as a preprocessing step. In our early experiments, we note that Byte Pair Encoding (BPE) works better than UNK replacement techniques. For our baseline system, we learn separate vocabularies for Hindi and English each with 32k merge operations. For our multilingual model, we learn a joint vocabulary for Hindi and Gujarati & a separate vocabulary for English. With the help of BPE, the vocabulary size is reduced drastically and we no longer need to prune the vocabularies. After the translation, we do an extra post processing step to convert the target language subword units back to normal words. We found this approach to be very helpful in handling rare word representations.

4.4 Script Conversion

India is a linguistically rich country having 22 constitutional languages, written in different scripts. Indian languages are highly inflectional with a rich morphology, default sentence structure as subject object verb (SOV) and relatively free word order. Many of them are structurally similar, also called as sibling languages. Hindi & Gujarati languages are such siblings. That is why, we have chosen Hindi as an assisting language for our multilingual model.

Although, there are many linguistic similarities between Gujarati & Hindi, both of these languages are written in different scripts. So, to make a strong multilingual NMT model, we converted the script of the Gujarati side of the parallel corpus to Hindi (Devanagari script). We used Indic NLP Library's transliteration script for this purpose. We found this approach to be very helpful in enabling better sharing between languages on the encoder side. BPE also enhances the usage of script conversion technique. We used script conversion only with our additional Multilingual NMT experiments based on Transformer architecture.

4.5 Training Details

The structure of our NMT model is same as in Luong et al. (2015), an RNN based encoder-decoder model with Global Attention mechanism. We used an LSTM based Bi-directional encoder and a uni-directional decoder. We kept 4 layers in both the encoder & decoder with embedding size set to 512. The batch size was set to 64 and a dropout rate of 0.3. We used Adam optimizer (Kingma and Ba, 2014) for our experiments. Our multilingual model is trained with all the same hyperparameters as our baseline model except that the training data is a combination of Hindi-English & Gujarati-English parallel data.

5 Results

In this section, we report the BLEU (Papineni et al., 2002) scores on the test sets provided in WMT19. Our simple NMT model which is an attention-based LSTM encoder-decoder model achieves a BLEU score of 6.2 on the test set. Our multilingual model which is trained with the help of Hindi-English parallel corpus attains a BLEU score of 9.8, showing a gain of +3.6 BLEU points on the same test set.

Table 2: WMT19 evaluation of our systems

System	BLEU
encoder-decoder + attention	6.2
Multilingual model	**9.8(+3.6)**

6 Additional Transformer Experiments

In this section, we present a set of experiments and results post WMT19 shared task involving the Transformer (Vaswani et al., 2017) architecture. We used the Transformer-Base architecture in this set of experiments with the rest of the pipeline being kept same as described before. We used 6 layers in both the encoder decoder with embedding size set to 512. The batch size was 2048 tokens & a dropout of 0.3. We used Adam optimizer for our experiments. During inference time, we averaged the checkpoints of the model at different epochs to obtain better results than a single checkpoint. In the multilingual Transformer experiments, we employ script conversion technique for its merits described before.

In table 3, we provide the results of our Transformer experiments and also compare it to other systems submitted to WMT19.

Table 3: Our Transformer models vs other systems at WMT19

System	BLEU
Transformer	4.28
Multilingual Transformer	15.78 (+11.5)
+ Averaging	**16.49 (+0.71)**
NICT (Unsupervised MT)	9.6
NICT (Transfer Learning)	18.6
NEU (WMT19 Best)	26.5

7 Conclusion & Future Work

We believe that NMT is a promising approach for Machine Translation for low resource languages. But we need various techniques to handle the data scarcity problem. Transfer Learning and Multilingual Machine Translation are two important areas of research that tackles this problem. In this paper, we showed that how Multilingual MT models are more effective than the individually trained MT models for a low resource language pair. We presented our results on the Gujarati→English language pair and achieved significant BLEU improvements. The Multilingual NMT model we presented in this paper is a many-to-one model. In future, we will work on building effective one-to-many Multilingual NMT systems.

References

Mikel Artetxe, Gorka Labaka, Eneko Agirre, and Kyunghyun Cho. 2017. Unsupervised neural machine translation. *arXiv preprint arXiv:1710.11041*.

Dzmitry Bahdanau, Kyunghyun Cho, and Yoshua Bengio. 2014. Neural machine translation by jointly learning to align and translate. *arXiv preprint arXiv:1409.0473*.

Daxiang Dong, Hua Wu, Wei He, Dianhai Yu, and Haifeng Wang. 2015. Multi-task learning for multiple language translation. In *Proceedings of the 53rd Annual Meeting of the Association for Computational Linguistics and the 7th International Joint Conference on Natural Language Processing (Volume 1: Long Papers)*, volume 1, pages 1723–1732.

Orhan Firat, Kyunghyun Cho, and Yoshua Bengio. 2016. Multi-way, multilingual neural machine translation with a shared attention mechanism. *arXiv preprint arXiv:1601.01073*.

Thanh-Le Ha, Jan Niehues, and Alexander Waibel. 2016. Toward multilingual neural machine translation with universal encoder and decoder. *arXiv preprint arXiv:1611.04798*.

Di He, Yingce Xia, Tao Qin, Liwei Wang, Nenghai Yu, Tieyan Liu, and Wei-Ying Ma. 2016. Dual learning for machine translation. In *Advances in Neural Information Processing Systems*, pages 820–828.

Melvin Johnson, Mike Schuster, Quoc V Le, Maxim Krikun, Yonghui Wu, Zhifeng Chen, Nikhil Thorat, Fernanda Viégas, Martin Wattenberg, Greg Corrado, et al. 2017. Googles multilingual neural machine translation system: Enabling zero-shot translation. *Transactions of the Association for Computational Linguistics*, 5:339–351.

Diederik P Kingma and Jimmy Ba. 2014. Adam: A method for stochastic optimization. *arXiv preprint arXiv:1412.6980*.

Tom Kocmi and Ondřej Bojar. 2018. Trivial transfer learning for low-resource neural machine translation. *arXiv preprint arXiv:1809.00357*.

Philipp Koehn, Hieu Hoang, Alexandra Birch, Chris Callison-Burch, Marcello Federico, Nicola Bertoldi, Brooke Cowan, Wade Shen, Christine Moran, Richard Zens, et al. 2007. Moses: Open source toolkit for statistical machine translation. In *Proceedings of the 45th annual meeting of the ACL on interactive poster and demonstration sessions*, pages 177–180. Association for Computational Linguistics.

Anoop Kunchukuttan, Pratik Mehta, and Pushpak Bhattacharyya. 2017. The iit bombay english-hindi parallel corpus. *arXiv preprint arXiv:1710.02855*.

Guillaume Lample, Alexis Conneau, Ludovic Denoyer, and Marc'Aurelio Ranzato. 2017. Unsupervised machine translation using monolingual corpora only. *arXiv preprint arXiv:1711.00043*.

Guillaume Lample, Myle Ott, Alexis Conneau, Ludovic Denoyer, and Marc'Aurelio Ranzato. 2018. Phrase-based & neural unsupervised machine translation. *arXiv preprint arXiv:1804.07755*.

Minh-Thang Luong, Hieu Pham, and Christopher D Manning. 2015. Effective approaches to attention-based neural machine translation. *arXiv preprint arXiv:1508.04025*.

Toan Q Nguyen and David Chiang. 2017. Transfer learning across low-resource, related languages for neural machine translation. *arXiv preprint arXiv:1708.09803*.

Kishore Papineni, Salim Roukos, Todd Ward, and Wei-Jing Zhu. 2002. Bleu: a method for automatic evaluation of machine translation. In *Proceedings of the 40th annual meeting on association for computational linguistics*, pages 311–318. Association for Computational Linguistics.

Rico Sennrich, Barry Haddow, and Alexandra Birch. 2015a. Improving neural machine translation models with monolingual data. *arXiv preprint arXiv:1511.06709*.

Rico Sennrich, Barry Haddow, and Alexandra Birch. 2015b. Neural machine translation of rare words with subword units. *arXiv preprint arXiv:1508.07909*.

Ashish Vaswani, Noam Shazeer, Niki Parmar, Jakob Uszkoreit, Llion Jones, Aidan N Gomez, Łukasz Kaiser, and Illia Polosukhin. 2017. Attention is all you need. In *Advances in Neural Information Processing Systems*, pages 5998–6008.

Lijun Wu, Yingce Xia, Li Zhao, Fei Tian, Tao Qin, Jianhuang Lai, and Tie-Yan Liu. 2017. Adversarial neural machine translation. *arXiv preprint arXiv:1704.06933*.

Barret Zoph and Kevin Knight. 2016. Multi-source neural translation. *arXiv preprint arXiv:1601.00710*.

Barret Zoph, Deniz Yuret, Jonathan May, and Kevin Knight. 2016. Transfer learning for low-resource neural machine translation. *arXiv preprint arXiv:1604.02201*.

Kingsoft's Neural Machine Translation System for WMT19

Xinze Guo, Chang Liu, Xiaolong Li, Yiran Wang
Guoliang Li, Feng Wang, Zhitao Xu, Liuyi Yang, Li Ma
Changliang Li*
Kingsoft AI Lab
{guoxinze,liuchang10,lixiaolong2,wangyiran3,liguoliang,
wangfeng5,xuzhitao,yangliuyi,mali5,lichangliang}@kingsoft.com

Abstract

This paper describes the Kingsoft AI Lab's submission to the WMT2019 news translation shared task. We participated in two language directions: English→Chinese and Chinese→English. For both language directions, we trained several variants of Transformer models using the provided parallel data enlarged with a large quantity of back-translated monolingual data. The best translation result was obtained with ensemble and reranking techniques. According to automatic metrics (BLEU) our Chinese→English system reached the second highest score, and our English→Chinese system reached the second highest score for this subtask.

1 Introduction

In recent years, the development of sequence-to-sequence (seq2seq) models have changed the field of machine translation a lot. This kind of models replaced traditional statistical approaches with neural machine translation (NMT) systems which is based on the encoder-decoder framework. Two years ago, the Transformer model, which is based on the multi-head attention mechanism and feedforward networks, has further advanced the field of NMT by improving the translation quality and speed of convergence (Vaswani et al., 2017; Ahmed et al., 2017). Until now, a variety of NMT models and advanced techniques have been proposed, leading to better performance of machine translation. We participated in the WMT19 shared task: the machine translation of news on English↔Chinese language pairs. This paper describes the NMT systems we submitted for the WMT19 Chinese→English and English→Chinese machine translation tasks. For data augmentation, we selected a subset of

monolingual corpus as additional datasets and applied back translation to augment our training corpus. The baseline model in our system was based on the Transformer architecture. In order to improve the single system's performance, we experimented with some research findings such as Transformer with Relative Position Attention (Shaw et al., 2018) and Dynamic Convolution Networks (Wu et al., 2019).

We also proposed our own model architectures and applied them in the tasks. These architectures improve translation quality a lot and will be described in the next section. For further improvement, we tried different multi-system based techniques, such as model ensembling and model reranking. These techniques can improve translation performance on the basis of a very strong single system. At the same time, we also designed some specific strategies to deal with problems during ensembling, such as the overflow of memory space and the slow decoding speed. As a result, our Chinese→English system achieved the second highest cased BLEU score among all 15 submitted constrained systems, and our English→Chinese system ranked the second out of 12 submitted systems.

2 Model Features

This section describes five different model architectures applied to translation tasks. Two of them come from public research works, while the other three come from our works. The Transformer was used as our baseline system.

2.1 Transformer with Relative Position

We used relative position representation in self-attention mechanism (Shaw et al., 2018) of both the encoder side and decoder side. Originally, the Transformer only uses the absolute position information that calculated by sinusoidal functions,

---

*Corresponding author

Proceedings of the Fourth Conference on Machine Translation (WMT), Volume 2: Shared Task Papers (Day 1) pages 196–202
Florence, Italy, August 1-2, 2019. ©2019 Association for Computational Linguistics

lacking of considering the relative position representation efficiently. Thus, it is an alternative approach to incorporate relative position representation in self-attention mechanism. In contrast to the absolute position, the relative position representation is invariant to the sentence length. We compared the translation results between whether using this feature or not, and found that model with relative position representation performs better. We conducted an implement in Fairseq[1] as an additional architecture with precise tuning. Experiments showed that this architecture leads to faster convergence and better performance.

2.2 Dynamic Convolution Network

Different from Transformer based on self-attention mechanism, Dynamic Convolution Network (Wu et al., 2019) uses a convolution network to replace the self-attention mechanism in the model framework. It predicts separate convolution kernels based solely on the current time-step in order to determine the importance of context elements. In other word, a Dynamic Convolution Network has kernels that vary over time as a learned function of the individual time steps. Experiments showed that Dynamic Convolution Network got better performance and decoded faster than the original Transformer. This architecture has already been implemented in Fairseq.

2.3 Linear Combination Transformer

For the better use of each layer's output in the Transformer, we proposed a new architecture called Linear Combination. In the original Transformer, each encoder layer only transfers its output to the next layer and the decoder only accepts the output of the final encoder layer. In this condition, some grammar or semantics information may be lost even residual connections are applied in each layer. Therefore, we collect each layer's output and calculate them as the final output of the encoder through a weight-sum function. After this operation, the final output is transferred to the decoder. Additionally, it only increases a few parameters which are the same as the number of encoder layers. The experimental results showed that the linear combination function leads the model to perform better.

---

[1] https://github.com/pytorch/fairseq

2.4 Transformer with Layer Aggregation

For further research of gaining information of each layers, we used layer aggregation mechanism both in the encoder side and decoder side, iterative deep aggregation for the encoder side, hierarchical deep aggregation for the decoder side (Yu et al., 2018), and the linear operation for the encoder side and decoder side. Hierarchical deep aggregation requires the number of layers to be the power of 2, so the number of layers in decoder was set to be 8. Originally, the Transformer only utilizes the top layer' output of the encoder and decoder, which misses the opportunity to exploit the useful information in other layers. Some recent studies reveal that simultaneously exposing all layer representations performs better for natural language processing tasks (Peters et al., 2018; Shen et al., 2018; Dou et al., 2018). In our experiments, we compared the translation results about whether using layer aggregation or not, and found that models with the layer aggregation performed better.

2.5 Encoder Branches with SE-pre in Transformer

Increasing the width of network can improve the model performance effectively and recent works such as Evolved Transformer (So et al., 2019) have proved this idea. Inspired by this, we proposed a new architecture using multi branches mechanism in the encoder side, self-attention for one branch and depthwise separable convolutions (Kaiser et al., 2017) for the other. The outputs of different branches are aggregated by gating unit or just averaging them. We also tried to use SE-pre method (Hu et al., 2018) to replace residual connection and gained a better performance. To reduce the number of parameters, we shared the parameter of different layers in depthwise separable convolutions. In source side, the model has a stack of 6 layers and each layer contains a self-attention sub-layer, a depthwise separable convolution sbulayer, a gating unit and a FFN sub-layer. In target side, we used the same structure as vanilla decoder in Transformer. Compared with vanilla Transformer, our novel structure outperformed significantly in EN-ZH translation task.

3 Experiment Techniques

3.1 Back Translation

Since Sennrich et al. proposed a method which can translate target side monolingual corpora into source side to add synthetic data and exploit large corpora, back translation has become a routine operation to build a state-of-art system in translation tasks. Target-side monolingual data plays an important role in neural machine translation systems, so we investigated the use of monolingual data for NMT. In general, we translated monolingual English sentences into Chinese sentences using our English→Chinese baseline system and translated monolingual Chinese sentences into English sentences using our Chinese→English baseline system. To improve the quality of the synthetic corpus, we also conducted a strict data filter which was also used in data preprocessing to exclude bad sentences with low sentence score.

To select sentences for back-translation, we trained unsupervised neural language models with Transformer architectures on target-side bilingual corpora and used them to score these monolingual sentences. We chose News-Discuss corpora 2017 and News-Discuss corpora 2018 which contained about 0.3B sentences totally as our target-side monolingual corpora in Chinese→English translation tasks. We first selected about 80M English sentences from the target-side monolingual corpus based on language model scores, which reflected their similarity to the in-domain corpus. Then we translated them into Chinese sentences and got about 80M sentence pairs. After that, we trained another translation model with Transformer architecture on original bilingual corpora. To calculate bilingual scores for those synthetic sentence pairs, we used the model to translate source-side synthetic sentences and scored their losses with target-side sentences. Finally, we selected 8M sentence pairs with high LM scores and low translation losses and added them to the original corpus.

For English-Chinese translation task, we used XMU monolingual corpus[2] instead of News-Discuss corpora, because XMU corpus contained more in-domain and higher-quality Chinese-side sentences than other monolingual corpora. All other filter operation was same as Chinese-English translation task. Finally, We got 3M synthetic data adding to original corpus.

3.2 Fine-tuning

The Transfer Learning had been used in the field of Computer Vision for a long time, and it had generated significant results (Razavian et al., 2014;

Shelhamer et al., 2017; He et al., 2016; Huang et al., 2017). Recent Researches have shown that transfer learning can be extended to natural language processing (NLP) and reinforcement learning. Several papers have indicated that transfer learning and fine-tuning has achieved great success in NLP. (McCann et al., 2017; Peters et al., 2017, 2018; Howard and Ruder, 2018)

In our work of the WMT19, the News-Commentary-v14 was chosen as the in-domain corpus, and the rest of training dataset and the monolingual back-translation corpus were used as the out-domain corpus. In order to enlarge the in-domain corpus, we exploited the algorithm detailed in Duh et al.; Axelrod et al.. Three methods were used to select sentence pairs from large out-domain corpus that are similar to the in-domain corpus, and these sentence pairs were added into the in-domain corpus. Then these new in-domain corpus we got were used to fine-tune the baseline model by continuing training a few steps. The three methods to select similar sentence pairs in our experiments as follows: the KenLM, the Transformer language model, and the tf-idf algorithm.

N- Language Model: According to the work of Deng et al., the in-domain corpus was set as I and the out-domain corpus was set as O. A smaller out-domain corpus o was got from the out-domain corpus by random sampling, and this corpus has similar size with corpus I. Then the KenLM was used to train 3-gram language models on the source side and target side of the corpus I and o respectively (H_{I-src}, H_{I-tgt}, H_{o-src} and H_{o-tgt}). After that, all the sentence pairs s from out-domain corpus O were passed into these language models, and scored by using the bilingual cross-entropy difference:

$$[H_{I-src(s)} - H_{I-tgt(s)}] + [H_{o-src(s)} - H_{o-tgt(s)}]$$

At last, the top 20 sentence pairs with lowest scores were add into the in-domain corpus to fine-tune the translation model.

Transformer Language Model: Similar to the above method, the language model with Transformer architecture from Tensor2tensor[3] was used to train the source side and target side of the corpus I and o respectively. The bilingual cross-entropy difference was used to get top 20 similar sentence

---

[2]http://nlp.nju.edu.cn/cwmt-wmt/

[3]https://github.com/tensorflow/tensor2tensor

pairs from the out-domain corpus to generate new in-domain corpus.

TF-IDF Algorithm: The tf-idf algorithm was chosen to calculate the similarity of the sentences in the in-domain corpus and out-domain corpus. Then we got top 20 similar sentence pairs from out-domain corpus by using the tf-idf scores.

3.3 Ensemble

Ensemble learning, which trains multiple learners and combines them, is a widely used technique in many real-world tasks. Model ensemble has been successfully applied to neural machine translation system, it combines the full probability distribution over the target vocabulary of different models at each step during sequence prediction. We implemented model ensemble module in Tensor2tensor and Fairseq, obtained an improvement of up to 1.2 bleu over the highest single model result. Noticed that simply increasing the size of an ensemble does not necessarily improve translation performance, and brute-force search of all models is unrealistic. As the number of models increases, the decoding of ensemble will take more time than single model, and exceed the limits of computer resource capacity. So we developed an approach that is capable of verifying model combination fast and effectively.

In our algorithm, all the ensemble models are firstly sorted by performance with beam_size = 4. At the first iteration, we selected the best N models and combined them. While it is known that enlarging beam_size can improve decoding performance, in order to verify model combination speedily, beam_size was chosen as 1. After that, we selected the M best model combinations, and decoding them with beam_size = 4 again to further reduce the combination size. Once the first iteration was finished, we added two or four new models to the existed model combination, and then put them into a standard ensemble process described above in the second iteration. The iteration loop will continue until all the models have joined ensemble process. If the number of models is too large, decoding with CPU can be an alternative. Finally, we chose the optimal model combinations, and then increased beam_size and modified the length penalty to gain better translation performance.

Model and data diversity are important factors for ensemble system, so we trained diverse models depending on different parameters, different model architectures, and different training data sets. In order to boost the ensemble performance, all the models have been fine-tuned. For model ensemble strategy, it seems intuitive to employ NMT ensembles by assigning same weights to different models or simply selecting the maximum output probability distributions. In this competition, we adopted a log-avg model ensemble strategy. Both of the max and avg strategy described above we have tried, there was no better result observed.

3.4 Rerank

Reranking is a technique to improve translation quality by choosing potentially better results from the N-Best list. In order to avoid an N-Best list with too many noises, we used strong ensemble systems to generate it. We got an N-Best list with a size of 200+. Then we used 30+ models to score the N-Best list. The models details will be described below. These scores make up several features to represent a sentence in an N-Best list. These features we used including:

Word-alignment feature: These features are generated by using fast-align tools[4] to score the N-Best list and their source sentence.

Language model features: These features are generated by using KenLM and neural language model to score the N-Best list.

Translation models features: Translation model can generate sentences from left to right (L2R) and right to left (R2L), and both source to target (S2T) and target to source (T2S) models can be used to get features. Therefore, there are four kinds (S2T-L2R, T2S-L2R, S2T-R2L, T2S-R2L) of translation model features. In order to get features that can represent the N-Best list more comprehensively, we used translation models that trained with three kinds of frameworks (Tensor2tensor, Fairseq and Sockeye[5]) to generate features.

After getting these features, K-batched MIRA algorithm(Cherry and Foster, 2012) which was implemented in Moses was introduced to the development dataset to get a set of weights. At last, we used these weights to rescore the N-Best list and got final translation results.

---

[4]https://github.com/clab/fast_align
[5]https://github.com/awslabs/sockeye

4 Experiments Settings and Results

4.1 Data

The WMT18 English↔Chinese translation task contains 24.22M raw data, and the WMT19 English↔Chinese translation task contains 26.17M raw data. There are three high-quality development set: *newstest2017, newsdev2017* and *newstest2018*.

4.2 Pre-processing and Post-processing

Firstly, we tokenized the English sentences by using NLTK[6] toolkit and segmented the Chinese sentences with Pkuseg[7] which was produced by Peking University. As a routine operation, we applied BPE (Sennrich et al., 2016b) using Sentencepiece [8] to enable an open vocabulary which contained about 50k words and subwords. For the data selection, we removed duplications in the training data, and designed a filter to exclude bad sentences according to the sentence score obtained by language models and translation models. The final amount of our training data is about 24M bilingual sentence pairs for EN-ZH tasks, and about 22M bilingual sentence pairs for ZH-EN tasks.

We applied post-processing on the outputs of these translation tasks. For EN-ZH translation task, we normalized the punctuations of outputs through converting the single byte character to double byte character and removed the space between Chinese characters. For ZH-EN translation task, we de-tokenized the outputs by Moses toolkit.

4.3 Training Details

All models were trained on 8 GPUs using floating point 16 precision and gradients accumulating (Ott et al., 2018) to employ a bigger batch size as large as 128 GPUs'. We batched sentence pairs by approximate length, limited the number of input and output tokens per batch to 3584 per GPU and re-shuffled the training corpus between epochs. Each training batch contained approximately 450K source tokens and 450K target tokens. We also applied a cosine learning rate schedule (Kingma and Ba, 2015; Loshchilov and Hutter, 2017) where the learning rate is first linearly warmed up for 10K steps from 10^{-7} to 10^{-3} and then annealed following a cosine rate with a single

System	Newsdev2017	Newstest2018
baseline	35.32	
+Data filtering	36.62	
+Back translation	40.23	42.52
+Model enhancement	40.73	42.98
+fine-tuning	41.33	44.10
+ensemble	41.93	46.10
+rerank	42.20	46.40

Table 1: English→Chinese Systems BLEU results on *newsdev2017* and *newstest2018*. As for *newsdev2017* ensemble step, we only mannually selected two models for ensembling test but for *newstest2018*, we applied our ensemble algorithm on all models.

cycle. During training, the label smoothing was employed with $\epsilon_{ls} = 0.1$ and the dropout rate was set from 0.1 to 0.3 (Hinton et al., 2012; Pereyra et al., 2017). The baseline system was trained for about 25 epochs and saved the last 15 epochs to perform checkpoint averaging. At last, we validated the model every 1000 mini-batches against BLEU on the WMT 17 news translation test set.

4.4 English→Chinese Systems

Table 1 shows the English→Chinese translation results on the validation set (WMT18 testset). We reported character-level BLEU scores calculated with Moses *mteval-v13a.pl* script [9]. For the baseline system with data filtering, it gained 1.3 BLEU scores compared to the result without filtering. After applying back translation, a single baseline model can improve by about 3.6 BLEU scores. That means synthetic data plays an important role in the success of our system. When it comes to model enhancement, Table 3 shows that each advanced model architecture got a better performance compared to the baseline model. After applying different combinations of the techniques described in Section 2 and 3, we got 11 systems. Thanks to these varieties of model architectures and different data selection strategies, our ensemble system gained a lot and improved about 2 points in term of BLEU. Then we rescored 200+ n-best lists decoding from different single and ensemble systems and finally achieved an improvement of 0.3 BLEU score.

4.5 Chinese→English Systems

Table 2 shows the Chinese→English translation results on the validation set. All results are re-

---

[6] https://github.com/nltk/nltk
[7] https://github.com/lancopku/pkuseg-python
[8] https://github.com/google/sentencepiece

[9] https://github.com/moses-smt/mosesdecoder/blob/master/scripts/generic/mteval-v13a.pl

System	Newstest2017
baseline	
+Data filtering	
+Back translation	26.41
+Model enhancement	27.00
+fine-tuning	28.49
+ensemble	29.62
+rerank	29.92

Table 2: Chinese→English Systems BLEU results on *newstest2017*.

Models	EN-ZH	ZH-EN
	dev17	test17
Baseline model(Transformer)	40.23	26.41
Relative Transformer	40.73	26.60
Dynamic Convolution Networks	40.10	26.51
Linear Combination Transformer	40.70	27.00
Layer Aggregation Transformer	40.73	26.93
SE-pre in Transformer	40.51	26.72

Table 3: BLEU results for different model architectures. For EN-ZH, It represents the results on *newsdev2017* and for ZH-EN, it represents the results on *newstest2017*. All models are trained with synthetic data after back translation.

ported with cased BLEU scores. We followed exactly the same settings with the English→Chinese translation system. In this case, the fine-tuning method brought a substantial improvement about 1.4 BLEU scores, showing the advantages of using high-quality in-domain data. For model enhancement, each model architecture got nearly the same BLEU score improvement. Finally, we applied ensemble and reranking techniques, which provided 1.5 BLEU improvements totally over the best single model.

5 Conclusion

We present our NMT systems for WMT19 Chinese↔English news translation tasks. For both translation directions, our final systems achieved substantial improvements up by $4 \sim 5$ BLEU score over baseline systems by integrating the following technique:

1. Data filtering and model enhancements
2. Back translate the target monolingual data set
3. Fine-tuning with in-domain data
4. System combination and reranking.

As a result, our submitted Chinese→English system achieved the second highest cased BLEU score among all 15 submitted constrained systems and our English→Chinese system ranked the second out of 12 submitted systems.

References

Karim Ahmed, Nitish Shirish Keskar, and Richard Socher. 2017. Weighted transformer network for machine translation. *CoRR*, abs/1711.02132.

Amittai Axelrod, Xiaodong He, and Jianfeng Gao. 2011. Domain adaptation via pseudo in-domain data selection. In *Proceedings of the 2011 Conference on Empirical Methods in Natural Language Processing, EMNLP 2011, 27-31 July 2011, John McIntyre Conference Centre, Edinburgh, UK, A meeting of SIGDAT, a Special Interest Group of the ACL*, pages 355–362.

Colin Cherry and George F. Foster. 2012. Batch tuning strategies for statistical machine translation. In *Human Language Technologies: Conference of the North American Chapter of the Association of Computational Linguistics, Proceedings, June 3-8, 2012, Montréal, Canada*, pages 427–436.

Yongchao Deng, Shanbo Cheng, Jun Lu, Kai Song, Jingang Wang, Shenglan Wu, Liang Yao, Guchun Zhang, Haibo Zhang, Pei Zhang, Changfeng Zhu, and Boxing Chen. 2018. Alibaba's neural machine translation systems for WMT18. In *WMT (shared task)*, pages 368–376. Association for Computational Linguistics.

Zi-Yi Dou, Zhaopeng Tu, Xing Wang, Shuming Shi, and Tong Zhang. 2018. Exploiting deep representations for neural machine translation. *arXiv preprint arXiv:1810.10181*.

Kevin Duh, Graham Neubig, Katsuhito Sudoh, and Hajime Tsukada. 2013. Adaptation data selection using neural language models: Experiments in machine translation. In *Proceedings of the 51st Annual Meeting of the Association for Computational Linguistics, ACL 2013, 4-9 August 2013, Sofia, Bulgaria, Volume 2: Short Papers*, pages 678–683.

Kaiming He, Xiangyu Zhang, Shaoqing Ren, and Jian Sun. 2016. Deep residual learning for image recognition. In *2016 IEEE Conference on Computer Vision and Pattern Recognition, CVPR 2016, Las Vegas, NV, USA, June 27-30, 2016*, pages 770–778.

Geoffrey E. Hinton, Nitish Srivastava, Alex Krizhevsky, Ilya Sutskever, and Ruslan Salakhutdinov. 2012. Improving neural networks by preventing co-adaptation of feature detectors. *CoRR*, abs/1207.0580.

Jeremy Howard and Sebastian Ruder. 2018. Universal language model fine-tuning for text classification. In *Proceedings of the 56th Annual Meeting of the Association for Computational Linguistics, ACL 2018, Melbourne, Australia, July 15-20, 2018, Volume 1: Long Papers*, pages 328–339.

Jie Hu, Li Shen, and Gang Sun. 2018. Squeeze-and-excitation networks. In *Proceedings of the IEEE conference on computer vision and pattern recognition*, pages 7132–7141.

Gao Huang, Zhuang Liu, Laurens van der Maaten, and Kilian Q. Weinberger. 2017. Densely connected convolutional networks. In *2017 IEEE Conference on Computer Vision and Pattern Recognition, CVPR 2017, Honolulu, HI, USA, July 21-26, 2017*, pages 2261–2269.

Lukasz Kaiser, Aidan N Gomez, and Francois Chollet. 2017. Depthwise separable convolutions for neural machine translation. *arXiv preprint arXiv:1706.03059*.

Diederick P Kingma and Jimmy Ba. 2015. Adam: A method for stochastic optimization. In *International Conference on Learning Representations (ICLR)*.

Ilya Loshchilov and Frank Hutter. 2017. SGDR: stochastic gradient descent with warm restarts. In *5th International Conference on Learning Representations, ICLR 2017, Toulon, France, April 24-26, 2017, Conference Track Proceedings*.

Bryan McCann, James Bradbury, Caiming Xiong, and Richard Socher. 2017. Learned in translation: Contextualized word vectors. In *Advances in Neural Information Processing Systems 30: Annual Conference on Neural Information Processing Systems 2017, 4-9 December 2017, Long Beach, CA, USA*, pages 6297–6308.

Myle Ott, Sergey Edunov, David Grangier, and Michael Auli. 2018. Scaling neural machine translation. In *Proceedings of the Third Conference on Machine Translation: Research Papers, WMT 2018, Belgium, Brussels, October 31 - November 1, 2018*, pages 1–9.

Gabriel Pereyra, George Tucker, Jan Chorowski, Lukasz Kaiser, and Geoffrey E. Hinton. 2017. Regularizing neural networks by penalizing confident output distributions. In *5th International Conference on Learning Representations, ICLR 2017, Toulon, France, April 24-26, 2017, Workshop Track Proceedings*.

Matthew E. Peters, Waleed Ammar, Chandra Bhagavatula, and Russell Power. 2017. Semi-supervised sequence tagging with bidirectional language models. In *Proceedings of the 55th Annual Meeting of the Association for Computational Linguistics, ACL 2017, Vancouver, Canada, July 30 - August 4, Volume 1: Long Papers*, pages 1756–1765.

Matthew E. Peters, Mark Neumann, Mohit Iyyer, Matt Gardner, Christopher Clark, Kenton Lee, and Luke Zettlemoyer. 2018. Deep contextualized word representations. In *Proceedings of the 2018 Conference of the North American Chapter of the Association for Computational Linguistics: Human Language Technologies, NAACL-HLT 2018, New Orleans, Louisiana, USA, June 1-6, 2018, Volume 1 (Long Papers)*, pages 2227–2237.

Ali Sharif Razavian, Hossein Azizpour, Josephine Sullivan, and Stefan Carlsson. 2014. Cnn features off-the-shelf: An astounding baseline for recognition. In *Proceedings of the 2014 IEEE Conference on Computer Vision and Pattern Recognition Workshops*, CVPRW '14, pages 512–519, Washington, DC, USA. IEEE Computer Society.

Rico Sennrich, Barry Haddow, and Alexandra Birch. 2016a. Improving neural machine translation models with monolingual data. In *Proceedings of the 54th Annual Meeting of the Association for Computational Linguistics (Volume 1: Long Papers)*, pages 86–96, Berlin, Germany. Association for Computational Linguistics.

Rico Sennrich, Barry Haddow, and Alexandra Birch. 2016b. Neural machine translation of rare words with subword units. In *Proceedings of the 54th Annual Meeting of the Association for Computational Linguistics (Volume 1: Long Papers)*, pages 1715–1725, Berlin, Germany. Association for Computational Linguistics.

Peter Shaw, Jakob Uszkoreit, and Ashish Vaswani. 2018. Self-attention with relative position representations. In *Proceedings of the 2018 Conference of the North American Chapter of the Association for Computational Linguistics: Human Language Technologies, Volume 2 (Short Papers)*, pages 464–468, New Orleans, Louisiana. Association for Computational Linguistics.

Evan Shelhamer, Jonathan Long, and Trevor Darrell. 2017. Fully convolutional networks for semantic segmentation. *IEEE Trans. Pattern Anal. Mach. Intell.*, 39(4):640–651.

Yanyao Shen, Xu Tan, Di He, Tao Qin, and Tie-Yan Liu. 2018. Dense information flow for neural machine translation. *arXiv preprint arXiv:1806.00722*.

David R. So, Chen Liang, and Quoc V. Le. 2019. The evolved transformer. *CoRR*, abs/1901.11117.

Ashish Vaswani, Noam Shazeer, Niki Parmar, Jakob Uszkoreit, Llion Jones, Aidan N Gomez, Ł ukasz Kaiser, and Illia Polosukhin. 2017. Attention is all you need. In I. Guyon, U. V. Luxburg, S. Bengio, H. Wallach, R. Fergus, S. Vishwanathan, and R. Garnett, editors, *Advances in Neural Information Processing Systems 30*, pages 5998–6008. Curran Associates, Inc.

Felix Wu, Angela Fan, Alexei Baevski, Yann N. Dauphin, and Michael Auli. 2019. Pay less attention with lightweight and dynamic convolutions. *CoRR*, abs/1901.10430.

Fisher Yu, Dequan Wang, Evan Shelhamer, and Trevor Darrell. 2018. Deep layer aggregation. In *Proceedings of the IEEE Conference on Computer Vision and Pattern Recognition*, pages 2403–2412.

The AFRL WMT19 Systems: Old Favorites and New Tricks

Jeremy Gwinnup, Grant Erdmann, Timothy Anderson
Air Force Research Laboratory
{jeremy.gwinnup.1, grant.erdmann, timothy.anderson.20}@us.af.mil

Abstract

This paper describes the Air Force Research Laboratory (AFRL) machine translation systems and the improvements that were developed during the WMT19 evaluation campaign. This year, we refine our approach to training popular neural machine translation toolkits, experiment with a new domain adaptation technique and again measure improvements in performance on the Russian–English language pair.

1 Introduction

As part of the 2019 Conference on Machine Translation (Bojar et al., 2019) news-translation shared task, the AFRL Human Language Technology team participated in the Russian–English portion of the competition. We build on our strategies from last year (Gwinnup et al., 2018), adding additional language ID based data processing and optimizing subword segmentation strategies. For Russian–English we again submitted an entry comprising our best systems trained with Marian (Junczys-Dowmunt et al., 2018), Sockeye (Hieber et al., 2017) with Elastic Weight Consolidation (EWC) (Thompson et al., 2019), OpenNMT (Klein et al., 2018), and Moses (Koehn et al., 2007) combined using the Jane system combination method (Freitag et al., 2014).

2 Data and Preprocessing

2.1 Data Preparation

We used and preprocess data as outlined in Gwinnup et al. (2018). For all systems trained, we applied either byte-pair encoding (BPE) (Sennrich et al., 2016) or SentencePiece (Kudo and Richardson, 2018) subword strategies to address the vocabulary-size problem.

For this year, we also employed a language ID filtering step for the BPE-based systems. Using the pre-built language ID model developed by the authors of fastText (Joulin et al., 2016a,b), we developed a utility that examined the source and target sentence pairs and discarded that pair if either side fell below 0.8[1] probability of the desired language. We applied this filtering to all provided parallel corpora, removing 33.7% of lines. This process was particularly effective when used to filter the Paracrawl corpus where 57.1% of lines were removed. Pre and post-filtering line counts for various corpora are shown in Table 1.

Corpus	Total	Retained
CommonCrawl	723,256	655,069
newscommentary	290,866	264,089
Yandex	1,000,000	901,307
ParaCrawl	12,061,155	5,173,675
UN2016	11,365,709	9,871,406
Total Lines	25,440,968	16,865,546

Table 1: Training corpus total and retained lines after fastText filtering

testset	wmt18preproc	wmt19filt
newstest2014	33.0	34.1
newstest2015	28.6	29.6
newstest2016	28.4	29.4
newstest2017	30.8	31.8
newstest2018	26.9	27.9

Table 2: Test set comparison for non-filtered WMT18 training corpus and filtered WMT19 training corpus measured by SacreBLEU.

A comparison with the organizer-provided parallel training data used in our WMT18 system

---

[1] We chose this value arbitrarily; future work will explore varying this threshold.

Proceedings of the Fourth Conference on Machine Translation (WMT), Volume 2: Shared Task Papers (Day 1) pages 203–208
Florence, Italy, August 1-2, 2019. ©2019 Association for Computational Linguistics

(which is largely the same as the provided parallel data for WMT19 in the Russian–English language pair) on baseline Marian transformer systems with identical training conditions show that aggressive language ID based filtering yields an approximate +1 BLEU point improvement as measured by SacreBLEU (Post, 2018). These results are shown in Table 2.

2.2 Exploration of Byte-Pair Encoding Merge Sizes

One of the problems faced when addressing the closed-vocabulary problem is the granularity of the subword units either produced by SentencePiece or BPE. To that end, we examined varying the number of BPE merge operations in order to determine an optimal setting to maximize performance for the Russian–English language pair.

For the OpenNMT-based systems, a vocabulary size of 32k entries was employed during training of a SentencePiece segmentation model[2]. This vocabulary size was determined empirically from the training data.

Alternatively, for the BPE-based systems, we systematically examined varying sizes of BPE merge operations and vocabulary sizes in 10k increments from 30k to 80k. Results in Table 3 show that 40k BPE merge operations perform best across all test sets decoded for this language pair. All subsequent Marian experiments in this work utilize this 40k BPE training corpus.

3 MT Systems

This year, we focused system-building efforts on the Marian, Sockeye, OpenNMT, and Moses toolkits, having explored a variety of parameters, data, and conditions. While most of our experimentation builds off of previous years' efforts, we did examine domain adaptation via continued training, including Elastic Weight Consolidation (EWC) (Thompson et al., 2019).

3.1 Marian

As with last year's efforts, we train multiple Marian (Junczys-Dowmunt et al., 2018) models with both University of Edinburgh's "bi-deep" (Miceli Barone et al., 2017; Sennrich et al., 2017) and Google's transformer (Vaswani et al., 2017)

architectures. Network hyperparameters are the same as detailed in Gwinnup et al. (2018). We again use `newstest2014` as the validation set during training.

Utilizing the best-performing BPE parameters from Section 2.2, we first trained a baseline system in each of the two network architectures, noting the Transformer system's better performance of +0.82 BLEU on average across decoded test sets. An additional six distinct transformer models were then independently[3] trained for use in ensemble decoding. We then ensemble decoded test sets with all eight models.

Marian typically assigns each model used in ensemble decoding a feature weight of 1.0; thus each model contributes equally to the decoding process. Borrowing from our Moses training approach, we utilize a multi-iteration decode and optimize feature weights using the "Expected Corpus BLEU" (ECB) metric with the Drem optimizer (Erdmann and Gwinnup, 2015). We experimented using `newstest2014` and `newstest2017` as tuning sets – 2017 did not help performance, but using 2014 did improve performance by up to +0.9 BLEU[4] over the non-tuned ensemble.

Scores for all the above-mentioned systems are shown in Table 4. The best-performing ensemble (ensemble tune14) was used in system combination.

3.2 Sockeye

For our Sockeye (Hieber et al., 2017) systems, we experimented with continued training (Luong and Manning, 2015; Sennrich et al., 2015) – a means to specialize a model in a new domain after a period of training on a general domain. One downside of utilizing continued training is the model adapts "too-well" to the new domain at the expense of performance in the original domain (Freitag and Al-Onaizan, 2016). One method to mitigate this performance drop is to prevent certain parameters of the network from changing with Elastic Weight Consolidation (EWC) (Kirkpatrick et al., 2017). Thompson et al. (2019) conveniently provides an implementation of this technique in Sockeye.

That work illustrated a use case where the original domain is news articles, while the new domain is text of patent applications – a marked dif-

---

[2]SentencePiece was used in part to provide diversity between our OpenNMT and other systems trained with BPE data.

[3]Identical training data and starting parameters except for random seed.

[4]This may be due to the choice of newstest2014 for validation during training.

System	newstest2014	newstest2015	newstest2016	newstest2017	newstest2018
bpe30k	33.7	28.9	28.7	31.4	27.6
bpe40k	**34.1**	**29.6**	**29.4**	**31.8**	**27.9**
bpe50k	33.9	29.2	29.1	31.6	27.8
bpe60k	33.4	29.1	28.7	31.3	27.6
bpe70k	33.0	28.8	28.8	31.2	26.9
bpe80k	32.6	28.7	28.2	31.1	26.9

Table 3: Cased, detokenized BLEU for various test sets and BPE merge-value treatments. Best scores for each test set are denoted with bold text.

System	newstest2014	newstest2015	newstest2016	newstest2017	newstest2018
single bi-deep	32.7	29.0	28.7	31.3	27.0
single transformer	34.1	29.6	29.4	31.8	27.9
untuned ensemble	36.2	**31.6**	30.5	34.2	29.7
ensemble tune17	35.3	31.1	30.2	34.2	29.7
ensemble tune14	**37.1**	31.3	**31.2**	**34.5**	**30.5**

Table 4: Test set comparison for baseline bi-deep, transformer, untuned and tuned ensembles for various test sets measured in cased, detokenized BLEU. Best scores for each test set are denoted with bold text.

ference in style and content. Here, we created a news subdomain corpus from the newstest2014 through newstest2017 test sets. The intuition is that more current events will be discussed in these test sets than the remainder of the provided training corpora, allowing better adaptation of new events in the newest test sets (newstest2018 and newstest2019.)

We first trained a baseline transformer system using the best-performing BPE parameters from Section 2.2, 512-dimension word embeddings, 6 layer encoder and decoder, 8 attention heads, label smoothing and transformer attention dropout of 0.1. We then continue-train a model on the adaptation set described above. We also followed the Sockeye EWC training procedure, producing a model more resilient to overfitting due to continued training. Results for these systems are shown in Table 5.

We see that the baseline Sockeye transformer model performs similarly to the baseline single-model Marian transformer system shown in Table 4. The continued-training system (con't train) system predictably overfit on newstest2014 as expected, since that test set is a part of the adaptation set. Likewise, performance on the out-of-domain newstest2018 also dropped as a result of overfitting. The best-performing EWC system[5]

actually improved performance on 2018 with less-pronounced overfitting on 2014.

System	newstest2014	newstest2018
baseline	33.4	27.6
con't train	89.3	24.3
best EWC	48.5	29.5

Table 5: Sockeye system scores for newstest2014 (in-domain) and newstest2018 (out-of-domain) test sets for various training conditions measured in Sacre-BLEU.

For system combination outlined later in Section 4, we decoded test sets with an ensemble of the four highest-scoring model checkpoints from the best EWC training run.

3.3 OpenNMT-T

Our first Open-NMT system was trained using the Transformer architecture with the default "TransformerBig" settings as described in Vaswani et al. (2017): 6 layers of 1024 units, 16 attention heads. Dropout rates of 0.3 for layers and 0.1 for attention heads and relu's. Training data for this system utilized the training corpus from our WMT17 Russian–English system (Gwinnup et al., 2017) consisting of provided parallel and backtranslated

---

[5]EWC applied with weight-decay of 0.001 and learning-rate of 0.00001

data. This data was then processed with a joint 32k word vocabulary SentencePiece model.

3.4 OpenNMT-G

For our second OpenNMT system, we first trained language-specific, 32k word vocabularies using SentencePiece. WMT news test data from all years except 2014 and 2017 were used to train SentencePiece. These data, with the addition of the language ID filtered ParaCrawl corpus outlined in Section 2.1, were used for training the system. WMT news test data from 2014 was used for validation. OpenNMT-tf was used to create the system, using the stock "Transformer" model.

3.5 Moses

As in previous years, we trained a phrase-based Moses (Koehn et al., 2007) system with the same data as the Marian system outlined in Section 3.1 in order to provide diversity for system combination. This system employed a hierarchical reordering model (Galley and Manning, 2008) and 5-gram operation sequence model (Durrani et al., 2011). The 5-gram English language model was trained with KenLM on all permissable monolingual English news-crawl data. The BPE model used was applied to both the parallel training data and the language modeling corpus. System weights were tuned with the Drem (Erdmann and Gwinnup, 2015) optimizer using the "Expected Corpus BLEU" (ECB) metric.

4 System Combination

Jane system combination (Freitag et al., 2014) was employed to combine outputs from the best systems from each approach outlined above. Individual component system and final combination scores are shown in Table 6 for cased, detokenized BLEU and BEER 2.0 (Stanojević and Sima'an, 2014) .

5 Submission Systems

We submitted the final 5-system combination outlined in Section 4 and the four-checkpoint EWC ensemble detailed in Section 3.2 to the Russian–English portion of the WMT19 news task evaluation. Selected newstest2019 automatic scores from the WMT Evaluation Matrix[6] are shown in Table 7.

---

[6]`http://matrix.statmt.org`

System	BLEU	BEER
1. Marian	30.47	0.5995
2. Sockeye EWC	29.43	0.5968
3. OpenNMT-T	26.22	0.5737
4. OpenNMT-G	30.05	0.6017
5. Moses	27.33	0.5836
Syscomb-5	32.12	0.6072

Table 6: System combination and input system scores measured in cased, detokenized BLEU and BEER on the `newstest2018` test set.

System	BLEU	BEER
afrl-syscomb19	37.2	0.627
afrl-ewc	34.3	0.613

Table 7: Final submission system scores measured in cased BLEU and BEER on the `newstest2019` test set.

6 Conclusion

We presented a series of improvements to our Russian–English systems, including improved preprocessing and domain adaptation. Clever remixing of older techniques from the phrase-based MT era enabled improvements in ensembled neural decoding. Lastly, we performed system combination to leverage benefits from these new techniques and favorite approaches from previous years.

References

Ondřej Bojar, Christian Federmann, Mark Fishel, Yvette Graham, Barry Haddow, Matthias Huck, Philipp Koehn, Christof Monz, Mathias Müller, and Matt Post. 2019. Findings of the 2019 conference on machine translation (wmt19). In *Proceedings of the Fourth Conference on Machine Translation, Volume 2: Shared Task Papers*, Florence, Italy. Association for Computational Linguistics.

Nadir Durrani, Helmut Schmid, and Alexander Fraser. 2011. A joint sequence translation model with integrated reordering. In *Proc. of the 49th Annual Meeting of the Association for Computational Linguistics (ACL '11)*, pages 1045–1054, Portland, Oregon.

Grant Erdmann and Jeremy Gwinnup. 2015. Drem: The AFRL submission to the WMT15 tuning task.

In *Proc. of the Tenth Workshop on Statistical Machine Translation*, pages 422–427, Lisbon, Portugal.

Markus Freitag and Yaser Al-Onaizan. 2016. Fast Domain Adaptation for Neural Machine Translation. *CoRR*, abs/1612.06897.

Markus Freitag, Matthias Huck, and Hermann Ney. 2014. Jane: Open source machine translation system combination. In *Conference of the European Chapter of the Association for Computational Linguistics*, pages 29–32, Gothenburg, Sweden.

Michel Galley and Christopher D. Manning. 2008. A simple and effective hierarchical phrase reordering model. In *Proceedings of the Conference on Empirical Methods in Natural Language Processing*, EMNLP '08, pages 848–856.

Jeremy Gwinnup, Tim Anderson, Grant Erdmann, and Katherine Young. 2018. The AFRL WMT18 systems: Ensembling, continuation and combination. In *Proceedings of the Third Conference on Machine Translation: Shared Task Papers*, pages 394–398. Association for Computational Linguistics.

Jeremy Gwinnup, Timothy Anderson, Grant Erdmann, Katherine Young, Michaeel Kazi, Elizabeth Salesky, Brian Thompson, and Jonathan Taylor. 2017. The AFRL-MITLL WMT17 systems: Old, new, borrowed, BLEU. In *Proceedings of the Second Conference on Machine Translation, Volume 2: Shared Task Papers*, pages 303–309, Copenhagen, Denmark. Association for Computational Linguistics.

Felix Hieber, Tobias Domhan, Michael Denkowski, David Vilar, Artem Sokolov, Ann Clifton, and Matt Post. 2017. Sockeye: A toolkit for neural machine translation. *arXiv preprint arXiv:1712.05690*.

Armand Joulin, Edouard Grave, Piotr Bojanowski, Matthijs Douze, Hérve Jégou, and Tomas Mikolov. 2016a. Fasttext.zip: Compressing text classification models. *arXiv preprint arXiv:1612.03651*.

Armand Joulin, Edouard Grave, Piotr Bojanowski, and Tomas Mikolov. 2016b. Bag of tricks for efficient text classification. *arXiv preprint arXiv:1607.01759*.

Marcin Junczys-Dowmunt, Roman Grundkiewicz, Tomasz Dwojak, Hieu Hoang, Kenneth Heafield, Tom Neckermann, Frank Seide, Ulrich Germann, Alham Fikri Aji, Nikolay Bogoychev, André F. T. Martins, and Alexandra Birch. 2018. Marian: Fast neural machine translation in C++. In *Proceedings of ACL 2018, System Demonstrations*, pages 116–121, Melbourne, Australia. Association for Computational Linguistics.

James Kirkpatrick, Razvan Pascanu, Neil Rabinowitz, Joel Veness, Guillaume Desjardins, Andrei A. Rusu, Kieran Milan, John Quan, Tiago Ramalho, Agnieszka Grabska-Barwinska, Demis Hassabis, Claudia Clopath, Dharshan Kumaran, and Raia Hadsell. 2017. Overcoming catastrophic forgetting in neural networks. *Proceedings of the National Academy of Sciences*, 114(13):3521–3526.

Guillaume Klein, Yoon Kim, Yuntian Deng, Vincent Nguyen, Jean Senellart, and Alexander Rush. 2018. OpenNMT: Neural machine translation toolkit. In *Proceedings of the 13th Conference of the Association for Machine Translation in the Americas (Volume 1: Research Papers)*, pages 177–184. Association for Machine Translation in the Americas.

Philipp Koehn, Hieu Hoang, Alexandra Birch, Chris Callison-Burch, Marcello Federico, Nicola Bertoldi, Brooke Cowan, Wade Shen, Christine Moran, Richard Zens, Chris Dyer, Ondřej Bojar, Alexandra Constantin, and Evan Herbst. 2007. Moses: Open source toolkit for statistical machine translation. In *Proc. of the 45th Annual Meeting of the ACL on Interactive Poster and Demonstration Sessions*, ACL '07, pages 177–180.

Taku Kudo and John Richardson. 2018. SentencePiece: A simple and language independent subword tokenizer and detokenizer for neural text processing. In *Proceedings of the 2018 Conference on Empirical Methods in Natural Language Processing: System Demonstrations*, pages 66–71, Brussels, Belgium. Association for Computational Linguistics.

Minh-Thang Luong and Christopher D. Manning. 2015. Stanford Neural Machine Translation Systems for Spoken Language Domain. In *International Workshop on Spoken Language Translation*, Da Nang, Vietnam.

Antonio Valerio Miceli Barone, Jindřich Helcl, Rico Sennrich, Barry Haddow, and Alexandra Birch. 2017. Deep architectures for neural machine translation. In *Proceedings of the Second Conference on Machine Translation*, pages 99–107. Association for Computational Linguistics.

Matt Post. 2018. A call for clarity in reporting BLEU scores. In *Proceedings of the Third Conference on Machine Translation: Research Papers*, pages 186–191. Association for Computational Linguistics.

Rico Sennrich, Alexandra Birch, Anna Currey, Ulrich Germann, Barry Haddow, Kenneth Heafield, Antonio Valerio Miceli Barone, and Philip Williams. 2017. The University of Edinburgh's neural MT systems for WMT17. In *Proceedings of the Second Conference on Machine Translation, Volume 2: Shared Task Papers*, pages 389–399, Copenhagen, Denmark. Association for Computational Linguistics.

Rico Sennrich, Barry Haddow, and Alexandra Birch. 2015. Improving neural machine translation models with monolingual data. *arXiv preprint arXiv:1511.06709*.

Rico Sennrich, Barry Haddow, and Alexandra Birch. 2016. Neural machine translation of rare words with subword units. In *Proceedings of the 54th Annual*

Meeting of the Association for Computational Linguistics (Volume 1: Long Papers), pages 1715–1725. Association for Computational Linguistics.

Miloš Stanojević and Khalil Sima'an. 2014. Fitting sentence level translation evaluation with many dense features. In *Proceedings of the 2014 Conference on Empirical Methods in Natural Language Processing (EMNLP)*, pages 202–206, Doha, Qatar. Association for Computational Linguistics.

Brian Thompson, Jeremy Gwinnup, Huda Khayrallah, Kevin Duh, and Philipp Koehn. 2019. Overcoming catastrophic forgetting during domain adaptation of neural machine translation. In *Proceedings of the 2019 Conference of the North American Chapter of the Association for Computational Linguistics: Human Language Technologies, Volume 2 (Short Papers)*, volume 2, page to appear.

Ashish Vaswani, Noam Shazeer, Niki Parmar, Jakob Uszkoreit, Llion Jones, Aidan N Gomez, Łukasz Kaiser, and Illia Polosukhin. 2017. Attention is all you need. In *Advances in Neural Information Processing Systems*, pages 6000–6010.

Evaluating the Supervised and Zero-shot Performance of Multi-lingual Translation Models

Chris Hokamp and **John Glover** and **Demian Gholipour**

Aylien Ltd.

Dublin, Ireland

`<first-name>@aylien.com`

Abstract

We study several methods for full or partial sharing of the decoder parameters of multilingual NMT models. Using only the WMT 2019 shared task parallel datasets for training, we evaluate both fully supervised and zero-shot translation performance in 110 unique translation directions. We use additional test sets and re-purpose evaluation methods recently used for unsupervised MT in order to evaluate zero-shot translation performance for language pairs where no gold-standard parallel data is available. To our knowledge, this is the largest evaluation of multi-lingual translation yet conducted in terms of the total size of the training data we use, and in terms of the number of zero-shot translation pairs we evaluate. We conduct an in-depth evaluation of the translation performance of different models, highlighting the trade-offs between methods of sharing decoder parameters. We find that models which have task-specific decoder parameters outperform models where decoder parameters are fully shared across all tasks.

1 Introduction

Multi-lingual translation models, which can map from multiple source languages into multiple target languages, have recently received significant attention because of the potential for positive transfer between high- and low-resource language pairs, and because of the potential efficiency gains enabled by translation models which share parameters across many languages (Dong et al., 2015; Ha et al., 2016; Firat et al., 2016; Johnson et al., 2016; Blackwood et al., 2018; Sachan and Neubig, 2018; Aharoni et al., 2019). Multi-lingual models which share parameters across tasks can also perform zero-shot translation, translating between language pairs for which no parallel training data is available (Wu et al., 2016; Ha et al., 2016; Johnson et al., 2016).

Although multi-task models have recently been shown to achieve positive transfer for some combinations of NLP tasks, in the context of MT, multi-lingual models do not universally outperform models trained to translate in a single direction when sufficient training data is available. However, the ability to do zero-shot translation may be of practical importance in many cases, as parallel training data is not available for most language pairs (Wu et al., 2016; Johnson et al., 2016; Aharoni et al., 2019). Therefore, small decreases in the performance of supervised pairs may be admissible if the corresponding gain in zero-shot performance is large. In addition, zero-shot translation can be used to generate synthetic training data for low- or zero- resource language pairs, making it a practical alternative to the bootstrapping by back-translation approach that has recently been used to build completely unsupervised MT systems (Firat et al., 2016; Artetxe et al., 2018; Lample et al., 2018a,b). Therefore, understanding the trade-offs between different methods of constructing multi-lingual MT systems is still an important line of research.

Deep sequence to sequence models have become the established state-of-the-art for machine translation. The dominant paradigm continues to be models divided into roughly three high-level components: *embeddings*, which map discrete tokens into real-valued vectors, *encoders*, which map sequences of vectors into an intermediate representation, and *decoders*, which use the representation from an encoder, combined with a dynamic representation of the current state, and output a sequence of tokens in the target language conditioned upon the encoder's representation of the input. For multi-lingual systems, any combination of encoder and/or decoder parameters can potentially be shared by groups of tasks, or duplicated and kept private for each task.

Proceedings of the Fourth Conference on Machine Translation (WMT), Volume 2: Shared Task Papers (Day 1) pages 209–217
Florence, Italy, August 1-2, 2019. ©2019 Association for Computational Linguistics

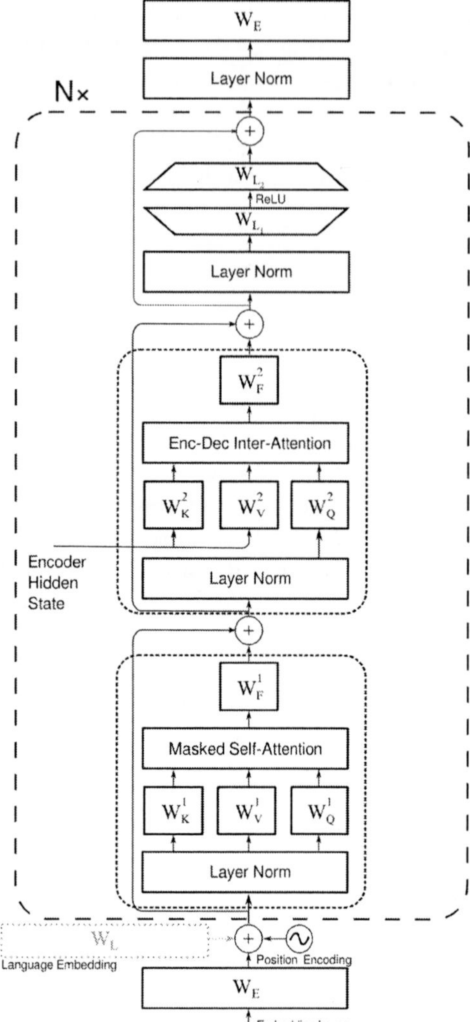

Figure 1: The decoder component of the transformer model (Vaswani et al., 2017). We can share all parameters across all target tasks, or we can create a unique set of decoder parameters for each task (outer dashed line). Alternatively, we can create unique attention parameters for each task, while sharing the final feed-forward layers (inner dotted lines). The possiblility of including an embedding for the target task is visualized at the bottom of the diagram. Illustration modeled after Sachan and Neubig (2018).

Our work builds upon recent research on many-to-one, one-to-many, and many-to-many translation models. We are interested in evaluating many-to-many models under realistic conditions, including:

1. A highly imbalanced amount of training data available for different language pairs.

2. A very diverse set of source and target languages.

3. Training and evaluation data from many domains.

We focus on multi-layer transformer models (Vaswani et al., 2017), which achieve state-of-the-art performance on large scale MT and NLP tasks (Devlin et al., 2018; Bojar et al., 2018). We study four ways of building multi-lingual translation models. Importantly, all of the models we study can do zero-shot translation: translating between language pairs for which no parallel data was seen at training time. The models use training data from 11 distinct languages[1], with supervised data available from the WMT19 news-translation task for 22 of the 110 unique translation directions[2]. This leaves 88 translation directions for which no parallel data is available. We try to evaluate zero-shot translation performance on all of these additional directions.

Target Language Specification Although the embedding and encoder parameters of a multilingual system may be shared across all languages without any special modification to the model, *decoding* from a multi-lingual model requires a means of specifying the desired output language. Previous work has accomplished this in different ways:

- pre-pending a special target-language token to the input (Wu et al., 2016)

- using an additional embedding vector for the target language (Lample and Conneau, 2019)

- using unique decoders for each target language (Luong et al., 2016; Firat et al., 2016)

- partially sharing some of the decoder parameters while keeping others unique to each target language (Sachan and Neubig, 2018; Blackwood et al., 2018)

However, to the best of our knowledge, no side-by-side comparison of these approaches has been conducted. We therefore train models which are identical except for the way that decoding into different target languages is handled, and conduct

---

[1] CS, DE, EN, FI, FR, GU, KK, LT, RU, TR and ZH

[2] Note we do not consider auto-encoding, thus the number of translation directions is $11^2 - 11 = 110$.

a large-scale evaluation. We use only the language pairs and official parallel data released by the WMT task organisers, meaning that all of our systems correspond to the constrained setting of the WMT shared task, and our experimental settings should thus be straightforward to replicate.

2 Multi-Task Translation Models

This section discusses the key components of the transformer-based NMT model, focusing on the various ways to enable translation into many target languages. We use the terms source/target *task* and *language* interchangeably, to emphasize our view that multi-lingual NMT is one instantiation of the more general case of multi-task sequence to sequence learning.

2.1 Shared Encoders and Embeddings

In this work, we are only interested in ways of providing target task information to the model – information about the source task is never given explicitly, and the encoder is always completely shared across all tasks. The segmentation model and embedding parameters are also shared between all source and target tasks (see below for more details).

2.2 Multi-lingual Decoder Configurations

Figure 1 visualizes the decoder component of the transformer model, with dashed and dotted lines indicating the parameter sets that we can replicate or share across target tasks.

2.2.1 Target Task Tokens (PREPEND)

Wu et al. (2016) showed that, as long as a mechanism exists for specifying the target task, it is possible to share the decoder module's parameters across all tasks. In the case where all parameters are shared, the decoder model must therefore learn to operate in a number of distinct modes which are triggered by some variation in the input. A simple way to achive this variation is by pre-pending a special "task-token" to each input. We refer to this method as **PREPEND**.

2.2.2 Task Embeddings (EMB)

An alternative to the use of a special task token is to treat the target task as an additional input feature, and to train a unique embedding for each target task (Lample and Conneau, 2019), which is combined with the source input. This technique has the advantage of explicitly decoupling target task information from source task input, introducing a relatively small number of additional parameters. This approach can be seen as adding an additional token-level *feature* which is the same for all tokens in a sequence (Sennrich and Haddow, 2016). We refer to this setting as **EMB**.

2.2.3 Task-specific Decoders (DEC)

In general, any subset of decoder parameters may be replicated for each target language, resulting in parameter sets which are specific to each target task. At one extreme, the entire decoder module may be replicated for each target language, a setting which we label **DEC** (Dong et al., 2015).

2.2.4 Task-specific Attention (ATTN)

An approach somewhere in-between EMB and DEC is to partially share some of the decoder parameters, while keeping others unique to each task. Recent work proposed creating unique attention modules for every target task, while sharing the other decoder parameters (Sachan and Neubig, 2018; Blackwood et al., 2018). The implementation of their approaches differ significantly – we propose to create completely unique attention parameters for each task. This means that for each of our 11 languages, we have unique context- and self-attention parameters in each layer of the transformer decoder. We refer to this setting as **ATTN**.

3 Experiments

All experiments are conducted using the transformer-base configuration of Vaswani et al. (2017) with the relevant modifications for each system discussed in the previous section. We use a shared sentencepiece[3] segmentation model with 32000 pieces. We use all available parallel data from the WMT19 news-translation task for training, with the exception of commoncrawl, which we found to be very noisy after manually checking a sample of the data, and paracrawl, which we use only for EN-FI and EN-LT[4].

We train each model on two P100 GPUs with an individual batch size of up to 2048 tokens. Gradients are accumulated over 8 mini-batches and parameters are updated synchronously, meaning that our effective batch size is $2 * 2048 * 4 = 16384$ tokens per iteration. Because the task pair for

---

[3]https://github.com/google/sentencepiece

[4]Turkish (TR) is included from the 2018 language pairs because the task-organizers suggest the possibility of using TR data to improve KK performance

	# seen	# available	# epochs	% budget
EN-CS	3,466,692	51,136,198	0.06	10.7
EN-DE	2,678,808	3,054,632	0.88	8.3
EN-FI	3,466,692	6,457,071	0.54	10.7
EN-GU	1,260,615	137,905	9.14	3.9
EN-KK	1,181,827	158,067	7.47	3.7
EN-LT	3,624,269	2,283,272	1.59	11.2
EN-RU	5,042,462	11,391,126	0.44	15.6
EN-TR	1,575,769	207,678	7.58	4.9
EN-ZH	5,846,104	14,549,833	0.40	18.1
DE-FR	4,097,000	1,980,332	2.06	12.7
TOTAL	32,240,238	91,356,114	-	100

Table 1: Training dataset statistics for our multilingual NMT experiments. **# seen** is the total number of segments seen during training. **# available** is the number of unique segments available in the parallel training datasets. **# epochs** is the number of passes made over the available training data – when this is < 1, the available training data was only partially seen. **% budget** is the percentage of the training budget allocated to this pair of tasks.

each mini-batch is sampled according to our policy weights and (fixed) random seed, and each iteration consists of 8 unique mini-batches, a single parameter update can potentially contain information from up to 8 unique task pairs. We train each model for 100,000 iterations without early stopping, which takes about 40 hours per model. When evaluating we always use the final model checkpoint (i.e. the model parameters saved after 100,000 iterations). We use our in-house research NMT system, which is heavily based upon OpenNMT-py (Klein et al., 2017).

The sampling policy weights were specified manually by looking at the amount of available data for each pair, and estimating the difficulty of each translation direction. The result of the sampling policy is that lower resource language pairs are upsampled significantly. Table 1 summarizes the statistics for each language pair. Note that the data in each row represents a *pair* of tasks, i.e. the total number of segments seen for EN-CS is split evenly between EN→CS, and CS→EN. Because we train for only 100,000 iterations, we do not see all of the available training data for some high-resource language pairs.

With the exception of the system which prepends a target task token to each input, the input to each model is identical. Each experimental setting is mutually exclusive, i.e. in the EMB setting we do not prepend task tokens, and in the ATTN setting we do not use task embeddings.

Figure 2 plots the validation performance during training on one of our validation datasets. The language embeddings from the EMB system are visualized in figure 3.

3.1 Results

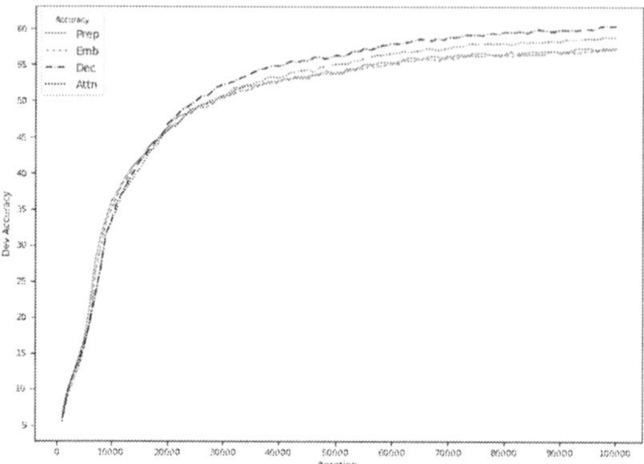

Figure 2: Word-level accuracy on WMT EN-DE 2014 dev set as training progresses. The model which has a DE-specific decoder achieves the highest accuracy on this dev set.

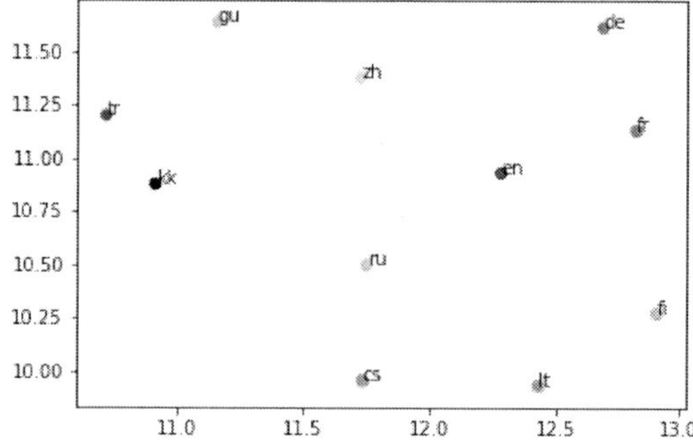

Figure 3: Language embeddings of the EMB system projected with UMAP (McInnes et al., 2018).

We evaluate the performance of our models in four ways. First, we check performance on the supervised pairs using dev and test sets from the WMT shared task. We then try to evaluate zero-shot translation performance in several ways. We use the TED talks multi-parallel dataset (Ye et al., 2018) to create gold sets for all zero-shot pairs that occur in the TED talks corpus, and evaluate on those pairs. We also try two ways of evaluating zero-shot translation without gold data. In the first, we do round-trip translation SRC $\rightarrow$ PIVOT $\rightarrow$ $\widehat{\text{SRC}}$, and measure performance on the $(\widehat{\text{SRC}}, \text{SRC})$ pair – this method is labeled

	Evaluation Dataset
EN-CS	newstest2018
EN-DE	newstest2018
EN-FI	newstest2018
EN-GU	newsdev2019
EN-KK	newsdev2019
EN-LT	newsdev2019
EN-RU	newstest2018
EN-TR	newstest2018
EN-ZH	newstest2018
DE-FR	euelections_dev2019

Table 2: The WMT evaluation dataset used for each language pair.

	PREPEND	EMB	DEC	ATTN
SUPERVISED	23.4	23.4	24.0	**24.1**
ZERO-SHOT-TED	10.6	7.8	**12.6**	12.4
ZERO-SHOT-PIVOT	16.9	**18.1**	14.0	15.1
ZERO-SHOT-PARALLEL-PIVOT	13.1	11.9	12.8	**13.2**

Table 3: Overall results for supervised and zero-shot tasks. Tokenized BLEU scores are computed by concatenating all of the hypotheses for all translation directions, and computing BLEU with respect to the concatenated references. We use the sentencepiece-segmented hypotheses and references to avoid issues with tokenization of multi-lingual hypotheses and references.

	PREPEND	EMB	DEC	ATTN
CS-EN	20.2	20.2	**20.9**	20.9
EN-CS	12.4	12.7	**13.7**	13.3
DE-EN	26.2	26.1	**27.4**	27.1
EN-DE	23.2	23.4	**25.7**	25.2
FI-EN	13.7	13.5	**14.4**	14.2
EN-FI	8.3	8.0	**9.4**	9.2
GU-EN	15.4	15.4	**15.7**	15.4
EN-GU	**8.1**	7.8	5.1	7.3
KK-EN	**14.4**	14.0	14.3	13.9
EN-KK	**5.6**	5.2	1.9	4.6
LT-EN	18.6	18.9	**19.3**	19.0
EN-LT	12.8	13.0	**14.4**	13.7
RU-EN	20.8	20.6	21.3	**21.3**
EN-RU	15.5	15.9	**17.0**	16.7
TR-EN	14.8	15.0	**15.2**	15.1
EN-TR	10.3	10.0	10.9	**11.3**
ZH-EN	13.5	13.7	**14.1**	13.7
EN-ZH	24.2	24.4	**25.6**	25.4
FR-DE	18.6	18.4	**19.9**	19.3
DE-FR	21.2	22.1	21.7	**22.6**

Table 4: Results for all task pairs in the WMT 2019 news-translation shared task where parallel training data is available.

ZERO-SHOT PIVOT. In the second, we use parallel evaluation datasets from the WMT shared tasks (consisting of (SRC, REF) pairs), and translate $\text{SRC} \rightarrow \text{PIVOT} \rightarrow \widehat{\text{TRG}}$, then measure performance on the resulting $(\widehat{\text{TRG}}, \text{REF})$ pairs (see below for more details), where the pivot and target language pair is a zero-shot translation task – this method is labeled ZERO-SHOT PARALLEL PIVOT.

Table 2 lists the WMT evaluation dataset that we use for each language pair. In the ZERO-SHOT PIVOT setting, the reference side of the dataset is used as input.

Table 3 shows global results for all parallel tasks and all zero-shot tasks, by system. Global scores are obtained by concatenating the segmented outputs for each translation direction, and computing the BLEU score against the corresponding concatenated, segmented reference translations. The results in table 3 are thus *tokenized* BLEU scores.

3.2 Parallel Tasks

In the following results, we report BLEU scores on de-tokenized output, and compute scores using sacrebleu [5]. Therefore, we expect BLEU scores to be equivalent to those used in the WMT automatic evaluation.

We note that across all but the lowest-resource tasks, the model with a unique decoder for each language outperforms all others. However, for EN→GU and EN→KK, the lowest-resource translation directions, the unique decoder model fails completely, probably because the unique parameters for KK and GU were not updated by a sufficient number of mini-batches (approximately 15,600 for EN→GU and 14,800 for EN→KK).

3.3 Zero-shot Translation Tasks

In order to test our models in the zero-shot setting, we adapt an evaluation technique that has recently been used for unsupervised MT – we translate from the source language into a pivot language, then back into the source language, and evaluate the score of the resulting source-language hypotheses against the original source (Lample

[5]
```
BLEU+case.mixed+
lang.<src-lang>-<trg-lang>+
numrefs.1+smooth.exp+tok.<trg-lang>+
version.1.2.19
```

	PREPEND	EMB	DEC	ATTN
RU→CS→RU	20.9	**23.8**	20.8	21.0
RU→DE→RU	14.6	11.9	**16.4**	15.6
RU→EN→RU*	21.7	22.2	**23.9**	23.2
RU→FI→RU	11.2	**17.0**	12.1	11.6
RU→FR→RU	13.8	**15.4**	14.1	15.1
RU→GU→RU	**10.3**	9.6	3.5	5.1
RU→KK→RU	~~5.8~~	~~19.6~~	~~1.0~~	~~2.2~~
RU→LT→RU	16.9	**22.0**	16.5	16.6
RU→TR→RU	7.9	**10.2**	7.4	7.7
RU→ZH→RU	8.8	**10.5**	9.1	8.5

Table 5: Zero-shot translation results for RU→*→RU Note that BLEU scores are computed by translating $SRC \rightarrow PIVOT \rightarrow \widehat{SRC}$, and computing the score between SRC and $\widehat{SRC}$. Systems which do not pass the language identification filter are struck-through and removed from global evaluation. Note that parallel training data was available for RU→EN.

	PREPEND	EMB	DEC	ATTN
# Failed Pivot Tasks	3	31	1	1

Table 6: Out of 110 pivot translation tasks, how many failed the language identification check?

et al., 2018a). This technique allows us to evaluate for all possible translation directions in our multi-directional model.

Aware of the risk that the model simply copies through the original source segment instead of translating, we assert that at least 95% of pivot translations' language code is correctly detected by `langid`[6], and pairs which do not meet this criteria for any system are removed from the evaluation for all systems (not just for the system that failed). For all models except EMB only RU→KK→RU FI→LT→FI, and ZH→GU→ZH failed this test, but for the EMB model 31 of the 110 translation directions failed (see tables 6 and 7[7]. This result indicates that models which use language embeddings may have a more "fuzzy" representation of the output task, and are much more prone to copying than other approaches to multi-lingual MT. However, even for the languages which passed the language identification filter, we suspect that some copying is occurring

for the EMB system, because of the mismatch in results between the ZERO-SHOT PIVOT task and the SUPERVISED, ZERO-SHOT TED, and ZERO-SHOT PARALLEL PIVOT tasks (see table 3). Table 7 (in appendix) contains the results for all possible translation directions and all models in the ZERO-SHOT PIVOT evaluation setting.

3.3.1 Zero-Shot Evaluation on TED Talks Corpus

We conduct an additional evaluation on some of the language pairs from the TED Talks multi-parallel corpus (Ye et al., 2018), which has recently been used for the training and evaluation of multi-lingual models. We filter the dev and test sets of this corpus to find segments which have translations for all of EN, FR, RU, TR, DE, CS, LT, FI, and are at least 20 characters long, resulting in 606 segments. Because this corpus is preprocessed, we first de-tokenize and de-escape punctuation using `sacremoses`[8]. We then evaluate zero-shot translation for all possible pairs which do not occur in our parallel training data, aggregate results are shown in the third row of table 3.

3.4 Discussion

Our results show that a models with either (1) a completely unique decoders for each target language or (2) unique decoder attention parameters for each target language clearly outperform models with fully shared decoder parameters in our setting.

It is plausible that the language-independence of encoder output could be correlated with the amount of sharing in the decoder module. Because most non-English target tasks only have parallel training data in English, a unique decoder for those tasks only needs to learn to decode from English, not from every possible source task. However, our results show that the ATTN model, which partially shares parameters across target languages only slightly outperforms the DEC model globally, because of the improved performance of the ATTN model on the lowest-resource tasks (Table 4, Table 7 (in appendix)).

4 Related Work

Dong et al. (2015); Firat et al. (2016); Ha et al. (2016); Johnson et al. (2016) and others have

---

[6] https://github.com/saffsd/langid.py

[7] We conduct round trip translation on all 110 directions, but we only use directions that are (1) not available in the parallel training data, and (2) pass the language identification test to compute the global zero-shot translation performance

[8] https://github.com/alvations/sacremoses

shown that multi-way NMT systems can be created with minimal modification to the approach used for single-language-pair systems. Johnson et al. (2016) showed that simply prepending a target-task token to source inputs is enough to enable zero-shot translation between language pairs for which no parallel training data is available.

Our work is most similar to Sachan and Neubig (2018), where many different strategies for sharing decoder parameters are investigated for one-to-many translation models. However, their evaluation setting is constrained to one-to-many models which translate from English into two target languages, whereas our setting is more ambitious, performing multi-way translation between 11 languages. Blackwood et al. (2018) showed that using separate attention parameters for each task can improve the performance of multi-task MT models – this work was the inspiration for the ATTN setting in our experiments.

Several recent papers focus specifically upon improving the zero-shot performance of multilingual MT models (Chen et al., 2017; Arivazhagan et al., 2019; Gu et al., 2019; Lu et al., 2018; Al-Shedivat and Parikh, 2019; Sestorain et al., 2019).

Concurrently with this work, (Aharoni et al., 2019) evaluated a multiway MT system on a large number of language pairs using the TED talks corpus. However, they focus upon EN-* and *-EN, and do not test different model variants.

5 Conclusions and Future Work

We have presented results which are consistent with recent smaller-scale evaluations of multilingual MT systems, showing that assigning unique attention parameters to each target language in a multi-lingual NMT system is optimal when evaluating such a system globally. However, when evaluated on the individual task level, models which have unique decoder parameters for every target task tend to outperform other configurations, except when the amount of available training data is extremely small. We have also introduced two methods of evaluating zero-shot translation performance when parallel data is not available, and we conducted a large-scale evaluation of translation performance across all possible translation directions in the constrained setting of the WMT19 news-translation task.

In future work, we hope to continue studying how multi-lingual translation systems scale to realistic volumes of training data and large numbers of source and target tasks.

References

Roee Aharoni, Melvin Johnson, and Orhan Firat. 2019. Massively multilingual neural machine translation. In *Proceedings of the 2019 Conference of the North American Chapter of the Association for Computational Linguistics: Human Language Technologies, Volume 1 (Long and Short Papers)*, pages 3874–3884, Minneapolis, Minnesota. Association for Computational Linguistics.

Maruan Al-Shedivat and Ankur Parikh. 2019. Consistency by agreement in zero-shot neural machine translation. In *Proceedings of NAACL*.

Naveen Arivazhagan, Ankur Bapna, Orhan Firat, Roee Aharoni, Melvin Johnson, and Wolfgang Macherey. 2019. The missing ingredient in zero-shot neural machine translation. *arXiv preprint arXiv:1903.07091*.

Mikel Artetxe, Gorka Labaka, Eneko Agirre, and Kyunghyun Cho. 2018. Unsupervised neural machine translation. In *Proceedings of the Sixth International Conference on Learning Representations*.

Graeme Blackwood, Miguel Ballesteros, and Todd Ward. 2018. Multilingual neural machine translation with task-specific attention. In *Proceedings of the 27th International Conference on Computational Linguistics*, pages 3112–3122, Santa Fe, New Mexico, USA. Association for Computational Linguistics.

Ondřej Bojar, Christian Federmann, Mark Fishel, Yvette Graham, Barry Haddow, Matthias Huck, Philipp Koehn, and Christof Monz. 2018. Findings of the 2018 conference on machine translation (wmt18). In *Proceedings of the Third Conference on Machine Translation, Volume 2: Shared Task Papers*, pages 272–307, Belgium, Brussels. Association for Computational Linguistics.

Yun Chen, Yang Liu, Yong Cheng, and Victor O.K. Li. 2017. A teacher-student framework for zero-resource neural machine translation. In *Proceedings of the 55th Annual Meeting of the Association for Computational Linguistics (Volume 1: Long Papers)*, pages 1925–1935, Vancouver, Canada. Association for Computational Linguistics.

Jacob Devlin, Ming-Wei Chang, Kenton Lee, and Kristina Toutanova. 2018. Bert: Pre-training of deep bidirectional transformers for language understanding. *arXiv preprint arXiv:1810.04805*.

Daxiang Dong, Hua Wu, Wei He, Dianhai Yu, and Haifeng Wang. 2015. Multi-task learning for multiple language translation. In *Proceedings of the*

53rd Annual Meeting of the Association for Computational Linguistics and the 7th International Joint Conference on Natural Language Processing (Volume 1: Long Papers), pages 1723–1732, Beijing, China. Association for Computational Linguistics.

Orhan Firat, Kyunghyun Cho, and Yoshua Bengio. 2016. Multi-way, multilingual neural machine translation with a shared attention mechanism. In *Proceedings of the 2016 Conference of the North American Chapter of the Association for Computational Linguistics: Human Language Technologies*, pages 866–875, San Diego, California. Association for Computational Linguistics.

Jiatao Gu, Yong Wang, Kyunghyun Cho, and Victor O. K. Li. 2019. Improved zero-shot neural machine translation via ignoring spurious correlations.

Thanh-Le Ha, Jan Niehues, and Alexander H. Waibel. 2016. Toward multilingual neural machine translation with universal encoder and decoder. *CoRR*, abs/1611.04798.

Melvin Johnson, Mike Schuster, Quoc V. Le, Maxim Krikun, Yonghui Wu, Zhifeng Chen, Nikhil Thorat, Fernanda Viégas, Martin Wattenberg, Greg Corrado, Macduff Hughes, and Jeffrey Dean. 2016. Google's multilingual neural machine translation system: Enabling zero-shot translation. Technical report, Google.

Guillaume Klein, Yoon Kim, Yuntian Deng, Jean Senellart, and Alexander M. Rush. 2017. Open-NMT: Open-source toolkit for neural machine translation. In *Proc. ACL*.

Guillaume Lample and Alexis Conneau. 2019. Cross-lingual language model pretraining. *arXiv preprint arXiv:1901.07291*.

Guillaume Lample, Alexis Conneau, Ludovic Denoyer, and Marc'Aurelio Ranzato. 2018a. Unsupervised machine translation using monolingual corpora only. In *6th International Conference on Learning Representations, ICLR 2018, Vancouver, BC, Canada, April 30 - May 3, 2018, Conference Track Proceedings*.

Guillaume Lample, Myle Ott, Alexis Conneau, Ludovic Denoyer, and Marc'Aurelio Ranzato. 2018b. Phrase-based & neural unsupervised machine translation. In *Proceedings of the 2018 Conference on Empirical Methods in Natural Language Processing (EMNLP)*.

Yichao Lu, Phillip Keung, Faisal Ladhak, Vikas Bhardwaj, Shaonan Zhang, and Jason Sun. 2018. A neural interlingua for multilingual machine translation. In *Proceedings of the Third Conference on Machine Translation: Research Papers*, pages 84–92, Belgium, Brussels. Association for Computational Linguistics.

Thang Luong, Quoc V. Le, Ilya Sutskever, Oriol Vinyals, and Lukasz Kaiser. 2016. Multi-task sequence to sequence learning. In *International Conference on Learning Representations*.

Leland McInnes, John Healy, Nathaniel Saul, and Lukas Grossberger. 2018. Umap: Uniform manifold approximation and projection. *The Journal of Open Source Software*, 3(29):861.

Devendra Sachan and Graham Neubig. 2018. Parameter sharing methods for multilingual self-attentional translation models. In *Proceedings of the Third Conference on Machine Translation: Research Papers*, pages 261–271, Belgium, Brussels. Association for Computational Linguistics.

Rico Sennrich and Barry Haddow. 2016. Linguistic Input Features Improve Neural Machine Translation. In *Proceedings of the First Conference on Machine Translation*, pages 83–91, Berlin, Germany. Association for Computational Linguistics.

Lierni Sestorain, Massimiliano Ciaramita, Christian Buck, and Thomas Hofmann. 2019. Zero-shot dual machine translation.

Ashish Vaswani, Noam Shazeer, Niki Parmar, Jakob Uszkoreit, Llion Jones, Aidan N Gomez, Ł ukasz Kaiser, and Illia Polosukhin. 2017. Attention is all you need. In I. Guyon, U. V. Luxburg, S. Bengio, H. Wallach, R. Fergus, S. Vishwanathan, and R. Garnett, editors, *Advances in Neural Information Processing Systems 30*, pages 5998–6008. Curran Associates, Inc.

Yonghui Wu, Mike Schuster, Zhifeng Chen, Quoc V. Le, Mohammad Norouzi, Wolfgang Macherey, Maxim Krikun, Yuan Cao, Qin Gao, Klaus Macherey, Jeff Klingner, Apurva Shah, Melvin Johnson, Xiaobing Liu, Łukasz Kaiser, Stephan Gouws, Yoshikiyo Kato, Taku Kudo, Hideto Kazawa, Keith Stevens, George Kurian, Nishant Patil, Wei Wang, Cliff Young, Jason Smith, Jason Riesa, Alex Rudnick, Oriol Vinyals, Greg Corrado, Macduff Hughes, and Jeffrey Dean. 2016. Google's neural machine translation system: Bridging the gap between human and machine translation. *CoRR*, abs/1609.08144.

Qi Ye, Sachan Devendra, Felix Matthieu, Padmanabhan Sarguna, and Neubig Graham. 2018. When and why are pre-trained word embeddings useful for neural machine translation. In *HLT-NAACL*.

	CS	DE	EN	FI	FR	GU	KK	LT	RU	TR	ZH
PREPEND	CS	15.7	19.6	11.4	11.1	8.7	3.6	16.6	17.4	7.8	7.5
EMB		9.3	19.9	~~24.4~~	12.4	9.3	3.3	~~28.4~~	15.8	~~10.2~~	7.5
DEC		17.7	21.3	11.5	13.3	3.3	0.7	14.0	17.8	6.7	7.5
ATTN		17.5	21.6	11.6	13.8	4.5	1.8	14.4	17.4	7.2	7.6
PREPEND	22.3	DE	27.1	16.4	25.3	11.2	5.3	18.3	18.1	12.4	12.3
EMB	~~41.5~~		27.6	~~38.0~~	25.1	~~19.4~~	8.5	~~40.7~~	23.6	~~29.9~~	~~19.6~~
DEC	23.4		29.8	15.6	25.8	4.0	0.9	16.2	19.1	11.2	12.2
ATTN	22.8		29.0	15.9	26.3	6.4	2.7	17.1	18.0	11.2	12.1
PREPEND	35.4	37.1	EN	24.6	34.5	22.1	9.3	29.2	32.9	23.3	25.6
EMB	36.5	37.4		25.9	~~35.0~~	21.5	9.3	30.4	33.9	24.2	26.6
DEC	35.8	37.5		25.8	32.6	10.1	1.6	29.7	33.2	22.8	26.3
ATTN	36.9	36.6		25.9	34.4	15.7	6.2	30.3	33.9	23.6	26.8
PREPEND	12.1	11.0	14.3	FI	7.2	5.6	2.6	~~13.1~~	9.2	6.6	6.2
EMB	~~19.9~~	~~7.9~~	14.7		8.2	6.2	4.2	~~23.8~~	11.1	~~12.0~~	~~6.8~~
DEC	11.2	11.7	15.4		9.8	3.0	0.5	10.7	9.9	6.2	5.8
ATTN	12.2	11.5	15.0		10.0	4.2	1.7	10.9	9.8	6.5	5.8
PREPEND	25.6	32.7	31.9	17.8	FR	17.1	7.8	20.5	22.9	16.0	15.3
EMB	26.0	32.0	~~36.5~~	20.4		12.4	5.0	~~24.5~~	22.5	15.6	14.1
DEC	25.7	32.9	33.9	18.4		5.9	1.5	20.2	23.6	14.4	15.1
ATTN	26.0	33.2	34.3	19.5		8.5	4.5	21.0	24.6	15.5	15.4
PREPEND	5.1	5.7	8.2	4.2	4.0	GU	2.0	5.3	5.2	3.5	3.9
EMB	~~5.3~~	4.6	7.6	5.4	4.4		1.6	~~6.2~~	3.6	4.2	3.7
DEC	3.5	3.5	5.5	3.2	3.2		0.5	3.6	3.4	2.9	2.7
ATTN	4.9	5.1	7.6	4.4	4.5		1.0	4.6	4.5	4.0	4.0
PREPEND	4.9	4.8	7.1	3.4	2.8	4.3	KK	4.6	4.9	4.4	3.9
EMB	3.4	3.4	6.4	3.8	3.5	~~1.9~~		3.9	~~3.6~~	4.5	2.4
DEC	1.7	1.8	2.2	1.6	1.5	1.1		1.5	1.7	1.7	1.2
ATTN	3.9	4.0	5.3	3.2	3.2	2.3		3.6	3.9	4.3	3.2
PREPEND	18.8	14.5	17.9	13.8	10.4	9.9	4.7	LT	16.8	10.0	9.0
EMB	~~30.5~~	~~12.0~~	18.3	~~30.7~~	10.8	10.6	~~6.8~~		18.2	~~19.7~~	13.7
DEC	16.7	13.6	18.9	12.8	11.6	3.7	0.9		16.1	8.0	8.5
ATTN	17.0	13.9	18.8	12.5	12.4	5.5	1.9		15.7	8.7	9.2
PREPEND	20.9	14.6	21.7	11.2	13.8	10.3	~~5.8~~	16.9	RU	7.9	8.8
EMB	23.8	11.9	22.2	17.0	15.4	9.6	~~19.6~~	~~22.0~~		10.2	10.5
DEC	20.8	16.4	23.9	12.1	14.1	3.5	~~1.0~~	16.5		7.5	9.1
ATTN	21.0	15.6	23.2	11.6	15.2	5.1	~~2.2~~	16.6		7.7	8.5
PREPEND	9.1	8.2	13.3	7.4	7.4	8.8	5.6	8.9	7.1	TR	6.4
EMB	~~12.7~~	7.2	12.6	~~14.6~~	7.5	6.7	4.1	~~17.3~~	6.6		6.4
DEC	7.2	7.6	13.1	6.5	6.8	2.5	0.7	6.4	5.6		5.3
ATTN	7.3	8.1	13.4	6.6	7.3	3.9	1.9	6.7	5.6		5.3
PREPEND	20.4	19.6	29.0	17.1	17.4	~~18.2~~	8.4	20.2	19.5	17.4	ZH
EMB	20.1	16.9	29.4	19.6	17.8	11.9	6.6	22.8	18.3	16.7	
DEC	19.2	19.4	30.2	16.6	17.6	7.2	2.2	19.5	20.1	16.3	
ATTN	19.8	20.4	30.0	16.7	18.2	11.0	5.0	18.6	19.4	17.1	

Table 7: Pivot-based translation results in all directions, for all models. Rows indicate source language, columns indicate pivot language. For example, cell $(1, 2)$ contains the results for CS→DE→CS. Runs which did not pass the language identification filter are struck-through. The MT-matrix (http://matrix.statmt.org/matrix) was the inspiration for this rendering.

The MLLP-UPV Supervised Machine Translation Systems for WMT19 News Translation Task

Javier Iranzo-Sánchez, Gonçal V. Garcés Díaz-Munío, Jorge Civera, Alfons Juan
Machine Learning and Language Processing (MLLP) research group
Valencian Research Institute for Artificial Intelligence (VRAIN)
Universitat Politècnica de València
Camí de Vera s/n, 46022, València, Spain
`{jairsan,ggarces,jcivera,ajuan}@vrain.upv.es`

Abstract

This paper describes the participation of the MLLP research group of the Universitat Politècnica de València in the WMT 2019 News Translation Shared Task. In this edition, we have submitted systems for the German ↔ English and German ↔ French language pairs, participating in both directions of each pair. Our submitted systems, based on the Transformer architecture, make ample use of data filtering, synthetic data and domain adaptation through fine-tuning.

1 Introduction

In this paper we describe the supervised Statistical Machine Translation (MT) systems developed by the MLLP research group of the Universitat Politècnica de València for the News Translation Shared Task of the *ACL 2019 Fourth Conference on Machine Translation* (WMT19). For this year's edition, we participated in both directions of the German ↔ English and German ↔ French language pairs, using Neural Machine Translation (NMT) models following the Transformer (Vaswani et al., 2017) architecture. Following the lessons learned from last year, we have continued working on data filtering, and we have experimented with additional synthetic data techniques and bigger neural network architectures trained with multi-GPU machines.

This paper is organized as follows. Section 2 describes the data processing steps (including data filtering and synthetic data generation) carried out prior to system training. Section 3 describes the architecture and settings used for our NMT models, and the different experiments and evaluations performed are detailed in Section 4. Our conclusions for this shared task are outlined in Section 5.

2 Data preparation

Data preprocessing, corpus filtering and data augmentation are described in the following sections.

2.1 Corpus preprocessing

The data was processed using the standard Moses pipeline (Koehn et al., 2007). Specifically, we normalized punctuation, and tokenized and true-cased data. Additionally, we applied 40K BPE operations (Sennrich et al., 2016b), learned jointly over the source and target languages, and excluded from the vocabulary all subwords that did not appear at least 10 times in the training data. BPE operations are learned before adding the data extracted using corpus filtering, described in Section 2.2. Sentences longer than 100 subwords were excluded from the training data.

2.2 Corpus filtering

The addition of the ParaCrawl corpus to the WMT shared tasks has placed an increasing importance in filtering and data selection techniques in order to take advantage of this additional data. This is highlighted by the fact that a majority of participating systems in the WMT18 News Translation Task (Bojar et al., 2018) apply filtering techniques to ParaCrawl. Additionally, the experiments carried out for our 2018 submission (Iranzo-Sánchez et al., 2018) show that using a noisy corpus such as ParaCrawl without filtering can result in a worse performance compared with a baseline system that simply excludes the noisy corpus from the training data.

We have compared two different approaches to corpus filtering:

- **LM-based filtering** (Iranzo-Sánchez et al., 2018): This approach uses language models for estimating the quality of a sentence pair, under the assumption that a low-perplexity

Proceedings of the Fourth Conference on Machine Translation (WMT), Volume 2: Shared Task Papers (Day 1) pages 218–224
Florence, Italy, August 1-2, 2019. ©2019 Association for Computational Linguistics

sentence is more likely to be an adequate sentence for training. Using in-domain data, we train one language model for each language, and then use them to score the corresponding side of the sentence pair, giving us perplexity scores (s, t). The score (perplexity) of a sentence pair is the geometric mean $\sqrt{s \cdot t}$. We select sentence pairs with the lowest score. This is the approach we used for our WMT18 submission.

- **Dual Conditional Cross-Entropy filtering** (Junczys-Dowmunt, 2018): This approach computes the sentence pair score by means of a product of a series of partial scores.

$$f(x, y) = \prod_i f_i(x, y) \qquad (1)$$

We have used the same configuration sent for the WMT18-filtering task, which uses 3 partial scores: a language identification score (*lang*), a dual conditional cross-entropy score (*adq*), and a cross-entropy difference score (*dom*) with a cut-off value of 0.25. The full details of each of these partial scores is given in Junczys-Dowmunt (2018). The translation models for the *adq* score are Transformer Base models trained with the Europarl portion of WMT19. In terms of the data for the *dom* score, we randomly sampled 1M sentences from NewsCrawl 2016 as in-domain data, and 1M sentences from ParaCrawl as out-of-domain data.

We carried out a series of comparisons between the two techniques, and found out that the cross-entropy model provides better performance than the LM-based filtering model. This is consistent with the fact that the cross-entropy filtering was the winning submission to the WMT18 Shared Task on Parallel Corpus Filtering (Koehn et al., 2018). As a result, we have elected to use the cross-entropy filtering method for filtering the different versions of the ParaCrawl corpus present in all language pairs.

2.3 Synthetic source sentences

The use of synthetic data produced by means of the backtranslation technique (Sennrich et al., 2016a) is an effective way of benefiting from additional monolingual data. Further improvements are possible if the data is from the same domain as the test data. For this reason, we have produced synthetic data for all the language pairs we have participated in.

We used the following configuration:

- German → English: We have used 20M sentences from our WMT18 submission (Iranzo-Sánchez et al., 2018), and an additional 24M sentences generated using a system with the same configuration as WMT18, but trained with 3 GPUs instead of 1. The monolingual sentences were randomly sampled from News Crawl 2017.

- English → German: We have generated 18M sentences using our German → English system submitted to WMT18, with monolingual sentences randomly sampled from News Crawl 2017.

- German → French: We have generated 10M synthetic sentences, using the reverse direction baseline system described in Section 3. The monolingual sentences were sampled from News Crawl 2015-2018.

- French → German: We have generated 18M synthetic sentences, using the reverse direction baseline system described in Section 3. The monolingual sentences were sampled from News Crawl 2017.

Prior to selecting sentences, we filtered out from the German News Crawl 2017 all sentences that were written in a language different from German, using the `langid` tool (Lui and Baldwin, 2012). When combining bilingual and synthetic data, the original bilingual data was upsampled in order to achieve a 1:1 ratio.

3 System description

This section describes the configuration and decisions adopted for training our NMT systems. We will first begin by describing the details that are common to all systems, and we will then move on to specific details for each of the considered translation directions.

Our models follow the Transformer architecture (Vaswani et al., 2017), and are configured based on the Transformer Base and Transformer Big settings.

The Transformer Base models are trained with a batch size of 3000 tokens per GPU, whereas the Transformer Big models use a batch size of 2300 tokens per GPU. We store a checkpoint every 10 000 updates, and inference is carried out by averaging the last 8 checkpoints.

We used the Adam optimizer (Kingma and Ba, 2015) with $\beta_1 = 0.9, \beta_2 = 0.98$. The learning rate was updated following an inverse square-root schedule, with an initial learning rate of 0.0005, and 4000 warm-up updates. All models use 0.1 label smoothing (Szegedy et al., 2016) and 0.1 dropout (Srivastava et al., 2014), with the exception of the German ↔ French models, that use 0.3 dropout due to having less training data.

The systems from our WMT18 submission and this year's baseline systems were built using the Sockeye toolkit (Hieber et al., 2017). The rest of the systems were built using the fairseq toolkit (Ott et al., 2019), in order to train using Half Precision and gradient accumulation like in Ott et al. (2018).

3.1 Finetuning

Finetuning (training on a new set of data after system convergence) has been widely used as a method for domain-adaptation in NMT systems (Luong and Manning, 2015; Sennrich et al., 2016a). Due to the different data sources provided in the competition, and possible domain mismatch between training and test data, we have decided to carry out finetuning in order to improve model performance. The goal of adapting our models to the domain of the test data is achieved by using test sets from previous years as in-domain data for finetuning.

To carry out finetuning, we set the learning rate to the value that was being used when training finished, and we reduced the checkpoint interval in order to store a checkpoint every 20 updates. Finetuning continues as long as the performance does not decrease in the appropriate dev set. For the German ↔ English systems, we follow the setup of Schamper et al. (2018), and use test sets from previous years (newstest08-16) as training data for the finetuning step. Since this is the first time the German ↔ French language pair is included in WMT, we do not have available test sets from previous editions, so we resort to using the dev1 set as training data, and stop finetuning when performance drops in dev2 (see Section 4).

4 Experimental evaluation

This section describes the experiments and evaluation carried out for each of the language directions, with special emphasis placed in the German ↔ English systems.

For the German ↔ English systems, we have used newstest2017 as dev set, and newstest2018 as test set. Additionally, we report results on this year's test set, newstest 2019. For the German ↔ French systems, we splitted in half the supplied euelections dev set into two sets, dev 1 and dev 2, and used the former as dev set and the latter as test set. We also report the results obtained in the official test set newstest2019. We report BLEU scores (Papineni et al., 2002) computed using SacreBLEU (Post, 2018).

4.1 German → English

Table 1 shows the results obtained by our systems trained for the German → English direction. As baselines, we take our WMT18 system, trained with 1 GPU (this is the configuration that was used for our WMT18 submission), and the same setup trained with 3 GPUs. The increase in effective batch size from 3000 to 9000 tokens results in an improvement of 1.7 BLEU in newstest2018 and 2.0 BLEU in newstest2019 without any other change in hyperparameters.

We began our WMT19 experiments by building a system following the Transformer Big architecture, trained in a 4-GPU machine and using the 20M backtranslations produced for WMT18. This results in an increase of 0.3 BLEU in newstest2018 and 0.6 BLEU in newstest2019. We then applied gradient accumulation by setting the Update Frequency (UF) to 2. Under this setting, the model's weights are updated every two steps (this simulates a batch size equivalent to training on 8 GPUs). This model obtains a significant improvement in the dev (+0.7 BLEU), and test sets (+1.4 BLEU), however the performance decreases by 0.7 BLEU when evaluating on newstest2019. We have found no explanation for this phenomenon. Finetuning on the news in-domain data results improves all previous results, resulting in 47.8 BLEU in newstest2018 and 39.4 BLEU in newstest2019.

For our final submission, we trained a system with noisy backtranslations, following the work of Edunov et al. (2018). We used the previous 20M backtranslations and appended an additional 24M generated with the system in row 2 of Table 1. We

System	GPUs	BLEU	
		newstest2018	newstest2019
WMT18 (Transformer Base)	1	44.2	35.6
WMT18 (Transformer Base)	3	45.9	37.6
Transformer Big, 20M backtrans	4	46.2	38.3
+ UF=2	4	47.6	37.7
+ finetuned	4	47.8	39.4
+ 24M backtrans, noise (non-converged)	4	47.5	39.9
+ finetuned	4	48.0	39.3
+ 24M backtrans, noise (converged)	4	48.0	40.2
+ finetuned	4	47.9	40.1

Table 1: Evaluation results of German $\rightarrow$ English systems

added noise to the source side of the synthetic sentence pairs using the technique described by Lample et al. (2018). Following the setup of Edunov et al. (2018), bilingual data was not upsampled, resulting in a ratio of around 1:3 original to synthetic sentences. The system had not converged at the time of the shared task deadline, so we report results both from our submission, which was generated when the system was still training, as well as the results from the converged system, obtained after the competition ended.

The system trained with noisy backtranslation obtains 47.5 BLEU in newstest2018 and 39.9 BLEU in newstest2019. An additional finetuning step improves the results in newstest2018 by 0.5 BLEU. Due to having obtained the best results in the test set, this was the system we submitted to the competition. However, when evaluating the finetuned version with this year's test set, we find a decrease of 0.6 BLEU. Allowing the system to train for additional epochs leaves us with a final result of 48.0 BLEU and 40.2 BLEU in newstest2018 and newstest2019, and 47.9 and 40.1 BLEU, respectively, after finetuning.

We observe that, in the case of the noisy system, finetuning seems to obtain mixed results, in contrast with other trained systems and language directions (see Sections 4.2, 4.3 and 4.4), where finetuning achieves a performance increase in all cases. We theorize this could be due to the fact that the system was first trained with a ratio that included 3 times as many noisy sentences as clean data, but the finetuning was carried out only with clean data, without any added noise.

4.2 English $\rightarrow$ German

Table 2 shows the results obtained by our systems trained for the English $\rightarrow$ German direction. We began with a baseline system trained using our WMT18 configuration and data, plus an additional 18M backtranslations. This system obtains 45.2 BLEU in newstest2018 and 39.3 BLEU in newstest2019. For our WMT19 submission, we trained a Transformer Big model, using the WMT19 data (including 10M filtered sentences from ParaCrawl), as well as the already mentioned 18M backtranslations. This system was trained with 2 GPUs and an Update Frequency of 2, giving us an effective batch size equivalent to 4 GPUs. This system obtains an improvement of 0.4 BLEU in newstest2018 and 0.1 BLEU in newstest2019 over the baseline. Increasing the number of GPUs from 2 to 4 shows no significant differences in either newstest2018 or newstest2019. Our final submission was generated after applying a finetuning step to the previous configuration. This finetuning resulted in an increase of 2.4 BLEU in newstest2018 and 2.3 BLEU in newstest2019 when compared with the non-finetuned model.

4.3 German $\rightarrow$ French

Table 3 shows the results obtained by our systems trained for the German $\rightarrow$ French direction. Our baseline system is a Transformer Base model trained with all the WMT19 data excluding ParaCrawl. This system obtains 31.3 BLEU in dev2 and 32.1 BLEU in newstest2019. We then moved on to training a Transformer Big model, adding 1M sentences filtered from ParaCrawl, and 10M backtranslations generated with the French $\rightarrow$ German baseline system. This system was trained with 2 GPUs and an Update Frequency

System	GPUs	BLEU	
		newstest2018	newstest2019
WMT18 (Transformer Base), 18M backtrans	3	45.2	39.3
Transformer Big, 18M backtrans, UF=2	2	45.6	39.4
+ GPU=4	4	45.7	39.4
+ finetuned	4	48.1	41.7

Table 2: Evaluation results of English → German systems

System	GPUs	BLEU	
		dev2	nt2019
WMT19 - {ParaCrawl}	1	31.1	32.1
Transformer Big, UF=2	2	33.3	34.4
+ finetuning	2	33.5	34.5

Table 3: Evaluation results of German → French systems

System	GPUs	BLEU	
		dev2	nt2019
WMT19 - {ParaCrawl}	1	22.8	25.7
Transformer Big, UF=2	2	24.9	26.9
+ finetuning	2	25.4	27.5

Table 4: Evaluation results of French → German systems

of 2. This results in an increase of 2.2 BLEU in dev2 and 2.3 BLEU in newstest2019. An additional finetuning step, carried out using the dev1 data, results in an increase of 0.2 BLEU in dev2 and 0.1 BLEU in newstest2019, and constituted our submission to the competition.

4.4 French → German

Table 4 shows the results obtained by our systems trained for the French → German direction. The approach and configurations for this language directions mirror those of the German → French direction (Section 4.3). We began with a baseline Transformer Base model, that obtains 22.8 BLEU in dev2 and 25.7 BLEU in newstest2019. The Transformer Big model obtains an improvement of 2.1 BLEU in dev2 and 1.2 BLEU in newstest2019, and the finetuning step results in an additional increase of 0.5 BLEU in dev2 and 0.6 BLEU in newstest2019.

5 Conclusions

The experiments carried out this year have allowed us to explore one of the missing pieces of our WMT18 submission, which is the interaction between the Transformer architecture and different batch sizes. The results show that the performance of models following the Transformer architecture is highly dependent on the batch size used to train the model, requiring multiple GPUs or gradient accumulation in order to fully take advantage of this architecture. This result is consistent with other works such as Popel and Bojar (2018).

As future work, we would like to look further into using massive amounts of synthetic data jointly with noise, as our experiments this year have not provided conclusive results. Overall, the finetuning steps loos like an effective way of obtaining translation improvements, at the expense of only a small amount of computation. This domain adaptation step can be carried out as long as we have some amount of in-domain data available. More work needs to be carried out to explore the interaction between finetuning and adding noise to the data. Another avenue for improvement is to look into the optimal amount of filtered data to extract from ParaCrawl, as well as the upsampling ratio to mix bilingual and synthetic data. These aspects were not explored in our WMT19 submission due to time constraints.

Acknowledgments

The research leading to these results has received funding from the European Union's Horizon 2020 research and innovation programme under grant agreement no. 761758 (X5gon); the Government of Spain's research project Multisub, ref. RTI2018-094879-B-I00 (MCIU/AEI/FEDER, EU); and the Universitat Politècnica de València's PAID-01-17 R&D support programme.

References

Ondrej Bojar, Christian Federmann, Mark Fishel, Yvette Graham, Barry Haddow, Philipp Koehn, and Christof Monz. 2018. Findings of the 2018 conference on machine translation (WMT18). In *Proceedings of the Third Conference on Machine Translation: Shared Task Papers, WMT 2018, Belgium, Brussels, October 31 - November 1, 2018*, pages 272–303.

Sergey Edunov, Myle Ott, Michael Auli, and David Grangier. 2018. Understanding back-translation at scale. In *Proceedings of the 2018 Conference on Empirical Methods in Natural Language Processing, Brussels, Belgium, October 31 - November 4, 2018*, pages 489–500.

Felix Hieber, Tobias Domhan, Michael Denkowski, David Vilar, Artem Sokolov, Ann Clifton, and Matt Post. 2017. Sockeye: A Toolkit for Neural Machine Translation. *arXiv preprint arXiv:1712.05690*.

Javier Iranzo-Sánchez, Pau Baquero-Arnal, Gonçal V. Garcés Díaz-Munío, Adria A. Martinez-Villaronga, Jorge Civera, and Alfons Juan. 2018. The MLLP-UPV german-english machine translation system for WMT18. In *Proceedings of the Third Conference on Machine Translation: Shared Task Papers, WMT 2018, Belgium, Brussels, October 31 - November 1, 2018*, pages 418–424.

Marcin Junczys-Dowmunt. 2018. Dual conditional cross-entropy filtering of noisy parallel corpora. In *Proceedings of the Third Conference on Machine Translation: Shared Task Papers, WMT 2018, Belgium, Brussels, October 31 - November 1, 2018*, pages 888–895.

Diederik P. Kingma and Jimmy Ba. 2015. Adam: A Method for Stochastic Optimization. In *Proceedings of the 3rd International Conference for Learning Representations*, San Diego, California, USA.

Philipp Koehn, Hieu Hoang, Alexandra Birch, Chris Callison-Burch, Marcello Federico, Nicola Bertoldi, Brooke Cowan, Wade Shen, Christine Moran, Richard Zens, Chris Dyer, Ondrej Bojar, Alexandra Constantin, and Evan Herbst. 2007. Moses: Open source toolkit for statistical machine translation. In *ACL 2007, Proceedings of the 45th Annual Meeting of the Association for Computational Linguistics, June 23-30, 2007, Prague, Czech Republic*.

Philipp Koehn, Huda Khayrallah, Kenneth Heafield, and Mikel L. Forcada. 2018. Findings of the WMT 2018 shared task on parallel corpus filtering. In *Proceedings of the Third Conference on Machine Translation: Shared Task Papers, WMT 2018, Belgium, Brussels, October 31 - November 1, 2018*, pages 726–739.

Guillaume Lample, Alexis Conneau, Ludovic Denoyer, and Marc'Aurelio Ranzato. 2018. Unsupervised machine translation using monolingual corpora only. In *6th International Conference on Learning Representations, ICLR 2018, Vancouver, BC, Canada, April 30 - May 3, 2018, Conference Track Proceedings*.

Marco Lui and Timothy Baldwin. 2012. langid.py: An off-the-shelf language identification tool. In *The 50th Annual Meeting of the Association for Computational Linguistics, Proceedings of the System Demonstrations, July 10, 2012, Jeju Island, Korea*, pages 25–30.

Minh-Thang Luong and Christopher D. Manning. 2015. Stanford neural machine translation systems for spoken language domain. In *International Workshop on Spoken Language Translation*.

Myle Ott, Sergey Edunov, Alexei Baevski, Angela Fan, Sam Gross, Nathan Ng, David Grangier, and Michael Auli. 2019. fairseq: A fast, extensible toolkit for sequence modeling. *arXiv preprint arXiv:1904.01038*.

Myle Ott, Sergey Edunov, David Grangier, and Michael Auli. 2018. Scaling neural machine translation. In *Proceedings of the Third Conference on Machine Translation: Research Papers, WMT 2018, Belgium, Brussels, October 31 - November 1, 2018*, pages 1–9.

Kishore Papineni, Salim Roukos, Todd Ward, and Wei-Jing Zhu. 2002. Bleu: a method for automatic evaluation of machine translation. In *Proceedings of the 40th Annual Meeting of the Association for Computational Linguistics, July 6-12, 2002, Philadelphia, PA, USA.*, pages 311–318.

Martin Popel and Ondřej Bojar. 2018. Training tips for the transformer model. *The Prague Bulletin of Mathematical Linguistics*, 110(1):43–70.

Matt Post. 2018. A call for clarity in reporting BLEU scores. In *Proceedings of the Third Conference on Machine Translation: Research Papers*, pages 186–191. Association for Computational Linguistics.

Julian Schamper, Jan Rosendahl, Parnia Bahar, Yunsu Kim, Arne Nix, and Hermann Ney. 2018. The RWTH aachen university supervised machine translation systems for WMT 2018. In *Proceedings of the Third Conference on Machine Translation: Shared Task Papers, WMT 2018, Belgium, Brussels, October 31 - November 1, 2018*, pages 496–503.

Rico Sennrich, Barry Haddow, and Alexandra Birch. 2016a. Improving neural machine translation models with monolingual data. In *Proceedings of the 54th Annual Meeting of the Association for Computational Linguistics, ACL 2016, August 7-12, 2016, Berlin, Germany, Volume 1: Long Papers*.

Rico Sennrich, Barry Haddow, and Alexandra Birch. 2016b. Neural machine translation of rare words with subword units. In *Proceedings of the 54th Annual Meeting of the Association for Computational Linguistics, ACL 2016, August 7-12, 2016, Berlin, Germany, Volume 1: Long Papers*.

Nitish Srivastava, Geoffrey E. Hinton, Alex Krizhevsky, Ilya Sutskever, and Ruslan Salakhutdinov. 2014. Dropout: a simple way to prevent neural networks from overfitting. *Journal of Machine Learning Research*, 15(1):1929–1958.

Christian Szegedy, Vincent Vanhoucke, Sergey Ioffe, Jonathon Shlens, and Zbigniew Wojna. 2016. Rethinking the inception architecture for computer vision. In *2016 IEEE Conference on Computer Vision and Pattern Recognition, CVPR 2016, Las Vegas, NV, USA, June 27-30, 2016*, pages 2818–2826.

Ashish Vaswani, Noam Shazeer, Niki Parmar, Jakob Uszkoreit, Llion Jones, Aidan N. Gomez, Lukasz Kaiser, and Illia Polosukhin. 2017. Attention is all you need. In *Advances in Neural Information Processing Systems 30: Annual Conference on Neural Information Processing Systems 2017, 4-9 December 2017, Long Beach, CA, USA*, pages 6000–6010.

Microsoft Translator at WMT 2019:
Towards Large-Scale Document-Level Neural Machine Translation

Marcin Junczys-Dowmunt
Microsoft
One Microsoft Way
Redmond, WA 98052, USA
`marcinjd@microsoft.com`

Abstract

This paper describes the Microsoft Translator submissions to the WMT19 news translation shared task for English-German. Our main focus is document-level neural machine translation with deep transformer models. We start with strong sentence-level baselines, trained on large-scale data created via data-filtering and noisy back-translation and find that back-translation seems to mainly help with translationese input. We explore fine-tuning techniques, deeper models and different ensembling strategies to counter these effects. Using document boundaries present in the authentic and synthetic parallel data, we create sequences of up to 1000 subword segments and train transformer translation models. We experiment with data augmentation techniques for the smaller authentic data with document-boundaries and for larger authentic data without boundaries. We further explore multi-task training for the incorporation of document-level source language monolingual data via the BERT-objective on the encoder and two-pass decoding for combinations of sentence-level and document-level systems. Based on preliminary human evaluation results, evaluators strongly prefer the document-level systems over our comparable sentence-level system. The document-level systems also seem to score higher than the human references in source-based direct assessment.

1 Introduction

This paper describes the Microsoft Translator submissions to the WMT19 news translation shared task (Bojar et al., 2019) for English-German. Our main focus is document-level neural machine translation with deep transformer models.

We first explore strong sentence-level systems, trained on large-scale data created via data-filtering and noisy back-translation and investigate the interaction of both with the translation direction of the development sets. We find that back-translation seems to mainly help with translationese input. Next, we explore fine-tuning techniques, deeper models and different ensembling strategies to counter these effects. Using document boundaries present in the authentic and synthetic parallel data, we create sequences of up to 1000 subword segments and train transformer translation models. We experiment with data augmentation techniques for the smaller authentic data with document-boundaries and for larger authentic data without boundaries.

We further explore multi-task training for the incorporation of document-level source language monolingual data via the BERT-objective on the encoder, and two-pass decoding for combinations of sentence-level and document-level systems. We find that current transformer models are perfectly capable of translating whole documents with up to 1000 subword segments with improved quality over comparable sentence-level systems. Deeper models seem to benefit more from the added context.

Based on preliminary human evaluation results, evaluators strongly prefer the document-level systems over comparable sentence-level systems. The document-level systems also seem to score higher than the human references in source-based direct assessment.

2 Sentence-Level Baselines

Before moving on to building our document-level systems, we first start with a baseline sentence-level system. We try to combine the strengths of last year's two dominating systems for the English-German news translation task – FAIR's submission with large-scale noisy back-translation (Edunov et al., 2018) and our own, based on dual cross-entropy data-filtering (Junczys-Dowmunt, 2018b,a). For the current WMT19 shared task for

Proceedings of the Fourth Conference on Machine Translation (WMT), Volume 2: Shared Task Papers (Day 1) pages 225–233
Florence, Italy, August 1-2, 2019. ©2019 Association for Computational Linguistics

English-German, evaluation is carried out on a test set where the source side consists of original English content only, the target side is a translation. To inform our system choices, we create a similar dev set out of test2016, test2017 and test2018 by splitting the test sets by original language and concatenating the respective splits, each about 4500 sentences. We report results on both splits of our new dev set as well as on the joint dev set. We further report results on the original test sets for comparison. We use SacreBLEU[1] (Post, 2018) for all reported scores.

It is currently not quite clear to us how to interpret results on the split test sets. One would assume that improvements on the original source language indicate actual translation quality improvements, but here we might be suffering from reference bias towards non-native target content. This might indicate higher adequacy but effectively penalize more fluent output. Conversely, higher results on the split with original target language might indicate higher fluency, but the reduced complexity of the non-native source language might make the translation task easier and result in false confidence in generally better translation quality. It is also unclear at this point if the model is able to tell apart native and non-native input and if possible data separation occurs. In that case the improvements on one side of the split might not be carried over to the other side. We currently assume the following strategy: we try to achieve high scores on the originally-English side without sacrificing too much quality on the originally-German side. We pretend that high scores on the originally-English side indicate adequacy while high scores on the originally-German side indicate fluency. This is a shot in the dark and we hope the results of the shared task will bring more clarity in this regard.

2.1 Model and Training

We use the Marian toolkit (Junczys-Dowmunt et al., 2018) for all our experiments. We train vanilla transformer-big models (Vaswani et al., 2017) when training 6-layer models. For 12-layer models we modify an idea from Radford et al. (2019) and initialize residual layers with Glorot uniform weights (Glorot and Bengio, 2010) multiplied by $1/\sqrt{i}$ where i is the number of the i-th layer from the bottom. Radford et al. (2019) used $1/\sqrt{d}$ where

---

[1]BLEU+case.mixed+lang.en-de+numrefs.1
+smooth.exp+test.wmt18+tok.13a
+version.1.3.0

d is the total depth of the transformer stack. We found that their method helped with perplexity, but hurt BLEU. We did not see detrimental effects for our progressive multiplier. Omitting the multiplier led to problems with convergence for deep models. We use the same SentencePiece vocabulary for all models (Kudo and Richardson, 2018).

For the purpose of the task, we extended the Marian toolkit with fp16 training, BERT-models (Devlin et al., 2018) and multi-task training. Similar to Edunov et al. (2018) we use mixed-precision training with fp16, an optimizer delay of 16 before updating the gradients. We train on 8 Voltas with 16GB each. Training of one model takes between 2 and 4 days on a single machine. In terms of words per second we reach about 180K target words per second for 6-layer sentence-level systems and 120K target labels for 6-layer document-level systems with long sequences.

2.2 Data-Filtering

Table 1 summarizes our experiments with a single transformer model. We also recomputed numbers for a single model from our WMT18 submission, and quoted results from FAIR's submission where available. Our WMT18 model used a combination of data-filtering and about 10M "clean" back-translated sentences. Transformer models are the same. It seems that the data-quality of the English-German training data (in particular of Paracrawl) improved from WMT18 to WMT19 as we are not seeing the strongly detrimental effects of adding unfiltered Paracrawl data to the training data mix anymore. Data-filtering still improves the results, but apparently only on the originally German side. Since there is barely any loss on the originally-English side we hope this shows a general improvement in fluency or a domain-adaptation effect due the language model scores used in filtering.

2.3 Noisy Back-Translation

We mostly reproduce the results from Edunov et al. (2018) and back-translate the entire German News-Crawl data with noisy back-translation. Similar to Edunov et al. (2018)'s best method, we use output sampling as the noising approach. This has been implemented in Marian with the Gumbel softmax trick. We end up with about 550M sentences of back-translated data. We up-sample the original parallel filtered data to match the size of the back-translated data and concatenate. Results on the split test set are interesting, to say the least. It seems we

	Separated by origin			Original test sets		
	en	de	both	2016	2017	2018
WMT18-Microsoft (single model)	41.1	35.5	39.1	38.6	31.3	46.5
WMT18-FAIR (single model)	–	–	–	–	32.7	44.9
6-layers: sentence-level parallel data only	41.8	32.5	38.2	37.7	30.3	46.5
+ filtering based on WMT18	41.7	34.0	39.0	38.3	31.1	46.6
+ large-scale noisy back-translation	38.9	40.4	39.7	38.9	32.8	46.3
+ fine-tuning	42.2	39.2	41.2	40.6	33.6	48.9
12-layers: sentence-level parallel data only	–	–	–	–	–	–
+ (a) filtering based on WMT18	41.6	33.4	38.4	38.2	30.5	45.7
+ (b) large-scale noisy back-translation	38.1	42.5	40.1	39.2	33.5	46.6
+ (c) fine-tuning	42.1	40.4	41.7	41.3	34.2	48.9

Table 1: SacreBLEU results for sentence-level systems on new devset (concatenated test2016, test2017, test2018) split by source language and combined. 6-layers denotes transformer models with 6 blocks, 12-layers with 12 blocks. For comparison, we also provide results on the original test sets although we did not use these numbers to inform our choices. Results have been computed for a single chosen model and may vary with different random initializations, but generally follow this pattern.

are losing a lot of quality on the originally-English side while gaining on the originally-German side. The general improvement on the unsplit WMT test sets hides this effect. In a setting where systems are going to be evaluated on originally-English data this seems unfortunate.

2.4 Fine-Tuning

To counter the quality loss on the originally-English side, we fine-tune on our filtered data only. We keep the same settings as in the first training pass, only substitute data and keep training until BLEU scores on the originally-English dev set stop improving. This seems to be a very successful strategy which restores and even improves quality on the originally-English split and retains most of the quality gains from back-translation on the originally-German half. At this point our single 6-layer model strongly outperforms a single model from our WMT18 submission.

2.5 Deeper Models

We also experiment with deeper models and increase the number of blocks in encoder and decoder to 12. Interestingly, we see mostly gains on the originally-German side. Since there is no loss on the originally-English half, we choose to use the 12-layer models for the following experiments. We did not see further improvements from even deeper models at this point, we tried 18 and 24

blocks, but there might have been problems with hyper-parameters.

2.6 Ensembling

In Table 2 we explore different ensembling strategies to further control for higher quality on the originally-English side without sacrificing too much quality on the other half. We experiment with (a) models that have been trained on filtered parallel data only and (c) models that have been trained with back-translated data and then fine-tuned on parallel filtered data. All models are 12-layer models, have been trained with the same training procedure and only differ in data and random initialization. We did not explore adding (b) models that were trained with back-translated data but without fine-tuning. After submission we found that small gains could be achieved by adding these to the mix as well. Unless stated differently, all models are weighted equally.

Unsurprisingly, adding more homogeneous models to the ensemble improves quality across all indicators in similar degree; gains become smaller when adding more models, but it seems we do not reach saturation with 4 models of the same type. Ensembling heterogeneous models – mixing type (a) and type (c) – results in more interesting behavior. The two-model ensemble (a) + (c) is stronger on the originally-English half than both homogeneous two-model ensembles (2×a) or (2×c) and

	Separated by origin			Original test sets		
	en	de	both	2016	2017	2018
WMT18-Microsoft (ensemble)	42.5	36.2	40.1	39.6	31.9	48.3
WMT18-FAIR (ensemble)	–	–	–	–	33.4	46.5
(a)	41.6	33.4	38.4	38.2	30.5	45.7
(2×a)	42.0	34.3	39.0	38.8	31.0	46.5
(4×a)	42.5	34.5	39.4	39.1	31.2	47.2
(c)	42.1	40.4	41.7	41.3	34.2	48.9
(2×c)	42.7	41.6	42.6	42.0	34.9	50.1
(4×c)	43.2	41.3	42.8	42.2	34.8	50.5
(a) + (c)	43.2	38.6	41.7	41.6	33.4	49.6
(2×a) + (2×c)	43.8	39.0	42.1	41.9	33.9	49.9
(4×a) + (4×c)	44.0	38.5	42.0	41.8	33.5	49.9
0.3 · (a) + 1.0 · (c)	42.6	40.6	42.2	41.7	34.3	49.6
0.3 · (2×a) + 1.0 · (2×c)	43.5	40.6	42.7	42.3	34.6	50.3
0.3 · (4×a) + 1.0 · (4×c) (submitted)	**43.8**	**40.3**	**42.7**	**42.4**	**34.4**	**50.4**

Table 2: SacreBLEU results for various ensembles of 12-layer sentence-level systems on new dev set (concatenated test2016, test2017, test2018) split by source language and combined. Ensembles are weighted equally when no weights are shown. (a) refers to a single model trained on filtered parallel data only, (c) refers to a models trained with back-translated data, fine-tuned on filtered parallel data.

loses quality on the originally-German part. The same is true when we compare heterogeneous four-model ensembles to their homogeneous counter-parts. Adding all eight models to a single ensemble (4×a) + (4×c) results in the strongest numbers on the originally-English side, but the loss on the other half remains. We try to mitigate this effect by weighting the model components by type.

We find that down-weighting type (a) models trained only with parallel data allows us to regain part of the quality on the originally-German dev set with acceptable losses on the originally-English side. We empirically choose a weight of 0.3 for type (a) models, using a weight of 1 for type (c) models. In hindsight, an ensemble of 8 models of type (c) might have been the better choice, however, we did not train that many models of type (c). Our final sentence-level model is the 0.3 · (4×a) + 1.0 · (4×c) ensemble; we submit this model as our pure sentence-level model.

3 Document-Level Systems

Our work is inspired rather by recent results on long-sequence language modelling than by previous document-level machine translation approaches. However, Tiedemann and Scherrer (2017) needs to be emphasized as an important precursor to this paper. They explore the influence of a limited number of context sentences by simply concatenating up to two sentences in source or target. We drop the limits and consume full documents if their total length stays below 1000 subword units. These sequences can easily consist of 20 or more sentences.

Recent work by Devlin et al. (2018) and Radford et al. (2019) have shown significant impact by training deeper models on large data sets with long-sequence context. In terms of architecture, the language modeling work relies on standard transformer architectures with small variations, this is true for BERT as well as for GPT-2. Document-level context is mostly handled by increasing training-sequence length, increasing model depth and adding sentence-embeddings. BERT also adds a cost-criterion that classifies if sentences belong to the same document or are random concatenations. We adopt the long-sequence training and increased model-depth in our experiments. For co-training of the encoder we also use the BERT masked-LM training criterion in a multi-task learning setting. We do not use sentence embeddings (this remains to be explored in the future).

```
<BEG> Toys R Us Plans to Hire Fewer Holiday Season Workers<SEP> Toys R Us says it
won't hire as many holiday season employees as it did last year, but the toy and
baby products retailer says it will give current employees and seasonal workers a
chance to work more hours.<SEP> The company said it plans to hire 40,000 people to
work at stores and distribution centers around the country, down from the 45,000
hired for the 2014 holiday season.<SEP> Most of the jobs will be part-time.<SEP> The
company said it will start interviewing applicants this month, with staff levels
rising from October through December.<SEP> While the holidays themselves are months
away, holiday shopping season is drawing closer and companies are preparing to hire
temporary employees to help them staff stores and sell, ship and deliver
products.<SEP><END>
```

Figure 1: Example document from validation set with mark-up.

3.1 Data and Data Preparation

Previous work on document-level MT was also limited by the availability of document-level parallel data. This year, for a subset (Europarl, Rapid, News-Commentary) of the parallel data document boundaries have been restored, the rest is provided without boundaries. The available monolingual news crawl data contains document boundaries for all its content, both in German and English. All three types of data are assembled into real and fake documents with varying degrees of data augmentation.

3.1.1 Document-level Mark-up

We use given document boundaries to concatenate parallel sentences into document-level sequences; parallel documents consist of the same number of sentences on both sides. We want to ensure that the models produce as many output sentences per document as input sentences were provided when we simply break on predicted separators to revert back to the sentence-level for evaluation. As a fail-safe mechanism, we sentence-align the sentence-broken document-level output with a sentence-level translation. The sentence-level translation serves as a template in which we replace all 1-1-aligned sentences with their document-level counterparts. This mechanism proved useful for early or intermediate models. For all our submissions, the document-level systems would correctly predict sentence boundaries and the fail-safe could be skipped. This by itself is noteworthy.

Figure 1 contains an example document from the validation set with added mark-up. We add symbols for document start (<BEG>) and end (<END>) and for sentence separators (<SEP>). In cases where documents exceed our length limit of 1000 sub-word tokens, we use a break symbol (<BRK>) instead of <END> and start the next sequence with a continuation symbol (<CNT>) instead of <BEG>. When breaking parallel documents due to the length restriction, we break consistently across languages. All training and validation data is marked up in the same way.

3.1.2 Parallel Data with Boundaries

In the case of original parallel data with document boundaries, we use all available content without data filtering. This set of original documents is quite small (about 200K documents) compared to the back-translated data, so we increase the size of the corpus by adding randomly chosen continuous parallel sub-documents to the original data set, but not more than 10 possible sub-document per full document. Allowing all possible sub-documents would heavily skew the distribution towards longer documents. We repeat the process until the size of the corpus matches about half the size of the back-translated data. Every repetition is created with different random sub-documents.

3.1.3 Parallel Data without Boundaries

The majority of authentic parallel data does not come with documents boundaries. Here, we shuffle the filtered parallel sentences and randomly add document boundaries. This results in fake documents that consist of unrelated but parallel sentences with consistent sentence boundaries inside the documents. Again, we repeat the process with random shuffles resulting in new fake documents until we reach a size close to half of the back-translated data.

3.1.4 Back-translated Documents

We back-translated the entire available news crawl data for our sentence-level system and can use the present boundaries to assemble parallel documents. Due to the large amount of monolingual data, we do not use any document-level data-augmentation besides back-translation.

	Separated by origin			Original test sets		
	en	de	both	2016	2017	2018
12-layers: Document-level	–	–	–	–	–	–
+ filtering based on WMT18	–	–	–	–	–	–
+ large-scale noisy back-translation	39.3	42.0	40.8	40.0	34.2	47.0
+ fine-tuning	41.4	41.7	41.8	*	34.5	48.6
12-layers: Document-level with BERT	–	–	–	–	–	–
+ (A) filtering based on WMT18	42.6	32.5	38.3	*	*	*
+ (B) large-scale noisy back-translation	40.3	40.7	40.8	39.8	33.7	47.3
+ (C) fine-tuning	42.7	39.2	41.5	41.3	34.2	48.4

Table 3: SacreBLEU results for document-level systems on new devset. Missing numbers marked as * were not computed during our experiments.

3.1.5 Monolingual English Documents

The English monolingual news-crawl also contains document boundaries. We simply assemble our long sequences from this data for our multi-task training.

3.2 Experiments

We train our document-level models with similar hyper-parameters as our sentence-level models, increasing the maximum allowed training sequence length to 1024.

3.2.1 Baseline Document-level Models

We compiled our results for the training of single document-level models in Table 3. The BLEU scores follow largely the results for the sentence-level systems, including improved scores for deeper models. Document-level models with capital letters (A), (B), (C) have been trained on similar data sets as sentence-level systems (a), (b), (c) respectively. Both (C) and (c) have undergone similar fine-tuning procedures. It is interesting to see that decoding very long sequences of up to 1000 tokens does not seem to degrade translation performance compared to sentence-level systems.

3.2.2 Multi-Task Training with BERT

We also experiment with multi-task training in the hope of improving the quality of our encoder. We are training on large amounts of back-translated data and much smaller parallel data that has been augmented to match the size of the back-translated data. It is unclear how much content in the authentic data is actual native English. Hence we add a BERT-style encoder over monolingual English source documents that is being trained in parallel to the sequence-to-sequence transformer model on separately fed parallel data. The BERT-style encoder is trained with the masked LM cost criterion from Devlin et al. (2018) and a masking factor of 20%. This encoder shares all parameters and structure with the encoder of the translation model. BERT masked LM cost is simply added to the cross-entropy cost of the translation model. During translation, the BERT encoder is not being constructed, the output layer of the masked LM is dropped. During fine-tuning, the BERT encoder is also being trained, but on the parallel source data, not on a separate monolingual data stream.

In Table 3, when training with large-scale back-translated documents, we seem to observe a shift towards higher quality on the originally-English side when comparing to training without the BERT criterion. This persists during fine-tuning, but it is generally unclear if this is an actual improvement. Based on our strategy of preferring improvements on the originally-English side, we use the multi-task trained models from now on.

3.2.3 Second-Pass Decoding

We also briefly experiment with second-pass decoding for the purpose of "up-casting" sentence-level translations to document-level translations. The initial idea was to have the potentially higher adequacy of sentence-level translations (due to more easily aligned sentence-boundaries) and then smooth it out with document-level knowledge. This would also allow to ensemble the sentence-level system output via the second pass with other document-level systems. In hindsight, for ensembling purposes, it might have been better to train a copy model that provides a document-level prob-

	Separated by origin			Original test sets		
	en	de	both	2016	2017	2018
1st-sent-level: (c)	42.1	40.4	41.7	41.3	34.2	48.9
2nd-doc-level: (P_A)	42.5	*	*	39.8	32.5	47.3
2nd-doc-level: (P_C)	42.2	*	*	41.5	33.8	48.6
1st-sent-level: $0.3 \cdot (4 \times a) + 1.0 \cdot (4 \times c)$	43.8	40.3	42.7	42.4	34.4	50.4
2nd-doc-level: (P_A)	43.4	36.9	40.9	40.5	32.5	47.8
2nd-doc-level: (P_C)	42.6	40.1	41.7	41.5	33.8	48.7

Table 4: SacreBLEU results for second-pass decoding of single fine-tuned sentence-level model (c) and best sentence-level ensemble. We pass both sentence level models through two second pass models. Missing numbers marked as * were not computed during our experiments.

	Separated by origin			Original test sets		
	en	de	both	2016	2017	2018
WMT18-Microsoft (ensemble, submission)	42.5	36.2	40.1	39.6	31.9	48.3
WMT18-FAIR (ensemble, submission)	–	–	–	–	33.4	46.5
(C)	42.7	39.2	41.5	41.3	34.2	48.4
(4×C) (submitted)	**44.0**	**40.1**	**42.5**	**42.2**	**34.5**	**50.2**
(2×A) + (4×C)	44.8	38.0	42.1	41.6	33.7	49.3
(2×A) + (4×C) + (P_A) + (P_C) (submitted)	**45.2**	**38.8**	**42.6**	**42.5**	**34.1**	**50.3**

Table 5: SacreBLEU results various for ensembles of 12-layer document-level systems on new devset

ability distribution for unmodified concatenated sentence-level input.

We forward-translated most of our training corpus with sampling (future work should examine the effects of this) to produce the first-pass output and next we trained a dual-encoder document-level transformer model following exactly Junczys-Dowmunt and Grundkiewicz (2018) as an automatic post-editing system. The three inputs being original source data and first-pass translation on the source and original target data. We train a second-pass system on original parallel data only (P_A) and on all data (P_C).

In Table 4, we apply the second pass models separately to a single fine-tuned sentence-level model (c) and to our best sentence-level ensemble. In both cases we see degradation in the second pass in terms of BLEU, but the second-pass seems to follow the improved quality of the sentence-level inputs. The two second-pass models over the strong sentence-level ensemble are actually among the better single document-level models we have trained (ignoring at this point that these are a different kind of ensemble or system combination).

3.3 Stacking and Ensembling

Following our ensembling efforts for sentence-level models, we also combine the diverse document-level models into larger ensembles. We see that a pure document-level system with four fine-tuned 12-layer models seems to be a promising candidate. We can further increase the quality on the originally-English side (while losing comparable quality on the originally-German half) by ensembling all eight models trained on diverse data sources. The last ensemble can be thought of as a hybrid sentence/document-level system as it includes two second-pass models.

4 Submissions

We submitted four systems in total, our original system from WMT18 applied to the new WMT19 test set, our best sentence-level ensemble, our best document-level ensemble (without second-pass decoding) and our best hybrid system, the document-level system ensemble that includes second-pass decoding systems. Cased BLEU scores from the WMT-matrix page are listed in Table 6. Our

System	en	de	2019
WMT18-Microsoft	42.5	36.2	41.9
Pure sentence-level	43.8	40.3	43.0
Pure document-level	44.0	40.1	43.9
Hybrid document-level	45.2	38.8	43.9

Table 6: Results from the WMT-Matrix on test 2019 for our submitted systems. We also include BLEU scores for our split dev set for comparison.

Ave.	Ave. z	System
90.3	0.347	Facebook-FAIR
93.0	**0.311**	**Microsoft-WMT19-sent-doc**
92.6	**0.296**	**Microsoft-WMT19-doc-level**
90.3	0.240	HUMAN
87.6	0.214	MSRA-MADL
		. . .
84.2	0.094	online-B
86.6	**0.094**	**Microsoft-WMT19-sent-level**
87.3	0.081	JHU
		. . .
82.4	0.132	TartuNLP-c
76.3	0.400	online-X
43.3	1.769	en-de-task

Table 7: Preliminary human evaluation results shared by the organizers. Our system submissions are marked with bold font. There was a total of 23 submissions, we selected highest and lowest scoring systems in each cluster and systems surrounding our own submissions.

document-level systems score second behind the highest submission of MSRA in terms of BLEU.

Table 7 contains preliminary human evaluation results shared by the organizers, see Bojar et al. (2019) for a full version and discussion. Our document systems are two out of three submissions that seem to outperform the human references in terms of quality (although non-significantly in the case of our systems when based on normalized z-scores). What is very encouraging is the large performance gain of the document-level systems over the sentence-level system which was not obvious when looking at BLEU scores. Since these systems are very comparable in terms of raw data, model size and training setting, the strong improvements seem to stem from the large context. However, more work and rigorous ablation testing is required to confirm this conclusion.

Finally, we would like to cast a bit of doubt at the (preliminary) ranking in Table 7. The large discrepancy between average raw scores and normalized z-scores for the top three systems seems disconcerting. At Microsoft, we base our deployment decisions on raw scores as z-scores proved unreliable. In our experience, a change of 3 percent points in terms of raw scores would usually indicate paradigm-shifts and drastically improved systems, especially at quality levels beyond 90%. We are curious to see the final ranking and comments by the organizers addressing this issue.

References

Ondřej Bojar, Christian Federmann, Mark Fishel, Yvette Graham, Barry Haddow, Matthias Huck, Philipp Koehn, Christof Monz, Mathias Müller, and Matt Post. 2019. Findings of the 2019 Conference on Machine Translation (WMT19). In *Proceedings of the Fourth Conference on Machine Translation, Volume 2: Shared Task Papers*, Florence, Italy. Association for Computational Linguistics.

Jacob Devlin, Ming-Wei Chang, Kenton Lee, and Kristina Toutanova. 2018. BERT: pre-training of deep bidirectional transformers for language understanding. *CoRR*, abs/1810.04805.

Sergey Edunov, Myle Ott, Michael Auli, and David Grangier. 2018. Understanding back-translation at scale. In *Proceedings of the 2018 Conference on Empirical Methods in Natural Language Processing*, pages 489–500, Brussels, Belgium. Association for Computational Linguistics.

Xavier Glorot and Yoshua Bengio. 2010. Understanding the difficulty of training deep feedforward neural networks. In *JMLR W&CP: Proceedings of the Thirteenth International Conference on Artificial Intelligence and Statistics (AISTATS 2010)*, volume 9, pages 249–256.

Marcin Junczys-Dowmunt. 2018a. Dual conditional cross-entropy filtering of noisy parallel corpora. In *Proceedings of the Third Conference on Machine Translation: Shared Task Papers*, pages 888–895, Belgium, Brussels. Association for Computational Linguistics.

Marcin Junczys-Dowmunt. 2018b. Microsoft's submission to the WMT2018 news translation task: How I learned to stop worrying and love the data. In *Proceedings of the Third Conference on Machine Translation: Shared Task Papers*, pages 425–430, Belgium, Brussels. Association for Computational Linguistics.

Marcin Junczys-Dowmunt and Roman Grundkiewicz. 2018. MS-UEdin submission to the WMT2018 APE shared task: Dual-source transformer for automatic post-editing. In *Proceedings of the Third Conference on Machine Translation: Shared Task Papers*, pages 822–826, Belgium, Brussels. Association for Computational Linguistics.

Marcin Junczys-Dowmunt, Roman Grundkiewicz, Tomasz Dwojak, Hieu Hoang, Kenneth Heafield, Tom Neckermann, Frank Seide, Ulrich Germann, Alham Fikri Aji, Nikolay Bogoychev, André F. T. Martins, and Alexandra Birch. 2018. Marian: Fast neural machine translation in C++. In *Proceedings of ACL 2018, System Demonstrations*, pages 116–121, Melbourne, Australia. Association for Computational Linguistics.

Taku Kudo and John Richardson. 2018. SentencePiece: A simple and language independent subword tokenizer and detokenizer for neural text processing. In *Proceedings of the 2018 Conference on Empirical Methods in Natural Language Processing: System Demonstrations*, pages 66–71, Brussels, Belgium. Association for Computational Linguistics.

Matt Post. 2018. A call for clarity in reporting BLEU scores. In *Proceedings of the Third Conference on Machine Translation: Research Papers*, pages 186–191, Belgium, Brussels. Association for Computational Linguistics.

Alec Radford, Jeff Wu, Rewon Child, David Luan, Dario Amodei, and Ilya Sutskever. 2019. Language models are unsupervised multitask learners.

Jörg Tiedemann and Yves Scherrer. 2017. Neural machine translation with extended context. In *Proceedings of the Third Workshop on Discourse in Machine Translation*, pages 82–92, Copenhagen, Denmark. Association for Computational Linguistics.

Ashish Vaswani, Noam Shazeer, Niki Parmar, Jakob Uszkoreit, Llion Jones, Aidan N Gomez, Ł ukasz Kaiser, and Illia Polosukhin. 2017. Attention is all you need. In I. Guyon, U. V. Luxburg, S. Bengio, H. Wallach, R. Fergus, S. Vishwanathan, and R. Garnett, editors, *Advances in Neural Information Processing Systems 30*, pages 5998–6008. Curran Associates, Inc.

CUNI Submission for Low-Resource Languages in WMT News 2019

Tom Kocmi   **Ondřej Bojar**

Charles University, Faculty of Mathematics and Physics
Institute of Formal and Applied Linguistics
Malostranské náměstí 25, 118 00 Prague, Czech Republic
`<surname>@ufal.mff.cuni.cz`

Abstract

This paper describes the CUNI submission to the WMT 2019 News Translation Shared Task for the low-resource languages: Gujarati-English and Kazakh-English. We participated in both language pairs in both translation directions. Our system combines transfer learning from different high-resource language pair followed by training on backtranslated monolingual data. Thanks to the simultaneous training in both directions, we can iterate the backtranslation process. We are using the Transformer model in a constrained submission.

1 Introduction

Recently, the rapid development of Neural Machine Translations (NMT) systems led to the claims, that human parity has been reached (Hassan et al., 2018) on a high-resource language pair Chinese-English. However, NMT systems tend to be very data hungry as Koehn and Knowles (2017) showed the NMT lacks behind phrase based approaches in the low-resource scenarios. This lead to the rise of attention in the low-resource NMT in recent years, where the goal is to improve the performance of a language pair that have only a limited available parallel data.

In this paper, we describe our approach to low-resource NMT. We use standard Transformer-big model (Vaswani et al., 2017) and apply two techniques to improve the performance on the low-resource language, namely transfer learning (Kocmi and Bojar, 2018) and iterative backtranslation (Hoang et al., 2018).

A model trained solely on the authentic parallel data of the low-resource NMT model has poor performance, thus using it directly for the backtranslation of monolingual data lead to poor translation. Hence the transfer learning is as a great tool to first improve the performance of the NMT system later used for backtranslating the monolingual data.

The structure of this paper is organized as follows. First, we describe the transfer learning and backtranslation, followed by a description of used datasets and the NMT model architecture. Next, we present our experiments, final submissions, and followup analysis of synthetic training data usage. The paper is concluded in Section 5.

2 Background

In this chapter, we first describe the technique of transfer learning and iterative backtranslation, followed by our training procedure that combines both approaches.

2.1 Transfer learning

Kocmi and Bojar (2018) presented a trivial method of transfer learning that uses a high-resource language pair to train the parent model. After the convergence, the parent training data are replaced with the training data of the low-resource language pair, and the training continues as if the replacement would not happen. The training continues without changing any parameters nor resetting moments or learning rate.

This technique of fine-tuning the model parameters is often used in a domain adaptation scenario on the same language pair. However, when using for different language pairs, there emerges a problem with vocabulary mismatch. Kocmi and Bojar (2018) overcome this problem by preparing the shared vocabulary for all languages in both language pairs in advance. Their approach is to prepare mixed vocabulary from training corpora of both languages and generate wordpiece vocabulary (Vaswani et al., 2017) from it.

We use the *balanced vocabulary* approach, that combines an equal amount of parallel data from both training corpora, low-resource as well as the same amount from high-resource language pair. Hence the low-resource language subwords are

Proceedings of the Fourth Conference on Machine Translation (WMT), Volume 2: Shared Task Papers (Day 1) pages 234–240
Florence, Italy, August 1-2, 2019. ©2019 Association for Computational Linguistics

Corpora	Language pair	Sentence pairs	Words 1st lang.	Words in English
Commoncrawl	Russian-English	878k	17.4M	18.8M
News Commentary	Russian-English	235k	5.0M	5.4M
UN corpus	Russian-English	11.4M	273.2M	294.4M
Yandex	Russian-English	1000k	18.7M	21.3M
CzEng 1.7	Czech-English	57.4M	546.2M	621.9M
Crawl	Kazakh-English	97.7k	1.0M	1.3M
News commentary	Kazakh-English	9.6k	174.1k	213.2k
Wiki titles	Kazakh-English	112.7k	174.9k	204.5k
Bible	Gujarati-English	7.8k	198.6k	177.1k
Dictionary	Gujarati-English	19.3k	19.3k	28.8k
Govincrawl	Gujarati-English	10.7k	121.2k	150.6k
Software	Gujarati-English	107.6k	691.5k	681.3k
Wiki texts	Gujarati-English	18.0k	317.9k	320.4k
Wiki titles	Gujarati-English	9.2k	16.6k	17.6k

Table 1: The parallel training corpora used to train our models with counts of the total number of sentences as well as the number of words (segmented on space). More details on the individual corpora can be obtained at `http://statmt.org/wmt19/`.

represented in the vocabulary in the roughly same amount as the high-resource language pair.

As Kocmi and Bojar (2018), showed the language pair does not have to be linguistically related, and the most important criteria is the amount of parent parallel data. For this reason, we have selected Czech-English as a parent language pair for Gujarati-English and Russian-English as a parent for the Kazakh-English. The Russian was selected due to the use of Cyrillic and being a high-resource language pair. All language pairs share English. We prepare Gujarati-English and Kazakh-English systems separately from each other.

2.2 Backtranslation

The amount of available monolingual data typically exceeds the amount of available parallel data. The standard technique of using monolingual data in NMT is called backtranslation (Sennrich et al., 2016). It uses a second model trained in the reverse direction to translate monolingual data to the source language of the first model.

Backtranslated data are aligned with their monolingual sentences to create synthetic parallel corpora. The standard practice is to mix the authentic parallel corpora to the synthetic. Although it is not the only approach. (Popel, 2018) proposed a scenario of alternating the training between using only synthetic and only authentic corpora instead of mixing them.

This new corpus is used to train the first model by using backtranslated data as the source and the monolingual as the target side of the model.

Hoang et al. (2018) showed that backtranslation can be iterated and with the second round of backtranslation, we improve the performance of both models. However, the third round of backtranslation does yield better results.

The performance of the backtranslation model is essential. Especially in the low-resource scenario, the baseline models trained only on the authentic parallel data have a poor score (2.0 BLEU for English→Gujarati) generate very low quality backtranslated data. We have improved the baseline with the transfer learning to improve performance and generate the synthetic data of better quality.

2.3 Training procedure

We are training two models in parallel, one for each translation direction. Our training procedure is as follows. We train four parent models on the high-resource language pair until convergence: two models, one for each direction, for both directions. We stop training the models if there was no improvement bigger than 0.1 BLEU in the last 20% of the training time.

At this point, we run a hyperparameter search on the Gujarati→English and update the parameters for all following steps of all language pairs.

Afterward, we apply transfer learning on the authentic dataset of the corresponding low-resource language pair. We preserve the English side, thus Czech→English is a parent to Gujarati→English

Corpora	Lang.	Sent.	Words
News crawl 2018	EN	15.4M	344.3M
Common Crawl	KK	12.5M	189.2M
News commentary	KK	13.0k	218.7k
News crawl	Kk	772.9k	10.3M
Common Crawl	GU	3.7M	67.3M
Newscrawl	GU	244.9k	3.3M
Emille	GU	273.2k	11.4M

Table 2: Statistics of all monolingual data used for the backtranslation. It shows the number of sentences in each corpus and the number of words segmented on space. We mixed together all corpora for each language separately.

and English→Czech to English→Gujarati, likewise for the Russian-Kazakh.

After transfer learning, we select one of the translation directions to translate monolingual data. As a starting system for the backtranslation process, we have selected the English→Gujarati and Kazakh→English. This decision is motivated by choosing the better performing model in Kazakh-English language pair, and since the Gujarati-English have a similar score for both directions, we decided to select a model with English target side in contrast to Kazakh-English.

Following the backtranslation, we create synthetic data by mixing them with authentic parallel data and using to improve the performance of the second system. We continue repeating this process: Use the better system to backtranslate the data, and use this data in order to build an even better system in reverse direction.

We make two rounds of backtranslation for both directions on Gujarati-English and only one round of backtranslation on Kazakh-English due to the time consumption of the NMT translation process.

At last, we take the model with the highest BLEU score on the devset and average it with seven previous checkpoints to create final model.

3 Datasets and Model

In this section, we describe the datasets used to train our final models. All our models were trained only on the data allowed for the WMT 2019 News shared task. Hence our submission is constrained.

All used training data are presented in Table 1. We used all available parallel corpora allowed and accessible by WMT 2019 except for the Czech-English language pair, where we used only the

CzEng 1.7. We have not clean any of the parallel corpora except deduplication and removing pairs with the same source and target translations in Wiki Titles dataset.

We used official WMT testsets from previous years as a development set. The year 2013 for Czech-English and Russian-English. For the Gujarati-English, we used the official 2019 development set. Lastly, for the Kazakh-English, the organizers do not provide any development set. Therefore we separated the first 2000 sentence pairs from the News Commentary training set and used as our development set.

The monolingual data used for the backtranslation are shown in Table 2. We use all available monolingual data for Gujarati and Kazakh. For the English, we did not use all available English monolingual data due to the backtranslation process being time-consuming, therefore we use only the 2018 News Crawl.

The available monolingual corpora are usually of high quality. However, we noticed that the Common Crawl contains many sentences in a different language and also long paragraphs, that are not useful for sentence level translation.

Therefore, we used language identification tool by Lui and Baldwin (2012) on the Common Crawl corpus and dropped all sentences automatically annotated as a different language than Gujarati or Kazakh respectively. Followed by splitting the remaining sentences that are longer than 100 words on all full stops, which led to an increase of sentences.

3.1 Model

The Transformer model seems superior to other NMT approaches as documented by several language pairs in the manual evaluation of WMT18 (Bojar et al., 2018).

We are using version 1.11 of sequence-to-sequence implementation of Transformer called tensor2tensor[1]. We are using the Transformer "big single GPU" configuration as described in (Vaswani et al., 2017), model which translates through an encoder-decoder with each layer involving an attention network followed by a feed-forward network. The architecture is much faster than other NMT due to the absence of recurrent layers.

---

[1] https://github.com/tensorflow/tensor2tensor

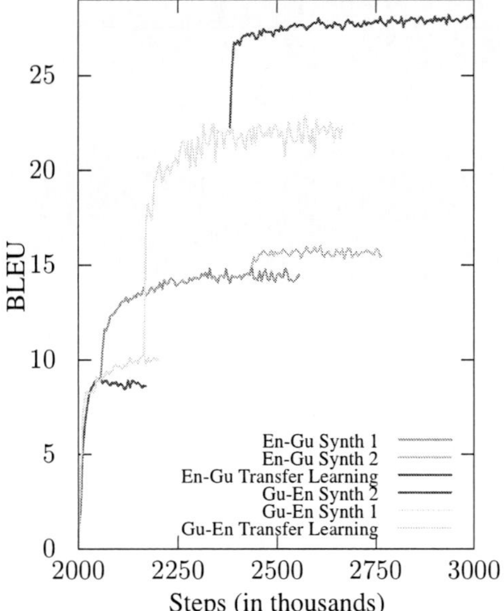

Figure 1: Learning curves for both directions of Gujarati-English models. The BLEU score is uncased and computed on the development set.

Popel and Bojar (2018) documented best practices to improve the performance of the model. Based on their observation, we are using as an optimizer Adafactor with inverse square root decay. Based on our previous experiments (Kocmi et al., 2018) we set the maximum number of subwords in a sentence to 100, which drops less than 0.1 percent of training sentences. However, it allows increasing the maximum size of the batch to 4500 for our GPU. The experiments are trained on a single GPU NVidia GeForce 1080 Ti.

4 Experiments

In this section, we describe our experiments starting with hyperparameter search, our training procedure, and supporting experiments.

All reported results are calculated over the test-set of WMT 2019 and evaluated with case sensitive SacreBLEU (Post, 2018)[2] if not specified otherwise.

4.1 Hyperparameter search

Before the first step of transfer learning, we have done a hyperparameter search on Gujarati→English over the set of parameters that are not fixed from the parent (like dimensions of matrices or structure of layers). We examined the following hyperparameters: learning rate, dropout, layer prepostprocess dropout, label smoothing, and attention dropout.

The performance before hyperparameter search was 9.8 BLEU[3] for Gujarati→English, this score was improved to 11.0 BLEU. Based on the hyperparameter search we set the layer prepostprocess dropout and label smoothing both to 0.2 in the setup of Transformer-big.

These improvements show that transfer learning is not strictly associated with parent setup and that some parameters are possible to change. Although it must be noted, that we experimented only with a small subset of all hyperparameters and it is possible that other parameters could also be changed without damaging the parent model.

In this paper, we are using these parameters for all experiments (except for the parent models). Although applying hyperparameter search on each model separately or even between before each dataset switch is an interesting question, it is over the scope of this paper.

4.2 Problems with backtranslation

The synthetic data have a quality similar with the model by which they were produced. Since the low-resource scenario has an overall low quality, we observed, that the synthetic data contain many relics:

- Repeated sequence of words: The State Department has made no reference in statements, statements, statements, statements ...
- Sentences in Czech or Russian, most probably due to the parent model.
- Source sentences generated untranslated.

To avoid these problems, we cleaned all synthetic data in the following way. We had dropped all sentences, that contained any repetitive sequence of words. Then we checked the sentences by language identification tool (Lui and Baldwin, 2012) and dropped all sentences automatically annotated as a wrong language. The second step also filtered out some remaining gibberish translations.

We have not used beam search during backtranslation of monolingual data in order to speed up the translation process roughly 20 times compared to the beam search of 8.

---

[2]The SacreBLEU signature is BLEU + case.mixed + numrefs.1 + smooth.exp + tok.13a + version.1.2.12.

[3]This score is computed over devset with averaging of 8 latest models distanced one and half hour of training time.

Training dataset	EN→GU	GU→EN	EN→KK	KK→EN
Authentic (baseline)	2.0	1.8	0.5	4.2
Parent dataset	0.7	0.1	0.7	0.6
Authentic (transfer learning)	① 9.1	9.2	6.2	① 14.4
Synth generated by model ①	-	② 14.2	② 8.3	-
Synth generated by model ②	③ 13.4	-	-	17.3
Synth generated by model ③	-	④ 16.2	-	-
Synth generated by model ④	13.7	-	-	-
Averaging + beam 8	14.3	17.4	8.7	18.5

Table 3: Testset BLEU scores of our setup. Except for the baseline, each column shows improvements obtained after fine-tuning a single model on different datasets beginning with the score on a trained parent model.

4.3 Final models

Following the training procedure describe in Section 2.3, we trained the parent models for two million steps. One exception from the described approach is that we used a subset of 2M monolingual English data for the first round of backtranslation by the English→Gujarati model to cut down on the total consumed time.

Figure 1 shows the progress of training Gujarati-English models in both directions. The learning curves start at two millionth step as a visualization of the parent model training. We can notice that after each change of parallel data, there is a substantial increment of the performance. The learning curve is visualized on the development data, exact numbers for the testsets are in Table 3.

The baseline model in Table 3 is trained on the authentic data only, and it seems that the amount of parallel data is not sufficient to train the NMT model for the investigated language pairs. The rest of the rows shows incremental improvements of the models based on an undertaken step. The last step of model averaging takes the best performing model and averages it with the previous seven checkpoints that are distanced on average one and half hour of training time between each other.

We see that the transfer learning can be combined with iterated backtranslation on a low-resource language to obtain an improvement of 12.3 BLEU compared to the baseline in Gujarati→English and 15.6 in English→Gujarati.

For the final submission, we have selected models at following steps: step 2.99M for English→Gujarati, step 3.03M for Gujarati→English, step 2.48M for English→Kazakh and step 2.47M for Kazakh→English

4.4 Ratio of parallel data

Poncelas et al. (2018) showed that the balance between the synthetic and authentic data matters, and there should always be a part of authentic parallel data. We started our experiments with this intuition. However, the low-resource scenario complicates the setup since the amount of authentic data is several times smaller than synthetic. In order to balance the authentic and synthetic parallel data, we duplicated the authentic data several times.

We notice that the performance did not change from the setup that is using only synthetic data. Thus we prepare an experiment, where we do a second round of backtranslation on Gujarati→English with a various ratio of authentic and synthetic parallel data. For this experiment, we duplicated the full authentic parallel corpora of 173k sentences into a subsampled synthetic parallel corpus used in the second round of backtranslation. We have randomly selected 3.6M sentences from the synthetic corpora. The number of sentences is equal to 20x size of synthetic corpora. Therefore, we can present the ratio between authentic and synthetic corpora in percentage. The ratio in the legend of Figure 2 represent the actual ratio in the final corpus and not how much times the corpus has been duplicated. The synthetic is never duplicated, we only duplicate the authentic corpora. For example, the ratio "authentic:synthetic 1:2" means that the authentic has been multiplied ten times because the synthetic is twenty times bigger than the authentic corpora.

In Figure 2, we can see the difference between the amount of synthetic and authentic data. It seems that using only synthetic data generates the best performance, and whenever we increase the authentic part, the performance slowly decreases, contrary to the Poncelas et al. (2018). It could be

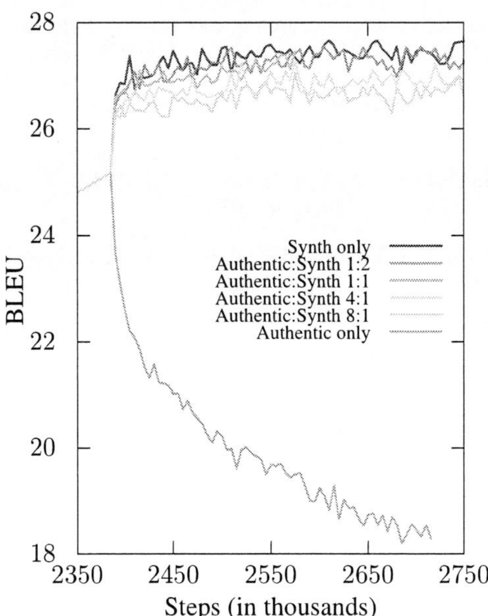

Figure 2: Comparison of different ratio of authentic and synthetic data.

due to the noise in the data, which implies that synthetic data are cleaner and more suitable for training the model.

4.5 Synthetic from Scratch

In the previous section, we have shown that during the iterative backtranslation of low-resource languages, the authentic data hurt the performance. In this section, we use the various ratios of training data and train the model from scratch without transfer learning or other backtranslation. Notably, all the parameters, as well as the wordpiece vocabulary, are the same.

Table 4 present the result of using synthetic data directly without any adaptation. It shows that having more authentic data hurt the low-resource languages. However, the most surprising fact is that training from scratch leads to significantly better model than the model trained by transfer learning and two rounds of the backtranslation by 0.7 (cased) BLEU. Unfortunately, we proposed this experiment after the submission. Therefore our final system has worse performance.

We believe it could be a result of unconscious overfitting to the development set because the performance on the development set is higher for our final model 26.9 BLEU compared to the performance of 25.8 BLEU for the synthetic only train-

Training dataset	cased	uncased
Authentic (baseline)	1.8	2.2
Synthetic only	**16.9**	**18.7**
Auth:Synth 1:1	16.8	18.4
Auth:Synth 2:1	16.3	17.8
Auth:Synth 4:1	15.2	16.8
Final model	16.2	17.9

Table 4: BLEU scores for training English→Gujarati from scratch on synthetic data from the second round of backtranslation. Neither of models uses the averaging or beam search. Thus the final model is our submitted model before averaging and beam search (the model ③). The scores are equal to those from `http://matrix.statmt.org`.

ing. It could have been because we used development set three times during the training of the final model: first to select the best model from the transfer learning, then when selecting the best performing model in the first round of backtranslation and then third times during the second round of backtranslation. On the other hand, training on synthetic data from scratch used the development set only once for selection of the best performing model to evaluate.

Another possible explanation is that the final model is already overspecialized on the data from the first round of backtranslation, that it is not able to adapt to the improved second synthetic data.

5 Conclusion

We participated in four translation directions on a low-resource language pairs in the WMT 2019 News translation Shared Task. We combined transfer learning with the iterated backtranslation and obtained significant improvements.

We showed that mixing authentic data and backtranslated data in a low-resource scenario does not affect the performance of the model: synthetic data is far more critical. This is a different result from what Poncelas et al. (2018) observed on higher-resource language pairs.

Lastly, in some scenarios, it is better to train the model on backtranslated data from scratch instead of fine-tuning the previous model.

In the future work, we want to investigate, why the training from scratch on backtranslated has led to better results. One of the reviewers suggested keep mixing the Czech→English corpus even during later stages of training as an additional source of parallel data, which we would like to compare.

239

Acknowledgments

This study was supported in parts by the grants SVV 260 453 of the Charles University, 18-24210S of the Czech Science Foundation and 825303 (Bergamot) of the European Union. This work has been using language resources and tools stored and distributed by the LINDAT/CLARIN project of the Ministry of Education, Youth and Sports of the Czech Republic (LM2015071).

References

Ondřej Bojar, Christian Federmann, Mark Fishel, Yvette Graham, Barry Haddow, Matthias Huck, Philipp Koehn, and Christof Monz. 2018. Findings of the 2018 conference on machine translation (wmt18). In *Proceedings of the Third Conference on Machine Translation, Volume 2: Shared Task Papers*, pages 272–307, Belgium, Brussels. Association for Computational Linguistics.

Hany Hassan, Anthony Aue, Chang Chen, Vishal Chowdhary, Jonathan Clark, Christian Federmann, Xuedong Huang, Marcin Junczys-Dowmunt, William Lewis, Mu Li, Shujie Liu, Tie-Yan Liu, Renqian Luo, Arul Menezes, Tao Qin, Frank Seide, Xu Tan, Fei Tian, Lijun Wu, Shuangzhi Wu, Yingce Xia, Dongdong Zhang, Zhirui Zhang, and Ming Zhou. 2018. Achieving human parity on automatic chinese to english news translation. *CoRR*, abs/1803.05567.

Vu Cong Duy Hoang, Philipp Koehn, Gholamreza Haffari, and Trevor Cohn. 2018. Iterative back-translation for neural machine translation. In *Proceedings of the 2nd Workshop on Neural Machine Translation and Generation*, pages 18–24.

Tom Kocmi and Ondřej Bojar. 2018. Trivial Transfer Learning for Low-Resource Neural Machine Translation. In *Proceedings of the 3rd Conference on Machine Translation (WMT): Research Papers*, Brussels, Belgium.

Tom Kocmi, Roman Sudarikov, and Ondřej Bojar. 2018. Cuni submissions in wmt18. In *Proceedings of the Third Conference on Machine Translation, Volume 2: Shared Task Papers*, pages 435–441, Belgium, Brussels. Association for Computational Linguistics.

Philipp Koehn and Rebecca Knowles. 2017. Six challenges for neural machine translation. In *Proceedings of the First Workshop on Neural Machine Translation*, pages 28–39, Vancouver. Association for Computational Linguistics.

Marco Lui and Timothy Baldwin. 2012. langid.py: An off-the-shelf language identification tool. In *Proceedings of the ACL 2012 System Demonstrations*, pages 25–30, Jeju Island, Korea. Association for Computational Linguistics.

Alberto Poncelas, Dimitar Shterionov, Andy Way, Gideon Maillette de Buy Wenniger, and Peyman Passban. 2018. Investigating backtranslation in neural machine translation. *arXiv preprint arXiv:1804.06189*.

Martin Popel. 2018. Machine translation using syntactic analysis. *Univerzita Karlova*.

Martin Popel and Ondej Bojar. 2018. Training Tips for the Transformer Model. *The Prague Bulletin of Mathematical Linguistics*, 110(1):43–70.

Matt Post. 2018. A Call for Clarity in Reporting BLEU Scores. *arXiv preprint arXiv:1804.08771*.

Rico Sennrich, Barry Haddow, and Alexandra Birch. 2016. Improving neural machine translation models with monolingual data. In *Proceedings of the 54th Annual Meeting of the Association for Computational Linguistics (Volume 1: Long Papers)*, pages 86–96, Berlin, Germany. Association for Computational Linguistics.

Ashish Vaswani, Noam Shazeer, Niki Parmar, Jakob Uszkoreit, Llion Jones, Aidan N Gomez, Łukasz Kaiser, and Illia Polosukhin. 2017. Attention is all you need. In I. Guyon, U. V. Luxburg, S. Bengio, H. Wallach, R. Fergus, S. Vishwanathan, and R. Garnett, editors, *Advances in Neural Information Processing Systems 30*, pages 6000–6010. Curran Associates, Inc.

CUNI Systems for the Unsupervised News Translation Task in WMT 2019

Ivana Kvapilíková   Dominik Macháček   Ondřej Bojar

Charles University, Faculty of Mathematics and Physics
Institute of Formal and Applied Linguistics
Malostranské náměstí 25, 118 00 Prague, Czech Republic
<surname>@ufal.mff.cuni.cz

Abstract

In this paper we describe the CUNI translation system used for the unsupervised news shared task of the ACL 2019 Fourth Conference on Machine Translation (WMT19). We follow the strategy of Artetxe et al. (2018b), creating a seed phrase-based system where the phrase table is initialized from cross-lingual embedding mappings trained on monolingual data, followed by a neural machine translation system trained on synthetic parallel data. The synthetic corpus was produced from a monolingual corpus by a tuned PBMT model refined through iterative back-translation. We further focus on the handling of named entities, i.e. the part of vocabulary where the cross-lingual embedding mapping suffers most. Our system reaches a BLEU score of 15.3 on the German-Czech WMT19 shared task.

1 Introduction

Unsupervised machine translation is of particular significance for low-resource language pairs. In contrast to traditional machine translation, it does not rely on large amounts of parallel data. When parallel data is scarce, both neural machine translation (NMT) and phrase-based machine translation (PBMT) systems can be trained using large monolingual corpora (Artetxe et al., 2018b,c; Lample et al., 2018).

Our translation systems submitted to WMT19 were created in several steps. Following the strategy of Artetxe et al. (2018b), we first train monolingual phrase embeddings and map them to the cross-lingual space. Secondly, we use the mapped embeddings to initialize the phrase table of the PBMT system which is first tuned and later refined with back-translation. We then translate the Czech monolingual corpus by the PBMT system to produce several synthetic parallel German-Czech corpora. Finally, we train a supervised NMT system

on a filtered synthetic data set, where we exclude sentences tagged as "not Czech", shuffle the word order and handle mistranslated name entities. The training pipeline is illustrated in Figure 1.

The structure of this paper is the following. The existing approaches used to build our system are described in Section 2. The data for this shared task is described in Section 3. Section 4 gives details on phrase embeddings. Section 5 describe the phrase-based model and how it was used to create synthetic corpora. Section 6 proceeds to the neural model trained on the synthetic data. Section 7 introduces our benchmarks and Section 8 reports the results of the experiments. Finally, Section 9 summarizes and concludes the paper.

2 Background

Unsupervised machine translation has been recently explored by Artetxe et al. (2018c,b) and Lample et al. (2018). They propose unsupervised training techniques for both the PBMT model and the NMT model as well as a combination of the two in order to extract the necessary translation information from monolingual data. For the PBMT model (Lample et al., 2018; Artetxe et al., 2018b), the phrase table is initialized with an n-gram mapping learned without supervision. For the NMT model (Lample et al., 2018; Artetxe et al., 2018c), the system is designed to have a shared encoder and it is trained iteratively on a synthetic parallel corpus which is created on-the-fly by adding noise to the monolingual text (to learn a language model by de-noising) and by adding a synthetic source side created by back-translation (to learn a translation model by translating from a noised source).

The key ingredient for functioning of the above mentioned systems is the initial transfer from a monolingual space to a cross-lingual space without using any parallel data. Zhang et al. (2017)

Proceedings of the Fourth Conference on Machine Translation (WMT), Volume 2: Shared Task Papers (Day 1) pages 241–248
Florence, Italy, August 1-2, 2019. ©2019 Association for Computational Linguistics

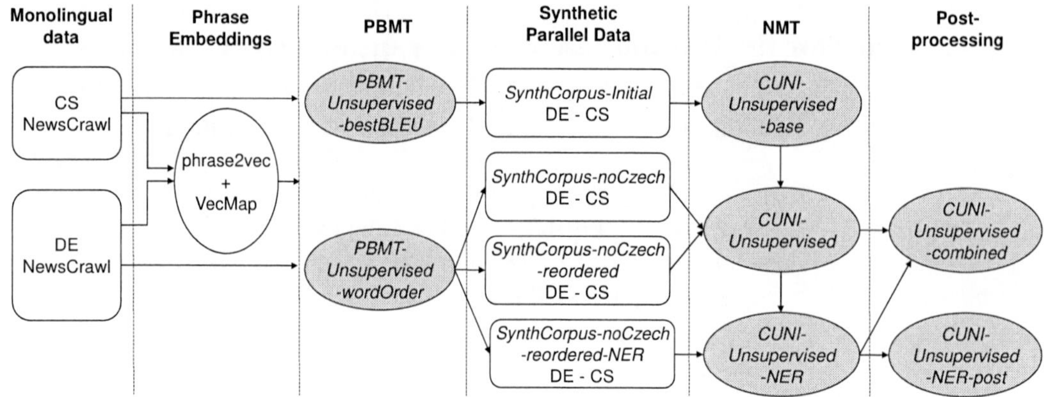

Figure 1: The training pipeline and an overview of our resulting systems. Corpora are displayed as rounded rectangles, MT systems as grey ovals.

and Conneau et al. (2018) have inferred a bilingual dictionary in an unsupervised way by aligning monolingual embedding spaces through adversarial training. Artetxe et al. (2018a) propose an alternative method of mapping monolingual embeddings to a shared space by exploiting their structural similarity and iteratively improving the mapping through self-learning.

3 Data

In line with the rules of the WMT19 unsupervised shared task, we trained our models on the NewsCrawl[1] corpus of newspaper articles collected over the period of 2007 to 2018.

We tokenized and truecased the text using standard Moses scripts. Sentences with less than 3 or more than 80 tokens were removed and the resulting monolingual corpora used for training of the unsupervised PBMT system consisted of 70M Czech sentences and 267M German sentences.

We performed further filtering of the Czech corpus before the NMT training stage. Since there are a lot of Slovak sentences in the Czech NewsCrawl corpus, we used a language tagger `langid.py` (Lui and Baldwin, 2012) to tag all sentences and remove the ones which were not tagged as Czech. After cleaning the corpus, the resulting Czech training set comprises 62M sentences.

Since small parallel data was allowed to tune the unsupervised system, we used newstest2013 for development of the PBMT system. Finally, we used newstest2012 to select the best PBMT

model and newstest2010 as the validation set for the NMT model.

4 Phrase Embeddings

The first step towards unsupervised machine translation is to train monolingual n-gram embeddings and infer a bilingual dictionary by learning a mapping between the two embedding spaces. The resulting mapped embeddings allow us to derive the initial phrase table for the PBMT model.

4.1 Training

We first train phrase embeddings (up to trigrams) independently in the two languages. Following Artetxe et al. (2018b), we use an extension of the word2vec skip-gram model with negative sampling (Mikolov et al., 2013) to train phrase embeddings. We use a window size of 5, embedding size of 300, 10 negative samples, 5 iterations and no subsampling. We restricted the vocabulary to the most frequent 200,000 unigrams, 400,000 bigrams and 400,000 trigrams.

Having trained the monolingual phrase embeddings, we use *VecMap* (Artetxe et al., 2018a) to learn a linear transformation to map the embeddings to a shared cross-lingual space.

4.2 Output: Unsupervised Phrase Table

The output of this processing stage is the unsupervised phrase table which is filled with source and target n-grams. For the sake of a reasonable phrase table size, only the 100 nearest neighbors are kept as translation candidates for each source phrase. The phrase translation probabilities are de-

---

[1] `http://data.statmt.org/news-crawl/`

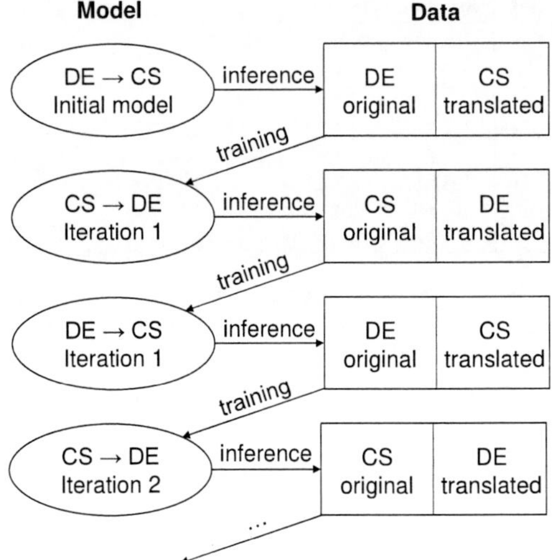

Figure 2: Step-by-step illustration of the iterative back-translation procedure.

rived from a softmax function over the cosine similarities of their respective mapped embeddings (Artetxe et al., 2018a).

5 PBMT Model

We followed the Monoses[2] pipeline of Artetxe et al. (2018b) for our unsupervised phrase-based system. The initial translation model is estimated based on the unsupervised phrase table induced from the mapped embeddings and the language model is estimated on the monolingual data. The reordering model is not used in the first step. The initial model is tuned and later iteratively refined by back-translation (Sennrich et al., 2016).

5.1 Training

The models are estimated using Moses (Koehn et al., 2007), with KenLM (Heafield, 2011) for 5-gram language modelling and fast_align (Dyer et al., 2013) for alignments. The feature weights of the log-linear model are tuned using Minimum Error Rate Training.

The back-translation process is illustrated in Figure 2. Both de→cs and cs→de systems are needed at this step. The de→cs system is used to translate a portion of the German monolingual corpus to Czech and create a synthetic parallel data set, which is then used to train the cs→de system and the procedure continues the other way around.

We note that we do not make use of the initial model for cs→de. Once the synthetic parallel data set is created, the problem turns into a supervised one and we can use standard PBMT features, including the standard phrase table extraction procedure and the reordering model estimated on the aligned data sets.

Since back-translation is computationally demanding, we experimented with using a synthetic data set of 2 and 4 million sentences for back-translation rather than translating the whole monolingual corpus.

5.2 Output: PBMT Systems (cs→de)

We evaluated various PBMT models to select the best candidate to translate the whole monolingual corpus from Czech to German. The translation quality was measured on newstest2012.

We experimented with tuning the model both on an authentic parallel development set (3K sentence pairs) and a synthetic back-translated development set (10K sentence pairs). In the first scenario, possibly as a result of a smaller development set, the model started diverging after the first round of back-translation. In the second scenario, the best result is achieved after two and three rounds of back-translation for the cs→de and de→cs model, respectively (see the results in Table 1).

PBMT-Unsupervised-bestBLEU system

We selected the cs→de model with the highest BLEU of 14.22 for creating the synthetic corpus for the initial training of the NMT system. This PBMT model was tuned on a synthetic development set with two rounds of back-translation).

PBMT-Unsupervised-wordOrder system

However, after reviewing the translations and despite the BLEU results, we kept also the cs→de model with a BLEU score of 12.06 which was tuned on authentic parallel data. The translations were superior especially in terms of the word order.

5.3 Output: Synthetic Corpora

The training data sets for our NMT models were created by translating the full target monolingual corpus (filtered as described in Section 3) from Czech to German using the best performing cs→de PBMT models. Due to time constraints, we were gradually improving our PBMT models

---

Iteration No.	Authentic Dev Set		Synthetic Dev Set	
	de→cs	cs→de	de→cs	cs→de
Initial model	9.44	11.46	9.06	11.06
1	11.11	*12.06	4.61	12.92
2	7.26	6.78	11.70	**14.22
3	1.06	2.32	12.06	14.07
4	-	-	5.65	13.67
5	-	-	11.69	14.18
6	-	-	11.56	13.96

Table 1: Results of the PBMT models on newstest2012. The systems in left two columns were tuned on the parallel newstest2013 (3K sentence pairs) and iteratively refined on 2M sentence pairs. The ones in the right two columns were tuned on a synthetic set (10K back-translated sentence pairs) and iteratively refined on 4M sentence pairs. ** indicates the model selected for creating the synthetic training data for the initial training of the NMT model (*PBMT-Unsupervised-bestBLEU*). * indicates the model selected for creating the synthetic training data for further fine-tuning of the NMT model (*PBMT-Unsupervised-wordOrder*).

and already training the NMT model on the synthetic data. As a result, the final NMT model used synthetic data sets of increasing quality in four training stages.

5.3.1 Frequent Errors in Synthetic Corpora

We read through the translations to detect further error patterns which are not easily detectable by BLEU but have a significant impact on human evaluation. We noticed three such patterns:

- wrong word order (e.g. in contrast to the Czech word order, verbs in subordinate clauses and verbs following a modal verb are at the end of a sentence in German)

- unknown Czech words copied to German sentences during translation

- randomly mistranslated named entities (NEs) (e.g. *king Ludvik* translated as *king Harold* or *Brno* translated as *Kraluv Dvur*);

5.3.2 Heuristics to Improve Synthetic Corpora

In order to reduce the detrimental effects of the above errors, we created several variations of the synthetic corpora. Here we summarize the final versions of the corpora that served in the subsequent NMT training:

SynthCorpus-Initial

The *PBMT-Unsupervised-bestBLEU* model was used for creating the data set for the initial training of the model. All submitted systems were trained on this initial training set.

SynthCorpus-noCzech

This time we translated the Czech corpus by the *PBMT-Unsupervised-wordOrder* model. Despite its lower BLEU, the translations produced by this model seem more fluent. In order to remove Czech words from German sentences in the synthetic corpus, we identified words with Czech diacritics and replaced them on the German side with the *unk* token. As a result, the models trained on this corpus do not learn to simply copy unknown words and therefore, the German translations produced by such models rarely contain copied Czech words.

SynthCorpus-noCzech-reordered

The *SynthCorpus-noCzech* was further treated to improve the word order in the synthetic corpus. We shuffled words in the synthetic German sentences within a 5-word window and mixed the reordered sentences into the original ones. We essentially doubled the size of the training corpus by first reordering odd-indexed sentences while keeping even-indexed sentences intact and then vice versa.

The motivation for this augmentation was to support the NMT system in learning to handle word reordering less strictly, essentially to improve its word order denoising capability. Ideally, the model should learn that German word order need not be strictly followed when translating to Czech. This feature is easy to observe in authentic parallel texts but the synthetic corpora are too monotone. We are aware of the fact that a 5-word window is not sufficient to illustrate the reordering necessary for German verbs but we did not want to introduce too language-specific components to our technique.

SynthCorpus-noCzech-reordered-NER

The *SynthCorpus-noCzech-reordered* was further treated to alleviate the problem of mistranslated NEs present in the data.

NEs were identified in the monolingual Czech corpus by a NE recognition tagger NameTag[3] (Straková et al., 2014). The model was trained on the training portion of the Czech Named Entity Corpus 2.0[4] which uses a detailed two-level named entity hierarchy. We then used automatic word alignments (fast_align) between the Czech side and the synthetic German side of the corpus and checked the German counterparts of automatically-identified Czech NEs. If the German counterpart was close enough (Levenshtein distance of at most 3) to the Czech original, we trusted the translation. In other cases, we either copied the NE from the source or we used *unk* on the German side, preventing the subsequent NMT system from learning a mistranslation. Instead, the *unk* should never match any input and the NMT system should be forced to fall back to its standard handling of unknown words. Ideally, this would be to copy the word, but since there is no copy mechanism in our NMT setups, the more probable solution of the system would be to somehow circumvent or avoid the NE in the target altogether.

Named entity types and their treatment are listed in Table 2. Mistranslated NEs were treated in two stages. First during improving the synthetic corpora and then during post-processing, as described in Section 6.2.

6 NMT Model

6.1 Model and Training

We use the Transformer architecture by Vaswani et al. (2017) implemented in Marian framework (Junczys-Dowmunt et al., 2018) to train an NMT model on the synthetic corpus produced by the PBMT model. The model setup, training and decoding hyperparameters are identical to the CUNI Marian systems in English-to-Czech news translation task in WMT19 (Popel et al., 2019), but in this case, due to smaller and noisier training data, we set the dropout between Transformer layers to 0.3. We use 8 Quadro P5000 GPUs with 16GB memory.

Named Entity Type	Pre-treatment	Post-treatment
Numbers in addresses	copied	copied
Geographical names	removed	copied
Institutions	copied	ignored
Media names	copied	ignored
Number expressions	copied	copied
Artifact names	copied	ignored
Personal names	copied	copied
Time expressions	copied	ignored

Table 2: Named Entity types extracted from Czech Named Entity Corpus 2.0. and their treatment during pre-processing and post-processing. During *pre-treatment* (creation of the synthetic corpus), the NEs were identified in the Czech corpus and their translation on the German synthetic side was either *removed*, *copied* from the source Czech side or completely *ignored*. During *post-treatment* (post-processing of the final NMT outputs), the NEs were identified in the Czech translations and either *copied* from the source German side or *ignored*.

6.2 Post-processing

During post-processing of the translated Czech test set, we always adjusted quotation marks to suit Czech standards. Some systems were subject to further post-processing as indicated in the following section.

6.3 Output: NMT Systems

Our resulting systems share the same architecture and training parameters but they emerged from different stages of the training process as illustrated in Figure 1. The entire training process included training the system on the initial training corpus, fine-tuning on other corpora and final post-processing.

CUNI-Unsupervised-base

This system was trained on the initial synthetic data set *SynthCorpus-Initial* until convergence. We used early stopping after 100 non-improvements on validation cross-entropy, with validation step 1 000. The training finished after 3 days and 11 hours at 249 000 steps. Then we selected the checkpoint with the highest `bleu-detok`, which was at 211 000 steps, in epoch 3.

No further fine-tuning was performed. This system was not submitted to WMT19.

CUNI-Unsupervised

This system was fine-tuned on the *SynthCorpus-noCzech* corpus for 4 hours, when it reached

---

[3] http://ufal.mff.cuni.cz/nametag
[4] http://ufal.mff.cuni.cz/cnec/cnec2.0

System Name	BLEU uncased	BLEU cased	TER	BEER 2.0	CharacTER
CUNI-Unsupervised-base	13.6	13.3	0.799	0.482	0.688
CUNI-Unsupervised*	15.3	15.0	0.784	0.489	0.672
CUNI-Unsupervised-NER*	14.6	14.3	0.786	0.487	0.675
CUNI-Unsupervised-NER-post**	14.4	14.1	0.788	0.485	0.677
CUNI-Unsupervised-combined*	14.9	14.6	0.785	0.488	0.674
Benchmark-Supervised	19.3	18.8	0.719	0.517	0.636
Benchmark-TransferEN	13.6	13.3	0.793	0.482	0.683

Table 3: Our systems and their performance on newstest2019 (* indicates our WMT submissions and ** indicates our primary system).

a maximum, and for another 4 hours on *SynthCorpus-noCzech-reordered*.

CUNI-Unsupervised-NER

This system is a result of additional 4 hours of fine-tuning of the *CUNI-Unsupervised* system on the *SynthCorpus-noCzech-reordered-NER* corpus. Although the effect of this fine-tuning on the final translation might not be significant in terms of BLEU points, the problem of mistranslated named entities is perceived strongly by human evaluators and warrants an improvement.

CUNI-Unsupervised-NER-post

The translations produced by *CUNI-Unsupervised-NER* were post-processed to tackle the remaining problem with named entities. We first trained GIZA++ (Och and Ney, 2003) alignments on 30K sentences. We used NameTag to tag NEs in Czech sentences and using the alignments, we copied personal names, geographical names and numbers from the German source to the Czech target.

CUNI-Unsupervised-combined

We translated the test set by two models and combined the results. We used NameTag to tag Czech sentences with named entities and translated the tagged sentences by *CUNI-Unsupervised-NER*. The sentences with no NEs were translated by the *CUNI-Unsupervised* system.

7 Benchmarks

For comparison, we created a NMT system using the same model architecture as above but training it in a supervised way on the German-Czech parallel corpus from Europarl (Koehn, 2005) and OpenSubtitles2016 (Tiedemann, 2012), after some cleanup pre-processing and character normalization provided by Macháček (2018). As far as we know, these are the only publicly available parallel data for this language pair. They consist of 8.8M sentence pairs and 89/78M tokens on the German and the Czech side, respectively. The system *Benchmark-Supervised* was trained from scratch for 8 days until convergence.

Our other comparison system, *Benchmark-TransferEN*, was first trained as an English-to-Czech NMT system (see *CUNI Transformer Marian* for the English-to-Czech news translation task in WMT19 by Popel et al. (2019)) and then fine-tuned for 6 days on the *SynthCorpus-noCzech-reordered-NER*. The vocabulary remained unchanged, it was trained on the English-Czech training corpus. This simple and effective transfer learning approach was suggested by Kocmi and Bojar (2018).

The scores of the systems on newstest2019 are reported in Table 3.

8 Final Evaluation

The systems submitted to WMT19 are listed in Table 3 along with our benchmarks. In addition to BLEU, we also report BEER (Stanojević and Sima'an, 2014) and CharacTER (Wang et al., "2016") scores.

Table 5 summarizes the improvement we gained by introducing a special named entity treatment. We manualy evaluated three systems, *CUNI-Unsupervised, CUNI-Unsupervised-NER* and *CUNI-Unsupervised-NER-post* on a stratified subset of the validation data set created by randomly selecting 100 sentences with NEs and 100 sentences without NEs. The results are presented in two steps, the first table shows that fine-tuning the system *CUNI-Unsupervised-NER* on a synthetic corpus with amended NEs proved beneficial in 52% of tested sentences which included NEs and it did not harm in 20% of sentences. When comparing the two systems on sentences

Source	Phrase
Original	Der Lyriker **Werner Söllner** ist IM **Walter**.
Reference	Básník **Werner Söllner** je tajný agent **Walter**.
CUNI-Unsupervised	Prozaik **Filip Bubeníček** je agentem StB **Josefem**.
CUNI-Unsupervised-NER	Prozaik **Filip Söllner** je agentem StB **Ladislavem Bártou**.
CUNI-Unsupervised-NER-post	Prozaik **Werner Söllner** je agentem StB **Walter**.

Table 4: Sample translations showing that fine-tuning on synthetic corpus with cleaned NEs (*CUNI-Unsupervised-NER*) alleviates a part of the NE problem while post-processing can handle the rest. However, note the imperfect translation of *Lyriker* as *novelist* rather than *poet* and the extra word *StB* which was not tagged as a NE and therefore not treated during post-processing.

Winning Systems	Sentences with NEs	Sentences with no NEs
CUNI-Unsup	28%	26%
CUNI-Unsup-NER	52%	28%
No winner	20%	46%

Winning Systems	Sentences with NEs	Sentences with no NEs
CUNI-Unsup-NER	14%	0%
CUNI-Unsup-NER-post	18%	0%
No winner	68%	100%

Table 5: Results of manual evaluation of three systems on a stratified subset of the validation data set created by randomly selecting 100 sentences with NEs and 100 sentences without NEs.

with no NEs, their performance is very similar.

Furthermore, adjusting NEs during post-processing proved useful in 18% of sentences with NEs and it did not harm in 68% of sentences. Post-processing introduced two types of errors: copying German geographical names into Czech sentences (e.g. translating *Norway* as *Norwegen* instead of *Norsko*) and replacing a Czech named entity with a word which does not correspond to it due to wrong alignments (e.g. translating *Miss Japan* as *Miss Miss*). On the other hand, when alignments were correct, the post-processing was able to fix remaining mismatches in named entities. See Table 4 for a sample translation.

9 Conclusion

This paper contributes to recent research attempts at unsupervised machine translation. We tested the approach of Artetxe et al. (2018b) on a different language pair and faced new challenges for this type of translation caused by the non-similar nature of the two languages (e.g. different word order, unrelated grammar rules).

We identified several patterns where the ini-

tial translation models systematically failed and we focused on alleviating such issues during fine-tuning of the system and final post-processing. The most severe type of a translation error, in our opinion, was a large number of randomly mistranslated named entities which left a significant impact on the perceived translation quality. We focused on alleviating this problem both during fine-tuning of the NMT system and during the post-processing stage. While our treatment is far from perfect, we believe that an omitted named entity or a non-translated named entity causes less harm than a random name used instead.

While the performance of our systems still lags behind the supervised benchmark, it is impressive that the translations reach their quality without ever seeing an authentic parallel corpus.

Acknowledgments

This study was supported in parts by the grants SVV 260 453, 1050119 of the Charles University Grant Agency, 18-24210S of the Czech Science Foundation and the EU grant H2020-ICT-2018-2-825460 (ELITR).

This work has been using language resources and tools stored and distributed by the LINDAT/CLARIN project of the Ministry of Education, Youth and Sports of the Czech Republic (LM2015071).

References

Mikel Artetxe, Gorka Labaka, and Eneko Agirre. 2018a. A robust self-learning method for fully unsupervised cross-lingual mappings of word embeddings. In *Proceedings of the 56th Annual Meeting of the Association for Computational Linguistics: Volume 1, Long Papers*.

Mikel Artetxe, Gorka Labaka, and Eneko Agirre. 2018b. Unsupervised statistical machine translation. In *Proceedings of the 2018 Conference on Empirical Methods in Natural Language Processing*.

Mikel Artetxe, Gorka Labaka, Eneko Agirre, and Kyunghyun Cho. 2018c. Unsupervised neural machine translation. In *Proceedings of the Sixth International Conference on Learning Representations*.

Alexis Conneau, Guillaume Lample, Marc'Aurelio Ranzato, Ludovic Denoyer, and Herv Jgou. 2018. Word translation without parallel data. In *International Conference on Learning Representations*.

Chris Dyer, Victor Chahuneau, and Noah A. Smith. 2013. A simple, fast, and effective reparameterization of IBM model 2. In *Proceedings of the 2013 Conference of the North American Chapter of the Association for Computational Linguistics: Human Language Technologies*.

Kenneth Heafield. 2011. KenLM: Faster and smaller language model queries. In *Proceedings of the Sixth Workshop on Statistical Machine Translation*.

Marcin Junczys-Dowmunt, Roman Grundkiewicz, Tomasz Dwojak, Hieu Hoang, Kenneth Heafield, Tom Neckermann, Frank Seide, Ulrich Germann, Alham Fikri Aji, Nikolay Bogoychev, André F. T. Martins, and Alexandra Birch. 2018. Marian: Fast neural machine translation in C++. In *Proceedings of the 56th Annual Meeting of the Association for Computational Linguistics: System Demonstrations*.

Tom Kocmi and Ondřej Bojar. 2018. Trivial transfer learning for low-resource neural machine translation. In *Proceedings of the Third Conference on Machine Translation: Research Papers*.

Philipp Koehn. 2005. Europarl: A Parallel Corpus for Statistical Machine Translation. In *Conference Proceedings: the tenth Machine Translation Summit*.

Philipp Koehn, Hieu Hoang, Alexandra Birch, Chris Callison-Burch, Marcello Federico, Nicola Bertoldi, Brooke Cowan, Wade Shen, Christine Moran, Richard Zens, Chris Dyer, Ondrej Bojar, Alexandra Constantin, and Evan Herbst. 2007. Moses: Open source toolkit for statistical machine translation. In *Proceedings of the 45th Annual Meeting of the Association for Computational Linguistics Companion Volume Proceedings of the Demo and Poster Sessions*.

Guillaume Lample, Myle Ott, Alexis Conneau, Ludovic Denoyer, and Marc'Aurelio Ranzato. 2018. Phrase-based & neural unsupervised machine translation. In *Proceedings of the 2018 Conference on Empirical Methods in Natural Language Processing*.

Marco Lui and Timothy Baldwin. 2012. langid.py: An off-the-shelf language identification tool. In *Proceedings of the 50th Annual Meeting of the Association for Computational Linguistics: System Demonstrations*.

Dominik Macháček. 2018. Enriching Neural MT through Multi-Task Training. Master's thesis, Institute of Formal and Applied Linguistics, Charles University.

Tomas Mikolov, Ilya Sutskever, Kai Chen, Greg S Corrado, and Jeff Dean. 2013. Distributed representations of words and phrases and their compositionality. In C. J. C. Burges, L. Bottou, M. Welling, Z. Ghahramani, and K. Q. Weinberger, editors, *Advances in Neural Information Processing Systems 26*. Curran Associates, Inc.

Franz Josef Och and Hermann Ney. 2003. A systematic comparison of various statistical alignment models. *Computational Linguistics*, 29(1).

Martin Popel, Dominik Macháček, Michal Aueršperger, Ondřej Bojar, and Pavel Pecina. 2019. English-czech systems in wmt19: Document-level transformer. In *Proceedings of the Fourth Conference on Machine Translation: Volume 2, Shared Task Papers*.

Rico Sennrich, Barry Haddow, and Alexandra Birch. 2016. Improving neural machine translation models with monolingual data. In *Proceedings of the 54th Annual Meeting of the Association for Computational Linguistics: Volume 1, Long Papers*.

Miloš Stanojević and Khalil Sima'an. 2014. Fitting sentence level translation evaluation with many dense features. In *Proceedings of the 2014 Conference on Empirical Methods in Natural Language Processing*.

Jana Straková, Milan Straka, and Jan Hajič. 2014. Open-Source Tools for Morphology, Lemmatization, POS Tagging and Named Entity Recognition. In *Proceedings of 52nd Annual Meeting of the Association for Computational Linguistics: System Demonstrations*.

Jörg Tiedemann. 2012. Parallel data, tools and interfaces in opus. In *Proceedings of the 8th International Conference on Language Resources and Evaluation*.

Ashish Vaswani, Noam Shazeer, Niki Parmar, Jakob Uszkoreit, Llion Jones, Aidan N Gomez, Ł ukasz Kaiser, and Illia Polosukhin. 2017. Attention is all you need. In I. Guyon, U. V. Luxburg, S. Bengio, H. Wallach, R. Fergus, S. Vishwanathan, and R. Garnett, editors, *Advances in Neural Information Processing Systems 30*. Curran Associates, Inc.

Weiyue Wang, Jan-Thorsten Peter, Hendrik Rosendahl, and Hermann Ney. "2016". Character: Translation edit rate on character level. In *"Proceedings of the First Conference on Machine Translation, Volume 2: Shared Task Papers"*.

Meng Zhang, Yang Liu, Huanbo Luan, and Maosong Sun. 2017. Adversarial training for unsupervised bilingual lexicon induction. In *Proceedings of the 55th Annual Meeting of the Association for Computational Linguistics: Volume 1, Long Papers*.

A Comparison on Fine-grained Pre-trained Embeddings for the WMT19 Chinese-English News Translation Task

Zhenhao Li
Department of Computing
Imperial College London, UK
zhenhao.li18@imperial.ac.uk

Lucia Specia
Department of Computing
Imperial College London, UK
l.specia@imperial.ac.uk

Abstract

This paper describes our submission to the WMT 2019 Chinese-English (zh-en) news translation shared task. Our systems are based on RNN architectures with pre-trained embeddings which utilize character and sub-character information. We compare models with these different granularity levels using different evaluating metics. We find that a finer granularity embeddings can help the model according to character level evaluation and that the pre-trained embeddings can also be beneficial for model performance marginally when the training data is limited.

1 Introduction

Neural Machine Translation (NMT) systems are mostly based on an encoder-decoder architecture with attention. Given a sentence x in source language, the model predicts a corresponding output sentence y in target language, which maximizes the conditional probability $p(y|x)$. The attention-based Recurrent Neural Network (RNN) version of this architecture has been a very popular approach to NMT (Bahdanau et al., 2015; Luong et al., 2015). Despite the success of these models, they still suffer from problems such as out-of-vocabulary (OOV) words, i.e. words that have not been seen at training. To alleviate the OOV problem, we follow the methods used in word representation and segment words into smaller units. In some morphorlogically rich languages such as Chinese, a word can be divided into characters and then the characters can be further divided into smaller components called *glyphs*. Both character and glyph might contain semantic information and therefore utilizing such information might help alleviate the OOV problem.

Based on the RNN attention-based model (Bahdanau et al., 2015), we experiment with different granularity levels on the WMT19 Chinese-English

(zh-en) news translation shared task. This paper describes our submitted systems with embeddings pre-trained on monolingual corpora. The two submitted systems use pre-trained embeddings enhanced by character and sub-character information respectively. The preprocessing methods include Chinese word segmentation, tokenization, data filtering based on rules and Byte Pair Encoding (BPE). Our baseline model is based on RNNSearch (Bahdanau et al., 2015) operating on word level and we use Long Short-Term Memory (LSTM) (Hochreiter and Schmidhuber, 1997) as encoder and decoder. For character level word embeddings, we use the Character-Enhanced Word Embedding (CWE) proposed by Chen et al. (2015). For the sub-character level embeddings, we use the Joint Learning Word Embedding (JWE) proposed by Yu et al. (2017). We use various metrics, namely BLEU (Papineni et al., 2002), METEOR (Denkowski and Lavie, 2011), TER (Snover et al., 2006) and CharacTER (Wang et al., 2016) for evaluation.

When compared with our baseline model, the models with pre-trained sub-character level embeddings on monolingual corpus show better performance, achieving an increase of +0.53 BLEU score with the sub-character level embeddings. We ran additional experiments on the character and subcharacter level pre-trained embeddings and found that the use of these embeddings can benefit the model when the training corpus size is limited.

This paper is structured as follows: Section 2 introduces the related work including the model architecture and pre-trained embeddings used in our experiment. In Section 3, data selection and preprocessing methods are described. Section 4 introduces the model architectures and hyperparameter settings. Section 5 shows the evaluation results on models with different granularity levels. Section 6

Proceedings of the Fourth Conference on Machine Translation (WMT), Volume 2: Shared Task Papers (Day 1) pages 249–256
Florence, Italy, August 1-2, 2019. ©2019 Association for Computational Linguistics

shows additional experiments to better understand our models.

2   Related Work

NMT has been an important task in Natural Language Processing. A translation system aims to find the corresponding target sentence $\mathbf{y} = \{y_1, y_2, ..., y_m\}$ given a sentence $\mathbf{x} = \{x_1, x_2, ..., x_n\}$ in source language, in a probabilistic manner, represented as $\max_y P(\mathbf{y}|\mathbf{x})$. Most NMT models are based on the sequence-to-sequence approach, and the RNN-based architecture (Sutskever et al., 2014) with attention (Bahdanau et al., 2015) is a popular version of such an approach. The attention mechanism functions as a dynamic calculation of the context vector. At each decoding step, a probability distribution is calculated based on the current decoder hidden state and all encoder hidden states. This distribution is defined as the attention score, representing the importance of each input token at current decoding time step. The context vector is calculated as a weighted average of all encoder hidden state vector, where the attention score is the weight. With the introduction of attention, the model does not need to rely on a single context vector to represent the whole sentence and thus can better handle long sentences.

In recent years model architectures based on convolutional neural networks (Gehring et al., 2017) and transformers (Vaswani et al., 2017) have shown competitive or better performance than RNN-based architectures. In addition, strategies such as back translation (Sennrich et al., 2016a), reranking (Neubig et al., 2015) and model ensembling have led to improvements in translation quality. In our experiments, we only experiment with RNN architectures and focus on the effect of using character and sub-character level embeddings and only use ensembling for comparison purposes.

We use the CWE model proposed by Chen et al. (2015) and the JWE model proposed by Yu et al. (2017) for pre-trained embeddings training. Both models are based on the word2vec proposed by Mikolov et al. (2013). Based on Continuous-Bag-of-Word (CBOW), the CWE model construct a new word representation by summing the word embeddings with character embeddings (see Eq 1). Chen et al. also proposed a multi-prototype character embeddings where characters are tagged with additional factors, such as position and con-

text cluster, for character disambiguation.

$$x_j = w_j \oplus \frac{1}{N_j} \sum_{k=1}^{N_j} c_k \qquad (1)$$

where w_j is the word embeddings and c_k is the embeddings of the k-th character in x_j. $\oplus$ is the composition operator (either addition or concatenation).

The JWE model proposed by Yu et al. (2017) is also based on CBOW and it utilizes character and sub-character level information. They construct a dictionary that maps each Chinese character to its sub-character components. As Figure 1 shows, words together with the characters and sub-character components within the context window are all used to predict the target word. The additional semantic information provided by character and subcharacters are shown to improve over word representation, especially in addressing out-of-vocabulary words.

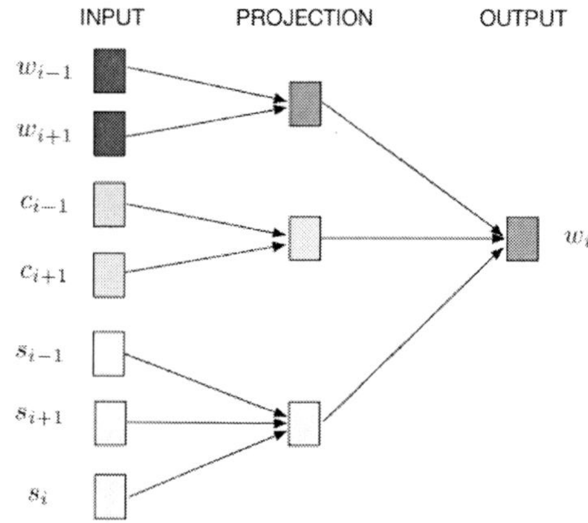

Figure 1: Illustration of JWE embedding taken from (Yu et al., 2017). w_{i-1} and w_{i+1} are context words. c_{i-1} and c_{i+1} represent characters in context words. s_{i-1} and s_{i+1} represent sub-characters of context characters and s_i is the sub-character of target word w_i.

3   Data and Preprocessing

We use all the parallel data provided by WMT for the zh-en translation task, including the News Commentary v14, UN Parallel Corpus V1.0 and the CWMT corpora. In addition, the Common Crawl Corpus from WMT is used as monolingual data to pre-train the embeddings. We use the newsdev2018 and newsdev2017 as validation set and the newstest2019 as our test data. We tokenize English sentences with the Moses tokenizer (Koehn et al., 2007). On the Chinese side we use Jieba for Chinese word segmentation.[1] The data preprocessing consists of filtering sentences to be added to the parallel training corpus by rules and by alignment score. Following the preprocessing criteria from submissions in previous years (Xu and Carpuat, 2018; Stahlberg et al., 2018; Haddow et al., 2018), we filter the training data based on the following criteria:

- The length of sentences in both languages must be between 4 and 50.

- The maximum length ratio of sentence pairs is 1.3.

- Chinese sentences with no Chinese character are filtered out.

- English sentences with no English character are filtered out.

- Same source and target sentences are removed.

- Sentences should not contains HTML tags.

- Sentence pairs with alignment score above -65 are removed.[2]

The `fast_align` toolkit[3] is used to calculate the alignment score for the parallel data. After the filtering, 10.38M sentence pairs are used as training data. We apply Byte-pair Encoding (BPE) (Sennrich et al., 2016b) with 30,000 merge operations on the English sentences. For Chinese sentences, we segment them into different granularity levels, including words, subwords via BPE and characters. In the character level setting, only Chinese words are separated and each character is treated as a single token. The training texts for models with pre-trained embeddings is the same as baseline, which use words as basic units.

4 Models

4.1 Baseline

The baseline model is based on the bidirectional RNN architecture with attention (Bahdanau et al.,

2015). Our models are built with OpenNMT-py (Klein et al., 2017). We follow the hyperparameter setting of Deep RNN from Xu and Carpuat (2018) and use a four-layer LSTM for both the encoder and decoder. The embeddings and hidden layer size are limited to 512. We use the Adam optimizer (Kingma and Ba, 2015) with initial learning rate of 0.0005. We apply label smoothing (Szegedy et al., 2016) and dropout (Srivastava et al., 2014) of 0.1 to avoid overfitting. We use the multi-layer perception (mlp) attention as in (Bahdanau et al., 2015). The batch size is 4096 tokens per batch and the models are selected based on best performance on the validation set. All our models are trained on a GTX 1080Ti GPU.

4.2 Pre-trained Embeddings

We apply pre-trained embeddings to the two submitted systems. The character level and sub-character level pre-trained embeddings are trained with CWE (Chen et al., 2015) and JWE (Yu et al., 2017) respectively. We trained the embeddings on the Common Crawl Corpus provided by WMT19 and fine-tuned them on the task data when training the RNN. The preprocessing for monolingual data includes Chinese word segmentation and removal of non-Chinese characters. Apart from the pre-trained embeddings, the hyperparameters of the two submissions are the same as in the baseline system.

5 Result and Analysis

We use the `CharacTER.py`[4] script for CharacTER score calculation and `multeval`[5] (Clark et al., 2011) to calculate BLEU, METEOR and TER scores. The evaluation results for models on word, subword and character level are presented in Table 1.

The model with BPE applied on both source and target languages (bpe2bpe) achieves higher score than other single models, with an increase of +1.18 BLEU score over the baseline system. The two models (baseline+cwe, baseline+jwe) utilizing character and sub-character information are based on pre-trained embeddings with CWE and JWE as described in Section 2. We use the source training text for the pre-trained embeddings to prevent the introduction of noise. As we can see from the BLEU scores, the model with JWE pre-

---

[1] https://github.com/fxsjy/jieba
[2] We tried different filter strategies and found this criterion gives a better performance than others.
[3] https://github.com/clab/fast_align
[4] https://github.com/rwth-i6/CharacTER
[5] https://github.com/jhclark/multeval

Granularity	Model	BLEU	METEOR	TER	CharacTER
word	baseline	16.90	**23.0**	**64.0**	0.717
	baseline+cwe	16.59	22.8	64.4	0.716
	baseline+jwe	**16.91**	**23.0**	**64.0**	0.712
subword	bpe2bpe	**18.08**	24.2	62.1	0.678
	bpe2bpe+cwe	17.97	24.2	62.4	**0.677**
char	char2bpe	15.80	22.5	64.9	**0.705**
word	apprentice-c*	16.94	23.0	63.7	0.713
	apprentice-g*	16.54	23.0	63.7	0.717
	apprentice-g(best)	**17.43**	**23.2**	**63.4**	**0.710**
	ensemble(jwe)	**18.16**	23.5	62.9	**0.702**

Table 1: Model performance on different granularity levels. The two models with a star are the official systems submitted to the WMT19 zh-en news translation shared task, where the pre-trained embeddings is trained on extra monolingual data.

trained embeddings shows similar performance to the baseline system while the model with CWE embeddings on character level shows a marginal decrease. The METEOR and TER score presents similar trends to BLEU, whereas from the evaluation of CharacTER scores the introduction of pre-trained embeddings on both character and sub-character levels shows better performance than the baseline.

It can also be seen from the comparison on BPE-based models that the model with CWE embeddings performs slightly worse than the bpe2bpe model, which operates on BPE on both source and target languages. The results according to CharacTER show that finer granularity embeddings can benefit the model in character level evaluations. The char2bpe model shows the worst performance according to BLEU scores, whereas the CharacTER score of this model is higher than that of other word level models. Finally, when we ensemble the baseline and four models with JWE embeddings pre-trained on different iterations, the BLEU score shows an increase of +1.26 BLEU over the baseline.

The two models with stars (apprentice-c and apprentice-g) are our official shared task submissions, with the first one operating on character level and the second, on glyph (sub-character) level. The apprentice-c model uses the CWE pre-trained embeddings while the apprentice-g uses JWE embeddings. For the first, we train the pre-trained embeddings on the monolingual data (Common Crawl) and then fine-tune it on filtered parallel data during the training of RNN models. Note that we did not use back-translation to aug-

ment the training data and due to time limit we apply a relatively larger learning rate than previous work to boost training speed, therefore our systems achieve relatively lower score than the previous work (Xu and Carpuat, 2018). The CWE-based model shows a better BLEU score than the baseline model. The lower performance for the apprentice-g model might have resulted from insufficient training epochs for the JWE embeddings. Due to time restrictions, we did not submit the system with the best word embeddings. In the additional experiments after the task deadline, we fine-tuned the models on the best word embeddings version and achieve a higher BLEU score of 17.43 for the apprentice-g(best) model. The CharacTER score for the fine-tuned model is lower than other models except the two with BPE. Generally, the sub-character level models perform better than the word level and character level models.

6 Additional Experiments

6.1 Evaluating Embeddings

We have tried additional experiments to evaluate the effect of character and subcharacter level pre-trained embeddings. Table 2 presents the model performance with respect to the embeddings performance in traditional word similarity and analogy tasks. We use the wordsim-240 and wordsim-297 dataset and the analogy dataset from Chen et al. (2015) for word similarity and analogy evaluation respectively. We use the evaluation script in JWE[6] for both evaluations.

From Table 2, we can see that among all models with JWE pre-trained embeddings, the one with

---

[6] https://github.com/HKUST-KnowComp/JWE

Model	BLEU	wordsim-240	wordsim-297	analogy
baseline	16.90	/	/	/
baseline+jwe5	16.43	0.4880	0.5833	0.4680
baseline+jwe10	**16.91**	0.5099	0.5985	**0.5293**
baseline+jwe20	16.82	**0.5152**	0.6037	0.5205
baseline+jwe50	16.37	0.5048	**0.6075**	0.4786
baseline+cwe5	16.59	0.4569	0.5769	0.2820
baseline+cwe10	16.47	0.4593	0.5742	0.3585
baseline+cwe20	16.52	0.4610	0.5764	0.3754
baseline+cwe50	16.49	0.4528	0.5765	0.3443

Table 2: Comparison of model performance and word embeddings performance. The evaluation on wordsim-240 and wordsim-297 test set shows Spearman correlation between the pre-trained embedding and human judgements. The performance on analogy indicates accuracy on analogy reasoning in "a:b::c:?" format. The number after the embeddings type represents number of training iterations.

10 iterations performs the best. When the embeddings are trained over 20 iterations, the BLEU score starts to decrease. The same pattern can be found on the CWE-based models. However, the model with 5-iteration embeddings achieves the highest BLEU score among all CWE-based models. From the embeddings performance on the analogy task, excluding the cwe5 model, we find that the embeddings performance correlates with BLEU scores. When comparing the CWE-based models with the JWE-based models, we see that on both translation quality and word embeddings evaluations, the model on finer granularity performs best.

6.2 Effect of Corpus Size

Another experiment was done to compare the effect of pre-trained embeddings on different corpora sizes. We train the word embeddings with best iteration setting and train the RNN model on different corpora sizes. Smaller corpora are created by taking 25% and 50% of the original corpus. Table 3 presents the BLEU scores for models on smaller corpora.

Model/data size	25%	50%	100%
baseline	15.95	15.95	16.90
baseline+cwe5	16.00	15.82	16.59
baseline+jwe10	16.04	15.95	16.91

Table 3: BLEU score with different training data sizes.

It can be seen from Table 3 that with smaller parallel training corpora the introduction of the pre-trained word embeddings has a more marked positive influence. When the dataset is reduced to half, all the three models show a decrease in BLEU score. However, the gap between the baseline and the cwe-based model is smaller. When the dataset is further limited to 25%, both models with pre-trained embeddings perform better than the baseline, whose score does not change. Although it seems that the pre-trained embeddings, even with sub-character level semantic information involved, could only benefit marginally on the whole training data, the introduction of extra semantic information might play a more important role when the parallel training resources are limited.

6.3 Effect of Sentence Length

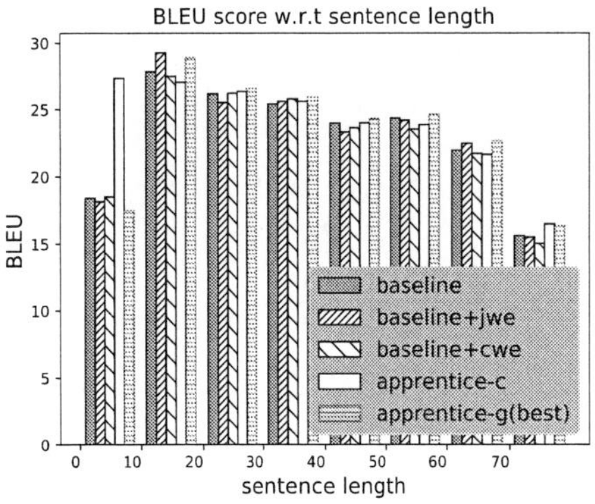

Figure 2: BLEU score of models w.r.t sentence length.

Here we measure the performance of models with varying sentence lengths, as shown in Figure 2. The test set is seperated into 8 subsets based on the sentence lengths and models are evaluated on each subset, the x-axis in Figure 2 represents sentence length intervals. We see that the two models with embeddings trained on a larger

monolingual corpus perform better than the other
models in medium-length sentences (between 30
and 50). The apprentice-c model, which uses
CWE embeddings operating on character level,
greatly outperforms the other models on short sentences with length less than 10. Since the sentence length is short, the tokens in the sentence are
mostly composed of one or two characters, thus
the model with character-based embeddings has
an advantage. Regarding the two models with embeddings trained without extra monolingual data,
both models show good performance on medium
length sentences but perform poorly on long sentences. The introduction of pre-trained embeddings can increase the models' preference to generate shorter sentences, resulting in the model
achieving lower BLEU score on long sentences.

6.4 Analysis of Model Perplexity

In order to understand the effect of pre-trained embedding on target language model, we calculate
the model perplexity on the test data with models on different corpus size. The result is represented in Table 4. The model with JWE pre-
trained embeddings performs better on all corpus
sizes, having a lower perplexity, though the difference is marginal. Similar result as the BLEU evaluation shows that the pre-trained embeddings benefit model performance on smaller corpus sizes.

Model	Perplexity	Corpus size
baseline	2.947	
+cwe	3.005	100%
+jwe	**2.932**	
baseline	3.049	
+cwe	3.046	50%
+jwe	**3.023**	
baseline	2.860	
+cwe	2.847	25%
+jwe	**2.836**	

Table 4: Model perplexity on test set.

6.5 Transformer Models

Besides the RNN model, we also experimented
with pre-trained embeddings and the transformer
architecture. We follow the hyperparameter setting from Vaswani et al. (2017), limiting the embeddings to 512 dimensions. We compare the
transformer models with and without pre-trained
embeddings. The results are presented in Table 5.

From the evaluation results on BLEU and Charac-
TER, the transformer models without pre-trained
embeddings show better performance. We find
it interesting that the embedding pre-trained with
CWE decrease the performance severely, leading to a reduction of -3.85 BLEU score from the
model without it. The introduction of finer granularity embeddings might not benefit the transformer performance. We hypothesize that the pre-
trained embedding enhanced by character and sub-
character infomation might conflict with the fixed
positional encoding used in transformer.

Model	BLEU	CharacTER
transformer	17.82	0.692
transformer+cwe	13.97	0.754
transformer+jwe	17.59	0.695

Table 5: BLEU and CharacTER for transformer models.

7 Conclusion

This paper describes our NMT models with pre-
trained embeddings operating on character and
sub-character levels. We participated in the
WMT19 zh-en news translation shared task and
submitted two systems with embeddings trained
on monolingual corpus. We experimented with
the effect of using fine-grained pre-trained embeddings and showed the potential benefit of using
them. In additional experiments, we find that using pre-trained embeddings can better benefit the
translation models when the parallel training data
is limited.

References

Dzmitry Bahdanau, Kyunghyun Cho, and Yoshua Bengio. 2015. Neural machine translation by jointly
learning to align and translate. In *3rd International Conference on Learning Representations,
ICLR 2015, San Diego, CA, USA, May 7-9, 2015,
Conference Track Proceedings*.

Xinxiong Chen, Lei Xu, Zhiyuan Liu, Maosong Sun,
and Huanbo Luan. 2015. Joint learning of character
and word embeddings. In *Twenty-Fourth International Joint Conference on Artificial Intelligence*.

Jonathan H. Clark, Chris Dyer, Alon Lavie, and
Noah A. Smith. 2011. Better hypothesis testing for
statistical machine translation: Controlling for optimizer instability. In *Proceedings of the 49th Annual Meeting of the Association for Computational
Linguistics: Human Language Technologies*, pages

176–181, Portland, Oregon, USA. Association for Computational Linguistics.

Michael Denkowski and Alon Lavie. 2011. Meteor 1.3: Automatic metric for reliable optimization and evaluation of machine translation systems. In *Proceedings of the Sixth Workshop on Statistical Machine Translation*, pages 85–91, Edinburgh, Scotland. Association for Computational Linguistics.

Jonas Gehring, Michael Auli, David Grangier, Denis Yarats, and Yann N Dauphin. 2017. Convolutional Sequence to Sequence Learning. *ArXiv e-prints*.

Barry Haddow, Nikolay Bogoychev, Denis Emelin, Ulrich Germann, Roman Grundkiewicz, Kenneth Heafield, Antonio Valerio Miceli Barone, and Rico Sennrich. 2018. The university of edinburghs submissions to the wmt18 news translation task. In *Proceedings of the Third Conference on Machine Translation, Volume 2: Shared Task Papers*, pages 403–413, Belgium, Brussels. Association for Computational Linguistics.

Sepp Hochreiter and Jürgen Schmidhuber. 1997. Long short-term memory. *Neural computation*, 9(8):1735–1780.

Diederik P. Kingma and Jimmy Ba. 2015. Adam: A method for stochastic optimization. In *ICLR*.

Guillaume Klein, Yoon Kim, Yuntian Deng, Jean Senellart, and Alexander M. Rush. 2017. Open-NMT: Open-source toolkit for neural machine translation. In *Proc. ACL*.

Philipp Koehn, Hieu Hoang, Alexandra Birch, Chris Callison-Burch, Marcello Federico, Nicola Bertoldi, Brooke Cowan, Wade Shen, Christine Moran, Richard Zens, Chris Dyer, Ondrej Bojar, Alexandra Constantin, and Evan Herbst. 2007. Moses: Open source toolkit for statistical machine translation. In *Proceedings of the 45th Annual Meeting of the Association for Computational Linguistics Companion Volume Proceedings of the Demo and Poster Sessions*, pages 177–180, Prague, Czech Republic. Association for Computational Linguistics.

Thang Luong, Hieu Pham, and Christopher D. Manning. 2015. Effective approaches to attention-based neural machine translation. In *Proceedings of the 2015 Conference on Empirical Methods in Natural Language Processing*, pages 1412–1421, Lisbon, Portugal. Association for Computational Linguistics.

Tomas Mikolov, Kai Chen, Greg Corrado, and Jeffrey Dean. 2013. Efficient estimation of word representations in vector space. *arXiv preprint arXiv:1301.3781*.

Graham Neubig, Makoto Morishita, and Satoshi Nakamura. 2015. Neural reranking improves subjective quality of machine translation: NAIST at WAT2015. In *Proceedings of the 2nd Workshop on Asian Translation (WAT2015)*, pages 35–41, Kyoto, Japan. Workshop on Asian Translation.

Kishore Papineni, Salim Roukos, Todd Ward, and Wei-Jing Zhu. 2002. Bleu: a method for automatic evaluation of machine translation. In *Proceedings of the 40th annual meeting on association for computational linguistics*, pages 311–318. Association for Computational Linguistics.

Rico Sennrich, Barry Haddow, and Alexandra Birch. 2016a. Improving neural machine translation models with monolingual data. In *Proceedings of the 54th Annual Meeting of the Association for Computational Linguistics (Volume 1: Long Papers)*, pages 86–96, Berlin, Germany. Association for Computational Linguistics.

Rico Sennrich, Barry Haddow, and Alexandra Birch. 2016b. Neural machine translation of rare words with subword units. In *Proceedings of the 54th Annual Meeting of the Association for Computational Linguistics (Volume 1: Long Papers)*, pages 1715–1725, Berlin, Germany. Association for Computational Linguistics.

Matthew Snover, Bonnie Dorr, Richard Schwartz, Linnea Micciulla, and John Makhoul. 2006. A study of translation edit rate with targeted human annotation. In *Proceedings of association for machine translation in the Americas*, volume 200.

Nitish Srivastava, Geoffrey Hinton, Alex Krizhevsky, Ilya Sutskever, and Ruslan Salakhutdinov. 2014. Dropout: a simple way to prevent neural networks from overfitting. *The Journal of Machine Learning Research*, 15(1):1929–1958.

Felix Stahlberg, Adri de Gispert, and Bill Byrne. 2018. The university of cambridges machine translation systems for wmt18. In *Proceedings of the Third Conference on Machine Translation, Volume 2: Shared Task Papers*, pages 508–516, Belgium, Brussels. Association for Computational Linguistics.

Ilya Sutskever, Oriol Vinyals, and Quoc V Le. 2014. Sequence to sequence learning with neural networks. In *Advances in neural information processing systems*, pages 3104–3112.

Christian Szegedy, Vincent Vanhoucke, Sergey Ioffe, Jon Shlens, and Zbigniew Wojna. 2016. Rethinking the inception architecture for computer vision. In *Proceedings of the IEEE conference on computer vision and pattern recognition*, pages 2818–2826.

Ashish Vaswani, Noam Shazeer, Niki Parmar, Jakob Uszkoreit, Llion Jones, Aidan N Gomez, Łukasz Kaiser, and Illia Polosukhin. 2017. Attention is all you need. In *Advances in neural information processing systems*, pages 5998–6008.

Weiyue Wang, Jan-Thorsten Peter, Hendrik Rosendahl, and Hermann Ney. 2016. Character: Translation edit rate on character level. In *Proceedings of the First Conference on Machine Translation: Volume 2, Shared Task Papers*, volume 2, pages 505–510.

Weijia Xu and Marine Carpuat. 2018. The university of maryland's chinese-english neural machine translation systems at wmt18. In *Proceedings of the Third Conference on Machine Translation, Volume 2: Shared Task Papers*, pages 539–544, Belgium, Brussels. Association for Computational Linguistics.

Jinxing Yu, Xun Jian, Hao Xin, and Yangqiu Song. 2017. Joint embeddings of chinese words, characters, and fine-grained subcharacter components. In *Proceedings of the 2017 Conference on Empirical Methods in Natural Language Processing*, pages 286–291.

The NiuTrans Machine Translation Systems for WMT19

Bei Li[1], Yinqiao Li[1], Chen Xu[1], Ye Lin[1], Jiqiang Liu[1], Hui Liu[1],
Ziyang Wang[1], Yuhao Zhang[1], Nuo Xu[1], Zeyang Wang[1], Kai Feng[1],
Hexuan Chen[1], Tengbo Liu[1], Yanyang Li[1], Qiang Wang[1],
Tong Xiao[12] and Jingbo Zhu[12]
[1]NLP Lab, Northeastern University, Shenyang, China
[2]NiuTrans Co.,Ltd., Shenyang, China
`libei_neu@outlook.com, {xiaotong, zhujingbo}@mail.neu.edu.cn`

Abstract

This paper described NiuTrans neural machine translation systems for the WMT 2019 news translation tasks. We participated in 13 translation directions, including 11 supervised tasks, namely EN↔{ZH, DE, RU, KK, LT}, GU→EN and the unsupervised DE↔CS subtrack. Our systems were built on deep Transformer and several back-translation methods. Iterative knowledge distillation and ensemble+reranking were also employed to obtain stronger models. Our unsupervised submissions were based on NMT enhanced by SMT. As a result, we achieved the highest BLEU scores in {KK↔EN, GU→EN} directions, ranking 2nd in {RU→EN, DE↔CS} and 3rd in {ZH→EN, LT→EN, EN→RU, EN↔DE} among all constrained submissions.

1 Introduction

Our NiuTrans team participated in 13 WMT19 shared news translation tasks, including 11 supervised and 2 unsupervised sub-tracks. We reused some effective approaches of our WMT18 submissions (Wang et al., 2018), including back-translation by beam search (Sennrich et al., 2016b), BPE (Sennrich et al., 2016c) and further strengthened our systems by exploiting some new techniques this year.

For our supervised task submissions, all the language pairs shared similar model architectures and training flow. We proposed four novel Deep-Transformer architectures based on (Wang et al., 2019) as our baseline, which outperformed the standard `Transformer-Big` significantly in terms of both translation quality and convergence speed.

As for the data augmentation aspect, we experimented several back-translation methods (Sennrich et al., 2016b), including beam search, unrestricted sampling and sampling-topK proposed by Edunov et al. (2018), to leverage the target-side monolingual data. We also applied iterative knowledge distillation (Freitag et al., 2017) to leverage the source-side monolingual data.

Our system also employed the conventional combination methods including ensemble and feature-based re-ranking to further improve the translation quality. We proposed a simple greedy search algorithm to find the best ensemble combination effectively and efficiently. Hypothesis combination (Hassan et al., 2018) was also adopted to generate more diverse hypotheses for better re-ranking.

For unsupervised tasks, we mainly investigated the methodology of unsupervised SMT (Artetxe et al., 2019) and NMT (Lample and Conneau, 2019) to build our baselines, then presented a joint training strategy on top of these baselines to boost their performances.

This paper was structured as follows: we described the details of our novel Deep-Transformer in Section 2, then in Section 3 we presented an overview of our universal training flow for all supervised language pairs and the unsupervised methods. The experiment settings and main results were shown in Section 4.

2 Deep Transformer

Neural machine translation models based on multi-layer self-attention (Vaswani et al., 2017) has shown strong results on several large-scale tasks. Enlarging the model capacity is an effective way to obtain stronger networks, including widening the hidden representation or deepening the model layers. Bapna et al. (2018) has shown that learning deeper networks is not easy for vanilla Transformer due to the gradient vanishing/exploding problem.

Proceedings of the Fourth Conference on Machine Translation (WMT), Volume 2: Shared Task Papers (Day 1) pages 257–266
Florence, Italy, August 1-2, 2019. ©2019 Association for Computational Linguistics

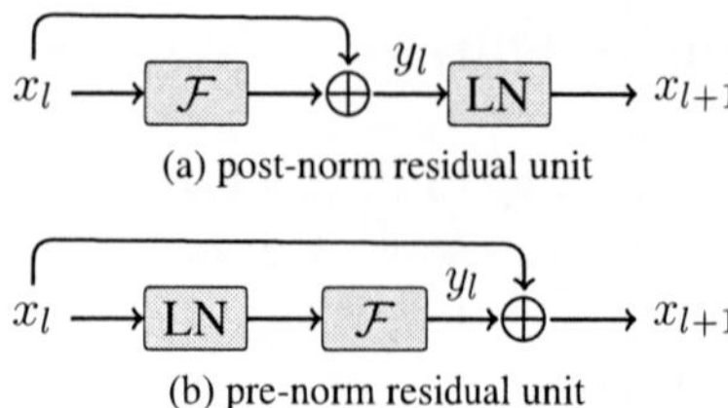

(a) post-norm residual unit

(b) pre-norm residual unit

Figure 1: Examples of pre-norm residual unit and post-norm residual unit. $\mathcal{F}$ = sub-layer, and LN = layer normalization.

Wang et al. (2019) emphasized that the location of layer normalization played a vital role when training deep Transformer. In early versions of Transformer (Vaswani et al., 2017), layer normalization was placed after the element-wise residual addition (see Figure 1(a)). While in recent implementations (Vaswani et al., 2018), layer normalization was applied to the input of every sub-layer(see Figure 1(b)), which can provide a direct way to pass error gradient from top to bottom. In this way pre-norm Transformer is more efficient for training than post-norm (vanilla Transformer) when the model goes deeper. Remarkably, a dynamic linear combination of previous layers method[1] can further improve the translation quality. Note that we built our deep self-attentional counterparts in pre-norm way as default. In this section we described the details about our deep architectures as below:

Pre-Norm Transformer: In recent Tensor2Tensor implementations[2], layer normalization (Lei Ba et al., 2016) was applied to the input of every sub-layer which the computation sequence could be expressed as: *normalize→Transform→dropout→residual-add*. In this way we could successfully train a deeper pre-norm Transformer within comparable performance with `Transformer-Big` or even better, only one fourth training cost.

Pre-Norm Transformer-RPR: We found Transformer-RPR (Shaw et al., 2018) which simultaneously incorporating relative position information with sinusoidal position encodings for sequences in pre-norm style could outperform the pre-norm Transformer with the same encoder depth. We used clipping distance $k = 20$ with the

---

[1] We called it as Transformer-DLCL in the subsequent sections

[2] `https://github.com/tensorflow/tensor2tensor`

unique edge representations per layer and head.

Pre-Norm Transformer-DLCL: The Transformer-DLCL employed direct links with all the previous layers and offered efficient access to lower-level representations in a deep stack. An additional weight matrix $W_{l+1} \in R^{L \times L}$ was used to weigh each incoming layer in a linear manner. This method can be formulated as:

$$\Psi(y_0, y_1...y_l) = \sum_{k=0}^{l} W_k^{l+1} LN(y_k) \qquad (1)$$

Eq.1 provided a way to learn preference of layers in different levels of the stack, $\Psi(y_0, y_1...y_l)$ was the combination of previous layer representation. Furthermore, this method is model architecture free which we can integrate with either pre-norm Transformer or pre-norm Transformer-RPR for further enhancement. The details can be seen in Wang et al. (2019).

3 System Overview

3.1 Data Filter

Previous work (Junczys-Dowmunt, 2018; Wang et al., 2018; Stahlberg et al., 2018) indicated that rigorous data filtering scheme is crucial, or it will lead to catastrophic loss in quality, especially in EN↔DE and EN↔RU. For most language pairs, we filter the training bilingual corpus with the following rules:

- Normalize punctuation with Moses scripts except the ZH ↔ EN language pair.

- Filter out the sentences longer than 100 words, or exceed 40 characters in a single word.

- Filter out the sentences which contain HTML tags or duplicated translations.

- Filter out the sentences which both the source and the target side are identical language.

- Filter out the sentences whose alignment scores obtained by fast-align[3] are lower than -6.

- The word ratio between the source and the target must not exceed 1:3 or 3:1.

After several data augmentation methods to leverage monolingual data in order to further boost translation quality, the same data filter strategy was employed.

---

[3] `https://github.com/clab/fast_align`

258

3.2 Back Translation

Back-translation (Sennrich et al., 2016b) is an essential method to integrate the target side monolingual synthetic knowledge when building a state-of-the-art NMT system. Especially for low-resource language tasks, it's indispensable to augment the training data by mixing the pseudo corpus with the parallel part, in that the target side lexicon coverage is insufficient, such as EN $\leftrightarrow$ {KK, GU} only consist of 0.11M and 0.5M bilingual data, respectively.

How to select the appropriate sentences from the abundant monolingual data is a crucial issue due to the limitation of equipment and huge overhead time. We trained a 5-gram language model based on the mixture of development set and bilingual-target side data to score the monolingual sentences. In addition, considering the impact of sequence length, we set a threshold range from 10 to 50.

Recent work (Edunov et al., 2018) has shown that different methods of generating pseudo corpus made discrepant influence on translation performance. Edunov et al. (2018) indicated that sampling or noisy synthetic data gives a much stronger training signal than data generated by beam or greedy search. This year we attempted several data augmentation methods as follows:

- Beam search: Generated target translation by beam search with beam 4.

- Sampling: Selected a word randomly from the whole distribution each step which increases the diversity of pseudo corpus compared with beam search, but low precision.

- Sampling Top-K: Selected a word in a restricted way that only top-K (we set K as 10) words can be chosen.

It's worthy noting that experimental results on different language pairs behaved inconsistent: sampling is more helpful when it comes to low-resource problem like Kazakh, Gujarati and Lithuanian. Oppositely, we observed that language pairs with abundant parallel corpus like ZH$\leftrightarrow$EN are insensitive to sampling method, and slight improvement by restricted sampling which selected from top-10 candidates. We used different strategies to leverage monolingual resource for specific task which we will show detail description in Section4.

3.3 Greedy Based Ensemble

Ensemble decoding is an effective system combination method to boost machine translation quality via integrating the predictions of several single models at each decode step. It has been proved effective in the past few years' WMT tasks (Wang et al., 2018; Deng et al., 2018; Junczys-Dowmunt, 2018; Sennrich et al., 2016a). We enhanced the single model by employing deep self-attentional models. Note that the improvement is poor if the single models performed strong enough and no significant benefits from increasing the participant quantity. So it's necessary to utilize the models sufficiently to search for a better combination on the development set. We adopted an easily operable greedy-base strategy as the following:

Algorithm 1 An Simple ensemble algorithm based on greedy search

---

Input:
  a model list Ω_{cand} sorted by the development scores.
Output:
  a final model list Φ_{final}.
1: **for all** $4\_model\_combination$ that $model \in top - 8\ models$ **do**
2:     Ensemble decoding to get the score
3: **end for**
4: Choose the best 4model combination as the initial Φ_{final} .
5: **repeat**
6:     Shift the single model from the rest of Ω_{cand} to the Φ_{final} which performs better when combined with Φ_{final}.
7: **until** there is tiny improvement as the model number increases

---

To ensure the diversity among the candidate models, we constructed a single model from several perspectives, such as different initialization seed, training epochs, model sizes and network architectures described in Section 2. On the development set, this algorithm can consistently improve nearly 1-1.5 BLEU scores over the best single model across all the tasks in which we have participated.

3.4 Iterative Knowledge Distillation

A natural idea to further boost the performance of the ensemble model obtained in Section 3.3 is to alternate knowledge distillation (Hinton et al.,

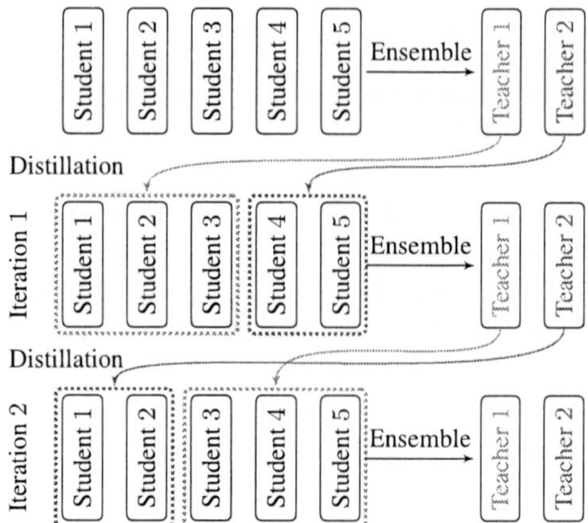

Figure 2: A simple example of Iterative Knowledge Distillation with 5 students, 2 teachers and 2 iterations

2015; Freitag et al., 2017) and ensemble iteratively. The naive approach started with a list of single model candidates as the students and the best 4 models combination retrieved from Algorithm 1 as the teacher. Sequence-level knowledge distillation (Kim and Rush, 2016) was then applied to fine-tune each student model with additional source data. With these enhanced student models, a stronger 4 models combination can be produced through Algorithm 1. We iterated this process until less than 0.1 BLEU improvement on the validation set.

However, in the preliminary experiments we found that such iteration didn't yield good results as we expected. We attributed this phenomenon to the deficiency of model diversity, due to the fact that all students were collapsed to a similar optimum induced by the same teacher they learnt from, which limited the potential gain from iteration. To avoid this, in each step of the iteration, we split the candidates into 4 subsets randomly and assign each subset a distinct teacher model sampled from the top-4 models combinations, then fine-tuned each model within the same subset with its corresponding teacher model. Moreover, we added additional 2M source-side monolingual data in each step to better preserve the model diversity. Figure 2 shows an example.

3.5 Feature Reranking

This year we adopted an hypothesis combination strategy to pick up a potentially better translation from the N-best consisting of several different ensemble outputs. For example we generated 96 hypothesises by 8 different ensemble systems, and set the beam size as 12 during the decoding procedure instead of obtaining all 96 outputs from a sin-

gle but best ensemble model. The oracle computed by sentence-level BLEU script on development set indicated that hypothesis combination achieved 5 BLEU scores higher compared with the single ensemble output. Our reranking features would be described on five aspects as follows:

Right-to-Left Models: NMT models generate the target translations in a left to right fashion, so it's obvious that incorporating models which generate the target sentences in reverse order can be complementary (Stahlberg et al., 2018). We trained four deep Transformer-DLCL models with different hyper-parameter settings by reversing the target side sentence, followed by ensemble knowledge distillation method to enhance the single model performance. Experiment results showed that the accuracy of the reverse model was extremely necessary, or you may even get worse results.

Target-to-Source Models: Re-scoring between the hypothesis and the source input by target-to-source systems. In addition Target-to-Source-Right-to-Left models were needed.

Language Model: We both used a 5-gram language model and a deep self-attention language model trained on target monolingual data.

Cross-lingual Sentence Similarity: We mixed the source-to-target and target-to-source training data about 1:1 to train a cross-lingual translation model, in order to compute the cosine similarity between the n-best hypothesis and the source sentence-level vectors (Hassan et al., 2018) .

Sentence-Align Score: We used fast-align tool to evaluate the alignment probability between the source and the target.

Translation Coverage: A SMT phrase-table to obtain the top-50 translation for each source-to-target word pair. In this way, the translation coverage score can be easily gained with respect to the dual direction hits in the dictionary with length normalization.

We rescored 96-best outputs generated by several ensemble systems using a rescoring model consisting of features above by K-batched MIRA (Cherry and Foster, 2012) algorithm which is widely used in Moses[4].

---

[4]`https://github.com/moses-smt/mosesdecoder`

3.6 Unsupervised NMT

We also participated in the unsupervised translation tasks with only the monolingual data provided by WMT organizer. We both attempted the unsupervised SMT and NMT, then combined them for better results. To train SMT models, the unsupervised tuning (Artetxe et al., 2019) was applied to further enhance the unsupervised SMT system, which employed a small pseudo generated by the target-to-source system to adjust weights of the source-to-target system. We followed Artetxe et al. (2019) to exploit subword information into unsupervised SMT system, which two additional weights were added to the initial phrase-table. The new features employed a character-level similarity function instead of word translation probabilities, which are analogous to the lexical weightings.

For unsupervised NMT, the techniques we used were based on the recently proposed method for unsupervised machine translation (Lample and Conneau, 2019), including proper initialization, leveraging a strong language model and iterative back-translation (Lample et al., 2018). Our systems were initiated by cross-lingual masked language model, which brought significant improvement than cross-lingual embedding method. After that, the standard NMT architecture can be trained by only leveraging monolingual data using combining denoising auto-encoding and iterative back-translation. We adopted two training strategies combining both NMT and SMT models to further enhance our unsupervised system:

- Generate the pseudo corpus by SMT and warmup the NMT models restricted in first 1000 training steps, then we used the pseudo corpus generated by NMT systems for the remained training.

- We mixed the pseudo corpus consisting of NMT and SMT outputs in 1:1 at the beginning, and we increased the ratio of NMT pseudo corpus iteratively until there was no significantly improvement on validation set.

4 Experiments and Results

For all supervised tasks, we used deep self-attentional models as our baseline, and we also experimented the shallow and wide counterparts to verify its effectiveness with the same training corpus. Preliminary experiments indicated that our deep models can even outperform the standard `Transformer-Big` by 0.7-1.3 BLEU scores on different language pairs. All of our experiments employed 25/30 encoder layers and 6 decoder layers, both embedding and hidden size have a dimension of 512, 8 heads for the self-attention and encoder-decoder attention mechanisms. We shared the target-side embedding and softmax matrix. All BLEU scores were reported with mteval-v13a.pl[5]. Next, we will show details for different language pairs in the following subsections.

4.1 Experiment setting

We implemented deep fashion models based on Tensor2Tensor, all models were trained on eight 1080Ti GPUs. We used the Adam optimizer with $\beta_1 = 0.97$, $\beta_2 = 0.997$ and $\epsilon = 10^{-6}$ as well as gradient accumulation due to the high GPU memory consumption. The training data was re-shuffled after finishing each training epoch, and we batched sentence pairs by target-side sentences lengths, with 8192 tokens per GPU. Large learning rate and warmup-steps were chosen for faster convergence. We set max learning rate as 0.002 and warmup-steps as 8000 for most language pairs including EN↔{ZH, RU, KK, LT}. Specifically in EN↔DE task, 16000 warmup-steps achieved better results. During training, we also employed label smoothing with a confidence score 0.9 and all the dropout probabilities were set to 0.1. Furthermore, we averaged the last 15 checkpoints of a single training process for all language pairs. The models were saved and validated every 20 minutes.

4.2 English ↔ Chinese

For ZH ↔ EN system, our parallel corpus included CWMT, wikititles-v1, NewsCommentary-v14, and 30% randomly sampled data from UN corpus. All parallel data were segmented by NiuTrans (Xiao et al., 2012) word segmentation toolkit. After the preprocessing, we trained BPE (Sennrich et al., 2016c) models with $32,000$ merge operations for both sides respectively.

For back-translation, we trained 25-layers transformer models using WMT18 (Wang et al., 2018) training data for both directions. We selected 10M NewsCrawl2018 monolingual data for ZH→EN and the combination of XinHua and XMU data

---

[5]`https://github.com/mosessmt/`
`mosesdecoder/blob/master/scripts/`
`generic/mtevalv13a.pl`

for EN→ZH. Experimental results from table 1 showed that generating the pseudo corpus by beam search brought significant improvement on *newstest2018* for ZH↔EN. Meanwhile, for EN→ZH system, additional pseudo corpus[6] by sampling-top10 could obtain +0.7 BLEU scores on *newstest2018*, but exhibited negative impact on *newstest2019*.

For ZH→EN, we trained 12 models with different configurations, e.g., layers, batch size, filters, seed, etc. The best performance on our development set *newstest2018* gained +1.6 BLEU improvement over `Transformer-Base`, even +0.7 BLEU higher than that of `Transformer-Big`. Iterative Knowledge Distillation with 4 teachers, 3 iterations and 1 epoch per iteration gave +1.6 BLEU improvement over the best single model. To this end, almost +4 BLEU improvement was observed on *newstest2019*. Through greedy based ensemble algorithm, we selected the best 8-model combination on *newstest2018* and boosted our system performance by +0.8 BLEU. Our reranking model contained 27 features, including 4 L2R-Ensemble, 4 R2L-Ensemble, 4 T2S-Ensemble, 4 T2S-R2L-Ensemble and other features mentioned in Section 3.5.

For EN→ZH, we used the same training settings to obtain our best system. The results after applying each component are reported in Table 1. Surprisingly, adding pseudo corpus hindered our system improvement on *newstest2019*, yet gained +3.7 BLEU improvement on *newstest2018*. One possible explanation is that the construction of test set in this year is different from those in previous years.

System	EN-ZH		ZH-EN	
	18test	19test	18test	19test
Base	38.3	35.7	24.2	-
+Beam	41.3	36.1	26.2	27.0
+S-TopK	42.0	35.9	-	-
Big	43.2	37.1	27.1	27.7
DLCL25RPR	43.9	38.2	27.8	29.1
+EKD	44.6	39.3	29.6	33.0
+Ensemble	45.1	39.8	30.4	34.0
+Reranking	45.6	39.9	30.9	34.2

Table 1: Results for EN↔ZH on official WMT test

---

[6] We mixed the sampling-topk corpus with the parallel one to fine-tune each single model

4.3 English ↔ German

Table 2 presents the BLEU scores on *newstest2018* and *newstest2019* for EN↔DE tasks. All parallel training data released were used and we adopted the dual conditional cross-entropy method (Junczys-Dowmunt, 2018) to filter out the noise data in ParaCrawl corpus, resulting in 10M bilingual sentence pairs. A joint BPE model was applied in both directions with $32,000$ merge operations. Moreover, we selected shared vocabulary for both language pairs.

The target-side monolingual data played an important role in the success of this language pairs. We back-translated 10M monolingual in-domain data from the collection of NewsCrawl2016-2018 filtered by XenC (Rousseau, 2013). We observed that generating pseudo corpus via random sampling is much more effective than beam search with the same volume of monolingual sentences, resulting in 2.5/3.7 BLEU improvement on *newstest2018* for EN→DE and DE→EN respectively. `Transformer-DLCL` with 25 encoder layers and 4096 filters obtained +2.5/1.7 BLEU improvement. Iterative Knowledge Distillation and 8 models combination yielded another +0.8/1.4 BLEU scores. Unfortunately, we failed to identify any significant improvement from reranking in terms of validation BLEU scores. Perhaps the features we used were not strong enough to score the n-best properly. It's worth noting that we re-normalized the quotes in German for the additional 1.8 BLEU improvement on EN→DE.

System	EN-DE		DE-EN	
	18test	19test	18test	19test
Base	41.4	38.3	40.8	42.3
+Paracrawl	43.2	39.5	42.7	44.7
+Beam	44.0	39.7	46.2	45.0
+Sampling	45.7	40.7	46.4	45.5
DLCL25filter4096	48.2	42.7	48.1	47.0
+EKD	48.6	44.2	47.0	47.6
+Ensemble	49.4	45.5	48.4	48.3

Table 2: Results for EN↔DE on official WMT test set

4.4 English ↔ Russian

For EN↔RU, we used the following resource provided by WMT, including News Commentary-v14, ParaCrawl-v3, CommonCrawl and Yandex Corpus. The parallel corpus we used was comprised of 7.66M sentences after removing the bad case mentioned in Section 3.1. We experiment-ed different BPE code size, ranging from $30,000$ to $80,000$, inspired by the morphology richness of Russian. Considering the efficiency and performance, we finally chose $50,000$ for both directions. We used the same data selection strategy as in EN↔DE and retained only 16M monolingual data from NewsCrawl2015-2018[7]. The selected sentences were then divided into two equal parts. We generated the pseudo corpus from the first part with beam search sized 4 and trained our NMT models with this corpus together with the parallel ones. The other 8M data were back-translated by random sampling and used to fine-tune each model.

Our final submissions consisted of four Deep Transformer models strengthened by Knowledge Distillation, including DLCL25, DLCL30, DLCL25RPR and DLCL30RPR for EN→RU. The reverse direction contained DLCL25, DLCL25RPR with 4096 filters, DLCL30RPR and DLCL30Filter with 4096 filters. The overall results of our system were reported in Table 3. We observed the same phenomenon as in EN→ZH, where back-translation could yield better results on *newstest2018* but inferior ones on *newstest2019*.

	EN-RU		RU-EN	
System	18test	19test	18test	19test
Base	29.0	27.8	30.9	38.2
+Beam	30.4	28.9	33.0	37.8
+Sampling	32.2	28.3	33.6	37.5
DLCL25RPR	33.4	29.8	34.9	38.9
+EKD	34.1	33.1	35.9	39.5
+Ensemble	35.1	33.8	36.5	40.0
+Reranking	35.5	34.0	36.7	40.0

Table 3: Results for EN↔RU on official WMT test set

4.5 English ↔ Kazakh

This section described our EN↔KK submissions, where we ranked No. 1 in both directions. This task was different from the above three language pairs, whose bilingual data, including News Commentary-v14 and English-Kazakh crawled corpus, contained only $97,000$ sentences after filtering. It was not possible to train a large NMT model, with only 2.6/10.1 BLEU on *newsdev2019*

as shown in Table 4. We used Russian as the pivotal language to construct the additional EN↔KK bilingual corpus from the crawled RU↔KK corpus as well as the RU↔EN one provided by WMT organizers, resulting in 3.78M high-quality bilingual data[8].

For back-translation, we generated the pseudo corpus via random sampling from 2M monolingual data selected by Xenc in the collection of Common Crawl, News Commentary, News crawl and Wiki dumps. This pseudo corpus was extremely effective for our system.

For KK→EN system, we adopted the same training procedure, except that we chose 4M English monolingual sentences from News crawl 2015-2018 instead, which consisted of 2M indomain sentences selected by Xenc and 2M randomly sampled. The detailed experiment results could be seen in Table 4.

	EN-KK		KK-EN	
System	19dev	19test	19dev	19test
Big	2.6	1.9	10.1	11.5
+Pivot	14.9	7.8	23.4	19.8
+Sampling	19.7	10.3	26.2	28.8
DLCL25	20.5	10.7	26.3	29.0
+RPR	-	-	26.6	30.1
+Ensemble	21.3	11.1	26.8	30.5

Table 4: Results for EN↔KK on official WMT test set

4.6 English ↔ Lithuanian

For EN ↔ LT tasks, we used all parallel data available as follows: Europarl-v9, ParaCrawl-v3 and Rapid corpus of EU press releases. Through data filtering mentioned in Section3-1, 1.93M bilingual corpus were remained. Lithuanian monolingual resources containing Common Crawl, Europarl, News crawl and Wiki dumps were back-translated to strengthen the EN→LT translation quality by sampling approach. Similarly, News Crawl from 2015 to 2018 were used for the reverse direction pair. We adopted the same performance improvement pipelines mentioned above, including various deep self-attentional architectures, greedy based ensemble and knowledge distillation teacher, except for feature reranking. We showed the detailed experiment results in Table 5.

---

[7]All monolingual data from NewsCrawl2015-2018 were selected for both directions

[8]The training data we used included the pseudo corpus as well as the provided parallel corpus

System	EN-LT		LT-EN	
	19dev	19test	19dev	19test
Base	18.3	11.5	27.1	29.2
+Pseudo	24.8	13.8	32.2	30.2
DLCL25	25.1	14.0	33.2	31.5
+EKD	26.1	15.0	34.6	33.8
+Ensemble	26.7	15.2	35.1	34.3

Table 5: Results for EN↔LT on official WMT test set

4.7 Gujarati → English

Our GU→EN system was based on Bible Corpus, crawled corpus, OPUS and wikipedia, a total of 0.5M sentence pairs. Additionally, 1.5M HindEn-Corp corpus were converted to GU→EN bilingual corpus in terms of the alphabet mapping between Gujarati and Hindi languages. Due to the grammar divergence in the two languages, we built a baseline model by bilingual data to score the corpus and removed the bad cases in which the scores were inferior to the threshold predefined. Preliminary experiments have shown that data filtering was extremely crucial, for noisy signals in training data did harm to our translation quality. Only 0.98 bilingual pairs were remained after strict data cleaning, including parallel corpus provided by WMT and pivot pairs originated from HindEnrop corpus.

We used the same approach to select pseudo corpus with KK→EN task, while different generation approach were applied. Our pseudo corpus consisted of two parts: 2M pseudo data by beam search within $(1.2, 10)$ for alpha and beam size respectively and another 1M through randomly sampling. From Table 6 we found that the data quantity was the key factor to enhance the translation quality in this task, and deep DLCL25RPR took full advantage of deep encoder layers to extract more expressive representations.

4.8 German ↔ Czech

This section demonstrated our unsupervised result on DE↔CS, Table 7 presents the BLEU scores on *newstest2013* and *newstest2019*. We removed the duplicated sentences and the sentences with exceptional length ratio. As a result, we used 24.38M Czech monolingual data and 24.36M German monolingual data for each direction respectively from News Crawl2007-2018. All texts were segmented with scripts provides by Moses, and $60,000$ BPE merge operations were applied to un-

System	GU-EN	
	19dev	19test
Base	3.1	3.0
+Pivot	16.3	12.5
+Beam	30.7	19.7
+Sampling	32.5	21.3
DLCL25RPR	34.2	22.8
+EKD	34.9	23.8
+Ensemble	35.5	24.6
+Reranking	36.1	24.9

Table 6: Results for EN→GU on official WMT test set

supervised NMT systems.

We used the Transformer architecture as described in Lample and Conneau (2019) that we revised the `Transformer-Big` with 8 attention heads, learned positional embedding and GELU activation functions. From Table 7 we observed that through several techniques, the unsupervised SMT has gained significantly improvement on *newstest2013* and *newstest2019*. Moreover, leveraging the pseudo corpus generated by unsupervised-SMT system can bring furthermore enhancement though the unsupervised SMT was inferior to NMT system. We both experimented the training strategies mentioned in Section 3.6, and the iterative training method was more efficient. We only fused two single models in decoding procedure and there is no significant improvement on both valid and test sets. Note that we fixed the quotes in both directions.

System	DE-CS		CS-DE	
	13test	19test	13test	19test
SMT Base	9.3	7.9	10.5	9.1
+weight-tune	10.0	8.2	11.2	9.5
+sub-word	11.0	9.2	12.4	10.7
+iterative-BT	13.3	11.7	14.7	12.7
NMT Base	17.8	15.8	18.8	16.2
+warmup	20.0	17.4	20.6	17.8
+iteration	20.1	17.6	21.0	18.0
Ensemble	20.3	17.6	21.2	18.1
+fix quotes*	-	18.9	-	17.7

Table 7: Unsupervised results for DE↔CS on official WMT test set, note that the *newstest2019* contains 1997 sentence pairs for both directions

5 Conclusion

This paper described all 13 tasks of NiuTrans systems in WMT19 news shared translation tasks including both supervised and unsupervised sub tracks, showing that we could adopt an universal training strategies to gain promising achievement. We built our final submissions considering two mainstreams:

- Neural architecture improvement by employing several deep self-attentional based models.

- Taking full advantage of both additional source and target monolingual data by knowledge distillation and back-translation, respectively.

In addition, a greed-based ensemble algorithm was helpful to search for a robust combination of models, and we adopted hypothesis combination strategy for more diverse re-ranking. Our systems performed strongly among all the constrained submissions: we ranked 1st in EN→KK, KK→EN and GU→EN respectively, and stayed Top-3 for the remained language pairs.

References

Mikel Artetxe, Gorka Labaka, and Eneko Agirre. 2019. An effective approach to unsupervised machine translation. *arXiv preprint arXiv:1902.01313*.

Ankur Bapna, Mia Chen, Orhan Firat, Yuan Cao, and Yonghui Wu. 2018. Training deeper neural machine translation models with transparent attention. In *Proceedings of the 2018 Conference on Empirical Methods in Natural Language Processing*, pages 3028–3033, Brussels, Belgium. Association for Computational Linguistics.

Colin Cherry and George Foster. 2012. Batch tuning strategies for statistical machine translation. In *Proceedings of the 2012 Conference of the North American Chapter of the Association for Computational Linguistics: Human Language Technologies*, pages 427–436. Association for Computational Linguistics.

Yongchao Deng, Shanbo Cheng, Jun Lu, Kai Song, Jingang Wang, Shenglan Wu, Liang Yao, Guchun Zhang, Haibo Zhang, Pei Zhang, Changfeng Zhu, and Boxing Chen. 2018. Alibaba's neural machine translation systems for wmt18. In *Proceedings of the Third Conference on Machine Translation, Volume 2: Shared Task Papers*, pages 372–380, Belgium, Brussels. Association for Computational Linguistics.

Sergey Edunov, Myle Ott, Michael Auli, and David Grangier. 2018. Understanding back-translation at scale. In *Proceedings of the 2018 Conference on Empirical Methods in Natural Language Processing*, pages 489–500, Brussels, Belgium. Association for Computational Linguistics.

Markus Freitag, Yaser Al-Onaizan, and Baskaran Sankaran. 2017. Ensemble distillation for neural machine translation. *arXiv preprint arXiv:1702.01802*.

Hany Hassan, Anthony Aue, Chang Chen, Vishal Chowdhary, Jonathan Clark, Christian Federmann, Xuedong Huang, Marcin Junczys-Dowmunt, William Lewis, Mu Li, et al. 2018. Achieving human parity on automatic chinese to english news translation. *arXiv preprint arXiv:1803.05567*.

Geoffrey Hinton, Oriol Vinyals, and Jeff Dean. 2015. Distilling the knowledge in a neural network. *arXiv preprint arXiv:1503.02531*.

Marcin Junczys-Dowmunt. 2018. Microsoft's submission to the wmt2018 news translation task: How i learned to stop worrying and love the data. In *Proceedings of the Third Conference on Machine Translation, Volume 2: Shared Task Papers*, pages 429–434, Belgium, Brussels. Association for Computational Linguistics.

Yoon Kim and Alexander M. Rush. 2016. Sequence-level knowledge distillation. In *Proceedings of the 2016 Conference on Empirical Methods in Natural Language Processing*, pages 1317–1327, Austin, Texas. Association for Computational Linguistics.

Guillaume Lample and Alexis Conneau. 2019. Cross-lingual language model pretraining. *arXiv: Computation and Language*.

Guillaume Lample, Myle Ott, Alexis Conneau, Ludovic Denoyer, and Marc'Aurelio Ranzato. 2018. Phrase-based & neural unsupervised machine translation. *arXiv preprint arXiv:1804.07755*.

Jimmy Lei Ba, Jamie Ryan Kiros, and Geoffrey E Hinton. 2016. Layer normalization. *arXiv preprint arXiv:1607.06450*.

Anthony Rousseau. 2013. Xenc: An open-source tool for data selection in natural language processing. *The Prague Bulletin of Mathematical Linguistics*, (100):73–82.

Rico Sennrich, Barry Haddow, and Alexandra Birch. 2016a. Edinburgh neural machine translation systems for wmt 16. *arXiv preprint arXiv:1606.02891*.

Rico Sennrich, Barry Haddow, and Alexandra Birch. 2016b. Improving neural machine translation models with monolingual data. In *Proceedings of the 54th Annual Meeting of the Association for Computational Linguistics (Volume 1: Long Papers)*, pages 86–96, Berlin, Germany. Association for Computational Linguistics.

Rico Sennrich, Barry Haddow, and Alexandra Birch. 2016c. Neural machine translation of rare words with subword units. In *Proceedings of the 54th Annual Meeting of the Association for Computational Linguistics (Volume 1: Long Papers)*, pages 1715–1725, Berlin, Germany. Association for Computational Linguistics.

Peter Shaw, Jakob Uszkoreit, and Ashish Vaswani. 2018. Self-attention with relative position representations. *arXiv preprint arXiv:1803.02155*.

Felix Stahlberg, Adria de Gispert, and Bill Byrne. 2018. The university of cambridge's machine translation systems for wmt18. In *Proceedings of the Third Conference on Machine Translation, Volume 2: Shared Task Papers*, pages 508–516, Belgium, Brussels. Association for Computational Linguistics.

Ashish Vaswani, Samy Bengio, Eugene Brevdo, Francois Chollet, Aidan N Gomez, Stephan Gouws, Llion Jones, Łukasz Kaiser, Nal Kalchbrenner, Niki Parmar, et al. 2018. Tensor2tensor for neural machine translation. *arXiv preprint arXiv:1803.07416*.

Ashish Vaswani, Noam Shazeer, Niki Parmar, Jakob Uszkoreit, Llion Jones, Aidan N Gomez, Łukasz Kaiser, and Illia Polosukhin. 2017. Attention is all you need. In *Advances in neural information processing systems*, pages 5998–6008.

Qiang Wang, Bei Li, Jiqiang Liu, Bojian Jiang, Zheyang Zhang, Yinqiao Li, Ye Lin, Tong Xiao, and Jingbo Zhu. 2018. The niutrans machine translation system for wmt18. In *Proceedings of the Third Conference on Machine Translation, Volume 2: Shared Task Papers*, pages 532–538, Belgium, Brussels. Association for Computational Linguistics.

Qiang Wang, Bei Li, Tong Xiao, and Jingbo Zhu. 2019. Learning deep transformer models for machine translation. In *Proceedings of the 57th Annual Meeting of the Association for Computational Linguistics (Volume 1: Long Papers)*, Italy, Florence. Association for Computational Linguistics.

Tong Xiao, Jingbo Zhu, Hao Zhang, and Qiang Li. 2012. Niutrans: An open source toolkit for phrase-based and syntax-based machine translation. In *Proceedings of the ACL 2012 System Demonstrations*, ACL '12, pages 19–24, Stroudsburg, PA, USA. Association for Computational Linguistics.

Multi-Source Transformer for
Kazakh-Russian-English Neural Machine Translation

Patrick Littell   Chi-kiu Lo   Samuel Larkin   Darlene Stewart

NRC-CNRC

National Research Council of Canada

1200 Montreal Road, Ottawa, Ontario K1A 0R6, Canada

{Patrick.Littell|Chikiu.Lo|Samuel.Larkin|Darlene.Stewart}@nrc-cnrc.gc.ca

Abstract

We describe the neural machine translation (NMT) system developed at the National Research Council of Canada (NRC) for the Kazakh-English news translation task of the Fourth Conference on Machine Translation (WMT19). Our submission is a multi-source NMT system taking both the original Kazakh sentence and its Russian translation as input for translating into English.

1 Introduction

The WMT19 (Bojar et al., 2019) Kazakh-English News Translation task presented a machine translation scenario in which parallel resources between the two languages (~200k sentences) were considerably fewer than parallel resources between these languages and a third language, Russian (~14M English-Russian sentence pairs and ~5M Kazakh-Russian pairs).

The NRC team therefore explored machine translation pipelines that utilized the Russian resources, including:

1. "Pivoting" through Russian: training an MT system from Kazakh to Russian, and another system from Russian to English (Fig. 1a).

2. Creating a synthetic Kazakh-English parallel corpus by training a Russian-Kazakh MT system and using it to "cross-translate"[1] the Russian-English corpus (Fig. 1b).

3. Training a multi-encoder (Libovický and Helcl, 2017; Libovický et al., 2018) Transformer system (Vaswani et al., 2017) from

Kazakh/Russian to English that subsumes both of these approaches (Fig. 1c).

Techniques (1) and (2) both involve the translation of genuine data into a synthetic translation (into Russian in the first case, and into Kazakh in the second case). It is, however, possible to attend to *both* the original sentence and its translation using multi-source techniques (Zoph and Knight, 2016; Libovický and Helcl, 2017; Nishimura et al., 2018); we hypothesized that giving the system both the originals and "cross-translations", in both directions (Kazakh-to-Russian and Russian-to-Kazakh), would allow the system to make use of the additional information available by seeing the sources before translation.

Our multi-encoder Transformer approach performed best among our submitted systems by a considerable margin, outperforming pivoting by 4.2 BLEU and augmentation by one-way cross-translation by 10.2 BLEU.[2]

2 Multilingual data

2.1 Kazakh-English

The raw bilingual Kazakh-English data provided for the constrained news translation task consists of web-crawled data, news commentary data and Wikipedia article titles. In total, they account for ~200k sentence pairs. All these data were used to train the foundation systems for back-translation. Since the web-crawled data is very noisy, we removed all the web-crawled portion from the training data before training our final submitted system.

For tuning and evaluating, we used the `newsdev2019-kken` data set; for SMT, we

---

[1] We term synthetic data creation by translation between source languages "cross-translation" to distinguish it from "back-translation" in the sense of Sennrich et al. (2016). Nishimura et al. (2018), which also uses source$_1$-to-source$_2$ translation, calls both kinds of synthetic data creation "back-translation", but because our pipeline uses both kinds we distinguish them with separate terms.

[2] However, these systems, as submitted, are not directly comparable due to some additional data filtering in our final submitted system; we will be releasing more direct comparisons and a more thorough description of the architecture in a companion article.

Proceedings of the Fourth Conference on Machine Translation (WMT), Volume 2: Shared Task Papers (Day 1) pages 267–274
Florence, Italy, August 1-2, 2019. ©2019 Association for Computational Linguistics

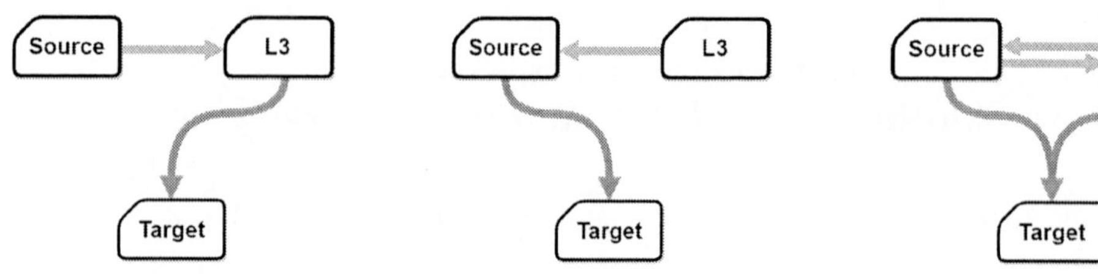

(a) "Pivoting": two systems (source-to-L3 and L3-to-target) executed in a pipeline

(b) Augmentation of source/target corpus with "cross-translated" synthetic data

(c) Multi-source system with augmentation by cross-translation in both directions

Figure 1: Approaches to utilizing a third language ("L3") in machine translation.

split it into two sets as our internal dev and devtest; dev contains 1266 sentence pairs and devtest contains the remaining 800 sentence pairs.

2.2 Kazakh-Russian

The raw bilingual Kazakh-Russian data provided to assist in the news translation task is web-crawled data. In total, they account for ~5M sentence pairs. All these data were used to train the foundation systems for cross-translation.

For tuning and evaluating, we randomly selected 1000 sentence pairs each for the dev and devtest sets from the provided bilingual data. The remaining bilingual data is de-duplicated against the bag of 6-grams collected from the dev and devtest sets. The de-duplicated bilingual data has ~4.2M sentence pairs.

2.3 Russian-English

The raw bilingual Russian-English data we used in our systems consists of web-crawled data, news commentary data and Wikipedia article titles. In total they account for ~14M sentence pairs. All these data were used to train the foundation systems for back-translation. Since the Paracrawl portion of the bilingual data is very noisy, before training our final submitted system we ran our parallel corpus filtering pipeline (Lo et al., 2018) with YiSi-2 as the scoring function (instead of MT + YiSi-1) and trimmed the size of the Paracrawl portion from 12M sentence pairs to 4M sentence pairs.

For tuning and evaluating, we used the `newstest2017-enru` data set as the dev set and the `newstest2018-enru` data set as the devtest set.

3 Data preparation

3.1 Cleaning and tokenization

Our preprocessing pipeline begins by cleaning the UTF-8 with both Moses' cleaning script[3] and an in-house script that performs additional white-space, hyphen, and control character normalization. We then proceed to normalize and tokenize the sentences with Moses' punctuation normalization[4] and tokenization scripts[5].

3.2 Transliteration

To mitigate some of the overall complexity, and allow greater sharing in joint BPE models and weight tying, we first converted the Kazakh and Russian text from Cyrillic to Roman, using official Romanization standards using spm_normalize (Kudo, 2018) and transliteration tables from Wiktionary for Kazakh[6] and Russian[7].

3.3 Byte-pair encoding

Our BPE model is a joint one across transliterated Kazakh, transliterated Russian, and English. Using fastBPE[8], we created a 90k-operation BPE model, balancing the three languages with ~8.2M sentences of each, using:

- all available Kazakh from bilinugual kk-en;
- all available Kazakh from bilinugual kk-ru;

---

[3] `github.com/moses-smt/`
`mosesdecoder/scripts/tokenizer/`
`remove-non-printing-char.perl`
[4] `github.com/moses-smt/mosesdecoder/`
`scripts/tokenizer/normalize-punctuation.`
`perl`
[5] `github.com/moses-smt/mosesdecoder/`
`scripts/tokenizer/tokenizer.perl`
[6] `en.wiktionary.org/wiki/Module:`
`kk-translit`
[7] `en.wiktionary.org/wiki/Module:`
`ru-translit`
[8] `github.com/glample/fastBPE`

- all monolingual Kazakh news and wiki data;

- all available English from bilingual kk-en;

- a sample of ˜8M English sentences from bilingual ru-en and monolingual en;

- all available Russian from bilinugual kk-ru;

- a sample of ˜3.2M Russian sentences from bilingual ru-en and monolingual ru.

A separate vocabulary was extracted for each language using the corpora used to create the BPE model. The BPE model was then applied to all training, dev and devtest data.

4 Multi-encoder transformer

We implemented a multi-source Transformer (Vaswani et al., 2017) architecture, in the Sockeye (Hieber et al., 2017) framework, that combines the output of two encoders (one for Kazakh, one for Russian); this architecture will be described in greater detail in a companion paper.

Our encoder combination takes place during attention (that is, the attention step in which information from the decoder and encoders are combined, rather than the self-attention steps inside each encoder and decoder); Figure 2 illustrates the position in which the multiple sources are combined into a single representation.

First, we perform multi-head scaled dot-product attention between the the decoder and each encoder separately.

$$C^{(s)} = \text{MultiHead}^{(s)}\left(D, H^{(s)}, H^{(s)}\right) \quad (1)$$

$$\text{MultiHead}^{(s)}\left(Q, K, V\right) = \sum_i^h \text{Head}_i^{(s)} W_i^{O(s)} \quad (2)$$

$$\text{Head}_i^{(s)}\left(Q, K, V, d_k\right) =$$
$$\mathcal{A}(QW_i^{Q(s)}, KW_i^{K(s)}, VW_i^{V(s)}, d_k) \quad (3)$$

$$\mathcal{A}\left(Q, K, V, d_k\right) = \text{softmax}\left(\frac{QK^\top}{\sqrt{d_k}}\right) V \quad (4)$$

where $D = (d_1, d_2, \cdots, d_n)$, $d_i \in \mathbb{R}^{d_{model}}$ represents the decoder states, $H = (h_1, h_2, \cdots, h_m)$, $h_i \in \mathbb{R}^{d_{model}}$ represents the outputs of the encoder's final self-attention layer, $W_i^{Q(s)} \in \mathbb{R}^{d_{model} \times d_k}$, $W_i^{K(s)} \in \mathbb{R}^{d_{model} \times d_k}$, $W_i^{V(s)} \in$

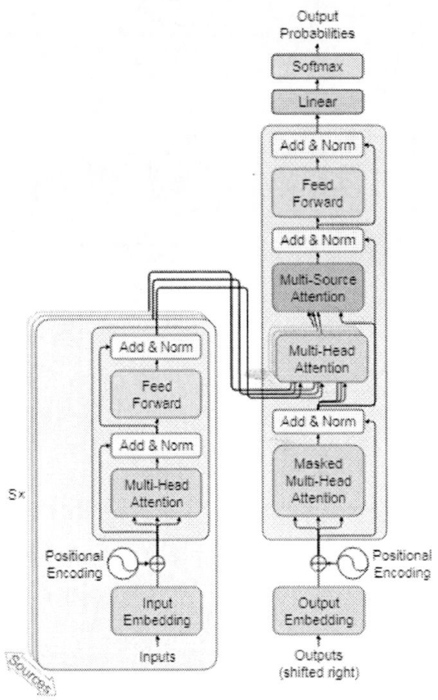

Figure 2: Multi-source attention on S sources. Each output from the S encoders is attended to by a separate multi-head attention layer (Eqs. 1-4), and then the outputs of these attention layers are combined (Eq. 5).

$\mathbb{R}^{d_{model} \times d_k}$ and $W_i^{O(s)} \in \mathbb{R}^{d_k \times d_{model}}$ are trainable parameter matrices which project the key, query and value into a smaller dimensionality. Together with $d_k = d_{model}/h$, we have $C^{(s)} \in \mathbb{R}^{n \times d_{model}}$.

Next, we combine the outputs from the different encoders with a simple projection and sum, similar to what Libovický et al. (2018) refer to as "parallel":

$$\tilde{C} = \sum_i^S C^{(i)} W^{C(i)} \quad (5)$$

As this is essentially the same operation as the multi-head combination in Equation (2), and no nonlinearities intervene, we can also conceptualize Equations (1)-(5) as if they were a single multi-head attention layer with $S * h$ heads (in this case $2 * 8$ heads), in which each group of h heads is constrained to attend to the output of one encoder.

We also experimented with a hierarchical attention mechanism along the lines of Libovický and Helcl (2017) and Libovický et al. (2018), but as this did not outperform the simpler combination mechanism in (5) in internal testing, our submitted systems utilized the latter.

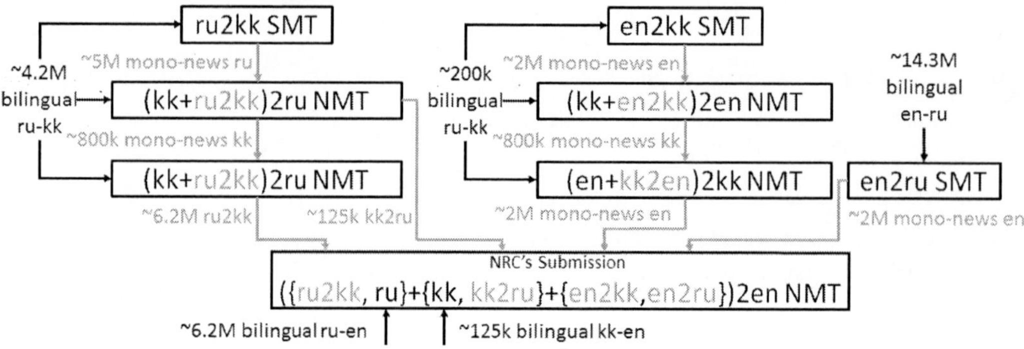

Figure 3: The relations of all the MT systems involved in building the NRC final submitted system.

5 Experiments and results

5.1 NMT Setup

Our code extends sockeye-1.18.72 from Hieber et al. (2017). Each source encoder has 6 layers and our decoder also has 6 layers, with a model dimension of $d_{model} = 512$ and 2048 hidden units sub-layer feed-forward networks. We use weight tying, where the source embeddings, the target embeddings and the target softmax weights are tied, which implies a shared vocab. We trained employing a cross-entropy loss with Adam (Kingma and Ba, 2014), $\beta_1 = 0.9$, $\beta_2 = 0.999$, $\epsilon = 1e - 8$ and an initial learning rate of 0.0001, decreasing the learning by 0.7 each time the development-set BLEU did not improve for 8 checkpoints. We optimized against BLEU using newsdev2019-kken as the development set, stopping early if BLEU did not improve for 32 checkpoints of 1000 updates each. The inputs and output lengths were restricted to a maximum of 60 tokens, and mini-batches were of variable size depending on sentence length, with each mini-batch containing up to 4096 words.

5.2 SMT Setup

We trained en2kk, ru2kk and en2ru SMT systems using Portage (Larkin et al., 2010), a conventional log-linear phrase-based SMT system, using the corresponding BPEed parallel corpora prepared as described in Section 3. The translation model of each SMT system uses IBM4 word alignments (Brown et al., 1993) with grow-diag-final- and phrase extraction heuristics (Koehn et al., 2003). The systems each have two n-gram language models: a 5-gram language model (LM) (a mixture LM in the kk2en case) trained on the target-side of the corresponding parallel corpora

using SRILM (Stolcke, 2002), and a pruned 6-gram LM trained on the monolingual training corpora (for en2ru, trained just on news using KenLM (Heafield, 2011); for ru2kk and en2kk, a static mixture LM trained on all monolingual Kazakh data using SRILM). Each SMT system also includes a hierachical distortion model, a sparse feature model consisting of the standard sparse features proposed in Hopkins and May (2011) and sparse hierarchical distortion model features proposed in Cherry (2013), and a neural network joint model, or NNJM, with 3 words of target context and 11 words of source context, effectively a 15-gram LM (Vaswani et al., 2013; Devlin et al., 2014). The parameters of the log-linear model were tuned by optimizing BLEU on the development set using the batch variant of the margin infused relaxed algorithm (MIRA) by Cherry and Foster (2012). Decoding uses the cube-pruning algorithm of Huang and Chiang (2007) with a 7-word distortion limit.

We then used these SMT systems to back-translate a ~2M sentence subselection of monolingual English news into Kazakh and Russian, and a ~5M sentence subselection of monolingual Russian news into Kazakh, as well as cross-translating the Russian of the ru-en parallel corpora into Kazakh.

5.3 Building the NRC Submission System

Our final submission involved several SMT components and several NMT components to produce back-translations and cross-translations needed for our multi-source submission system, as shown in Figure 3.

Available Resources	Training			Dev./Test		BLEU	
	Source 1	Source 2	Att. Comb.	Source 1	Source 2	Dev.	Test
kk-en	kk+en2kk	–	–	kk	–	12.8	9.9
kk-en, ru-en	kk+ru+en2kk	–	–	kk	–	15.4	12.6
kk-en, kk-ru, ru-en	kk+ru2kk+en2kk	–	–	kk	–	17.9	14.8
kk-ru, ru-en	pivoting					19.3	20.8
kk-en, kk-ru, ru-en	kk+ru2kk+en2kk	kk2ru+ru+en2ru	Parallel	kk	kk2ru	19.6	**24.2 /25.0***

Table 1: BLEU scores on WMT19 Kazakh-English news translation. en2kk denotes synthetic Kazakh back-translated from English. ru2kk denotes synthetic Kazakh cross-translated from Russian. en2ru denotes synthetic Russian back-translated from English. kk2ru denotes synthetic Russian cross-translated from Kazakh. * denotes an unofficial post-competition result, a fully-trained version of our top system, which had only been partially trained due to time constraints.

5.3.1 Synthetic cross-translations

To synthesize cross-translations, we trained 3 systems using our filtered ˜4.2M sentences of bilingual Russian-Kazakh data. First, we trained a Russian-to-Kazakh (ru2kk) SMT system and then used it to generate ˜5M sentences of synthetic Kazakh. Augmenting the bilingual data with the Kazakh back-translations, we trained a Kazakh-to-Russian NMT system to back translate ˜800k sentences of monolingual Kazakh news for a ru2kk NMT system and to cross translate ˜125k kk-en sentences for one component of our final system. Finally, we trained a Russian-to-Kazkah NMT system using the bilingual data and the synthetic Russian to cross translate ˜6M for our second component of the final system.

5.3.2 Synthetic back-translation

A stack of another three MT systems was used to synthesize Kazakh from English using ˜200k of available English-Kazakh bilingual data for training. Starting with an English-to-Kazakh SMT system, ˜2M English sentences were back-translated to Kazakh. Augmenting the bilingual data with the newly generated Kazakh, we trained a NMT Kazakh-to-English system and back translated ˜800k sentences of Kazakh news. The last English-to-Kazakh NMT system in that stack was trained using the bilingual data enlarged with the ˜800k previously generated back-translations. It generated our en2kk back-translation of ˜2M sentences of English news.

Our final component was accomplished by training an English-to-Russian SMT system using ˜14.3M bilingual sentences and back translating the ˜2M sentence subselection of English news into Russian.

5.3.3 Putting it all together

The box labelled "NRC's Submission" in Figure 3 depicts how each sub-corpus was assembled into the final bilingual corpora used to train our multi-source NMT submission system. Each set of curly braces surrounds a pair of corresponding Kazakh and Russian sources. The first pair represents Kazakh and its cross-translation to Russian, the second is the cross-translation of Russian-to-Kazakh with the original Russian, and lastly we have our sub-selected corpus back-translated into both Kazakh and Russian.

5.4 Results

We can see in Table 1 that the full multi-source, multi-encoder system with two-way cross-translation (both Kazakh-to-Russian and Russian-to-Kazakh) is significantly better than our other systems, outperforming the pivoting system (on the fourth line) by 4.2 BLEU and augmentation by one-way cross-translation (on the third line) by 10.2 BLEU.

We believe this improvement over the other two methods is due to the model being able to attend to additional original data, to which the other systems do not have direct access. Both pivoting and one-way synthetic augmentation involve "discarding" genuine data, in that some of the original sentences – Kazakh sentences in the former, and Russian sentences in the later – are never seen by the downstream system, since they are only encountered in translation. Multi-source methods allow a system to attend to the original data in both directions, thus capturing information that would otherwise be lost in translation.

Notable in this table is the comparative improvement of the test scores over the dev scores, between the pivoting (line 4) and multi-source (line 5) systems. This can be explained, we

System	BLEU	YiSi-1	YiSi-1_srl
NEU	30.5	79.19	76.97
rug-morfessor	27.9	77.70	75.47
talp-upc-2019	24.9	75.07	72.74
NRC-CNRC	**24.9**	**75.76**	**73.41**
Frank-s-MT	19.8	76.17	73.87

Table 2: Automatic evaluation results for the top 5 constrained systems in WMT19

System	Ave	Ave. B
NEU	70.1	0.218
rug-morfessor	69.7	0.189
talp-upc-2019	67.1	0.113
NRC-CNRC	**67.0**	**0.092**
Frank-s-MT	65.8	0.066

Table 3: Human evaluation results for the top 5 constrained systems in WMT19

think, by a domain difference between the dev and test sets, where the dev set was sampled from the same news commentary dataset as the training data, whereas the test set comes from actual newswire text. The scores appear to show that the multi-source system has managed to generalize better to newswire text, possibly because it has seen synthetic newswire text (synthesized from the English-Russian dataset) and can respond more appropriately to it.[9]

Tables 2 and 3 compare our multi-source system to the other official submissions in the top 5 of the WMT19 competition. In automatic evaluation by BLEU, we were tied for third place, although with a slight edge when measured by YiSi-1 (Lo, 2019); in human evaluation, we were in a statistical tie for second place. Notably, our multi-source system was the top non-ensemble pure NMT system, with other higher-scoring systems either being ensembles or SMT/NMT hybrids.

6 Conclusion and future work

We present the NRC submission to the WMT19 Kazakh-English news translation shared task. Our submitted system is a multi-source, multi-encoder neural machine translation system that takes Russian as the second source in the system. The ad-

vantages of using the multi-source NMT architecture are that it incorporates additional information obtained from 1) the Russian-English training data cross translated into Kazakh, and 2) the Russian cross translated from Kazakh in the Kazakh-Russian training data.

The drawback of this approach is the comparative complexity of the pipeline, with separate systems being trained to create back-translations and cross-translations (including back-translations to train those systems themselves). This complexity was difficult for a human team to manage when considered for three languages; it would be prohibitive (without additional automation) when making systems that involve four or more languages. Making use of the multi-source architecture itself for creating back- and cross-translations together, and sharing encoders and decoders between systems that share languages, would considerably lessen the the complexity of the pipeline and the number of distinct systems that need to be trained.

In other future work, we want to consider additional methods of multi-source attention, as well as other means of creating cross-linguistic synthetic data beyond machine translation, for lower-resource language pairs that do not have substantial parallel data but may be, for example, closely related.

References

Ondřej Bojar, Christian Federmann, Mark Fishel, Yvette Graham, Barry Haddow, Matthias Huck, Philipp Koehn, Christof Monz, Mathias Müller, and Matt Post. 2019. Findings of the 2019 conference on machine translation (wmt19). In *Proceedings of the Fourth Conference on Machine Translation, Volume 2: Shared Task Papers*, Florence, Italy. Association for Computational Linguistics.

Peter F. Brown, Stephen Della Pietra, Vincent J. Della Pietra, and Robert L. Mercer. 1993. The mathematics of statistical machine translation: Parameter estimation. *Computational Linguistics*, 19(2):263–311.

Colin Cherry. 2013. Improved reordering for phrase-based translation using sparse features. In *Human Language Technologies: Conference of the North American Chapter of the Association of Computational Linguistics, Proceedings, June 9-14, 2013, Westin Peachtree Plaza Hotel, Atlanta, Georgia, USA*, pages 22–31. The Association for Computational Linguistics.

Colin Cherry and George F. Foster. 2012. Batch tuning strategies for statistical machine translation. In

---

[9]Note that, although we did perform additional filtering on the training data of the multi-source system, we do not believe this is the cause of the better performance on the test compared to the pivoting system. In later tests, we found the pivoting system to be relatively insensitive to this filtering process, giving similar BLEU on both dev and test.

Human Language Technologies: Conference of the North American Chapter of the Association of Computational Linguistics, Proceedings, June 3-8, 2012, Montréal, Canada, pages 427–436. The Association for Computational Linguistics.

Jacob Devlin, Rabih Zbib, Zhongqiang Huang, Thomas Lamar, Richard M. Schwartz, and John Makhoul. 2014. Fast and robust neural network joint models for statistical machine translation. In *Proceedings of the 52nd Annual Meeting of the Association for Computational Linguistics, ACL 2014, June 22-27, 2014, Baltimore, MD, USA, Volume 1: Long Papers*, pages 1370–1380. The Association for Computer Linguistics.

Kenneth Heafield. 2011. KenLM: faster and smaller language model queries. In *Proceedings of the EMNLP 2011 Sixth Workshop on Statistical Machine Translation*, pages 187–197, Edinburgh, Scotland, United Kingdom.

Felix Hieber, Tobias Domhan, Michael Denkowski, David Vilar, Artem Sokolov, Ann Clifton, and Matt Post. 2017. Sockeye: A toolkit for neural machine translation. *CoRR*, abs/1712.05690.

Mark Hopkins and Jonathan May. 2011. Tuning as ranking. In *Proceedings of the 2011 Conference on Empirical Methods in Natural Language Processing, EMNLP 2011, 27-31 July 2011, John McIntyre Conference Centre, Edinburgh, UK, A meeting of SIGDAT, a Special Interest Group of the ACL*, pages 1352–1362. ACL.

Liang Huang and David Chiang. 2007. Forest rescoring: Faster decoding with integrated language models. In *ACL 2007, Proceedings of the 45th Annual Meeting of the Association for Computational Linguistics, June 23-30, 2007, Prague, Czech Republic*. The Association for Computational Linguistics.

Diederik P. Kingma and Jimmy Ba. 2014. Adam: A method for stochastic optimization. Cite arxiv:1412.6980Comment: Published as a conference paper at the 3rd International Conference for Learning Representations, San Diego, 2015.

Philipp Koehn, Franz Josef Och, and Daniel Marcu. 2003. Statistical phrase-based translation. In *Human Language Technology Conference of the North American Chapter of the Association for Computational Linguistics, HLT-NAACL 2003, Edmonton, Canada, May 27 - June 1, 2003*. The Association for Computational Linguistics.

Taku Kudo. 2018. Subword regularization: Improving neural network translation models with multiple subword candidates. *CoRR*, abs/1804.10959.

Samuel Larkin, Boxing Chen, George Foster, Ulrich Germann, Eric Joanis, Howard Johnson, and Roland Kuhn. 2010. Lessons from nrc's portage system at wmt 2010. In *Proceedings of the Joint Fifth Workshop on Statistical Machine Translation and MetricsMATR*, WMT '10, pages 127–132, Stroudsburg,

PA, USA. Association for Computational Linguistics.

Jindřich Libovický and Jindřich Helcl. 2017. Attention strategies for multi-source sequence-to-sequence learning. In *Proceedings of the 55th Annual Meeting of the Association for Computational Linguistics (Volume 2: Short Papers)*, pages 196–202, Vancouver, Canada. Association for Computational Linguistics.

Jindřich Libovický, Jindřich Helcl, and David Mareček. 2018. Input combination strategies for multi-source transformer decoder. In *Proceedings of the Third Conference on Machine Translation: Research Papers*, pages 253–260, Belgium, Brussels. Association for Computational Linguistics.

Chi-kiu Lo. 2019. YiSi - A unified semantic MT quality evaluation and estimation metric for languages with different levels of available resources. In *Proceedings of the Fourth Conference on Machine Translation, Volume 2: Shared Task Papers*, Florence, Italy. Association for Computational Linguistics.

Chi-kiu Lo, Michel Simard, Darlene Stewart, Samuel Larkin, Cyril Goutte, and Patrick Littell. 2018. Accurate semantic textual similarity for cleaning noisy parallel corpora using semantic machine translation evaluation metric: The NRC supervised submissions to the parallel corpus filtering task. In *Proceedings of the Third Conference on Machine Translation: Shared Task Papers*, pages 908–916, Belgium, Brussels. Association for Computational Linguistics.

Yuta Nishimura, Katsuhito Sudoh, Graham Neubig, and Satoshi Nakamura. 2018. Multi-source neural machine translation with data augmentation. *CoRR*, abs/1810.06826.

Rico Sennrich, Barry Haddow, and Alexandra Birch. 2016. Improving neural machine translation models with monolingual data. In *Proceedings of the 54th Annual Meeting of the Association for Computational Linguistics (Volume 1: Long Papers)*, pages 86–96, Berlin, Germany. Association for Computational Linguistics.

Andreas Stolcke. 2002. SRILM - an extensible language modeling toolkit. In *7th International Conference on Spoken Language Processing, IC-SLP2002 - INTERSPEECH 2002, Denver, Colorado, USA, September 16-20, 2002*. ISCA.

Ashish Vaswani, Noam Shazeer, Niki Parmar, Jakob Uszkoreit, Llion Jones, Aidan N Gomez, Łukasz Kaiser, and Illia Polosukhin. 2017. Attention is all you need. In *Advances in neural information processing systems*, pages 5998–6008.

Ashish Vaswani, Yinggong Zhao, Victoria Fossum, and David Chiang. 2013. Decoding with large-scale neural language models improves translation. In *Proceedings of the 2013 Conference on Empirical*

Methods in Natural Language Processing, EMNLP 2013, 18-21 October 2013, Grand Hyatt Seattle, Seattle, Washington, USA, A meeting of SIGDAT, a Special Interest Group of the ACL, pages 1387–1392. ACL.

Barret Zoph and Kevin Knight. 2016. Multi-source neural translation. In *Proceedings of NAACL-HLT*, pages 30–34.

Incorporating Word and Subword Units in Unsupervised Machine Translation Using Language Model Rescoring

Zihan Liu*, Yan Xu*, Genta Indra Winata, Pascale Fung
Center for Artificial Intelligence Research (CAiRE)
Department of Electronic and Computer Engineering
The Hong Kong University of Science and Technology, Clear Water Bay, Hong Kong
{zliurc,yxucb,giwinata}@connect.ust.hk, pascale@ece.ust.hk

Abstract

This paper describes CAiRE's submission to the unsupervised machine translation track of the WMT'19 news shared task from German to Czech. We leverage a phrase-based statistical machine translation (PBSMT) model and a pre-trained language model to combine word-level neural machine translation (NMT) and subword-level NMT models without using any parallel data. We propose to solve the morphological richness problem of languages by training byte-pair encoding (BPE) embeddings for German and Czech separately, and they are aligned using MUSE (Conneau et al., 2018). To ensure the fluency and consistency of translations, a rescoring mechanism is proposed that reuses the pre-trained language model to select the translation candidates generated through beam search. Moreover, a series of pre-processing and post-processing approaches are applied to improve the quality of final translations.

1 Introduction

Machine translation (MT) has achieved huge advances in the past few years (Bahdanau et al., 2015; Gehring et al., 2017; Vaswani et al., 2017, 2018). However, the need for a large amount of manual parallel data obstructs its performance under low-resource conditions. Building an effective model on low resource data or even in an unsupervised way is always an interesting and challenging research topic (Gu et al., 2018; Radford et al., 2016; Lee et al., 2019). Recently, unsupervised MT (Artetxe et al., 2018b,a; Conneau et al., 2018; Lample et al., 2018b; Wu et al., 2019), which can immensely reduce the reliance on parallel corpora, has been gaining more and more interest.

Training cross-lingual word embeddings (Conneau et al., 2018; Artetxe et al., 2017) is always the first step of the unsupervised MT models which produce a word-level shared embedding space for both the source and target, but the lexical coverage can be an intractable problem. To tackle this issue, Sennrich et al. (2016b) provided a subword-level solution to overcome the out-of-vocabulary (OOV) problem.

In this work, the systems we implement for the German-Czech language pair are built based on the previously proposed unsupervised MT systems, with some adaptations made to accommodate the morphologically rich characteristics of German and Czech (Tsarfaty et al., 2010). Both word-level and subword-level neural machine translation (NMT) models are applied in this task and further tuned by pseudo-parallel data generated from a phrase-based statistical machine translation (PBSMT) model, which is trained following the steps proposed in Lample et al. (2018b) without using any parallel data. We propose to train BPE embeddings for German and Czech separately and align those trained embeddings into a shared space with MUSE (Conneau et al., 2018) to reduce the combinatorial explosion of word forms for both languages. To ensure the fluency and consistency of translations, an additional Czech language model is trained to select the translation candidates generated through beam search by rescoring them. Besides the above, a series of post-processing steps are applied to improve the quality of final translations. Our contribution is two-fold:

- We propose a method to combine word and subword (BPE) pre-trained input representations aligned using MUSE (Conneau et al., 2018) as an NMT training initialization on a morphologically-rich language pair such as German and Czech.

- We study the effectiveness of language model

---

*These two authors contributed equally.

Proceedings of the Fourth Conference on Machine Translation (WMT), Volume 2: Shared Task Papers (Day 1) pages 275–282
Florence, Italy, August 1-2, 2019. ©2019 Association for Computational Linguistics

rescoring to choose the best sentences and unknown word replacement (UWR) procedure to reduce the drawback of OOV words.

This paper is organized as follows: in Section 2, we describe our approach to the unsupervised translation from German to Czech. Section 3 reports the training details and the results for each steps of our approach. More related work is provided in Section 4. Finally, we conclude our work in Section 5.

2 Methodology

In this section, we describe how we built our main unsupervised machine translation system, which is illustrated in Figure 1.

2.1 Unsupervised Machine Translation

2.1.1 Word-level Unsupervised NMT

We follow the unsupervised NMT in Lample et al. (2018b) by leveraging initialization, language modeling and back-translation. However, instead of using BPE, we use MUSE (Conneau et al., 2018) to align word-level embeddings of German and Czech, which are trained by FastText (Bojanowski et al., 2017) separately. We leverage the aligned word embeddings to initialize our unsupervised NMT model.

The language model is a denoising autoencoder, which is trained by reconstructing original sentences from noisy sentences. The process of language modeling can be expressed as minimizing the following loss:

$$L^{lm} = \lambda * \{E_{x \sim S}[-log P_{s \to s}(x|N(x))] +$$
$$E_{y \sim T}[-log P_{t \to t}(x|N(y))]\}, \quad (1)$$

where N is a noise model to drop and swap some words with a certain probability in the sentence x, $P_{s \to s}$ and $P_{t \to t}$ operate on the source and target sides separately, and λ acts as a weight to control the loss function of the language model. a Back-translation turns the unsupervised problem into a supervised learning task by leveraging the generated pseudo-parallel data. The process of back-translation can be expressed as minimizing the following loss:

$$L^{bt} = E_{x \sim S}[-log P_{t \to s}(x|v^*(x))] +$$
$$E_{y \sim T}[-log P_{s \to t}(y|u^*(y))], \quad (2)$$

where $v^*(x)$ denotes sentences in the target language translated from source language sentences S, $u^*(y)$ similarly denotes sentences in the source language translated from the target language sentences T and $P_{t \to s}$, and $P_{s \to t}$ denote the translation direction from target to source and from source to target respectively.

2.1.2 Subword-level Unsupervised NMT

We note that both German and Czech (Tsarfaty et al., 2010) are morphologically rich languages, which leads to a very large vocabulary size for both languages, but especially for Czech (more than one million unique words for German, but three million unique words for Czech). To overcome OOV issues, we leverage subword information, which can lead to better performance.

We employ subword units (Sennrich et al., 2016a) to tackle the morphological richness problem. There are two advantages of using the subword-level. First, we can alleviate the OOV issue by zeroing out the number of unknown words. Second, we can leverage the semantics of subword units from these languages. However, German and Czech are distant languages that originate from different roots, so they only share a small fraction of subword units. To tackle this problem, we train FastText word vectors (Bojanowski et al., 2017) separately for German and Czech, and apply MUSE (Conneau et al., 2018) to align these embeddings.

2.1.3 Unsupervised PBSMT

PBSMT models can outperform neural models in low-resource conditions. A PBSMT model utilizes a pre-trained language model and a phrase table with phrase-to-phrase translations from the source language to target languages, which provide a good initialization. The phrase table stores the probabilities of the possible target phrase translations corresponding to the source phrases, which can be referred to as $P(s|t)$, with s and t representing the source and target phrases. The source and target phrases are mapped according to inferred cross-lingual word embeddings, which are trained with monolingual corpora and aligned into a shared space without any parallel data (Artetxe et al., 2017; Conneau et al., 2018).

We use a pre-trained n-gram language model to score the phrase translation candidates by providing the relative likelihood estimation $P(t)$, so that the translation of a source phrase is derived from: $argmax_t P(t|s) = argmax_t P(s|t) P(t)$.

Back-translation enables the PBSMT models

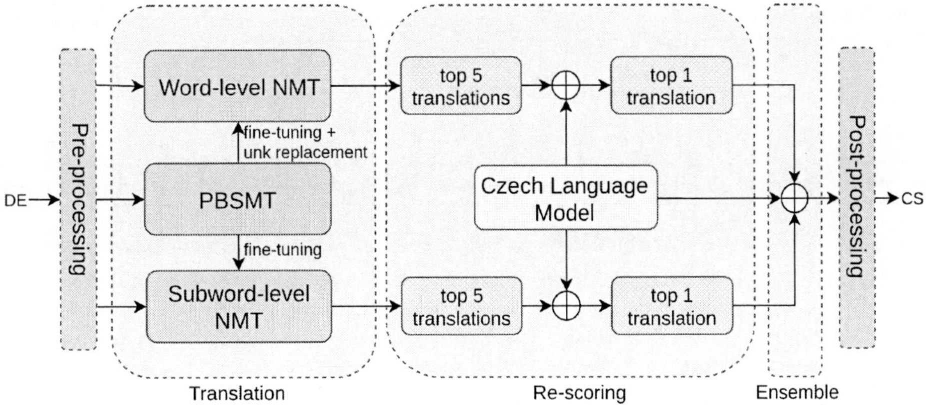

Figure 1: The illustration of our system. The translation procedure can be divided into five steps: (a) pre-processing, (b) translation generation (§2.1) from word-level NMT, subword-level NMT, and PBSMT. In the training, we fine-tune word-level and subword-level NMT models with pseudo-parallel data from NMT models and the best PBSMT model. Moreover, an unknown word replacement mechanism (§2.2) is applied to the translations generated from the word-level NMT model, (c) translation candidate rescoring, (d) construction of an ensemble of the translations from NMT models, and (e) post-processing.

to be trained in a supervised way by providing pseudo-parallel data from the translation in the reverse direction, which indicates that the PBSMT models need to be trained in dual directions so that the two models trained in the opposite directions can promote each other's performance.

In this task, we follow the method proposed by Lample et al. (2018b) to initialize the phrase table, train the KenLM language models (Heafield, 2011)[1] and train a PBSMT model, but we make two changes. First, we only initialize a uni-gram phrase table because of the large vocabulary size of German and Czech and the limitation of computational resources. Second, instead of training the model in the *truecase* mode, we maintain the same pre-processing step (see more details in §3.1) as the NMT models.

2.1.4 Fine-tuning NMT

We further fine-tune the NMT models mentioned above on the pseudo-parallel data generated by a PBSMT model. We choose the best PBSMT model and mix the pseudo-parallel data from the NMT models and the PBSMT model, which are used for back-translation. The intuition is that we can use the pseudo-parallel data produced by the PBSMT model as the supplementary translations in our NMT model, and these can potentially boost the robustness of the NMT model by increasing the variety of back-translation data.

2.2 Unknown Word Replacement

Around 10% of words found in our NMT training data are unknown words (<UNK>), which immensely limits the potential of the word-level NMT model. In this case, replacing unknown words with reasonable words can be a good remedy. Then, assuming the translations from the word-level NMT model and PBSMT model are roughly aligned in order, we can replace the unknown words in the NMT translations with the corresponding words in the PBSMT translations. Compared to the word-level NMT model, the PBSMT model ensures that every phrase will be translated without omitting any pieces from the sentences. We search for the word replacement by the following steps, which are also illustrated in Figure 2:

Step 1 For every unknown word, we can get the context words with a context window size of two.

Step 2 Each context word is searched for in the corresponding PBSMT translation. From our observation, the meanings of the words in Czech are highly likely to be the same if only the last few characters are different. Therefore, we allow the last two characters to be different between the context words and the words they match.

Step 3 If several words in the PBSMT translation match a context word, the word that is closest to the position of the context word in the PBSMT translation will be selected and put into the can-

---

[1]The code can be found at https://github.com/kpu/kenlm

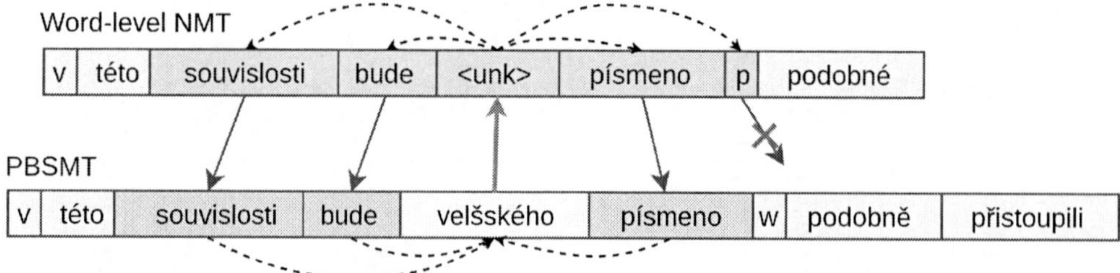

Figure 2: The illustration of the unknown word replacement (UWR) procedure for word-level NMT. The words of the PBSMT model translation in the pink boxes match the context words of the unknown word <UNK> in the word-level NMT model translation in the blue boxes. Finally, we choose a possible target word, in the yellow box, from the PBSMT model translation to replace the unknown word in the green box.

didate list to replace the corresponding <UNK> in the translation from the word-level NMT model.

Step 4 Step 2 and Step 3 are repeated until all the context words have been searched. After removing all the punctuation and the context words in the candidate list, the replacement word is the one that most frequently appears in the candidate list. If no candidate word is found, we just remove the <UNK> without adding a word.

2.3 Language Model Rescoring

Instead of direct translation with NMT models, we generate several translation candidates using beam search with a beam size of five. We build the language model proposed by Merity et al. (2018b,a) trained using a monolingual Czech dataset to rescore the generated translations. The scores are determined by the perplexity (PPL) of the generated sentences and the translation candidate with the lowest PPL will be selected as the final translation.

2.4 Model Ensemble

Ensemble methods have been shown very effective in many natural language processing tasks (Park et al., 2018; Winata et al., 2019). We apply an ensemble method by taking the top five translations from word-level and subword-level NMT, and rescore all translations using our pre-trained Czech language model mentioned in §2.3. Then, we select the best translation with the lowest perplexity.

3 Experiments

3.1 Data Pre-processing

We note that in the corpus, there are tokens representing quantity or date. Therefore, we delex-

icalize the tokens using two special tokens: (1) <NUMBER> to replace all the numbers that express a specific quantity, and (2) <DATE> to replace all the numbers that express a date. Then, we retrieve these numbers in the post-processing. There are two advantages of data pre-processing. First, replacing numbers with special tokens can reduce vocabulary size. Second, the special tokens are more easily processed by the model.

3.2 Data Post-processing

Special Token Replacement In the pre-processing, we use the special tokens <NUMBER> and <DATE> to replace numbers that express a specific quantity and date respectively. Therefore, in the post-processing, we need to restore those numbers. We simply detect the pattern <NUMBER> and <DATE> in the original source sentences and then replace the special tokens in the translated sentences with the corresponding numbers detected in the source sentences. In order to make the replacement more accurate, we will detect more complicated patterns like <NUMBER> / <NUMBER> in the original source sentences. If the translated sentences also have the pattern, we replace this pattern <NUMBER> / <NUMBER> with the corresponding numbers in the original source sentences.

Quotes Fixing The quotes are fixed to keep them the same as the source sentences.

Recaser For all the models mentioned above that work under a lower-case setting, a recaser implemented with Moses (Koehn et al., 2007) is applied to convert the translations to the real cases.

Patch-up From our observation, the ensemble NMT model lacks the ability to translate name entities correctly. We find that words with capital characters are named entities, and those named entities in the source language may have the same form in the target language. Hence, we capture and copy these entities at the end of the translation if they does not exist in our translation.

3.3 Training

Unsupervised NMT The settings of the word-level NMT and subword-level NMT are the same, except the vocabulary size. We use a vocabulary size of 50k in the word-level NMT setting and 40k in the subword-level NMT setting for both German and Czech. In the encoder and decoder, we use a transformer (Vaswani et al., 2017) with four layers and a hidden size of 512. We share all encoder parameters and only share the first decoder layer across two languages to ensure that the latent representation of the source sentence is robust to the source language. We train auto-encoding and back-translation during each iteration. As the training goes on, the importance of language modeling become a less important compared to back-translation. Therefore the weight of auto-encoding (λ in equation (1)) is decreasing during training.

Unsupervised PBSMT The PBSMT is implemented with Moses using the same settings as those in Lample et al. (2018b). The PBSMT model is trained iteratively. Both monolingual datasets for the source and target languages consist of 12 million sentences, which are taken from the latest parts of the WMT monolingual dataset. At each iteration, two out of 12 million sentences are randomly selected from the the monolingual dataset.

Language Model According to the findings in Cotterell et al. (2018), the morphological richness of a language is closely related to the performance of the model, which indicates that the language models will be extremely hard to train for Czech, as it is one of the most complex languages. We train the QRNN model with 12 million sentences randomly sampled from the original WMT Czech monolingual dataset, [2] which is also pre-processed in the way mentioned in §3.1. To maintain the quality of the language model, we enlarge the vocabulary size to three million by including all the words that appear more than 15 times. Finally, the PPL of the language model on the test set achieves 93.54.

---

²http://www.statmt.org/wmt19/

Recaser We use the recaser model provided in Moses and train the model with the two million latest sentences in the Czech monolingual dataset. After the training procedure, the recaser can restore words to the form in which the maximum probability occurs.

3.4 PBSMT Model Selection

The BLEU (cased) score of the initialized phrase table and models after training at different iterations are shown in Table 1. From comparing the results, we observe that back-translation can improve the quality of the phrase table significantly, but after five iterations, the phrase table has hardly improved. The PBSMT model at the sixth iteration is selected as the final PBSMT model.

Model	BLEU Cased
Unsupervised PBSMT	
Unsupervised Phrase Table	3.8
+ Back-translation Iter. 1	6.6
+ Back-translation Iter. 2	7.3
+ Back-translation Iter. 3	7.5
+ Back-translation Iter. 4	7.6
+ Back-translation Iter. 5	7.7
+ Back-translation Iter. 6	**7.7**

Table 1: Results of PBSMT at different iterations

3.5 Results

The performances of our final model and other baseline models are illustrated in Table 2. In the baseline unsupervised NMT models, subword-level NMT outperforms word-level NMT by around a 1.5 BLEU score. Although the unsupervised PBSMT model is worse than the subword-level NMT model, leveraging generated pseudo-parallel data from the PBSMT model to fine-tune the subword-level NMT model can still boost its performance. However, this pseudo-parallel data from the PBSMT model can not improve the word-level NMT model since the large percentage of OOV words limits its performance. After applying unknown words replacement to the word-level NMT model, the performance improves by a BLEU score of around 2. Using the Czech language model to re-score helps the model improve by around a 0.3 BLEU score each time. We also use this language model to create an ensemble of the best word-level and subword-level NMT model and achieve the best performance.

Model	BLEU	BLEU Cased	TER	BEER 2.0	CharacterTER
Unsupervised PBSMT					
Unsupervised phrase table	4	3.8	-	0.384	0.773
+ Back-translation Iter. 6	8.3	7.7	0.887	0.429	**0.743**
Unsupervised NMT					
Subword-level NMT	9.4	9.1	-	0.419	0.756
+ fine-tuning	9.8	9.5	0.832	0.424	0.756
+ fine-tuning + rescoring	10.3	10	0.833	0.426	0.749
Word-level NMT	7.9	7.6	-	0.412	0.823
+ fine-tuning	7.9	7.7	-	0.413	0.819
+ fine-tuning + UWR	10.1	9.6	**0.829**	**0.432**	0.766
+ fine-tuning + UWR + rescoring	10.4	9.9	**0.829**	**0.432**	0.764
Model Ensemble					
Best Word-level + Subword-level	**10.6**	**10.2**	**0.829**	0.429	0.755
+ patch-up	**10.6**	**10.2**	0.833	0.430	0.757

Table 2: Unsupervised translation results. We report the scores of several evaluation methods for every step of our approach. Except the result that is listed on the last line, all results are under the condition that the translations are post-processed without patch-up.

4 Related Work

4.1 Unsupervised Cross-lingual Embeddings

Cross-lingual word embeddings can provide a good initialization for both the NMT and SMT models. In the unsupervised senario, Artetxe et al. (2017) independently trained embeddings in different languages using monolingual corpora, and then learned a linear mapping to align them in a shared space based on a bilingual dictionary of a negligibly small size. Conneau et al. (2018) proposed a fully unsupervised learning method to build a bilingual dictionary without using any foregone word pairs, but by considering words from two languages that are near each other as pseudo word pairs. Lample and Conneau (2019) showed that cross-lingual language model pre-training can learn a better cross-lingual embeddings to initialize an unsupervised machine translation model.

4.2 Unsupervised Machine Translation

In Artetxe et al. (2018b) and Lample et al. (2018a), the authors proposed the first unsupervised machine translation models which combines an auto-encoding language model and back-translation in the training procedure. Lample et al. (2018b) illustrated that initialization, language modeling, and back-translation are key for both unsupervised neural and statistical machine translation. Artetxe et al. (2018a) combined back-translation and MERT (Och, 2003) to iteratively refine the SMT model. Wu et al. (2019) proposed to discard back-translation. Instead, they extracted and edited the nearest sentences in the target language to construct pseudo-parallel data, which was used as a supervision signal.

5 Conclusion

In this paper, we propose to combine word-level and subword-level input representation in unsupervised NMT training on a morphologically rich language pair, German-Czech, without using any parallel data. Our results show the effectiveness of using language model rescoring to choose more fluent translation candidates. A series of pre-processing and post-processing approaches improve the quality of final translations, particularly to replace unknown words with possible relevant target words.

Acknowledgments

We would like to thank our colleagues Jamin Shin, Andrea Madotto, and Peng Xu for insightful discussions. This work has been partially funded by ITF/319/16FP and MRP/055/18 of the Innovation Technology Commission, the Hong Kong SAR Government.

References

Mikel Artetxe, Gorka Labaka, and Eneko Agirre. 2017. Learning bilingual word embeddings with (almost) no bilingual data. In *Proceedings of the 55th Annual Meeting of the Association for Computational Linguistics (Volume 1: Long Papers)*, pages 451–462.

Mikel Artetxe, Gorka Labaka, and Eneko Agirre. 2018a. Unsupervised statistical machine translation. In *Proceedings of the 2018 Conference on Empirical Methods in Natural Language Processing*, pages 3632–3642.

Mikel Artetxe, Gorka Labaka, Eneko Agirre, and Kyunghyun Cho. 2018b. Unsupervised neural machine translation. In *International Conference on Learning Representations*.

Dzmitry Bahdanau, Kyunghyun Cho, and Yoshua Bengio. 2015. Neural machine translation by jointly learning to align and translate. In *3rd International Conference on Learning Representations, ICLR 2015, San Diego, CA, USA, May 7-9, 2015, Conference Track Proceedings*.

Piotr Bojanowski, Edouard Grave, Armand Joulin, and Tomas Mikolov. 2017. Enriching word vectors with subword information. *Transactions of the Association for Computational Linguistics*, 5:135–146.

Alexis Conneau, Guillaume Lample, Marc'Aurelio Ranzato, Ludovic Denoyer, and Hervé Jégou. 2018. Word translation without parallel data. In *International Conference on Learning Representations (ICLR)*.

Ryan Cotterell, Sebastian J Mielke, Jason Eisner, and Brian Roark. 2018. Are all languages equally hard to language-model? In *Proceedings of the 2018 Conference of the North American Chapter of the Association for Computational Linguistics: Human Language Technologies, Volume 2 (Short Papers)*, pages 536–541.

Jonas Gehring, Michael Auli, David Grangier, Denis Yarats, and Yann N Dauphin. 2017. Convolutional sequence to sequence learning. In *Proceedings of the 34th International Conference on Machine Learning-Volume 70*, pages 1243–1252. JMLR. org.

Jiatao Gu, Hany Hassan, Jacob Devlin, and Victor OK Li. 2018. Universal neural machine translation for extremely low resource languages. In *Proceedings of the 2018 Conference of the North American Chapter of the Association for Computational Linguistics: Human Language Technologies, Volume 1 (Long Papers)*, pages 344–354.

Kenneth Heafield. 2011. Kenlm: Faster and smaller language model queries. In *Proceedings of the sixth workshop on statistical machine translation*, pages 187–197. Association for Computational Linguistics.

Philipp Koehn, Hieu Hoang, Alexandra Birch, Chris Callison-Burch, Marcello Federico, Nicola Bertoldi, Brooke Cowan, Wade Shen, Christine Moran, Richard Zens, et al. 2007. Moses: Open source toolkit for statistical machine translation. In *Proceedings of the 45th Annual Meeting of the Association for Computational Linguistics Companion Volume Proceedings of the Demo and Poster Sessions*, pages 177–180.

Guillaume Lample and Alexis Conneau. 2019. Cross-lingual language model pretraining. *arXiv preprint arXiv:1901.07291*.

Guillaume Lample, Alexis Conneau, Ludovic Denoyer, and Marc'Aurelio Ranzato. 2018a. Unsupervised machine translation using monolingual corpora only. In *International Conference on Learning Representations*.

Guillaume Lample, Myle Ott, Alexis Conneau, Ludovic Denoyer, and Marc'Aurelio Ranzato. 2018b. Phrase-based & neural unsupervised machine translation. In *Proceedings of the 2018 Conference on Empirical Methods in Natural Language Processing (EMNLP)*.

Nayeon Lee, Zihan Liu, and Pascale Fung. 2019. Team yeon-zi at semeval-2019 task 4: Hyperpartisan news detection by de-noising weakly-labeled data. In *Proceedings of the 13th International Workshop on Semantic Evaluation*, pages 1052–1056.

Stephen Merity, Nitish Shirish Keskar, and Richard Socher. 2018a. An Analysis of Neural Language Modeling at Multiple Scales. *arXiv preprint arXiv:1803.08240*.

Stephen Merity, Nitish Shirish Keskar, and Richard Socher. 2018b. Regularizing and optimizing LSTM language models. In *International Conference on Learning Representations*.

Franz Josef Och. 2003. Minimum error rate training in statistical machine translation. In *Proceedings of the 41st Annual Meeting on Association for Computational Linguistics-Volume 1*, pages 160–167. Association for Computational Linguistics.

Ji Ho Park, Peng Xu, and Pascale Fung. 2018. Plusemo2vec at semeval-2018 task 1: Exploiting emotion knowledge from emoji and# hashtags. In *Proceedings of The 12th International Workshop on Semantic Evaluation*, pages 264–272.

Alec Radford, Luke Metz, and Soumith Chintala. 2016. Unsupervised representation learning with deep convolutional generative adversarial networks. *4th International Conference on Learning Representations, ICLR 2016, San Juan, Puerto Rico, May 2-4, 2016, Conference Track Proceedings*.

Rico Sennrich, Barry Haddow, and Alexandra Birch. 2016a. Improving neural machine translation models with monolingual data. In *Proceedings of the*

54th Annual Meeting of the Association for Computational Linguistics (Volume 1: Long Papers), volume 1, pages 86–96.

Rico Sennrich, Barry Haddow, and Alexandra Birch. 2016b. Neural machine translation of rare words with subword units. In *Proceedings of the 54th Annual Meeting of the Association for Computational Linguistics (Volume 1: Long Papers)*, volume 1, pages 1715–1725.

Reut Tsarfaty, Djamé Seddah, Yoav Goldberg, Sandra Kübler, Marie Candito, Jennifer Foster, Yannick Versley, Ines Rehbein, and Lamia Tounsi. 2010. Statistical parsing of morphologically rich languages (spmrl): what, how and whither. In *Proceedings of the NAACL HLT 2010 First Workshop on Statistical Parsing of Morphologically-Rich Languages*, pages 1–12. Association for Computational Linguistics.

Ashish Vaswani, Samy Bengio, Eugene Brevdo, Francois Chollet, Aidan Gomez, Stephan Gouws, Llion Jones, Łukasz Kaiser, Nal Kalchbrenner, Niki Parmar, et al. 2018. Tensor2tensor for neural machine translation. In *Proceedings of the 13th Conference of the Association for Machine Translation in the Americas (Volume 1: Research Papers)*, volume 1, pages 193–199.

Ashish Vaswani, Noam Shazeer, Niki Parmar, Jakob Uszkoreit, Llion Jones, Aidan N Gomez, Łukasz Kaiser, and Illia Polosukhin. 2017. Attention is all you need. In *Proceedings of the 31st International Conference on Neural Information Processing Systems*, pages 6000–6010. Curran Associates Inc.

Genta Indra Winata, Andrea Madotto, Zhaojiang Lin, Jamin Shin, Yan Xu, Peng Xu, and Pascale Fung. 2019. CAiRE_HKUST at SemEval-2019 task 3: Hierarchical attention for dialogue emotion classification. In *Proceedings of the 13th International Workshop on Semantic Evaluation*, pages 142–147, Minneapolis, Minnesota, USA. Association for Computational Linguistics.

Jiawei Wu, Xin Wang, and William Yang Wang. 2019. Extract and edit: An alternative to back-translation for unsupervised neural machine translation. In *Proceedings of the 2019 Conference of the North American Chapter of the Association for Computational Linguistics: Human Language Technologies, Volume 1 (Long and Short Papers)*, pages 1173–1183.

JUMT at WMT2019 News Translation Task: A Hybrid approach to Machine Translation for Lithuanian to English

Sainik Kumar Mahata, Avishek Garain, Adityar Rayala,
Dipankar Das, Sivaji Bandyopadhyay
Computer Science and Engineering
Jadavpur University, Kolkata, India
sainik.mahata@gmail.com, avishekgarain@gmail.com, mailsofadityar@gmail.com,
dipankar.dipnil2005@gmail.com, sivaji_cse_ju@yahoo.com

Abstract

In the current work, we present a description of the system submitted to WMT 2019 News Translation Shared task. The system was created to translate news text from Lithuanian to English. To accomplish the given task, our system used a Word Embedding based Neural Machine Translation model to post edit the outputs generated by a Statistical Machine Translation model. The current paper documents the architecture of our model, descriptions of the various modules and the results produced using the same. Our system garnered a BLEU score of 17.6.

1 Introduction

Machine Translation (MT) is automated translation of one natural language to another using a computer. Translation, itself, is a very tough task for both humans as well as a computer. It requires a thorough understanding of the syntax and semantics of both the languages under consideration. For producing good translations, a MT system needs good quality and sufficient amount of parallel corpus (Mahata et al., 2016, 2017).

In the modern context, MT systems can be categorized into **S**tatistical **M**achine **T**ranslation (SMT) and **N**eural **M**achine **T**ranslation (NMT). SMT has had its share in making MT very popular among the masses. It includes creating statistical models, whose input parameters are derived from the analysis of bilingual text corpora, created by professional translators (Weaver, 1955). The state-of-art for SMT is Moses Toolkit[1], created by Koehn et al. (2007), incorporates subcomponents like Language Model generation, Word Alignment and Phrase Table generation. Various works have been done in SMT (Lopez, 2008; Koehn, 2009) and it has shown good results for many language pairs.

On the other hand NMT (Bahdanau et al., 2014), though relatively new, has shown considerable improvements in the translation results when compared to SMT (Mahata et al., 2018b). This includes better fluency of the output and better handling of the Out-of-Vocabulary problem. Unlike SMT, it doesnt depend on alignment and phrasal unit translations (Kalchbrenner and Blunsom, 2013). On the contrary, it uses an Encoder-Decoder approach incorporating Recurrent Neural Cells (Cho et al., 2014). As a result, when given sufficient amount of training data, it gives much more accurate results when compared to SMT (Doherty et al., 2010; Vaswani et al., 2013; Liu et al., 2014).

For the given task[2], we attempted to create a MT system that can translate sentences from Lithuanian to English. Since, using only SMT or NMT models leads to some or the other disadvantages, we tried to use both in a pipeline. This leads to an improvement of the results over the individual usage of either SMT or NMT. The main idea was to train a SMT model for translating Lithuanian language to English. Thereafter, a test set was translated using this model. Then, a word embedding based NMT model was trained to learn the mappings between the SMT output (in English) and the gold standard data (in English).

The organizers provided the required parallel corpora, consisting of 9,62,022 sentence pairs, for training the translation model. Among this, 7,62,022 pairs was used to train the SMT system and 2,00,000 pairs were used to test the SMT system and then train the NMT system. The statistics of the parallel corpus is depicted in 1.

The remainder of the paper is organized as follows. Section 2 will describe the methodology of creating the SMT and the NMT model and will in-

---

[1] http://www.statmt.org/moses/

[2] http://www.statmt.org/wmt19/translation-task.html

Proceedings of the Fourth Conference on Machine Translation (WMT), Volume 2: Shared Task Papers (Day 1) pages 283–286
Florence, Italy, August 1-2, 2019. ©2019 Association for Computational Linguistics

# sentences in Lt corpus	9,62,022
# sentences in En corpus	9,62,022
# words in Lt corpus	1,16,65,937
# words in En corpus	1,56,22,488
# word vocab size for Lt corpus	4,88,593
# word vocab size for En corpus	2,27,131

Table 1: Statistics of the Lithuanian-English parallel corpus provided by the organizers. "#" depicts No. of. "Lt" and "En" depict Lithuanian and English, respectively. "vocab" means vocabulary of unique tokens.

clude the preprocessing steps, a brief summary of the encoder-decoder approach and the architecture of our system. This will be followed by the results and conclusion in Section 3 and 4, respectively.

2 Methodology

2.1 SMT

For designing the model we followed some standard preprocessing steps on 7,62,022 sentence pairs, which are discussed below.

2.1.1 Preprocessing

The following steps were applied to preprocess and clean the data before using it for training our Statistical machine translation model. We used the NLTK toolkit[3] for performing the steps.

- **Tokenization**: Given a character sequence and a defined document unit, tokenization is the task of chopping it up into pieces, called tokens. In our case, these tokens were words, punctuation marks, numbers. NLTK supports tokenization of Lithuanian as well as English texts.

- **Truecasing**: This refers to the process of restoring case information to badly-cased or non-cased text (Lita et al., 2003). Truecasing helps in reducing data sparsity.

- **Cleaning**: Long sentences (of tokens > 80) were removed.

2.1.2 Moses

Moses is a statistical machine translation system that allows you to automatically train translation models for any language pair, when trained with a large collection of translated texts (parallel corpus). Once the model has been trained, an efficient

search algorithm quickly finds the highest probability translation among the exponential number of choices.

We trained Moses using 7,62,022 sentence pairs provided by WMT2019, with Lithuanian as the source language and English as the target language. For building the Language Model we used KenLM[4] (Heafield, 2011) with 7-grams from the target corpus. The English monolingual corpus from WMT2019 was used to build the language model

Training the Moses statistical MT system resulted in generation of Phrase Model and Translation Model that helps in translating between source-target language pairs. Moses scores the phrase in the phrase table with respect to a given source sentence and produces best scored phrases as output.

2.2 NMT

Neural machine translation (NMT) is an approach to machine translation that uses neural networks to predict the likelihood of a sequence of words. The main functionality of NMT is based on the sequence to sequence (seq2seq) architecture, which is described in Section 2.2.1.

2.2.1 Sequence to Sequence Model

Sequence to Sequence learning is a concept in neural networks, that helps it to learn sequences. Essentially, it takes as input a sequence of tokens (words in our case)

$$X = \{x_1, x_2, ..., x_n\}$$

and tries to generate the target sequence as output

$$Y = \{y_1, y_2, ..., y_m\}$$

where x_i and y_i are the input and target symbols respectively.

Sequence to Sequence architecture consists of two parts, an Encoder and a Decoder.

The encoder takes a variable length sequence as input and encodes it into a fixed length vector, which is supposed to summarize its meaning and taking into account its context as well. A **Long Short Term Memory** (LSTM) cell was used to achieve this. The uni-directional encoder reads the words of the Lithuanian texts, as a sequence from one end to the other (left to right in our case),

$$\vec{h}_t = \vec{f}_{enc}(E_x(x_t), \vec{h}_{t-1})$$

---

[3] https://www.nltk.org/

[4] https://kheafield.com/code/kenlm/

Here, E_x is the input embedding lookup table (dictionary), $\vec{f}_{enc}$ is the transfer function for the LSTM recurrent unit. The cell state h and context vector C is constructed and is passed on to the decoder.

The decoder takes as input, the context vector C and the cell state h from the encoder, and computes the hidden state at time t as,

$$s_t = f_{dec}(E_y(y_{t\text{-}1}), s_{t\text{-}1}, c_t)$$

Subsequently, a parametric function out_k returns the conditional probability using the next target symbol k.

$$(y_t = k \mid y < t, X) = \frac{1}{Z} exp(out_k(E_y(y_t - 1), s_t, c_t))$$

Z is the normalizing constant,

$$\sum_j exp(out_j(E_y(y_t - 1), s_t, c_t))$$

The entire model can be trained end-to-end by minimizing the log likelihood which is defined as

$$L = -\frac{1}{N} \sum_{n=1}^{N} \sum_{t=1}^{Ty^n} logp(y_t = y_t{}^n, y_{jt}{}^n, X^n)$$

where N is the number of sentence pairs, and X^n and $y_t{}^n$ are the input sentence and the t-th target symbol in the n-th pair respectively.

The input to the decoder was one hot tensor (embeddings at word level) of 2,00,000 English sentences while the target data was identical, but with an offset of one time-step ahead.

2.3 Architecture

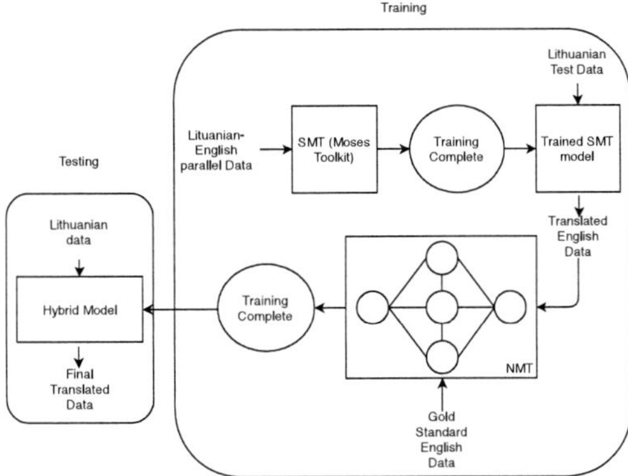

Figure 1: Architecture

2.3.1 Training

For the training purpose, 7,62,202 , preprocessed, Lituanian-English sentence pairs were fed to Moses Toolkit. This created a SMT translation model with Lithuanian as the source language and English as the target language. Thereafter, we had 2,00,000 Lithuanian-English sentence pairs, from which the Lithuanian sentences were given as input to the SMT model and it gave 2,00,000 translated English sentences as output. Now, this 2,00,000 translated English sentences and the respective gold standard 2,00,000 sentences, from the Lithuanian-English sentence pair, were given as input to a word embedding based NMT model. As a result, this constituted our Hybrid model.

2.3.2 Testing

For the testing purpose, 10k Lithuanian Sentences were fed to the Hybrid model, and the output, when checked using BLEU (Papineni et al., 2002), resulted in an accuracy of 21.6. The training and testing architecture is shown in Figure 1

3 Results

WMT2019 provided us with a test set of Lithuanian sentences in .SGM format. This file was parsed and fed to our hybrid system. The output file was again converted to .SGM format and submitted to the organizers. Our system garnered a BLEU Score of 17.6, when it was scored using automated accuracy metrics. Other accuracy scores are mentioned in Table 2.

Metric	Score
BLEU	17.6
BLEU-cased	16.6
TER	0.762
BEER 2.0	0.497
CharactTER	0.718

Table 2: Accuracy scores calculated using various autmoated evaluation metrics.

4 Conclusion

The paper presents the working of the translation system submitted to WMT 2019 News Translation shared task. We have used Word Embedding based NMT on top of SMT, for our proposed system. We have used a single LSTM layer as an encoder as well as a decoder. As a future prospect, we plan to use more LSTM layers in our model. We plan to create another model that incrementally trains both the SMT and NMT systems in a pipeline to improve the translation quality.

Acknowledgement

The reported work is supported by Media Lab Asia, MeitY, Government of India, under the Visvesvaraya PhD Scheme for Electronics & IT.

References

Dzmitry Bahdanau, Kyunghyun Cho, and Yoshua Bengio. 2014. Neural machine translation by jointly learning to align and translate. *arXiv preprint arXiv:1409.0473*.

Ondřej Bojar, Christian Federmann, Mark Fishel, Yvette Graham, Barry Haddow, Matthias Huck, Philipp Koehn, and Christof Monz. 2018. Findings of the 2018 conference on machine translation (WMT18). In *Proceedings of the Third Conference on Machine Translation, Volume 2: Shared Task Papers*, Brussels, Belgium. Association for Computational Linguistics.

Kyunghyun Cho, Bart Van Merriënboer, Dzmitry Bahdanau, and Yoshua Bengio. 2014. On the properties of neural machine translation: Encoder-decoder approaches. *arXiv preprint arXiv:1409.1259*.

Stephen Doherty, Sharon O?Brien, and Michael Carl. 2010. Eye tracking as an mt evaluation technique. *Machine translation*, 24(1):1–13.

Kenneth Heafield. 2011. KenLM: faster and smaller language model queries. In *Proceedings of the EMNLP 2011 Sixth Workshop on Statistical Machine Translation*, pages 187–197, Edinburgh, Scotland, United Kingdom.

Nal Kalchbrenner and Phil Blunsom. 2013. Recurrent continuous translation models. In *EMNLP*, volume 3, page 413.

Philipp Koehn. 2009. *Statistical machine translation.* Cambridge University Press.

Philipp Koehn, Hieu Hoang, Alexandra Birch, Chris Callison-Burch, Marcello Federico, Nicola Bertoldi, Brooke Cowan, Wade Shen, Christine Moran, Richard Zens, et al. 2007. Moses: Open source toolkit for statistical machine translation. In *Proceedings of the 45th annual meeting of the ACL on interactive poster and demonstration sessions*, pages 177–180. Association for Computational Linguistics.

Jason Lee, Kyunghyun Cho, and Thomas Hofmann. 2016. Fully character-level neural machine translation without explicit segmentation. *CoRR*, abs/1610.03017.

Wang Ling, Isabel Trancoso, Chris Dyer, and Alan W. Black. 2015. Character-based neural machine translation. *CoRR*, abs/1511.04586.

Lucian Vlad Lita, Abe Ittycheriah, Salim Roukos, and Nanda Kambhatla. 2003. Truecasing. In *Proceedings of the 41st Annual Meeting on Association for Computational Linguistics-Volume 1*, pages 152–159. Association for Computational Linguistics.

Shujie Liu, Nan Yang, Mu Li, and Ming Zhou. 2014. A recursive recurrent neural network for statistical machine translation.

Adam Lopez. 2008. Statistical machine translation. *ACM Computing Surveys (CSUR)*, 40(3):8.

Sainik Mahata, Dipankar Das, and Santanu Pal. 2016. Wmt2016: A hybrid approach to bilingual document alignment. In *WMT*, pages 724–727.

Sainik Kumar Mahata, Dipankar Das, and Sivaji Bandyopadhyay. 2017. Bucc2017: A hybrid approach for identifying parallel sentences in comparable corpora. *ACL 2017*, page 56.

Sainik Kumar Mahata, Dipankar Das, and Sivaji Bandyopadhyay. 2018a. Jucbnmt at wmt2018 news translation task: Character based neural machine translation of finnish to english. In *Proceedings of the Third Conference on Machine Translation: Shared Task Papers*, pages 445–448.

Sainik Kumar Mahata, Dipankar Das, and Sivaji Bandyopadhyay. 2018b. Mtil2017: Machine translation using recurrent neural network on statistical machine translation. *Journal of Intelligent Systems*, pages 1–7.

Sainik Kumar Mahata, Soumil Mandal, Dipankar Das, and Sivaji Bandyopadhyay. 2018c. Smt vs nmt: A comparison over hindi & bengali simple sentences. *arXiv preprint arXiv:1812.04898*.

Kishore Papineni, Salim Roukos, Todd Ward, and Wei-Jing Zhu. 2002. Bleu: a method for automatic evaluation of machine translation. In *Proceedings of the 40th annual meeting on association for computational linguistics*, pages 311–318. Association for Computational Linguistics.

Ashish Vaswani, Yinggong Zhao, Victoria Fossum, and David Chiang. 2013. Decoding with large-scale neural language models improves translation. In *EMNLP*, pages 1387–1392.

Warren Weaver. 1955. Translation. *Machine translation of languages*, 14:15–23.

Johns Hopkins University Submission for WMT News Translation Task

Kelly Marchisio
Center for Language and
Speech Processing
Johns Hopkins University
kmarchi1@jhu.edu

Yash Kumar Lal
Department of
Computer Science
Johns Hopkins University
yash@jhu.edu

Philipp Koehn
Center for Language and
Speech Processing
Johns Hopkins University
phi@jhu.edu

Abstract

We describe the work of Johns Hopkins University for the shared task of news translation organized by the Fourth Conference on Machine Translation (2019). We submitted systems for both directions of the English-German language pair. The systems combine multiple techniques – sampling, filtering, iterative backtranslation, and continued training – previously used to improve performance of neural machine translation models. At submission time, we achieve a BLEU score of 38.1 for De-En and 42.5 for En-De translation directions on newstest2019. Post-submission, the score is 38.4 for De-En and 42.8 for En-De. Various experiments conducted in the process are also described.

1 Introduction

This paper describes the Johns Hopkins University (JHU) submission to the Fourth Conference on Machine Translation (WMT19) news translation shared task (Bojar et al., 2019). We built systems for both German-English and English-German. Our attempts are based on previous year's submissions by Edinburgh (model architectures) (Sennrich et al., 2017), Microsoft (data filtering) (Junczys-Dowmunt, 2018), Facebook (backtranslation using sampling) (Edunov et al., 2018), and JHU (continued training on previous years' test sets) (Koehn et al., 2018).

Our models leverage several techniques popular in neural machine translation – backtranslation, continued training (Luong and Manning, 2015) and sentence filtering. We use Transformer-big (Vaswani et al., 2017) models trained on available bitext to generate backtranslations via sampling. These backtranslations are then scored and filtered using dual conditional cross-entropy and cross-entropy difference scores, then added to up-sampled bitext (x2). ParaCrawl[1] and Common Crawl[2] are filtered similarly, and added to form the training set for the final models. We refine each final model by performing continued training on the test sets of previous years of WMT. We then perform ensemble decoding using multiple models for each language. Finally, translations are reranked using separately-trained models to obtain the final output. In the De-En direction, scores from a language model also contribute to reranking. In the automatic evaluation, we scored 38.1 on De-En and 42.5 on En-De at submission time. Post-submission, we ensembled more similar models and scored 38.4 on De-En and 42.8 on En-De.

We built our systems using the Marian and Fairseq toolkits.

1.1 Marian

Marian[3] (Junczys-Dowmunt et al., 2018) is a purely C++11 toolkit that allows for creation and training of neural machine translation models efficiently. Most of our models were built using Marian and the sample scripts therein.

1.2 Fairseq

Fairseq[4] (Ott et al., 2019) is a sequence-to-sequence learning toolkit created with a focus on neural machine translation. It contains implementations for various standard NMT architectures and system components. Using this toolkit allows us to use sampling as a method for inference (Edunov et al., 2018).

---

[1] https://ParaCrawl.eu/index.html
[2] http://CommonCrawl.org
[3] https://marian-nmt.github.io/
[4] https://github.com/pytorch/fairseq

Proceedings of the Fourth Conference on Machine Translation (WMT), Volume 2: Shared Task Papers (Day 1) pages 287–293
Florence, Italy, August 1-2, 2019. ©2019 Association for Computational Linguistics

2 Motivation

Our work was motivated by three submissions to the news translation task at WMT18. Namely, we combined critical parts of Junczys-Dowmunt (2018), Edunov et al. (2018) and Koehn et al. (2018), and iterated upon them to create our system. Junczys-Dowmunt (2018) was based off of Edinburgh's WMT17 submission (Sennrich et al., 2017).

Our contributions are using filtered backtranslation data and performing hyperparameter search to improve BLEU score gain when performing continued training using previous years' test sets. Models were slightly different for the En-De and De-En directions, which is noted in the subsequent sections.

3 Model Description

Our reproduction of Junczys-Dowmunt (2018), follows the example at `https://github.com/marian-nmt/marian-examples/tree/master/wmt2017-transformer`, using the same data and similar preprocessing. The data is the parallel training bitext provided in the WMT17 shared task, excluding Rapid. Punctuation normalization, tokenization, corpus cleaning and truecasing was applied using Moses (Koehn et al., 2007). The truecaser applied to the clean bitext was trained over the punctuation normalized, tokenized, and cleaned bitext, whereas the truecaser applied to other data, such as the data to backtranslate, was trained on ParaCrawl. We deviated slightly from the example and applied a joint byte pair encoding (BPE) (Sennrich et al., 2016) model that was trained previously over the ParaCrawl German-English bitext to form 32,000 subword units. For the 10 million lines of German monolingual news data to backtranslate, any sentences longer than 100 tokens as well as pairs with source/target length ratio exceeding 9 were discarded after BPE was applied using Moses' `clean-corpus-n.perl`.

Just as Junczys-Dowmunt (2018) replicated Edinburgh's WMT17 results for En-De and upgraded to using the Transformer, we have replicated Junczys-Dowmunt (2018)'s replication with the Transformer-base model. The models were trained on upsampled WMT17 bitext (x2) plus 10M lines of backtranslated German monolingual data. The vocabulary was a joint vocabulary created from the WMT17 bitext and contained 36000 subword units.

Our models for the replication of Junczys-Dowmunt (2018) were trained on a single GPU. For Transformer-base models, we added –maxi-batch-sort src[5]. We additionally added an optimizer delay of 4, and changed the beam size to 6 and the –normalize hyperparameter to 0.6[6]. We trained our Transformer-base models until convergence with early stopping, which was implemented based on Marian word-wise normalized cross-entropy with a patience of 5 and validation occurring every 5000 steps. The maximum training epochs was set to 10. Inference was done using the model with best BLEU score during training.

Model	BLEU
Microsoft Transformer-base (x1)	28.8
+Ensemble	29.4
Our Transformer-base (x1)	29.5
+Ensemble	30.2

Table 1: Reproduction of Microsoft's replication of the University of Edinburgh's submission to WMT17, using the Transformer-base model. Scores are reported on newstest2017. Our single model performance ranged from 28.3-28.6.

Next, we filtered the ParaCrawl data by removing sentence pairs that scored below e^-4 based on dual conditional cross-entropy filtering, then kept the top 8 million based on cross-entropy difference filtering[7] (Junczys-Dowmunt, 2018). This model's vocabulary included the WMT17 bitext and backtranslated data. The WMT17 bitext was also cleaned after BPE was applied for this model. It achieved a BLEU score of 30.6 on newstest2017, as evidence of the benefit of adding filtered ParaCrawl data.

We also replicated the backtranslation model from Facebook's WMT18 submission in order to use inference by sampling. We first preprocess data in the manner described by Edunov et al. (2018) and then train a Transformer-big model for backtranslation using all available bitext. We used the same hyperparameters mentioned in the original work. The learning rate was set to 0.0001, which is suitable for large batches.

---

[5] `https://github.com/marian-nmt/marian-dev/issues/184`

[6] Marcin Junczys-Dowmunt, personal communication

[7] Marcin Junczys-Dowmunt, personal communication

All models for the replication of Facebook's submission were trained on a single GPU, which makes it difficult to match results achieved on a large number of GPUs. Fairseq has a training flag to simulate training on multiple GPUs (update-freq) which accumulates updates for a certain number of batches and applies them all at once. Here, the flag was set to 16 (even though it does not replicate the exact settings of the original work). Table 2 shows BLEU scores on newstest2017 for our replication of Facebook AI Research's (FAIR) submission last year.

	Train Set	FAIR '18	Replication
En-De	Bitext	29.5	27.0
	Bitext+top10	32.1	29.6
De-En	Bitext	-	27.8
	Bitext+top10	-	30.6

Table 2: FAIR 2018 Replication

The discrepancy may be due to different batching in the original work and our replication, as the Transformer-big is very sensitive to batch sizes and updates. Edunov et al. (2018) used word batching that we could not match due to memory shortage in the machines we were using. It is likely that this difference in batch size and the distributed versus single-machine training can explain the discrepancies in the numbers. For ideal sampling, we desire a model with as high a BLEU score as possible when translating using beam search, and simultaneously as low a BLEU score as possible when translating using sampling[8].

4   System Components

Our basic training architecture was based off Junczys-Dowmunt (2018), which itself was based of Sennrich et al. (2017).

4.1   Transformer architectures

Using Fairseq, a Transformer-big model was trained over all processed bitext. It was used to translate the prepared monolingual data, employing top-10 sampling (Edunov et al., 2018). Typically, beam search is used to create backtranslated data. Sampling from the model's distribution to create this data allows more room for diverse examples to be generated. Edunov et al. (2018) argue that synthetic data created using this technique

sends a "stronger training signal than data generated by beam or greedy search".

Top-10 sampling creates effective, noisy samples and it takes far less time to translate the entire monolingual set than unrestricted sampling.

4.2   Filtering Methods

We applied dual conditional cross-entropy filtering (Junczys-Dowmunt, 2018) and cross-entropy difference filtering (Moore and Lewis, 2010; Junczys-Dowmunt, 2018) to filter our backtranslated data, ParaCrawl, and Common Crawl. ParaCrawl and Common Crawl were combined into a single corpus before filtering.

For both the backtranslation data as well as ParaCrawl and Common Crawl, we first sorted each corpus by "adequacy score", which corresponds to dual conditional cross-entropy filtering. We then removed the lowest-scoring sentences[9], corresponding to an adequecy score threshold of approximately e^{-5} for the backtranslated data, and e^{-4} for ParaCrawl and Common Crawl. Next, we sorted by "domain score", which corresponds to cross-entropy difference filtering, and kept the top 60% of data backtranslated from German, and the top 80% of data backtranslated from English. For ParaCrawl and Common Crawl, we kept the top 50% of data. This data was domain-scored for the target domain. Thus, when the data would be used to train an En-De model, the domain scores were based on cross-entropy difference filtering using models trained with German data, vice-versa for De-En.

Translation models used in dual conditional cross-entropy filtering were shallow RNNs trained on a 1 million line random sample of all available constrained bitext for 2019, excluding ParaCrawl and Common Crawl. The "in-domain" language model for cross-entropy difference filtering was trained on a 1 million line random sample of monolingual News crawl data from WMT16-18, and the "out-of-domain" model was trained on a random 1 million lines from the concatenation of ParaCrawl and Common Crawl.

We discovered a small error in our in-domain language models for cross-entropy difference filtering after submission whereby we had unintentionally filtered out many WMT18 German-side monolingual sentences before creating the language models (LMs). These LMs were used to

---

[8] Sergey Edunov, personal communication

[9] Marcin Junczys-Dowmunt, personal communication

score both backtranslation as well as ParaCrawl and Common Crawl data.

In total, the filtering methods above resulted in:

- 10.3M lines of ParaCrawl + Common Crawl

- 20.1M lines backtranslated from German

- 13.7M lines backtranslated from English

The filtered data (backtranslations, ParaCrawl, and Common Crawl) was concatenated with 2x upsampled bitext. This results in a final dataset of 40.3M for En-De and 33.9M for De-En. Multiple Transformer-base models were trained over this data using Marian to serve as the primary translation models. A similar method was used to create training data for reranking models, except for these, we reused models whose backtranslations had been generated using beam search. The filtering methods described above resulted in slightly smaller subsets of backtranslated German and English data for the reranking models. Furthermore, the training set for the De-En reranking models was generated by exploiting iterative backtranslation (Hoang et al., 2018; Koehn et al., 2018) along with the filtering methods described. The adequacy score threshold used to filter backtranslations generated via beam search was e^{-4}.

4.3 Continued Training

We fine-tuned the models on newstest2015-18, which closely mirrors the data in the test set. Due to continued training, our models gained up to 1 BLEU point for De-En and up to 1.5 BLEU points for En-De. Multiple such models were then ensembled to perform translations.

5 Training Setup

For our submissions to WMT19, we use similar preprocessing techniques as described for the reproduction of Junczys-Dowmunt (2018), but this time using WMT19 bitext. As a result, 5.2M sentences were obtained. For our submission, we apply Moses' `clean-corpus-n.perl` to the bitext before use.

For backtranslation, we ran a similar preprocessing method on WMT18 News crawl monolingual data. Any sentences with greater than 100 BPE tokens were discarded, leaving us with 34M German monolingual and 24M English monolingual sentences.

Similar to (Sennrich et al., 2017) and (Junczys-Dowmunt, 2018), our training regimen can be divided into these steps:

- Train a Transformer-big model for backtranslation with Fairseq using the clean bitext.

- Backtranslate monolingual data from WMT18 using top-10 sampling.

- Filter backtranslations using domain and adequacy scores.

- Use backtranslated data, upsampled bitext, and filtered ParaCrawl + Common Crawl to train Transformer-base translation models.

- Perform continued training.

- Ensemble decode using translation models.

- Rerank translations using Transformer-base translation models for both language directions, and a language model for De-En.

Reranking models were trained similar to Junczys-Dowmunt (2018) and Sennrich et al. (2017). Our training recipe is as follows:

- Train a shallow RNN model with Marian for backtranslation using clean bitext

- Backtranslate News crawl monolingual data from WMT18 using beam search

- Filter backtranslations using domain and adequacy scores.

- Use backtranslated data, upsampled bitext, and filtered ParaCrawl + Common Crawl to train Transformer-base reranking models.

- Perform continued training.

Since we reused previously-trained models for reranking, the De-En reranking models had additionally undergone filtered iterative backtranslation. The secondary model for backtranslation was a Transformer-base model in the En-De language direction, trained on the upsampled bitext plus the filtered WMT18 News crawl backtranslation data produced by the shallow RNN in the De-En direction. Backtranslations were produced using beam search by the secondary model, concatenated with 2x the clean bitext and the filtered ParaCrawl + Common Crawl, and used to train Transformer-base De-En reranking models.

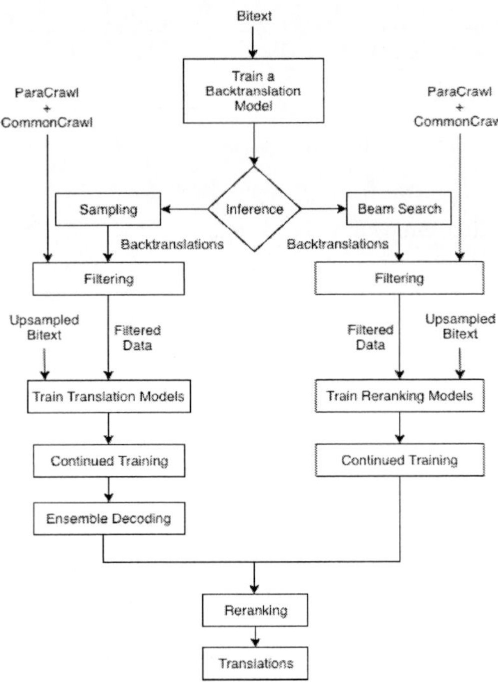

Figure 1: System Architecture. For peculiarities in models of each direction, see Sections 5.1 and 5.2.

BLEU (Papineni et al., 2002) was calculated using the multi-bleu-detok.perl script in Moses.

An overview of our architecture can be found in Figure 1. In the figure, filtered data is comprised of filtered backtranslations, and filtered ParaCrawl and Common Crawl data. All models were trained on a single NVIDIA GeForce GTX 1080Ti GPU.

5.1 English→German

Following the training regimen described above, we first train a Transformer-big model over the original bitext. Hyperparameters used here are the same as the ones used when replicating FAIR. This is used to perform backtranslation of monolingual German data via sampling. The generated data was filtered to the top 60% using both domain and adequacy scoring as described in Section 4.2, before being concatenated with twice the bitext and the filtered ParaCrawl and Common Crawl. Finally, this is used to train two Transformer-base models which are continued trained. We run continued training for 5 epochs at an increased learning rate of 0.001, without the use of a learning rate scheduler. These models are ensembled and used to generate translations which are finally reranked by the reranking models.

For reranking, we replicate the same models

mentioned above, except that backtranslations are generated using standard beam search. We retain the same percentage of the backtranslated data. Four such models are created and undergo continued training as described above.

For this direction of the language pair, we corrected the quotation marks of the German translations in a post-processing step.

5.2 German→English

Translation and reranking models for this direction of the language pair were trained the similarly as En-De. We retain the top 80% of the backtranslations by domain score as described in Section 4.2; the ones generating using sampling are used to train the primary translation models, whereas the ones generatd by beam search are used to train the reranking models. We train three Transformer-base translation models that we adapt to previous years' test sets. They run for 5 epochs at an increased learning rate of 0.0005, without the use of a learning rate scheduler. These models are then ensembled to produce a 12-best list of translations.

For reranking in this language direction, we trained our reranking models using iterative backtranslation. We first trained a De-En backtranslation model and used beam search to generate backtranslations for monolingual data from WMT18. The filtered backtranslation data was used along with upsampled bitext to train a second-round En-De backtranslation model. Beam search backtranslations generated using this model, along with clean bitext, ParaCrawl and Common Crawl was used to train the final reranking models. Three of these models were used as the reranking models in conjuction with the three primary models mentioned earlier.

A Transformer-base language model trained on 100M lines of English monolingual data from WMT16-18 also contributed to rescoring the translations for this language direction.

6 Results and Evaluation

A critical component of our system is continued training (CT). To demonstrate the effectiveness of this method, we continue training using newstest2014-18, excluding newstest2017, using the learning rates mentioned in the previous section. The scores presented in Table 3 are reported on newstest2017.

Ensembling multiple models is a common way

System	Before CT	CT	CT-Ensemble
De-En	37.3	38.3	39.0 (x3)
En-De	30.8	32.3	32.6 (x2)

Table 3: Effect of continued training and ensembling, reported on newstest2017.

to improve performance of a NMT system. In Table 3, we observe a +0.74 improvement when ensembling 3 models (De-En) and +0.38 when ensembling 2 models (En-De).

M1	M2	M3	M1+M3	Ensemble (all)
30.8	29.7	30.8	32.6	32.3

Table 4: Results of ensembling En-De models, reported on newstest2017. Ensembling with the lower-performing model #2 (M2) degrades performance versus ensembling only models #1 and #3 (M1 and M3).

Table 4 shows the effects of ensembling En-De models with identical training setups, labeled M1, M2, and M3. M2 converged earlier than expected, and we observe that ensembling with this lower-performing model causes lower BLEU score than just ensembling the better performing models. As such, we exclude M2 from the final submission.

System	Our Submission	Highest Score
De-En	38.1	42.8 (MSRA)
En-De	42.5	44.9 (MSRA)

Table 5: BLEU-cased score on newstest2019.

For submission, we perform continued training using newstest2014-18 and ensemble multiple models with the same vocabulary for translation. We then employ reranking models on the 12-best lists produced from the ensembles.

6.1 Post-Submission Work

We built additional En-De and De-En translation models using the same training regimen described in this work. This allowed use to ensemble more models to boost performance. Results are seen in Table 6. Each post-submission ensemble was comprised of four models.

7 Conclusion

We began by replicating various top-scoring submissions from WMT 2018 (Bojar et al., 2018):

System	Submission Score	Final Score
De-En	38.1	**38.4**
En-De	42.5	**42.8**

Table 6: BLEU-cased score on newstest2019.

Microsoft (Junczys-Dowmunt, 2018) and FAIR (Edunov et al., 2018). We were unable to match all the numbers from latter, perhaps due to our limited compute and differing hyperparameters.

Our system is built on various components from these submissions and JHU's 2018 submission (Koehn et al., 2018). We use clean bitext to train a backtranslation model (Transformer-big) and translate monolingual data using sampling inference. We filter the backtranslations, ParaCrawl, and Common Crawl, according to the domain and adequacy scores described in Junczys-Dowmunt (2018). We concatenate the filtered data with upsampled clean bitext to train Transformer-base translation models, and perform continued training over previous years' test sets.

An ensemble of such models are used to decode the test set, and translations are reranked using reranking models (Transformer-base) that are trained on a concatenation of upsampled bitext and filtered beam search backtranslated data. The reranking models also undergo equivalent continued training. On the De-En side, we also use a language model trained on 100 million monolingual English sentences to this effect. At the time of submission, we achieve a BLEU score of 38.1 for De-En and 42.5 for En-De. Our post-submission system consisting of 4-model ensembles scores 38.4 for De-En and 42.8 for En-De.

It is likely that effective training of Transformer-big models would have further boosted scores for our system, had we been able to do so on our single-GPU setup in time for this year's shared task.

Acknowledgements

The authors would like to thank Huda Khayrallah and Dan Povey for assistance with this project. We also appreciate the advice of Marcin Junczys-Dowmunt on filtering and hyperparameter optimization, Brian Thompson for guidance regarding continued training, and Mitchell Gordon for help with post-processing. We also thank our anonymous reviewers for their helpful comments.

References

Ondřej Bojar, Christian Federmann, Mark Fishel, Yvette Graham, Barry Haddow, Philipp Koehn, and Christof Monz. 2018. Findings of the 2018 conference on machine translation (WMT18). In *Proceedings of the Third Conference on Machine Translation: Shared Task Papers*, pages 272–303, Belgium, Brussels. Association for Computational Linguistics.

Ondřej Bojar, Christian Federmann, Mark Fishel, Yvette Graham, Barry Haddow, Matthias Huck, Philipp Koehn, Christof Monz, Mathias Müller, and Matt Post. 2019. Findings of the 2019 conference on machine translation (wmt19). In *Proceedings of the Fourth Conference on Machine Translation, Volume 2: Shared Task Papers*, Florence, Italy. Association for Computational Linguistics.

Sergey Edunov, Myle Ott, Michael Auli, and David Grangier. 2018. Understanding Back-Translation at Scale. In *Proceedings of the 2018 Conference on Empirical Methods in Natural Language Processing*, pages 489–500, Brussels, Belgium. Association for Computational Linguistics.

Vu Cong Duy Hoang, Philipp Koehn, Gholamreza Haffari, and Trevor Cohn. 2018. Iterative back-translation for neural machine translation. In *Proceedings of the 2nd Workshop on Neural Machine Translation and Generation*, pages 18–24, Melbourne, Australia. Association for Computational Linguistics.

Marcin Junczys-Dowmunt. 2018. Microsoft's Submission to the WMT2018 News Translation Task: How I Learned to Stop Worrying and Love the Data. In *Proceedings of the Third Conference on Machine Translation: Shared Task Papers*, pages 425–430, Belgium, Brussels. Association for Computational Linguistics.

Marcin Junczys-Dowmunt, Roman Grundkiewicz, Tomasz Dwojak, Hieu Hoang, Kenneth Heafield, Tom Neckermann, Frank Seide, Ulrich Germann, Alham Fikri Aji, Nikolay Bogoychev, André F. T. Martins, and Alexandra Birch. 2018. Marian: Fast Neural Machine Translation in C++. In *Proceedings of ACL 2018, System Demonstrations*, pages 116–121, Melbourne, Australia. Association for Computational Linguistics.

Philipp Koehn, Kevin Duh, and Brian Thompson. 2018. The JHU Machine Translation Systems for WMT 2018. In *Proceedings of the Third Conference on Machine Translation: Shared Task Papers*, pages 438–444.

Philipp Koehn, Hieu Hoang, Alexandra Birch, Chris Callison-Burch, Marcello Federico, Nicola Bertoldi, Brooke Cowan, Wade Shen, Christine Moran, Richard Zens, Chris Dyer, Ondřej Bojar, Alexandra Constantin, and Evan Herbst. 2007. Moses: Open Source Toolkit for Statistical Machine Translation. In *Proceedings of the 45th Annual Meeting of the ACL on Interactive Poster and Demonstration Sessions*, ACL '07.

Minh-Thang Luong and Christopher D. Manning. 2015. Neural Machine Translation Systems for Spoken Language Domains. In *International Workshop on Spoken Language Translation*.

Robert C. Moore and William Lewis. 2010. Intelligent Selection of Language Model Training Data. In *Proceedings of the ACL 2010 Conference Short Papers*, ACLShort '10, pages 220–224, Stroudsburg, PA, USA. Association for Computational Linguistics.

Myle Ott, Sergey Edunov, Alexei Baevski, Angela Fan, Sam Gross, Nathan Ng, David Grangier, and Michael Auli. 2019. fairseq: A Fast, Extensible Toolkit for Sequence Modeling. In *Proceedings of NAACL-HLT 2019: Demonstrations*.

Kishore Papineni, Salim Roukos, Todd Ward, and Wei-Jing Zhu. 2002. BLEU: A Method for Automatic Evaluation of Machine Translation. In *Proceedings of the 40th Annual Meeting on Association for Computational Linguistics*, ACL '02, pages 311–318.

Rico Sennrich, Alexandra Birch, Anna Currey, Ulrich Germann, Barry Haddow, Kenneth Heafield, Antonio Valerio Miceli Barone, and Philip Williams. 2017. The University of Edinburgh's Neural MT Systems for WMT17. *arXiv preprint arXiv:1708.00726*.

Rico Sennrich, Barry Haddow, and Alexandra Birch. 2016. Neural Machine Translation of Rare Words with Subword Units. In *Proceedings of the 54th Annual Meeting of the Association for Computational Linguistics (Volume 1: Long Papers)*, pages 1715–1725, Berlin, Germany. Association for Computational Linguistics.

Ashish Vaswani, Noam Shazeer, Niki Parmar, Jakob Uszkoreit, Llion Jones, Aidan N Gomez, Lukasz Kaiser, and Illia Polosukhin. 2017. Attention is All you Need. In *Advances in Neural Information Processing Systems*, pages 5998–6008.

NICT's Unsupervised Neural and Statistical Machine Translation Systems for the WMT19 News Translation Task

Benjamin Marie[1*], **Haipeng Sun**[2,1*], **Rui Wang**[1†], **Kehai Chen**[1],
Atsushi Fujita[1], **Masao Utiyama**[1], **and Eiichiro Sumita**[1]

1 National Institute of Information and Communications Technology (NICT)

2 Harbin Institute of Technology

{bmarie, sun.haipeng, wangrui, khchen, atsushi.fujita, mutiyama, eiichiro.sumita}@nict.go.jp

Abstract

This paper presents the NICT's participation in the WMT19 unsupervised news translation task. We participated in the unsupervised translation direction: German-Czech. Our primary submission to the task is the result of a simple combination of our unsupervised neural and statistical machine translation systems. Our system is ranked first for the German-to-Czech translation task, using only the data provided by the organizers ("constraint"), according to both BLEU-cased and human evaluation. We also performed contrastive experiments with other language pairs, namely, English-Gujarati and English-Kazakh, to better assess the effectiveness of unsupervised machine translation in for distant language pairs and in truly low-resource conditions.

1 Introduction

This paper describes the unsupervised neural (NMT) and statistical machine translation (SMT) systems built for the participation of the National Institute of Information and Communications Technology (NICT) to the WMT19 shared News Translation Task. Only one translation direction was proposed in the unsupervised track of task: German-to-Czech (de-cs). Our submitted systems are constrained, in other words, we used only the provided monolingual data for training our models and the provided parallel data for development, i.e., validation and tuning. We trained unsupervised NMT (UNMT) and unsupervised SMT (USMT) systems, and combined them through training a pseudo-supervised NMT model with merged pseudo-parallel corpora and n-best list

reranking using different informative features as proposed by Marie and Fujita (2018a). This simple combination method performed the best among unsupervised MT systems at WMT19 by BLEU [1] and human evaluation (Bojar et al., 2019). In addition to the official track, we also present the unsupervised systems for English-Gujariti and English-Kazakh for contrastive experiments with much more distant language pairs.

The remainder of this paper is organized as follows. In Section 2, we introduce the data preprocessing. In Section 3, we describe the details of our UNMT, USMT, and pseudo-supervised MT systems. Then, the combination of pseudo-supervised NMT and USMT is described in Section 4. Empirical results produced with our systems are shown and analyzed in Section 6 and 7, and Section 8 concludes this paper.

2 Data and Preprocessing

2.1 Data

As monolingual training data to train our de-cs UNMT and USMT systems, we randomly extracted 50 million sentences from WMT monolingual News Crawl datasets.[2] Bilingual development data (16.6K sentences) from "last years' parallel dev and test sets"[3] were also officially provided "for bootstrapping" the UNMT systems.[4] Among the large number of possible approaches for exploiting the development data, we only used it for tuning USMT, validate UNMT models, train a reranking system, and finally to fine-tune our pseudo-supervised NMT systems.

---

*Equal contribution in alphabetical order. This work was conductd when Haipeng Sun visited NICT as an internship student.

†Corresponding author.

[1]http://matrix.statmt.org/matrix/
systems_list/1897

[2]http://data.statmt.org/news-crawl/

[3]http://data.statmt.org/wmt19/
translation-task/dev.tgz

[4]http://www.statmt.org/wmt19/
translation-task.html

Proceedings of the Fourth Conference on Machine Translation (WMT), Volume 2: Shared Task Papers (Day 1) pages 294–301
Florence, Italy, August 1-2, 2019. ©2019 Association for Computational Linguistics

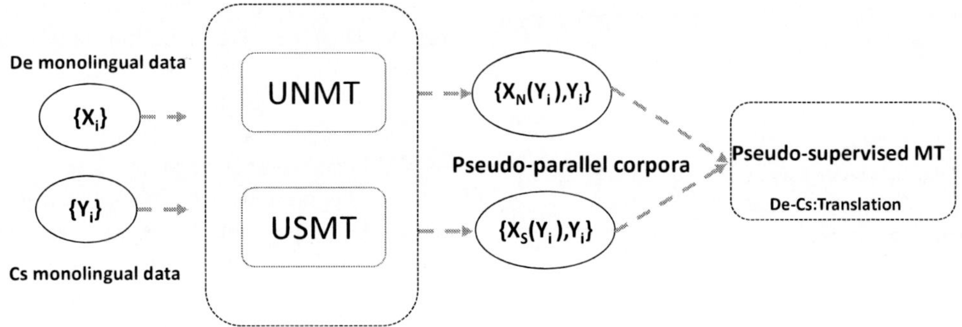

Figure 1: Our training framework. UNMT can generate the pseudo-parallel corpora $\{X_N(Y_i), Y_i\}$; USMT can generate the pseudo-parallel corpora $\{X_S(Y_i), Y_i\}$. These pseudo-parallel corpora were merged to train the pseudo-supervised MT system.

2.2 Tokenization, Truecasing, and Cleaning

We used `Moses` tokenizer (Koehn et al., 2007)[5] and truecaser for both languages. The truecaser was trained on one million tokenized lines extracted randomly from the monolingual data. Truecasing was then performed on all the tokenized data. For cleaning, we only applied the `Moses` script `clean-corpus-n.perl` to remove lines in the monolingual data containing more than 50 tokens, and replaced characters forbidden by `Moses`. Note that we did not perform any punctuation normalization.

3 Systems

Our entire system is illustrated in Figure 1.

3.1 Unsupervised NMT

To build competitive UNMT systems, we chose to rely on the Transformer-based UNMT initialized by a pre-trained cross-lingual language model (Lample and Conneau, 2019) since it had been shown to outperform UNMT initialized with word embeddings, in quality and efficiency. In order to limit the size of the vocabulary of the UNMT model, we segmented tokens in the training data into sub-word units via byte pair encoding (BPE) (Sennrich et al., 2016b). We determined 60k BPE operations jointly on the training monolingual data for German and Czech, and used a shared vocabulary for both languages with 60k tokens based on BPE.

We used 50M monolingual corpora to train a

```
--lgs 'cs-de' --mlm_steps
'cs,de' --emb_dim
1024 --n_layers 6
--n_heads 8 --dropout 0.1
--attention_dropout 0.1
--gelu_activation true
--batch_size 32 --bptt 256
--optimizer adam,lr=0.0001
```

Table 1: Parameters for training XLM.

cross-lingual language model using XLM[6] in order to pre-train the UNMT model. We used the accumulate gradient method to train the language model on 1 GPU[7] to solve the out-of-memory problem caused by big batch. The accumulate size was set to 8. The other parameters for training the language model were set as listed in Table 1. Then we trained a Transformer-based UNMT model with the pre-trained cross-lingual language model using XLM toolkit.

The auto-encoder of UNMT architecture cannot learn useful knowledge without some constraints; it would merely become a copying task that learns to copy the input words one by one (Lample et al., 2018). To alleviate this issue, we utilized a denoising auto-encoder (Vincent et al., 2010), and added noise in the form of random token swapping in input sentences to improve the model learning ability (Hill et al., 2016; He et al., 2016).

The denoising auto-encoder acts as a language model that has been trained in one language and

---

[5]`https://github.com/moses-smt/mosesdecoder`

[6]`https://github.com/facebookresearch/XLM`

[7]NVIDIA @ Tesla @ P100 16Gb.

```
--lgs 'cs-de' --ae_steps
'cs,de' --bt_steps
'cs-de-cs,de-cs-de'
--word_shuffle 3
--word_dropout 0.1
--word_blank 0.1 --lambda_ae
'0:1,100000:0.1,300000:0'
--encoder_only false
--emb_dim 1024 --n_layers
6 --n_heads 8 --dropout
0.1 --attention_dropout
0.1 --gelu_activation
true --tokens_per_batch
2000 --batch_size 32
--bptt 256 --optimizer
adam_inverse_sqrt,beta1=0.9,
beta2=0.98,lr=0.0001
--eval_bleu true
```

Table 2: Parameters for training UNMT.

does not consider the final goal of translating across different languages. Therefore, back-translation (Sennrich et al., 2016a) was adapted to train a translation system in a true translation setting based on monolingual corpora. The pseudo-parallel sentence pairs generated by the model at the previous iteration is used to train the new translation model.

We used 50M monolingual corpora to train the UNMT model for 50000 iterations. The de-cs UNMT system was trained on 4 GPUs, with the parameters listed in Table 2.

3.2 Unsupervised SMT

Previous work has shown that USMT performs similarly or better than UNMT (Artetxe et al., 2018c). Marie and Fujita (2018b) has also shown that USMT can be used to train a standard NMT system to obtain significant improvements in translation quality while the whole training framework remains unsupervised.

We built USMT systems using a framework similar to the one proposed in Marie and Fujita (2018b). The first step of USMT consists in inducing a phrase table from the monolingual corpora. We first collected phrases of up to six tokens from the monolingual News Crawl corpora using `word2phrase`.[8] As phrases,

we also considered all the token types in the corpora. Then, we selected the 300k most frequent phrases in the monolingual corpora to be used for inducing a phrase table. All possible phrase pairs are scored, as in Marie and Fujita (2018b), using bilingual word embeddings (BWE), and the 300 target phrases with the highest scores were kept in the phrase table for each source phrase. In total, the induced phrase table contains 90M phrase pairs. BWE of 512 dimensions were obtained using word embeddings trained with `fastText`[9] and aligned in the same space using unsupervised `Vecmap` (Artetxe et al., 2018b)[10] for this induction. In total four scores, to be used as features in the phrase table, for each of these phrase pairs were computed to mimic phrase-based SMT: forward and backward phrase and lexical translation probabilities. Then, the phrase table was plugged into a `Moses` system that was tuned on the development data using `KB-MIRA`. We performed four refinement steps to improve the system using at each step 3M synthetic parallel sentences generated by the forward and backward translation systems, instead of using only either forward (Marie and Fujita, 2018b) or backward translations (Artetxe et al., 2018c). We report on the performance of the systems obtained after the fourth refinement step.

3.3 Pseudo-supervised MT

As shown in Marie and Fujita (2018b), pseudo-parallel data generated by unsupervised MT can be directly used as training data to train a standard NMT system with a significantly better translation quality. We adopted the same strategy for our unsupervised systems. We generated pseudo-parallel corpora with our USMT and UNMT systems. Then we trained a Transformer-based NMT model (Vaswani et al., 2017) on these pseudo-parallel corpora. Since the pseudo-parallel corpora generated by USMT and UNMT are of very different nature, and that USMT and UNMT perform similarly in translation quality, we can expect that the complementarity of both data will be useful to train a better NMT system in contrast to using only data generated either by USMT or UNMT. Our synthetic parallel corpora for training this system was composed of 6M sentence pairs generated by USMT and 20M

---

[8] `https://code.google.com/archive/p/word2vec/`

[9] `https://github.com/facebookresearch/fastText`

[10] `https://github.com/artetxem/vecmap`

```
--type transformer
--max-length  100
--transformer-dim-ffn   4096
--dim-vocabs   50000   50000
-w  12000   --mini-batch-fit
--valid-freq 5000 --save-freq
5000 --disp-freq 500
--valid-metrics   ce-mean-words
perplexity   translation
--quiet-translation
--sync-sgd --beam-size
12 --normalize=1
--valid-mini-batch 16
--keep-best   --early-stopping
20 --cost-type=ce-mean-words
--enc-depth 6 --dec-depth
6  --tied-embeddings
--transformer-dropout
0.1 --label-smoothing
0.1   --learn-rate   0.0003
--lr-warmup   16000
--lr-decay-inv-sqrt
16000 --lr-report
--optimizer-params   0.9
0.98  1e-09 --clip-norm   5
--exponential-smoothing
```

Table 3: Parameters for training `Marian`.

sentence pairs generated by UNMT. To train this pseudo-supervised NMT (PNMT) system, we chose `Marian` (Junczys-Dowmunt et al., 2018)[11] since it supports state-of-the-art features and is one of the fastest NMT frameworks publicly available. Specifically, the pseudo-supervised NMT system for de-cs was trained on 4 GPUs for 300,000 iterations, with the parameters listed by Table 3.

4   Combination of PNMT and USMT

Our primary submission for the task was the result of a simple combination of PNMT and USMT similarly to what we did last year in our participation to the supervised News Translation Task of WMT18 (Marie et al., 2018). As demonstrated by Marie and Fujita (2018a), and despite the simplicity of the method used, combining NMT and SMT makes MT more robust and can significantly improve translation quality, even though SMT greatly underperforms

NMT. Following Marie and Fujita (2018a), our combination of PNMT and USMT works as follows.

4.1   Generation of n-best Lists

We first independently generated the 100-best and 12-best translation hypotheses[12] with N PNMT models, independently trained, and also with the ensemble of these N PNMT models. We also generated 100-best translation hypotheses with our USMT system. We then merged all these lists generated by different systems, without removing duplicated hypotheses, which resulted in a list of $(N+2)*100+(N+1)*12$ translation hypotheses for each source sentence. Finally, we rescored all the hypotheses in the list with a reranking framework using features to better model the fluency and the adequacy of each hypothesis. This method can find a better hypothesis in these merged n-best lists than the one-best hypothesis originated by the individual systems.

4.2   Reranking Framework and Features

We chose `KB-MIRA` (Cherry and Foster, 2012) as a rescoring framework and used a subset of the features proposed in Marie and Fujita (2018a). All the following features we used are described in details by Marie and Fujita (2018a). It includes the scores given by N PNMT models independently trained. We computed sentence-level translation probabilities using the lexical translation probabilities learned by `mgiza` during the training of our USMT system. We also used two 4-gram language models to compute two features for each hypothesis. One is the same language model used by our USMT system while the other is a small model trained on all the development data from which we removed the data used to train the reranking framework. To account for hypotheses length, we added the difference, and its absolute value, between the number of tokens in the translation hypothesis and the source sentence.

The reranking framework was trained on n-best lists generated by decoding the first 3k sentence pairs of the development data that we also used to validate the training of UNMT and PNMT systems and to tune the weights of USMT models.

---

[11]https://marian-nmt.github.io/

[12]We generated n-best with different beam size for decoding since translation quality can decrease with larger beam size (Koehn and Knowles, 2017).

#	Methods	de-cs
1	Single UNMT system	15.5
2	Single USMT system	11.1
3	Single NMT system pseudo-supervised by UNMT	15.9
4	Single NMT system pseudo-supervised by USMT	15.3
5	Single Pseudo-supervised MT system	16.2
6	Ensemble Pseudo-supervised MT system	16.5
7	Re-ranking Pseudo-supervised MT system	17.0
8	Fine-tuning Pseudo-supervised MT system	18.7
9	Fine-tuning Pseudo-supervised MT system + fixed quotes	19.6
10	Fine-tuning + re-ranking Pseudo-supervised MT system + fixed quotes	20.1

Table 4: BLEU scores of UMT. #10 is our primary system submitted to the organizers.

5   Fine-tuning and Post-processing

Fine-tuning (Luong and Manning, 2015; Sennrich et al., 2016a) is a conventional method for NMT on low-resource language pairs and domain-specific tasks (Chu et al., 2017; Chu and Wang, 2018; Wang et al., 2017a,b). The PNMT model only relying on monolingual corpora was further trained on the parallel development data to improve translation performance. Finally, fixed quotes method was applied to the final Czech translation.

6   Results on the German-to-Czech Task

The results of our systems computed for the Newstest2019 test set are presented in Table 4. As Table 4 shows, UNMT systems significantly outperformed our best USMT system according to BLEU. However, compared with pseudo-supervised MT model trained only on pseudo-parallel corpora generated by either UNMT (#3) or USMT (#4), merging pseudo-parallel corpora generated by UNMT and USMT (#5) can improve translation performance. Reranking `Moses` 100-best hypotheses using PNMT models (#7) significantly improved the translation quality. Another methods such as ensemble, fine-tuning, and fixed quotes also could improve translation performance.

7   Contrastive Experiments on English-Gujarati and English-Kazakh

To obtain a better picture of the feasibility of unsupervised MT, we also set up unsupervised MT for two truly low-resource and distant language pairs: English-Gujarati (en-gu) and English-Kazakh (en-kk).[13]   As shown by previous work (Søgaard et al., 2018), we can expect unsupervised word embeddings to be challenging to train for distant language pairs, and subsequently to obtain unsupervised MT systems with a very poor translation quality.

Note that for these experiments, we did not train any UNMT systems. We present results only for USMT and NMT pseudo-supervised by USMT. Since training unsupervised BWE for these language pairs is particularly challenging, we also present configurations using supervised BWE trained using the approach described by Artetxe et al. (2018a) on a bilingual word lexicon extracted from the development data provided by the organizers. Our configuration of USMT and PNMT are the same as for de-cs.

As English training data, we only used all the provided News Crawl corpora as they are large in-domain corpora.   For Gujarati and Kazakh, we used Common Crawl and News Crawl corpora, in addition to the provided News Commentary corpus for Kazakh. Statistics of the data preprocessed with `Moses` are presented in Table 5.

Our results are presented in Table 6. In contrast to what we observed for de-cs, unsupervised BWE are too noisy to be used in phrase table induction for USMT. For both en-gu and en-kk, we obtained unexploitable results confirming the conclusions of Søgaard et al. (2018).

Switching to supervised BWE improved significantly the translation quality of USMT but

---

[13]These language pairs were proposed for the supervised News Translation Task.

Corpus		en-gu		en-kk	
		en	gu	en	kk
Monolingual	#lines	187.50M	3.39M	187.50M	9.03M
	#tokens	4.39B	50.52M	4.39B	141.06M
Development	#lines	1,998	1,998	2,066	2,066
	#tokens	42,264	38,963	53,451	42,910

Table 5: Statistics of preprocessed monolingual and development data used for en-gu and en-kk.

System		en-gu		en-kk	
		$\rightarrow$	$\leftarrow$	$\rightarrow$	$\leftarrow$
Unsupervised BWE	USMT	< 1.0	< 1.0	< 1.0	< 1.0
Supervised BWE	USMT	5.7	6.2	1.4	4.7
	Pseudo-supervised NMT	8.1	8.8	2.1	5.7
	Supervised NMT	10.5	17.2	6.4	26.2

Table 6: BLEU scores of our USMT and NMT pseudo-supervised by USMT systems. Note that we did not conduct experiments with pseudo-supervised NMT using USMT initialized with unsupervised BWE as the generated pseudo-parallel data were not useful to train a NMT system at all. The results of our supervised systems (last row) submitted for the News Translation Task are presented for comparison.

remains below 10 BLEU points in all our experiments. Compared with our best supervised system, the difference in translation quality appears very large especially when translating into English.

These results show that while we obtained a reasonable translation quality for de-cs, unsupervised MT is far from being useful for real world applications, i.e., truly low-resource distant language pairs. Training useful bilingual weakly-supervised/unsupervised BWE for distant language pairs remains one of the main challenges.

8 Conclusion

We participated in the unsupervised translation direction and compared USMT and UNMT performances. We achieved the best results through the combination of both approaches thanks to an NMT framework pseudo-supervised by UNMT and USMT. We also showed that reranking of the n-best lists in this unsupervised settings can bring additional improvements in translation quality. While we achieved a reasonable translation quality for German-to-Czech, a language pair for which there exists plenty of bilingual data, our results for English-Gujarati and English-Kazakh highlighted that unsupervised machine translation is still very far from exploitable for low-resource distant language pairs.

Acknowledgments

We thank the organizers for providing the datasets and the reviewers for their valuable suggestions for improving this paper. This work was conducted under the program "Research and Development of Enhanced Multilingual and Multipurpose Speech Translation Systems" of the Ministry of Internal Affairs and Communications (MIC), Japan. Rui Wang was partially supported by JSPS grant-in-aid for early-career scientists (19K20354): "Unsupervised Neural Machine Translation in Universal Scenarios."

References

Mikel Artetxe, Gorka Labaka, and Eneko Agirre. 2018a. Generalizing and improving bilingual word embedding mappings with a multi-step framework of linear transformations. In *Proceedings of the Thirty-Second AAAI Conference on Artificial Intelligence*, pages 5012–5019, New Orleans, Louisiana, USA. AAAI Press.

Mikel Artetxe, Gorka Labaka, and Eneko Agirre. 2018b. A robust self-learning method for fully unsupervised cross-lingual mappings of word embeddings. In *Proceedings of the 56th Annual Meeting of the Association for Computational Linguistics (Volume 1: Long Papers)*, pages

789–798, Melbourne, Australia. Association for Computational Linguistics.

Mikel Artetxe, Gorka Labaka, and Eneko Agirre. 2018c. Unsupervised statistical machine translation. In *Proceedings of the 2018 Conference on Empirical Methods in Natural Language Processing*, pages 3632–3642, Brussels, Belgium. Association for Computational Linguistics.

Ondřej Bojar, Christian Federmann, Mark Fishel, Yvette Graham, Barry Haddow, Matthias Huck, Philipp Koehn, Christof Monz, Mathias Müller, and Matt Post. 2019. Findings of the 2019 conference on machine translation (WMT19). In *Proceedings of the Fourth Conference on Machine Translation, Volume 2: Shared Task Papers*, Florence, Italy. Association for Computational Linguistics.

Colin Cherry and George Foster. 2012. Batch tuning strategies for statistical machine translation. In *Proceedings of the 2012 Conference of the North American Chapter of the Association for Computational Linguistics: Human Language Technologies*, pages 427–436, Montréal, Canada. Association for Computational Linguistics.

Chenhui Chu, Raj Dabre, and Sadao Kurohashi. 2017. An empirical comparison of domain adaptation methods for neural machine translation. In *Proceedings of the 55th Annual Meeting of the Association for Computational Linguistics (Volume 2: Short Papers)*, pages 385–391, Vancouver, Canada. Association for Computational Linguistics.

Chenhui Chu and Rui Wang. 2018. A survey of domain adaptation for neural machine translation. In *Proceedings of the 27th International Conference on Computational Linguistics*, pages 1304–1319, Santa Fe, New Mexico, USA. Association for Computational Linguistics.

Di He, Yingce Xia, Tao Qin, Liwei Wang, Nenghai Yu, Tie-Yan Liu, and Wei-Ying Ma. 2016. Dual learning for machine translation. In *Advances in Neural Information Processing Systems 29: Annual Conference on Neural Information Processing Systems 2016*, pages 820–828, Barcelona, Spain. Curran Associates, Inc.

Felix Hill, Kyunghyun Cho, and Anna Korhonen. 2016. Learning distributed representations of sentences from unlabelled data. In *Proceedings of the 2016 Conference of the North American Chapter of the Association for Computational Linguistics: Human Language Technologies*, pages 1367–1377, San Diego California, USA. Association for Computational Linguistics.

Marcin Junczys-Dowmunt, Roman Grundkiewicz, Tomasz Dwojak, Hieu Hoang, Kenneth Heafield, Tom Neckermann, Frank Seide, Ulrich Germann, Alham Fikri Aji, Nikolay Bogoychev, André F. T. Martins, and Alexandra Birch. 2018. Marian: Fast neural machine translation in C++. In

Proceedings of ACL 2018, System Demonstrations, pages 116–121, Melbourne, Australia. Association for Computational Linguistics.

Philipp Koehn, Hieu Hoang, Alexandra Birch, Chris Callison-Burch, Marcello Federico, Nicola Bertoldi, Brooke Cowan, Wade Shen, Christine Moran, Richard Zens, Chris Dyer, Ondrej Bojar, Alexandra Constantin, and Evan Herbst. 2007. Moses: Open source toolkit for statistical machine translation. In *Proceedings of the 45th Annual Meeting of the Association for Computational Linguistics Companion Volume Proceedings of the Demo and Poster Sessions*, pages 177–180, Prague, Czech Republic. Association for Computational Linguistics.

Philipp Koehn and Rebecca Knowles. 2017. Six challenges for neural machine translation. In *Proceedings of the First Workshop on Neural Machine Translation*, pages 28–39, Vancouver, Canada. Association for Computational Linguistics.

Guillaume Lample and Alexis Conneau. 2019. Cross-lingual language model pretraining. *CoRR*, abs/1901.07291.

Guillaume Lample, Alexis Conneau, Ludovic Denoyer, and Marc'Aurelio Ranzato. 2018. Unsupervised machine translation using monolingual corpora only. In *Proceedings of the Sixth International Conference on Learning Representations*, Vancouver, Canada. OpenReview.net.

Minh-Thang Luong and Christopher D. Manning. 2015. Stanford neural machine translation systems for spoken language domain. In *International Workshop on Spoken Language Translation*, Da Nang, Vietnam.

Benjamin Marie and Atsushi Fujita. 2018a. A smorgasbord of features to combine phrase-based and neural machine translation. In *Proceedings of the 13th Conference of the Association for Machine Translation in the Americas (Volume 1: Research Papers)*, pages 111–124, Boston, MA. Association for Machine Translation in the Americas.

Benjamin Marie and Atsushi Fujita. 2018b. Unsupervised neural machine translation initialized by unsupervised statistical machine translation. *CoRR*, abs/1810.12703.

Benjamin Marie, Rui Wang, Atsushi Fujita, Masao Utiyama, and Eiichiro Sumita. 2018. NICT's neural and statistical machine translation systems for the WMT18 news translation task. In *Proceedings of the Third Conference on Machine Translation: Shared Task Papers*, pages 449–455, Belgium, Brussels. Association for Computational Linguistics.

Rico Sennrich, Barry Haddow, and Alexandra Birch. 2016a. Improving neural machine translation models with monolingual data. In *Proceedings of the 54th Annual Meeting of the Association for Computational Linguistics (Volume 1: Long Papers)*, pages 86–96, Berlin, Germany. Association for Computational Linguistics.

Rico Sennrich, Barry Haddow, and Alexandra Birch. 2016b. Neural machine translation of rare words with subword units. In *Proceedings of the 54th Annual Meeting of the Association for Computational Linguistics (Volume 1: Long Papers)*, pages 1715–1725, Berlin, Germany. Association for Computational Linguistics.

Anders Søgaard, Sebastian Ruder, and Ivan Vulić. 2018. On the limitations of unsupervised bilingual dictionary induction. In *Proceedings of the 56th Annual Meeting of the Association for Computational Linguistics (Volume 1: Long Papers)*, pages 778–788, Melbourne, Australia. Association for Computational Linguistics.

Ashish Vaswani, Noam Shazeer, Niki Parmar, Jakob Uszkoreit, Llion Jones, Aidan N. Gomez, Łukasz Kaiser, and Illia Polosukhin. 2017. Attention is all you need. In *Advances in Neural Information Processing Systems 30: Annual Conference on Neural Information Processing Systems 2017*, pages 6000–6010, Long Beach, CA, USA. Curran Associates, Inc.

Pascal Vincent, Hugo Larochelle, Isabelle Lajoie, Yoshua Bengio, and Pierre-Antoine Manzagol. 2010. Stacked denoising autoencoders: Learning useful representations in a deep network with a local denoising criterion. *Journal of Machine Learning Research*, 11:3371–3408.

Rui Wang, Andrew Finch, Masao Utiyama, and Eiichiro Sumita. 2017a. Sentence embedding for neural machine translation domain adaptation. In *Proceedings of the 55th Annual Meeting of the Association for Computational Linguistics (Volume 2: Short Papers)*, pages 560–566, Vancouver, Canada. Association for Computational Linguistics.

Rui Wang, Masao Utiyama, Lemao Liu, Kehai Chen, and Eiichiro Sumita. 2017b. Instance weighting for neural machine translation domain adaptation. In *Proceedings of the 2017 Conference on Empirical Methods in Natural Language Processing*, pages 1482–1488, Copenhagen, Denmark. Association for Computational Linguistics.

PROMT Systems for WMT 2019 Shared Translation Task

Alexander Molchanov
PROMT LLC
17E Uralskaya str. building 3, 199155,
St. Petersburg, Russia
Alexander.Molchanov@promt.ru

Abstract

This paper describes the PROMT submissions for the WMT 2019 Shared News Translation Task. This year we participated in two language pairs and in three directions: English-Russian, English-German and German-English. All our submissions are MarianNMT-based neural systems. We use significantly more data compared to the last year. We also present our improved data filtering pipeline.

1 Introduction

This paper provides an overview of the PROMT submissions for the WMT 2019 Shared News Translation Task. This year we participate with neural MT systems for the second time. We participate in two language pairs and in three directions (English-Russian, English-German and German-English). We describe our data preparation pipelines, models training setups and present the results on the newstest sets.

The paper is organized as follows: Section 2 is a brief overview of the submitted systems. Section 3 describes the data preparation, preprocessing and statistics in detail. Section 4 provides a detailed description of the systems. In Section 5 we present and discuss the results. Section 6 concludes the paper.

2 Systems overview

We submitted three systems based on the MarianNMT (Junczys-Dowmunt et al., 2018) toolkit: English-Russian, English-German and German-English. All systems are unconstrained (we use the allowed data, private data and publicly available unconstrained data like OpenSubtitles). The English-German and German-English have the same architecture. The English-Russian system is slightly different as we use separate vocabularies.

3 Data

We use all data provided by the WMT organizers, private in-house parallel data and other publicly available data, mainly from the OPUS website (Tiedemann, 2012).

The Tatoeba sets as our validation sets and the newstest2018 is our test set. The reason why we choose the Tatoeba corpus for validation is that we aim at building general-domain (and not just news-domain) models. Besides, the Tatoeba corpus is available for many language pairs beyond the scope of the WMT Translation Task.

We select a small subset from training data and mix it with monolingual news with its back-translations for fine-tuning. This will be described in detail in Section 3.4 below.

3.1 Data filtering

There are several stages in our data filtering pipeline. The statistics for the final training data are shown in Table 1 (English-Russian) and Table 2 (English-German).

Basic filtering

This includes some simple length-based and source-target length ratio-based heuristics, removing tags, lines with low amount of alphabetic symbols etc. We also remove lines which appear to be emails or web-addresses. In addition, we remove lines with rare words from the Bookshop and the OpenSubtitles corpora (using frequency lists built on large monolingual corpora including all monolingual data from WMT, private data and Wikipedia dumps).

Proceedings of the Fourth Conference on Machine Translation (WMT), Volume 2: Shared Task Papers (Day 1) pages 302–307
Florence, Italy, August 1-2, 2019. ©2019 Association for Computational Linguistics

Deduplication

We remove duplicate translations and keep only the most frequent translation for the source sentence if it repeats more than two times. This procedure is applied to some corpora, e.g. OpenSubtitles and MultiUN which contain a lot of various (and often incorrect) translations for common phrases. For example, the English phrase '*No.*' is encountered almost 100k times in the source side of the English-Russian OpenSubtitles corpus. It has more than 78k unique translations, second most popular among which is '*Да.*' ('*Yes.*' in Russian).

Corpus	#sent	#tokens EN	#tokens RU
MultiUN	14.9	440.6	415.1
Private data	12.4	120.1	96.2
OpenSubtitles	10.9	104.9	90.5
ParaCrawl	3.0	64.3	55.9
WikiPedia	1.0	21.2	18.7
Yandex corpus	0.6	16.8	15.4
CommonCrawl	0.4	10.3	9.5
NewsCommentary	0.3	6.2	5.9
TED Talks	0.1	2.4	2.1
Total	**43.6**	**786.8**	**709.3**

Table 1: Statistics for the filtered parallel English-Russian data in millions of sentences (#sent) and tokens.

Language detection

The algorithm is a fairly simple ensemble of three tools: `pycld2`[1], `langid` (Lui and Baldwin, 2012), `langdetect`[2].

Parallel segments filtering

We apply this step to low-quality data (basically, OpenSubtitles, CommonCrawl, ParaCrawl, Bookshop). We use `Hunalign` (Varga et al., 2005) to obtain basic sentence pair scores. We also extract about 30 additional features from sentence pairs and apply inhouse classifier to discard unparallel sentence pairs. It is a simple SVM classifier, and the features include source and target lengths in tokens, average token length in symbols, number of punctuation symbols in

source and target etc. We do not use any categorical features.

Corpus	#sent	#tokens EN	#tokens DE
ParaCrawl	20.3	424.8	403.4
OpenSubtitles	10.5	97.3	91.1
Private data	9.2	101.3	94.5
DGT	3.2	72.9	55.4
Europarl	2.0	57.7	54.7
CommonCrawl	1.4	31.4	29.9
EUBookshop	1.3	28.6	27.1
Rapid	1.3	22.9	22.0
EMEA	1.2	12.0	11.5
JRC-Acquis	0.7	34.1	30.7
NewsCommentary	0.3	6.2	6.4
MultiUN	0.2	6.2	5.7
TED Talks	0.1	2.4	2.3
ECB	0.1	3.1	2.8
Total	**51.8**	**900.9**	**837.5**

Table 2: Statistics for the filtered parallel English-German data in millions of sentences (#sent) and tokens.

Data filtering using language models

As last year, we use the modified bilingual Moore-Lewis data selection algorithm (Axelrod et al., 2011). However, this time we apply it all training corpora. We use the English and Russian news 2018 corpora from statmt.org as the in-domain corpora. The idea is that the news corpora can be seen as high quality general-domain data. So using them in this scenario allows to remove some noisy outlying data.

We also substitute numbers and alphanumeric sequences with placeholders and sort the data according to language models scores. We use Levenshtein distance (set to a rather low threshold) to remove similar sentence pairs with similar scores. We regard such sentence pairs as useless (or even harmful) duplicates which can prevent our translation models from better and faster converging. We remove up to 15% of data using this procedure.

3.2 Data preprocessing

BPE

We use byte pair encoding (BPE) (Sennrich et al., 2016b) to encode our data to subword units. This year we use a different preprocessing scheme compared to the last year's systems. We noticed

---

[1] https://pypi.org/project/pycld2/
[2] https://pypi.org/project/langdetect/

that the BPE algorithm from the `OpenNMT` toolkit (Klein et al., 2017) gives better results compared to the default script `learn_bpe.py` from the MarianNMT toolkit. We see two reasons for that: 1) the BPE merge operations are learnt to distinguish subword units at the beginning, in the middle and at the end of the word and 2) the BPE merge operations can be learnt in case-insensitive mode (OpenNMT architecture supports features, so a feature can be used to handle case). Case-insensitive BPE model is very useful when dealing with a lot of different and sometimes noisy data (like, for example, OpenSubtitles where uppercase is often used to communicate emphasis). This is also crucial when dealing with legal and financial data where specific terms are written in title case or uppercase. News headlines are also often written in title case or uppercase.

As MarianNMT does not support features yet, we decided to perform a 'trick' similar to the one described in (Tamchyna et al., 2017): instead of using a feature we insert special tokens <C> and <U> after sequences in title case or uppercase. For example, a source sentence

World Championships 2017: Neil Black praises Scottish members of Team GB

is converted to

world <C> championships <C> 2017 : neil <C> black <C> pra@@ ises scottish <C> members of team <C> gb <U>

We do not use truecaser in our pipeline as it is redundant. All data is tokenized using the `Moses` toolkit (Koehn et al., 2007) tokenizer with aggressive tokenization, then the OpenNMT BPE-splitter is applied, after that we convert the case feature to separate tokens.

English-Russian system

Same as last year, we train the model with separate vocabularies due to the Cyrillic nature of Russian alphabet. Therefore we use separate BPE models for source and target with 35k and 45k merge operations respectively. We experimented with shared vocabulary following the procedure for the English-Russian pair described in (Sennrich et al., 2016b) but did not get improvements. This year, however, we train much smaller BPE models as we noticed that our NMT systems do not handle large vocabularies (70-90k) well and generate many OOVs in the output.

English-German and German-English systems

We train a joint BPE model for the English-German pair with 40k merge operations. We use a shared vocabulary and tie all embeddings of the translation models. The human parallel data for the German-English system is exactly the same as for the English-German system, the two systems only have different synthetic back-translated data.

3.3 Synthetic data

There are two types of additional synthetic training data described in detail below. The final size of the training data for the submitted systems is roughly 4 times the total size of the filtered data in Tables and 2.

Back-translated data

Back-translations (Sennrich et al., 2016a) are a common way to improve NMT models quality. As we aim at building general-domain models, we use data from Wikipedia dumps and news from statmt.org. We shuffle the Wikipedia data and randomly select a subset of appropriate size. The selected Wikipedia subset and the news subset are roughly equal in size. The size of the whole corpus used for back-translation is approximately equivalent to the size of human training data.

For the English-Russian pair we train a baseline Russian-English transformer model using the data prepared for the last year's WMT news task (Molchanov, 2018). For the German-English we also trained a transformer model using some data from OPUS as is: Europarl, DGT, JRC-Acquis, EMEA, ECB, NewsCommentary, TED2013, GlobalVoices. We use the Tatoeba corpus as our validation set in both cases. We use our final English-German model to obtain back-translations for the German-English model.

The trained systems were used to back-translate the 2017, 2018 news corpora from statmt.org and data selected from Wikipedia in Russian, German and English respectively.

Replicated data with unknown words

We apply the technique described in (Pinnis et al., 2017) to create a synthetic parallel corpus. The procedure includes the following steps: first, we perform word-alignment of our initial parallel training corpus using the fast-align tool (Dyer et al., 2013). Then, we randomly replace from one to three unambiguously (one-to-one) aligned tokens in both source and target parallel sentences with the special <UNK> placeholder. The same pipeline is applied to both the initial and back-translated data. We train our models to reproduce the <UNK> placeholder in various contexts and use this feature for handling named entities described in Section 4.2 below.

3.4 Data for fine-tuning

We again apply the modified bilingual Moore-Lewis data selection algorithm. We use the news 2018 corpora as our in-domain data. We select 1M sentences from the human training data (excluding MultiUN and OpenSubtitles). We also randomly select 1M sentences from the news 2018 corpus with their back-translations. The same procedure is applied to both English-Russian and English-German pairs.

4 Systems architecture

This section describes the trained systems in detail. We train transformer (Vaswani et al., 2017) models for all submitted systems. We use the recipe available at the MarianNMT website[3]. The system configuration, hyperparameters and training steps follow those in the recipe. There are two minor differences: 1) we check the validation translation less frequently and set a higher early-stopping threshold to allow the model iterate over the training data a bit longer; 2) we do not use shared vocabulary for the English-Russian system because of the different alphabets in English and Russian as we mentioned earlier. For this reason we do not tie all embeddings and only tie the target embeddings to the output layer.

We trained two models - Model1 and Model2 - for the English-Russian pair with different seeds for almost five epochs each. The training data for the two models is slightly different: 1) we did not use the deduplication scheme described in Section 3.1 above for Model1; 2) we found about 350k English sentences in the Russian news 2018 corpus. These were removed from the synthetic data only before training Model2.

We trained single models for the English-German and German-English. Both models were trained for two epochs.

4.1 Back-off to RBMT

We fall back to our rule-based system (RBMT) in several cases:

- if the NMT model output's language is other than expected. For example, we noticed that the English-Russian model sometimes generates English text (less than 1% of the test set sentences). The reasons for this were the 350k English sentences in Russian news 2018 corpus that we used for back-translation. We did not apply language filtering to the news-crawl corpora because they had been filtered by the WMT organisers until 2018. The English output is handled by the inhouse language detection tool.

- If the output contains recurring words or n-grams.

- If the output is much shorter or longer compared to the input sentence. We use simple rules based on source-translation length ratio to detect such cases.

- We also fall back to RBMT to translate very short strings (one or two words).

4.2 Handling named entities

We preserve several types of named entities (NEs): numbers, emails, alphanumeric sequencies etc. in the following way. First, we produce the baseline NMT translation without any processing. Then we validate the translation of NEs by comparing the system's output to the source sentence. The validation is simple: we search for the corresponding strings (numbers, emails etc.) in the system's output. If some of the NEs are not translated or are translated incorrectly, we replace the entities with the <UNK> placeholder in the source sentence and translate the sentence again allowing the decoder to generate unknown words in the output. Finally, we substitute the <UNK> placeholders in the output with their initial value. If the number of the <UNK> placeholders in the NMT system's output is not equal to the number of the placeholders in the source sentence, we fall back to the baseline NMT translation without NEs processing. We do not do any specific processing for proper names this time as they are handled much better by our current systems compared to our last year's submissions.

---

[3] https://github.com/marian-nmt/marian-examples/tree/master/wmt2017-transformer

4.3 Models configuration

We use an ensemble of two fine-tuned models as our final translation system for the English-Russian pair.

We use a single fine-tuned model for the English-German system; the German-English system is a single baseline model.

We use the beam of size 12 and the `--normalize` parameter is set to 1.

5 Results and discussion

In this section we present the BLEU (Papineni et al., 2002) scores for our systems on two test sets and the analysis of the results.

The scores are presented in Table 4. Calculation is done using the `multi-bleu-detok.perl` script from the `Moses` toolkit.

System	newstest2018	newstest2019
English-Russian		
Model2018	27.4	24.7
Model1	30.4	27.7
Model2	32.1	29.6
Model1 fine-tuned	31.9	29.1
Model2 fine-tuned	32.5	30.4
Model1+Model2 fine-tuned	**32.9**	**30.8**
English-German		
Model (baseline)	40.0	38.1
Model fine-tuned	**40.4**	**38.4**
German-English		
Model (baseline)	**40.1**	**32.1**

Table 4: Results for different systems. The submitted systems are marked in bold. Model2018 stands for our last year's submitted system which we consider the baseline. Model1 and Model2 are described in Section 4 above.

We significantly outperform the baseline for the English-Russian pair - our last year's submission for the News Task, an ensemble of 4 models. The results for Model1 and Model2 show us that better data filtering leads to better translation quality.

Fine-tuning does not give us significant improvements in terms of BLEU. We should probably try new approaches to data selection for domain adaptation.

We should also note the lower quality of the German-English model compared to our models and other participants. We think this must be connected with the fact that the data used for training the German-English model was in fact filtered for training the English-German model (thus, we paid less attention to the English side of the data).

6 Conclusions and Future work

In this paper we have described our submissions for the WMT 2019 Shared News Translation Task. Overall we have made three submissions: English-Russian, English-German and German-English.

We have documented the methodology used to prepare the training data, system training set-ups, the pipelines for handling NEs and using RBMT.

We show competitive results in two out of three language pairs.

We plan our future research in several directions. First of all, data filtering improvement (especially when training models in both directions). Second, handling proper names translation into Russian. Finally, exploring other language pairs including the Chinese and Kazakh languages.

References

Amittai Axelrod, Xiaodong He, and Jianfeng Gao. 2011. Domain adaptation via pseudo in-domain data selection. In *Proceedings of the ACL Conference on Empirical Methods in Natural Language Processing (EMNLP)*, pages 355–362, Edinburgh, Scotland, UK.

Anna Currey, Antonio Valerio Miceli Barone, and Kenneth Heafield. 2017. Copied monolingual data improves low-resource neural machine translation. In *Proceedings of the Second Conference on Machine Translation*, pages 148–156, Copenhagen, Denmark.

Chris Dyer, Victor Chahuneau, and Noah A Smith. 2013. A Simple, Fast, and Effective Reparameterization of IBM Model 2. In *Proceedings of NAACL HLT 2013*, pages 644–648, Atlanta, USA.

Marcin Junczys-Dowmunt, Roman Grundkiewicz, Tomasz Dwojak, Hieu Hoang, Kenneth Heafield, Tom Neckermann, Frank Seide, Ulrich Germann, Alham Fikri Aji, Nikolay Bogoychev, André F. T. Martins, and Alexandra Birch. 2018. Marian: Fast Neural Machine Translation in C++. In *Proceedings of ACL 2018, System Demonstrations*, pages 116–121, Melbourne, Australia.

Guillaume Klein, Yoon Kim, Yuntian Deng, Jean Senellart, Alexander M. Rush. 2017. OpenNMT: Open-Source Toolkit for Neural Machine

Translation. *Computing Research Repository*, arXiv:1701.02810. Version 2.

Marco Lui and Timothy Baldwin. 2012. langid.py: An Off-the-shelf Language Identification Tool. In *Proceedings of ACL 2012, System Demonstrations*, pages 25–30, Jeju, Republic of Korea.

Philipp Koehn, Hieu Hoang, Alexandra Birch, Chris Callison-Burch, Marcello Federico, Nicola Bertoldi, Brooke Cowan, Wade Shen, Christine Moran, Richard Zens, Chris Dyer, Ondrej Bojar, Alexandra Constantin, and Evan Herbst. 2007. Moses: open source toolkit for statistical machine translation. In *Proceedings of the 45th Annual Meeting of the ACL on Interactive Poster and Demonstration Sessions, ACL 07*, pages 177–180, Stroudsburg, PA, USA.

Alexander Molchanov. 2018. PROMT Systems for WMT 2018 Shared Translation Task. In *Proceedings of the Third Conference on Machine Translation*, pages 460–464, Brussels, Belgium.

Kishore Papineni, Salim Roukos, Todd Ward, and WeiJing Zhu. 2002. Bleu: a method for automatic evaluation of machine translation. In *Proceedings of the 40th Annual Meeting of the Association for Computational Linguistics (ACL 02)*, pages 311–318, Philadelphia, PA, USA.

Marcis Pinnis, Rihards Krišlauks, Daiga Deksne, and Toms Miks. 2017. Neural Machine Translation for Morphologically Rich Languages with Improved Sub-word Units and Synthetic Data. In *Proceedings of the 20th International Conference of Text, Speech and Dialogue (TSD2017)*, pages 237–245, Prague, Czechia.

Rico Sennrich, Barry Haddow, and Alexandra Birch. 2016a. Improving Neural Machine Translation Models with Monolingual Data. In *Proceedings of the 54th Annual Meeting of the Association for Computational Linguistics (ACL 2016)*, Berlin, Germany.

Rico Sennrich, Barry Haddow, and Alexandra Birch. Neural machine translation of rare words with subword units. 2016b. In *Proceedings of the 54th Annual Meeting of the Association for Computational Linguistics (ACL 2016)*, pages 35–40, Berlin, Germany.

Michel Simard, Cyril Goutte, and Pierre Isabelle. 2007. Statistical phrase-based post-editing. In *Proceedings of The North American Chapter of the 342 Association for Computational Linguistics Conference (NAACL-07)*, pages 508–515, Rochester, NY, USA.

Aleš Tamchyna, Marion Weller-Di Marco and Alexander Fraser. 2017. Modeling Target-Side Inflection in Neural Machine Translation. In *Proceedings of the Second Conference on Machine Translation*, pages 32–42, Copenhagen, Denmark.

Jorg Tiedemann. 2012. Parallel data, tools and interfaces in opus. In *Proceedings of the Eight International Conference on Language Resources and Evaluation (LREC'12)*, pages 2214–2218, Istanbul, Turkey.

Dániel Varga, László Németh, Péter Halácsy, András Kornai, Viktor Trón, Viktor Nagy. 2005. Parallel corpora for medium density languages. In *Proceedings of the RANLP 2005*, pages 590–596, Borovets, Bulgaria.

Ashish Vaswani, Noam Shazeer, Niki Parmar, Jakob Uszkoreit, Llion Jones, Aidan N. Gomez, Lukasz Kaiser, and Illia Polosukhin. 2017. Attention is all you need. In *Proceedings of the Annual Conference on Neural Information Processing Systems (NIPS 2017)*, Long Beach, CA, USA.

JU-Saarland Submission in the WMT2019 English–Gujarati Translation Shared Task

Riktim Mondal[1,*], Shankha Raj Nayek[1,*], Aditya Chowdhury[1,*]
Santanu Pal[2], Sudip Kumar Naskar[1], Josef van Genabith[2]
[1]Jadavpur University, Kolkata, India
[2]Saarland University, Germany
{riktimrules,shankharaj29,adityachowdhury21}@gmail.com
{santanu.pal,josef.vangenabith}@uni-saarland.de
sudip.naskar@cse.jdvu.ac.in

Abstract

In this paper we describe our joint submission (JU-Saarland) from Jadavpur University and Saarland University in the WMT 2019 news translation shared task for English–Gujarati language pair within the translation task sub-track. Our baseline and primary submissions are built using a Recurrent neural network (RNN) based neural machine translation (NMT) system which follows attention mechanism followed by fine-tuning using in-domain data. Given the fact that the two languages belong to different language families and there is not enough parallel data for this language pair, building a high quality NMT system for this language pair is a difficult task. We produced synthetic data through back-translation from available monolingual data. We report the automatic evaluation scores of our English–Gujarati and Gujarati–English NMT systems trained at word, byte-pair and character encoding levels where RNN at word level is considered as the baseline and used for comparison purpose. Our English–Gujarati system ranked in the second position in the shared task.

1 Introduction

Neural Machine translation (NMT) is an approach to machine translation (MT) that uses artificial neural network to directly model the conditional probability $p(y|x)$ of translating a source sentence $(x_1,x_2,...,x_n)$ into a target sentence $(y_1,y_2,...,y_m)$. NMT has consistently performed better than the phrase-based statistical MT (PB-SMT) approaches and has provided state-of-the-art results in the last few years. However, one of the major constraints of using supervised NMT is that it is not suitable for low resource language pairs. Thus, to use supervised NMT, low resource pairs need to resort to other techniques

to increase the size of the parallel training dataset. In the WMT 2019 news translation shared task, one such resource scarce language pair is English-Gujarati. Due to insufficient volume of parallel corpora available to train an NMT system for these language pairs, creation of more actual/synthetic parallel data for low resources languages such as Gujarati, is an important issue.

In this paper, we described our joint participation of Jadavpur University and Saarland University in the WMT 2019 news translation task for English–Gujarati and Gujarati–English. The released training data set is completely different in-domain compared to the development set and the size is not anywhere close to the sizable amount of training data which is typically required for the success of NMT systems. We use additional synthetic data produced through back-translation from the monolingual corpus. This provides significant improvements in translation performance for both our English–Gujarati and Gujarati–English NMT systems. Our English–Gujarati system was ranked second in terms of BLEU (Papineni et al., 2002) and TER (Snover et al., 2006) in the shared task.

2 Related Works

Dungarwal et al. (Dungarwal et al., 2014) developed a statistical method for machine translation, where phrase based method for Hindi-English and factored based method for English-Hindi SMT system was used. They had shown improvements to the existing SMT systems using pre-procesing and post-processing components that generated morphological inflections correctly. Imankulova et al. (Imankulova et al., 2017) showed how back-translation and filtering from monolingual data can be used to build an effective translation system for a low-resourse language pair like Japanese-

---

* These three authors have contributed equally.

Proceedings of the Fourth Conference on Machine Translation (WMT), Volume 2: Shared Task Papers (Day 1) pages 308–313
Florence, Italy, August 1-2, 2019. ©2019 Association for Computational Linguistics

Dataset	Pairs
Parallel Corpora	192,367
Cleaned Parallel Corpora	64,346
Back-translated Data	219,654
Development Data	1,998
Gujarati Test Data	1,016
English Test Data	998

Table 1: Data Statistics of WMT 2019 English–Gujarati translation shared task.

Russian. Sennrich et al. (Sennrich et al., 2016a) shown how back-translation of monolingual data can improve the NMT system. Ramesh et al. (Ramesh and Sankaranarayanan, 2018) demonstrated how an existing model like bidirectional recurrent neural network can be used to generate parallel sentences for non-English languages like English-Tamil and English-Hindi, which belong to low-resource language pair, to improve the SMT and the NMT systems. Choudhary et al. (Choudhary et al., 2018) has shown how to build NMT system for low resource parallel corpus language pair like English-Tamil using techniques like word embeddings and Byte-Pair-Encoding (Sennrich et al., 2016b) to handle Out-Of-Vocabulary Words.

3   Data Preparation

For our experiments we used both parallel and monolingual corpus released by the WMT 2019 Organizers. We back-translate the monolingual corpus and use it as additional synthetic parallel corpus to train our NMT system. The detailed statistics of the corpus is given in Table 1.

We performed our experiments on two datasets, one using the parallel corpus provided by WMT 2019 for the Gujarati–English news translation shared task, and the other using the parallel corpus combined with back translated sentences from provided monolingual corpus (only News crawl corpus was used for back translation) for the same language pair.

Since the released parallel corpus was very noisy, containing redundant sentences, we cleaned the parallel corpus, the procedure of which is described in section 3.1.

In the next step we shuffle the whole corpus as it reduces variance and makes sure that our model overfits less. We then split the dataset into three parts: training, validation and test set. Shuffling

is important in the splitting part too as it is important to choose the test and validation set from the same distribution and must be chosen randomly from the available data. Here, test set was also shuffled as this dataset was used for our internal assessment. After cleaning, we randomly selected 64,346 sentence pairs for training, 1,500 sentence pairs for validation and 1,500 sentences as test data. It is to be noted that our validation and test corpus is taken from the released parallel data to setup a baseline model. Later when WMT19 Organizers released the development set, we continued training our models by considering WMT19 development set as our test set and the new development set consisting of 3,000 sentences which were obtained after combining 1,500 sentences from the validation and the testing set (both were from the parallel corpus as stated above). While training our final model, the released development set was used. After cleaning it was obvious that the amount of training data is not enough to train a neural system for such a low resource language pair. Therefore, preparation for large volume of parallel corpus is required which can be produced either by manual translation by professional translators or scraping parallel data from the internet. However, these processes are costly, tedious and sometimes inefficient (in case of scraping from internet).

As the released data was insufficient, to generate more training data, we use back-translation. For back-translation we applied two methods, first, using unsupervised statistical machine translation as described in (Artetxe et al., 2018) and second, using Doc translation API[1] (The API uses Google translator as of April 2019). We have explained the extraction of sentences and the corresponding results using the above methods in section 4.2. The synthetic dataset which we have generated can be found here.[2]

3.1   Data Preprocessing

To train an efficient machine translation system, it is required to clean the available raw parallel corpus for the system to produce consistent and reliable translations. The released version of the raw parallel corpus consisted of redundant pairs which needs to be removed to obtain better results

---

[1] https://www.onlinedoctranslator.com/en/

[2] https://github.com/riktimmondal/Synthetic-Data-WMT19-for-En-Gu-Language-pair

as demonstrated in previous works (Johnson et al., 2017) which are of types as given below:

- The source is same for different targets.

- The source is different for the same target.

- Repeated identical sentence pair

The redundancy in the translation pairs makes the model prone to overfitting and hence prevents it from recognizing new features. Thus, one of the sentence pair is kept while the other redundant pairs are removed. Some sentence pairs had combinations of both language pairs which were also identified as redundant. These pairs strictly need elimination as the vocabularies of the individual languages consist of alphanumeric characters of the other language which results in inconsistent encoding and decoding during encoder-decoder application steps on the considered language pair. We tokenize the English side using Moses (Koehn et al., 2007) tokenizer and for Gujarati, we use the Indic NLP library tokenization tool[3]. Punctuation normalization was also done.

3.2 Data Postprocessing

Postprocessing, such as detokenization (Klein et al., 2017), punctuation normalization[4] (Koehn et al., 2007), was performed on our translated data (on the test set) to produce the final translated data.

4 Experiment Setup

We have explained our experimental setups in the next two sections. The first section contains the setup used for our final submission and the next section describes all the other supporting experimental setups. We use the OpenNMT toolkit (Klein et al., 2017) for our experiments.
We performed several experiments where the parallel corpus is sent to the model as space separated character format, space separated word format, and space separated Byte Pair Encoding (BPE) format (Sennrich et al., 2016b). For our final (i.e., primary) submission for the English–Gujarati task, the source input words were converted to BPE whereas the Gujarati words were kept as it is. For our Gujarati–English submission, both the source and the target were in simple word level format.

[3]http://anoopkunchukuttan.github.io/indic_nlp_library/

[4]punctuation_normalization.perl

4.1 Primary System description

Our primary NMT systems are based on attention-based uni-directional RNN (Cho et al., 2014) for Gujarati–English and bi-directional RNN (Cheng et al., 2016) for English–Gujarati.

hyper-parameter	Value
Model-type	text
Model-dtype	fp32
Attention-layer	2
Attention-Head/layer	8
Hidden-layers	500
Batch-Size	256
Training-steps	160,000
Source vocab-size	50,000
Target vocab-size	50,000
learning-rate	warm-up+decay*
global-attention function	softmax
tokenization-strategy	wordpiece
RNN-type	LSTM

Table 2: Hyper-parameter configurations for Gujarati–English translation using unidirectional RNN (Cho et al., 2014)), *learning-rate was initially set to 1.0.

Table 2 shows the hyper-parameter configurations for our Gujarati–English translation system. We initially trained our model with the cleaned parallel corpus provided by WMT 2019 up to 100K training steps. Thereafter, we fine-tune our generic model on domain specific corpus (containing 219K sentences back-translated using Doc Translator API) changing the learning rate to 0.5 and decay started from 130K training steps with a decay factor of 0.5 and keeping the other hyper-parameters same as mentioned in Table 2.

hyper-parameter	Value
Model-type	text
Model-dtype	fp32
Encoder-type	BRNN
Attention-layer	2
Attention-Head/layer	8
Hidden-layers	512
Batch-Size	256
Training-steps	135,000
Source vocab-size	26,859
Target vocab-size	50,000
learning-rate	warm-up+decay
global-attention function	softmax
tokenization-strategy	Byte-pair Encoding
RNN-type	LSTM

Table 3: Hyper-parameter configurations for English–Gujarati translation using bi-directional RNN (Cheng et al., 2016).

To build our English–Gujarati translation system, we initially trained a generic model like our

Gujarati–English translation system. However, in this case we use different hyper-parameter configurations as mentioned in Table 3. Additionally, here, we use byte-pair encoding on the English side with 32K merge operations. We do not perform BPE operation on the Gujarati corpus; we keep the original word format for Gujrati. Our generic model was trained with up to 100K training steps and then fine-tuned our model on domain specific parallel corpus having English side as BPE and Gujarati side as word level format. During fine-tuning, we reduce the learning rate from 1.0 to 0.25 and started decaying from 120K training steps with a decay factor of 0.5. The other hyper-parameter configurations remain unchanged. The respective hyperparameters used for the English–Gujarati task in our primary system submission were also tested for the reverse direction; however, it did not perform as good as the primary system and hence the final system is modified accordingly.

4.2 Other Supporting Experiments

In this section we describe all the supporting experiments that we performed for this shared task starting from Statistical MT to NMT with both supervised and unsupervised settings.

All the results and experiments discussed below are tested on the released development set (considering this as the test set). These models were not tested with the released test set as they provided poor BLEU scores on the development set.

We used uni-directional RNN having LSTM units trained on 64,346 pre-processed sentences (cf. Section 3) with 120K training steps and learning rate of 1.0. For English–Gujarati where input was space separated words for both sides, we achieved highest BLEU score of **4.15** after fine-tuning with 10K sentences selected from the cleaned parallel corpus whose total number of tokens(words) was exceeding 8.The BLEU score dropped to **3.56** while applying BPE on the both sides. For the other direction (Gujarati–English) of the language pair, we got highest BLEU scores of **5.13** and **5.09** at word level and BPE level respectively.

We also tried transformer-based NMT model (Vaswani et al., 2017) which however gave extremely poor results on similar experimental settings. The highest BLEU we achieved was **0.74** for Gujarati–English and **0.96** for English–

Gujarati. The transformer model was trained until 100K training steps, with 64 batch size in a single GPU and positional encoding layers size was set to 2.

Since the the training data size was not enough, we used backtranslation to generate additional synthetic sentence pairs from the monolingual corpus released in WMT 2019. We initially used *monoses* (Artetxe et al., 2018), which is based on unsupervised statistical phrase based machine translation, to translate the monolingual sentences from English to Gujarati. We used 2M English sentences to train the monoses system. The training process took around 6 days in our modest 64 GB server. However, the results were extremely poor with a BLEU score of **0.24** for English–Gujarati and **0.01** for the opposite direction, without using preprocessed parallel corpus. Moreover, after adding preprocessed parallel corpus, the BLEU score dropped significantly. This motivated us to use online document translator, in our case Google translation API, for back-translating sentence pairs from the released monolingual dataset. The back-translated data was later combined with our preprocessed parallel corpus for our final model.

Additionally, we also tried a simple unidirectional RNN model on character level, however, this also fails to contribute in terms of improving performance. We have compiled all the results in table 4.

5 Primary System Results

Our primary submission for English–Gujarati using bidirectional RNN model with BPE at English side (see Section 4.1) and word format at Gujarati side gave the best result. On the other hand, the Gujarati-English primary submission, based on an uni-directional RNN model with both English and Gujarati in word format, gave the best result. Before submission, we performed punctuation normalization, unicode normalization, and detokenization for each runs. Table 5 shows the published results of our primary submissions on WMT 2019 Test set. Table 6 shows our hands on experimental results on the development set.

6 Conclusion and Future Work

In this paper, we applied NMT to one of the most challenging language pair, English–Gujarati, as the availability of parallel corpus is really scarce

Language pair	Model used	Tokenization Strategy	BLEU
EN-GU	RNN	Word	4.15
EN-GU	RNN	BPE	3.56
GU-EN	RNN	Word	5.13
GU-EN	RNN	BPE	5.09
EN-GU	Transformer	Word	0.96
GU-EN	Transformer	Word	0.74
EN-GU	Monoses	Word	0.24
GU-EN	Monoses	Word	0.01

Table 4: Results of supporting experiments.

Language pair	BLEU	BLEU-cased	TER	BEER2.0	characTER
EN-GU	21.9	21.9	0.688	0.529	0.647
GU-EN	12.8	11.8	0.796	0.422	0.891

Table 5: WMT 2019 evaluation for EN-GU and GU-EN on test set.

Language pair	BLEU	BLEU-cased
EN-GU	22.3	22.3
GU-EN	17.6	16.8

Table 6: WMT 2019 evaluation for EN-GU and GU-EN on development set released by WMT 2019.

for this language pair. In this scenario, collecting and preprocessing of data play very crucial role to increase the dataset as well as to obtain quality result using NMT. In this paper we show how increasing the parallel data through back-translation via Google translation API can increase the overall performance. Our primary result also exceeded Google translate (which gave a BLEU of 13.7) by a margin of around 8.0 absolute BLEU points. Our method is not just limited to English–Gujarati translation task; it can also be useful in various scarce-resource language pairs and domains.

We did not make use of any ensemble mechanism in this task, otherwise we could have achieved higher BLEU scores. Therefore, in future we will try to ensemble several models, increasing more useful back-translated data using existing state-of-the-art model. In future, we would also like to explore cross-lingual BERT (Devlin et al., 2018) to enhance the performance.

Acknowledgments

We want to thank Google Colab where we trained all our models. Santanu Pal is supported in part by the German research foundation (DFG) under grant number GE 2819/2-1 (project MMPE) and the German Federal Ministry of Education and Research (BMBF) under funding code 01IW17001 (project Deeplee). The responsibility for this publication lies with the authors. Sudip Kumar Naskar is partially supported by Digital India Corporation (formerly Media Lab Asia), MeitY, Government of India, under the Young Faculty Research Fellowship of the Visvesvaraya PhD Scheme for Electronics IT. We also want to thank the reviewers for their valuable input, and the organizers of the shared task.

References

Mikel Artetxe, Gorka Labaka, and Eneko Agirre. 2018. Unsupervised statistical machine translation. In *Proceedings of the 2018 Conference on Empirical Methods in Natural Language Processing*, pages 3632–3642, Brussels, Belgium. Association for Computational Linguistics.

Yong Cheng, Shiqi Shen, Zhongjun He, Wei He, Hua Wu, Maosong Sun, and Yang Liu. 2016. Agreement-based joint training for bidirectional attention-based neural machine translation. In *Proceedings of the Twenty-Fifth International Joint Conference on Artificial Intelligence*, IJCAI'16, pages 2761–2767. AAAI Press.

Kyunghyun Cho, Bart van Merrienboer, Caglar Gulcehre, Dzmitry Bahdanau, Fethi Bougares, Holger Schwenk, and Yoshua Bengio. 2014. Learning phrase representations using RNN encoder–decoder for statistical machine translation. In *Proceedings of the 2014 Conference on Empirical Methods in Natural Language Processing (EMNLP)*, pages 1724–1734, Doha, Qatar. Association for Computational Linguistics.

Himanshu Choudhary, Aditya Kumar Pathak, Rajiv Ratan Saha, and Ponnurangam Kumaraguru. 2018. Neural machine translation for English-Tamil. In *Proceedings of the Third Conference on Machine Translation: Shared Task Papers*, pages 770–775, Belgium, Brussels. Association for Computational Linguistics.

Jacob Devlin, Ming-Wei Chang, Kenton Lee, and Kristina Toutanova. 2018. BERT: pre-training of deep bidirectional transformers for language understanding. *CoRR*, abs/1810.04805.

Piyush Dungarwal, Rajen Chatterjee, Abhijit Mishra, Anoop Kunchukuttan, Ritesh Shah, and Pushpak Bhattacharyya. 2014. The IIT Bombay Hindi-English translation system at WMT 2014. In *Proceedings of the Ninth Workshop on Statistical Machine Translation*, pages 90–96, Baltimore, Maryland, USA. Association for Computational Linguistics.

Aizhan Imankulova, Takayuki Sato, and Mamoru Komachi. 2017. Improving low-resource neural machine translation with filtered pseudo-parallel corpus. In *Proceedings of the 4th Workshop on Asian Translation (WAT2017)*, pages 70–78, Taipei, Taiwan. Asian Federation of Natural Language Processing.

Melvin Johnson, Mike Schuster, Quoc V. Le, Maxim Krikun, Yonghui Wu, Zhifeng Chen, Nikhil Thorat, Fernanda Viégas, Martin Wattenberg, Greg Corrado, Macduff Hughes, and Jeffrey Dean. 2017. Google's multilingual neural machine translation system: Enabling zero-shot translation. *Transactions of the Association for Computational Linguistics*, 5:339–351.

Guillaume Klein, Yoon Kim, Yuntian Deng, Jean Senellart, and Alexander M. Rush. 2017. OpenNMT: Open-source toolkit for neural machine translation. In *Proc. ACL*.

Philipp Koehn, Hieu Hoang, Alexandra Birch, Chris Callison-Burch, Marcello Federico, Nicola Bertoldi, Brooke Cowan, Wade Shen, Christine Moran, Richard Zens, Chris Dyer, Ondřej Bojar, Alexandra Constantin, and Evan Herbst. 2007. Moses: Open source toolkit for statistical machine translation. In *Proceedings of the 45th Annual Meeting of the ACL on Interactive Poster and Demonstration Sessions*, ACL '07, pages 177–180, Stroudsburg, PA, USA. Association for Computational Linguistics.

Kishore Papineni, Salim Roukos, Todd Ward, and Wei-Jing Zhu. 2002. Bleu: A method for automatic evaluation of machine translation. In *Proceedings of the 40th Annual Meeting on Association for Computational Linguistics*, ACL '02, pages 311–318, Stroudsburg, PA, USA. Association for Computational Linguistics.

Sree Harsha Ramesh and Krishna Prasad Sankaranarayanan. 2018. Neural machine translation for low resource languages using bilingual lexicon induced from comparable corpora. In *Proceedings of the 2018 Conference of the North American Chapter of the Association for Computational Linguistics: Student Research Workshop*, pages 112–119, New Orleans, Louisiana, USA. Association for Computational Linguistics.

Rico Sennrich, Barry Haddow, and Alexandra Birch. 2016a. Improving neural machine translation models with monolingual data. In *Proceedings of the 54th Annual Meeting of the Association for Computational Linguistics (Volume 1: Long Papers)*, pages 86–96, Berlin, Germany. Association for Computational Linguistics.

Rico Sennrich, Barry Haddow, and Alexandra Birch. 2016b. Neural machine translation of rare words with subword units. In *Proceedings of the 54th Annual Meeting of the Association for Computational Linguistics (Volume 1: Long Papers)*, pages 1715–1725, Berlin, Germany. Association for Computational Linguistics.

Matthew Snover, Bonnie Dorr, Richard Schwartz, Linnea Micciulla, and John Makhoul. 2006. A study of translation edit rate with targeted human annotation. In *In Proceedings of Association for Machine Translation in the Americas*, pages 223–231.

Ashish Vaswani, Noam Shazeer, Niki Parmar, Jakob Uszkoreit, Llion Jones, Aidan N Gomez, Ł ukasz Kaiser, and Illia Polosukhin. 2017. Attention is all you need. In I. Guyon, U. V. Luxburg, S. Bengio, H. Wallach, R. Fergus, S. Vishwanathan, and R. Garnett, editors, *Advances in Neural Information Processing Systems 30*, pages 5998–6008. Curran Associates, Inc.

Facebook FAIR's WMT19 News Translation Task Submission

Nathan Ng, Kyra Yee, Alexei Baevski, Myle Ott, Michael Auli, Sergey Edunov
Facebook AI Research,
Menlo Park, CA & New York, NY.

Abstract

This paper describes Facebook FAIR's submission to the WMT19 shared news translation task. We participate in four language directions, English ↔ German and English ↔ Russian in both directions. Following our submission from last year, our baseline systems are large BPE-based transformer models trained with the FAIRSEQ sequence modeling toolkit. This year we experiment with different bitext data filtering schemes, as well as with adding filtered back-translated data. We also ensemble and fine-tune our models on domain-specific data, then decode using noisy channel model reranking. Our system improves on our previous system's performance by 4.5 BLEU points and achieves the best case-sensitive BLEU score for the translation direction English→Russian.

1 Introduction

We participate in the WMT19 shared news translation task in two language pairs and four language directions, English→German (En→De), German→English (De→En), English→Russian (En→Ru), and Russian→English (Ru→En). Our methods are based on techniques and approaches used in our submission from last year (Edunov et al., 2018), including the use of subword models, (Sennrich et al., 2016), large-scale back-translation, and model ensembling. We train all models using the FAIRSEQ sequence modeling toolkit (Ott et al., 2019). Although document level context for En→De is now available, all our systems are pure sentence level systems. In the future, we expect better results from leveraging this additional context information.

Compared to our WMT18 submission, we also decide to compete in the En↔Ru and De→En translation directions. Although all four directions are considered high resource settings where lar-ge amounts of bitext data is available, we demonstrate that leveraging high quality monolingual data through back-translation is still very important. For all language directions, we back-translate the Newscrawl dataset using a reverse direction bitext system. In addition to back-translating the relatively clean Newscrawl dataset, we also experiment with back-translating portions of the much larger and noisier Commoncrawl dataset. For our final models, we apply a domain-specific fine-tuning process and decode using noisy channel model reranking (Anonymous, 2019).

Compared to our WMT18 submission in the En→De direction, we observe substantial improvements of 4.5 BLEU. Some of these gains can be attributed to differences in dataset quality, but we believe most of the improvement comes from larger models, larger scale back-translation, and noisy channel model reranking with strong channel and language models.

2 Data

For the En↔De language pair we use all available bitext data including the bicleaner version of Paracrawl. For our monolingual data we use English and German Newscrawl. Although our language models were trained on document level data, we did not use document level boundaries in our final decoding step, so all our systems are purely sentence level systems.

For the En↔Ru language pair we also use all available bitext data. For our monolingual data we use English and Russian Newscrawl as well as a filtered portion of Russian Commoncrawl. We choose to use Russian Commoncrawl to augment our monolingual data due to the relatively small size of Russian Newscrawl compared to English and German.

Proceedings of the Fourth Conference on Machine Translation (WMT), Volume 2: Shared Task Papers (Day 1) pages 314–319
Florence, Italy, August 1-2, 2019. ©2019 Association for Computational Linguistics

2.1 Data Preprocessing

Similar to last year's submission for En→De, we normalize punctuation and tokenize all data with the Moses tokenizer (Koehn et al., 2007). For En↔De we use joint byte pair encodings (BPE) with 32K split operations for subword segmentation (Sennrich et al., 2016). For En↔Ru, we learn separate BPE encodings with 24K split operations for each language. Systems trained with this separate BPE encoding performed significantly better than those trained with joint BPE.

2.2 Data Filtering

2.2.1 Bitext

Large datasets crawled from the internet are naturally very noisy and can potentially decrease the performance of a system if they are used in their raw form. Cleaning these datasets is an important step to achieving good performance on any downstream tasks.

We apply language identification filtering (`langid`; Lui et al., 2012), keeping only sentence pairs with correct languages on both sides. Although not the most accurate method of language identification (Joulin et al., 2016), one side effect of using `langid` is the removal of very noisy sentences consisting of mostly garbage tokens, which are classified incorrectly and filtered out.

We also remove sentences longer than 250 tokens as well as sentence pairs with a source/target length ratio exceeding 1.5. In total, we filter out about 30% of the original bitext data. See Table 1 for details on the bitext dataset sizes.

2.2.2 Monolingual

For monolingual Newscrawl data we also apply `langid` filtering. Since the monolingual Newscrawl corpus for Russian is significantly smaller than that of German or English, we augment our monolingual Russian data with data from the commoncrawl corpus. Commoncrawl is the largest monolingual corpus available for training but is also very noisy. In order to select a limited amount of high quality, in-domain sentences from the larger corpus, we adopt the method of Moore and Lewis (2010) for selecting in-domain data (§3.2.1).

	En-De	En-Ru
No filter	38.8M	38.5M
+ length filter	35.7M	33.4M
+ `langid` filter	27.7M	26.0M

Table 1: Number of sentences in bitext datasets for different filtering schemes

3 System Overview

3.1 Base System

Our base system is based on the big Transformer architecture (Vaswani et al., 2017) as implemented in FAIRSEQ. We experiment with increasing network capacity by increasing embed dimension, FFN size, number of heads, and number of layers. We find that using a larger FFN size (8192) gives a reasonable improvement in performance while maintaining a manageable network size. All subsequent models, including ensembles, use this larger FFN Transformer architecture.

We trained all our models using FAIRSEQ (Ott et al., 2019) on 128 Volta GPUs, following the setup described in Ott et al. (2018)

3.2 Large-scale Back-translation

Back-translation is an effective and commonly used data augmentation technique to incorporate monolingual data into a translation system. Back-translation first trains an intermediate target-to-source system that is used to translate monolingual target data into additional synthetic parallel data. This data is used in conjunction with human translated bitext data to train the desired source-to-target system.

In this work we used back-translations obtained by sampling (Edunov et al., 2018) from an ensemble of three target-to-source models. We found that models trained on data back-translated using an ensemble instead of a single model performed better (Table 2). Previous work also found that upsampling the bitext data can improve back-translation (Edunov et al., 2018). We adopt this method to tune the amount of bitext and synthetic data the model is trained on. We find a ratio of 1:1 synthetic to bitext data to perform the best.

3.2.1 Back-translating Commoncrawl

The amount of monolingual Russian data available in the Newscrawl dataset is significantly smaller than that of English and German (Table 3). In

	En→Ru	
	Single Model	Ensemble
newstest15	35.98	36.32
newstest16	32.78	33.28
newstest17	36.57	36.77
newstest18	34.72	34.72

Table 2: SacreBLEU for English-Russian models trained with data back-translated using a single model vs. an ensemble of two models

	En	De	Ru
Newscrawl	434M	559M	80M
+ `langid` filter	424M	521M	76M
Commoncrawl	-	-	1.2B
+ `KenLM` filter	-	-	60M
Total	424M	521M	136M

Table 3: Number of sentences in monolingual datasets available for back-translation

order to increase the amount of monolingual Russian data for back-translation, we experiment with incorporating Commoncrawl data. Commoncrawl is a much larger and noisier dataset compared to Newscrawl, and is also non-domain specific. We experiment with methods to identify a subset of Commoncrawl that is most similar to Newscrawl. Specifically, we use the in-domain filtering method described in Moore and Lewis (2010).

Given an in domain corpus I, in this case Newscrawl, and a non-domain specific corpus N, in this case Commoncrawl, we would like the find the subcorpus N_I that is drawn from the same distribution as I. For any given sentence s, we can calculate, using Bayes' rule, the probability a sentence s in N is drawn from N_I

$$P(N_I|s, N) = \frac{P(s|N_I)P(N_I|N)}{P(s|N)} \quad (1)$$

We ignore the $P(N_I|N)$ term, since it will be constant for any given I and N, and use $P(s|I)$ instead of $P(s|N_I)$, since I and N_I are drawn from the same distribution. Moving into the log domain, we can calculate the probability score for a sentence s by $\log P(N_I|s, N) = \log P(s|I) - \log P(s|N)$, or after normalizing for length, $H_I(s) - H_N(s)$, where $H_I(s)$ and $H_N(s)$ are the word-normalized cross entropy scores for a sentence s according to language models L_I and

	En-**De**	De-**En**	En-**Ru**	Ru-**En**
newstest12	26.7	28.0	-	-
newstest13	27.8	27.6	42.7	27.6
newstest14	21.4	24.0	32.3	22.4
newstest15	25.1	24.6	34.7	21.8
newstest16	24.5	22.0	35.5	19.4
newstest17	25.0	21.9	37.9	19.5
newstest18	25.1	26.0	39.3	20.0

Table 4: Perplexity scores for language models on bolded target languages in all translation directions

L_N trained on I and N respectively.

Our corpora are very large and we therefore use an n-gram model (Heafield, 2011) rather than a neural language model which would be much slower to train and evaluate. We train two language models L_I and L_N on Newscrawl and Commoncrawl respectively, then score every sentence s in Commoncrawl by $H_I(s) - H_N(s)$. We select a cutoff of 0.01, and use all sentences that score higher than this value for back-translation, or about 5% of the entire dataset.

3.3 Fine-tuning

Fine-tuning with domain-specific data is a common and effective method to improve translation quality for a downstream task. After completing training on the bitext and back-translated data, we train for an additional epoch on a smaller in-domain corpus. For De→En, we fine-tune on test sets from previous years, including newstest2012, newstest2013, newstest2015, and newstest2017. For En→De, we fine-tune on previous test sets as well as the News-Commentary dataset. For En↔Ru we fine-tune on a combination of News-Commentary, newstest2013, newstest2015, and newstest2017. The other test sets are held out for other tuning procedures and evaluation metrics.

3.4 Noisy Channel Model Reranking

N-best reranking is a method of improving translation quality by scoring and selecting a candidate hypothesis from a list of n-best hypotheses generated by a source-to-target, or forward model. For our submissions, we rerank using a noisy channel model approach (Anonymous, 2019).

Given a target sequence y and a source sequence x, the noisy channel approach applies Bayes' rule to model

$$P(y|x) = \frac{P(x|y)P(y)}{P(x)} \qquad (2)$$

Since $P(x)$ is constant for a given source sequence x, we can ignore it. We refer to the remaining terms $P(y|x)$, $P(x|y)$, and $P(y)$, as the forward model, channel model, and language model respectively. In order to combine these scores for reranking, we calculate for every one of our n-best hypotheses:

$$\log P(y|x) + \lambda_1 \log P(x|y) + \lambda_2 \log P(y) \qquad (3)$$

The weights λ_1 and λ_2 are determined by tuning them with a random search on a validation set and selecting the weights that give the best performance. In addition, we also tune a length penalty.

For all translation directions, our forward models are ensembles of fine-tuned and back-translated models. Since we compete in both directions for both language pairs, for any given translation direction we can use the forward model for the reverse direction as the channel model. Our language models for each of the target languages English, German, and Russian, are big Transformer decoder models with FFN 8192. We train the language models on the monolingual Newscrawl dataset, and use document level context for the English and German models. Perplexity scores for the language models on the bolded target language of each translation direction are shown in table 4. With a smaller amount of monolingual Russian data available, we observe that our Russian language model performs worse than the German and English language models.

To select the length penalty and weights, λ_1 and λ_2, for decoding, we use random search, choosing values in the range $[0, 2)$ for the weights and values in the range $[0, 1)$ for the length penalty. For all language directions, we choose the weights that give the highest BLEU score on a combined dataset of newstest2014 and newstest2016.

To run our final decoding step, we first use the forward model with beam size 50 to generate an n-best list. We then use the channel and language models to score each of these hypotheses, using the weights and length penalty tuned previously. Finally, we select the hypothesis with the highest score as our output.

| System | En→De | |
	news2017	news2018
baseline	30.90	45.40
+ langid filtering	30.78	46.43
+ ffn 8192	31.15	46.28
+ ensemble	31.55	47.09
+ BT	33.62	46.66
+ fine tuning	-	47.61
+ ensemble	-	49.27
+ reranking	-	50.63
WMT'18 submission	-	46.10
WMT'19 submission	**42.7**	

Table 5: SacreBLEU scores on English→German.

3.5 Postprocessing

For En→De and En→Ru, we also change the standard English quotation marks (" ... ") to German-style quotation marks (,, ... ").

4 Results

Results and ablations for En→De are shown in Table 5, De→En in Table 6, En→Ru in Table 7 and Ru→En in Table 8. We report case-sensitive SacreBLEU scores using SacreBLEU (Post, 2018)[1], using international tokenization for En→Ru. In the final row of each table we also report the case-sensitive BLEU score of our submitted system on this year's test set. All single models and individual models within ensembles are averages of the last 10 checkpoints of training. Our baseline systems are big Transformers as described in (Vaswani et al., 2017). The baselines were trained with minimally filtered data, removing only those sentences longer than 250 words and exceeding a source/target length ratio of 1.5 This setup gave us a reasonable baseline to evaluate data filtering.

4.1 English→German

For En→De, `langid` filtering, larger FFN, and ensembling improve our baseline performance on news2018 by about 1.5 BLEU. Note that our best

---

[1] SacreBLEU signatures:
BLEU+case.mixed+lang.en-de+numrefs.1+smooth.exp+test.wmt{17/18}+tok.13a+version.1.2.11,
BLEU+case.mixed+lang.de-en+numrefs.1+smooth.exp+test.wmt{17/18}+tok.13a+version.1.2.11,
BLEU+case.mixed+lang.ru-en+numrefs.1+smooth.exp+test.wmt{17/18}+tok.13a+version.1.2.11,
BLEU+case.mixed+lang.en-ru+numrefs.1+smooth.exp+test.wmt{17/18}+tok.intl+version.1.2.11

System	De→En	
	news2017	news2018
baseline	37.28	45.32
+ langid and ffn 8192	38.45	46.16
+ ensemble	38.82	46.76
+ BT	41.08	48.78
+ fine tuning	-	49.07
+ ensemble	-	49.60
+ reranking	-	51.13
WMT'19 submission	**40.8**	

Table 6: SacreBLEU scores on German→English.

bitext only systems already outperforms our system from last year by 1 BLEU point. This is perhaps due to the addition of higher quality bitext data and improved data filtering techniques. The addition of back-translated (BT) data improves single model performance by only 0.3 BLEU, but combining this with fine-tuning and ensembling gives us a total of 3 BLEU. Finally, applying reranking on top of these strong ensembled systems gives another 1.4 BLEU.

4.2 German→English

For De→En, as with En→De, we see similar improvements with `langid` filtering, larger FFN, and ensembling on the order of 1.4 BLEU. Compared to En→De however, we also observe that the addition of back-translated data is much more significant, improving single model performance by over 2.5 BLEU. Fine-tuning, ensembling, and reranking add an additional 2.4 BLEU, with reranking contributing 1.5 BLEU, a majority of the improvement.

4.3 English→Russian

For En→Ru, we observe large improvements of 2.4 BLEU over a bitext-only model after applying `langid` filtering, larger FFN, and ensembling. Since we start with a lower quality initial En↔Ru bitext dataset, we observe a large improvement of 3.5 BLEU by adding back-translated data. Augmenting this back-translated data with Commoncrawl adds an additional 0.2 BLEU. Finally, applying fine-tuning, ensembling, and reranking adds 2.2 BLEU, with reranking contributing 1 BLEU.

System	En→Ru	
	news2017	news2018
baseline	35.42	31.53
+ langid filtering	35.69	31.77
+ ffn 8192	36.66	33.49
+ ensemble	37.42	33.93
+ BT NC	40.09	37.07
+ BT NC + CC	40.42	37.3
+ fine tuning	-	37.74
+ ensemble	-	38.59
+ reranking	-	39.53
WMT'19 submission	**36.3**	

Table 7: SacreBLEU scores on English→Russian

System	Ru→En	
	news2017	news2018
baseline	37.07	32.69
+ langid and ffn 8192	37.72	33.44
+ ensemble	38.69	34.29
+ BT	41.68	36.49
+ fine tuning	-	38.54
+ ensemble	-	38.96
+ reranking	-	40.16
WMT'19 submission	**40.0**	

Table 8: SacreBLEU scores on Russian→English

4.4 Russian→English

For Ru→En, we observe similar trends to En↔De, with `langid` filtering, larger FFN, and ensembling improving performance of a bitext-only system by 1.6 BLEU. Backtranslation adds 3 BLEU, again most likely due to the lower quality bitext data available. Fine-tuning, ensembling, and reranking add almost 4 BLEU, with reranking contributing 1.2 BLEU.

4.5 Reranking

For every language direction, reranking gives a significant improvement, even when applied on top of an ensemble of very strong back-translated models. We also observe that the biggest improvement of 1.5 BLEU comes in the De→En language direction, and the smallest improvement of 1 BLEU in the En→Ru direction. This is perhaps due to the relatively weak Russian language model, which is trained on significantly less data compared to English and German. Improving our language models may lead to even greater improvements with reranking.

5 Conclusions

This paper describes Facebook FAIR's submission to the WMT19 news translation task. For all four translation directions, En↔De and En↔Ru, we use the same strategy of filtering bitext data, back-translating monolingual data, then training strong individual models on a combination of this data. Each of these models is fine-tuned and ensembled into a final system that is used for decoding with noisy channel model reranking. We demonstrate the effectiveness of our reranking approach, even when applied on top of very strong systems, and achieve the best case-sensitive BLEU score for En→Ru and competitive results in all other directions.

References

Sergey Edunov, Myle Ott, Michael Auli, and David Grangier. 2018. Understanding back-translation at scale. In *Proceedings of the 2018 Conference on Empirical Methods in Natural Language Processing*, pages 489–500.

Kenneth Heafield. 2011. Kenlm: faster and smaller language model queries. In *Proceedings of the Sixth Workshop on Statistical Machine Translation*, pages 187–197.

Armand Joulin, Edouard Grave, Piotr Bojanowski, and Tomas Mikolov. 2016. Bag of tricks for efficient text classification. *arXiv preprint arXiv:1607.01759*.

Philipp Koehn, Hieu Hoang, Alexandra Birch, Chris Callison-Burch, Marcello Federico, Nicola Bertoldi, Brooke Cowan, Wade Shen, Christine Moran, Richard Zens, Chris Dyer, Ondrej Bojar, Alexandra Constantin, and Evan Herbst. 2007. Moses: Open source toolkit for statistical machine translation. In *ACL Demo Session*.

Marco Lui and Timothy Baldwin. 2012. langid. py: An off-the-shelf language identification tool. In *Proceedings of the ACL 2012 system demonstrations*, pages 25–30. Association for Computational Linguistics.

Robert Moore and William Lewis. 2010. Intelligent selection of language model training data. In *Proceedings of the ACL 2010 Conference Short Papers*, pages 220–224.

Myle Ott, Sergey Edunov, Alexei Baevski, Angela Fan, Sam Gross, Nathan Ng, David Grangier, and Michael Auli. 2019. fairseq: A fast, extensible toolkit for sequence modeling. In *Proceedings of NAACL-HLT 2019: Demonstrations*.

Myle Ott, Sergey Edunov, David Grangier, and Michael Auli. 2018. Scaling neural machine translation. In *Proc. of WMT*.

Matt Post. 2018. A call for clarity in reporting BLEU scores. In *Proceedings of the Third Conference on Machine Translation: Research Papers*, pages 186–191. Association for Computational Linguistics.

Rico Sennrich, Barry Haddow, and Alexandra Birch. 2016. Neural machine translation of rare words with subword units. In *Proceedings of the 54th Annual Meeting of the Association for Computational Linguistics*, pages 1715–1725.

Ashish Vaswani, Noam Shazeer, Niki Parmar, Jakob Uszkoreit, Llion Jones, Aidan Gomez, ukasz Kaiser, and Illia Polosukhin. 2017. Attention is all you need. In *Proceedings of the 31st Conference on Neural Information Processing Systems*.

eTranslation's Submissions to the WMT 2019 News Translation Task

Csaba Oravecz
IRIS Luxembourg
oravecz.csaba@gmail.com

Katina Bontcheva
Sogeti Luxembourg
katina.bontcheva@sogeti.lu

Adrien Lardilleux
C-Dev Luxembourg
adrien.lardilleux@c-dev.eu

László Tihanyi
IRIS Luxembourg
tihanyi1123@gmail.com

Andreas Eisele
DGT, European Commission
andreas.eisele@ec.europa.eu

Abstract

This paper describes the submissions of the eTranslation team to the WMT 2019 news translation shared task. The systems have been developed with the aim of identifying and following rather than establishing best practices, under the constraints imposed by a low resource training and decoding environment normally used for our production systems. Thus most of the findings and results are transferable to systems used in the eTranslation service. Evaluations suggest that this approach is able to produce decent models with good performance and speed without the overhead of using prohibitively deep and complex architectures.

1 Introduction

The European Commission's eTranslation[1] project, a building block of the Connecting Europe Facility (CEF), has been set up to help European and national public administrations exchange information across language barriers in the EU. It provides secure access to machine translation (both formatted documents and text snippets) between all 26 official languages of the EU and the EEA for translators and officials in EU and national authorities. In addition it enables multilinguality in all Digital Service Infrastructures of CEF.

CEF eTranslation builds on the previous machine translation service of the European Commission, MT@EC (Eisele, 2017), developed by the Directorate-General for Translation (DGT)

---

[1]https://ec.europa.eu/cefdigital/wiki/display/CEFDIGITAL/eTranslation

since 2010. MT@EC translation engines were trained using the vast Euramis translation memories (Steinberger et al., 2014), comprising over 1 billion sentences in the 24 official EU languages, produced by the translators of the EU institutions over the past decades. While this large set of training data provides very good coverage of the type of language used in official EU documents, recent usage of the service is trending towards texts from other domains. The eTranslation team is working to widen the scope of the service and improve the coverage in more general types of texts. Given this background, the participation of eTranslation in this year's shared task on news translation is an early, but important step on a longer path towards a more generic MT service.

We participated in the task with 4 different language pairs: English→German, French→German, English→Lithuanian and Russian→English, in order to find best practices that guarantee the production of a solid system in a constrained resource environment.

2 Data Preparation

In this section we describe the data sets, the selection, and filtering methods that we applied to the provided parallel and monolingual data in order to increase the quality of trained models. We primarily focused on constrained submissions and made limited experiments with unconstrained resources, which we briefly describe later in Section 4.5.

2.1 Data Selection and Filtering

In most cases we used all of the provided original parallel data to build baseline models for back-

Proceedings of the Fourth Conference on Machine Translation (WMT), Volume 2: Shared Task Papers (Day 1) pages 320–326
Florence, Italy, August 1-2, 2019. ©2019 Association for Computational Linguistics

Data set	En→De	Fr→De	En→Lt	Ru→En
Europarl v9	1.80M	1.72M	0.63M	–
Common Crawl	2.32M	0.62M	–	0.88M
News Commentary v14	0.32M	0.26M	–	0.29M
Rapid Corpus	1.47M	–	0.21M	–
Wiki Titles v1	1.25M	–	0.13M	1.00M
Yandex	–	–	–	1.00M
Total (unique):	7.16M (6.85M)	2.60M (2.59M)	0.97M (0.84M)	3.2M (2.1M)

Table 1: Number of segments in the filtered parallel data used for baseline models.

translation as well as for cross-entropy based filtering. The domain distribution of these data sets is not uniform across language pairs, which had some effect on the workflows we applied to specific language pairs. The basic procedure of data cleaning, however, was similar in all cases.

As a general clean-up, we performed the following steps on the parallel data:

- language identification with Python's `langid` module,

- segment deduplication with masked numerals,

- deletion of segments where source/target token ratio exceeds 1:3 (or 3:1),

- deletion of segments longer than 110 tokens,

- exclusion of segments without alphabetic characters.

The above steps reduced the data set by about 10%. However, we filtered out 65% of the Ru→En Wiki Titles corpus with an additional rule of having a minimum sum of 12 tokens in a segment pair. The number of segments in the base filtered data is shown in Table 1.

For the three language pairs[2] where we used monolingual data to build language models or create synthetic parallel text, we chose the recent target language News Crawl data sets, except for the 2018 German set, which contained a large number of segments with suspiciously scrambled characters in all words. Therefore, we discarded this version and made use of the 2016 and 2017 sets. In addition, for Fr→De we experimented with the 2014 and 2016 News Crawl as candidate data for the topic modeling based data selection (see Section 3.2). In the monolingual data used for back-translation we performed some additional filtering; we set a threshold on the maximum length of a token (40) and the minimum ratio of letters to digits in a segment (4).

We applied dual conditional cross-entropy filtering (Junczys-Dowmunt, 2018a) to the provided ParaCrawl and CommonCrawl parallel datasets using the baseline translation models. This significantly reduced the size of these data sets without a major decrease in BLEU score for the high resource language pairs. For En→De the reduction in ParaCrawl was from 31M to 18M segments and in CommonCrawl from 2.3M to 1.4M segments with a drop of 0.2 BLEU points compared to using the full sets[3]. No additional cleaning was applied to the Fr→De and Ru→En Common Crawl since these already contained fewer than 1M segments. Experiments with the filtered (7.5M) and full (11M) ParaCrawl for Fr→De showed that the scores on the development test set were also almost identical. Therefore, we worked with this reduced data in the experiments to save time and resources. The parallel data for En→Lt was very small and we found that the unfiltered ParaCrawl was more beneficial than the filtered one. For Ru→En we used only the filtered ParaCrawl because we did not have time for more experiments.

Depending on data availability we opted for different ways of creating development and test data sets. For En→De we used the 2017 test set as validation set in the trainings and the 2018 test set as the test set to evaluate the trained models. For Fr→De we used the 2008–2014 test sets and

---

[2] Four minus Ru→En.

[3] This suggests that version 3 of the ParaCrawl is significantly less noisy than previous versions: we did not experience any improvement from filtering contrary to some of last year's experiments (Pham et al., 2018; Junczys-Dowmunt, 2018b).

randomly extracted 2000 segments for validation and 3000 segments for test, while the rest (about 13000) was kept for fine-tuning. For En→Lt we used a small random subset of the training data for validation and the provided development test for testing. For Ru→En we used the 2018 test set for testing and for validation we randomly extracted 3000 segments from the 2016 and 2017 newstests. The rest of the development data was used for fine-tuning.

2.2 Pre- and Postprocessing

The in-house translation workflow in the MT environment of eTranslation contains a fairly complex pre- and postprocessing pipeline, where standard steps (tokenization, normalization, placeholder replacement) are tailored to the Euramis data. It thus does not altogether fit the more heterogenous domain of WMT news data. This was confirmed in a few early baseline experiments on WMT 2018 parallel data where we simply used SentencePiece (Kudo, 2018), which allows raw text input/output within the the Marian toolkit (Junczys-Dowmunt et al., 2018). Since it proved to be superior to other (external) pre- and postprocessing workflows, we opted for this approach[4] in the 2019 experiments.

3 Trainings

Due to our low resource environment (no large-scale computing facilities), we did not have much room for experimenting with either a wide range of scenarios or much tuning of hyperparameters. Therefore, we decided to stick to simple setups and training procedures. In all experiments we used Marian, which is also the core of our standard NMT framework in the eTranslation service. All trainings were run as multi-GPU trainings on 4 NVIDIA P100 GPUs with 16GB RAM.

3.1 NMT Models

We trained only base transformer models (Vaswani et al., 2017) in all language pairs except for Fr→De and En→Lt, where we also tried experimenting with a big transformer.[5] We discarded the idea of building large ensembles

of big transformers for high resource language pairs in the beginning due to the constrained environment. For most of the hyperparameters we used the default settings for the base transformer architecture in Marian[6] with dynamic batching and tying all embeddings. To save time and resources we stopped the trainings if sentence-wise normalized cross-entropy on the validation set did not improve in 5 consecutive validation steps. In the big transformer experiments, following recommended settings for Marian, we doubled the filter size and the number of heads, decreased the learning rate from 0.0003 to 0.0002 and halved the update value for `--lr-warmup` and `--lr-decay-inv-sqrt`.

Based on the results of previous experiments we set 30k joint SentencePiece vocabulary for En→De. We did not run additional trainings to test the effect of other vocabulary sizes, except for Ru→En, where we ran a baseline model experiment with separate 60k vocabularies. However, this resulted in a loss of 0.7 BLEU points on the 2018 test set.[7] Therefore, we kept the 30k joint setting through all language pairs.

3.2 Improving Baseline Models

In this section we describe the methods we experimented with to improve baseline models such as building an additional synthetic data set with back-translation (Sennrich et al., 2016), using the development data (where available) to fine-tune converged models with continued trainings and building ensembles out of a few variants of the best models originally trained from different seeds. We report the evaluation scores in Section 4.

3.2.1 Synthetic Data

Back-translation (Sennrich et al., 2016) has become a widely used data augmenting technique in NMT but at the same time significantly extends the search space for best settings as far as the amount of data, ratio of bitext to back-translation data or methods to generate the synthetic source are concerned (Edunov et al., 2018).

In the En→De system we experimented with adding 10M and 20M back-translated segments from the 2017 News Crawl to the available bitext. The latter setting yielded no improvement, in ef-

---

[4]We used default settings for Marian's built-in Sentence-Piece: unigram model, built-in normalization and no subword regularization.

[5]However, the difference between the base and big transformer models for Fr→De and En→Lt was not significant. We decided to submit the big models in the hope of their better performance on the shared task test set.

[6]See eg. `https://github.com/marian-nmt/marian-examples/tree/master/transformer`.

[7]Confirmed post-submission with a loss of 1.9 BLEU points on the 2019 test set.

fect it was slightly worse so for the final systems the 10M data set was used. We had no time and resources for more fine-grained experiments to find the optimal setups with back-translation data.

For Fr→De we tuned our models towards the topic defined in the task by making use of guided topic modeling[8]. We manually created a seed word list with around 100 tokens from a few German news articles on elections, then we classified the documents in the 2014 and 2016 German News Crawl data sets into different topics.[9] We finally selected about 170k doc units from News Crawl 2014 and 186k doc units from News Crawl 2016 as candidate data for back-translation. We also experimented with back-translation of 2.5M randomly selected segments from News Crawl 2017. This synthetic data brought some improvement but not as much as the synthetic data obtained from topic modeling.

For En→Lt we back-translated all of the provided monolingual data with the exception of Common Crawl. We filtered Common Crawl using a language model built on the only in-domain resource for this language pair, 2018 News Crawl. We took the top 500k segments and back-translated them but this did not result in any improvement (we used, however, a transformer type language model built on 2018 News Crawl for later models (cf. Section 3.2.3)).

3.2.2 Fine-tuning with In-domain Data

For language pairs where a substantial amount of test data from previous years' tasks is available a possible direction to improve performance is to continue training with this data as domain adaptation (Luong and Manning, 2015). For En→De we used the 2008–2017 development sets (30k segments) in the experiments and for the final submission we extended it with the 2018 test set. For Ru→En we used a set of about 18k segments from the news test sets from 2012 onwards, with the exception of the data used for testing and validation.

In the Fr→De system we used a set of about 13k segments (cf. Section 2.1). It yielded improvements on our test set, which was selected randomly rather than through topic modeling. Since we tuned the system this way towards the more general news domain it is not surprising that for the 2019 test set this fine tuning proved to be harm-

ful. Unfortunately, we submitted the fine-tuned model, which, although it did not alter our position in the rankings, still led to a loss of 0.8 BLEU points (cf. Table 3 in Section 4.2).

3.2.3 Ensembles

For the final En→De submission we created a 3 model ensemble trained with the same (best) configuration but with different seeds. We also built an ensemble with a transformer type language model from the 2016 and 2017 German News Crawl (117M segments) which we trained for 2 epochs. We set the weight of the language model to 0.1 and the weight of the translation models to 1.0 to get the largest improvement.[10]

For the Fr→De and En→Lt final submissions, we also created ensembles from the best single models trained from different seeds but here we only had time to experiment with 2 models. For En→Lt we added a transformer type language model from filtered 2018 news (375k) to the ensemble. Similarly to En→De, the translation models had a weight of 1.0, while the language model had a weight of 0.1.

3.2.4 Ineffective Methods

We make a brief mention of the methods that we tried but did not seem to work. In particular, for En→De oversampling the original parallel data did not yield any improvement so we stopped the experiments in this direction. Since for Ru→En the addition of the UN corpus did not increase model quality, we left it out from the training data.[11] Another technique that seemed promising but did not give any improvement was incremental iterative back-translation (Hoang et al., 2018; Marie et al., 2018). For En→Lt, where the available data set was in general much smaller, we had time to experiment with this technique but we did not manage to generate better models.

4 Results

We submitted one model for each of the four language pairs. In this section we provide evaluation scores for models at important stages in the experiments which reflect how the models got better as

---

[8]https://github.com/vi3k6i5/guidedlda

[9]We tokenized the text and used stopword list but no lemmatization in creating the document-term matrices.

[10]It might be worth noting that the ensemble of a single translation model and the language model did not give any improvement; a small increase in the final score could only be obtained by adding the language model to the 3 member ensemble.

[11]Some WMT 2018 participants had similar experience in the En→Ru direction (Deng et al., 2018).

we tried various methods for improvement. All results are reported in detokenized BLEU.[12]

4.1 English→German

System	Parallel data	2018	2019
M1 Baseline	6.8M	41.3	38.1
M2 M1+PC	24M	44.6	39.9
M3 M2+BT	34M	45.4	38.7
M4 M3 ens.	34M	46.0	40.1
M5 M4+LM	34M	46.3	40.3
M6 M5+FT	34+0.03M	**47.8**	**42.4**

Table 2: Results for En→De models. The 2019 results are post-submission.

Table 2 summarizes the scores for the En→De models. Model 1 as our baseline used only the original parallel data (Table 1). In Model 2 we extended this data with filtered ParaCrawl (PC) v3 data, which led to a substantial improvement (although less so on the 2019 test set). For Model 3 we added the synthetic data (BT), which seemed to improve the quality on the 2018 test set but to our great surprise resulted in a performance drop on the 2019 test set. This might suggest that the synthetic data already introduces some unwanted noise into the model that could have a detrimental effect depending on the input to be translated. Model 4 is an ensemble of three Model 3 setups and this proved to be a very efficient choice with respect to the 2019 test set. Some small additional improvement could be gained by adding the language model (LM) to the ensemble (Model 5) but the largest positive effect came from the fine tuning (FT) as seen in Model 6.

4.2 French→German

Table 3 gives the scores for the Fr→De models. The 2008-14D column contains the scores on our development test set (cf. Section 2.1). The baseline Model 1 is built from the original parallel data (Table 1). In Model 2 we added a small amount of back-translated data, which was generated from the monolingual Europarl and News Commentary. From this data set we filtered out the segments that overlap with the original parallel data. This step led to a moderate improvement. For Model 3

System	Parallel data	2008-14D	2019
M1 Baseline	2.6M	20.8	26.1
M2 M1+BT1	3.2M	21.4	27.8
M3 M2+PC	6.9M	22.4	29.4
M4 M3+BT2	11.6	22.8	33.1
M5 M4+FT	11.6M+13k	23.8	32.4
M6 M4 ens.	11.6M	22.7	**33.5**
M7 M5 ens.	11.6+13k	**24.3**	32.7

Table 3: Results for Fr→De models. The 2019 results are post-submission.

we added filtered ParaCrawl v3 data, again with a moderate improvement. In Model 4 we included the topic selected synthetic data, which improved the quality minimally on the development set but significantly on the 2019 test set. In Model 5 we fine-tuned Model 4, which gave yet again a moderate improvement on the development set but resulted in a decrease on the 2019 test set (cf. Section 3.2.2). At this stage, we decided to test big transformers from Model 4. We only had time to train 2 models and even they could not reach convergence in time. Model 6 is an ensemble of the 2 big transformers, each with a weight of 1.0, while for Model 7 we ensembled the fine-tuned models of Model 6. Unsurprisingly, Model 7 was better than Model 6 on the development set but worse on the 2019 test data (cf. Section 3.2.2). For this language pair, the most beneficial step was the addition of topic-selected back-translated data.

4.3 English→Lithuanian

System	Parallel data	2019D	2019
M1 Baseline	0.84M	15.5	11.4
M2 M1+PC	2.2M	19.4	12.5
M3 M2+BT	4.7M	25.7	16.6
M4 M3+OS	5.9M	25.8	15.9
M5 M4+LM	5.9M	26.1	16.0
M6 M5 ens.	5.9M	**27.0**	**17.1**

Table 4: Results for En→Lt models. The 2019 results are post-submission.

Table 4 presents the scores for En→Lt. The 2019D column is for the scores on the provided development set (cf. Section 2.1). Model 1 is the baseline with the original parallel data (Table 1). In Model 2 we added the full ParaCrawl

---

[12]sacreBLEU signatures: `BLEU+case.mixed+lang.en-de+numrefs.1+smooth.exp+tok.13a+version.1.3.0`

v3 data, which led to a substantial improvement on the 2019 development set but just a moderate one on the 2019 test set. In Model 3 we further added the synthetic data (back-translation of all monolingual data except Common Crawl). This resulted in a big boost in the quality on both test sets. For Model 4 we oversampled (OS) 2 times the Rapid corpus from the parallel data and the domain-relevant back-translated data (2018 News Crawl). Model 5 is a $(1, 0.1)$ ensemble of Model 4 with a transformer-type language model, with a minimal improvement on the 2018 development set but a drop of 0.6-0.7 BLEU points on the 2019 test set. Since this was unknown in the development stage, we decided to build big transformer models on the same training data as Model 4. Model 6 is an ensemble of these 2 big transformers and the language model. The improvement on the 2019 test set was significant.

4.4 Russian→English

System	Parallel data	2018	2019
M1 Baseline	2.1M	27.3	32.4
M2 M1+PC	5.9M	29.5	35.9
M3 M2+FT	5.9M+17.8k	**32.9**	**37.4**

Table 5: Results for Ru→En models. The 2019 results are post-submission.

We made fewer experiments with the Ru→En system. The scores in Table 5 give the outcome of the evaluation of three simple single transformer models: (i) Model 1 built on the original parallel data (excluding the UN corpus); (ii) Model 2 with filtered ParaCrawl added; (iii) Model 3, which is fine-tuned on domain-specific data. This shows that it is possible to produce reasonable models in very constrained conditions.

4.5 Experiments with Unconstrained Models

We ran a few experiments with unconstrained models making use of the Euramis (Steinberger et al., 2014) data set. This data contains millions of segments for 3 of the 4 language pairs we worked with and offers itself as a natural resource to build unconstrained models from. At the same time it is in general quite distant from the news domain. Thus for the high resource language pairs (En→De, Fr→De) we first tried to use only those subsets which might be closer to the shared task domain. We extracted additional training data using language models built from monolingual news corpora as reference in-domain text with the XenC toolkit (Rousseau, 2013). For Fr→De we built the language model from the topic modeling based selection and also experimented with extracting Euramis data using the same guided LDA process as described in Section 3.2.1. We re-ran the trainings of the best constrained models by adding 2M and later 3M Euramis segments to the training data but as we cannot report on any improvement, we stopped this line of experiments and did not submit the unconstrained systems.

For En→Lt, we trained 3 non-constrained models by adding to the best constrained system (i) all our Euramis data, (ii) 1M and (iii) 2M segment subsets selected as described above. This resulted in a very small improvement of less than 0.5 BLEU points for the models with selected Euramis subsets, while the model with the full Euramis data was almost 2 BLEU points worse. We thus decided not to submit any of the 3 systems.

5 Conclusion

For the first participation in WMT 2019, the eTranslation team submitted four systems to the news translation shared task. We experimented with different settings for each task but the development of all systems shared the common goal of maximizing efficiency in a relatively low-resource production environment. For this reason, our systems relied on simple architectures, and we focused instead on finding the most appropriate combination of standard techniques and tools, which can thus directly be ported to production systems. In particular, we could confirm that a careful selection of the training data, back-translation and fine-tuning were generally the most rewarding techniques, allowing all our systems to perform decently and to end up in the first half of the rankings, despite the limitations imposed by our low resource environment.

References

Yongchao Deng, Shanbo Cheng, Jun Lu, Kai Song, Jingang Wang, Shenglan Wu, Liang Yao, Guchun Zhang, Haibo Zhang, Pei Zhang, Changfeng Zhu, and Boxing Chen. 2018. Alibaba's neural machine translation systems for WMT18. In *Proceedings of the Third Conference on Machine Translation*, pages 372–380, Belgium, Brussels. Association for Computational Linguistics.

Sergey Edunov, Myle Ott, Michael Auli, and David Grangier. 2018. Understanding back-translation at scale. In *Proceedings of the 2018 Conference on Empirical Methods in Natural Language Processing*, pages 489–500, Brussels, Belgium. Association for Computational Linguistics.

Andreas Eisele. 2017. Machine translation at the European Commission. In Jörg Porsiel, editor, *Machine Translation: What Language Professionals Need to Know*, pages 209–220. BDÜ Fachverlag, Berlin.

Vu Cong Duy Hoang, Philipp Koehn, Gholamreza Haffari, and Trevor Cohn. 2018. Iterative back-translation for neural machine translation. In *Proceedings of the 2nd Workshop on Neural Machine Translation and Generation*, pages 18–24. Association for Computational Linguistics.

Marcin Junczys-Dowmunt. 2018a. Dual conditional cross-entropy filtering of noisy parallel corpora. In *Proceedings of the Third Conference on Machine Translation*, pages 901–908, Belgium, Brussels. Association for Computational Linguistics.

Marcin Junczys-Dowmunt. 2018b. Microsoft's submission to the WMT2018 news translation task: How I learned to stop worrying and love the data. In *Proceedings of the Third Conference on Machine Translation*, pages 429–434, Belgium, Brussels. Association for Computational Linguistics.

Marcin Junczys-Dowmunt, Roman Grundkiewicz, Tomasz Dwojak, Hieu Hoang, Kenneth Heafield, Tom Neckermann, Frank Seide, Ulrich Germann, Alham Fikri Aji, Nikolay Bogoychev, André F. T. Martins, and Alexandra Birch. 2018. Marian: Fast neural machine translation in C++. In *Proceedings of ACL 2018, System Demonstrations*, pages 116–121. Association for Computational Linguistics.

Taku Kudo. 2018. Subword regularization: Improving neural network translation models with multiple subword candidates. In *Proceedings of the 56th Annual Meeting of the Association for Computational Linguistics (Volume 1: Long Papers)*, pages 66–75. Association for Computational Linguistics.

Minh-Thang Luong and Christopher Manning. 2015. Stanford neural machine translation systems for spoken language domains. In *Proceedings of the International Workshop on Spoken Language Translation (IWSLT)*, pages 76–79.

Benjamin Marie, Rui Wang, Atsushi Fujita, Masao Utiyama, and Eiichiro Sumita. 2018. NICT's neural and statistical machine translation systems for the WMT18 news translation task. In *Proceedings of the Third Conference on Machine Translation*, pages 453–459, Belgium, Brussels. Association for Computational Linguistics.

Ngoc-Quan Pham, Jan Niehues, and Alexander Waibel. 2018. The Karlsruhe Institute of Technology systems for the news translation task in WMT 2018.

In *Proceedings of the Third Conference on Machine Translation*, pages 471–476, Belgium, Brussels. Association for Computational Linguistics.

Anthony Rousseau. 2013. XenC: An open-source tool for data selection in natural language processing. *The Prague Bulletin of Mathematical Linguistics*, 100:73–82.

Rico Sennrich, Barry Haddow, and Alexandra Birch. 2016. Improving neural machine translation models with monolingual data. In *Proceedings of the 54th Annual Meeting of the Association for Computational Linguistics (Volume 1: Long Papers)*, pages 86–96, Berlin, Germany. Association for Computational Linguistics.

Ralf Steinberger, Mohamed Ebrahim, Alexandros Poulis, Manuel Carrasco-Benitez, Patrick Schlüter, Marek Przybyszewski, and Signe Gilbro. 2014. An overview of the European Union's highly multilingual parallel corpora. *Language Resources and Evaluation*, 48(4):679–707.

Ashish Vaswani, Noam Shazeer, Niki Parmar, Jakob Uszkoreit, Llion Jones, Aidan N Gomez, Ł ukasz Kaiser, and Illia Polosukhin. 2017. Attention is all you need. In I. Guyon, U. V. Luxburg, S. Bengio, H. Wallach, R. Fergus, S. Vishwanathan, and R. Garnett, editors, *Advances in Neural Information Processing Systems 30*, pages 5998–6008. Curran Associates, Inc.

Tilde's Machine Translation Systems for WMT 2019

Mārcis Pinnis and **Rihards Krišlauks** and **Matīss Rikters**
Tilde / Vienibas gatve 75A, Riga, Latvia
`{firstname.lastname}@tilde.lv`

Abstract

The paper describes the development process of Tilde's NMT systems for the WMT 2019 shared task on news translation. We trained systems for the English-Lithuanian and Lithuanian-English translation directions in constrained and unconstrained tracks. We build upon the best methods of the previous year's competition and combine them with recent advancements in the field. We also present a new method to ensure source domain adherence in back-translated data. Our systems achieved a shared first place in human evaluation.

1 Introduction

Since the paradigm-shifting success of neural machine translation (NMT) systems at the 2016 Conference on Machine Translation (WMT) (Bojar et al., 2016), NMT methods and neural network architectures applied in NMT have been annually improved. In 2016, the best-performing systems were based on recurrent neural networks with gated recurrent units (GRU) (Sennrich et al., 2016; Bojar et al., 2016). In 2017, deep GRU models (Sennrich et al.) and models based on shallow multiplicative long short-term memory units (MLSTM; (Pinnis et al., 2017b)) allowed achieving the best results (Bojar et al., a). In 2018, the majority of best-performing systems were based on self-attentional (Vaswani et al., 2017) (Transformer) models (Bojar et al., b).

A year has passed, and the majority of best-performing systems submitted to the shared task on news translation of WMT 2019 are still based on Transformer networks. However, improvements are evident in other areas (e.g., usage of document-level context, very deep models, distillation by ensemble teachers, etc.)[1]. Quite a few of the submissions indicate that substantial amounts of computational resources may have been utilised in order to achieve such results. As we do not have access to large GPU clusters, our strategy for participating at the shared task on news translation of the 2019 Conference on Machine Translation was comprised of combining different methods that showed promising results in scientific publications published in 2018, and analysing whether the methods allowed increasing the overall quality of NMT systems when training NMT models using just modest hardware (with access to one or two graphical processing units) and with the goal of producing models suitable for production.

In our experiments, we investigated methods for corpora filtering (the Tilde MT parallel data filtering (TMTF) and normalisation workflow (Pinnis, 2018) together with dual conditional cross-entropy filtering (DCCEF) (Junczys-Dowmunt, 2018)), training data pre-processing using the methods described by Pinnis et al. (2018a), a new optimisation method, the quasi-hyperbolic Adam, proposed by Ma and Yarats (2018), back-translation with sampling-based decoding (e.g., as done by Edunov et al. (2018)) and by targeting rare words (Fadaee and Monz, 2018) and in-domain subsets of the monolingual data, and automatic linguistically informed post-editing of named entities and non-translatable phrases.

This year, Tilde participated in the shared task on news translation for the English↔Lithuanian language pair. We trained constrained and unconstrained systems for both translation directions.

The paper is further structured as follows: Section 2 describes the data used for training, Section 3 describes the main NMT model training experiments, Section 4 describes our experiments on automatic post-editing of named entities, Section 5 summarises our automatic evaluation results, and the paper is concluded in Section 6.

---

[1] http://matrix.statmt.org

Proceedings of the Fourth Conference on Machine Translation (WMT), Volume 2: Shared Task Papers (Day 1) pages 327–334
Florence, Italy, August 1-2, 2019. ©2019 Association for Computational Linguistics
">

2   Data

Similarly to the year before, we used both constrained data, which were provided by the organisers of the shared task, as well as unconstrained data, which comprised publicly available parallel and monolingual corpora as well as proprietary data from the Tilde Data Library[2]. For language model (LM) training and back-translation, we used news data provided by the organisers. For the unconstrained systems, we used a proprietary news corpus. The raw statistics of data available are provided in Table 1. For validation, we used the first 1000 sentences of the NewsDev2019 data set. Evaluation was performed on NewsTest 2019.

2.1   Data Filtering

For data filtering, we applied the parallel data filtering methods of Tilde MT (Pinnis et al., 2018b; Pinnis, 2018) for both constrained and unconstrained systems. The filters address potential issues that arise from misalignment of parallel data , incomplete translation, various types of data corruption, and other types of data quality issues. However, these filters do not perform data selection. Therefore, we applied also data filtering using DCCEF proposed by Junczys-Dowmunt (2018). As it uses an in-domain LM to discard out-of-domain sentence pairs, it performs the task of data selection. Because for the constrained systems the data-set was not sufficiently large, we applied the filter with a threshold of > 0. For the unconstrained systems, we set the threshold to 11 million[3] highest scored sentence pairs.

For monolingual data, we filtered out all sentences that: 1) were redundant, 2) exceeded 128 tokens or 1000 characters, 3) contained tokens over 50 characters, and 4) contained corrupt characters. See Table 1 for statistics of data filtering.

2.2   Data Pre-Processing

This year, we did not change the parallel and monolingual data pre-processing workflows that we used for our WMT 2018 submissions (Pinnis et al., 2018a).

Similarly to last year, the training corpora were supplemented with synthetic data where up to three words in each sentence were replaced with unknown word identifiers on both source and target sides to ensure that the NMT models are able to handle rare and unknown phenomena during translation (Pinnis et al., 2017a). The statistics of the parallel corpora after supplementing them with synthetic data sets are provided in Table 1.

3   NMT Systems

We took an iterative approach to validating the methods we selected for use in NMT system training. At each step, we either accepted or rejected a method for further use based on its performance compared to a baseline. When moving on, we would often use the previously selected method as a baseline for the next method (which we would combine with the previous method) and so on. More specifically, we conducted the experiments as follows: 1) Filtering (Section 3.1), 2) ~QHAdam (Section 3.2.1), 3) regular back-translation, 4) large batches (Section 3.3), 5.a) back-translation using beam search or sampling (Section 3.4.2), 5.b) back-translation using rare or random data (Section 3.4.1, the results weren't used further), 6) QHAdam (Section 3.2), 7) Source domain adherence (Section 3.4.3), 8) Transformer-big (Section 3.5). The outline of this section loosely follows the above timeline.

As a result of the iterative approach, the evaluation of the training methods was mostly non-exhaustive – meaning that it was usually done only for a single translation direction (most often En $\rightarrow$ Lt) testing only a few possible configurations (e.g., different model hyper-parameters, back-translated data-set size, etc.). Also, for some experiments we did not methodically test the effect of each of the compounding changes to the experiment's configuration, e.g., in ~QHAdam experiments (in Section 3.2) along with adopting the new optimiser we also selected a new learning-rate and learning-rate schedule without confirming that the baseline optimiser would not also benefit from these changes. As a result, for some experiments we cannot confirm with certainty that the selected method is better than the baseline, only that the selected method with a given set of hyper-parameters is better. The above choices were primarily motivated by resource and time constraints.

All NMT systems described further used the Transformer architecture (Vaswani et al., 2017) and were trained using the Marian NMT toolkit (Junczys-Dowmunt et al., 2018). Unless noted

---

[2]www.tilde.com/products-and-services/data-library

[3]The threshold was empirically identified by training multiple models with thresholds set at 8 to 12 million.

	Lang. pair	Parallel data (sentence pairs)					Monolingual data (sentences)		
		Raw Total	Raw Unique	+TMTF	+Synth. data	+DCCEF	Raw Total	Filtered Unique	For LM Unique
(U)	en-lt	42.9M	30.5M	15.0M	28.6M	11.0M	82.5M	61.3M	4.7M
	lt-en						63.9M	61.0M	4.9M
(C)	en-lt	2.4M	2.3M	1.5M	3.0M	1.7M	103.5M	75.5M	0.7M
	lt-en						63.5M	60.9M	2.0M

Table 1: Training data statistics (TMTF - Tilde MT filtering, DCCEF - dual conditional cross-entropy filtering)

otherwise, we used the *base model* configuration for the model hyper-parameters.

3.1 Filtering

Since DCCEF achieved the best results in the shared task on parallel corpus filtering at WMT 2018 (Koehn et al., 2018), we decided to test whether the combination of our filtering methods (i.e., TMTF) and DCCEF allows acquiring better models. Therefore, we filtered the parallel corpora using DCCEF. For this, we trained two NMT models using the data that were already filtered using TMTF and four language models (two in-domain models that were trained on news corpora and two models trained using the parallel data), and trained several NMT systems. Figure 1 shows the training progress for En → Lt. It is evident that the combination of the methods works better only for the unconstrained systems. We suspect that it is because the unconstrained data sets are large enough to leave enough training data remaining in the filtered data sets. Further, all experiments for unconstrained systems will be performed using data filtered with TMTF and DCCEF and for constrained systems – only TMTF.

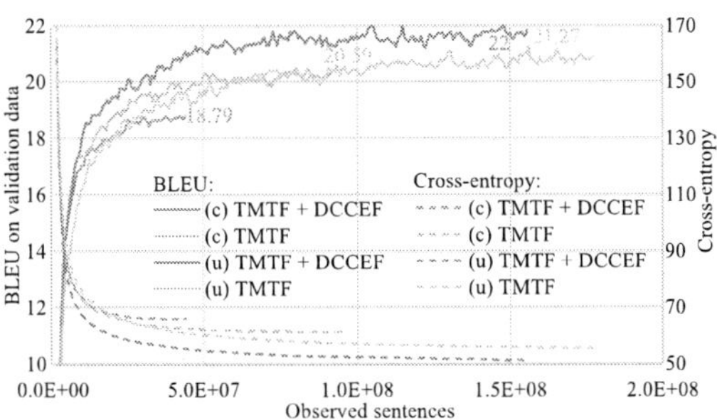

Figure 1: En → Lt systems trained on datasets filtered using the TMTF and DCCEF methods

3.2 QHAdam

We used two versions of the Quasi-Hyperbolic Adam (QHAdam) optimiser (Ma and Yarats, 2018) to train our systems – a version as described in the original paper, and a modified version (~QHAdam) as described below. The modified version was due to an error in our initial implementation of the optimiser but it performed well enough for us to use it to train the majority of the systems during the period of the competition.

3.2.1 ~QHAdam

We define the ~QHAdam's update step in (1). The definitions for g'_t, s'_t, v_1 and v_2 are the same as in the original paper.

The comparison of ~QHAdam and the baseline system for the constrained En → Lt track is given in Figure 2. ~QHAdam was tested with different combinations of settings for the learning rate and the number of warm-up steps used. In our initial experiments, we found that setting the learning rate to 5×10^{-4} and using 48k warm-up steps worked best. A workspace size of 9 GB on 2 GPUs was used in Marian which resulted in an effective batch-size of around 255 sentences.

3.3 Using Large Batches

As shown by Popel and Bojar (2018) and Ott et al. (2018), using a large batch size in conjunction with increasing the learning rate allows to train better-performing NMT systems. We confirm these findings. We trained the same system described in Section 3.2.1 except training it with a workspace size of 14 GB on 8 GPUs (simulated using the *--optimizer-delay* option in Marian) which resulted in an effective batch size of ~1263 sentences. Additionally we increased the learning rate to 7.3×10^{-4} roughly keeping to the rule of scaling the learning rate by a factor of $\sqrt{n}$ when the batch size has increased by a factor of n (Hoffer et al., 2017). The results are given in Figure 3. These experiments were done using back-translated data (see Section 3.4). When using non-back-translated data, we saw overfitting occur.

$$\theta_{t+1} \leftarrow \theta_t - \alpha \left[(1 - v_1) \cdot \nabla \hat{L}_t(\theta_t) + \frac{v_1 \cdot g'_{t+1}}{\sqrt{(1 - v_2)(\nabla \hat{L}_t(\theta_t))^2 + v_2 \cdot s'_{t+1} + \epsilon}} \right] \tag{1}$$

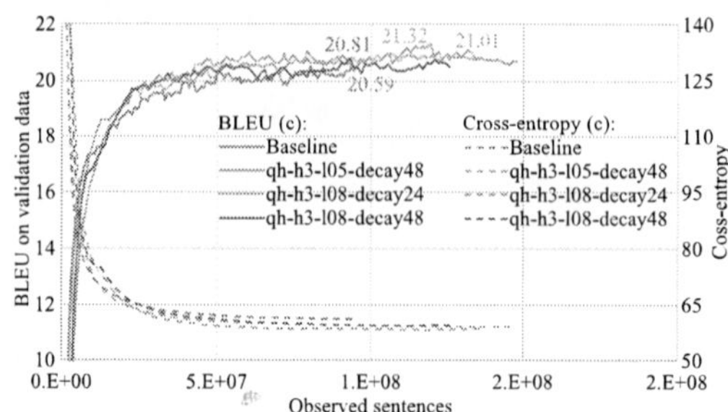

Figure 2: Training progress for the baseline and ~QHAdam systems in the En $\rightarrow$ Lt translation direction.

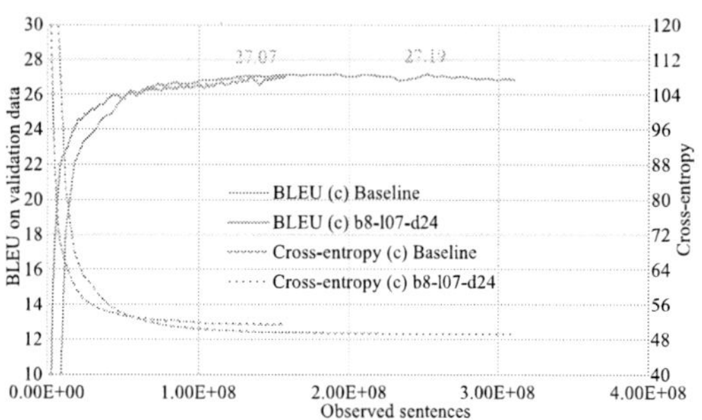

Figure 3: Training progress for ~QHAdam systems comparing effects of different batch sizes and learning rates in the En $\rightarrow$ Lt translation direction.

3.4 Experiments with Back-translation

We used NMT model adaptation through back-translation (Sennrich et al., 2015) to adapt NMT systems to the news domain. We applied two iterations of back-translation and the subsequent system training to incrementally improve the back-translated data set (Rikters, 2018). We also analysed methods for selection of the data for back-translation. The methods are discussed further. In the figures further, if not specified in the name of each system, the proportion between parallel and back-translated data is 1-to-1.

3.4.1 Rare vs. Random Data for Back-Translation

Fadaee and Monz (2018) showed that adaptation through back-translation works better if the data for back-translation can be considered rare or difficult. Therefore, we compared two types of data selection - random selection and selection by target-

ing rare words (as proposed by Fadaee and Monz (2018)), back-translated the data sets using beam search, and trained NMT models. Figure 4 depicts the training progress of the En $\rightarrow$ Lt and Lt $\rightarrow$ En systems. The results suggest that targeting of sentences containing rare words did not help. We believe that this is due to the fact that what is rare in the target language may not be relevant for speakers of the source language. Therefore, there is no guarantee that the method will work. We stopped here and did not pursue this method further.

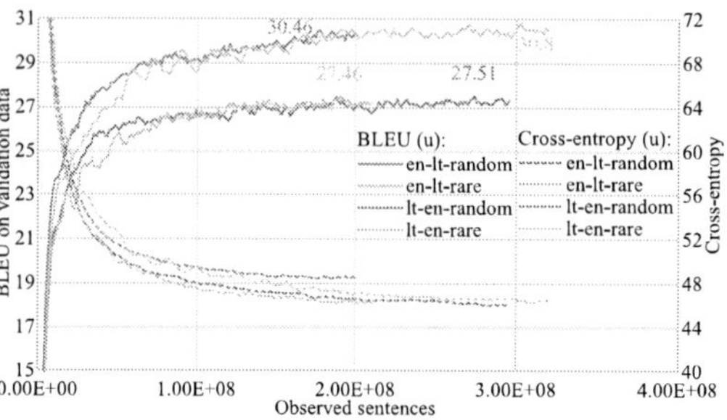

Figure 4: Training progress of systems trained on randomly selected data for back-translation and data selected by targeting rare words

3.4.2 Beam vs. Sampling

As suggested by Edunov et al. (2018), when back-translating data for domain adaptation, better-performing models can be acquired when using sampling instead of beam search. Therefore, we trained several systems on different amounts of back-translated data. The training progress of the systems is depicted in Figure 5.

For the final training iteration, we used sampling instead of beam-search during decoding for all but one system.

3.4.3 Source Domain Adherence

When adapting a system to a specific domain, it is important to use data from that specific domain. However, since we use a monolingual corpus from the target language to adapt an NMT system for source content, there may still be a domain mismatch, because how people write and what they write about in the target language may be (to higher or lower extent) irrelevant for the

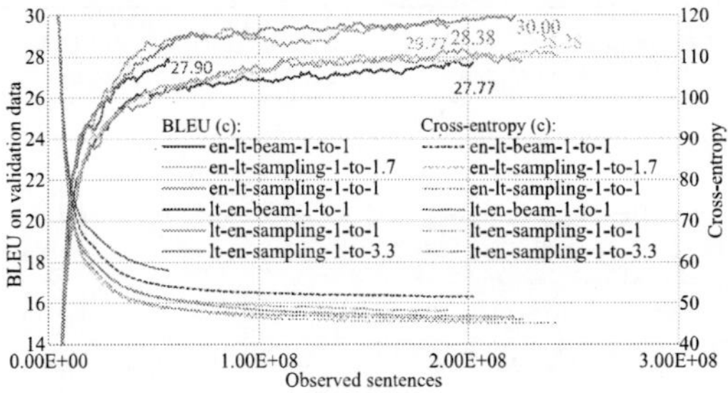

Figure 5: Training progress of systems trained on back-translated data that was acquired using beam search and sampling.

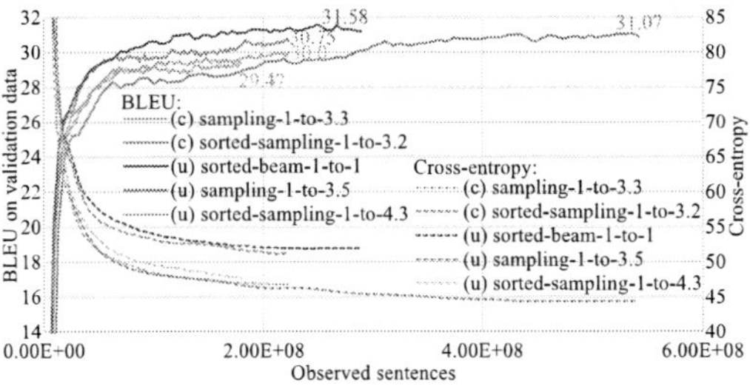

Figure 6: Training progress of systems trained on randomly selected data and data selected using LMs for back-translation.

people writing in the source language. Therefore, we performed an experiment where we translated the in-domain source data into the target side using an NMT system, trained a language model on the translations, scored each sentence of the target side's monolingual corpus, and used only the top-scored sentences for back-translation. Comparison between systems trained on randomly selected data for back-translation and data selected using LMs (with *sorted* in the name) is given in Figure 6.

3.5 Transformer Big

When training the unconstrained systems on the second iteration of back-translated data, we trained a variant for both translation directions using the *transformer-big* configuration (Vaswani et al., 2017). While doing so, we also adjusted the learning rate. Due to time constraints and technical difficulties we were not able to run these experiments to completion. Nonetheless, the *transformer-big* configuration still managed to surpass the baseline. For results see Figure 7.

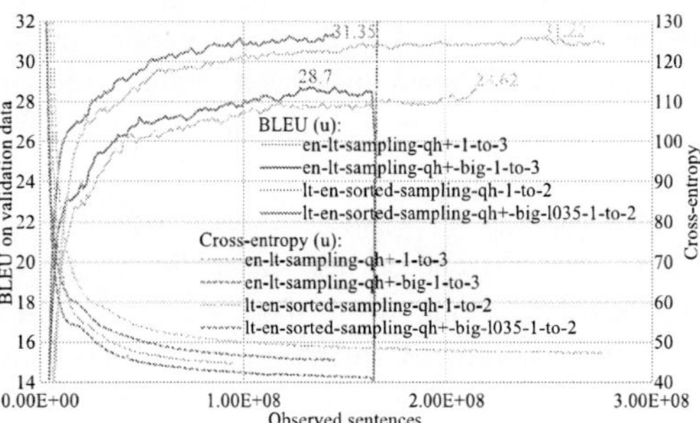

Figure 7: Training progress for the *transformer-big* systems comparing them to QHAdam baselines.

4 Automatic Named Entity Post-Editing

In our submissions for WMT 2018, we introduced an automatic named entity (NE) post-editing (ANEPE) workflow (Pinnis et al., 2018a), which allowed to fix translations of NEs (consisting of one word) and non-translatable words after NMT decoding. The method depends on the quality of word alignments. Because then we did not have methods to extract reliable word alignments from Transformer models, we had to rely on external word alignment using *fast_align* (Dyer et al., 2013). This resulted in many mis-alignments and unalignments, and incorrect post-edits. This year, we trained all models using the guided alignment method implemented in Marian (Junczys-Dowmunt et al., 2018). Although we still had to pre-process training data using *fast_align*, the NMT models learned to produce more reliable word alignments. We also extended the ANEPE method to support multi-word NEs and non-translatable phrases.

The method works as described further. Using collections of NEs and non-translatable phrases, we perform dictionary-based NE recognition in the source text. Then, for each recognised unit, we analyse whether the NMT translation contains a valid translation of the source unit. In order to support morphologically rich languages (as is Lithuanian), stemming of tokens is performed. However, NEs can already be included in surface forms in the NE collections to account for possible stemming-related issues. If a valid translation is not found, we analyse whether we can identify, which target words the source unit was translated into. If the words are next to each other (i.e., there is no gap between the target words), we replace the target words (except trailing stop-words) with the most similar (according to Levenshtein distance (Levenshtein, 1966)) translation equivalent (except trailing stop-words) found in the NE collection. Stop-words are excluded as the word alignment extracted from the NMT model commonly aligns stop-words to content words when stop-words (dis)appear in the target language. Using ANEPE, we improved the translation quality by 0.04 to 0.1 BLEU points for all submissions. Statistics also show that out of 408 named entities and non-translatable phrases identified in the Lithuanian validation set, 322 already had valid translations, 26 were post-edited, and the remaining 60 either had alignment issues or the target words were too dissimilar from the entries in the NE collection. We applied ANEPE for all our submissions.

5 Results

Automatic evaluation results of our final systems using BLEU[4] (Papineni et al., 2002) are given in Table 2. To acquire final translations, we performed also ensembling of the best-performing individual models. For submission, we selected the best-performing models for both translation directions and both scenarios. However, it is evident that other models were able to translate the NewsTest 2019 evaluation set better (for 3 out of 4 submissions). Although this can be expected, when deciding, which systems to submit, we did not account for the change of the evaluation strategy, i.e., the fact that the evaluation set contained only texts originally written in the source language (which is different from previous years). The results clearly show that the models that are more source domain adherent (e.g., the '(u) so-beam-~qh-1-to-1' unconstrained system for Lt → En) even surpass the quality of our ensemble models.

6 Conclusion

The paper presented Tilde's efforts on developing NMT systems for the WMT 2019 shared task on news translation. We built upon our methods from the previous year and investigated other novel methods proposed in 2018. Our experiments showed that improvements in translation quality could be achieved by using improved filtering by combining TMTF and DCCEF, sampling-based back-translation (although not for all sys-

tems), and the quasi-hyperbolic Adam optimiser. We also introduced a new method that allows to boost the quality of back-translation by ensuring source domain adherence of the data selected for back-translation, as well as described improvements upon our automatic named entity post-editing method. Our systems achieved a shared first place in human evaluation.

Acknowledgements

The research has been supported by the European Regional Development Fund within the research project "Multilingual Artificial Intelligence Based Human Computer Interaction" No. 1.1.1.1/18/A/148. We thank the High Performance Computing Center of Riga Technical University for providing access to their GPU computing infrastructure.

System	NewsDev (2019a)	NewsTest (2019)
English-Lithuanian		
(u) best 4 ens.	**27.18**	18.84
(u) best 2 ens.	27.03	**19.53**
(c) best 5 ens.	**26.70**	17.86
(u) sa-~qh-1-to-3	26.66	18.76
(u) sa-qh+-big-1-to-3	26.61	19.13
(c) best 3 ens.	26.54	**18.59**
(c) sa-qh+-1-to-3.3	26.42	18.14
(c) sa-~qh-1-to-1.7	26.19	18.17
(c) sa-~qh-1-to-1	26.16	17.83
Lithuanian-English		
(u) best 5 ens.	**30.41**	31.55
(c) best 5 ens.	**29.76**	**30.21**
(u) so-beam-~qh-1-to-1	29.43	**31.67**
(u) so-sa-qh+-big-l035-1-to-2	29.12	30.09
(u) so-sa-qh-1-to-2	28.99	29.60
(c) so-sa-~qh-1-to-3.2	28.84	29.30
(c) so-sa-qh-1-to-3.2	28.66	28.93
(c) sa-1-to-3.3	28.17	28.94

Table 2: Evaluation results - BLEU scores (submitted models are underlined, bold marks best results for both scenarios, (c) - constrained scenario, (u) - unconstrained scenario, 'ens.' - ensembles of models, 'sa' - sampling-based back-translation, 'so' - source domain adherence, 'qh' - quasi-hyperbolic Adam, '~qh' - modified version of 'qh', 'qh+' - 'qh' with tuned parameters, 'M-to-N' - the proportion of parallel and back-translated data)

---

[4]BLEU scores were obtained using SacreBLEU (Post, 2018), checksum: BLEU+case.mixed+numrefs.1 +smooth.exp+tok.13a+version.1.2.7.

References

Ondřej Bojar, Rajen Chatterjee, Christian Federmann, Yvette Graham, Barry Haddow, Shujian Huang, Matthias Huck, Philipp Koehn, Qun Liu, Varvara Logacheva, Christof Monz, Matteo Negri, Matt Post, Raphael Rubino, Lucia Specia, and Marco Turchi. a. findings of the 2017 conference on machine translation (wmt17).

Ondřej Bojar, Rajen Chatterjee, Christian Federmann, Yvette Graham, Barry Haddow, Matthias Huck, Antonio Jimeno Yepes, Philipp Koehn, Varvara Logacheva, Christof Monz, Matteo Negri, Aurelie Neveol, Mariana Neves, Martin Popel, Matt Post, Raphael Rubino, Carolina Scarton, Lucia Specia, Marco Turchi, Karin Verspoor, and Marcos Zampieri. 2016. Findings of the 2016 Conference on Machine Translation. In *Proceedings of the First Conference on Machine Translation*, pages 131–198, Berlin, Germany. Association for Computational Linguistics.

Ondřej Bojar, Christian Federmann, Mark Fishel, Yvette Graham, Barry Haddow, Matthias Huck, Philipp Koehn, and Christof Monz. b. findings of the 2018 conference on machine translation.

Chris Dyer, Victor Chahuneau, and Noah A Smith. 2013. A Simple, Fast, and Effective Reparameterization of IBM Model 2. In *Proceedings of the Conference of the North American Chapter of the Association for Computational Linguistics: Human Language Technologies (NAACL HLT 2013)*, June, pages 644–648, Atlanta, USA.

Sergey Edunov, Myle Ott, Michael Auli, and David Grangier. 2018. Understanding Back-Translation at Scale. In *Proceedings of the 2018 Conference on Empirical Methods in Natural Language Processing*, pages 489–500.

Marzieh Fadaee and Christof Monz. 2018. Back-Translation Sampling by Targeting Difficult Words in Neural Machine Translation. In *Proceedings of the 2018 Conference on Empirical Methods in Natural Language Processing*, pages 436–446.

Elad Hoffer, Itay Hubara, and Daniel Soudry. 2017. Train Longer, Generalize Better: Closing the Generalization Gap in Large Batch Training of Neural Networks. In I. Guyon, U. V. Luxburg, S. Bengio, H. Wallach, R. Fergus, S. Vishwanathan, and R. Garnett, editors, *Advances in Neural Information Processing Systems 30*, pages 1731–1741. Curran Associates, Inc.

Marcin Junczys-Dowmunt. 2018. Dual conditional cross-entropy filtering of noisy parallel corpora. In *Proceedings of the Third Conference on Machine Translation, Volume 2: Shared Task Papers*, pages 901–908, Belgium, Brussels. Association for Computational Linguistics.

Marcin Junczys-Dowmunt, Roman Grundkiewicz, Tomasz Dwojak, Hieu Hoang, Kenneth Heafield, Tom Neckermann, Frank Seide, Ulrich Germann, Alham Fikri Aji, Nikolay Bogoychev, André F. T. Martins, and Alexandra Birch. 2018. Marian: Fast Neural Machine Translation in C++. In *Proceedings of ACL 2018, System Demonstrations*, pages 116–121, Melbourne, Australia. Association for Computational Linguistics.

Philipp Koehn, Huda Khayrallah, Kenneth Heafield, and Mikel L. Forcada. 2018. Findings of the WMT 2018 Shared Task on Parallel Corpus Filtering. In *Proceedings of the Third Conference on Machine Translation, Volume 2: Shared Task Papers*, pages 739–752, Belgium, Brussels. Association for Computational Linguistics.

Vladimir I Levenshtein. 1966. Binary Codes Capable of Correcting Deletions, Insertions, and Reversals. *Soviet Physics Doklady*, 10(8):707–710.

Jerry Ma and Denis Yarats. 2018. Quasi-Hyperbolic Momentum and Adam for Deep Learning. *arXiv preprint arXiv:1810.06801*.

Myle Ott, Sergey Edunov, David Grangier, and Michael Auli. 2018. Scaling Neural Machine Translation. *arXiv:1806.00187 [cs]*. ArXiv: 1806.00187.

Kishore Papineni, Salim Roukos, Todd Ward, and Wei-Jing Zhu. 2002. BLEU: a Method for Automatic Evaluation of Machine Translation. In *Proceedings of the 40th annual meeting on association for computational linguistics*, pages 311–318. Association for Computational Linguistics.

Mārcis Pinnis. 2018. Tilde's parallel corpus filtering methods for wmt 2018. In *Proceedings of the Third Conference on Machine Translation, Volume 2: Shared Task Papers*, pages 952–958, Belgium, Brussels. Association for Computational Linguistics.

Mārcis Pinnis, Rihards Krišlauks, Daiga Deksne, and Toms Miks. 2017a. Neural Machine Translation for Morphologically Rich Languages with Improved Sub-word Units and Synthetic Data. In *Proceedings of the 20th International Conference of Text, Speech and Dialogue (TSD2017)*, volume 10415 LNAI, Prague, Czechia.

Mārcis Pinnis, Rihards Krišlauks, Toms Miks, Daiga Deksne, and Valters Šics. 2017b. Tilde's Machine Translation Systems for WMT 2017. In *Proceedings of the Second Conference on Machine Translation (WMT 2017), Volume 2: Shared Task Papers*, pages 374–381, Copenhagen, Denmark. Association for Computational Linguistics.

Mārcis Pinnis, Matīss Rikters, and Rihards Krišlauks. 2018a. Tilde's machine translation systems for wmt 2018. In *Proceedings of the Third Conference on Machine Translation, Volume 2: Shared Task Papers*, pages 477–485, Belgium, Brussels. Association for Computational Linguistics.

Mārcis Pinnis, Andrejs Vasiļjevs, Rihards Kalniņš, Roberts Rozis, Raivis Skadiņš, and Valters Šics. 2018b. Tilde MT Platform for Developing Client Specific MT Solutions. In *Proceedings of the Eleventh International Conference on Language Resources and Evaluation (LREC 2018)*, Miyazaki, Japan. European Language Resources Association (ELRA).

Martin Popel and Ondej Bojar. 2018. Training Tips for the Transformer Model. *The Prague Bulletin of Mathematical Linguistics*, 110(1):43–70. ArXiv: 1804.00247.

Matt Post. 2018. A Call for Clarity in Reporting BLEU Scores. In *Proceedings of the Third Conference on Machine Translation: Research Papers*, pages 186–191, Belgium, Brussels. Association for Computational Linguistics.

Matīss Rikters. 2018. Impact of Corpora Quality on Neural Machine Translation. In *In Proceedings of the 8th Conference Human Language Technologies - The Baltic Perspective (Baltic HLT 2018)*, Tartu, Estonia.

Rico Sennrich, Alexandra Birch, Anna Currey, Ulrich Germann, Barry Haddow, Kenneth Heafield, Antonio Valerio Miceli Barone, and Philip Williams. the university of edinburgh's neural mt systems for wmt17.

Rico Sennrich, Barry Haddow, and Alexandra Birch. 2015. Improving Neural Machine Translation Models with Monolingual Data. *arXiv preprint arXiv:1511.06709*.

Rico Sennrich, Barry Haddow, and Alexandra Birch. 2016. Edinburgh neural machine translation systems for wmt 16. In *Proceedings of the First Conference on Machine Translation*, pages 371–376, Berlin, Germany. Association for Computational Linguistics.

Ashish Vaswani, Noam Shazeer, Niki Parmar, Jakob Uszkoreit, Llion Jones, Aidan N Gomez, Łukasz Kaiser, and Illia Polosukhin. 2017. Attention Is All You Need. In *Advances in Neural Information Processing Systems*, pages 5998–6008.

Apertium-fin-eng—Rule-based shallow machine translation for WMT 2019 shared task

Tommi A Pirinen
Universität Hamburg
Hamburger Zentrum für Sprachkorpora
`tommi.antero.pirinen@uni-hamburg.de`

Abstract

In this paper I describe a rule-based, bi-directional machine translation system for the Finnish—English language pair. The original system is based on the existing data of FinnWordNet, omorfi and apertium-eng. I have built the disambiguation, lexical selection and translation rules by hand. The dictionaries and rules have been developed based on the shared task data. I describe in this article the use of the shared task data as a kind of a test-driven development workflow in RBMT development and show that it suits perfectly to a modern software engineering continuous integration workflow of RBMT and yields big increases to BLEU scores with minimal effort. The system described in the article is mainly developed during shared tasks.

1 Introduction

This paper describes our submission for Finnish—English language pair to the machine translation shared task of the *Fourth conference on machine translation* (WMT19) at ACL 2019. Traditionally *rule-based machine translation* (RBMT) is not in the focus for WMT shared tasks, however, there are two reasons I experimented with this system this year. One is that we have had an extensively large amount of lesser used resources for this pair: omorfi[1] (Pirinen, 2015) has well over 400,000 lexemes[2], apertium-eng[3] has over 40,000 lexemes and apertium-fin-eng[4] over 160,000 lexeme-to-lexeme translations. One of our key interests in the shared task like this is that it provides an ideal data for test-driven development of lexical resources.

One concept I experimented with the shared task is various degrees of automation—expert supervision for the lexical data enrichment. In this experiment I used automatic methods to refine the lexical selection of the machine translation, and semi-automatised workflows for the generation of the lexical data, as well as some expert-driven development of the more grammatical rules like noun phrase chunking and determiner generation. It might be noteworthy that this machine translator I describe in the article is not actively developed outside the shared tasks, so the article is moreso motivated as an exploration of the workflow and methods on semi-automatically generated shallow RBMT than a description of a fully developed RBMT.

The rest of the article is organised as follows: In Section 2 I describe the components of our RBMT pipeline, in Section 3 I describe the development workflow and in Section 4 I show the shared task results and I perform error analysis and discuss the results and finally in Section 5 we summarise the findings.

2 System description and setup

The morphological analyser for Finnish is based on omorfi (Pirinen, 2015), a large morphological lexical database for Finnish. Data from omorfi has been converted into Apertium format and is freely available in the apertium-style format in the github repository apertium-fin[5]. For English I have used Apertium's standard English analyser apertium-eng[6]. Both analysers were downloaded from github in the beginning of the shared task and we have updated and further developed them based on the development data during the shared

---

[1] `https://github.com/flammie/omorfi`
[2] `https://flammie.github.io/omorfi/statistics.html`
[3] `http://wiki.apertium.org/wiki/English`
[4] `https://github.com/apertium/apertium-fin-eng`

[5] `https://github.com/apertium/apertium-fin`
[6] `https://github.com/apertium/apertium-eng`

Proceedings of the Fourth Conference on Machine Translation (WMT), Volume 2: Shared Task Papers (Day 1) pages 335–341
Florence, Italy, August 1-2, 2019. ©2019 Association for Computational Linguistics

Dictionary	Lexemes	Manual rules
Finnish	426,425	143
English	40,185	187
Finnish-English	164,501	273

Table 1: Sizes of dictionaries. The numbers are numbers of unique word entries or translation entries as defined in the dictionary, e.g., homonymy judgements have been made by the dictionary writers. The rule counts are combined counts of all sorts of linguistic rules: disambiguation, lexical selection, transfer and so forth.

task. I developed the Apertium's Finnish-English[7] dictionary initially based on the FinnWordNet's translated data, which was over 260,000 Wordnet-style lexical items; of these I discarded most which had multiple spaces in them or didn't match any source or target words in Finnish and English dictionaries, ending with around 150,000 lexical translations. The size of dictionaries at the time of writing is summarized in Table 1, however more up-to-date numbers can be found in Apertium's Wiki [8]

The system is based on the Apertium[9] machine translation platform (Forcada et al., 2011), a shallow transfer rule-based machine translation toolkit. For morphological analysis and generation, HFST[10] (Lindn et al., 2011) is used and for morphological disambiguation VISL CG-3 [11] is used. The whole platform as well as all the linguistic data are licensed under the GNU General Public Licence (GPL).

Apertium is a modular NLP system based on UNIX command-line ideology. The source text is processed step-by-step to form a shallow analysis (morphological analysis), then translated (lexical transfer) and re-arranged (structural transfer) to target language analyses and finally generated (morphological generation). Each of the steps can be processed with arbitrary command-line tool that transforms the input in expected formats. All of the steps also involve ambiguity or one-to-many mappings, that requires a decision, and while these decisions can be made using expert written rules, the writing of the rules is also a demanding task, and it is interesting to see how much can be achieved by simply bootstrapping the rulesets using automatic rule acquisition.

To illuminate how apertium does RBMT in Finnish—English, and the kinds of ambiguities I resolve, I show in Table 3 examples of the ambiguities with an example sentence. The ambiguity of source morphology is the true ambiguity rate of the language (according to the morphological analyser), i.e. how many potential interpretation each word has. It is no surprise that Finnish has relatively high ambiguity rate, however, English is nearly unambiguous is more due to limitation of apertium's English dictionary than feature of English per se, given that English has a bit of productive zero-derivations, e.g. verbing nouns and vice versa. The lexical selection ambiguity is the translation dictionary's rate of choices per source word, and FinnWordNet on average has 5 synonyms per word to suggest. The target morphology ambiguity is the rate of allomorphy or free variation, in Finnish as target language there's some systematic problems, such as plural genitives and partitives, whereas English literally has two incidents in the whole dev set: *sown / sowed* and *fish / fishes*. Assuming a perfect RBMT system would keep all options open, until final decision, the number of hypotheses at the end would be at least $\mathrm{MA_{SL}} \times \mathrm{LS_{SL \to TL}} \times \mathrm{MA_{TL}}$, where MA is morphological ambiguity rate, LS is lexical selection ambiguity rate, SL is source language and TL is target language. For Finnish—English I show the example figures of the ambiguities based on the development and test sets in Table 2.

The rule-based machine translation process as it is performed by apertium is shown in Table 3. The first step of the RBMT here is morphological analysis, in apertium this covers both tokenisation and morphological analysis as seen here; in apertium-eng the expression 'in front of' is considered to be a single token and is packaged as a preposition (we have also omitted an ambiguity between attributive and nominal reading of the house, since the distinction does not currently make difference in English to Finnish translation, in order to fit the table in the paper). The morphological analysis in apertium is performed by finite-state morphological analysis as defined in Beesley and Karttunen (2003) and implemented in open source format

---

[7] https://github.com/apertium/apertium-fin-eng

[8] http://wiki.apertium.org/wiki/List_of_dictionaries

[9] https://github.com/apertium

[10] https://hfst.github.io

[11] http://visl.sdu.dk/cg3.html

Feature:	**Source morphology**	**Lexical** selection	**Target** morphology	*Total*
Corpus				
Finnish dev set	1.68	5.04	1.0002	8.46
Finnish test set	1.69	4.80	1.0003	8.13
English dev set	1.04	1.15	1.0013	1.19
English test set	1.03	1.12	1.0006	1.15

Table 2: Ambiguity influencing RBMT Finnish-to-English and English-to-Finnish

by Lindn et al. (2011). After analysis, the next step is to disambiguate, i.e. pick 1-best lists of morphological analyses; in apertium this is done by constraint grammar, as described by Karlsson (1990) and implemented in open source by VISL CG 3.[12]. In lexical translation phase, each lemma is looked up from the translation dictionary, and in lexical selection the translation that is most suitable by the context and statistics is selected. In the structural transfer phase a number of things is performed: the English morphological analyses are rewritten into Finnish analyses, e.g. the adjective and noun will receive a genitive case tag due to the adposition, and the adposition is moved before the noun phrase since it is a preposition in Finnish and postposition in English, and the article is just removed, as the use of articles is non-standard in Finnish. Finally the Finnish analysis is generated into a surface string using a finite-state morphological analyser, since they are inherently bidirectional this needs no extra software or algorithms.

3 RBMT development workflow

I present here different levels of automation in the RBMT workflow: in Subsection 3.1 I have automated the generation of rules, in Subsection 3.2 I have a semi-automated workflow and finally in Subsection 3.3 I have an expert-driven development workflow.

3.1 Lexical selection training

One of the key components of this experiment was to try automatic rule-creation mechanisms for the converted Wordnet dictionary refinement. A large number of translation quality issues in the initial converted Wordnet dictionary was a high number of low-frequency 'synonyms' in translations. To overcome this some automatic methods were used. For automatic bootstrapping of the lexical selec-

tion rules I used Europarl corpus (Koehn, 2005) data and the methods demonstrated by Tyers et al. (2012). Since the result of this training seemed also insufficient, I experimented with another system to generate more rules for lexical selection.[13] On top of that, I have updated the lexical selection with some manual rules, that were either not covered by Europarl hits or skewed wrongly for the news domain, for example, the word 'letter' seemed to mainly have translations of *kirje* (a message written on paper), while in the development set all the sentences I sampled, a more suitable translation would of been *kirjain* (a character of alphabet). The resulting lexical selection rule sets are summarised in the table 4. The first method of creating rules is based on n-gram patterns, due to restricted time and processing resources I have only included bigrams into this model, and the second model only considers unigrams. The results are added up in the table lines + *bigrams* and + *unigrams* respectively.

3.2 Lexicon development workflow

One of the key components of this experiment is to show that a *shared-task driven development* (STDD) is a usable workflow for the development of the lexical data in rule-based machine translation system. As such, a 'training' phase in the RBMT development has been replaced by a very simple semi-automated native speaker - driven project workflow consisting of following:

1. Collect all lexemes unknown to source language dictionary, and add them with necessary morpholexical information

2. Collect all lexemes unknown to bilingual translation dictionary, and add their translations

---

[12] http://visl.sdu.dk/cg3.html

[13] https://svn.code.sf.net/p/apertium/
svn/trunk/apertium-swe-nor/dev/
lex-learn-unigram.sh

Input:	In front of the big house
Morphological analysis:	In front of.PREP the.DET.DEF.SP big.ADJ house.N.SG
Morphological disambiguation:	In front of.PREP the.DET.DEF.SP big.ADJ house.N.SG
Lexical translation:	In front of.PREP→Edessä.POST the.DET.DEF.SP→se.DET.DEF.SP big.ADJ→iso~raju~paha~kova~…jalomielinen.ADJ house.N.SG→huone~talo~suku~…edustajainhuone.N.SG
Lexical selection:	Edessä.POST se.DET.DEF.SP iso.ADJ talo.N.SG
Structural transfer:	iso.ADJ.POS.SG.GEN talo.N.SG.GEN Edessä.POST
Finnish translation:	ison talon Edessä

Table 3: Translation process for the English phrase 'In front of the big house'

Orig. Fin-Eng	18,066
+ bigrams	24,662
+ unigrams	30,049
Orig. Eng-Fin	22
+ bigrams	24,631
+ unigrams	25,748

Table 4: Lexical selection rules statistically generated

Corpus	BLEU-cased	CharacTER
MSRA.NAO	27.4	0.515
HelsinkiNLP RBMT	8.9	0.650
apertium-eng-fin	4.3	0.756
USYD	33.0	0.494
apertium-fin-eng	7.6	0.736

Table 5: automatic scores from `http://matrix.statmt.org`, we show our scores (boldfaced), the highest ranking RBMT and the highest ranking NMT for reference.

3. Collect all lexemes unknown to the target language dictionary, and add them to the dictionary with necessary morpholexical information

The semi-automation that I have developed lies in collecting the different unknown lexemes or *out-of-vocabulary* items (OOVs), and guessing a lexical entry or multiple plausible entries for them and have the dictionary writer select and correct them.

3.3 Grammar development

An expert-driven part of the RBMT workflow in our current methodology is the grammar development. This consists manually reading the sentences produced by the MT system to spot systematic errors caused by grammatical differences between languages. For the purposes of this shared task and the workshop, the linguistics or grammar are not a central concept, so I will not detail it here in detail. In practice this concerns of such grammatical rules as mapping between no articles in Finnish to articles in English, mapping between case or possessive suffixes and their corresponding lexical representations in English and so forth.

The details can be seen in the code that is available in github.

4 Evaluation, error analysis and discussion

The automatic measurements as used by the shared task are given in the table 5. I show here the BLEU (Papineni et al., 2002) and the CharacTER scores. BLEU, as it is a kind of industry standard, and CharacTER (Wang et al., 2016) as it is maybe more suited for morphologically complex languages. As the automatic scores show, the rule-based system has still room for improvement.

I find that a linguistic error analysis is one of the most interesting part of this experiment. The reason for this is is that the experiment's scientific contribution lies more in the extension of linguistic resources and workflows than machine learning algorithm design. It is noteworthy, that in the sustainable workflow I demonstrate in this article, error analysis is a part of the workflow, namely, adding of the lexical data and rules follows the

Error	count
OOVs in Finnish	763
OOVs in English	943
OOVs in FinEng	2696

Table 6: Classification of mainly lexical errors in apertium-fin-eng submissions for 2019

Corpus		BLEU-cased
apertium-eng-fin	2015	2.9
	2017	3.5
	2019	4.3
apertium-fin-eng	2015	6.9
	2017	6.3
	2019	7.6

Table 7: Progress of apertium-fin-eng over the years using only the WMT shared task driven development method.

layout given in Section 3 and is the same for development and error analysis phase. I have, to that effect, categorised the errors in translations along the workflow:

1. OOV in source language dictionary (including typos and non-words)

2. OOV in bilingual dictionary

3. OOV in target language dictionary

4. disambiguation or lexical selection fail

5. structural failure or higher level

The OOV's can be calculated automatically from the corpus data, but the higher level failures need human annotation. A summary of the errors can be seen in the table 6, this is based on the errors that were fixed as a part of error analysis process. As a result of this workflow, I have improved the BLEU points of apertium-fin-eng over the years, as can be seen in the table 7.

The OOV numbers might look moderately large but a major part falls under proper nouns, which are generally low frequency and do not cause a large problem in translation pipeline, the untranslated proper noun is recognisable and the mapping of adpositions and case inflections will fail where applicable. The task of adding proper nouns to the dictionaries is also simplest, they are easy to gather from the text, and for English and bilingual dictionaries no further classification is necessary; for the Finnish dictionary entry generation, paradigm guessing is necessary, although the paradigms used in foreign names are much more limited than with other parts-of-speech to be added. In the *newstest 2019* data there was a number of words that I decided not to add to our dictionaries, unlike our usual workflow where I aim at virtual 100 % coverage with gold corpora. The unadded words were for example words like "Toimiluvanmuodossatoteutettavajulki-senjayksityisensektorinkumppanuus", which seems to have a large number of missing spaces and extra hyphen, these as well as extraneous spaces were quite common in the data in our error analysis as well as 'words' like 'OIet', 'OIi', 'OIin', 'OIisi', 'OIIut', i.e. forms of 'olla' (to be) where lowercase L has been replaced with uppercase I. While I do account for common spelling mistakes in our dictionaries, these kind of errors are probably more suited for robustness testing and implemented with spelling correction methods for specific problematic generated text, such as OCR. We will look into implementing spelling correction into our pipeline in the future. Comparing the performance of RBMT to NMT, it can be clearly seen that contemporary NMT is better suited for error tolerance, in part because it can be more character-based than token-based, in part because any large training data set will actually have some OCR errors and run-in tokens.

After OOV-errors one of the biggest easily solvable problems is ambiguity, so word sense disambiguation and lexical selection. For lexical selection I found about 200 lexical translations that were still badly wrong and could be solved without coming up complex context conditions. For disambiguation problems, a surprisingly common problem was sentence-initial proper noun that is a common noun as well, as a high frequency example, for the word 'trump' meaning a winning suit in card games (= Finnish 'valtti') would get selected over the POTUS, plausibly when most of the training and development before WMT 2019 did not contain so many proper noun Trumps. Also rather common problem still is the ambiguity in English verb forms, and between English zero derivations.

In the structural transfer a large number of errors are caused by long-distance re-ordering.

For example for Finnish to English proper noun phrases regardless of length of the phrase, the Finnish shows case in last word or postposition after the last word, English has preposition before the word, but when phrase gets chunked partially the adpositions or case suffixes end up in the middle with a rather jarring effect to the translated sentence. The same applies for other effects where generating correct language depends on correct chunk detection, e.g. the article generation is very limited in the current code because the articles need to be generated from nothing, when translating from Finnish to English, only at the very beginning of specific noun phrases.

Finally a number of problems were caused for such grammatical differences between languages that do not have a good solution in lexical rule-based machine translation, such as difference between English noun phrases and corresponding Finnish compound nouns or for example the common English class of -able suffixed adjectives that does not have accurate lexical Finnish translation at all.

In terms of where RBMT is perhaps more usable than NMT, one important factor is how predictable and systematic the errors are when they appear. For example just looking at the first page of the top-ranking system in Finnish-to-English[14] one can see the Finnish "Aika nopeasti saatiin hommat sovittua, Kouki sanoi" translated into "Pretty quickly we got the gays agreed, Kouki said." whereas the correct translation is "We reached a pretty quick agreement, Kouki said.", the big problem with the neural translation is that it is deceptively fluent language but conveys something completely different, comparing to the rule-based version: "Kinda swiftly let jobs agreed, Kouki said." which is not fluent at all, but doesn't hallucinate gays there so it may be more usable for post-editing. For further research in the problems of NMT for real-world use, see for example Moorkens et al. (2018).

In comparison to neural and statistical systems, the rule-based approach does not generally fare well as measured with automatic metrics like BLEU, for a human evaluation refer to (Bojar et al., 2019). However, the experiment I describe here is also not the most actively developed machine translators, rather I use the experiment to gauge the effects the described workflow has to quality of semi-automatically generated RBMT, to see how more developed systems fare on the same task you should also refer to (Hurskainen and Tiedemann, 2017; Kolachina and Ranta, 2015).

5 Concluding remarks

In this article I've shown a workflow of *shared task driven development* for rule-based machine translations, namely the lexicons and rules. I show that a small effort to update lexical data based on yearly released gold corpora increases BLEU points and enlarges dictionaries as well as improves rulesets sizes and qualities by a significant amount. In future I aim to build more automatisation for the workflow to make it trivially usable with continuous integration.

The systems are all available as free/libre opensource software under the GNU GPL licence, and can be downloaded from the internet.

Acknowledgements

This work has been written while employed in the *Hamburger Zentrum für Sprachkorpora* by CLARIN-D. Thanks to all contributors of the related projects: omorfi, FinnWordNet, Apertium, and everyone helping with apertium-fin, apertium-eng and apertium-fin-eng.

References

Kenneth R Beesley and Lauri Karttunen. 2003. *Finite State Morphology*. CSLI publications.

Ondřej Bojar, Christian Federmann, Mark Fishel, Yvette Graham, Barry Haddow, Matthias Huck, Philipp +Koehn, Christof Monz, Mathias Müller, and Matt Post. 2019. Findings of the 2019 conference on machine translation (wmt19). In *Proceedings of the Fourth Conference on Machine Translation, Volume 2: Shared Task Papers*, Florence, Italy. Association for Computational Linguistics.

Mikel L Forcada, Mireia Ginestí-Rosell, Jacob Nordfalk, Jim ORegan, Sergio Ortiz-Rojas, Juan Antonio Pérez-Ortiz, Felipe Sánchez-Martínez, Gema Ramírez-Sánchez, and Francis M Tyers. 2011. Apertium: a free/open-source platform for rule-based machine translation. *Machine translation*, 25(2):127–144.

Arvi Hurskainen and Jörg Tiedemann. 2017. Rule-based machine translation from english to finnish. In *Proceedings of the Second Conference on Machine Translation*, pages 323–329.

---

[14]`http://matrix.statmt.org/matrix/output/1903?score_id=39757`

Fred Karlsson. 1990. Constraint grammar as a framework for parsing unrestricted text. In *Proceedings of the 13th International Conference of Computational Linguistics*, volume 3, pages 168–173, Helsinki.

Philipp Koehn. 2005. Europarl: A parallel corpus for statistical machine translation. In *MT summit*, volume 5, pages 79–86.

Prasanth Kolachina and Aarne Ranta. 2015. Gf wide-coverage english-finnish mt system for wmt 2015. In *Proceedings of the Tenth Workshop on Statistical Machine Translation*, pages 141–144.

Krister Lindn, Erik Axelson, Sam Hardwick, Tommi A Pirinen, and Miikka Silfverberg. 2011. Hfstframework for compiling and applying morphologies. *Systems and Frameworks for Computational Morphology*, pages 67–85.

Joss Moorkens, Antonio Toral, Sheila Castilho, and Andy Way. 2018. Translators perceptions of literary post-editing using statistical and neural machine translation. *Translation Spaces*, 7(2):240–262.

Kishore Papineni, Salim Roukos, Todd Ward, and Wei-Jing Zhu. 2002. Bleu: a method for automatic evaluation of machine translation. In *Proceedings of the 40th annual meeting on association for computational linguistics*, pages 311–318. Association for Computational Linguistics.

Tommi A Pirinen. 2015. Development and use of computational morphology of finnish in the open source and open science era: Notes on experiences with omorfi development. *SKY Journal of Linguistics*, 28.

Francis M Tyers, Felipe Sánchez-Martínez, Mikel L Forcada, et al. 2012. Flexible finite-state lexical selection for rule-based machine translation.

Weiyue Wang, Jan-Thorsten Peter, Hendrik Rosendahl, and Hermann Ney. 2016. Character: Translation edit rate on character level. In *Proceedings of the First Conference on Machine Translation: Volume 2, Shared Task Papers*, volume 2, pages 505–510.

English-Czech Systems in WMT19: Document-Level Transformer

Martin Popel, Dominik Macháček, Michal Auersperger, Ondřej Bojar and **Pavel Pecina**
Charles University, Faculty of Mathematics and Physics,
Institute of Formal and Applied Linguistics,
Malostranské náměstí 25, 118 00 Prague, Czech Republic
surname@ufal.mff.cuni.cz

Abstract

We describe our NMT systems submitted to the WMT19 shared task in English→Czech news translation. Our systems are based on the Transformer model implemented in either Tensor2Tensor (T2T) or Marian framework.

We aimed at improving the adequacy and coherence of translated documents by enlarging the context of the source and target. Instead of translating each sentence independently, we split the document into possibly overlapping multi-sentence segments. In case of the T2T implementation, this "document-level"-trained system achieves a +0.6 BLEU improvement ($p < 0.05$) relative to the same system applied on isolated sentences. To assess the potential effect document-level models might have on lexical coherence, we performed a semi-automatic analysis, which revealed only a few sentences improved in this aspect. Thus, we cannot draw any conclusions from this week evidence.

1 Introduction

Neural machine translation has reached a point, where the quality of automatic translation measured on isolated sentences is similar on average to the quality of professional human translations. Hassan et al. (2018) report achieving a "human parity" on Chinese→English news translation. Bojar et al. (2018, p. 291) report that our last year's English→Czech system (Popel, 2018) was evaluated as significantly better ($p < 0.05$) than the human reference. However, it has been shown (Läubli et al., 2018; Toral et al., 2018) that evaluating the quality of translation of news articles on isolated sentences without the context of the whole document is not sufficient. It can bias the evaluation results because systems that ignore the context are not penalized in the evaluation for these context-related errors; and vice versa: systems (or humans) that take the context into account may be unfairly penalized. Läubli et al. (2018) show that while the difference between human and machine translation in adequacy is not significant when evaluated on isolated sentences, it is significant (humans are better) when evaluated on whole documents. This suggests that there are some inter-sentential phenomena where MT applied on isolated sentences is lacking.

Since assessing the performance of document-level systems is one of the goals of WMT19 (Barrault et al., 2019), we decided to build NMT systems trained for translation of longer segments than single sentences. In this paper, we describe our five NMT systems submitted to WMT19 English→Czech news translation task (see Table 1). They are based on the Transformer model (Vaswani et al., 2017) and on our submission from WMT18 (Popel, 2018). Our new contributions are (i) adaptation of the baseline single-sentence models to translate multiple adjacent sentences in a document at once, so the Transformer can attend to inter-sentence relations and achieve better document-level translation quality, as was already showed to be effective by Jean et al. (2017); and (ii) reimplementation of our last year's submission in the Marian framework (Junczys-Dowmunt et al., 2018).

This paper is organized as follows: In Section 2, we describe our training data and its augmentation to overlapping multi-sentence sequences. We describe also the hyper-parameters of our models in the two frameworks. Section 3 follows with a description of the document-level decoding strategies. Section 4 reports and discusses the results of automatic (BLEU) evaluation.

Proceedings of the Fourth Conference on Machine Translation (WMT), Volume 2: Shared Task Papers (Day 1) pages 342–348
Florence, Italy, August 1-2, 2019. ©2019 Association for Computational Linguistics

official name	description
CUNI DocTransformer T2T	Document level trained Transformer in T2T.
CUNI DocTransformer Marian	Document level trained Transformer in Marian.
CUNI Transformer T2T 2019	Same model as CUNI DocTransformer T2T, but applied on single sentences (i.e. with no cross-sentence context).
CUNI Transformer T2T 2018	Same model as in the last year (Popel, 2018).
CUNI Transformer Marian	Reimplementation of the last year's model in Marian.

Table 1: Brief descriptions of our WMT19 systems. In the rest of the paper, we omit the CUNI (Charles University) prefix for brevity.

data set	sentence pairs (k)	words (k) EN	words (k) CS
CzEng 1.7	57 065	618 424	543 184
Europarl v7	647	15 625	13 000
News Commentary v12	211	4 544	4 057
CommonCrawl	162	3 349	2 927
WikiTitles	361	896	840
EN NewsCrawl 2016–17	47 483	934 981	
CS NewsCrawl 2007–17	65 383		927 348
CS NewsCrawl 2018	12 983		181 004
total	184 295	1 577 819	1 672 360

Table 2: Training data sizes (in thousands).

2 Experimental Setup

2.1 Data sources

Our training data (see Table 2) are constrained to the data allowed in the WMT2019 shared task. "Transformer T2T 2018" and "Transformer Marian" use only the data allowed in WMT2018, which does not include CS NewsCrawl 2018 and WikiTitles. All the data were preprocessed, filtered and backtranslated by the same process as in Popel (2018). We selected the originally English part of newstest2016 for validation, following the idea of CZ/nonCZ tuning in Popel (2018), but excluding the CZ tuning because the WMT2019 test set was announced to contain only original English sentences and no translationese.

2.2 Training Data Context Augmentation

In WMT19, all the training data from Table 2 are available with document boundaries (and unlike in previous years the sentences are not shuffled).[1] We extracted all sequences of consecutive sentences with at most 1000 characters.[2] Our context-augmented data consists of pairs of such sequences, where the source sequence has always the same number of sentences as the target sentence. We separate the sentences in each sequence with a special token,[3] so that we can easily extract sentence alignment after decoding. We randomly shuffle the augmented training sequences, but we keep separately the authentic parallel and synthetic (backtranslated) data, so that we can apply *concat backtranslation* (Popel, 2018).

Note that this particular way of context augmentation implicitly upsamples sentences from longer documents relative to sentences from shorter documents. We leave the analysis of this effect and possible alternative samplings for future work.

2.3 Model Hyper-parameters

2.3.1 Tensor2Tensor

Our three systems with "T2T" in the name are implemented in the Tensor2Tensor framework (Vaswani et al., 2018), version 1.6.0. The model and training parameters this year are identical to our last year's (WMT18) submission (Popel, 2018), with just two exceptions: First, we trained on 10 GPUs instead of 8 GPUs, thus using the effective batch size of 29k subwords instead of 23k subwords. Second, we used `max_length=200` instead of 150. This means we discard all training sequences longer than 200 subwords. With our 32k joint subword vocabulary, a word contains on average 1.5 subwords. Thus effectively, the sequence-length limit used in T2T training was in most cases lower than 1000 characters – on average it was 785 characters.

2.3.2 Marian

Our two systems with "Marian" in the name use the Marian framework (Junczys-Dowmunt et al., 2018), in the latest stable version 1.7.6. We chose

---

[1] In WikiTitles, each pair of titles is considered a separate document. We decided to upsample this source 23 times, but we have not evaluated the effect of this on the final quality.

[2] The limit of 1000 characters was chosen rather arbitrarily. A 1000-characters long sequence from our training data contains on average about 15 sentences (165 English and 144 Czech words).

[3] Any token not present in the training data can be used, but it should be included in the subword vocabulary.

343

Marian for its fast and efficient training and decoding. Due to the good results of "CUNI Transformer" in WMT18 evaluation and lack of time and resources for exhaustive parameter search, we reconstructed all its hyperparameters in Marian wherever possible. Therefore, we trained with the following options:

```
--type transformer --enc-depth 6
--dec-depth 6 --dim-emb 1024
--transformer-dim-ffn 4096
--transformer-heads 16
--transformer-dropout 0.0
--transformer-dropout-attention 0.1
--transformer-dropout-ffn 0.1
--lr-warmup 20000
--lr-decay-inv-sqrt 20000
--optimizer-params 0.9 0.98 1e-09
--clip-norm 5 --label-smoothing 0.1
--learn-rate 0.0002
--exponential-smoothing
```

We used the same learning rate as T2T and estimated the number of warmup training steps so the model consumed approximately the same number of sentences as T2T in warmup. Instead of T2T's default SubwordTextEncoder, we used SentencePiece (Kudo and Richardson, 2018) with its default parameters to obtain a shared vocabulary of 32,000 entries from untokenized training data. We set the maximal sentence length to 150 and decoded with beam size 4.

We could not use Adafactor (Shazeer and Stern, 2018) optimizer as in T2T, because it is not implemented in Marian. We used Adam instead.

We did not set the batch size manually, but used the `--mini-batch-fit` parameter to determine the mini-batch size automatically based on sentence lengths to fit the available memory. We estimated the workspace memory to 13,900 MB as the largest possible on our hardware. We shuffled the training data before training and did not use any advanced reordering to fit more non-padding tokens into a training batch as in T2T.

Another difference is the checkpoint averaging: while our T2T models are (uniform) averages of the last 8 checkpoints from the last 8 hours of training, our Marian models use the exponential moving average regularization method (`--exponential-smoothing`) applied after each update, as suggested by the Marian authors.

2.4 Training

The summary of hardware used for training is in Table 3. First, we trained a non-document models on single sentences, on concatenation of out-domain authentic data and in-domain synthetic

systems	#GPUs	GPU memory	GPU type
T2T 2018	8	11GB	GTX 1080 Ti
T2T 2019	10	11GB	GTX 1080 Ti
Marian	8	16GB	Quadro P5000

Table 3: Hardware used for our systems.

datasets. We trained "Transformer Marian" model for 17 days until the epoch 18. We observed the last improvement in validation BLEU at 15 days and 18 hours of training, in step 1,266M, which we selected as the final model "Transformer Marian". The "DocTransformer T2T" model was trained for 9 days (660k steps).

3 Document-Level Systems

Our document-level models were created by training on the context-augmented data described in Section 2.2. We used different strategies for document-level decoding in Marian and in T2T.

3.1 Decoding in Marian

For"DocTransformer Marian" decoding, we decided to reduce the context to up to three consecutive sentences because decoding of longer contexts was time-consuming and our time was constrained. Each sentence appeared as the first, second or third sentence in a 3-sentence context (1st/3, 2nd/3, 3rd/3) if possible.[4] We experimented also with a 2-sentence context (1st/2, 2nd/2) and no context (1st/1, i.e. the baseline).

We compared dev-set BLEU scores of these six setups and selected the following strategy for the selection of the final translation: For each sentence, if possible and if the translation is "valid", use 2nd/3. If not possible or "valid", use 1st/3, followed by 2nd/2, 1st/2 and 1st/1.

We consider a translation "valid" if it contains the same number of sentences (delimited by a special sentence-boundary character) as the input. We excluded translations containing a given word more than 20 times and translations with a word longer than 49 characters. This rule detected non-meaningful outputs that we observed in validation. We decided to not use 3rd/3 because these translations were the least accurate ones.

Based on the validation BLEU scores, we selected two checkpoints for the final document-level translation. The checkpoint at 2,044M steps

---

[4] For the first sentence in a document only 1st/3 is possible, for the second sentence only 1st/3 or 2nd/3 is possible, etc.

was used for 1st/3, 2nd/3 and 2nd/2. The checkpoint at 1,775M steps was used elsewhere (1st/2 and 1st/1).

3.2 Decoding in T2T

In an initial experiment, we split the test set into non-overlapping sequences of sentences with at most 1000 characters, following the maximum sequence length used in training. We realized that the translation quality is very low, especially close to the end of each translated sequence. Sometimes the number of output sentences (detected based on the special separator character) was different than the number of input sentences. We hypothesized that the reason of low quality is that there are not enough 1000-character sequences in the training data (cf. Section 2.2). With non-overlapping splits, we achieved the best dev-set BLEU, when lowering the limit to about 700 characters.

We further experimented with overlapping splits, where each sequence to be translated consists of

- pre-context: sentences which are ignored in the translation and serve only as a context for better translation of the main content,

- main content: sentences which are used for the final translation,

- post-context: sentences which are ignored, similarly to the pre-context.

Based on a small dev-set BLEU hyperparameter search, we selected the following length limits: pre-context of up to 200 characters (splitting on word boundaries), main content of up to 500 characters (whole sentences only) and post-context of up to 900 characters minus the length of the pre-context and main content (whole sentences only). After the main decoding, we joined together the translations of main contents of all sequences. In rare cases (8 sentences out of 3611), when there were not enough sentences in the translated sequence, we used a single-sentence translation as a backup.

3.3 Post-processing

For T2T systems, we used the same postprocessing as last year (Popel, 2018): We deleted the repetitions of phrases of one to four words appearing directly after each other more than two times, and converted the quotation symbols to

system	BLEU uncased	BLEU cased	chrF2 cased
DocTransformer T2T	**31.03**	**29.94**	*0.5628*
Transformer T2T 2018	*30.93*	*29.86*	**0.5630**
Transformer T2T 2019	30.42	29.39	0.5552
DocTransformer Marian	29.17	28.14	0.5466
Transformer Marian	29.20	28.13	0.5474
UEdin	29.00	27.89	0.5516

Table 4: Automatic evaluation on `newstest2019`. Significantly different BLEU scores ($p < 0.05$ bootstrap resampling) are separated by a horizontal line.

„lower and upper". This is considered as standard in Czech formal texts. For Marian, we applied only the conversion of quotation symbols.

4 Results

4.1 Automatic Evaluation

Table 4 reports the automatic metrics of our English→Czech systems submitted to WMT2019, plus the best other system – UEdin (Marian system trained by University of Edinburgh). The automatic metrics are calculated using sacreBLEU 1.3.2 (Post, 2018) and their signatures are:

- BLEU+case.mixed+lang.en-cs+numrefs.1+smooth.exp+tok.13a,

- BLEU+case.lc+lang.en-cs+numrefs.1+smooth.exp+tok.intl and

- chrF2+case.mixed+lang.en-cs+numchars.6+numrefs.1+space.False.

4.2 Explaining the Difference of T2T and Marian

The two comparable systems using the closest possible settings we were able to achieve and identical data, "Transformer Marian" and "Transformer T2T 2018", did not perform equally. The last year's T2T system was around 1.73 BLEU better at the point, where both systems had enough training time to converge. We hypothesize this was caused by the parameters, in which they differ: (i) Marian uses Adam optimizer, T2T Adafactor; (ii) Marian had 8 16GB GPUs and T2T 8 11GB GPUs, it means 128GB vs 88GB in total. We assume Marian is not as effective in memory usage, or we used bigger than optimal memory (and thus batch) size; (iii) Marian uses different batch ordering; (iv) in Marian, we used the exponential moving average, T2T used uniform averaging of the last 8 checkpoints.

4.3 Doc-Level Evaluation

We hypothesized that by providing the translation model with larger attendable context, the resulting translations display larger lexical consistency. We could demonstrate it by finding less examples where an English polysemous word is translated to two or more Czech non-synonymous lemmata within one document.

To evaluate the hypothesis, we word-aligned the source and target sentences using `fast_align` (Dyer et al., 2013).[5] We then lemmatized the aligned words (both English and Czech) using MorphoDiTa (Straková et al., 2014) and considered all instances where a single English lemma was aligned to at least two Czech lemmata in a single document. Since our focus was on evaluating the difference between non-context and document-level models, we selected only the English lemmata with different number of aligned Czech lemmata in the two types of systems. Two pairs of models were compared: "DocTransformer T2T" vs. "Transformer T2T 2019" and "Doc-Transformer Marian" vs. "Transformer Marian". The final pool of examples was evaluated manually.

We found only one and three instances for the Marian and T2T models, respectively, where the document-level variant performed better than the non-context variant. The examples are shown in Table 5. We also found a possible counter-example where the document-level model performed worse than the non-context model, but the evaluation is not clear-cut. The example is shown in Table 6.

Because there are too few examples for any meaningful quantitative analysis, we conclude more data is needed to evaluate the potential benefit a document-level model could have on lexical consistency. By doing manual evaluation, we found the cases where the inter-sentential context is necessary for determining the correct meaning of a polysemous word are rare.

5 Conclusion

We were not able to replicate our last year's T2T system in Marian, but we acknowledge several differences in the setup. We were not able to im-prove the sentence-level Marian system BLEU by adding a context of up to three sentences. Our document-level trained T2T system achieved an insignificant improvement (+0.1 BLEU) over our last year's sentence-level T2T system, but applying this system on sentences led to a significant worsening (−0.6 BLEU).

Acknowledgments

This research was supported by the Czech Science Foundation (grant n. 19-26934X) and the Grant Agency of Charles University (grant n. 978119). The experiments were conducted using language resources distributed by the LINDAT/CLARIN project of the Ministry of Education, Youth and Sports of the Czech Republic (LM2015071).

References

Loïc Barrault, Ondřej Bojar, Marta R. Costa-jussà, Christian Federmann, Mark Fishel, Yvette Graham, Barry Haddow, Matthias Huck, Philipp Koehn, Shervin Malmasi, Christof Monz, Mathias Müller, Santanu Pal, Matt Post, and Marcos Zampieri. 2019. Findings of the 2019 conference on machine translation (wmt19). In *Proceedings of the Fourth Conference on Machine Translation, Volume 2: Shared Task Papers*, Florence, Italy. Association for Computational Linguistics.

Ondřej Bojar, Christian Federmann, Mark Fishel, Yvette Graham, Barry Haddow, Matthias Huck, Philipp Koehn, and Christof Monz. 2018. Findings of the 2018 conference on machine translation (wmt18). In *Proceedings of the Third Conference on Machine Translation, Volume 2: Shared Task Papers*, pages 272–307, Belgium, Brussels. Association for Computational Linguistics.

Chris Dyer, Victor Chahuneau, and Noah A. Smith. 2013. A simple, fast, and effective reparameterization of IBM model 2. In *Proceedings of the 2013 Conference of the North American Chapter of the Association for Computational Linguistics: Human Language Technologies*, pages 644–648, Atlanta, Georgia. Association for Computational Linguistics.

Hany Hassan, Anthony Aue, Chang Chen, Vishal Chowdhary, Jonathan Clark, Christian Federmann, Xuedong Huang, Marcin Junczys-Dowmunt, William Lewis, Mu Li, Shujie Liu, Tie-Yan Liu, Renqian Luo, Arul Menezes, Tao Qin, Frank Seide, Xu Tan, Fei Tian, Lijun Wu, Shuangzhi Wu, Yingce Xia, Dongdong Zhang, Zhirui Zhang, and Ming Zhou. 2018. Achieving human parity on automatic chinese to english news translation. *CoRR*, abs/1803.05567.

---

[5] To improve the reliability of automatic word alignments, we trained them on the translations together with the first 500k sentences of CzEng 1.7. Only the intersection of the source-to-target and target-to-source alignments was considered.

Sebastien Jean, Stanislas Lauly, Orhan Firat, and Kyunghyun Cho. 2017. Does neural machine translation benefit from larger context?

Marcin Junczys-Dowmunt, Roman Grundkiewicz, Tomasz Dwojak, Hieu Hoang, Kenneth Heafield, Tom Neckermann, Frank Seide, Ulrich Germann, Alham Fikri Aji, Nikolay Bogoychev, André F. T. Martins, and Alexandra Birch. 2018. Marian: Fast neural machine translation in C++. In *Proceedings of ACL 2018, System Demonstrations*, pages 116–121, Melbourne, Australia. Association for Computational Linguistics.

Taku Kudo and John Richardson. 2018. Sentence-Piece: A simple and language independent subword tokenizer and detokenizer for neural text processing. In *Proceedings of the 2018 Conference on Empirical Methods in Natural Language Processing: System Demonstrations*, pages 66–71, Brussels, Belgium. Association for Computational Linguistics.

Samuel Läubli, Rico Sennrich, and Martin Volk. 2018. Has machine translation achieved human parity? a case for document-level evaluation. In *Proceedings of the 2018 Conference on Empirical Methods in Natural Language Processing*, pages 4791–4796, Brussels, Belgium. Association for Computational Linguistics.

Martin Popel. 2018. Cuni transformer neural mt system for wmt18. In *Proceedings of the Third Conference on Machine Translation, Volume 2: Shared Task Papers*, pages 486–491, Belgium, Brussels. Association for Computational Linguistics.

Matt Post. 2018. A Call for Clarity in Reporting BLEU Scores. *CoRR*, arXiv/1804.08771.

Noam Shazeer and Mitchell Stern. 2018. Adafactor: Adaptive Learning Rates with Sublinear Memory Cost. *CoRR*, arXiv/1804.04235.

Jana Straková, Milan Straka, and Jan Hajič. 2014. Open-Source Tools for Morphology, Lemmatization, POS Tagging and Named Entity Recognition. In *Proceedings of 52nd Annual Meeting of the Association for Computational Linguistics: System Demonstrations*, pages 13–18, Baltimore, Maryland. Association for Computational Linguistics.

Antonio Toral, Sheila Castilho, Ke Hu, and Andy Way. 2018. Attaining the unattainable? reassessing claims of human parity in neural machine translation. In *Proceedings of the Third Conference on Machine Translation, Volume 1: Research Papers*, pages 113–123, Belgium, Brussels. Association for Computational Linguistics.

Ashish Vaswani, Samy Bengio, Eugene Brevdo, Francois Chollet, Aidan N. Gomez, Stephan Gouws, Llion Jones, Łukasz Kaiser, Nal Kalchbrenner, Niki Parmar, Ryan Sepassi, Noam Shazeer, and Jakob Uszkoreit. 2018. Tensor2tensor for neural machine translation. *CoRR*, abs/1803.07416.

Ashish Vaswani, Noam Shazeer, Niki Parmar, Jakob Uszkoreit, Llion Jones, Aidan N Gomez, Łukasz Kaiser, and Illia Polosukhin. 2017. Attention is all you need. In *Advances in Neural Information Processing Systems 30*, pages 6000–6010. Curran Associates, Inc.

6 Appendix

source	[...] to meet Craig Halkett's header across goal. The hosts were content to let Rangers play in front of them, knowing they could trouble the visitors at set pieces. And that was the manner in which the crucial **goal** came. Rangers conceded a free-kick [...]
T2T	A to byl způsob, jakým přišel rozhodující **cíl** (*aim*).
T2T-doc	A to byl způsob, jakým přišel rozhodující **gól** (*goal*).
source	Elizabeth Warren Will Take "Hard Look" At Running For President in 2020, Massachusetts Senator Says Massachusetts Senator Elizabeth Warren said on Saturday she would take a "hard look" at running for president following the midterm elections. During a town hall in Holyoke, Massachusetts, Warren confirmed she'd consider **running**. "It's time for women to go to Washington and fix our broken government and that includes a woman at the top," she said, according to The Hill. [...]
T2T	Na radnici v Holyoke v Massachusetts Warrenová potvrdila, že uvažuje o **útěku** (*escape*).
T2T-doc	Na radnici v Holyoke ve státě Massachusetts Warrenová potvrdila, že o **kandidatuře** (*candidacy*) uvažuje.
source	At 6am, just as Gegard Mousasi and Rory MacDonald were preparing to face each other, viewers in the UK were left stunned when the coverage changed to Peppa Pig. Some were unimpressed after they had stayed awake until the early hours especially for the **fight**. [...]
T2T	Na některé to neudělalo žádný dojem, když zůstali vzhůru až do časných ranních hodin, zvláště kvůli **rvačce** (*crawl*).
T2T-doc	Na některé to neudělalo žádný dojem, když zůstali vzhůru až do ranních hodin, zejména kvůli **zápasu** (*match*).
source	[...] she felt "terrified of retaliation" and was worried about "being publicly humiliated." The 34-year-old says she is now seeking to overturn the **settlement** as she continues to be traumatized by the alleged incident. [...]
Marian	Čtyřiatřicetiletá žena tvrdí, že se nyní snaží o zrušení **osady** (*village*), protože je nadále traumatizována údajným incidentem.
Marian-doc	34letá žena tvrdí, že nyní usiluje o zrušení **vyrovnání** (*compensation*), protože je nadále traumatizována údajným incidentem.

Table 5: Examples of non-context model errors corrected by the document-level models.

source	New cancer vaccine can teach the immune system to 'see' rogue cells New cancer vaccine can teach the immune system to 'see' rogue cells and kill them Vaccine teaches immune system to recognise rogue cells as part of treatment Method involves extracting immune cells from a **patient**, altering them in lab They can then 'see' a protein common to many cancers and then reinjected A trial vaccine is showing promising results in **patients** with a range of cancers. One woman treated with the vaccine, which teaches the immune system to recognise rogue cells, saw her ovarian cancer disappear for more than 18 months. The method involves extracting immune cells from a **patient**, altering them in the laboratory so they can "see" a protein common to many cancers called HER2, and then reinjecting the cells.
T2T	Nová protinádorová vakcína může naučit imunitní systém „vidět" zlovolné buňky Nová protinádorová vakcína může naučit imunitní systém „vidět" zlovolné buňky a zabít je. Vakcína učí imunitní systém rozpoznávat zlovolné buňky jako součást léčby Metoda zahrnuje odebrání imunitních buněk z **pacienta** a jejich změnu v laboratoři. Pak mohou vidět protein, který je společný mnoha nádorům, a znovu ho vstříknout. Zkušební vakcína vykazuje slibné výsledky u **pacientů** s řadou nádorových onemocnění. Jedna žena léčená vakcínou, která učí imunitní systém rozeznávat zlovolné buňky, byla svědkem vymizení rakoviny vaječníků na více než 18 měsíců. Metoda spočívá v odebrání imunitních buněk z **pacienta**, jejich přeměně v laboratoři, aby mohli „vidět" protein, který je společný mnoha nádorům nazývaným HER2, a poté reinjekci buněk.
T2T-doc	Nová protinádorová vakcína může naučit imunitní systém „vidět" zlovolné buňky Nová protinádorová vakcína může naučit imunitní systém „vidět" zlovolné buňky a zabít je Vakcína učí imunitní systém rozpoznávat zlovolné buňky jako součást léčby Metoda zahrnuje extrakci imunitních buněk z **pacienta**, jejich změnu v laboratoři Poté mohou „vidět" bílkovinu společnou mnoha nádorových onemocněním a poté ji znovu nasadit Zkušební vakcína vykazuje slibné výsledky u **pacientů** s řadou nádorových onemocnění. Jedna žena léčená touto vakcínou, která učí imunitní systém rozpoznávat zlovolné buňky, byla svědkem vymizení rakoviny vaječníků na více než 18 měsíců. Tato metoda zahrnuje odebrání imunitních buněk od **pacientky** (*female patient*), jejich změnu v laboratoři, aby mohly „vidět" bílkovinu, která je společná mnoha nádorům nazývaným HER2, a poté reinjekci buněk.

Table 6: The example of an error introduced by a document-level model.

The RWTH Aachen University
Machine Translation Systems for WMT 2019

Jan Rosendahl, Christian Herold, Yunsu Kim, Miguel Graça,
Weiyue Wang, Parnia Bahar, Yingbo Gao and Hermann Ney
Human Language Technology and Pattern Recognition Group
Computer Science Department
RWTH Aachen University
D-52056 Aachen, Germany
`<surname>@i6.informatik.rwth-aachen.de`

Abstract

This paper describes the neural machine translation systems developed at the RWTH Aachen University for the De→En, Zh→En and Kk→En news translation tasks of the *Fourth Conference on Machine Translation* (WMT19). For all tasks, the final submitted system is based on the Transformer architecture. We focus on improving data filtering and fine-tuning as well as systematically evaluating interesting approaches like unigram language model segmentation and transfer learning. For the De→En task, none of the tested methods gave a significant improvement over last years winning system and we end up with the same performance, resulting in 39.6% BLEU on `newstest2019`. In the Zh→En task, we show 1.3% BLEU improvement over our last year's submission, which we mostly attribute to the splitting of long sentences during translation. We further report results on the Kk→En task where we gain improvements of 11.1% BLEU over our baseline system. On the same task we present a recent transfer learning approach, which uses half of the free parameters of our submission system and performs on par with it.

1 Introduction

The RWTH Aachen University developed three systems for the German→English, Chinese→English and Kazakh→English WMT19 news translation tasks.

For the language pairs De→En and Zh→En there is a lot of training data available, however it consists partially of low quality data. Therefore we improve our data filtering techniques and the preprocessing of the data. We also studied different settings for the fine-tuning and ensembling steps of the final models.

For the low resource Kk→En task we furthermore make use of additional Ru−En/Kk parallel data, exploiting the similarities between the Russian and Kazakh languages.

This paper is organized as follows: In Section 2, we describe our data preprocessing. Our translation software and baseline setups are explained in Section 3. The results of the experiments for the various language pairs are summarized in Section 4.

2 Preprocessing

For English, German and Kazakh data, we use a simple preprocessing pipeline consisting of minor text normalization steps (such as removing some special UTF-8 characters), followed by frequent casing from the Jane toolkit (Vilar et al., 2010). We remove all the spaces in the Chinese data and applied a dictionary to convert traditional to simplified Chinese characters (including quotation marks). The Kk→En experiments also use the Moses tokenizer (Koehn et al., 2007) as an intermediate step.

In this work, we consider two variants of byte-pair encoding (BPE): (i) the original approach as proposed by Sennrich et al. (2016) (further denoted as pure BPE) and (ii) the unigram language model (ULM) approach by Kudo (2018) (further denoted as ULM-BPE). We apply the ULM implementation from Kudo and Richardson (2018) (SentencePiece) to segment words into subwords for De→En and Zh→En (Kudo, 2018). The segmentation model is trained jointly for the De→En task with a vocabulary size of 50k, and it is trained separately for the Zh→En task with a vocabulary size of 32k. For De→En, we use data from CommonCrawl, Europarl, NewsCommentary and Rapid. For Zh→En, we use 12M out of the 25M sentence pairs to train the segmentation model. When applying the ULM-BPE model, we employ a 30-best list for Chinese→English and try differ-

Proceedings of the Fourth Conference on Machine Translation (WMT), Volume 2: Shared Task Papers (Day 1) pages 349–355
Florence, Italy, August 1-2, 2019. ©2019 Association for Computational Linguistics

ent n-best sizes for German→English explained in Section 4. For Kk→En, we use joint pure BPE with 50k operations unless otherwise stated.

3 MT Systems

The final systems submitted by RWTH Aachen are based on the Transformer architecture implemented in the Sockeye sequence-to-sequence framework for neural machine translation (NMT) (Hieber et al., 2017) which is built on top of MXNet (Chen et al., 2015).

Our models resemble the 'big' architecture as presented by Vaswani et al. (2017) consisting of 6 layers in both encoder and decoder with 16 heads in all multi-head attention layers. We train our models using the Adam optimizer (Kingma and Ba, 2014) with a learning rate ranging from 0.0001 and 0.0003. We employ a learning rate scheduling scheme which scales down the learning rate if no improvement in perplexity on the development set has been observed for several consecutive evaluation checkpoints. A warmup period with constant or increasing learning rate was not used. During training we apply dropout ranging from 0.1 to 0.3. All batch sizes are specified on the token level and are chosen to be as big as the memory of the GPUs allows. In case of the utilization of multiple GPUs we use synchronized training, i.e. we increase the effective batch size. In the Kk→En scenarios, the parameters of the word embeddings and output layer projection are shared and 8 attention heads are used throughout the model.

Our fine-tuning strategy involves re-starting training with a lower learning rate on an in-domain data set, using the optimal parameters from the larger data set as initialization.

We perform experiments using the workflow manager Sisyphus (Peter et al., 2018).

4 Experimental Evaluation

In this section, we present our results on the three translation tasks in which we participated. We report case-sensitive BLEU (Papineni et al., 2002) scores as well as results on the TER (Snover et al., 2006) and CTER (Wang et al., 2016) measures. All reported scores are given in percentage and the specific options of the tools are set to be consistent with the calculations of the organizers.

Segmentation	n_best	vocab	newstest2015 (dev)		
			BLEU	TER	CTER
pure BPE	-	≈ 50k	32.1	54.2	50.2
ULM-BPE	10	20k	32.2	54.1	49.5
	10	30k	32.2	54.2	49.5
	10	50k	32.2	54.3	49.7
	30	50k	**32.6**	**52.8**	**49.2**
	120	50k	32.2	54.2	49.4
+ not joint	10	50k	31.9	54.7	49.9

Table 1: Results in percentage of our comparison of the ULM-BPE to pure BPE on the De→En task. If not stated otherwise the operations are learned jointly.

4.1 German→English

For experiments on the De→En task we use the Transformer architecture as described in Section 3 with `newstest2015` as the development set. We compare the performance of the SentencePiece implementation of the ULM-BPE to that of pure BPE. For these experiments, we train a system using the same architecture as the 'base' Transformer (see Vaswani et al. (2017)), but without tied embedding weights, on the data from Common-Crawl, Europarl, NewsCommentary and Rapid i.e. about 6M sentence pairs. We train a baseline with 50k pure joint BPE merge operations same as last year's winning system and try different vocabulary and nbest sizes for the segmentation based on a unigram language model. As can be seen in Table 1, there are only minor differences in performance. For all follow-up experiments, we use a segmentation based on the unigram language model from the SentencePiece segmenter with a vocabulary size of 50k and unigram language model with a 30-best list since it performs best with an improvement of 0.5% BLEU over the pure BPE baseline.

The main results of the De→En task are presented in Table 2. We start with a 'base' Transformer on all parallel data except the ParaCrawl resulting in a BLEU score of 32.6% on `newstest2015`.

We filter ParaCrawl based on the word-to-token ratio, average-word-length, source-target-length ratio, and source-target Levenshtein distance measures as presented in Rossenbach et al. (2018). The remaining corpus of 23M sentence pairs is scored using a count-based KenLM (Heafield, 2011) 5-gram language model on the target side and we select the top 50% as described by Schamper et al. (2018).

We train a 'big' Transformer in the En→De

direction and back-translate the deduplicated NewsCrawl 2018 monolingual corpus. This back-translation system is trained on CommonCrawl, Europarl, NewsCommentary, Rapid and on the 23M sentence pairs from the filtered version of ParaCrawl as well as on 18M synthetic sentence pairs from a back-translated NewsCrawl 2017 corpus. It achieves 31.3% BLEU and 29.9% BLEU on the En→De task on `newstest2015` and `newstest2017` respectively.

To filter out sentence pairs that were copied instead of translated by the system, we apply a filtering method based on the Levenshtein distance between source and target sentences (Rossenbach et al., 2018). This has further reduced the synthetic corpus size to 15.9M sentence pairs which are used to train our final systems.

We oversample CommonCrawl, Europarl, NewsCommentary and Rapid by a factor of 3 and end up with a corpus of roughly 47M lines (18M oversampled, 1M Wikititles, 16M synthetic, 11M ParaCrawl). Training a 'big' Transformer on this corpus leads to a performance of 36.3% BLEU on the dev set as is shown in Table 2. Finetuning on the test sets from previous years (excluding only `newstest2015` and `newstest2017`) adds another 0.9% BLEU. We train two models with this configuration and experiment with different ensembles. For our final submission we pick the 3 best checkpoints out of the 2 training runs, apply finetuning to them and use a linear ensemble of them for decoding with a beam size of 12. The final performance of the ensemble is 37.4% BLEU on the dev set and 39.6% BLEU on `newstest2019`.

4.2 Chinese→English

The original Chinese-English training set contains 25.8M sentence pairs. After applying the preprocessing steps described in Section 2, we first filter out 1.1M sentence pairs which contain a large number of illegal characters (on either side). This step is performed using a Gaussian mixture model, which uses UTF-8 blocks as feature vectors and is trained on the Chinese and English development data sets. Then we apply deduplication on both sides, which further removes around 5.8M sentence pairs. From the remaining 18.9M sentence pairs we sampled 12M sentences from each side to follow the SentencePiece approach as described in Section 2. Note that we did not use any additional

tools to pre-segement the Chinese data.

We also use the provided Chinese and English monolingual data and apply the same pre-proceesing procedure. After the filtering, the Chinese and English monolingual data sets contain 27.5M and 52.9M sentences respectively. We train LSTM-based Chinese and English language models on these monolingual data sets, as well as a big Transformer-based Chinese→English translation model on the 18.9M bilingual data set. Note that here the Chinese language model uses characters and the English language model uses sub words. The concatenation of the `newsdev2017` and `newstest2017` data sets are used as the development set for training. Then we apply the language models to score the Chinese and English training sentence pairs. The translation model is used to decode the entire training set and then we calculate the CHRF score (Popović, 2015) of each hypothesis. Then the remaining 18.9M sentence pairs are further filtered according to the language model perplexities and CHRF scores. Only sentence pairs that satisfy the following three conditions are retained:

- The CHRF score is higher than 0.55;

- The Chinese language model log-perplexity is lower than 5;

- The English language model log-perplexity is lower than 7.

Only about 13.7M parallel sentence pairs from the training data is retained after this round of filtering.

The English language model is also used to score the English monoligual data. We randomly sub-sample 10M English sentences from the filtered monolingual data for back-translation. The synthetic data is generated by a big Transformer-based En→Zh translation model trained on the 18.9M sentence pairs, i.e. before the last round of filtering.

We train the following Transformer-based translation models on the final 23.7M parallel sentences (each batch contains 4k tokens if not stated):

1. Transformer big architecture (Vaswani et al., 2017);

2. Transformer big architecture with 7 encoder and 7 decoder layers, gradient accumulation of 2 batches, which yields an effective batch size of 8k tokens;

	Systems	newstest2015 (dev)			newstest2017			newstest2019		
		BLEU	TER	CTER	BLEU	TER	CTER	BLEU	TER	CTER
1	Transformer Base	32.6	53.7	49.2	33.8	53.0	49.9	35.7	52.2	49.9
2	Transformer Big + Paracrawl + BT	36.3	50.2	45.5	38.3	48.9	45.8	37.5	50.7	46.6
3	+ fine-tuning	37.2	49.4	45.0	39.5	47.8	44.8	38.9	49.2	45.3
4	Ensemble†	37.4	49.1	44.7	39.9	47.4	44.6	39.6	48.4	44.7

Table 2: Main results for the German→English task measured in BLEU [%], TER [%] and CTER [%] †: Submitted system.

3. Transformer big architecture with gradient accumulation of 4 batches, which yields an effective batch size of 16k tokens;

4. Transformer big architecture with BLEU as metric for the learning rate reduction scheme;

5. Self-attentive encoder + LSTM decoder network (Chen et al., 2018).

All models are trained for around 14 epochs and during decoding we use a beam size of 16. As can be seen in Table 3 the first four systems show about equal performance while the LSTM decoder stays 0.4% BLEU behind the baseline on the dev set and 0.7% BLEU on `newstest2018`. Ensembling of the four strongest models provides 1.3% BLEU improvement over the baseline on the dev set.

In addition, we found that there are many long source samples in the test set. As during training we eliminate all samples which are longer than 100 subwords, our system does not perform well in the translation of longer samples. To tackle this problem, we first split all samples, which include '.', '!', '?' or ';' characters, into shorter sentences. If there are still sentences which contain more than 80 subwords, we split them on ',' once, in a way that keeps the lengths of the two separated sentences as equal as possible. This splitting brings up to 1.1% BLEU improvements on `newstest2018`. The final submitted system achieves a BLEU score of 31.7% on `newstest2019`.

4.3 Kazakh→English

We tackle the low-resource Kazakh→English task by leveraging additional mono- and bilingual data via back-translation, language modeling and transfer learning. Our main results are summarized in Table 4 and we deviate from the system described in Section 3 by using model dimensions of 512 and

internal projections 2,048, which we further denote as the base model. A larger variant is used for Systems 4-7 with a model dimension of 1,024. A batch size of 10k words or 8k subwords is used for the smaller and larger models, respectively. This is achieved by accumulating gradients over 4 smaller batches.

In total, we leverage 24M synthetic sentence pairs and over-sample all available Kk−En data to obtain a ratio of 1:4 (authentic:synthetic) for systems 2-3 and 1:2 for systems 4-7. The Kk→En data consists of 224k training samples. For the synthetic data, we make use of the Ru-En bilingual data: the Yandex and News Commentary corpora plus 10M sentences from the UN corpus. Further, the organizers supply a crawled Kk-Ru corpus, from which we remove redundant sentences by using the technique described by Rossenbach et al. (2018). Finally, 10M sentences are sub-sampled from News Crawl 2017 for back-translation. As in-domain data, we make use of the 2014-2018 Ru-En test sets of past competitions.

The Russian side of the Kk-Ru corpus is translated to English using the small model variant and 50k joint pure BPE operations. The Russian side of the Ru-En corpus is translated to Kazakh by the former setup on the crawled corpus. Back-translations are generated using a bilingual base model (System 1), i.e. that shares parameters between both translation directions, trained with 20k joint pure BPE operations. The model itself includes 4M back-translated sentences from News Crawl 2017 and is fine-tuned on the News Commentary corpus of the Kk-Ru corpus.

We also experiment with transfer learning as presented by Kim et al. (2019). In this framework, we train a Ru→En model with non-joint pure BPE vocabularies[1] on the corresponding WMT 2018 translation task. Kazakh word embeddings are then trained on all available monolingual data,

---

[1] 20k operations for Russian, 50k operations for English

	Systems	dev			newstest2018	
		BLEU	TER	CTER	BLEU	CTER
1	Transformer 'big'	25.2	65.8	60.6	25.8	63.3
2	+ 7th layer + grad-acc 2	25.4	65.6	60.2	25.8	62.7
3	+ grad-acc 4	25.5	65.0	60.0	25.9	62.6
4	+ optimize on BLEU	25.4	65.6	60.6	26.0	63.3
5	+ LSTM decoder	24.8	66.3	61.4	25.5	63.5
6	Ensemble [1,2,3,4]	26.5	64.2	58.9	26.9	61.4
7	+ Split long sentences[†]	-	-	-	**28.0**	**60.4**

Table 3: Results for Zh→En measured in BLEU [%], TER [%] and CTER [%]. The development set is the concatenation of `newsdev2017` and `newstest2017`. TER computation fails on `newstest2018`.
†: Submitted systems.

	Systems	Size	newsdev2019			newstest2019		
			BLEU	TER	CTER	BLEU	TER	CTER
1	Baseline	base	15.9	75.8	74.8	12.8	78.6	76.7
2	Transfer	base	21.6	72.8	64.1	23.6	69.0	62.5
3	+ fine-tuning		22.0	72.2	63.9	23.9	67.9	60.5
4	Scratch	large	21.5	72.9	64.8	23.2	68.9	62.7
5	+ fine-tuning		22.2	72.0	63.9	23.3	68.8	61.2
6	+ search tuning[†]		22.8	71.1	64.9	24.2	66.8	61.2
7	+ LM[†]		23.6	71.2	67.2	23.1	69.9	66.2

Table 4: Results measured in BLEU [%], TER [%] and CTER [%] for Kk→En. †: Submitted systems.

processed with 20k pure BPE operations, and are mapped to the same distribution as the Russian embeddings via an unsupervised mapping (Conneau et al., 2017). Finally, training is initialized with the replaced parameters and fine-tuned on the Kk-En task (System 2+3). We expect a bigger model to perform better on the Ru→En task and therefore transfer better to this task, but time constraints prohibited this.

Fine-tuning on the translated news test sets from the Ru→En task (System 5) improves performance by 0.7% BLEU on the development set but does not generalize to test set improvements. The length penalty and beam size hyperparameters were tuned to maximize the difference of BLEU and TER on `newsdev2019` (System 6). Finally, we experiment with adding a 5-gram modified Kneser-Ney language model (Chen and Goodman, 1999) during inference using KenLM (Heafield, 2011) (System 7). We perform a log-linear combination and re-run the optimization grid search as before with the additional language model scaling factor. This improves the development set performance but considerably decreases the test set performance. In hindsight, our experimental setup was flawed due to not having unseen test data and therefore overfitting on the development set, clearly seen by comparing Systems 6 and 7.

5 Conclusion

This paper describes the RWTH Aachen University's submission to the WMT 2019 news translation task. For all language pairs we use the Transformer architecture. Different methods for data filtering, preprocessing and synthetic data creation were tested. We experiment with different segmentation schemes, model depth, language modelling during search and transfer learning. Our De→En system performs on par with our 2018 submission and our Zh→En model shows an 1.3% BLEU improvement over our last year's submission. For the Kk→En system we gain improvements of 11.4% BLEU over a standard semi-supervised baseline resulting in a final performance of 24.2% BLEU on `newstest2019`.

Acknowledgements

This work has received funding from the European Research Council (ERC) (under the European Union's Horizon 2020 research and innovation programme, grant agreement No 694537, project "SEQCLAS") and the Deutsche Forschungsgemeinschaft (DFG; grant agreement NE 572/8-1, project "CoreTec"). The work reflects only the authors' views and none of the funding agencies is responsible for any use that may be made of the information it contains.

References

Mia Xu Chen, Orhan Firat, Ankur Bapna, Melvin Johnson, Wolfgang Macherey, George Foster, Llion Jones, Mike Schuster, Noam Shazeer, Niki Parmar, Ashish Vaswani, Jakob Uszkoreit, Lukasz Kaiser, Zhifeng Chen, Yonghui Wu, and Macduff Hughes. 2018. The best of both worlds: Combining recent advances in neural machine translation. In *Proceedings of the 56th Annual Meeting of the Association for Computational Linguistics*, pages 76–86, Melbourne, Australia.

Stanley F Chen and Joshua Goodman. 1999. An empirical study of smoothing techniques for language modeling. *Computer Speech & Language*, 13(4):359–394.

Tianqi Chen, Mu Li, Yutian Li, Min Lin, Naiyan Wang, Minjie Wang, Tianjun Xiao, Bing Xu, Chiyuan Zhang, and Zheng Zhang. 2015. MXNet: A flexible and efficient machine learning library for heterogeneous distributed systems. *arXiv preprint arXiv:1512.01274*. Version 1.

Alexis Conneau, Guillaume Lample, Marc'Aurelio Ranzato, Ludovic Denoyer, and Hervé Jégou. 2017. Word translation without parallel data. *arXiv preprint arXiv:1710.04087*.

Kenneth Heafield. 2011. KenLM: Faster and smaller language model queries. In *Proceedings of the EMNLP 2011 Sixth Workshop on Statistical Machine Translation*, pages 187–197, Edinburgh, Scotland, United Kingdom.

Felix Hieber, Tobias Domhan, Michael Denkowski, David Vilar, Artem Sokolov, Ann Clifton, and Matt Post. 2017. Sockeye: A toolkit for neural machine translation. *arXiv preprint arXiv:1712.05690*. Version 2.

Yunsu Kim, Yingbo Gao, and Hermann Ney. 2019. Effective cross-lingual transfer of neural machine translation models without shared vocabularies. In *Annual Meeting of the Assoc. for Computational Linguistics*, Florence, Italy.

Diederik P Kingma and Jimmy Ba. 2014. Adam: A method for stochastic optimization. *arXiv preprint arXiv:1412.6980*. Version 9.

Philipp Koehn, Hieu Hoang, Alexandra Birch, Chris Callison-Burch, Marcello Federico, Nicola Bertoldi, Brooke Cowan, Wade Shen, Christine Moran, Richard Zens, et al. 2007. Moses: Open source toolkit for statistical machine translation. In *Proceedings of the 45th annual meeting of the ACL on interactive poster and demonstration sessions*, pages 177–180. Association for Computational Linguistics.

Taku Kudo. 2018. Subword regularization: Improving neural network translation models with multiple subword candidates. In *Proceedings of the 56th Annual Meeting of the Association for Computational Linguistics*, pages 66–75, Melbourne, Australia.

Taku Kudo and John Richardson. 2018. Sentencepiece: A simple and language independent subword tokenizer and detokenizer for neural text processing. *arXiv preprint arXiv:1808.06226*.

Kishore Papineni, Salim Roukos, Todd Ward, and Wei-Jing Zhu. 2002. BLEU: A method for automatic evaluation of machine translation. In *Proceedings of the 41st Annual Meeting of the Association for Computational Linguistics*, pages 311–318, Philadelphia, Pennsylvania, USA.

Jan-Thorsten Peter, Eugen Beck, and Hermann Ney. 2018. Sisyphus, a workflow manager designed for machine translation and automatic speech recognition. In *Proceedings of the 2018 Conference on Empirical Methods in Natural Language Processing (EMNLP 2018)*, pages 84–89.

Maja Popović. 2015. CHRF: charactern-gram f-score for automatic mt evaluation. In *Proceedings of the Tenth Workshop on Statistical Machine Translation*, pages 392–395, Lisboa, Portugal.

Nick Rossenbach, Jan Rosendahl, Yunsu Kim, Miguel Graça, Aman Gokrani, and Hermann Ney. 2018. The rwth aachen university filtering system for the wmt 2018 parallel corpus filtering task. In *Proceedings of the Third Conference on Machine Translation: Shared Task Papers*, pages 946–954.

Julian Schamper, Jan Rosendahl, Parnia Bahar, Yunsu Kim, Arne Nix, and Hermann Ney. 2018. The rwth aachen university supervised machine translation systems for wmt 2018. In *Proceedings of the Third Conference on Machine Translation: Shared Task Papers*, pages 496–503.

Rico Sennrich, Barry Haddow, and Alexandra Birch. 2016. Neural machine translation of rare words with subword units. In *Proceedings of the 54th Annual Meeting of the Association for Computational Linguistics (Volume 1: Long Papers)*, volume 1, pages 1715–1725.

Matthew Snover, Bonnie Dorr, Richard Schwartz, Linnea Micciulla, and John Makhoul. 2006. A study of translation edit rate with targeted human annotation. In *Proceedings of the 7th Conference of the Association for Machine Translation in the Americas*, pages 223–231, Cambridge, Massachusetts, USA.

Ashish Vaswani, Noam Shazeer, Niki Parmar, Jakob Uszkoreit, Llion Jones, Aidan N Gomez, Łukasz Kaiser, and Illia Polosukhin. 2017. Attention is all you need. In *Advances in Neural Information Processing Systems*, pages 5998–6008.

David Vilar, Daniel Stein, Matthias Huck, and Hermann Ney. 2010. Jane: Open source hierarchical translation, extended with reordering and lexicon models. In *Proceedings of the Joint Fifth Workshop on Statistical Machine Translation and MetricsMATR*, pages 262–270. Association for Computational Linguistics.

Weiyue Wang, Jan-Thorsten Peter, Hendrik Rosendahl, and Hermann Ney. 2016. Character: Translation edit rate on character level. In *Proceedings of the First Conference on Machine Translation: Volume 2, Shared Task Papers*, volume 2, pages 505–510.

The Universitat d'Alacant submissions to the English-to-Kazakh news translation task at WMT 2019

Víctor M. Sánchez-Cartagena, Juan Antonio Pérez-Ortiz, Felipe Sánchez-Martínez
Departament de Llenguatges i Sistemes Informàtics
Universitat d'Alacant, Spain
`{vmsanchez, japerez, fsanchez}@dlsi.ua.es`

Abstract

This paper describes the two submissions of Universitat d'Alacant to the English-to-Kazakh news translation task at WMT 2019. Our submissions take advantage of monolingual data and parallel data from other language pairs by means of iterative backtranslation, pivot backtranslation and transfer learning. They also use linguistic information in two ways: morphological segmentation of Kazakh text, and integration of the output of a rule-based machine translation system. Our systems were ranked 2nd in terms of chrF++ despite being built from an ensemble of only 2 independent training runs.

1 Introduction

This paper describes the Universitat d'Alacant submissions to the WMT 2019 news translation task. Our two submissions address the low-resource English-to-Kazakh language pair, for which only a few thousand in-domain parallel sentences are available.

In order to build competitive neural machine translation (NMT) systems, we generated synthetic training data. We took advantage of the available English–Russian (`en-ru`) and Kazakh–Russian (`kk-ru`) parallel data by means of pivot backtranslation and transfer learning, and integrated monolingual data by means of iterative backtranslation.

In addition, we used linguistic information in two different ways: we morphologically segmented the Kazakh text to make the system generalize better from the training data; and we built a hybrid system combining NMT and the Apertium English-to-Kazakh rule-based machine translation (RBMT) system (Forcada et al., 2011; Sundetova et al., 2015).

The rest of the paper is organized as follows. Section 2 describes how corpora were filtered and preprocessed, and the steps followed to train NMT systems from them. Section 3 outlines the process

corpus	pair	raw	cleaned
News Commentary	en-kk	7.7k	7.4k
Wikititles	en-kk	117k	113k
web crawled	en-kk	97.6k	27.2k
web crawled	kk-ru	4.5M	4.4M
concatenation of WMT19 data	en-ru	31.7M	31.1M

Table 1: Number of segments in the parallel corpora used for training.

followed to obtain synthetic training data. Sections 4 and 5 describe respectively morphological segmentation and hybridization with Apertium. The model ensembles we submitted are then presented in Section 6. The paper ends with some concluding remarks.

2 Data preparation and training details

In our submissions, we only used the corpora allowed in the constrained task. Parallel corpora were cleaned with the script `clean-corpus-n.perl` shipped with Moses (Koehn et al., 2007), that removes unbalanced sentence pairs and those with at least one side longer than 80 tokens. Additional filtering steps, described below, were applied to the web crawled corpora. Tables 1 and 2 depict the number of segments in the parallel and monolingual corpora used, and their sizes after cleaning.

The English–Kazakh web crawled corpus allowed in the constrained task presented a high proportion of parallel segments that were not translation of each other. We filtered it with Bicleaner (Sánchez-Cartagena et al., 2018). We applied the *hardrules* and the detection of misaligned sentences described by Sánchez-Cartagena et al. (2018), but not the fluency filtering.[1]

---

[1] We extracted probabilistic bilingual dictionaries from the

Proceedings of the Fourth Conference on Machine Translation (WMT), Volume 2: Shared Task Papers (Day 1) pages 356–363
Florence, Italy, August 1-2, 2019. ©2019 Association for Computational Linguistics

corpus	lang.	raw	cleaned
News Crawl	kk	783k	783k
Wiki dumps	kk	1.7M	1.7M
Common Crawl	kk	10.9M	5.4M
News Crawl	en	200M	200M

Table 2: Number of segments in the monolingual corpora used for training.

The Kazakh–Russian crawled corpus was cleaned in a shallower way: we just removed those sentence pairs that contained less than 50% of alphabetic characters in either side, as we did not consider them fluent enough to be useful for NMT training. The same filtering was applied to the monolingual Kazakh Common Crawl corpus. In addition, inspired by Iranzo-Sánchez et al. (2018), we ranked its sentences by perplexity computed by a character-based 7-gram language model and discarded the half of the corpus with the highest perplexity. The language model was trained[2] on the high-quality Kazakh monolingual News Commentary corpus.

Training corpora were tokenized and truecased with the Moses scripts. Truecaser models were learned independently for each trained system from the very same training parallel corpus. Unless otherwise specified, for each trained system, words were split with 50 000 byte pair encoding (BPE; Sennrich et al., 2016c) operations learned from the concatenation of the source-language (SL) and target-language (TL) training corpora.

As described in Section 6, our submissions were ensembles of Transformer (Vaswani et al., 2017) and recurrent neural network (RNN; Bahdanau et al., 2015) NMT models trained with the Marian toolkit (Junczys-Dowmunt et al., 2018). We used the Transformer hyperparameters[3] described by Sennrich et al. (2017) and the RNN hyperparameters[4] described by Sennrich et al. (2016a). Early stopping was based on perplexity and patience was set to 5. We selected the checkpoint that obtained the highest BLEU (Papineni et al., 2002) score on

the development set.

Since the only evaluation corpus made available was `newsdev2019`, we split it in two halves, and we respectively used them as development and test set in all the training runs previous to the submission (those reported in all sections but Section 6). Throughout the paper, we report BLEU (Papineni et al., 2002) and chrF++ (Popović, 2017) scores.[5] The latter is known to correlate better than BLEU with human judgements when the TL is highly inflected (Bojar et al., 2017), as is the case. Where reported, we assess whether differences between systems' outputs are statistically significant for $p < 0.05$ with 1 000 iterations of paired bootstrap resampling (Koehn, 2004).

3 Data augmentation

This section describes the process followed to select the best strategy to take advantage of parallel corpora from other language pairs (Section 3.1) and monolingual corpora (Section 3.2).

3.1 Data from other language pairs

In order to take advantage of the parallel corpora listed in Table 1 for other language pairs, we applied the transfer learning approach proposed by Kocmi and Bojar (2018). We experimented with the *parent* models listed next (models trained on other high-resource language pairs) and used the concatenation of the genuine English–Kazakh parallel data as the *child* corpus (corpus of a low-resource language pair used to continue training a parent model):[6]

- A Russian-to-Kazakh model trained on the crawled parallel corpus depicted in Table 1.

- An English-to-Russian model trained on all the available parallel data for the English–Russian language pair in this year's news translation task (depicted in Table 1).

- A multilingual system (Johnson et al., 2017) trained on the concatenation of the corpora of the two previous models. This strategy aims at making the most of the data available for related language pairs.

We also explored pivot backtranslation (Huck and Ney, 2012): we translated the Russian side of the crawled Kazakh–Russian parallel corpus with

---

Wikititles parallel corpus and extracted the positive and negative training examples from News Commentary. We kept those sentences with a classifier score above 0.6.

[2] The language model was trained with KenLM (Heafield, 2011) with modified Kneser-Ney smoothing (Ney et al., 1994).

[3] `https://github.com/marian-nmt/marian-examples/tree/master/wmt2017-transformer`

[4] `https://github.com/marian-nmt/marian-examples/tree/master/training-basics`

[5] Following Popović (2017), we set β to 2.

[6] In the 3 set-ups evaluated, BPE models were trained from the concatenation of the parent and the child corpora.

a Russian-to-English NMT system to produce a synthetic English–Kazakh parallel corpus. The NMT system was a Transformer trained on the English–Russian parallel data depicted in Table 1. We concatenated the pivot-backtranslated corpus to the genuine English–Kazakh parallel data and fine-tuned the resulting system only on the latter.

The results of the evaluation of these strategies, reported in the upper part of Table 3, show that the multilingual/transfer learning strategy outperforms the pure transfer learning approaches, probably because it takes advantage of more resources. Moreover, it performs similarly to pivot backtranslation, which we chose for our submission. All the strategies evaluated clearly outperformed the system trained only on the genuine parallel data.

As a Kazakh-to-English MT system is needed to backtranslate the Kazakh monolingual data (see Section 3.2), we also explored the best strategy for taking advantage of data from other language pairs for that direction. We experimented only with transfer learning and discarded pivot backtranslation since we wanted to avoid training a system on a parallel corpus with a synthetic TL side.

We evaluated the same parent-child configurations as in the English-to-Kazakh experiments, but we inverted their direction to ensure that either the SL of the parent corpora is Kazakh or the TL is English. Results are reported in the lower part of Table 3 and show that, as in the opposite direction, transfer learning brings a clear improvement over training only on the genuine parallel data, and the best parent model is the multilingual one.

3.2 Monolingual data: iterative backtranslation

Backtranslation (Sennrich et al., 2016b) is a widespread method for integrating TL monolingual corpora into NMT systems. In order to integrate the available Kazakh monolingual data into our submission, we need a Kazakh-to-English MT system as competitive as possible, since the quality of a system trained on backtranslated data is usually correlated with the quality of the system that perform the backtranslation (Hoang et al., 2018, Sec. 3). We followed the iterative backtranslation algorithm (Hoang et al., 2018) outlined below with the aim of obtaining strong English-to-Kazakh and Kazakh-to-English systems using monolingual English and monolingual Kazakh corpora:

1. The best strategies from Section 3.1 were applied to build systems in both directions without backtranslated monolingual data.

2. English and Kazakh monolingual data were backtranslated with the previous systems.

3. Systems in both directions were trained on the combination of the backtranslated data and the parallel data.

4. Steps 2–3 were re-executed 2 more times. Backtranslation in step 2 was always carried out with the systems built in the most recent execution of step 3.

The Kazakh monolingual corpus used was the concatenation of the corpora listed in Table 2, while the English monolingual corpus was a subset of the News Crawl corpus in the same table. The size of the subset was duplicated after each backtranslation and started at 5 million sentences in the first one. The objective of the first 2 executions of steps 2–3 (from now on, *iterations*) was building a strong Kazakh-to-English system. The remainder of this section explains how MT systems were trained in these 2 iterations. The objective of the 3rd iteration, in which only English-to-Kazakh systems were trained, was building the submissions, and the corresponding details are described in Section 6.

We explored different ways of training NMT systems with backtranslated data. First, we carried out transfer learning from the multilingual models described in Section 3.1. In this case, the child model was trained on a parallel corpus built from the concatenation of the genuine parallel data and the backtranslated data. The genuine parallel data was oversampled to match the size of the backtranslated data (Chu et al., 2017).

As an alternative to transfer learning, we experimented with corpus concatenation and fine-tuning. For the English-to-Kazakh direction, we concatenated the backtranslated data to the pivot-backtranslated corpus and the genuine parallel corpora, trained a model from scratch, and fine-tuned it only on the genuine parallel data. For the opposite direction, we trained a system only on the concatenation of the backtranslated and the genuine parallel data, and fine-tuned it on the latter (note that in this set-up we dispensed with parallel data from other language pairs).

Table 4 shows the automatic evaluation scores obtained in the 1st iteration by the strategies being evaluated. Only the best performing strategies in the 1st iteration were used in the subsequent ones; the scores obtained on the 2nd iteration are also depicted. The results show the positive impact of the introduction of backtranslated data in both directions. Concatenation plus fine-tuning outperformed

strategy	BLEU	chrF++
en→kk		
only parallel en→kk	4.36	27.80
transfer from ru→kk	10.22	39.93
transfer from en→ru	9.66	39.67
transfer from en→ru,ru→kk	11.81	42.87
pivot backtranslation	11.80	42.86
kk→en		
only parallel kk→en	8.15	30.43
transfer from kk→ru	17.03	42.90
transfer from ru→en	15.77	41.33
transfer from ru→en,kk→ru	20.58	46.24

Table 3: Results obtained by the different strategies evaluated for combining the available parallel corpora.

strategy	it.	BLEU	chrF++
en→kk			
transfer learning	0	11.80	42.86
transfer learning	1	12.63	44.46
concatenate + fine-tune	1	13.46	44.99
concatenate + fine-tune	2	13.79	45.24
kk→en			
transfer learning	0	20.58	46.24
transfer learning	1	21.58	47.65
concatenate + fine-tune	1	22.66	48.91
concatenate + fine-tune	2	23.28	49.45

Table 4: Results obtained by the different strategies evaluated for combining parallel corpora and the back-translated data.

transfer learning in both directions. This result is surprising for Kazakh-to-English, where the transfer learning strategy makes use of more resources. One possible explanation could be that, with concatenation plus fine-tuning, the system is trained mostly on data from the news domain, as the English monolingual data is extracted only from News Crawl. Finally, the repetition of steps 2–3 helped to further improve translation quality.

4 Morphological segmentation

Morphological segmentation is a strategy for segmeting words into sub-word units that consists in splitting them into a *stem*, that carries out the meaning of the word, and a *suffix* or sequence of suffixes that contain morphological and syntatic information. When that strategy has been followed to segment the training corpus for an NMT system, it has been reported to outperform BPE for highly inflected languages such as Finnish (Sánchez-Cartagena and Toral, 2016), German (Huck et al., 2017) or Basque (Sánchez-Cartagena, 2018).

In our submissions, we morphologically segmented the Kazakh text with the Apertium Kazakh morphological analyzer.[7] For each word, the analyzer provides a set of candidate analyses made of a lemma and morphological information. Those analyses in which the lemma is a prefix of the word are considered valid analyses for segmentation and involve that the word can be morphologically segmented into the lemma and the remainder of the word.[8] When there are multiple valid analyses for a word, they are disambiguated as explained below. When a word has no valid analyses for segmentation, we generate as many segmentation candidates as known suffixes match the word (plus the empty suffix, since a possible option could be no segmenting at all). Known suffixes are extracted in advance from those words with a single valid analysis.

Multiple segmentation candidates (either coming from multiple valid analyses or from suffix matching) are disambiguated by means of the strategy described by Sánchez-Cartagena (2018), which relies on the semi-supervised morphology learning method Morfessor (Virpioja et al., 2013). We trained the Morfessor model on all the available Kazakh corpora listed in Tables 1 and 2. Finally, as suggested by Huck et al. (2017), we applied BPE splitting with a model learned on the concatenation of all training corpora after performing the morphological segmentation.

Table 5 depicts some examples of Kazakh words, their analyses and their morphological segmentation. The first word is the genitive form of университет (*university*). The morphological segmentation allows the NMT system to generalize to other inflected forms of the same word, while BPE does not split it because it is a rather frequent term in the corpus. The second word is an inflected form of the verb жаса (*to do*), although it is also analyzed as a inflected form of жасал due to an error in the analyzer. The Morfessor model preferred the wrong analysis, but the plain BPE segmentation made translation even more difficult for the MT system by choosing the prefix жас, which means *young*. BPE introduced more ambiguity, as the token жас can encode both the verb *to do* and the adjective *young*.

---

[7] `https://github.com/apertium/apertium-eng-kaz`

[8] We can safely apply this strategy because in Kazakh the stem usually corresponds to the lemma.

word	analyses	morph. seg.	plain BPE
университетінің	университет- n.px3sp.gen	университет@@ інің	университетінің
жасалмайды	жаса-v.tp.n.p3 жасал-v.i.n.p3*	жасал@@ майды	жас@@ алмайды

Table 5: Examples of Kazakh words, their morphological analyses, and their segmentation.

system	BLEU	chrF++
RNN	10.13	40.54
hybrid RNN	10.53	**41.03**
Transformer	11.71	42.65
hybrid Transformer	11.20	42.23
Apertium	1.59	26.60

Table 6: Results obtained by the different strategies evaluated for integrating the Apertium English-to-Kazakh rule-based machine translation system into an NMT system. Scores of hybrid systems are shown in bold if they outperform the corresponding pure NMT system by a statistically significant margin.

5 Hybridization with rule-based machine translation

The Apertium platform contains an English-to-Kazakh RBMT system (Sundetova et al., 2015) that may encode knowledge that is not present in the corpora available in the constrained task. In order to take advantage of that knowledge, we built a hybrid system by means of multi-source machine translation (Zoph and Knight, 2016). Our hybrid system is a multi-source NMT system with two inputs: the English sentence to be translated, and its translation into Kazakh provided by Apertium. This very same set-up has been successfully followed in the WMT automated post-editing task (Junczys-Dowmunt and Grundkiewicz, 2018).

In order to assess the viability of this approach, we trained and automatically evaluated multi-source and single-source English-to-Kazakh systems on the concatenation of the genuine English–Kazakh parallel corpora and the backtranslation of the Kazakh monolingual corpora News Crawl and Wiki dumps.[9]

Results, depicted in Table 6, show that the multi-source system is able to outperform the single-source one only with the RNN architecture (the difference is statistically significant for chrF++). Apertium output seems to be of very low quality

according to the scores reported in the table.[10] Despite that, the multi-source RNN is able to extract useful information from it. The poor performance of the multi-source Transformer architecture could be related to the low quality of the Apertium output. In order to prevent that the errors in the Apertium translation are propagated to the output, the decoder should focus mostly on the SL input. However, according to the analysis of attention carried out by Libovický et al. (2018), in the serial multi-source architecture of Marian the output seems to be built with information from all inputs. We plan to explore more multi-source architectures in the future. Due to the poor performance of the Transformer multi-source architecture, we used only the multi-source RNN in our submission, as explained in the next section.

6 Final submissions

We submitted a constrained and an unconstrained ensemble for the English-to-Kazakh direction. This section describes how the individual models of the ensembles were trained and selected, and presents the results of an automatic evaluation.

Training details. All the ensembled models were trained on the genuine parallel corpora, the pivot-backtranslated corpus, and the backtranslated corpus obtained in the 3rd iteration, in a similar way to what has been described in Section 3.2. Preprocessing steps and training parameters were those described in Section 2, with the following exceptions: we applied morphological segmentation to the Kazakh text as described in Section 4, we used the full `newsdev2019` as the development corpus, and we oversampled the News Commentary parallel corpus for fine-tuning to match the size of the concatenation of all the other genuine English–Kazakh parallel corpora.

Ensemble building. Our constrained submission was an ensemble of 2 transformer models and 2 RNN models. For each architecture, the 2 models

---

[9] We backtranslated with the best system from Section 3.1.

[10] Sundetova et al. (2015) state that the system is only able to translate simple sentences and questions.

were checkpoints from the same training run, thus our submission only contained models from 2 independent training runs. In both cases, the first model in the ensemble was the last saved checkpoint of the main training run (that was carried out on the concatenation of all the corpora), after being fine-tuned on the genuine parallel corpora. The second model in the ensemble was the checkpoint of the main training run which, after being fine-tuned on the genuine parallel corpora and ensembled with the first model, maximized chrF++ on the development set. We gave the Transformer and RNN models different weights on the final ensemble, which were also optimized on the development set. Our unconstrained submission was created in a similar way, but the two RNN models were multi-source models such as those described in Section 5. Additionally, we built an ensemble of 5 independently trained Transformer models that could not be submitted due to time constraints.

Automatic evaluation. Table 7 shows the values of the BLEU and chrF++ automatic evaluation metrics obtained by our systems on the `newstest2019` test set. In order to assess the impact of the enhancements applied, we also show scores for single models, and for alternatives without morphological segmentation and without the additional RBMT input. We can observe that morphological segmentation slightly improves the results. In line with the results in Section 5, adding the additional Apertium input to a single model also brings an improvement according to both evaluation metrics. However, that gain vanishes when we compare the ensembles, probably because the scores obtained by the RNN models are far below those obtained by the Transformer models. Moreover, the ensemble of 5 independently trained Transformers outperforms our submitted systems, which were ensembles of only 2 independent training runs.

Comparison with other teams. Table 7 also depicts the scores obtained by the top 3 constrained systems submitted by other teams with the highest chrF++. In comparison with them, our constrained submission is ranked in 2nd position in terms of chrF++ and 3rd in terms of BLEU. Our ensemble of 5 Transformer models, built after the submission deadline, reaches the 1st position in terms of chrF++. There are no statistically significant differences for any of the evaluation metrics between our 5-Transformer ensemble and the best performing contestant.

system	BLEU	chrF++
single Transformer	9.25	39.48
+ morph. seg.	9.57	39.76
single RNN + morph. seg.	8.43	37.24
+ Apertium	8.68	37.99
constrained submission	9.97	40.28
unconstrained submission	9.90	40.31
ensemble 5 Transformer	10.65	41.00
`NEU`	11.11	40.78
`CUNI-T2T-transfer-enkk`	8.70	39.30
`rug_enkk_bpe`	10.30	37.65

Table 7: Results obtained by our submissions, single-model alternatives, and systems submitted by other teams, computed on `newstest2019`. There are no statistically significant differences for any of the evaluation metrics between our 5-Transformer ensemble and the `NEU` submission.

7 Concluding remarks

We have presented the Universitat d'Alacant submissions to the WMT 2019 news translation shared task for the English-to-Kazakh language pair. As it is a low-resource pair, we took advantage of parallel corpora from other language pairs via pivot backtranslation and transfer learning. We also iteratively backtranslated monolingual data and made the most of the noisy, crawled corpora after filtering it with automatic classifiers and language models. We morphologically segmented Kazakh text to improve the generalization capacity of the NMT system and successfully used multi-source machine translation to build a hybrid system that integrates the Apertium RBMT English-Kazakh RBMT engine. Our constrained submission was ranked 2nd in terms of chrF++.

We plan to continue exploring the hybridization of NMT and RBMT. More multi-source Transformer architectures need to be evaluated to better fit the nature of the RBMT input. Another research line involves using RBMT to generate synthetic training data.

Acknowledgments

We would like to thank Mikel L. Forcada for its contribution to the morphological segmentation algorithm, and Barry Haddow for the advice on iterative backtranslation. This work has been funded by European Union's Horizon 2020 research and innovation programme under grant agreement No 825299 (GoURMET project).

References

Dzmitry Bahdanau, Kyunghyun Cho, and Yoshua Bengio. 2015. Neural Machine Translation by Jointly Learning to Align and Translate. In *Proceedings of ICLR 2015*, San Diego, CA, USA.

Ondřej Bojar, Yvette Graham, and Amir Kamran. 2017. Results of the WMT17 Metrics Shared Task. In *Proceedings of the Second Conference on Machine Translation, Volume 2: Shared Task Papers*, pages 489–513, Copenhagen, Denmark. Association for Computational Linguistics.

Chenhui Chu, Raj Dabre, and Sadao Kurohashi. 2017. An empirical comparison of domain adaptation methods for neural machine translation. In *Proceedings of the 55th Annual Meeting of the Association for Computational Linguistics (Volume 2: Short Papers)*, pages 385–391.

Mikel L Forcada, Mireia Ginestí-Rosell, Jacob Nordfalk, Jim O'Regan, Sergio Ortiz-Rojas, Juan Antonio Pérez-Ortiz, Felipe Sánchez-Martínez, Gema Ramírez-Sánchez, and Francis M Tyers. 2011. Apertium: a free/open-source platform for rule-based machine translation. *Machine translation*, 25(2):127–144.

Kenneth Heafield. 2011. KenLM: faster and smaller language model queries. In *Proceedings of the EMNLP 2011 Sixth Workshop on Statistical Machine Translation*, pages 187–197, Edinburgh, Scotland, United Kingdom.

Vu Cong Duy Hoang, Philipp Koehn, Gholamreza Haffari, and Trevor Cohn. 2018. Iterative backtranslation for neural machine translation. In *Proceedings of the 2nd Workshop on Neural Machine Translation and Generation*, pages 18–24, Melbourne, Australia. Association for Computational Linguistics.

Matthias Huck and Hermann Ney. 2012. Pivot lightly-supervised training for statistical machine translation. In *Proc. 10th Conf. of the Association for Machine Translation in the Americas*, pages 50–57.

Matthias Huck, Simon Riess, and Alexander Fraser. 2017. Target-side word segmentation strategies for neural machine translation. In *Proceedings of the Second Conference on Machine Translation*, pages 56–67.

Javier Iranzo-Sánchez, Pau Baquero-Arnal, Gonçal V. Garcés Díaz-Munío, Adrià Martínez-Villaronga, Jorge Civera, and Alfons Juan. 2018. The MLLP-UPV German-English machine translation system for WMT18. In *Proceedings of the Third Conference on Machine Translation, Volume 2: Shared Task Papers*, pages 422–428, Belgium, Brussels. Association for Computational Linguistics.

Melvin Johnson, Mike Schuster, Quoc V Le, Maxim Krikun, Yonghui Wu, Zhifeng Chen, Nikhil Thorat, Fernanda Viégas, Martin Wattenberg, Greg Corrado, et al. 2017. Google's multilingual neural machine translation system: Enabling zero-shot translation. *Transactions of the Association for Computational Linguistics*, 5:339–351.

Marcin Junczys-Dowmunt and Roman Grundkiewicz. 2018. MS-UEdin submission to the WMT2018 APE shared task: Dual-source transformer for automatic post-editing. In *Proceedings of the Third Conference on Machine Translation: Shared Task Papers*, pages 822–826, Belgium, Brussels. Association for Computational Linguistics.

Marcin Junczys-Dowmunt, Roman Grundkiewicz, Tomasz Dwojak, Hieu Hoang, Kenneth Heafield, Tom Neckermann, Frank Seide, Ulrich Germann, Alham Fikri Aji, Nikolay Bogoychev, André F. T. Martins, and Alexandra Birch. 2018. Marian: Fast neural machine translation in C++. In *Proceedings of ACL 2018, System Demonstrations*, pages 116–121, Melbourne, Australia. Association for Computational Linguistics.

Tom Kocmi and Ondřej Bojar. 2018. Trivial transfer learning for low-resource neural machine translation. In *Proceedings of the Third Conference on Machine Translation, Volume 1: Research Papers*, pages 244–252, Belgium, Brussels. Association for Computational Linguistics.

Philipp Koehn. 2004. Statistical significance tests for machine translation evaluation. In *Proceedings of the 2004 conference on empirical methods in natural language processing*.

Philipp Koehn, Hieu Hoang, Alexandra Birch, Chris Callison-Burch, Marcello Federico, Nicola Bertoldi, Brooke Cowan, Wade Shen, Christine Moran, Richard Zens, et al. 2007. Moses: Open source toolkit for statistical machine translation. In *Proceedings of the 45th annual meeting of the association for computational linguistics companion volume proceedings of the demo and poster sessions*, pages 177–180.

Jindřich Libovický, Jindřich Helcl, and David Mareček. 2018. Input combination strategies for multi-source transformer decoder. In *Proceedings of the Third Conference on Machine Translation: Research Papers*, pages 253–260.

Hermann Ney, Ute Essen, and Reinhard Kneser. 1994. On structuring probabilistic dependences in stochastic language modelling. *Computer Speech & Language*, 8(1):1 – 38.

Kishore Papineni, Salim Roukos, Todd Ward, and Wei-Jing Zhu. 2002. BLEU: a method for automatic evaluation of machine translation. In *Proceedings of the 40th annual meeting on association for computational linguistics*, pages 311–318. Association for Computational Linguistics.

Maja Popović. 2017. chrF++: words helping character n-grams. In *Proceedings of the second conference on machine translation*, pages 612–618.

Víctor M Sánchez-Cartagena. 2018. Prompsit's Submission to the IWSLT 2018 Low Resource Machine Translation Task. In *Proceedings of the 15th International Workshop on Spoken Language Translation*.

Víctor M. Sánchez-Cartagena, Marta Bañón, Sergio Ortiz-Rojas, and Gema Ramírez-Sánchez. 2018. Prompsit's submission to wmt 2018 parallel corpus filtering shared task. In *Proceedings of the Third Conference on Machine Translation, Volume 2: Shared Task Papers*, Brussels, Belgium. Association for Computational Linguistics.

Víctor M Sánchez-Cartagena and Antonio Toral. 2016. Abu-matran at WMT 2016 translation task: Deep learning, morphological segmentation and tuning on character sequences. In *Proceedings of the First Conference on Machine Translation: Volume 2, Shared Task Papers*, volume 2, pages 362–370.

Rico Sennrich, Alexandra Birch, Anna Currey, Ulrich Germann, Barry Haddow, Kenneth Heafield, Antonio Valerio Miceli Barone, and Philip Williams. 2017. The University of Edinburgh's Neural MT Systems for WMT17. In *Proceedings of the Second Conference on Machine Translation, Volume 2: Shared Task Papers*, pages 389–399, Copenhagen, Denmark. Association for Computational Linguistics.

Rico Sennrich, Barry Haddow, and Alexandra Birch. 2016a. Edinburgh Neural Machine Translation Systems for WMT 16. In *Proceedings of the First Conference on Machine Translation*, pages 371–376, Berlin, Germany. Association for Computational Linguistics.

Rico Sennrich, Barry Haddow, and Alexandra Birch. 2016b. Improving neural machine translation models with monolingual data. In *Proceedings of the 54th Annual Meeting of the Association for Computational Linguistics (Volume 1: Long Papers)*, volume 1, pages 86–96.

Rico Sennrich, Barry Haddow, and Alexandra Birch. 2016c. Neural machine translation of rare words with subword units. In *Proceedings of the 54th Annual Meeting of the Association for Computational Linguistics (Volume 1: Long Papers)*, volume 1, pages 1715–1725.

Aida Sundetova, Mikel Forcada, and Francis Tyers. 2015. A free/open-source machine translation system for English to Kazakh. In *Proceedings of the International Conference Turkic Languages Processing (Turk-Lang 2015)*, pages 78–90, Kazan, Tatarstan, Russia.

Ashish Vaswani, Noam Shazeer, Niki Parmar, Jakob Uszkoreit, Llion Jones, Aidan N Gomez, Łukasz Kaiser, and Illia Polosukhin. 2017. Attention is all you need. In *Advances in neural information processing systems*, pages 5998–6008.

Sami Virpioja, Peter Smit, Stig-Arne Grönroos, and Mikko Kurimo. 2013. Morfessor 2.0: Python implementation and extensions for morfessor baseline. D4 julkaistu kehittämis- tai tutkimusraportti tai -selvitys.

Barret Zoph and Kevin Knight. 2016. Multi-source neural translation. In *Proceedings of the 2016 Conference of the North American Chapter of the Association for Computational Linguistics: Human Language Technologies*, pages 30–34.

CUED@WMT19:EWC&LMs

Felix Stahlberg[†] and **Danielle Saunders**[†] and **Adrià de Gispert**[‡] and **Bill Byrne**[†‡]

[†]Department of Engineering, University of Cambridge, UK
[‡]SDL Research, Cambridge, UK

{fs439, ds636, wjb31}@cam.ac.uk, {agispert, bbyrne}@sdl.com

Abstract

Two techniques provide the fabric of the Cambridge University Engineering Department's (**CUED**) entry to the **WMT19** evaluation campaign: elastic weight consolidation (**EWC**) and different forms of language modelling (**LMs**). We report substantial gains by fine-tuning very strong baselines on former WMT test sets using a combination of checkpoint averaging and EWC. A sentence-level Transformer LM and a document-level LM based on a modified Transformer architecture yield further gains. As in previous years, we also extract n-gram probabilities from SMT lattices which can be seen as a source-conditioned n-gram LM.

1 Introduction

Both fine-tuning and language modelling are techniques widely used for NMT. Fine-tuning is often used to adapt a model to a new domain (Luong and Manning, 2015), while ensembling neural machine translation (NMT) with neural language models (LMs) is an effective way to leverage monolingual data (Gulcehre et al., 2015, 2017; Stahlberg et al., 2018a). Our submission to the WMT19 news shared task relies on ideas from these two lines of research, but applies and combines them in novel ways. Our contributions are:

- Elastic weight consolidation (Kirkpatrick et al., 2017, EWC) is a domain adaptation technique that aims to avoid degradation in performance on the original domain. We report large gains from fine-tuning our models on former English-German WMT test sets with EWC. We find that combining fine-tuning with checkpoint averaging (Junczys-Dowmunt et al., 2016b,a) yields further significant gains. Fine-tuning is less effective for German-English.

- Inspired by the shallow fusion technique by Gulcehre et al. (2015, 2017) we ensemble our neural translation models with neural language models. While this technique is effective for single models, the gains are diminishing under NMT ensembles trained with large amounts of back-translated sentences.

- To incorporate document-level context in a light-weight fashion, we propose a modification to the Transformer (Vaswani et al., 2017) that has separate attention layers for inter- and intra-sentential context. We report large perplexity reductions compared to sentence-level LMs under the new architecture. Our document-level LM yields small BLEU gains on top of strong NMT ensembles, and we hope to benefit even more from it in document-level human evaluation.

- Even though the performance gap between NMT and traditional statistical machine translation (SMT) is growing rapidly on the task at hand, SMT can still improve very strong NMT ensembles. To combine NMT and SMT we follow Stahlberg et al. (2017a, 2018b) and build a specialized n-gram LM for each sentence that computes the risk of hypotheses relative to SMT lattices.

- While data filtering was central in last year's evaluation (Koehn et al., 2018b; Junczys-Dowmunt, 2018b), in our experiments this year we found that a very simple filtering approach based on a small number of crude heuristics can perform as well as dual conditional cross-entropy filtering (Junczys-Dowmunt, 2018a,b).

- We confirm the effectiveness of source-side noise for scaling up back-translation as proposed by Edunov et al. (2018).

Proceedings of the Fourth Conference on Machine Translation (WMT), Volume 2: Shared Task Papers (Day 1) pages 364–373
Florence, Italy, August 1-2, 2019. ©2019 Association for Computational Linguistics

2   Document-level Language Modelling

MT systems usually translate sentences in isolation. However, there is evidence that humans also take context into account, and judge translations from humans with access to the full document higher than the output of a state-of-the-art sentence-level machine translation system (Läubli et al., 2018). Common examples of ambiguity which can be resolved with cross-sentence context are pronoun agreement or consistency in lexical choice. This year's WMT competition encouraged submissions of translation systems that are sensitive to cross-sentence context. We explored the use of document-level language models to enhance a sentence-level translation system. We argue that this is a particularly light-weight way of incorporating document-level context. First, the LM can be trained independently on monolingual target language documents, i.e. no parallel or source language documents are needed. Second, since our document-level decoder operates on the n-best lists from a sentence-level translation system, existing translation infrastructure does not have to be changed – we just add another (document-level) decoding pass. On a practical note, this means that, by skipping the second decoding pass, our system would work well even for the translation of isolated sentences when no document context is available.

Our document-level LMs are trained on the concatenations of all sentences in target language documents, separated by special sentence boundary tokens. Training a standard Transformer LM (Vaswani et al., 2017) on this data already yields significant reductions in perplexity compared to sentence-level LMs. However, the attention layers have to capture two kinds of dependencies – the long-range cross-sentence context and the short-range context within the sentence. Our modified Intra-Inter Transformer architecture (Fig. 1) splits these two responsibilities into two separate layers using masking. The "Intra-Sentential Attention" layer only allows to attend to the previous tokens in the current sentence, i.e. the intra-sentential attention mask activates the tokens between the most recent sentence boundary marker and the current symbol. The "Inter-Sentential Attention" layer is restricted to the tokens in all previous *complete* sentences, i.e. the mask enables all tokens from the document beginning to the most recent sentence boundary

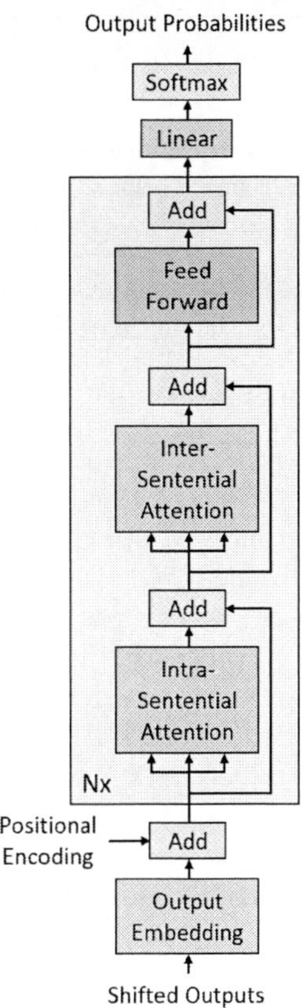

Figure 1: Our modified Intra-Inter Transformer architecture with two separate attention layers.

marker. As usual (Vaswani et al., 2017), during training the attention masks are also designed to prevent attending to future tokens. Fig. 2 shows an example of the different masks. Note that as illustrated in Fig. 1, both attention layers are part of the same layer stack which allows a tight integration of both types of context. An implication of this design is that they also use the same positional embedding – the positional encoding for the first unmasked item for intra-sentential attention may not be zero. For example, 'Lonely' has the position 10 in Fig. 2 although it is the first word in the current sentence.

We use our document-level LMs to rerank n-best lists from a sentence-level translation system. Our initial document is the first-best sentence hypotheses. We greedily replace individual sentences with lower-ranked hypotheses (according to the translation score) to drive up a combination of translation and document LM scores. We start with the sentence with the minimum difference between the first- and second-best translation scores.

	Vinyl	destination	:	who	is	actually	buying	records	?	< /s >	Lonely	,	middle-aged	men	love	'???'
Position	0	1	2	3	4	5	6	7	8	9	10	11	12	13	14	15
Intra-sentential	0	0	0	0	0	0	0	0	0	0	1	1	1	1	1	-
Inter-sentential	1	1	1	1	1	1	1	1	1	1	0	0	0	0	0	-

Figure 2: Intra-sentential and inter-sentential attention masks for an English example from `news-test2017`. Document-level context helps to predict the next word ('vinyl').

We stop when the translation score difference to the first-best translation exceeds a threshold.[1]

3 Experimental Setup

Our experimental setup is essentially the same as last year (Stahlberg et al., 2018b): Our preprocessing includes Moses tokenization, punctuation normalization, truecasing, and joint subword segmentation using byte pair encoding (Sennrich et al., 2016c) with 32K merge operations. We compute cased BLEU scores with `mteval-v13a.pl` that are directly comparable with the official WMT scores.[2] Our models are trained with the TensorFlow (Abadi et al., 2016) based Tensor2Tensor (Vaswani et al., 2018) library and decoded with our SGNMT framework (Stahlberg et al., 2017b, 2018c). We delay SGD updates (Saunders et al., 2018) to use larger training batch sizes than our technical infrastructure[3] would normally allow with vanilla SGD by using the `MultistepAdam` optimizer in Tensor2Tensor. We use Transformer (Vaswani et al., 2017) models in two configurations (Tab. 1). Preliminary experiments are carried out with the 'Base' configuration while we use the 'Big' models for our final system. We use `news-test2017` as development set to tune model weights and select checkpoints and `news-test2018` as test set.

3.1 ParaCrawl Corpus Filtering

Junczys-Dowmunt (2018a,b) reported large gains from filtering the ParaCrawl corpus. This year, the WMT organizers made version 3 of the ParaCrawl corpus available. We compared two different filtering approaches on the new data set. First, we implemented dual cross-entropy filtering (Junczys-Dowmunt, 2018a,b), a sophisticated data selection criterion based on neural

	Base	**Big**
T2T HParams set	`trans._base`	`trans._big`
# physical GPUs	4	4
Batch size	4,192	2,048
SGD delay factor	2	4
# training iterations	300K	1M
Beam size	4	8

Table 1: Transformer setups.

language model and neural machine translation model scores in both translation directions. In addition, we used the "naive" filtering heuristics proposed by Stahlberg et al. (2018b):

- Language detection (Nakatani, 2010) in both source and target language.

- No words contain more than 40 characters.

- Sentences must not contain HTML tags.

- The minimum sentence length is 4 words.

- The character ratio between source and target must not exceed 1:3 or 3:1.

- Source and target sentences must be equal after stripping out non-numerical characters.

- Sentences must end with punctuation marks.

Tab. 2 indicates that our systems benefit from ParaCrawl even without filtering (rows 1 vs. 2). Our best 'Base' model uses both dual and naive filtering. However, the difference between filtering techniques diminishes under stronger 'Big' models with back-translation (rows 6 and 7).

4 Results

4.1 Back-translation

Back-translation (Sennrich et al., 2016b) is a well-established technique to use monolingual target language data for NMT. The idea is to automatically generate translations into the source language with an inverse translation model, and add these synthetic sentence pairs to the training data. A major limitation of vanilla back-translation is that the amount of synthetic data

---

[1]Tensor2Tensor implementation: `https://github.com/fstahlberg/ucam-scripts/blob/master/t2t/t2t_refine_with_glue_lm.py`

[2]`http://matrix.statmt.org/`

[3]The Cambridge HPC service (`http://www.hpc.cam.ac.uk/`) allows parallel training on up to four physical P100 GPUs.

	Model	ParaCrawl	Naive filtering	BLEU			
				test15	test16	test17	test18
1	Base	No		29.3	34.1	27.8	41.9
2	Base	Full		30.0	35.3	28.2	43.1
3	Base	Full	✓	30.3	35.6	28.6	43.5
4	Base	Dual x-ent filtering		30.2	35.5	28.7	43.6
5	Base	Dual x-ent filtering	✓	30.6	35.7	28.8	43.8
6	Big (with back-translation)	Full	✓	32.4	38.5	31.2	46.6
7	Big (with back-translation)	Dual x-ent filtering	✓	32.7	38.1	31.1	46.6

Table 2: Comparison of ParaCrawl filtering techniques. The rest of the training data is over-sampled to roughly match the size of the filtered ParaCrawl corpus. In the 'Dual x-ent filtering' experiments we selected the 15M best sentences according the dual cross-entropy filtering criterion of Junczys-Dowmunt (2018a).

	news-2016 (35M sentences)	news-2017 (20M sentences)	news-2018 (37M sentences)	Noise	BLEU			
					test15	test16	test17	test18
1					30.2	35.7	28.7	43.8
2		✓			30.8	36.2	29.8	44.3
3			✓		30.4	35.8	29.4	43.2
4		✓	✓		30.3	35.9	29.5	43.1
5		✓		✓	31.0	36.6	29.7	44.8
6			✓	✓	30.7	36.6	29.5	44.7
7		✓	✓	✓	30.6	36.6	29.5	44.4
8	✓	✓	✓	✓	31.3	37.4	30.0	45.2
9	✓	✓	✓	✓	31.3	37.3	30.3	45.2

Table 3: Using different corpora for back-translation. We back-translated with a 'base' model for `news-2017` and the big single Transformer model of Stahlberg et al. (2018b) for `news-2016` and `news-2018`.

	Fine-tuning	Checkpoint averaging	BLEU (test18)	
			En-De	De-En
1	No		46.7	46.5
2	No	✓	46.6	46.4
3	Cont'd train.		47.1	46.6
4	Cont'd train.	✓	47.3	46.8
5	EWC		47.1	46.4
6	EWC	✓	47.8	46.8

Table 4: Fine-tuning our models on former WMT test sets using continued training and EWC.

has to be balanced with the amount of real parallel data (Sennrich et al., 2016b,a; Poncelas et al., 2018). Edunov et al. (2018) had overcome this limitation by adding random noise to the synthetic source sentences. Tab. 3 shows that using noise improves the BLEU score by between 0.5 and 1.5 points on the `news-test2018` test set (rows 2-4 vs. 5-7).[4] Our final model uses a very large number (92M) of (noisy) synthetic sentences (row 9), although the same performance could already be reached with fewer sentences (row 8).

4.2 Fine-tuning with EWC and Checkpoint Averaging

Fine-tuning (Luong and Manning, 2015) is a domain adaptation technique that first trains a model until it converges on a training corpus A, and then continues training on a usually much smaller corpus B which is close to the target domain. Similarly to Schamper et al. (2018); Koehn et al. (2018a), we fine-tune our models on former WMT test sets (2008-2016) to adapt them to the target domain of high-quality news translations. Due to the very small size of corpus B, much care has to be taken to avoid over-fitting. We experimented with different techniques that keep the model parameters in the fine-tuning phase close to the original ones. First, we fine-tuned our models for about 1K-2K iterations (depending on the performance on the `news-test2017` dev set) and dumped checkpoints every 500 steps. Averaging all fine-tuning checkpoints together with the last unadapted checkpoint yields minor gains over fine-tuning without averaging (rows 3 vs. 4 in Tab. 4). However, we obtain the best results by combining checkpoint averaging with another regularizer – elastic weight consolidation (Kirkpatrick et al., 2017, EWC) – that explicitly penalizes the distance of the model parameters θ to the optimized but unadapted model parameters θ_A^*. The regularized training objective according EWC is:

$$L(\theta) = L_B(\theta) + \lambda \sum_i F_i(\theta_i - \theta_{A,i}^*)^2 \quad (1)$$

---

[4] We use Sergey Edunov's `addnoise.py` script available at `https://gist.github.com/edunov/d67d09a38e75409b8408ed86489645dd`

Model	Context	Perplexity (per subword)							
		German				English			
		test15	test16	test17	test18	test15	test16	test17	test18
Standard (Big)	Sentence-level	36.23	35.69	36.17	34.77	39.94	37.19	35.34	42.38
Standard(Big)	Document-level	26.63	27.85	25.43	28.36	43.37	34.55	31.27	39.74
Intra-Inter (Big)	Document-level	23.54	22.39	22.05	22.56	34.25	31.16	29.31	34.47

Table 5: Language model perplexities of different neural language models. 'Intra-Inter' denotes our modified Transformer architecture from Sec. 2. The standard model has 448M parameters, Intra-Inter has 549M parameters.

		English-German			German-English		
		Base	Big (with EWC)		Base	Big (with EWC)	
		Single	Single	4-Ensemble	Single	Single	4-Ensemble
1	Using back-translation?	No	Yes	Yes	No	Yes	Yes
2	NMT	43.8	47.8	48.8	40.7	47.4	48.3
3	+ Sentence-level LM	44.7	47.8	48.8	41.4	47.6	48.3
4	+ PBSMT (MBR-based)	45.1	48.0	49.1	42.1	47.6	48.5
5	+ Document-level Intra-Inter LM	45.7	47.6	49.3	42.1	47.3	48.6

Table 6: Using different kinds of language models for translation on `news-test2018`. The PBSMT baseline gets 26.7 BLEU on English-German and 27.5 BLEU on German-English.

where $L_B(\theta)$ is the normal cross-entropy training loss on task B and $F_i = \mathbb{E}\big[\nabla^2 L_A(\theta_i)\big]$ is an estimate of task A Fisher information, which represents the importance of parameter θ_i to A. On English-German, fine-tuning with EWC and checkpoint averaging yields an 1.1 BLEU improvement (rows 1 vs. 6 in Tab. 4). Gains are generally smaller on German-English.

4.3 Language modelling

We introduced our new Intra-Inter Transformer architecture for document-level language modelling in Sec. 2. Tab. 5 shows that our architecture achieves much better perplexity than both a sentence-level language model and a document-level vanilla Transformer model. Tab. 6 summarizes our translation results with various kinds of language models. Adding a Transformer sentence-level LM to NMT helps for the single Base model without back-translation, but is less effective on top of (ensembles of) Big models with back-translation (row 2 vs. 3). Extracting n-gram probabilities from traditional PBSMT lattices as described by Stahlberg et al. (2017a) and using them as source-conditioned n-gram LMs yields gains even on top of our ensembles (row 4). Our document-level Intra-Inter language models improve the ensembles and the single En-De Base model, but hurt performance slightly for the single Big models (row 5).

5 Related Work

Regularized fine-tuning Our approach to fine-tuning is a combination of EWC (Kirkpatrick

et al., 2017) and checkpoint averaging (Junczys-Dowmunt et al., 2016b,a). In our context, both methods aim to avoid *catastrophic forgetting*[5] (Goodfellow et al., 2013; French, 1999) and over-fitting by keeping the adapted model close to the original, and can thus be seen as *regularized* fine-tuning techniques. Khayrallah et al. (2018); Dakwale and Monz (2017) regularized the output distributions during fine-tuning using techniques inspired by knowledge distillation (Bucilu et al., 2006; Hinton et al., 2014; Kim and Rush, 2016). Barone et al. (2017) applied standard L2 regularization and a variant of dropout to domain adaptation. EWC as generalization of L2 regularization has been used for NMT domain adaptation by Thompson et al. (2019); Saunders et al. (2019). In particular, Saunders et al. (2019) showed that EWC is not only more effective than L2 in reducing catastrophic forgetting but even yields gains on the general domain when used for fine-tuning on a related domain.

Document-level MT Various techniques have been proposed to provide the translation system with inter-sentential context, for example by initializing encoder or decoder states (Wang et al., 2017a), using multi-source encoders (Bawden et al., 2018; Jean et al., 2017), as additional decoder input (Wang et al., 2017a), with memory-augmented neural networks (Tu et al., 2018; Maruf and Haffari, 2018; Kuang et al., 2017), hierar-

---

[5]Catastrophic forgetting occurs when the performance on the specific domain is improved after fine-tuning, but the performance of the model on the general domain has decreased drastically.

chical attention (Miculicich et al., 2018; Maruf et al., 2019), deliberation networks (Xiong et al., 2018), or by simply concatenating multiple source and/or target sentences (Tiedemann and Scherrer, 2017; Bawden et al., 2018). Context-aware extensions to Transformer encoders have been proposed by Voita et al. (2018); Zhang et al. (2018). Techniques also differ in whether they use source context only (Jean et al., 2017; Wang et al., 2017a; Voita et al., 2018; Zhang et al., 2018), target context only (Tu et al., 2018; Kuang et al., 2017), or both (Bawden et al., 2018; Maruf and Haffari, 2018; Miculicich et al., 2018; Tiedemann and Scherrer, 2017; Maruf et al., 2019). Several studies on document-level NMT indicate that automatic and human sentence-level evaluation metrics often do not correlate well with improvements in discourse level phenomena (Bawden et al., 2018; Läubli et al., 2018; Müller et al., 2018). Our document-level LM approach is similar to the work of Xiong et al. (2018) in that cross-sentence context is only used in a second pass to improve translations from a sentence-level MT system. Our method is light-weight as, similarly to Tiedemann and Scherrer (2017), we do not modify the architecture of the core NMT system.

NMT-SMT hybrid systems Popular examples of combining a fully trained SMT system with independently trained NMT are rescoring and reranking methods (Neubig et al., 2015; Stahlberg et al., 2016b; Khayrallah et al., 2017; Grundkiewicz and Junczys-Dowmunt, 2018; Avramidis et al., 2016; Marie and Fujita, 2018; Zhang et al., 2017), although these models may be too constraining if the neural system is much stronger than the SMT system. Loose combination schemes include the edit-distance-based system of Stahlberg et al. (2016a) or the minimum Bayes-risk approach of Stahlberg et al. (2017a) we adopted in this work. NMT and SMT can also be combined in a cascade, with SMT providing the input to a post-processing NMT system (Niehues et al., 2016; Zhou et al., 2017) or vice versa (Du and Way, 2017). Wang et al. (2017b, 2018) interpolated NMT posteriors with word recommendations from SMT and jointly trained NMT together with a gating function which assigns the weight between SMT and NMT scores dynamically. The AMU-UEDIN submission to WMT16 let SMT take the lead and used NMT as a feature in phrase-based MT (Junczys-Dowmunt et al.,

English-German		German-English	
Team	**BLEU**	**Team**	**BLEU**
MSRA	44.9	MSRA	42.8
Microsoft	43.9	Facebook FAIR	40.8
NEU	43.5	NEU	40.5
UCAM	**43.0**	**UCAM**	**39.7**
Facebook FAIR	42.7	RWTH	39.6
JHU	42.5	MLLP-UPV	39.3
eTranslation	41.9	DFKI	38.8
8 more...		*4 more...*	

Table 7: English-German and German-English primary submissions to the WMT19 shared task.

Year	Best in competition	This work	Δ
2017	28.3	32.8	**+4.5**
2018	48.3	49.3	**+1.0**
2019	44.9	43.0	**-1.9**

Table 8: Comparison of our English-German system with the winning submissions over the past two years.

2016b). In contrast, Long et al. (2016) translated most of the sentence with an NMT system, and just used SMT to translate technical terms in a post-processing step. Dahlmann et al. (2017) proposed a hybrid search algorithm in which the neural decoder expands hypotheses with phrases from an SMT system.

6 Conclusion

Our WMT19 submission focused on regularized fine-tuning and language modelling. With our novel Intra-Inter Transformer architecture for document-level LMs we achieved significant reductions in perplexity and minor improvements in BLEU over very strong baselines. A combination of checkpoint averaging and EWC proved to be an effective way to regularize fine-tuning. Our systems are competitive on both English-German and German-English (Tab. 7), especially considering the immense speed with which our field has been advancing in recent years (Tab. 8).

Acknowledgments

This work was supported by the U.K. Engineering and Physical Sciences Research Council (EPSRC) grant EP/L027623/1 and has been performed using resources provided by the Cambridge Tier-2 system operated by the University of Cambridge Research Computing Service[6] funded by EPSRC Tier-2 capital grant EP/P020259/1.

---

[6]http://www.hpc.cam.ac.uk

References

Martín Abadi, Paul Barham, Jianmin Chen, Zhifeng Chen, Andy Davis, Jeffrey Dean, Matthieu Devin, Sanjay Ghemawat, Geoffrey Irving, Michael Isard, et al. 2016. TensorFlow: A system for large-scale machine learning. In *Proceedings of the 12th USENIX conference on Operating Systems Design and Implementation*, pages 265–283. USENIX Association.

Eleftherios Avramidis, Vivien Macketanz, Aljoscha Burchardt, Jindrich Helcl, and Hans Uszkoreit. 2016. Deeper machine translation and evaluation for German. In *Proceedings of the 2nd Deep Machine Translation Workshop*, pages 29–38. ÚFAL MFF UK.

Antonio Valerio Miceli Barone, Barry Haddow, Ulrich Germann, and Rico Sennrich. 2017. Regularization techniques for fine-tuning in neural machine translation. In *Proceedings of the 2017 Conference on Empirical Methods in Natural Language Processing*, pages 1489–1494, Copenhagen, Denmark. Association for Computational Linguistics.

Rachel Bawden, Rico Sennrich, Alexandra Birch, and Barry Haddow. 2018. Evaluating discourse phenomena in neural machine translation. In *Proceedings of the 2018 Conference of the North American Chapter of the Association for Computational Linguistics: Human Language Technologies, Volume 1 (Long Papers)*, pages 1304–1313, New Orleans, Louisiana. Association for Computational Linguistics.

Cristian Bucilu, Rich Caruana, and Alexandru Niculescu-Mizil. 2006. Model compression. In *Proceedings of the 12th ACM SIGKDD international conference on Knowledge discovery and data mining*, pages 535–541. ACM.

Leonard Dahlmann, Evgeny Matusov, Pavel Petrushkov, and Shahram Khadivi. 2017. Neural machine translation leveraging phrase-based models in a hybrid search. In *Proceedings of the 2017 Conference on Empirical Methods in Natural Language Processing*, pages 1411–1420, Copenhagen, Denmark. Association for Computational Linguistics.

Praveen Dakwale and Christof Monz. 2017. Fine-tuning for neural machine translation with limited degradation across in-and out-of-domain data. *Proceedings of the XVI Machine Translation Summit*, page 117.

Jinhua Du and Andy Way. 2017. Neural pre-translation for hybrid machine translation. *In Proceedings of MT Summit XVI*, 1:27–40.

Sergey Edunov, Myle Ott, Michael Auli, and David Grangier. 2018. Understanding back-translation at scale. In *Proceedings of the 2018 Conference on Empirical Methods in Natural Language Processing*, pages 489–500.

Robert M French. 1999. Catastrophic forgetting in connectionist networks. *Trends in cognitive sciences*, 3(4):128–135.

Ian J Goodfellow, Mehdi Mirza, Da Xiao, Aaron Courville, and Yoshua Bengio. 2013. An empirical investigation of catastrophic forgetting in gradient-based neural networks. *arXiv preprint arXiv:1312.6211*.

Roman Grundkiewicz and Marcin Junczys-Dowmunt. 2018. Near human-level performance in grammatical error correction with hybrid machine translation. In *Proceedings of the 2018 Conference of the North American Chapter of the Association for Computational Linguistics: Human Language Technologies, Volume 2 (Short Papers)*, pages 284–290, New Orleans, Louisiana. Association for Computational Linguistics.

Caglar Gulcehre, Orhan Firat, Kelvin Xu, Kyunghyun Cho, Loic Barrault, Huei-Chi Lin, Fethi Bougares, Holger Schwenk, and Yoshua Bengio. 2015. On using monolingual corpora in neural machine translation. *arXiv preprint arXiv:1503.03535*.

Caglar Gulcehre, Orhan Firat, Kelvin Xu, Kyunghyun Cho, and Yoshua Bengio. 2017. On integrating a language model into neural machine translation. *Computer Speech & Language*, 45:137 – 148.

Geoffrey Hinton, Oriol Vinyals, and Jeff Dean. 2014. Distilling the knowledge in a neural network. In *NIPS Deep Learning Workshop*.

Sebastien Jean, Stanislas Lauly, Orhan Firat, and Kyunghyun Cho. 2017. Does neural machine translation benefit from larger context? *arXiv preprint arXiv:1704.05135*.

Marcin Junczys-Dowmunt. 2018a. Dual conditional cross-entropy filtering of noisy parallel corpora. In *Proceedings of the Third Conference on Machine Translation: Shared Task Papers*, pages 888–895, Belgium, Brussels. Association for Computational Linguistics.

Marcin Junczys-Dowmunt. 2018b. Microsoft's submission to the WMT2018 news translation task: How I learned to stop worrying and love the data. In *Proceedings of the Third Conference on Machine Translation: Shared Task Papers*, pages 425–430. Association for Computational Linguistics.

Marcin Junczys-Dowmunt, Tomasz Dwojak, and Hieu Hoang. 2016a. Is neural machine translation ready for deployment? A case study on 30 translation directions. In *International Workshop on Spoken Language Translation IWSLT*.

Marcin Junczys-Dowmunt, Tomasz Dwojak, and Rico Sennrich. 2016b. The AMU-UEDIN submission to the WMT16 news translation task: Attention-based NMT models as feature functions in phrase-based SMT. In *Proceedings of the First Conference on Machine Translation*, pages 319–325, Berlin, Germany. Association for Computational Linguistics.

Huda Khayrallah, Gaurav Kumar, Kevin Duh, Matt Post, and Philipp Koehn. 2017. Neural lattice search for domain adaptation in machine translation. In *Proceedings of the Eighth International Joint Conference on Natural Language Processing (Volume 2: Short Papers)*, pages 20–25, Taipei, Taiwan. Asian Federation of Natural Language Processing.

Huda Khayrallah, Brian Thompson, Kevin Duh, and Philipp Koehn. 2018. Regularized training objective for continued training for domain adaptation in neural machine translation. In *Proceedings of the 2nd Workshop on Neural Machine Translation and Generation*, pages 36–44, Melbourne, Australia. Association for Computational Linguistics.

Yoon Kim and Alexander M. Rush. 2016. Sequence-level knowledge distillation. In *Proceedings of the 2016 Conference on Empirical Methods in Natural Language Processing*, pages 1317–1327, Austin, Texas. Association for Computational Linguistics.

James Kirkpatrick, Razvan Pascanu, Neil Rabinowitz, Joel Veness, Guillaume Desjardins, Andrei A Rusu, Kieran Milan, John Quan, Tiago Ramalho, Agnieszka Grabska-Barwinska, et al. 2017. Overcoming catastrophic forgetting in neural networks. *Proceedings of the national academy of sciences*, 114(13):3521–3526.

Philipp Koehn, Kevin Duh, and Brian Thompson. 2018a. The JHU machine translation systems for WMT 2018. In *Proceedings of the Third Conference on Machine Translation: Shared Task Papers*, pages 438–444, Belgium, Brussels. Association for Computational Linguistics.

Philipp Koehn, Huda Khayrallah, Kenneth Heafield, and Mikel L. Forcada. 2018b. Findings of the WMT 2018 shared task on parallel corpus filtering. In *Proceedings of the Third Conference on Machine Translation: Shared Task Papers*, pages 726–739, Belgium, Brussels. Association for Computational Linguistics.

Shaohui Kuang, Deyi Xiong, Weihua Luo, and Guodong Zhou. 2017. Cache-based document-level neural machine translation. *arXiv preprint arXiv:1711.11221*.

Samuel Läubli, Rico Sennrich, and Martin Volk. 2018. Has machine translation achieved human parity? A case for document-level evaluation. In *Proceedings of the 2018 Conference on Empirical Methods in Natural Language Processing*, pages 4791–4796.

Zi Long, Takehito Utsuro, Tomoharu Mitsuhashi, and Mikio Yamamoto. 2016. Translation of patent sentences with a large vocabulary of technical terms using neural machine translation. In *Proceedings of the 3rd Workshop on Asian Translation (WAT2016)*, pages 47–57. The COLING 2016 Organizing Committee.

Minh-Thang Luong and Christopher D Manning. 2015. Stanford neural machine translation systems for spoken language domains. In *Proceedings of the International Workshop on Spoken Language Translation*, pages 76–79.

Benjamin Marie and Atsushi Fujita. 2018. A smorgasbord of features to combine phrase -based and neural machine translation. In *Proceedings of AMTA Workshop on MT Research and the Translation Industry*, Boston, US.

Sameen Maruf and Gholamreza Haffari. 2018. Document context neural machine translation with memory networks. In *Proceedings of the 56th Annual Meeting of the Association for Computational Linguistics (Volume 1: Long Papers)*, pages 1275–1284, Melbourne, Australia. Association for Computational Linguistics.

Sameen Maruf, André F. T. Martins, and Gholamreza Haffari. 2019. Selective attention for context-aware neural machine translation. In *Proceedings of the 2019 Conference of the North American Chapter of the Association for Computational Linguistics: Human Language Technologies, Volume 1 (Long and Short Papers)*, pages 3092–3102, Minneapolis, Minnesota. Association for Computational Linguistics.

Lesly Miculicich, Dhananjay Ram, Nikolaos Pappas, and James Henderson. 2018. Document-level neural machine translation with hierarchical attention networks. In *Proceedings of the 2018 Conference on Empirical Methods in Natural Language Processing*, pages 2947–2954, Brussels, Belgium. Association for Computational Linguistics.

Mathias Müller, Annette Rios, Elena Voita, and Rico Sennrich. 2018. A large-scale test set for the evaluation of context-aware pronoun translation in neural machine translation. In *Proceedings of the Third Conference on Machine Translation: Research Papers*, pages 61–72, Belgium, Brussels. Association for Computational Linguistics.

Shuyo Nakatani. 2010. Language detection library for Java.

Graham Neubig, Makoto Morishita, and Satoshi Nakamura. 2015. Neural reranking improves subjective quality of machine translation: NAIST at WAT2015. In *Proceedings of the 2nd Workshop on Asian Translation (WAT2015)*, pages 35–41, Kyoto, Japan. Workshop on Asian Translation.

Jan Niehues, Eunah Cho, Thanh-Le Ha, and Alex Waibel. 2016. Pre-translation for neural machine translation. In *Proceedings of COLING 2016, the 26th International Conference on Computational Linguistics: Technical Papers*, pages 1828–1836. The COLING 2016 Organizing Committee.

Alberto Poncelas, Dimitar Shterionov, Andy Way, Gideon Maillette de Buy Wenniger, and Peyman Passban. 2018. Investigating backtranslation in neural machine translation. *arXiv preprint arXiv:1804.06189*.

Danielle Saunders, Felix Stahlberg, Adrià de Gispert, and Bill Byrne. 2018. Multi-representation ensembles and delayed SGD updates improve syntax-based NMT. In *Proceedings of the 56th Annual Meeting of the Association for Computational Linguistics (Volume 2: Short Papers)*, pages 319–325. Association for Computational Linguistics.

Danielle Saunders, Felix Stahlberg, Adrià de Gispert, and Bill Byrne. 2019. Domain adaptive inference for neural machine translation. In *Proceedings of the 57th Annual Meeting of the Association for Computational Linguistics (Volume 2: Short Papers)*. Association for Computational Linguistics.

Julian Schamper, Jan Rosendahl, Parnia Bahar, Yunsu Kim, Arne Nix, and Hermann Ney. 2018. The RWTH Aachen university supervised machine translation systems for WMT 2018. In *Proceedings of the Third Conference on Machine Translation: Shared Task Papers*, pages 496–503, Belgium, Brussels. Association for Computational Linguistics.

Rico Sennrich, Barry Haddow, and Alexandra Birch. 2016a. Edinburgh neural machine translation systems for WMT 16. In *Proceedings of the First Conference on Machine Translation*, pages 371–376, Berlin, Germany. Association for Computational Linguistics.

Rico Sennrich, Barry Haddow, and Alexandra Birch. 2016b. Improving neural machine translation models with monolingual data. In *Proceedings of the 54th Annual Meeting of the Association for Computational Linguistics (Volume 1: Long Papers)*, pages 86–96. Association for Computational Linguistics.

Rico Sennrich, Barry Haddow, and Alexandra Birch. 2016c. Neural machine translation of rare words with subword units. In *Proceedings of the 54th Annual Meeting of the Association for Computational Linguistics (Volume 1: Long Papers)*, pages 1715–1725, Berlin, Germany. Association for Computational Linguistics.

Felix Stahlberg, James Cross, and Veselin Stoyanov. 2018a. Simple fusion: Return of the language model. In *Proceedings of the Third Conference on Machine Translation: Research Papers*, pages 204–211. Association for Computational Linguistics.

Felix Stahlberg, Adrià de Gispert, and Bill Byrne. 2018b. The University of Cambridge's machine translation systems for WMT18. In *Proceedings of the Third Conference on Machine Translation: Shared Task Papers*, pages 504–512. Association for Computational Linguistics.

Felix Stahlberg, Adrià de Gispert, Eva Hasler, and Bill Byrne. 2017a. Neural machine translation by minimising the Bayes-risk with respect to syntactic translation lattices. In *Proceedings of the 15th Conference of the European Chapter of the Association for Computational Linguistics: Volume 2, Short Papers*, pages 362–368. Association for Computational Linguistics.

Felix Stahlberg, Eva Hasler, and Bill Byrne. 2016a. The edit distance transducer in action: The University of Cambridge English-German system at WMT16. In *Proceedings of the First Conference on Machine Translation: Volume 2, Shared Task Papers*, pages 377–384. Association for Computational Linguistics.

Felix Stahlberg, Eva Hasler, Danielle Saunders, and Bill Byrne. 2017b. SGNMT – A flexible NMT decoding platform for quick prototyping of new models and search strategies. In *Proceedings of the 2017 Conference on Empirical Methods in Natural Language Processing: System Demonstrations*, pages 25–30. Association for Computational Linguistics.

Felix Stahlberg, Eva Hasler, Aurelien Waite, and Bill Byrne. 2016b. Syntactically guided neural machine translation. In *Proceedings of the 54th Annual Meeting of the Association for Computational Linguistics (Volume 2: Short Papers)*, pages 299–305. Association for Computational Linguistics.

Felix Stahlberg, Danielle Saunders, Gonzalo Iglesias, and Bill Byrne. 2018c. Why not be versatile? Applications of the SGNMT decoder for machine translation. In *Proceedings of the 13th Conference of the Association for Machine Translation in the Americas (Volume 1: Research Papers)*, pages 208–216. Association for Machine Translation in the Americas.

Brian Thompson, Jeremy Gwinnup, Huda Khayrallah, Kevin Duh, and Philipp Koehn. 2019. Overcoming catastrophic forgetting during domain adaptation of neural machine translation. In *Proceedings of the 2019 Conference of the North American Chapter of the Association for Computational Linguistics: Human Language Technologies, Volume 1 (Long and Short Papers)*, pages 2062–2068, Minneapolis, Minnesota. Association for Computational Linguistics.

Jörg Tiedemann and Yves Scherrer. 2017. Neural machine translation with extended context. In *Proceedings of the Third Workshop on Discourse in Machine Translation*, pages 82–92, Copenhagen, Denmark. Association for Computational Linguistics.

Zhaopeng Tu, Yang Liu, Shuming Shi, and Tong Zhang. 2018. Learning to remember translation history with a continuous cache. *Transactions of the Association for Computational Linguistics*, 6:407–420.

Ashish Vaswani, Samy Bengio, Eugene Brevdo, Francois Chollet, Aidan N. Gomez, Stephan Gouws, Llion Jones, Łukasz Kaiser, Nal Kalchbrenner, Niki Parmar, Ryan Sepassi, Noam Shazeer, and Jakob Uszkoreit. 2018. Tensor2tensor for neural machine translation. *CoRR*, abs/1803.07416.

Ashish Vaswani, Noam Shazeer, Niki Parmar, Jakob Uszkoreit, Llion Jones, Aidan N Gomez, Łukasz Kaiser, and Illia Polosukhin. 2017. Attention is all you need. In *Advances in Neural Information Processing Systems*, pages 5998–6008.

Elena Voita, Pavel Serdyukov, Rico Sennrich, and Ivan Titov. 2018. Context-aware neural machine translation learns anaphora resolution. In *Proceedings of the 56th Annual Meeting of the Association for Computational Linguistics (Volume 1: Long Papers)*, pages 1264–1274, Melbourne, Australia. Association for Computational Linguistics.

Longyue Wang, Zhaopeng Tu, Andy Way, and Qun Liu. 2017a. Exploiting cross-sentence context for neural machine translation. In *Proceedings of the 2017 Conference on Empirical Methods in Natural Language Processing*, pages 2826–2831, Copenhagen, Denmark. Association for Computational Linguistics.

Xing Wang, Zhengdong Lu, Zhaopeng Tu, Hang Li, Deyi Xiong, and Min Zhang. 2017b. Neural machine translation advised by statistical machine translation. In *AAAI*, pages 3330–3336.

Xing Wang, Zhaopeng Tu, and Min Zhang. 2018. Incorporating statistical machine translation word knowledge into neural machine translation. *IEEE/ACM Transactions on Audio, Speech, and Language Processing*, 26(12):2255–2266.

Hao Xiong, Zhongjun He, Hua Wu, and Haifeng Wang. 2018. Modeling coherence for discourse neural machine translation. *arXiv preprint arXiv:1811.05683*.

Jiacheng Zhang, Huanbo Luan, Maosong Sun, Feifei Zhai, Jingfang Xu, Min Zhang, and Yang Liu. 2018. Improving the Transformer translation model with document-level context. In *Proceedings of the 2018 Conference on Empirical Methods in Natural Language Processing*, pages 533–542, Brussels, Belgium. Association for Computational Linguistics.

Jingyi Zhang, Masao Utiyama, Eiichro Sumita, Graham Neubig, and Satoshi Nakamura. 2017. Improving neural machine translation through phrase-based forced decoding. In *Proceedings of the Eighth International Joint Conference on Natural Language Processing (Volume 1: Long Papers)*, pages 152–162, Taipei, Taiwan. Asian Federation of Natural Language Processing.

Long Zhou, Wenpeng Hu, Jiajun Zhang, and Chengqing Zong. 2017. Neural system combination for machine translation. In *Proceedings of the 55th Annual Meeting of the Association for Computational Linguistics (Volume 2: Short Papers)*, pages 378–384. Association for Computational Linguistics.

Baidu Neural Machine Translation Systems for WMT19

Meng Sun, Bojian Jiang, Hao Xiong, Zhongjun He, Hua Wu, Haifeng Wang

Baidu Inc. No. 10, Shangdi 10th Street, Beijing, 100085, China

`{sunmeng09,jiangbojian,xionghao05,`
`hezhongjun,wu_hua,wanghaifeng}@baidu.com`

Abstract

In this paper we introduce the systems Baidu submitted for the WMT19 shared task on Chinese↔English news translation. Our systems are based on the Transformer architecture with some effective improvements. Data selection, back translation, data augmentation, knowledge distillation, domain adaptation, model ensemble and re-ranking are employed and proven effective in our experiments. Our Chinese→English system achieved the highest case-sensitive BLEU score among all constrained submissions, and our English→Chinese system ranked the second in all submissions.

1 Introduction

The Transformer model (Vaswani et al., 2017), which exploits self-attention mechanism both in the encoder and decoder, has significantly improved the translation quality in recent years. It is also adopted by most participants as the basic Neural Machine Translation (NMT) system in the previous translation campaigns (Bojar et al., 2018; Niehues et al., 2018). In this year's translation task, we focus on the improvement of single system, and propose three novel Transformer variants:

- Pre-trained Transformer: We train a big Transformer language model (Radford et al., 2018; Devlin et al., 2018; Dai et al., 2019; Sun et al., 2019) on monolingual corpora, and use the language model as the encoder of the Transformer model.

- Deeper Transformer: We increase the encoder layers to better learn the representation of the source sentences. Specifically, we increase the number of encoder layers from 6 to 30 for the base version, and from 6 to 15 layers for the big version.

- Bigger Transformer: According to the previous experiments, the performance of the Transformer model is largely dependent on the dimensions of feed forward network. To further improve the performance, we increase the inner dimension of feed-forward network from 4,096 to 15,000 for big version.

In addition, we develop effective approaches to exploit additional monolingual data and generate augmented bilingual data. To use the monolingual data, back translation (Sennrich et al., 2015a) is employed on large corpora including News Corpus and Gigaword. We also use an iterative approach (Zhang et al., 2018) to extend the back translation method by jointly training source-to-target and target-to-source NMT models. For bilingual data augmentation, a target-to-source baseline system is used to translate the target of the bilingual corpus as the synthetic data. Moreover, the sequence-level knowledge distillation (Hassan et al., 2018) mechanism is employed to boost the performance by means of using the model decoding from right to left (Right-to-Left) and the aforementioned Transformer variants to generate synthetic data for training the NMT model (Wang et al., 2018).

The remainder of paper is structured as follows: Section 2 describes the detailed overview of our training strategy. Section 3 shows the experimental settings and results. Finally, we conclude our work in Section 4.

2 System Overview

Figure 1 depicts the overall process of our submissions in this year's evaluation task, in which we train our advanced Transformer models on the bilingual corpus together with synthetic corpora, fine-tune them on the well-selected in-domain data, and generate the ensemble model for the final

Proceedings of the Fourth Conference on Machine Translation (WMT), Volume 2: Shared Task Papers (Day 1) pages 374–381
Florence, Italy, August 1-2, 2019. ©2019 Association for Computational Linguistics

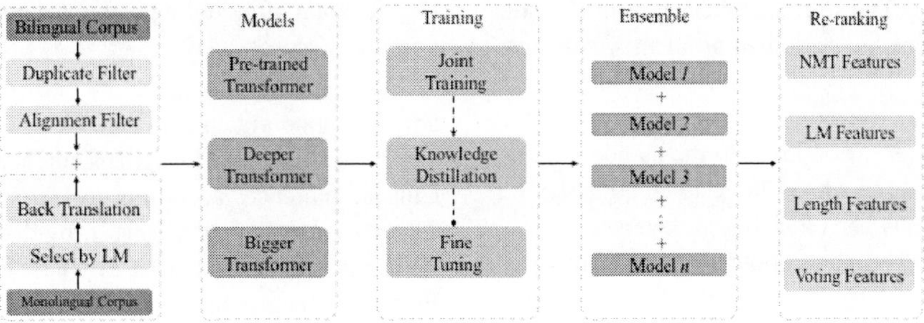

Figure 1: Architecture of Baidu NMT system

re-ranking strategy. In this section, we will introduce each step in details.

It is worth noting that our advanced Transformer model requires larger GPU memory to train due to the large number of training parameters. Hence we train our models on machines with 8 NVIDIA V100 GPUs each of which has 32 GB memory, to avoid out-of-memory issues. In training phase, we limit the number of source and target tokens per batch to 4,096 per GPU for deeper and bigger Transformer models (at most 526,052,128 parameters), while the token batch size is 3,072 for pre-trained Transformer model due to GPU memory limitation.

2.1 Pre-trained Transformer

Recent empirical improvements with language models have showed that unsupervised pre-training (Peters et al., 2018; Radford et al., 2018; Devlin et al., 2018; Dai et al., 2019; Sun et al., 2019) on very large corpora is an integral part of many NLP tasks. We implement a big Transformer language model using PaddlePaddle[1], an end-to-end open source deep learning platform developed by Baidu. It provides a complete suite of deep learning libraries, tools and service platforms to make the research and development of deep learning simple and reliable. The language model is pre-trained only with masked language model task (Taylor, 1953; Devlin et al., 2018; Sun et al., 2019) on a monolingual corpus of the source language.

We use all the available resources of WMT19 as the pre-training corpus. For the Chinese language model, we use the concatenation of Chinese Gigaword, Chinese News Crawl, XMU and the Chinese part of CWMT and UN corpus. For the English language model, we use the concatenation of English Gigaword, English News Crawl and the English part of CWMT and UN corpus. There are 45 million Chinese sentences and 170 million English sentences in our pre-training corpora.

To use the pre-trained language model as encoder of NMT and enable the open-vocabulary translation, we learn a BPE (Sennrich et al., 2015b) model with 30K merge operations. We use Adam with learning rate of 1e-4, $\beta_1 = 0.9$, $\beta_2 = 0.999$, L2 weight decay of 0.001, and learning rate warmup over the 10,000 steps. We train the big Transformer language model with 24 layers, setting the hidden size to 1,024 and the number of self-attention heads to 16. Both Chinese and English pre-training took 7 days to complete.

In the fine-tuning procedure of the translation task, we employ a pre-trained language model as encoder of NMT, and the parameters of decoders are learned during fine-tuning. The decoder has 6 self-attention layers, and the hidden size is 1024, which is same with the decoder of standard big Transformer. During fine-tuning, we only fix the parameters of the language model for the first 10,000 steps.

2.2 Deeper Transformer

According to the previous literatures, the model tends to specialize in word sense disambiguation and tends to focus on local dependencies in lower layers but finds long dependencies on higher ones while increasing the size of layers in the encoder (Tang et al., 2018; Domhan, 2018; Raganato and Tiedemann, 2018). Meanwhile, inspired by the success of pre-trained Transformer, that translation results can benefit from very deep architectures of encoder, we introduce the deeper Transformer. But vanishing-gradient problem is encountered by just increasing the encoder depth,

---

[1] https://github.com/paddlepaddle/paddle

the standard Transformer failed to train. To alleviate the vanishing-gradient problem, we design a particular residual connections. Specifically, the outputs of all preceding layers are used as inputs for each layer, as opposed to the standard Transformer model in which the residual connection is employed between two adjacent layers.

In our experiments, both the big Transformer with 15 encoder layers and the base transformer with 30 encoder layers obtain significant improvements compared with the standard big Transformer on Chinese→English translation task, whereas the improvement is not remarkable on English→Chinese translation task.

2.3 Bigger Transformer

Motivated by the success of increasing the model size on the language modeling (Devlin et al., 2018) and NMT (Vaswani et al., 2017) tasks, we propose bigger Transformer which has larger inner dimension of feed-forward network than the standard big Transformer. Specifically, we increase the inner dimension of feed-forward network from 4,096 to 15,000 constrained by the GPU memory capacity. To overcome the overfitting problem, we set attention dropout and relu dropout from 0.1 to 0.3, increasing the value of label smoothing from 0.1 to 0.2. Note that the specific settings are only employed for the bigger Transformer.

In addition, we explore the effectiveness of increasing hidden size with respect to the Transformer model. However, the results indicate that the model with increased hidden size performs worse than the model with big feed-forward network. Nevertheless, we retain the model with different hidden size as one diverse system for the generation of the final ensemble model, which has shown effective performance in our further experiments.

2.4 Large-scale Back-Translation

In recent work, Edunov et al. (2018) proposed an effective approach to improve the translation quality by exploiting back-translation mechanism on the large-scale monolingual corpus. Following their work, we also train our model on the synthetic bilingual corpus to further improve the performance. However, the provided monolingual data contains a certain amount of noise and out-of-domain data which may affect the translation quality implicitly. Therefore, we use a language model to select high-quality and in-domain data from the large amount of monolingual data according to the perplexity score.

After training language models on different types of monolingual data (i.e., News crawl, Gigaword), we select 96M English sentences and 23M Chinese sentences according to LM scores, since Chinese monolingual corpus provided by WMT 19 is much less than that of English. The selected English sentences are translated and divided into 12 portions. For the 23M Chinese sentences, we translate and divide the sentences into 3 portions, resulting in 8M synthetic parallel sentence pairs in each portion. We further evaluate the performance of the similar model training on a different bilingual corpus which consists of the original bilingual corpus and the generated synthetic bitext. According to the BLEU score of translation results on the WMT 18 news translation dev set, we select the top 4 most effective portions for training Chinese→English system and the top 2 portions for training English→Chinese system. In the final submission, the selected synthetic portions are used to enhance individual baseline models by the following joint training technique, respectively.

2.5 Joint Training and Data Augmentation

In the work of Zhang et al. (2018), they proposed a novel method for better usage of monolingual data from both source side and target side by jointly optimizing a source-to-target (S2T) model and a target-to-source (T2S) model, training with several iterations. In each iteration, the T2S model is responsible for generating synthetic parallel training data for S2T model using target-side monolingual data, while S2T model is employed to generate synthetic parallel training data for T2S model using source-side monolingual data. After training on the additional synthetic data, the performance of both T2S model and S2T model can be further improved. In the next iteration, the two improved models can potentially generate better synthetic parallel data. This procedure can be applied in several iterations until no further improvement can be obtained.

In addition, we also augment the training data by exploring the bilingual corpus rather than the monolingual corpus. Specifically, we translate the sentences in the target language back into the source language by diverse training models, such as Left-to-right model and Right-to-left model. This procedure can be viewed as one alternative solution for alleviating the exposure bias problem (Ranzato et al., 2016).

2.6 Knowledge Distillation

The early adoption of knowledge distillation (Kim and Rush, 2016) is for model compression, where the goal is to deliver a compact student model that matches the accuracy of a large teacher model or the ensemble of models. In our knowledge distillation approach, we translate the source side of the bilingual data with a Right-to-Left (R2L) (Liu et al., 2016) model teacher and different architecture NMT teachers to use the translations as additional training data for the student network. Considering that distillation from a bad teacher model is likely to hurt the student model and thus result in inferior accuracy, we selectively use distillation in the training process. In particular, the sentences generated by a teacher model are filtered if BLEU scores are below a threshold τ. According to our previous empirical results, we select English translations with BLEU score higher than 30 and Chinese translations with BLEU score higher than 42.

There are two kinds of teacher models to help a student model improve translation performance:

- R2L Teacher: The idea is to reverse the target sentences of bilingual corpus and train a R2L model. Then we employ R2L model to translate the source sentences of the bilingual corpus and reverse the translated sentences. The pseudo corpus is added to the real bilingual corpus in order to enhance the L2R model. The paradigm can be regarded as a kind of knowledge transfer method which provides complementary information for student model to learn.

- Hybrid Heterogeneous Teacher: Pre-trained Transformer, deeper Transformer and bigger Transformer represent a source sentence at different granularities, therefore it is intuitive that each model can learn effective knowledge from other models. For each individual model, we use the other two models as the teacher model to further improve the performance.

2.7 Fine-tuning with In-domain Data

Domain adaptation plays an important role in improving the performance towards given testing

Source	Chn→En	En→Chn
CWMT	6.7M	6.7M
UN	9M	3.5M
Wiki Titles	-	0.6M
Total	15.7M	10.8M

Table 1: Statistics of the bilingual training data (Chn indicates Chinese while En indicates English).

data. The dominant approach for domain adaptation is training on large-scale out-of-domain data and then fine-tuning on the in-domain data (Luong and Manning, 2015). Thus the effectiveness of the domain adaptation depends on the selected in-domain data.

According to our previous empirical results, using the WMT 18 dev set to fine-tune the models straightforwardly achieves the best results. In our final submission, we set the batch size to 1,024 and fine-tune the model for a few iterations on the WMT 18 dev set. It is surprising to find a gain of almost +2 BLEU improvement on WMT 18 Chinese→English test set. However, on WMT 18 English→Chinese test set, the improvement is not significant.

In WMT 17 and 18, the source side of both dev set and test set are composed of two parts: documents created originally in Chinese and documents created originally in English. We split both the dev set and test set into original Chinese part and original English part according to tag attributes of SGM files. Finally, we translate each specific test part with the model fine-tuned on the corresponding dev set. Experiments show significant improvement with this method, that is, 2.23 BLEU improvements on Chinese→English test set and 0.5 BLEU improvements on English→Chinese test set. This indicates that the translation quality is affected by the original sources of the language. Consider the English→Chinese task, if the English sentences are created from native English corpus, then the corresponding Chinese sentences are translation style, so the model fine-tuned on these parallel sentences is more inclined to decode with translation style. Similarly, if the Chinese sentences are created from native Chinese corpus, the fine-tuned English→Chinese model decodes with more native style.

In the final submission, we take the following steps to avoid overfitting: 1) We employ the en-

Settings	Big Transformer	Pre-trained Transformer	Deeper Transformer	Bigger Transformer
Baseline	25.86	-	-	-
+ Back Translation	26.72	27.68	26.83	27.54
+ Joint Training	26.95	27.79	27.01	27.61
+ Knowledge Distillation	27.4	28.11	27.43	27.88
+ Fine-tuning	29.39	29.87	29.82	30.11
+ Ensemble	31.59			
+ Re-ranking*	31.83			

Table 2: BLEU evaluation results on the WMT 2018 Chinese→English test set (* denotes the submitted system).

semble models to translate the WMT 19 test set, and use the translations as additional synthetic fine-tuning corpus. 2) We fine-tune the final system on the mixture of the additional synthetic corpus and the selected in-domain corpus.

2.8 Model Ensemble

Model ensemble is a widely used technique to boost the performance by combining the predictions of several models at each decoding step. In our previous experiments, we find that the improvement is slight while integrating the predictions of multiple models with similar model architecture. Instead, we train our models with different model architectures training on different versions of training data, increasing the model diversity for the model ensemble. The experimental results indicate that this method achieves absolute improvements over the single system (at most a 1.7 BLEU point improvements).

2.9 Re-ranking

In order to get better translation results, we generate n-best hypotheses with an ensemble model and then train a re-ranker using k-best MIRA (Cherry and Foster, 2012) on the validation set. K-best MIRA is a version of MIRA (Chiang et al., 2008) that works with a batch tuning to learn a re-ranker for the n-best hypotheses. The features we use for re-ranking are:

- NMT Features: Ensemble model score and Right-to-Left model score.

- Language Model Features: Multiple n-gram language models and backward n-gram language models.

- Length Features: Length ratio and length difference between source sentences and hypotheses.

- Weighted Voting Features: Average of BLEU scores calculated between each hypothesis and the other hypotheses.

3 Experiments and Results

All of our experiments are carried out on 32 machines with 8 NVIDIA V100 GPUs each of which have 32 GB memory. For all models, we average the last 20 checkpoints to avoid overfitting. We use cased BLEU scores calculated with Moses[2] mteval-v12a.pl script as evaluation metric. Following the organizers' suggestion, News dev 2018 is used as the development set and News test 2018 as the test set.

3.1 Pre-processing and Post-processing

The Chinese data has been tokenized using the Jieba tokenizer[3]. For English data, punctuation normalization, aggressive tokenization and truecasing are applied orderly to all sentences with the scripts provided in Moses. We also filter the parallel sentences which are duplicated or bad alignment scores obtained by fast-align (Dyer et al., 2013), and then we have a preprocessed bilingual training data consisting of 18M parallel sentences.

In post-processing phase, the English translations are true-cased and de-tokenized with the scripts provided in Moses. We use simple rules to normalize the punctuations and Arabic numerals in the Chinese translations.

3.2 Chinese→English

For Chinese→English task, we do not use all of the 18M preprocessed parallel sentences, in that there is much out-of-domain data in UN corpus. Table 1 shows that the 6.7M CWMT corpus and 9M UN corpus which are selected ran-

[2]http://www.statmt.org/moses/
[3]https://github.com/fxsjy/jieba

Settings	Big Transformer	Pre-trained Transformer	Deeper Transformer	Bigger Transformer
Baseline	39.2	-	-	-
+ Back Translation	43.33	43.7	42.19	44
+ Joint Training	43.86	44.12	42.5	44.78
+ Knowledge Distillation	44.25	44.6	42.86	45.27
+ Fine-tuning	44.72	44.75	42.94	45.79
+ Ensemble	46.42			
+ Re-ranking*	46.51			

Table 3: BLEU evaluation results on the WMT 2018 English→Chinese test set (* denotes the submitted system).

domly are used as our bilingual training set for Chinese→English task. We learn a BPE (Sennrich et al., 2015b) model with 30K merge operations, in which 46.4K and 31K sub-word tokens are adopted as Chinese and English vocabularies separately. We set beam size to 12 and alpha to 1.1 during decoding.

12 portions of sentences are selected from huge volumes of English monolingual data, and we carry out a large number of experiments in which the Transformer models are trained with each portion. And then 4 most effective portions are selected. Due to the extensive training time and the approaching deadline for submissions, pre-trained transformer, deep Transformer(base Transformer with 30 encoder layers) and bigger Transformer are trained on the combination of real bilingual data and the synthetic data directly. For each different architecture model, we train 4 more systems with different portions of monolingual data and different parameters in order to obtain more diverse models. For comparison, we only report results on the WMT 2018 test set with the same portion of monolingual data.

Table 2 shows that the translation quality is largely improved using proposed techniques. We observe solid improvement of 0.86 BLEU for the baseline system after back translation. Joint training and knowledge distillation yield improvements over all the different architecture models, approximating 0.34-0.68 BLEU improvements toward single models. It is also clear that the fine-tuning technique brings substantial improvements compared with the baseline systems.

In our experiments, the ensemble models consists of 8 single models: 1 Transformer, 2 pre-trained Transformers, 2 deeper Transformers and 3 bigger Transformers. As shown in the Table 2, the ensemble models also outperform the best single model by 1.49 BLEU score. However, the improvement of re-ranking is relatively slight, and we attribute this to the strong performance of ensemble models. Our WMT 2019 Chinese→English submission achieves a cased BLEU score of 38.0, winning the first place among all submissions.

3.3 English→Chinese

As listed in the Table 1, the parallel training data for English→Chinese translation task consists of about 6.7M sentence pairs from the filtered CWMT Corpus, 3.5M sentence pairs from the UN Parallel Corpus, 0.6M sentence pairs from the Wiki Titles Corpus. For the UN data, we train a 5-gram KN language model on the Chinese sides of the CWMT data and select 3.5M sentence pairs according to their perplexities. The size of the English vocabulary and the Chinese vocabulary are 31K and 48.6K respectively after BPE operation. We use beam search with a beam size of 12, and set alpha 0.8.

From the Table 3, we can observe: 1) We obtain +4.13 BLEU score when adding the synthetic parallel data to the training set of the Transformer. 2) We further gain +0.92 BLEU score after applying joint training and knowledge distillation for the Transformer system. 3) The improvement from the fine-tuning technique is relative slight for the pre-trained Transformer and deeper Transformer, whereas it is effective for the Transformer and bigger Transformer, with about 0.5 BLEU score improvements.

Notably, the ensemble models consist of pre-trained Transformers and bigger Transformers. We omit the deeper Transformer model due to its worse performance on this translation task. On the WMT 2019 English→Chinese task, our submission achieves 42.4 cased BLEU score, winning the second place in the translation task.

4 Conclusion

This paper presents the Baidu NMT systems for WMT 2019 Chinese↔English news translation tasks. We investigate various different architectures of Transformer to build numerous strong single systems. We exploit effective strategies to better utilize parallel data as well as monolingual data. We find significant gains from combining multiple heterogeneous systems due to the diversity. Finally, our submission of Chinese→English news task achieves the highest cased BLEU score and our submission of English→Chinese achieves the second best cased BLEU score among all the constrained submissions.

5 Acknowledgements

We thank Shikun Feng at Baidu for providing the pre-trained language model. We thank the anonymous reviews for their careful reading and their thoughtful comments.

References

Ondřej Bojar, Christian Federmann, Mark Fishel, Yvette Graham, Barry Haddow, Philipp Koehn, and Christof Monz. 2018. Findings of the 2018 conference on machine translation (WMT18). In *Proceedings of the Third Conference on Machine Translation: Shared Task Papers*, pages 272–303, Belgium, Brussels. Association for Computational Linguistics.

Colin Cherry and George Foster. 2012. Batch tuning strategies for statistical machine translation. In *Proceedings of the 2012 Conference of the North American Chapter of the Association for Computational Linguistics: Human Language Technologies*, pages 427–436. Association for Computational Linguistics.

David Chiang, Yuval Marton, and Philip Resnik. 2008. Online large-margin training of syntactic and structural translation features. In *Proceedings of the conference on empirical methods in natural language processing*, pages 224–233. Association for Computational Linguistics.

Zihang Dai, Zhilin Yang, Yiming Yang, William W Cohen, Jaime Carbonell, Quoc V Le, and Ruslan Salakhutdinov. 2019. Transformer-xl: Attentive language models beyond a fixed-length context. *arXiv preprint arXiv:1901.02860.*

Jacob Devlin, Ming-Wei Chang, Kenton Lee, and Kristina Toutanova. 2018. Bert: Pre-training of deep bidirectional transformers for language understanding. *arXiv preprint arXiv:1810.04805.*

Tobias Domhan. 2018. How much attention do you need? a granular analysis of neural machine translation architectures. In *Proceedings of the 56th Annual Meeting of the Association for Computational Linguistics (Volume 1: Long Papers)*, pages 1799–1808.

Chris Dyer, Victor Chahuneau, and Noah A Smith. 2013. A simple, fast, and effective reparameterization of ibm model 2. In *Proceedings of the 2013 Conference of the North American Chapter of the Association for Computational Linguistics: Human Language Technologies*, pages 644–648.

Sergey Edunov, Myle Ott, Michael Auli, and David Grangier. 2018. Understanding back-translation at scale. In *Proceedings of the 2018 Conference on Empirical Methods in Natural Language Processing*, pages 489–500, Brussels, Belgium. Association for Computational Linguistics.

Hany Hassan, Anthony Aue, Chang Chen, Vishal Chowdhary, Jonathan Clark, Christian Federmann, Xuedong Huang, Marcin Junczys-Dowmunt, William Lewis, Mu Li, et al. 2018. Achieving human parity on automatic chinese to english news translation. *arXiv preprint arXiv:1803.05567.*

Yoon Kim and Alexander M Rush. 2016. Sequence-level knowledge distillation. *arXiv preprint arXiv:1606.07947.*

Lemao Liu, Masao Utiyama, Andrew Finch, and Eiichiro Sumita. 2016. Agreement on target-bidirectional neural machine translation. In *Proceedings of the 2016 Conference of the North American Chapter of the Association for Computational Linguistics: Human Language Technologies*, pages 411–416.

Minh-Thang Luong and Christopher D Manning. 2015. Stanford neural machine translation systems for spoken language domains. In *Proceedings of the International Workshop on Spoken Language Translation*, pages 76–79.

Jan Niehues, Ronaldo Cattoni, Sebastian Stüker, Mauro Cettolo, Marco Turchi, and Marcello Federico. 2018. The iwslt 2018 evaluation campaign. In *International Workshop on Spoken Language Translation (IWSLT) 2018.*

Matthew E Peters, Mark Neumann, Mohit Iyyer, Matt Gardner, Christopher Clark, Kenton Lee, and Luke Zettlemoyer. 2018. Deep contextualized word representations. *arXiv preprint arXiv:1802.05365.*

Alec Radford, Karthik Narasimhan, Tim Salimans, and Ilya Sutskever. 2018. Improving language understanding by generative pre-training. *URL https://s3-us-west-2. amazonaws. com/openai-assets/research-covers/languageunsupervised/language understanding paper. pdf.*

Alessandro Raganato and Jörg Tiedemann. 2018. An analysis of encoder representations in transformer-based machine translation. In *Proceedings of the 2018 EMNLP Workshop BlackboxNLP: Analyzing and Interpreting Neural Networks for NLP*, pages 287–297.

Marc'Aurelio Ranzato, Sumit Chopra, Michael Auli, and Wojciech Zaremba. 2016. Sequence level training with recurrent neural networks. In *International Conference on Learning Representations*.

Rico Sennrich, Barry Haddow, and Alexandra Birch. 2015a. Improving neural machine translation models with monolingual data. *arXiv preprint arXiv:1511.06709*.

Rico Sennrich, Barry Haddow, and Alexandra Birch. 2015b. Neural machine translation of rare words with subword units. *arXiv preprint arXiv:1508.07909*.

Yu Sun, Shuohuan Wang, Yukun Li, Shikun Feng, Xuyi Chen, Han Zhang, Xin Tian, Danxiang Zhu, Hao Tian, and Hua Wu. 2019. Ernie: Enhanced representation through knowledge integration. *arXiv preprint arXiv:1904.09223*.

Gongbo Tang, Mathias Müller, Annette Rios, and Rico Sennrich. 2018. Why self-attention? a targeted evaluation of neural machine translation architectures. *arXiv preprint arXiv:1808.08946*.

Wilson L Taylor. 1953. "cloze procedure": A new tool for measuring readability. *Journalism Bulletin*, 30(4):415–433.

Ashish Vaswani, Noam Shazeer, Niki Parmar, Jakob Uszkoreit, Llion Jones, Aidan N Gomez, Łukasz Kaiser, and Illia Polosukhin. 2017. Attention is all you need. In *Advances in neural information processing systems*, pages 5998–6008.

Mingxuan Wang, Li Gong, Wenhuan Zhu, Jun Xie, and Chao Bian. 2018. Tencent neural machine translation systems for WMT18. In *Proceedings of the Third Conference on Machine Translation: Shared Task Papers*, pages 522–527, Belgium, Brussels. Association for Computational Linguistics.

Zhirui Zhang, Shujie Liu, Mu Li, Ming Zhou, and Enhong Chen. 2018. Joint training for neural machine translation models with monolingual data. In *Thirty-Second AAAI Conference on Artificial Intelligence*.

University of Tartu's Multilingual Multi-domain WMT19 News Translation Shared Task Submission

Andre Tättar   Elizaveta Korotkova   Mark Fishel

Institute of Computer Science

University of Tartu, Estonia

{andre.tattar,elizaveta.korotkova,fishel}@ut.ee

Abstract

This paper describes the University of Tartu's submission to the news translation shared task of WMT19, where the core idea was to train a single multilingual system to cover several language pairs of the shared task and submit its results. We only used the constrained data from the shared task. We describe our approach and its results and discuss the technical issues we faced.

1 Introduction

Typically the majority of WMT news translation shared task submissions are based on language pair-specific machine translation (MT) systems (Bojar et al., 2016, 2017, 2018). However, recently several multilingual approaches to MT have been proposed (e.g. Johnson et al., 2017; Vázquez et al., 2018; Aharoni et al., 2019). With them as inspiration, the goal of this paper is to describe our submission to the WMT'2019 news translation shared task, where we trained a single multilingual translation system using the constrained parallel and monolingual data for several language pairs.

In addition to multilinguality we wanted to incorporate the multiple text domains that constitute the constrained set of parallel corpora in the WMT shared task. We approach multi-domain NMT using the method of (Tars and Fishel, 2018): namely, by treating domains as separate languages, therefore creating a "double-multilingual" system.

In addition to multilinguality and multi-domain NMT our submission has more common features, like data filtering, ensembles of several models and fine-tuning on back-translated monolingual data.

Below we describe the architecture of our approach in Section 2, experimental setup in Sec-

tion 3, results and analysis in Section 4 and conclude the paper in Section 5.

2 Architecture

Our model is a neural MT system based on autoregressive self-attention in the encoder and decoder (Vaswani et al., 2017). We achieve multilinguality in a similar fashion to (Johnson et al., 2017): using an additional input specifying the output language, so that the system would know which language to generate. Differently from Johnson et al. (2017), who include the output language into the input segment itself, we use word factors (Hieber et al., 2017) and specify the output language as a factor of each input token.

In addition to multilinguality, our NMT system also uses the information on which domain the parallel or monolingual corpora come from. The WMT data consist of a variety of text domains (parliamentary speeches, crawled web and news texts, press releases, Wikipedia titles, etc.) and it has been shown (Tars and Fishel, 2018) that multi-domain NMT can get much better results than the default approach of mixing heterogeneous corpora together, as well as yield more efficient solutions than fine-tuning to each domain separately. Our solution is to specify the output text domain as another word factor.

One peculiarity of multilingual NMT is that the model performs back-translation for itself, therefore avoiding the necessity of training more than one translation system.

3 Experiments

3.1 Model Setup

We use the Sockeye (Hieber et al., 2017) machine translation framework for our experiments. The main reason behind this choice is that Sockeye

Proceedings of the Fourth Conference on Machine Translation (WMT), Volume 2: Shared Task Papers (Day 1) pages 382–385
Florence, Italy, August 1-2, 2019. ©2019 Association for Computational Linguistics

	CZ-EN	DE-EN	DE-FR	EN-FI	EN-LT	TOTAL
NEWS	2534352	5985498	4372033	2656508	1803323	17351714
OFF	11462432	1797854	1687074	1725792	615219	17288371
SUBS	37251088	-	-	-	-	37251088
OTHER	10932478	34457911	7585341	4012589	1290931	58279250
TOTAL	62180350	42241263	13644448	8394889	3709473	130170423

Table 1: Dataset sizes after filtering. Shown number of parallel sentences.

implements word factors together with the Transformer.

We use traditional transformer NMT architecture with 6 layers for both encoder and decoder, with the transformer model size 1024, transformer attention heads 16, batch size 6000, with a shared byte-pair encoded (BPE) (Sennrich et al., 2015) vocabulary of size 90000. SentencePiece[1] are used to extract BPE vocabulary. The embedding size for source factors is 8. There are 6 different language factors and 4 different domain factors. All other parameters were kept as default.

Models are trained on 4 Tesla V100 GPUs.

3.2 Data

All of the available WMT constrained data for all languages was downloaded and then fed through a data pipeline. The data pipeline consisted of 6 steps:

1. **Filtering** Data filtering included several steps: it filtered out empty/too long sentences, sentences with too many non-alphanumeric characters, sentences where the length difference was too big, and also sentences automatically identified as a different language than the expected one.

2. **Tokenization** The data was tokenized with MosesTokenizer.

3. **Truecasing** A Truecasing model was trained for every language separately, then applied on all the data.

4. **SentencePiece** A SentencePiece model was trained on one big text file which included all data, low-resource language pairs like EN-LT were upscaled and high-resource language pairs like CZ-EN were downscaled. In total 50M lines of text were used for SentencePiece model with vocabulary size 90K.

5. **Factoring** Then the source factors for target domain and target language were generated for all data.

6. **Sharding** Sockeye uses shards to handle massive datasets, which means that a big dataset is divided into more manageable dataset sizes. Each shard is of equal size. A shard size of 1M was used.

Due to time constraints we deviated from the original plan of including all WMT'2019 language pairs and only included languages that use the Latin script in our submissions. The final data set sizes are shown in Table 1.

In order to generate the domain factors we grouped some of the domains by the apparent similarity of texts, additionally grouping smaller corpora together:

- **News** - Rapid2019, Rapid2016, EESC, dev dataset from previous years, EMEA2016, ECB2017, news (from CzEng), News-commentary

- **Subs** - Subtitles from the CzEng corpus

- **Off** - Parts of the CzEng corpus, Europarl

- **Other** - Everything else

Additionally, monolingual data was extracted for back-translation and fine-tuning, mainly News Crawl corpora was used. For every language pair 3M sentences were extracted, with the exception of Lithuanian, where the news crawl size is smaller, and thus other monolingual data like Wiki dumps and Europarl were used.

4 Results and Analysis

Results are presented in Table 2. We separate the results of our **baseline** system, trained on parallel data only, and the **fine-tuned** system that was trained further on monolingual data, back-translated by the baseline system.

[1] https://github.com/google/sentencepiece

	Baseline	Fine-tune
EN-CS	22.8	-
DE-EN	29.9	-
EN-DE	39.6	-
DE-FR	32.4	30.7
EN-FI	18.6	-
EN-LT	12.7	-
FI-EN	22.1	24.8
FR-DE	25.9	-
LT-EN	24.5	25.3

Table 2: Results of our multilingual baseline model, trained on parallel data and the fine-tuned model that was further trained on back-translated monolingual data.

	#Sents	#Baseline Wrong	#Ensemble Wrong
DE-EN	33650	214	18596
DE-FR	1698	3	117
EN-CS	9917	256	10137
EN-DE	8853	85	6396
F EN-FI	2606	221	2799
EN-LT	1056	11	1066
FI-EN	4105	8	76
FR-DE	2705	6	843
Total	65684	809	40054
%		1.22	60.24

Table 3: Number of sentences which are classified as having a wrong language after translation using the FastText language classifier.

Our baseline performed reasonably well, however the goal was to achieve state-of-the-art results after doing fine-tuning on back-translated news data. As a result of this second step unexpectedly the model started confusing the output language and generating the output in a different language than requested: for example generating Czech or English instead of Finnish. Automatic language identification with FastText[2] shows the baseline model only produced output in the wrong language in 1.22% of cases, whereas after just a day of fine-tuning on in-domain data, the percentage of translations our model got wrong jumped up to 60.24%. Mostly our ensemble model got English right and other languages wrong. Our ensemble model was done by using 2 snapshots of baseline model and 2 snapshots of fine-tuned model.

For human evaluations published in (Bojar et al., 2019) our model (called TartuNLP-c) performed similarly to other multilingual systems noted as Online-X in the findings paper. Online systems are freely available online systems like Google Translate, Bing Translate etc. Our models performed worse than single language pair NMT systems.

We suspect that the reason for the wrong language output lies in two factors:

- wrong language segments in monolingual crawled data. This mainly occurs in non-English languages like Czech, Finnish and Lithuanian and affects the output side of back-translated data. Before the submission deadline we did not have language-filtering in the data preparation pipeline, which might have caused this effect.

- wrong language output by our model. This affects the input side of the back-translated data. While this does not occur often, filtering out the wrong-language translations should still help learn a more precise translation model.

We are investigating alternative explanations to this behavior further.

5 Conclusions and Future Work

We have described a multilingual multi-domain neural machine translation approach that can be trained on a mixture of different language pairs and text domains.

Our results are modest, mainly due to failing to properly fine-tune the systems on back-translated news texts. Precise reasons for failing the fine-tuning are under investigation.

Other future work includes including more languages and domains, testing online continuous back-translation and experimenting with other ways of providing the output language and domain information to the NMT model.

Acknowledgments

This work was supported in part by funding from the European Union's Horizon 2020 research and innovation programme under grant agreement No. 825303, Estonian Research Council grant no. 1226 and the AWS Cloud Credits for Research program.

[2] https://github.com/facebookresearch/fastText

References

Roee Aharoni, Melvin Johnson, and Orhan Firat. 2019. Massively multilingual neural machine translation. In *Proceedings of NAACL 2019*, page (accepted), Minneapolis, MN, USA.

Ondřej Bojar, Rajen Chatterjee, Christian Federmann, Yvette Graham, Barry Haddow, Shujian Huang, Matthias Huck, Philipp Koehn, Qun Liu, Varvara Logacheva, Christof Monz, Matteo Negri, Matt Post, Raphael Rubino, Lucia Specia, and Marco Turchi. 2017. Findings of the 2017 conference on machine translation (WMT17). In *Proceedings of the Second Conference on Machine Translation*, pages 169–214, Copenhagen, Denmark.

Ondřej Bojar, Rajen Chatterjee, Christian Federmann, Yvette Graham, Barry Haddow, Matthias Huck, Antonio Jimeno Yepes, Philipp Koehn, Varvara Logacheva, Christof Monz, Matteo Negri, Aurelie Neveol, Mariana Neves, Martin Popel, Matt Post, Raphael Rubino, Carolina Scarton, Lucia Specia, Marco Turchi, Karin Verspoor, and Marcos Zampieri. 2016. Findings of the 2016 conference on machine translation. In *Proceedings of the First Conference on Machine Translation*, pages 131–198, Berlin, Germany.

Ondřej Bojar, Christian Federmann, Mark Fishel, Yvette Graham, Barry Haddow, Matthias Huck, Philipp Koehn, and Christof Monz. 2018. Findings of the 2018 conference on machine translation (WMT18). In *Proceedings of WMT'18: the Third Conference on Machine Translation*, Brussels, Belgium.

Ondřej Bojar, Christian Federmann, Mark Fishel, Yvette Graham, Barry Haddow, Matthias Huck, Philipp Koehn, and Christof Monz. 2019. Findings of the 2019 conference on machine translation (wmt19). In *Proceedings of the Fourth Conference on Machine Translation, Volume 2: Shared Task Papers*, Florence, Italy. Association for Computational Linguistics.

Felix Hieber, Tobias Domhan, Michael Denkowski, David Vilar, Artem Sokolov, Ann Clifton, and Matt Post. 2017. Sockeye: A toolkit for neural machine translation. *CoRR*, abs/1712.05690.

Melvin Johnson, Mike Schuster, Quoc V. Le, Maxim Krikun, Yonghui Wu, Zhifeng Chen, Nikhil Thorat, Fernanda Viégas, Martin Wattenberg, Greg Corrado, Macduff Hughes, and Jeffrey Dean. 2017. Google's multilingual neural machine translation system: Enabling zero-shot translation. *Transactions of the Association for Computational Linguistics*, 5:339–351.

Rico Sennrich, Barry Haddow, and Alexandra Birch. 2015. Neural machine translation of rare words with subword units. *CoRR*, abs/1508.07909.

Sander Tars and Mark Fishel. 2018. Multi-domain neural machine translation. In *Proceedings of EAMT*, pages 259 – 268, Alicante, Spain.

Ashish Vaswani, Noam Shazeer, Niki Parmar, Jakob Uszkoreit, Llion Jones, Aidan N Gomez, Łukasz Kaiser, and Illia Polosukhin. 2017. Attention is all you need. In *Proceedings of NIPS*, pages 5998–6008, Long Beach, CA, USA.

Raúl Vázquez, Alessandro Raganato, Jörg Tiedemann, and Mathias Creutz. 2018. Multilingual NMT with a language-independent attention bridge. *CoRR*, abs/1811.00498.

Neural Machine Translation for English–Kazakh with Morphological Segmentation and Synthetic Data

Antonio Toral† Lukas Edman‡ Galiya Yeshmagambetova‡ Jennifer Spenader‡
†Center for Language and Cognition, ‡Institute for Artificial Intelligence
University of Groningen
The Netherlands

a.toral.ruiz@rug.nl,{j.l.edman,g.yeshmagambetova}@student.rug.nl, j.spenader@ai.rug.nl

Abstract

This paper presents the systems submitted by the University of Groningen to the English–Kazakh language pair (both translation directions) for the WMT 2019 news translation task. We explore potential benefits from using (i) morphological segmentation (both unsupervised and rule-based), given the agglutinative nature of Kazakh, (ii) data from two additional languages (Turkish and Russian), given the scarcity of English–Kazakh data, and (iii) synthetic data, both for the source and for the target language. Our best submissions ranked second for Kazakh→English and third for English→Kazakh in terms of the BLEU automatic evaluation metric.

1 Introduction

This paper presents the neural machine translation (NMT) systems submitted by the University of Groningen to the WMT 2019 news translation task.[1] We participated in the English↔Kazakh (henceforth referred to as EN↔KK) constrained tasks.

Because of the inherent characteristics of this language pair and the current state-of-the-art of related techniques, we focused on two main research questions (RQs):

- RQ1. Does morphological segmentation help? Recent research in NMT for agglutinative languages found that morphological segmentation outperforms the most widely used segmentation technique, byte-pair encoding (BPE, using character sequence frequencies) (Sennrich et al., 2016). Rule-based segmentation improved English-to-Finnish translation (Sánchez-Cartagena and Toral,

2016) and unsupervised segmentation improved Turkish-to-English translation (Ataman et al., 2017). Because Kazakh belongs to the same language family as Turkish, the work by Ataman et al. (2017) is particularly relevant. Their training data had fewer than 300,000 sentence pairs and they trained an NMT system under the recurrent sequence-to-sequence with attention paradigm (Bahdanau et al., 2015). Our training data is considerably bigger and we use a non-recurrent attention-based system (Vaswani et al., 2017). Does the advantage of morphological segmentation over BPE also hold in our experimental setup?

- RQ2. Does the use of additional languages improve outcomes? Due to the scarcity of parallel data for EN–KK, we investigate if using data from two additional languages is useful, Russian (RU) and Turkish (TR). Even though RU is not related to either EN or KK, it seems a sensible choice due to the availability of large amounts of EN–RU and RU–KK parallel data. TR is related to KK and there are limited amounts of EN–TR data available. Does this additional data improve the performance, and is more data from an unrelated language (RU) better than less data from a related language (TR)?

The rest of the paper is organized as follows. Section 2 describes the datasets and tools used. Then Section 3 details our experiments. Finally, Section 4 outlines our conclusions and plans for future work.

2 Datasets and Tools

We preprocessed all the corpora used (training, validation and test sets) with scripts from the

---

[1]http://www.statmt.org/wmt19/translation-task.html

Proceedings of the Fourth Conference on Machine Translation (WMT), Volume 2: Shared Task Papers (Day 1) pages 386–392
Florence, Italy, August 1-2, 2019. ©2019 Association for Computational Linguistics

Moses toolkit (Koehn et al., 2007). The following operations were performed sequentially: punctuation normalisation, tokenisation,[2] truecasing and escaping of problematic characters. The truecaser was lexicon-based and it was trained on all the monolingual data available for each language. In addition, we removed sentence pairs where either side was empty or longer than 80 tokens from the parallel corpora . Tables 1 to 4 show the parallel datasets used for training for each translation direction after preprocessing. The corpora Kazakhtv (EN–KK) and crawl (KK–RU) were provided with sentence-level scores; we sorted their files according to these scores and a native KK speaker proficient in both EN and RU identified a threshold where alignments were roughly 90% correct. This led to discarding the bottom 27% of the data for EN–KK's Kazakhtv and the bottom 3% for KK–RU's crawl.

Corpus	Sentences (k)	Words (M)	
		EN	KK
Kazakhtv	67.7	1.00	0.82
News-comm.	7.5	0.19	0.16
Wikititles	117.0	0.23	0.19

Table 1: Preprocessed EN–KK parallel training data.

Corpus	Sentences (k)	Words (M)	
		EN	RU
Common crawl	871.8	20.82	19.97
News-comm.	278.2	7.17	6.86
Paracrawl	11,881.0	189.90	166.50
Yandex	997.3	24.06	22.00

Table 2: Preprocessed EN–RU parallel training data.

Corpus	Sentences (k)	Words (M)	
		KK	RU
Crawl	4,861.5	99.34	105.16

Table 3: Preprocessed KK–RU parallel training data.

All our NMT systems are trained with Marian (Junczys-Dowmunt et al., 2018).[3] We used the `transformer` model type (Vaswani et al., 2017)

---

[2]Moses does not contain a tokeniser for KK. KK texts were tokenised with the RU model, as both languages are written in the cyrillic alphabet. The resulting tokenisation was inspected and validated by a KK native speaker.

[3]https://marian-nmt.github.io/

Corpus	Sentences (k)	Words (M)	
		EN	TR
newstest2016-18	9.0	0.20	0.17
SETimes	207.4	5.12	4.61

Table 4: Preprocessed EN–TR parallel training data.

in all experiments, except for a few experiments where the training data was very limited, where we used the `s2s` model type (Bahdanau et al., 2015).

During development, we evaluated our systems on the development sets provided. We used two automatic evaluation metrics: BLEU (Papineni et al., 2002) and CHRF (Popović, 2015). CHRF is our primary evaluation metric for EN→KK, due to the fact that this metric has been shown to correlate better than BLEU with human evaluation when the target language is agglutinative (Stanojević et al., 2015). BLEU is our primary evaluation metric for KK→EN systems, as the correlations with human evaluation of BLEU and CHRF are roughly on par for EN as the target language. Prior to evaluation the MT output is detruecased and detokenized with Moses' scripts.

3 Experiments

3.1 Cyrilization and Turkish

Since KK is a low-resourced language, multilingual NMT (Johnson et al., 2017) was used. Following Neubig and Hu (2018), we have chosen TR as a helper source language, because it is related to KK (both belong to the same language family) and TR is higher-resourced than KK. However, TR uses a Latin-script alphabet, while KK uses a Cyrillic-script alphabet, which means their vocabularies do not match as they are. For this reason, we decided to transliterate TR into Cyrillic (*cyrillization*). However, some characters in KK's alphabet are not present in existing transliterators. Therefore, we created a cyrillizer that matches KK's alphabet exactly.

We trained a {KK, TR}→EN system in two steps. First, we use as training data the concatenation of the EN–KK and EN–TR corpora (Tables 1 and 4) and when the model converged, we resume training using only the EN–KK dataset. We compared models that used the original TR versus cyrillized. These models were trained with the `s2s` architecture using 32,000 joining operations in BPE and dropout of 0.05.

Training data	BLEU
EN–KK	6.61
+ EN–TR	11.15
+ cyrillizer	10.34

Table 5: BLEU scores on the development set for KK→EN using additional EN–TR data.

As it is shown in Table 5, the addition of EN–TR data proves very beneficial (absolute improvement of 4.5 BLEU points), which is not surprising since the amount of training data more than doubles (cf. Tables 1 and 4). However, cyrillising TR decreases the BLEU score by 0.8 points.

3.2 Backtranslation and Russian

Given the small amount of EN–KK parallel data (see Table 1) and the large amount of EN–RU and KK–RU datasets, we introduced RU as a pivot language, using backtranslation (Sennrich et al., 2015) to derive bigger datasets where the source side is synthetic. For KK→EN, we trained a RU→KK auxiliary system on the available KK–RU data (Table 3), and used this to translate the RU portion of the EN–RU (Table 2) data into KK, creating a synthetic EN–KK' dataset. This was then used, along the original EN–KK data (Table 1) to train the KK→EN model.

For EN→KK, we trained a RU→EN auxiliary model on the available EN–RU data, and used this model to translate the RU portion of the KK–RU data into EN, creating a synthetic EN'–KK dataset. This synthetic dataset, alongside the original EN–KK data, was then used to train the EN→KK model.

Table 6 shows the results for EN→KK and KK→EN without and with the backtranslated data. The addition of backtranslated data results in massive improvements: +17.9 CHRF points for EN→KK and +14.2 BLEU points for KK→EN. This is expected given the very small size of EN–KK data and the much larger EN–RU and KK–RU datasets. The improvements are considerably larger than those obtained with additional EN–TR data (see Table 5).

Backtranslation	EN→KK	KK→EN
No	27.75	6.61
Yes	45.67	20.17

Table 6: Performance of MT systems with and without backtranslation for EN→KK (CHRF) and KK→EN (BLEU).

3.3 Corpus Filtering and Target Synthetic Data

Since most of our training data is crawled, we applied corpus filtering to remove noisy sentence pairs. Following Artetxe and Schwenk (2018a), we removed sentences shorter than 3 words and longer than 80 words, and sentence pairs where either sentence is classified as another language using the FastText language identifier (Joulin et al., 2016a,b).[4] We also removed sentence pairs with a token overlap of 50% or higher.

We identify and remove misaligned sentence pairs (where the meanings of the source and target sentences do not match), using the LASER system, a 93-language BiLSTM encoder (Artetxe and Schwenk, 2018b).[5] This encodes the sentences in each side, and uses the cosine similarity between the embeddings of the two sentences as a filtering threshold (where sentences below the threshold are removed).

This filtering is applied after backtranslation (see Section 3.2). For KK→EN, we filter the EN–KK' data, i.e. the EN–RU corpora whose RU side had been translated into KK. The thresholds (determined manually, as previously mentioned in Section 2) and number of sentence pairs kept are shown in Table 7.

Corpus	Threshold	Pairs left (k)
CommonCrawl	0.7323	568.50
News Comm.	0.7314	254.79
ParaCrawl	0.8031	4056.28
Yandex	0.7220	887.76

Table 7: Cosine similarity thresholds used to filter out EN–RU corpora and resulting corpus sizes after all filtering steps are applied.

We quantify the impact on translation performance of each filtering step, cumulatively, in Table 8. Each filtering step improves the BLEU score, corroborating previous research, e.g. (Koehn et al., 2018), that has shown that noisy sentence pairs indeed cause a drop in translation performance.

---

[4]https://fasttext.cc/docs/en/language-identification.html
[5]https://github.com/facebookresearch/LASER

Filtering	BLEU	# sent. pairs
none	20.17	15.1
language identification	20.76	9.8
+cosine	21.60	6.9
+3-80 & overlap	22.26	5.4

Table 8: BLEU scores for KK→EN systems adding one filtering mechanism at a time. The table also shows the number of sentence pairs (millions) that make up the training data for each system.

In the opposite direction, EN→KK, we filter the EN'–KK data, i.e. the RU–KK corpora whose RU side has been translated into EN. The threshold and number of sentence pairs kept are shown in Table 9.

Corpus	Threshold	Pairs left (k)
Crawl	0.1463	4494.10

Table 9: Sentence pairs left in the EN'–KK dataset after filtering.

By manual inspection, we noticed that the biggest dataset used for EN→KK (the KK–RU crawl corpus, see Table 3) is domain-specific and rather unrelated to the domain of the test set (news). Due to this, we decided to experiment with target synthetic data by translating the EN–RU corpora, which are not domain-specific, into KK and adding a subset of the resulting EN–KK' data to our EN→KK system. We experimented with two similarity thresholds: a more conservative one (0.8) and a less conservative one (0.75). The thresholds and number of sentence pairs kept are shown in Table 10.

Corpus	Pairs left (k)	
	sim $\geq$ 0.75	sim $\geq$ 0.80
CommonCrawl	80.49	30.47
News Comm.	15.41	3.71
ParaCrawl	739.16	320.98
Yandex	83.16	31.65

Table 10: Sentence pairs left in the EN–KK' dataset after filtering using the similarity thresholds 0.75 and 0.8.

Table 11 shows the impact of adding target synthetic data on translation performance. Adding a small amount using a conservative threshold (0.8) results in an absolute improvement of 1.15 CHRF points. Adding more data using a less conservative threshold (0.75) results in a bigger improvement of

1.6 points. An even lower threshold was not tested due to time constraints.

Target synthetic data	CHRF
None	45.67
similarity>0.80	46.82
similarity>0.75	47.27

Table 11: Impact of adding target synthetic data on translation performance (CHRF) for the translation direction EN→KK

3.4 Segmentation

Data is segmented with BPE (Sennrich et al., 2016) on all the languages involved in our experiments (EN, KK, RU and TR). In addition, we perform two types of morphological segmentation on KK: unsupervised and rule-based.

Unsupervised morphological segmentation is performed with LMVR (Ataman et al., 2017),[6] a variant of Morfessor (Virpioja et al., 2013) that allows a fixed vocabulary size to be defined. LMVR was trained on the KK side of the RU–KK parallel data as well as on the monolingual KK data. We experimented using vocabulary sizes of 8, 16, 24, and 32 thousand. The trained LMVR models are used to segment the KK portion of the RU–KK data and the synthetic KK derived from the EN-RU data created with a RU-KK system (see Section 3.2).

For rule-based segmentation, `Apertium-kaz` (Washington et al., 2014) was used.[7] A transducer that provides multiple segmentation variants was set up four our purpose,[8] from these variants we decided to pick the one that segments into the smallest units, because this one, as observed by manual inspection, tends to be correct more often. Some segmentations do not correspond to the original word when joined, which we attribute to the fact that Apertium is not doing pure segmentation but also analysis. We do not pick these variants. We also observed that some words were out-of-vocabulary (OOV), i.e. not found in Apertium's transducer, so those were left unsegmented.

As can be seen in Table 12, Apertium segmenter leads to lower automatic metric scores, while BPE and LVMR are on par. This could be attributed

---

[6] https://github.com/d-ataman/lmvr
[7] http://wiki.apertium.org/wiki/Apertium-kaz
[8] This is a version of the regular transducer that does not delete the morpheme boundary in the morphophonological rules, and is therefore more suitable for segmentation.

to the morphological ambiguity issues described above and to the fact that some words were not segmented (OOV).

Segmentation	EN→KK	KK→EN
BPE	45.67	22.26
LVMR	45.47	22.36
Apertium	42.21	-

Table 12: Performance of MT systems using different segmentations (BPE, LVMR and Apertium) for EN→KK (CHRF) and KK→EN (BLEU). Apertium was not used for the KK→EN due to time constraints.

Besides these quantitative results, we also performed qualitative analyses of the segmentations. Table 13 shows examples of words that result in ambiguous segmentations with Apertium. Table 14 shows a KK sentence segmented with BPE and LVMR. Morphological segmentation results in a better segmentation, which has a direct impact on the quality of the resulting EN translation.

3.5 Final Submissions

We took the best performing systems from previous experiments and carried out fine-tuning by resuming training after convergence using solely the EN–KK data (i.e. without any data whose source or target is synthetic). Finally, we ran ensembles of the best performing systems (with and without fine-tuning) and chose those that perform best on the development set. Those constitute our submissions to the shared task.

For KK→EN, we consider systems segmented with BPE and with LVMR since their BLEU scores are roughly on par: 22.26 and 22.36, respectively. The fine-tuned KK→EN system with BPE segmentation reaches 23.11. We built an ensemble on four BPE-based models, the two top performing ones without fine tuning (21.9 and 22.26) and the two top performing ones with fine tuning (22.99 and 23.11). The ensemble attains 23.37. We then tried different length-penalty values for the decoder (parameter `normalize` in Marian), using 0.9 (instead of the default 0.6) we reach 23.47.

The fine-tuned KK→EN with LVMR reaches a BLEU score of 23.26, thus slightly outperforming the fine-tuned system with BPE (23.11). We also performed fine-tuning including the synthetic data but including the non-synthetic data four times (i.e. synthetic to non-synthetic ratio of 1:4). This

system reaches 22.65. We built an ensemble of the two fine-tuned models. This ensemble achieves a BLEU score of 23.71, which using a length normalisation penalty of 0.9 increases to 23.84.

For EN→KK we submitted systems based on BPE segmentation only. Our best of these systems achieves 47.27 CHRF while the best LVMR-based system yields 45.27.[9] We build an ensemble made of five models: the two top performing ones using target synthetic data with threshold 0.8 (CHRF scores 46.48 and 46.79), the two top performing ones using target synthetic data with threshold 0.75 (CHRF scores 47.07 and 47.27), and the top performing fine-tuned model with threshold 0.75 (CHRF score 47.57). The ensemble attains a CHRF score of 48.43.

4 Conclusions

This paper has reported on the systems submitted by the University of Groningen to the English↔Kazakh translation directions of the news shared task at WMT 2019.

Our results show quantitative evidence that, for an agglutinative language such as Kazakh, morphological segmentation is on par with segmentation based on the frequency of character sequences (in terms of automatic evaluation metrics) and qualitative evidence that it can result in better translations due to segmenting at the right morpheme boundaries. In addition, we show that the addition of data from an additional language, be it related or not, improves the performance notably, corroborating previous results. Finally, the use of synthetic data (both for the source and target languages), filtered with a state-of-the-art system based on language-independent similarity, improved the performance of our systems further.

As for future work, we plan to work along three lines. First, related to morphological segmentation, we note that Kazakh uses vowel harmony, which should be useful to model as part of the segmentation. Second, we would like to explore the contribution of synthetic target data in further detail. Third, given the unexpected negative results of cyrillization, we plan to analyse cyrillization's effects in detail.

---

[9]The BPE-based system uses target synthetic data while the LVMR-based system does not. The BPE-based system without target synthetic data reaches 45.67 CHRF, thus on par with the LVMR-based system (45.27 CHRF). We did not build a LVMR-based system with target synthetic data due to time constraints.

Original word	Segmentations
осыдан	осыдан | <u>осынан</u>
тіркелмеген	тіркелмеген | тіркел→ген емес
құжаттардың	құжат→тар→дың | құжатта→р→дың
өнерін	өнер→ін | өн→ер→ін

Table 13: Examples of morphological ambiguity challenges faced using Apertium's segmenter. The segmentation variants shown include those that when joined do not match the original word (underlined).

Segmentation	Sentence and System output
None	Қауіптің алдын алуға жәрдемдесетін мұндай құрылғыларды көптеп дайындауға облыс әкімдігі мен Қорқыт ата атындағы Қызылорда Мемлекеттік <u>университетінің</u> басшылығы ұсыныс білдіріпті.
BPE	Қауіп→тің алдын алуға жәрдемде→сетін мұндай құрылғыларды көпте→п дайындауға облыс әкімдігі мен Қорқы→т ата атындағы Қызылорда Мемлекеттік уни→верси→те→тінің басшыл→ығы ұсыныс білдір→іп→ті. In addition, the regional administration and the Kyzylorda State <u>Universum</u> named after the Fund named after the President of the Republic of Kazakhstan are ready to provide assistance in the prevention of the threat.
LVMR	Қауіп→тің алды→н ал→уға жәрдемде→сетін мұн→дай құр→ылғы→ларды көп→теп дайын да→уға облыс әкім→дігі мен Қорқыт ата ат→ындағы Қызыл→орда Мемлеке→ттік уни→верситет→інің басшылығы ұсыныс білдір→іпті. According to the Governor's Office of the region and the leadership of the Kyzylorda State <u>University</u> named after the Foundation of the First President of Kazakhstan, such devices are ready to help in the prevention of the threat.
English reference	Regional Akimat and Management of Kyzylorda State <u>University</u> named after Korkyt ata proposed to fabricate such safety devices assisting in <u>prevention</u> of danger in large quantities.

Table 14: Segmentation examples of BPE and unsupervised morphological segmentation (LVMR) systems for KK→EN. Arrows represent boundaries between the morphs in which a word is split. Note that the word "университетінің" is segmented differently in both systems. The MT system with LVMR segmentation translates it correctly as *"University"*, while the MT system with BPE segmentation produces *"Universum"* because of incorrect segmentation. This word, its segmentations and its translations are underlined.

Acknowledgments

We would like to thank Jonathan Washington and Francis Tyers for setting up for us a custom segmenter for `Apertium-kaz` tailored to morphological segmentation.

References

Mikel Artetxe and Holger Schwenk. 2018a. Margin-based Parallel Corpus Mining with Multilingual Sentence Embeddings. *arXiv preprint arXiv:1811.01136*.

Mikel Artetxe and Holger Schwenk. 2018b. Massively Multilingual Sentence Embeddings for Zero-Shot Cross-Lingual Transfer and Beyond. *arXiv preprint arXiv:1812.10464*.

Duygu Ataman, Matteo Negri, Marco Turchi, and Marcello Federico. 2017. Linguistically motivated vocabulary reduction for neural machine translation from Turkish to English. *The Prague Bulletin of Mathematical Linguistics*, 108(1):331–342.

Dzmitry Bahdanau, Kyunghyun Cho, and Yoshua Bengio. 2015. Neural machine translation by jointly learning to align and translate. In *3rd International Conference on Learning Representations, ICLR 2015, San Diego, CA, USA, May 7-9, 2015, Conference Track Proceedings*.

Melvin Johnson, Mike Schuster, Quoc V Le, Maxim Krikun, Yonghui Wu, Zhifeng Chen, Nikhil Thorat, Fernanda Viégas, Martin Wattenberg, Greg Corrado, et al. 2017. Google's multilingual neural machine translation system: Enabling zero-shot translation. *Transactions of the Association for Computational Linguistics*, 5:339–351.

Armand Joulin, Edouard Grave, Piotr Bojanowski, Matthijs Douze, Hérve Jégou, and Tomas Mikolov. 2016a. FastText.zip: Compressing text classification models. *arXiv preprint arXiv:1612.03651*.

Armand Joulin, Edouard Grave, Piotr Bojanowski, and Tomas Mikolov. 2016b. Bag of Tricks for Efficient Text Classification. *arXiv preprint arXiv:1607.01759*.

Marcin Junczys-Dowmunt, Roman Grundkiewicz, Tomasz Dwojak, Hieu Hoang, Kenneth Heafield, Tom Neckermann, Frank Seide, Ulrich Germann, Alham Fikri Aji, Nikolay Bogoychev, André F. T. Martins, and Alexandra Birch. 2018. Marian: Fast neural machine translation in C++. In *Proceedings of ACL 2018, System Demonstrations*, pages 116–121, Melbourne, Australia. Association for Computational Linguistics.

Philipp Koehn, Hieu Hoang, Alexandra Birch, Chris Callison-Burch, Marcello Federico, Nicola Bertoldi, Brooke Cowan, Wade Shen, Christine Moran, Richard Zens, Chris Dyer, Ondřej Bojar, Alexandra Constantin, and Evan Herbst. 2007. Moses: Open source toolkit for statistical machine translation. In *Proceedings of the 45th Annual Meeting of the ACL on Interactive Poster and Demonstration Sessions*, ACL '07, pages 177–180, Stroudsburg, PA, USA. Association for Computational Linguistics.

Philipp Koehn, Huda Khayrallah, Kenneth Heafield, and Mikel L. Forcada. 2018. Findings of the WMT 2018 shared task on parallel corpus filtering. In *Proceedings of the Third Conference on Machine Translation, Volume 2: Shared Task Papers*, pages 739–752, Belgium, Brussels. Association for Computational Linguistics.

Graham Neubig and Junjie Hu. 2018. Rapid adaptation of neural machine translation to new languages. *arXiv preprint arXiv:1808.04189*.

Kishore Papineni, Salim Roukos, Todd Ward, and Wei-Jing Zhu. 2002. Bleu: a method for automatic evaluation of machine translation. In *Proceedings of the 40th Annual Meeting of the Association for Computational Linguistics*, pages 311–318, Philadelphia. Association for Computational Linguistics.

Maja Popović. 2015. chrf: character n-gram F-score for automatic MT evaluation. In *Proceedings of the Tenth Workshop on Statistical Machine Translation*, pages 392–395, Lisbon, Portugal. Association for Computational Linguistics.

Víctor M. Sánchez-Cartagena and Antonio Toral. 2016. Abu-MaTran at WMT 2016 translation task: Deep learning, morphological segmentation and tuning on character sequences. In *Proceedings of the First Conference on Machine Translation*, pages 362–370, Berlin, Germany. Association for Computational Linguistics.

Rico Sennrich, Barry Haddow, and Alexandra Birch. 2015. Improving neural machine translation models with monolingual data. *arXiv preprint arXiv:1511.06709*.

Rico Sennrich, Barry Haddow, and Alexandra Birch. 2016. Neural machine translation of rare words with subword units. In *Proceedings of the 54th Annual Meeting of the Association for Computational Linguistics (Volume 1: Long Papers)*, pages 1715–1725, Berlin, Germany. Association for Computational Linguistics.

Miloš Stanojević, Amir Kamran, Philipp Koehn, and Ondřej Bojar. 2015. Results of the WMT15 metrics shared task. In *Proceedings of the Tenth Workshop on Statistical Machine Translation*, pages 256–273, Lisbon, Portugal. Association for Computational Linguistics.

Ashish Vaswani, Noam Shazeer, Niki Parmar, Jakob Uszkoreit, Llion Jones, Aidan N Gomez, Ł ukasz Kaiser, and Illia Polosukhin. 2017. Attention is all you need. In I. Guyon, U. V. Luxburg, S. Bengio, H. Wallach, R. Fergus, S. Vishwanathan, and R. Garnett, editors, *Advances in Neural Information Processing Systems 30*, pages 5998–6008. Curran Associates, Inc.

Sami Virpioja, Peter Smit, Stig-Arne Grönroos, Mikko Kurimo, et al. 2013. Morfessor 2.0: Python implementation and extensions for morfessor baseline.

Jonathan Washington, Ilnar Salimzyanov, and Francis Tyers. 2014. Finite-state morphological transducers for three Kypchak languages. In *Proceedings of the Ninth International Conference on Language Resources and Evaluation (LREC'14)*, Reykjavik, Iceland. European Language Resources Association (ELRA).

The LMU Munich Unsupervised Machine Translation System for WMT19

Dario Stojanovski, Viktor Hangya, Matthias Huck and **Alexander Fraser**
Center for Information and Language Processing
LMU Munich
{stojanovski,hangyav,mhuck,fraser}@cis.lmu.de

Abstract

We describe LMU Munich's machine translation system for German→Czech translation which was used to participate in the WMT19 shared task on unsupervised news translation. We train our model using monolingual data only from both languages. The final model is an unsupervised neural model using established techniques for unsupervised translation such as denoising autoencoding and online back-translation. We bootstrap the model with masked language model pretraining and enhance it with back-translations from an unsupervised phrase-based system which is itself bootstrapped using unsupervised bilingual word embeddings.

1 Introduction

In this paper we describe the system we developed at the LMU Munich Center for Information and Language Processing, which we used to participate in the unsupervised track of the news translation task at WMT19. The system builds on our last year's submission to the unsupervised shared task (Stojanovski et al., 2018) and previous work on unsupervised machine translation (Lample et al., 2018a; Artetxe et al., 2018c; Lample et al., 2018b; Lample and Conneau, 2019). We submitted system runs for the German→Czech translation direction. The goal of the unsupervised track is to train machine translation models without access to any bilingual or comparable monolingual data.

Supervised neural machine translation (NMT) has achieved state-of-the-art results (Bahdanau et al., 2015). With the introduction of the Transformer (Vaswani et al., 2017) the quality of automatic translations has been significantly improved. However, a prerequisite for high performance has been access to large scale bilingual data. Naturally, this is not available for many language pairs and specific domains. Moreover, Koehn and

Knowles (2017) also show that in low-resource setups neural models fail to match traditional phrase-based systems in terms of quality. This is the motivation for the unsupervised track at WMT19.

The system we use to participate in the shared task is multipart and borrows on existing techniques for unsupervised learning. We make use of bilingual word embeddings (BWE), phrase-based translation (PBT), cross-lingual masked language models (MLM) and NMT models, all trained in an unsupervised way. Lample et al. (2018a) and Artetxe et al. (2018c) showed that, given proper bootstrapping, it is possible to train unsupervised NMT models by making use of two general techniques, denoising autoencoding and online back-translation. Lample et al. (2018b) and Artetxe et al. (2018b) further showed that this is also possible for phrase-based statistical machine translation. A key technique that enables this is obtaining word-by-word translations by utilizing unsupervised bilingual word embeddings. Lample et al. (2018b) further simplified the bootstrapping step by showing that jointly trained BPE-level (Sennrich et al., 2016) embeddings are a better alternative, assuming closely related languages that potentially share surface forms. Lample et al. (2018b) also showed that a single shared encoder and decoder are sufficient for learning both translation directions. A general trend in NLP recently has been unsupervised masked language model pretraining. Devlin et al. (2018) showed that a wide range of NLP tasks are significantly improved by fine-tuning large MLM. They propose a way to train a Transformer language model which has access to left and right context as opposed to traditional LM which only have left context access. Lample and Conneau (2019) extended the approach to a multilingual setting and showed that this vastly outperforms the previous approaches for bootstrapping NMT models.

Proceedings of the Fourth Conference on Machine Translation (WMT), Volume 2: Shared Task Papers (Day 1) pages 393–399
Florence, Italy, August 1-2, 2019. ©2019 Association for Computational Linguistics

The model we used to participate in the shared task makes use of several of the aforementioned techniques. We train unsupervised BWEs and use them to bootstrap an unsupervised PBT model. We use large scale German and Czech monolingual NewsCrawl data to train a cross-lingual masked language model in order to bootstrap our unsupervised NMT model which itself is trained using denoising autoencoding and online back-translation. We combine all of these techniques and obtain competitive results in the shared task.

2   Bilingual Word Embeddings

Recently, many works showed that good quality bilingual word embeddings can be produced by using only monolingual resources (Conneau et al., 2017; Artetxe et al., 2018a; Dou et al., 2018). Most of these techniques follow a two-step approach involving (i) training monolingual vector spaces for both languages using large amount of monolingual data and (ii) projecting them to a shared bilingual space. We use the approach of (Conneau et al., 2017) which employs adversarial training to build bilingual word embeddings for the initialization of the phrase table used by our PBT system.

A general approach to measure word similarity in embedding spaces is to calculate their *cosine* similarity. A disadvantage of this approach is caused by the so called hubness problem of high dimensional spaces (Dinu et al., 2015), i.e., some words are similar to a high proportion of other words although their meaning is not necessarily close. To overcome the problem, the cosine similarity based *Cross-Domain Similarity Local Scaling* (CSLS) metric was proposed (Conneau et al., 2017). In short, this metric adjusts the similarity values of a word based on the density of the area where it lies, i.e., it increases similarity values for a word lying in a sparse area and decreases values for a word in a dense area. We use CSLS to create a dictionary of the 100 nearest target words for each source language word with their similarities which we convert to a phrase table. For more details on phrase-table creation see Section 3.

One problem with the approach arises when translating German compound words which are combinations of two or more words that function as a single unit of meaning. In most of the cases, these words should be translated into multiple Czech words, but our generated dictionary contains only 1-to-1 translations. In our previous work (Stojanovski et al., 2018), we experimented with bigrams in addition to unigrams in order to overcome this issue. We looked for frequent bigrams in the non-German side of the monolingual input data and trained separate embeddings for bigrams. Similarly, in the system of Artetxe et al. (2018c) embeddings for word n-grams are learned. The disadvantage of this approach is the lack of ability to represent previously unseen n-grams. It also significantly increases the size of the vocabulary. Since new compounds are constantly created in the German language, this could cause problems when using the system in the long run. To tackle the problem we applied the inverse of the approach and used compound splitting on all the German data. In this way we kept the vocabulary size relatively low and our system can handle novel compound words. A negative aspect of our approach is that non-compositional nouns could be incorrectly translated.

3   Unsupervised Phrase-based Translation

We build on the BWEs to create an unsupervised phrase-based translation system using the Moses decoder (Koehn et al., 2007).

In an initial step (*iteration 0*), a bilingual word-based translation lexicon is obtained from the embeddings space and stored in a format compatible with Moses' phrase table. The BWE cosine similarities serve as translation feature scores. We include multiple single-word target-side translation candidates per source-side token, given as the nearest neighbors in the bilingual embeddings space. An n-gram language model trained on target-side monolingual data is provided to Moses as another feature function. Moses then decodes with a variant of a beam search algorithm. We tune scaling factors to combine the feature functions.[1]

In a next step (*iteration 1*), synthetic parallel data is produced in order to acquire multi-word phrase table entries and improve over the initial simple word-based Moses translation system. To this end, we prepare an *iteration 0* Moses setup for the inverse translation direction (cs→de) as well and use it to translate a larger-sized Czech monolingual corpus (NewsCrawl 2018) into German. The Czech side of the resulting synthetic bitext is

---

[1] Note that a small parallel corpus (newstest2009) is utilized to tune the scaling factors.

original human-created data, whereas the German side is noisy machine translation output from our *iteration 0* Czech→German unsupervised PBT engine. When machine-translating the monolingual corpus, we let the Moses decoder also write out the word alignment information. From this synthetic German-Czech bitext, a phrase table for the German→Czech translation direction can be extracted and a new German→Czech Moses PBT system can be built in the usual manner. We opted to switch off reordering in the *iteration 0* setup, but now allow for reordering in *iteration 1*. We also add word penalty, phrase penalty, and distance-based distortion cost feature functions and tune the scaling factors again.

The process of producing synthetic parallel data can be repeated, which we do for one more step (*iteration 2*). The idea here is to also improve the inverse translation system by means of building an *iteration 1* system for the Czech→German direction as well through machine-translating German monolingual training data (the German NewsCrawl 2018 corpus) to Czech using the initial German→Czech unsupervised PBT engine. The improved inverse-direction system is then applied to back-translate the Czech monolingual training corpus once again and achieve better quality of the synthetic bitext. The *iteration 2* German→Czech is trained with a phrase table extracted from that higher-quality synthetic bitext. The systems in the two translation directions can benefit from each other in the course of the reciprocal re-training procedure. Translation quality in both directions is gradually improved.

4 Unsupervised Neural Translation

4.1 Masked Language Model Pretraining

We use the MLM approach proposed in Lample and Conneau (2019) to pretrain our NMT model. The MLM is trained by masking a percentage of the tokens which then the model is tasked to predict. Lample and Conneau (2019) extend MLM in a multilingual context by adding language-specific embeddings and using monolingual data from multiple languages. We train a MLM with German and Czech monolingual data. We randomly sample 15% of the input tokens and mask 80% of those with [MASK], swap 10% with a random token and in 10% of cases we keep the original token. We train a 6-layer Transformer with

8 attention heads, and an embedding and layer size of 1024. The size of the position-wise feed-forward neural network is 4096. We use dropout of 0.1, GELU activations (Hendrycks and Gimpel, 2017) and learned positional embeddings. The model is trained with batches of 32 streams of continuous sentences composed of 256 tokens. For further details, we refer to Lample and Conneau (2019). The model was trained for 7 days and subsequently used to initialize the encoder and decoder of the NMT model.

4.2 Denosing Autoencoding and Online Back-translation

As with previous work (Artetxe et al., 2018c; Lample et al., 2018a,b; Lample and Conneau, 2019) we train an unsupervised NMT model with denoising autoencoding and online back-translation. It is important to properly bootstrap this model in order to enable the model to get off the ground. In previous work this was made possible by using word-by-word translations or jointly trained BPE-level word embeddings. We bootstrap the model with the pretrained cross-lingual MLM as in Lample and Conneau (2019).

Although we initialize the model with a pretrained cross-lingual MLM, it is still necessary to use denoising autoencoding. Since the LM is trained with the masked LM objective, it is reasonable to assume that it has not learned language-specific reorderings which are key for machine translation. The denoising autoencoding is trained by feeding in a noisy version of a sentence and trying to reconstruct the original version. The noisy sentences are created by dropping words with probability of 0.1, shuffling words within a range of 3 and masking them with a probability of 0.1. In this way, the model is trained to produce fluent output. Furthermore, denoising autoencoding enables the model to learn important reorderings, insertions and deletions.

The translation component of the network is trained by first using the model in inference mode to produce back-translations. The back-translations are coupled with the original sentences to create pseudo-parallel data and train the model in a traditional fashion.

We train a single joint model using both techniques on both language directions. The goal is to end up with a model capable of translating from German into Czech. However, since the model depends on having quality German→Czech translations, it is important to be able to produce German back-translations from Czech. As a result, we train the model in both language directions.

The model has a single shared encoder and decoder, each equipped with 6 layers and 8 attention heads per layer. The batch size is 1600 tokens. We apply dropout of 0.1. We share the source, target and output embeddings and also share them across the two languages.

4.3 Incorporating PBT Synthetic Data

The training curriculum to enable this model to work is to first pretrain a cross-lingual MLM. Subsequently, one can further bootstrap this model with back-translations from an unsupervised phrase-based system and finally, fine-tune this model with the unsupervised neural criteria. However, due to time constraints we first fine-tune the pretrained MLM with the NMT system. After several iterations of training, we include additional back-translations from the phrase-based system. We only used pseudo-parallel German→Czech translations. We continue using online back-translation during this fine-tuning stage, but not denoising autoencoding. For the primary submission at WMT19, we used back-translations from *iteration 0* from the phrase-based system. In subsequent experiments, we also trained a model with data from *iteration 1*.

5 Experiments and Empirical Evaluation

5.1 Data and Preprocessing

As monolingual data in this work we used German and Czech NewsCrawl articles from 2007 to 2018. In the case of both languages the corpora contained a small set of sentences coming from foreign languages which we filtered out using a language detection tool[2]. The datasets were tokenized and truecased with the standard scripts from the Moses toolkit (Koehn et al., 2007).

For the bilingual word embeddings used by our PBT system we compound split the German corpus using `compound-splitter.perl` from the Moses toolkit with the following parameters: minimum word size 4; minimum count 5; maximum count 1000. To train monolingual word embeddings we used *fasttext* (Bojanowski et al., 2017), instead of *word2vec* (Mikolov et al., 2013),

which performs better on morphological rich languages by employing subword information. We used 300 dimensional embeddings and default values for the rest of the parameters. For the unsupervised mapping we used *MUSE* (Conneau et al., 2017) with default parameters, but restricting the vocabulary size for both source and target languages to the most frequent $200K$ words due to memory considerations.

We used BPE segments in the case of our neural system. The segmentation was computed jointly on all the NewsCrawl data available for both languages using $32K$ merge operations. We train the cross-lingual MLM with German NewsCrawl 2017-2018, and Czech NewsCrawl 2007-2018 monolingual data. For the unsupervised NMT model, we use NewsCrawl 2018 for German and NewsCrawl 2013-2018 for Czech. In this way, both models are trained with roughly equal amounts of German and Czech data. Details on the training data is in Table 1. For the NMT experiments, we use the code from (Lample and Conneau, 2019)[3].

In the following we perform evaluation for both our unsupervised phrase-based and neural machine translation systems. We report BLEU scores on the detokenized translations of newstest2013 and newstest2019 using *sacreBLEU*[4] (Post, 2018).

model	de	cs
BWE	270M	67M
MLM	75M	67M
PBT	270M	67M
NMT	37M	41M

Table 1: Training data sizes in number of sentences.

5.2 PBT Experiments

As mentioned earlier we initialize our PBT system with BWEs trained on compound split data. In Table 2 we show baseline word-by-word (*wbw*) results, i.e., we greedily translate each source word independently of the others using the most similar target word, according to the BWE-based dictionary, without any reordering. We compare BWEs trained with and without compound split data. The results of both approaches are low, which is due to the morphological richness of the target lan-

---

[2] `https://github.com/indix/whatthelang`

[3] `https://github.com/facebookresearch/XLM`

[4] `https://github.com/mjpost/sacreBLEU`

	newstest2013 de→cs
wbw	4.2
wbw+comp. split	4.3
unsup. PBT iter. 0	6.0
unsup. PBT iter. 1	7.9
unsup. PBT iter. 2	8.4

Table 2: Baseline results (BLEU) with word-by-word translations (wbw) and unsupervised phrase-based translations (PBT) on newstest2013. We compare wbw results with and without compound splitting on the German language side. For the unsupervised PBT experiments, German is compound-split.

guage. On one hand, based on manual investigation[5] of the BWE-based dictionary and the sentence translations, we conclude that the various inflected forms of the correct Czech stems are often the most similar translations of given German words. On the other hand, without the context it is much harder to pick the right form as opposed to some other language pairs such as German and English. Compound splitting resulted in performance increase of the system which is due to the translation of German compounds to multiple Czech words. In addition, it also helped lowering the number of Out-Of-Vocabulary (OOV) words which is partly due to limiting the size of the vocabulary.

Table 2 also presents the results from our PBT system. At *iteration 0* the model obtains 6.0 BLEU on newstest2013. The score increased to 7.9 BLEU at *iteration 1* and to 8.4 at *iteration 2*.

5.3 NMT Experiments

We show the results from our unsupervised neural model and the combination with synthetic data from the phrase-based system. Our primary submission at WMT19 has achieved competitive results despite using a single model with no ensembling. The model for the primary submission was trained for ~12h due to time constraints. For the contrastive experiments we present in Table 3 we further trained this model for ~62h overall. We train the models on 8 Nvidia GTX 1080 Ti with 12 GB RAM.

We present results on newstest2013. For model selection we used newstest2009. The first row in Table 3 shows our baseline unsupervised neural

---

[5]Note that none of the authors speak the target language.

	newstest2013 de→cs
unsup. NMT	17.0
unsup. NMT + PBT iter. 0	18.5
+ fine-tune no PBT	18.3
+ fine-tune PBT iter. 1	18.8
unsup. NMT + PBT iter. 1	19.1

Table 3: BLEU scores with the unsupervised NMT systems on newstest2013.

	newstest2019 de→cs
unsup. NMT	16.2
*unsup. NMT + PBT iter. 0	17.0
‡unsup. NMT + PBT iter. 0	17.6
+ fine-tune no PBT	17.4
+ fine-tune PBT iter. 1	17.8
unsup. NMT + PBT iter. 1	17.8

Table 4: BLEU scores with the unsupervised NMT systems on newstest2019. * - primary submission, trained for ~12h. ‡- trained for ~62h.

system. This model achieves significant improvements over the word-by-word approach and PBT system. All results except for the *unsup. NMT* baseline are obtained by applying compound splitting to the German input from newstest2013. We present the result for the baseline without compound splitting because the initial cross-lingual MLM and unsupervised NMT system were trained with German monolingual data which was not compound split. However, the BWEs and PBT system were trained with compound split German monolingual data and as a result the German back-translations we obtain from the PBT system were compound split. Consequently, all contrastive models where we fine-tune the original unsupervised NMT system are trained with compound split German monolingual data. However, we do not observe any adverse effects on translation quality. Furthermore, the results from the fine-tuned models show that very similar results are obtained with both versions of the test set.

When fine-tuning our model with PBT synthetic data, we disable denoising autoencoding, but continue to do online back-translation. Even though we used PBT synthetic data from *iteration 0*, we observe significant improvements. We fine-tune the model for ~62h and BLEU score was improved from 17.0 to 18.5. We use this model for the primary submission, but a version which was trained for ~12h only. We intuitively assumed that removing this data and continuing training with online back-translation only would further improve performance. However, we observe that BLEU score decreased to 18.3.

We also experimented with adding PBT synthetic data from *iteration 1*. We tried adding this data as we did with the back-translations from *iteration 0*. Furthermore, we also tried fine-tuning the model trained on *iteration 0* data with data from *iteration 1*. For this setup, the data from *iteration 0* was removed. It is interesting that fine-tuning the initial unsupervised NMT obtains better performance than fine-tuning the model trained with *iteration 0* data. The best score we managed to obtain was 19.1 by fine-tuning the initial unsupervised NMT with *iteration 1* data and translating a compound split version of newstest2013.

In Table 4 we show the results on newstest2019. Our primary submission obtained 17.0 BLEU. Further training and including synthetic data from *iteration 1* increased the score to 17.8 BLEU.

6 Conclusion

In this work, we present LMU Munich's unsupervised system for German→Czech news translations. We developed unsupervised BWEs, phrase-based and neural systems and studied different ways of combining them. We show that an unsupervised neural model pretrained with large cross-lingual masked language model is superior to unsupervised phrase-based model for this language pair. Despite working on a Germanic-Slavic language pair, the unsupervised methods for machine translation work well and provide for a relatively good translation quality.

Acknowledgments

We would like to thank the anonymous reviewers for their valuable input. This project has received funding from the European Research Council (ERC) under the European Union's Horizon 2020 research and innovation programme (grant agreement № 640550).

References

Mikel Artetxe, Gorka Labaka, and Eneko Agirre. 2018a. A robust self-learning method for fully unsupervised cross-lingual mappings of word embeddings. In *Proceedings of the 56th Annual Meeting of the Association for Computational Linguistics (Volume 1: Long Papers)*, pages 789–798.

Mikel Artetxe, Gorka Labaka, and Eneko Agirre. 2018b. Unsupervised statistical machine translation. In *Proceedings of the 2018 Conference on Empirical Methods in Natural Language Processing*, pages 3632–3642, Brussels, Belgium. Association for Computational Linguistics.

Mikel Artetxe, Gorka Labaka, Eneko Agirre, and Kyunghyun Cho. 2018c. Unsupervised Neural Machine Translation. In *International Conference on Learning Representations*.

Dzmitry Bahdanau, Kyunghyun Cho, and Yoshua Bengio. 2015. Neural Machine Translation by Jointly Learning to Align and Translate. In *Proceedings of the 3rd International Conference on Learning Representations*, ICLR '15. ArXiv: 1409.0473.

Piotr Bojanowski, Edouard Grave, Armand Joulin, and Tomas Mikolov. 2017. Enriching Word Vectors with Subword Information. *Transactions of the Association for Computational Linguistics*, 5:135–146.

Alexis Conneau, Guillaume Lample, Marc'Aurelio Ranzato, Ludovic Denoyer, and Hervé Jégou. 2017. Word Translation Without Parallel Data. *CoRR*, abs/1710.04087.

Jacob Devlin, Ming-Wei Chang, Kenton Lee, and Kristina Toutanova. 2018. Bert: Pre-training of deep bidirectional transformers for language understanding. In *NAACL-HLT*.

Georgiana Dinu, Angeliki Lazaridou, and Marco Baroni. 2015. Improving Zero-Shot Learning by Mitigating the Hubness Problem. In *Proceedings of the International Conference on Learning Representations: Workshop Track*.

Zi-Yi Dou, Zhi-Hao Zhou, and Shujian Huang. 2018. Unsupervised Bilingual Lexicon Induction via Latent Variable Models. In *Proceedings of the 2018 Conference on Empirical Methods in Natural Language Processing*, pages 621–626.

Dan Hendrycks and Kevin Gimpel. 2017. Bridging nonlinearities and stochastic regularizers with gaussian error linear units. *CoRR*, abs/1606.08415.

Philipp Koehn, Hieu Hoang, Alexandra Birch, Chris Callison-Burch, Marcello Federico, Nicola Bertoldi, Brooke Cowan, Wade Shen, Christine Moran, Richard Zens, et al. 2007. Moses: Open Source Toolkit for Statistical Machine Translation. In *Proceedings of the 45th annual meeting of the ACL on interactive poster and demonstration sessions*, pages 177–180. Association for Computational Linguistics.

Philipp Koehn and Rebecca Knowles. 2017. Six Challenges for Neural Machine Translation. In *Proceedings of the First Workshop on Neural Machine Translation*, pages 28–39.

Guillaume Lample and Alexis Conneau. 2019. Cross-lingual language model pretraining. *CoRR*, abs/1901.07291.

Guillaume Lample, Alexis Conneau, Ludovic Denoyer, and Marc'Aurelio Ranzato. 2018a. Unsupervised Machine Translation Using Monolingual Corpora Only. In *International Conference on Learning Representations*.

Guillaume Lample, Myle Ott, Alexis Conneau, Ludovic Denoyer, and Marc'Aurelio Ranzato. 2018b. Phrase-Based & Neural Unsupervised Machine Translation. *arXiv preprint arXiv:1804.07755*.

Tomas Mikolov, Ilya Sutskever, Kai Chen, Greg S Corrado, and Jeff Dean. 2013. Distributed Representations of Words and Phrases and their Compositionality. In *Advances in Neural Information Processing Systems 26*, pages 3111–3119. Curran Associates, Inc.

Matt Post. 2018. A Call for Clarity in Reporting BLEU Scores. In *Proceedings of the Third Conference on Machine Translation: Research Papers*, pages 186–191.

Rico Sennrich, Barry Haddow, and Alexandra Birch. 2016. Neural machine translation of rare words with subword units. In *Proceedings of the 54th Annual Meeting of the Association for Computational Linguistics (Volume 1: Long Papers)*, pages 1715–1725, Berlin, Germany. Association for Computational Linguistics.

Dario Stojanovski, Viktor Hangya, Matthias Huck, and Alexander Fraser. 2018. The LMU Munich Unsupervised Machine Translation Systems. In *Proceedings of the Third Conference on Machine Translation, Volume 2: Shared Task Papers*, pages 517–525, Brussels, Belgium. Association for Computational Linguistics.

Ashish Vaswani, Noam Shazeer, Niki Parmar, Jakob Uszkoreit, Llion Jones, Aidan N Gomez, Łukasz Kaiser, and Illia Polosukhin. 2017. Attention is all you need. In *Advances in Neural Information Processing Systems*, pages 6000–6010.

Combining Local and Document-Level Context: The LMU Munich Neural Machine Translation System at WMT19

Dario Stojanovski and **Alexander Fraser**
Center for Information and Language Processing
LMU Munich
{stojanovski,fraser}@cis.lmu.de

Abstract

We describe LMU Munich's machine translation system for English→German translation which was used to participate in the WMT19 shared task on supervised news translation. We specifically participated in the document-level MT track. The system used as a primary submission is a context-aware Transformer capable of both rich modeling of limited contextual information and integration of large-scale document-level context with a less rich representation. We train this model by fine-tuning a big Transformer baseline. Our experimental results show that document-level context provides for large improvements in translation quality, and adding a rich representation of the previous sentence provides a small additional gain.

1 Introduction

In this paper we describe the system we developed at the LMU Munich Center for Information and Language Processing, which we used to participate in the news translation task at WMT19. We submitted system runs for the English→German translation direction and specifically focus on the document-level translation track. The goal of the document-level track is to train machine translation models capable of taking into account larger context or even entire documents when translating sentences.

Supervised NMT has achieved state-of-the-art results (Bahdanau et al., 2015; Vaswani et al., 2017). Several works have claimed translation quality on a level similar to human translation. Wu et al. (2016) report translation quality on par with average bilingual human translators and Hassan et al. (2018) argue for parity to professional human translators on news translation from Chinese to English. However, these claims have been challenged in several ways with recent work (Läubli

et al., 2018; Toral et al., 2018). One challenge is that these evaluations were done without giving evaluators access to the whole document-level context. They further show that human translations are preferred over automatic ones if evaluators are given document-level context. This is precisely the motivation for the document-level MT track in this year's WMT19.

One of the reasons for the failure of NMT in these context-dependent cases is not being able to model discourse-level phenomena. The straightforward reason for this is that traditional NMT does not have access to the context. As a result, it fails to account for several discourse-level phenomena, prominent ones being coreference resolution and coherence.

Coreference resolution has a particular impact on English→German translation, specifically for pronoun translation. English has only one third person singular pronoun that is routinely used for non-human references ("it"), while German has three, each representing a specific gender: masculine, feminine and neuter. Consider the following sentence: *We know it won't change students' behaviour instantly.* The translation of *it* into German can be, *er*, *sie* or *es* depending on the gender of the noun the English *it* is referencing. Since traditional NMT is working on the sentence-level, it has no way of ascertaining the appropriate gender and usually falls back to the data-driven prior, which is the neuter *es*.

Coherence is important in order to provide coherent translations across the whole given document. It is usually undesirable to produce translations with different meanings within a single document for the same ambiguous word.

Taking into account the whole document when generating translations will address some of the relevant discourse-level phenomena. An implicit effect that one could expect by modeling the whole

Proceedings of the Fourth Conference on Machine Translation (WMT), Volume 2: Shared Task Papers (Day 1) pages 400–406
Florence, Italy, August 1-2, 2019. ©2019 Association for Computational Linguistics

document is also modeling the underlying domain. On an abstract level, one can presume that this is happening in sentence-level models as well, however access to larger context is likely to improve the ability to implicitly identify the domain. Domain adaptation and multi-domain NMT have been extensively studied (Kobus et al., 2017; Freitag and Al-Onaizan, 2016; Farajian et al., 2017; Sajjad et al., 2017; Zhang and Xiong, 2018; Chen et al., 2017; Tars and Fishel, 2018). However, most previous works assume that the domain of each sentence is known at training time, which is often not the case.

Taking into consideration different discourse-level phenomena, we develop a Transformer (Vaswani et al., 2017) which can richly model the previous sentence, but also takes advantage of larger context. We borrow on previous work on context-aware NMT (Stojanovski and Fraser, 2018; Voita et al., 2018; Miculicich et al., 2018; Zhang et al., 2018) and add additional parameters in the encoder and decoder to account for the previous sentence. We limit the context since we want this part of the model to be able to do coreference resolution which very often can be addressed by looking at the first previous sentence. We additionally take the 10 previous sentences and create a simple document representation by averaging their embeddings. This embedding is subsequently added to each source token in the sentence to be translated in the same fashion as positional embeddings are added to the token-level embeddings in the Transformer. We assume that this representation can help provide a clear domain signal.

The remainder of the paper outlines the model in detail, and presents the experimental setup and obtained results.

2 Related Work

There are large number of works in NMT focusing on integrating document-level information into otherwise sentence-level models (Jean et al., 2017; Wang et al., 2017; Tiedemann and Scherrer, 2017; Bawden et al., 2018; Voita et al., 2018; Zhang et al., 2018; Stojanovski and Fraser, 2018; Miculicich et al., 2018; Tu et al., 2018; Maruf and Haffari, 2018). These works have shown that improvements in pronoun translation are achieved by better handling coreference resolution. Smaller improvements are observed for coherence and cohesion. The main intuition behind the models in

these works is that they employ an additional encoder for contextual sentences and integrate the information in the encoder or decoder using a gating mechanism. Our model is similar to the context-aware Transformer models proposed in these works with some specifics which we discuss in Section 3.

We also extend the Transformer model with a simple document representation which we assume provides for a domain signal. This could be useful for domain disambiguation and improved coherence and cohesion. This model is similar to previous work on domain adaptation for NMT (Kobus et al., 2017; Tars and Fishel, 2018) where special domain tokens are either added to the beginning of the sentence or concatenated as additional features to the token-level embeddings. However, they assume a set of known domains in advance which is not the case in our work. We model the domain implicitly.

3 Model

In this work we develop two models: a previous-sentence and document-level context-aware Transformer. For our primary submission, we use a joint model combining both approaches into a single model. We use source side context only, both at training and testing time.

3.1 Previous-sentence context-aware Transformer

This context-aware model is in line with previous works on context-aware NMT (Voita et al., 2018; Stojanovski and Fraser, 2018; Miculicich et al., 2018; Zhang et al., 2018). The standard Transformer is extended to be able to receive an additional sentence as input. In this work we only use the first previous sentence. We feed this context sentence through the Transformer encoder. As suggested in Voita et al. (2018), we share the encoder for the main and context sentence. In order to provide information as to what is being encoded, we add a special token at the beginning of the context sentence. We share the encoder layers up to and including the penultimate layer. Unlike Voita et al. (2018), we do not integrate the context in the encoder, but rather in the decoder. As a result, the last encoder layer is the standard Transformer encoder, but it is not shared across the main and context sentence.

We modify the decoder by adding an additional

multi-head attention (MHA) sublayer on the context representation. As in the standard Transformer decoder layer, at training time, we first compute self-attention over the target sentence and use this to compute the MHA representation c_i over the main sentence. The output of this step is used to condition the MHA c_i^c over the context. Subsequently, the outputs of the MHA over the main and context representations, c_i and c_i^c, are merged using a gated sum. The use of the gate is similar to previous work (Wang et al., 2017; Voita et al., 2018). It is conditioned on c_i and c_i^c. The output is computed as follows:

$$s_i = g_i \otimes c_i + (1 - g_i) \otimes c_i^c$$

and the gate is computed as:

$$g_i = \sigma(W_e c_i + W_c c_i^c)$$

where σ represents sigmoid activation and $\otimes$ element-wise multiplication. The gate enables the model to control how much information should be used from the main sentence and from the context sentence. Finally, the output of the gated sum is passed through a feed-forward neural network.

3.2 Document-level context-aware Transformer

We also extend the model with the ability to consume larger context. Miculicich et al. (2018) proposed a model capable of using large context using hierarchical attention. They tackle the memory requirements of such models by reusing already computed sentence representations. This introduces limitations as to how the random batching usually used to train NMT works, since it is necessary to have the previous sentences of a given sentence in a document already processed. Furthermore, Miculicich et al. (2018) report that they fail to obtain significant improvements as the context increases. They do not improve results beyond context sizes of 2 or 3 sentences.

As a result, we make a simple modification to the Transformer which enables it to handle large context sizes. In this work we use up to 10 sentences of context, all of which are previous sentences (but it would also be possible to use the following sentences as well). We take the embeddings of all tokens within the context and simply average them. This averaged document representation is then passed through a feed-forward network. The final document-level representation

is then added to all token-level source embeddings in the sentence to be translated in the same manner as the positional embeddings are added in the Transformer. A similar approach was proposed by Kobus et al. (2017) for domain adaptation in RNN-based NMT. The work differs since they have special tokens which indicate the domain and they concatenate them instead of adding them to the token-level embeddings. Our approach is more flexible since it only relies on having access to contextual information and does not require explicit domain knowledge. Our intuition with this approach is that the document representation should be informative of the type or domain of the document being translated.

We share all source, target, output and context embeddings. We freeze them in the continued training phase with the context-aware model in order for the model to be more memory efficient.

4 Experimental Setup

4.1 Preprocessing

The data is preprocessed by normalizing punctuation, tokenizing and truecasing with the scripts from Moses. We apply BPE splitting (Sennrich et al., 2016b) with 32K merge operations. BPE is computed jointly on both languages.

Corpus	sentences
CommonCrawl	2.1M x2
Europarl	1.5M x2
NewsCommentary	0.3M x2
Rapid	1.4M x2
WikiTitles	1.3M x2
ParaCrawl	13.5M
NewsCrawl	9.3M
NewsCrawl v2	16.9M

Table 1: Training data sizes after filtering. x2 - oversampling factor.

4.2 Data filtering

Samples where the length of the source, target or first previous sentence before BPE-splitting is over 50 tokens are removed. For the purposes of our document-level model, we also use larger context. In our experiments, we restrict the model to access only the 10 previous sentences at most. Samples where the total length of these sentences exceeds 500 are also removed. After applying BPE splitting, an additional length filtering step is applied with a maximum length allowed of 100 for the source, target and first previous sentence. Document-level context is limited to 800.

WMT provides the large ParaCrawl corpus which is very noisy. In previous years at WMT, high scoring systems showed that it is necessary to perform aggressive filtering. We reuse some of the data selection steps proposed in Stahlberg et al. (2018). We run language identification and remove non-English and non-German sentences. Furthermore, all sentences are removed where one of the following conditions is met: a word is over 40 characters long, HTML tags in text, sentence length less than 4 words, character ratio between source and target sentence is over 1:3 or 3:1, source or target sentence is not identical after removing non-numerical characters and sentence does not end in a punctuation mark. As a result, the size of the ParaCrawl corpus was reduced from 30M to 13.5M sentences. Unfortunately, due to time constraints, we were not able to reproduce the data filtering and data selection suggested by Junczys-Dowmunt (2018) which obtained the top BLEU scores at WMT18. They showed that the optimal number of sentences is 8M. We assume that the higher number of presumably noisy sentences is affecting our initial baseline.

4.3 Backtranslation

As shown in previous years, using backtranslations (Sennrich et al., 2016a) is essential for strong translation quality. We train a German→English small Transformer and use it to backtranslate NewsCrawl data. Due to time constraints, we were not able to use the backtranslated data in the initial training of the English→German model. As a result, we fine-tune the already trained baseline with the backtranslated data mixed in with the parallel WMT data.

4.4 Hyperparameters

We train a big Transformer as a baseline. Embedding and hidden dimension size in the encoder and decoder is 1024. All attention sublayers use dot product attention and have 16 attention heads. The size of the feed-forward neural networks is 4096. The hidden dimension size of the context-aware encoder and context attention sublayer in the decoder is 512. All context-related attention sublayers have 8 attention heads. All models have 6 encoder and decoder layers. We use sinusoidal positional embeddings which are added

to the token-level embeddings. In the case of the document-level model, we further add the average of all large-context embeddings. We apply residual dropout of 0.1 as in (Vaswani et al., 2017). Additionally, dropout of 0.1 is applied to the multi-head attention and feed-forward network. We also use label smoothing of value 0.1.

4.5 Training

We train the Transformer baseline with a warmup period and a learning rate of 10^{-4}. In all cases of continued training in the paper, we set the learning rate to 10^{-5}. We train the models with early-stopping based on the perplexity on the development set. We checkpoint the model every 4000 updates. The learning rate is reduced by a factor of 0.7 if no improvements are observed for 8 checkpoints. Training converges if no improvements are observed after 32 checkpoints. We train our context-aware models by continued training on the converged baseline. All parameters relating only to the context-aware parts of the architecture are randomly initialized. The batch size is set to 4096 tokens.

Model	parameters
baseline	217M
previous-sentence context	253M
document-level context	225M
joint model	261M

Table 2: Number of model parameters. All models are big Transformer models.

The number of parameters for all models are presented in Table 2. We train the models on 4 GTX 1080 Ti GPUs with 12GB RAM. We use Sockeye[1] (Hieber et al., 2018) to train the baseline and our context-aware models.

5 Empirical Evaluation

We present the results we obtain with our models in Table 3. We report results on the English→German newstest2017, newstest2018 and newstest2019. We report BLEU scores using sacreBLEU[2] (Post, 2018) on detokenized text. For the final submission, we processed quotation marks to match the German style.

We train our baseline on the data presented in Table 1. We initially train on the ParaCrawl

---

[1] https://github.com/awslabs/sockeye
[2] https://github.com/mjpost/sacreBLEU

dataset and an oversampled version of the other datasets. We train this baseline until convergence with early-stopping based on the perplexity on the development set. As a development set, we use newstest2018. After convergence, we fine-tune with 9.3M NewsCrawl backtranslations in addition to the dataset we used for the initial baseline. This baseline is used to initialize all the other context-aware models. It is interesting to observe that fine-tuning with NewsCrawl backtranslations and WMT data improves on newstest2017 and newstest2018, but significantly decreases the BLEU score on newstest2019.

| | en→de | | |
Model	nt17	nt18	nt19
baseline	29.8	45.3	39.5
baseline*	30.3	45.6	38.5
previous-sentence*	30.5	46.0	38.6
document-level*	30.5	45.7	39.3
document-level	**31.1**	47.0	40.0
joint	**31.1**	**47.1**	**40.3**

Table 3: BLEU scores on newstest2017, newstest2018 and newstest2019. * - model trained with NewsCrawl backtranslations. All context-aware models fine-tuned on baseline*.

For training the context-aware models, we ignore the ParaCrawl data and use the remaining datasets. Depending on the setup, we either use the 16.9M NewsCrawl backtranslations with document boundaries or completely ignore them. Our previous sentence context-aware Transformer trained with NewsCrawl backtranslations do not provide for significant improvements. It increases the BLEU score from 38.5 to 38.6. However, the document-level model with averaging context embeddings obtains a BLEU score of 39.3.

We also remove the NewsCrawl backtranslations when fine-tuning our average context embedding Transformer. This proves to be very helpful and we manage to obtain 40.0 BLEU. It is interesting that this model also substantially improves the BLEU score on newstest2017 and newstest2018. One possible explanation of the adverse effect of using backtranslations is that our document-level model is more sensitive to noisy input. We leave a further examination of the issue for future work.

Finally, we train a joint model where we combine the average context embedding approach with the previous-sentence context-aware Transformer where we employ a separate encoder and modify the decoder. This further pushes the BLEU score to 40.3 on newstest2019 and slightly improves results on the other test sets. This is the system we used for the primary submission.

We also tried ensembling context-aware joint models. However, due to time constraints we only managed to train a single baseline. Therefore, all context-aware models were trained by fine-tuning on top of the single baseline. As a result, these models were not diverse enough and ensembling did not help. After the evaluation period, we also tried averaging the last 5 checkpoints of a single run of the joint model. This improved the score on newstest2019 to 40.8 BLEU.

6 Conclusion

In this work, we presented our system which we used to participate in the English→German news translation task at WMT19. We proposed two modifications to the standard Transformer architecture. We propose a context-aware Transformer which has a separate encoder and a modified decoder in order to provide for a fine-grained access to a limited context. We further extend this model by proposing to average the context token-level embeddings and add them to the main sentence embeddings. This enables access to large scale context. We show that the latter modification provides for large improvements with regards to a baseline and that combining both approaches leads to a further performance increase.

Acknowledgments

We would like to thank the anonymous reviewers for their valuable input. This project has received funding from the European Research Council (ERC) under the European Union's Horizon 2020 research and innovation programme (grant agreement № 640550).

References

Dzmitry Bahdanau, Kyunghyun Cho, and Yoshua Bengio. 2015. Neural Machine Translation by Jointly Learning to Align and Translate. In *Proceedings of the 3rd International Conference on Learning Representations*, ICLR '15.

Rachel Bawden, Rico Sennrich, Alexandra Birch, and Barry Haddow. 2018. Evaluating discourse phenomena in neural machine translation. In *Proceedings of the 2018 Conference of the North American*

Chapter of the Association for Computational Linguistics: Human Language Technologies, Volume 1 (Long Papers), pages 1304–1313, New Orleans, Louisiana. Association for Computational Linguistics.

Boxing Chen, Colin Cherry, George Foster, and Samuel Larkin. 2017. Cost weighting for neural machine translation domain adaptation. In *Proceedings of the First Workshop on Neural Machine Translation*, pages 40–46. Association for Computational Linguistics.

M. Amin Farajian, Marco Turchi, Matteo Negri, and Marcello Federico. 2017. Multi-domain neural machine translation through unsupervised adaptation. In *Proceedings of the Second Conference on Machine Translation*, pages 127–137. Association for Computational Linguistics.

Markus Freitag and Yaser Al-Onaizan. 2016. Fast domain adaptation for neural machine translation. *CoRR*, abs/1612.06897.

Hany Hassan, Anthony Aue, Chang Chen, Vishal Chowdhary, Jonathan Clark, Christian Federmann, Xuedong Huang, Marcin Junczys-Dowmunt, William Lewis, Mu Li, et al. 2018. Achieving Human Parity on Automatic Chinese to English News Translation. *arXiv preprint arXiv:1803.05567*.

Felix Hieber, Tobias Domhan, Michael Denkowski, David Vilar, Artem Sokolov, Ann Clifton, and Matt Post. 2018. The sockeye neural machine translation toolkit at AMTA 2018. In *Proceedings of the 13th Conference of the Association for Machine Translation in the Americas (Volume 1: Research Papers)*, pages 200–207, Boston, MA. Association for Machine Translation in the Americas.

Sebastien Jean, Stanislas Lauly, Orhan Firat, and Kyunghyun Cho. 2017. Does neural machine translation benefit from larger context? *arXiv preprint arXiv:1704.05135*.

Marcin Junczys-Dowmunt. 2018. Microsoft's submission to the WMT2018 news translation task: How i learned to stop worrying and love the data. In *Proceedings of the Third Conference on Machine Translation, Volume 2: Shared Task Papers*, pages 429–434, Brussels, Belgium. Association for Computational Linguistics.

Catherine Kobus, Josep Crego, and Jean Senellart. 2017. Domain control for neural machine translation. In *Proceedings of the International Conference Recent Advances in Natural Language Processing, RANLP 2017*, pages 372–378. INCOMA Ltd.

Samuel Läubli, Rico Sennrich, and Martin Volk. 2018. Has machine translation achieved human parity? a case for document-level evaluation. In *Proceedings of the 2018 Conference on Empirical Methods in Natural Language Processing*, pages 4791–4796, Brussels, Belgium. Association for Computational Linguistics.

Sameen Maruf and Gholamreza Haffari. 2018. Document context neural machine translation with memory networks. In *Proceedings of the 56th Annual Meeting of the Association for Computational Linguistics (Volume 1: Long Papers)*, pages 1275–1284, Melbourne, Australia. Association for Computational Linguistics.

Lesly Miculicich, Dhananjay Ram, Nikolaos Pappas, and James Henderson. 2018. Document-level neural machine translation with hierarchical attention networks. In *Proceedings of the 2018 Conference on Empirical Methods in Natural Language Processing*, pages 2947–2954. Association for Computational Linguistics.

Matt Post. 2018. A Call for Clarity in Reporting BLEU Scores. In *Proceedings of the Third Conference on Machine Translation: Research Papers*, pages 186–191.

Hassan Sajjad, Nadir Durrani, Fahim Dalvi, Yonatan Belinkov, and Stephan Vogel. 2017. Neural machine translation training in a multi-domain scenario. *CoRR*, abs/1708.08712.

Rico Sennrich, Barry Haddow, and Alexandra Birch. 2016a. Improving neural machine translation models with monolingual data. In *Proceedings of the 54th Annual Meeting of the Association for Computational Linguistics (Volume 1: Long Papers)*, pages 86–96, Berlin, Germany. Association for Computational Linguistics.

Rico Sennrich, Barry Haddow, and Alexandra Birch. 2016b. Neural machine translation of rare words with subword units. In *Proceedings of the 54th Annual Meeting of the Association for Computational Linguistics (Volume 1: Long Papers)*, pages 1715–1725, Berlin, Germany. Association for Computational Linguistics.

Felix Stahlberg, Adri de Gispert, and Bill Byrne. 2018. The University of Cambridges machine translation systems for WMT18. In *Proceedings of the Third Conference on Machine Translation, Volume 2: Shared Task Papers*, pages 508–516, Brussels, Belgium. Association for Computational Linguistics.

Dario Stojanovski and Alexander Fraser. 2018. Coreference and coherence in neural machine translation: A study using oracle experiments. In *Proceedings of the Third Conference on Machine Translation, Volume 1: Research Papers*, pages 49–60, Brussels, Belgium. Association for Computational Linguistics.

Sander Tars and Mark Fishel. 2018. Multi-domain neural machine translation. *arXiv preprint arXiv:1805.02282*.

Jörg Tiedemann and Yves Scherrer. 2017. Neural machine translation with extended context. In *Proceedings of the Third Workshop on Discourse in Machine Translation*, pages 82–92.

Antonio Toral, Sheila Castilho, Ke Hu, and Andy Way. 2018. Attaining the unattainable? Reassessing claims of human parity in neural machine translation. In *Proceedings of the Third Conference on Machine Translation, Volume 1: Research Papers*, pages 113–123, Brussels, Belgium. Association for Computational Linguistics.

Zhaopeng Tu, Yang Liu, Shuming Shi, and Tong Zhang. 2018. Learning to remember translation history with a continuous cache. *Transactions of the Association for Computational Linguistics*, 6:407–420.

Ashish Vaswani, Noam Shazeer, Niki Parmar, Jakob Uszkoreit, Llion Jones, Aidan N Gomez, Łukasz Kaiser, and Illia Polosukhin. 2017. Attention is all you need. In *Advances in Neural Information Processing Systems*, pages 6000–6010.

Elena Voita, Pavel Serdyukov, Rico Sennrich, and Ivan Titov. 2018. Context-Aware Neural Machine Translation Learns Anaphora Resolution. In *Proceedings of the 56th Annual Meeting of the Association for Computational Linguistics (Volume 1: Long Papers)*, pages 1264–1274, Melbourne, Australia.

Longyue Wang, Zhaopeng Tu, Andy Way, and Qun Liu. 2017. Exploiting cross-sentence context for neural machine translation. In *Proceedings of the 2017 Conference on Empirical Methods in Natural Language Processing*, pages 2826–2831.

Yonghui Wu, Mike Schuster, Zhifeng Chen, Quoc V. Le, Mohammad Norouzi, Wolfgang Macherey, Maxim Krikun, Yuan Cao, Qin Gao, Klaus Macherey, Jeff Klingner, Apurva Shah, Melvin Johnson, Xiaobing Liu, Lukasz Kaiser, Stephan Gouws, Yoshikiyo Kato, Taku Kudo, Hideto Kazawa, Keith Stevens, George Kurian, Nishant Patil, Wei Wang, Cliff Young, Jason Smith, Jason Riesa, Alex Rudnick, Oriol Vinyals, Greg Corrado, Macduff Hughes, and Jeffrey Dean. 2016. Google's neural machine translation system: Bridging the gap between human and machine translation. *CoRR*, abs/1609.08144.

Jiacheng Zhang, Huanbo Luan, Maosong Sun, Feifei Zhai, Jingfang Xu, Min Zhang, and Yang Liu. 2018. Improving the transformer translation model with document-level context. In *Proceedings of the 2018 Conference on Empirical Methods in Natural Language Processing*, pages 533–542. Association for Computational Linguistics.

Shiqi Zhang and Deyi Xiong. 2018. Sentence weighting for neural machine translation domain adaptation. In *Proceedings of the 27th International Conference on Computational Linguistics*, pages 3181–3190. Association for Computational Linguistics.

IITP-MT System for Gujarati-English News Translation Task at WMT 2019

Sukanta Sen, Kamal Kumar Gupta, Asif Ekbal, Pushpak Bhattacharyya
Department of Computer Science and Engineering
Indian Institute of Technology Patna
{sukanta.pcs15,kamal.pcs17,asif,pb}@iitp.ac.in

Abstract

We describe our submission to WMT 2019 News translation shared task for Gujarati-English language pair. We submit constrained systems, i.e, we rely on the data provided for this language pair and do not use any external data. We train Transformer based subword-level neural machine translation (NMT) system using original parallel corpus along with synthetic parallel corpus obtained through back-translation of monolingual data. Our primary systems achieve BLEU scores of 10.4 and 8.1 for Gujarati→English and English→Gujarati, respectively. We observe that incorporating monolingual data through back-translation improves the BLEU score significantly over baseline NMT and SMT systems for this language pair.

1 Introduction

In this paper, we describe the system that we submit to the WMT 2019[1] news translation shared task (Bojar et al., 2019). We participate in Gujarati-English language pair and submit two systems: English→Gujarati and Gujarati→English. Gujarati language belongs to Indo-Aryan language family and is spoken predominantly in the Indian state of Gujarat. It is a low-resource language as only a few thousands parallel sentences are available, which are not enough to train a neural machine translation (NMT) system as well statistical machine translation (SMT) system. Gujarati-English is a distant language pair and they have different linguistic properties including syntax, morphology, word order etc. English follows subject-verb-object order while Gujarati follows subject-object-verb order.

NMT (Kalchbrenner and Blunsom, 2013; Cho et al., 2014; Sutskever et al., 2014; Bahdanau et al., 2015) has recently become dominant paradigm for machine translation (MT) achieving state-of-the-art on standard benchmark data sets for many language pairs. As opposed to SMT, NMT systems are trained in an end-to-end manner. Training an effective NMT requires a huge amount of high-quality parallel corpus and in absence of that, an NMT system tends to perform poorly (Koehn and Knowles, 2017). However, back-translation (Sennrich et al., 2016) has been shown to improve NMT systems in such a situation. In this work, we train a SMT system and an NMT system for both English→Gujarati and Gujarati→English using the original training data. SMT systems are also used to generate synthetic parallel corpora through back-translation of monolingual data from English news crawl and Gujarati Wikipedia dumps. These corpora along with the original training corpora are used to improve the baseline NMT systems. All the SMT and NMT systems are trained at subword level.

Our SMT systems are standard phrase-based SMT systems (Koehn et al., 2003), and NMT systems are based on Transformer (Vaswani et al., 2017) architecture. Experiments show that NMT systems achieve BLEU (Papineni et al., 2002) scores of 10.4 and 8.1 for Gujarati→English and English→Gujarati, respectively, outperforming the baseline SMT systems even in the absence of enough-sized parallel data.

Rest of the paper is arranged in following manner: Section 2 gives brief introduction of the Transformer architecture that we used for NMT training, Section 3 describes the task, Section 4 describes the submitted systems, Section 5 gives various evaluation scores for English-Gujarati translation pair, and finally, Section 6 concludes the work.

---

[1] http://www.statmt.org/wmt19/translation-task.html

Proceedings of the Fourth Conference on Machine Translation (WMT), Volume 2: Shared Task Papers (Day 1) pages 407–411
Florence, Italy, August 1-2, 2019. ©2019 Association for Computational Linguistics

2 Transformer Architecture

Recurrent neural network based encoder-decoder NMT architecture (Cho et al., 2014; Sutskever et al., 2014; Bahdanau et al., 2015) deals with input/output sentences word-by-word sequentially, which prevents the model from parallel computation. Vaswani et al. (2017) came up with a highly parallelizable architecture called Transformer which uses the self-attention to better encode a sequences. Self-attention is used in the architecture to calculate attention between a word and the other words in the sentence itself. Encoder and decoder both are stack of 6 identical layers. Each layer in encoder has two sub-layers: *i.* multi-head self attention mechanism and *ii.* position wise feed forward network. Each sub-layer is associated with residual connections, followed by layer normalization. Multi-head attention computes the attention multiple times for each word. Since their is no sequence to sequence encoding, positional encoding is used to encode the sequence information.

3 Task Description

This task focuses on translating news domain corpus and this year, Gujarati language is introduced for the first time in a WMT shared task. Gujarati is a low-resource language and not many results have been reported in machine translation involving this language. Also, there was no standard test set for this language pair. So introduction of this language pair will help in further research for this language pair.

As Gujarati does not have enough parallel data, the data that are provided for this shared task are mainly from WikiTitles which consists of only 11,671 parallel titles. Apart from that, few publicly available domain specific parallel data that are provided are: Bible corpus (Christodouloupoulos and Steedman, 2015); a localization extracted from OPUS[2]; parallel corpus extracted from Wikipedia; crawled corpus produced for this task; and monolingual Wikipedia dumps.

4 System Description

We participated in Gujarati-English pair only and we submit for both directions: English→Gujarati

and Gujarati→English. As Gujarati is a low-resource language and only a little amount of parallel data is available, we explore the back-translation technique for this pair. Also our models are based on Transformer as it has become state of the art for machine translation for many language pairs. We train systems at subword level. For back-translation, we train a phrase-based SMT (Koehn et al., 2003) system for each system in reverse direction. Using these SMT systems, monolingual sentences (for both Gujarati and English) are translated to create synthetic parallel data having original monolingual sentences at target and translated sentences at source side. These synthetic parallel data, along with the original parallel data are used to train a transformer based NMT system for each direction.

4.1 Dataset

Sources	#Sentences
Parallel	
Bible	7,807
govin-clean.gu-en.tsv	10,650
opus.gu-en.tsv	107,637
wikipedia.gu-en.tsv	18,033
wikititles-v1.gu-en.tsv	11,671
Total	155,798
Monolingual	
Gujarati (Wikipedia dump)	382,881
English (News crawl)	1,000,000

Table 1: Training data sources and number of sentences.

The datasets that we use for training are shown in the Table 1, which combine to a total of 155,798 parallel sentences. These parallel data are compiled from different sources. The compiled datasets are Bible[3], govin-clean.gu-en.tsv[4], opus.gu-en.tsv[5], wikipedia.gu-en.tsv[6] and wikititles-v1.gu-en.tsv[7]. We use *newsdev2019* for tuning the model, which has 1,998 parallel sentences.

---

[2]http://opus.nlpl.eu

[3]http://data.statmt.org/wmt19/translation-task/bible.gu-en.tsv.gz

[4]http://data.statmt.org/wmt19/translation-task/govin-raw.gu-en.tsv.gz

[5]http://data.statmt.org/wmt19/translation-task/opus.gu-en.tsv.gz

[6]http://data.statmt.org/wmt19/translation-task/wikipedia.gu-en.tsv.gz

[7]http://data.statmt.org/wikititles/v1/wikititles-v1.gu-en.tsv.gz

System	BLEU	BLEU-cased	TER	CharactTER
English→Gujarati				
PBSMT	5.2	5.2	0.987	0.782
Transformer	4.0	4.0	1.005	0.884
Transformer + Synth	8.1	8.1	0.919	0.763
Gujarati→English				
PBSMT	7.3	6.3	0.883	0.817
Transformer	5.5	5.1	0.905	0.859
Transformer + Synth	10.4	9.4	0.828	0.774

Table 2: BLEU scores of different SMT and NMT based systems. Synth: Synthetic data

Apart from these parallel data, we use monolingual English (news crawl) and Gujarati (Wikipedia dumps) sentences for synthetic parallel data creation. After training two models i.e. English→Gujarati and Gujarati→English using the parallel data mentioned in Table 1, English and Gujarati monolingual sentences are back translated respectively.

4.2 Experimental Setup

We train phrase based statistical system (PB-SMT) (Koehn et al., 2003) as well as Transformer (Vaswani et al., 2017) based neural system for comparing their performance under low-resource conditions. In addition to that, PBSMT are used to genrate synthetic parallel data. PBSMT systems are trained only on original training data, while neural based models are trained on original training data (*Transfomer* in Table 2), and also with synthetic parallel data in addition to original data (*Transfomer+Synth* in Table 2). Synthetic parallel data are obtained through back-translation of a target monolingual corpus into source using PB-SMT system. We use Moses (Koehn et al., 2007) toolkit for PBSMT training and Sockeye (Hieber et al., 2017) toolkit for NMT training. Some pre-processing of data is required before using it for experiment. English data is tokenized using moses tokenizer, and truecased. For tokenizing Gujarati data, we use indic_nlp_library[8]. After tokeninzation and truecasing, we subword (Sennrich et al., 2015) all original data. We apply 10,000 BPE merge operations over English and Gujarati data independently.

For back-translation of monolingual data, two PBSMT models English→Gujarati and Gujarati→English are trained over original available parallel subworded corpora. 4-gram language model is trained using KenLM (Heafield, 2011). For word alignment, we use GIZA++ (Och and Ney, 2003) with grow-diag-final-and heuristics. Model is tuned with Minimum Error Rate Training (Och, 2003). After these two models are trained, monolingual subworded data from both English and Gujarati are back-translated using English→Gujarati and Gujarati→English PB-SMT model, respectively. We merge the back translated data with original parallel data to have larger parallel corpora for Gujarati→English and English→Gujarati translation directions.

Finally, with the augmented parallel corpora, we train one Transformer based NMT model for each direction. We use the following hyper-parameters values of Sockeye toolkit: 6 layers in both encoder and decoder, word embedding size of 512, hidden size of 512, maximum input length of 50 tokens, Adam optimizer, word batch size 1000, attention type is dot, learning rate of 0.0002. The rest of the hyper-parameters are set to the default values in Sockeye. We use early stopping criteria for terminating the training on the validation set of 1,998 parallel sentences.

5 Results

The official automatic evaluation uses the following metrics: BLEU (Papineni et al., 2002), TER (Snover et al., 2006), CharactTER (Wang et al., 2016). The official scores are shown in the Table 2. Phrase-base SMT (PBSMT) obtains BLEU scores of 5.2 and 7.3 for English→Gujarati and Gujarati→Englsih, respectively. Whereas, baseline NMT (*Transformer*) obtains lower BLEU scores of 4.0 and 5.5 for the same directions. Though, SMT systems outperforms baseline NMT systems trained using small amount of original parallel data only. We observe from the Table 2 that Transformer with synthetic (*Transformer +*

---

[8]https://github.com/anoopkunchukuttan/indic_nlp_library

Gujarati→English

Ave.	Ave. z	System
64.8	0.210	NEU
61.7	0.126	UEDIN
59.4	0.100	GTCOM-Primary
60.8	0.090	CUNI-T2T-transfer
59.4	0.066	aylien-mt-multilingual
59.3	0.044	NICT
51.3	−0.189	online-G
50.9	−0.192	IITP-MT
48.0	−0.277	UdS-DFKI
47.4	−0.296	IIITH-MT
41.1	−0.598	Ju-Saarland

English→Gujarati

Ave.	Ave. z	System
73.1	0.701	HUMAN
72.2	0.663	online-B
66.8	0.597	GTCOM-Primary
60.2	0.318	MSRA-CrossBERT
58.3	0.305	UEDIN
55.9	0.254	CUNI-T2T-transfer
52.7	−0.079	Ju-Saarland-clean-num-135-bpe
35.2	−0.458	IITP-MT
38.8	−0.465	NICT
39.1	−0.490	online-G
33.1	−0.502	online-X
33.2	−0.718	UdS-DFKI

Table 3: Preliminary official results of WMT 2019 news translation task for Gujarati-English pair. Systems ordered by DA score z-score; systems within a cluster are considered tied; lines indicate clusters according to Wilcoxon rank-sum test p < 0.05; grayed entry indicates resources that fall outside the constraints provided.

Synth) data obtained through back-translation of monolingual data, outperforms the baseline SMT systems with a margin of 2.9 and 3.1 BELU points. Also, as a result of augmenting back-translated data with original training data, we obtain improvement of of 4.7 and 5.3 BLEU points over baseline NMT for English→Gujarati and Gujarati→English, respectively. The official preliminary human evaluation results are shown in the Table 3.

6   Conclusion

In this paper, we described our submission to the WMT 2019 News translation shared task for Gujarati-English language pair. This is the first time Gujarati language is introduced in a WMT shared task. We submit Transformer based NMT systems for English-Gujarati language pair. Since the number of parallel sentences in training set are very less and many sentences have length of only 2-3 tokens, BLEU scores for English-Gujarati pair using only available parallel corpus are very low (4.0 and 5.1 for English→Gujarati and Gujarati→English, respectively). So we use monolingual sentences for both languages to create synthetic parallel data through back-translation, and merged them with original parallel data. We obtained improved BLEU scores of 8.1 and 10.4, respectively.

References

Dzmitry Bahdanau, Kyunghyun Cho, and Yoshua Bengio. 2015. Neural Machine Translation by Jointly Learning to Align and Translate. In *Proceedings of the 3rd International Conference on Learning Representation (ICLR 2015)*.

Ondřej Bojar, Christian Federmann, Mark Fishel, Yvette Graham, Barry Haddow, Matthias Huck, Philipp Koehn, Christof Monz, Mathias Müller, and Matt Post. 2019. Findings of the 2019 conference on machine translation (wmt19). In *Proceedings of the Fourth Conference on Machine Translation, Volume 2: Shared Task Papers*, Florence, Italy. Association for Computational Linguistics.

Kyunghyun Cho, Bart Van Merriënboer, Dzmitry Bahdanau, and Yoshua Bengio. 2014. On the Properties of Neural Machine Translation: Encoder-decoder Approaches. In *Proceedings of SSST-8, Eighth Workshop on Syntax, Semantics and Structure in Statistical Translation*, pages 103–111.

Christos Christodouloupoulos and Mark Steedman. 2015. A massively parallel corpus: the Bible in 100 languages. *Language resources and evaluation*, 49(2):375–395.

Kenneth Heafield. 2011. Kenlm: Faster and smaller language model queries. In *Proceedings of the Sixth Workshop on Statistical Machine Translation*, pages 187–197. Association for Computational Linguistics.

Felix Hieber, Tobias Domhan, Michael Denkowski, David Vilar, Artem Sokolov, Ann Clifton, and Matt Post. 2017. Sockeye: A toolkit for neural machine translation. *arXiv preprint arXiv:1712.05690*.

Nal Kalchbrenner and Phil Blunsom. 2013. Recurrent Continuous Translation Models. In *Proceedings of the 2013 Conference on Empirical Methods in Natural Language Processing (EMNLP 2013)*, pages 1700–1709.

Philipp Koehn, Hieu Hoang, Alexandra Birch, Chris Callison-Burch, Marcello Federico, Nicola Bertoldi, Brooke Cowan, Wade Shen, Christine Moran, Richard Zens, et al. 2007. Moses: Open source toolkit for statistical machine translation. In *Proceedings of the 45th annual meeting of the ACL on interactive poster and demonstration sessions*, pages 177–180. Association for Computational Linguistics.

Philipp Koehn and Rebecca Knowles. 2017. Six challenges for neural machine translation. In *Proceedings of the First Workshop on Neural Machine Translation*, pages 28–39, Vancouver. Association for Computational Linguistics.

Philipp Koehn, Franz Josef Och, and Daniel Marcu. 2003. Statistical phrase-based translation. In *Proceedings of the 2003 Conference of the North American Chapter of the Association for Computational Linguistics on Human Language Technology-Volume 1*, pages 48–54. Association for Computational Linguistics.

Franz Josef Och. 2003. Minimum error rate training in statistical machine translation. In *Proceedings of the 41st Annual Meeting on Association for Computational Linguistics-Volume 1*, pages 160–167. Association for Computational Linguistics.

Franz Josef Och and Hermann Ney. 2003. A systematic comparison of various statistical alignment models. *Computational linguistics*, 29(1):19–51.

Kishore Papineni, Salim Roukos, Todd Ward, and Wei-Jing Zhu. 2002. BLEU: a Method for Automatic Evaluation of Machine Translation. In *Proceedings of the 40th annual meeting on association for computational linguistics*, pages 311–318, Philadelphia, Pennsylvania.

Rico Sennrich, Barry Haddow, and Alexandra Birch. 2015. Neural machine translation of rare words with subword units. *arXiv preprint arXiv:1508.07909*.

Rico Sennrich, Barry Haddow, and Alexandra Birch. 2016. Improving neural machine translation models with monolingual data. In *Proceedings of the 54th Annual Meeting of the Association for Computational Linguistics, ACL 2016, August 7-12, 2016, Berlin, Germany*.

Matthew Snover, Bonnie Dorr, Richard Schwartz, Linnea Micciulla, and John Makhoul. 2006. A study of translation edit rate with targeted human annotation. In *Proceedings of association for machine translation in the Americas*, volume 200.

Ilya Sutskever, Oriol Vinyals, and Quoc V Le. 2014. Sequence to Sequence Learning with Neural Networks. In *Proceedings of Advances in neural information processing systems (NIPS 2014)*, pages 3104–3112.

Ashish Vaswani, Noam Shazeer, Niki Parmar, Jakob Uszkoreit, Llion Jones, Aidan N Gomez, Łukasz Kaiser, and Illia Polosukhin. 2017. Attention is all you need. In *Advances in neural information processing systems*, pages 5998–6008.

Weiyue Wang, Jan-Thorsten Peter, Hendrik Rosendahl, and Hermann Ney. 2016. Character: Translation edit rate on character level. In *Proceedings of the First Conference on Machine Translation: Volume 2, Shared Task Papers*, volume 2, pages 505–510.

The University of Helsinki submissions to the WMT19 news translation task

Aarne Talman,[*][†] **Umut Sulubacak,**[*] **Raúl Vázquez,**[*] **Yves Scherrer,**[*] **Sami Virpioja,**[*]
Alessandro Raganato,[*][†] **Arvi Hurskainen**[*] and **Jörg Tiedemann**[*]

[*]University of Helsinki
[†]Basement AI
{name.surname}@helsinki.fi

Abstract

In this paper, we present the University of Helsinki submissions to the WMT 2019 shared task on news translation in three language pairs: English–German, English–Finnish and Finnish–English. This year, we focused first on cleaning and filtering the training data using multiple data-filtering approaches, resulting in much smaller and cleaner training sets. For English–German, we trained both sentence-level transformer models and compared different document-level translation approaches. For Finnish–English and English–Finnish we focused on different segmentation approaches, and we also included a rule-based system for English–Finnish.

1 Introduction

The University of Helsinki participated in the WMT 2019 news translation task with four primary submissions. We submitted neural machine translation systems for English-to-Finnish, Finnish-to-English and English-to-German, and a rule-based machine translation system for English-to-Finnish.

Most of our efforts for this year's WMT focused on data selection and pre-processing (Section 2), sentence-level translation models for English-to-German, English-to-Finnish and Finnish-to-English (Section 3), document-level translation models for English-to-German (Section 4), and a comparison of different word segmentation approaches for Finnish (Section 3.3). The final submitted NMT systems are summarized in Section 5, while the rule-based machine translation system is described in Section 3.4.

2 Pre-processing, data filtering and back-translation

It is well known that data pre-processing and selection has a huge effect on translation quality in neural machine translation. We spent substantial effort on filtering data in order to reduce noise—especially in the web-crawled data sets—and to match the target domain of news data.

The resulting training sets, after applying the steps described below, are for 15.7M sentence pairs for English–German, 8.5M sentence pairs for English–Finnish, and 12.3M–26.7M sentence pairs (different samplings of back-translations) for Finnish–English.

2.1 Pre-processing

For each language, we applied a series of pre-processing steps using scripts available in the Moses decoder (Philipp Koehn, 2007):

- replacing unicode punctuation,
- removing non-printing characters,
- normalizing punctuation,
- tokenization.

In addition to these steps, we replaced a number of English contractions with the full form, *e.g.* *"They're"* → *"They are"*. After the above steps, we applied a Moses truecaser model trained for individual languages, and finally a byte-pair encoding (BPE) (Sennrich et al., 2016b) segmentation using a set of codes for either language pair.

For English–German, we initially pre-processed the data using only punctuation normalization and tokenization. We subsequently trained an English truecaser model using all monolingual English data as well as the English side of all parallel English–German datasets except the Rapid corpus (in which non-English characters were missing from a substantial portion of the German sentences). We also repeated the same for German. Afterwards, we used a heuristic cleanup script[1] in

---

[1]Shared by Marcin Junczys-Dowmunt. Retrieved

Proceedings of the Fourth Conference on Machine Translation (WMT), Volume 2: Shared Task Papers (Day 1) pages 412–423
Florence, Italy, August 1-2, 2019. ©2019 Association for Computational Linguistics

order to filter suspicious samples out of Rapid, and then truecased all parallel English–German data (including the filtered Rapid) using these models. Finally, we trained BPE codes with 35 000 symbols jointly for English–German on the truecased parallel sets. For all further experiments with English–German data, we applied the full set of tokenization steps as well as truecasing and BPE segmentation.

For English–Finnish, we first applied the standard tokenization pipeline. For English and Finnish respectively, we trained truecaser models on all English and Finnish monolingual data as well as the English and Finnish side of all parallel English–Finnish datasets. As we had found to be optimal in our previous year submission (Raganato et al., 2018), we trained a BPE model using a vocabulary of 37 000 symbols, trained jointly only on the parallel data. Furthermore, for some experiments, we also used domain labeling. We marked the datasets with 3 different labels: ⟨NEWS⟩ for the development and test data from 2015, 2016, 2017, ⟨EP⟩ for Europarl, and ⟨WEB⟩ for ParaCrawl and Wikititles.

2.2 Data filtering

For data filtering we applied four types of filters: (i) rule-based heuristics, (ii) filters based on language identification, (iii) filters based on word alignment models, and (iv) language model filters.

Heuristic filters: The first step in cleaning the data refers to a number of heuristics (largely inspired by (Stahlberg et al., 2018)) including:

- removing all sentence pairs with a length difference ratio above a certain threshold: for CommonCrawl, ParaCrawl and Rapid we used a threshold of 3, for WikiTitles a threshold of 2, and for all other data sets a threshold of 9;

- removing pairs with short sentences: for CommonCrawl, ParaCrawl and Rapid we required a minimum number of four words;

- removing pairs with very long sentences: we restricted all data to a maximum length of 100 words;

- removing sentences with extremely long words: We excluded all sentence pairs with words of 40 or more characters;

- removing sentence pairs that include HTML or XML tags;

- decoding common HTML/XML entities;

- removing empty alignments (while keeping document boundaries intact);

- removing pairs where the sequences of non-zero digits occurring in either sentence do not match;

- removing pairs where one sentence is terminated with a punctuation mark and the other is either missing terminal punctuation or terminated with another punctuation mark.

Language identifiers: There is a surprisingly large amount of text segments in a wrong language in the provided parallel training data. This is especially true for the ParaCrawl and Rapid data sets. This is rather unexpected as a basic language identifier certainly must be part of the crawling and extraction pipeline. Nevertheless, after some random inspection of the data, we found it necessary to apply off-the-shelf language identifiers to the data for removing additional erroneous text from the training data. In particular, we applied the Compact Language Detector version 2 (CLD2) from the Google Chrome project (using the Python interface from *pycld2*[2]), and the widely used *langid.py* package (Lui and Baldwin, 2012) to classify each sentence in the ParaCrawl, CommonCrawl, Rapid and Wikititles data sets. We removed all sentence pairs in which the language of one of the aligned sentences was not reliably detected. For this, we required the correct language ID from both classifiers, the reliable-flag set to "True" by CLD2 with a reliability score of 90 or more, and the detection probability of *langid.py* to be at least 0.9.

Word alignment filter: Statistical word alignment models implement a way of measuring the likelihood of parallel sentences. IBM-style alignment models estimate the probability $p(f \mid a, e)$ of a foreign sentence f given an "emitted" sentence e and an alignment a between them. Training word alignment models and aligning large corpora is very expensive using traditional methods and implementations. Fortunately, we can rely on *eflomal*[3], an efficient word aligner based on Gibbs sampling (Östling and Tiedemann, 2016). Recently, the software has been updated to allow the storage of model priors that makes it possible to initialize the aligner with previously stored model parameters. This is handy for our filtering needs as we can now train a model on clean parallel data and apply that model to estimate alignment probabilities of noisy data sets.

We train the alignment model on Europarl and news test sets from previous WMTs for English–Finnish, and NewsCommentary for English–German. For both language pairs, we train a Bayesian HMM alignment model with fertilities in both directions and estimate the model priors from the symmetrized alignment. We then use those priors to run the alignment of the noisy data sets using only a single iteration of the final model to avoid a strong influence of the noisy data on alignment parameters. As it is intractable to estimate a fully normalized conditional probability of a sentence pair under the given higher-level word alignment model, eflomal estimates a score based on the maximum unnormalized log-probability of links in the last sampling iteration. In practice, this seems to work well, and we take that value to rank sentence pairs by their alignment quality. In our experiments, we set an arbitrary threshold of 7 for that score, which seems to balance recall and precision well according to some superficial inspection of the ranked data. The word alignment filter is applied to all web data as well as to the back-translations of monolingual news.

Language model filter: The most traditional data filtering method is probably to apply a language model. The advantage of language models is that they can be estimated from monolingual data, which may be available in sufficient amounts even for the target domain. In our approach, we opted for a combination of source and target language models and focused on the comparison between scores coming from both models. The idea is to prefer sentence pairs for which not only the cross-entropy of the individual sentences ($H(S, q_s)$ and $H(T, q_t)$) is low with respect to in-domain LMs, but also the absolute difference between the cross-entropies ($abs(H(S, q_s) - H(T, q_t))$) for aligned source and target sentences

is low. The intuition is that both models should be roughly similarly surprised when observing sentences that are translations of each other. In order to make the values comparable, we trained our language models on parallel data sets.

For English–Finnish, we used news test data from 2015-2017 as the only available in-domain parallel training data, and for English–German we added the NewsCommentary data set to the news test sets from 2008-2018. As both data sets are small, and we aimed for an efficient and cheap filter, we opted for a traditional n-gram language model in our experiments. To further avoid data sparseness and to improve comparability between source and target language, we also based our language models on BPE-segmented texts using the same BPE codes as for the rest of the training data. *VariKN* (Siivola et al., 2007b,a)[4] is the perfect toolkit for the purposes of estimating n-gram language models with subword units. It implements Kneser-Ney growing and revised Kneser-Ney pruning methods with the support of n-grams of varying size and the estimation of word likelihoods from text segmented in subword units. In our case, we set the maximum n-gram size to 20, and the pruning threshold to 0.002. Finally, we computed cross-entropies for each sentence in the noisy parallel training data and stored 5 values as potential features for filtering: $H(S, q_s)$, $H(T, q_t)$, $avg(H(S, q_s), H(T, q_t))$, $max(H(S, q_s), H(T, q_t))$ and $abs(H(S, q_s) - (T, q_t))$. Based on some random inspection, we selected a threshold of 13 for the average cross-entropy score, and a threshold of 4 for the cross-entropy difference score. For English–Finnish, we opted for a slightly more relaxed setup to increase coverage, and set the average cross-entropy to 15 and the difference threshold to 5. We applied the language model filter to all web data and to the back-translations of monolingual news.

Applying the filter to WMT 2019 data: The impact of our filters on the data provided by WMT 2019 is summarized in Tables 1, 2 and 3.

We can see that the ParaCrawl corpus is the one that is the most affected by the filters. A lot of noise can be removed, especially by the language model filter. The strict punctuation filter also has a strong impact on that data set. Naturally, web data does not come with proper com-

---

[3]Software available from `https://github.com/robertostling/eflomal`

[4]VariKN is available from `https://vsiivola.github.io/variKN/`

	EN–DE	EN–FI
CommonCrawl	3.2%	
Europarl	0.8%	2.8%
News-Commentary	0.2%	
ParaCrawl	0.6%	
Rapid	13.2%	5.2%
WikiTitles	8.0%	4.0%

Table 1: Basic heuristics for filtering – percentage of lines removed. For English–Finnish the statistics for ParaCrawl are not available because the cleanup script was applied after other filters.

		% rejected	
Filter	CC	ParaCrawl	Rapid
LM average CE	31.9%	62.0%	12.7%
LM CE diff	19.0%	12.7%	6.9%
Source lang ID	4.0%	30.7%	7.3%
Target lang ID	8.0%	22.7%	6.2%
Wordalign	46.4%	3.1%	8.4%
Number	15.3%	16.0%	5.0%
Punct	0.0%	47.4%	18.7%
total	66.7%	74.7%	35.1%

Table 2: Percentage of lines rejected by each filter for English–German data sets. Each line can be rejected by several filters. The total of rejected lines is the last row of the table.

	% rejected			
	ParaCrawl		Rapid	
Filter	strict	relax	strict	relax
LM avg CE	62.5%	40.0%	50.7%	21.4%
LM CE diff	35.4%	25.7%	44.8%	31.1%
Src lang ID	37.2%	37.2%	11.9%	11.9%
Trg lang ID	29.1%	29.1%	8.5%	8.5%
Wordalign	8.3%	8.3%	8.3%	8.3%
Number	16.8%	16.8%	6.7%	6.7%
Punct	54.6%	3.3%	23.7%	7.6%
total	87.9%	64.2%	62.2%	54.8%

Table 3: Percentage of lines rejected by each filter for English–Finnish data sets. The strict version is the same as for English–German, and the relax version applies relaxed thresholds.

plete sentences that end with proper final punctuation marks, and the filter might remove quite a bit of the useful data examples. However, our fi-nal translation scores reflect that we do not seem to lose substantial amounts of performance even with the strict filters. Nevertheless, for English–Finnish, we still opted for a more relaxed setup to increase coverage, as the strict version removed over 87% of the ParaCrawl data.

It is also interesting to note the differences of individual filters on different data sets. The word alignment filter seems to reject a large portion of the CommonCrawl data set whereas it does not affect other data sets that much. The importance of language identification can be seen with the ParaCrawl data whereas other corpora seem to be much cleaner with respect to language.

2.3 Back-translation

We furthermore created synthetic training data by back-translating news data. We translated the monolingual English news data from the years 2007–2018, from which we used a filtered and sampled subset of 7M sentences for our Finnish–English systems, and the Finnish data from years 2014–2018 using our WMT 2018 submissions. We also used the back-translations we generated for the WMT 2017 news translation task, where we used an SMT model to create 5.5M sentences of back-translated data from the Finnish news2014 and news2016 corpora (Östling et al., 2017).

For the English–German back-translations, we trained a standard transformer model on all the available parallel data and translated the monolingual German data into English. The BLEU score for our back-translation model is 44.24 on newstest 2018. We applied our filtering pipeline to the back-translated pairs, resulting in 10.3M sentence pairs. In addition to the new back-translations, we also included back-translations from the WMT16 data by Sennrich et al. (2016a).

3 Sentence-level approaches

In this section we describe our sentence-level translation models and the experiments in the English-to-German, English-to-Finnish and Finnish-to-English translation directions.

3.1 Model architectures

We experimented with both NMT and rule-based systems. All of our neural sentence-level models are based on the transformer architecture (Vaswani et al., 2017). We used both the OpenNMT-py (Klein et al., 2017) and MarianNMT (Junczys-

Dowmunt et al., 2018) frameworks. Our experiments focused on the following:

- Ensemble models: using ensembles with a combination of independent runs and save-points from a single training run.

- Left-to-right and right-to-left models: Transformer models with decoding of the output in left-to-right and right-to-left order.

The English-to-Finnish rule-based system is an enhanced version of the WMT 2018 rule-based system (Raganato et al., 2018).

3.2 English–German

Our sentence-level models for the English-to-German direction are based on ensembles of independent runs and different save-points as well as save-points fine-tuned on in-domain data. For our submission, we used an ensemble of 9 models containing:

- 4 save-points with the lowest development perplexity taken from a model trained for 300 000 training steps.

- 5 independent models fine-tuned with in-domain data.

All our sentence-level models for the English–German language pair are trained on filtered versions of Europarl, NewsCommentary, Rapid, CommonCrawl, ParaCrawl, Wikititles, and back-translations. For in-domain fine-tuning, we use newstest 2011–2016. Our submission is composed of transformer-big models implemented in OpenNMT-py with 6 layers of hidden size 4096, 16 attention heads, and a dropout of 0.1. The differences in development performance between the best single model, an ensemble of save-points of a single training run and our final submission are reported in Table 4. We gain 2 BLEU points with the ensemble of save-points, and an additional 0.8 points by adding in-domain fine-tuned models into the ensemble. This highlights the well-known effectiveness of ensembling and domain adaptation for translation quality.

Furthermore, we trained additional models using MarianNMT with the same training data and fine-tuning method. In this case, we also included right-to-left decoders that are used as a complement in the standard left-to-right decoders in rescoring approaches. In total, we also end up with 9 models including:

	BLEU news2018
Single model	44.61
5 save-points	46.65
5 save-points + 4 fine-tuned	**47.45**

Table 4: English–German development results comparing the best single model, an ensemble of 5 save-points, and an ensemble of 5 save-points and 4 independent runs fine-tuned on in-domain data.

- 3 independent models trained for left-to-right decoding,

- 3 independent models trained for right-to-left decoding,

- 3 save-points based on continued training of one of the left-to-right decoding models.

The save-points were added later as we found out that models kept on improving when using larger mini-batches and less frequent validation in early stopping. Table 5 lists the results of various models on the development test data from 2018.

	BLEU news2018	
Model	Basic	Fine-tuned
L2R run 1	43.63	45.31
L2R run 2	43.52	45.14
L2R run 3	43.33	44.93
L2R run3 cont'd 1	43.65	45.11
L2R run3 cont'd 2	43.76	45.43
L2R run3 cont'd 3	43.53	45.67
Ensemble all L2R	44.61	46.34
Rescore all L2R		46.49
R2L run 1	42.14	43.80
R2L run 2	41.96	43.67
R2L run 3	42.17	43.91
Ensemble all R2L	43.03	44.70
Rescore all R2L		44.73
Rescore all L2R+R2L		**46.98**

Table 5: English–German results from individual MarianNMT transformer models and their combinations (cased BLEU).

There are various trends that are interesting to point out. First of all, fine-tuning gives a consistent boost of 1.5 or more BLEU points. Our initial runs were using a validation frequency of 5 000 steps and a single GPU with dynamic mini-batches that fit in 13G of memory. The stopping criterion was set to 10 validation steps without improving cross-entropy on heldout data (newstest 2015 + 2016). Later on, we switched to multi-GPU training with two GPUs and early stopping of 20 validation steps. The dynamic batching method of MarianNMT produces larger minibatches once there is more memory available, and multi-GPU settings simply multiply the working memory for that purpose. We realized that this change enabled the system to continue training substantially, and Table 5 illustrates the gains of that process for the third L2R model.

Another observation is that right-to-left decoding models in general work less well compared to the corresponding left-to-right models. This is also apparent with the fine-tuned and ensemble models that combine independent runs. The difference is significant with about 1.5 BLEU points or more. Nevertheless, they still contribute to the overall best score when re-scoring n-best lists from all models in both decoding directions. In this example, re-scoring is done by simply summing individual scores. Table 5 also shows that re-scoring is better than ensembles for model combinations with the same decoding direction because they effectively increase the beam size as the hypotheses from different models are merged before re-ranking the combined and re-scored n-best lists.

The positive effect of beam search is further illustrated in Figure 1. All previous models were run with a beam size of 12. As we can see, the general trend is that larger beams lead to improved performance, at least until the limit of 64 in our experiments. Beam size 4 is an exception in the left-to-right models.

3.3 English–Finnish and Finnish–English

The problem of open-vocabulary translation is particularly acute for morphologically rich languages like Finnish. In recent NMT research, the standard approach consists of applying a word segmentation algorithm such as BPE (Sennrich et al., 2016b) or SentencePiece (Kudo and Richardson, 2018) during pre-processing. In recent WMT editions, various alternative segmentation approaches were examined for Finnish: hybrid models that back off to character-level representations (Östling et al., 2017), and variants of the Morfessor unsupervised morphology algorithm (Grönroos et al., 2018). This year, we exper-

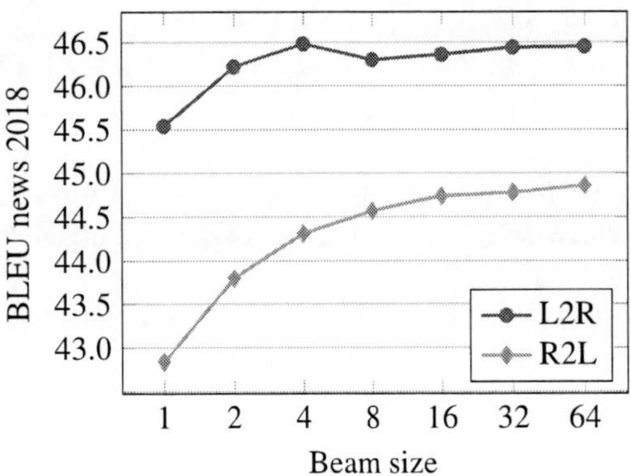

Figure 1: The effect of beam size on translation performance. All results use model ensembles and the scores are case-sensitive.

imented with rule-based word segmentation based on Omorfi (Pirinen, 2015). Omorfi is a morphological analyzer for Finnish with a large-coverage lexicon. Its segmentation tool[5] splits a word form into morphemes as defined by the morphological rules. In particular, it distinguishes prefixes, infixes and suffixes through different segmentation markers:

Intia→ ←*n ja   Japani*→ ←*n pää*→ ←*ministeri*→
India   GEN and Japan   GEN prime minister

←*t tapaa*→ ←*vat Tokio*→ ←*ssa*
PL   meet   3PL   Tokyo   INE

While Omorfi provides word segmentation based on morphological principles, it does not rely on any frequency cues. Therefore, the standard BPE algorithm is run over the Omorfi-segmented text in order to split low-frequency morphemes.

In this experiment, we compare two models for each translation direction:

- One model segmented with the standard BPE algorithm (joint vocabulary size of 50 000, vocabulary frequency threshold of 50).

- One model where the Finnish side is presegmented with Omorfi, and both the Omorfi-segmented Finnish side and the English side are segmented with BPE (same parameters as above).

All models are trained on filtered versions of Europarl, ParaCrawl, Rapid, Wikititles, newsdev2015 and newstest2015 as well as backtranslations. Following our experiments at WMT

---

[5]`https://flammie.github.io/omorfi/pages/usage-examples.html#morphological-segmentation`

2018 (Raganato et al., 2018), we also use domain labels ($\langle EP \rangle$ for Europarl, $\langle Web \rangle$ for ParaCrawl, Rapid and Wikititles, and $\langle NEWS \rangle$ for newsdev, newstest and the back-translations). We use newstest2016 for validation. All models are trained with MarianNMT, using the standard Transformer architecture.

Figures 2 and 3 show the evolution of BLEU scores on news2016 during training. For English–Finnish, the Omorfi-segmented system shows slightly higher results during the first 40 000 training steps, but is then outperformed by the plain BPE-segmented system. For Finnish–English, the Omorfi-segmented system obtains higher BLEU scores much longer, until both systems converge after about 300 000 training steps.

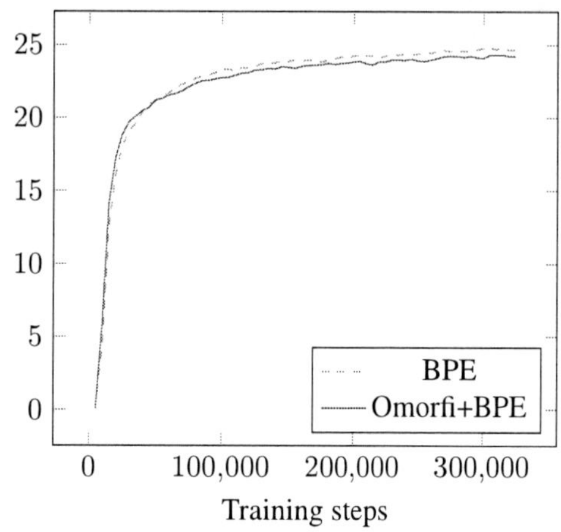

Figure 2: Evolution of English–Finnish BLEU scores (on y-axis) during training.

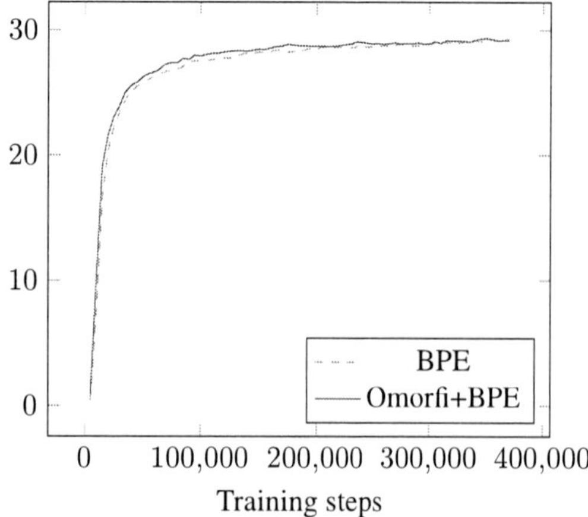

Figure 3: Evolution of Finnish–English BLEU scores (on y-axis) during training.

Table 6 compares BLEU scores for the 2017 to 2019 test sets. The Omorfi-based system shows consistent improvements when used on the source side, *i.e.* from Finnish to English. However, due to timing constraints, we were not able to integrate the Omorfi-based segmentation into our final submission systems. In any case, the difference observed in the news2019 set after submission deadline is within the bounds of random variation.

Data set	Δ BLEU EN-FI	Δ BLEU FI-EN
news2017	-0.47	$+0.36$
news2018	-0.61	$+0.38$
news2019	$+0.19$	$+0.04$

Table 6: BLEU score differences between Omorfi-segmented and BPE-segmented models. Positive values indicate that the Omorfi+BPE model is better, negative values indicate that the BPE model is better.

We tested additional transformer models segmented with the SentencePiece toolkit, using a shared vocabulary of 40k tokens trained only on the parallel corpora. We do this with the purpose of comparing the use of a software tailored specifically for Finnish language (Omorfi) with a more general segmentation one. These models were trained with the same specifications as the previous ones, including the transformer hyperparameters, the train and development data and the domain-labeling. Since we used OpenNMT-py to train these models, it is difficult to know whether the differences come from the segmentation or the toolkit. We, however, find it informative to present these results. Table 7 presents the obtained BLEU scores with both systems.

We notice that both systems yield similar scores for both translation directions. SentencePiece models are consistently ahead of Omorfi+BPE, but this difference is so small that it cannot be considered convincing nor significant.

Our final models for English-to-Finnish are standard transformer models with BPE-based segmentation, trained using MarianNMT with the same settings and hyper-parameters as the other experiments. We used the filtered training data using the relaxed settings of the language model filter to obtain better coverage for this language pair. The provided training data is much smaller and we also have less back-translated data at our disposal, which motivated us to lower the threshold

Model		news 2017	news 2019
SentencePiece	EN-FI	25.60	20.60
Omorfi+BPE	EN-FI	25.50	20.13
SentencePiece	EN-FI	31.50	25.00
Omorfi+BPE	FI-EN	31.21	24.06

Table 7: BLEU scores comparison between Sentence-Piece and Omorfi+BPE-segmented models.

of taking examples from web-crawled data. Domain fine-tuning is done as well using news test sets from 2015, 2016 and 2018. The results on development test data from 2017 are listed in Table 8.

| Model | BLEU news2017 | |
	L2R	R2L
Run 1	27.68	28.01
Run 2	28.64	28.77
Run 3	28.64	28.41
Ensemble	29.54	29.76
Rescored	29.60	29.72
– L2R+R2L	**30.66**	
Top matrix	21.7	

Table 8: Results from individual MarianNMT transformer models and their combinations for English to Finnish (cased BLEU). The *top matrix* result refers to the best system reported in the on-line evaluation matrix (accessed on May 16, 2019).

A striking difference to English–German is that right-to-left decoding models are on par with the other direction. The scores are substantially higher than the currently best (post-WMT 2017) system reported in the on-line evaluation matrix for this test set, even though this also refers to a transformer with a similar architecture and back-translated monolingual data. This system does not contain data derived from ParaCrawl, which was not available at the time, and the improvements we achieve demonstrate the effectiveness of our data filtering techniques from the noisy on-line data.

For Finnish-to-English, we trained MarianNMT models using the same transformer architecture as for the other language pairs. Table 9 shows the scores of individual models and their combinations on the development test set of news from WMT 2017. All models are trained on the same filtered training data using the strict settings of the language model filter including the back-translations produced for English monolingual news.

| Model | BLEU news2017 | |
	L2R	R2L
Run 1	32.26	31.70
Run 2	31.91	31.83
Run 3	32.68	31.81
Ensemble	33.23	33.03
Rescored	33.34	32.98
– L2R+R2L	**33.95**	
Top (with ParaCrawl)	34.6	
Top (without ParaCrawl)	25.9	

Table 9: Results from individual MarianNMT transformer models and their combinations for Finnish to English (cased BLEU). Results denoted as top refer to the top systems reported at the on-line evaluation matrix (accessed on May 16, 2019), one trained with the 2019 data sets and one with 2017 data.

In contrast to English-to-German, models in the two decoding directions are quite similar again and the difference between left-to-right and right-to-left models is rather small. The importance of the new data sets from 2019 are visible again and our system performs similarly, but still slightly below the best system that has been submitted this year to the on-line evaluation matrix on the 2017 test set.

3.4 The English–Finnish rule-based system

Since the WMT 2018 challenge, there has been development in four areas of translation process in the rule-based system for English–Finnish:

1. The standard method in handling English noun compounds was to treat them as multiword expressions (MWE). This method allows many kinds of translations, even multiple translation, which can be handled in semantic disambiguation. However, because noun compounding is a common phenomenon, also a default handling method was developed for such cases, where two or more consecutive nouns are individually translated and glued together as a single word. The system works so that if the noun combination is not handled as MWE, the second strategy is applied (Hurskainen, 2018a).

2. The translation of various types of questions has been improved. Especially the translation of indirect questions was defective, because the use of *if* in the role of initiating the indirect question was not implemented. The conjunction *if* is ambiguous, because it is used also for initiating the conditional clause (Hurskainen, 2018b).

3. Substantial rule optimizing was carried out. When rules are added in development process, the result is often not optimal. There are obsolete rules and the rules may need new ordering. As a result, a substantial number of rules (30%) were removed and others were reordered. This has effect on translation speed but not on translation result (Hurskainen, 2018c).

4. Temporal subordinate clauses, which start with the conjunction *when* or *while*, can be translated with corresponding subordinate clauses in Finnish. However, such clauses are often translated with participial phrase constructions. Translation with such constructions was tested. The results show that although they can be implemented, they are prone to mistakes (Hurskainen, 2018d).

These improvements to the translation system contribute to fluency and accuracy of translations.

4 Document-level approaches

To evaluate the effectiveness of various document-level translation approaches for the English–German language pair, we experimented with a number of different approaches which are described below. In order to test the ability of the system to pick up document-level information, we also created a shuffled version of the news data from 2018. We then test our systems on both the original test set with coherent test data divided into short news documents and the shuffled test set with broken coherence.

4.1 Concatenation models

Some of the previously published approaches use concatenation of multiple source-side sentences in order to extend the context of the currently translated sentence (Tiedemann and Scherrer, 2017). In addition to the source-side concatenation model, we also tested an approach where we concatenate the previously translated sentence with the current source sentence. The concatenation approaches we tested are listed below.

- MT-concat-source: (2+1) Concatenating previous source sentence with the current source sentence (Tiedemann and Scherrer, 2017). (3+1a) Concatenating the previous two sentences with the current source sentence. (3+1b) Concatenating the previous, the current and the next sentence in the source languages.

- MT-concat-target: (1t+1s+1) Concatenating the previously translated (target) sentence with the current source sentence.

- MT-concat-source-target: (2+2) Concatenating the previous with the current source sentence and translate into the previous and the current target sentence (Tiedemann and Scherrer, 2017). Only the second sentence in the translation will be kept for evaluation of the translation quality.

Extended context models only make sense with coherent training data. Therefore, we ran experiments only with the training data that contain translated documents, *i.e.* Europarl, NewsCommentary, Rapid and the back-translations of the German news from 2018. Hence, the baseline is lower than a sentence-level model on the complete data sets provided by WMT. Table 10 summarizes the results on the development test data (news 2018).

System	BLEU news2018	
	Shuffled	Coherent
Baseline	38.96	38.96
2+1	36.62	37.17
3+1a	33.90	34.30
3+1b	34.14	34.39
1t+1s+1	36.82	37.24
2+2	38.53	**39.08**

Table 10: Comparison of concatenation approaches for English–German document-level translation.

The results overall are rather disappointing. All but one of the concatenation models underperform and cannot beat the sentence-level baseline. Note that the concat-target model (1t+1s+1) even refers to an oracle experiment in which the reference translation of the previous sentence is fed into the translation model for translating the current source sentence. As this is not very successful, we did not even try to run a proper evaluation with system output provided as target context during testing. Besides the shortcomings, we can nevertheless see a consistent pattern that the extended context models indeed pick up information from discourse. For all models we observe a gain of about half a BLEU point when comparing the shuffled to the non-shuffled versions of the test set. This is interesting and encourages us to study these models further in future work, possibly with different data sets, training procedures and slightly different architectures.

4.2 Hierarchical attention models

A number of approaches have been developed to utilize the attention mechanism to capture extended context for document-level translation. We experimented with the two following models:

- NMT-HAN: Sentence-level transformer model with a hierarchical attention network to capture the document-level context (Miculicich et al., 2018).

- selectAttn: Selective attention model for context-aware neural machine translation (Maruf et al., 2019).

For testing the selectAttn model, we used the same data with document-level information as we applied in the concatenation models. For NMT-HAN we had to use a smaller training set due to lack of resources and due to the implementation not supporting data shards. For NMT-HAN we used only Europarl, NewsCommentary and Rapid for training. Table 11 summarizes the results on the development test data. Both of the tested models need to be trained on sentence-level first, before tuning the document-level components.

Model	Sentence-level	Document-level
NMT-HAN	35.03	31.73
selectAttn	35.26	34.75

Table 11: Results (case-sensitive BLEU) of the hierarchical attention models on the coherent newstest 2018 dataset.

The architecture of the selective attention model is based on the general transformer model but with quite a different setup in terms of hyperparameters and dimensions of layer components etc. We applied the basic settings following the documentation of the software. In particular, the model includes 4 layers and 8 attention heads, and the dimensionality of the hidden layers is 512. We applied a sublayer and attention dropout of 0.1 and trained the sentence-level model for about 3.5 epochs. We selected monolingual source-side context for our experiments and hierarchical document attention with sparse softmax. Otherwise, we also apply the default parameters suggested in the documentation with respect to optimizers, learning rates and dropout. Unfortunately, the results do not look very promising as we can see in Table 11. The document-level model does not even reach the performance of the sentence-level model even though we trained until convergence on development data with patience of 10 reporting steps, which is quite disappointing. Overall, the scores are below the standard transformer models of the other experiments, and hence, we did not try to further optimize the results using that model.

For the NMT-HAN model we used the implementation of Miculicich et al. (2018) with the recommended hyperparameter values and settings. The system is based on the OpenNMT-py implementation of the transformer. The model includes 6 hidden layers on both the encoder and decoder side with a dimensionality of 512 and the multi-head attention has 8 attention heads. We applied a sublayer and attention dropout of 0.1. The target and source vocabulary size is 30K. We trained the sentence-level model for 20 epochs after which we further fine-tuned the encoder side hierarchical attention for 1 epoch and the joint encoder-decoder hierarchical attention for 1 epoch. The results for the NMT-HAN model are disappointing. The document-level model performs significantly worse than the sentence-level model.

5   Results from WMT 2019

Table 12 summarizes our results from the WMT 2019 news task. We list the official score from the submitted systems and post-WMT scores that come from models described above. For Finnish–English and English–Finnish, the submitted systems correspond to premature single models that did not converge yet. Our submitted English–German model is the ensemble of 9 models described in Section 3.2.

Language pair	Model	BLEU
English–German	submitted	41.4
	L2R+R2L	42.95
Finnish–English	submitted	26.7
	L2R+R2L	27.80
English–Finnish	submitted	20.8
	rule-based	8.9
	L2R+R2L	23.4

Table 12: Final results (case-sensitive BLEU scores) on the 2019 news test set; partially obtained after the deadline.

The ensemble results clearly outperform those results but were not ready in time. We are still below the best performing system from the official participants of this year's campaign but the final models perform in the top-range of all the three tasks. For English–Finnish, our final score would end up on a third place (12 submissions from 8 participants), for Finnish–English it would be the fourth-best participant (out of 9), and English–German fifth-best participant (out of 19 with 28 submissions).

6 Conclusions

In this paper, we presented our submission for the WMT 2019 news translation task in three language pairs: English–German, English–Finnish and Finnish–English.

For all the language pairs we spent considerable time on cleaning and filtering the training data, which resulted in a significant reduction of training examples without a negative impact on translation quality.

For English–German we focused both on sentence-level neural machine translation models as well as document-level models. For English–Finnish, our submissions consists of an NMT system as well as a rule-based system whereas the Finnish–English system is an NMT system. For the English–Finnish and Finnish–English language pairs, we compared the impact of different segmentation approaches. Our results show that the different segmentation approaches do not significantly impact BLEU scores. However, our experiments highlight the well-known fact that ensembling and domain adaptation have a significant positive impact on translation quality.

One surprising finding was that none of the document-level approaches really worked, with some even having a negative effect on translation quality.

Acknowledgments

The work in this paper was supported by the FoTran project, funded by the European Research Council (ERC) under the European Union's Horizon 2020 research 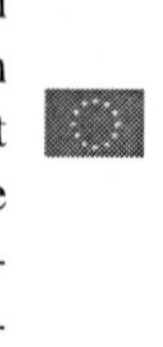 and innovation programme (grant agreement No 771113), and the MeMAD project funded by the European Union's Horizon 2020 Research and Innovation Programme under grant agreement No 780069.

The authors gratefully acknowledge the support of the Academy of Finland through project 314062 from the ICT 2023 call on Computation, Machine Learning and Artificial Intelligence and project 270354/273457.

References

Stig-Arne Grönroos, Sami Virpioja, and Mikko Kurimo. 2018. Cognate-aware morphological segmentation for multilingual neural translation. In *Proceedings of the Third Conference on Machine Translation: Shared Task Papers*, pages 386–393, Belgium, Brussels. Association for Computational Linguistics.

Arvi Hurskainen. 2018a. Compound nouns in English to Finnish machine translation. Technical Reports in Language Technology 32, University of Helsinki.

Arvi Hurskainen. 2018b. Direct and indirect questions in English to Finnish machine translation. Technical Reports in Language Technology 33, University of Helsinki.

Arvi Hurskainen. 2018c. Optimizing rules in English to Finnish machine translation. Technical Reports in Language Technology 34, University of Helsinki.

Arvi Hurskainen. 2018d. Participial phrases in English to Finnish machine translation. Technical Reports in Language Technology 35, University of Helsinki.

Marcin Junczys-Dowmunt, Roman Grundkiewicz, Tomasz Dwojak, Hieu Hoang, Kenneth Heafield, Tom Neckermann, Frank Seide, Ulrich Germann, Alham Fikri Aji, Nikolay Bogoychev, André F. T. Martins, and Alexandra Birch. 2018. Marian: Fast neural machine translation in C++. In *Proceedings of ACL 2018, System Demonstrations*, pages 116–121, Melbourne, Australia. Association for Computational Linguistics.

Guillaume Klein, Yoon Kim, Yuntian Deng, Jean Senellart, and Alexander M. Rush. 2017. Open-NMT: Open-source toolkit for neural machine translation. In *Proc. ACL*.

Taku Kudo and John Richardson. 2018. Sentence-Piece: A simple and language independent subword tokenizer and detokenizer for neural text processing. In *Proceedings of the 2018 Conference on Empirical Methods in Natural Language Processing: System Demonstrations*, pages 66–71, Brussels, Belgium. Association for Computational Linguistics.

Marco Lui and Timothy Baldwin. 2012. langid.py: An off-the-shelf language identification tool. In *Proceedings of the ACL 2012 System Demonstrations*, pages 25–30, Jeju Island, Korea. Association for Computational Linguistics.

Sameen Maruf, André F. T. Martins, and Gholamreza Haffari. 2019. Selective attention for context-aware neural machine translation. In *Proceedings of the 2019 Conference of the North American Chapter of the Association for Computational Linguistics: Human Language Technologies, Volume 1 (Long and Short Papers)*, pages 3092–3102, Minneapolis, Minnesota. Association for Computational Linguistics.

Lesly Miculicich, Dhananjay Ram, Nikolaos Pappas, and James Henderson. 2018. Document-level neural machine translation with hierarchical attention networks. In *Proceedings of the Conference on Empirical Methods in Natural Language Processing (EMNLP)*.

Robert Östling, Yves Scherrer, Jörg Tiedemann, Gongbo Tang, and Tommi Nieminen. 2017. The Helsinki neural machine translation system. In *Proceedings of the Second Conference on Machine Translation*, pages 338–347, Copenhagen, Denmark. Association for Computational Linguistics.

Robert Östling and Jörg Tiedemann. 2016. Efficient word alignment with Markov Chain Monte Carlo. *Prague Bulletin of Mathematical Linguistics*, 106:125–146.

Alexandra Birch Chris Callison-Burch Marcello Federico Nicola Bertoldi Brooke Cowan Wade Shen Christine Moran Richard Zens Chris Dyer Ondrej Bojar Alexandra Constantin Evan Herbst Philipp Koehn, Hieu Hoang. 2007. Moses: Open source toolkit for statistical machine translation. *CoRR*, Annual Meeting of the Association for Computational Linguistics (ACL).

Tommi A. Pirinen. 2015. Omorfi — free and open source morphological lexical database for Finnish. In *Proceedings of the 20th Nordic Conference of Computational Linguistics (NODALIDA 2015)*, pages 313–315, Vilnius, Lithuania. Linköping University Electronic Press, Sweden.

Alessandro Raganato, Yves Scherrer, Tommi Nieminen, Arvi Hurskainen, and Jörg Tiedemann. 2018.

The University of Helsinki submissions to the WMT18 news task. In *Proceedings of the Third Conference on Machine Translation: Shared Task Papers*, pages 488–495, Belgium, Brussels. Association for Computational Linguistics.

Rico Sennrich, Barry Haddow, and Alexandra Birch. 2016a. Improving neural machine translation models with monolingual data. In *Proceedings of the 54th Annual Meeting of the Association for Computational Linguistics (Volume 1: Long Papers)*, volume 1, pages 86–96.

Rico Sennrich, Barry Haddow, and Alexandra Birch. 2016b. Neural machine translation of rare words with subword units. In *Proceedings of the 54th Annual Meeting of the Association for Computational Linguistics (Volume 1: Long Papers)*, pages 1715–1725, Berlin, Germany. Association for Computational Linguistics.

Vesa Siivola, Mathias Creutz, and Mikko Kurimo. 2007a. Morfessor and VariKN machine learning tools for speech and language technology. In *8th Annual Conference of the International Speech Communication Association (Interspeech 2007), Antwerp, Belgium, August 27-31, 2007*, pages 1549–1552. ISCA.

Vesa Siivola, Teemu Hirsimäki, and Sami Virpioja. 2007b. On growing and pruning Kneser-Ney smoothed n-gram models. *IEEE Trans. Audio, Speech & Language Processing*, 15(5):1617–1624.

Felix Stahlberg, Adriá de Gispert, and Bill Byrne. 2018. The University of Cambridge's machine translation systems for WMT18. In *Proceedings of the Third Conference on Machine Translation, Volume 2: Shared Task Papers*, pages 508–516, Belgium, Brussels. Association for Computational Linguistics.

Jörg Tiedemann and Yves Scherrer. 2017. Neural machine translation with extended context. In *Proceedings of the Third Workshop on Discourse in Machine Translation*.

Ashish Vaswani, Noam Shazeer, Niki Parmar, Jakob Uszkoreit, Llion Jones, Aidan N Gomez, Ł ukasz Kaiser, and Illia Polosukhin. 2017. Attention is all you need. In I. Guyon, U. V. Luxburg, S. Bengio, H. Wallach, R. Fergus, S. Vishwanathan, and R. Garnett, editors, *Advances in Neural Information Processing Systems 30*, pages 5998–6008. Curran Associates, Inc.

Microsoft Research Asia's Systems for WMT19

Yingce Xia, Xu Tan, Fei Tian, Fei Gao,
Weicong Chen, Yang Fan, Linyuan Gong, Yichong Leng,
Renqian Luo, Yiren Wang, Lijun Wu, Jinhua Zhu,
Tao Qin*, Tie-Yan Liu
Microsoft Research Asia

Abstract

We Microsoft Research Asia made submissions to 11 language directions in the WMT19 news translation tasks. We won the first place for 8 of the 11 directions and the second place for the other three. Our basic systems are built on Transformer, back translation and knowledge distillation. We integrate several of our rececent techniques to enhance the baseline systems: multi-agent dual learning (MADL), masked sequence-to-sequence pre-training (MASS), neural architecture optimization (NAO), and soft contextual data augmentation (SCA).

1 Introduction

We participated in the WMT19 shared news translation task in 11 translation directions. We achieved first place for 8 directions: German↔English, German↔French, Chinese↔English, English→Lithuanian, English→Finnish, and Russian→English, and three other directions were placed second (ranked by teams), which included Lithuanian→English, Finnish→English, and English→Kazakh.

Our basic systems are based on Transformer, back translation and knowledge distillation. We experimented with several techniques we proposed recently. In brief, the innovations we introduced are:

Multi-agent dual learning (MADL) The core idea of dual learning is to leverage the duality between the primal task (mapping from domain $\mathcal{X}$ to domain $\mathcal{Y}$) and dual task (mapping from domain $\mathcal{Y}$ to $\mathcal{X}$) to boost the performances of both tasks. MADL (Wang et al., 2019) extends the dual learning (He et al., 2016; Xia et al., 2017a) framework by introducing multiple primal and dual models. It was integrated into our submitted systems for

German↔English and German↔French translations.

Masked sequence-to-sequence pretraining (MASS) Pre-training and fine-tuning have achieved great success in language understanding. MASS (Song et al., 2019), a pre-training method designed for language generation, adopts the encoder-decoder framework to reconstruct a sentence fragment given the remaining part of the sentence: its encoder takes a sentence with randomly masked fragment (several consecutive tokens) as input, and its decoder tries to predict this masked fragment. It was integrated into our submitted systems for Chinese→English and English→Lithuanian translations.

Neural architecture optimization (NAO) As well known, the evolution of neural network architecture plays a key role in advancing neural machine translation. Neural architecture optimization (NAO), our newly proposed method (Luo et al., 2018), leverages the power of a gradient-based method to conduct optimization and guide the creation of better neural architecture in a continuous and more compact space given the historically observed architectures and their performances. It was applied in English↔Finnish translations in our submitted systems.

Soft contextual data augmentation (SCA) While data augmentation is an important trick to boost the accuracy of deep learning methods in computer vision tasks, its study in natural language tasks is relatively limited. SCA (Zhu et al., 2019) softly augments a randomly chosen word in a sentence by its contextual mixture of multiple related words, i.e., replacing the one-hot representation of a word by a distribution provided by a language model over the vocabulary. It was applied in Russian→English translation in our submitted systems.

---

*Corresponding author. This work was conducted at Microsoft Research Asia.

Proceedings of the Fourth Conference on Machine Translation (WMT), Volume 2: Shared Task Papers (Day 1) pages 424–433
Florence, Italy, August 1-2, 2019. ©2019 Association for Computational Linguistics

2 Our Techniques

2.1 Multi-agent dual learning (MADL)

MADL is an enhanced version of dual learning (He et al., 2016; Wang et al., 2018). It leverages N primal translation models f_i and N dual translation models g_j for training, and eventually outputs one f_0 and one g_0 for inference, where $f_i : \mathcal{X} \mapsto \mathcal{Y}, g_j : \mathcal{Y} \mapsto \mathcal{X}, i, j \in \{0, 1, \cdots, N-1\}$. All these models are pre-trained on bilingual data . The i-th primal model f_i has a non-negative weight α_i and the j-th dual model g_i has a non-negative weight β_j. All the $\alpha.$'s and $\beta.$'s are hyperparameters. Let F_α denote a combined translation model from $\mathcal{X}$ to $\mathcal{Y}$, and G_β a combined translation model from $\mathcal{Y}$ to $\mathcal{X}$,

$$F_\alpha = \sum_{i=0}^{N-1} \alpha_i f_i, \quad G_\beta = \sum_{j=0}^{N-1} \beta_j g_j;$$

$$\text{s.t.} \sum_{i=0}^{N-1} \alpha_i = 1; \quad \sum_{j=0}^{N-1} \beta_j = 1. \tag{1}$$

F_α and G_β work as follows: for any $x \in \mathcal{X}$ and $y \in \mathcal{Y}$,

$$F_\alpha(x) : \hat{y} = \operatorname{argmax}_{\tilde{y} \in \mathcal{Y}} \sum_{i=0}^{N-1} \alpha_i \log P(\tilde{y}|x; f_i);$$

$$G_\alpha(y) : \hat{x} = \operatorname{argmax}_{\tilde{x} \in \mathcal{X}} \sum_{j=0}^{N-1} \beta_j \log P(\tilde{x}|y; g_j).$$

Let $\mathcal{B}$ denote the bilingual dataset. Let $\mathcal{M}_x$ and $\mathcal{M}_y$ denote the monolingual data of $\mathcal{X}$ and $\mathcal{Y}$. The training objective function of MADL can be written as follows:

$$\min_{f_0, g_0} -\frac{1}{|\mathcal{B}|} \sum_{(x,y) \in \mathcal{B}} \log P(y|x; f_0)$$

$$-\frac{1}{|\mathcal{B}|} \sum_{(x,y) \in \mathcal{B}} \log P(x|y; g_0)$$

$$-\frac{1}{|\mathcal{M}_x|} \sum_{x \in \mathcal{M}_x} \log P(x|G_\beta(F_\alpha(x))) \tag{2}$$

$$-\frac{1}{|\mathcal{M}_y|} \sum_{y \in \mathcal{M}_y} \log P(y|F_\alpha(G_\beta(y))).$$

Note that $f_{>0}$ and $g_{>0}$ will not be optimized during training and we eventually output f_0 and g_0 for translation. More details can be found in (Wang et al., 2019).

2.2 Masked sequence-to-sequence pre-training (MASS)

MASS is a pre-training method for language generation. For machine translation, it can leverage monolingual data in two languages to pre-train a translation model. Given a sentence $x \in \mathcal{X}$, we denote $x^{\backslash u:v}$ as a modified version of x where its fragment from position u to v are masked, $0 < u < v < m$ and m is the number of tokens of sentence x. We denote $k = v - u + 1$ as the number of tokens being masked from position u to v. We replace each masked token by a special symbol $[\mathbb{M}]$, and the length of the masked sentence is not changed. $x^{u:v}$ denotes the sentence fragment of x from u to v.

MASS pre-trains a sequence to sequence model by predicting the sentence fragment $x^{u:v}$ taking the masked sequence $x^{\backslash u:v}$ as input. We use the log likelihood as the objective function:

$$L(\theta; \mathcal{X}) = \frac{1}{|\mathcal{X}|} \Sigma_{x \in \mathcal{X}} \log P(x^{u:v}|x^{\backslash u:v}; \theta),$$

$$L(\theta; \mathcal{Y}) = \frac{1}{|\mathcal{Y}|} \Sigma_{y \in \mathcal{Y}} \log P(y^{u:v}|y^{\backslash u:v}; \theta), \tag{3}$$

where $\mathcal{X}, \mathcal{Y}$ denote the source and target domain. We also extend MASS to supervised setting where bilingual sentence pair $(x, y) \in (\mathcal{X}, \mathcal{Y})$ can be leveraged for pre-training. The log likelihood in the supervised setting is as follows:

$$L(\theta; (\mathcal{X}, \mathcal{Y})) = \Sigma_{(x,y) \in (\mathcal{X}, \mathcal{Y})} (\log P(y|x^{\backslash u:v}; \theta)$$

$$+ \log P(x|y^{\backslash u:v}; \theta)$$

$$+ \log P(x^{u:v}|[x^{\backslash u:v}; y^{\backslash u:v}]; \theta)$$

$$+ \log P(y^{u:v}|[x^{\backslash u:v}; y^{\backslash u:v}]; \theta)$$

$$+ \log P(y^{u:v}|x^{\backslash u:v}; \theta) + \log P(x^{u:v}|y^{\backslash u:v}; \theta)). \tag{4}$$

where $[\cdot ; \cdot]$ represents the concatenation operation. $P(y|x^{\backslash u:v}; \theta)$ and $P(x|y^{\backslash u:v}; \theta)$ denote the probability of translating a masked sequence to another language, which encourage the encoder to extract meaningful representations of unmasked input tokens in order to predict the masked output sequence. $P(x^{u:v}|[x^{\backslash u:v}; y^{\backslash u:v}]; \theta)$ and $P(y^{u:v}|[x^{\backslash u:v}; y^{\backslash u:v}]; \theta)$ denote the probability of generating the masked source/target segment given both the masked source and target sequences, which encourage the model to extract cross-lingual information. $P(y^{u:v}|x^{\backslash u:v}; \theta)$ and $P(x^{u:v}|y^{\backslash u:v}; \theta)$ denote the probability of generating the masked fragment given only the masked sequence in another language. More details about MASS can be found in Song et al. (2019).

2.3 Neural architecture optimization (NAO)

NAO (Luo et al., 2018) is a gradient based neural architecture search (NAS) method. It contains three key components: an encoder, an accuracy predictor, and a decoder, and optimizes a network architecture as follows. (1) The encoder maps a network architecture x to an embedding vector e_x in a continuous space $\mathcal{E}$. (2) The predictor, a function f, takes $e_x \in \mathcal{E}$ as input and predicts the dev set accuracy of the architecture x. We perform a gradient ascent step, i.e., moving e_x along the direction specified via the gradient $\frac{\partial f}{\partial e_x}$, and get a new embedding vector $e_{x'}$:

$$e_{x'} = e_x + \eta \frac{\partial f}{\partial e_x}, \tag{5}$$

where η is the step size. (3) The decoder is used to map $e_{x'}$ back to the corresponding architecture x'. The new architecture x' is assumed to have better performance compared with the original one x due to the property of gradient ascent. NAO repeats the above three steps, and sequentially generates better and better architectures.

To learn high-quality encoder, decoder and performance prediction function, it is essential to have a large quantity of paired training data in the form of (x, y), where y is the dev set accuracy of the architecture x. To reduce computational cost, we share weights among different architectures (Pham et al., 2018) to aid the generation of such paired training data.

We use NAO to search powerful neural sequence-to-sequence architectures. The search space is illustrated in Fig. 1. Specifically, each *network* is composed of N encoder layers and N decoder layers. We set $N = 6$ in our experiments. Each encoder *layer* further contains 2 *nodes* and each decoder layer contains 3 nodes. The *node* has two branches, respectively taking the output of other node as input, and applies a particular operator (OP), for example, identity, self-attention and convolution, to generate the output. The outputs of the two branches are added together as the output of the *node*. Each encoder layer contains two nodes while each decoder layer has three. For each layer, we search: 1) what is the operator at each branch of every node. For a comprehensive list of different OPs, please refer to the Appendix of this paper; 2) the topology of connection between nodes within each layer. In the middle part of Fig. 1, we plot possible connections within the nodes of a layer specified by all candidate architectures, with a particular highlight of Transformer (Vaswani et al., 2017).

To construct the final network, we do not adopt the typically used way of stacking the same layer multiple times. Instead we assume that layers in encoder/decoder could have different architectures and directly search such personalized architecture for each layer. We found that such a design significantly improves the performance due to the more flexibility.

2.4 Soft contextual data augmentation (SCA)

SCA is a data augmentation technology for NMT (Zhu et al., 2019), which replaces a randomly chosen word in a sentence with its *soft version*. For any word $w \in V$, its soft version is a distribution over the vocabulary of $|V|$ words: $P(w) = (p_1(w), p_2(w), ..., p_{|V|}(w))$, where $p_j(w) \geq 0$ and $\sum_{j=1}^{|V|} p_j(w) = 1$.

Given the distribution $P(w)$, one may simply sample a word from this distribution to replace the original word w. Different from this method, we directly use this distribution vector to replace the randomly chosen word w from the original sentence. Suppose E is the embedding matrix of all the $|V|$ words. The embedding of the soft version of w is

$$e_w = P(w)E = \sum_{j=0}^{|V|} p_j(w)E_j, \tag{6}$$

which is the expectation of word embeddings over the distribution.

In our systems, we leverage a pre-trained language model to compute $P(w)$ and condition on all the words preceding w. That is, for the t-th word x_t in a sentence, we have

$$p_j(x_t) = LM(v_j | x_{<t}),$$

where $LM(v_j | x_{<t})$ denotes the probability of the j-th word v_j in the vocabulary appearing after the sequence $x_1, x_2, \cdots, x_{t-1}$. The language model is pre-trained using the monolingual data.

3 Submitted Systems

3.1 English↔German

We submit constrained systems to both English to German and German to English translations, with the same techniques.

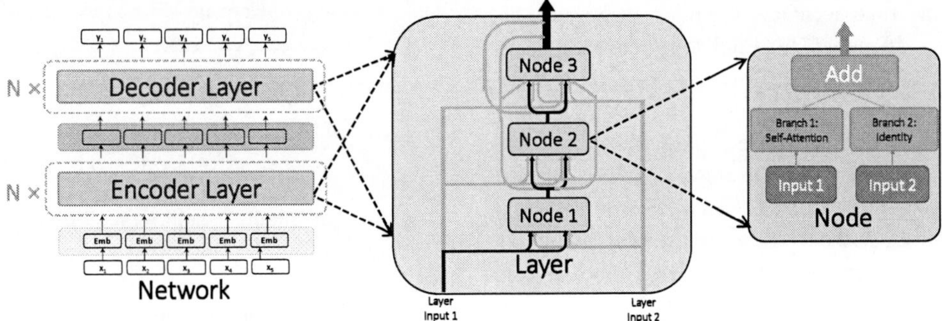

Figure 1: Visualization of different levels of the search space, from the *network*, to the *layer*, to the *node*. For each of the different layers, we search its unique *layer* space. The lines in the middle part denote all possible connections between the three nodes (constituting the *layer* space) as specified via each architecture, while among them the deep black lines indicate the particular connection in *Transformer*. The right part similarly contains the two branches used in Node2 of *Transformer*.

Dataset We concatenate "Europarl v9", "News Commentary v14", "Common Crawl corpus" and "Document-split Rapid corpus" as the basic bilingual dataset (denoted as $\mathcal{B}_0$). Since "Paracrawl" data is noisy, we select 20M bilingual data from this corpus using the script `filter_interactive.py`[1]. The two parts of bilingual data are concatenated together (denoted as $\mathcal{B}_1$). We clean $\mathcal{B}_1$ by normalizing the sentences, removing non-printable characters, and tokenization. We share a vocabulary for the two languages and apply BPE for word segmentation with 35000 merge operations. (We tried different BPE merge operations but found no significant differences.) For monolingual data, we use $120M$ English sentences (denoted as $\mathcal{M}_{\text{en}}$) and $120M$ German sentences (denoted as $\mathcal{M}_{\text{de}}$) from Newscrawl, and preprocess them in the same way as bilingual data. We use newstest 2016 and the validation set and newstest 2018 as the test set.

Model Configuration We use the PyTorch implementation of Transformer[2]. We choose the *Transformer_big* setting, in which both the encoder and decoder are of six layers. The dropout rate is fixed as 0.2. We set the batchsize as 4096 and the parameter `--update-freq` as 16. We apply Adam (Kingma and Ba, 2015) optimizer with learning rate 5×10^{-4}.

Training Pipeline The pipeline consists of three steps:

1. Pre-train two English→German translation models (denoted as $\bar{f}_1$ and $\bar{f}_2$) and

two German→English translation models (denoted as $\bar{g}_1$ and $\bar{g}_2$) on $\mathcal{B}_1$; pre-train another English→German (denoted as $\bar{f}_3$) and German→English (denoted as $\bar{g}_3$) on $\mathcal{B}_0$.

2. Apply back translation following (Sennrich et al., 2016a; Edunov et al., 2018). We back-translate $\mathcal{M}_{\text{en}}$ and $\mathcal{M}_{\text{de}}$ using $\bar{f}_3$ and $\bar{g}_3$ with beam search, add noise to the translated sentences (Edunov et al., 2018), merge the synthetic data with $\mathcal{B}_1$, and train one English→German model f_0 and one German→English model g_0 for seven days on eight V100 GPUs.

3. Apply MADL to f_0 and g_0. That is, the F_α in Eqn.(2) is specified as the combination of $f_0, \bar{f}_1, \bar{f}_2$ with equal weights; and G_β consists of $g_0, \bar{g}_1, \bar{g}_2$. During training, we will only update f_0 and g_0. To speed up training, we randomly select $20M$ monolingual English and German sentences from $\mathcal{M}_{\text{en}}$ and $\mathcal{M}_{\text{de}}$ respectively instead of using all monolingual sentences. The eventual output models are denoted as f_1 and g_1 respectively. This step takes 3 days on four P40 GPUs.

Table 1: Results of English↔German by sacreBLEU.

	En→De		De→En	
	news16	news18	news16	news18
baseline	37.4	45.6	41.9	44.9
BT	39.2	47.4	45	47.1
MADL	41.9	50.4	47.4	49.1

Results The results are summarized in Table 1, which are evaluated by sacreBLEU[3]. The baseline

---

[1] Scripts at `https://tinyurl.com/yx9fpoam`
[2] `https://github.com/pytorch/fairseq`
[3] `https://github.com/mjpost/sacreBLEU`

is the average accuracy of models using only bitext, i.e., $\bar{f}_1$ and $\bar{f}_2$ for English$\rightarrow$German translation and $\bar{g}_1$ and $\bar{g}_2$ for German$\rightarrow$English, and BT is the accuracy of the model after back-translation training. As can be seen, back translation improves accuracy. For example, back-translation boosts the BLEU score from 45.6 to 47.4 on news18 English$\rightarrow$German translation, which is 1.8 point improvement. MADL further boosts BLEU to 50.4, obtaining another 3-point improvement, demonstrating the effectiveness of our method.

For the final submission, we accumulate many translation models (trained using bitext, back translation, and MADL, with different random seeds) and do knowledge distillation on the source sentences from WMT14 to WMT19 test sets. Take English$\rightarrow$German translation as an example. Denote the English inputs as $\mathcal{T} = \{s_i\}_{i=1}^{N_T}$, where N_T is the size of the test set. For each s in $\mathcal{T}$, we translate s to d' using M English$\rightarrow$German models and eventually obtain

$$\mathcal{E} = \{(s_i, f^{(j)}(s_i)) | s \in \mathcal{T}\}_{i,j}, i \in [N_T], j \in [M],$$

where $f^{(j)}$ is the j-th translation model we accumulated, $\mathcal{T}$ is the combination of inputs from WMT14 to WMT19. After obtaining $\mathcal{E}$, we randomly select $N_T M$ bitext pairs (denoted as $\mathcal{B}_2$) from $\mathcal{B}_1$ and finetune model f_1 on $\mathcal{B}_2 \cup \mathcal{E}$. We stop tuning when the BLEU scores of WMT16 (i.e., the validation set) drops.

We eventually obtain 44.9 BLEU score for English$\rightarrow$German and 42.8 for German$\rightarrow$English on WMT19 test sets and are ranked in the first place in these two translation tasks.

3.2 German$\leftrightarrow$French

For German$\leftrightarrow$French translation, we follow a similar process as the one used to English$\leftrightarrow$German tasks introduced in Section 3.1. We merge the "commoncrawl", "europarl-v7" and part of "de-fr.bicleaner07" selected by `filter_interactive.py` as the bilingual data. We collect $20M$ monolingual sentences for French and $20M$ for German from newscrawl. The data pre-processing rule and training procedure are the same as that used in Section 3.1. We split $9k$ sentences from the "dev08_14" as the validation set and use the remaining ones as the test set.

The results of German$\leftrightarrow$French translation on the test set are summarized in Table 2.

Table 2: Results of German$\leftrightarrow$French by sacreBLEU.

	De$\rightarrow$Fr	Fr$\rightarrow$De
baseline	29.5	23.4
MADL	31.5	24.9

Again, our method achieves significant improvement over the baselines. Specifically, MADL boosts the baseline of German$\rightarrow$French and French$\rightarrow$German by 2 and 1.5 points respectively.

Our submitted German$\rightarrow$French is a single system trained by MADL, achieving 37.3 BLEU on WMT19. The French$\rightarrow$German is an ensemble of three independently trained models, achieving 35.0 BLEU score. Our systems are ranked in the first place for both German$\rightarrow$French and French$\rightarrow$German in the leaderboard.

3.3 Chinese$\rightarrow$English

Dataset For Chinese$\rightarrow$English translation, we use all the bilingual and monolingual data provided by the WMT official website, and also extra bilingual and monolingual data crawled from the web. We filter the total 24M bilingual pairs from WMT using the script `filter_interactive.py` as described in Section 3.1 and get 18M sentence pairs. We use the Chinese monolingual data from XMU monolingual corpus[4] and English monolingual data from News Crawl as well as the English sentences from all English-XX language pairs in WMT. We use 100M additional parallel sentences drawn from UN data, Open Subtitles and Web crawled data, which is filtered using the same filter rule described above, as well as fast align and in/out-domain filter. Finally we get 38M bilingual pairs. We also crawled 80M additional Chinese monolingual sentences from Sougou, China News, Xinhua News, Sina News, Ifeng News, and 2M English monolingual sentences from China News and Reuters. We use newstest2017 and newstest2018 on Chinese-English as development datasets.

We normalize the Chinese sentence from SBC case to DBC case, remove non-printable characters and tokenize with both Jieba[5] and PKUSeg[6] to increase diversity. For English sentences, we remove non-printable characters and tokenize with

---

[4] http://nlp.nju.edu.cn/cwmt-wmt/
[5] https://github.com/fxsjy/jieba
[6] https://github.com/lancopku/PKUSeg-python

Moses tokenizer[7]. We follow previous practice (Hassan et al., 2018) and apply Byte-Pair Encoding (BPE) (Sennrich et al., 2016b) separately for Chinese and English, each with 40K vocabulary.

MASS Pre-training We pre-train MASS (Transfomer_big) with both monolingual and bilingual data. We use 100M Chinese and 300M English monolingual sentences for the unsupervised setting (Equation 3), and with a total of 56M bilingual sentence pairs for the supervised setting (Equation 4). We share the encoder and decoder for all the losses in Equation 3 and 4. We then fine-tune the MASS pre-trained model on both 18M and 56M bilingual sentence pairs to get the baseline translation model for both Chinese→English and English→Chinese.

Back Translation and Knowledge Distillation We randomly choose 40M monolingual sentences for Chinese and English respectively for back translation following (Sennrich et al., 2016a; He et al., 2016) and sequence-level knowledge distillation following (Kim and Rush, 2016). We iterate back translation and knowledge distillation multiple times, to gradually boost the performance of the model.

Results The results on newstest2017 and newstest2018 are shown in Table 3. We list two baseline Transformer_big systems which use 18M bilingual data (constraint) and 56M bilingual data (unconstraint) respectively. The pre-trained model achieves about 1 BLEU point improvement after fine-tuning on both 18M and 56M bilingual data. After iterative back translation (BT) and knowledge distillation (KD), as well as re-ranking, our system achieves 30.8 and 30.9 BLEU points on newstest2017 and newstest2018 respectively.

System	newstest17	newstest18
Baseline (18M)	24.2	24.5
+ MASS (18M)	25.2	25.4
Baseline (56M)	26.9	27.0
+ MASS (56M)	28.0	27.8
+ Iterative BT/KD	30.4	30.5
+ Reranking	30.8	30.9

Table 3: BLEU scores on Chinese→English test sets.

---

[7]https://github.com/moses-smt/mosesdecoder/blob/master/scripts/tokenizer/tokenizer.perl

WMT19 Submission For the WMT19 submission, we conduct fine-tuning and speculation to further boost the accuracy by using the source sentences in the WMT19 test set. We first filter the bilingual as well as pseudo-generated data according to the relevance to the source sentences. We use the filter method in Deng et al. (2018) and continue to train the model on the filtered data. Second, we conduct speculation on the test source sentences following the practice in Deng et al. (2018). The final BLEU score of our submission is 39.3, ranked in the first place in the leaderboard.

3.4 English↔Lithuanian

For English↔Lithuanian translation, we follow the similar process as that for Chinese→English task introduced in Section 3.3. We use all the WMT bilingual data, which is 2.24M after filtration. We use the same English monolingual data as used in Chinese-English. We select 100M Lithuanian monolingual data from official commoncrawl and use all the wiki and news Lithuanian monolingual data provided by WMT. In addition, we crawl 5M Lithuanian news data from LRT website[8]. We share the BPE vocabulary between English and Lithuanian, and the vocabulary size is 65K.

All the bilingual and monolingual data are used for MASS pre-training, and all the bilingual data are used for fine-tuning. For iterative back translation and knowledge distillation, we split 24M English monolingual data as well as 12M Lithuanian monolingual data into 5 parts through sampling with replacement, to get different models independently so as to increase diversity in re-ranking/ensemble. Each model uses 8M English monolingual data and 6M Lithuanian monolingual data. For our WMT19 submission, different from zh-en, speculation technology is not used.

The BLEU scores on newsdev19 are shown in Table 4. Our final submissions for WMT19 achieves 20.1 BLEU points for English→Lithuanian translation (ranked in the first place) and 35.6 for Lithuanian→English translation (ranked in the second place).

3.5 English↔Finnish

Preprocess We use the official English-Finnish data from WMT19, including both bilingual data and monolingual data. After de-duplicating, the

---

[8]https://www.lrt.lt/

System	En→Lt	Lt→En
Baseline	20.7	28.2
MASS + Fine-tune	21.5	28.7
+ Iterative BT/KD	28.3	33.6
+ Reranking	29.1	34.2

Table 4: BLEU scores for English↔Lithuanian on the newsdev19 set.

bilingual data contains $8.8M$ aligned sentence pairs. We share the vocabulary for English and Finnish with $46k$ BPE units. We use the WMT17 and WMT18 English-Finnish test sets as two development datasets, and tune hyper-parameters based on the concatenation of them.

Architecture search We use NAO to search sequence-to-sequence architectures for English-Finnish translation tasks, as introduced in subsection 2.3. We use PyTorch for our implementations. Due to time limitations, we are not targeting at finding better neural architectures than Transformer; instead we target at models with comparable performance to Transformer, while providing diversity in the reranking process. The whole search process takes 2.5 days on 16 P40 GPU cards and the discovered neural architecture, named as NAONet, is visualized in the Appendix.

Train single models The final system for English-Finnish is obtained through reranking of three strong model checkpoints, respectively from the Transformer model decoding from left to right (L2R Transformer), the Transformer model decoding from right to left (R2L Transformer) and NAONet decoding from left to right. All the models have 6-6 layers in encoder/decoder, and are obtained using the same process which is detailed as below.

Step 1: Base models. Train two models $P_1(x|y)$ and $P_1(y|x)$ based on all the bilingual dataset (8.8M), respectively for English→Finnish and Finnish→English translations.

Step 2: Back translation. Do the normal back translation (Sennrich et al., 2016a; He et al., 2016) using P_1 and P_2. Specifically we choose $10M$ monolingual English corpus, use $P_1(y|x)$ to generate the $10M$ pseudo bitext with beam search (beam size is set to 5), and mix it with the bilingual data to continue the training of $P_1(x|y)$. The ratio of mixing is set as 1 : 1 through up-sampling. The model obtained through such a process is de-

noted as $P_2(x|y)$. The same process is applied to the opposite direction and the new model $P_2(y|x)$ is attained.

Step 3: Back translation + knowledge distillation. In this step we generate more pseudo bitext by sequence level knowledge distillation (Kim and Rush, 2016) apart from using back translation. To be more concrete, as the first step, similar to Step 2, we choose $15M$ monolingual English and Finnish corpus, and generate the translations using $P_2(y|x)$ and $P_2(x|y)$, respectively. The resulting pseudo bitext is respectively denoted as $D_{x\to y}$ and $D_{y\to x}$. Then we concatenate all the bilingual data, $D_{x\to y}$ and $D_{y\to x}$, and use the whole corpus to train a new English-Finnish model *from scratch*. The attained model is denoted as $P_3(y|x)$.

Step 4: Finetune. In this step we try a very simple data selection method to handle the domain mismatch problem in WMT. We remove all the bilingual corpus from Paracrawl which is generally assumed to be quite noisy (Junczys-Dowmunt, 2018) and use the remaining bilingual corpus $(4.5M)$ to finetune $P_3(y|x)$ for one epoch. The resulting model is denoted as $P_4(y|x)$ which is set as the final model checkpoint.

	newstest17	newstest18
Baseline	26.09	16.07
+BT	28.84	18.54
+BT & KD	29.76	19.13
+Finetune	30.19	19.46

Table 5: BLEU scores of L2R Transformer on English→Finnish test sets.

	newstest17	newstest18
L2R Transformer	30.19	19.46
R2L Transformer	30.40	19.73
NAONet	30.54	19.58

Table 6: The final BLEU scores on English→Finnish test sets, for the three models: L2R Transformer, R2L Transformer and NAONet, after the four steps of training.

To investigate the effects of the four steps, we record the resulting BLEU scores on WMT17 and WMT18 test sets in Table 5, taking the L2R Transformer model as an example. Furthermore, we report the final BLEU scores of the three models after the four steps in Table 6. All the results are obtained via beam size 5 and length penalty 1.0.

The similar results for Finnish-English translation are shown in Table 7.

	newstest17	newstest18
L2R Transformer	35.66	25.56
R2L Transformer	35.31	25.56
NAONet	36.18	26.38

Table 7: The final BLEU scores on Finnish→English test sets, for the three models: L2R Transformer, R2L Transformer and NAONet, after the four steps of training.

Re-ranking We use n-best re-ranking to deliver the final translation results using the three model checkpoints introduced in the last subsection. The beam size is set as 12. The weights of the three models, as well as the length penalty in generation, are tuned on the WMT-18 test sets. The results are shown in the second row of Table 8.

We would also like to investigate what is the influence of the NAONet to the re-ranking results. To achieve that, in re-ranking we replace NAONet with another model from L2R Transformer, trained with the same process in subsection 3.5 with the difference only in random seeds, while maintain the other two models unchanged. The results are illustrated in the last row of Table 8. From the comparison of the two rows in Table 8, we can see the new architecture NAONet discovered via NAO brings more diversity in the ranking, thus leading to better results. We also report the similar results for Finnish-English tasks in Table 9.

Our systems achieve 27.4 for and 31.9 for English→Finnish and Finnish→English, ranked in the first place and second place (by teams), respectively.

3.6 Russian→English

Dataset We use the bitext data from the several corpora: ParaCrawl, Common Crawl, News Commentary, Yandex Corpus, and UN Parallel Corpus.

	news17	news18	news19
Re-ranking w/ NAONet	31.48	21.21	27.4
Re-ranking w/o NAONet	30.82	20.79	/

Table 8: English→Finnish BLEU scores of re-ranking using the three models. "news" is short for "newstest".

	news17	news18	news19
Re-ranking w/ NAONet	37.54	27.51	31.9
Re-ranking w/o NAONet	36.83	26.99	/

Table 9: Finnish→English BLEU scores of re-ranking using the three models.

We also use News Crawl corpora as monolingual data. The data is filtered by rules such as sentence length, language identification, resulting a training dataset with 16M bilingual pairs and 40M monolingual sentences (20M for English and 20M for Russian). We use WMT17 and WMT18 test set as development data. The two languages use separate vocabularies, each with 50K BPE merge operations.

Our system Our final system for Russian→English translation is a combination of Transformer network (Vaswani et al., 2017), back translation (Sennrich et al., 2016a), knowledge distillation (Kim and Rush, 2016), soft contextual data augmentation (Zhu et al., 2019), and model ensemble. We use Transformer_big as network architecture. We first train two models, English→Russian and Russian→English respectively, on bilingual pairs as baseline model. Based on these two models, we perform back translation and knowledge distillation on monolingual data, generating 40M synthetic data. Combining both bilingual and synthetic data, we get a large train corpus with 56M pairs in total. We upsample the bilingual pairs and shuffle the combined corpus to ensure the balance between bilingual and synthetic data. Finally, we train the Russian→English model from scratch. During the training, we also use soft contextual data augmentation to further enhance training. Following the above procedures, 5 different models are trained and ensembled for final submission.

Results Our final submission achieves 40.1 BLEU score, ranked first in the leaderboard. Table 10 reports the results of our system on the development set.

3.7 English→Kazakh

Dataset We notice that most of the parallel data are out of domain. Therefore, we crawl some external data:

	newstest17	newstest18
Baseline	36.5	32.6
+BT & KD	40.9	35.2
+SCA	41.7	35.6

Table 10: Russian→English BLEU scores.

(1) We crawl all news articles from `inform.kz`, a Kazakh-English news website. Then we match an English new article to a Kazakh one by matching their images with image hashing. In this way, we find 10K pairs of bilingual news articles. We use their title as additional parallel data. These data are in-domain and useful in training.

(2) We crawl 140K parallel sentence pairs from `glosbe.com`. Although most of these sentences are out-of-domain, they significantly extended the size of our parallel dataset and lead to better results.

Because most of our parallel training data are noisy, we filter these data with some rules: (1) For the *KazakhTV* dataset, we remove any sentence pair with an alignment score less than 0.05. (2) For the *Wiki Titles* dataset, we remove any sentence pair that starts with *User* or *NGC*. (3) For all datasets, we remove any sentence pair in which the English sentence contains no lowercase alphabets. (4) For all datasets, we remove any sentence pair where the length ratio is greater than 2.5:1.

We tokenize all our data using the Moses Decoder. We learn a shared BPE (Sennrich et al., 2016b) from all our data (including all WMT19 parallel data, WMT19 monolingual data[9], glosbe, inform.kz news titles, and inform.kz news contents) and get a shared vocabulary of 49,152 tokens. Finally, our dataset consists of 300K bilingual sentence pairs, 700K Kazakh monolingual sentences, and many English monolingual sentences.

Our system Our model is based on the Transformer (Vaswani et al., 2017). We vary the hyper-parameters to increase the diversity of our model. Our models usually have 6 encoder layers, 6/7 decoder layers, ReLU/GELU (Hendrycks and Gimpel, 2016) activation function, and an embedding dimension of 640.

We train 4 English-Kazakh models and 4 Kazakh-English models with different random seeds and hyper-parameters. Then we apply back-translation (Edunov et al., 2018) and knowledge distillation (Kim and Rush, 2016) for 6 rounds. In each round, we

1. Sample 4M sentences from English monolingual data and back-translate them to Kazakh with the best EN-KK model (on the dev set) in the previous round.

2. Back-translate all Kazakh monolingual data to English with the best KK-EN model in the previous round.

3. Sample 200K sentences from English monolingual data and translate them to Kazakh using the ensemble of all EN-KK models in the previous round.

4. Train 4 English-Kazakh models with BT data from step 2 and KD data from step 3. We up-sample bilingual sentence pairs by 2x.

5. Train 4 Kazakh-English models with BT data from step 1. We up-sample bilingual sentence pairs by 3x.

Result Our final submission achieves 10.6 BLEU score, ranked second by teams in the leaderboard.

4 Conclusions

This paper describes Microsoft Research Asia's neural machine translation systems for the WMT19 shared news translation tasks. Our systems are built on Transformer, back translation and knowledge distillation, enhanced with our recently proposed techniques: multi-agent dual learning (MADL), masked sequence-to-sequence pre-training (MASS), neural architecture optimization (NAO), and soft contextual data augmentation (SCA). Due to time and GPU limitations, we only apply each technique to a subset of translation tasks. We believe combining them together will further improve the translation accuracy and will conduct experiments in the future. Furthermore, some other techniques such as deliberation learning (Xia et al., 2017b), adversarial learning (Wu et al., 2018b), and reinforcement learning (He et al., 2017; Wu et al., 2018a) could also hep and are worthy of exploration.

Acknowledgments

This work is supported by Microsoft Machine Translation team.

---

[9]When we learn BPE, English monolingual data is down-sampled to make the number of English sentences roughly the same as the number of Kazakh sentences.

References

Yongchao Deng, Shanbo Cheng, Jun Lu, Kai Song, Jingang Wang, Shenglan Wu, Liang Yao, Guchun Zhang, Haibo Zhang, Pei Zhang, et al. 2018. Alibaba's neural machine translation systems for wmt18. In *Proceedings of the Third Conference on Machine Translation: Shared Task Papers*, pages 368–376.

Sergey Edunov, Myle Ott, Michael Auli, and David Grangier. 2018. Understanding back-translation at scale. *2018 Conference on Empirical Methods in Natural Language Processing*.

Hany Hassan, Anthony Aue, Chang Chen, Vishal Chowdhary, Jonathan Clark, Christian Federmann, Xuedong Huang, Marcin Junczys-Dowmunt, William Lewis, Mu Li, et al. 2018. Achieving human parity on automatic chinese to english news translation. *arXiv preprint arXiv:1803.05567*.

Di He, Hanqing Lu, Yingce Xia, Tao Qin, Liwei Wang, and Tie-Yan Liu. 2017. Decoding with value networks for neural machine translation. In *Advances in Neural Information Processing Systems*, pages 178–187.

Di He, Yingce Xia, Tao Qin, Liwei Wang, Nenghai Yu, Tie-Yan Liu, and Wei-Ying Ma. 2016. Dual learning for machine translation. In *Advances in Neural Information Processing Systems*, pages 820–828.

Dan Hendrycks and Kevin Gimpel. 2016. Bridging nonlinearities and stochastic regularizers with gaussian error linear units. *CoRR*, abs/1606.08415.

Marcin Junczys-Dowmunt. 2018. Microsoft's submission to the wmt2018 news translation task: How i learned to stop worrying and love the data. In *Proceedings of the Third Conference on Machine Translation (WMT), Volume 2: Shared Task Papers*, pages 429–434.

Yoon Kim and Alexander M. Rush. 2016. Sequence-level knowledge distillation. In *Proceedings of the 2016 Conference on Empirical Methods in Natural Language Processing*, pages 1317–1327, Austin, Texas. Association for Computational Linguistics.

Diederik P Kingma and Jimmy Ba. 2015. Adam: A method for stochastic optimization. *International Conference on Learning Representation (ICLR)*.

Renqian Luo, Fei Tian, Tao Qin, Enhong Chen, and Tie-Yan Liu. 2018. Neural architecture optimization. In S. Bengio, H. Wallach, H. Larochelle, K. Grauman, N. Cesa-Bianchi, and R. Garnett, editors, *Advances in Neural Information Processing Systems 31*, pages 7816–7827. Curran Associates, Inc.

Hieu Pham, Melody Y. Guan, Barret Zoph, Quoc V. Le, and Jeff Dean. 2018. Efficient neural architecture search via parameters sharing. *international conference on machine learning*, pages 4092–4101.

Rico Sennrich, Barry Haddow, and Alexandra Birch. 2016a. Improving neural machine translation models with monolingual data. In *Proceedings of the 54th Annual Meeting of the Association for Computational Linguistics (Volume 1: Long Papers)*, volume 1, pages 86–96.

Rico Sennrich, Barry Haddow, and Alexandra Birch. 2016b. Neural machine translation of rare words with subword units. *54th Annual Meeting of the Association for Computational Linguistics (ACL)*.

Kaitao Song, Xu Tan, Tao Qin, Jianfeng Lu, and Tie-Yan Liu. 2019. Mass: Masked sequence to sequence pre-training for language generation. In *International Conference on Machine Learning*, pages 5926–5936.

Ashish Vaswani, Noam Shazeer, Niki Parmar, Jakob Uszkoreit, Llion Jones, Aidan N Gomez, Łukasz Kaiser, and Illia Polosukhin. 2017. Attention is all you need. In *Advances in neural information processing systems*, pages 5998–6008.

Yijun Wang, Yingce Xia, Li Zhao, Jiang Bian, Tao Qin, Guiquan Liu, and Tie-Yan Liu. 2018. Dual transfer learning for neural machine translation with marginal distribution regularization. In *Thirty-Second AAAI Conference on Artificial Intelligence*.

Yiren Wang, Yingce Xia, Tianyu He, Fei Tian, Tao Qin, ChengXiang Zhai, and Tie-Yan Liu. 2019. Multi-agent dual learning. In *International Conference on Learning Representations*.

Lijun Wu, Fei Tian, Tao Qin, Jianhuang Lai, and Tie-Yan Liu. 2018a. A study of reinforcement learning for neural machine translation. In *Proceedings of the 2018 Conference on Empirical Methods in Natural Language Processing*, pages 3612–3621.

Lijun Wu, Yingce Xia, Fei Tian, Li Zhao, Tao Qin, Jianhuang Lai, and Tie-Yan Liu. 2018b. Adversarial neural machine translation. In *Asian Conference on Machine Learning*, pages 534–549.

Yingce Xia, Tao Qin, Wei Chen, Jiang Bian, Nenghai Yu, and Tie-Yan Liu. 2017a. Dual supervised learning. In *Proceedings of the 34th International Conference on Machine Learning-Volume 70*, pages 3789–3798. JMLR. org.

Yingce Xia, Fei Tian, Lijun Wu, Jianxin Lin, Tao Qin, Nenghai Yu, and Tie-Yan Liu. 2017b. Deliberation networks: Sequence generation beyond one-pass decoding. In *Advances in Neural Information Processing Systems*, pages 1784–1794.

Jinhua Zhu, Fei Gao, Lijun Wu, Yingce Xia, Tao Qin, Wengang Zhou, Xueqi Cheng, and Tie-Yan Liu. 2019. Soft contextual data augmentation for neural machine translation. In *ACL 2019*.

The En-Ru Two-way Integrated Machine Translation System Based on Transformer

Anonymous ACL submission

Abstract

Machine translation is one of the most popular areas in natural language processing. WMT is a conference to assess the level of machine translation capabilities of organizations around the world, which is the evaluation activity we participated in. In this review we participated in a two-way translation track from Russian to English and English to Russian. We used official training data, 38 million parallel corpora, and 10 million monolingual corpora. The overall framework we use is the Transformer(Vaswani et al., 2017) neural machine translation model, supplemented by data filtering, post-processing, reordering and other related processing methods. The BLEU(Papineni et al., 2002) value of our final translation result from Russian to English is 38.7, ranking 5th, while from English to Russian is 27.8, ranking 10th.

1 Introduction

Neural machine translation has been widely used in the field of machine translation, because it is more accurate than statistical machine translation in most cases. The proposed attention mechanism brought a new revolution in the neural machine translation, making the overall effect of translation much better than before. Then, the Transformer that makes full use of the attention mechanism , both in terms of performance and effectiveness. Up to now, most of the work has been carried out on Transformer, and its superiority has been widely recognized.

From the beginning of machine translation research, there has been the development of two-way translation between Russian and English. As early as 1954, Georgetown University in the United States under the IBM company completed the English-Russian machine translation experiment with IBM-701 computer, which opened the

prelude of machine translation research. During the period, there are three core technologies, rule-based machine translation, statistical machine translation(Koehn et al., 2007) and neural machine translation(Bahdanau et al., 2014), which continue to develop. However, as the application fields of machine translation become more and more complex, the limitations of different technologies begin to appear. Because of the more application scenarios and the higher requirements for accuracy, the problem of model optimization appeared.

The translation between Russian and English is extremely difficult because their linguistic features are distinguished and the lexical composition and grammatical structure of Russian are more complicated than English. Early statistical machine translations were hoped to be implemented through phrase-based methods(Marcu and Wong, 2002), including rule-based lexical, phrase analysis systems, and related techniques for language models and translation models. These methods have solved the translation problem between Russian and English to a certain extent. However, at the same time, there is still a problem that the time cost is long and the translation result is not good enough.

Therefore, the emergence of neural machine translation has brought a new dawn for the translation between Russian and English. The basic modeling framework for neural machine translation is an end-to-end sequence generation model, a framework and method for transforming input sequences into output sequences. There are two points in the core part. One is to represent the input sequence through the encoder, and the other is to obtain the output sequence through the decoder. In addition, for machine translation, neural machine translation not only includes encoding and decoding, but also uses RNN(Sutskever et al., 2014) or other methods to encode sentence

Proceedings of the Fourth Conference on Machine Translation (WMT), Volume 2: Shared Task Papers (Day 1) pages 434–439
Florence, Italy, August 1-2, 2019. ©2019 Association for Computational Linguistics

pairs. It also introduces an additional mechanism, the attention mechanism(Luong et al., 2015), to help us to convert sequences. The translation results thus obtained more expectations than before. Later, Transformer appeared, which greatly enhances neural machine translation in terms of performance and effect.

This paper is based on Transformer, a neural machine translation network structure, to develop a two-way evaluation task between Russian and English. Taking into account the language characteristics of Russian and English, we have done appropriate operations in data preprocessing, including removing duplicates, deleting unreasonable sentence pairs, lowercase and Latinization operations, and judging sentence alignment problems, removing the parallel corpus with problems. The filtered parallel corpus is then sent to the model for training and the training results are tested. After getting the trained model, we start to consider using the back-translation operation to augment the data, continuing to filter the generated artificial corpus, and put it into the model training together with the original parallel corpus.

Finally, ensemble(Dietterich, 2000), average and rerank(Shen et al., 2004) operations are implemented on different models to improve the overall performance of the translation system.

2 Background

Neural network machine translation is based on a sequence-to-sequence overall structure consisting of an encoder and a decoder. The encoder converts the source language sentence into an intermediate sequence result, and the decoder converts the intermediate sequence result into a target language sentence. There is also the Attention mechanism to help make the results perform better. In the construction of the overall translation system, we used a lot of excellent methods proposed by the predecessors.

The basic model used here is Transformer. This is a paper published by Google in 2017 titled Attention Is All You Need, an attention-based structure proposed to deal with sequence model related issues, such as machine translation. Traditional neural machine translation mostly uses RNN or CNN as the model base of encoder-decoder, and Google's latest Attention-based Transformer model abandons the inherent formula and does not use any CNN or RNN structure. The model works in

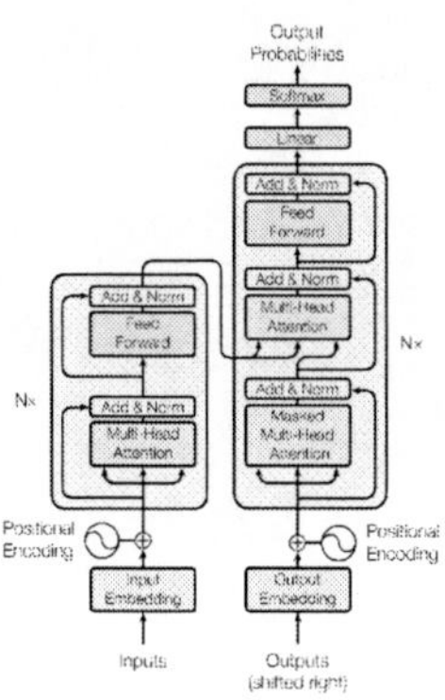

Figure 1: Transformer Structure

high-level parallel process, so training speed is also extremely fast while improving translation performance.

The structure of Transformer is shown in Figure 1. The model is divided into two parts: the encoder and the decoder. The encoder is stacked by six identical layers, each with two more sub-layers. The first sub-layer is a long self-attention mechanism, and the second sub-layer is a simple fully connected feed forward network. A residual connection is added outside the two layers, and then layer normalization is performed. The output dimensions of all sub-layers and embedding layers of the model are d_{models}; the decoder also stacks six identical layers. However, in addition to the two layers in the encoder, the decoder also adds a third sub-layer, as shown in the figure which also uses the residual and layer normalization.

3 Experiment

For this evaluation task, we start from the data preprocessing, through the data augmentation operation, get the parallel corpus that needs to be trained, input the Transformer model for training, and test the training results, and finally ensemble results according to the model generated by different strategies, average and rerank operations, for the best results. Next, the experimental content will be elaborated separately. The overall experimental process is shown in Figure 2.

3.1 Data Preprocessing

The first is data preprocessing, which is crucial for the translation of the model. The sentences used in this evaluation with data preprocessing method to filter out include parallel sentence pairs with

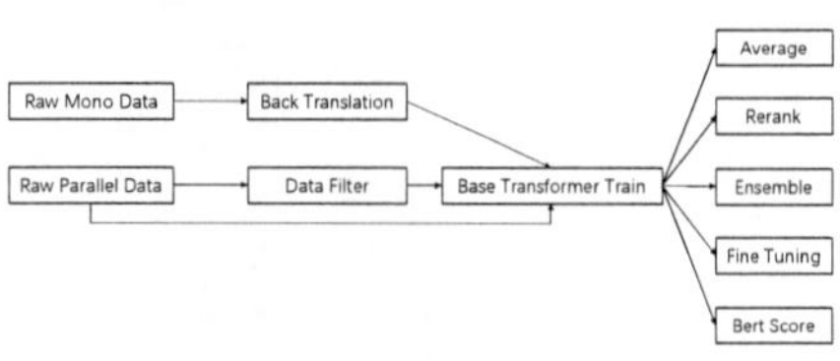

Figure 2: Project Process

high repetition rate, length mismatch and alignment problems. The amount of data given by the official at the beginning was about 38 million lines. After data filtering, 33 million lines were left, and 5 million lines were deleted, accounting for 0.13 of the original quantity. This result is in line with expectations and acceptable.

The sentence with higher repetition rate has little meaning in the training corpus, which increases the burden of the model and affects the translation effect, so it needs to perform deduplication operation. The method used here is to calculate the cosine distance of the SimHash value between each row of data. When the difference is less than 0.2, we believe it is repeated, and can be deleted. Because the amount of data is large and the global deduplication time is too long, so here is a simple calculation of three sentences before and after current line, that is, using a window of size 7 to check the sentence repetition, which also conforms to the principle of local consistency.

From the practical experience and linguistic knowledge, the length of sentences generated by the two languages expressing the same meaning is not too different, especially for Russian and English. So we also screened the length of the sentence. In the experimental processing, we control the ratio of the source language and the target language length to 1/2-2/1, which means that the sentence lengths of the two languages are not more than twice as large. The length of the sentence is calculated by the number of tokens. The parallel sentence pairs thus obtained are also reasonable in length ratio.

Sentence alignment is a very important factor to measure the quality of parallel sentence pairs from the perspective of sentence meaning. Different from the previous method, it needs to enter sentences themselves and judge whether the data

pairs are reasonable according to the correspondence between words in the two languages. The gize++ tool(Gao and Vogel, 2008) is used here to help check for data alignment issues. By reading Russian-English vocabulary and Russian-English parallel corpus information, creating a new dictionary, building an IBM model 1, making EM algorithm iteration, generating word alignment information, and obtaining a calculated sentence pair for each data. We generate alignment scores and eliminate sentence pairs with scores less than the threshold 10e-10 for better alignment data.

3.2 Back Translation

In the process of data augmentation, the back-translation strategy(Edunov et al., 2018) plays a crucial role. The auxiliary translation system from the target language to the source language first trains on the available parallel data and then uses to generate translations from the monolingual corpus of the large target. The pairs of these translations and their corresponding reference targets are then used as additional training data for the original translation system. Using this strategy can greatly increase the data required for training and improve the translation effect of the model. In the back-translation, we trained a translation model from the target language to the source language based on the existing corpus. By inputting the target language corpus into the model, the corresponding source language corpus can be obtained, and the two are combined to obtain a new parallel corpus.

The data set size of this trial is not too large and it is stipulated that external parallel corpus expansion cannot be used, so we use the back translation method to increase the amount of training data.

Using back translation extended corpus in NMT is a common data enhancement technique. We trained a translation model from the target language to the source language based on the existing corpus. By inputting the target language corpus into the model, the corresponding source language corpus can be obtained and combined to get a new parallel corpus.

External data is not allowed in this competition, so we use the mono part of the original corpus to generate para data. However, there is a problem with this approach that there may be duplication between the new parallel corpus and the original corpus. To solve this problem, we added some random noise on the decoding side to avoid this situation.

We selected 10 million Russian and English sentences respectively from the official monolingual corpus as raw data for back translation operations. The model obtained through the training of the existing parallel corpus translated this part of the monolingual corpus and obtained 10 million pseudo-parallel corpora. Then, we filter this part of the data according to the data filtering and noise strategy mentioned in the previous section. Finally, 8 million individual parallel corpora are obtained and the filtered parallel corpus input model is used for training operations.

3.3 Model training

Considering the hardware cost and time cost of the experiment, the model we selected for this experiment is the basic version of Transformer. The encoder and decoder have 6 sub-layers and the multihead attention mechanism has 8 headers. The word vector size is 512. Guaranteed to get the best results in a limited time in a laboratory environment. The development environment for evaluation is MXNET, which is the deep learning library that Amazon chose.

The input model needs to be further processed before training, including generating the corresponding token for the sentence. The tool used here is the commonly used tokenizer.perl, which can separate the words and punctuation in English and convert the special symbols to keep the same symbol. Russian is the same. In addition, the BPE method is needed to generate the subword vocabulary to reduce the vocabulary size during the model training and improve the performance of the model.

After the above processing, the data can be divided to obtain a training set, a test set and a verification set, the training set is used for model training, the verification set is used for performance detection in the training process, and the test set is used for evaluating the result of model trained.

For the evaluation task, the following experiment was designed:

1. Baseline Model

Use the official 38 million parallel corpus without screening and direct it into the model for training and testing. The results of the base model are used to compare with different strategy results and generate reverse translation data to extend the cor-

pus and continue training. The purpose is to maintain the generalization ability and robustness of the model to the greatest extent, and to provide reference for other model training results.

2. Filter Model

The data preprocessing operation is used to screen the official data and the ideal training corpus is obtained. The 33 million filtered parallel sentences are trained to obtain a data filtering model. Because the quality of the data used for training is higher, the effect of model translation is better than the basic model.

3. Back Model

10 million is extracted from the official monolingual corpus as the source language input to the baseline model for translation, and the artificial parallel corpus based on the baseline model translation is obtained. Since the effect of the baseline model is not good enough, the generated corpus needs to be further filtered, and the method is also the data preprocessing operation mentioned above. After screening, we got about 8 million good quality artificial data and then combined the artificial parallel corpus with the previously filtered official parallel corpus and input them into the model for training. Then we got the Back translation model. Because artificial corpus has been added, the translation effect and the robustness is improved.

4. Fine-tuning Model

Fine-tuning a trained model using small-scale corpus is a commonly used strategy in the field of machine learning. It can make the model more sensitive to specific domain scenarios, thus reflecting better results. Here, we select a corpus with much similarity to the test set from the training set to fine-tune the trained model. The similarity scores between the test corpus and the training corpus are sorted and ranked. Then the parallel sentence pairs with higher scores are found and the corpus is extracted as a fine-tuning corpus. In this way, about 5,000 pieces of data are obtained and this part of the corpus is input into the previously trained model to obtain the result of fine-tuning the model, so that it can perform better on the test set.

5. Ensemble Model

Ensemble is a method that combines the results of multiple models. The purpose of this is to complement the advantages of different models, make up for the problems that fall into the local optimum and get the results of the machine translation model with better comprehensive effects. For the sake of simplicity, only different initialization random seed parameters are set for the same model. So training of multiple models is performed, generally two or three models, and finally the results of all models are subjected to ensemble operation. By composing and complementing multiple models, we obtain the comprehensive optimal results of data translation.

6. Average Model

The Average operation is similar in thought to ensemble, but it operates on different training parameters of the same model. The parameters in these training results are subjected to the average operation, and a set of training results are comprehensively obtained from the best training parameters of the single model. Top 5 of the model training results is selected for averaging to prevent a certain result from falling into the local optimum and a plurality of parameters are integrated to obtain an averaged optimal solution. This results in the best combination of different training parameters in the same model, thereby improving the performance of a single model.

7. Nbest and Rerank Model

Extracting only one of the highest-scoring statements from the translation results of the model as an output is not necessarily the best result. So this strategy can be used to extract the best three from each translation model result as a candidate set. Then use some rules to rerank and get the best one as the output result. The translated content thus obtained is the comprehensive output of multiple results of each model, which is theoretically optimal. The rules used here include weighted summation of beam search score and the language model scores. The first one is based on the beam score returned during decoding, but different models have different performances, so it is difficult to sort under a uniform metric. So we introduced different weights for different models. Using beam score weight as the final score for each translation result, the final result was obtained by screening. The second one gives scores of the generated translations using the pre-trained language model. They are judged from the linguistics itself and the sentences with the highest scores are selected. The final result is an output that combines the highest scores of the two methods described above.

The above models also had different batch sizes, comparison of the number of graphics cards and

Name	Pair	Bleu	Improve
base-re	RU-EN	34.8	0
filter-re	RU-EN	36.1	+1.3
average-filter-re	RU-EN	36.2	+1.4
rerank-re	**RU-EN**	**37.5**	**+2.7**
vote-re	RU-EN	36.1	+1.3
base-er	EN-RU	25.6	0
filter-er	EN-RU	26.6	+1.0
average-filter-er	EN-RU	26.8	+1.2
rerank-er	**EN-RU**	**27.8**	**+2.2**
vote-er	EN-RU	26.5	+0.9

Table 1: Experiment Result.

vocabulary sizes in the training process. We extracted them for the optimal results. Finally, the output is simply post-processed. In order to comply with normal text habits. However, due to the limitations of time and hardware resources, not every experiment has been refined and detailed totally, so there is still improvement of results in the future.

3.4 Results Analysis

The above experimental results are presented in the Table 1. It should be noted that only the better and more complete results in the experiment are given here. We can see that the BLEU values of the Baseline Model form English to Russian is 25.9, while from Russian to English is 35.2, respectively as a benchmark, to provide reference for the following models. The results after filtration are 27.0 and 36.5, which has 1.0 or so improvement over baseline. The results obtained by the Average strategy are 27.2 and 36.5, which is basically no improvement. The strategy of obtaining nbest for translation results and reranking according to the reference rules worked very well, which got 28.2 and 38.0, from 2 to 3 points higher than baseline. Back Model, Fine-tuning and Ensemble strategies are not very completed in detail, so they are not shown here.

4 Conclusion

In this evaluation task, we established a Russian-English two-way machine translation system based on Transformer. Through data preprocessing, model training, data post-processing and other optimization strategies, the evaluation results were finally from English to Russian BLEU value 28.2, while from Russian to English 38.0, which was about 3 points higher than the baseline result. In the final list, we got 5th in Ru-En, and 10th in En-Ru. Good results have been obtained in limited time and hardware resources, which is also in line with the industry's demands for service construction. In the whole experiment process, we also learned a lot of experience in data processing and experimental design, which will be of great help in later research and study. We will continue to improve the previous experiments, strive to get better results, and see what rankings can eventually be achieved, in preparation for the next year.

References

Dzmitry Bahdanau, Kyunghyun Cho, and Yoshua Bengio. 2014. Neural machine translation by jointly learning to align and translate. *arXiv preprint arXiv:1409.0473*.

Thomas G Dietterich. 2000. Ensemble methods in machine learning. In *International workshop on multiple classifier systems*, pages 1–15. Springer.

Sergey Edunov, Myle Ott, Michael Auli, and David Grangier. 2018. Understanding back-translation at scale. *arXiv preprint arXiv:1808.09381*.

Qin Gao and Stephan Vogel. 2008. Parallel implementations of word alignment tool. *Software engineering, testing, and quality assurance for natural language processing*, pages 49–57.

Philipp Koehn, Hieu Hoang, Alexandra Birch, Chris Callison-Burch, Marcello Federico, Nicola Bertoldi, Brooke Cowan, Wade Shen, Christine Moran, Richard Zens, et al. 2007. Moses: Open source toolkit for statistical machine translation. In *Proceedings of the 45th annual meeting of the association for computational linguistics companion volume proceedings of the demo and poster sessions*, pages 177–180.

Minh-Thang Luong, Hieu Pham, and Christopher D Manning. 2015. Effective approaches to attention-based neural machine translation. *arXiv preprint arXiv:1508.04025*.

Daniel Marcu and Daniel Wong. 2002. A phrase-based, joint probability model for statistical machine translation. In *Proceedings of the 2002 Conference on Empirical Methods in Natural Language Processing (EMNLP 2002)*.

Kishore Papineni, Salim Roukos, Todd Ward, and Wei-Jing Zhu. 2002. Bleu: a method for automatic evaluation of machine translation. In *Proceedings of the 40th annual meeting on association for computational linguistics*, pages 311–318. Association for Computational Linguistics.

Libin Shen, Anoop Sarkar, and Franz Josef Och. 2004. Discriminative reranking for machine translation. In *Proceedings of the Human Language Technology Conference of the North American Chapter of the Association for Computational Linguistics: HLT-NAACL 2004*.

Ilya Sutskever, Oriol Vinyals, and Quoc V Le. 2014. Sequence to sequence learning with neural networks. In *Advances in neural information processing systems*, pages 3104–3112.

Ashish Vaswani, Noam Shazeer, Niki Parmar, Jakob Uszkoreit, Llion Jones, Aidan N Gomez, Łukasz Kaiser, and Illia Polosukhin. 2017. Attention is all you need. In *Advances in neural information processing systems*, pages 5998–6008.

DFKI-NMT Submission to the WMT19 News Translation Task

Jingyi Zhang[1], Josef van Genabith[1,2]
[1]German Research Center for Artificial Intelligence (DFKI),
Saarbrücken, Germany
[2]Department of Language Science and Technology,
Saarland University, Germany
Jingyi.Zhang@dfki.de, Josef.Van_Genabith@dfki.de

Abstract

This paper describes the DFKI-NMT submission to the WMT19 News translation task. We participated in both English-to-German and German-to-English directions. We trained standard Transformer models and adopted various techniques for effectively training our models, including data selection, back-translation, in-domain fine-tuning and model ensemble. We show that these training techniques improved the performance of our Transformer models up to 5 BLEU points. We give a detailed analysis of the performance of our system.

1 Introduction

This paper describes the DFKI-NMT submission to the WMT19 News translation task. We participated in both English-to-German and German-to-English directions. We trained Transformer models (Vaswani et al., 2017) using Sockeye[1] (Hieber et al., 2017). Compared to RNN-based translation models (Bahdanau et al., 2014), Transformer models can be trained very fast due to parallelizable self-attention networks. We applied several very useful techniques for effectively training our models.

Data Selection The parallel training data provided for German-English is quite large (38M sentence pairs). Most of the parallel data is crawled from the Internet and is not in News domain. Out-of-domain training data can hurt the translation performance on News test sets (Wang et al., 2017) and also significantly increase training time. Therefore, we trained neural language models on a large monolingual News corpus to perform data selection (Schamper et al., 2018).

Back-translation Large monolingual data in the News domain is provided for both German and English, which can be back-translated as additional parallel training data for our system (Sennrich et al., 2016a; Fadaee and Monz, 2018). The back-translated parallel data is in the News domain, which is a big advantage compared to out-of-domain parallel training data provided for the News task.

In-domain Fine-tuning The Transformer models were finally fine-tuned using the small in-domain parallel data provided for the News task (Luong and Manning, 2015; Schamper et al., 2018). Note that the large back-translated parallel data is also in-domain, but it has relatively low quality due to translation errors.

Model Ensemble We trained two Transformer models with different sizes, Transformer-base and Transformer-big. Our final submission is an ensemble of both models (Schamper et al., 2018). The ensemble of both models outperformed a single base or big model most likely because the two models can capture somewhat different features for the translation task.

2 System Details

2.1 Data Selection

The parallel data provided for the German-to-English and English-to-German tasks includes Europarl v9, ParaCrawl v3, Common Crawl corpus, News Commentary v14, Wiki Titles v1 and Document-split Rapid corpus. We also used old test sets (*newstest2008* to *newstest2017*) for training our systems. We consider News Commentary v14 and old test sets as in-domain data and the rest as out-of-domain data. Compared to the in-domain data (356k sentence pairs), the size of the out-of-domain data (38M sentence pairs) is quite large, which makes the training process relatively slow and may also hurt the translation per-

---

[1]https://github.com/awslabs/sockeye

Proceedings of the Fourth Conference on Machine Translation (WMT), Volume 2: Shared Task Papers (Day 1) pages 440–444
Florence, Italy, August 1-2, 2019. ©2019 Association for Computational Linguistics

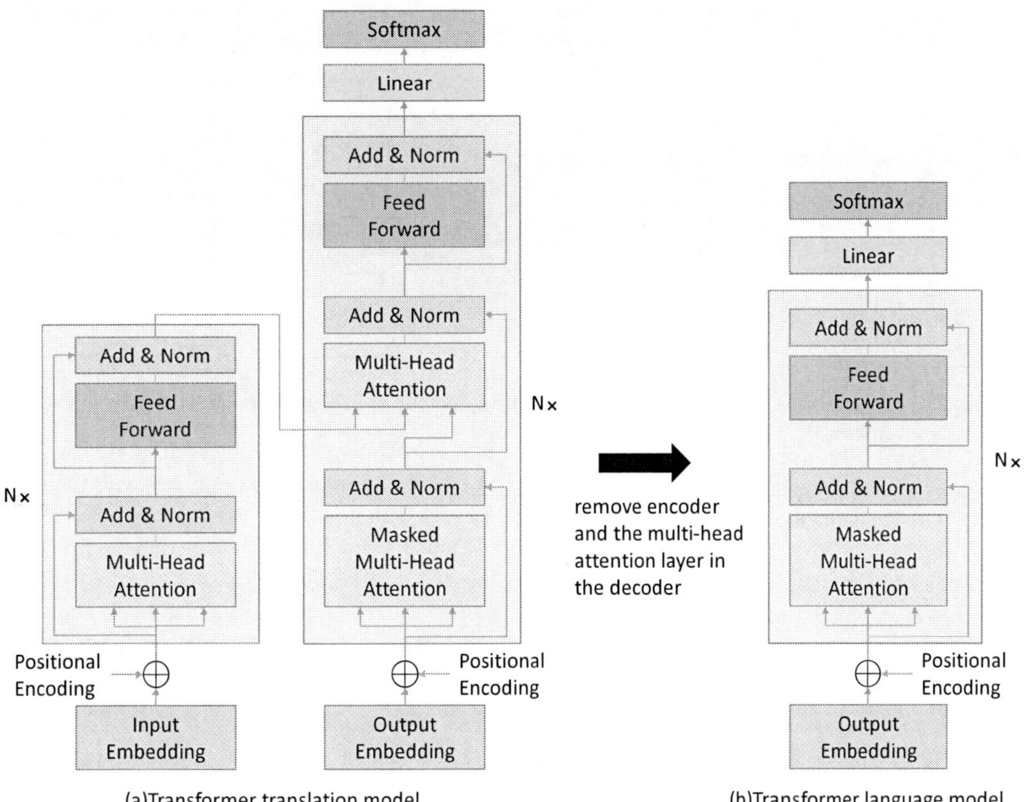

Figure 1: Structures of Transformer translation models and Transformer language models used in our experiments.

formance due to domain dismatch. Therefore, we performed data selection on out-of-domain data.

Inspired by Schamper et al. (2018)'s work which used KenLM (Heafield, 2011) for data selection, we trained two neural language models based on self-attention networks using the 2018 part of the large monolingual *News crawl* corpus for English and German, respectively. Because these neural language models are trained on the News domain, we can use them to score out-of-domain data. Sentences with higher probabilities are more likely to be in News domain. Equation 1 is used to score each sentence pair in the out-of-domain corpus. In Equation 1, P_s is the language model probability of the source sentence; N_s is the length of the source sentence; P_t is the language model probability of the target sentence; N_t is the length of the target sentence. We selected the top 15M scored sentence pairs from out-of-domain data for training our systems.

$$\frac{\log P_s}{N_s} + \frac{\log P_t}{N_t} \qquad (1)$$

The neural language models trained for data

selection in our experiments are based on self-attention networks which can be trained very fast. Figure 1 (a) shows the structure of the standard Transformer translation model (Vaswani et al., 2017) and we removed the encoder and the attention layer in the decoder from the Transformer translation model to create our Transformer language model as shown in Figure 1 (b). For training efficiency, we used byte pair encoding (Sennrich et al., 2016b) to learn a vocabulary of 50k for English and German respectively.

2.2 Back-translation

We back-translated the 2018 part of the large monolingual in-domain *News crawl* data as additional training data for our translation systems. Fadaee and Monz (2018) showed that it is more beneficial to back-translate sentences that contain difficult words. In our experiments, we consider words which occur less than 1000 times in the bilingual training data as difficult words. Then we randomly selected 10M sentences which contain difficult words for back-translation. The mod-

	in-domain 356k	out-of-domain 15M	back-translated 10M
Stage 1	✓	✓	
Stage 2	✓	✓	✓
Stage 3	✓		

Table 1: Training data used in different training stages.

	en-de		de-en	
	base	big	base	big
Stage 1	7.3	7.6	6.6	6.8
Stage 2	0.3	0.4	0.8	1.4
Stage 3	18.5	18.5	12.4	12.4

Table 2: Training epochs for different training stages.

els used for back-translating monolingual data are baseline Transformers (Vaswani et al., 2017) trained on the bilingual data after data selection as described before. During back-translation, we used greedy search instead of beam search for efficiency.

2.3 Model and Training

We trained two Transformer models for each translation task as Transformer-base and Transformer-big. The settings of Transformer-base is the same as the baseline Transformer in Vaswani et al. (2017)'s work. For Transformer-big, we changed word embedding size into 1024 and kept other parameters unchanged. A joint vocabulary of 50k for German and English is learned by byte pair encoding (BPE) (Sennrich et al., 2016b).[2] We set dropout to 0.1 for both Transformer-base and Transformer-big. We used adam (Kingma and Ba, 2014) for optimization. We used *newstest2018* as the validation set for model training. The training processes for both Transformer-base and Transformer-big consist of three stages.

Stage 1 We first trained the Transformers using bilingual training data, including all in-domain data and selected out-of-domain data as described in section 2.1. Note that the back-translated data was not used in this stage. Each training batch contains 8192 words and the validation frequency is 2000 batches. We set the initial learning rate to be 2.00e-04. We reduced the learning rate by a factor of 0.70 whenever the validation score does not

---

[2] For preprocessing, we used Moses (Koehn et al., 2007) scripts *normalize-punctuation.perl*, *tokenizer.perl*, *lower-case.perl*. We trained a recaser using *train-recaser.perl* to recase translations.

	en-de		de-en	
	base	big	base	big
Stage 1	44.24	45.03	45.34	45.75
Stage 2	46.42	47.10	47.84	48.65
Stage 3	47.80	48.83	48.65	49.33
Ensemble	49.45		49.75	

Table 3: Case-insensitive BLEU scores on *newstest2018*. "Ensemble" means ensemble both Transformer-base and Transformer-big after Stage 3.

improve 8 times. We stopped the training process after 5 times of learning rate reduction.

Stage 2 We used all bilingual training data used in the first training stage together with the back-translated monolingual data to continue training the models which had converged in the first training stage. We kept the batch size to be 8192 words and changed the validation frequency to 1000 batches. We set the initial learning rate to be 1.00e-05 and stopped the training process when the validation score does not improve 8 times.

Stage 3 For fine-tuning, we used the small parallel in-domain data as described in section 2.1 to continue training the models which had converged in the second training stage. We changed batch size to be 1024 words and validation frequency to be 100 batches. We set the initial learning rate to be 1.00e-06 and stopped the training process when the validation score does not improve 8 times.

Table 1 shows training data used in different training stages. The models trained in the first training stage were used to back-translate monolingual data as described in section 2.2. In Stage 2, we continued training the models which had converged in Stage 1 instead of training models with random initialization in order to reduce the training time of Stage 2.

2.4 Results and Analysis

Table 2 shows the numbers of training epochs for different training stages and Table 3 shows the performance of our systems after different training stages. As we can see, back-translation (Stage 2) and in-domain fine-tuning (Stage 3) both improved the translation quality on a significant level. An ensemble of Stage 3 Transformer-base and Transformer-big achieved further improvements. We also tried to ensemble different checkpoints of Transformer-big, but achieved little improvement, likely because different checkpoints of

Example 1	
Src	wei@@ dez@@ aun@@ projekt ist element@@ ar
Ref	past@@ ure fence project is fundamental
Ours	electric sound project is elementary
Example 2	
Src	jetzt nimmt sich das weiße haus von trump die freiheits@@ statue vor
Ref	now trump 's white house is targeting the statue of liberty
Ours	now trump 's white house takes the statue of liberty

Table 4: Translation examples. "@@" means segmented by *byte pair encoding*.

the same model are very similar.

In addition, we give some translation examples in Table 4 to analyze when and why our translation system makes mistakes. The translations in Table 4 are produced by our best system, i.e., ensemble of Transformer-base and Transformer-big after training stage 3. In Example 1, "wei@@ dez@@ aun@@ projekt" (pasture fence project) is wrongly translated into "electric sound project", likely because "weidezaunprojekt" is a unknown word and does not occur in the training data. Although BPE can help to relieve data sparsity by using smaller and more frequent sub-word units, the automatic BPE segmentation "wei@@ dez@@ aun@@ projekt" is a bad segmentation with linguistically meaningless sub-word pieces. A better segmentation "weide@@(pasture) zaun@@(fence) projekt" may help to reduce data sparsity and get better translation. Example 2 does not contain rare words, but "nimmt vor" is still wrongly translated into "takes". This is likely because "nimmt vor" has different translations in the training data and the correct translation here "targeting" is relatively uncommon. We find many translation mistakes of our system are caused by rare words or uncommon usages of words as shown in Table 4, which we will work on in the future.

3 Conclusion

This paper describes the DFKI-NMT submission to the WMT19 English-to-German and German-to-English News translation tasks. We trained standard Transformer models and adopted various techniques for effectively training our models, including data selection, back-translation, in-domain fine-tuning and model ensemble. We show that effective training techniques can improve the performance of standard Transformer models up to 5 BLEU points.

Acknowledgments

This work is supported by the German Federal Ministry of Education and Research (BMBF) under the funding code 01IW17001 (Deeplee). Responsibility for the content of this publication is with the authors.

References

Dzmitry Bahdanau, Kyunghyun Cho, and Yoshua Bengio. 2014. Neural machine translation by jointly learning to align and translate. *arXiv preprint arXiv:1409.0473*.

Marzieh Fadaee and Christof Monz. 2018. Back-translation sampling by targeting difficult words in neural machine translation. In *Proceedings of the 2018 Conference on Empirical Methods in Natural Language Processing*, pages 436–446.

Kenneth Heafield. 2011. KenLM: Faster and smaller language model queries. In *Proceedings of the Sixth Workshop on Statistical Machine Translation*, pages 187–197.

Felix Hieber, Tobias Domhan, Michael Denkowski, David Vilar, Artem Sokolov, Ann Clifton, and Matt Post. 2017. Sockeye: A toolkit for neural machine translation. *arXiv preprint arXiv:1712.05690*.

Diederik P Kingma and Jimmy Ba. 2014. Adam: A method for stochastic optimization. *arXiv preprint arXiv:1412.6980*.

Philipp Koehn, Hieu Hoang, Alexandra Birch, Chris Callison-Burch, Marcello Federico, Nicola Bertoldi, Brooke Cowan, Wade Shen, Christine Moran, Richard Zens, Chris Dyer, Ondrej Bojar, Alexandra Constantin, and Evan Herbst. 2007. Moses: Open source toolkit for statistical machine translation. In *Proceedings of the 45th Annual Meeting of the Association for Computational Linguistics Companion Volume Proceedings of the Demo and Poster Sessions*, pages 177–180.

Minh-Thang Luong and Christopher D Manning. 2015. Stanford neural machine translation systems for spoken language domains. In *Proceedings of the In-*

ternational Workshop on Spoken Language Transla-tion, pages 76–79.

Julian Schamper, Jan Rosendahl, Parnia Bahar, Yunsu Kim, Arne Nix, and Hermann Ney. 2018. The RWTH aachen university supervised machine trans-lation systems for WMT 2018. In *Proceedings of the Third Conference on Machine Translation: Shared Task Papers*, pages 496–503.

Rico Sennrich, Barry Haddow, and Alexandra Birch. 2016a. Improving neural machine translation mod-els with monolingual data. In *Proceedings of the 54th Annual Meeting of the Association for Compu-tational Linguistics (Volume 1: Long Papers)*, pages 86–96.

Rico Sennrich, Barry Haddow, and Alexandra Birch. 2016b. Neural machine translation of rare words with subword units. In *Proceedings of the 54th An-nual Meeting of the Association for Computational Linguistics (Volume 1: Long Papers)*, pages 1715–1725.

Ashish Vaswani, Noam Shazeer, Niki Parmar, Jakob Uszkoreit, Llion Jones, Aidan N Gomez, Łukasz Kaiser, and Illia Polosukhin. 2017. Attention is all you need. In *Advances in neural information pro-cessing systems*, pages 5998–6008.

Rui Wang, Andrew Finch, Masao Utiyama, and Ei-ichiro Sumita. 2017. Sentence embedding for neural machine translation domain adaptation. In *Proceed-ings of the 55th Annual Meeting of the Association for Computational Linguistics (Volume 2: Short Pa-pers)*, pages 560–566.

Linguistic evaluation of German-English Machine Translation using a Test Suite

Eleftherios Avramidis, Vivien Macketanz, Ursula Strohriegel and Hans Uszkoreit
German Research Center for Artificial Intelligence (DFKI), Berlin, Germany
`firstname.lastname@dfki.de`

Abstract

We present the results of the application of a grammatical test suite for German→English MT on the systems submitted at WMT19, with a detailed analysis for 107 phenomena organized in 14 categories. The systems still translate wrong one out of four test items in average. Low performance is indicated for idioms, modals, pseudo-clefts, multi-word expressions and verb valency. When compared to last year, there has been a improvement of function words, non verbal agreement and punctuation. More detailed conclusions about particular systems and phenomena are also presented.

1 Introduction

For decades, the development of Machine Translation (MT) has been based on either automatic metrics or human evaluation campaigns with the main focus on producing scores or comparisons (rankings) expressing a generic notion of quality. Through the years there have been few examples of more detailed analyses of the translation quality, both automatic (HTER (Snover et al., 2009), Hjerson (Popović, 2011)) and human (MQM Lommel et al., 2014). Nevertheless, these efforts have not been systematic and they have only focused on few shallow error categories (e.g. morphology, lexical choice, reordering), whereas the human evaluation campaigns have been limited by the requirement for manual human effort. Additionally, previous work on MT evaluation focused mostly on the ability of the systems to translate test sets sampled from generic text sources, based on the assumption that this text is representative of a common translation task (Callison-Burch et al., 2007).

In order to provide more systematic methods to evaluate MT in a more fine-grained level, recent research has relied to the idea of test suites (Guillou and Hardmeier, 2016; Isabelle et al., 2017).

The test suites are assembled in a way that allows testing particular issues which are the focus of the evaluation. The evaluation of the systems is not based on generic text samples, but from the perspective of fulfilling a priori quality requirements.

In this paper we use the DFKI test suite for German→English MT (Burchardt et al., 2017) in order to analyze the performance of the 16 MT Systems that took part at the translation task of the Fourth Conference of Machine Translation. The evaluation focuses on 107 mostly grammatical phenomena organized in 14 categories. In order to apply the test suite, we follow a semi-automatic methodology that benefits from regular expressions, followed by minimal human refinement (Section 3). The application of the suite allows us to form conclusions on the particular grammatical performance of the systems and perform several comparisons (Section 4).

2 Related Work

Several test suites have been presented as part of the Test Suite track of the Third Conference of Machine Translation (Bojar et al., 2018a). Each test suite focused on a particular phenomenon, such as discourse (Bojar et al., 2018b), morphology (Burlot et al., 2018), grammatical contrasts (Cinkova and Bojar, 2018), pronouns (Guillou et al., 2018) and word sense disambiguation (Rios et al., 2018). In contrast to the above test suites, our test suite is the only one that does such a systematic evaluation of more than one hundred phenomena. A direct comparison can be done with the latter related paper, since it focuses at the same language direction. Its authors use automated methods to extract text items, whereas in our test suite the test items are created manually.

Proceedings of the Fourth Conference on Machine Translation (WMT), Volume 2: Shared Task Papers (Day 1) pages 445–454
Florence, Italy, August 1-2, 2019. ©2019 Association for Computational Linguistics

3 Method

The test suite is a manually devised test set whose contents are chosen with the purpose to test the performance of the MT system on specific phenomena or requirements related to quality. For each phenomenon a subset of relevant test sentences is chosen manually. Then, each MT system is requested to translate the given subset and the performance of the system on the particular phenomenon is calculated based on the percentage of the phenomenon instances that have been properly translated.

For this paper we use the latest version of the DFKI Test Suite for MT on German to English. The test suite has been presented in (Burchardt et al., 2017) and applied extensively in last year's shared task (Macketanz et al., 2018b). The current version contains 5560 test sentences in order to control 107 phenomena organised in 14 categories. It is similar to the method used last year, with few minor corrections. The number of the test instances per phenomenon varies, ranging between a 20 and 180 sentences. A full list of the phenomena and their categories can be seen as part of the results in the Appendix. An example list of test sentences with correct and incorrect translations is available on GitHub[1].

3.1 Construction and application of the test suite

The construction and the application of the test suite follows the steps below, also indicated in Figure 1:

(a) Produce paradigms: A person with good knowledge of German and English grammar devises or selects a set of source language sentences that may trigger translation errors related to particular phenomena. These sentences may be written from scratch, inspired from previous observations on common MT errors or drawn from existing resources (Lehmann et al., 1996).

(b) Fetch sample translations: The source sentences are given as an input to easily accessible MT systems and their outputs are fetched.

(c) Write regular expressions: By inspecting the MT output for every given sentence, the annotator writes rules that control whether the output contains a correct translation regarding the respective phenomenon. The rules are written as positive or

Lexical Ambiguity	
Das Gericht gestern Abend war lecker.	
The court last night was delicious.	fail
The dish last night was delicious.	pass
Conditional	
Er würde einkaufen gehen, wenn die Geschäfte nicht geschlossen hätten.	
He would go shopping if the stores didn't close.	fail
He would go shopping if the shops hadn't closed.	pass
Passive voice	
Es wurde viel gefeiert und getanzt.	
A lot was celebrated and danced.	fail
There was a lot of celebration and dancing.	pass

Table 1: Examples of passing and failing MT outputs

negative regular expressions, that signify a correct or an incorrect translation respectively.

(d) Fetch more translations: When the test suite contains a sufficient number of test items with the respective control rules, the test suite is ready for its broad application. The test items are consequently given to a large number of MT systems. This is done in contact with their developers or through the submission process of a shared task, as is the case described in this paper.

(e) Apply regular expressions: The control rules are applied on the MT outputs in order to check whether the relevant phenomena have been translated properly. When the MT output matches a positive regular expression, the translation is considered correct (*pass*) whereas when the MT output matches a negative regular expression, the translation is considered incorrect (*fail*). Examples can be seen in Table 1. In case an MT output does not match either a positive or a negative regular expression, or in case these contradict to each other, the automatic evaluation results in a uncertain decision (*warning*).

(f) Resolve warnings and refine regular expressions: The *warnings* are given to the annotator, so that they manually resolve them and if possible refine the rules to address similar cases in the future. Through the iterative execution of steps (e) and (f) (which are an extension of steps (c) and (d) respectively) the rules get more robust and attain a better coverage. If needed, the annotator can add full sentences as rules, instead of regular expressions.

For every system we calculate the phenomenon-specific translation accuracy as the the number of the test sentences for the phenomenon which were translated properly, divided by the number of all test sentences for this phenomenon:

---

[1] https://github.com/DFKI-NLP/TQ_AutoTest

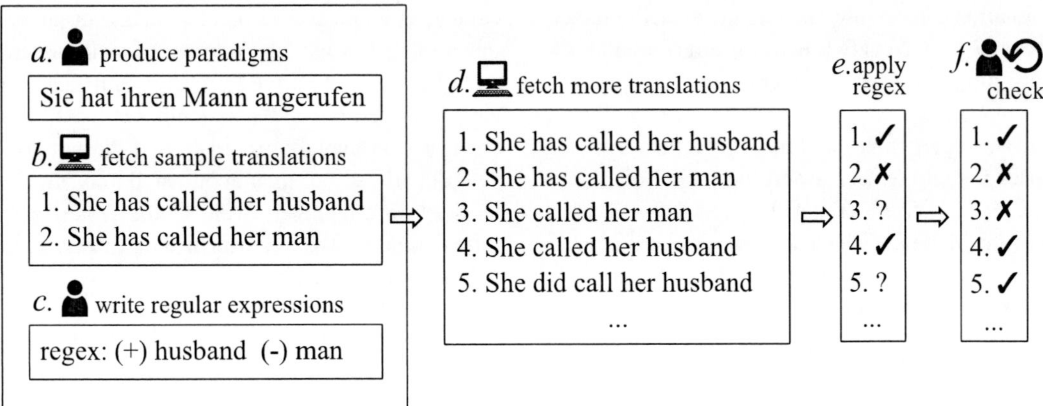

Figure 1: Example of the preparation and application of the test suite for one test sentence

$$accuracy = \frac{correct\ translations}{sum\ of\ test\ sentences}$$

When doing comparisons, the significance of every comparison is confirmed with a one-tailed Z-test with $\alpha = 0.95$.

3.2 Experiment Setup

In the evaluation presented in the paper, MT outputs are obtained from the 16 systems that are part of the *news translation task* of the Fourth Conference on Machine Translation (WMT19). According to the details that the developers have published by the time this paper is written, 10 of the systems are declared to be Neural Machine Translation (NMT) systems and 9 of them confirm that they follow the Transformer paradigm, whereas for the rest 6 systems no details were given. For the evaluation of the MT outputs the software TQ-AutoTest (Macketanz et al., 2018a) was used.

After processing the MT output for the 5560 items of the test suite, the automatic application of the regular expressions resulted to about 10% warnings. Consequently, one human annotator (student of linguistics) committed about 70 hours of work in order to reduce the warnings to 3%. The final results were calculated using 5393 test items, which, after the manual inspection, did not have any warning for any of the respective MT-outputs.

Since we applied the same test suite as last year, this year's automatic evaluation is profiting from the manual refinement of the regular expressions that took place then. The first application of the test suite in 2018 resulted in about 10-45% of warnings depending on the system, whereas after this year's application, we only had 8-28%. This year's

results are therefore based on 16% more valid test items, as compared to last year.

4 Results

The results of the test suite evaluation can be seen in Tables 3 and 4, where the significantly best systems for every category or phenomenon are bold-faced. The average accuracy per system is calculated either based on all test items (with the assumption that all items have equal importance) or based on the categories (with the assumption that all categories have equal importance). In any case, since the averages are calculated on an artificial test suite and not on a sample test set, one must be careful with their interpretation.

4.1 Linguistic categories

Despite the significant progress of NMT and the recent claims for human parity, the results in terms of the test suite are somewhat mediocre. The MT systems achieve 75.6% accuracy in average for all given test items, which indicates that one out of four test items is not translated properly. If one considers the categories separately, only five categories have an accuracy of more than 80%: **negation**, where there are hardly any mistakes, followed by **composition**, **function word**, **subordination** and **non-verbal agreement**. The lowest-performing categories are the **multi-word expressions** (MWE) and the **verb valency** with about 66% accuracy.

4.2 Linguistic phenomena

Most MT systems seem to struggle with **idioms**, since they could only translate properly only 11.6% of the ones in our test set, whereas a similar situation can be observed with resultative predicates (17.8%). **Negated modal pluperfect** and **modal pluperfect** have an accuracy of only 23-28%. Some of the phenomena have an accuracy of about 50%, in particular the domain-specific terms, the pseudo-cleft sentences and the modal of pluperfect subjunctive II (negated or not). We may assume that these phenomena are not correctly translated because they do not occur often enough in the training and development corpora.

On the other side, for quite a few phenomena an accuracy of more than 90% has been achieved. This includes several cases of verbs declination concerning the transitive, intransitive and ditransitive verbs mostly on perfect and future tenses, the passive voice, the polar question, the infinitive clause, the conditional, the focus particles, the location and the phrasal verbs.

4.3   Comparison between systems

As seen in Table 3, the system that significantly wins most categories is Facebook with 11 categories and an average of 87.5% (if all categories counted equally), followed by DFKI and RWTH which are in the best cluster for 10 categories. When it comes to averaging all test items, the best systems are RWTH and Online-A. On specific categories, the most clear results come in **punctuation** where NEU has the best performance with 100% accuracy, whereas Online-X has the worst with 31.7%. Concerning **ambiguity**, Facebook has the highest performance with 92.6% accuracy. In **verb tense/aspect/mood**, RWTH Aachen and Online-A have the highest performance with 84% accuracy, whereas in this category, MSRA.MADL has the lowest performance with 60.4%. For the rest of the categories there are small differences between the systems, since more than five systems fall into the same significance cluster of the best performance.

When looking into particular phenomena (Table 4), Facebook has the higher accuracy concerning **lexical ambiguity** with an accuracy of 93.7%. NEU and MSRA.MADL do best with more than 95% on **quotation marks**. The best system for translating **modal pluferect** is online-A with 75.6%, whereas at the same category, Online-Y and Online-G perform worse, with less than 2.2%. On **modal negated - preterite**, the best systems are RWTH and UCAM with more than 95%. On the contrary, MSRA.MADL achieves the worst ac-

curacy, as compared to other systems, in phenomena related to modals (perfect, present, preterite, negated modal Future I), where it mistranslates half of the test items. One system, Online-X, was the worst on quotation marks, as it did not convey properly any of them, compared to other systems that did relatively well. Online-Y also performs significantly worse than the other systems on domain-specific terms.

4.4   Comparison with last year's systems

One can attempt to do a vague comparison of the statistics between two consequent years (Table 2). Here, the last column indicates the percentage of improvement from the average accuracy of all systems from last year's shared task[2] to the average accuracy of all systems of this year. Although this is not entirely accurate, since different systems participate, we assume that the large amount of the test items allows some generalisations to this direction. When one compares the overall accuracy, there has been an improvement of about 6%. When focusing on particular categories, the biggest improvements are seen at function words (+12.5%), non-verbal agreement (+9.7%) and punctuation (+8%). The smallest improvement is seen at named entity and terminology (+0.3%).

We also attempt to perform comparisons of the systems which were submitted with the same name both years. Again, the comparison should be done under the consideration that the MT systems are different in many aspects, which are not possible to consider at the time this paper is written. The highest improvement is shown by the system Online-G, which has an average accuracy improvement of 18.7%, with most remarkable the one concerning negation, function words and non-verbal agreement. Online-A has also improved at composition, verb issues and non-verbal agreement and RWTH and UEDIN at punctuation. On the contrary, we can notice that UCAM deteriorated its accuracy for several categories, mostly for coordination and ellipsis (-13.1%), verb issues (-7.6%) and composition (-4.7%). JHU and Online-G and RWTH show some deterioration for three categories each, whereas Online-A seems to have worsened considerably regarding punctuation (-21.6%) and UEDIN regarding negation (-10.5%).

---

[2] unsupervised systems excluded

category	#	JHU	MLLP	onlA	onlB	onlG	onlY	RWTH	UCAM	UEDIN	avg
Ambiguity	74	-2.7	21.6	4.1	0.0	4.1	10.8	-1.3	2.7	12.1	6.9
Composition	42	4.8	0.0	14.3	0.0	9.5	2.4	-2.4	-4.7	7.1	5.2
Coordination and ellipsis	23	8.7	-4.4	0.0	0.0	13.1	0.0	0.0	-13.1	0.0	7.3
False friends	34	-3.0	5.8	0.0	3.0	-5.9	23.6	5.9	-5.8	14.7	6.8
Function word	41	-2.5	7.3	4.9	0.0	41.4	0.0	-7.4	-2.4	9.7	12.5
LDD & interrogatives	38	10.6	10.6	-2.7	0.0	5.3	0.0	0.0	5.3	7.9	5.6
MWE	53	5.6	7.5	5.7	0.0	1.9	1.9	3.8	-1.8	3.8	4.7
Named entity and terminology	34	5.9	3.0	5.9	0.0	-3.0	-5.9	8.9	0.0	5.9	0.3
Negation	19	0.0	0.0	0.0	0.0	42.1	0.0	0.0	0.0	-10.5	6.6
Non-verbal agreement	48	12.5	10.4	12.5	0.0	22.9	2.1	-2.1	0.0	12.5	9.7
Punctuation	51	5.9	2.0	-21.6	0.0	-7.9	1.9	27.5	0.0	23.5	8.0
Subordination	31	3.3	6.5	-6.5	3.2	19.4	3.2	6.5	0.0	0.0	5.0
Verb tense/aspect/mood	3995	-4.0	-5.9	12.9	0.2	19.8	1.6	5.6	-7.6	5.1	6.0
Verb valency	30	10.0	0.0	0.0	0.0	13.4	6.6	0.0	0.0	3.4	5.8
average (items)	4513	-3.1	-4.3	11.6	0.2	18.7	2.0	5.3	-6.8	5.4	6.1
average (categories)		3.9	4.6	2.1	0.5	12.6	3.4	3.2	-2.0	6.8	6.5

Table 2: Percentage (%) of accuracy improvement or deterioration between WMT18 and WMT19 for all the systems submitted (averaged in last column) and the systems submitted with the same name

5 Conclusion and Further Work

The application of the test suite results in a multitude of findings of minor or major importance. Despite the recent advances, state-of-the-art German→English MT still translates erroneously one out of four test items of our test suite, indicating that there is still room for improvement. For instance, one can note the low performance on MWE and verb valency, whereas there are issues with idioms, resultative predicates and modals. Function words, non verbal agreement and punctuation on the other side have significantly improved.

One potential benefit of the test suite would be to investigate the implication of particular development settings and design decisions on particular phenomena. For some superficial issues, such as punctuation, this would be relatively easy, as pre- and post-processing steps may be responsible. But for more complex phenomena, further comparative analysis of settings is needed. Unfortunately, this was hard to achieve for this shared task due to the heterogeneity of the systems, but also due to the fact that at the time this paper was written, no exact details about the systems were known. We aim at looking further on such an analysis in future steps.

Acknowledgments

This research was supported by the German Federal Ministry of Education and Research through the projects DEEPLEE (01IW17001) and BBDC2 (01IS18025E).

References

Ondej Bojar, Rajen Chatterjee, Christian Federmann, Mark Fishel, Yvette Graham, Barry Haddow, Matthias Huck, Antonio Jimeno Yepes, Philipp Koehn, Christof Monz, Matteo Negri, Aurélie Névéol, Mariana Neves, Matt Post, Lucia Specia, Marco Turchi, and Karin Verspoor, editors. 2018a. *Proceedings of the Third Conference on Machine Translation*. Association for Computational Linguistics, Belgium, Brussels.

Ondej Bojar, Jií Mírovský, Kateina Rysová, and Magdaléna Rysová. 2018b. EvalD Reference-Less Discourse Evaluation for WMT18. In *Proceedings of the Third Conference on Machine Translation*, pages 545–549, Belgium, Brussels. Association for Computational Linguistics.

Aljoscha Burchardt, Vivien Macketanz, Jon Dehdari, Georg Heigold, Jan-Thorsten Peter, and Philip Williams. 2017. A Linguistic Evaluation of Rule-Based, Phrase-Based, and Neural MT Engines. *The Prague Bulletin of Mathematical Linguistics*, 108:159–170.

Franck Burlot, Yves Scherrer, Vinit Ravishankar, Ondej Bojar, Stig-Arne Grönroos, Maarit Koponen, Tommi Nieminen, and François Yvon. 2018. The WMT'18 Morpheval test suites for English-Czech, English-German, English-Finnish and Turkish-English. In *Proceedings of the Third Conference on Machine Translation*, pages 550–564, Belgium, Brussels. Association for Computational Linguistics.

Chris Callison-Burch, Cameron Fordyce, Philipp Koehn, Christof Monz, and Josh Schroeder. 2007. (Meta-) evaluation of machine translation. In *Proceedings of the Second Workshop on Statistical Machine Translation*, pages 136–158, Prague, Czech Republic. Association for Computational Linguistics.

Silvie Cinkova and Ondej Bojar. 2018. Testsuite on Czech–English Grammatical Contrasts. In *Proceedings of the Third Conference on Machine Translation*, pages 565–575, Belgium, Brussels. Association for Computational Linguistics.

Liane Guillou and Christian Hardmeier. 2016. PROTEST: A Test Suite for Evaluating Pronouns in Machine Translation. *Tenth International Conference on Lan- guage Resources and Evaluation (LREC 2016)*.

Liane Guillou, Christian Hardmeier, Ekaterina Lapshinova-Koltunski, and Sharid Loáiciga. 2018. A Pronoun Test Suite Evaluation of the English–German MT Systems at WMT 2018. In *Proceedings of the Third Conference on Machine Translation*, pages 576–583, Belgium, Brussels. Association for Computational Linguistics.

Pierre Isabelle, Colin Cherry, and George Foster. 2017. A Challenge Set Approach to Evaluating Machine Translation. In *EMNLP 2017: Conference on Empirical Methods in Natural Language Processing*, Copenhagen, Denmark. Association for Computational Linguistics.

Sabine Lehmann, Stephan Oepen, Sylvie Regnier-Prost, Klaus Netter, Veronika Lux, Judith Klein, Kirsten Falkedal, Frederik Fouvry, Dominique Estival, Eva Dauphin, Herve Compagnion, Judith Baur, Lorna Balkan, and Doug Arnold. 1996. TSNLP - Test Suites for Natural Language Processing. *Proceedings of the 16th ...*, page 7.

Arle Lommel, Aljoscha Burchardt, Maja Popović, Kim Harris, Eleftherios Avramidis, and Hans Uszkoreit. 2014. Using a new analytic measure for the annotation and analysis of MT errors on real data. In *Proceedings of the 17th Annual Conference of the European Association for Machine Translation*, pages 165–172. Croatian Language Technologies Society, European Association for Machine Translation.

Vivien Macketanz, Renlong Ai, Aljoscha Burchardt, and Hans Uszkoreit. 2018a. TQ-AutoTest An Automated Test Suite for (Machine) Translation Quality. In *Proceedings of the Eleventh International Conference on Language Resources and Evaluation. International Conference on Language Resources and Evaluation (LREC-2018), 11th, May 7-12, Miyazaki, Japan*. European Language Resources Association (ELRA).

Vivien Macketanz, Eleftherios Avramidis, Aljoscha Burchardt, and Hans Uszkoreit. 2018b. Fine-grained evaluation of German-English Machine Translation based on a Test Suite. In *Proceedings of the Third Conference on Machine Translation (WMT18)*, Brussels, Belgium. Association for Computational Linguistics.

Maja Popović. 2011. Hjerson: An Open Source Tool for Automatic Error Classification of Machine Translation Output. *The Prague Bulletin of Mathematical Linguistics*, 96(-1):59–68.

Annette Rios, Mathias Müller, and Rico Sennrich. 2018. The Word Sense Disambiguation Test Suite at WMT18. In *Proceedings of the Third Conference on Machine Translation*, pages 594–602, Belgium, Brussels. Association for Computational Linguistics.

Matthew Snover, Nitin Madnani, Bonnie J Dorr, and Richard Schwartz. 2009. Fluency, adequacy, or HTER?: exploring different human judgments with a tunable MT metric. In *Proceedings of the Fourth Workshop on Statistical Machine Translation*, number March in StatMT '09, pages 259–268, Stroudsburg, PA, USA. Association for Computational Linguistics.

A Appendices

	#	DFKI	FB	JHU	MMLP	MSRA	NEU	onlA	onlB	onlG	onlX	onlY	PROMT	RWTH	Tartu	UCAM	UEDIN	avg
Ambiguity	81	70.4	**92.6**	64.2	76.5	80.2	75.3	69.1	76.5	72.8	50.6	76.5	48.1	77.8	60.5	75.3	59.3	70.4
Composition	48	**93.8**	**97.9**	87.5	85.4	83.3	87.5	**93.8**	**95.8**	83.3	58.3	**93.8**	81.2	85.4	81.2	**89.6**	87.5	86.6
Coordination & ellipsis	74	**85.1**	**89.2**	**78.4**	**85.1**	75.7	**81.1**	**85.1**	**85.1**	60.8	**79.7**	**78.4**	74.3	**86.5**	68.9	**78.4**	**81.1**	79.6
False friends	36	72.2	75.0	55.6	63.9	63.9	55.6	72.2	**77.8**	72.2	72.2	**91.7**	72.2	72.2	55.6	58.3	66.7	68.6
Function word	60	**88.3**	**91.7**	78.3	**91.7**	83.3	**90.0**	**88.3**	80.0	**90.0**	65.0	**88.3**	**85.0**	83.3	76.7	**88.3**	**88.3**	84.8
LDD & interrogatives	160	**82.5**	**85.0**	79.4	**82.5**	81.2	81.2	73.1	**78.8**	66.2	63.1	75.6	71.2	**83.8**	76.2	**85.0**	69.4	77.1
MWE	77	68.8	**77.9**	64.9	66.2	66.2	67.5	67.5	70.1	68.8	48.1	**71.4**	55.8	**70.1**	61.0	**63.6**	62.3	65.7
Named entity & terminology	87	**80.5**	**82.8**	**83.9**	81.6	82.8	79.3	81.6	**85.1**	66.7	48.3	**82.8**	64.4	**85.1**	79.3	**80.5**	**83.9**	78.0
Negation	20	100.0	100.0	100.0	100.0	95.0	100.0	100.0	95.0	100.0	100.0	100.0	90.0	100.0	100.0	100.0	90.0	98.1
Non-verbal agreement	61	85.2	**91.8**	83.6	**88.5**	86.9	78.7	83.6	86.9	80.3	65.6	80.3	70.5	**82.0**	80.3	78.7	**82.0**	81.6
Punctuation	60	85.0	**93.3**	70.0	68.3	95.0	**100.0**	76.7	76.7	58.3	31.7	80.0	83.3	88.3	91.7	58.3	90.0	77.9
Subordination	168	**89.3**	**89.9**	88.7	**89.9**	88.1	85.7	75.6	85.7	83.3	70.8	86.3	79.2	**88.7**	83.9	**89.9**	76.2	84.4
Verb tense/aspect/mood	4375	77.1	79.4	70.3	78.8	60.4	77.1	**84.1**	74.3	66.2	70.2	72.7	75.4	**83.9**	71.7	79.2	81.4	75.1
Verb valency	86	**72.1**	**79.1**	68.6	**67.4**	70.9	66.3	67.4	68.6	67.4	55.8	**66.3**	54.7	**72.1**	62.8	**68.6**	60.5	66.8
average (items)	5393	78.0	80.9	71.6	79.2	64.3	77.7	**82.8**	75.5	67.5	68.4	74.1	74.4	**83.6**	72.3	79.2	80.2	75.6
average (categories)	5393	82.2	**87.5**	76.7	80.4	79.5	80.4	79.9	81.2	74.0	62.8	81.7	71.8	82.8	75.0	78.1	77.0	78.2

Table 3: Accuracies of successful translations for 16 systems and 14 categories. Boldface indicates significantly best systems in each row

	#	DFKI	FB	JHU	MLLP	MSRA	NEU	onlA	onlB	onlG	onlX	onlY	PROMT	RWTH	Tartu	UCAM	UEDIN	avg
Ambiguity	81	70.4	**92.6**	64.2	76.5	80.2	75.3	69.1	76.5	72.8	50.6	76.5	48.1	77.8	60.5	75.3	59.3	70.4
Lexical ambiguity	63	73.0	**93.7**	65.1	77.8	81.0	74.6	73.0	82.5	79.4	55.6	82.5	50.8	81.0	58.7	76.2	66.7	73.2
Structural ambiguity	18	61.1	**88.9**	61.1	**72.2**	**77.8**	**77.8**	55.6	55.6	50.0	33.3	55.6	38.9	**66.7**	**66.7**	**72.2**	33.3	60.4
Composition	48	**93.8**	**97.9**	87.5	85.4	83.3	87.5	**93.8**	**95.8**	83.3	58.3	**93.8**	81.2	85.4	81.2	**89.6**	87.5	86.6
Compound	28	**92.9**	**96.4**	82.1	78.6	78.6	82.1	**92.9**	**96.4**	82.1	50.0	**89.3**	67.9	82.1	85.7	**92.9**	78.6	83.0
Phrasal verb	20	95.0	**100.0**	95.0	95.0	90.0	95.0	95.0	95.0	85.0	70.0	**100.0**	**100.0**	90.0	75.0	85.0	**100.0**	91.6
Coordination & ellipsis	74	**85.1**	**89.2**	78.4	**85.1**	75.7	**81.1**	**85.1**	**85.1**	60.8	**79.7**	**78.4**	74.3	**86.5**	68.9	**78.4**	**81.1**	79.6
Gapping	19	**94.7**	**100.0**	**94.7**	**100.0**	**100.0**	89.5	89.5	89.5	57.9	89.5	73.7	73.7	**94.7**	78.9	**94.7**	89.5	88.2
Right node raising	20	**80.0**	**85.0**	80.0	75.0	55.0	85.0	85.0	85.0	50.0	70.0	75.0	70.0	80.0	60.0	60.0	60.0	72.2
Sluicing	18	88.9	88.9	83.3	88.9	88.9	88.9	88.9	88.9	83.3	77.8	88.9	83.3	88.9	88.9	88.9	88.9	87.2
Stripping	17	76.5	**82.4**	52.9	76.5	58.8	58.8	76.5	76.5	52.9	**82.4**	76.5	70.6	**82.4**	47.1	70.6	**88.2**	70.6
False friends	36	72.2	75.0	55.6	63.9	63.9	55.6	72.2	**77.8**	72.2	72.2	**91.7**	72.2	72.2	55.6	58.3	66.7	68.6
Function word	60	**88.3**	**91.7**	78.3	**91.7**	83.3	**90.0**	**88.3**	80.0	**90.0**	65.0	**88.3**	**85.0**	83.3	76.7	**88.3**	**88.3**	84.8
Focus particle	20	95.0	**100.0**	95.0	90.0	**100.0**	95.0	85.0	95.0	90.0	85.0	95.0	85.0	95.0	95.0	95.0	**100.0**	93.4
Modal particle	22	**81.8**	**81.8**	**81.8**	**86.4**	72.7	**81.8**	**81.8**	77.3	**90.9**	63.6	**81.8**	**86.4**	68.2	**77.3**	**77.3**	68.2	78.7
Question tag	18	88.9	**94.4**	55.6	**100.0**	77.8	**94.4**	**100.0**	66.7	88.9	44.4	**88.9**	83.3	88.9	55.6	**94.4**	**100.0**	82.6
LDD & interrogatives	160	**82.5**	**85.0**	79.4	**82.5**	81.2	81.2	73.1	**78.8**	66.2	63.1	75.6	71.2	**83.8**	76.2	**85.0**	69.4	77.1

	#	DFKI	FB	JHU	MLLP	MSRA	NEU	onlA	onlB	onlG	onlX	onlY	PROMT	RWTH	Tartu	UCAM	UEDIN	avg
Extended adjective construction	18	83.3	83.3	66.7	83.3	61.1	77.8	66.7	66.7	44.4	38.9	66.7	61.1	83.3	61.1	72.2	66.7	67.7
Extraposition	18	44.4	61.1	55.6	55.6	72.2	66.7	55.6	61.1	50.0	50.0	61.1	66.7	61.1	55.6	61.1	55.6	58.3
Multiple connectors	20	90.0	85.0	80.0	80.0	80.0	85.0	75.0	75.0	65.0	80.0	55.0	85.0	85.0	85.0	85.0	70.0	78.8
Pied-piping	19	84.2	84.2	89.5	78.9	89.5	84.2	78.9	73.7	73.7	52.6	84.2	73.7	84.2	68.4	94.7	73.7	79.3
Polar question	19	100.0	100.0	100.0	100.0	100.0	89.5	84.2	100.0	84.2	100.0	94.7	94.7	100.0	100.0	100.0	84.2	95.7
Scrambling	17	76.5	88.2	70.6	76.5	76.5	70.6	52.9	70.6	64.7	29.4	70.6	29.4	64.7	70.6	88.2	35.3	64.7
Topicalization	18	83.3	83.3	77.8	83.3	77.8	72.2	61.1	77.8	66.7	66.7	66.7	61.1	88.9	66.7	83.3	55.6	73.3
Wh-movement	31	90.3	90.3	87.1	93.5	87.1	93.5	93.5	93.5	74.2	74.2	93.5	83.9	93.5	90.3	90.3	93.5	88.9
MWE	77	68.8	77.9	64.9	66.2	66.2	67.5	67.5	70.1	68.8	48.1	71.4	55.8	70.1	61.0	63.6	62.3	65.7
Collocation	19	68.4	94.7	57.9	68.4	78.9	73.7	78.9	84.2	78.9	52.6	89.5	57.9	73.7	63.2	57.9	63.2	71.4
Idiom	20	15.0	20.0	15.0	5.0	15.0	5.0	15.0	15.0	10.0	10.0	10.0	5.0	20.0	10.0	5.0	10.0	11.6
Prepositional MWE	19	100.0	100.0	100.0	94.7	89.5	100.0	84.2	94.7	94.7	57.9	89.5	73.7	100.0	78.9	100.0	89.5	90.5
Verbal MWE	19	94.7	100.0	89.5	100.0	84.2	94.7	94.7	89.5	94.7	73.7	100.0	89.5	89.5	94.7	94.7	89.5	92.1
Named entity & terminology	87	80.5	82.8	83.9	81.6	82.8	79.3	81.6	85.1	66.7	48.3	82.8	64.4	85.1	79.3	80.5	83.9	78.0
Date	20	85.0	90.0	90.0	95.0	95.0	90.0	95.0	95.0	50.0	55.0	95.0	50.0	90.0	95.0	95.0	95.0	85.0
Domainspecific term	19	57.9	68.4	63.2	52.6	57.9	52.6	52.6	68.4	42.1	21.1	47.4	36.8	68.4	52.6	57.9	57.9	53.6
Location	20	95.0	95.0	100.0	95.0	90.0	90.0	100.0	90.0	80.0	65.0	90.0	90.0	95.0	90.0	95.0	100.0	91.2
Measuring unit	19	84.2	84.2	94.7	89.5	89.5	89.5	89.5	89.5	89.5	63.2	100.0	89.5	94.7	78.9	78.9	100.0	87.8
Proper name	9	77.8	66.7	55.6	66.7	77.8	66.7	55.6	77.8	77.8	22.2	77.8	44.4	66.7	77.8	66.7	44.4	63.9
Negation	20	100.0	100.0	100.0	100.0	95.0	100.0	100.0	95.0	100.0	100.0	100.0	90.0	100.0	100.0	100.0	90.0	98.1
Non-verbal agreement	61	85.2	91.8	83.6	88.5	86.9	78.7	83.6	86.9	80.3	65.6	80.3	70.5	82.0	80.3	78.7	82.0	81.6
Coreference	20	75.0	85.0	75.0	80.0	80.0	65.0	75.0	70.0	65.0	45.0	65.0	65.0	65.0	70.0	70.0	80.0	70.6
External possessor	21	85.7	95.2	76.2	90.5	81.0	76.2	81.0	90.5	81.0	61.9	81.0	57.1	85.7	81.0	71.4	71.4	79.2
Internal possessor	20	95.0	95.0	100.0	95.0	100.0	95.0	95.0	100.0	95.0	90.0	95.0	90.0	95.0	90.0	95.0	95.0	95.0
Punctuation	60	85.0	93.3	70.0	68.3	95.0	100.0	76.7	76.7	58.3	31.7	80.0	83.3	88.3	91.7	58.3	90.0	77.9
Comma	20	100.0	100.0	100.0	95.0	95.0	100.0	100.0	95.0	95.0	95.0	100.0	100.0	100.0	95.0	100.0	95.0	97.8
Quotation marks	40	77.5	90.0	55.0	55.0	95.0	100.0	65.0	67.5	40.0	0.0	70.0	75.0	82.5	90.0	37.5	87.5	68.0
Subordination	168	89.3	89.9	88.7	89.9	88.1	85.7	75.6	85.7	83.3	70.8	86.3	79.2	88.7	83.9	89.9	76.2	84.4
Adverbial clause	20	90.0	90.0	95.0	90.0	95.0	90.0	85.0	90.0	90.0	75.0	95.0	90.0	95.0	80.0	90.0	85.0	89.1
Cleft sentence	19	94.7	94.7	94.7	94.7	100.0	94.7	84.2	89.5	84.2	84.2	84.2	78.9	100.0	94.7	100.0	89.5	91.4
Free relative clause	18	94.4	83.3	83.3	94.4	94.4	94.4	94.4	88.9	88.9	94.4	88.9	94.4	94.4	88.9	88.9	94.4	91.3
Indirect speech	19	73.7	84.2	89.5	89.5	73.7	68.4	42.1	94.7	84.2	57.9	73.7	63.2	78.9	42.1	84.2	36.8	71.1
Infinitive clause	20	100.0	100.0	95.0	90.0	100.0	90.0	85.0	95.0	95.0	90.0	100.0	90.0	100.0	100.0	100.0	85.0	94.7
Object clause	20	95.0	100.0	90.0	95.0	95.0	95.0	85.0	95.0	95.0	85.0	90.0	85.0	95.0	85.0	95.0	90.0	91.9
Pseudo-cleft sentence	18	66.7	72.2	66.7	72.2	61.1	55.6	22.2	50.0	55.6	22.2	61.1	44.4	55.6	77.8	61.1	22.2	54.2
Relative clause	18	94.4	83.3	83.3	94.4	77.8	83.3	83.3	77.8	77.8	83.3	94.4	83.3	83.3	88.9	88.9	88.9	85.4
Subject clause	16	93.8	100.0	100.0	87.5	93.8	100.0	100.0	87.5	75.0	37.5	87.5	81.2	93.8	100.0	100.0	93.8	89.5
Verb tense/aspect/mood	4375	77.1	79.4	70.3	78.8	60.4	77.1	84.1	74.3	66.2	70.2	72.7	75.4	83.9	71.7	79.2	81.4	75.1
Conditional	19	100.0	89.5	84.2	100.0	89.5	100.0	94.7	100.0	89.5	68.4	100.0	94.7	100.0	84.2	100.0	100.0	93.4
Ditransitive - future I	36	100.0	100.0	100.0	100.0	97.2	83.3	100.0	100.0	91.7	100.0	100.0	100.0	100.0	94.4	83.3	100.0	96.9
Ditransitive - future I subjunctive II	36	100.0	100.0	91.7	100.0	100.0	80.6	100.0	97.2	97.2	100.0	100.0	97.2	100.0	88.9	83.3	97.2	95.8
Ditransitive - future II	36	83.3	100.0	58.3	100.0	86.1	83.3	86.1	100.0	72.2	63.9	50.0	77.8	100.0	97.2	83.3	80.6	82.6
Ditransitive - future II subjunctive II	36	83.3	100.0	100.0	100.0	94.4	83.3	83.3	100.0	80.6	100.0	100.0	97.2	100.0	91.7	83.3	77.8	92.2

	#	DFKI	FB	JHU	MLLP	MSRA	NEU	onlA	onlB	onlG	onlX	onlY	PROMT	RWTH	Tartu	UCAM	UEDIN	avg
Ditransitive - perfect	36	86.1	**97.2**	**100.0**	**100.0**	**100.0**	83.3	**100.0**	**100.0**	88.9	**94.4**	**97.2**	**100.0**	**100.0**	**100.0**	83.3	**100.0**	95.7
Ditransitive - pluperfect	35	48.6	**100.0**	51.4	60.0	82.9	57.1	91.4	45.7	25.7	25.7	20.0	51.4	91.4	80.0	77.1	74.3	61.4
Ditransitive - pluperfect subjunctive II	36	83.3	**100.0**	**97.2**	**94.4**	**100.0**	86.1	**100.0**	77.8	88.9	**100.0**	**94.4**	**94.4**	**100.0**	86.1	83.3	**94.4**	92.5
Ditransitive - present	36	**94.4**	**100.0**	**97.2**	86.1	**97.2**	86.1	**100.0**	**100.0**	61.1	88.9	72.2	63.9	**97.2**	66.7	77.8	**100.0**	86.8
Ditransitive - preterite	35	80.0	**94.3**	71.4	68.6	65.7	71.4	68.6	**85.7**	77.1	60.0	**85.7**	62.9	**85.7**	74.3	65.7	62.9	73.8
Ditransitive - preterite subjunctive II	36	69.4	75.0	63.9	58.3	63.9	58.3	58.3	69.4	69.4	52.8	72.2	58.3	72.2	72.2	55.6	52.8	63.9
Imperative	20	**70.0**	**85.0**	**70.0**	65.0	65.0	**70.0**	**70.0**	**85.0**	**85.0**	60.0	**85.0**	50.0	80.0	60.0	**65.0**	60.0	70.3
Intransitive - future I	36	**97.2**	**97.2**	**97.2**	**97.2**	88.9	**97.2**	**100.0**	**100.0**	**100.0**	**100.0**	**100.0**	**100.0**	**97.2**	**97.2**	**97.2**	**94.4**	97.6
Intransitive - future I subjunctive II	36	**100.0**	**100.0**	80.6	**100.0**	77.8	**100.0**	**100.0**	**100.0**	**100.0**	**100.0**	**100.0**	**100.0**	**100.0**	91.7	**100.0**	**100.0**	96.9
Intransitive - future II	42	92.9	**100.0**	57.1	90.5	85.7	92.9	**97.6**	81.0	88.1	78.6	**100.0**	**97.6**	95.2	85.7	85.7	85.7	88.4
Intransitive - future II subjunctive II	36	**97.2**	**100.0**	83.3	75.0	88.9	91.7	**100.0**	**100.0**	77.8	**100.0**	**100.0**	**100.0**	88.9	83.3	75.0	83.3	90.3
Intransitive - perfect	80	**97.5**	92.5	90.0	**97.5**	88.8	93.8	**98.8**	**98.8**	**97.5**	**100.0**	**100.0**	**97.5**	**98.8**	85.0	**98.8**	90.0	95.3
Intransitive - pluperfect	36	**83.3**	77.8	30.6	75.0	58.3	66.7	**94.4**	47.2	19.4	44.4	16.7	55.6	**83.3**	63.9	80.6	80.6	61.1
Intransitive - pluperfect subjunctive II	36	**97.2**	**100.0**	77.8	**100.0**	91.7	**94.4**	**100.0**	**100.0**	88.9	**100.0**	**97.2**	86.1	**94.4**	72.2	91.7	80.6	92.0
Intransitive - present	36	**100.0**	**100.0**	**97.2**	**100.0**	52.8	**100.0**	**97.2**	**97.2**	**97.2**	**100.0**	**97.2**	**94.4**	**100.0**	91.7	**100.0**	**94.4**	95.0
Intransitive - preterite	65	80.0	**96.9**	70.8	73.8	67.7	76.9	81.5	86.2	80.0	69.2	**96.9**	75.4	**93.8**	69.2	89.2	72.3	80.0
Intransitive - preterite subjunctive II	35	**65.7**	**80.0**	**60.0**	**62.9**	51.4	**68.6**	62.9	65.7	**71.4**	42.9	**71.4**	54.3	**62.9**	51.4	**71.4**	**65.7**	63.0
Modal - future I	180	76.1	**77.2**	75.6	71.1	61.1	**84.4**	80.0	74.4	65.0	**79.4**	**78.3**	80.0	**78.3**	73.3	**79.4**	**80.0**	75.9
Modal - future I subjunctive II	173	74.6	71.7	76.9	71.7	38.7	**81.5**	**82.7**	71.1	65.3	79.2	72.3	72.8	**82.7**	61.3	77.5	**87.9**	73.0
Modal - perfect	168	88.7	73.2	72.6	83.3	34.5	83.9	62.5	69.0	73.2	42.3	91.7	85.7	**98.8**	78.0	79.2	66.1	73.9
Modal - pluperfect	179	20.1	29.1	11.2	40.2	7.3	22.9	**76.5**	30.7	1.7	7.3	2.2	34.1	49.7	17.9	46.4	58.1	28.5
Modal - pluperfect subjunctive II	178	**57.3**	52.8	**55.6**	**59.6**	41.0	**59.6**	**59.6**	52.2	42.7	52.2	**49.4**	60.7	56.2	52.8	59.0	**59.6**	54.4
Modal - present	179	90.5	**94.4**	92.2	**93.3**	48.6	86.6	**94.4**	**96.6**	59.8	**94.4**	77.7	88.8	**95.0**	85.5	**92.7**	**96.1**	86.7
Modal - preterite	179	95.5	**97.2**	86.6	96.6	52.0	89.4	93.9	95.0	89.4	95.0	**99.4**	89.4	**99.4**	86.0	**99.4**	81.6	90.4
Modal - preterite subjunctive II	173	**75.7**	**76.3**	**72.8**	**73.4**	48.6	**73.4**	**78.6**	**72.8**	**71.7**	**77.5**	**74.0**	**74.0**	**80.3**	64.7	**71.7**	**76.9**	72.7
Modal negated - future I	177	**76.3**	**78.0**	**75.7**	**75.1**	45.8	**81.4**	**80.2**	70.1	69.5	**80.2**	70.1	**80.2**	**78.5**	**75.7**	**79.7**	**81.4**	74.9
Modal negated - future I subjunctive II	175	78.3	71.4	76.6	77.7	60.6	83.4	84.0	69.7	67.4	81.7	72.0	78.9	81.7	69.7	81.7	**90.9**	76.6
Modal negated - perfect	175	93.1	73.1	80.6	92.6	65.1	83.4	91.4	69.1	68.0	77.1	70.9	86.9	**97.1**	76.6	79.4	89.7	80.9
Modal negated - pluperfect	173	10.4	13.9	0.0	34.7	8.7	6.4	**97.1**	16.8	0.0	20.8	0.0	15.6	46.2	9.2	16.2	80.3	23.5
Modal negated - pluperfect subjunctive II	170	51.2	60.0	32.9	**64.1**	51.2	63.5	**68.8**	33.5	38.2	43.5	50.0	**64.1**	65.3	58.8	**68.8**	**70.6**	55.3
Modal negated - present	177	**99.4**	96.0	90.4	**97.7**	71.2	96.6	**97.2**	68.9	72.3	77.4	67.2	92.7	96.6	83.6	**98.9**	96.0	87.6
Modal negated - preterite	178	93.8	96.6	83.7	98.3	79.8	89.3	98.3	96.1	81.5	93.8	94.4	88.2	**100.0**	91.0	**99.4**	83.1	91.7
Modal negated - preterite subjunctive II	171	66.7	**74.3**	64.9	**69.6**	67.3	**73.7**	**76.6**	**72.5**	66.1	**75.4**	69.0	70.2	**77.2**	**73.7**	**73.7**	**77.8**	71.8
Progressive	20	65.0	**85.0**	60.0	**70.0**	**80.0**	45.0	50.0	**60.0**	**60.0**	55.0	**80.0**	45.0	55.0	**65.0**	**70.0**	**60.0**	62.8
Reflexive - future I	32	**87.5**	**93.8**	**87.5**	**90.6**	**87.5**	**87.5**	81.2	**93.8**	81.2	65.6	**90.6**	81.2	**81.2**	75.0	**84.4**	**90.6**	85.0
Reflexive - future I subjunctive II	36	75.0	**88.9**	72.2	**80.6**	**80.6**	83.3	69.4	**91.7**	83.3	**80.6**	**91.7**	77.8	66.7	72.2	**80.6**	75.0	79.3
Reflexive - future II	33	75.8	**84.8**	33.3	78.8	66.7	**90.9**	69.7	**87.9**	48.5	33.3	81.8	57.6	**97.0**	72.7	81.8	**90.9**	72.0
Reflexive - future II subjunctive II	34	**82.4**	**94.1**	70.6	70.6	67.6	**85.3**	67.6	**88.2**	61.8	47.1	**88.2**	70.6	76.5	73.5	**82.4**	64.7	74.4
Reflexive - perfect	32	**96.9**	**90.6**	68.8	**90.6**	**84.4**	**93.8**	78.1	**93.8**	68.8	68.8	**87.5**	68.8	**87.5**	81.2	**84.4**	**96.9**	83.8
Reflexive - pluperfect	31	74.2	80.6	71.0	80.6	67.7	**96.8**	74.2	**93.5**	67.7	22.6	80.6	64.5	**83.9**	**93.5**	77.4	**90.3**	76.2
Reflexive - pluperfect subjunctive II	34	76.5	**79.4**	**79.4**	76.5	67.6	**79.4**	61.8	76.5	**79.4**	47.1	**79.4**	61.8	70.6	67.6	**79.4**	**82.4**	72.8
Reflexive - present	35	80.0	**82.9**	77.1	65.7	65.7	**91.4**	**82.9**	**94.3**	54.3	57.1	80.0	57.1	68.6	71.4	80.0	**82.9**	74.5
Reflexive - preterite	32	75.0	**96.9**	50.0	78.1	56.2	71.9	68.8	**84.4**	**84.4**	25.0	**87.5**	46.9	75.0	75.0	81.2	68.8	70.3

	#	DFKI	FB	JHU	MLLP	MSRA	NEU	onlA	onlB	onlG	onlX	onlY	PROMT	RWTH	Tartu	UCAM	UEDIN	avg
Reflexive - preterite subjunctive II	34	**70.6**	**88.2**	47.1	**73.5**	44.1	61.8	58.8	**76.5**	**73.5**	20.6	**82.4**	47.1	**76.5**	**73.5**	**73.5**	58.8	64.2
Transitive - future I	41	100.0	100.0	100.0	100.0	97.6	100.0	100.0	100.0	100.0	100.0	100.0	100.0	100.0	100.0	100.0	100.0	99.8
Transitive - future I subjunctive II	36	100.0	100.0	97.2	100.0	100.0	100.0	100.0	100.0	100.0	100.0	100.0	100.0	100.0	97.2	100.0	100.0	99.7
Transitive - future II	36	**100.0**	**100.0**	86.1	**100.0**	94.4	**100.0**	**100.0**	**100.0**	**100.0**	91.7	**100.0**	**100.0**	**100.0**	94.4	**100.0**	**97.2**	97.7
Transitive - future II subjunctive II	36	**100.0**	**100.0**	**100.0**	83.3	94.4	**100.0**	**100.0**	**100.0**	**100.0**	**94.4**	**100.0**	**100.0**	**100.0**	94.4	**100.0**	83.3	96.9
Transitive - perfect	41	**95.1**	**100.0**	**100.0**	**100.0**	**100.0**	97.6	**100.0**	**100.0**	**100.0**	92.7	**100.0**	87.8	**100.0**	**100.0**	**100.0**	**100.0**	98.3
Transitive - pluperfect	36	**100.0**	**100.0**	72.2	69.4	**100.0**	80.6	**100.0**	72.2	44.4	91.7	41.7	83.3	**100.0**	91.7	**100.0**	88.9	83.5
Transitive - pluperfect subjunctive II	36	**94.4**	**100.0**	**97.2**	**97.2**	**100.0**	**100.0**	**100.0**	**94.4**	**97.2**	**97.2**	**100.0**	**97.2**	**100.0**	91.7	**100.0**	**97.2**	97.7
Transitive - present	48	**100.0**	**100.0**	**100.0**	**100.0**	97.9	**100.0**	97.9	**100.0**	93.8	**97.9**	95.8	**97.9**	**100.0**	85.4	**100.0**	**100.0**	97.9
Transitive - preterite	36	86.1	**97.2**	80.6	80.6	69.4	77.8	72.2	83.3	**97.2**	72.2	**97.2**	80.6	**100.0**	83.3	86.1	72.2	83.5
Transitive - preterite subjunctive II	36	47.2	**83.3**	58.3	61.1	47.2	**66.7**	55.6	58.3	**75.0**	30.6	**63.9**	52.8	**63.9**	44.4	**75.0**	58.3	58.9
Verb valency	86	**72.1**	**79.1**	**68.6**	67.4	**70.9**	66.3	67.4	**68.6**	67.4	55.8	66.3	54.7	**72.1**	62.8	**68.6**	60.5	66.8
Case government	27	77.8	**96.3**	**81.5**	74.1	**81.5**	74.1	70.4	74.1	77.8	63.0	70.4	55.6	**81.5**	70.4	70.4	63.0	73.8
Mediopassive voice	20	85.0	85.0	70.0	75.0	80.0	75.0	80.0	75.0	70.0	60.0	80.0	60.0	80.0	65.0	80.0	70.0	74.4
Passive voice	20	**100.0**	**100.0**	95.0	**100.0**	**100.0**	95.0	**100.0**	**100.0**	95.0	80.0	90.0	95.0	**100.0**	95.0	**100.0**	95.0	96.2
Resultative predicates	19	21.1	26.3	21.1	15.8	15.8	15.8	15.8	21.1	21.1	15.8	21.1	5.3	21.1	15.8	21.1	10.5	17.8
average (items)	5393	78.0	80.9	71.6	79.2	64.3	77.7	**82.8**	75.5	67.5	68.4	74.1	74.4	**83.6**	72.3	79.2	80.2	75.6

Table 4: Accuracies (%) of successful translations for 16 systems and 107 phenomena organized in 14 categories. Boldface indicates the significantly best systems in each row.

A Test Suite and Manual Evaluation of Document-Level NMT at WMT19

Kateřina Rysová, Magdaléna Rysová, Tomáš Musil, Lucie Poláková and **Ondřej Bojar**
Charles University, Faculty of Mathematics and Physics
Institute of Formal and Applied Linguistics
Malostranské náměstí 25, 118 00 Prague, Czech Republic
`{rysova, magdalena.rysova, musil, polakova, bojar}@ufal.mff.cuni.cz`

Abstract

As the quality of machine translation rises and neural machine translation (NMT) is moving from sentence to document level translations, it is becoming increasingly difficult to evaluate the output of translation systems.

We provide a test suite for WMT19 aimed at assessing discourse phenomena of MT systems participating in the News Translation Task. We have manually checked the outputs and identified types of translation errors that are relevant to document-level translation.

1 Introduction

Currently, the level of machine translation systems can be very good or excellent. For some languages, the systems are on par with humans when evaluated *at the level of individual sentences*, see Hassan et al. (2018) for Chinese-to-English and Bojar et al. (2018) for English-to-Czech translation at WMT18. The main criterion for distinguishing MT systems' quality thus has to shift from evaluating individual sentences to larger units. Ideally, the translated text should be now evaluated as a whole.

We believe that the fundamental criterion of the quality of manual or automatic translation is the extent to which the translation is functional in human communication. These days, the critical basic level in this criterion has been already reached by multiple machine translation systems covering a wide range of language pairs. While the reader of an automatically translated text may be groping at some points in the text, the overall quality of the translation is already so high that the main content of the text and the author's communicative intention is mostly conveyed.

Still, the reader of an MT output takes a higher effort to understand the translated text. For example, morphological errors, shortcomings in the word order, incorrect syntactic relations, failure in translating terminology, or the choice of inappropriate synonyms can hinder the speed and accuracy of text understanding.

In this paper, we first provide a test suite for WMT19 aimed at assessing translation quality of English to Czech NMT systems regarding document-level language phenomena. As qualitative analyses of document-level errors in MT outputs are up-to-date quite rare, this paper further aims at identification, manual annotation and linguistic description of these types of errors relevant to English-Czech NMT and a comparison of performance of the submitted systems in the given areas. We compare NMT systems that translate one sentence at a time with systems that have more than one sentence on input and therefore have potential to translate document-level phenomena better.

After an overview of detected translation errors from various levels of language description, the paper zooms in on three document-level, or coherence-related, phenomena: topic-focus articulation (information structure), discourse connectives and alternative lexicalizations of connectives.[1] We assume that translation systems might have difficulties with these phenomena, as they are related to the previous context and go beyond (or are affected by the phenomena across) the sentence boundary. In this way, they contribute to the overall coherence of the text that should (as a whole) function as an independent unit of human communication.

---

[1]This work does not address in detail errors in coreference, pronoun and gender translation, as these phenomena have been already widely accounted for, e.g. Guillou et al. (2016); Novák (2016).

Proceedings of the Fourth Conference on Machine Translation (WMT), Volume 2: Shared Task Papers (Day 1) pages 455–463
Florence, Italy, August 1-2, 2019. ©2019 Association for Computational Linguistics

2 Data

The evaluations in this paper are conducted on a selection of 101 documents from the parallel Prague Czech-English Dependency Treebank (PCEDT, Hajič et al. (2012)), and we also used discourse annotations of the same texts in the Penn Discourse Treebank 3.0 (PDTB, for details see Webber et al. (2019)).

2.1 Prague Czech-English Dependency Treebank

The Prague Czech-English Dependency Treebank is a parallel corpus consisting of English original texts and their Czech translations. The PCEDT contains 1.2 million running words in almost 50,000 sentences in each part.

The English texts come from the Penn Treebank (Wall Street Journal Section; Marcus et al., 1993). They were manually translated into Czech by trained linguists without any support of MT and proofread. The PCEDT is manually annotated on the tectogrammatical (deep-syntactic) layer in both languages. The sentences are represented by dependency structures of content words. The nodes in the tree structures are provided with syntactico-semantic labels as, e.g., predicate, actor, patiens, addressee or locative. Also, the valency frames of verbs (argument structure) are captured, as well as elliptical structures and anaphoric relations.

In addition, the Czech part is automatically tagged and parsed as surface-syntactic dependency trees on the analytical layer. The English part also preserves the original phrase-structure annotation of the Penn Treebank. Also, the annotation of discourse relations, connectives and Altlexes from the Penn Discourse Treebank was extracted and added to our PCEDT dataset.

3 NMT Systems

We evaluated 5 NMT systems from those participating in WMT19 in English-to-Czech translation. In particular, we selected those of the highest quality as estimated by automatic scoring at matrix.statmt.org.[2]

`CUNI-Transf-2018` is last year submission by Popel (2018). It is a neural machine translation model based on the Transformer architecture

and trained on parallel and back-translated monolingual data. It translates one sentence at a time.

`CUNI-DocTransf-T2T` is a Transformer model following Popel (2018), but trained on WMT19 document-level parallel and monolingual data. During decoding, each document was split into overlapping multi-sentence segments, where only the "middle" sentences in each segment are used for the final translation. `CUNI-Transf-T2T` is the same system as `CUNI-DocTransf-T2T`, just applied on separate sentences during decoding.

`CUNI-DocTransf-Marian` is document-level trained Transformer in Marian framework following Popel (2018), but finetuned on document-level parallel and monolingual data by translating triples of adjacent sentences at once. If possible, only the middle sentence is considered for the final translation hypothesis, otherwise a double or single sentence context is used.

`Online-B` is an anonymized online system which we know also from several previous years of WMT.

`Reference` is the Czech side of the PCEDT corpus.

4 Annotation Design

The 101 PCEDT documents selected for translation and manual evaluation belong to the "essay" and "letter" genre labels according to the classification of PDTB given in Webber (2009). At the same time, the selected texts have a length of 20–50 sentences. These documents were submitted as an additional test suite for Machine Translation of News shared task at the WMT 2019. Because we are interested in document-level translation and the effect of context on the translation, we only selected documents with cross-sentence discourse relations.

We have created a simple annotation interface (see Figure 1), which allows the annotator to mark the items that were translated correctly.

Specifically, several types of cross-sentence discourse relations are considered on the source side (reusing the annotations available in the Penn Discourse Treebank 3.0).

The target side was validated by trained linguists. For each of the observed connectives / AltLex, the annotators indicated whether:
(1) the given expression/phrase in the source fulfills the function of a connective – according to the

---

[2] `http://matrix.statmt.org/matrix/systems_list/1896`

President Bush and Soviet leader Mikhail Gorbachev will hold an informal meeting in early December, a move that should give both leaders a political boost at home. | Prezident Bush a sovětský vůdce Michail Gorbačov uspořádají na začátku prosince neformální setkání, ktere by mělo dát oběma vůdcům politickou podporu doma.

⊳ The White House is purposely not calling the meeting a summit so that there won't be any expectation of detailed negotiations or agreements ⊲. | Bílý dům úmyslně neříká schůzku summitem, takže nebude žádné očekávání podrobných jednání či dohod.

Rather, senior administration officials said ⊳ that the unexpected meeting was scheduled at Mr. Bush's request because of his preference for conducting diplomacy through highly personal and informal meetings with other leaders ⊲. | Úředníci vyšších správních úřadů uvedli, že nečekané setkání bylo naplánováno na žádost pana Bushe kvůli jeho preferenci vést diplomacii prostřednictvím vysoce osobních a neformálních setkání s ostatními vůdci.

1 Exp Expansion.Substitution.Arg2-as-subst

| Původní vztah: | ○ Ano ○ Ne | poznámky |
| Zachován v překladu: | ○ Ano ○ Ne | |

⊳ The two leaders will meet on Dec. 2 and 3, alternating the two days of meetings between a U.S. and a Soviet naval vessel in the Mediterranean Sea ⊲. | Oba vůdci se sejdou 2. a 3. prosince a střídají dva dny schůzek mezi USA a sovětským námořním plavidlem ve Středozemním moři.

⊳ The unusual seaborne meeting won't disrupt plans for a formal summit meeting next spring or summer, at which an arms-control treaty is likely to be completed ⊲. | Neobvyklé námořní setkání nenaruší plány na formální summit na jaře nebo v létě, na kterém bude pravděpodobně uzavřena smlouva o kontrole zbraní.

2 Ent

| Původní vztah: | ○ Ano ○ Ne | poznámky |
| Zachován v překladu: | ○ Ano ○ Ne | |

In announcing the meeting yesterday, Mr. Bush told reporters at the White House that neither he nor Mr. Gorbachev expects any "substantial decisions or agreements." Instead, he said that the purpose is simply for the two to get "better acquainted" and discuss a wide range of issues without a formal agenda. | Bush oznámil včera v Bílém domě novinářům, že ani on, ani pan Gorbačov neočekávají žádná „podstatná rozhodnutí nebo dohody". Místo toho, on říkal, že účelem je jednoduše, aby se dva „lépe seznámit" a diskutovat o široké škále otázek, aniž by formální agendu.

⊳ Despite the informal nature of the session and the calculated effort to hold down expectations, the meeting could pay significant political dividends for both leaders ⊲. | Navzdory neformální povaze zasedání a vypočtené snaze držet se nad očekáváním by se na setkání mohli zúčastnit významné politické dividendy pro oba vůdce.

⊳ ⊳ Mr. Gorbachev badly needs a diversion from the serious economic problems and ethnic unrest he faces at home ⊲ ⊲. | Pan Gorbačov špatně potřebuje odklon od vážných ekonomických problemů a etnickych nepokojů, kterým čelí doma.

3 Imp Contingency.Cause.Reason

| Původní vztah: | ○ Ano ○ Ne | poznámky |
| Zachován v překladu: | ○ Ano ○ Ne | |

American officials have said ⊳ that a meeting with the leader of the U.S. could help bolster his stature among Soviet politicians and academics, whose support he needs ⊲. | Američtí představitele uvedli, že setkání s vůdcem USA by mohlo pomoci posilit jeho postavení mezi sovětskými politiky a akademiky, jejichž podporu potřebuje.

4 Imp Contingency.Cause.Result

| Původní vztah: | ○ Ano ○ Ne | poznámky |
| Zachován v překladu: | ○ Ano ○ Ne | |

⊳ For his part, Mr. Bush has been criticized regularly at home for moving too slowly and cautiously in reacting to Mr. Gorbachev's reforms and the historic moves away from communism in Eastern Europe ⊲. | Pan Bush byl pravidelně kritizován doma za to, že se příliš pomalu a opatrně pohyboval v reakci na reformy pana Gorbačova a na historické posuny od komunismu ve východní Evropě.

⊳ A face-to-face meeting with Mr. Gorbachev should damp such criticism, though it will hardly eliminate it ⊲. | Tváří v tvář osobnímu setkání s panem Gorbačovem by tato kritika měla být vlhká, i když ji sotva odstraní.

5 Imp Contingency.Cause.Result

Figure 1: Screenshot of the annotation interface.

annotator, or the function of AltLex – according to the original English annotation displayed. If yes, then whether its Czech translation is (2):

- adequate and correctly placed,[3]
- adequate but incorrectly placed,
- omitted and it does not harm the output
- omitted and it harms the output
- not adequate.

The questionnaire for word order annotation is analogous, compare the description of tables with results below in Section 7. The original translation into Czech from PCEDT could serve as a reference translation but similarly to Bojar et al. (2018), we opted for a bilingual evaluation, showing the annotators always the source and the candidate translation. The benefit is that the human translation can be evaluated using the same criteria as the MT system outputs.

There were 6 annotators, all of them students of linguistics. Each annotator evaluated 8 documents in the first round. For each document, they

evaluated the output of one MT system (without knowing which MT system produced the output). To measure the inter-annotator agreement, we organized a second round of evaluation, where each annotator was given documents and systems combination that was in the first round evaluated by another annotator. Details on the IAA are given in Section 7.

5 Linguistic Analysis of Translations Errors across Language Levels

We carried out a complex linguistic analysis of a sample of the translated texts and revealed that even the best translations contained cca 15–20 linguistic issues (per text of 35 sentences). This means that although the content reliability and linguistic level of (the best) MT systems is very high, they still do not reach communication skills of humans. This fact may be challenging for their authors, as there are still possibilities for improvement. However, a systematic improvement of MT systems is rather difficult due to non-systematic nature of language errors found in the analysis – e.g. if there appeared an untypical word order in a

---

[3]for Altlexes: and preserves the original discourse meaning

sentence, it does not mean that word order errors are also present in the rest of the translated text. It turned out, on the contrary, that the errors / problematic issues appear individually, as singularities.

In the following part, we discuss the problematic places in a sample of translated texts. We tried to select the best or (at least) good MT systems to demonstrate that even in such an advanced translation, there are still issues requiring improvement.

5.1 Morphology

We were able to detect errors from various levels of language description. Some problematic issues concerned even such basic phenomena as e.g. the use of a verbal mood or other morphological issues (*It's as if France decided to give only French history questions to students in a European history class, and when everybody aces the test, they say their kids are good in European history – Je to, jako by se Francie rozhodla dávat studentům evropských hodin dějepisu jen otázky z francouzštiny, a když všichni v testu excelují, říkají, že jejich děti jsou v evropských dějinách dobré*; the Czech translation is not consistent in maintaining potentiality: the intended content should be translated into Czech as: *jako kdyby se Francie..., a až by všichni v textu excelovali, řekli by...*) with the obligatory conditional morpheme *by*, also as a part of the conjunction *kdyby*, used in past (unreal) conditions.

5.2 Lexicon

Other issues concerned the choice of vocabulary. The individual translations included e.g. inappropriate repetition of the same word (ie. the MT systems produced a non-natural output by not attempting to use a synonym, cf. *in test-coaching workbooks and worksheets — v pracovních sešitech a pracovních sešitech "in test-coaching workbooks and in test-coaching workbooks"*). In some of them, there also appeared incorrect literal translations of terms (cf. *a joint venture of McGraw-Hill Inc. and Macmillan's **parentt**, Britain's Maxwell Communication Corp – společným podnikem McGraw-Hill Inc. a Macmillanovým **rodičem**, britskou společností Maxwell Communication Corp*).

Another lexical issue was the use of an inaccurate synonym in a given context (cf. *but he doesn't deny that some items are similar – ale nepopírá, že některé předměty jsou podobné*; the word *předměty* may be a synonym to the original *items* but not in this context, the Czech word here means rather tangible *objects*).

Generally, the MT systems succeed in translating basic words or phrases but sometimes they fail in translating terms or technical words and in lexical variety (often resulting in word repetition and failure to use an appropriate synonym).

5.3 Syntax

The translations also exhibit signs of incorrect syntactic relations, e.g. excessive genitive accumulation, which is untypical for Czech (cf. *About 20,000 sets of Learning Materials teachers' binders have also been sold in the past four years. – Asi 20 000 souborů (Noun in Gen) učebních materiálů (NP in Gen) učitelských pořadačů (NP in Gen) bylo také prodáno v posledních čtyřech letech.*). Another typical syntactic error appears in translation of syntactically potentially homonymous phrases, as in the example above in 5.1 the phrase *European history class*, translated wrongly as *evropských hodin dějepisu* (European classes of history).

Also, a large problematic area was revealed in word order configurations. Some translations contained the word order adopted from English, where it is untypical or even incorrect in Czech. This issue is related to sentence information structure or topic-focus articulation, as the word order is connected with contextual boundness (cf. *... says "well over 10 million" of its Scoring High test-preparation books have been sold since their introduction 10 years ago – uvádí, že "více než 10 milionů" jeho testovacích knih Scoring High se prodalo od jejich zavedení před 10 lety*; the expression *"více než 10 milionů"* is the focus of the sentence and therefore it should be placed in the final position in Czech). Similar issue (concerning topic-focus articulation) may be observed in the sentence *Scoring High and Learning Materials are the best-selling preparation tests. – Scoring High and Learning Materials jsou nejprodávanější přípravné testy.* Again, the expression *Scoring High and Learning Materials* should be (as focus proper of the sentence) placed in the final sentence position in Czech.

5.4 Semantics

Semantic issues (to a certain extent) are already partly included in the incorrect translations of terms as discussed above. Other are related especially to factual inaccuracy, e.g. the expression

French history questions was incorrectly translated as *otázky z francouzštiny* "questions from French".

In some cases, even a whole part of the original text was completely omitted in the translation – the meaning of the sentence was thus negatively affected (*... and Harcourt Brace Jovanovich Inc.'s Metropolitan Achievement Test and Stanford Achievement Test – ... a Harcourt Brace Jovanovich*).

5.5 Discourse

Further issues in translations also appeared on higher levels of language description, crossing the sentence boundary and mostly affecting text understanding as a whole. These discourse-related phenomena include especially coreference and discourse (semantico-pragmatic) relations, largely expressed by discourse connectives or their paraphrases (AltLexes). A detailed analysis of discourse-related translation errors is given below in Section 6.1.

6 Linguistic Analysis of Selected Document-Level Errors

6.1 Selected coherence phenomena

A comprehensive linguistic analysis of a sample of translated texts showed that even the best translations are not completely error-free (the best ones contained about 15–20 errors per text). These errors were further analyzed – they appear across individual levels of language description. Unfortunately, the main common feature of the errors seems to be the fact that they are not systematic. The key to a good distinction of translation quality is thus their complex linguistic analysis. For the annotation, we have chosen three document-level types of the errors discovered in the output analysis, namely those concerning **topic-focus articulation, discourse connectives** and the meanings they convey and **alternative lexicalizations of connectives** (AltLexes). The annotators then assessed them on a larger sample of translated data from all the systems and the reference translation. The finding are analyzed linguistically in the rest of this Section and quantitatively below in Section 7.

6.1.1 Topic-focus articulation and word order

First, we observed the phenomenon of topic-focus articulation (we follow this phenomenon as presented within the Functional Generative Description, see Sgall (1967) or Sgall et al. (1986)). In our experiment, we took advantage of the fact that English and Czech have a different word order system in combination with topic-focus articulation and contextual boundness.[4] While English has a fixed word order, strongly influenced by grammar, Czech has a free word order mainly influenced by the contextual boundness of individual sentence constituents. It is thus necessary to harmonize the word order in a Czech sentence always with respect to the previous (con)text.

In the annotation of the translated texts, we focused on the word order of the subject. While the subject is typically at the beginning of the sentence in English, it can occupy various positions in Czech, depending on whether it is contextually bound or not. We were wondering how individual MT-systems reflect this word order issue.

We automatically selected English original sentences from the PCEDT that contained a noun used with an indefinite article in the subject position and its Czech counterparts in evaluated translated texts. It is assumed that this subject is contextually non-bound (not deductible from the previous context, it is "new" information) and is thus expected elsewhere than at the beginning of the sentence, most likely to follow the predicate in Czech. Moreover, this subject (or the constituent corresponding to it in Czech) could be also so-called *focus proper* standing at the very end of the Czech sentence in written texts.

For Czech translations, it was necessary to check whether the Czech equivalent of the English subject was retained as a contextually non-bound sentence constituent and whether it was appropriately located in the Czech sentence, see the following example.

English text: *What is the best-selling preparation test? A NEW LANGUAGE TEST is the best-selling preparation test.*

Expected Czech translation: *Co je nejprodávanějším přípravným testem? Ne-*

---

[4]For definitions of terms related to topic-focus articulation and contextual boundness see Hajičová et al. (1998).

jprodávanějším přípravným testem je NEW LANGUAGE TEST.

6.1.2 Discourse connectives and their sentence positions

The second phenomenon assessed in the annotation were discourse connectives. Discourse connectives are rather short function words (e.g. *but, therefore, nevertheless, because,* or *and*) that connect two text units while expressing a discourse (semantico-pragmatic) relation between them, thus ensuring text to a large extent text coherence and cohesion. Here, the problematic issues included the use of a wrong Czech equivalent – both from the semantic and grammatical point of view (e.g. the positions of connectives in a sentence etc.). An example of a wrong connective translation is as follows. *Since chalk first touched slate, schoolchildren have wanted to know: What's on the test? – *Protože se křída poprvé dotkla břidlice, žáci chtěli vědět: Co je na testu?*

The English connective *since* is homonymous and its meaning may be causal or temporal. In the example, it was translated as causal (by the Czech connective *protože – because*) in a temporal context (the correct Czech translation here would be *od okamžiku, kdy* (from the moment when...). Such an incorrect translation of a discourse connective demonstrates nicely the potential huge impact on overall comprehensibility.

From the word order perspective, even these cohesive devices have their typical positions in a clause – according to their part-of-speech classification. Coordinating conjunctions typically stand between two discourse units (*I play the flute and I dance. / Hraju na flétnu a tančím.*) both in English and Czech. Subordinating conjunctions typically occur at the beginning of the discourse unit to which they belong syntactically (*Because it rains, I'm not going out. I won't go out because it rains. / Protože prší, nepůjdu ven. Nepůjdu ven, protože prší.*). Connectives of adverbial origin have looser positions in some cases;[5] they can occur e.g. in the first and second position in the sentence (*For me it is easier to not lose a game than to win it, thus I produce better results in stronger tournaments. Both umpires claimed that they were unsighted, and were thus forced to give Somny the benefit of the doubt. / Pro mě je snazší neztratit*

hru, než ji vyhrát, **proto** dosahuji lepších výsledků v silnějších turnajích. Oba rozhodčí tvrdili, že neviděli, byli **proto** nuceni dát Somnymu výhodu pochybovat.).*

In some word-order positions of discourse connectives, English and Czech differ. In other words, a Czech translation should not copy the connective ordering from an English original. In English, some discourse connectives can occur e.g. at the very end of the sentence (cf. *too, as well, instead, nevertheless* etc.), which is not typical for Czech.

To better compare the quality of the individual translations, we observed especially the translation equivalents of multi-word connectives like *as long as* or *as much as* that could be problematic due to their idiomatic character.

6.1.3 Alternative lexicalizations of discourse connectives (AltLexes)

In addition to discourse connectives, discourse relations can also be expressed by their alternatives called AltLexes, see Prasad et al. (2010). Alternative lexicalizations of connectives are often multi-word phrases such as *for this reason*. Since these cohesive structures often have an idiomatic character and they generally do not achieve such degree of grammaticalization as connectives, their forms in languages may vary to a large extent.

For example, the AltLex *for this reason* is not translated into Czech literary as *pro tento důvod* 'lit. for this reason', but as *z tohoto důvodu* 'lit. from this reason'. Other examples of English AltLexes are *that's all, that's largely due to, attributed that to, it will cause* etc. A list of AltLexes in English is given in Prasad et al. (2007), multi-word connective expressions in Czech are described and presented in Rysová (2018). Due to their high lexical variety and lower degree of grammaticalization, AltLexes were selected for the annotation as potentially interesting expressions for translation.

7 Results

In this section, we present the results of the evaluation.

7.1 Inter-annotator agreement

The inter-annotator agreement was measured pairwise, it ranges from 66 % to 93 % with an average of 80 %. The agreement was on average 69 % for AltLexes, 87 % for connectives and 79 % for questions concerning word order.

---

[5] For more information see Rysová and Rysová (2018).

7.2 AltLexes

The annotation interface for alternative lexicalizations contained identical questions to those for connective assessment (described above in Section 4), with the exception of their (in)correct placement, as this question is irrelevant for such non-grammaticalized phrases. There were 23 queries in average for each of the evaluated translations. The results for adequacy of AltLex translations in each system output AND the reference are summed up in Table 1.

A source AltLex was assessed as an appropriate connecting device in accordance with the original discourse annotation in 130 cases (Yes), and inappropriate in 42 cases (No). The proportion of negative answers is surprisingly high, but a closer look on the data reveals that the annotators, quite in unity (but in contrast to the PDTB notion of AltLex), resist treating **verbs** as a specific form of connecting devices. This mostly concerns causative verbs like *to explain, to strengthen* or *to blame*. They might be in fact right, these verbs are mostly translated well and their role in discourse coherence is a rather supplementary one. Apart from this issue, Table 1 demonstrates that once an AltLex is approved as a connecting device, it is in vast majority of cases translated correctly (rarely incorrectly), the original discourse meaning is preserved and it is not omitted in the translation. This applies quite equally across all systems, with a small decrease for CUNI-DocTransf-Marian system and the reference (!). A potential explanation is the typically looser human translation (and possibly the context-aware Marian system).

7.3 Connectives

As for connectives, there were 52 queries in average for each of the evaluated translations. The results for adequacy of connective translations in each system output and the reference are summed up in Table 2. A source connective candidate was assessed as an factual connecting device in 303 cases (Yes), and not a connective in 30 cases (No). This proportion seems to be correct, the non-connective readings of some expressions are relevant, e.g. several times for *as much as* in the function (and position) of a quantifier. Once a connective candidate is approved as an actual connective, it translated always correctly (compare column "n" in Table 2), but it is possibly incorrectly placed in the translation (column "ax"). The result

figures indicate that there are no significant differences across the systems in translating the traced connectives.

7.4 Word order

The word order evaluation focused the translation of contextually non-bound subjects (representing a new information in the sentence). The annotators first determined, which of the automatically preselected sentences from the English source indeed contain a contextually non-bound subject (85 Yes, 10 No). If yes, they traced whether the subject in the Czech translation also contextually non-bound. The results of manual annotation demonstrate that MT systems in general preserve the contextual non-boundness of the subjects. The figures are comparable across the systems, only the Marian system and the reference achieved a slightly worse scores:

	yes	no
CUNI-Transf-2018	11	1
CUNI-DocTransf-Marian	17	3
online-B	6	1
CUNI-DocTransf-T2T	17	1
CUNI-Transf-2019	6	1
reference	19	4

In a second task, we observed whether the subject in the English original the focus proper of the given sentence. Again, the annotators first filtered out relevant sentences (10 Yes, 36 No). Then they looked at whether the subject in the Czech translation is also the focus proper of the sentence. Similarly as in the previous task, the Marian system's performance is worse, and the performance of CUNI-DocTransf-T2T drops. However, the results here are less significant, as there were only few occurrences of the annotated tokens:

	yes	no
CUNI-Transf-2018	2	0
CUNI-DocTransf-Marian	5	3
online-B	0	1
CUNI-DocTransf-T2T	1	2
CUNI-Transf-2019	0	1
reference	1	6

Next, we followed the systems' ability to place the Czech equivalents of the original English subjects correctly into the Czech output sentence. Here, a correct placement according to the Czech word order rules was mostly achieved by all systems. There was not enough data collected for the online-B system, but the rest is comparable, with both context-aware systems performing slightly

	adequate	missing	wrong
CUNI-Transf-2018	★★★★½	☆☆☆☆☆	½☆☆☆☆
CUNI-DocTransf-Marian	★★★½☆	½☆☆☆☆	★☆☆☆☆
online-B	★★★★☆	☆☆☆☆☆	★☆☆☆☆
CUNI-DocTransf-T2T	★★★★☆	☆☆☆☆☆	★☆☆☆☆
CUNI-Transf-2019	★★★★☆	☆☆☆☆☆	★☆☆☆☆
reference	★★★½☆	☆☆☆☆☆	★½☆☆☆

Table 1: Results for AltLex annotations. Each ★ represents 20 % and the results are rounded to the nearest half-star.

	a	ax	m	n
CUNI-Transf-2018	★★★★½	½☆☆☆☆	☆☆☆☆☆	☆☆☆☆☆
CUNI-DocTransf-Marian	★★★★☆	★☆☆☆☆	☆☆☆☆☆	☆☆☆☆☆
online-B	★★★★½	½☆☆☆☆	☆☆☆☆☆	☆☆☆☆☆
CUNI-DocTransf-T2T	★★★★½	½☆☆☆☆	☆☆☆☆☆	☆☆☆☆☆
CUNI-Transf-2019	★★★★½	½☆☆☆☆	☆☆☆☆☆	☆☆☆☆☆
reference	★★★★☆	☆☆☆☆☆	☆☆☆☆☆	½☆☆☆☆

Table 2: Results for connectives annotations. The columns are: (a) adequate and correctly placed, (ax) adequate but incorrectly placed, (m) omitted and it does not harm the output, and (n) not adequate. Each ★ represents 20 % and the results are rounded to the nearest half-star.

worse than others:

	yes	no
CUNI-Transf-2018	14	0
CUNI-DocTransf-Marian	14	5
online-B	3	1
CUNI-DocTransf-T2T	13	3
CUNI-Transf-2019	6	0
reference	19	3

8 Conclusion

In this paper, we have described a test suite of parallel English-Czech texts provided for WMT19 with the aim to assess discourse phenomena in output of MT systems participating in the News Translation Task. We have carried out an extensive manual annotation of the MT outputs and identified types of translation errors relevant to document-level translation. We also compared the systems' performance with respect to the observed phenomena.

In general, the recent NMT systems have achieved such a high level of translation quality that it has become difficult to evaluate their output in a systematic fashion. Most of the errors in the translation cannot be found by a simple comparison with the reference translation, a bilingual evaluation is needed. Moreover, for the observed phenomena, the systems performed with only a minor differences among each other and they reached the quality of the reference. In fact, the reference translation was in some aspects evaluated as worse, which is likely caused by the greater literal adherence of the automatic translations to the original and it does not mean that the reference is incorrect. Contrary to our assumptions, the two context-aware systems did not outperform the others in translating the followed document-level phenomena. This can be attributed to the fact that the systems perform good enough on this task already, and also partly because the evaluation can change a lot using just a slightly different annotation setting, e.g. if we traced also other (ambiguous) connective expressions or anaphoric items. The actual errors are difficult to predict from scratch and they occur randomly. More specifically, while the translations of AltLexes and discourse connectives showed quite satisfactory (at least of those observed here), the most errors (equally across systems) were detected in the area of word order and contextual (non-)boundness of the subjects. The systems prefer to keep the original word also in the translations, not really accounting for the impact of information structure.

Acknowledgement

We acknowledge support from the Czech Science Foundation project no. GA17-06123S (Anaphoricity in Connectives: Lexical Description and Bilingual Corpus Analysis) and the EU project H2020-ICT-2018-2-825460 (ELITR). This study has utilized language resources distributed by the LINDAT/CLARIN project of the Ministry of Education, Youth and Sports of the Czech Republic (project LM2015071). This research was partially supported by SVV project number 260 453.

References

Ondřej Bojar, Christian Federmann, Mark Fishel, Yvette Graham, Barry Haddow, Matthias Huck, Philipp Koehn, and Christof Monz. 2018. Findings of the 2018 Conference on Machine Translation (WMT18). In *Proceedings of the Third Conference on Machine Translation, Volume 2: Shared Task Papers*, Brussels, Belgium. Association for Computational Linguistics.

Liane Guillou, Christian Hardmeier, Preslav Nakov, Sara Stymne, Jörg Tiedemann, Yannick Versley, Mauro Cettolo, Bonnie Webber, and Andrei Popescu-Belis. 2016. Findings of the 2016 WMT shared task on cross-lingual pronoun prediction. In *Proceedings of the First Conference on Machine Translation: Volume 2, Shared Task Papers*, volume 2, pages 525–542.

Jan Hajič, Eva Hajičová, Jarmila Panevová, Petr Sgall, Ondřej Bojar, Silvie Cinková, Eva Fučíková, Marie Mikulová, Petr Pajas, Jan Popelka, Jiří Semecký, Jana Šindlerová, Jan Štěpánek, Josef Toman, Zdeňka Urešová, and Zdeněk Žabokrtský. 2012. Announcing Prague Czech-English Dependency Treebank 2.0. In *Proceedings of the Eighth International Language Resources and Evaluation Conference (LREC'12)*, pages 3153–3160, Istanbul, Turkey. ELRA, European Language Resources Association.

Eva Hajičová, Barbara H Partee, and Petr Sgall. 1998. *Topic-focus articulation, tripartite structures and semantic content*. Kluwer, Dordrecht.

Hany Hassan, Anthony Aue, Chang Chen, Vishal Chowdhary, Jonathan Clark, Christian Federmann, Xuedong Huang, Marcin Junczys-Dowmunt, William Lewis, Mu Li, Shujie Liu, Tie-Yan Liu, Renqian Luo, Arul Menezes, Tao Qin, Frank Seide, Xu Tan, Fei Tian, Lijun Wu, Shuangzhi Wu, Yingce Xia, Dongdong Zhang, Zhirui Zhang, and Ming Zhou. 2018. Achieving Human Parity on Automatic Chinese to English News Translation. https://www.microsoft.com/en-us/research/uploads/prod/2018/03/final-achieving-human.pdf.

M. P. Marcus, B. Santorini, and M. A. Marcinkiewicz. 1993. Building a large annotated corpus of English: the Penn treebank. *Computational Linguistics*, 19:313–330.

Michal Novák. 2016. Pronoun prediction with linguistic features and example weighing. In *Proceedings of the First Conference on Machine Translation: Volume 2, Shared Task Papers*, volume 2, pages 602–608.

Martin Popel. 2018. Cuni transformer neural mt system for wmt18. In *Proceedings of the Third Conference on Machine Translation: Shared Task Papers*, pages 482–487.

Rashmi Prasad, Aravind Joshi, and Bonnie Webber. 2010. Realization of discourse relations by other means: Alternative lexicalizations. In *Proceedings of the 23rd International Conference on Computational Linguistics: Posters*, pages 1023–1031. Association for Computational Linguistics.

Rashmi Prasad, Eleni Miltsakaki, Nikhil Dinesh, Alan Lee, Aravind Joshi, Livio Robaldo, and Bonnie L Webber. 2007. The penn discourse treebank 2.0 annotation manual.

Magdaléna Rysová and Kateřina Rysová. 2018. Primary and secondary discourse connectives: Constraints and preferences. *Journal of Pragmatics*, 130:16–32.

Magdaléna Rysová. 2018. *Diskurzní konektory v češtině: Od centra k periferii*. Institute of Formal and Applied Linguistics, Praha, Czechia.

Petr Sgall. 1967. Functional sentence perspective in a generative description. *Prague studies in mathematical linguistics*, 2(203-225).

Petr Sgall, Eva Hajičová, and Jarmila Panevová. 1986. *The meaning of the sentence in its semantic and pragmatic aspects*. Springer Science & Business Media.

Bonnie Webber. 2009. Genre distinctions for discourse in the Penn TreeBank. In *Proceedings of the Joint Conference of the 47th Annual Meeting of the ACL and the 4th International Joint Conference on Natural Language Processing of the AFNLP: Volume 2- Volume 2*, pages 674–682. Association for Computational Linguistics.

Bonnie Webber, Rashmi Prasad, Alan Lee, and Aravind Joshi. 2019. The penn discourse treebank 3.0 annotation manual.

Evaluating conjunction disambiguation on English-to-German and French-to-German WMT 2019 translation hypotheses

Maja Popović
ADAPT Centre
Dublin City University
Ireland
maja.popovic@adaptcentre.ie

Abstract

We present a test set for evaluating an MT system's capability to translate ambiguous conjunctions depending on the sentence structure. We concentrate on the English conjunction "but" and its French equivalent "mais" which can be translated into two different German conjunctions. We evaluate all English-to-German and French-to-German submissions to the WMT 2019 shared translation task. The evaluation is done mainly automatically, with additional fast manual inspection of unclear cases.

All systems almost perfectly recognise the target conjunction "aber", whereas accuracies for the other target conjunction "sondern" range from 78% to 97%, and the errors are mostly caused by replacing it with the alternative conjunction "aber". The best performing system for both language pairs is a multilingual Transformer *TartuNLP* system trained on all WMT 2019 language pairs which use the Latin script, indicating that the multilingual approach is beneficial for conjunction disambiguation. As for other system features, such as using synthetic back-translated data, context-aware, hybrid, etc., no particular (dis)advantages can be observed.

Qualitative manual inspection of translation hypotheses shown that highly ranked systems generally produce translations with high adequacy and fluency, meaning that these systems are not only capable of capturing the right conjunction whereas the rest of the translation hypothesis is poor. On the other hand, the low ranked systems generally exhibit lower fluency and poor adequacy.

1 Introduction

Ambiguous words are often difficult to translate automatically, even by the current state-of-the-art neural machine (NMT) systems. Whereas NMT systems produce more fluent (grammatical and natural) translations than the previous state-of-the-art statistical phrase-based (PBMT) models, the semantic faithfulness of the translation to the original (adequacy) is still often problematic (Castilho et al., 2017; Klubička et al., 2018). Adequacy is even more problematic for ambiguous words which have two or more meanings depending on the context. Whereas the ambiguity of nouns, verbs and pronouns has been evaluated extensively in the recent years (Burchardt et al., 2017; Müller et al., 2018; Rios Gonzales et al., 2017, 2018), no results for conjunctions have been reported so far, and conjunctions can be ambiguous, too. It should be noted, though, that the conjunction ambiguity is more structural than lexical: it is mainly related to certain aspects of grammar involving the arrangement of words and word types. Therefore, the conjunction ambiguity is related more to fluency than to adequacy. The only work dealing with conjunctions and machine translation (Huang, 1983) explores conjunction scope for rule-based MT systems and does not address the ambiguity.

Our aim is to enable quantitative analysis of translating ambiguous conjunctions in a reproducible and semi-automatic way and to compare different types of systems in this respect. Our test sets for WMT 2019 are designed for the English ambiguous conjunction "but" and its French equivalent "mais", each of which can be translated into two different German conjunctions, "aber" or "sondern". The content is mainly based on general domain from subtitles (Tiedemann, 2012). Instead of comparing the translation hypotheses with a reference translation, we base the evaluation on the presence or absence of the correct conjunction in the target language. For unclear cases (about 1% of segments), manual inspection is carried out. We report results on all English→German and French→German submissions to the WMT 2019 shared translation task.

Proceedings of the Fourth Conference on Machine Translation (WMT), Volume 2: Shared Task Papers (Day 1) pages 464–469
Florence, Italy, August 1-2, 2019. ©2019 Association for Computational Linguistics

In addition to German, the test sets can be used for any target language which has these two variants of the conjunction "but" (for example Spanish or Croatian).

2   German equivalents of "but"/"mais"

The English coordinating conjunction "but" and its French equivalent "mais" are ambiguous when translated into certain target languages such as German. In German, there are two possible variants, "aber" and "sondern". "Aber" can be used after either a positive or a negative clause. On the other hand, "sondern" is only used after a negative clause when expressing a contradiction. The first clause in the sentence must contain a negation marker, and the second part of the sentence must contradict the first part of the sentence.

Three examples can be seen in Table 1. The sentences on the left have the same context, same or similar meanining, and contain similar words as the sentences on the right. Nevertheless, the conjunction "but" in all sentences on the left should be translated as "aber" and in those on the right as "sondern". This illustrates the statement from the previous section about the structural nature of conjunction ambiguity.

Generally, sentences with "aber" can be found more frequently in the data. Table 2 presents the distribution of the two types of sentences in the WMT 2019 News Commentary training corpus. In addition, it can be noted that both types of sentences occure rarely in the News corpus (less than 4% in total).

3   Test sets

3.1 Preparation

The test sets are generated semi-automatically using the bilingual subtitles corpora[1] according to the following requirements: (i) include only short segments (up to 20 words) (ii) remove all noise (iii) avoid complex words and rare name entities which could introduce additional effects.

First step was to extract all short segments containing the desired conjunctions in the source (English and French) and the target (German) language, and the second step was manual elimination or rephrasing complex and noisy parts. In this way, about 1000 sentences for each of the source

languages were prepared, containing about 800 instances of "sondern" and 200 instances of "aber". Since our preliminary experiments shown that the sentences requiring "aber" are less difficult for MT systems, we concentrate more on the performance for the conjunction "sondern".

A detailed corpus statistics is presented in Table 3. It can be seen that the segments are relatively short, and the vocabulary size relatively low – the vocabulary size of the standard English test set from WMT 2018 is more than double, about 5000 distinct words, and the average sentence length is 22.5. Apart from this, it can be seen that the average segment length of the easier "aber" instances is slightly lower.

It should be noted that, although the basis for the generation of the test sets was a bilingual corpus, the resulting test sets do not contain any reference translations. The reason for this is twofold: on the one hand, bilingual manual filtering of noisy and complex content would be very time and resource consuming. On the other hand, reference translations are not really needed – since we are interesting only in conjunction disambiguation, checking the conjunction in the translation hypothesis is sufficient and it can be carried out without a reference translation.

3.2 Evaluation

The vast majority of checks is performed automatically, however for a small number of sentences (usually 1-2%) a manual inspection is needed. For each sentence, there are four possible outcomes of the automatic evaluation:

- only the correct conjunction is found

  $\Rightarrow$ correct

- only the opposite conjunction is found

  $\Rightarrow$ incorrect

- both conjunctions are found

  $\Rightarrow$ manual inspection

- none of the two conjunctions is found

  $\Rightarrow$ manual inspection

Manual inspection is carried out in the following way: if the structure of a sentence with additional or without any conjunctions is correct, then the sentence is considered correct. All errors which are not related to the conjunction are ignored, both by automatic and by manual evaluation.

---

[1] http://opus.nlpl.eu/OpenSubtitles-v2018.php

"aber"	"sondern"
You're apologizing to me, but you should apologize to her.	Don't apologize to me, but to her.
The child wanted to go to the park, but we went home.	The child didn't want to go home, but to the park.
You should never speak but you can write.	You should never speak but only write.

Table 1: Examples of difference between the two German conjunctions.

lang. pair	aber	sondern
En-De	8230 (2.4%)	4389 (1.3%)
Fr-De	5498 (2.1%)	3369 (1.3%)

Table 2: Distribution of sentences requiring each of the two German conjunctions in the News Commentary training corpus for WMT 2019: number of sentences and percentage in the whole corpus.

4   MT Systems

4.1   English-to-German

All English-to-German systems are trained on the constraint data except *en-de-task* and *PROMT-NMT*. For the *en-de-task* system, as well as the *Microsoft-doc/sent level* systems, no additional information is available.

All other systems are based on the Transformer architecture, and *UCAM* uses the phrase-based approach too, thus being the only hybrid system.

All systems used BPE[2] segmentation except *eTranslation* which used SentencePiece[3] segmentation.

MSRA.MADL, *TartuNLP* and *UdS-DFKI* were trained only on natural parallel data, whereas all other systems used synthetic back-translated data, too. *JHU*, *NEU* and *UCAM* performed back-translation more than once.

The *LMU* and *UdS-DFKI* systems are context aware, *UdS-DFKI* being coreference aware.

MSRA.MADL used multi-agent dual learning (MADL)[4].

The only multilingual system is *TartuNLP*, one and the same Transformer system trained on all WMT language pairs which use Latin script.

4.2   French-to-German

All French-to-German systems are based on the Transformer architecture and used the constrained data.

All systems used BPE units except *eTranslation* which used SentencePiece units.

MSRA.MADL and *TartuNLP* are trained only on natural parallel data, whereas *eTranslation, LIUM* and *MLLP-UPV* used additional synthetic back-translated data.

MSRA.MADL again used multi-agent dual learning (MADL).

TartuNLP is again the only multilingual system, the same one used for the English-to-German task.

5   Results

The results are presented in Table 4 in the form of percentage of sentences automatically identified as correct ("aut."), identified as correct after both automatic check and manual inspection ("full"), and automatically identified as incorrect because the source conjunction is translated into the opposite conjunction ("opposite"). The systems are ranked by the full accuracy of the conjunction "sondern".

5.1   General observations

Generally, the same tendencies are observed for both language pairs.

First of all, in can be noted that the results of our preliminary experiments mentioned in Section 2 are confirmed on the large scale: translating sentences requiring the conjunction "aber" is not problematic for any of the systems: the percentage of correct sentences is 100%, or in the worst cases, close to 100%, for both language pairs and all systems.

As for the "difficult" conjunction "sondern", the majority of the systems translates it correctly in 90-95% of cases, and the predominant problem for the rest is translating it as "aber" (5-10%). Other types of errors are found in only very small number of cases (for example, parts of the sentences left untranslated, or completely incorrect sentence structure).

For the sentences with both conjunctions or without any of the two conjunctions, manual in-

[2]https://github.com/rsennrich/subword-nmt
[3]https://github.com/google/sentencepiece
[4]https://openreview.net/pdf?id=HyGhN2A5tm

source language	target conjunction	number of sentences	number of running words	vocabulary size	average sent. length
English	all	1066	13655	2252	12.8
	"sondern"	858	11058	2043	12.9
	"aber"	208	2597	560	12.5
French	all	1010	12963	2162	12.8
	"sondern"	806	10478	1823	13.0
	"aber"	98.1	2485	673	12.2

Table 3: Statistics of the test sets: number of sentences, number of running words, vocabulary size and average sentence length.

language pair	system	"sondern" correct aut.	"sondern" correct full	"sondern" opposite ("aber")	"aber" correct aut.	"aber" correct full	"aber" opposite ("sondern")
En→De	TartuNLP	97.2	97.3	2.7	98.6	99.0	1.0
	NEU	96.1	96.1	3.8	100	100	0
	HelsinkiNLP	95.3	95.6	4.3	99.0	99.5	0
	MSRA.MADL	94.5	94.6	5.1	99.5	99.5	0
	dfki-nmt	94.0	94.6	5.2	99.0	99.5	0.5
	online-A	94.3	94.4	5.3	99.0	99.0	1.0
	eTranslation	94.0	94.3	5.5	100	100	0
	Microsoft-sent-level	93.8	93.9	6.1	99.5	100	0
	Facebook-Fair	93.6	93.7	6.2	100	100	0
	Microsoft-doc-level	93.6	93.6	6.3	100	100	0
	UdS-DFKI	92.8	92.8	6.7	99.0	99.0	0
	LMU	91.6	91.8	7.8	95.2	95.7	1.0
	UCAM	91.7	91.7	8.2	99.0	99.0	1.0
	JHU	91.4	91.7	8.2	100	100	0
	MLLP-UPV	91.0	91.2	8.4	100	100	0
	online-Y	90.3	90.3	9.6	99.5	99.5	0.5
	PROMT-NMT	89.4	89.4	9.9	100	100	0
	online-B	88.8	89.4	10.2	99.0	99.5	0
	online-G	89.0	89.2	10.7	100	100	0
	online-X	86.0	86.0	13.7	99.5	99.5	0.5
	en-de-task	78.2	78.2	21.3	95.2	95.7	3.4
Fr→De	TartuNLP	96.9	96.9	3.1	97.5	98.5	0.5
	eTranslation	93.0	93.4	6.6	100	100	0
	online-G	87.6	93.4	6.7	100	100	0
	MSRA.MADL	93.2	93.3	6.7	100	100	0
	online-A	88.5	92.8	6.7	100	100	0
	MLLP-UPV	92.0	92.4	7.4	99.5	99.5	0.5
	LIUM	91.3	91.7	8.3	100	100	0
	online-B	87.3	89.7	10.5	100	100	0
	online-Y	67.9	88.7	10.5	100	100	0
	online-X	86.8	86.8	13.2	100	100	0

Table 4: Percentage of correct conjunctions retrieved automatically and by full evaluation, and percentage of opposite conjunctions.

source:	*However*, this is not Agnes,
	but her daughter.
output:	Das ist *aber* nicht Agnes,
	sondern ihre Tochter.
source:	The time, *however*, is not thirty
	years ago, **but** now.
output:	Die Zeit is *aber* nicht dreissig
	Jahre her, **sondern** jetzt.

Table 5: Examples of correct translations with both German conjunctions.

spection is carried out. For English-to-German systems, only a small number of sentences fall into these two categories, so that manual inspection has no or very little effect on ranking. For four "on-line" French-to-German systems, online-A, -B, -G and -Y, however, a larger number of sentence without conjunctions is found.

Both conjunctions: Manual inspection revealed that this is not problematic: it can happen if "however", "yet" or similar word which can be translated as "aber" is present in the source sentence. Two examples can be seen in Table 5.

No conjunctions: For the English source, it can happen for a small number of sentences with structure "not only X, but Y, too", whereas for the French source a number of other sentence structures was paraphrased, too. Some of these paraphrased translations are perfect, whereas some of them are not as fluent as they would be if the construction with conjunction were used, but are nevertheless considered as correct. Two examples can be seen in Table 6.

5.2 Differences between the systems

The first and very interesting observation is that the best performing system for both language pairs is the multilingual *TartuNLP* system. The advantage of a multilingual system is probably its ability to get a signal for different structures from many languages, so that the information about different variants of the target conjunction necessary for different source sentence structures is better captured.

As for other system features, no particular differences can be spotted. For example, the best system *TartuNLP* is trained only on natural parallel data, the other system without back-translation *MSRA.MADL* performed very well, one system using multiple back-translation *NEU* is ranked

source	Ce n'est pas un robot,
	mais un humain.
source (en gloss)	It is not a robot,
	but a human.
output	Er ist kein Roboter,
	er ist ein Mensch.
output (en gloss)	He is not a robot,
	he is a human.
source	Ce n'taient pas des mots,
	mais des actes.
source (gloss en)	It were not the words,
	but the deeds.
output	Es waren keine Worte,
	es waren Taten.
output (en gloss)	It was not words,
	it was deeds.

Table 6: Examples of correct translations without any of the two German conjunctions (mostly occuring in French-to-German systems).

as second and two other such systems *JHU* and *UCAM* in the middle, so no (dis)advantage of synthetic parallel data can be observed. Furthermore, two context-aware English-to-German systems *LMU* and *UdS-DFKI* as well as the hybrid *UCAM* system are ranged in the middle, thus no clear (dis)advangates of either of the approaches can be noted.

Qualitative analysis of overall performance

In order to check whether the best ranked systems maybe produce generally poor translations and only capture the conjunctions correctly, as well as other way round (maybe the lowest ranked systems produce fluent and adequate translations), we carried out a manual qualitative inspection of five highest and five lowest ranked hypotheses. The most important finding is that the best ranked systems produce decent translations both in terms of adequacy and fluency, meaning that these systems are not only capable of choosing the right conjunction while generating poor translations. As for the low ranked systems, they all have much lower fluency and adequacy, especially the lowest ranked *en-de-task* system with very low adequacy and a number of non-existing words.

Of course, to draw stabler conclusions, a systematic quantitative analysis of correlation between conjunction disambiguation and adequacy/fluency should be carried out in future work.

6 Conclusions

We present a targeted evaluation of 21 English-to-German and 10 French-to-German MT systems regarding their performance in lexical choice for ambiguous source conjunction "but"/"mais". We observe that all systems almost perfectly recognise the target conjunction "aber", whereas accuracies for the other target conjunction "sondern" range from 78% to 97%, and the errors are mostly caused by replacing it with the alternative conjunction "aber".

The best performing system on the "difficult" target variant "sondern" for both source languages is based on the multilingual transformer model trained on all WMT language pairs using Latin script. The advantage of a multilingual system might be a better ability to learn the relation between different sentence structures and corresponding conjunctions. Apart of this, there are no other clear differences between the systems.

Qualitative analysis of translation hypotheses shown that highly ranked systems generally produce translations with high adequacy and fluency, meaning that they are not only capable of capturing the right conjunction whereas the rest of the translation hypothesis is poor. On the other hand, the low ranked systems generally exhibit lower fluency and poor adequacy. Quantitative analysis of correlation between the conjunction disambiguation and overall performance should be a part of future work.

The current study is focused on only one ambiguous conjunction and only one target language. In future, we plan to extend the test set with more conjunctions (and variants), and possibly, to more language pairs.

Acknowledgments

This research was supported by the ADAPT Centre for Digital Content Technology at Dublin City University, funded under the Science Foundation Ireland Research Centres Programme (Grant 13/RC/2106) and co-funded under the European Regional Development Fund.

References

Aljoscha Burchardt, Vivien Macketanz, Jonathan Dehdari, Georg Heigold, Jan-Thorsten Peter, and Philip Williams. 2017. A Linguistic Evaluation of Rule-Based, Phrase-Based, and Neural MT Engines. *The Prague Bulletin of Mathematical Linguistics*, 108(1):159–170.

Sheila Castilho, Joss Moorkens, Federico Gaspari, Rico Sennrich, Vilelmini Sosoni, Yota Georgakopoulou, Pintu Lohar, Andy Way, Antonio Miceli Barone, and Maria Gialama. 2017. A comparative quality evaluation of pbsmt and nmt using professional translators. In *Proceedings of MT Summit XVI*, pages 116–131.

Xiuming Huang. 1983. Dealing with Conjunctions in a Machine Translation Environment. In *Proceedings of the 1st Conference on European Chapter of the Association for Computational Linguistics (EACL 1983)*, pages 81–85, Pisa, Italy.

Filip Klubička, Antonio Toral, and Víctor M. Sánchez-Cartagena. 2018. Quantitative fine-grained human evaluation of machine translation systems: A case study on english to croatian. *Machine Translation*, 32(3):195–215.

Mathias Müller, Annette Rios Gonzales, Elena Voita, and Rico Sennrich. 2018. A Large-Scale Test Set for the Evaluation of Context-Aware Pronoun Translation in Neural Machine Translation. In *Proceedings of the 3rd Conference on Machine Translation (WMT 2018)*, pages 61–72, Belgium, Brussels. Association for Computational Linguistics.

Annette Rios Gonzales, Laura Mascarell, and Rico Sennrich. 2017. Improving word sense disambiguation in neural machine translation with sense embeddings. In *Proceedings of the 2nd Conference on Machine Translation (WMT 2017)*, pages 11–19, Copenhagen, Denmark.

Annette Rios Gonzales, Mathias Mller, and Rico Sennrich. 2018. The word sense disambiguation test suite at wmt18. In *Proceedings of the 3rd Conference on Machine Translation (WMT 2018)*, pages 594–602, Belgium, Brussels. Association for Computational Linguistics.

Jörg Tiedemann. 2012. Parallel data, tools and interfaces in OPUS. In *Proceedings of the 8th International Conference on Language Resources and Evaluation (LREC 2012)*, pages 2214–2218, Istanbul, Turkey.

The MᴜCᴏW test suite at WMT 2019:
Automatically harvested multilingual contrastive word sense disambiguation test sets for machine translation

Alessandro Raganato[*][†], Yves Scherrer[*] and Jörg Tiedemann[*]

[*]University of Helsinki   [†]Basement AI
`{name.surname}@helsinki.fi`

Abstract

Supervised Neural Machine Translation (NMT) systems currently achieve impressive translation quality for many language pairs. One of the key features of a correct translation is the ability to perform word sense disambiguation (WSD), i.e., to translate an ambiguous word with its correct sense. Existing evaluation benchmarks on WSD capabilities of translation systems rely heavily on manual work and cover only few language pairs and few word types. We present Mᴜ-CᴏW, a multilingual contrastive test suite that covers 16 language pairs with more than 200 000 contrastive sentence pairs, automatically built from word-aligned parallel corpora and the wide-coverage multilingual sense inventory of BabelNet. We evaluate the quality of the ambiguity lexicons and of the resulting test suite on all submissions from 9 language pairs presented in the WMT19 news shared translation task, plus on other 5 language pairs using pretrained NMT models. The MᴜCᴏW test suite is available at `http://github.com/Helsinki-NLP/MuCoW`.

1 Introduction

Neural Machine Translation (NMT) has provided impressive advances in translation quality, leading to a discussion whether translations produced by professional human translators can still be distinguished from the output of NMT systems, and to what extent automatic evaluation measures can reliably account for these differences (Hassan Awadalla et al., 2018; Läubli et al., 2018; Toral et al., 2018). One answer to this question lies in the development of so-called *test suites* (Burchardt et al., 2017) or *challenge sets* (Isabelle et al., 2017) that focus on particular linguistic phenomena that are known to be difficult to evaluate with simple reference-based metrics such as BLEU. Existing test suites focus e.g. on morphosyntactic and syn-

tactic divergences between source and target language (Burchardt et al., 2017; Burlot and Yvon, 2017; Isabelle et al., 2017; Sennrich, 2017; Burlot et al., 2018; Macketanz et al., 2018) or on discourse phenomena (Guillou and Hardmeier, 2016; Bawden et al., 2018; Müller et al., 2018; Guillou et al., 2018).

Another linguistic phenomenon that is challenging for translation is lexical ambiguity (Liu et al., 2018; Marvin and Koehn, 2018), i.e., words of the source language that have multiple translations in the target language representing different meanings. Recently, Rios Gonzales et al. (2017) introduced a lexical ambiguity benchmark called ContraWSD that is based on contrastive translation pairs: a sentence containing an ambiguous source word is paired with the correct reference translation and with a modified translation in which the ambiguous word has been replaced by a word of a different sense. Contrastive evaluation makes use of the ability of NMT systems to score given translations: a contrast is considered successfully detected if the reference translation obtains a higher score than an artificially modified translation.

However, all these test suites require significant amounts of expert knowledge and manual work for identifying the divergences and compiling the examples, which typically limits their coverage to a small number of language pairs and directions. For example, the test sets built by Rios Gonzales et al. (2017) cover only 65 ambiguous words for two language pair directions.

In this paper, we present a language-independent method for automatically building ContraWSD-style test suites. It involves the following steps: (1) identify ambiguous source words and their translations; (2) cluster the translations into senses; (3) select sentences with ambiguous words and create contrast pairs.

The setup proposed by Rios Gonzales et al.

Proceedings of the Fourth Conference on Machine Translation (WMT), Volume 2: Shared Task Papers (Day 1) pages 470–480
Florence, Italy, August 1-2, 2019. ©2019 Association for Computational Linguistics

177 input	26 documents	9 system
50 typing	21 petition	8 entered
29 entering	17 data	8 command
28 entry	14 submission	7 display
27 loading	13 the	7 to
26 enter	11 inputting	...

Table 1: English words aligned with the German word *Eingabe* and their alignment frequencies. Words with frequency < 10 are discarded from further processing.

Petition, Antrag, Gesuch, Eingabe	**petition**, request, postulation
Produktionsfaktor, Ressource, Eingabe	factors of production, **input**, resource
Eingabe (Computer), Dateneingabe, Input	**input**, data entry

Table 2: Three bilingual German–English clusters for the German word *Eingabe*, as obtained from BabelNet. Intersected words with Table 1 are displayed in bold. The second and third clusters are merged because of the shared English word *input*.

(2017) has shown a certain number of drawbacks. First, it cannot be used in conjunction with online systems (which do not provide an API for scoring) or with rule-based systems. Second, it is unclear to what extent the score of an MT system reflects its quality, as it might never have generated that particular sentence. Third, it requires the explicit construction of contrastive sentences, which is not trivial, especially for morphologically rich languages. For these reasons, the WMT test suite calls focus on *translation test suites*, where the participants are asked to produce translations of the source sentence instead of scoring given hypotheses. Following Rios et al. (2018) and Macketanz et al. (2018), who proposed small-scale translation test suites targeting WSD, we participated at WMT with modified versions of MUCOW. The modifications only concern step (3).

As a result, we make available two variants of MUCOW, a **mu**ltilingual **co**ntrastive **w**ord sense disambiguation test suite for machine translation. The scoring variant covers 11 language pairs with a total of almost 240 000 sentence pairs. The translation variant covers 9 language pairs with a total of 15 600 sentences. The data and scoring scripts are available at `https://github.com/Helsinki-NLP/MuCoW`.

2 Building MUCOW

In this section, we describe the three steps needed to create a MUCOW test suite and illustrate them with some German→English examples.

2.1 Step 1: Identify ambiguous source words and their translations

We first compile a list of source language words that have a large number of distinct translations. For this, we apply the *eflomal* word alignment tool (Östling and Tiedemann, 2016) on a collection of parallel corpora, keeping only those source words that were aligned at least 10 times each with at least two distinct target words. We use parallel corpora from the OPUS collection (Tiedemann, 2012),[1] counting only one-to-one word alignment links. Table 1 provides an example.

2.2 Step 2a: Cluster target words via BabelNet

For each source word of the previous step, those target words that potentially share the same meaning (for example synonyms) are clustered together. To this end, we exploit BabelNet (Navigli and Ponzetto, 2012), a wide-coverage multilingual encyclopedic dictionary obtained automatically from various resources (WordNet and Wikipedia, among others). BabelNet 4.0 covers 284 languages with almost 16 million entries, called Babel synsets. Each entry represents a given meaning and includes a set of synonyms (synset) in different languages. Conveniently, it provides inter-resource mappings in multiple languages, which enables us to translate words and senses between several languages.

We query BabelNet with each source word and take the intersection of the alignment-inferred target words and the BabelNet-inferred target words. Crucially, we group the remaining target words according to the BabelNet sense clusters. Finally, we combine those clusters that share at least one common target word. Table 2 shows an example.

---

[1] We use the following corpora: Books v1, EU Bookshop Corpus v2, Europarl v7 (Koehn, 2005), MultiUN v1 (Eisele and Chen, 2010), News-Commentary v11, OpenSubtitles v2018 (Lison and Tiedemann, 2016), SETIMES v2 (Tyers and Alperen, 2010), Tatoeba v2, TED2013 v1.1 (Cettolo et al., 2013).

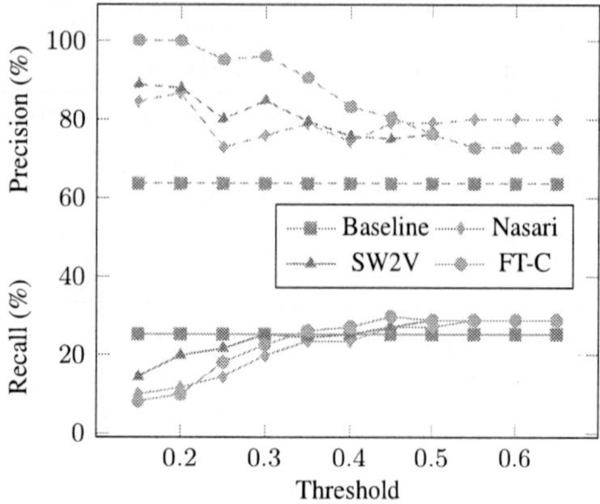
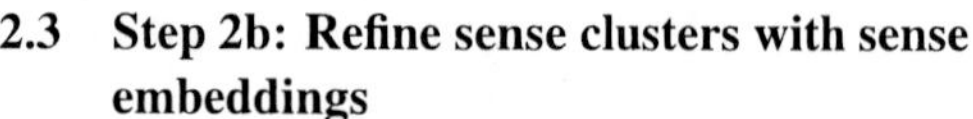

Figure 1: Precision (dashed) and recall (solid lines) values for different sense embeddings and thresholds.

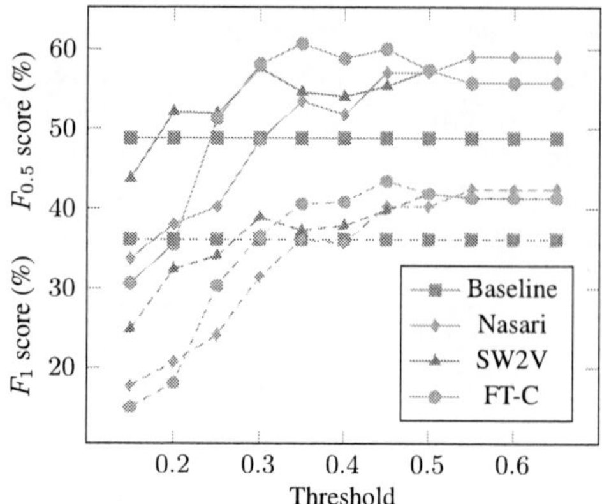

Figure 2: F_1-scores (dashed) and $F_{0.5}$-scores (solid lines) for different sense embeddings and thresholds.

2.3 Step 2b: Refine sense clusters with sense embeddings

It is known that lexical resources such as Babel-Net tend to suffer from overly fine granularity of their sense inventory (Navigli, 2006; Palmer et al., 2007). We therefore introduce an additional merging step: i) we associate each Babel synset with an embedding, ii) compute pairwise cosine similarities between synsets, iii) and merge them if their embedding similarity is higher than a threshold γ.

Choosing a good Babel synset embedding and an optimal threshold is a difficult task. We evaluated three Babel synset vector representations, using the existing German$\rightarrow$English ContraWSD test suite as gold standard:

Nasari (Camacho-Collados et al., 2016) is a vector representation built by combining the knowledge from Wikipedia and WordNet with word embeddings.

SW2V (Mancini et al., 2017) is a neural model that learns word and synset embeddings in a shared vector space exploiting a shallow graph-based disambiguation algorithm.

FastText-Centroid (FT-C): We also include a synset embedding representation by looking up the FastText word embeddings (Bojanowski et al., 2017) for all words in a synset and computing their centroid.

Note that Nasari and SW2V embeddings are tied to the (language-independent) BabelNet synset IDs and can therefore be applied in a straightforward way to non-English target languages.[2] As a baseline, we use the synset clusters obtained from Section 2.2.

We compute precision and recall scores for all three embedding methods with γ threshold values ranging from 0.15 to 0.65 with a 0.05 step size. An inferred synset was considered correct if all its lexicalisations (if present) occurred in a single gold synset, and no lexicalisations of a gold synset were found in a different inferred synset. In other words, an inferred synset was considered wrong if it had been falsely merged or if it had falsely been kept separate from another one. Figure 1 shows the precision and recall curves. All refinement methods improve precision, whereas recall only decreases at low thresholds. Figure 2 shows F_1 and $F_{0.5}$ scores; we deem the latter more sensible in the present setting as high precision is more important to us than high recall. The FT-C and SW2V methods perform best at lower thresholds, while Nasari works best at high thresholds.

An additional manual evaluation was carried out with 50 random German words[3] and four settings that obtained high F_1 or $F_{0.5}$ scores. As shown in Table 3, the SW2V method with a threshold set at 0.3 obtained the highest precision value by a large margin and therefore also the best $F_{0.5}$ score. We chose this setting for all languages. Source words that end up with a single synset as a result of this step are discarded.

---

[2] For both embeddings, we use the pre-trained 300-dimensional Babel synset representation trained on the UMBC corpus.

[3] All words were associated with at least two synsets by the baseline model, but only 18 out of them (36%) contained two or more synsets according to a human annotator.

Method	Threshold	Prec.	Rec.	F_1	$F_{0.5}$
Baseline		33%	**48%**	39%	35%
Nasari	0.55	54%	31%	39%	47%
SW2V	0.3	**67%**	28%	40%	**52%**
	0.5	46%	42%	**44%**	45%
FT-C	0.35	54%	27%	36%	45%
	0.45	50%	35%	41%	46%

Table 3: Manual evaluation results for selected parameter settings.

2.4 Step 3: Selecting sentences and creating contrast pairs (Scoring variant only)

We use the synset lexicon built in the previous step to guide the creation of contrast pairs. We extract sentence pairs from the parallel corpora and group them by source word and target word sense. We restrict the extraction process to sentences longer than 10 words and skip sentences in which the source or target item occurs more than once. From this set, we randomly choose 20 instances of each sense from various corpus sources.

For each extracted sentence pair, a contrastive sentence pair is produced by keeping the source sentence identical, but replacing the target word in the target sentence by another lexicalisation from a different synset.

While this entirely automatic setup could give rise to inconsistencies which would require manual correction as in Rios Gonzales et al. (2017), we argue that BabelNet constraints already provide some filtering (for example mostly keeping number constant). Given our aim to scale up to a large number of languages, the need for human intervention would make the creation of a large scale multilingual benchmark difficult and costly.

2.5 Statistics

We apply the three steps presented above to all to-English translation directions that were part of the Conference of Machine Translation (WMT) news translation task over the last years. Table 4 summarizes the statistics of these resources. The average number of senses per source word ranges between 2.0 and 2.11 (2.36–2.4 for ContraWSD). The lexicons for the Baltic languages are small due to the small size of available parallel corpora.

3 Measuring machine translation WSD capability with MᴜCoW

The aim of MᴜCoW is to examine the ability of current machine translation systems to choose the

Language pair	Corpus Sentence pairs	Lexicon Source words	Lexicon Target synsets	Lexicon Target words	Test suite Sentence pairs
CS–EN	44M	107	223	412	11470
DE–EN	35M	259	548	1086	33077
ES–EN	81M	515	1090	2398	72295
ET–EN	14M	34	68	89	2500
FI–EN	31M	176	367	610	16326
FR–EN	68M	456	963	2152	64369
LT–EN	2.5M	10	20	31	922
LV–EN	1.6M	5	10	12	318
RO–EN	52M	129	263	496	14258
RU–EN	38M	113	234	396	12378
TR–EN	46M	107	220	420	11795

Table 4: Sizes of the parallel corpora used for lexicon extraction, the inferred and filtered ambiguity lexicons, and the resulting test suite corpora.

Lg. pair	Model	ContraWSD	MᴜCoW	BLEU
DE–EN	LSTM	77.55	60.50	30.3
	Transformer	86.42	66.98	33.3
	Nematus	86.72	68.80	35.1
CS–EN	Nematus		78.77	30.9
RO–EN	Nematus		62.86	33.3
RU–EN	Nematus		72.36	30.8
TR–EN	Nematus		62.69	20.1

Table 5: Comparison of MᴜCoW and ContraWSD accuracy scores and BLEU scores computed on the WMT news2017 test set (news2016 for RO–EN).

correct target sense of ambiguous source words. Here, we give some baseline results obtained with supervised NMT systems. Following Rios Gonzales et al. (2017), we score both reference and contrastive translations with the same NMT system. A correct decision is detected when the score of the reference is higher than the scores from all contrastive translations. The final test suite score corresponds to the accuracy over all decisions.

Three models are examined for German→English: a 6-layer bi-LSTM model and a Transformer model[4] trained on the provided training data from WMT17 plus backtranslations from Sennrich et al. (2016b), and the University of Edinburgh's WMT17 submission, a deep LSTM model with additional synthetic data trained with Nematus (Sennrich et al., 2017b).[5] The upper half of Table 5 reports ContraWSD

---

[4]Sentences are encoded using Byte-Pair Encoding (Sennrich et al., 2016c), with 32,000 merge operations for each language. For the Bi-LSTM model we use embedding layers and hidden units of 512 dimensions. For the Transformer, we use the *base* version (Vaswani et al., 2017).

[5]`data.statmt.org/wmt17_systems/`

and MuCoW accuracy scores as well as BLEU scores computed on the WMT17 test set. The ranking of the three models is consistent across the three tasks. Interestingly, the Transformer model (trained on far less data than the Nematus model) scores much better on the two test suites than the BLEU score would suggest, confirming the findings by Tang et al. (2018).

The University of Edinburgh also makes available their NMT models for other WMT16 and WMT17 language pairs.[6] MuCoW accuracy scores of these models are shown in the lower half of Table 5 together with the WMT test set BLEU scores reported by the authors (Sennrich et al., 2016a, 2017a).

Even though we only assess the confidence of an NMT system in detecting the right sense of a single word within a sentence, the results show that WSD is still an issue in MT – even in state-of-the-art-systems – that requires further study.

4 Translation test suites for WMT 2019

As mentioned in Section 1, the WMT test suite call requires a different setup that does not rely on scoring capabilities of the participating systems. Therefore, we modified step (3) of our method to conform with these requirements, analogously to the modification of ContraWSD by Rios et al. (2018). As a beneficial side effect, we were also able to include language pairs with non-English target languages.[7] The changes to step (3) are the following:

- The sentence pairs were filtered more aggressively. We only kept sentence pairs in which both the source and target words were tagged as NOUNs by the respective UDPipe part-of-speech tagger (Straka and Straková, 2017).

- Source sentences stemming from one of the WMT training corpora were excluded. We only used sentences from the following OPUS corpora: *Books, Tatoeba, TED2013, EUBookstore* and *OpenSubtitles2018*.

- We only kept synsets for which we found at least 4 example sentences, and we retained at most 10 example sentences per sense.

Language pair	Source words	Target synsets	In-dom synsets	Out-dom synsets	Sentences
DE–EN	217	461	329	132	4268
FI–EN	109	231	91	140	2117
LT–EN	6	12	5	7	99
RU–EN	67	138	59	79	1223
EN–CS	98	200	29	171	1843
EN–DE	176	362	220	142	3337
EN–FI	48	97	22	75	830
EN–LT	4	8	3	5	69
EN–RU	97	199	40	163	1814

Table 6: Sizes of the MuCoW data sets compiled for WMT19.

- If as a result of the above filters, all but one senses of a source word were removed, we removed the source word entirely.

- We distinguished between in-domain and out-of-domain synsets. A synset is considered out-of-domain if more than half of its example sentences come from *OpenSubtitles2018*. The intuition behind this distinction is that most participating systems will be tuned towards the news domain and thus will not handle features of colloquial speech reliably.

- We disregarded the automatically generated contrastive sentences.

We built the translation variant of MuCoW for 9 translation directions of the news task. Table 6 shows some statistics.

The resulting test suites contain sentences of the source language together with the following metadata: the ambiguous source word, the list of correct target words (the correct target synset), the list of incorrect target words (the incorrect target synset), and information about the domain of the synsets. Table 7 shows an example. The source language sentences were sent (without metadata) to the WMT participants as part of the test set, and we received the translations for evaluation.

5 WMT 2019 test suite results

In order to assess the translation output of the WMT participants, we check whether any of the correct or incorrect target words listed in the metadata file can be identified in the tokenized and lowercased translation output.

Although the sentences have been selected to contain the uninflected base form both in the

<hr>

[6]`data.statmt.org/wmt{16,17}_systems/`

[7]We limited our work to from-English language pairs due to time restrictions, but the method would be generic enough to also work for French–German, German–French, and German–Czech.

Example containing **ambiguous word**	Correct translations	Incorrect translations
It occurred to me that my **watch** might be broken.	Armbanduhr, Uhr	*Wache*
I hope you didn't get distracted during your **watch**.	*Wache*	Armbanduhr, Uhr
In winter, the dry leaves fly around in the **air**.	Luft, Luftraum, Aura	Miene, Ausdruck
He remained silent for a moment, with a thoughtful but contented **air**.	Miene, Ausdruck	Luft, Luftraum, Aura
Harry had to back out of the competition because of a broken **arm**.	Arm	*Waffe*
So does the cop who left his side arm in a subway bathroom.	*Waffe*	Arm
Drain the pasta and return the pasta to the **pot**.	Blumentopf, Kochtopf, Topf, Nachttopf	*Marihuana, Gras*
Where did those idiots get all of this **pot** anyhow?	*Marihuana, Gras*	Blumentopf, Kochtopf, Topf, Nachttopf

Table 7: Examples of test suite instances of the English–German WMT test suite. The ambiguous (English) source word is highlighted in bold, and correct and incorrect (German) translations – as inferred by the MuCoW procedure – are given. Senses classified as out-of-domain are shown in italics. Note that some example sentences may further restrict the set of correct translations.

Language pair	Average coverage (tokenized)	Average coverage (with lemma backoff)
DE–EN	83.06%	84.51%
FI–EN	81.52%	82.14%
LT–EN	92.75%	93.48%
RU–EN	82.23%	82.85%
EN–CS	61.77%	74.87%
EN–DE	66.52%	69.26%
EN–FI	52.27%	67.55%
EN–LT	64.86%	79.71%
EN–RU	58.88%	73.29%

Table 8: Average coverage of target words among WMT19 primary submissions.

source and target languages, we cannot assume that all translation systems will output base forms. Hence, if neither correct nor incorrect target words can be identified, we lemmatize the translation output and search the target words again in the lemmatized version.[8] Depending on the target language, lemmatization allowed us to substantially increase the coverage (see Table 8).

We report precision, recall and F1-score for in-domain senses and out-of-domain senses, except for Lithuanian, where not enough examples are available. Precision and recall are computed as follows:[9]

$$\text{Precision} = \frac{\text{\# examples with correct target words}}{\text{\# examples with either correct or incorrect target words}}$$

$$\text{Recall} = \frac{\text{\# examples with correct target words}}{\text{\# total examples}}$$

For each language pair, EN→CS, EN↔DE, EN↔FI, EN↔RU and EN↔LT, results are shown respectively in Tables 9 to 13. Overall, we observe that systems perform quite well in WSD, achieving high precision overall. For some translation directions, there is a big gap between in-domain and out-of-domain synsets, showing clearly that systems tuned towards news translation struggle to identify the right sense when tested on a different domain. At the same time, online systems are more robust to domain mismatch, which is likely due to their use of a much larger variety of training data. Interestingly, the Czech–English task shows opposite results, with online systems performing better on in-domain synsets than research systems.

Interestingly enough, having English as source side yields better overall precision comparing with English as target side. One possible explanation could be found in the difficulty to obtain better encoder representations for morphologically rich languages. Recall is better with English on the target side due to higher coverage (Table 8).

It would have been instructive to compare the MuCoW results with automatic or manual evaluation scores on the official WMT19 test set, but unfortunately, such scores were not available in time for all systems.

6 Conclusion

In this paper, we have presented MuCoW, an automatically built WSD test suite for machine translation that relies on large parallel corpora, the multilingual lexical resource BabelNet and language-

---

[8]We used the Turku neural lemmatizer with pretrained models (Kanerva et al., 2019). For Lithuanian, as no pretrained model was available, we trained one using the respective available data from the Universal Dependencies project.

[9]Examples that contained both correct and incorrect target words were counted as incorrect.

independent synset embeddings. We used the proposed benchmark to assess the WSD ability of NMT systems following two evaluation protocols: scoring both reference and contrastive translations with pretrained NMT models, and as translation test suite for the WMT19 news shared task.

We find that state-of-the-art and fine-tuned NMT systems still present some drawbacks on handling ambiguous words, especially when evaluated on out-of-domain data and when the encoder has to deal with a morphologically rich language. It will be particularly instructive to see how well the WSD test suite results correlate with human evaluation scores and with recently proposed evaluation metrics that are based on semantic representations of the translations (Gupta et al., 2015; Shimanaka et al., 2018).

As future work we plan to further extend the test suite including more languages and parallel data, and make use of the contrastive sentences as adversarial examples during training.

Acknowledgments

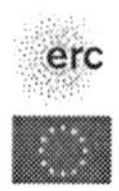 This work is part of the FoTran project, funded by the European Research Council (ERC) under the European Union's Horizon 2020 research and innovation programme (grant agreement No 771113).

The authors gratefully acknowledge the support of the Academy of Finland through project 314062 from the ICT 2023 call on Computation, Machine Learning and Artificial Intelligence. Finally, We would also like to acknowledge NVIDIA and their GPU grant.

References

Rachel Bawden, Rico Sennrich, Alexandra Birch, and Barry Haddow. 2018. Evaluating discourse phenomena in neural machine translation. In *Proceedings of the 2018 Conference of the North American Chapter of the Association for Computational Linguistics: Human Language Technologies, Volume 1 (Long Papers)*, pages 1304–1313. Association for Computational Linguistics.

Piotr Bojanowski, Edouard Grave, Armand Joulin, and Tomas Mikolov. 2017. Enriching word vectors with subword information. *Transactions of the Association for Computational Linguistics*, 5:135–146.

Aljoscha Burchardt, Vivien Macketanz, Jon Dehdari, Georg Heigold, Jan-Thorsten Peter, and Philip Williams. 2017. A linguistic evaluation of rule-based, phrase-based, and neural MT engines.

The Prague Bulletin of Mathematical Linguistics, 108:159–170.

Franck Burlot, Yves Scherrer, Vinit Ravishankar, Ondřej Bojar, Stig-Arne Grönroos, Maarit Koponen, Tommi Nieminen, and François Yvon. 2018. The WMT'18 morpheval test suites for English-Czech, English-German, English-Finnish and Turkish-English. In *Proceedings of the Third Conference on Machine Translation: Shared Task Papers*, pages 546–560, Belgium, Brussels. Association for Computational Linguistics.

Franck Burlot and François Yvon. 2017. Evaluating the morphological competence of machine translation systems. In *Proceedings of the Second Conference on Machine Translation*, pages 43–55. Association for Computational Linguistics.

José Camacho-Collados, Mohammad Taher Pilehvar, and Roberto Navigli. 2016. Nasari: Integrating explicit knowledge and corpus statistics for a multilingual representation of concepts and entities. *Artificial Intelligence*, 240:36–64.

Mauro Cettolo, Jan Niehues, Sebastian Stüker, Luisa Bentivogli, and Marcello Federico. 2013. Report on the 10th iwslt evaluation campaign. In *Proceedings of the International Workshop on Spoken Language Translation, Heidelberg, Germany*.

Andreas Eisele and Yu Chen. 2010. MultiUN: A multilingual corpus from united nation documents. In *Proceedings of the Seventh conference on International Language Resources and Evaluation (LREC'10)*, Valletta, Malta. European Languages Resources Association (ELRA).

Liane Guillou and Christian Hardmeier. 2016. PROTEST: A test suite for evaluating pronouns in machine translation. In *Proceedings of the Tenth International Conference on Language Resources and Evaluation (LREC 2016)*, pages 636–643. European Language Resources Association (ELRA).

Liane Guillou, Christian Hardmeier, Ekaterina Lapshinova-Koltunski, and Sharid Loáiciga. 2018. A pronoun test suite evaluation of the English–German MT systems at WMT 2018. In *Proceedings of the Third Conference on Machine Translation: Shared Task Papers*, pages 570–577, Belgium, Brussels. Association for Computational Linguistics.

Rohit Gupta, Constantin Orasan, and Josef van Genabith. 2015. ReVal: A simple and effective machine translation evaluation metric based on recurrent neural networks. In *Proceedings of the 2015 Conference on Empirical Methods in Natural Language Processing*, pages 1066–1072, Lisbon, Portugal. Association for Computational Linguistics.

Hany Hassan Awadalla, Anthony Aue, Chang Chen, Vishal Chowdhary, , Christian Federmann, Xuedong Huang, Marcin Junczys-Dowmunt, Will Lewis, Shujie Liu, Tie-Yan Liu, Renqian Luo, Arul Menezes,

	In-domain synsets			Out-of-domain synsets			All synsets		
Submission	Prec.	Recall	F1	Prec.	Recall	F1	Prec.	Recall	F1
CUNI-Trf-T2T-2018	96.76	84.75	90.36	**79.85**	**71.71**	**75.56**	**82.77**	74.01	**78.15**
CUNI-Trf-T2T-2019	95.60	85.66	90.36	79.58	71.57	75.36	82.38	**74.04**	77.99
CUNI-DocTrf-T2T	95.60	85.66	90.36	79.58	71.57	75.36	82.38	**74.04**	77.99
CUNI-DocTrf-Marian	96.00	85.71	90.57	72.45	68.51	70.42	76.61	71.69	74.07
uedin	96.30	83.27	89.31	72.96	67.85	70.31	77.02	70.70	73.72
online-Y	97.57	84.86	90.77	61.57	63.73	62.63	67.93	68.03	67.98
parfda	95.02	75.27	84.00	68.16	58.44	62.93	72.85	61.57	66.74
online-X	95.70	**87.81**	**91.59**	57.35	58.89	58.11	64.54	64.83	64.68
online-A	95.88	83.21	89.10	58.36	58.25	58.30	65.17	63.33	64.24
online-B	**97.93**	83.16	89.94	57.02	57.24	57.13	64.46	62.63	63.53

Table 9: Results for English–Czech.

	In-domain synsets			Out-of-domain synsets			All synsets		
Submission	Prec.	Recall	F1	Prec.	Recall	F1	Prec.	Recall	F1
German–English:									
Facebook_FAIR	**80.78**	**85.80**	**83.21**	**52.77**	**72.56**	**61.10**	**73.55**	**82.99**	**77.99**
online-B	77.88	83.81	80.73	45.50	66.51	54.04	69.58	80.31	74.56
online-G	77.62	83.76	80.57	45.62	65.43	53.76	69.48	80.02	74.38
online-Y	76.82	84.51	80.48	41.93	61.71	49.93	68.10	79.97	73.56
dfki-nmt	77.64	83.35	80.39	41.08	63.02	49.74	68.31	79.42	73.45
RWTH_Aachen	77.62	84.30	80.83	36.96	60.92	46.01	67.30	80.02	73.11
MSRA.MADL	77.95	84.36	81.03	36.73	56.26	44.44	67.78	79.08	73.00
UCAM	76.79	84.04	80.25	35.38	55.71	43.28	66.54	78.77	72.14
MLLP-UPV	77.26	83.24	80.14	35.85	54.92	43.38	67.02	77.93	72.06
online-A	75.77	83.08	79.26	37.47	63.15	47.04	65.87	79.40	72.00
NEU	75.26	83.50	79.16	32.49	55.93	41.11	64.49	78.58	70.84
JHU	74.94	83.68	79.07	31.56	51.38	39.10	64.31	77.79	70.41
uedin	74.26	81.62	77.77	32.21	45.89	37.85	64.28	74.70	69.10
PROMT_NMT	70.05	81.34	75.27	32.02	43.94	37.05	61.20	73.70	66.87
online-X	67.04	80.29	73.07	31.98	62.47	42.31	57.77	77.07	66.04
TartuNLP-c	71.11	77.22	74.04	29.29	46.31	35.88	60.68	71.48	65.64
English–German:									
Facebook_FAIR	**83.43**	76.99	**80.08**	**56.29**	**55.10**	**55.69**	**74.48**	**70.05**	**72.19**
Microsoft-sentence-level	83.18	**77.14**	80.05	52.81	51.92	52.36	73.31	69.27	71.23
online-B	83.37	74.78	78.85	51.92	50.66	51.28	73.04	67.30	70.05
Microsoft-document-level	81.76	75.68	78.60	47.21	48.11	47.65	70.54	67.29	68.88
online-Y	81.29	75.30	78.18	46.37	48.21	47.27	69.87	67.12	68.47
online-G	81.44	73.76	77.41	46.61	45.44	46.02	70.21	65.09	67.55
dfki-nmt	80.70	74.37	77.41	44.95	42.04	43.44	69.54	64.39	66.87
MLLP-UPV	79.90	73.60	76.62	44.03	39.63	41.72	68.90	63.01	65.82
lmu-ctx-tf-single	79.55	72.51	75.86	43.93	41.99	42.94	68.23	63.13	65.58
NEU	78.39	73.50	75.86	41.91	41.53	41.72	66.83	63.75	65.25
eTranslation	80.44	71.00	75.43	43.47	40.48	41.92	68.69	61.65	64.98
MSRA.MADL	80.53	71.97	76.01	41.79	35.63	38.46	68.88	60.67	64.51
UCAM	78.21	72.70	75.35	40.41	37.28	38.78	66.61	61.77	64.10
online-A	79.21	72.05	75.46	40.48	36.44	38.35	67.37	61.09	64.07
Helsinki-NLP	78.34	72.52	75.32	39.06	36.65	37.82	66.24	61.57	63.82
PROMT_NMT	78.08	72.40	75.13	36.99	34.16	35.52	65.61	60.77	63.10
JHU	77.80	71.48	74.50	37.77	29.35	33.04	66.47	58.08	61.99
UdS-DFKI	78.27	70.54	74.21	35.68	30.16	32.69	65.72	58.10	61.68
online-X	71.01	72.71	71.85	34.36	40.47	37.17	59.07	63.16	61.05
TartuNLP-c	77.32	66.29	71.38	33.02	26.13	29.17	64.34	53.85	58.63
en_de_task	64.54	23.14	34.06	38.41	5.64	9.84	59.43	16.62	25.97

Table 10: Results for German–English and English–German.

Submission	In-domain synsets			Out-of-domain synsets			All synsets		
	Prec.	Recall	F1	Prec.	Recall	F1	Prec.	Recall	F1
Finnish–English:									
online-G	78.00	84.17	80.97	**71.47**	81.65	**76.22**	**74.14**	**82.71**	**78.19**
online-Y	79.30	82.89	81.05	63.40	**81.73**	71.41	69.78	82.25	75.51
GTCOM-Primary	81.87	**84.81**	**83.31**	57.28	77.64	65.92	67.36	81.05	73.57
MSRA.NAO	**82.21**	83.79	82.99	57.26	77.86	65.99	67.42	80.70	73.46
USYD	80.05	83.43	81.71	56.18	71.50	62.92	66.20	77.09	71.23
parfda	77.89	78.66	78.27	55.16	66.01	60.10	64.71	71.86	68.10
online-B	77.55	82.01	79.72	52.10	66.97	58.61	62.88	74.07	68.02
online-A	76.16	78.70	77.41	52.85	69.02	59.87	62.46	73.57	67.56
Helsinki-NLP	76.65	78.53	77.58	48.52	62.86	54.77	60.37	70.37	64.99
online-X	68.92	76.68	72.59	51.39	67.75	58.45	58.63	71.81	64.56
TartuNLP-c	75.35	79.77	77.49	45.32	53.13	48.92	58.70	65.68	61.99
apertium-unconstrained	63.97	67.15	65.52	38.46	52.86	44.53	48.96	59.69	53.80
English–Finnish:									
online-G	93.71	75.25	83.47	**80.62**	**68.54**	**74.09**	**84.01**	**70.36**	**76.58**
online-Y	94.74	72.00	81.82	75.06	66.08	70.28	80.03	67.75	73.38
MSRA.NAO	**95.62**	**76.12**	**84.76**	68.47	66.60	67.52	75.44	69.42	72.31
GTCOM-Primary	94.81	73.00	82.49	66.24	67.97	67.09	73.25	69.49	71.32
online-X	84.14	65.95	73.94	62.22	61.95	62.08	67.56	63.11	65.26
NICT	90.32	72.54	80.46	57.62	59.35	58.48	66.06	63.42	64.71
online-B	88.75	74.74	81.14	59.02	56.38	57.67	67.12	61.85	64.38
Aalto-ORMFC	88.81	66.15	75.82	64.94	54.79	59.44	71.17	58.04	63.93
Helsinki-NLP	84.56	61.50	71.21	59.65	52.51	55.85	65.93	55.11	60.03
online-A	86.75	77.42	81.82	52.31	46.79	49.39	62.59	55.95	59.08
TartuNLP-c	93.29	70.20	80.12	53.83	43.49	48.11	65.24	51.61	57.63
Helsinki-NLP-rule-based	71.60	75.62	73.56	48.88	47.36	48.11	55.59	55.21	55.40
apertium-unconstrained	81.71	34.72	48.73	45.61	20.88	28.65	55.16	24.75	34.17

Table 11: Results for Finnish–English and English–Finnish.

Submission	In-domain synsets			Out-of-domain synsets			All synsets		
	Prec.	Recall	F1	Prec.	Recall	F1	Prec.	Recall	F1
Russian–English:									
online-G	**92.15**	89.63	**90.87**	**66.95**	**80.87**	**73.26**	**78.57**	**85.38**	**81.84**
Facebook_FAIR	89.98	**89.80**	89.89	56.67	77.30	65.40	72.12	84.07	77.64
online-B	89.55	87.58	88.55	56.41	74.07	64.04	71.81	81.34	76.28
online-A	87.93	87.58	87.76	50.97	73.16	60.08	68.09	81.15	74.05
online-Y	88.68	87.07	87.87	50.90	70.75	59.21	68.52	79.78	73.72
MSRA.SCA	86.22	85.33	85.77	50.27	72.45	59.35	66.76	79.57	72.60
NEU	87.19	86.48	86.83	47.89	72.15	57.57	65.97	80.23	72.40
afrl-syscomb19	86.85	85.42	86.13	44.40	65.41	52.90	64.26	76.78	69.96
eTranslation	87.71	84.15	85.89	43.82	62.73	51.60	64.41	74.91	69.27
rerank-re	87.71	84.15	85.89	43.23	61.99	50.94	64.14	74.62	68.99
online-X	82.39	87.90	85.06	35.99	65.06	46.35	57.66	78.71	66.56
TartuNLP-u	84.11	87.50	85.77	37.35	53.09	43.85	60.38	72.71	65.97
afrl-ewc	87.04	82.24	84.58	33.75	45.63	38.80	59.92	66.86	63.20
NICT	78.62	69.11	73.56	30.17	24.42	26.99	56.29	47.59	51.58
English–Russian:									
online-G	**95.56**	89.58	92.47	**75.11**	**74.85**	**74.98**	**80.05**	**78.58**	**79.31**
Facebook_FAIR	95.49	88.28	91.75	67.68	71.54	69.56	74.40	76.01	75.20
online-B	95.08	91.10	93.05	62.12	69.05	65.40	70.31	75.16	72.66
USTC-MCC	95.30	90.08	92.62	59.35	71.08	64.69	68.02	76.54	72.03
NEU	94.43	89.21	91.75	59.31	70.98	64.62	67.74	76.18	71.71
online-Y	95.37	91.38	**93.33**	57.47	69.02	62.72	66.80	75.51	70.89
online-A	91.14	89.40	90.26	55.29	68.28	61.10	64.00	74.35	68.79
PROMT_NMT	93.48	**91.49**	92.47	56.78	63.76	60.07	66.18	71.61	68.79
online-X	93.65	89.92	91.75	52.53	67.35	59.02	62.53	74.12	67.83
TartuNLP-u	90.91	84.01	87.32	51.44	56.17	53.70	61.41	64.11	62.73
rerank-er	94.98	78.91	86.20	55.54	33.78	42.01	68.17	45.36	54.47
NICT	89.19	25.52	39.68	46.99	5.88	10.46	63.90	10.33	17.78

Table 12: Results for Russian–English and English–Russian.

	All synsets					All synsets		
Submission	Prec.	Recall	F1		Submission	Prec.	Recall	F1
Lithuanian–English:					**English–Lithuanian:**			
tilde-c-nmt	**80.41**	97.50	**88.14**		MSRA.MASS	78.69	**85.71**	**82.05**
NEU	79.59	**98.73**	**88.14**		online-B	79.31	80.70	80.00
tilde-nc-nmt	79.38	97.47	87.50		tilde-nc-nmt	80.70	79.31	80.00
GTCOM-Primary	77.32	97.40	86.21		tilde-c-nmt	81.82	76.27	78.95
online-B	75.51	98.67	85.55		MSRA.MASS	78.95	78.95	78.95
MSRA.MASS	73.47	98.63	84.21		online-A	**83.02**	73.33	77.88
online-A	73.96	95.95	83.53		GTCOM-Primary	78.57	77.19	77.88
online-G	72.92	95.89	82.84		NEU	76.79	76.79	76.79
online-X	60.22	90.32	72.26		eTranslation	79.25	72.41	75.68
JUMT	71.62	67.95	69.74		TartuNLP-c	81.25	65.00	72.22
TartuNLP-c	64.86	65.75	65.31		online-X	70.37	71.70	71.03
					online-G	71.15	68.52	69.81

Table 13: Results for Lithuanian–English and English–Lithuanian.

Tao Qin, Frank Seide, Xu Tan, Fei Tian, Lijun Wu, Shuangzhi Wu, Yingce Xia, Dongdong Zhang, Zhirui Zhang, and Ming Zhou. 2018. Achieving human parity on automatic Chinese to English news translation. ArXiv:1803.05567.

Pierre Isabelle, Colin Cherry, and George Foster. 2017. A challenge set approach to evaluating machine translation. In *Proceedings of the 2017 Conference on Empirical Methods in Natural Language Processing*, pages 2486–2496, Copenhagen, Denmark. Association for Computational Linguistics.

Jenna Kanerva, Filip Ginter, and Tapio Salakoski. 2019. Universal lemmatizer: A sequence to sequence model for lemmatizing universal dependencies treebanks. *arXiv preprint arXiv:1902.00972*.

Philipp Koehn. 2005. Europarl: A parallel corpus for statistical machine translation. In *MT summit*, volume 5, pages 79–86.

Samuel Läubli, Rico Sennrich, and Martin Volk. 2018. Has machine translation achieved human parity? A case for document-level evaluation. In *Proceedings of the 2018 Conference on Empirical Methods in Natural Language Processing*, pages 4791–4796. Association for Computational Linguistics.

Pierre Lison and Jörg Tiedemann. 2016. OpenSubtitles2016: Extracting large parallel corpora from movie and TV subtitles. In *Proceedings of the Tenth International Conference on Language Resources and Evaluation (LREC 2016)*, pages 923–929, Portorož, Slovenia. European Language Resources Association (ELRA).

Frederick Liu, Han Lu, and Graham Neubig. 2018. Handling homographs in neural machine translation. In *Proceedings of the 2018 Conference of the North American Chapter of the Association for Computational Linguistics: Human Language Technologies, Volume 1 (Long Papers)*, volume 1, pages 1336–1345.

Vivien Macketanz, Eleftherios Avramidis, Aljoscha Burchardt, and Hans Uszkoreit. 2018. Fine-grained evaluation of German-English machine translation based on a test suite. In *Proceedings of the Third Conference on Machine Translation: Shared Task Papers*, pages 578–587, Belgium, Brussels. Association for Computational Linguistics.

Massimiliano Mancini, Jose Camacho-Collados, Ignacio Iacobacci, and Roberto Navigli. 2017. Embedding words and senses together via joint knowledge-enhanced training. In *Proceedings of the 21st Conference on Computational Natural Language Learning (CoNLL 2017)*, pages 100–111, Vancouver, Canada. Association for Computational Linguistics.

Rebecca Marvin and Philipp Koehn. 2018. Exploring word sense disambiguation abilities of neural machine translation systems (non-archival extended abstract). In *Proceedings of the 13th Conference of the Association for Machine Translation in the Americas (Volume 1: Research Papers)*, volume 1, pages 125–131.

Mathias Müller, Annette Rios, Elena Voita, and Rico Sennrich. 2018. A large-scale test set for the evaluation of context-aware pronoun translation in neural machine translation. In *Proceedings of the Third Conference on Machine Translation: Research Papers*, pages 61–72. Association for Computational Linguistics.

Roberto Navigli. 2006. Meaningful clustering of senses helps boost word sense disambiguation performance. In *Proceedings of the 21st International Conference on Computational Linguistics and the 44th annual meeting of the Association for Computational Linguistics*, pages 105–112. Association for Computational Linguistics.

Roberto Navigli and Simone Paolo Ponzetto. 2012. BabelNet: The automatic construction, evaluation and application of a wide-coverage multilingual semantic network. *Artificial Intelligence*, 193:217–250.

Robert Östling and Jörg Tiedemann. 2016. Efficient word alignment with Markov Chain Monte Carlo. *Prague Bulletin of Mathematical Linguistics*, 106:125–146.

Martha Palmer, Hoa Trang Dang, and Christiane Fellbaum. 2007. Making fine-grained and coarse-grained sense distinctions, both manually and automatically. *Natural Language Engineering*, 13(2):137–163.

Annette Rios, Mathias Müller, and Rico Sennrich. 2018. The word sense disambiguation test suite at WMT18. In *Proceedings of the Third Conference on Machine Translation: Shared Task Papers*, pages 588–596.

Annette Rios Gonzales, Laura Mascarell, and Rico Sennrich. 2017. Improving word sense disambiguation in neural machine translation with sense embeddings. In *Proceedings of the Second Conference on Machine Translation*, pages 11–19, Copenhagen, Denmark. Association for Computational Linguistics.

Rico Sennrich. 2017. How grammatical is character-level neural machine translation? Assessing MT quality with contrastive translation pairs. In *Proceedings of the 15th Conference of the European Chapter of the Association for Computational Linguistics: Volume 2, Short Papers*, pages 376–382, Valencia, Spain. Association for Computational Linguistics.

Rico Sennrich, Alexandra Birch, Anna Currey, Ulrich Germann, Barry Haddow, Kenneth Heafield, Antonio Valerio Miceli Barone, and Philip Williams. 2017a. The University of Edinburgh's neural MT systems for WMT17. In *Proceedings of the Second Conference on Machine Translation*, pages 389–399. Association for Computational Linguistics.

Rico Sennrich, Orhan Firat, Kyunghyun Cho, Alexandra Birch, Barry Haddow, Julian Hitschler, Marcin Junczys-Dowmunt, Samuel Läubli, Antonio Valerio Miceli Barone, Jozef Mokry, and Maria Nadejde. 2017b. Nematus: a toolkit for neural machine translation. In *Proceedings of the Software Demonstrations of the 15th Conference of the European Chapter of the Association for Computational Linguistics*, pages 65–68, Valencia, Spain. Association for Computational Linguistics.

Rico Sennrich, Barry Haddow, and Alexandra Birch. 2016a. Edinburgh neural machine translation systems for WMT 16. In *Proceedings of the First Conference on Machine Translation: Volume 2, Shared Task Papers*, pages 371–376. Association for Computational Linguistics.

Rico Sennrich, Barry Haddow, and Alexandra Birch. 2016b. Improving neural machine translation models with monolingual data. In *Proceedings of the 54th Annual Meeting of the Association for Computational Linguistics (Volume 1: Long Papers)*, volume 1, pages 86–96.

Rico Sennrich, Barry Haddow, and Alexandra Birch. 2016c. Neural machine translation of rare words with subword units. In *Proceedings of the 54th Annual Meeting of the Association for Computational Linguistics (Volume 1: Long Papers)*, volume 1, pages 1715–1725.

Hiroki Shimanaka, Tomoyuki Kajiwara, and Mamoru Komachi. 2018. RUSE: Regressor using sentence embeddings for automatic machine translation evaluation. In *Proceedings of the Third Conference on Machine Translation: Shared Task Papers*, pages 751–758, Belgium, Brussels. Association for Computational Linguistics.

Milan Straka and Jana Straková. 2017. Tokenizing, POS tagging, lemmatizing and parsing UD 2.0 with UDPipe. In *Proceedings of the CoNLL 2017 Shared Task: Multilingual Parsing from Raw Text to Universal Dependencies*, pages 88–99, Vancouver, Canada. Association for Computational Linguistics.

Gongbo Tang, Rico Sennrich, and Joakim Nivre. 2018. An analysis of attention mechanisms: The case of word sense disambiguation in neural machine translation. In *Proceedings of the Third Conference on Machine Translation: Research Papers*, pages 26–35. Association for Computational Linguistics.

Jörg Tiedemann. 2012. Parallel data, tools and interfaces in OPUS. In *Proceedings of the Eight International Conference on Language Resources and Evaluation (LREC'12)*, pages 2214–2218, Istanbul, Turkey. European Language Resources Association (ELRA).

Antonio Toral, Sheila Castilho, Ke Hu, and Andy Way. 2018. Attaining the unattainable? Reassessing claims of human parity in neural machine translation. In *Proceedings of the Third Conference on Machine Translation: Research Papers*, pages 113–123. Association for Computational Linguistics.

Francis M Tyers and Murat Serdar Alperen. 2010. South-east european times: A parallel corpus of balkan languages. In *Proceedings of the LREC Workshop on Exploitation of Multilingual Resources and Tools for Central and (South-) Eastern European Languages*, pages 49–53.

Ashish Vaswani, Noam Shazeer, Niki Parmar, Jakob Uszkoreit, Llion Jones, Aidan N Gomez, Łukasz Kaiser, and Illia Polosukhin. 2017. Attention is all you need. In *Advances in Neural Information Processing Systems*, pages 5998–6008.

SAO WMT19 Test Suite: Machine Translation of Audit Reports

Tereza Vojtěchová*   Michal Novák*   Miloš Klouček*[†]   Ondřej Bojar*

* Charles University, Faculty of Mathematics and Physics
Institute of Formal and Applied Linguistics
Malostranské náměstí 25, 118 00 Prague, Czech Republic

[†] Supreme Audit Office of the Czech Republic
Jankovcova 1518/2, 170 04 Prague, Czech Republic
{vojtechova, mnovak, kloucek, bojar}@ufal.mff.cuni.cz

Abstract

This paper describes a machine translation test set of documents from the auditing domain and its use as one of the "test suites" in the WMT19 News Translation Task for translation directions involving Czech, English and German.

Our evaluation suggests that current MT systems optimized for the general news domain can perform quite well even in the particular domain of audit reports. The detailed manual evaluation however indicates that deep factual knowledge of the domain is necessary. For the naked eye of a non-expert, translations by many systems seem almost perfect and automatic MT evaluation with one reference is practically useless for considering these details.

Furthermore, we show on a sample document from the domain of agreements that even the best systems completely fail in preserving the semantics of the agreement, namely the identity of the parties.

1 Introduction

Domain mismatch is often the main sources of machine translation errors. At the same time, it has been suggested in the speech recognition area that models trained on extremely large data can perform well across domains, i.e. without any particular domain adaptation (Narayanan et al., 2018).

We believe that for some of the language pairs annually tested in the WMT shared translation task, the best machine translation systems may have grown to sizes where the domain dependence may be less critical. At the same time, we know that most of current MT systems still operate at the level of individual sentences and therefore have no control over document-level coherence e.g. in terms of lexical choice.

To investigate the two questions, domain independence and document-level coherence, we cleaned and prepared a dedicated set of documents from the auditing domain and submitted it as one of the "test suites" to this year's WMT News Translation Task. The collection is called "SAO WMT19 Test Suite" after the Supreme Audit Office of the Czech Republic (SAO) who provided the original audit reports created in cooperation with other national supreme audit institutions (SAIs).[1]

This paper is organized as follows: In Section 2 we describe the source and our processing of the test documents. Section 3 provides automatic scores of WMT19 MT systems on the test suite and Section 4 presents the manual evaluation. One more document type, namely a sublease agreement, was evaluated separately, see Section 5. We release the test suite for public use, see Section 6, and we conclude in Section 7.

2 Composition of SAO Test Suite

The SAO Test Suite consists of 10 multi-language audit reports issued by the SAO. The reports describe investigations carried out jointly by SAO and one or more other national auditing institutions between the years 2004 and 2015. The reports were published in multiple language versions or as multilingual documents. They were created jointly by the co-operating SAIs in English and later on, they were translated by translation agencies and finally corrected by the authorized auditors from the respective countries. The end effect of this careful procedure is that from time to time, the different language versions slightly depart in the exact wording, including minor shifts of the conveyed meanings.

---

[1] We adhere to the convention that "SAO" refers solely to the Supreme Audit Office of the Czech Republic. For other supreme audit institutions, we use the acronym SAI.

Proceedings of the Fourth Conference on Machine Translation (WMT), Volume 2: Shared Task Papers (Day 1) pages 481–493
Florence, Italy, August 1-2, 2019. ©2019 Association for Computational Linguistics

Language	Count
Czech	10
English	10
Slovak	5
German	4
Polish	1
Total documents	30

Table 1: Number of languages in SAO Test Suite. Languages in bold were used in WMT19 Shared Translation Task.

Language Pair	Documents	MT Systems
en-cs	11	11
en-de	4	22
de-en	4	16
cs-de	4	7
de-cs	4	11

Table 2: Evaluated language pairs, documents and MT systems.

All the reports come in 3 different languages. All of them include Czech and English, the third used language differs. See Table 1 for a summary.

2.1 Creation of the SAO Test Suite

The audit reports were collected primarily from the website of SAO. It is important to note that while being publicly available, these documents did not make it to any of WMT19 constrained training data, probably because the texts appear on the web only in the form of PDFs. We double-checked that there is no overlap by searching the data for exact and near sentence matches. Very short segments like generic titles or section numbers were naturally present in the training data but we did not find any longer sentences, let alone more sentences from a test document.

First, we converted the documents from the PDF format to plain text. We note that some of the documents were bitmap PDFs (scans) and we had to use OCR to obtain the text. This was particularly tedious for multi-language documents with texts side by side in two or three columns.

The rest of the processing was applied only to Czech, English and German versions of the documents, because other languages were not considered in WMT19 News Translation Task.

The plain text versions were automatically segmented into sentences using the trainable tokenizer TrTok by Maršík and Bojar (2012). We then automatically aligned sentences in English and Czech versions using hunalign (Varga et al., 2005) and manually revised this alignment.

During the manual revision of sentence alignments, we removed footnotes, tables and graph captions, as well as occasional paragraphs not present in one of the languages. Sometimes, sentence segmentation had to be fixed as well.

In the final stage, we added the German side to the already sentence-aligned English-Czech files, creating a tri-parallel test set. In some cases, the segmentation into sentences was not exactly parallel and we had to break primarily the German sentences into clauses, or introduce blank segments in some of the files to allow for a better match. Once or twice even the order of the clauses in German was swapped compared to the aligned Czech and English.

2.2 SAO Test Suite in WMT19 Shared Task

We submitted our files as a "test suite" complementing the WMT19 News Translation Task. This means that all primary MT systems participating in the News Translation Task also translated our files.

The English→Czech and German↔English systems were *supervised*, i.e. trained on genuine parallel texts (and target-side monolingual data). The Czech↔German research systems were *unsupervised*, i.e. trained only on monolingual source and target texts, optionally using a small parallel development set of a few thousand sentence pairs. Our evaluation also includes several anonymized online systems ("online-...") the internals of which are not known. These online systems could in principle include our test suite as part of their training data.

The number of evaluated documents and MT systems for each examined language pair is in Table 2.

3 Automatic Evaluation

For automatic evaluation, we use several of common MT evaluation metrics (Papineni et al., 2002; Popović, 2015; Leusch and Ney, 2008; Wang et al., 2016; Snover et al., 2006). Metrics listed with the prefix "n" are reversed ($1 - $ score) so that higher numbers indicate a better translation in all the figures we report.

We calculate the score for each of the documents in our test suite separately and report the average score and the standard deviation.

The scores are detailed in Tables 3 to 7. In the subsequent tables, we sometimes abbreviate system names for typesetting reasons.

The main observation across the tables is that all the scores heavily vary across individual documents. The typical standard deviation is 3–5 for BLEU and similarly for other metrics.

The metrics do not always agree on the overall ranking of the systems, as indicated by "ι" in the tables, but these differences are much smaller that the variance due to the particular documents.

A big caveat should be taken when interpreting all automatic scores as an estimate of real translation quality, because they are all based on the single reference translation. See also the discussion in Section 4.2 below.

4 Manual Evaluation

Due to the specific terminology in the documents and domain knowledge needed to verify translation quality, we asked the SAO's employees serve as the annotators.[2] All of them were native Czech speakers with a high level of English and/or German proficiency.

We also attempted to find native German auditors but we were not successful so far. English→German and German→English translation was thus evaluated by a single SAO employee, a native Czech speaker with a great command of both English and German, including the specific auditing domain.

4.1 Establishing Evaluation Criteria

Our manual evaluation criteria are based on the criteria used for the scoring of essays in the Czech GCSE counterpart ("maturita") for the Czech language.

After a short test session with our prospective annotators, we realized how very narrow this specific field is and we simplified the original set of 7 criteria with 6 levels each to only 5 criteria and 4 levels each. This simplification definitely saved some annotation time and we also believe that it increased the inter-annotator agreement, although

we did not collect enough annotations to reliably measure it.

The final criteria to be used in the evaluation are as follows:

1) Language Resources – Spelling and Morphology
- 0 points: 10 or more spelling or morphology errors.
- 1 point: 9-6 spelling or morphology errors.
- 2 points: 5-3 spelling or morphology errors.
- 3 points: 2-0 spelling or morphology errors.

2) Vocabulary – Adequacy of Terms Used
- 0 points: Frequently, used terms are inappropriately chosen.
- 1 point: Sometimes, used terms are inappropriately chosen.
- 2 points: Rarely, used terms are inappropriately chosen.
- 3 points: There are no terms, which would be inappropriately chosen.

3) Vocabulary – Clarity of the Text in Terms of Used Words
- 0 points: The choice of words and phrases fundamentally impairs the understanding of the text.
- 1 point: The choice of words and phrases sometimes impairs the understanding of the text.
- 2 points: The choice of words and phrases rarely impairs the understanding of the text.
- 3 points: The choice of words and phrases does not impair the understanding of the text.

4) Syntax and Word Order
- 0 points: Syntactic shortcomings are high in the text.
- 1 point: Syntactic shortcomings occur in the text.
- 2 points: Syntactic shortcomings are rare in the text.
- 3 points: Syntactic shortcomings are almost absent from the text.

5) Coherence and Overall Understanding of the Text
- 0 points: The recipient is completely lost in the text. The text is incoherent and fails to fulfil its communication purpose (the addressee has completely misunderstood what the text expresses).
- 1 point: The orientation in the text is completely uncomfortable for the addressee, the text is at

---

[2] Relying on purely linguistic expertise proved insufficient after a discussion with SAO employees. While for the best systems, we could hardly notice any errors, the knowledge experts discussed term choice and even among themselves, they were carefully considering the logical implications of the particular terms.

	BLEU	chrF3	nCDER	nCharacTER	nPER	nTER	nWER
CUNI-Transformer-T2T-2018	30.21±6.22	58.49±4.14	50.69±6.48	50.27±9.47	58.04±7.70	46.20±9.04	44.11±8.79
CUNI-Transformer-T2T-2019	29.16±6.16	57.40±3.96	49.61±6.54	47.75±8.97	56.76±7.93	44.64±9.21	42.48±8.99
CUNI-DocTransformer-T2T	29.15±6.04	57.33±3.87	49.57±6.61	⟨48.38±9.31	56.34±7.53	44.53±8.93	42.45±8.78
uedin	29.15±5.94	57.31±3.84	⟨49.87±6.29	⟨48.73±8.25	⟨57.02±7.06	⟨45.53±8.53	⟨43.49±8.20
online-B	29.14±5.57	⟨57.36±3.39	49.74±5.78	48.44±8.23	⟨57.47±7.18	45.46±8.22	43.15±7.88
online-Y	28.53±5.57	57.34±3.56	49.44±6.10	45.00±7.78	56.89±7.48	45.04±8.47	42.92±8.14
CUNI-DocTransformer-Marian	25.86±4.57	54.65±3.11	46.73±5.45	-6.50±110.46	53.60±6.64	41.15±7.74	39.07±7.46
TartuNLP-c	25.12±4.94	54.57±3.00	46.21±5.80	⟨44.71±7.40	53.02±7.92	40.40±8.44	38.31±8.11
online-A	24.01±5.72	53.59±3.58	45.19±6.45	⟨44.80±8.27	52.84±7.52	40.27±9.03	38.19±8.74
online-G	23.84±4.64	⟨54.21±3.40	44.78±5.79	⟨45.91±9.40	52.83±7.02	40.16±7.88	38.02±7.58
online-X	19.61±3.43	50.42±2.69	41.07±4.22	41.39±6.72	47.54±6.78	34.62±6.81	32.79±6.65

Table 3: Automatic scores for English→Czech. "⟨" marks scores out of sequence.

	BLEU	chrF3	nCDER	nCharacTER	nPER	nTER	nWER
Microsoft-sent-level	22.06±3.61	55.57±2.24	42.62±4.68	38.22±4.08	44.83±5.04	30.23±5.91	28.37±5.89
Microsoft-doc-level	21.91±3.57	⟨55.84±2.07	42.52±4.50	⟨38.63±3.89	44.18±5.42	29.67±6.37	27.72±6.30
online-B	21.70±3.73	54.55±2.35	41.48±4.47	34.63±6.04	⟨46.25±5.41	⟨30.44±6.15	⟨28.61±6.17
Facebook_FAIR	21.52±4.21	⟨55.20±2.72	⟨42.24±5.17	⟨37.65±4.34	43.49±6.16	29.35±7.23	27.36±7.21
lmu-ctx-tf-single	21.52±3.77	54.72±2.11	41.91±4.42	37.50±4.86	⟨45.40±5.41	⟨30.20±6.11	⟨28.24±5.98
NEU	21.29±3.61	54.63±1.97	⟨42.11±4.62	⟨38.36±4.45	44.73±5.34	30.01±6.52	28.16±6.40
MSRA.MADL	21.23±3.82	53.96±2.07	41.20±4.65	37.14±3.24	44.07±5.99	29.07±6.68	27.29±6.59
Helsinki-NLP	20.57±3.39	53.35±1.84	41.09±4.56	36.16±3.96	⟨44.76±5.00	⟨29.51±5.99	⟨27.65±5.95
UCAM	20.52±4.00	53.14±2.37	41.02±4.96	35.72±4.07	44.67±5.47	29.32±6.52	27.38±6.42
online-Y	20.46±3.42	⟨53.72±1.79	⟨41.14±4.47	⟨37.22±4.83	44.53±5.48	⟨29.65±6.33	⟨27.75±6.14
dfki-nmt	20.30±3.11	⟨53.74±1.75	40.96±4.18	36.92±4.65	43.67±4.81	28.88±5.98	26.97±5.78
MLLP-UPV	20.30±3.47	53.45±2.00	40.75±4.57	36.75±4.49	⟨43.80±4.99	28.81±6.12	26.84±5.98
PROMT_NMT	20.16±2.88	53.27±1.26	40.46±3.69	36.41±4.84	⟨43.88±4.85	28.76±5.44	26.73±5.45
eTranslation	20.12±3.47	⟨53.45±2.00	⟨40.73±4.42	36.22±4.26	43.45±4.90	28.17±5.89	26.15±5.63
UdS-DFKI	20.05±3.31	51.41±1.40	39.39±3.89	33.37±8.07	⟨45.36±4.99	⟨28.80±5.62	⟨26.97±5.59
JHU	19.89±3.02	⟨52.93±1.64	⟨40.53±4.23	⟨36.20±5.19	44.09±4.83	⟨28.92±5.92	26.95±5.81
TartuNLP-c	19.67±3.33	52.72±1.31	39.93±4.11	36.15±5.01	⟨44.18±5.86	28.56±6.11	26.58±6.03
online-A	19.36±3.71	52.47±2.15	39.73±4.68	34.63±3.52	42.36±5.39	27.17±6.66	25.23±6.49
online-G	18.80±3.41	52.26±1.35	38.97±3.86	⟨34.89±4.93	⟨44.69±5.34	⟨28.53±5.84	⟨26.73±5.88
online-X	13.66±2.22	48.06±1.12	33.85±3.67	31.48±5.69	30.69±5.80	17.04±6.51	15.42±6.24
en_de_task	10.44±1.93	42.22±1.25	28.15±2.92	22.23±6.98	⟨34.90±5.05	16.85±5.52	15.15±5.50
Microsoft-sent_doc	0.00±0.00	0.12±0.02	0.00±0.00	-3408.43±471.13	0.00±0.00	0.00±0.00	0.00±0.00

Table 4: Automatic scores for English→German. "⟨" marks scores out of sequence.

times incoherent and barely serves its communication purpose (but the addressee believes that he or she understands the main content of the text more or less).

- 2 points: The recipient navigates the text, though not entirely comfortably. The text is coherent and more or less fulfils its communication purpose (the addressee is sure he understands the text as a whole).
- 3 points: The recipient is fully oriented in the text. The text is completely coherent, it serves its communication purpose excellently (the addressee fully and without difficulty understands the text as a whole).

4.2 Reference Effectively Useless

One observation that emerged from our consultation with the experts in the auditing field was that precise choice of terms is extremely important but that detailed knowledge of the respective legislation and practice is necessary to evaluate the translations. We, highly proficient speakers of English, but lacking any substantial information on taxation and other topics discussed in the documents, often could not see any lexical errors, because at the general level, the choice of words seemed acceptable. The experts discussed at length the various factual implications of using one of the near-synonyms over another.

Anecdotally, *voting* among our three consultants would not always work either. Without a chance to discuss a particular term, two of the consultants would label the choice of an MT system as wrong, but the third consultant, the most experienced expert in the very field actually approved it.

The reference translations proved effectively useless for these fine distinctions, because the particular term used in the single reference was often not the only possible one. As already mentioned, the careful revision applied to the reference translations has sometimes slightly shifted the meaning, preferring a better match with the factual knowledge over the literality of the translation.

4.3 Execution of Evaluation

As was mentioned above, the annotators were the employees of the SAO.

We decided to score not the complete docu-

	BLEU	chrF3	nCDER	nCharacTER	nPER	nTER	nWER
Facebook_FAIR	26.81±2.95	52.76±2.38	46.17±3.07	35.78±3.89	57.82±2.70	39.59±4.03	36.73±4.04
RWTH_Aachen	26.02±3.01	51.74±2.52	45.53±3.16	35.61±3.66	57.09±3.29	39.16±4.29	36.41±4.34
online-B	25.62±3.06	51.30±2.57	45.30±3.44	33.97±4.02	56.42±3.65	↻ 39.70±4.30	↻ 36.99±4.21
NEU	25.45±2.84	↻ 51.55±2.27	45.19±2.85	↻ 35.27±3.97	↻ 57.04±3.10	38.83±3.80	36.09±3.81
online-Y	25.27±3.26	51.30±2.40	↻ 45.38±3.34	35.01±3.58	56.52±3.46	↻ 39.77±4.20	↻ 36.93±4.11
dfki-nmt	25.00±2.90	50.89±2.18	44.64±2.89	34.67±3.47	56.21±3.18	38.34±3.96	35.65±3.94
UCAM	24.95±3.37	50.44±2.60	44.64±3.25	33.83±4.38	56.21±3.57	38.30±4.03	35.51±3.95
MSRA.MADL	24.86±3.59	↻ 50.73±2.65	44.38±3.32	33.17±4.24	55.73±4.53	36.23±5.93	33.37±5.83
JHU	24.82±2.97	50.56±1.94	44.38±2.84	↻ 33.98±3.74	↻ 55.92±2.83	↻ 36.90±3.62	↻ 34.14±3.61
MLLP-UPV	24.39±3.30	50.20±2.13	44.20±3.07	32.97±4.24	55.91±3.18	↻ 37.72±4.04	↻ 34.89±3.98
online-A	24.13±3.41	50.03±2.57	44.06±3.64	32.95±3.73	55.34±3.72	↻ 37.87±4.62	↻ 35.26±4.66
online-G	24.11±3.38	↻ 50.52±2.08	43.80±3.07	↻ 34.19±4.50	↻ 55.55±3.10	36.49±4.09	33.75±4.10
TartuNLP-c	23.82±2.80	50.46±2.27	↻ 43.83±3.15	33.30±3.31	54.88±3.31	↻ 38.45±3.50	↻ 35.56±3.57
PROMT_NMT	22.58±2.29	49.29±2.12	42.48±2.46	32.80±3.65	53.98±2.95	36.02±3.56	33.31±3.31
uedin	21.37±3.34	47.22±3.04	41.30±3.68	25.52±7.74	50.68±4.07	↻ 37.55±4.00	↻ 35.16±3.87
online-X	17.95±2.09	44.93±2.26	38.38±2.42	↻ 26.69±4.34	49.95±2.76	32.69±3.06	30.23±3.03

Table 5: Automatic scores for German→English. "↻" marks scores out of sequence.

	BLEU	chrF3	nCDER	nCharacTER	nPER	nTER	nWER
online-B	15.67±4.40	47.16±4.21	33.60±5.83	28.12±4.94	42.24±5.92	23.10±7.18	21.22±6.96
online-Y	15.55±4.20	↻ 47.71±3.97	↻ 34.32±6.06	↻ 31.75±5.20	39.59±6.17	21.96±7.47	20.22±7.17
online-A	13.15±3.38	45.45±3.65	31.95±5.28	27.51±4.77	35.61±5.13	18.19±6.39	16.57±6.07
online-G	12.69±3.25	45.36±3.34	31.29±4.92	↻ 28.96±4.62	↻ 36.98±5.60	↻ 18.80±6.67	↻ 17.01±6.39
NICT	10.61±2.39	43.24±2.48	29.49±4.24	27.46±3.84	27.13±4.75	11.51±5.88	10.04±5.58
NEU_KingSoft	9.34±2.80	40.09±2.04	27.38±4.87	22.78±3.86	26.39±6.29	10.11±7.21	8.71±6.93
Nanjing	6.85±2.15	35.73±2.20	24.02±4.17	19.40±5.42	23.37±5.10	6.68±5.63	5.41±5.24

Table 6: Automatic scores for Czech→German. "↻" marks scores out of sequence. Note that online systems use parallel data while the others use only monolingual data.

ments but rather selected segments of about 15 consecutive sentences. Each such segment takes something between a half and a full A4 page when printed.

For each evaluated page, the annotators were provided with another such page—the corresponding 15 sentences in the source language. We deliberately avoided providing reference translations for two reasons: (1) we included the reference as if it was one of the competing MT systems, (2) we know that the source and the reference occasionally departed from each other; judging MT systems based on the references would thus not be a fair comparison even if carried out by humans and not an automatic metric.

In a small probe, we estimated that the annotation of one such segment will take about 15 minutes.

Table 8 summarizes the number of annotated document segments and annotators providing the scores.

The actual evaluation of each segment was submitted by the annotators through a simple web interface, which recorded:

- the segment ID;
- points assigned to the evaluated categories;
- a free-form description of the most serious error(s);
- a free-form field for further comments;

- a check-box indicating whether the annotator is an expert in the given field of the segment (e.g. in the field of value-added tax, VAT).

4.4 Results of Manual Evaluation

We did not have enough human capacity to calculate an full-fledged inter-annotator agreement. To have at least some idea of how annotators agree, we let three of all segments be assessed by two different annotators. Comparison of the scores reveals that annotators often differ in their assessment, even though the assigned points are almost always neighbouring.

Somewhat surprisingly, except for a single segment, the annotators did not consider themselves experts in the field of the documents presented to them, even though they all should be professionals in the auditing field.

4.4.1 English-to-Czech Translation

Altogether, the English→Czech translations were evaluated by 5 annotators. They evaluated 48 segments randomly chosen from documents translated by 4 selected systems and the reference translation. The translation systems were selected based on their automatic scores in WMT19 and their results in the past years. TartuNLP-c was added as a representative of a system with an overall lower output quality, although it seemed to perform well in some of the observed phenomena.

	BLEU	chrF3	nCDER	nCharacTER	nPER	nTER	nWER
online-B	14.86±4.01	40.69±2.96	32.04±4.91	22.32±5.07	40.86±4.53	26.12±7.74	24.43±7.53
online-Y	14.69±3.82	40.68±2.92	⁊32.12±4.66	⁊24.69±4.88	⁊40.87±4.48	26.02±7.20	24.33±6.80
online-G	12.22±2.71	39.16±1.94	29.59±3.44	22.13±5.36	38.75±3.86	21.90±5.76	20.32±5.48
online-A	11.80±2.92	38.09±2.52	28.92±4.11	21.11±5.35	37.42±5.20	⁊22.17±7.38	⁊20.51±7.14
NICT	10.49±2.95	35.99±3.00	27.20±4.37	20.08±5.78	36.49±4.69	19.63±6.55	18.10±6.17
NEU_KingSoft	8.18±2.65	32.89±2.86	24.61±4.94	16.94±5.84	32.62±4.93	19.61±7.08	⁊18.36±6.75
lmu-unsup-nmt	7.40±2.49	31.69±2.46	22.96±4.14	13.86±4.88	30.72±4.27	18.00±6.07	16.91±5.90
CUNI-Unsupervised-NER-post	7.03±2.26	⁊32.40±2.46	22.76±4.18	⁊14.59±4.51	⁊31.46±4.42	17.43±6.11	16.13±5.77
Nanjing-6929	6.26±2.11	28.42±2.00	21.11±3.89	9.16±7.70	28.55±4.02	13.92±6.20	13.00±6.10
Nanjing-6935	6.26±2.11	28.42±2.00	21.11±3.89	9.16±7.70	28.55±4.02	13.92±6.20	13.00±6.10
CAiRE	5.85±2.05	26.75±2.21	20.13±3.41	4.52±7.22	⁊29.14±4.50	⁊14.16±5.07	⁊13.03±4.74

Table 7: Automatic scores for German→Czech. "⁊" marks scores out of sequence. Note that online systems use parallel data while the others use only monolingual data.

Langs.	# Doc Segments	# Annotators
en-cs	48	5
en-de	16	
de-en	16	1

Table 8: Summary of manual annotations.

Table 9 shows the mean scores and standard deviations collected on the translations according to the five criteria specified in Section 4.1.

As our mini-comparison of annotator agreement suggests mismatches in score assignments, we provide also a statistic that abstracts from the absolute values of assigned scores. Because the assigned scores are associated with a particular categorical description, we avoid the standard normalization of mean and variance. Instead, we take all the assessments produced by a single annotator and sort the systems by the average of scores assigned by him or her in a given criterion. Table 10 then shows the mean ordinal number of each of the systems across all the annotators. Unlike the scores in Table 9, the best ordinal number is 1 and it gets worse as it increases.

Even though some subtle differences occur in ordering of the systems in Tables 9 and 10, the main observations remain the same. Manual evaluation confirms the lower quality of TartuNLP-c measured by automatic metrics. On the other hand, online-B scored best and it appears on par with the human translation, whereas it was surpassed by CUNI systems in terms of the automatic metrics as well as in news translation (see the main Findings of WMT19 paper). Interestingly, apart from TartuNLP-c all the other MT systems seem to yield fewer spelling and morphology errors than the human translators, although the differences are within the standard deviation bounds. CUNI-DocTransformer-T2T stands out by being better even beyond the reported standard devia-

tion of the ordinal interpretation (see 1.40±0.80 in "Spell. & morpho." in Table 10).

Due to large values of standard deviations, the small sample size and the fact that the underlying set of evaluated document segments varied across the systems, it is difficult to draw reliable conclusions from these observations. Some counter-intuitive results can be thus attributed to pure randomness. For example, CUNI-Transformer-T2T-2019 differs from CUNI-DocTransformer-T2T only in the fact that it operates on triples of consecutive sentences. This should increase the adequacy of vocabulary chosen and should have no effect on spelling and morphology but we have seen the opposite.

The overall statement we *can* make is that for English-to-Czech, the specific domain of audit reports does not differ much from the general observations made in the main News Translation Task: the order of the systems generally matches and the better systems are very close to the human performance.

4.4.2 English↔German Translation

Manual evaluation of English→German translations was provided by a single annotator on 16 randomly selected segments, covering 3 systems and the human translation. In the opposite translation direction, also 16 segments were evaluated by the same annotator, this time covering 2 systems and the human translation. We chose the systems which are popular (online-B), expected to score among the best based on their (automatically assessed) performance on the News Translation Task (MSRA-MADL) or are provided by the European Commission as a service for EU institutions (eTranslation).

The mean scores in Tables 11 and 12 show that none of the systems outperforms human translation. The ordering of the systems remains the

	Spell. & morpho.	Vocab. – adequacy	Vocab. – clarity	Syntax & word order	Coher. & overall underst.
Reference	2.38±0.70	2.44±0.46	2.44±0.46	2.50±0.71	2.50±0.50
online-B	↲ 2.50±0.67	2.40±0.49	2.20±0.75	↲ 2.60±0.66	2.40±0.66
CUNI-DocTransformer-T2T	↲ 2.75±0.43	2.25±0.83	↲ 2.33±0.75	2.58±0.49	2.33±0.85
CUNI-Transformer-T2T-2019	2.60±0.49	↲ 2.50±0.67	2.30±0.78	2.40±0.49	2.30±0.78
TartuNLP-c	1.88±0.78	1.62±0.86	1.75±0.83	1.88±0.93	1.75±0.97

Table 9: Mean scores of English→Czech translation obtained in manual evaluation. The systems are sorted by the "coherence and overall understanding" criterion. Higher scores are better. "↲" marks scores out of sequence.

	Spell. & morpho.	Vocab. – adequacy	Vocab. – clarity	Syntax & word order	Coher. & overall underst.
online-B	1.80±0.98	1.60±0.80	2.00±1.10	1.40±0.80	1.80±0.75
Reference	2.75±1.09	1.75±0.83	↲ 1.75±0.83	2.00±1.22	2.00±0.71
CUNI-DocTransformer-T2T	↲ 1.40±0.80	2.60±1.62	2.00±1.55	2.20±0.75	2.20±1.47
CUNI-Transformer-T2T-2019	1.75±0.83	↲ 2.00±1.00	2.50±1.12	2.75±1.48	2.25±1.09
TartuNLP-c	3.40±1.96	4.00±0.63	3.00±0.89	3.00±1.41	3.20±1.47

Table 10: Mean ordinal numbers of English→Czech systems sorted by manual evaluation scores for each annotator. Lower numbers are better.

same across most of the evaluation criteria. Unlike in automatic evaluation, the human annotator considers the output of online-B in English→German translation of lower quality (except spelling and morphology) than the outputs of its competitors. In German→English translation, the ordering of the systems according to the manual evaluation agrees with the automatic one.

All in all, comparison of manual and automatic evaluation suggests that the systems achieving high automatic scores may be judged differently by human annotators. As the quality of translation decreases, it is sufficient to evaluate it automatically.

4.4.3 Most Common Mistakes

A part of the evaluation web interface was a free-form field for the description of the most serious error(s) encountered. We collected these comments and manually organized them into several categories. We found out that the most common mistakes were:

- fluency;
- wrong translation of terms;
- grammatical correctness (such as a wrong gender chosen for pronouns);
- non-translated abbreviations, or abbreviations which do not make sense in the Czech translation;
- outputs completely missing a half of the sentence. This was particularly likely after a punctuations such as the closing bracket in the middle of the sentence.

Table 13 summarizes the overall error counts by category. (The reference is included in these counts.) As mentioned above, we did not find any native German auditor who could annotate our

SAO Test Suite, so the annotation was done by a single Czech auditor. This could explain the relatively big differences between language pairs: with a single annotation, the annotator disagreements are not averaged out. For instance, it is possible that this marked some of the errors as wrong grammatical constructions while en→cs annotators could score it in fluency criterion.

We also have to take into account the absolute number of annotated document segments (48 for Czech, 16 for English↔German). Considering the average number of errors per one annotated document segment, German→English translation seems the worst, see the last line of Table 13.

5 Translation of Agreements

Aside from the SAO audit documents, we added one moderately long document from a very specific domain related to auditing: agreements.

As the source document, we used the English version of a sublease agreement, which was in fact a (non-professional) translation from Czech. The original Czech text was evaluated with all other WMT19 systems as if it was one of the systems.

Due to the different nature of the text, we decided to evaluate the translation of the sublease agreement differently from the evaluation of the main part of SAO Test Suite.

5.1 Manual Evaluation

The evaluation of this small set containing one source document, one human translation and 11 machine translated documents was done manually. The evaluation was partially blind. Technically, the candidate translations were not labelled with the system name, but the main annotator could

	Spell. & morpho.	Vocab. – adequacy	Vocab. – clarity	Syntax & word order	Coher. & overall underst.
Reference	3.00±0.00	3.00±0.00	3.00±0.00	3.00±0.00	3.00±0.00
MSRA-MADL	2.75±0.43	2.25±0.83	2.25±0.83	2.25±0.83	2.25±0.83
eTranslation	2.50±0.50	2.25±0.83	2.25±0.83	2.25±0.83	2.00±1.00
online-B	2.75±0.43	1.75±1.30	1.75±1.30	2.00±0.71	1.50±1.12

Table 11: Mean scores of English→German translation obtained in manual evaluation. The systems are sorted by the "coherence and overall understanding" criterion. Higher scores are better.

	Spell. & morpho.	Vocab. – adequacy	Vocab. – clarity	Syntax & word order	Coher. & overall underst.
Reference	2.60±0.49	2.60±0.49	2.60±0.49	2.60±0.49	2.60±0.49
online-B	2.33±0.47	2.17±0.69	1.83±0.69	2.00±0.58	1.83±0.69
MSRA-MADL	2.40±0.49	1.60±0.80	1.60±0.80	1.80±0.75	1.60±0.80

Table 12: Mean scores of German→English translation obtained in manual evaluation. The systems are sorted by the "coherence and overall understanding" criterion. Higher scores are better.

Errors in	en-cs	en-de	de-en
Wrong translation	20	14	28
Fluency	25	1	0
Untranslated	5	3	7
Abbreviations	6	4	4
Grammar	8	2	2
Missing words	4	0	2
Coherence	4	1	0
Added words	4	0	0
Word repetition	2	0	2
Spasm	1	0	0
Total	79	25	45
Avg. per Doc. Segm.	1.6	1.5	2.8

Table 13: Summary of errors found by SAO annotators.

guess some of the systems. Only the systems online-X, Y and G are truly blind, we do not know their identity even from past evaluations.

We are confident that even the knowledge of the MT system did not affect our evaluation because we fully focused on the hard criteria such as named entity preservation or term consistence throughout the document. The only soft criterion included was the "fluency" one. We have also included the reference document in the evaluation.

5.2 Establishing Evaluation Criteria

By inspecting several of the MT outputs, we first defined the assessment criteria. They generally fall into two categories: (1) target-only, and (2) source-based. Whereas in the former category, we consider only quality of the target texts on their own, regardless the source, in the latter we validate if the selected bits of information were preserved or corrupted during the translation process.

In the target-only category, we focused on the following:

- fluency;
- grammatical correctness (this is very strict and well defined in Czech; most errors were in morphological agreement and sometimes verb tense);
- casing errors (esp. in named entities);
- incomprehensibility of the segment;
- "spasm", i.e. the situation when the MT system gets stuck in repeating some tokens;
- superfluous words;
- missing words or a whole sentence.

As for the source-based category, we have focused on the errors, which were formed either by wrong translation of a very domain-specific term or an inconsistence of used terms throughout the whole document.

- Named Entities—here we checked mainly the preservation of the information:
  - Person (e.g. name and surname);
  - Address (e.g. street name and number);
  - Date (esp. whether the format has been kept consistent);
  - Numbers (if the transcription of numerals was correct);
  - Flat composition (the Czech-specific way is to count rooms and kitchens/kitchinette and indicate it as a compact string, here "1+1");
  - Wrong abbreviation;
  - Expanded abbreviation (e.g. in Czech, the "ZIP CODE" should be translated as "PSČ", which stands for "poštovní směrovací číslo", but this abbreviation is never spelled out in written text).
- Document-specific terms:
  - Tenant;
  - Lessee;
  - Supplement (of the agreement);
  - Sublease agreement;

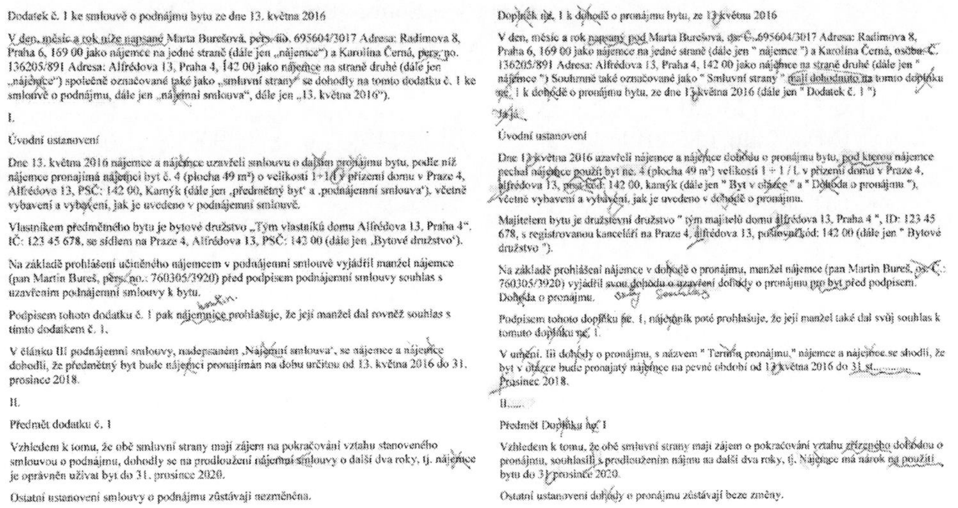

Figure 1: Samples from our annotation with one of the best scoring systems (CUNI-Transformer-T2T-2018) on the left and one of the worst ones (online-X) on the right. Crosses indicate errors in term translation, strange wordings are underlined, casing errors and other errors have their simple marks.

- Contracting parties;
- Apartment in question;
- Equipment (e.g. the kitchen);
- Amenities (e.g. a cellar or a segment of the garden);
- Housing cooperative;
- Team of owners;
- Term of the lease;
- The specification of the supplement ("no. 1").

In the category of "Document-specific terms", we focused on evaluation whether:

- the term is translated correctly, incorrectly (incl. not translated at all), or missing altogether;
- the target term is preserved in the document.

It should be noted that the MT system was often free to choose from several translation options of a term. At the same time, a very important criterion was whether the translation of each of the terms was consistent throughout the document and also whether it did not clash with other choices. For example, each of the terms "tenant" and "lessee" could be—depending on the particular situation—correctly translated as "pronajímatelka", "nájemkyně" or "podnájemkyně" (all are feminine variants of the words, because incidentally, it was women who were entering this sample agreement). If the two different parties however happened to have been referred to in any way that could lead to confusion, we marked this as a (serious) error.

In some cases, we had a strict expectation. For instance the term "sublease" could be translated into Czech in principle either as "pronájem" (which corresponds to the relationship between a landlord and a tenant) or as "podnájem" (which corresponds to the relationship between a tenant and a lessee). Based on the text of the agreement, it was however clear that the correct term is "podnájem" (the tenant is not the actual owner of the property), so we demanded the this particular choice.

5.3 Execution of Evaluation

Because of the relatively small amount of data, the evaluation was done on paper, see Figure 1.

The annotations of "source-based" error types were done with respect to the source text using a fixed set of "markables", i.e. the set of occurrences of words and expressions to annotate for correctness. The set of markables was identical for all the candidate translations. Each markable in each translation candidate received a label indicating if it was translated correctly, with an error, or if was fully missing.

The "target-only" error types were marked independently for each system, with no number of markable positions given apriori.

The question was how to deal with inconsistency in used terms. At the beginning it was not clear whether we should assume that the first occurrence of term "defines" it for the rest of the

System	Target-Only		Source-Based		Total	
	Errs	**(Miss)**	**Errs**	**(Miss)**	**Errs**	**(Miss)**
Reference	3	1	6	2	9	3
C-Trafo-T2T-2018	6	0	15	0	21	0
C-DocTrafo-T2T-2019	9	0	21	0	30	0
online-Y	10	0	20	0	30	0
C-Trafo-T2T-2019	5	2	26	2	31	4
online-B	15	1	27	0	42	1
uedin	9	2	34	12	43	14
online-A	19	0	30	0	49	0
C-DocTrafo-Marian	13	2	38	0	51	2
TartuNLP-c	14	1	37	1	51	2
online-G	34	0	28	0	62	0
online-X	48	7	77	0	125	7

Table 14: Total number of errors "Errs", and of those the cases when the output was completely missing "(Miss)", by English-Czech WMT19 news translation systems applied to the sublease agreement.

document or whether we should take the most frequent one as the "intended one" by the MT system and treat other translations as errors. After the first round of corrections, we chose the first option. Some terms, e.g. "tenant", "lessee" or "agreement" had always only one correct translation, but some, e.g. "sublease" could have had multiple possible translations. In these latter cases, we always marked the first occurrence as correct.

5.4 Results of Manual Evaluation

The summary of manual evaluation is presented in Table 14. Errors in the source-based categories are more frequent than in target-only. This is mainly due to the incorrect translation of the term "lessee" (see Section 5.4.2 below).

One thing worth mentioning is the 9 errors and 3 omissions in the reference translation. This can be partly attributed to Czech being in fact the original and English (i.e. the source for MT systems) its translation. What is a good Czech→English manual translation is not always literal enough when observed from the English side. Three errors were for instance incurred from one single case where the Czech text referred to the agreement itself one time less than the English text, but this "missing reference" (fully acceptable in the Czech→English direction) counted as several missing expressions. As for the true errors, there was one incorrect translation of term "lessee" and one mistake in the number of the Supplement.

The number of errors considerably varies across the systems. The best system (CUNI-

Transformer-T2T-2018) in our evaluation is also the winner on news in the evaluation last year. As Bojar et al. (2018) report, this system significantly outperformed humans *at the level of individual sentences* in that evaluation. In our setting, the number of errors by CUNI-Transformer-T2T-2018 is twice the number of errors in the reference, but aside from term choice discussed in Section 5.4.2, one could say that the translation is very good.

In the target-only category, we did not have any pre-defined items that could be correct or incorrect. Therefore the number of errors varies greatly across the systems. From the lowest number of errors in the CUNI-Transformer-T2T-2019 (5 errors) and in CUNI-Transformer-T2T-2018 (6 errors) to the very high numbers in online-X and online-G (48 and 34 errors, respectively).

As for the "(Miss)" counts, there were two types of situations: (1) only a single word was missing in the output and (2) the whole sentence or a half of a paragraph was not there. The second case often lead to a large increase in the "(Miss)" count because several markables from the source were supposed to appear in the lost part. The systems uedin and online-X were most affected by this.

Another interesting fact worth mentioning is that even though the system online-Y had a relatively low number of mistakes, those errors made the readability and the comprehensibility of the message substantially more difficult than e.g. the translation by online-B with a higher error count.

The point here is that the number of errors

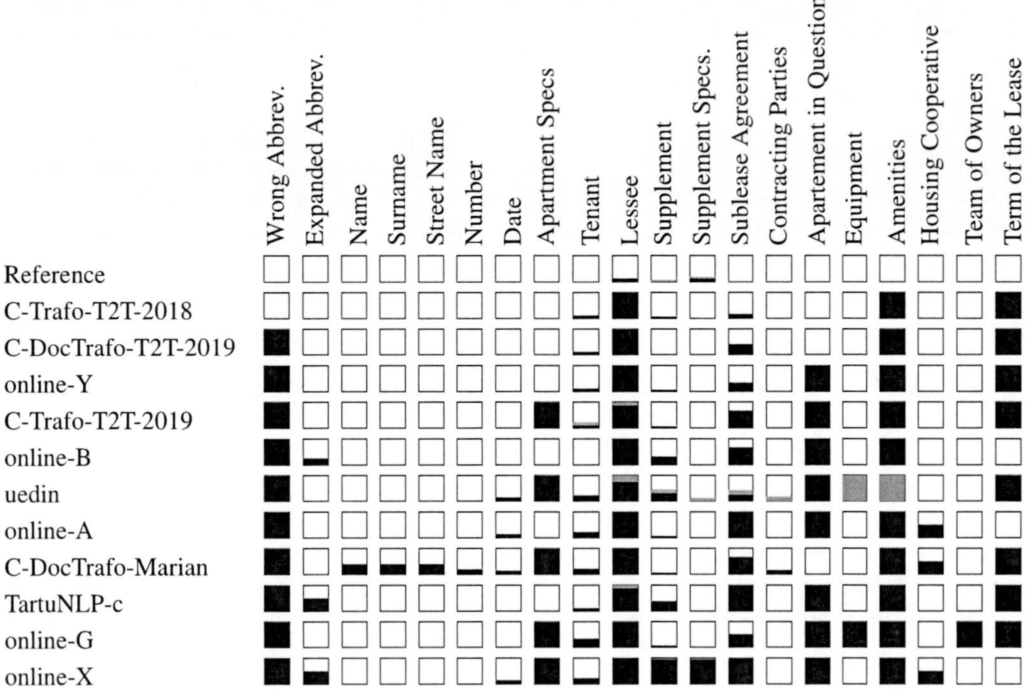

Table 15: Composition of source-based errors of individual MT systems. An empty box ( ) indicates no error. Black-filled portion corresponds to erroneous output and gray-filled output corresponds to missing output.

is important but their type can be critical, too. We already mentioned the missing sentences or "spasm", which accounted for the 14 missing term translations in the output of uedin. Another interesting case is a "misunderstanding" of the MT system. For instance, uedin system misunderstood "I." (the Roman numeral) for the pronoun "I" or mistranslated the "ZIP CODE" as "občanka" (personal ID card). It is exactly these types of errors, which are the most serious from the reader's point of view.

5.4.1 Detailed Error Counts

Table 15 provides further details on error types observed in the outputs of individual MT systems. The table is again sorted by the total number of errors as in Table 14. We see that the best system (CUNI-Transformer-T2T-2018) fully failed in the translation of the terms "lessee", "amenities" and "term of the lease". This system was also the only one which dealt well with abbreviations.

In contrast to all other systems, CUNI-DocTransformer-Marian struggled to translate several named entities correctly. This system used the same training data as CUNI-Transformer-T2T-2019 and both of these systems translate several

consecutive sentences at once in order to improve cross-sentence consistency but they somewhat differ in the details of the handling of multi-sentence input, and they also differ in the underlying MT system: Tensor2Tensor vs. Marian, see Popel et al. (2019) for more details. It is hard to explain why these sentences could adversely affect named entities, so the authors of the system should carefully look at this issue.

5.4.2 Referring to Contracting Parties

Our analysis so far does not sufficiently highlight the most severe flaw of all the MT systems. The problem concerns a clear way of referring to the contracting parties, i.e. the translation of the terms "tenant" and "lessee". All the systems translated almost all occurrences of these terms using one word only, "nájemce", which causes a lot of confusion to any reader (including native Czech speakers). The problem which occurred here arose from the fact that there are actually three common roles and two types of agreements in apartment renting. Commonly, the contracting parties are:

- landlord—tenant = pronajímatel—nájemce in the case when the landlord is the owner of the

	Correct	Clash	Non.	Oth.
Reference	16	1	-	-
online-B	9	8	-	-
C-DocTrafo-T2T-2019	8	7	2	-
online-Y	8	7	-	2
C-Trafo-T2T-2018	8	7	1	1
C-DocTrafo-Marian	8	6	1	2
TartuNLP-c	8	6	2	1
online-A	7	8	-	2
online-X	7	8	-	2
C-Trafo-T2T-2019	7	7	-	3
uedin	7	5	1	4
online-G	6	7	1	3

Table 16: How the systems were referring to the contracting parties. "Correct" indicates an appropriate and consistent translation. "Clash" indicates that the translation wrongly refers to the other party. "Non." are cases when the original English word appeared in MT output and "Oth." are other translations; these are also confusing because the identity with the correct party is not maintained.

property;

- tenant—lessee = nájemce—podnájemce for the sublease agreement, i.e. when the owner is not directly involved in the agreement.

The common translation in training corpora or dictionaries of the term "lessee" is apparently "nájemce" which is possible, but only if the term "tenant" is not used in the document as well. Should this happen, "lessee" needs to be translated as "podnájemce" to avoid confusion.

Table 16 details the performance of the systems in this respect. Each line sums up to 17 mentions of either of the two contracting parties. We see that the reference translation made only one error by using the wrong term while all the other systems cause a term clash (using the same term for both parties) in half of the cases. This, in fact, corresponds to all the mentions of the second party and *all these translations by all the systems* are thus completely wrong.

6 Test Suite Availability

SAO Test Suite is available under CC-BY-SA at:

> https://github.com/ELITR/
> wmt19-elitr-testsuite

7 Conclusion

We presented a test suite of Czech, English, German, Polish and Slovak documents from the au-diting domain and used its English-Czech-German tri-parallel part in the WMT19 Translation Shared Task. We also added one more document type, namely a sublease agreement.

Despite the fact that the participating MT systems were trained for a rather general domain of news articles, many of them perform very well *on general terms*. Our detailed manual evaluation used criteria similar to those used in the scoring of GCSE essays of the Czech language.

An important observation in our study was that a thorough domain knowledge is necessary to assess the correctness of the translation, esp. in terms of lexical choices, and that the reference translations are insufficient for the task. Our impression is that automatic MT evaluation is effectively useless for assessing terminological subtleties, esp. with one reference translation only. We find this observation particularly important for future research directions, because none of the MT systems are trained in a way which could directly address such subtle issues. Terminology lists may be a good help for both MT and MT evaluation but we anticipate that the only practically possible ultimate solution for translation would be an interactive system supporting a domain expert in manual correction of terminological choices.

As for the translations of the Sublease Agreement, even though the dispersion in the number of errors is huge—varying from 21 errors (CUNI-Transformer-T2T-2018) to 125 errors online-X—the number of errors alone is not as indicative of the practical usability of the translation. The main problem was that *all* the systems made the same (and from the readers' perspective, the most severe) translation error by translating the terms "tenant" and "lessee" using the same Czech word "nájemce", which made the whole text incomprehensible. Other observed mistakes needed rather cosmetic adjustments, except for the occasions where the system forgot a whole sentence or the rest of a paragraph.

We released the texts of the test suite for future use and we are also happy to share our annotation protocols, but as of now, we cannot provide any novel automatic evaluation of MT on this test suite.

Acknowledgments

This study was supported in parts by the grants H2020-ICT-2018-2-825460 (ELITR) and H2020-

ICT-2018-2-825303 (Bergamot) of the European Union and Czech Science Foundation (grant n. 19-26934X, NEUREM3).

We are very grateful to our colleagues and students Ivana Kvapilíková, Ján Faryad, Lukáš Kyjánek, and Simon Will for their help with the revision of the German alignment.

References

Ondřej Bojar, Christian Federmann, Mark Fishel, Yvette Graham, Barry Haddow, Matthias Huck, Philipp Koehn, and Christof Monz. 2018. Findings of the 2018 Conference on Machine Translation (WMT18). In *Proceedings of the Third Conference on Machine Translation, Volume 2: Shared Task Papers*, Brussels, Belgium. Association for Computational Linguistics.

Gregor Leusch and Hermann Ney. 2008. BLEUSP, INVWER, CDER: Three improved MT evaluation measures. In *NIST Metrics for Machine Translation Challenge*, Waikiki, Honolulu, Hawaii.

Jiří Maršík and Ondřej Bojar. 2012. TrTok: A Fast and Trainable Tokenizer for Natural Languages. *Prague Bulletin of Mathematical Linguistics*, 98:75–85.

Arun Narayanan, Ananya Misra, Khe Chai Sim, Golan Pundak, Anshuman Tripathi, Mohamed Elfeky, Parisa Haghani, Trevor Strohman, and Michiel Bacchiani. 2018. Toward domain-invariant speech recognition via large scale training. In *2018 IEEE Spoken Language Technology Workshop, SLT 2018, Athens, Greece, December 18-21, 2018*, pages 441–447.

Kishore Papineni, Salim Roukos, Todd Ward, and Wei-Jing Zhu. 2002. BLEU: a Method for Automatic Evaluation of Machine Translation. In *Proceedings of ACL 2002*, pages 311–318, Philadelphia, Pennsylvania.

Martin Popel, Dominik Macháček, Michal Auersperger, Ondřej Bojar, and Pavel Pecina. 2019. English-czech systems in wmt19: Document-level transformer. In *Proceedings of the Fourth Conference on Machine Translation: Volume 2, Shared Task Papers*.

Maja Popović. 2015. chrF: character n-gram F-score for automatic MT evaluation. In *Proceedings of the Tenth Workshop on Statistical Machine Translation*, pages 392–395, Lisbon, Portugal. ACL.

Matthew Snover, Bonnie Dorr, Richard Schwartz, Linnea Micciulla, and John Makhoul. 2006. A Study of Translation Edit Rate with Targeted Human Annotation. In *Proceedings AMTA*, pages 223–231.

Dániel Varga, László Németh, Péter Halácsy, András Kornai, Viktor Trón, and Viktor Nagy. 2005. Parallel corpora for medium density languages. In *Proceedings of the Recent Advances in Natural Language Processing RANLP 2005*, pages 590–596, Borovets, Bulgaria.

Weiyue Wang, Jan-Thorsten Peter, Hendrik Rosendahl, and Hermann Ney. 2016. CharacTER: Translation edit rate on character level. In *ACL 2016 First Conference on Machine Translation*, Berlin, Germany.

WMD$_O$: Fluency-based Word Mover's Distance for Machine Translation Evaluation

Julian Chow, **Pranava Madhyastha** and **Lucia Specia**
Department of Computing
Imperial College London, UK
{julian.chow16,pranava,l.specia}@imperial.ac.uk

Abstract

We propose WMD$_O$, a metric based on distance between distributions in the semantic vector space. Matching in the semantic space has been investigated for translation evaluation, but the constraints of a translation's word order have not been fully explored. Building on the Word Mover's Distance metric and various word embeddings, we introduce a fragmentation penalty to account for fluency of a translation. This word order extension is shown to perform better than standard WMD, with promising results against other types of metrics.

1 Introduction

Current metrics to automatically evaluate machine translations, such as the popular BLEU (Papineni et al., 2002), are heavily based on string matching. They claim to account for adequacy by checking for overlapping words between the machine translation output and reference translation, and fluency by rewarding matches in sequences of more than one word. This way of viewing adequacy is very limiting; comparing strings makes it harder to evaluate any deviation from the semantics of the original text in the reference or machine translation.

Meteor (Banerjee and Lavie, 2005) relaxes this constraint by allowing matching of lemmas, synonyms or paraphrases. However, this requires linguistic resources to lemmatise the data or lexical databases to fetch synonyms/paraphrases, which do not exist for most languages.

Character-based metrics like chrF (Popovic, 2015) and CharacTER (Wang et al., 2016) also relax the exact word match constraint by allowing the matching of characters. However, they ultimately still assume a surface-level similarity between reference and machine translation output.

Chen and Guo (2015) presented a number of experiments where both translation and reference sentences are compared in the embedding space rather than at surface level. They however simply extract these two embedding representations and measure the (cosine) similarity between them, which may account for some overall semantic similarity, but ignores other aspects of translation quality.

A version of Meteor has been proposed that also performs matches at the word embedding space (Servan et al., 2016). Two words are considered to match if their cosine distance in the embedding space is above a certain threshold. In other words, the embeddings are only used to provide this binary decision, rather than to measure overall semantic distance between two sentences. In a similar vein, bleu2vec and ngram2vec (Tttar and Fishel, 2017) are a direct modification of BLEU where fuzzy matches are added to strict matches. The fuzzy match score is implemented via token and n-gram embedding similarities. As we show in Section 4, these metrics do not perform well.

MEANT 2.0 (Lo, 2017) also relies on matching of words in the embedding space, but this is only used to score the similarity between pairs of words that have already been aligned based on their semantic roles, rather than to find the alignments between words.

We suggest a more general way of using distributional representations of words, where distance in the semantic space is viewed as a global decision between the entire machine and reference translations. More specifically, we propose an adaptation of a powerful and flexible metric that operates on the semantic space: Word Mover's Distance (WMD) (Kusner et al., 2015). WMD is an instance of the Earth Mover's Distance transportation problem that calculates the most efficient way to transform one distribution onto another.

Proceedings of the Fourth Conference on Machine Translation (WMT), Volume 2: Shared Task Papers (Day 1) pages 494–500
Florence, Italy, August 1-2, 2019. ©2019 Association for Computational Linguistics

Adjustments to EMD have been used previously to create evaluation metrics based on word embeddings and word positions (Echizen'ya et al., 2019). Likewise, using vector word embeddings as an indicator of similarity and the word embeddings of each text as a distribution, WMD gives the optimal method of transforming the words of one document to the words of another document. WMD does not take word order into account and rather focuses on semantic similarity of word meanings.

WMD has been recently used for the evaluation of image captioning models (Kilickaya et al., 2017; Madhyastha et al., 2019). It proved promising for image captioning evaluation, where word order is less relevant. The same image can be described similarly using different word orders as it is constrained by the image itself. We note that in machine translation evaluation, word order is more important, since the order is constrained by that of the source sentence.

In this paper, we propose WMD$_O$ – an extension to WMD that incorporates word order. We show that this metric outperforms the standard WMD and performs on par or better than most state-of-the-art evaluation metrics.

2 Method

In this section we describe the original WMD distance metric and its extension to account for word order.

2.1 WMD

Word Mover's Distance (WMD) (Kusner et al., 2015) makes use of vectorial relationships between word embeddings to compute distance between two text documents. In essence, WMD captures the minimal distance required to move words from the first document to words in the second document.

Let $X \in \mathcal{R}^{n \times d}$ be a d-dimensional word embedding matrix for a vocabulary of n words. Let $x_i \in \mathcal{R}^d$ be a d-dimensional representation of ith word. Assume two documents A and B with d^a and d^b as the normalized bag-of-words (BOW) vectors, k-dimensional vectors for the respective documents, where $d_j{}^a$ is the number of times word j occurs in A (normalized by all words appearing in A). Note that stop words are removed from documents; only content words are retained.

Kusner et al. (2015) propose the word travel cost, that is the cost of moving words from T_i^a to

T_j^b, as the measure of word dissimilarity, using the Euclidean distance between the embeddings corresponding to words. More precisely, the cost associated is defined as:

$$c(i,j) = \|x_i - x_j\|_2^2 \,, \tag{1}$$

This allows documents with many closely related words to have smaller distances than documents with very dissimilar words. WMD defines a transport matrix $T \in \mathcal{R}^{n \times n}$,

where T_{ij} contains information about the proportion of d_i^a that needs to be transported to d_j^b. Formally, WMD computes T that optimizes:

$$D(d^a, d^b) = \min_{T \geq 0} \sum_{i,j=1}^{n} T_{ij} c(i,j), \tag{2}$$

such that: $\sum_{j=1}^{n} T_{ij} = d_i^a$ and $\sum_{i=1}^{n} T_{ij} = d_j^b$, $\forall \, i, j$. Here, the normalized bag-of-words distribution of the documents d^a and d^b contains a combined vocabulary from d^a and d^b resulting in a square transport matrix T of dimensionality $n \times n$.

We note that Kusner et al. (2015) remove stop words and retain only content words before computing WMD, as stop words are generally less relevant for capturing content specific similarity between documents. In our implementation, we include the stop words in order to capture a more coherent distance.

2.2 WMD with word order

Evaluation of translation candidates generally takes into account fluency as well as adequacy to form a judgment. As described in previous section, the standard WMD does not take word order into account. We introduce a modified version which includes a specialized penalty that is intended to penalize for words occurring in a different order from the reference translation. This modification adds a notion of fluency on top of the original WMD metric, which is crucial in matching the multifaceted approach of human translation evaluation.

The word order penalty is applied after calculation of the standard WMD score. Our proposal for penalty is similar to the notion of fragmentation penalty of Meteor (Banerjee and Lavie, 2005), which separates word matches into chunks in order to prevent the metric from doubly-penalising a translation for having out of order consecutive words. These chunks are defined as a group of unigrams which are adjacent in both reference and machine translation. The longer each chain of n-grams is, the fewer the chunks, so if the entire machine translation matches the reference in consecutive order there is only one chunk. Figure 1 is an illustration of the use of chunks. The matched unigrams for "the president" and "spoke loudly" are in the same order in both sentences, giving two chunks for this translation, fragmented by the word "then".

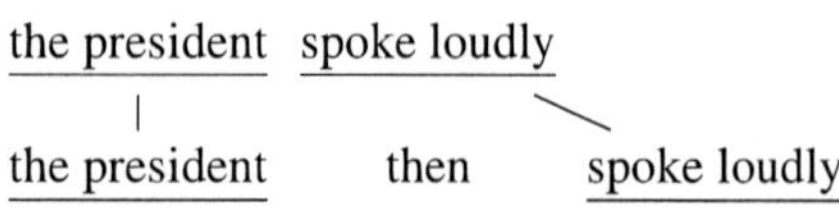

Figure 1: An example of chunks.

This type of word order penalty is necessary to deal with examples such as that of Figure 2. The sentence gets a perfect WMD score because all of its words align exactly to another one in the vector space, with no regard to its fluency. With a fragmentation penalty, this type of situation would see the score get worse because of its different sentence structure to the reference.

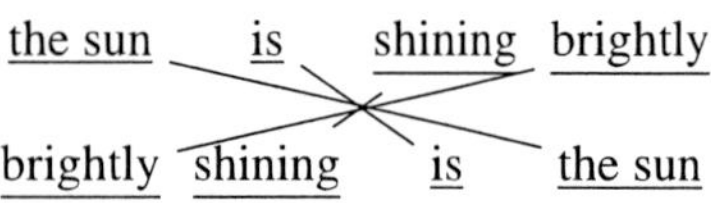

Figure 2: The WMD score for this sentence pair is 0.0.

The penalty is formulated as:

$$\text{Penalty} = \frac{c}{u_m} \qquad (3)$$

where c is the number of chunks and u_m is the number of unigrams in the machine translation.

This penalty is weighted by a value δ. and is formulated as:

$$\text{Weight} = \delta \times \text{Penalty} \qquad (4)$$

We also observed that, in many cases, the simple penalty in Equation 4 can further be augmented with a modification that rewards sentences which are largely contiguous. We modify Equation 4 such that sentences with fewer chunks are rewarded and sentences with more chunks are penalized. We empirically found that $\frac{1}{2}$ is optimal for such a realization. With this modification, our fluency based word mover's distance (WMD_O) is

defined as:

$$\text{WMD}_O = \text{WMD} - \delta(\frac{1}{2} - \text{Penalty}) \qquad (5)$$

We also observe that, in most cases, the optimal weight seems to be 0.2.

3 Experimental settings

We performed experiments to verify the performance of the proposed metric, comparing the metric's results against human annotations to measure a level of correlation. We used the PyEMD wrapper (Mayner, 2019) for calculating the WMD, based on (Pele and Werman, 2008, 2009). We did not remove any stopwords as these are important to fluency. We also use Cosine rather than Euclidean distance to calculate distance between word embeddings as magnitude of the vectors is not as important in such high dimensions.

3.1 Datasets

We used the WMT17 segment-level into-English datasets for our experiments (Bojar et al., 2017). This has data from seven different source languages, with 560 different texts each. Every text carries a reference translation and a machine translation, with a human annotation labelling how closely the machine translation relates to the reference.

3.2 Word embeddings

Many pre-trained word embeddings are available for English. Since word2vec embeddings have been shown to work well with WMD, this was our starting point as the embeddings used to develop the metric. We used a freely-available pre-trained model of 300 dimensions trained on approximately 100 billion words from news articles (Mikolov et al., 2013). This model had a vocabulary size of 3 million. While large, there were still many instances of out-of-vocabulary (OOV) words in the WMT17 dataset alone. Some of this can be attributed to incomplete translations; many of the missing words were foreign words in the source language. Other instances were proper nouns which had not been seen in the pre-trained embeddings vocabulary, as well as numerical values for the same reason.

To tackle OOV, we tried several different approaches. One was to assign a single random vector as an OOV vector, using the same vector for every instance of a missing word. For these experiments, we used the vector of all 0s, as this seemed the most neutral. Another was to have a random vector for each OOV word and store it in a dictionary, calling on the same value whenever the OOV word is encountered again. In the same vein, one setting was to generate this vector by taking an average of five random vectors in the embedding.

An alternative approach we also pursued was to use a different set of embeddings. FastText (Mikolov et al., 2018) is a type of embedding which is able to produce embeddings for words not part of the vocabulary. This utilises vectors from of substrings of characters contained in the missing word, adding them together so even vectors for misspelled words or a concatenation of words can be produced. Again, a pre-trained model, also of 300 dimensions and trained on news articles was used here. We also fine-tuned this model to produce another set of embeddings, using monolingual training data from the WMT19 news translation task. The experiments with these embeddings were done with and without the FastText character n-gram method of solving OOVs.

All of these approaches were used to test the metric against human scores, the results of which can be seen in Section 4.

4 Results

The results of these experiments are shown in Tables 1 to 4. Each row in a table corresponds to an experimental setting, while each column represents one of the seven language pairs. The value of each cell represents the Pearson correlation with of the metric's score with the given human score, with a higher value suggesting better agreement with the gold standard human evaluation.

Table 1 shows the results of the different OOV strategies, all using the pre-trained word2vec embedding and the standard WMD metric. Out of these strategies, the same random vector for all OOVs came out top by a small margin.

Table 2 looks at the effect of using different embeddings on results and OOV rate, including with and without the n-gram method of FastText to resolve OOVs. We can see that the pre-trained FastText vectors with the OOV resolution strategy of the same vector for all OOV had the best performance, but only marginally over a random vector for each OOV. A different vector choice might be better for different embeddings, but for the

purposes of further experiments with this dataset the zero vector was used. It also shows that the FastText embeddings perform better than the word2vec embedding with the same OOV resolution strategy, suggesting a difference in quality of vectors.

Table 3 presents the experimental results of WMD and the WMD word order metrics for different values of δ. These experiments used the pre-trained FastText vectors with a zero vector for all OOV. It shows that the WMD word order metric performs better than the standard WMD metric in the majority of language pairs.

Combining these results, we find that the best performing iteration of our metric for all language pairs is the word order version of WMD, with δ at 0.2. This is using the pre-trained FastText embedding, with the zero vector used for each OOV word. However, it should be noted that some language pairs perform slightly better with a higher or lower δ; this is reflected in the next table with the "ideal" parameter.

We compare this to the rest of the results from the WMT17 metrics task in Table 4; it shows that our metric performs at a similar level or better than most evaluation metrics. Of the metrics which do better than WMD_O. Blend and AutoDA are trained metrics, which are not the most practical when applied to larger datasets as they rely on human annotated training data. MEANT is a metric that does very well for most language combinations. It also uses word embeddings to score matching words, but it is not clear whether the benefit comes from this or from other components in the metric. Overall, this metric has a very large number of steps that rely on linguistic resources, and its code is not available.

5 Analysis

We plot two examples of the distributions of human and WMD_O metric scores in Figures 3 and 4. The results for Finnish-English were fairly strong, but those for Latvian-English had a few more anomalies.

The metric performs sufficiently with reference and machine translated outputs which were largely of a similar length, as the influence of each word was not overbearing on the metric's end result. This can be seen in the results for Finnish to English, which are quite consistent.

Our metric struggled more with bad translations

	cs-en	de-en	fi-en	lv-en	ru-en	tr-en	zh-en
Same vector for all OOV	0.513	0.531	0.689	0.505	0.562	0.561	0.595
Random vector per OOV	0.513	0.531	0.687	0.501	0.560	0.557	0.591
Average of 5 random vectors	0.500	0.534	0.678	0.492	0.563	0.557	0.572

Table 1: Performance of OOV strategies with standard WMD and word2vec.

	cs-en	de-en	fi-en	lv-en	ru-en	tr-en	zh-en	OOV (%)
Word2vec (same vector for all OOV)	0.513	0.531	0.689	0.505	0.562	0.561	0.595	0.10
FastText (same vector for all OOV)	0.521	0.536	0.704	0.530	0.571	0.566	0.607	0.22
FastText (random vector per OOV)	0.521	0.536	0.702	0.530	0.571	0.566	0.607	0.22
FastText (n-grams)	0.511	0.542	0.700	0.526	0.572	0.577	0.583	0
FastText finetuned (n-grams)	0.485	0.525	0.671	0.513	0.546	0.538	0.597	0

Table 2: Performance of different embeddings on standard WMD, including OOV rate.

	cs-en	de-en	fi-en	lv-en	ru-en	tr-en	zh-en
WMD	0.521	0.536	0.704	0.530	0.571	0.566	0.607
$\text{WMD}_O, \delta = 0.05$	0.528	0.544	0.709	0.537	0.580	0.585	0.616
$\text{WMD}_O, \delta = 0.1$	**0.531**	**0.546**	**0.710**	0.541	**0.585**	0.600	0.621
$\text{WMD}_O, \delta = 0.2$	0.530	0.542	0.705	**0.543**	**0.585**	0.620	**0.623**
$\text{WMD}_O, \delta = 0.3$	0.525	0.534	0.696	0.540	0.579	0.631	0.621
$\text{WMD}_O, \delta = 0.4$	0.518	0.525	0.686	0.535	0.572	**0.637**	0.616

Table 3: Performance of different WMD implementations with pre-trained FastText and same vector strategy. Bolded value signify the best performing metric for each language pair.

	cs-en	de-en	fi-en	lv-en	ru-en	tr-en	zh-en
AUTODA	0.499	0.543	0.673	0.533	0.584	0.625	0.583
BEER	0.511	0.530	0.681	0.515	0.577	0.600	0.582
BLEND	0.594	0.571	0.733	0.577	0.622	0.671	0.661
BLEU2VEC_SEP	0.439	0.429	0.590	0.386	0.489	0.529	0.526
CHRF	0.514	0.531	0.671	0.525	0.599	0.607	0.591
CHRF++	0.523	0.534	0.678	0.520	0.588	0.614	0.593
MEANT_2.0	**0.578**	**0.565**	0.687	**0.586**	**0.607**	0.596	**0.639**
MEANT_2.0-NOSRL	0.566	0.564	0.682	0.573	0.591	0.582	0.630
NGRAM2VEC	0.436	0.435	0.582	0.383	0.490	0.538	0.520
SENTBLEU	0.435	0.432	0.571	0.393	0.484	0.538	0.512
TREEAGGREG	0.486	0.526	0.638	0.446	0.555	0.571	0.535
UHH_TSKM	0.507	0.479	0.600	0.394	0.465	0.478	0.477
WMD	0.521	0.536	0.704	0.530	0.571	0.566	0.607
$\text{WMD}_O, \delta = 0.2$	0.530	0.542	0.705	0.543	0.585	0.620	0.623
$\text{WMD}_O, \delta = \text{IDEAL}$	0.531	0.546	**0.710**	0.543	0.585	**0.637**	0.623

Table 4: Performance of different metrics in the WMT17 shared task against the two proposed metrics. Our metrics are highlighted in blue. Trained/ensemble metrics are highlighted in grey. Bolded values signify the best performing non-trained metric for each language pair.

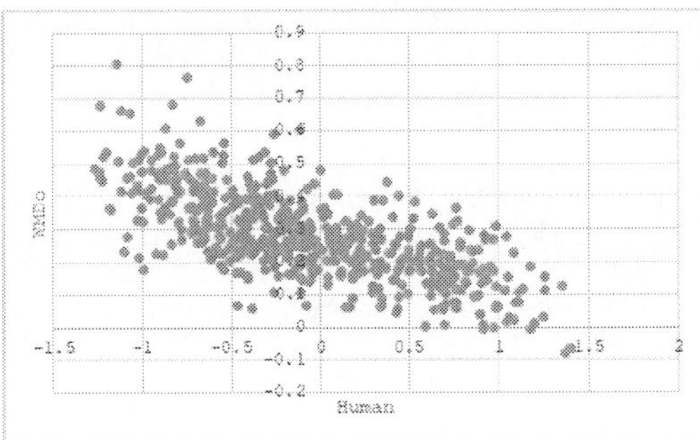

Figure 3: WMD$_O$ against human scores for fi-en

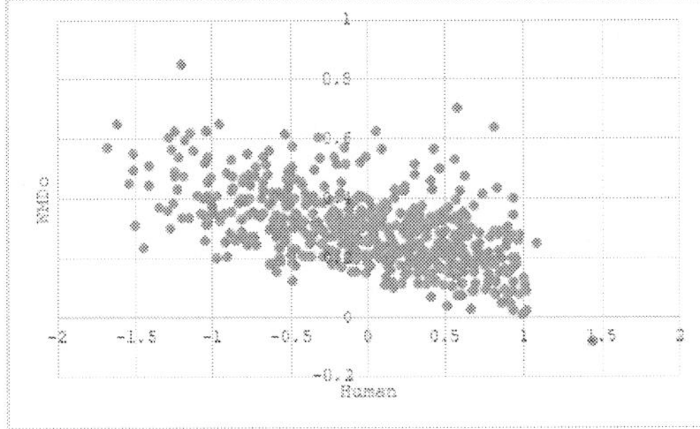

Figure 4: WMD$_O$ against human scores for lv-en

of sentences which were shorter, as each chunk became more pronounced in the penalty, which compounded the bad WMD scores of the nonsensical translation. This was especially evident with poor translations which were comprised largely of retained foreign words. An example of this is from the Latvian to English set; one of the machine translations was "Pann uzkars oil" for the reference "Heat oil in a frying-pan". The penalty could be adjusted in the future to account for sentence length.

6 Conclusions

We have proposed a novel method of evaluating machine translations, focusing on word embeddings and the semantic space. Our metric implementing a word order weighting achieved strong performance in relation to other state-of-the-art metrics and the standard WMD metric. From this we can conclude that semantic spaces are a viable approach to assessing machine translations.

In terms of experimental settings, we found that using the n-gram approach of FastText did not significantly outperform initialising a random vector for each OOV word, although the higher quality FastText embeddings proved to be more accurate

than the older word2vec embeddings. These settings, along with the value of δ, may vary for different datasets. This may be because the WMT17 dataset had a large number of foreign words, which would not make much sense to use n-grams to piece back together. In addition, the finetuned FastText embedding might have had suboptimal training parameters, leading to its poorer performance. It can also be seen that different values of δ work better on certain language pairs; this may have to be a value tuned per language pair rather than a catch-all value.

This work within semantic spaces can also be extended to other translation tasks; as comparisons of two segments are performed within the currently monolingual vector space, future translation evaluations could make use of cross-lingual word embeddings, which carry vectors for different languages in the same space. This could potentially allow translation evaluations to be done directly from the source text to the machine translation, without the human evaluation in between by using a vector space combining the source and target language. Work into cross-lingual embeddings has been growing in recent years (Conneau et al., 2017) and this metric could be used to leverage the potential of this area in the future of automatic translation evaluation. We will provide an open source implementation of WMD$_O$ (Chow, 2019).

References

Satanjeev Banerjee and Alon Lavie. 2005. ME-TEOR: An Automatic Metric for MT Evaluation with Improved Correlation with Human Judgments. Proceedings of the ACL Workshop on Intrinsic and Extrinsic Evaluation Measures for Machine Translation and/or Summarization, pages 65–72.

Ondrej Bojar, Yvette Graham, and Amir Kamran. 2017. Results of the wmt17 metrics shared task. Proceedings of the Second Conference on Machine Translation, page 489513.

Boxing Chen and Hongyu Guo. 2015. Representation based translation evaluation metrics. In Proceedings of the 53rd Annual Meeting of the Association for Computational Linguistics and the 7th International Joint Conference on Natural Language Processing (Volume 2: Short Papers), pages 150–155, Beijing, China. Association for Computational Linguistics.

Julian Chow. 2019. Wmdo. https://github.com/julianchow/WMDO.

Alexis Conneau, Guillaume Lample, Marc'Aurelio Ranzato, Ludovic Denoyer, and Hervé Jégou. 2017.

Word translation without parallel data. arXiv preprint arXiv:1710.04087.

Hiroshi Echizen'ya, Kenji Araki, and Eduard Hovy. 2019. Word embedding-based automatic mt evaluation metric using word position information. Proceedings of NAACL-HLT, page 18741883.

Mert Kilickaya, Aykut Erdem, Nazli Ikizler-Cinbis, and Erkut Erdem. 2017. Re-evaluating automatic metrics for image captioning. Proceedings of EACL 2017, pages 199–209.

Matt J Kusner, Yu Sun, Nicholas I Kolkin, and Kilian Q Weinberger. 2015. From word embeddings to document distances. Proceedings of the 32nd International Conference on International Conference on Machine Learning, 37:957–966.

Chi-kiu Lo. 2017. Meant 2.0: Accurate semantic mt evaluation for any output language. In Proceedings of the Second Conference on Machine Translation, Volume 2: Shared Task Papers, pages 589–597, Copenhagen, Denmark. Association for Computational Linguistics.

Pranava Madhyastha, Josiah Wang, and Lucia Specia. 2019. VIFIDEL: evaluating the visual fidelity of image descriptions. In Proceedings of Annual Meeting of the Association for Computational Linguistics (ACL).

William Mayner. 2019. Fast emd for python: a wrapper for pele and werman's c++ implementation of the earth mover's distance metric. https://github.com/wmayner/pyemd.

Tomas Mikolov, Kai Chen, Greg Corrado, and Jeffrey Dean. 2013. Efficient estimation of word representations in vector space. ICLR Workshop.

Tomas Mikolov, Edouard Grave, Piotr Bojanowski, Christian Puhrsch, and Armand Joulin. 2018. Advances in pre-training distributed word representations. In Proceedings of the International Conference on Language Resources and Evaluation (LREC 2018).

Kishore Papineni, Salim Roukos, Todd Ward, and Wei-Jing Zhu. 2002. BLEU: a Method for Automatic Evaluation of Machine Translation. Proceedings of the 40th Annual Meeting of the Association for Computational Linguistics, pages 311–318.

Ofir Pele and Michael Werman. 2008. A linear time histogram metric for improved sift matching. In Computer Vision–ECCV 2008, pages 495–508. Springer.

Ofir Pele and Michael Werman. 2009. Fast and robust earth mover's distances. In 2009 IEEE 12th International Conference on Computer Vision, pages 460–467. IEEE.

Maja Popovic. 2015. CHRF: character n-gram F-score for automatic MT evaluation. Proceedings of the Tenth Workshop on Statistical Machine Translation, pages 392–395.

Christophe Servan, Alexandre Berard, Zied El-loumi, Hervé Blanchon, and Laurent Besacier. 2016. Word2Vec vs DBnary: Augmenting METEOR using Vector Representations or Lexical Resources? Proceedings of COLING 2016, the 26th International Conference on Computational Linguistics: Technical Papers, pages 1159–1168.

Andre Tttar and Mark Fishel. 2017. bleu2vec: the painfully familiar metric on continuous vector space steroids. Proceedings of the Second Conference on Machine Translation, page 619622.

Weiyue Wang, Jan-Thorsten Peter, Hendrik Rosendahl, and Hermann Ney. 2016. CharacTER: Translation Edit Rate on Character Level. Proceedings of the First Conference on Machine Translation.

Meteor++ 2.0: Adopt Syntactic Level Paraphrase Knowledge into Machine Translation Evaluation

Yinuo Guo, Junfeng Hu[*]

Key Laboratory of Computational Linguistics, School of EECS, Peking University

{gyn0806, hujf}@pku.edu.cn

Abstract

This paper describes Meteor++ 2.0, our submission to the WMT19 Metric Shared Task. The well known Meteor metric improves machine translation evaluation by introducing paraphrase knowledge. However, it only focuses on the lexical level and utilizes consecutive n-grams paraphrases. In this work, we take into consideration syntactic level paraphrase knowledge, which sometimes may be skip-grams. We describe how such knowledge can be extracted from Paraphrase Database (PPDB) and integrated into Meteor-based metrics. Experiments on WMT15 and WMT17 evaluation datasets show that the newly proposed metric outperforms all previous versions of Meteor.

1 Introduction

Accurate evaluation of machine translation (MT) plays an important role in measuring improvement in system performance. Since human evaluation is time-consuming and expensive, automatic metrics for MT have received significant attention in the past few years. A lot of MT evaluation metrics from different perspective have been proposed to measure how close machine-generated translations are to professional human translations such as BLEU (Papineni et al., 2002), Meteor (Banerjee and Lavie, 2005), TER (Snover et al., 2006) etc. Because Meteor has the ability to employ various linguistic language features and resources easily, a lot of improved versions has been put forward continuously (Lavie and Denkowski, 2009; Denkowski and Lavie, 2010a,b, 2011, 2014; Guo et al., 2018). The Meteor-Next (Denkowski and Lavie, 2010a,b) extends the Meteor to phrase-level with the support of paraphrase tables. It's clear that this knowledge incorporated into matching procedure do help the metric reach a higher correlation with the human scores.

In previous work, phrases in paraphrase table are defaulted to be consecutive n-grams which mainly draw on the lexical level. What's more, skip n-gram (Huang et al., 1993) paraphrases whose components need not be consecutive also capture many meaning-preserving syntactic transformations. The original Meteor-based metrics only pay attention to consecutive string matching, they perform badly when reference-hypothesis pairs contain skip n-grams. Using the pair (**protect...from, protect...against**) for an example, the two different prepositions **from** and **against** will bring a miss-matching and then have a negative effect on the Meteor score. Obviously, these two words are equivalent when appearing simultaneously with the verb **protect**. What's more, **from** and **against** here mainly support the sentence structure and contribute little on semantic expression.

In this paper, we seek to directly address the problem mentioned before by adopting a syntactic-level language resource into Meteor. Taking advantage of the large Paraphrase Database (Ganitkevitch et al., 2013; Pavlick et al., 2015), we automatically extract a subset of syntax PPDB which contains skip n-grams. To demonstrate the efficacy of this knowledge, we raise an improved version of the Meteor incorporated with that via an extra parallel syntax stage. Our extended metric, Meteor++ 2.0, shows an improvement in the correlation with the human scores on most of the language pairs.

We organize the remainder of the paper as follows: Section 2 describes the traditional Meteor scoring. Section 3 presents the syntactic level paraphrase table acquisition and model details. Section 4 is devoted to the experiments and results. The conclusions follow in the final section.

2 Traditional Meteor Scoring

The Meteor metric based on a general concept of flexible unigram matching, unigram precision and unigram recall, including the match of words that

Proceedings of the Fourth Conference on Machine Translation (WMT), Volume 2: Shared Task Papers (Day 1) pages 501–506
Florence, Italy, August 1-2, 2019. ©2019 Association for Computational Linguistics

are simple morphological variants of each other by the identical stem and words that are synonyms of each other. For a single hypothesis-reference pair, the space of possible alignments is constructed by exhaustively identifying all possible matches between the sentences according to the following matchers with different weight.

- *Exact:* Words are matched if and only if their surface forms are identical.

- *Stem:* Words are stemmed using a language appropriate Snowball Stemmer (Porter, 2001) and matched if the stems are identical.

- *Synonym:* Words are matched if they are both members of a synonym set according to the WordNet (Miller, 1998) database.

- *Paraphrase:* Phrases are matched if they are listed as paraphrases in a paraphrase table.

Alignment resolution is conducted as a beam search using a heuristic based on the specified criteria.The final alignment is then resolved as the largest subset of all matches to meet the following criteria in order of importance:

1. Require each word in each sentence to be covered by zero or one match.

2. Maximize the number of covered words across both sentences.

3. Minimize the number of chunks, where a chunk is defined as a series of matches that is contiguous and identically ordered in both sentences.

4. Minimize the sum of absolute distances between match start indices in the two sentences. (Break ties by preferring to align phrases that occur at similar positions in both sentences.)

Once the final alignment is selected, the Meteor calculates weighted precision P and recall R. For each matcher (m_i), it counts the number of content and function words covered by matches of ith type in the hypothesis ($m_i(h_c)$, $m_i(h_f)$) and reference ($m_i(r_c)$, $m_i(r_f)$), $|h_f|$ and $|r_f|$ mean the total number of function words in hypothesis and reference, $|h_c|$ and $|r_c|$ mean the total number of content words in hypothesis and reference.

$$P = \frac{\sum_i w_i \cdot (\delta \cdot m_i(h_c) + (1 - \delta) \cdot m_i(h_f))}{\delta \cdot |h_c| + (1 - \delta) \cdot |h_f|} \tag{1}$$

$$R = \frac{\sum_i w_i \cdot (\delta \cdot m_i(r_c) + (1 - \delta) \cdot m_i(r_f))}{\delta \cdot |r_c| + (1 - \delta) \cdot |r_f|} \tag{2}$$

The parameterized harmonic mean of precision P and recall R then calculated:

$$F_{mean} = \frac{P \cdot R}{\alpha \cdot P + (1 - \alpha) \cdot R} \tag{3}$$

To account for gaps and differences in word order, a fragmentation penalty is calculated using the total number of matched words (m, averaged over hypothesis and reference) and number of chunks(ch):

$$Pen = \gamma \cdot (\frac{ch}{m})^\beta \tag{4}$$

The Meteor score is then calculated:

$$Score = (1 - Pen) \cdot F_{mean} \tag{5}$$

The parameters α, β, γ, δ and $w_i...w_n$ are tuned to maximize correlation with human judgments.

3 Our Approach

In this section, we firstly present the syntactic level paraphrase table acquisition in 3.1 and then we introduce how to integrate this knowledge resource into Meteor in 3.2.

Element A	Element B
assist _ in	help _ to
protect _ from	protect _ against
the turkish _	the _ of turkey
feel _ is	believe that _ is
_ administration	of _ management
give	provide _ with
ask _ to do	ask that _
depressing _ of	depressing _ from
issue	the _ number of

Table 1: Some examples of our extracted Syntactic Level Paraphrase Table. Note that '_' is the placeholder which can be skipped over.

3.1 Syntactic Level Paraphrase Table Acquisition

Syntactic paraphrases always capture meaning-preserving syntactic transformations but gain less attention than lexical paraphrases in Meteor-based metrics. In this work, we benefit from the widely

| Reference | We(0) will(1) get(2) the(3) boys(4) ready(5) to(6) go(7) again(8) said(9) donnelly(10) | | | |
| Hypothesis | We(0) will(1) prepare(2) the(3) boy(4) back(5) to(6) action(7) donnelly(8) promises(9) | | | |

Index	Reference	Hypothesis	Match Type	Match Weight
0	we(0)	we(0)	*Exact*	[1.0]
1	will(1)	will(1)	*Exact*	[1.0]
2	get(2) _ _ ready(5)	prepare(2)	*Syntax*	[0.4, 0, 0, 0.8]
3	the(3)	the(3)	*Exact*	[1.0]
4	boys(4)	boy(4)	*Synonym*	[0.8]
5	-	-	-	-
6	to(6)	to(6)	*Exact*	[1.0]
7	go(7)	-	-	-
8	again(8)	-	-	-
9	said(9)	-	-	-
10	donnelly(10)	donnelly(8)	*Exact*	[1.0]

Table 2: An example of alignment result between the reference-hypothesis pair. The weights of *Exact*, *Stem*, *Synonym*, *Paraphrase* and *Syntax* are set to be [1.0, 0.6, 0.8, 0.6, 0.4]

used paraphrase resource PPDB2.0 (Pavlick et al., 2015) and try to bring syntactic level knowledge into Meteor evaluation. Here we mainly focus on skip n-gram paraphrases whose components are not consecutive in appearance such as examples shown in Table 1. Note that here we filter those pairs in which both elements are consecutive n-grams because they will be duplicate with the pairs in existing paraphrase table of Meteor.

The PPDB divides the database into six sizes for several languages according to three perspectives, from *S* to *XXXL* on the lexical, phrasal and syntactic level. We build our own syntactic level paraphrase table using the *XXXL* syntax PPDB:Eng which contains over 140 million syntax paraphrase pairs. Then we use regular expressions to extract the skip n-gram paraphrases with the following criteria and hold out about 27 million pairs. The paraphrase pair in the following descriptions means two phrases which are listed as paraphrases in our syntactic level paraphrase shaped like (Element A, Element B) in Table 1.

- Each phrase in one paraphrase pair should be not consecutive in appearance .

- Each phrase in one paraphrase pair should contain at least one content word.

- The length difference between the two phrases in one paraphrase pair should less than the threshold.

Compared to the prior paraphrase tables, we list two principal differences between them:

- In appearance, we mainly focus on skip n-grams whose components need not be consecutive in the text. In our table, at least one element in each paraphrase pair should have a break by the placeholder '_' which means the position can be any word.

- Lots of pairs have **duplicate** words between the two elements in ours. For the reason that some meaning-preserving syntactic transformations just substitute function words and still have the same content words.

Therefore, treated this knowledge the same way with the previous is unreasonable, and we will discuss the details on how to leverage this language resources under the Meteor framework in the next section.

3.2 Meteor++ 2.0

Under the Meteor framework, Meteor++ 2.0 adds a parallel *Syntax* stage for possible syntactic level paraphrases matching. Due to its difference mentioned in 3.1, we discuss the following modified steps during the matching process.

3.2.1 Possible Alignment Construction

In the extended *Syntax* stage, phrases are matched if they are listed as a pair in our syntactic para-

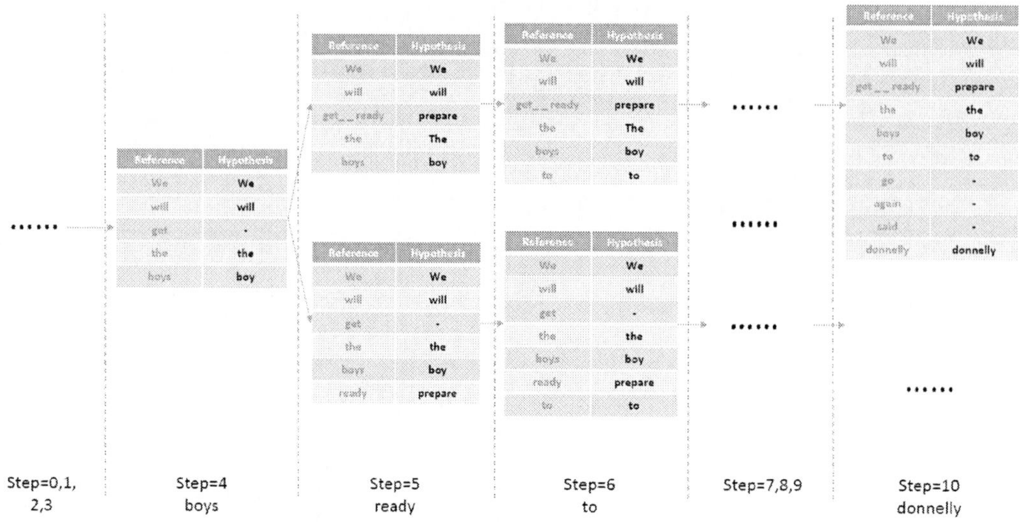

Figure 1: An example of the modified beam search.

phrase table (3.1). The position of the place-holder '_' can be any word which will be skipped over in this phrase matching. And we only keep those matching pairs with the absolute distances between match start indices in the reference and hypothesis less than the threshold.

In prior paraphrase stage, all words in both Element A and B are set with the same value. While in the *Syntax* stage, we set the different word with a different value in one element of the paraphrase pair. More generally, we set 1.0 as the weight of *Exact* stage and 0.4 as the weight of *Syntax* stage. Consider about the paraphrase pair (**protect _ from, protect _ against**), we suppose the two elements appear in the reference and hypothesis separately. If we assign the weight 0.4 for all the words in this paraphrase pair, there will be a bias with the other *Exact* matching pairs. Because the two **protect** would be an exact matching with the weight 1.0 if *Syntax* stage doesn't exist. In a word, as for the weight assignment in *Sytax* stage , we set the word exact weight if it appears in both elements, and set the word synonym weight if the other element includes its synonym and so on.

Table 2 shows a matching example in a reference-hypothesis pair. The weights of *Exact, Stem, Synonym, Paraphrase* and *Syntax* are set to be [1.0, 0.6, 0.8, 0.6, 0.4]. The (**get _ ready, prepare**) pair is matched in *Syntax* stage, the weight for words **ready** and **prepare** is 0.8, for the reason that they are synonym each other, in other word, it

would be matched in an *Synonym* stage if no *Syntax* stage here. And for the word **get**, only matched in the syntax stage, set with the *Syntax* weight 0.4.

3.2.2 Incorporate Syntactic knowledge into Beam Search

The incorporation of the syntactic level paraphrases will bring much more possible matches, therefore it requires a larger beam size which leads a low efficiency. Consider the trade-off between performance and efficiency, we add the syntactic matching pair into the current path until the last word appears during the beam search procedure. Then we look backward to check the state of the other words in this pair, if they are all free to match, we add it into our path.

Figure 1 shows an example in the modified beam search process. At step 4, **get** is an unmatched word in the reference. When comes to the word **ready** in next step, (**get _ ready, prepare**) is a syntax matching pair between the reference-hypothesis. Then we look backward and find that **get** hasn't been matched by others words before, finally, we add the paths with or without (**get _ ready, prepare**) into the current path queue.

4 Experiments

4.1 Setups

To evaluate the impact of our syntactic level paraphrase knowledge, We carry out experiments to compare the performance of Meteor++ 2.0 and

504

	lang-pair	de-en	fi-en	ru-en	cs-en	tr-en	lv-en	zh-en
WMT2015	Meteor	.615	**.638**	.629	.595	-	-	-
	Meteor++ 2.0 (syntax)	**.621**	.633	**.631**	**.606**	-	-	-
WMT2017	Meteor	.532	.719	**.621**	.555	**.628**	.555	.639
	Meteor++ 2.0 (syntax)	**.535**	**.722**	**.621**	**.561**	**.628**	**.556**	**.646**

Table 3: Comparison of segment-level Pearson correlation between Meteor and Meteor++ 2.0 (syntax) on WMT15 and WMT17 evaluation datasets. The weight of *Syntax* stage in Meteor++ 2.0 is set to be 0.4, other parameters are consistent with the Meteor Universal.

	lang-pair	de-en	fi-en	ru-en	cs-en	tr-en	lv-en	zh-en
WMT2015	Meteor++ (copy)	.630	**.652**	.625	.595	-	-	–
	Meteor++ 2.0 (copy + syntax)	**.634**	.647	**.628**	**.606**	-	-	-
WMT2017	Meteor++ (copy)	.525	.717	.625	.557	**.623**	.562	.644
	Meteor++ 2.0 (copy + syntax)	**.527**	**.721**	**.626**	**.563**	.621	**.565**	**.652**

Table 4: Comparison of segment-level Pearson correlation between Meteor++ (copy) and Meteor++ 2.0 (copy + syntax) on WMT15 and WMT17 evaluation datasets. The weight of *Syntax* stage in Meteor++ 2.0 is set to be 0.4, other parameters are consistent with the Meteor Universal.

other prior Meteor-based metrics using the evaluation datasets on WMT15 and WMT17 to-English pairs. And we tune the weight of *Syntax* stage to maximize the Pearson correlation with human scores on all WMT16 to-English datasets, other parameters are consist of the Meteor Universal. Table 5 shows statistics for each language-pair in WMT15-17, each dataset contains the source sentence, MT output, reference, and human score. And we calculate the Pearson correlation between metric scores and human scores for each language pair.

lang-pair	WMT15	WMT16	WMT17
de-en	500	560	561
fi-en	500	560	561
ru-en	500	560	561
ro-en	-	560	-
cs-en	500	560	561
tr-en	-	560	561
lv-en	-	-	561
zh-en	-	-	561

Table 5: Number of sentences for each language pairs in WMT15-17 evaluation sets.

4.2 Results

Table 3-4 show the Pearson correlation with direct assessment (DA) (Graham et al., 2013) on WMT15 and WMT17 evaluation sets at segment-level. Meteor++ is the previous work in WMT2018 (Guo et al., 2018) integrated with copy

knowledge, i.e. words that are likely to be preserved across all paraphrases of a sentence in a given language. Meteor++ 2.0 is the newly proposed one in this paper. In Table 3, we give the comparison between Meteor and Meteor++ 2.0, and Table 4 gives the comparison between Meteor++ and Meteor++ 2.0. **For both prior Meteor-based metrics, the incorporation of the syntactic paraphrase table has a positive influence on almost every to-English language pairs.** Apparently, Meteor++ 2.0 (copy + syntax), the combination with Guo et al. (2018) achieve the best performance in almost every language pair. Hence, we submit Meteor++ 2.0 (copy + syntax) to WMT19 Metric task to-English language pairs.

5 Conclusion

In this paper, we describe the submission of our proposed metric Meteor++ 2.0 for WMT19 Metrics task. Firstly, we extract a syntactic level paraphrase table from the syntax PPDB and list the principle differences between the two paraphrase tables. Secondly, we propose Meteor++ 2.0 incorporated with this language resource. Finally, our metric outperforms all prior Meteor-based metrics on almost every WMT15 and WMT17 to-English language pairs.

6 Future Work

According to the observation of the phrase matches contributed by syntactic level paraphrases, though we benefit a lot from this knowledge resource, some noises are brought at the meantime.

Firstly, in the perspective of the knowledge quality, despite filtering techniques, there are still some unusual, inaccurate or highly context-dependent paraphrases. High-frequency usage always indicates high confidence, so hope our metric can play a role of a quality estimator for paraphrase tables in the future.

Secondly, since the syntax-level knowledge pay more attention on sentence structure, mismatch can not always be avoid. With the help of syntactic tools such as parsing may help take better usage of this knowledge.

7 Acknowledgments

This paper is supported by the National Natural Science Foundation of China (Grant No. 61472017)

References

Satanjeev Banerjee and Alon Lavie. 2005. Meteor: An automatic metric for mt evaluation with improved correlation with human judgments. In *Proceedings of the acl workshop on intrinsic and extrinsic evaluation measures for machine translation and/or summarization*, pages 65–72.

Michael Denkowski and Alon Lavie. 2010a. Extending the meteor machine translation evaluation metric to the phrase level. In *Human Language Technologies: The 2010 Annual Conference of the North American Chapter of the Association for Computational Linguistics*, pages 250–253. Association for Computational Linguistics.

Michael Denkowski and Alon Lavie. 2010b. Meteor-next and the meteor paraphrase tables: Improved evaluation support for five target languages. In *Proceedings of the Joint Fifth Workshop on Statistical Machine Translation and MetricsMATR*, pages 339–342.

Michael Denkowski and Alon Lavie. 2011. Meteor 1.3: Automatic metric for reliable optimization and evaluation of machine translation systems. In *Proceedings of the sixth workshop on statistical machine translation*, pages 85–91. Association for Computational Linguistics.

Michael Denkowski and Alon Lavie. 2014. Meteor universal: Language specific translation evaluation for any target language. In *Proceedings of the ninth workshop on statistical machine translation*, pages 376–380.

Juri Ganitkevitch, Benjamin Van Durme, and Chris Callison-Burch. 2013. Ppdb: The paraphrase database. In *Proceedings of the 2013 Conference of the North American Chapter of the Association for Computational Linguistics: Human Language Technologies*, pages 758–764.

Yvette Graham, Timothy Baldwin, Alistair Moffat, and Justin Zobel. 2013. Continuous measurement scales in human evaluation of machine translation. In *Proceedings of the 7th Linguistic Annotation Workshop and Interoperability with Discourse*, pages 33–41.

Yinuo Guo, Chong Ruan, and Junfeng Hu. 2018. Meteor++: Incorporating copy knowledge into machine translation evaluation. In *Proceedings of the Third Conference on Machine Translation: Shared Task Papers*, pages 740–745.

Xuedong Huang, Fileno Alleva, Hsiao-Wuen Hon, Mei-Yuh Hwang, Kai-Fu Lee, and Ronald Rosenfeld. 1993. The sphinx-ii speech recognition system: an overview. *Computer Speech & Language*, 7(2):137–148.

Alon Lavie and Michael J Denkowski. 2009. The meteor metric for automatic evaluation of machine translation. *Machine translation*, 23(2-3):105–115.

George Miller. 1998. *WordNet: An electronic lexical database*. MIT press.

Kishore Papineni, Salim Roukos, Todd Ward, and Wei-Jing Zhu. 2002. Bleu: a method for automatic evaluation of machine translation. In *Proceedings of the 40th annual meeting on association for computational linguistics*, pages 311–318. Association for Computational Linguistics.

Ellie Pavlick, Pushpendre Rastogi, Juri Ganitkevitch, Benjamin Van Durme, and Chris Callison-Burch. 2015. Ppdb 2.0: Better paraphrase ranking, fine-grained entailment relations, word embeddings, and style classification. In *Proceedings of the 53rd Annual Meeting of the Association for Computational Linguistics and the 7th International Joint Conference on Natural Language Processing (Volume 2: Short Papers)*, volume 2, pages 425–430.

Martin F Porter. 2001. Snowball: A language for stemming algorithms.

Matthew Snover, Bonnie Dorr, Richard Schwartz, Linnea Micciulla, and John Makhoul. 2006. A study of translation edit rate with targeted human annotation. In *Proceedings of association for machine translation in the Americas*, volume 200.

YiSi - A unified semantic MT quality evaluation and estimation metric for languages with different levels of available resources

Chi-kiu Lo
NRC-CNRC
Multilingual Text Processing
National Research Council Canada
1200 Montreal Road, Ottawa, ON K1A 0R6, Canada
`chikiu.lo@nrc-cnrc.gc.ca`

Abstract

We present YiSi, a unified automatic semantic machine translation quality evaluation and estimation metric for languages with different levels of available resources. Underneath the interface with different language resources settings, YiSi uses the same representation for the two sentences in assessment. Besides, we show significant improvement in the correlation of YiSi-1's scores with human judgment is made by using contextual embeddings in multilingual BERT–Bidirectional Encoder Representations from Transformers to evaluate lexical semantic similarity. YiSi is open source and publicly available.

1 Introduction

A good automatic MT quality metric is one that closely reflect the usefulness of the translation, in terms of assisting human readers to understand the meaning of the input sentence. BLEU (Papineni et al., 2002) has long been shown not to correlate well with human judgment on translation quality (Machacek and Bojar, 2014; Stanojević et al., 2015; Bojar et al., 2016, 2017; Ma et al., 2018). However, it is still the most commonly used metric for reporting quality of machine translation systems. One of the major reasons is that BLEU is ready-to-deploy to all languages due to its simplicity. Semantic MT evaluation metrics, such as METEOR (Denkowski and Lavie, 2014) and MEANT (Lo, 2017), require additional linguistic resources to more accurately evaluate the meaning similarity between the MT output and the reference translation. The lower portability hinders the wide adoption of these metrics.

We, therefore, propose a unified framework, YiSi, for MT quality evaluation and estimation that take advantage of both metric paradigms by providing options to fallback to surface-level lexical similarity when semantic models are not available for the languages in assessment.

YiSi were first used in WMT 2018 metrics shared task (Ma et al., 2018) and performed well and consistently at segment-level across the tested language pairs in correlating with human judgment. An YiSi based system successfully served in WMT2018 parallel corpus filtering task (Lo et al., 2018).

This year, instead of using `word2vec` (Mikolov et al., 2013) to evaluate lexical semantic similarity in YiSi, we use BERT –Bidirectional Encoder Representation from Transformers (Devlin et al., 2018). YiSi is open source and publicly available.[1]

2 YiSi

YiSi[2] is a unified semantic MT quality evaluation and estimation metric for languages with different levels of available resources. Inspired by MEANT (Lo, 2017), YiSi-1 is a MT quality evaluation metric that measures the similarity between a machine translation and human references by aggregating the weighted distributional lexical semantic similarities and optionally incorporating shallow semantic structures. YiSi-0 is the degenerate version of YiSi-1 that is ready-to-deploy to any languages. It uses longest common character substring to measure the lexical similarity. YiSi-2 is the bilingual, reference-less version, which uses bilingual embeddings to evaluate crosslingual lexical semantic similarity between the input and MT output. Like YiSi-1, YiSi-2 can exploit shallow semantic structures as well.

YiSi-0 and YiSi-1 were first used in WMT 2018 metrics shared task (Ma et al., 2018) and performed well and consistently at segment-level

---

[1] http://chikiu-jackie-lo.org/home/index.php/yisi

[2] YiSi is the romanization of the Cantonese word 意思 ('meaning').

Proceedings of the Fourth Conference on Machine Translation (WMT), Volume 2: Shared Task Papers (Day 1) pages 507–513
Florence, Italy, August 1-2, 2019. ©2019 Association for Computational Linguistics

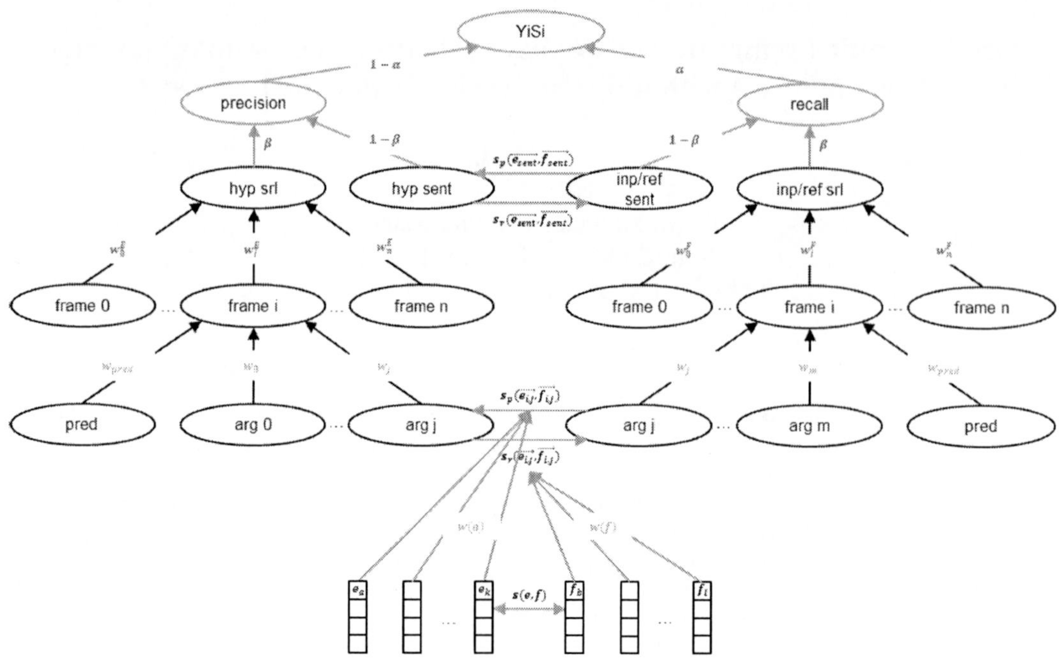

Figure 1: Graphical representation of the computation of YiSi.

across the tested language pairs in correlating with human judgment. While YiSi-1 also successfully served in WMT2018 parallel corpus filtering task, YiSi-2 showed comparable accuracy in our internal experiments (Lo et al., 2018).

2.1 Overview

Following the guiding principle that a good MT quality metric reflects how well human readers understand the meaning of the input sentence, YiSi is the weighted f-scores over corresponding semantic frames and role fillers in the two sentences E and F in assessment. The procedure of computing YiSi is described as follow:

1. Apply a shallow semantic parser to both E and F.

2. Apply the maximum weighted bipartite matching algorithm to align the semantic frames between E and F according to the lexical similarities of the predicates.

3. For each pair of aligned frames, apply the maximum weighted bipartite matching algorithm to align the arguments between E and F according to the lexical similarity of role fillers.

4. Compute the weighted f-score over the

matching role labels of these aligned predicates and role fillers according to the following definitions: (Figure 1 is the graphical representation of the following computation.)

$$w(e) = \text{lexical weight of } e$$
$$s(e, f) = \text{lexical similarity of } e \text{ and } f$$

where $s(e, f)$ is the lexical similarity and it is weighted by $w(e)$ and $w(f)$ for computing phrasal precision and recall respectively. Different variants of YiSi have different definition of lexical similarities and weights depend on the resources available for the assessment settings. By aggregating the weighted lexical similarities into n-gram similarities, we then align the bag of n-grams in the two sentences using maximum alignment on the n-gram similarities. The phrasal similarity precision, s_p, and recall, s_r, (as defined below) are the weighted average of the similarities of the aligned n-gram.

$$s_p(\overrightarrow{e}, \overrightarrow{f}) = \frac{\sum_a \max_b \sum_{k=0}^{n-1} w(e_{a+k}) \cdot s(e_{a+k}, f_{b+k})}{\sum_a \sum_{k=0}^{n-1} w(e_{a+k})}$$

$$s_r(\overrightarrow{e}, \overrightarrow{f}) = \frac{\sum_b \max_a \sum_{k=0}^{n-1} w(f_{b+k}) \cdot s(e_{a+k}, f_{b+k})}{\sum_b \sum_{k=0}^{n-1} w(f_{b+k})}$$

508

With the phrasal semantic precision and recall, we compute the structural semantic precision and recall as follow:

$$q_{i,j}^E = \text{argument } j \text{ of aligned frame } i \text{ in } E$$

$$q_{i,j}^F = \text{argument } j \text{ of aligned frame } i \text{ in } F$$

$$w_i^E = \frac{\#\text{units filled in aligned frame } i \text{ of } E}{\text{total \#units in } E}$$

$$w_i^F = \frac{\#\text{units filled in aligned frame } i \text{ of } F}{\text{total \#units in } F}$$

$$w_j = \text{count}\,(\text{argument } j \text{ in } \mathbb{F})$$

$$w_t = 0.25 * \text{count}\,(\text{predicate in } \mathbb{F})$$

$$\text{srl}_p = \frac{\sum_i w_i^e \dfrac{w_t s_p(\overrightarrow{e_{i,t}},\overrightarrow{f_{i,t}}) + \sum_j w_j s_p(\overrightarrow{e_{i,j}},\overrightarrow{f_{i,j}})}{w_t + \sum_j w_j |q_{i,j}^e|}}{\sum_i w_i^e}$$

$$\text{srl}_r = \frac{\sum_i w_i^f \dfrac{w_t s_r(\overrightarrow{e_{i,t}},\overrightarrow{f_{i,t}}) + \sum_j w_j s_r(\overrightarrow{e_{i,j}},\overrightarrow{f_{i,j}})}{w_t + \sum_j w_j |q_{i,j}^f|}}{\sum_i w_i^f}$$

where w_t is the weight of the lexical similarities of the aligned predicates in step 2. w_j is the weight of the phrasal similarities of the role fillers of the arguments of role type j of the aligned frames between the reference translations and the MT output in step 3 if their role types are matching. As in (Lo, 2017), we merge the semantic role labels into 8 role types (who, did, what, whom, when, where, why, how) for more robust performance. Thus, there is a total of 8 weights for the set of semantic role types in YiSi estimated by type counts in the document $\mathbb{F}$. The frame precision/recall is the weighted sum of the phrasal precision/recall of the aligned role fillers. The token coverage w_i^e and w_i^f estimate the importance of frame i in the sentence E and F. The structural semantic precision and recall is the weighted average of all the aligned frames in sentence E and F respectively.

Now, the overall precision and recall is the weighted sum of the phrasal precision and recall of the whole sentence of $\overrightarrow{e_{\text{sent}}}$ and $\overrightarrow{f_{\text{sent}}}$, like in the following:

$$\text{precision} = \beta \cdot \text{srl}_p + (1 - \beta) \cdot s_p(\overrightarrow{e_{\text{sent}}}, \overrightarrow{f_{\text{sent}}})$$

$$\text{recall} = \beta \cdot \text{srl}_r + (1 - \beta) \cdot s_r(\overrightarrow{e_{\text{sent}}}, \overrightarrow{f_{\text{sent}}})$$

It is important to note that the weight β should *NOT* be interpreted as the importance of the structural semantic similarity in YiSi because there is a

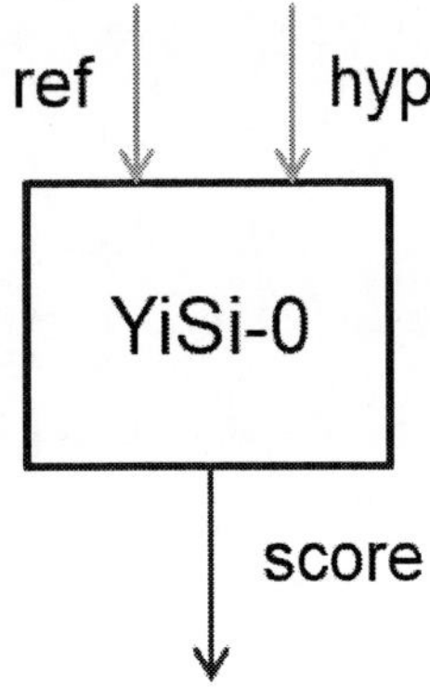

Figure 2: Resources used in YiSi-0.

huge overlap in the structural semantic similarity and the phrasal semantic similarity. Instead, we should pay attention to the significant difference in the performance of YiSi with and without structural semantic similarity, especially in YiSi-2, the crosslingual variant. In this experiment, β is set to 0.1.

Finally, the weight α for the precision and recall is introduced for different usages of YiSi. α should be set to 0.7 to make YiSi more recall-oriented when it is used for MT evaluation. When used for MT system optimization, α should be set to 0.5 to balance precision and recall.

$$\text{YiSi} = \frac{\text{precision} \cdot \text{recall}}{\alpha \cdot \text{precision} + (1 - \alpha) \cdot \text{recall}}$$

In the following, we describe how we estimate the lexical similarity $s(e, f)$ and lexical weight $w(e)$ under different resource conditions.

2.1.1 YiSi-0: quality evaluation metric for extremely low resource languages

YiSi-0 is the degenerate resource-free variant of YiSi for MT quality evaluation, where sentence E is the MT output and sentence F is the reference. Figure 2 shows the resources used in YiSi-0.

YiSi-0 uses the longest common character substring accuracy to evaluate lexical similarity between the MT output and human reference. Since the MT output and the human reference are both in the same language, the lexical weight $w(e)$ of word e in the translation and the lexical weight $w(f)$ of word f in the reference are both estimated by the inverse-document-frequency of those words in the reference document $\mathbb{F}$. Thus, formally YiSi-

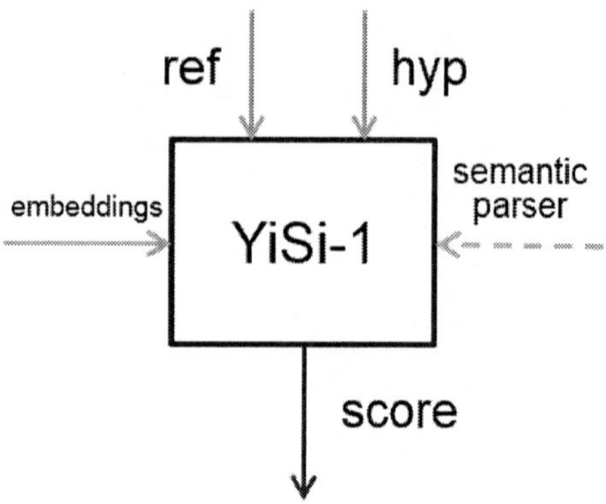

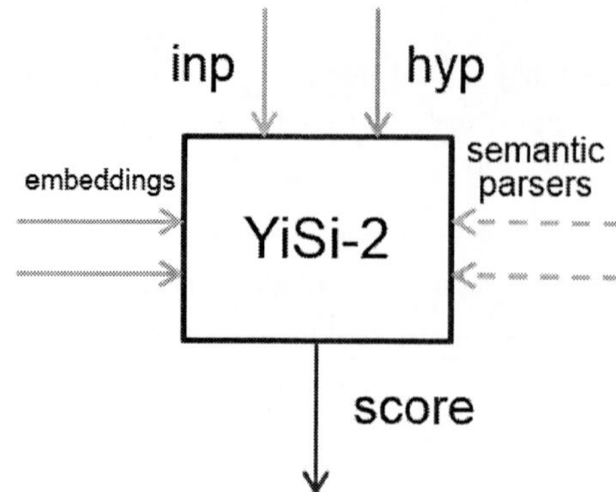

Figure 3: Resources used in YiSi-1. The dash arrow means that the semantic parser is optional.

Figure 4: Resources used in YiSi-2. Arrows in green depict resources in target language and arrows in orange depict resources in source language. The dash arrows mean that the semantic parsers are optional.

0 is defined as follow:

$$l(e, f) = \text{longest common substring of } e \text{ and } f$$
$$s_0(e, f) = \frac{2 * l(e, f)}{|e| + |f|}$$
$$w(e) = idf(e) = log(1 + \frac{|\mathbb{F}| + 1}{|\mathbb{F}_{\exists e}| + 1})$$
$$\text{YiSi-0} = \text{YiSi}(s{=}s_0, \beta{=}0.0, E{=}\text{MT}, F{=}\text{REF})$$

2.1.2 YiSi-1: quality evaluation metric with access to an embedding model

YiSi-1 is the monolingual variant of YiSi for MT quality evaluation, where sentence E is the MT output and sentence F is the reference. Figure 3 shows the resources used in YiSi-1.

YiSi-1 requires an embedding model to evaluate lexical semantic similarity and optionally requires a semantic role labeler in the output language for evaluating structural semantic similarity. The lexical semantic similarity is the cosine similarity of the embeddings from the lexical representation model. Similar to YiSi-0, the lexical weight $w(u)$ of word unit u in the MT and the reference are estimated by the inverse-document-frequency of that word in the reference document $\mathbb{F}$. Thus, formally YiSi-1 is defined as follow:

$$v(u) = \text{embedding of unit } u$$
$$s_1(e, f) = cos(v(e), v(f))$$
$$w(u) = idf(u) = log(1 + \frac{|\mathbb{F}| + 1}{|\mathbb{F}_{\exists u}| + 1})$$
$$\text{YiSi-1} = \text{YiSi}(s{=}s_1, \beta{=}0.0, E{=}\text{MT}, F{=}\text{REF})$$
$$\text{YiSi-1\_srl} = \text{YiSi}(s{=}s_1, \beta{=}0.1, E{=}\text{MT}, F{=}\text{REF})$$

2.1.3 YiSi-2: quality estimation metric for languages with access to a bilingual embedding model

YiSi-2 is the cross-lingual variant of YiSi for MT quality estimation, where sentence E is the MT output and sentence F is the input. Figure 4 shows the resources used in YiSi-2.

YiSi-2 requires a cross-lingual embedding model for evaluating cross-lingual lexical semantic similarity and optionally requires a semantic role labeler in both the input and the output languages for evaluating structural semantic similarity. The lexical semantic similarity is the cosine similarity of the embeddings from the cross-lingual lexical representation model. The lexical weight $w(e)$ of word unit e in the MT is estimated by the inversion-document-frequency of the word in the MT document $\mathbb{E}$ while the lexical weight $w(f)$ of word unit f in the MT is estimated by the inversion-document-frequency of the word in the MT document $\mathbb{F}$. Thus, formally YiSi-2 is defined as follow:

$$v(u) = \text{embedding of unit } u$$
$$s_2(e, f) = cos(v(e), v(f))$$
$$w(e) = idf(e) = log(1 + \frac{|\mathbb{E}| + 1}{|\mathbb{E}_{\exists e}| + 1})$$
$$w(f) = idf(f) = log(1 + \frac{|\mathbb{F}| + 1}{|\mathbb{F}_{\exists f}| + 1})$$
$$\text{YiSi-2} = \text{YiSi}(s{=}s_2, \beta{=}0.0, E{=}\text{MT}, F{=}\text{IN})$$
$$\text{YiSi-2\_srl} = \text{YiSi}(s{=}s_2, \beta{=}0.1, E{=}\text{MT}, F{=}\text{IN})$$

2.2 Using BERT for lexical unit semantic similarity

In WMT 2018 metrics shared task, YiSi-1 uses `word2vec` (Mikolov et al., 2013) to evaluate lexical semantic similarity between the MT output and the human reference at word level. The shortcomings of this kind of static embedding models (also including but not limited to `GloVe` (Pennington et al., 2014)) is that they provide the same embedding representation for the same word without reflecting context of different sentences. In contrast, BERT (Devlin et al., 2018) uses a bidirectional transformer encoder (Vaswani et al., 2017) to capture the sentence context in the output embeddings (at subword unit level), such that the embedding for the same word/subword unit in different sentences would be different and better represented in the embedding space. Zhang et al. (2019) provided an extensive study on the performance of the output embeddings of difference layers of BERT model in correlation with human adequacy. Following the recommendation from their studies, we use embeddings extracted from BERT models with the following settings:

- the 18th layer of the pretrained English cased BERT-Large model to represent the subword units in the reference and MT output in English for computing YiSi-1;

- the 9th layer of the pretrained Chinese BERT-Base model to represent the characters in the reference and MT output in Chinese for computing YiSi-1; and

- the 9th layer of the pretrained multilingual cased BERT-Base model to represent the subword units in the reference and MT output in languages other than Chinese and English for computing YiSi-1 and to represent the subword units in the original input and MT output in all language pairs for computing YiSi-2.

2.3 Using MATE/MATEPLUS for structural semantic similarity

There are a handful of shallow semantic parsers available publicly. `mate-tools` (Björkelund et al., 2009) is an SVM classifier based on features extracted from a dependency parse. Its successor `mateplus` (Roth and Woodsend, 2014) also uses features extracted from distributional word embeddings. `mate-tools` and `mateplus` are integrated into YiSi because of their support for languages other than English. We use `mateplus` for German's and English's semantic role labeling and `mate-tools` for Chinese's semantic role labeling.

3 Experiments and results

We use WMT 2018 metrics task evaluation set (Ma et al., 2018) for our development experiments.

The official human judgments of translation quality in WMT 2018 were collected using direct assessment. The direct assessment evaluation protocol in WMT2018 gave the annotators the reference and a MT output and asked them to evaluate the translation adequacy of the MT output on an absolute scale.

Due to space limitations, we only report the results of YiSi, chrF (Popović, 2015), BLEU and the best correlation in each of the individual language pairs. Since we use exactly the same correlation analysis as the official task for each of the test sets, our reported results are directly comparable with those reported in the task's overview paper. We summarize our observations in the following sections.

3.1 Correlation with human judgment at system-level

Table 1 shows the Pearson's correlation with WMT 2018 official aggregated human direct assessment of translation adequacy at system-level.

YiSi-0 performs more stably than chrF and BLEU in correlating with human on translation quality across all translation directions. YiSi-0 achieves comparable results with chrF and BLEU in most of the translation directions while significantly outperforms chrF and BLEU in correlating with human in evaluating Turkish-English and English-Turkish translations.

YiSi-1 beats all the WMT2018 participants in correlation with human at system level for evaluating Czech-English, German-English, Chines-English, English-German, English-Estonian, English-Finnish and English-Russian translations. In addition, YiSi-1_srl further improves YiSi-1's correlation with human at system level for evaluating German-English, Chinese-English translations.

For the quality estimation variants, YiSi-2 achieves reasonably good results (with less than

input lang.	cs	de	et	fi	ru	tr	zh	en	en	en	en	en	en	en
output lang.	en	en	en	en	en	en	en	cs	de	et	fi	ru	tr	zh
individual best	.981	.997	**.991**	**.996**	**.995**	**.958**	.982	**.999**	.991	.984	.974	.992	**.990**	**.983**
chrF	.966	.994	.981	.987	,990	.452	.960	.990	.990	.981	.969	.989	.948	.944
BLEU	.970	.971	.986	.973	.979	.657	.978	.995	.981	.975	.962	.983	.826	.947
YiSi-0	.962	.995	.982	.986	.985	.857	.972	.984	.989	.984	.954	.989	.980	.956
YiSi-1	**.990**	.998	.986	.994	.993	.830	.988	.993	**.995**	**.988**	**.979**	**.993**	.929	.977
YiSi-1_srl	.989	**.999**	.987	.993	.993	.793	**.989**	–	**.995**	–	–	–	–	.976
Quality estimation as a metric														
YiSi-2	.919	.946	.865	.927	.566	.061	.797	.710	.862	.156	.475	.204	.389	.417
YiSi-2_srl	–	.948	–	–	–	–	.781	–	.902	–	–	–	–	.472

Table 1: Pearson's correlation of the metric scores with WMT 2018 aggregated human direct assessment scores at system-level.

input lang.	cs	de	et	fi	ru	tr	zh	en	en	en	en	en	en	en
output lang.	en	en	en	en	en	en	en	cs	de	et	fi	ru	tr	zh
individual best	.347	.498	.368	.273	.311	.259	.218	.518	.696	.573	.525	.407	**.418**	.323
chrF	.288	.479	.328	.229	.269	.210	.208	.516	.677	.572	.520	.383	.409	.328
sentBLEU	.233	.415	.285	.154	.228	.145	.178	.389	.320	.414	.355	.330	.261	.311
YiSi-0	.308	.480	.330	.210	.284	.213	.216	.454	.670	.530	.468	.396	.362	.316
YiSi-1	.391	**.544**	**.397**	.299	**.352**	**.301**	**.254**	**.548**	**.734**	**.599**	**.549**	**.427**	.402	**.371**
YiSi-1_srl	**.396**	.543	.390	**.303**	.351	.297	.253	–	.719	–	–	–	–	.368
Quality estimation as a metric														
YiSi-2	.014	.279	.186	.151	.088	.066	.091	-.043	.359	.106	.172	.061	.103	.101
YiSi-2_srl	–	.281	–	–	–	–	.085	–	.380	–	–	–	–	.103

Table 2: Kendall's correlation of metric scores with the rankings at segment-level human direct assessment in WMT 2018.

0.1 degradation in correlation with human) in evaluating Czech-English , German-English, Finnish-English translation without using the human translation as reference. At the same time, YiSi-2_srl improves YiSi-2's correlation with human at system level for evaluating English-German, English-Chinese translations.

3.2 Correlation with human judgment at segment-level

Table 2 shows the Kendall's correlation with the rankings at segment-level human direct assessment obtained in the WMT 2018.

YiSi-0 achieves comparable results with chrF and BLEU for evaluating all translation directions at segment level. YiSi-1 beats all the WMT2018 participants in correlation with human at segment level for evaluating almost all translation directions, except English-Turkish. In addition, YiSi-1_srl further improves YiSi-1's correlation with human at segment level for evaluating Czech-English and Finnish-English translations.

For the quality estimation variants, YiSi-2 performs significantly worse than YiSi-1 due to the lacking of a reference translation in the same language for evaluating fluency. Therefore, We can see that as shown by the significant improvement in YiSi-2_srl for evaluating English-German trans-

lation without reference translation, using semantic parsers to extract the semantic frames of the input sentence and machine translation become very helping in evaluating translation fluency.

4 Conclusion

We have presented the on-going work in developing a unified semantic MT quality evaluation and estimation metric for languages with different levels of available resources. Initial experiment results show that the improved variants of YiSi that use BERT contextual embeddings correlate with human judgment significantly better than other trained metrics.

References

Anders Björkelund, Love Hafdell, and Pierre Nugues. 2009. Multilingual semantic role labeling. In *Proceedings of the Thirteenth Conference on Computational Natural Language Learning (CoNLL 2009): Shared Task*, pages 43–48, Boulder, Colorado. Association for Computational Linguistics.

Ondřej Bojar, Yvette Graham, and Amir Kamran. 2017. Results of the WMT17 metrics shared task. In *Proceedings of the Second Conference on Machine Translation*, pages 489–513, Copenhagen, Denmark. Association for Computational Linguistics.

Ondřej Bojar, Yvette Graham, Amir Kamran, and Miloš Stanojević. 2016. Results of the WMT16 Metrics Shared Task. In *Proceedings of the First Conference on Machine Translation*, pages 199–231, Berlin, Germany. Association for Computational Linguistics.

Michael Denkowski and Alon Lavie. 2014. METEOR universal: Language specific translation evaluation for any target language. In *9th Workshop on Statistical Machine Translation (WMT 2014)*.

Jacob Devlin, Ming-Wei Chang, Kenton Lee, and Kristina Toutanova. 2018. BERT: pre-training of deep bidirectional transformers for language understanding. *CoRR*, abs/1810.04805.

Chi-kiu Lo. 2017. MEANT 2.0: Accurate semantic MT evaluation for any output language. In *Proceedings of the Second Conference on Machine Translation*, pages 589–597, Copenhagen, Denmark. Association for Computational Linguistics.

Chi-kiu Lo, Michel Simard, Darlene Stewart, Samuel Larkin, Cyril Goutte, and Patrick Littell. 2018. Accurate semantic textual similarity for cleaning noisy parallel corpora using semantic machine translation evaluation metric: The NRC supervised submissions to the parallel corpus filtering task. In *Proceedings of the Third Conference on Machine Translation: Shared Task Papers*, pages 908–916, Belgium, Brussels. Association for Computational Linguistics.

Qingsong Ma, Ondřej Bojar, and Yvette Graham. 2018. Results of the WMT18 metrics shared task: Both characters and embeddings achieve good performance. In *Proceedings of the Third Conference on Machine Translation: Shared Task Papers*, pages 671–688, Belgium, Brussels. Association for Computational Linguistics.

Matous Machacek and Ondrej Bojar. 2014. Results of the WMT14 Metrics Shared Task. In *Proceedings of the Ninth Workshop on Statistical Machine Translation*, pages 293–301, Baltimore, Maryland, USA. Association for Computational Linguistics.

Tomas Mikolov, Ilya Sutskever, Kai Chen, Greg Corrado, and Jeffrey Dean. 2013. Distributed representations of words and phrases and their compositionality. In *Proceedings of the 26th International Conference on Neural Information Processing Systems*, NIPS'13, pages 3111–3119, USA. Curran Associates Inc.

Kishore Papineni, Salim Roukos, Todd Ward, and Wei-Jing Zhu. 2002. BLEU: a method for automatic evaluation of machine translation. In *40th Annual Meeting of the Association for Computational Linguistics (ACL-02)*, pages 311–318, Philadelphia, Pennsylvania.

Jeffrey Pennington, Richard Socher, and Christopher Manning. 2014. Glove: Global vectors for word representation. In *Proceedings of the 2014 Conference on Empirical Methods in Natural Language Processing (EMNLP)*, pages 1532–1543, Doha, Qatar. Association for Computational Linguistics.

Maja Popović. 2015. chrF: character n-gram f-score for automatic MT evaluation. In *Proceedings of the Tenth Workshop on Statistical Machine Translation*, pages 392–395, Lisbon, Portugal. Association for Computational Linguistics.

Michael Roth and Kristian Woodsend. 2014. Composition of word representations improves semantic role labelling. In *Proceedings of the 2014 Conference on Empirical Methods in Natural Language Processing (EMNLP)*, pages 407–413, Doha, Qatar. Association for Computational Linguistics.

Miloš Stanojević, Amir Kamran, Philipp Koehn, and Ondřej Bojar. 2015. Results of the WMT15 Metrics Shared Task. In *Proceedings of the Tenth Workshop on Statistical Machine Translation*, pages 256–273, Lisbon, Portugal. Association for Computational Linguistics.

Ashish Vaswani, Noam Shazeer, Niki Parmar, Jakob Uszkoreit, Llion Jones, Aidan N Gomez, Łukasz Kaiser, and Illia Polosukhin. 2017. Attention is all you need. In *Advances in neural information processing systems*, pages 5998–6008.

Tianyi Zhang, Varsha Kishore, Felix Wu, Kilian Q. Weinberger, and Yoav Artzi. 2019. Bertscore: Evaluating text generation with BERT. *CoRR*, abs/1904.09675.

EED: Extended Edit Distance Measure for Machine Translation

Peter Stanchev   **Weiyue Wang**   **Hermann Ney**

Human Language Technology and Pattern Recognition, Computer Science Department

RWTH Aachen University, 52056 Aachen, Germany

`<surname>@i6.informatik.rwth-aachen.de`

Abstract

Over the years a number of machine translation metrics have been developed in order to evaluate the accuracy and quality of machine-generated translations. Metrics such as BLEU and TER have been used for decades. However, with the rapid progress of machine translation systems, the need for better metrics is growing. This paper proposes an extension of the edit distance, which achieves better human correlation, whilst remaining fast, flexible and easy to understand.

1 Introduction

Machine Translation (MT) has been a popular research topic for the past few years. It deals with the paradigm of how to automatically translate a sentence or a set of sentences from a source language to a different target language. In statistical MT, this can be formally described as finding the translation $e_1^I = e_1 \ldots e_i \ldots e_I$ with the highest probability for a given source language sentence $f_1^J = f_1 \ldots f_j \ldots f_J$:

$$\hat{e}_1^{\hat{I}} = \underset{I, e_1^I}{\arg\max}\{p(e_1^I \mid f_1^J)\} \tag{1}$$

This approach models the translation task by defining it as a search for the sentence that best suits a given criterion. For example through log-linear models as described by Och and Ney, 2002.

However, all approaches have to be evaluated to quantify the quality and accuracy of the produced translations. Naturally, the best method would be to have human experts rate each produced translation in order to evaluate the whole MT system. This is quite a costly process and is not viable for development of MT systems. For this reason a number of metrics exist that automate the process and use different scoring methods to automatically evaluate the produced translation based on a reference sentence. Two of the earliest and most pop-

ular metrics are BLEU (Papineni et al., 2002) and TER (Snover et al., 2006).

This paper introduces a new MT metric: Extended Edit Distance (EED), based on an extension of the Levenshtein distance (Levenshtein, 1966). This metric follows a number of criteria:

- It is bound between zero and one.

- Its definition is kept simple, as it does not depend on external dictionaries or language analysis.

- It has competitive human correlation.

- It is fast to compute.

The remainder of this paper is structured as follows: first, related work is reviewed in Section 2; Section 3 introduces the concept of edit distance and the different existing extensions of it; Section 4 introduces the EED metric in detail; A comparison with other metrics regarding human correlation and speed is performed in Section 5; Finally, a conclusion is drawn in Section 6.

2 Background

MT metrics compute a score based on the output of a MT system, here called "candidate", and a "reference" sentence, which is provided. The reference is a valid translation of the original source sentence to the target language, usually obtained through a human expert. A metric aims to use the pair of reference and candidate to give a numerical value to the correctness of the translation. A naïve approach would be to directly compare the candidate and reference in order to consider the translation quality. This, however, cannot be a good evaluation criterion since human language has multiple ways of expressing the same idea, and thus there is seldom one unique translation of a sentence from one language to another.

Over the years, a number of metrics have been created based on a variety of ideas and principles.

514

Proceedings of the Fourth Conference on Machine Translation (WMT), Volume 2: Shared Task Papers (Day 1) pages 514–520

Florence, Italy, August 1-2, 2019. ©2019 Association for Computational Linguistics

Some examples for such principles can be seen in the count-based metrics (BLEU, CHRF (Popovic, 2015)) or the edit distance based metrics (TER, CHARACTER (Wang et al., 2016), CDER (Leusch et al., 2006)).

Count-based metrics compute the n-grams of both reference and candidate and then compare them with each other using a scoring function. One of the most used metrics – BLEU, uses word level n-grams as input to a modified version of precision to evaluate the translation accuracy. Furthermore, a brevity penalty is applied if the candidate is shorter than the reference. CHRF uses the F-score to produce a scoring based on character level n-grams. In most cases, the shift from word level n-grams to the character level results in better human correlation (Popovic, 2015).

Edit distance based metrics utilise the edit distance to express the difference between the candidate and the reference. Since written language allows for the word order to be changed without significant change in meaning, the pure edit distance is too restrictive and is often extended by additional operations. TER extends it by introducing "shifts" which allow for words or phrases to be moved from one position in the candidate to another with a certain cost.

CDER gives another solution to the problem by introducing the operation of jumps. These "jumps" allow for a more flexible alignment. Of course, as in the n-gram based metrics, it is possible to apply these methods at both the word and the character level. CHARACTER uses the edit distance at the character level while keeping the shift operations at the word level with suitably adjusted costs.

3 Edit Distance

Since the metric presented in this paper belongs to the category of the edit distance based metrics, a more thorough introduction to the concept of edit distance is needed. The goal of the Levenshtein distance is to find the minimum number of operations required to transform the candidate into the reference. The Levenshtein distance in its purest form consists of three basic operations:

- Substitution: the act of switching one symbol with another

- Deletion: the removal of a symbol

- Insertion: the addition of a symbol

All of the basic operations are defined as having an uniform cost of one. To not penalise matching symbols with substitutions, substitutions can be defined via the Kroneker delta: $1 - \delta(c_n, r_m)$ with c_n and r_m standing for the symbol at position $m \in \{1, 2 \ldots |r|\}, n \in \{1, 2 \ldots |c|\}$ for the candidate c and reference r, respectively. The edit distance is then computed as the sum of substitution, insertion and deletion operations made.

The edit distance can be efficiently computed via the dynamic programming algorithm by Wagner and Fischer, 1974. This allows for a computation in $\mathcal{O}(cr)$.

In MT, the Levenshtein distance is not usually used in its original definition since it does not provide the required flexibility. The reason is that written language allows for multiple ways to express the same concept or idea. To alleviate this problem extensions to the edit distance have been proposed.

The most prominent extension of the edit distance, implemented by both TER and CHARACTER, is the introduction of an additional operation prior to computing the edit distance on the candidate. Namely, to permute the words in the candidate to most closely match the reference. This permutation is termed *shift*. Since computing all possible shifts of a given sentence is quite costly, in practice, the beam search algorithm is used to reduce the search space.

Another possible extension of the edit distance is to define so called *jumps*. Jumps provide the opportunity to continue the edit distance computation from a different point. A more detailed explanation of the jumps is presented in the next section.

To obtain a final score, the edit distance is normalised either over the length of the candidate or over the length of the reference. Naturally, in the case where every symbol is wrong and the normalising term is the shorter one of the candidate and the reference, the resulting score may significantly exceed 1.0. This in turn results in scores which are not easily interpretable.

4 Extended Edit Distance

One aspect of each metric is its input which usually comes in tokenized form. Punctuation marks are separated from words via a white space and abbreviation dots are kept next to the word e.g. "e.g.". EED additionally adds a white space at both beginning and end of each sentence.

EED utilises the idea of jumps as an extension of the edit distance. EED operates at character level and is defined as follows:

$$\text{EED} = \min \left(\frac{(e + \alpha \cdot j) + \rho \cdot v}{|r| + \rho \cdot v}, 1 \right) \quad (2)$$

where e is the sum of the edit operation with uniform cost of 1 for insertions and substitutions and 0.2 for deletions. j denotes the number of jumps performed with the corresponding control parameter $\alpha = 2.0$. v defines the number of characters that have been visited multiple times or not at all and scales over $\rho = 0.3$. The parameter values have been optimised based on the average correlation scores (both from and to English) from WMT17 and WMT18 (Bojar et al., 2017; Ma et al., 2018). EED is normalised over the length of the reference $|r|$ and the coverage penalty. To keep it within the [0,1] boundary, the minimum between 1 and the metric score is taken. This makes the metric more robust in cases of extreme discrepancy between candidate and reference length.

Jumps are a way to move between characters or blocks thereof and can be incorporated into the dynamic programming algorithm for the Levenshtein distance (Leusch et al., 2006). This provides an optimal solution for the matching between candidate and reference in reasonable computation time. In EED jumps may only be performed when a blank in the reference is reached, allowing the metric to take word boundaries into account and restricting the inter-word jumps. Figure 1 illustrates the way jumps work. Here Die Fans from the reference are aligned with die Fans from the candidate via a jump, after which normal edit distance operations are performed. When the s is reached, another jump is made to the blank before n, in order to align nicht to Nicht. Finally another jump is performed to align the period and white spaces. In total, this results in two edit operation errors (from the difference in capitalisation) and three jumps.

To further refine the metric a coverage penalty is introduced that aims to penalise characters which are aligned to more than once or not at all in the candidate. This allows the metric to penalise repetition of words in the reference with more than just the jump costs. The sum v of visits for all characters visited more than once is computed and is added, after multiplication with a scaling factor ρ to the total cost. To keep the situations where 1

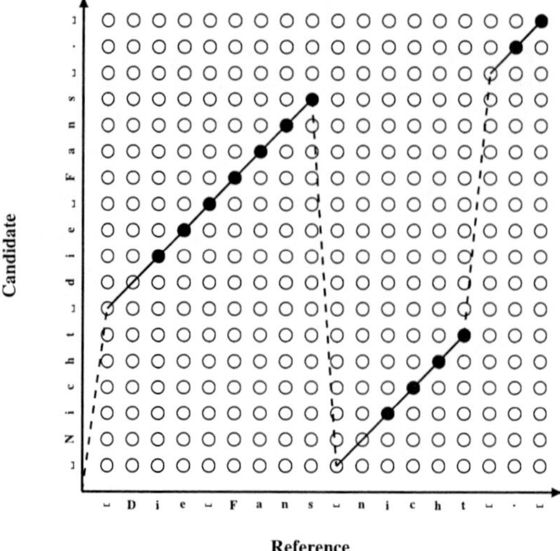

Figure 1: EED alignment lattice. Identity operations are marked with solid points, jumps with dashed lines, edit operations with full lines and blanks with ␣.

is chosen by the minimum in Equation (2) as few as possible, the coverage penalty is also used in the denominator.

Using only the length of the reference as part of the normalisation factor does not guarantee that the metric score is in the range [0,1]. This is undesirable since scores above one are not interpretable as an error measure. For this reason a number of strategies were considered to enforce this bound:

- Taking the maximum length between candidate and reference;

- Taking the average length between candidate and reference;

- Using just the candidate or just the reference;

- Cutting the score to 1.0 if it is above 1.0;

- Mapping the score to accuracy via the function $1/(1 - \text{EED})$ (Zhang et al., 2011).

Out of all of these methods, the simplest and most efficient method is to use the reference as normalisation and to cut the score if it is above one. In our experiments taking the maximum or average between candidate and reference leads to a decline in correlation. The use of accuracy mapping yields different results depending on the parameter setting of the metric and the test set used. For this reason EED uses the cut method for normalisation.

Although EED utilises the same movement technique as CDER, there are a few notable differences:

- Edit distance is performed on the character level;

- Jumps are performed only upon reaching a blank in the reference;

- An additional penalty for multiple matching of the same symbol (coverage cost) is applied

5 Results

EED is implemented in C++ and imported in python via a wrapper. This implementation retains the ease of use of python while getting the speed from a C++ implementation.

EED was evaluated via the scripts provided by Ma et al., 2018 as part of WMT18. The evaluation is done both on segment and system level. The data consists of about 3000 sentences per language pair as part of the newstest2018 test set and provides one reference per translation. In total there are 14 language pairs. For the system level evaluation, direct assessment (DA) (Graham et al., 2017) was used to obtain human scores and Pearson's r is used as the correlation coefficient. The segment level uses the relative ranking (RR) which is pooled from system level DA scores. This results in DARR. The correlation coefficient used for the segment level is the Kendall's τ like formulation defined by Graham et al., 2015.

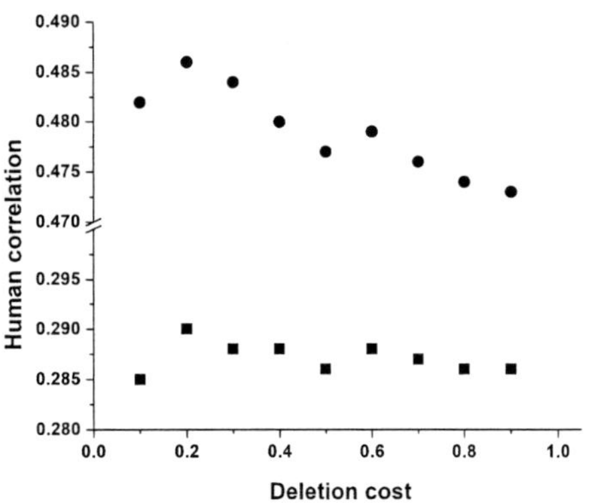

Figure 2: Human correlation variation as a function of deletion cost on WMT18 *to English* ■ and *from English* ● on segment-level.

To obtain the best possible human correlation, a parameter search was performed over ρ, α and the edit operation costs. For substitution and insertions there is no relevant correlation improvement. However, changes to the deletion cost parameter resulted in human correlation improve-

ment. Using the WMT18 segment level test set, a parameter search was performed. Since searching over the whole search space is infeasible, the parameter search was done in a sequential manner. The results of the search are shown in Figure 2. From these results, combined with the findings on WMT16 and WMT17 (Bojar et al., 2016, 2017), the deletion cost is set to 0.2.

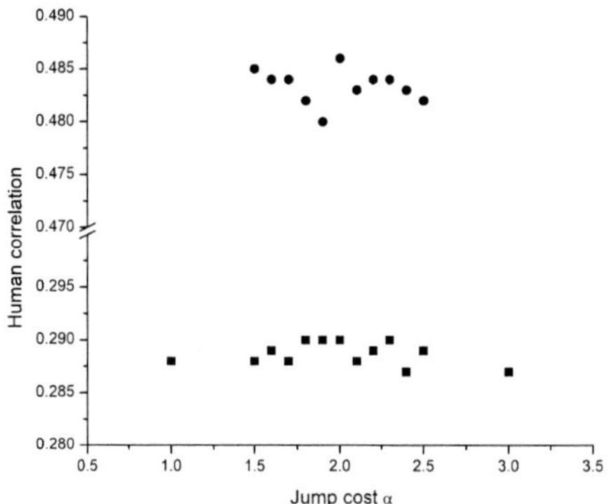

Figure 3: Human correlation variation as a function of jump cost on WMT18 *to English* ■ and *from English* ● on segment-level.

The error distribution of EED was skewed quite heavily towards performing jumps even after restricting jump operation only to blanks on the reference side. For this reason it was restricted further by increasing the jump costs. In order to determine the optimal jump penalty α, a parameter search was performed, which is presented Figure 3. It is evident that the optimal jump cost lie close to 2.0 for the *to English* direction. For the *from English* direction the optimum is clear, thus α is set to 2.0.

Similar to the deletion cost and the jump penalty, a parameter search was carried out for the coverage cost in order to increase human correlation. The results of the search are presented in Figure 4. The resulting optimum is $\rho = 0.3$.

After the parameter tuning, the performance of EED was measured by the human correlation achieved on the WMT18 test set. The results of this measurement obtained at the segment and system level and also in the directions *to English* and *from English* are presented in Tables 1 to 4. At the segment level, EED offers competitive results compared with the top-ranking metrics BEER, RUSE and CHRF +. On system level EED performs best for the *out of English* direction, fol-

	cs-en	**de-en**	**et-en**	**fi-en**	**ru-en**	**zh-en**	**Average**
# Sentences	5110	77811	56721	15648	10404	33357	33181
EED	0.297	0.486	0.335	0.227	0.284	**0.225**	0.309
BEER[1]	0.295	0.481	0.341	0.232	0.288	0.214	0.309
CHARACTER	0.256	0.450	0.286	0.185	0.244	0.202	0.271
CHRF+	0.288	0.479	0.332	0.234	0.279	0.207	0.303
ITER[2]	0.198	0.396	0.235	0.128	0.139	0.144	0.206
RUSE[3]	**0.347**	**0.498**	**0.368**	**0.273**	**0.311**	0.218	**0.336**
sentBLEU	0.233	0.415	0.285	0.154	0.228	0.178	0.248

Table 1: Segment-level human correlation measured through DARR to English on `newstest18` as part of WMT18 via absolute Kendall's τ.
[1] Stanojevic and Sima'an, 2014
[2] Panja and Naskar, 2018
[3] Shimanaka et al., 2018

	en-cs	**en-de**	**en-et**	**en-fi**	**en-ru**	**en-zh**	**Average**
# Sentences	5413	19711	32202	9809	22181	28602	19820
EED	0.508	0.674	0.572	0.503	**0.405**	**0.350**	**0.502**
BEER	**0.518**	**0.686**	0.558	0.511	0.403	0.302	0.496
CHARACTER	0.414	0.604	0.464	0.403	0.352	0.313	0.425
CHRF+	0.513	0.680	**0.573**	**0.525**	0.392	0.328	**0.502**
ITER	0.333	0.610	0.392	0.311	0.291	–	0.387
sentBLEU	0.389	0.620	0.414	0.355	0.330	0.311	0.403

Table 2: Segment-level human correlation measured through DARR from English on `newstest18` as part of WMT18 via absolute Kendall's τ.

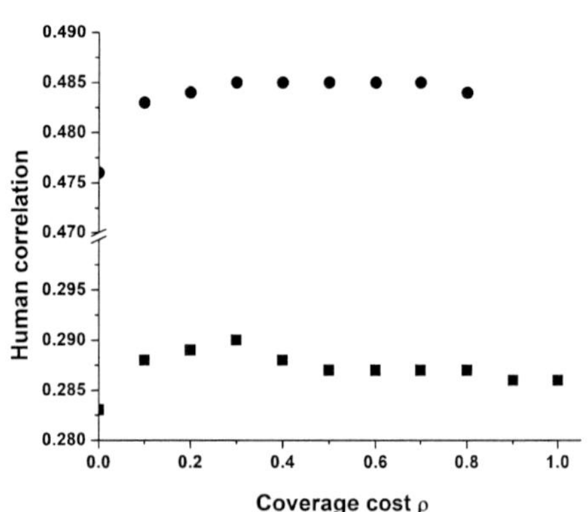

Figure 4: Human correlation variation as a function of coverage cost on WMT18 *to English* ■ and *from English* ● on segment-level.

lowed by CHARACTER and CDER. For the *to English* direction, EED is the second best after RUSE.

Apart from human correlation, EED was compared to the performance of the most common metrics. This measurement was performed by letting each metric evaluate 1M (10^6) sentence pairs

and tracking the time and memory needed to complete the task. The following metrics have been tested: BEER, BLEU, CHARACTER, CHRF, EED. The results of the resource usage test are summarised in Table 5. The fastest is BLEU followed by EED. Concerning memory usage all metrics have similar memory needs, except for the shift based metrics which needed considerably more. Since CHARACTER needs more memory, candidate sentences above 200 words were restricted to 200 words for this test.

6 Conclusion

A number of different metrics have been developed over the years to help evaluate MT. Metrics such as BLEU and TER have been used for some time, but are surpassed by others both in terms of speed and human correlation.

EED as a metric provides a fast and reliable way to measure human correlation. It achieves competitive human correlation in comparison to the best metrics – BEER and CHRF and surpasses the most used metrics – BLEU and TER. Due to its simplicity and low resource usage it can be used to

518

	cs-en	de-en	et-en	fi-en	ru-en	zh-en	Average
# Systems	5	16	14	9	8	14	11
BEER	0.958	0.994	0.985	0.991	0.982	0.976	0.981
BLEU	0.970	0.971	0.986	0.973	0.979	0.978	0.976
CDER	0.972	0.980	**0.990**	0.984	0.980	**0.982**	0.981
CHARACTER	0.970	0.993	0.979	0.989	0.991	0.950	0.979
CHRF +	0.966	0.993	0.981	0.989	0.990	0.964	0.981
EED	0.970	0.994	0.984	0.991	**0.993**	0.974	0.984
ITER	0.975	0.990	0.975	**0.996**	0.937	0.980	0.976
NIST[1]	0.954	0.984	0.983	0.975	0.973	0.968	0.973
RUSE	**0.981**	**0.997**	**0.990**	0.991	0.988	0.981	**0.988**
TER	0.950	0.970	**0.990**	0.968	0.970	0.975	0.971

Table 3: System-level human correlation as DA to English on `newstest18` as part of WMT18 via absolute Pearson's r.
[1] Doddington, 2002

	en-cs	en-de	en-et	en-fi	en-ru	en-zh	Average
# Systems	5	16	14	12	9	14	12
BEER	0.992	**0.991**	0.980	0.961	0.988	0.928	0.973
BLEU	0.995	0.981	0.975	0.962	0.983	0.947	0.973
CDER	0.997	0.986	**0.984**	0.964	0.984	0.961	0.979
CHARACTER	0.993	0.989	0.956	0.974	0.983	**0.983**	0.980
CHRF +	0.990	0.989	0.982	0.970	0.989	0.943	0.977
EED	0.988	0.990	0.983	**0.977**	**0.990**	0.955	**0.981**
ITER	0.915	0.984	0.981	0.973	0.975	−	0.966
NIST	**0.999**	0.986	0.983	0.949	**0.990**	0.950	0.976
TER	0.997	0.988	0.981	0.942	0.987	0.963	0.976

Table 4: System-level human correlation as DA from English on `newstest18` as part of WMT18 via absolute Pearson's r.

Metric	EED	BEER	CHRF ++	CHARACTER	BLEU	TER
Sentences/s	969.9	621.5	261.7	9.5	6410.2	316.6
Memory	1.3G	1.1G	0.3G	48.4G	0.3G	8.4G

Table 5: Speed and memory comparison between metrics, as sentences per second and memory in gigabyte. Measured on 1M sentences.

quickly evaluate a MT system's output during development.

Since there are a number of metrics based on some extensions of the Levenshtein distance, a more in-depth analysis of the field is required. Furthermore, the relationship between shifts and jumps will be investigated in the future.

Acknowledgments

This work has received funding from the European Research Council (ERC) (under the European Union's Horizon 2020 research and innovation programme, grant agreement No 694537, project "SEQCLAS") and the Deutsche Forschungsgemeinschaft (DFG; grant agreement NE 572/8-1, project "CoreTec"). The GPU cluster used for the experiments was partially funded by DFG Grant INST 222/1168-1. The work reflects only the authors' views and none of the funding agencies is responsible for any use that may be made of the information it contains.

References

Ondřej Bojar, Yvette Graham, and Amir Kamran. 2017. Results of the wmt17 metrics shared task. In *Proceedings of the Second Conference on Machine Translation*, pages 489–513.

Ondřej Bojar, Yvette Graham, Amir Kamran, and Miloš Stanojević. 2016. Results of the wmt16 metrics shared task. In *Proceedings of the First Conference on Machine Translation: Volume 2, Shared Task Papers*, volume 2, pages 199–231.

George Doddington. 2002. Automatic evaluation of machine translation quality using n-gram co-occurrence statistics. In *Proceedings of the Second International Conference on Human Language Technology Research*, pages 138–145. Morgan Kaufmann Publishers Inc.

Yvette Graham, Timothy Baldwin, and Nitika Mathur. 2015. Accurate evaluation of segment-level machine translation metrics. In *HLT-NAACL*, pages 1183–1191.

Yvette Graham, Timothy Baldwin, Alistair Moffat, and Justin Zobel. 2017. Can machine translation systems be evaluated by the crowd alone. *Natural Language Engineering*, 23(1):3–30.

Gregor Leusch, Nicola Ueffing, and Hermann Ney. 2006. Cder: Efficient mt evaluation using block movements. In *11th Conference of the European Chapter of the Association for Computational Linguistics*.

Vladimir I Levenshtein. 1966. Binary codes capable of correcting deletions, insertions, and reversals. In *Soviet physics doklady*, volume 10, pages 707–710.

Qingsong Ma, Ondřej Bojar, and Yvette Graham. 2018. Results of the wmt18 metrics shared task: Both characters and embeddings achieve good performance. In *Proceedings of the Third Conference on Machine Translation: Shared Task Papers*, pages 671–688.

Franz Josef Och and Hermann Ney. 2002. Discriminative training and maximum entropy models for statistical machine translation. In *Proceedings of the 40th annual meeting on association for computational linguistics*, pages 295–302. Association for Computational Linguistics.

Joybrata Panja and Sudip Kumar Naskar. 2018. Iter: Improving translation edit rate through optimizable edit costs. In *Proceedings of the Third Conference on Machine Translation, Volume 2: Shared Task Papers*, pages 759–763, Belgium, Brussels. Association for Computational Linguistics.

Kishore Papineni, Salim Roukos, Todd Ward, and Wei-Jing Zhu. 2002. BLEU: A method for automatic evaluation of machine targeted translation. In *Proceedings of the 40th annual meeting on association for computational linguistics*, pages 311–318. Association for Computational Linguistics.

Maja Popovic. 2015. CHRf: character n-gram f-score for automatic MT evaluation. In *WMT@ EMNLP*, pages 392–395.

Hiroki Shimanaka, Tomoyuki Kajiwara, and Mamoru Komachi. 2018. Ruse: Regressor using sentence embeddings for automatic machine translation evaluation. In *Proceedings of the Third Conference on Machine Translation: Shared Task Papers*, pages 751–758.

Matthew Snover, Bonnie Dorr, Richard Schwartz, Linnea Micciulla, and John Makhoul. 2006. A study of translation edit rate with targeted human annotation. In *Proceedings of Association for Machine Translation in the Americas*, volume 200.

Milos Stanojevic and Khalil Sima'an. 2014. BEER: Better evaluation as ranking. In *WMT@ ACL*, pages 414–419.

Robert A Wagner and Michael J Fischer. 1974. The string-to-string correction problem. *Journal of the ACM (JACM)*, 21(1):168–173.

Weiyue Wang, Jan-Thorsten Peter, Hendrik Rosendahl, and Hermann Ney. 2016. CharacTER: Translation edit rate on character level. In *Proceedings of the First Conference on Machine Translation: Volume 2, Shared Task Papers*, volume 2, pages 505–510.

Junsheng Zhang, Yunchuan Sun, Huilin Wang, and Yanqing He. 2011. Calculating statistical similarity between sentences. *Journal of Convergence Information Technology*, 6(2).

Filtering Pseudo-References by Paraphrasing
for Automatic Evaluation of Machine Translation

Ryoma Yoshimura   **Hiroki Shimanaka**   **Yukio Matsumura**
Hayahide Yamagishi   **Mamoru Komachi**
Tokyo Metropolitan University, Tokyo, Japan
{yoshimura-ryoma, shimanaka-hiroki, matsumura-yukio
yamagishi-hayahide}@ed.tmu.ac.jp, komachi@tmu.ac.jp

Abstract

In this paper, we introduce our participation in
the WMT 2019 Metric Shared Task.   We
propose a method to filter pseudo-references
by paraphrasing for automatic evaluation of
machine translation (MT). We use the outputs of off-the-shelf MT systems as pseudo-
references filtered by paraphrasing in addition to a single human reference (gold reference).   We use BERT fine-tuned with paraphrase corpus to filter pseudo-references by
checking the paraphrasability with the gold
reference.   Our experimental results of the
WMT 2016 and 2017 datasets show that our
method achieved higher correlation with human evaluation than the sentence BLEU (Sent-
BLEU) baselines with a single reference and
with unfiltered pseudo-references.

1 Introduction

In general, automatic evaluation of MT is based
on n-gram agreement between the system output
and a manually translated reference of the source
sentence. Therefore, automatic evaluation fails to
evaluate a semantically correct sentence if the surface of the system output differs from that in the
reference. To solve this problem, many automatic
evaluation methods allow the use of multiple references that potentially cover various surfaces; in
particular, Finch et al. (2004) reported that correlation between automatic evaluation results and
human evaluation increases when multiple references are used for evaluation. However, owing to
the time and costs involved in manually creating
references, many datasets only include one reference per source sentence, which leads to improper
translation evaluation, especially in the case of diverse machine translation systems.

In order to obtain cheap references without
any human intervention, Albrecht and Hwa (2008)
used the outputs of off-the-shelf MT systems as
pseudo-references; They showed that using mul-

tiple references consisting of gold and pseudo-
references may yield higher correlation with human evaluation than using a single gold reference.
However, because they did not consider the quality of the pseudo-references, this may result in using poor references. Thus, in some cases the correlation becomes worse when using multiple references consisting of gold and pseudo-references
relative to only using a gold reference.

To address the quality of pseudo-references, we
filtered pseudo-references by checking the paraphrasability to the gold reference. Our approach
can be applied to various MT evaluation metrics
which can be evaluated with multiple references.
The experimental results show that our method
achieves higher correlation with human evaluation
than the previous work.

2 Related Work

Albrecht and Hwa (2008) showed that using the
outputs of off-the-shelf MT systems as pseudo-
references in n-gram based metrics such as
BLEU (Papineni et al., 2002) and METEOR
(Denkowski and Lavie, 2011) may yield higher
correlation with human evaluation than using a
gold reference. They use the outputs of off-the-
shelf MT systems as they are, whereas we filter
them by paraphrasing the gold reference.

Kauchak and Barzilay (2006) proposed a
method to obtain a paraphrase of a gold reference
that is closer in wording to the system output
than the gold reference for MT evaluation. They
evaluated an MT system using only the generated
references, whereas we evaluated MT systems
using multiple references, including those obtained by adding generated references to the gold
reference. They generate a paraphrase of a gold
reference, whereas we translate source sentences
and identify whether the outputs are paraphrases
of gold references. That is, they used only gold
references whereas we used both source and gold

Proceedings of the Fourth Conference on Machine Translation (WMT), Volume 2: Shared Task Papers (Day 1) pages 521–525
Florence, Italy, August 1-2, 2019. ©2019 Association for Computational Linguistics

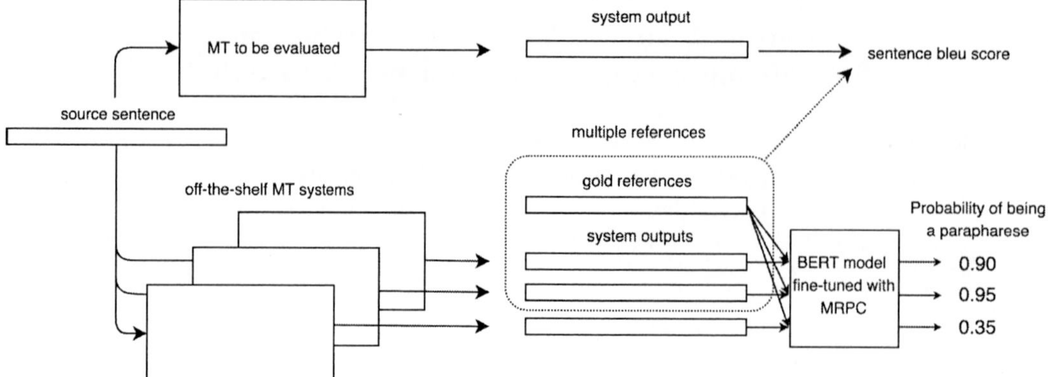

Figure 1: Overview of the proposed method.

reference information.

3 MT Evaluation Metric Using Filtered Multiple Pseudo-References

3.1 Overview

Figure 1 shows the overview of our proposed method. The procedure of our proposed method is as follows.

1. Prepare off-the-shelf MT systems for generating pseudo-references.

2. Translate the source sentence in the evaluation data using the abovementioned MT systems.

3. Filter the outputs of off-the-shelf MT systems by checking the paraphrasability of being a paraphrase to the single gold reference.

4. Calculate the sentence evaluation score with multiple references obtained by adding filtered pseudo-references to the single gold references.

3.2 Automatic pseudo-reference generation

Any MT system can be used as a pseudo-reference generation system except for the translation system to be evaluated. [1] There are no restrictions on the type of MT systems, such as neural machine translation (NMT) or statistical machine translation (SMT) systems, or the number of MT systems.

---

[1] If the system to be evaluated were used as a pseudo-reference generation system, the output would be used as a reference.

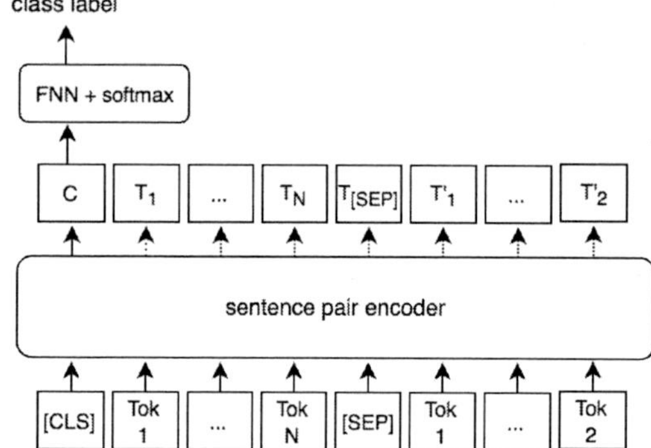

Figure 2: BERT model architecture for sentence pair classification.

3.3 Filtering by paraphrasing

We use Bidirectional Encoder Representations from Transformers (BERT) (Devlin et al., 2019) to filter pseudo-references by checking the paraphrasability with a gold reference. BERT is a new approach to pre-train language representations, and it obtains state-of-the-art results on a wide variety of natural language processing (NLP) tasks, including question answering (QA), semantic textual similarity (STS), natural language inference (NLI). The key to pre-training BERT is the prediction of masked words and of the next sentence. Masking words allows bidirectional learning, which improves joint training of language context relative to Embeddings from Language Models (ELMo) (Peters et al., 2018), which combines forward and backward training. Prediction of the next sentence leads to capturing the relationship between two sentences.

Figure 2 shows the BERT model architec-

	cs-en	de-en	fi-en	ru-en
single reference	0.557	0.484	0.448	**0.502**
single reference + pseudo-references	0.565	0.499	0.543	0.456
single reference + filtered references (MAS)	0.576	0.473	0.517	0.469
single reference + filtered references (BERT)	**0.589**	**0.519**	**0.572**	0.490

Table 1: Segment-level Pearson correlation between SentBLEU and human evaluation scores in WMT 2016.

	cs-en	de-en	fi-en	ru-en
single reference	0.435	0.433	0.571	0.484
single reference + pseudo-references	0.515	0.565	0.653	0.519
single reference + filtered references (MAS)	0.524	**0.586**	0.650	0.517
single reference + filtered references (BERT)	**0.555**	0.580	**0.671**	**0.545**

Table 2: Segment-level Pearson correlation between SentBLEU and human evaluation scores in WMT 2017.

corpus	train	dev	test	Accuracy
MRPC	3,669	408	1726	0.845

Table 3: Numbers of sentences in each split of MRPC and accuracy of BERT.

ture for sentence pair classification. In classification tasks where labels are attached to sentence pairs, BERT encodes sentence pairs together with a [CLS] token for classification and a [SEP] token for sentence boundaries; The output of the [CLS] token is used for the input of classifier of a feedforward neural network with softmax. BERT achieves state-of-the-art performance in a paraphrase identification task on the Microsoft Research Paraphrase Corpus (MRPC) (Dolan and Brockett, 2005) with this architecture.

For that reason, we use BERT to estimate the paraphrasability between pseudo-references and the gold reference. We fine-tune BERT with MRPC. The output of the classifier is the probability of the paraphrase from 0 to 1. We use pseudo-references whose paraphrase probability is greater than 0.5.

4 Experiments

4.1 Data

We used the segment-level evaluation datasets of Czech-English (cs-en), German-English (de-en), Finnish-English (fi-en), Russian-English (ru-en) language pair from WMT 2016 (Bojar et al., 2016) and 2017 (Bojar et al., 2017). The datasets consist of 560 pairs of sources and references,

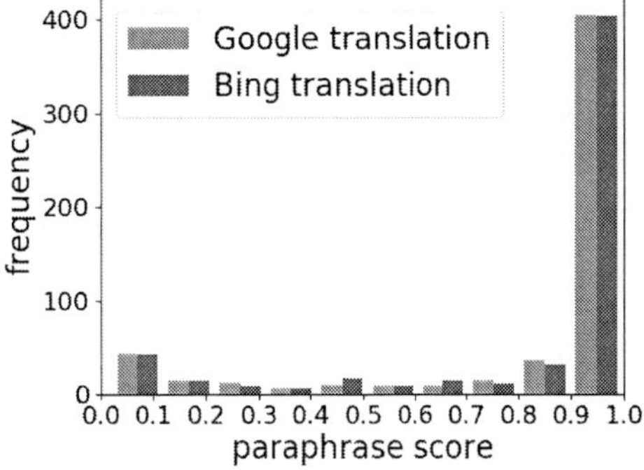

Figure 3: Histograms of paraphrase score of pseudo-references in the fi-en language pairs of WMT 2016.

along with the outputs of each system and human evaluation scores.

4.2 Off-the-shelf MT systems

We used Google Translation [2] and Bing Microsoft Translator [3] as MT systems to generate pseudo-references. We chose these two MT systems because they are widely used, easy to use, and well known to have good performance. We automatically translated source files using each translation API.

4.3 Fine-tuning BERT with MRPC

We use the pre-trained BERT-Base Uncased model [4], which has 12 layer, 768 hidden, 12 heads

---

[2] https://translate.google.com/
[3] https://www.bing.com/translator
[4] https://github.com/google-research/bert

system output	gymnastics and freestyle exercises - where bayles defends the title of world champion - lie in the veil .
gold reference	balance beam and floor exercise - where biles is the defending world champion - lay in wait .
pseudo-reference (Google)	gymnastics log and floor exercises - where biles defends the world champion title - lie in wait . (0.994)
pseudo-reference (Bing)	gymnastic log and freestyle exercises — where the bayles defends the title of world champion — lie in ambush . (0.215)
human score: -1.497; **SentBLEU**: single reference: -1.118, without filtering: -0.335, filtering: -1.662	

Table 4: Example of pseudo-references in ru-en language pair of WMT 2017; The value in parentheses at the end of each pseudo-reference indicates the paraphrase score by BERT. Each score is standardized according to the mean and standard deviation to compare human evaluation and each SentBLEU score.

and 110M parameters. We fine-tuned BERT with MRPC. MRPC is a dataset extracted from web news articles along with human annotations indicating whether each pair is a paraphrase. If the pair is paraphrase, the label is 1, if not, the label is 0. The original dataset consists of 4,077 sentences for training and 1,726 sentences for testing. We divided the test set in half and used it as development data. The numbers of sentences in each corpus and the accuracy of the fine-tuned BERT model are listed in Table 3.

Figure 3 shows the histogram of paraphrase score of pseudo-references in the fi-en language pair of WMT 2016. Due to the use of high quality MT systems, more than 50% of the pseudo-references have paraphrase scores between 0.9 and 1.0. The same trend was observed in all languages and years.

4.4 Evaluation

We calculated the SentBLEU score with system output and multiple references which consisted of a single gold reference and pseudo-references. The SentBLEU is computed using the sentence-bleu.cpp [5], a part of the Moses toolkit. It is a smoothed version of BLEU (Lin and Och, 2004). We followed the tokenization method for each year's dataset. We measured Pearson correlation identically to WMT 2016 and WMT 2017 between the automatic and human evaluation scores. In order to compare with our method, we also performed filtering by Maximum Alignment Similarity (MAS) (Song and Roth, 2015), which is one of the unsupervised sentence similarity measures based on alignments between word embeddings

and is known to achieve good performance on Semantic Textual Similarity (STS) task. We used GloVe [6] (Pennington et al., 2014) as word embeddings. We used pseudo-references whose MAS score is higher than 0.8.

5 Results

Tables 1 and 2 show the segment-level Pearson correlation coefficients between automatic and human evaluation scores. The result shows that our proposed method outperforms the baselines except in the case of the ru-en language pair in WMT 2016 and filtering by MAS does not produce any consistent result.

6 Discussion

Table 4 shows an example of pseudo-references with BERT's paraphrase score for the ru-en language pair in WMT 2017. The pseudo-reference from Bing translation has a low paraphrase score because "biles" in the gold reference remains as "bayles" in the pseudo-reference, and "floor exercise" became "freestyle exercise" in Bing translation. In the unfiltered method, the BLEU score is unreasonably high because the surface of the pseudo-reference from Bing translation is similar to the output sentence. Filtering the pseudo-references prevents the problem. The pseudo-reference from Google translation has different surfaces but carry the same meaning as in the gold reference. Our filtering method correctly retains the sentence because BERT assigned high paraphrase score.

---

[5] https://github.com/moses-smt/mosesdecoder/blob/master/mert/sentence-bleu.cpp

[6] https://nlp.stanford.edu/projects/glove/
Common Crawl (840B tokens, 2.2M vocab, cased, 300d vectors)

7 Conclusions

We proposed a method to filter pseudo-references in terms of paraphrasability with a gold reference that addresses the problem of using poor pseudo-references from previous work (Albrecht and Hwa, 2008). We use BERT finetuned with MRPC to filter pseudo-references. By filtering pseudo-references in terms of paraphrasability with a gold reference, we can keep the references having the same meaning with the gold reference but different surface and solve the problem of using poor pseudo-reference from previous work. The experimental results show that our method outperforms baselines.

Acknowledgement

We would like to thank Tomoyuki Kajiwara for providing a script to calculate the MAS score.

References

Joshua S. Albrecht and Rebecca Hwa. 2008. The role of pseudo references in MT evaluation. In *Proceedings of the Third Workshop on Statistical Machine Translation (WMT2008)*.

Ondřej Bojar, Yvette Graham, and Amir Kamran. 2017. Results of the WMT17 metrics shared task. In *Proceedings of the Second Conference on Machine Translation (WMT2017)*.

Ondřej Bojar, Yvette Graham, Amir Kamran, and Miloš Stanojević. 2016. Results of the WMT16 metrics shared task. In *Proceedings of the First Conference on Machine Translation (WMT2016)*.

Michael Denkowski and Alon Lavie. 2011. Meteor 1.3: Automatic metric for reliable optimization and evaluation of machine translation systems. In *Proceedings of the 2011 Conference on Empirical Methods in Natural Language Processing (EMNLP2011)*.

Jacob Devlin, Ming-Wei Chang, Kenton Lee, and Kristina Toutanova. 2019. BERT: pre-training of deep bidirectional transformers for language understanding. *Proceedings of the 2019 Conference of the North American Chapter of the Association for Computational Linguistics (NAACL2019)*.

William B. Dolan and Chris Brockett. 2005. Automatically constructing a corpus of sentential paraphrases. In *Proceedings of the Third International Workshop on Paraphrasing (IWP2005)*.

Andrew M Finch, Yasuhiro Akiba, and Eiichiro Sumita. 2004. How does automatic machine translation evaluation correlate with human scoring as the number of reference translations increases? In *Proceedings of the Fourth International Conference on Language Resources and Evaluation (LREC2004)*.

David Kauchak and Regina Barzilay. 2006. Paraphrasing for automatic evaluation. In *Proceedings of the Human Language Technology Conference of the North American Chapter of the ACL (NAACL2006)*.

Chin-Yew Lin and Franz Josef Och. 2004. ORANGE: a method for evaluating automatic evaluation metrics for machine translation. In *Proceedings of the 20th International Conference on Computational Linguistics (COLLING2004)*.

Kishore Papineni, Salim Roukos, Todd Ward, and Wei-Jing Zhu. 2002. BLEU: a method for automatic evaluation of machine translation. In *Proceedings of the 40th Annual Meeting of the Association for Computational Linguistics (ACL2002)*.

Jeffrey Pennington, Richard Socher, and Christopher D. Manning. 2014. Glove: Global vectors for word representation. In *Proceedings of the 2011 Conference on Empirical Methods in Natural Language Processing (EMNLP2014)*.

Matthew Peters, Mark Neumann, Mohit Iyyer, Matt Gardner, Christopher Clark, Kenton Lee, and Luke Zettlemoyer. 2018. Deep contextualized word representations. In *Proceedings of the 2018 Conference of the North American Chapter of the Association for Computational Linguistics (NAACL2018)*.

Yangqiu Song and Dan Roth. 2015. Unsupervised sparse vector densification for short text similarity. In *Proceedings of the Human Language Technology Conference of the North American Chapter of the ACL (NAACL2015)*.

Naver Labs Europe's Systems for the WMT19 Machine Translation Robustness Task

Alexandre Bérard   **Ioan Calapodescu**   **Claude Roux**

Naver Labs Europe
first.last@naverlabs.com

Abstract

This paper describes the systems that we submitted to the WMT19 Machine Translation robustness task. This task aims to improve MT's robustness to noise found on social media, like informal language, spelling mistakes and other orthographic variations. The organizers provide parallel data extracted from a social media website[1] in two language pairs: French-English and Japanese-English (in both translation directions). The goal is to obtain the best scores on unseen test sets from the same source, according to automatic metrics (BLEU) and human evaluation. We proposed one single and one ensemble system for each translation direction. Our ensemble models ranked first in all language pairs, according to BLEU evaluation. We discuss the pre-processing choices that we made, and present our solutions for robustness to noise and domain adaptation.

1   Introduction

Neural Machine Translation (NMT) has achieved impressive results in recent years, especially on high-resource language pairs (Vaswani et al., 2017; Edunov et al., 2018), and has even lead to some claims of human parity (Hassan et al., 2018).[2]

However, Belinkov and Bisk (2018) show that NMT is brittle, and very sensitive to simple character-level perturbations like letter swaps or keyboard typos. They show that one can make an MT system more robust to these types of synthetic noise, by introducing similar noise on the source side of the training corpus. Sperber et al. (2017) do similar data augmentation, but at the word level and so as to make an MT model more robust to Automatic Speech Recognition errors (within a speech translation pipeline). Cheng et al. (2018) propose an adversarial training approach

to make an encoder invariant to word-level noise. Karpukhin et al. (2019) propose to inject aggressive synthetic noise on the source side of training corpora (with random char-level operations: deletion, insertion, substitution and swap), and show that this is helpful to deal with natural errors found in Wikipedia edit logs, in several language pairs.

Michel and Neubig (2018) release MTNT, a real-world noisy corpus, to help researchers develop MT systems that are robust to natural noise found on social media. The same authors co-organized this task (Li et al., 2019), in which MTNT is the primary resource. Vaibhav et al. (2019) show that back-translation (with a model trained on MTNT) and synthetic noise (that emulates errors found in MTNT) are useful to make NMT models more robust to MTNT noise.

This task aims at improving MT's robustness to noise found on social media, like informal language, spelling mistakes and other orthographic variations. We present the task in more detail in Section 2. Then, we describe our baseline models and pre-processing in Section 3. We extend these baseline models with robustness and domain adaptation techniques that are presented in Section 4. Finally, in Section 5, we present and discuss the results of our systems on this task.

2   Task description

The goal of the task is to make NMT systems that are robust to noisy text found on Reddit, a social media, in two language pairs (French-English and Japanese-English) and both translation directions. The evaluation will be performed on a blind test set (obtained from the same source), using automatic metrics and human evaluation. We present our final BLEU scores in Section 5, while the human evaluation results are given in the shared task overview paper (Li et al., 2019).

MTNT   Michel and Neubig (2018) crawled monolingual data from Reddit in three languages:

---

[1] https://www.reddit.com
[2] These claims were discussed at WMT by Toral et al. (2018).

Proceedings of the Fourth Conference on Machine Translation (WMT), Volume 2: Shared Task Papers (Day 1) pages 526–532
Florence, Italy, August 1-2, 2019. ©2019 Association for Computational Linguistics

English, French and Japanese, which they filtered to keep only the "noisiest" comments (containing unknown words or with low LM scores).

Then, they tasked professional translators to translate part of the English data to French, and part of it to Japanese. The Japanese and French data was translated to English. The resulting parallel corpora were split into train, valid and test sets (see Table 1). The test sets were manually filtered so as to keep only good quality translations. The data that was not translated is made available as monolingual corpora (see Table 3).

Other data In addition to the provided in-domain training and evaluation data, we are allowed to use larger parallel and monolingual corpora (see Tables 2 and 3). For FR↔EN, any parallel or monolingual data from the WMT15 news translation task[3] is authorized. For JA↔EN, we are allowed the same data that was used by Michel and Neubig (2018): KFTT, TED and JESC.

Challenges Michel and Neubig (2018) identified a number of challenges for Machine Translation of MTNT data, which warrant the study of MT robustness. Here is an abbreviated version of their taxonomy:

- Spelling and grammar mistakes: e.g., their/they're, have/of.

- Spoken language and internet slang: e.g., lol, *mdr*, lmao, etc.

- Named entities: many Reddit posts link to recent news articles and evoke celebrities or politicians. There are also many references to movies, TV shows and video games.

- Code switching: for instance, Japanese text on Reddit contains many English words.

- Reddit jargon: words like "downvote", "upvote" and "cross-post",[4] and many acronyms like TIL (Today I Learned), OP (Original Poster), etc.

- Reddit markdown: characters like "~", "*" and "^" are extensively used for formatting. "!" is used to call macros.

- Emojis (☺) and emoticons (";-)").

Lang pair	Lines	Words	
		Source	Target
JA→EN	6 506	160k	155k
EN→JA	5 775	339k	493k
FR→EN	19 161	794k	763k
EN→FR	36 058	1 014k	1 152k

Table 1: Size of the MTNT training corpora. Word counts by Moses (fr/en) and Kytea (ja) tokenizers.

Lang pair	Lines	Words	
		Source	Target
JA↔EN	3.90M	48.42M	42.63M
FR↔EN	40.86M	1 392M	1 172M

Table 2: Size of the authorized out-of-domain parallel corpora in constrained submissions.

- Inconsistent capitalization: missing capital letters on proper names, capitalization for emphasis or "shouting", etc.

- Inconsistent punctuation.

Evaluation Automatic evaluation is performed with cased BLEU (Papineni et al., 2002), using SacreBLEU (Post, 2018).[5] For English and French, the latter takes as input the detokenized MT outputs and the untokenized reference data. For Japanese, the MT output and reference are first tokenized with Kytea[6] (Neubig et al., 2011) before being processed by SacreBLEU (because it does not know how to tokenize Japanese). The organizers will also collect subjective judgments from human annotators, and rank the participants accordingly.

Language	Corpus	Lines
Japanese	MTNT	32 042
French	MTNT	26 485
	news-discuss	3.84M
	news-crawl	42.1M
English	MTNT	81 631
	news-discuss	57.8M
	news-crawl	118.3M

Table 3: Authorized monolingual data.

---

[3]`http://www.statmt.org/wmt15/translation-task.html`

[4]The French-speaking Reddit community sometimes uses funny literal translations of these: "bas-vote", "haut-vote" and "croix-poteau".

[5]`BLEU+case.mixed+numrefs.1+smooth.exp+tok.13a+version.1.3.1`

[6]`kytea -model share/kytea/model.bin -out tok (v0.4.7)`

3 Baseline models

This section describes the pre-processing and hyper parameters of our baseline models. We will then detail the techniques that we applied for robustness and domain adaptation.

3.1 Pre-processing

CommonCrawl filtering We first spent efforts on filtering and cleaning the WMT data (in particular CommonCrawl).

We observed two types of catastrophic failures when training FR→EN models: source sentence copy, and total hallucinations.

The first type of error (copy) is due to having sentence pairs in the training data whose reference "translation" is a copy of the source sentence. Khayrallah and Koehn (2018) show that even a small amount of this type of noise can have catastrophic effects on BLEU. We solve this problem by using a language identifier (langid.py, Lui and Baldwin, 2012) to remove any sentence pair whose source or target language is not right.

Then, we observed that most of the hallucinations produced by our models were variants of the same phrases (see Table 5 for an example). We looked for the origin of these phrases in the training data, and found that they all come from CommonCrawl (Smith et al., 2013).

We tried several approaches to eliminate hallucinations, whose corresponding scores are shown in Table 4:

1. Length filtering (removing any sentence pair whose length ratio is greater than 1.8, or 1.5 for CommonCrawl): removes most hallucinations and gives the best BLEU score (when combined with LID filtering). This type of filtering is common in MT pipelines (Koehn et al., 2007).

2. Excluding CommonCrawl from the training data: removes all hallucinations, but gives worse BLEU scores, suggesting that, albeit noisy, CommonCrawl is useful to this task.[7]

3. Attention-based filtering: we observed that when hallucinating, an NMT model produces a peculiar attention matrix (see Figure 1), where almost all the probability mass is concentrated on the source EOS token. A similar matrix is produced during the forward pass of training when facing a misaligned sentence pair. We

LID	Len	CC	Att	FR	Hallu.	BLEU
			✓	126	46	34.4
				0	12	34.8
✓	✓			0	0	35.2
✓		✓		0	29	37.7
✓	✓	✓	✓	0	0	38.7
✓	✓	✓		0	10	39.6

Table 4: Number of hallucinations and French-language outputs (according to langid.py) when translating MTNT-test (FR→EN). LID: language identifier, Len: length filtering, CC: training data includes CommonCrawl, Att: attention-based filtering.

SRC	T'as trouvé un champion on dirait !
REF	You got yourself a champion it seems !
MT	I've never seen videos that SEXY !!!

Table 5: Example of hallucination by a FR→EN Transformer trained on WMT15 data without filtering.

filtered CommonCrawl as follows: we trained a baseline FR→EN model on WMT without filtering, then translated CommonCrawl while forcing the MT output to be the actual reference, and extracted the corresponding attention matrices. We computed statistics on these attention matrices: their entropy and proportion of French words with a total attention mass lower than 0.2, 0.3, 0.4 and 0.5. Then, we manually looked for thresholds to filter out most of the misalignments, while removing as little correctly aligned data as possible.

A combination of LID, length-based and attention-based filtering removed all hallucinations in the MT outputs, while obtaining excellent BLEU scores. The resulting corpus has 12% fewer lines.[8] We use this filtered data for both FR→EN and EN→FR. As the JA↔EN training data seemed much cleaner, we only did a LID filtering step.

SentencePiece We use SentencePiece (Kudo and Richardson, 2018) for segmentation into subword units.

An advantage of SentencePiece is that it does not require a prior tokenization step (it does its own coarse tokenization, based on whitespaces and changes of unicode categories). It also escapes all whitespaces (by replacing them with a meta

---

[7] And yet, CommonCrawl represents only 7.9% of all lines and 6.5% of all words in WMT.

[8] LID: -5%, length filtering: -6.7%, attention filtering: -0.5%.

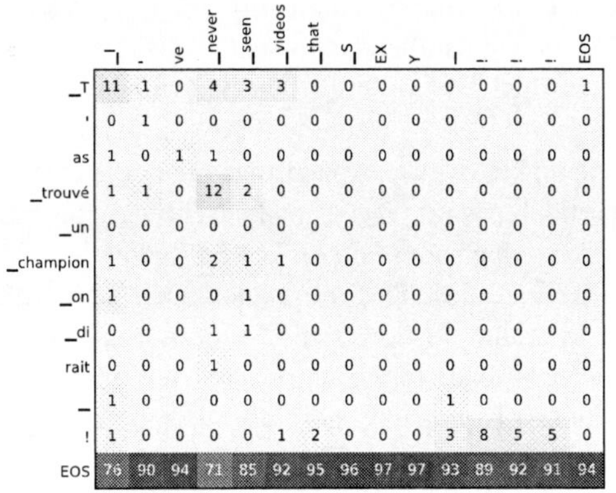

Figure 1: Attention matrix of a French (left) → English (top) Transformer when hallucinating. This is the average of the attention heads of the last decoder layer over the last encoder layer.

symbol), so that its tokenization is fully reversible. This is convenient for emoticons (e.g., ':-('), which Moses-style tokenization tends to break apart irreversibly.

SentencePiece also normalizes unicode characters using the NFKC rules (e.g., ½ → 1/2). It is useful for Japanese, which sometimes uses double-width variants of the ASCII punctuation symbols (e.g., "fullwidth question mark" in unicode table).

We tried different settings of SentencePiece, and settled with the BPE algorithm (Sennrich et al., 2016b),[9] with a joined model of 32k tokens for FR↔EN (with a vocabulary threshold of 100), and two separate models of size 16k for JA↔EN.

Japanese tokenization SentencePiece's tokenization is based mostly on whitespaces, which are very rare in Japanese. For this reason, a pre-tokenization step may be useful (as a way to enforce some linguistic bias and consistency in the BPE segmentation).

We tested several tokenizers for Japanese: MeCab (with IPA and Juman dictionaries),[10] Juman++,[11] and Kytea.[12] MeCab and KyTea gave comparable results, slightly better than when using no pre-tokenization (especially when Japanese is the target language), and Juman++ gave worse results. We settled with Kytea, which is the official tokenizer used on the EN→JA task.[13]

[9]SentencePiece also implements ULM (Kudo, 2018).
[10]http://taku910.github.io/mecab/
[11]https://github.com/ku-nlp/jumanpp
[12]http://www.phontron.com/kytea/
[13]We use the default model shipped with KyTea.

3.2 Model and hyper-parameters

We use Transformer Big for FR↔EN and JA→EN, and Transformer Base for EN→JA. We work with Fairseq, with essentially the same hyper-parameters as Ott et al. (2018).

For FR↔EN, we fit up to 3500 tokens in each batch, while training on 8 GPUs (with synchronous SGD). We accumulate gradients over 10 batches before updating the weights. This gives a theoretical maximum batch size of 280k tokens. These models are trained for 15 epochs, with a checkpoint every 2500 updates. We set the dropout rate to 0.1. The source and target embedding matrices are shared and tied with the last layer.

For JA↔EN, we fit 4000 tokens in each batch, and train on 8 GPUs without delayed updates, for 100 epochs with one checkpoint every epoch. We set the dropout rate to 0.3.

For both language pairs, we train with Adam (Kingma and Ba, 2015), with a max learning rate of 0.0005, and the same learning rate schedule as Ott et al. (2018); Vaswani et al. (2017). We also do label smoothing with a 0.1 weight. We average the 5 best checkpoints of each model according to their perplexity on the validation set. We do half precision training, resulting in a 3× speedup on V100 GPUs (Ott et al., 2018).

4 Robustness techniques

We now describe the techniques that we applied to our baseline models to make them more robust to the noise found in MTNT.

4.1 Case handling

One of the sources of noise in the MTNT data is capital letters. On the Web, capital letters are often used for emphasis (to stress one particular word, or for "shouting"). However, NMT models treat uppercase words or subwords as completely different entities than their lowercase counterparts. BPE even tends to over-segment capitalized words that were not seen in its training data.

One solution, used by Levin et al. (2017) is to do factored machine translation (Sennrich and Haddow, 2016; Garcia-Martinez et al., 2016), where words (or subwords) are set to lowercase and their case is considered as an additional feature.

In this work, we use a simpler technique that we call "inline casing", which consists in using special tokens to denote uppercase (<U>) or title case subwords (<T>), and including these tokens within the sequence right after the corresponding (lowercase) subword. For instance, *"They were SO TASTY!!"* → *"they <T> _were _so <U> _tas <U> ty <U> !!"*. SentencePiece is trained and applied on lowercase text and the case tokens are added after the BPE segmentation. We also force SentencePiece to split mixed-case words (e.g., *MacDonalds* → *_mac <T> donalds <T>*)

4.2 Placeholders

MTNT contains emojis, which our baseline MT models cannot handle (unicode defines over 3 000 unique emojis). We simply replace all emojis in the training and test data with a special <emoji> token. Models trained with this data are able to recopy <emoji> placeholders at the correct position.[14] At test time, we replace target-side placeholders with source-side emojis in the same order.

We use the same solution to deal with Reddit user names (e.g., /u/frenchperson) and subreddit names (e.g., /r/france). MT models sometimes fail to recopy them (e.g., /u/français). For this reason, we identify such names with regular expressions (robust to small variations: without leading / or with extra spaces), and replace them with <user> and <reddit> placeholders.

4.3 Natural noise

We extract noisy variants of known words from the MTNT monolingual data, thanks to French and English lexicons and an extended edit distance (allowing letter swaps and letter repetitions). We also manually build a list of noise rules, with the most common spelling errors in English (e.g., your/you're, it/it's) and French (e.g., ça/sa, à/a), punctuation substitutions, letter swaps, spaces around punctuation and accent removal. Then we randomly replace words with noisy variants and apply these noise rules on the source side of MTNT-train, CommonCrawl and News Commentary (MTNT-train, TED and KFTT for EN→JA), and concatenate these noised versions to the clean training corpus.

4.4 Back-translation

Back-translation (Sennrich et al., 2016a; Edunov et al., 2018) is a way to take advantage of large amounts of monolingual data. This is particularly useful for domain adaptation (when the parallel data is not in the right domain), or for low-resource MT (when parallel data is scarce).

In this task, we hope that back-translation can help on JA→EN, where we have less parallel data, and on FR↔EN to expand vocabulary coverage (in particular w.r.t. recent named entities and news topics which are often evoked on Reddit).

Table 3 describes the monolingual data which is available for constrained submissions. News-discuss (user comments on the Web about news articles) is probably more useful than news-crawl as it is closer to the domain. We use our baseline models presented in Section 3 to back-translate the monolingual data. Following Edunov et al. (2018), we do sampling instead of beam search, with a softmax temperature of $\frac{1}{0.9}$.

In all language pairs, we back-translate the target language MTNT monolingual data, with one different sampling for each epoch. We also back-translate the following data:

- JA→EN: $\frac{1}{20}$th of *news-discuss.en* per epoch (with rotation at the 21th epoch).

- FR→EN: $\frac{1}{5}$th of *news-discuss.en* per epoch (with rotation at the 6th epoch).

- EN→FR: *news-discuss.fr* with one different sampling for each epoch and $\frac{1}{5}$th of *news-crawl.fr* (with rotation at the 6th epoch).

4.5 Tags

We insert a tag at the beginning of each source sentence, specifying its type: <BT> for back-translations, <noise> for natural noise, <real> for real data, and <rev> for MTNT data in the reverse direction (e.g., for JA→EN MT, we concatenate MTNT JA→EN and "reversed" MTNT EN→JA). Like Vaibhav et al. (2019), we found that "isolating" the back-translated data with a different source-side tag gave better BLEU scores. At test time, we always use the <real> tag.

Like Kobus et al. (2017), we also use tags for domain adaptation. We prepend a tag to all source sentences specifying their corpus. For instance, sentences from MTNT get the <MTNT> tag and those from Europarl get the <europarl> tag. These "corpus" tags are used in conjunction with the "type" tags (e.g., MTNT back-translated sentences begin with <MTNT> <BT>). At test time, we use <MTNT> to translate MTNT-domain text, and no corpus tag at all to translate out-of-domain text.

We found that this method is roughly as good for domain adaptation as fine-tuning. We settle

---

[14] We ensure that there is always the same number of placeholders on both sides of the training corpus.

Model	Test	Valid	Blind
MTNT	6.7†	–	5.8
MTNT fine-tuned	9.8†	–	–
Transformer base + tags	13.5	11.2	13.7
+ Back-Translation (BT)	15.0	12.8	14.1
+ Trans. big architecture **	15.5	12.4	14.0
+ Ensemble of 4 *	**16.6**	**13.7**	**15.5**

Table 6: BLEU scores of the JA→EN models on MTNT-test, MTNT-valid and MTNT-blind.

Model	Test	Valid	Blind
MTNT	9.0†	–	8.4
MTNT fine-tuned	12.5†	–	–
Transformer base + tags	19.5	19.0	16.6
+ BT + natural noise **	19.4	19.4	16.8
+ Ensemble of 6 *	**20.7**	**21.2**	**17.9**

Table 7: BLEU scores of the EN→JA models.

with corpus tags (rather than fine-tuning), as it is more flexible, less tricky to configure and has better properties on out-of-domain text.

5 Results

Tables 6, 7, 8 and 9 give the BLEU scores of our models on the MTNT-valid, MTNT-test and MTNT-blind sets (i.e., final results of the task). For FR↔EN we also give BLEU scores on news-test 2014, to compare with the literature, and to measure general-domain translation quality after domain adaptation. For news-test, we use Moses' `normalize-punctuation.perl` on the MT outputs before evaluation.

"MTNT" and "MTNT fine-tuned" are the baseline models of the task organizers (Michel and Neubig, 2018). The models marked * and ** were submitted respectively to the competition as primary and secondary systems. Our primary ensemble models ranked first in all translation directions

Model	Test	News	Blind
MTNT	23.3†	–	25.6
MTNT fine-tuned	30.3†	–	–
Transformer big	39.1	39.3	40.9
+ MTNT + tags	43.1	39.2	45.0
+ BT + natural noise **	44.3	40.2	47.0
+ Ensemble of 4 *	**45.7**	**40.9**	**47.9**

Table 8: BLEU scores of the FR→EN models on MTNT-test, news-test 2014 and MTNT-blind.

Model	Test	News	Blind
MTNT	21.8†	–	22.1
MTNT fine-tuned	29.7†	–	–
Transformer big	33.1	40.7	37.0
+ MTNT + tags	38.8	40.2	39.0
+ BT + natural noise **	40.5	42.3	41.0
+ Ensemble of 4 *	**41.0**	**42.9**	**41.4**

Table 9: BLEU scores of the EN→FR models.

(with +0.7 up to +3.1 BLEU compared to the next best result). $\dagger$ means that different SacreBLEU parameters were used (namely "intl" tokenization).

The "robustness" techniques like inline casing, emoji/Reddit placeholders and natural noise had little to no impact on BLEU scores. They solve problems that are too rare to be accurately measured by BLEU. For instance, we counted 5 emojis and 36 "exceptionally" capitalized words in MTNT-test. Improvements could be measured with BLEU on test sets where these phenomena have been artificially increased: e.g., an all-uppercase test set, or the natural noise of Karpukhin et al. (2019).

Most of the BLEU gains were obtained thanks to careful data filtering and pre-processing, and thanks to domain adaptation: back-translation and integration of in-domain data with corpus tags.

Punctuation fixes We looked at the translation samples on the submission website, and observed that the French references used apostrophes (') and angle quotes (« and »). This is inconsistent with the training data (including MTNT), which contains mostly single quotes (') and double quotes ("). A simple post-processing step to replace quotes led to a BLEU increase of 5 points for EN→FR.[15]

6 Conclusion

We presented our submissions to the WMT Robustness Task. The goal of this task was to build Machine Translation systems that are robust to the types of noise found on social media, in two language pairs (French-English and Japanese-English). Thanks to careful pre-processing and data filtering, and to a combination of several domain adaptation and robustness techniques (special handling of capital letters and emojis, natural noise injection, corpus tags and back-translation), our systems ranked first in the BLEU evaluation in all translation directions.

---

[15]The organizers and participants were informed of this.

References

Yonatan Belinkov and Yonatan Bisk. 2018. Synthetic and Natural Noise Both Break Neural Machine Translation. In *ICLR*.

Yong Cheng, Zhaopeng Tu, Fandong Meng, Junjie Zhai, and Yang Liu. 2018. Towards Robust Neural Machine Translation. In *ACL*.

Sergey Edunov, Myle Ott, Michael Auli, and David Grangier. 2018. Understanding Back-Translation at Scale. In *EMNLP*.

Mercedes Garcia-Martinez, Loic Barrault, and Fethi Bougares. 2016. Factored Neural Machine Translation Architectures. In *IWSLT*.

Hany Hassan, Anthony Aue, Chang Chen, Vishal Chowdhary, Jonathan Clark, Christian Federmann, Xuedong Huang, Marcin Junczys-Dowmunt, William Lewis, Mu Li, Shujie Liu, Tie-Yan Liu, Renqian Luo, Arul Menezes, Tao Qin, Frank Seide, Xu Tan, Fei Tian, Lijun Wu, Shuangzhi Wu, Yingce Xia, Dongdong Zhang, Zhirui Zhang, and Ming Zhou. 2018. Achieving Human Parity on Automatic Chinese to English News Translation. *arXiv*.

Vladimir Karpukhin, Omer Levy, Jacob Eisenstein, and Marjan Ghazvininejad. 2019. Training on Synthetic Noise Improves Robustness to Natural Noise in Machine Translation. *arXiv*.

Huda Khayrallah and Philipp Koehn. 2018. On the Impact of Various Types of Noise on Neural Machine Translation. In *Proceedings of the Second Workshop on Neural Machine Translation and Generation (WNMT)*.

Diederik Kingma and Jimmy Ba. 2015. Adam: A Method for Stochastic Optimization. In *ICLR*.

Catherine Kobus, Josep Crego, and Jean Senellart. 2017. Domain Control for Neural Machine Translation. In *RANLP*.

Philipp Koehn, Hieu Hoang, Alexandra Birch, Chris Callison-Burch, Marcello Federico, Nicola Bertoldi, Brooke Cowan, Wade Shen, Christine Moran, Richard Zens, Chris Dyer, Ondřej Bojar, Alexandra Constantin, and Evan Herbst. 2007. Moses: Open Source Toolkit for Statistical Machine Translation. In *ACL*.

Taku Kudo. 2018. Subword Regularization: Improving Neural Network Translation Models with Multiple Subword Candidates. In *ACL*.

Taku Kudo and John Richardson. 2018. SentencePiece: A simple and language independent subword tokenizer and detokenizer for Neural Text Processing. In *EMNLP*.

Pavel Levin, Nishikant Dhanuka, and Maxim Khalilov. 2017. Machine Translation at Booking.com: Journey and Lessons Learned. In *EAMT*.

Xian Li, Paul Michel, Antonios Anastasopoulos, Yonatan Belinkov, Nadir K. Durrani, Orhan Firat, Philipp Koehn, Graham Neubig, Juan M. Pino, and Hassan Sajjad. 2019. Findings of the First Shared Task on Machine Translation Robustness. In *WMT*.

Marco Lui and Timothy Baldwin. 2012. langid.py: An Off-the-shelf Language Identification Tool. In *ACL*.

Paul Michel and Graham Neubig. 2018. MTNT: A Testbed for Machine Translation of Noisy Text. In *EMNLP*.

Graham Neubig, Yosuke Nakata, and Shinsuke Mori. 2011. Pointwise Prediction for Robust, Adaptable Japanese Morphological Analysis. In *ACL-HLT*.

Myle Ott, Sergey Edunov, David Grangier, and Michael Auli. 2018. Scaling Neural Machine Translation. In *WMT*.

Kishore Papineni, Salim Roukos, Todd Ward, and Wj Zhu. 2002. BLEU: a Method for Automatic Evaluation of Machine Translation. In *ACL*.

Matt Post. 2018. A Call for Clarity in Reporting BLEU Scores. In *WMT*.

Rico Sennrich and Barry Haddow. 2016. Linguistic Input Features Improve Neural Machine Translation. In *WMT*.

Rico Sennrich, Barry Haddow, and Alexandra Birch. 2016a. Improving Neural Machine Translation Models with Monolingual Data. In *ACL*.

Rico Sennrich, Barry Haddow, and Alexandra Birch. 2016b. Neural Machine Translation of Rare Words with Subword Units. In *ACL*.

Jason R Smith, Herve Saint-Amand, Magdalena Plamada, Philipp Koehn, Chris Callison-Burch, and Adam Lopez. 2013. Dirt Cheap Web-Scale Parallel Text from the Common Crawl. In *ACL*.

Matthias Sperber, Jan Niehues, and Alex Waibel. 2017. Toward Robust Neural Machine Translation for Noisy Input Sequences. In *IWSLT*.

Antonio Toral, Sheila Castilho, Ke Hu, and Andy Way. 2018. Attaining the Unattainable? Reassessing Claims of Human Parity in Neural Machine Translation. In *WMT*.

Vaibhav, Sumeet Singh, Craig Stewart, and Graham Neubig. 2019. Improving Robustness of Machine Translation with Synthetic Noise. In *NAACL*.

Ashish Vaswani, Noam Shazeer, Niki Parmar, Jakob Uszkoreit, Llion Jones, Aidan N. Gomez, Łukasz Kaiser, and Illia Polosukhin. 2017. Attention Is All You Need. In *NIPS*.

NICT's Supervised Neural Machine Translation Systems for the WMT19 Translation Robustness Task

Raj Dabre and **Eiichiro Sumita**

National Institute of Information and Communications Technology, Kyoto, Japan

`{raj.dabre,eiichiro.sumita}@nict.go.jp`

Abstract

In this paper we describe our neural machine translation (NMT) systems for Japanese↔English translation which we submitted to the translation robustness task. We focused on leveraging transfer learning via fine tuning to improve translation quality. We used a fairly well established domain adaptation technique called Mixed Fine Tuning (MFT) (Chu et al., 2017) to improve translation quality for Japanese↔English. We also trained bi-directional NMT models instead of uni-directional ones as the former are known to be quite robust, especially in low-resource scenarios. However, given the noisy nature of the in-domain training data, the improvements we obtained are rather modest.

1 Introduction

Neural machine translation (NMT) (Cho et al., 2014; Sutskever et al., 2014; Bahdanau et al., 2015) has enabled end-to-end training of a translation system without needing to deal with word alignments, translation rules, and complicated decoding algorithms, which are the characteristics of phrase-based statistical machine translation (PB-SMT) (Koehn et al., 2007). NMT performs well in resource-rich scenarios but badly in resource-poor ones (Zoph et al., 2016).

One such resource-poor scenario is the translation of noisy sentences which are often found on social media like Reddit, Facebook, Twitter etc. There are two main problems: (a) The type of noise (spelling mistakes, code switching, random characters, emojis) in the text is unpredictable (b) Scarcity of training data to capture all noise phenomena. One of the first works on dealing with noisy translation led to the development of the MTNT (Michel and Neubig, 2018) test suite for testing MT models that are robust

to noisy text. Fortunately, the problem of noisy text translation can be treated as a domain adaptation problem and there is an abundant amount of Japanese–English text that be leveraged for this purpose. In this paper, we describe the systems for Japanese↔English translation, that we developed and submitted for WMT 2019 under the team name "NICT". In particular our observations can be summarized as follows:

Japanese↔English translation dramatically fails given the limited amount of noisy training data.

Fine-Tuning is simple but has over-fitting risks.

Mixed-Fine-Tuning is a simple but effective way of performing domain adaptation via fine tuning where one does not have to worry about the possibility of quick over-fitting.

Kindly refer to the task overview paper (Li et al., 2019) for additional details about the task, an analysis of the results and comparisons of all submitted systems which we do not include in this paper.

2 Approaches

We used domain adaptation approaches on top of the transformer model.

2.1 The Transformer NMT Model

The Transformer (Vaswani et al., 2017) is the current state-of-the-art model for NMT. It is a sequence-to-sequence neural model that consists of two components: the *encoder* and the *decoder*. The encoder converts the input word sequence into a sequence of vectors. The decoder, on the other hand, produces the target word sequence by predicting the words using a combination of the previously predicted word and relevant parts of the

Proceedings of the Fourth Conference on Machine Translation (WMT), Volume 2: Shared Task Papers (Day 1) pages 533–536
Florence, Italy, August 1-2, 2019. ©2019 Association for Computational Linguistics

input sequence representations. The reader is encouraged to read the original paper (Vaswani et al., 2017) for a deeper understanding.

2.2 Mixed Fine Tuning for Domain Adaptation

The fastest way to adapt an out-of-domain model to an in-domain task is to first train a L1→L2 model on the large out-of-domain data and then fine tune it on the small in-domain data. However, given that NMT models overfit quickly on small data (Zoph et al., 2016), it is important to consider learning rate modification, regularization and sophisticated training schedules. All this can be avoided by performing Mixed-Fine-Tuning (MFT) (Chu et al., 2017) where the out-of-domain model is fine-tuned on a combination of both the out-of-domain data and the oversampled[1] in-domain data. When using this technique there is no risk of overfitting.

2.3 Bi-directional NMT Modeling

Multilingual models (Johnson et al., 2017) enable a model to learn multiple translation directions without increasing the model size. We concatenated the Japanese→English and English→Japanese training corpora after appending the tokens "2en" and "2ja" to the source sentences of the respective corpora. In addition to this, we did not modify the NMT model in any way.

3 Experimental Settings and Results

3.1 Datasets

We used the official Japanese→English and English→Japanese datasets provided by WMT. The out-of-domain (non noisy) datasets are KFTT, JESC and TED Talks, all of which are adequately described in the original MTNT paper (Michel and Neubig, 2018). The total number of out-of-domain sentence pairs is 3,900,772. As for the in-domain corpus, the number of training sentence pairs for Japanese→English translation is 6,506 pairs and for English→Japanese translation there are 5,775 pairs. Upon inspection of the English→Japanese data, we noted that many sentences were actually paragraphs which are almost useless for NMT training as they are trimmed to

avoid out-of-memory errors. We tried a naive paragraph splitting method where we split a paragraphs into sentences and keep the splits if there are an equal number of sentences. Upon manual investigation we found out that this splitting leads to correct splits most of the times. As a result, the number of training sentences for English→Japanese translation increases to 10,060 pairs. We pre-processed the Japanese text using KyTea (Neubig et al., 2011). Other than this, we do not perform any pre-processing.

3.2 Model Training Details

We used the tensor2tensor[2] version 1.6 implementation of the Transformer (Vaswani et al., 2017) model. We used the default hyperparameters in tensor2tensor for all our models with the exception of the number of training iterations. Unless mentioned otherwise we use the "base" transformer model hyperparameter settings with a $2^{15} = 32,768$ shared sub-word vocabulary which is learned using tensor2tensor's internal tokenization and sub-word segmentation mechanism. We used a shared sub-word vocabulary because we trained bi-directional models. This allows us to share embeddings between the encoder and the decoder. During training, a model checkpoint is saved every 1000 iterations. All models were trained till convergence on the development set BLEU score. We averaged the last 10 model checkpoints and used it for decoding the test sets. We chose a default beam size of 10 and length penalty of 0.8. We did not ensemble multiple models although it could possibly improve the translation quality even further. When we fine-tuned models, we simply resumed training the last model checkpoint on the noisy in-domain data. We did not change the optimizer nor any other hyperparameters. One might argue that this could lead to overfitting but tensor2tensor uses a learning rate decay by default which prevents this. Furthermore, MFT does not suffer from overfitting.

3.3 Systems

We first trained a (bidirectional) Japanese↔English model using the out-of-domain parallel corpus for 150,000 iterations on 1 GPU with a batch size of 2048 words. We did not train for a larger number of iterations

---

[1] To balance the highly skewed corpora ratio thereby ensuring that the model sees an equal number of training examples from both domains.

[2] https://github.com/tensorflow/tensor2tensor

Task	BLEU	BLEU cased	IGNORE BLEU (11b)	IGNORE BLEU-cased (11b)	IGNORE BLEU-cased-norm	BEER 2.0
English→Japanese	11.1	11.1	11.1	11.1	11.1	0.354
Japanese→English	8.1	7.4	8.1	7.4	7.8	0.352

Table 1: Results for Japanese↔English translation for the robustness task.

Approach	Ja→En	En→Ja
Bidirectional FT	9.6	10.5
Bidirectional MFT	9.2	**13.4**

Table 2: BLEU scores on the non-blind test set for Japanese–English translation. We show that MFT is either comparable to or significantly better than regular fine-tuning.

because the model had converged sufficiently by 150,000 iterations. We then used this model to perform Mixed-Fine-Tuning (MFT) which uses a combination of the out-of-domain and in-domain corpus. MFT is done for 50,000 iterations on 1 GPU with a batch size of 2048 words.

3.4 Results

Refer to Table 1 for the various automatic evaluation scores. For English→Japanese our submitted system's run achieved a cased BLEU score of 11.1. On the other hand, our Japanese→English system's run achieved a BLEU score of 8.1.

A surface level analysis of our translations showed that the implementation of the Transformer that we used is not well suited to handle noisy text. In most cases it does not handle emojis. We noted that emojis are always missing in the translation. Another problem we observed was that the default KyTea model does not give good morphological segmentations which we believe is one of the reasons for our poor performance in the task. In the future, we will incorporate better pre-processing mechanisms into the tensor2tensor implementation for better translation. Although, we did not mention it in the paper, we tried to use back-translation to translate the monolingual data in the MTNT dataset but were unable to achieve satisfactory results.

3.5 Comparison of Approaches

In Table 2 we give the BLEU scores of our bidirectional models using fine-tuning and mixed-fine tuning. We obtained these BLEU scores on the non-blind test set which was provided along with

the training data. We did not use this test set for training or tuning. The BLEU scores are obtained using SacreBLEU (Post, 2018). We can see that while the performance of Japanese to English slightly degrades (not statistically significant), English to Japanese translation improves by approximately 2 BLEU points. As such MFT is either comparable to or significantly better than regular fine-tuning and was the reason why we chose it for the final submission.

4 Conclusion

In this paper we have described our primary Japanese↔English systems whose translations we have submitted to the robustness translation task in WMT2019. In general, we found that bi-directional modeling and Mixed-Fine-Tuning (MFT) work reasonably well for this task although MFT is the main reason behind the improvements. However, these techniques only partially address the problem of training NMT models that are robust to noise. MFT is a robust training approach and does not actually deal with different sources of noise. In the future we will consider applying better pre-processing mechanisms, domain adaptation techniques and data augmentation techniques for even more robust translation systems.

Acknowledgements

We thank the organizers for providing the datasets and the reviewers for their valuable suggestions in improving this paper. This work was conducted under the program "Research and Development of Enhanced Multilingual and Multipurpose Speech Translation Systems" of the Ministry of Internal Affairs and Communications (MIC), Japan.

References

Dzmitry Bahdanau, Kyunghyun Cho, and Yoshua Bengio. 2015. Neural machine translation by jointly learning to align and translate. In *Proceedings of the 3rd International Conference on Learning Representations*, San Diego, USA.

Kyunghyun Cho, Bart van Merriënboer, Çaglar Gülçehre, Dzmitry Bahdanau, Fethi Bougares, Holger Schwenk, and Yoshua Bengio. 2014. Learning phrase representations using RNN encoder–decoder for statistical machine translation. In *Proceedings of the 2014 Conference on Empirical Methods in Natural Language Processing*, pages 1724–1734, Doha, Qatar.

Chenhui Chu, Raj Dabre, and Sadao Kurohashi. 2017. An empirical comparison of domain adaptation methods for neural machine translation. In *Proceedings of the 55th Annual Meeting of the Association for Computational Linguistics*, pages 385–391, Vancouver, Canada.

Melvin Johnson, Mike Schuster, Quoc Le, Maxim Krikun, Yonghui Wu, Zhifeng Chen, Nikhil Thorat, Fernanda Viégas, Martin Wattenberg, Greg Corrado, Macduff Hughes, and Jeffrey Dean. 2017. Google's multilingual neural machine translation system: Enabling zero-shot translation. *Transactions of the Association for Computational Linguistics*, 5:339–351.

Philipp Koehn, Hieu Hoang, Alexandra Birch, Chris Callison-Burch, Marcello Federico, Nicola Bertoldi, Brooke Cowan, Wade Shen, Christine Moran, Richard Zens, Chris Dyer, Ondrej Bojar, Alexandra Constantin, and Evan Herbst. 2007. Moses: Open source toolkit for statistical machine translation. In *Proceedings of the 45th Annual Meeting of the Association for Computational Linguistics Companion Volume Proceedings of the Demo and Poster Sessions*, pages 177–180, Prague, Czech Republic.

Xian Li, Paul Michel, Antonios Anastasopoulos, Yonatan Belinkov, Nadir K. Durrani, Orhan Firat, Philipp Koehn, Graham Neubig, Juan M. Pino, and Hassan Sajjad. 2019. Findings of the first shared task on machine translation robustness. In *Proceedings of the Fourth Conference on Machine Translation, Volume 2: Shared Task Papers*, Florence, Italy. Association for Computational Linguistics.

Paul Michel and Graham Neubig. 2018. MTNT: A testbed for machine translation of noisy text. In *Conference on Empirical Methods in Natural Language Processing (EMNLP)*, Brussels, Belgium.

Graham Neubig, Yosuke Nakata, and Shinsuke Mori. 2011. Pointwise prediction for robust, adaptable Japanese morphological analysis. In *Proceedings of the 49th Annual Meeting of the Association for Computational Linguistics: Human Language Technologies*, pages 529–533, Portland, Oregon, USA. Association for Computational Linguistics.

Matt Post. 2018. A call for clarity in reporting BLEU scores. In *Proceedings of the Third Conference on Machine Translation: Research Papers*, pages 186–191, Belgium, Brussels. Association for Computational Linguistics.

Ilya Sutskever, Oriol Vinyals, and Quoc V. Le. 2014. Sequence to sequence learning with neural networks. In *Proceedings of the 27th International Conference on Neural Information Processing Systems*, pages 3104–3112, Montréal, Canada.

Ashish Vaswani, Noam Shazeer, Niki Parmar, Jakob Uszkoreit, Llion Jones, Aidan N. Gomez, Łukasz Kaiser, and Illia Polosukhin. 2017. Attention is all you need. In *Proceedings of 30th Advances in Neural Information Processing Systems*, pages 5998–6008.

Barret Zoph, Deniz Yuret, Jonathan May, and Kevin Knight. 2016. Transfer learning for low-resource neural machine translation. In *Proceedings of the 2016 Conference on Empirical Methods in Natural Language Processing*, pages 1568–1575, Austin, USA.

System Description
– the submission of FOKUS to the WMT 19 robustness task –

Cristian Grozea
Fraunhofer FOKUS
`cristian.grozea@fokus.fraunhofer.de`

Abstract

This paper describes the systems of Fraunhofer FOKUS for the WMT 2019 machine translation robustness task. We have made submissions to the EN-FR, FR-EN, and JA-EN language pairs. The first two were made with a baseline translator, trained on clean data for the WMT 2019 biomedical translation task. These baselines improved over the baselines from the MTNT paper by 2 to 4 BLEU points, but where not trained on the same data. The last one used the same model class and training procedure, with induced typos in the training data to increase the model robustness.

1 Introduction

Our submissions to the robustness task (Li et al., 2019) aimed to investigate two questions: a) how robust are well-performing models that are trained on clean text and b) does making small intentional "typos" in the training data lead to robust models?

2 Methods

FR-EN, EN-FR

We reproduce here for the sake of self-containment the description of the baseline model we have developed for the biomedical translation task. In order to create a baseline for that task, we have tried to emulate a non-expert who uses a slightly modified NMT tutorial on the data listed in the competition page to compete (minimal effort). The tutorial our submissions are based on was written for the MT Marathon 2018 Labs and is available online [1]. It uses the Marian NMT system(Junczys-Dowmunt et al., 2018).

As training data we have used the UFAL medical corpus(UFA), from which we have removed the "Subtitles" pairs, as they are lower quality than the rest, less medically oriented – if at all, and with the wrong addressing (dialogue, as opposed to narration). As validation dataset we have used Khresmoi(Pecina et al., 2013), which we did not find to be included in UFAL, despite being mentioned as one of the sources.

The training was set to stop when either the cross-entropy or the the BLEU on the validation stalled for 5 training and evaluation cycles. One such cycle processed 10000 sentence pairs.

The model implemented by Marian NMT in the tutorial used here is Sequence2Sequence with shallow networks. The text data has been preprocessed with BPE. Here we deviated for efficiency reasons from the MOSES BPE(Koehn et al., 2007) and used FastBPE[2].

The vocabulary size for BPE was set to 85000, the workspace memory to be reserved on the GPU was reduced to 6 GB to avoid out of memory errors on GTX 1080 Ti. The tests were run on machines with 8 GPUs, the training process of a single language pair took in general a couple of days.

JA-EN

For the Japanese to English submission, we have employed the same models and training as above, but with a preprocessing intended to increase the robustness to typos of two types: missing letters, duplicated letters.

3 Results

The results are presented in Table 1

4 Discussion and Conclusion

The models trained on the UFAL medical corpus are fairly robust and generic, not excessively specialized for the biomedical domain. Despite being trained for the biomedical translation task,

---

[1] https://marian-nmt.github.io/examples/mtm2018-labs

[2] https://github.com/glample/fastBPE

Proceedings of the Fourth Conference on Machine Translation (WMT), Volume 2: Shared Task Papers (Day 1) pages 537–538
Florence, Italy, August 1-2, 2019. ©2019 Association for Computational Linguistics

Source	Target	BLEU un-cased	BLEU cased	WMT19 Biomed.
EN	FR	24.8	24.2	32.5
FR	EN	30.8	29.9	29.9
JA	EN	7.3	6.4	ZH2EN 16.7

Table 1: BLEU scores of our submissions, contrasted with the results of the same models on the biomedical translation task, except for JA-EN, where the result on the closest language pair is given, Chinese to English

the EN2FR and FR2EN models trained by us behaved reasonably well in the WMT ROBUSTNESS task, surpassing the NTMT paper baseline by 2.5 (EN2FR) and 4 (FR2EN) BLEU points, with the caveat of not being a constrained system, in the sense that the training has not been done on the data listed and intended for that task. Still, as Reddit is not among the sources of UFAL, this should not affect the validation results.

One choice that we made, and we think it is right for the biomedical task, to avoid dialogues and direct speech (the subtitles part of UFAL medical corpus) has probably influenced negatively the performance in the robustness task - the Reddit text used for evaluation contains often the first person and second person addressing modes.

In comparison with the performance on the biomedical text, the performance of FR-EN was apparently not affected by the noisy text, whereas for EN-FR there was a strong decrease of the BLEU score, 8.3 points from 32.5 down to 24.2. We did apply the postprocessing of the French text to fix the punctuation marks, thus there should be another explanation for the decrease of performance.

The performance of the JA-EN was very low. Visual inspection of the results shows typical early stage training RNN issues like this translation: Our model's translation: "It's very, very, ..." repeated 17 times. The reference translation was "Minpaku has such cool content and it was fun". In general, numbers are changed to other numbers or ignored completely by our JA-EN translation model. One can assume the training data was not sufficient in quantity to train a reliable Japanese to English translation model. In addition to that, due to an error, we have introduced the intentional typos not only in the source text but also in the target

text.

The quality of the FR-EN and EN-FR is on the surface better, but they miss fairly easy translations by translating too literally ("I'm **on the train**" translated as "Je suis **sur le train**") or by missing the correct sense of the word, probably because we didn't use the context at all ("I don't think we're are making any **trades** til the off season." translated as "Je ne pense pas que nous ne faisons aucun **métier** en dehors de la saison."). Meaning got changed ("tu crois vraiment qu'il n'y a vraiment **aucune solution que** la ségrégation ?" went to "Do you really believe that there is really **no solution to** segregation?"), coreference is not properly processed ("**Comme** Nelson Mandela ne voulait pas le pouvoir aux noirs(...), il voulait la fin du racisme." was translated "**As** Nelson Mandela(...)he wanted to see the end of racism.").

References

UFAL medical corpus 1.0. `https://ufal.mff.cuni.cz/ufal_medical_corpus`. Accessed: 2018-07-24.

Marcin Junczys-Dowmunt, Roman Grundkiewicz, Tomasz Dwojak, Hieu Hoang, Kenneth Heafield, Tom Neckermann, Frank Seide, Ulrich Germann, Alham Fikri Aji, Nikolay Bogoychev, André F. T. Martins, and Alexandra Birch. 2018. Marian: Fast neural machine translation in C++. In *Proceedings of ACL 2018, System Demonstrations*, pages 116–121, Melbourne, Australia. Association for Computational Linguistics.

Philipp Koehn, Hieu Hoang, Alexandra Birch, Chris Callison-Burch, Marcello Federico, Nicola Bertoldi, Brooke Cowan, Wade Shen, Christine Moran, Richard Zens, et al. 2007. Moses: Open source toolkit for statistical machine translation. In *Proceedings of the 45th annual meeting of the ACL on interactive poster and demonstration sessions*, pages 177–180. Association for Computational Linguistics.

Xian Li, Paul Michel, Antonios Anastasopoulos, Yonatan Belinkov, Nadir K. Durrani, Orhan Firat, Philipp Koehn, Graham Neubig, Juan M. Pino, and Hassan Sajjad. 2019. Findings of the first shared task on machine translation robustness. In *Proceedings of the Fourth Conference on Machine Translation, Volume 2: Shared Task Papers*, Florence, Italy. Association for Computational Linguistics.

Pavel Pecina, Ondřej Dušek, Jan Hajič, and Zdeňka Urešová. 2013. Khresmoi query translation test data 1.0. LINDAT/CLARIN digital library at the Institute of Formal and Applied Linguistics (ÚFAL), Faculty of Mathematics and Physics, Charles University.

CUNI System for the WMT19 Robustness Task

Jindřich Helcl and **Jindřich Libovický** and **Martin Popel**
Charles University, Faculty of Mathematics and Physics,
Institute of Formal and Applied Linguistics,
Malostranské náměstí 25, 118 00 Prague, Czech Republic
{helcl, libovicky, popel}@ufal.mff.cuni.cz

Abstract

We present our submission to the WMT19 Robustness Task. Our baseline system is the Charles University (CUNI) Transformer system trained for the WMT18 shared task on News Translation. Quantitative results show that the CUNI Transformer system is already far more robust to noisy input than the LSTM-based baseline provided by the task organizers. We further improved the performance of our model by fine-tuning on the in-domain noisy data without influencing the translation quality on the news domain.

1 Introduction

Machine translation (MT) is usually evaluated on text coming from news written by a professional journalist. However, in practice, MT should cover more domains, including informal and not carefully spelled text that we encounter in the online world.

Although machine translation quality increased dramatically in recent years (Bojar et al., 2018), several studies (Belinkov and Bisk, 2018; Khayrallah and Koehn, 2018) has shown that the current systems are sensitive to the source-side noise. It is also an issue that was not studied intensively in the past because neural systems appear to be more noise-sensitive than the previously used statistical systems (Khayrallah and Koehn, 2018).

Recently, Michel and Neubig (2018) prepared a dataset called Machine Translation of Noisy Text (MTNT) that focuses exclusively on translating texts from the online environment. This dataset is used for the WMT19 Robustness Task.

2 MTNT Dataset and Baselines

The MTNT dataset consists of sentences collected from Reddit[1] posts. Unlike the standard corpora which (in a major part) consist of formal language, often written by professionals, this dataset contains a substantial number of spelling errors, grammatical errors, emoticons, and profanities.

Manual translations are provided with the source sentences crawled from the web. The translators were asked to keep all the noise-related properties of the source sentence.

There are two language pairs included in the dataset: English-French and English-Japanese in both directions. The dataset comes in three splits, for training, validation, and testing. The English-French part consists of 36k examples in the training split, 852 examples for validation, 1020 examples for testing in the En→Fr direction, and 19k, 886, and 1022 examples for training, validation, and testing respectively in the opposite direction. For English-Japanese, the dataset is substantially smaller, with around 6k training examples in both directions. In our experiments, we focus solely on the translation between French and English.

We noticed that the MTNT dataset as provided for the task has some peculiarities that were probably caused inadvertently during the dataset building. Namely, the training and validation splits seem to come from a single alphabetically sorted file. This means that all validation source sentences start with the letter "Y", and anything that comes after "Y" in the alphabetical order. Because of this, the validation scores are unreliable. Moreover, a system trained on the training split will have a difficult time translating sentences beginning with e.g. the word "You", which is a commonly seen instance in the online discussion domain. This does not affect the test split.

The baseline system introduced with the dataset is a recurrent sequence-to-sequence model with attention (Bahdanau et al., 2014). The encoder is a bidirectional LSTM with two layers. The decoder is a two-layer LSTM. The hidden state dimension

---

[1] http://www.reddit.com

Proceedings of the Fourth Conference on Machine Translation (WMT), Volume 2: Shared Task Papers (Day 1) pages 539–543
Florence, Italy, August 1-2, 2019. ©2019 Association for Computational Linguistics

in the LSTMs is 1,024 and the word embedding size is 512.

The model that was used as a baseline for the Robustness Task was trained on the WMT15 parallel data. Additionally, simple fine-tuning using stochastic gradient descent on the MTNT data is shown to improve the translation quality by a large margin. The translation quality of the system is tabulated among our systems in Table 2.

3 Related Work

There have been several attempts to increase the robustness of MT systems in recent years.

Cheng et al. (2018) employ an adversarial training scheme in a multi-task learning setup in order to increase the system robustness. For each training example, its noisy counterpart is randomly generated. The network is trained to yield such input representations such that it is not possible to train a discriminator that decides (based on the input representation) which input is the noisy one. This method improves both the robustness and the translation quality on the clean data.

Liu et al. (2018) attempt to make the translation more robust towards noise from homophones. This type of noise is common in languages with non-phonetic writing systems and concerns words or phrases which are pronounced in the same way, but spelled differently. The authors of the paper train the word embeddings to capture the phonetic information which eventually leads not only to bigger robustness but also to improved translation quality in general.

To our knowledge, the only work that specifically uses the MTNT dataset attempts to improve the system robustness by emulating the noise in the clean data (Vaibhav et al., 2019). They introduce two techniques for noise induction, one employing hand-crafted rules, and one based on back-translation. The techniques offer a similar translation quality gains as fine-tuning on MTNT data.

4 The CUNI Transformer model

Our original plan was to train a system that would be robust by itself and would not require further fine-tuning on the MTNT dataset.

As the baseline model, we use the Transformer "Big" model (Vaswani et al., 2017) as implemented in Tensor2Tensor (Vaswani et al., 2018). We train the model using the procedure

Corpus		# Sentences
Parallel	10^9 English-French Corpus	22,520k
	Europarl	2,007k
	News Commentary	200k
	UN Corpus	12,886k
	Common Crawl	3,224k
Mono	French News Crawl ('08–'14)	37,320k
	English News Crawl ('11–'17)	127,554k

Table 1: Overview of the data used to train the CUNI Transformer baseline system.

described in Popel (2018) and Popel and Bojar (2018), which was the best-performing method for Czech-to-English and English-to-Czech translation at WMT18 News Translation shared task (Bojar et al., 2018).

We trained our model on all parallel data available for the WMT15 News Translation task (Bojar et al., 2015). We acquired additional synthetic data by back-translation of the WMT News Crawl corpora (from years 2008–2014 for French and 2011–2017 for English). We did not include the News Discussion corpus that we considered too noisy for training the system. Table 1 gives an overview of the training data composition.

5 Fine-Tuning

Similarly to the baseline experiments presented with the MTNT dataset (Michel and Neubig, 2018), we fine-tune our general-domain model on the MTNT dataset.

We continued the training of the models using the training part of the MTNT dataset. Unlike the original model, we used plain stochastic gradient descent with a constant learning rate for updating the weights. We executed several fine-tuning runs with different learning rates and observed that learning rates smaller than 10^{-5} do not change the model outputs at all and learning rates larger than 10^{-4} cause the models to diverge immediately. The models in our final submission were fine-tuned with a learning rate of 10^{-4}.

6 Results

We evaluate the results on four datasets. The first one is *neswtest2014* (Bojar et al., 2014), a standard WMT test set consisting of manually translated newspaper texts where one half is originally in English and the other half originally in French.

	English-French				French-English			
	WMT14	WMT15	MTNT	blind	WMT14	WMT15	MTNT	blind
MTNT baseline	33.5	33.0	21.8	22.1	28.9	30.8	23.3	25.6
+ fine-tuning	—	—	29.7	—	—	—	30.3	—
CUNI Transformer	43.6	41.6	34.0	37.0	42.9	39.6	39.9	42.6
+ fine-tuning	43.5	41.6	36.6	38.5	41.5	40.9	42.1	44.8

Table 2: BLEU scores of the baseline and CUNI models measured on several datasets.

	en-fr	fr-en
Naver Labs Europe	41.4	47.9
this work	38.5	44.8
Baidu & Oregon State Uni.	36.4	43.6
Johns Hopkins Uni.	—	40.2
Fraunhofer FOKUS – VISCOM	24.2	29.9
MTNT Baseline	22.1	25.6

Table 3: Quantiative comparison of the CUNI Transformer system + fine-tuning (this work) with other submitted systems.

Because of the large amount of training data available, even the statistical MT systems achieved high translation quality on the news domain. Because of that a slightly different test set, *newsdiscusstest2015*, was used as the evaluation test set for the WMT15 competition (Bojar et al., 2015). The test set consists of sentences from discussions under news stories from The Guardian and Le Monde. Even though the topics are the same as the news stories, the language used in the discussions is less formal and contains grammatical and spelling errors, which makes them somewhat closer to the MTNT dataset.

Finally, we evaluate the models on the test part of the MTNT dataset (described in Section 2) and the blind test set for the WMT19 Robustness Task, which was collected in the same way as the original MTNT dataset.

The quantitative results are shown in Table 2. The Transformer-based baseline outperforms the RNN-based MTNT baseline by a large margin on both WMT and MTNT test datasets.

The fine-tuning of the RNN-based models brings a substantial translation quality boost of 8 and 7 BLEU points in each direction respectively. This effect is much smaller with our stronger baseline and only improves the performance by around 2 BLEU points in either direction. This may in-

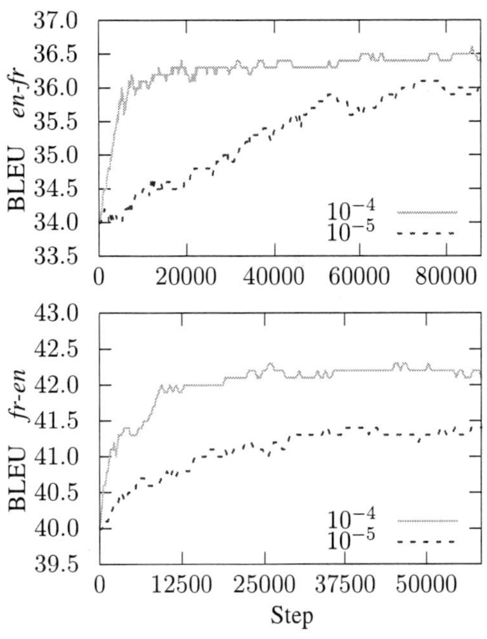

Figure 1: Learning curves showing the progress of fine-tuning on the MTNT test split for English-to-French (top) and French-to-English (bottom) systems with two different learning rates.

dicate that sufficiently strong models are robust enough and do not need further fine-tuning for the type of noise present in the MTNT dataset. Especially in French-to-English translation, the fine-tuning improvement is reached at the expense of decreased translation quality in the news domain.

We observe that the fine-tuning has only a small negative impact on the translation quality of our models on the general-domain data. It would be interesting to see how big impact made the fine-tuning of the MTNT baseline model, which gained such a large improvement on the domain-specific data. However, the authors of the baseline (Michel and Neubig, 2018) do not report these results.

We plot the learning curves from the progress of the system fine-tuning in Figure 1. Even though the fine-tuning improved the model performance on both language pairs by approximately the same margin, the courses of the fine-tuning differ fundamentally. For English-to-French translation, we see that the translation quality slowly increases until convergence. For the opposite direction, it improves immediately and keeps oscillating during the remaining training steps. We found that this effect was similar regardless of the learning rate.

Although we observed a strong effect of checkpoint averaging during the baseline model training, it has almost no effect on the fine-tuned models. Therefore, we report only the performance for parameter checkpoints with the highest validation BLEU scores.

Table 3 compares the automatic scores with other WMT19 Robustness Task participants. Our submission was outperformed by submissions by Naver Labs Europe in both translation directions. Their submission used the same architecture as our submission, but in addition, it employed corpus tags and synthetic noise generation. Details about other systems were not known at the time of our submission.

7 Conclusions

In our submission to the WMT19 Robustness Task, we experiment with fine-tuning of strong Transformer-based baselines for translation between English and French.

Our results show that when using a strong baseline, the effect of fine-tuning on a domain-specific dataset is much smaller than for weaker models introduced as a baseline with the MTNT dataset.

Acknowledgements

This research has been supported by the from the European Union's Horizon 2020 research and innovation programme under grant agreement No. 825303 (Bergamot), Czech Science Foundtion grant No. 19-26934X (NEUREM3), and Charles University grant No. 976518 and using language resources distributed by the LINDAT/CLARIN project of the Ministry of Education, Youth and Sports of the Czech Republic (LM2015071).

References

Dzmitry Bahdanau, Kyunghyun Cho, and Yoshua Bengio. 2014. Neural machine translation by jointly learning to align and translate. *CoRR*, abs/1409.0473.

Yonatan Belinkov and Yonatan Bisk. 2018. Synthetic and natural noise both break neural machine translation. In *6th International Conference on Learning Representations, ICLR 2018, Vancouver, BC, Canada, April 30 - May 3, 2018, Conference Track Proceedings*.

Ondrej Bojar, Christian Buck, Christian Federmann, Barry Haddow, Philipp Koehn, Johannes Leveling, Christof Monz, Pavel Pecina, Matt Post, Herve Saint-Amand, Radu Soricut, Lucia Specia, and Aleš Tamchyna. 2014. Findings of the 2014 workshop on statistical machine translation. In *Proceedings of the Ninth Workshop on Statistical Machine Translation*, pages 12–58, Baltimore, Maryland, USA. Association for Computational Linguistics.

Ondřej Bojar, Rajen Chatterjee, Christian Federmann, Barry Haddow, Matthias Huck, Chris Hokamp, Philipp Koehn, Varvara Logacheva, Christof Monz, Matteo Negri, Matt Post, Carolina Scarton, Lucia Specia, and Marco Turchi. 2015. Findings of the 2015 workshop on statistical machine translation. In *Proceedings of the Tenth Workshop on Statistical Machine Translation*, pages 1–46, Lisbon, Portugal. Association for Computational Linguistics.

Ondřej Bojar, Christian Federmann, Mark Fishel, Yvette Graham, Barry Haddow, Philipp Koehn, and Christof Monz. 2018. Findings of the 2018 conference on machine translation (WMT18). In *Proceedings of the Third Conference on Machine Translation: Shared Task Papers*, pages 272–303, Belgium, Brussels. Association for Computational Linguistics.

Yong Cheng, Zhaopeng Tu, Fandong Meng, Junjie Zhai, and Yang Liu. 2018. Towards robust neural machine translation. In *Proceedings of the 56th Annual Meeting of the Association for Computational Linguistics (Volume 1: Long Papers)*, pages 1756–1766, Melbourne, Australia. Association for Computational Linguistics.

Huda Khayrallah and Philipp Koehn. 2018. On the impact of various types of noise on neural machine translation. In *Proceedings of the 2nd Workshop on Neural Machine Translation and Generation*, pages 74–83, Melbourne, Australia. Association for Computational Linguistics.

Hairong Liu, Mingbo Ma, Liang Huang, Hao Xiong, and Zhongjun He. 2018. Robust neural machine translation with joint textual and phonetic embedding. *CoRR*, abs/1810.06729.

Paul Michel and Graham Neubig. 2018. MTNT: A testbed for machine translation of noisy text. In *Proceedings of the 2018 Conference on Empirical Meth-

ods in Natural Language Processing, pages 543–553, Brussels, Belgium. Association for Computational Linguistics.

Martin Popel. 2018. CUNI transformer neural MT system for WMT18. In *Proceedings of the Third Conference on Machine Translation: Shared Task Papers*, pages 482–487, Belgium, Brussels. Association for Computational Linguistics.

Martin Popel and Ondřej Bojar. 2018. Training Tips for the Transformer Model. *The Prague Bulletin of Mathematical Linguistics*, 110:43–70.

Vaibhav, Sumeet Singh, Craig Stewart, and Graham Neubig. 2019. Improving robustness of machine translation with synthetic noise. *CoRR*, abs/1902.09508.

Ashish Vaswani, Samy Bengio, Eugene Brevdo, Francois Chollet, Aidan Gomez, Stephan Gouws, Llion Jones, Łukasz Kaiser, Nal Kalchbrenner, Niki Parmar, Ryan Sepassi, Noam Shazeer, and Jakob Uszkoreit. 2018. Tensor2Tensor for neural machine translation. In *Proceedings of the 13th Conference of the Association for Machine Translation in the Americas (Volume 1: Research Papers)*, pages 193–199, Boston, MA. Association for Machine Translation in the Americas.

Ashish Vaswani, Noam Shazeer, Niki Parmar, Jakob Uszkoreit, Llion Jones, Aidan N Gomez, Łukasz Kaiser, and Illia Polosukhin. 2017. Attention is all you need. In *Advances in Neural Information Processing Systems 30*, pages 6000–6010, Long Beach, CA, USA. Curran Associates, Inc.

NTT's Machine Translation Systems for WMT19 Robustness Task

Soichiro Murakami[1]*, **Makoto Morishita**[2]*, **Tsutomu Hirao**[2] and **Masaaki Nagata**[2]

[1] Service Innovation Department, NTT DOCOMO, INC., Japan

[2] NTT Communication Science Laboratories, NTT Corporation, Japan

`souichirou.murakami.cr@nttdocomo.com`
`{makoto.morishita.gr, tsutomu.hirao.kp,`
`masaaki.nagata.et}@hco.ntt.co.jp`

Abstract

This paper describes NTT's submission to the WMT19 robustness task. This task mainly focuses on translating noisy text (e.g., posts on Twitter), which presents different difficulties from typical translation tasks such as news. Our submission combined techniques including utilization of a synthetic corpus, domain adaptation, and a placeholder mechanism, which significantly improved over the previous baseline. Experimental results revealed the placeholder mechanism, which temporarily replaces the non-standard tokens including emojis and emoticons with special placeholder tokens during translation, improves translation accuracy even with noisy texts.

1 Introduction

This paper describes NTT's submission to the WMT 2019 robustness task (Li et al., 2019). This year, we participated in English-to-Japanese (En-Ja) and Japanese-to-English (Ja-En) translation tasks with a constrained setting, i.e., we used only the parallel and monolingual corpora provided by the organizers.

The task focuses on the robustness of Machine Translation (MT) to noisy text that can be found on social media (e.g., Reddit, Twitter). The task is more challenging than a typical machine translation task like the news translation tasks (Bojar et al., 2018) due to the characteristics of noisy text and the lack of a publicly available parallel corpus (Michel and Neubig, 2018). Table 1 shows example comments from Reddit, a discussion website. Text on social media usually contains various noise such as (1) abbreviations, (2) grammatical errors, (3) misspellings, (4) emojis, and (5) emoticons. In addition, most provided parallel corpora are not related to our target domain,

---

(1) I'll let you know <u>bro, thx</u>
(2) She had <u>a ton of</u> rings.
(3) oh my god it's <u>beatiful</u>
(4) Thank you so much for all your advice!!👿💕
(5) <u>(\＊´∀`＊)</u> so cute

Table 1: Example of comments from Reddit.

and the amount of in-domain parallel corpus is still limited as compared with parallel corpora used in the typical MT tasks (Bojar et al., 2018).

To tackle this *non-standard* text translation with a low-resource setting, we mainly use the following techniques. First, we incorporated a placeholder mechanism (Crego et al., 2016) to correctly copy special tokens such as emojis and emoticons that frequently appears in social media. Second, to cope with the problem of the low-resource corpus and to effectively use the monolingual corpus, we created a synthetic corpus from a target-side monolingual corpus with a target-to-source translation model. Lastly, we fine-tuned our translation model with the synthetic and in-domain parallel corpora for domain adaptation.

The paper is organized as follows. In Section 2, we present a detailed overview of our systems. Section 3 shows experimental settings and main results, and Section 4 provides an analysis of our systems. Finally, Section 5 draws a brief conclusion of our work for the WMT19 robustness task.

2 System Details

In this section, we describe the overview and features of our systems:

- Data preprocessing techniques for the provided parallel corpora (Section 2.2).

- Synthetic corpus, back-translated from the

---

*Equal contribution.

Proceedings of the Fourth Conference on Machine Translation (WMT), Volume 2: Shared Task Papers (Day 1) pages 544–551
Florence, Italy, August 1-2, 2019. ©2019 Association for Computational Linguistics

	# sentences	# words
MTNT (for En-Ja)	5,775	280,543
MTNT (for Ja-En)	6,506	128,103
KFTT	440,288	9,737,715
JESC	3,237,376	21,373,763
TED	223,108	3,877,868

Table 2: The number of training sentences and words on the English side contained in the provided parallel corpora.

	# sentences	# words
MTNT (Japanese)	32,042	943,208
MTNT (English)	81,631	3,992,200

Table 3: The number of training sentences and words contained in the provided monolingual corpus.

provided monolingual corpus, and noisy data filtering for its data. (Section 2.3).

- Placeholder mechanism to handle tokens that should be copied from a source-side sentence (Section 2.4).

2.1 NMT Model

Neural Machine Translation (NMT) has been making remarkable progress in the field of MT (Bahdanau et al., 2015; Luong et al., 2015). However, most existing MT systems still struggle with noisy text and easily make mistranslations (Belinkov and Bisk, 2018), though the Transformer has achieved the state-of-the-art performance in several MT tasks (Vaswani et al., 2017).

In our submission system, we use the Transformer model (Vaswani et al., 2017) without changing the neural network architecture as our base model to explore strategies to tackle the robustness problem. Specifically, we investigate how its noise-robustness against the noisy text can be boosted by introducing preprocessing techniques and a monolingual corpus in the experiments.

2.2 Data Preprocessing

For an in-domain corpus, the organizers provided the MTNT (Machine Translation of Noisy Text) parallel corpus (Michel and Neubig, 2018), which is a collection of Reddit discussions and their manual translations. They also provided relatively large out-of-domain parallel corpora, namely KFTT (Kyoto Free Translation Task) (Neubig, 2011), JESC (Japanese-English Subtitle Corpus) (Pryzant et al., 2017), and TED talks (Cettolo et al., 2012). Table 2 shows the number of sentences and words on the English side contained in the provided parallel corpora.

Yamamoto and Takahashi (2016) pointed out that the KFTT corpus contains some inconsistent translations. For example, Japanese era names are only contained in the Japanese side and not translated into English. We fixed these errors by the script provided by Yamamoto and Takahashi (2016)[1].

We use different preprocessing steps for each translation direction. This is because we need to submit tokenized output for En-Ja translation, thus it seems to be better to tokenize the Japanese side in the same way as the submission in the preprocessing steps, whereas we use a relatively simple method for Ja-En direction.

For Ja-En, we tokenized the raw text into subwords by simply applying `sentencepiece` with the vocabulary size of 32,000 for each language side (Kudo, 2018; Kudo and Richardson, 2018). For En-Ja, we tokenized the text by KyTea (Neubig et al., 2011) and the Moses tokenizer (Koehn et al., 2007) for Japanese and English, respectively. We also truecased the English words by the script provided with Moses toolkits[2]. Then we further tokenized the words into subwords using joint Byte-Pair-Encoding (BPE) with 16,000 merge operations[3] (Sennrich et al., 2016b).

2.3 Monolingual Data

In addition to both the in-domain and out-of-domain parallel corpora, the organizers provided a MTNT monolingual corpus, which consists of comments from the Reddit discussions. Table 3 shows the number of sentences and words contained in the provided monolingual corpus.

As NMT can be trained with only parallel data, utilizing a monolingual corpus for NMT is a key

---

[1] https://github.com/kanjirz50/mt_ialp2016/blob/master/script/ja_prepro.pl

[2] https://github.com/moses-smt/mosesdecoder/blob/master/scripts/recaser/truecase.perl

[3] Normally, Japanese and English do not share any words, thus using joint BPE does not seem effective. However, for this dataset, we found that Japanese sentences often include English words (e.g., named entities), so we use joint BPE even for this language pair.

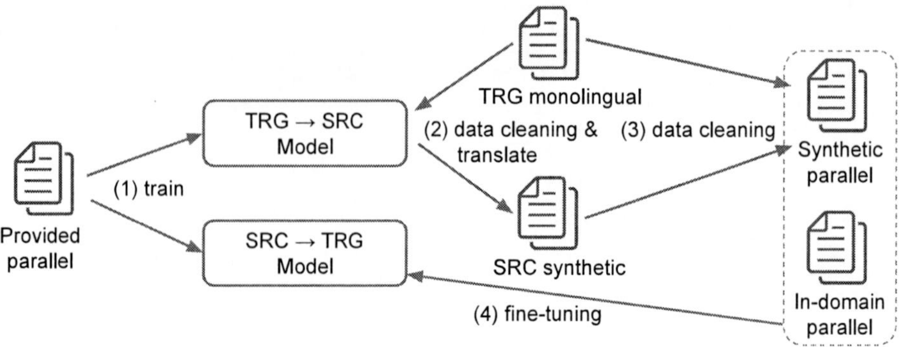

Figure 1: Overview of back-translation and fine-tuning.

challenge to improve translation quality for low-resource language pairs and domains. Sennrich et al. (2016a) showed that training with a synthetic corpus, which is generated by translating a monolingual corpus in the target language into the source language, effectively works as a method to use a monolingual corpus. Figure 1 illustrates an overview of the back-translation and fine-tuning processes we performed. (1) We first constructed both of source-to-target and target-to-source translation models with the provided parallel corpus. (2) Then, we created a synthetic parallel corpus through back-translation with the target-to-source translation model. (3) Next, we applied filtering techniques to the synthetic corpus to discard noisy synthetic sentences. (4) Finally, we fine-tuned the source-to-target model on both the synthetic corpus and in-domain parallel corpus.

Before the back-translation, we performed several data cleaning steps on the monolingual data to remove the sentences including ASCII arts and sentences that are too long or short. To investigate whether each sentence contains ASCII art or not, we use a word frequency-based method to detect ASCII arts. Since ASCII arts normally consist of limited types of symbols, the frequency of specific words in a sentence tends to be locally high if the sentence includes an ASCII art. Therefore, we calculate a standard deviation of word frequencies in each sentence of monolingual data to determine whether a sentence is like ASCII arts. More specifically, we first define a word frequency list $\mathbf{x_i}$ of the sentence i. For example, the word frequency list is denoted as $\mathbf{x}_i = [1, 1, 1, 1, 1]$ for the sentence i, *"That 's pretty cool ."* but as $\mathbf{x}_j = [1, 1, 1, 1, 3]$ for another sentence j, *"THIS IS MY LIFE ! ! !"*. Note that the length of the list $\mathbf{x}_i$ is equal to the vocabulary size of the sentence

i or j and each element of the list corresponds to the word frequency of a specific word. Second, we calculate the standard deviation σ_i of the word frequency list $\mathbf{x}_i$ for the sentence i. Finally, if σ_i is higher than a specific threshold, we assume that the sentence i contains an ASCII art and discard it from the monolingual data. We set the threshold to 6.0.

Moreover, since the provided monolingual data includes lines with more than one sentence, we first performed the sentence tokenization using the `spaCy`[4] toolkit. After that, we discarded the sentences that are either longer than 80 tokens or equal to 1 token.

Since a synthetic corpus might contain noisy sentence pairs, previous work shows that an additional filtering technique helps to improve accuracy (Morishita et al., 2018). We also apply a filtering technique to the synthetic corpus as illustrated in (3) in Figure 1. For this task, we use the `qe-clean`[5] toolkit, which filtered out the noisy sentences on the basis of a word alignment and language models by estimating how correctly translated and natural the sentences are (Denkowski et al., 2012). We train the word alignment and language models by using KFTT, TED, and MTNT corpora[6]. We use `fast_align` for word alignment and `KenLM` for language modeling (Dyer et al., 2013; Heafield, 2011).

2.4 Placeholder

Noisy text on social media often contains tokens that do not require translation such as emojis, "😄, 😎, 🖤", and emoticons, "m(_ _)m, (` · ω · ´),

---

[4]`https://spacy.io`
[5]`https://github.com/cmu-mtlab/qe-clean`
[6]Note that the JESC corpus is relatively noisy, thus we decided not to use it for cleaning.

$\backslash(\char`^o\char`^)/$". However, to preserve the meaning of the input sentence that contains emojis or emoticons, such tokens need to be output to the target language side. Therefore, we simply copy the emojis and emoticons from a source language to a target language with a placeholder mechanism (Crego et al., 2016), which aims at alleviating the rare-word problem in NMT. Both the source- and target-side sentences containing either emojis or emoticons need to be processed for the placeholder mechanism. Specifically, we use a special token "<PH>" as a placeholder and replace the emojis and emoticons in the sentences with the special tokens.

To leverage the placeholder mechanism, we need to recognize which tokens are corresponding to emojis or emoticons in advance. Emojis can easily be detected on the basis of Unicode Emoji Charts[7]. We detect emoticons included in both the source- and the target-side sentences with the `nagisa`[8] toolkit, which is a Japanese morphological analyzer that can also be used as an emoticon detector for Japanese and English text.

Moreover, we also replace ">" tokens at the beginning of the sentence with the placeholders because ">" is commonly used as a quotation mark in social media posts and emails and does not require translation.

2.5 Fine-tuning

Since almost all the provided corpora are not related to our target domain, it is natural to adapt the model by fine-tuning with the in-domain corpora. Whereas we use both the MTNT and synthetic corpora for Ja-En, we only use the MTNT corpus for En-Ja because the preliminary experiment shows that synthetic corpus does not help to improve accuracy for the En-Ja direction. We suspect this is due to the synthetic corpus not having sufficient quality to improve the model.

3 Experiments

3.1 Experimental Settings

We used the Transformer model with six blocks. Our model hyper-parameters are based on *transformer_base* settings, where the word embedding dimensions, hidden state dimensions, feedforward dimensions and number of heads are 512, 512, 2048, and 8, respectively. The model shares

the parameter of the encoder/decoder word embedding layers and the decoder output layer by three-way-weight-tying (Press and Wolf, 2017). Each layer is connected with a dropout probability of 0.3 (Srivastava et al., 2014). For an optimizer, we used Adam (Kingma and Ba, 2015) with a learning rate of 0.001, $\beta_1 = 0.9$, $\beta_2 = 0.98$. We use a root-square decay learning rate schedule with a linear warmup of 4000 steps (Vaswani et al., 2017). We applied mixed precision training that makes use of GPUs more efficiently for faster training (Micikevicius et al., 2018). Each mini-batch contains about 8000 tokens (subwords), and we accumulated the gradients of 128 mini-batches for an update (Ott et al., 2018). We trained the model for 20,000 iterations, saved the model parameters each 200 iterations, and took an average of the last eight models[9]. Training took about 1.5 days to converge with four NVIDIA V100 GPUs. We compute case-sensitive BLEU scores (Papineni et al., 2002) for evaluating translation quality[10]. All our implementations are based on the `fairseq`[11] toolkit (Ott et al., 2019).

After training the model with the whole provided parallel corpora, we fine-tuned it with in-domain data. During fine-tuning, we used almost the same settings as the initial training setup except we changed the model save interval to every three iterations and continued the learning rate decay schedule. For fine-tuning, we trained the model for 50 iterations, which took less than 10 minutes with four GPUs.

When decoding, we used a beam search with the size of six and a length normalization technique with $\alpha = 2.0$ and $\beta = 0.0$ (Wu et al., 2016). For the submission, we used an ensemble of three (En-Ja) or four (Ja-En) independently trained models[12].

3.2 Experimental Results

Table 4 shows the case-sensitive BLEU scores of provided blind test sets. Replacing the emoticons

---

[7]`https://unicode.org/emoji/charts`
[8]`https://github.com/taishi-i/nagisa`

[9]The number of iterations might seem to be too low. However, Ott et al. (2018) showed that we could train the model with a small number of iterations if we use a large mini-batching. We also confirmed the model had already converged with this number of iterations.

[10]We report the scores calculated automatically on the organizer's website `http://matrix.statmt.org/`.

[11]`https://github.com/pytorch/fairseq`

[12]Originally, we planned to submit an ensemble of four for both directions. However, we could train only three models for En-Ja in time. In this paper, we also report the score of ensembles of four for reference.

	Ja-En		En-Ja	
Baseline model	10.8		14.3	
+ placeholders	12.2	(+1.4)	15.0	(+0.7)
+ fine-tuning	11.9	(+1.1)	16.2	(+1.9)
+ synthetic	14.0	(+3.2)	—	
+ 4-model ensemble	14.9	(+4.1)	17.0	(+2.7)
Submission	14.8		17.0	

Table 4: Case-sensitive BLEU scores of provided blind test sets. The numbers in the brackets show the improvements from the baseline model.

	Improved	Degraded	Unchanged
Ja-En	9 (53%)	0 (0%)	8 (47%)
En-Ja	14 (82%)	1 (6%)	2 (12%)

Table 5: The number of improved/degraded sentences by applying the placeholder mechanism compared with the baseline model. We manually evaluated all sentences containing placeholders in terms of whether the emojis and emoticons are correctly copied to the output.

and emojis with the placeholders achieves a small gain over the baseline model, which was trained with the provided raw corpora. Also, additional fine-tuning with in-domain and synthetic corpora also leads to a substantial gain for both directions. For Ja-En, although we failed to improve the accuracy by fine-tuning the MTNT corpus only, we found that the fine-tuning on both the in-domain and synthetic corpora achieves a substantial gain. We suspect this is due to overfitting, and modifying the number of iterations might alleviate this problem. As described in Section 2.5, we did not use the synthetic corpus for the En-Ja direction. For the submission, we decoded using an ensemble of independently trained models, which boosts the scores.

4 Analysis

4.1 Effect of Placeholders

To investigate the effectiveness of using the placeholder mechanism, we compared the translation of the baseline to the model trained with the placeholders. We manually evaluated how correctly the emojis and emoticons were copied to the output. Table 5 shows the numbers of sentences on the MTNT test set that are improved/degraded by applying the placeholder mechanism. These result demonstrate that the placeholder mechanism could improve the translation of the noisy text, which frequently includes emojis and emoticons, almost without degradation.

Tables 6 and 7 show examples of translations in the Ja-En and En-Ja tasks, respectively. Both the emoji (😎) and the ">" token, which represents a quotation mark, were properly copied from the source text to the translation of *+placeholders*, whereas the baseline model did not output such tokens as shown in Tables 6 and 7. Thus, we can consider this to be the reason the placeholders contribute to improving case-sensitive BLEU scores over the baseline.

In our preliminary experiments, although we tried a method to introduce the placeholder technique to our systems at the fine-tuning phase, we found that it does not work properly with only the fine-tuning. This means that an NMT needs to be trained with the corpus pre-processed for the placeholder mechanism before the fine-tuning.

4.2 Effect of Fine-tuning

According to the comparison between *+fine-tuning* and *baseline* shown in Table 4, fine-tuning on the in-domain and synthetic corpus achieved a substantial gain in both directions. Accordingly, we can see that the sentence translated by *+fine-tuning* has a more informal style than those translated by *baseline* and *+placeholders* as presented in Tables 6 and 7.

4.3 Difficulties in Translating Social Media Texts

Challenges still remain to improving the model's robustness against social media texts such as Reddit comments. As we pointed out in Section 1, various abbreviations are often used. For example, the term, "東スポWeb" (literally *East Spo Web*) in

Input	Woah woah, hang on a minute, let's hear this guy out. Amazing title 😀
Reference	おいおい、ちょっと待てよ。こいつの言うことを聞いてみようぜ。凄いタイトルだ😀
Baseline	うわぁ ちょっと 待って こいつ の 話 を 聞いて みましょう 驚く ような 名前 だった わ ね (Well wait a minute let's listen to this story It was an amazing name)
+ placeholders	ちょっと 待って ください この 人 の 話 を 聞いて みましょう 素晴らしい タイトル だ😀 (Wait a minute, let's hear the story of this person It's a great title 😀.)
+ fine-tuning	うわー 、 うわー 、 ちょっと 待って 、 この 男 の 話 を 聞こうぜ 。 すごい タイトル だ😀 (Wow, wow, wait a minute and hear this guy talk. It's an amazing title 😀.)

Table 6: Translation results on the English-to-Japanese development set. English sentences corresponding to the Japanese translations are also given.

Input	>男同士で物言えない奴のただの逆恨み
Reference	>Just misguided resentment from some fellow who can't speak amongst other men.
Baseline	A mere grudge against a man who can't say anything.
+ placeholders	> It's just a grudge against guys who can't say anything between men.
+ fine-tuning	>it's just inverted resentment for guys who can't say anything between men.

Table 7: Translation results on the Japanese-to-English test set.

the MTNT dataset should be translated to *"Tokyo Sports Website"* according to its reference, but our model incorrectly translated it to *"East Spoweb"*. Such abbreviations that cannot be translated correctly without prior knowledge, such as "東スポWeb stands for 東京スポーツWebサイト (literally *Tokyo Sports Website*)", are commonly used on social media.

4.4 Use of Contextual Information

Some sentences need contextual information for them to be precisely translated. The MTNT corpus provides comment IDs as the contextual information to group sentences from the same original comment. We did not use the contextual information in our systems, but we consider that it would help to improve translation quality as in previous work (Tiedemann and Scherrer, 2017; Bawden et al., 2018). For example, in the following two sentences, *"Airborne school isn't a hard school."* and *"Get in there with some confidence!"*, which can be found in the MTNT corpus and have the same comment ID, we consider that leveraging their contextual information would help to clarify what *"there"* means in the latter and to translate it more accurately.

5 Conclusion

In this paper, we presented NTT's submission to the WMT 2019 robustness task. We participated in the Ja-En and En-Ja translation tasks with constrained settings. Through experiments, we showed that we can improve translation accuracy by introducing the placeholder mechanism, performing fine-tuning on both in-domain and synthetic corpora, and using ensemble models of Transformers. Moreover, our analysis indicated that the placeholder mechanism contributes to improving translation quality.

In future work, we will explore ways to use monolingual data more effectively, introduce contextual information, and deal with a variety of noisy tokens such as abbreviations, ASCII-arts, and grammar errors.

Acknowledgments

We thank two anonymous reviewers for their careful reading and insightful comments and suggestions.

References

Dzmitry Bahdanau, Kyunghyun Cho, and Yoshua Bengio. 2015. Neural machine translation by jointly learning to align and translate. In Proceedings of the 3rd International Conference on Learning Representations (ICLR).

Rachel Bawden, Rico Sennrich, Alexandra Birch, and Barry Haddow. 2018. Evaluating discourse phenomena in neural machine translation. In Proceedings of the 2018 Conference of the North American Chapter of the Association for Computational Linguistics: Human Language Technologies (NAACL HLT), pages 1304–1313.

Yonatan Belinkov and Yonatan Bisk. 2018. Synthetic and natural noise both break neural machine translation. In Proceedings of the 6th International Conference on Learning Representations (ICLR).

Ondřej Bojar, Christian Federmann, Mark Fishel, Yvette Graham, Barry Haddow, Matthias Huck, Philipp Koehn, and Christof Monz. 2018. Findings of the 2018 conference on machine translation (WMT18). In Proceedings of the 3rd Conference on Machine Translation (WMT), pages 272–303.

Mauro Cettolo, Christian Girardi, and Marcello Federico. 2012. WIT3: web inventory of transcribed and translated talks. In Proceedings of the 16th Annual Conference of the European Association for Machine Translation (EAMT), pages 261–268.

Josep Crego, Jungi Kim, Guillaume Klein, Anabel Rebollo, Kathy Yang, Jean Senellart, Egor Akhanov, Patrice Brunelle, Aurelien Coquard, Yongchao Deng, Satoshi Enoue, Chiyo Geiss, Joshua Johanson, Ardas Khalsa, Raoum Khiari, Byeongil Ko, Catherine Kobus, Jean Lorieux, Leidiana Martins, Dang-Chuan Nguyen, Alexandra Priori, Thomas Riccardi, Natalia Segal, Christophe Servan, Cyril Tiquet, Bo Wang, Jin Yang, Dakun Zhang, Jing Zhou, and Peter Zoldan. 2016. Systran's pure neural machine translation systems. arXiv preprint arXiv:1610.05540.

Michael Denkowski, Greg Hanneman, and Alon Lavie. 2012. The cmu-avenue french-english translation system. In Proceedings of the 7th Workshop on Statistical Machine Translation (WMT), pages 261–266.

Chris Dyer, Victor Chahuneau, and Noah A. Smith. 2013. A simple, fast, and effective reparameterization of IBM model 2. In Proceedings of the 2013 Conference of the North American Chapter of the Association for Computational Linguistics: Human Language Technologies (NAACL HLT), pages 644–648.

Kenneth Heafield. 2011. KenLM: Faster and smaller language model queries. In Proceedings of the 6th Workshop on Statistical Machine Translation (WMT), pages 187–197.

Diederik Kingma and Jimmy Ba. 2015. Adam: A method for stochastic optimization. In Proceedings of the 3rd International Conference on Learning Representations (ICLR).

Philipp Koehn, Hieu Hoang, Alexandra Birch, Chris Callison-Burch, Marcello Federico, Nicola Bertoldi, Brooke Cowan, Wade Shen, Christine Moran, Richard Zens, Chris Dyer, Ondrej Bojar, Alexandra Constantin, and Evan Herbst. 2007. Moses: Open source toolkit for statistical machine translation. In Proceedings of the 45th Annual Meeting of the Association for Computational Linguistics (ACL), pages 177–180.

Taku Kudo. 2018. Subword regularization: Improving neural network translation models with multiple subword candidates. In Proceedings of the 56th Annual Meeting of the Association for Computational Linguistics (ACL), pages 66–75.

Taku Kudo and John Richardson. 2018. SentencePiece: A simple and language independent subword tokenizer and detokenizer for neural text processing. In Proceedings of the Conference on Empirical Methods in Natural Language Processing (EMNLP), pages 66–71.

Xian Li, Paul Michel, Antonios Anastasopoulos, Yonatan Belinkov, Nadir K. Durrani, Orhan Firat, Philipp Koehn, Graham Neubig, Juan M. Pino, and Hassan Sajjad. 2019. Findings of the first shared task on machine translation robustness. In Proceedings of the 4th Conference on Machine Translation (WMT).

Minh-Thang Luong, Hieu Pham, and Christopher D. Manning. 2015. Effective approaches to attention-based neural machine translation. In Proceedings of the Conference on Empirical Methods in Natural Language Processing (EMNLP), pages 1412–1421.

Paul Michel and Graham Neubig. 2018. MTNT: A testbed for machine translation of noisy text. In Proceedings of the Conference on Empirical Methods in Natural Language Processing (EMNLP), pages 543–553.

Paulius Micikevicius, Sharan Narang, Jonah Alben, Gregory F. Diamos, Erich Elsen, David García, Boris Ginsburg, Michael Houston, Oleksii Kuchaiev, Ganesh Venkatesh, and Hao Wu. 2018. Mixed precision training. In Proceedings of the 6th International Conference on Learning Representations (ICLR).

Makoto Morishita, Jun Suzuki, and Masaaki Nagata. 2018. NTT's neural machine translation systems for WMT 2018. In Proceedings of the 3rd Conference on Machine Translation (WMT), pages 461–466.

Graham Neubig. 2011. The Kyoto free translation task. http://www.phontron.com/kftt.

Graham Neubig, Yosuke Nakata, and Shinsuke Mori. 2011. Pointwise prediction for robust, adaptable Japanese morphological analysis. In Proceedings of the 49th Annual Meeting of the Association for Computational Linguistics (ACL), pages 529–533.

Myle Ott, Sergey Edunov, Alexei Baevski, Angela Fan, Sam Gross, Nathan Ng, David Grangier, and Michael Auli. 2019. fairseq: A fast, extensible toolkit for sequence modeling. In Proceedings of the 2019 Conference of the North American Chapter of the Association for Computational Linguistics: Human Language Technologies (NAACL HLT), pages 48–53.

Myle Ott, Sergey Edunov, David Grangier, and Michael Auli. 2018. Scaling neural machine translation. In Proceedings of the 3rd Conference on Machine Translation (WMT), pages 1–9.

Kishore Papineni, Salim Roukos, Todd Ward, and Wei-Jing Zhu. 2002. BLEU: a method for automatic evaluation of machine translation. In Proceedings of the 40th Annual Meeting of the Association for Computational Linguistics (ACL), pages 311–318.

Ofir Press and Lior Wolf. 2017. Using the output embedding to improve language models. In Proceedings of the 15th European Chapter of the Association for Computational Linguistics (EACL), pages 157–163.

R. Pryzant, Y. Chung, D. Jurafsky, and D. Britz. 2017. JESC: Japanese-English Subtitle Corpus. arXiv preprint arXiv:1710.10639.

Rico Sennrich, Barry Haddow, and Alexandra Birch. 2016a. Improving neural machine translation models with monolingual data. In Proceedings of the 54th Annual Meeting of the Association for Computational Linguistics (ACL), pages 86–96.

Rico Sennrich, Barry Haddow, and Alexandra Birch. 2016b. Neural machine translation of rare words with subword units. In Proceedings of the 54th Annual Meeting of the Association for Computational Linguistics (ACL), pages 1715–1725.

Nitish Srivastava, Geoffrey Hinton, Alex Krizhevsky, Ilya Sutskever, and Ruslan Salakhutdinov. 2014. Dropout: A simple way to prevent neural networks from overfitting. Journal of Machine Learning Research, 15:1929–1958.

Jörg Tiedemann and Yves Scherrer. 2017. Neural machine translation with extended context. In Proceedings of the 3rd Workshop on Discourse in Machine Translation, pages 82–92.

Ashish Vaswani, Noam Shazeer, Niki Parmar, Jakob Uszkoreit, Llion Jones, Aidan N. Gomez, Lukasz Kaiser, and Illia Polosukhin. 2017. Attention is all you need. In Proceedings of the 31st Annual Conference on Neural Information Processing Systems (NIPS), pages 6000–6010.

Yonghui Wu, Mike Schuster, Zhifeng Chen, Quoc V. Le, Mohammad Norouzi, Wolfgang Macherey, Maxim Krikun, Yuan Cao, Qin Gao, Klaus Macherey, Jeff Klingner, Apurva Shah, Melvin Johnson, Xiaobing Liu, Łukasz Kaiser, Stephan Gouws, Yoshikiyo Kato, Taku Kudo, Hideto Kazawa, Keith Stevens, George Kurian, Nishant Patil, Wei Wang, Cliff Young, Jason Smith, Jason Riesa, Alex Rudnick, Oriol Vinyals, Greg Corrado, Macduff Hughes, and Jeffrey Dean. 2016. Google's neural machine translation system: Bridging the gap between human and machine translation. arXiv preprint arXiv:1609.08144.

Kazuhide Yamamoto and Kanji Takahashi. 2016. Japanese orthographical normalization does not work for statistical machine translation. In Proceedings of the 20th International Conference on Asian Language Processing (IALP), pages 133–136.

JHU 2019 Robustness Task System Description

Matt Post and **Kevin Duh**
Johns Hopkins University
Baltimore, Maryland
USA

Abstract

We describe the JHU submissions to the French–English, Japanese–English, and English–Japanese Robustness Task at WMT 2019. Our goal was to evaluate the performance of baseline systems on both the official noisy test set as well as news data, in order to ensure that performance gains in the latter did not come at the expense of general-domain performance. To this end, we built straightforward 6-layer Transformer models and experimented with a handful of variables including subword processing (FR–EN) and a handful of hyperparameters settings (JA↔EN). As expected, our systems performed reasonably.

1 Introduction

The team at JHU submitted three systems to the WMT19 Robustness task: French–English, Japanese–English, and English–Japanese. Our goal was to evaluate the performance of reasonable state-of-the-art systems against both the robustness test set as well as more standard "general domain" test sets. We believe this is an important component of evaluating for actual robustness. In this way, we ensure that performance gains on robustness data are not purchased at the expense of this general-domain performance. Our systems used no monolingual data and relatively straightforward state-of-the-art techniques, and produced systems of roughly average performance.

2 French-English Systems

2.1 Training Data

We constrained our data use to the officially supplied data, comprising the WMT15 English–French parallel data (Bojar et al., 2015). For French, we experimented with three data settings:

- all of Europarl and News Commentary;

- the best million lines each of CommonCrawl, Gigaword, and the UN corpus; and

- the MTNT training data.

Data sizes are indicated in Table 1.

dataset	segments	words
Europarl	2.0m	50.2m
News Commentary	200k	4.4m
Common Crawl	820k	17.4m
FR–EN Gigaword	1m	26.1m
UN Doc	106k	1.1m
$\text{MTNT}_{EN \to FR}$	36k	841k
$\text{MTNT}_{FR \to EN}$	19k	634k

Table 1: Training datasets for French–English systems. Common Crawl, Gigaword, and the UN data are post-filtering.

To filter the data, we applied dual cross-entropy filtering (Junczys-Dowmunt, 2018). We trained two smaller 4-layer Transformer models, one each for EN–FR and FR–EN, and used them to score the data according to the formula:

$$\exp(-(|s_1 - s_2| + 0.5 * (s_1 + s_2)))$$

where s_1 is the score (a negative logprob) from the forward FR–EN model and s_2 the score from the reverse EN–FR model. We then uniqued this data, sorted by score, and took a random sample of one million lines from the set of all sentence pairs with a score greater than 0.1.[1] For all but FR–EN Gigaword, what remained was well less than a million lines. We did this both because prior work has indicated the utility of filtering, and to make our

---

[1] We determined this threshold by eyeballing where in the ranked list the garbage started to thin out.

Proceedings of the Fourth Conference on Machine Translation (WMT), Volume 2: Shared Task Papers (Day 1) pages 552–558
Florence, Italy, August 1-2, 2019. ©2019 Association for Computational Linguistics

training data sizes more manageable. We therefore did not compare against a model trained on all of the filtered data.

We experimented with two preprocessing regimes. In the first, we applied standard preprocessing techniques from the Moses pipeline[2] (Koehn et al., 2007), followed by subword splitting with BPE (Sennrich et al., 2016) using 32k merge operations. In the second scenario, we did not use any data preparation, instead applying `sentencepiece` (Kudo and Richardson, 2018) with subword regularization (Kudo, 2018) directly to the raw text. In this latter setting, we varied the size of the learned subword models, experimenting with 8k, 16k, 24k, and 32k.

2.2 Models

We used Sockeye (Hieber et al., 2017), a sequence to sequence transduction framework written in Python and based on MXNet. Our models were variations of the Transformer architecture (Vaswani et al., 2017), mostly using default settings supplied with Sockeye: an embedding and model size of 512, a feed-forward layer size of 2048, 8 attention heads, and three-way tied embeddings. We used batch sizes of 4,096 words, checkpointed every 5,000 updates, and stopped training with the best-perplexity checkpoint when validation perplexity had failed to improve for 10 consecutive checkpoints. The initial learning rate was set to 0.0002, the Sockeye default.

2.3 Scoring

At test time, we decoded with beam search using a beam of size 12.

We scored with sacreBLEU (Post, 2018), with international tokenization.[3] In the spirit of the robustness task, we measure BLEU not just on the reddit dataset, but also on the WMT15 newstest dataset, in order to examine how experimental variables vary in both in- and out-of-domain settings. We believe that testing both in- and out-of-domain data is essential to measuring robustness.

2.4 Results & Discussion

Table 2 contains BLEU scores.

---

[2]Calling `normalize-punctuation.perl`, `remove-non-printing-char.perl`, and `tokenizer.perl` with flags `-no-escape`.

[3]BLEU+case.mixed+refs.1+smooth.exp+tok.intl+v1.2.20

	WMT15	MTNT18
4 layers (BPE)	31.6	27.9
6 layers (BPE)	32.7	27.9
+ MTNT	32.6	32.9
+ filter	36.4	33.7
+ both	37.2	39.9
sp_{24k} + filter	36.5	34.5
sp_{24k} + both	37.2	40.0

Table 2: French–English translation results.

size	WMT15		MTNT18	
	filter	both	filter	both
8k	36.0	36.5	33.9	38.7
16k	36.2	36.9	33.9	39.7
24k	36.5	37.2	34.5	40.0

Table 3: BLEU scores with the sentencepiece models and no other preprocessing.

Observation 1 *Improvements are to be had both from more data and from better (in-domain) data.* Adding the large filtered dataset to the 6 layer model improved BLEU more (27.9 → 33.7, +5.8) than adding the MTNT training data (27.9 → 32.9, +5), but the gains from both were even greater (+12).

Observation 2 In order to ensure that our models did not increase accuracy on the MTNT data at the expense of in-domain data, we report scores on both WMT and MTNT test sets. In only one situation was there a problem: For the 6-layer Transformer, adding the MTNT data alone (without the large amount of filtered bitext) helped on $MTNT_18$ (+5) but caused a small drop on WMT15 (-0.1).

Observation 3 In all situations, the sentencepiece model (with no other preprocessing) was just as good as the BPE model (with the Moses preprocessing pipeline). In one situation (adding the filtered data alone), it caused a gain of 0.8 over its BPE counterpart.

We further conducted a small experiment varying the sentencepiece model size (Table 3). Larger sentencepiece models were consistently better in this relatively large-data setting.

Our score on the official MTNT2019 blind test set was 40.2.

3 Japanese-English Systems

3.1 Training Data

We trained systems using only the bitext data allowed in the shared task constrained setting:

- The in-domain Reddit dataset–MTNT version 1.1 (Michel and Neubig, 2018)[4]– consists of approximately 6k segments for training (which we label Train-MTNT) and 900 segments for validation (Valid-MTNT) in both JA→EN and EN→JA language directions. Additionally we use the included "test set" (which we label Test18-MTNT) for internal BLEU benchmarks prior to submitting results for the official 2019 blindtest. We did not use the monolingual part of MTNT.

- The out-of-domain data consists of KFTT (Wikipedia articles), TED Talks, and JESC Subtitles.[5] We concatenate these out-of-domain training data with Train-MTNT to create Train-ALL; similarly we concatenate the out-of-domain validation data with Valid-MTNT to create Valid-ALL.

Dataset sizes are shown in Table 4.

JA→EN dataset	segments	words
Train-ALL	3.9m	42.7m
Train-MTNT	6506	155k
Valid-ALL	5416	88k
Valid-MTNT	965	23k
Test18-MTNT	1001	13k

EN→JA dataset	segments	words
Train-ALL	3.9m	42.9m
Train-MTNT	5775	333k
Valid-ALL	5405	111k
Valid-MTNT	954	46k
Test18-MTNT	1002	13k

Table 4: Datasets for English–Japanese systems. Word counts are source side only.

For preprocessing on the English side, we apply the standard Moses pipeline in the same fashion as the French–English system. For preprocessing on the Japanese side, we first performed word segmentation by Kytea (Neubig et al., 2011)[6], then ran the English Moses preprocessing pipeline to handle potential code-switched English/Japanese in the data. Finally, we induced BPE subword units with 10k, 30k, and 50k merge operations, independently for each side on the bitexts (JA→EN Train-ALL and EN→JA Train-ALL). Unlike the French-English systems, the Japanese-English systems do not use shared BPE and embeddings.

3.2 Models

We use the Sockeye Transformer models for both JA→EN and EN→JA directions, similar to our French-English systems. The hyperparameter settings are different, however. We performed random search in the following hyperparameter space (see Table 5):

- Initial learning rate (**LR**) for the ADAM optimizer: 0.001, 0.0003, 0.0006

- Number of attention heads (**head**): 8, 16

- Number of layers (**layer**): 2, 4

- Feed-forward layer size (**ffsize**): 1024, 2048

- Embedding and model size (**embedding**): 256, 518, 1024

The training process follows a continued-training procedure (c.f. Koehn et al. (2018); Khayrallah et al. (2018)): In Stage 1, we train systems from scratch on Train-ALL, and perform early stopping on Valid-ALL. This represents a mixed corpus with both in-domain and out-of-domain bitexts. For all models, we used batch sizes of 4,096 words, checkpointed every 2,000 updates, and stopped training with the best-perplexity checkpoint when validation perplexity on Valid-ALL had failed to improve for 16 consecutive checkpoints.

In Stage 2, we fine-tuned the above systems by training on Train-MTNT, and perform early stopping on Valid-MTNT. Effectively, we initialize a new model with Stage 1 model weights, reset the optimizer's learning rate schedule, and train on only in-domain data. To prevent overfitting to the small Train-MTNT bitext, we now checkpoint

---

[4] http://www.cs.cmu.edu/~pmichel1/mtnt/

[5] The data is also downloaded in pre-packaged form from the MTNT website via https://github.com/pmichel31415/mtnt/releases/download/v1.1/clean-data-en-ja.tar.gz, but do not confuse these with the MTNT data, which is in the Reddit domain.

[6] v0.4.7: http://www.phontron.com/kytea/

more frequently, saving a checkpoint after every 50 updates, and stopped training either when the perplexity on Valid-MTNT fails to improve for 16 consecutive checkpoints or when we reached 30 checkpoints (i.e., $30 \times 50 = 1500$ updates of 4,096 word batches), to prevent fitting excessively on the Train-MTNT bitext.

3.3 Scoring

At test time, we decoded with beam search using a beam of size 5. We scored with sacreBLEU (Post, 2018), with international tokenization.[7] Per organizer suggestion, we applied Kytea to Japanese output prior to scoring. We measure BLEU on both VALID-ALL and Test18-MTNT in order to compare the results on mixed and in-domain corpora.

3.4 Results & Discussion

The BLEU results for Stage 1 models are shown in Table 5. We performed random search in hyperparameter space, training approximately 40 models in each language-pair. The table is sorted by Test18-MTNT BLEU score and shows the top 5 models in terms of BLEU (id=a,b,c,d,e; id=z,y,x,w,v) as well as another 5 randomly selected model (id=e,f,g,h,i,j; id=u,t,s,r,q).

Observation 1: Despite the relatively narrow range of hyperparameter settings, there is a comparatively large range of BLEU scores in the table. For example in JA→EN, the best Test18-MTNT BLEU is 11.1, 2.7 points better than the worst BLEU (8.4) in the table; there are other poorer performing systems, not sampled for the table. This suggests that hyperparameter search is important in practice, even for relatively standard hyperparameters.

Additionally, we note it is difficult to make posthoc recommendations on the "best" hyperparameter settings, as there are no clear trends in the data. For example, from the top 5 JA→EN models, it appears that 30k BPE merge operations is good, but there is an competitive outlier with 10k BPE (id=c). In the results (not all shown in the table), most 10k BPE models achieve Test18-MTNT BLEU in the 8-10 range, so it is difficult to explain the strong BLEU score of id=c. Also, it does appear that layer=4 is consistently better than layer=2 in the JA→EN results, but the results are more mixed in the EN→JA direction.

Observation 2: There is some correlation between the BLEU scores of Valid-ALL and Test18-MTNT; the system rankings are relatively similar. But we note that there are a few outliers, e.g. the top 5 models in EN→JA perform similarly on Test18-MTNT, but there are noticeable degradations for id=x and id=v on Valid-ALL. Similarly, id=b and id=c perform close on Test18-MTNT but not on Valid-ALL. With the goal of robustness, we think these kinds of BLEU gaps due to domain differences deserve more investigation.

Continued Training: Next, we perform continued training on the top 5 models. The results on Test18-MTNT are shown in Table 6. We observe consistent BLEU gains in these Stage 2 models, close to 2 or 3 points across all systems. This re-affirms the surprising effectiveness of a simple procedure such as continued training; but we should also note that preliminary efforts on English-French did not yield similar gains.

Note that we do not measure Valid-ALL in this case since we now expect the models to be optimized specifically for MTNT; it is likely Valid-ALL scores will degrade due to catastrophic forgetting (Thompson et al., 2019).

Final Submission: In the final official submission, we performed an 4-ensemble of the Stage 2 Continued Training models of id=a,b,d,e for JA→EN and id=z,y,w,v for EN→JA. Note that the ensemble method in Sockeye currently assumes the same vocabulary, so BPE needs to be the same for all models in the ensemble. This is a reasonable assumption, but in the spirit of subword regularization (Kudo, 2018), we think it may be interesting to explore whether ensembles of systems with diverse BPE will lead to more robust outputs.

For JA→EN, the ensemble achieved 14.6 BLEU on Test18-MTNT (N-gram precisions: 43.9/19.3/10.1/5.5, Brevity Penalty: 0.991, Length ratio: 0.991). The official MTNT2019 blindtest cased-BLEU is 11.4.

For EN→JA, the ensemble achieved 15.0 BLEU on Test18-MTNT (N-gram precisions: 45.2/19.2/10.3/5.7, Brevity Penalty: 1.0, Length ratio: 1.122). The official MTNT2019 blindtest case-BLEU is 14.8.

4 Conclusion

We constructed reasonably-scoring systems on three language pairs without too much effort. Our

---

[7]BLEU+case.mixed+refs.1+smooth.exp+tok.intl+v1.2.14

id	JA→EN Systems Hyperparameter Setting						BLEU (EN output)	
	BPE	**LR**	**head**	**layer**	**ffsize**	**embed**	**Valid-ALL**	**Test18-MTNT**
a	30k	0.0003	8	4	2048	512	17.1	11.1
b	30k	0.0006	16	4	2048	512	16.5	10.7
c	10k	0.0006	16	4	2048	512	15.7	10.5
d	30k	0.0006	16	4	2048	256	16.4	10.1
e	30k	0.0003	8	4	1024	256	16.0	10.0
f	50k	0.0003	8	4	1024	512	16.4	10.0
g	30k	0.0006	8	2	2048	512	15.9	9.9
h	50k	0.0006	8	2	1024	256	14.4	9.1
i	10k	0.0006	8	2	2048	256	14.0	8.6
j	30k	0.0006	16	2	1024	1024	13.9	8.4

id	EN→JA Systems Hyperparameter Setting						BLEU (JA output)	
	BPE	**LR**	**head**	**layer**	**ffsize**	**embed**	**Valid-ALL**	**Test18-MTNT**
z	50k	0.0006	8	4	2048	256	17.0	12.7
y	50k	0.0003	16	4	2048	512	17.5	12.7
x	30k	0.0003	8	2	2048	512	16.6	12.6
w	50k	0.0006	16	4	2048	512	17.1	12.5
v	50k	0.001	8	4	2048	512	16.5	12.5
u	10k	0.0003	8	4	1024	512	16.4	12.3
t	30k	0.001	16	4	1024	256	16.0	12.1
s	50k	0.001	8	4	1024	256	15.8	12.1
r	10k	0.0006	16	2	1024	512	15.3	11.9
q	10k	0.0006	8	2	1024	256	14.5	10.6

Table 5: JA→EN and EN→JA Results for Stage 1 models. For each language pair, we show the top 5 models (according to Test18-MTNT) and another random selection of 5 models from randomized hyperparameter search.

id	Stage 1	Stage 2	Improvement
JA→EN			
a	11.1	13.4	+2.3
b	10.7	13.4	+2.7
c	10.5	13.1	+2.6
d	10.1	13.1	+3.0
e	10.0	13.2	+3.2
EN→JA			
z	12.7	14.5	+1.8
y	12.7	14.4	+1.7
x	12.6	14.5	+1.9
w	12.5	14.4	+1.9
v	12.5	14.3	+1.8

Table 6: Continued Training BLEU results on Test18-MTNT. Stage 1 results are from Table 5. Continued Training (Stage 2) consistently improves BLEU.

scores fell into roughly the middle tier among those reported on `matrix.statmt.org`. It is certain that much higher gains could be had by adding even known techniques to our pipeline, such as backtranslating monolingual data (Sennrich et al., 2016).

We also believe that our approach of evaluating on multiple test sets is essential to the robustness task. Without this, the task reduces to domain adaptation, and one has no assurance that high scores on the out-of-domain data do not come at the expense of general-domain performance.

References

Ondřej Bojar, Rajen Chatterjee, Christian Federmann, Barry Haddow, Matthias Huck, Chris Hokamp, Philipp Koehn, Varvara Logacheva, Christof Monz, Matteo Negri, Matt Post, Carolina Scarton, Lucia Specia, and Marco Turchi. 2015. Findings of the 2015 workshop on statistical machine translation. In *Proceedings of the Tenth Workshop on Statistical Machine Translation*, pages 1–46, Lisbon, Portugal. Association for Computational Linguistics.

Felix Hieber, Tobias Domhan, Michael Denkowski, David Vilar, Artem Sokolov, Ann Clifton, and Matt Post. 2017. Sockeye: A toolkit for neural machine translation. *CoRR*, abs/1712.05690.

Marcin Junczys-Dowmunt. 2018. Dual conditional cross-entropy filtering of noisy parallel corpora. In *Proceedings of the Third Conference on Machine Translation: Shared Task Papers*, pages 888–895, Belgium, Brussels. Association for Computational Linguistics.

Huda Khayrallah, Brian Thompson, Kevin Duh, and Philipp Koehn. 2018. Regularized training objective for continued training for domain adaptation in neural machine translation. In *Proceedings of the 2nd Workshop on Neural Machine Translation and Generation*, pages 36–44. Association for Computational Linguistics.

Philipp Koehn, Kevin Duh, and Brian Thompson. 2018. The jhu machine translation systems for wmt 2018. In *Proceedings of the Third Conference on Machine Translation, Volume 2: Shared Task Papers*, pages 442–448, Belgium, Brussels. Association for Computational Linguistics.

Philipp Koehn, Hieu Hoang, Alexandra Birch, Chris Callison-Burch, Marcello Federico, Nicola Bertoldi, Brooke Cowan, Wade Shen, Christine Moran, Richard Zens, Chris Dyer, Ondrej Bojar, Alexandra Constantin, and Evan Herbst. 2007. Moses: Open source toolkit for statistical machine translation. In *Proceedings of the 45th Annual Meeting of the Association for Computational Linguistics Companion Volume Proceedings of the Demo and Poster Sessions*, pages 177–180, Prague, Czech Republic. Association for Computational Linguistics.

Taku Kudo. 2018. Subword regularization: Improving neural network translation models with multiple subword candidates. In *Proceedings of the 56th Annual Meeting of the Association for Computational Linguistics (Volume 1: Long Papers)*, pages 66–75, Melbourne, Australia. Association for Computational Linguistics.

Taku Kudo and John Richardson. 2018. SentencePiece: A simple and language independent subword tokenizer and detokenizer for neural text processing. In *Proceedings of the 2018 Conference on Empirical Methods in Natural Language Processing: System Demonstrations*, pages 66–71, Brussels, Belgium. Association for Computational Linguistics.

Paul Michel and Graham Neubig. 2018. MTNT: A testbed for machine translation of noisy text. In *Proceedings of the 2018 Conference on Empirical Methods in Natural Language Processing*, pages 543–553, Brussels, Belgium. Association for Computational Linguistics.

Graham Neubig, Yosuke Nakata, and Shinsuke Mori. 2011. Pointwise prediction for robust, adaptable Japanese morphological analysis. In *Proceedings of the 49th Annual Meeting of the Association for Computational Linguistics: Human Language Technologies*, pages 529–533, Portland, Oregon, USA. Association for Computational Linguistics.

Matt Post. 2018. A call for clarity in reporting BLEU scores. In *Proceedings of the Third Conference on Machine Translation: Research Papers*, pages 186–191, Belgium, Brussels. Association for Computational Linguistics.

Rico Sennrich, Barry Haddow, and Alexandra Birch. 2016. Neural machine translation of rare words with subword units. In *Proceedings of the 54th Annual Meeting of the Association for Computational Linguistics (Volume 1: Long Papers)*, pages 1715–1725, Berlin, Germany. Association for Computational Linguistics.

Brian Thompson, Huda Khayrallah Jeremy Gwinnup, Kevin Duh, and Philipp Koehn. 2019. Overcoming catastrophic forgetting during domain adaptation of neural machine translation. In *Proceedings of the 2019 Conference of the North American Chapter of the Association for Computational Linguistics: Human Language Technologies, Volume 2 (Short Papers)*. Association for Computational Linguistics.

Ashish Vaswani, Noam Shazeer, Niki Parmar, Jakob Uszkoreit, Llion Jones, Aidan N Gomez, Ł ukasz Kaiser, and Illia Polosukhin. 2017. Attention is all you need. In I. Guyon, U. V. Luxburg, S. Bengio, H. Wallach, R. Fergus, S. Vishwanathan, and R. Garnett, editors, *Advances in Neural Information Processing Systems 30*, pages 5998–6008. Curran Associates, Inc.

Robust Machine Translation with Domain Sensitive Pseudo-Sources:
Baidu-OSU WMT19 MT Robustness Shared Task System Report

Renjie Zheng [*‡]   **Hairong Liu** [*†]   **Mingbo Ma** [†]   **Baigong Zheng** [†]   **Liang Huang** [†,‡]

[†]Baidu Research, Sunnyvale, CA
[‡]School of EECS, Oregon State University, Corvallis, OR
`{zrenjll, lhrbss, cosmmb, zbgzbg2007, liang.huang.sh}@gmail.com`

Abstract

This paper describes the machine translation system developed jointly by Baidu Research and Oregon State University for WMT 2019 Machine Translation Robustness Shared Task. Translation of social media is a very challenging problem, since its style is very different from normal parallel corpora (e.g. News) and also include various types of noises. To make it worse, the amount of social media parallel corpora is extremely limited. In this paper, we use a domain sensitive training method which leverages a large amount of parallel data from popular domains together with a little amount of parallel data from social media. Furthermore, we generate a parallel dataset with pseudo noisy source sentences which are back-translated from monolingual data using a model trained by a similar domain sensitive way. We achieve more than 10 BLEU improvement in both En-Fr and Fr-En translation compared with the baseline methods.

1 Introduction

Translation of social media is very challenging. First, there are various types of noises, such as abbreviations, spelling errors, obfuscated profanities, inconsistent capitalization, Internet slang and emojis (Michel and Neubig, 2018). Second, the amount of parallel data is limited. These characteristics of social media make existing neural machine translation systems extremely vulnerable.

The noise issue of social media has been investigated in some previous work (Baldwin et al., 2013; Eisenstein, 2013). Most recently, Belinkov and Bisk (2017) demonstrated the vulnerability of neural machine translation system to both synthetic and natural noises. However, the noises tested in (Belinkov and Bisk, 2017) are not real noises in social media. To our best knowledge, there seems

to be a lack of translation methods systematically targeting noises in social media.

Existing neural machine translation systems are famous for their hungry of data. However, the amount of parallel data in social media domain is very limited. Just recently, a dataset collected from Reddit has been published and attracted a lot of attention (Michel and Neubig, 2018). The amount of data in this dataset is still very small, compared to the large amount of data from News domain. Naturally, how to utilize the large amount of parallel data from the News domain become a central problem in improving the translation of social meida.

In this paper, inspired by the success of back-translation technique (Sennrich et al., 2015a), we propose to learn a model to generate "social-media-style" translation in source language from clean sentences in target language. Since the amount of parallel data in social media domain is limited, we utilize the large amount of parallel data in News domain to help the training. With this model, large mount of parallel data for back-translation can be generated from monolingual data in target language. In the final translation model, a special "domain" symbol is added to indicate which domain the source sentence belonging to.

The contributions of this paper are multifold, and some important ones are highlighted below:

1. We found that "social-media-style" sentences can be generated by training a translation model with different "start-of-sentence" symbols for sentences in different domains in the decoder side. The model is trained with data from all domains, especially News domain, which has a large amount of parallel data, but also adapted to the style in the domain of social media, even the amount of

* Equal contribution

Proceedings of the Fourth Conference on Machine Translation (WMT), Volume 2: Shared Task Papers (Day 1) pages 559–564
Florence, Italy, August 1-2, 2019. ©2019 Association for Computational Linguistics

parallel data in social media is limited. As demonstrated by our experiments, generating "social-media-style" sentences is crucial in the effectiveness of back-translation for training a translation model suitable for translating social media.

2. We illustrated that adding a domain symbol in source sentence improves the robustness of the model. This may be because the encoder learns some domain-specific features from input sentences.

2 Methods

Noisy text translation is short of in-domain training data. In this section, we present approaches to leverage a large amount of out-of-domain (e.g. News) dataset and monolingual data paired with pseudo noisy source data from back-translation.

2.1 Domain Sensitive Data Mixing

To improve the translation model from limited parallel data, we want to make the use of larger amount of out-of-domain data. However, simply mixing the clean and noisy data will make the whole training set unbalanced. To differentiate the data from different domain, we use different start symbol in source side.

The intuition of injecting domain label in source side is based on the noise occurrence statistics from (Michel and Neubig, 2018), which shows much more spelling and grammar errors in the source side of noisy text translation dataset. Thus the clean and noisy start symbols work as a meaningful sign of source text style for encoder. Compared with the source side sentences, the human translation of target side sentences are less noisier with less spelling and grammar errors.

2.2 Noisy Pseudo-Sources Generation with Back-Translation

To further make the use of monolingual data, we regard them as target data and generate it's corresponding source data by back-translation (Sennrich et al., 2015a). However, different from Sennrich et al. (2015a) who uses this method in both clean source and target sentences, the source side sentences in our test set is much noisier than target side (as mentioned in previous subsection). Therefore, we reverse the source and target sentences where the noisy source sentences becomes target and cleaner target sentences becomes source. For

example, to generate noisy pseudo French source sentences for English monolingual data, we train a En-Fr translation model which takes the noisy French source sentences in Fr-En noisy dataset as target, and the corresponding paralleled English target sentences as source. In this way, the model will learned how to inject noise into the target side. Similar to previous domain sensitive method, we include out-of-domain clean data during the training of this noisy translation model and differentiate them by different start symbol int target side.

2.3 Ensemble

In our experiments with relatively small training dataset, the translation qualities of models with different initializations can vary notably. To make the performance much more stable and improve the translation quality, we ensemble different models during decoding to achieve better translation.

To ensemble, we take the average of all model outputs:

$$\hat{y}_t = \sum_{i=1}^{N} \frac{\hat{y}_t^i}{N} \tag{1}$$

where $\hat{y}_t^i$ denotes the output distribution of ith model at position t. Similar to Zhou et al. (2017) and Zheng et al. (2018c), we can ensemble models trained with different architectures and training algorithms.

3 Experiments

To investigate the empirical performances of our proposed methods, we conduct experiments on MTNT dataset (Michel and Neubig, 2018) using Transformer (Vaswani et al., 2017).

We first apply BPE (Sennrich et al., 2015b) on both sides in order to reduce the vocabulary for both source and target sides. We then exclude the sentences pairs whose length are longer than 256 words or subwords. We use length reward (Huang et al., 2017) to find the optimal target length.

Our implementation is adapted from PyTorch-based OpenNMT (Klein et al., 2017). Our Transformer's parameters are as the same as the base model's parameter settings in the original paper (Vaswani et al., 2017).

In all experiments, our evaluation uses sacre-BLEU [1], a standardized BLEU score evaluation

---

[1] https://github.com/mjpost/sacreBLEU

	Training	Validation	Test
Clean	2,207,962	-	-
Monolingual	26,485	-	-
Noisy	36,058	852	1,020

Table 1: Statistics of En2Fr Dataset. Monolingual data is French only.

	Training	Validation	Test
Clean	2,207,962	-	-
Monolingual	2,244,020	-	-
Noisy	19,161	886	1,022

Table 2: Statistics of Fr2En Dataset, Monolingual data is English only.

	En2Fr	Fr2En
Domain Insensitive	31.3	34.6
Domain Sensitive	35.7	39.5

Table 3: Results of noisy data generation. We reverse the source and target direction of MTNT Fr2En (En2Fr) dev-set to evaluate the ability of noisy data generation for En2Fr (Fr2En).

tool by Post (2018). We specify the `intl` tokenization option during BLEU evaluation. We also uses detokenization and normalization tools in Moses.

Table 1 and 2 show statistics of En2Fr and Fr2En datasets. For both En-Fr and Fr-En dataset, the clean parallel data is from WMT15 news translation task. The noisy data is from (Michel and Neubig, 2018) collected from social network. Except the French and English monolingual data from WMT15 news translation task, we also make the use of English portion of parallel data from KFTT, TED and JESC used in (Michel and Neubig, 2018).

3.1 Noisy Data Generation

To make use of monolingual target data, we want to generate the corresponding parallel pseudo noisy source data and put them into training set. Table 3 shows the performance of our noisy data generation models. In this experiment, we mix the clean and noisy dataset as the training set, but use the target sentences in reversed direction of noisy dataset (training, validation, test) set as source and source sentences as target. The domain insensitive method simply mix the clean and noisy dataset in training while the domain sensitive method differentiate the clean and noisy dataset in target side by

starting with different symbol (e.g. < `clean_s` >, < `noisy_s` >). The experiment shows that the domain sensitive method can outperform the domain insensitive method with a large margin.

3.2 Methods Comparison

Table 4 shows the final results of different methods on test set. Similar with the previous experiments, the domain insensitive methods simply mix all the clean, noisy training data. The performance has a little improvement in En-Fr by adding the monolingual data paired with the pseudo source data generated by the model trained in previous experiments. To differentiate the clean and noisy dataset, we assign different label at the start of them and the performance is thus boosted about 3 to 4 BLEU score. We further generate pseudo noisy source data from the monolingual target with the model using the domain sensitive method in previous experiment. By adding these noisy back-translation data, we achieve more than 2 BLEU improvement. Our final submission ensembles 5 models trained with the domain sensitive method and including the noisy back translation data.

3.3 Final Results

Table 5 and Table 6 show the final results of our submission in Fr-En and En-Fr. Our system ranks third in both directions. Table 7 shows the human judgments over all submitted systems which are done by Li et al. (2019) who also analyze and discuss all submitted systems.

4 Related Work

The method proposed in this paper is a kind of domain adaptation technique. There are many previous work on domain adaptation for machine translation (Britz et al., 2017; Wang et al., 2017; Chu et al., 2017; Chu and Wang, 2018), which leverages out-of-domain parallel corpora and in-domain monolingual corpora to improve translation. The difference between our method and previous work lies in that we use back-translation (Sennrich et al., 2015a) for domain adaptation. Different from some previous work using adversarial training (Liu et al., 2017) or different attention (Zheng et al., 2018a) to differentiate multiple tasks, we simply assign different starting symbol for multiple tasks (Lample et al., 2018).

A similar method was proposed in (Xie et al.,

	Methods	En-Fr	Fr-En
Baseline	MTNT †	21.8	23.3
	+ tuning †	29.7	30.3
Domain Insensitive	Mix training	33.4	34.5
	+ Back translation	33.7	34.3
Domain Sensitive	Mix training	36.3	38.7
	+ Noisy back translation	38.4	41.0
	+ Ensemble	40.4	42.3

Table 4: Results of different methods on test-set. †(Michel and Neubig, 2018)

	BLEU	BLEU-cased	BEER	CharacTER
NLE	48.8	47.9	0.676	0.364
CUNI	45.8	44.8	0.654	0.395
BD-OSU*	44.5	43.6	0.641	0.499
JHU	41.2	40.2	0.624	-
CMU	32.8	32.2	0.573	0.514
FOKUS†	30.8	29.9	0.530	0.574
MTNT	26.2	25.6	0.529	0.550
IITP-MT	25.5	20.8	0.499	0.594

Table 5: Semi-blind test results of Fr-En. *Our submission. †Unconstrained.

	BLEU	BLEU-cased	BEER	CharacTER
NLE	42.0	41.4	0.626	0.446
CUNI	39.1	38.5	0.605	0.483
BD-OSU*	37.0	36.4	0.599	0.512
FOKUS†	24.8	24.2	0.515	0.619
MTNT	22.5	22.1	0.498	0.621
CMU	20.8	20.4	0.488	0.622
IITP-MT	20.7	19.2	0.492	0.619
SFU	19.4	19.1	0.491	0.614

Table 6: Semi-blind test results of En-Fr. *Our submission. †Unconstrained.

	En-Fr	En-Fr	Fr-En	Fr-En
	Score	Rank	BLEU	Rank
BD-OSU*	71.5	2	80.6	3
CMU	-	-	58.2	6
CUNI	66.3	3	82.0	2
JHU	-	-	76.3	4
NaverLabs	75.5	1	85.3	1
FOKUS†	52.5	4	62.6	5

Table 7: Human judgments over all submitted systems (the higher the better) *Our submission. †Unconstrained.

2018) in the context of grammar correction, where a model is trained to add noises on original sentences to produce noisy sentences. However, instead of learn how to generate arbitrary "noises", our goal is to learn "social-media-style" translations. Singh et al. (2019) injects artificial noise in the clean data according to the distribution of noisy data. Liu et al. (2019a) propose to leverage phonetic information to reduce the noises in data.

Another group of work related to this paper is data augmentation in machine translation. Although data augmentation is very popular in general learning tasks, such as image processing, it is non-trivial to do so in machine translation because even slight modifications of sentences can make huge difference in semantics. To our best knowledge, there are two categories of successful data augmentation approaches for machine translation. The first one is based on back-translation ((Sennrich et al., 2015a)) which augments monolingual data into training set. The second one is based on word replacement, such as (Sennrich et al., 2016) and (Wang et al., 2018). Zheng et al. (2018b) make the use of multiple references and generates even more pseudo-references and achieve improvement in both machine translation and image captioning.

5   Conclusions and Future Work

In this paper, we proposed a method to improve the translation of social media. The style of social media is very unique, and is very different from the style of widely researched News sentences. The core part of our method is to generate useful parallel data for back-translation, that is, generating synthetic in-domain parallel data. To achieve this goal, we proposed a method to generate "social-media-style" source sentences from monolingual target sentences. We also distinguish the domain of source sentences by inserting a domain symbol into source sentences. Both techniques are proven to be extremely useful in the scenario of translating social media. Finally, we utilized the ensemble to further boosts the translation performance.

The noises in social media are mostly introduced by human mistakes. There are some other cases that noises in source side are introduced by systems, such as ASR in speech-to-text translation (Liu et al., 2019b). We plan to further investigate this domain sensitive method on these tasks, even on speech-to-text simultaneous translation (Ma et al., 2018; Zheng et al., 2019).

References

Timothy Baldwin, Paul Cook, Marco Lui, Andrew MacKinlay, and Li Wang. 2013. How noisy social media text, how diffrnt social media sources? In *Proceedings of the Sixth International Joint Conference on Natural Language Processing*, pages 356–364.

Yonatan Belinkov and Yonatan Bisk. 2017. Synthetic and natural noise both break neural machine translation. *arXiv preprint arXiv:1711.02173*.

Denny Britz, Quoc Le, and Reid Pryzant. 2017. Effective domain mixing for neural machine translation. In *Proceedings of the Second Conference on Machine Translation*, pages 118–126.

Chenhui Chu, Raj Dabre, and Sadao Kurohashi. 2017. An empirical comparison of simple domain adaptation methods for neural machine translation. *arXiv preprint arXiv:1701.03214*.

Chenhui Chu and Rui Wang. 2018. A survey of domain adaptation for neural machine translation. *arXiv preprint arXiv:1806.00258*.

Jacob Eisenstein. 2013. What to do about bad language on the internet. In *Proceedings of the 2013 conference of the North American Chapter of the association for computational linguistics: Human language technologies*, pages 359–369.

Liang Huang, Kai Zhao, and Mingbo Ma. 2017. When to finish? optimal beam search for neural text generation (modulo beam size). In *Proceedings of the 2017 Conference on Empirical Methods in Natural Language Processing*, pages 2134–2139.

G. Klein, Y. Kim, Y. Deng, J. Senellart, and A. M. Rush. 2017. OpenNMT: Open-Source Toolkit for Neural Machine Translation. *ArXiv e-prints*.

Guillaume Lample, Myle Ott, Alexis Conneau, Ludovic Denoyer, et al. 2018. Phrase-based & neural unsupervised machine translation. In *Proceedings of the 2018 Conference on Empirical Methods in Natural Language Processing*, pages 5039–5049.

Xian Li, Paul Michel, Antonios Anastasopoulos, Yonatan Belinkov, Nadir K. Durrani, Orhan Firat, Philipp Koehn, Graham Neubig, Juan M. Pino, and Hassan Sajjad. 2019. Findings of the first shared task on machine translation robustness. In *Proceedings of the Fourth Conference on Machine Translation, Volume 2: Shared Task Papers*, Florence, Italy. Association for Computational Linguistics.

Hairong Liu, Mingbo Ma, Liang Huang, Hao Xiong, and Zhongjun He. 2019a. Robust neural machine translation with joint textual and phonetic embedding. *ACL*.

Pengfei Liu, Xipeng Qiu, and Xuanjing Huang. 2017. Adversarial multi-task learning for text classification. In *Proceedings of the 55th Annual Meeting of the Association for Computational Linguistics (Volume 1: Long Papers)*, pages 1–10.

Yuchen Liu, Hao Xiong, Zhongjun He, Jiajun Zhang, Hua Wu, Haifeng Wang, and Chengqing Zong. 2019b. End-to-end speech translation with knowledge distillation. *arXiv preprint arXiv:1904.08075*.

Mingbo Ma, Liang Huang, Hao Xiong, Renjie Zheng, Kaibo Liu, Baigong Zheng, Chuanqiang Zhang, Zhongjun He, Hairong Liu, Xing Li, Hua Wu, and Haifeng Wang. 2018. Stacl: Simultaneous translation with integrated anticipation and controllable latency. *ACL*.

Paul Michel and Graham Neubig. 2018. Mtnt: A testbed for machine translation of noisy text. *arXiv preprint arXiv:1809.00388.*

Matt Post. 2018. A call for clarity in reporting bleu scores. *arXiv preprint arXiv:1804.08771.*

Rico Sennrich, Barry Haddow, and Alexandra Birch. 2015a. Improving neural machine translation models with monolingual data. *arXiv preprint arXiv:1511.06709.*

Rico Sennrich, Barry Haddow, and Alexandra Birch. 2015b. Neural machine translation of rare words with subword units. *arXiv preprint arXiv:1508.07909.*

Rico Sennrich, Barry Haddow, and Alexandra Birch. 2016. Edinburgh neural machine translation systems for wmt 16. *arXiv preprint arXiv:1606.02891.*

Sumeet Singh, Craig Stewart, Graham Neubig, et al. 2019. Improving robustness of machine translation with synthetic noise. *arXiv preprint arXiv:1902.09508.*

Ashish Vaswani, Noam Shazeer, Niki Parmar, Jakob Uszkoreit, Llion Jones, Aidan N Gomez, Łukasz Kaiser, and Illia Polosukhin. 2017. Attention is all you need. In *Advances in Neural Information Processing Systems 30.*

Rui Wang, Masao Utiyama, Lemao Liu, Kehai Chen, and Eiichiro Sumita. 2017. Instance weighting for neural machine translation domain adaptation. In *Proceedings of the 2017 Conference on Empirical Methods in Natural Language Processing*, pages 1482–1488.

Xinyi Wang, Hieu Pham, Zihang Dai, and Graham Neubig. 2018. Switchout: an efficient data augmentation algorithm for neural machine translation. *arXiv preprint arXiv:1808.07512.*

Ziang Xie, Guillaume Genthial, Stanley Xie, Andrew Ng, and Dan Jurafsky. 2018. Noising and denoising natural language: Diverse backtranslation for grammar correction. In *Proceedings of the 2018 Conference of the North American Chapter of the Association for Computational Linguistics: Human Language Technologies, Volume 1 (Long Papers)*, pages 619–628.

Baigong Zheng, Renjie Zheng, Mingbo Ma, and Liang Huang. 2019. Simultaneous translation with flexible policy via restricted imitation learning. *ACL.*

Renjie Zheng, Junkun Chen, and Xipeng Qiu. 2018a. Same representation, different attentions: shareable sentence representation learning from multiple tasks. In *Proceedings of the 27th International Joint Conference on Artificial Intelligence*, pages 4616–4622. AAAI Press.

Renjie Zheng, Mingbo Ma, and Liang Huang. 2018b. Multi-reference training with pseudo-references for neural translation and text generation. In *Proceedings of the 2018 Conference on Empirical Methods in Natural Language Processing*, pages 3188–3197.

Renjie Zheng, Yilin Yang, Mingbo Ma, and Liang Huang. 2018c. Ensemble sequence level training for multimodal mt: Osu-baidu wmt18 multimodal machine translation system report. In *Proceedings of the Third Conference on Machine Translation: Shared Task Papers*, pages 632–636.

Long Zhou, Wenpeng Hu, Jiajun Zhang, and Chengqing Zong. 2017. Neural system combination for machine translation. In *Proceedings of the 55th Annual Meeting of the Association for Computational Linguistics (Volume 2: Short Papers)*, volume 2, pages 378–384.

Improving Robustness of Neural Machine Translation
with Multi-task Learning

Shuyan Zhou, Xiangkai Zeng, Yingqi Zhou
Antonios Anastasopoulos, Graham Neubig

Language Technologies Institute, School of Computer Science
Carnegie Mellon University
{shuyanzh,xiangkaz,yingqiz,aanastas,gneubig}@cs.cmu.edu

Abstract

While neural machine translation (NMT) achieves remarkable performance on clean, in-domain text, performance is known to degrade drastically when facing text which is full of typos, grammatical errors and other varieties of noise. In this work, we propose a multi-task learning algorithm for transformer-based MT systems that is more resilient to this noise. We describe our submission to the WMT 2019 Robustness shared task (Li et al., 2019) based on this method. Our model achieves a BLEU score of 32.8 on the shared task French to English dataset, which is 7.1 BLEU points higher than the baseline vanilla transformer trained with clean text[1].

1 Introduction

Real world data, especially in the realm of social media, often contains noise such as mis-spellings, grammar errors, or lexical variations. Even though humans do not have much difficulty in recognizing and translating noisy or ungrammatical sentences, neural machine translation (NMT; Bahdanau et al. (2015); Vaswani et al. (2017)) systems are known to degrade drastically when confronted with noisy data (Belinkov and Bisk, 2017; Khayrallah and Koehn, 2018; Anastasopoulos et al., 2019). Thus, there is increasing need to build robust NMT systems that are resilient to naturally occurring noise.

In this work, we attempt to enhance the robustness of the NMT system through multi-task learning. Our model is a transformer-based model (Vaswani et al., 2017) augmented with two decoders, with each decoder bound to different learning objectives. It has a cascade architecture (Niehues et al., 2016; Anastasopoulos and Chiang, 2018) where the first decoder reads in the output of the encoder and the second decoder reads in the

output of both encoder and the first decoder. The objective of the first decoder, namely the denoising decoder, is to recover from the noisy sentence and generate the corresponding clean sentence. Given both the noisy and clean sentence, the objective of the second decoder, namely the translation decoder, is to correctly translate the sentence to the target language. This framework should be beneficial in two ways: 1) Since the model is trained with noisy text, it should inherently better generalize to noisy text. 2) The translation decoder could potentially take advantage of the recovered clean sentence while maintaining specific varieties of noise (e.g. emoji) by referring to the original noisy sentence. This framework requires triplets of clean and noisy source sentences, along with target translations, so we also follow Vaibhav et al. (2019) and design a back-translation strategy that synthesizes noisy data.

Our proposed model outperforms the baseline vanilla transformer trained with clean text by 4.6 BLEU points on the WMT 2019 Robustness shared task (Li et al., 2019) French to English dataset. The fine-tuning process brings an additional 2.5 points improvement. According to our analysis, however, the improvements can mainly be attributed to introducing noisy data during training rather than the multi-task learning objective.

2 Multi-task Transformer

In this section, we describe in detail the architecture of our proposed multi-task transformer. It is a transformer-based (Vaswani et al., 2017) cascade multi-task framework (Niehues et al., 2016; Anastasopoulos and Chiang, 2018).

2.1 Detailed Architecture

As illustrated in Figure 1, the model consists of one transformer encoder and two transformer de-

---

[1]The code is available at https://github.com/shuyanzhou/multitask_transformer

565

Proceedings of the Fourth Conference on Machine Translation (WMT), Volume 2: Shared Task Papers (Day 1) pages 565–571
Florence, Italy, August 1-2, 2019. ©2019 Association for Computational Linguistics

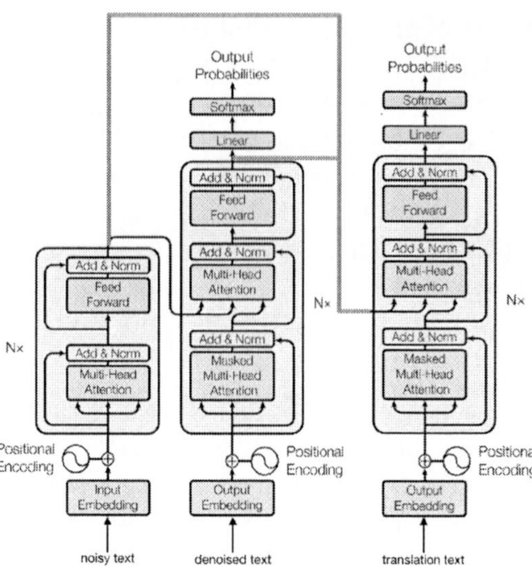

Figure 1: Multitask transformer architecture. Bold grey lines represent parts we add on top of the vanilla transformer.

coders. The dataset consists of triplets: $\mathbf{T} = \{\mathbf{t}_n, \mathbf{t}_c, \mathbf{t}_t\}$ where $\mathbf{t}_n$ is the noisy source sentence, $\mathbf{t}_c$ is the clean source sentence and $\mathbf{t}_t$ is the target translation. Each $\mathbf{t}$ consists of a sequence of words $[w_1, w_2, ..., w_l]$, where l is the length of the corresponding text. By looking up the word and position embedding lookup tables, each $\mathbf{t}$ is converted to a representation matrix $\mathbf{x} = \{e_1, e_2, ..., e_l\}$ and thus result in $\mathbf{X} = \{\mathbf{x}_n, \mathbf{x}_c, \mathbf{x}_t\}$.

The encoder reads in noisy text $\mathbf{x}_n$ and generates the encoded representation $\mathbf{M}_n$. The layers of the first decoder (denoising decoder) first attends to $\mathbf{x}_c$ (self-attention) and then attends to $\mathbf{M}_n$ from the encoder. After N layers, this decoder generates another representation $\mathbf{M}_c$ which represents the clean rather than the noisy source text. Now, the layers of the second decoder (translation decoder) first perform self-attention as usual, and then attend to both $\mathbf{M}_n$ and $\mathbf{M}_c$ simultaneously. After repeating this process N times, the translation decoder generates $\mathbf{M}_t$ which is then passed on to a position-wise feed-forward network followed by a softmax layer. The output of the model is a probability matrix $P \in \mathbb{R}^{l \times V}$, where V is the vocabulary size and l is the length of translated sentence.

As the description above, the denoising decoder is exactly the same as the decoder of the vanilla transformer. The only difference is that for the translation decoder each layer needs to attend to

both encoder outputs $\mathbf{M}_n$ and denoising decoder outputs $\mathbf{M}_c$ after self-attention. Therefore, the translation decoder receives two contexts, namely from the encoder attention $\mathbf{A}_n$ and the denoising decoder attention $\mathbf{A}_c$. In our model, we design the final attention context as the linear transformation of the concatenation of these two attention states:

$$\mathbf{A}_t = \mathbf{W}[\mathbf{A}_n; \mathbf{A}_c] + \mathbf{b}$$

Where $\mathbf{W} \in \mathbb{R}^{d \times 2d}$ and $\mathbf{b} \in \mathbb{R}^d$.

Following Tu et al. (2017); Anastasopoulos and Chiang (2018), the first objective is to maximize the log likelihood of the clean text $\mathbf{t}_c$ and the second objective is to maximize that of the translated text $\mathbf{t}_t$. The importance of these two objectives are controlled by a hyper-parameter λ:

$$\mathcal{L}(\theta) = \lambda \log P(\mathbf{t}_c | \mathbf{t}_n; \theta) + \qquad (1)$$
$$(1 - \lambda) \log P(\mathbf{t}_t | \mathbf{t}_n, \mathbf{t}_c; \theta)$$

2.2 Two Phase Beam Search

Following Anastasopoulos and Chiang (2018), we use two separate beam search processes to decode the final translation. Let N_{beam} be the size of the beam-search. The process is outlined here for clarity. Given a sentence $\mathbf{t}_n$, the denoising decoder produces a N_{beam} outputs, each consisting of a denoised hypothesis $\hat{\mathbf{t}}_c$, the probability of the hypothesis $P(\hat{\mathbf{t}}_c | \mathbf{x}_n; \theta)$, and corresponding hidden state matrix $\hat{\mathbf{M}}_c$. For each hypothesis from this first decoder, the second decoder also produces N_{beam} tuples, each including a translation hypothesis $\hat{\mathbf{t}}_t$ and its probability $P(\hat{\mathbf{t}}_t | \mathbf{t}_n, \hat{\mathbf{t}}_c; \theta)$. At the end of the second phase, we will have $N_{\text{beam}} \times N_{\text{beam}}$ translation hypotheses. We rank these hypothesis by their scores defined in Equation 1.

3 Training Triple Generation

As mentioned in Section 2, the desired training data for our multi-task transformer is a collection of triples $\mathbf{T} = \{\mathbf{t}_n, \mathbf{t}_c, \mathbf{t}_t\}$. However, datasets of this kind are very rare; the available amounts of data are less than enough to train such a model with enormous number of parameters. Inspired by Vaibhav et al. (2019), we instead use a back-translation strategy to synthesize these triples. Our proposed strategy is flexible and it could be used as long as we have at least one element of the $\mathbf{T}$ triple.

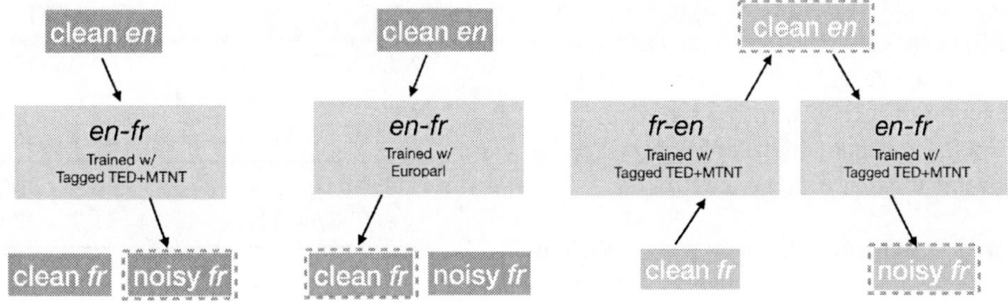

Figure 2: Training data synthesis. Blocks rounded by dash rectangle are synthetic while others are real.

Depending on which part of triple is available, we select the proper NMT model and synthesize the missing ones. In Figure 2, we show 3 ways that we did this in this work. Note that because we focus on the translation from French to English where the French text mostly consists of MTNT-style noise (Michel and Neubig, 2018), we specify the source language as `fr`, the target language as `en` and the noise style as `MTNT`; however, our approach could be used for all other language pairs with different noise distributions.

Clean fr & Clean en: This is the most common parallel corpus that could be obtained from many existing resources. The only missing text is the noisy French text. In this case, we synthesize the noisy text with the help of the NMT model trained with both TED and MTNT training data. During training, we add a tag showing the source of this pair at the beginning of each English sentence (Kobus et al., 2017; Vaibhav et al., 2019). By adding this tag, the model could potentially better distinguish TED data and MTNT data. To generate the noisy French text, we add an MTNT tag at the beginning of each sentence and feed them to this NMT model. Ideally, besides the inherent noise as a result of imperfect translations, the translated French sentences could also possess a similar noise distribution as MTNT.

Noisy fr & Clean en: This kind of parallel text can be found in the MTNT training data. Note that even though the manually translated English sentences contain some level of "noise" (e.g. emoji), we treat them as clean English text. In this scenario, we leverage a pre-trained NMT system provided by fairseq (Ott et al., 2019) to translate English sentences back to French. Considering its good performance over other benchmarks (e.g. WMT newstest datasets) we assume that the trans-

lated French sentences are of high quality and thus treat them as clean French text.

Clean fr: To make our back-translation strategy more generalized to settings where the above parallel data is not enough to train the model, we also design a pipeline to utilize monolingual data which is likely to be available most of the time. In this case, we first translate these sentences to English and then translate them back to French. Both NMT models are trained with TED and MTNT data as we describe above. Similarly, in both directions, we add the MTNT tag in the beginning of the sentences. Note that alternatively one could use an off-the-shelf NMT model to generate clean English text.[2]

4 Experiments

In this section, we first describe in detail our data pre-processing scheme, as well as the choice of hyperparameters. Then we compare our system with the baseline model (a vanilla transformer trained on clean French and clean English parallel data). Finally, we carry out a case study by comparing the output of our model with the baseline model.

4.1 Data Pre-processing

Because of time limitations, we did not use all three kinds of training triples. We only used the first two triples introduced in Section 3.

Clean fr & Clean en: The clean data consists of europarl-v7[3] and news-commentary-v10 copora.[4] We filter out sentences whose length is greater

---

[2] We did not attempt this due to time restrictions.
[3] http://www.statmt.org/europarl/v7/fr-en.tgz
[4] http://www.statmt.org/wmt15/training-parallel-nc-v10.tgz

than 50. We apply a pretrained Byte Pair Encoding (BPE, Gage (1994)) model with 16k subword units to both source and target sentences. The process of synthesizing noisy French sentences is described in the corresponding paragraph of Section 3. We denote this set of triples as $\mathbf{T}_{\text{europarl}}$.

Noisy fr & Clean en: As mentioned in the corresponding paragraph of Section 3, both noisy French and clean English come from MTNT training data and we create clean French through back-translation. This set of triples is denoted as $\mathbf{T}_{\text{mtnt}}$.

4.2 Hyperparameters

We follow the transformer-base setting of Vaswani et al. (2017), using $N = 6$ layers for both encoder and decoder, $h = 8$ heads for self-attention, and d_k, d_v are both set to 64. The hidden size of the model d_{model} is set to 512 and the hidden size of the feed forward network is set to 2048. The smoothing rate ϵ is set to 0.1 and the dropout rate is set to 0.1. For our multi-task transformer specifically, the weight λ in Equation 1 is set to 0.5. The implementation of the model is based on fairseq (Ott et al., 2019)[5].

4.3 Results

The baseline model is the vanilla transformer trained with clean French and clean English. In our experiment, it contains pairs $\mathbf{T}_1 = \{\mathbf{t}_c, \mathbf{t}_t\}$ that are extracted from $\mathbf{X}_{\text{europarl}}$. On the other hand, our model is the multitask transformer trained with $\mathbf{X}_{\text{europarl}}$. The same number of pairs and triples are used during training. We evaluate these two models on two MTNT datasets, one of them comes from the original paper (Michel and Neubig, 2018) while the other one is provided by WMT Robustness shared task (Li et al., 2019). The BLEU score of these two models are shown in the first and the third column of Table 1.

Compared to the vanilla transformer, our proposed multi-task transformer yields 2.5 and 4.6 BLEU points improvement on two MTNT datasets. However, the component that leads to the success of this model is unclear as there are mainly two differences: 1) our proposed model utilizes an auxiliary decoder to recover from the noisy text, it could potentially benefit the translation process with cleaner data 2) our model is further trained on

---

⁵ `https://github.com/pytorch/fairseq/tree/master/fairseq`

Model	BLEU	
Vanilla Transformer	22.0	25.7
+FT w/ synthetic noise	24.6	27.1
+FT w/ MTNT	**34.1**	**36.0**
Our Model	24.5	30.3
+FT w/ MTNT	31.7	32.8

Table 1: BLEU score of different models. The second column shows the score in MTNT test dataset introduced in Michel and Neubig (2018) and the third column shows the score in the MTNT test dataset provided by WMT Robustness share task (Li et al., 2019).

noisy data, presumably overcoming any domain-adaptation issues.

We investigate this issue by fine-tuning the baseline model with another set of pairs $\mathbf{T}_2 = \{\mathbf{t}_n, \mathbf{t}_t\}$ that are extracted from $\mathbf{T}_{\text{europarl}}$. We load the pre-trained model and continue training for an extra epoch. With this fine-tuning process, the baseline model sees exact the same number of data as our proposed model. The fine-tuning result is shown in the second row of Table 1.

The performance of the fine-tuned baseline system is very close to that of our proposed model on the original MTNT test data and is 3.2 BLEU points lower on the shared task dataset. This result suggest that while the inclusion of synthetic noisy sentences is generalizable among datasets, using the denoising decoder might be beneficial only in specific settings.

Further, to investigate model's potential when in possession of in-domain training data, we fine tune both models with MTNT parallel training data. The data we use here is the same as the MTNT data we use to train auxiliary NMT systems to generate triples (Section 3). During the fine-tuning process, hence, we do not introduce new parallel data. The performance of the fine-tuned systems are shown in the third and the last row of Table 1 respectively.

Even vanilla transformer could not beat the multi-task transformer on both datasets before fine-tuned with in-domain data, it performs significantly better and outperforms our proposed model on both datasets after the fine-tuning process. The results suggest the potential of vanilla transformer in fitting in-domain data. It is notable, of course, that the fine-tuning process leads to a 9.5/8.9 BLEU points improvement for the vanilla transformer and 7.2/1.5 points for our proposed model respectively. This again shows the power of domain adaptation for building a robust NMT system.

4.4 Case Study

Table 2 shows example outputs of original MTNT test dataset from different models. The denoised source is the sentence generated by the denoising decoder in our proposed model.

The first example contains special characters '>' and the word 'xQc'. All models fail to correctly copy the special character > and generate a replacement. On the other hand, the word 'xQc' confuses the two baseline models and they fail to correctly copy this word. Our model, however, correctly copies the word and generates a reasonable translation. The denoised sentence seems to not bring benefit and, in fact, it attempts to denoise 'xQc' to 'XVC'. The translation decoder then seems to combine the two versions, copying the word from the source noisy sentence but uppercasing it just like the denoised version.

The second example contains the acronym 'PC' and our model does not produce a correct translation. It is interesting that the translated word 'pellets' is also not the corresponding translation of 'peloton' in the denoised sentence. Somewhat similar to the first example, this suggests that the translation decoder mostly ignores the context from the denoisy decoder. In terms of performance of vanilla transformer, although the baseline model also fails, the fine-tuned model deals with 'PC' correctly and procures a good translation. This indicates that explicitly having attention to both noisy and clean sentences does not always lead to better translation quality.

In the last example, the noise lies in a typo in the phrase corresponding to the phrase ``double negative''. None of the models produces a good translation of this phrase. Similar to the first case, the denoised sentence has a negative effect as it falsely "corrects" ``ngation'' to ``voie'' ("way" in English), which changes the meaning of the word and results in the bad translation 'track'. This demonstrates that all models still need to address issues regarding rare and misspelled words.

The main takeaway from a manual inspection of the outputs, is that the first (denoising) decoder does not really properly deal with noise in the desired way, and the translation decoder generally

ignores its output. We suspect that this issue is caused by the data synthesis process which results in low quality triples. Other further improvements could be possibly achieved by constraining the output of the denoising decoder, such that it produces minimal, non-meaning-altering edits. We leave these investigations as future work.

5 Related Work

Here, we discuss how the MT community handles the noise problem. In general, there are mainly two kinds of approaches: the first attempts to denoise text, and the second proposes training with noisy texts.

Denoising text: Sakaguchi et al. (2017) proposes semi-character level recurrent neural network (scRNN) to correct words with scrambling characters. Each word is represented as a vector with elements corresponding to the characters' position. Heigold et al. (2018) investigates the robustness of character-based word embeddings in machine translation against word scrambling and random noise. The experiments show that the noise has a larger influence on character-based models than BPE-based models. To minimize the influence of word structure, Belinkov and Bisk (2017) proposes to represent word as its average character embeddings, which is invariant to these kinds of noise. The proposed method enables the MT system to be more robust to scrambling noise even training the model with clean text. Instead of handling noise at the word level, we try to recover the clean text from the noisy one at the sentence level. Besides noise like word scrambling, the sentence level denoising could potentially better deal with more complex noise like grammatical errors.

Training with noisy data: Li et al. (2017) designs methods to generate noise in the text, mainly focusing on syntactic noise and semantic noise. (Sperber et al., 2017) proposes a noise model based on automatic speech recognizer (ASR) error types, which consists of substitutions, deletions and insertions. Their noise model samples the positions of words that should be altered in the source sentence. Even training with synthetic noise data brings a large improvement in translating noisy data, Belinkov and Bisk (2017) shows that models mainly perform well on the same kind of noise that is introduced at training time, and they mostly fail to generalize to text with other

Source	> Tu veux dire comme xQc?
Target	> Do you mean like xQc?
Baseline	'You want to call it al-Qc?'
Baseline FT	— Do you mean asylum-seekers?
Denoised Source	— Avez-vous lintention de parler de XVC?
Our model	— Do you intend to refer to as XQC?
Source	Si tu joues sur pc, a-t-il t bien adapt?
Target	If you play on PC, has it been well adapted?
Baseline	If you are playing on a pile, has it been adequate?
Baseline FT	If you play on pc, has it been properly adapted?
Denoised Source	Si vous jouez au peloton, a-t-il t bien adapt?
Our model	If you play on pellets, has you been well adapted?
Source	Les franais sont les champions de la double-ngation.
Target	French people are the champions of the double negative.
Baseline	The French are the champions of dual-nation.
Baseline FT	The French are the champions of double-nutrition.
Denoised Source	Les Franais sont les champions de la double voie.
Our model	The French are the champions of the double-track.

Table 2: Comparison of baseline, baseline FT w/ synthetic noise and our model in MTNT fr-en.

kinds of noise. Similar findings were outlined in Anastasopoulos et al. (2019) and Anastasopoulos (2019), which evaluated MT systems on natural and natural-like grammatical noise, specifically on English produced by non-native speakers. Natural noise appears to be richer and more complex compared to synthetic noise, making it challenging to manually design a comprehensive set of noise to approximate real world settings. In our work, we follow (Vaibhav et al., 2019) and synthesize the noisy text through back-translation. There is no need to manually control the distribution of noise.

In terms of multi-task learning for machine translation, Tu et al. (2017) proposes to add a reconstructor on top of the decoder. The auxiliary objective is to reconstruct the source sentence from the hidden layers of the translation decoder. This encourages the decoder to embed complete source information, which helps improve the translation performance. This approach was found to be helpful in low-resource MT scenarios also by Niu et al. (2019). Anastasopoulos and Chiang (2018) proposes a tied multitask learning model architecture to improve the speech translation task. The intuition is that, speech transcription as an intermediate task, should improve the performance of speech translation if the speech translation is based on both the input speech and its transcription.

6 Conclusion

In this work, we propose a multi-task transformer architecture that tries to not only denoisy the noisy source text but also translate it. We design a strategy for synthesizing data triplets for this architecture. Our model could be viewed as a combination of denoising source text and domain adaptation, both of which are popular approaches for designing robust NMT systems. Compared to the baseline vanilla transformer that is trained on clean data only, our proposed model with fine tuning enjoys 7.1 BLEU points improvement on the WMT Robustness shared task French to English dataset. However, this improvement is most likely attributed to the noisy text we add to the training process (hence, due to better domain adaptation), and not due to the denoising multi-task strategy.

Acknowledgements We thank AWS Educate program for donating computational GPU resources used in this work. We also thank Daniel Clothiaux and Junxian He for their insightful comments. This material is based upon work supported in part by the Defense Advanced Research Projects Agency Information Innovation Office (I2O) Low Resource Languages for Emergent Incidents (LORELEI) program under Contract No. HR0011-15-C0114 and the National Science Foundation under grant 1761548. The views and conclusions contained in this document are those of the authors and should not be interpreted as representing the official policies, either expressed or implied, of the U.S. Government. The U.S. Government is authorized to reproduce and distribute reprints for Government purposes notwithstanding any copyright notation here on.

References

Antonios Anastasopoulos. 2019. An analysis of source-side grammatical errors in nmt. In *Proc. BlackboxNLP*. To appear.

Antonios Anastasopoulos and David Chiang. 2018. Tied multitask learning for neural speech translation. In *Proceedings of the 2018 Conference of the North American Chapter of the Association for Computational Linguistics: Human Language Technologies, Volume 1 (Long Papers)*, pages 82–91.

Antonios Anastasopoulos, Alison Lui, Toan Q. Nguyen, and David Chiang. 2019. Neural machine translation of text from non-native speakers. In *Proc. NAACL-HLT*.

Dzmitry Bahdanau, Kyunghyun Cho, and Yoshua Bengio. 2015. Neural machine translation by jointly learning to align and translate. In *International Conference on Learning Representations*.

Yonatan Belinkov and Yonatan Bisk. 2017. Synthetic and natural noise both break neural machine translation. In *International Conference on Learning Representations*.

Philip Gage. 1994. A new algorithm for data compression. *The C Users Journal*, 12(2):23–38.

Georg Heigold, Stalin Varanasi, Günter Neumann, and Josef Genabith. 2018. How robust are character-based word embeddings in tagging and mt against wrod scramlbing or randdm nouse? In *Proceedings of the 13th Conference of the Association for Machine Translation in the Americas (Volume 1: Research Papers)*, volume 1, pages 68–80.

Huda Khayrallah and Philipp Koehn. 2018. On the impact of various types of noise on neural machine translation. In *Proceedings of the 2nd Workshop on Neural Machine Translation and Generation*, pages 74–83.

Catherine Kobus, Josep Crego, and Jean Senellart. 2017. Domain control for neural machine translation. In *Proceedings of the International Conference Recent Advances in Natural Language Processing, RANLP 2017*, pages 372–378.

Xian Li, Paul Michel, Antonios Anastasopoulos, Yonatan Belinkov, Nadir K. Durrani, Orhan Firat, Philipp Koehn, Graham Neubig, Juan M. Pino, and Hassan Sajjad. 2019. Findings of the first shared task on machine translation robustness. In *Proceedings of the Fourth Conference on Machine Translation, Volume 2: Shared Task Papers*, Florence, Italy. Association for Computational Linguistics.

Yitong Li, Trevor Cohn, and Timothy Baldwin. 2017. Robust training under linguistic adversity. In *Proceedings of the 15th Conference of the European Chapter of the Association for Computational Linguistics: Volume 2, Short Papers*, volume 2, pages 21–27.

Paul Michel and Graham Neubig. 2018. Mtnt: A testbed for machine translation of noisy text. In *Proceedings of the 2018 Conference on Empirical Methods in Natural Language Processing*.

Jan Niehues, Eunah Cho, Thanh-Le Ha, and Alex Waibel. 2016. Pre-translation for neural machine translation. In *Proceedings of COLING 2016, the 26th International Conference on Computational Linguistics: Technical Papers*, pages 1828–1836, Osaka, Japan. The COLING 2016 Organizing Committee.

Xing Niu, Weijia Xu, and Marine Carpuat. 2019. Bi-directional differentiable input reconstruction for low-resource neural machine translation. In *Proc. NAACL-HLT*.

Myle Ott, Sergey Edunov, Alexei Baevski, Angela Fan, Sam Gross, Nathan Ng, David Grangier, and Michael Auli. 2019. fairseq: A fast, extensible toolkit for sequence modeling. In *Proceedings of NAACL-HLT 2019: Demonstrations*.

Keisuke Sakaguchi, Kevin Duh, Matt Post, and Benjamin Van Durme. 2017. Robsut wrod reocginiton via semi-character recurrent neural network. In *Thirty-First AAAI Conference on Artificial Intelligence*.

Matthias Sperber, Jan Niehues, and Alex Waibel. 2017. Toward robust neural machine translation for noisy input sequences. In *International Workshop on Spoken Language Translation (IWSLT), Tokyo, Japan*.

Zhaopeng Tu, Yang Liu, Lifeng Shang, Xiaohua Liu, and Hang Li. 2017. Neural machine translation with reconstruction. In *Thirty-First AAAI Conference on Artificial Intelligence*.

Vaibhav, Sumeet Singh, Craig Stewart, and Graham Neubig. 2019. Improving robustness of machine translation with synthetic noise. In *Meeting of the North American Chapter of the Association for Computational Linguistics (NAACL)*, Minneapolis, USA.

Ashish Vaswani, Noam Shazeer, Niki Parmar, Jakob Uszkoreit, Llion Jones, Aidan N Gomez, Łukasz Kaiser, and Illia Polosukhin. 2017. Attention is all you need. In *Advances in Neural Information Processing Systems*, pages 5998–6008.

Author Index